A Concise Encyclopaedia

S. V. UTECHIN, the editor, and, together with his wife Patricia Utechin, the principal contributor to *A Concise Encyclopaedia of Russia*, is Senior Research Officer in Soviet Studies at the London School of Economics and Political Science. Dr. Utechin was born in Russia in 1921 and lived there until 1943. He studied at Moscow University from 1939 to 1941 and after the war studied at Kiel and Oxford Universities.

A CONCISE ENCYCLOPAEDIA OF RUSSIA was first published in 1961.

A CONCISE ENCYCLOPAEDIA OF RUSSIA

by
S. V. UTECHIN

A Dutton  Paperback

NEW YORK
E. P. DUTTON & CO., INC.
1964

FOR KOLYA

who did not demand attention
over many, many weekends

ILLUSTRATIONS

PREFACE

THIS BOOK is a co-operative effort: the entries on painting and sculpture have been written by V. Gregoriy, on the cinema by Hugh Lunghi, on architecture by D. Makaroff, on music, ballet and opera by G. R. Seaman, and the entry 'Theatre' by David Tutaev. The rest of the book owes a great deal to the collaboration of my wife, Patricia Utechin, to the extent that it is impossible to single out her contribution.

The aim of the book is to provide easily accessible information upon the principal aspects of contemporary Russia and its historical background. It may go some way towards filling the gap which exists in the literature between, on the one hand, detailed studies aimed at the specialist reader, and on the other those popular writings on Russia which are now so numerous and which only too often reflect a very fleeting acquaintance with the subject. It would, of course, be absurd to claim intimate knowledge of all the fields I have dealt with, and in particular the entries on science and technology and on military matters are pure compilations, though I hope from the best available sources, both Russian and foreign. On the other hand, many of the entries in the fields of society, modern history, political theory and education are to a considerable extent based upon my own academic work.

The selection of the material has been determined by what I have thought a prospective reader is likely to want to know, by what I think he ought to know, and by the limitations which the available information and the present state of research impose. The book is not primarily intended for the specialist in any particular field, although I hope it may be of use to him for reference. In no case is previous knowledge of any subject in its Russian context assumed; conversely, no attempt is made to deal with the general aspects of such subjects as, for example, communism or the Orthodox Church—they are treated only in relation to Russia.

A few technical points. 'The party' always means the Communist Party, and 'the Central Committee,' unless otherwise

vii

stated, always means the Central Committee of the Communist Party. In biographical entries the ethnic origin of an individual where known is specified if it is not Great Russian. In a very few cases it has not been possible to discover the full names, date of birth or date of death of certain individuals; these gaps usually occur where the individual concerned is at present and has been for some time regarded as an 'un-person' in the Soviet Union, thus making biographical details difficult to come by. The bibliographies at the end of entries are as a general rule confined to publications in the English language, but exception is made for a few outstanding or useful works in Russian, French and German. The bibliographies are not exhaustive, but are intended to include standard works and the more important recent works; the place of publication is given only if it is outside Great Britain. References to articles in periodicals are sometimes included in the bibliographies when there are no books on the subject concerned or when the articles are of recent date. On the question of transcription I have decided in favour of transliteration rather than phonetical transcription. There is unfortunately no universally accepted system of transliteration of Russian in English-speaking countries; however, there is a standard system for geographical names—that recommended by the Permanent Committee on Geographical Names—and it seemed convenient, in the interest of uniformity, to use this system throughout the book. The only exceptions are those proper names, such as Eisenstein or Tchaikovsky, for which there is an established tradition of spelling in English. The names of Ukrainian nationalist political figures are given in their Ukrainian form. The use of the systematic list of entries at the beginning of the book may on occasion present some difficulties. In some closely related subject categories, especially those of history and politics, law and government, and society, the decision to include an entry in one or another section had often to be almost arbitrary; thus if a particular matter is not found in one such section of the list it is advisable to look for it under one of the allied headings.

I owe very sincere thanks to the following friends and colleagues for advice and assistance, including reading parts of the manuscript: Dr N. Andreyev, Professor Max Beloff, Mr David Footman, Mr H. M. Hayward, Dr R. Hingley, Dr G. Katkov, Mr Walter Kolarz, Professor I. Lapenna, Mr M. Mackintosh, Mr A. Nove, my father-in-law Brigadier R. B. Rathbone, Mr L. B.

Schapiro and Dr F. Sternfeld. None of them is of course responsible for the views expressed or for any factual errors that may
be found. I should also like to express my gratitude to my
publishers, Messrs J. M. Dent & Sons Ltd, and in particular to
the Editorial Director, Mr E. F. Bozman, for his patience and
constant encouragement.

Oxford,   S. V. UTECHIN.
   May 1960.

SYSTEMATIC LIST OF ENTRIES

ARTS

ECONOMY

EDUCATION

ETHNOGRAPHY AND LINGUISTICS

GEOGRAPHY

HISTORY AND POLITICS

LAW AND GOVERNMENT

LITERATURE

MILITARY

PHILOSOPHY (including Political Theory)

RELIGION

SCIENCE AND TECHNOLOGY

SOCIETY

MOSCOW AREA

Zagorsk
Tushino · Khimki
Khristishchi
Babushkin · Mytishchi
Noginsk
MOSCOW
Moskva · Kuntsevo · Perovo
Lyublino · Pavlovsky Posad
Lyubertsy · Orekhovo-Zuyevo
Podol'sk · Elektrostall'
Moskva
Yegor'yevsk
Kolomna
Serpukhov · Oka
MILES
0 10 20 30

TASHKENT
XIV
Chirchik
Chirchik
Angren
XII
LENINABAD

A E R E C T E I C

Barents Sea
Novaya Zemlya
Kara Sea

MURMANSK · Pechenga
Kandalaksha · Kirovsk
White Sea
PETROZAVODSK
L. Onega
Mezen'
Nar'yan-Mar
Vorkuta
Salekhard
Dudinka
Igarka

TALLINN
KALININGRAD
II
III
I
GRODNO
Kaunas
PSKOV
NOVGOROD
VILNIUS · MINSK
BREST
MOGILEV
GOMEL
UZHGOROD
L'VOV
ZHITOMIR
CHERNIGOV
CHERNOVTSY
VINNITSA
KIEV
ORËL
KURSK
POLTAVA
LIPETSK
TAMBOV
KISHINEV
CHERKASSY
KHAR'KOV
VORONEZH
ODESSA
NIKOLAYEV
KHERSON
Krivoy Rog
DNEPROPETROVSK
ZAPOROZH'YE
DONETSK
LUGANSK
SIMFEROPOL'
Sevastopol'
Yalta
Kerch
Novorossiysk
Sochi
KRASNODAR
STAVROPOL'
CHERKESSK
Pyatigorsk
ELISTA
ORDZHONIKIDZE
GROZNY
MAKHACHKALA
TBILISI
YEREVAN
Kirovabad
NAKHICHEVAN'
Derbent
Sumgait
BAKU
MOSCOW
YAROSLAVL'
KOSTROMA
IVANOVO
VOLOGDA
KALININ
SMOLENSK
TULA
RYAZAN'
GOR'KIY
CHEBOKSARY
KAZAN'
UL'YANOVSK
KUYBYSHEV
UFA
PENZA
SARATOV
STALINGRAD
Sterlitamak
ORENBURG
URAL'SK
AKTYUBINSK
GUR'YEV
ASTRAKHAN'
SYKTYVKAR
Ukhta
Kotlas
Sukhona
Kama
SVERDLOVSK
CHELYABINSK
KURGAN
Tobol'sk
Khanty-Mansiysk
Serëzovo
KUSTANAY
KOKCHETAV
AKMOLINSK
Turgay
Atbasar
Temir-Tau
KARAGANDA
SEMIPALATINSK
PAVLODAR
OMSK
NOVOSIBIRSK
BARNAUL
Kulunda
GORNO-ALTAYSK
UST'-KAMENOGORSK
Zaysan
Ayaguz
Aktogay
Balkhash
L. Balkhash
KZYL-ORDA
Turkestan
CHIMKENT
DZHAMBUL
FRUNZE
ALMA-ATA
NAMANGAN
ANDIZHAN
FERGANA
XIII
West Siberian Plain
Ob
Irtysh
Yenisey
XV

Ust'-Urt Plateau
Aral Sea
Kungrad
NUKUS
URGENCH
Khiva
TASHAUZ
Krasnovodsk
Nebit-Dag
ASHKHABAD
X
CHARDZHOU
MARY
BUKHARA
SAMARKAND
TASHKENT
XI
XII
STALINABAD
KHOROG
TERMEZ

LEGEND

Railways .... ┼┼┼┼┼
Important trunk roads .....
International boundaries .. ▬ ▬ ▬
Union Republic boundaries ─ ─ ─ ─
Mountainous areas
Capitals of Union Republics, ... **FRUNZE**
Administrative centres of oblasts, krays or autonomous oblasts
or capitals of autonomous republics....KUSTANAY
Other towns .... Kungrad

REPUBLICS

I Estonia, II Latvia, III Lithuania.
IV Belorussia, V Moldavia,
VI Ukraine, VII Georgia, VIII Azerbaydzhan
IX Armenia, X Turkmenia,
XI Uzbekistan, XII Tadzhikistan,
XIII Kirgizia, XIV Kazakhstan, XV R.S.F.S.R.

Map of the U.S.S.R.

FERGANA VALLEY

MILES
0 10 20 30 40 50

XIII

XI

NAMANGAN
Syr-Dar'ya
ANDIZHAN

Kokand
Margelan
OSH
FERGANA
XIII

MILES
0 200 400 600 800

O C E A N
Bering Str.
Wrangel I.
Gulf of
Anadyr'
ANADYR'

Severnaya
Zemlya
New
Siberian
Is.
Ambarchik
Markovo
Penzhino

East Siberian
Sea
Laptev Sea
Russkoye
Ust'ye
Kazach'ya
Stredne-
Kolymsk
Cherskiy Range
PALANA

Tiksi
Verkhoyansk
Ust'Nera
Susuman
Seymchan

Vilyuy Range
Oymyakon
MAGADAN
PETROPAVLOVSK-
KAMCHATSKIY

Central
Siberian
Vilyuysk
YAKUTSK
Okhotsk
Sea

Tunguska
Tura
Suntar
Olekminsk
Use-Maya
of Okhotsk

Highlands
Mirnyy
Ayan

Yuzhno-
Yeniseyskiy
Patom
Highlands
Bodaybo
Stanovoy Mts.
Komsomol'sk

Kansk
Kirensk
KHABAROVSK
Korsakov

Tayshet
Nizhneudinsk
Zheleznogorsk
CHITA

Sayan Mts.
ULAN-UDE
Nerchinsk
Spassk-Dal'niy
Artem
Suchan
Nakhodka
VLADIVOSTOK

Sea of
Japan

DONETS BASIN

MILES
0 10 20 30 40

Slavyansk
Kramatorsk
Northern
Donets
Kadiyevka
Kamensk-
Shakhtinskiy

Konstantinovka
Artemovsk
Voroshilovsk
LUGANSK

Gorlovka
Yenakiyevo
VI
Krasnyy Luch
XV

Makeyevka
Chistyakovo

STALINO
Novoshakhtinsk
Shakhty

Novocherkassk

POPULATION OF TOWNS

Over 1 million .... ■
500,000 to 1 million .... ⊙
100,000 to 500,000 .... •
50,000 to 100,000 .... o
Less than 50,000 .... ▫

A

Abakan, town on the Yenisey in southern Siberia, administrative centre of the Khakas Autonomous Oblast and cultural centre of the Minusinsk Basin. Population (1959) 56,000, mainly Russian. It is an important junction on the Southern Siberian Railway, and has saw-milling and food industries and an airport. Abakan was founded as a Russian fort in 1707, was later a village and became a town in 1931.

Abakumov, Viktor Semënovich (*d.* 1954), security official. In 1930 he was on the staff of Stalin's private secretariat, then head of the N.K.V.D. administration in Rostov-on-Don. He was Commissar for Internal Affairs for a short time in 1941, then Beria's deputy, then head of Smersh (q.v.), and 1946–52 Minister of State Security (*see* M.G.B.). In 1954 he was accused of complicity with Beria, tried and shot; it was later stated that one of the main charges against him was the fabrication, at the instigation of Malenkov, of the 'Leningrad Case' (q.v.)

Abaza, Caucasian-speaking people who live in the Karachay-Circassian Autonomous Oblast of the North Caucasus, numbering (1959) 20,000. They are bilingual in Abaza and Circassian.

Abdullah Khan, most outstanding and popular ruler of the Bukhara Khanate (q.v.), 1557–98. He transferred the capital from Samarkand to Bukhara, and united under his rule all parts of Central Asia dominated by Uzbeks, including Khorezm and Tashkent. He is remembered as a great protector of agriculture, crafts, commerce and learning, and as a benefactor of his people.

Abkhazia, Autonomous Republic within Georgia, situated in the north-west of Georgia between the main Caucasian range and the Black Sea, with a subtropical climate on the shore; it has deposits of coal. Area 3,300 sq. m.; population (1959) 400,000 (37 per cent urban), mainly Georgians, also Abkhazians and Russians. Tobacco, citrus and other fruits, and tea are cultivated, cattle raised and bees kept, and there are tobacco, food and coal-mining industries. There are many health resorts on the seashore. The capital of the republic is Sukhumi. In antiquity Abkhazia belonged to Colchis, Pontus, Rome and Byzantium; in 756 it became independent and in 985 was merged in the all-Georgian state. It became a separate principality in the 16th century, falling under Turkish rule in 1578, under Russian in 1810, and being abolished in 1864. Uprisings against Russian rule occurred and resulted in the emigration of many Abkhazians to Turkey. The Autonomous Republic was established in 1921. *See* W. Kolarz, *Russia and her Colonies,* 1952.

Abkhazians, Caucasian-speaking people related to the Circassians, numbering (1959) 74,000, who live in Abkhazia where they form about 15 per cent of the population. They are mainly fruit, vine and tobacco growers, and are partly Muslims, partly Orthodox Christians.

1

For history *see* ABKHAZIA. Before 1864 there were several hundred thousand Abkhazians living in their historical territory, but the majority of them soon emigrated to Turkey. In the period 1938–53 they were subjected to a policy of assimilation by the Georgian authorities.

Abortion is legal in Russia provided it is carried out by a doctor. It was permitted free of charge in 1920 as a concession to 'moral survivals of the past and the difficult economic conditions of the present.' The number of abortions was particularly great in the early 1930's (in Moscow and some other cities it was higher than the number of births), reflecting the social misery caused by the collectivization of agriculture (q.v.). Abortion was prohibited in 1936 in pursuance of the general policy of the restoration of traditional norms, though a public discussion showed that a majority of those participating favoured the retention of the freedom of abortion. Women's legal responsibility was abolished in 1954, and abortion was again made legal in 1956, though a charge is now made. *See* H. J. Berman, *Justice in Russia*, Cambridge, Mass., 1950; W. W. Kulski, *The Soviet Regime*, Syracuse, 1954.

Abrikosov, Aleksey Ivanovich (1875–1955), professor of pathological anatomy at the First Moscow Medical Institute, member of the Academy of Sciences and the Academy of Medical Sciences and director of the latter's Institute for Normal and Pathological Morphology, author of many works on pathological anatomy.

Academy of Pedagogical Sciences of the R.S.F.S.R., central research institution in the field of education, founded in 1943. In 1957 it had 32 full members and 53 corresponding members, and a research staff numbering about 1,000 working in eight specialized institutes attached to the academy. Other departments of the academy include the State Library of Education (over 820,000 volumes), the Museum of Public Education, a toy museum, a publishing house and a small number of experimental schools. The monthly journal *Soviet Pedagogics* is published by the academy. From 1943 until his death in 1946 the then Minister of Education, V. P. Potëmkin, was president of the academy; since then, I. A. Kairov.

Academy of Sciences, of the U.S.S.R. (until 1917 IMPERIAL ACADEMY OF SCIENCES, then until 1925 ACADEMY OF SCIENCES OF RUSSIA), highest academic institution in the country, subordinated since 1934 to the Council of People's Commissars (since 1946 Council of Ministers). It consists of nine departments: physics and mathematics, chemistry, biology, geology and geography, technology, history, economics, philosophy and law, literature and language. The governing body of the academy, according to its statute, is the general meeting of full members, which elects new members and the presidium and president (currently N. A. Nesmeyanov). The elections are to a greater or lesser extent controlled by the science department of the Central Committee of the party, the greatest degree of control being exercised over the election of humanists; in philosophy the only members are party propagandists. In 1958 there were 167 full members and 361 corresponding members. The members are heavily concentrated in the department of technology, and to a lesser extent in those of the natural sciences, while the humanistic departments are very small. There are about 200 institutes and other research institutions managed by the academy, employing about 18,000 research workers. There are branches of the academy in the Urals (Sverdlovsk), Kazan', Bashkiria (Ufa), Daghestan (Makhachkala), Karelia (Petrozavodsk), Moldavia (Kishinëv), the Komi Autonomous Republic (Syktyvkar) and the Kola Peninsula. In 1957 a Siberian division of the academy was set up which is a kind of regional academy for Siberia and the Far East. The Union Republics (except the R.S.F.S.R. and Moldavia) have their own academies, all of which, except in the Ukraine and Belorussia, grew out of branches of the U.S.S.R. Academy. In addition to its other functions, the U.S.S.R. Academy of Sciences acts as a kind of Ministry of Science, co-ordinating the work of the Union Republic academies. Membership of the academy carries with it an honorarium of Rs. 5,000 (pre-1961) per month, though it is not necessarily a full-time job. The title of academician confers on the holder a very high status in the official social hierarchy, and academicians enjoy genuine prestige of a very high order.

The Academy of Sciences was founded in 1726, the scheme having been prepared for Peter the Great by Leibnitz. Most outstanding Russian scholars of the past became academicians, though there were notable exceptions, and the Czar's refusal, for political reasons, to permit the election of Maksim Gor'kiy in 1902 created a scandal and caused the resignation in protest of Chekhov and Korolenko. From the Bolshevik seizure of power until 1925 the academy, under its aged and eminent president Karpinskiy, managed by and large to ignore the Soviet Government. During the next five years the Communist authorities took possession of the academy's apparatus and transformed it into an organ of the Soviet system; a number of high-ranking Communists, e.g. Bukharin, were made academicians. In 1934 the academy was transferred from Leningrad to Moscow, and the fusion in 1936 of the institutions of the Communist Academy with the Academy of Sciences completed its reorganization. The Great Purge (q.v.) took a heavy toll in the academy. It has played a key role in the recent spectacular Russian scientific achievements. The academy has not remained unaffected by the ideological unrest of the post-Stalin period. See G. C. Guins, 'The Academy of Sciences of the U.S.S.R.,' Russian Review, vol. xii, No. 4, Oct. 1953; A. S. Vucinich, The Soviet Academy of Sciences, Stanford, California, 1956. A complete 'cover-to-cover' translation of the journal Bulletin of the Academy of Sciences of the U.S.S.R. exists in English.

Academy of Social Sciences, highest institution in the system of party education, attached to the Central Committee of the party. Only party members who have completed higher education and who have experience in the party, government or trade union apparatus are admitted, on the recommendation of republic or oblast party committees. All students receive grants. The full course lasts three years, during which the students do graduate work in such subjects as philosophy, political economy and party history, and are expected to prepare a thesis for a candidate's degree (see DEGREES), which the academy is empowered to award. The main purpose of the academy is to provide teachers of these subjects for higher educational establishments and theoretically well-qualified personnel for high positions in the party apparatus. The academy was founded in 1946 and can be regarded as a successor of the Institute of Red Professorship (q.v.).

Achinsk, town in the Krasnoyarsk Kray (central Siberia), situated on the River Chulym and the Trans-Siberian Railway about 90 m. west of Krasnoyarsk. Population (1956) 42,400. It has manganese mining, dairy and flour-milling industries, and cement factories are under construction. It is an important railway junction, the starting point of a line to the mouth of the Angara which is now being built. Achinsk was founded as a Russian fort in 1642, was later a village, became a town in 1782 and is now the centre of a rapidly developing industrial area.

Activist, word used for a person who voluntarily assists the Communist Party in its directing and supervisory tasks in all organized spheres of life. *See* A. Inkeles and R. A. Bauer, *The Soviet Citizen*, 1959.

Administrative Territorial Divisions. Russia is formally a federal state, the Union of Soviet Socialist Republics (U.S.S.R.), consisting of 15 Union Republics (q.v.). The larger of these are divided into provinces called *oblast* or *kray* (qq.v.), and some of them also include Autonomous Soviet Socialist Republics (A.S.S.R., *see* AUTONOMOUS REPUBLIC) and Autonomous Oblasts (A.O., q.v.); some oblasts include National Okrugs (*see* OKRUG). The following table shows the administrative territorial divisions and population in 1963.

Division	Area (sq. m.)	Population (thousands)	Administrative Centre
I. *Russian Soviet Federative Socialist Republic*	6,567,500	123,441	Moscow
A. North-West		12,026 (total)	
Archangel Oblast	229,700	1,352	Archangel
Kaliningrad Oblast	5,800	645	Kaliningrad
Karelian A.S.S.R.	66,300	673	Petrozavodsk
Komi A.S.S.R.	160,000	903	Syktyvkar
Leningrad Oblast	33,000	4,860	Leningrad
Murmansk Oblast	55,700	649	Murmansk
Novgorod Oblast	21,300	726	Novgorod
Pskov Oblast	21,300	904	Pskov
Vologda Oblast	56,100	1,314	Vologda
B. Centre		25,357 (total)	
Bryansk Oblast	13,400	1,571	Bryansk
Ivanovo Oblast	9,200	1,345	Ivanovo
Kalinin Oblast	32,200	1,769	Kalinin
Kaluga Oblast	11,500	957	Kaluga
Kostroma Oblast	23,100	897	Kostroma
Moscow Oblast	18,100	11,472	Moscow
Ryazan' Oblast	11,400	1,457	Ryazan'
Smolensk Oblast	19,200	1,106	Smolensk

[1] Slight disparity between republic figures and those for the divisions within republics is due to rounding.

Division	Area (sq. m.)	Population (thousands)	Administrative Centre
Tula Oblast	9,900	1,928	Tula
Vladimir Oblast	11,100	1,463	Vladimir
Yaroslavl' Oblast	14,000	1,392	Yaroslavl'
C. Volga-Vyatka Area		8,288 (total)	
Chuvash A.S.S.R.	7,000	1,143	Cheboksary
Gor'kiy Oblast	28,800	3,660	Gor'kiy
Kirov Oblast	46,400	1,821	Kirov
Mari A.S.S.R.	8,900	657	Yoshkar-Ola
Mordva A.S.S.R.	10,100	1,007	Saransk
D. Central Black-Earth Area		8,902 (total)	
Belgorod Oblast	10,400	1,255	Belgorod
Kursk Oblast	11,500	1,510	Kursk
Lipetsk Oblast	9,300	1,190	Lipetsk
Orël Oblast	9,500	945	Orël
Tambov Oblast	13,200	1,548	Tambov
Voronezh Oblast	20,100	2,454	Voronezh
E. Volga Area		13,224 (total)	
Astrakhan' Oblast	17,000	762	Astrakhan'
Kuybyshev Oblast	20,700	2,447	Kuybyshev
Penza Oblast	16,600	1,539	Penza
Saratov Oblast	38,500	2,289	Saratov
Tatar A.S.S.R.	26,100	3,011	Kazan'
Ul'yanovsk Oblast	15,100	1,153	Ul'yanovsk
Volgograd Oblast	43,900	2,023	Volgograd
F. North Caucasus		12,998 (total)	
Chechen-Ingush A.S.S.R.	6,800	922	Groznyy
Daghestan A.S.S.R.	19,300	1,222	Makhachkala
Kabarda-Balkar A.S.S.R.	4,800	485	Nal'chik
Kalmyk A.S.S.R.	29,200	219	Elista
Krasnodar Kray,	32,200	4,036	Krasnodar
including Adyge A.O.	2,900	343	Maykop
North Ossetian A.S.S.R.	3,100	487	Ordzhonikidze
Rostov Oblast	38,800	3,587	Rostov-on-Don
Stavropol' Kray,	31,000	2,040	Stavropol'
including Karachay-Circassian A.O.	5,100	308	Cherkessk
G. Urals		19,750 (total)	
Bashkir A.S.S.R.	59,100	3,603	Ufa
Chelyabinsk Oblast	33,800	3,190	Chelyabinsk
Kurgan Oblast	27,300	1,067	Kurgan
Orenburg Oblast	47,700	1,991	Orenburg
Perm' Oblast	61,800	3,081	Perm'
Sverdlovsk Oblast	74,900	4,258	Sverdlovsk
Tyumen' Oblast	552,100	1,183	Tyumen'
Udmurt A.S.S.R.	16,200	1,377	Izhevsk
H. Western Siberia		10,794 (total)	
Altay Kray,	100,700	2,832	Barnaul
including Mountainous Altay A.O.	35,600	166	Gorno-Altaysk
Kemerovo Oblast	36,000	2,980	Kemerovo
Novosibirsk Oblast	68,500	2,450	Novosibirsk

Division	Area (sq. m.)	Population (thousands)	Administration Centre
Omsk Oblast	53,700	1,768	Omsk
Tomsk Oblast	121,900	764	Tomsk
I. Eastern Siberia		7,535 (total)	
Buryat A.S.S.R.	135,100	737	Ulan-Ude
Chita Oblast	166,000	1,067	Chita
Irkutsk Oblast	295,300	2,155	Irkutsk
Krasnoyarsk Kray,	923,700	2,801	Krasnoyarsk
including Khakas A.O.	23,800	442	Abakan
Tuva A.O.	66,000	198	Kyzyl
Yakut A.S.S.R.	1,193,500	577	Yakutsk
J. Far East		4,567 (total)	
Amur Oblast	139,900	742	Blagoveshchensk
Kamchatka Oblast	181,700	246	Petropavlovsk-Kamchatskiy
Khabarovsk Kray,	317,200	1,206	Khabarovsk
including Jewish, A.O.	13,800	167	Birobidzhan
Magadan Oblast	461,200	279	Magadan
Maritime Kray	63,800	1,467	Vladivostok
Sakhalin Oblast	33,900	627	Yuzhno-Sakhalinsk
II. Ukrainian S.S.R.	231,200	44,054	Kiev
Cherkassy Oblast	7,900	1,486	Cherkassy
Chernigov Oblast	12,100	1,570	Chernigov
Chernovtsy Oblast	3,100	814	Chernovtsy
Crimean Oblast	9,800	1,392	Simferopol'
Dnepropetrovsk Oblast	12,300	2,963	Dnepropetrovsk
Donetsk Oblast	10,200	4,555	Donetsk
Ivano-Frankovsk Oblast	5,300	1,171	Ivano-Frankovsk
Khar'kov Oblast	12,200	2,601	Khar'kov
Kherson Oblast	10,400	897	Kherson
Khmel'nitskiy Oblast	8,000	1,627	Khmel'nitskiy
Kiev Oblast	11,100	3,034	Kiev
Kirovograd Oblast	9,300	1,252	Kirovograd
Lugansk Oblast	10,300	2,648	Lugansk
L'vov Oblast	8,400	2,267	L'vov
Nikolayev Oblast	9,600	1,053	Nikolayev
Odessa Oblast	12,800	2,131	Odessa
Poltava Oblast	11,200	1,662	Poltava
Rovno Oblast	7,800	990	Rovno
Sumy Oblast	9,300	1,529	Sumy
Ternopol' Oblast	5,300	1,134	Ternopol'
Transcarpathian Oblast	4,900	999	Uzhgorod
Vinnitsa Oblast	10,300	2,164	Vinnitsa
Volhynia Oblast	7,700	939	Lutsk
Zaporozh'ye Oblast	10,400	1,576	Zaporozh'ye
Zhitomir Oblast	11,500	1,600	Zhitomir
III. Belorussian S.S.R.	79,800	8,413	Minsk
Brest Oblast	12,500	1,211	Brest
Gomel' Oblast	15,500	1,436	Gomel'
Grodno Oblast	9,600	1,104	Grodno
Minsk Oblast	15,700	2,153	Minsk
Mogilëv Oblast	11,000	1,196	Mogilëv
Vitebsk Oblast	15,400	1,313	Vitebsk

Division	Area (sq. m.)	Population (thousands)	Administration Centre
IV. *Moldavian S.S.R.*	13,000	3,172	Kishinev
V. *Lithuanian S.S.R.*	25,400	2,878	Vilnius
VI. *Latvian S.S.R.*	24,500	2,187	Riga
VII. *Estonian S.S.R.*	17,300	1,244	Tallinn
VIII. *Georgian S.S.R.*, including Abkhaz	26,800	4,342	Tiflis
A.S.S.R.	3,300	442	Sukhumi
Adzhar A.S.S.R.	1,200	273	Batumi
South Ossetian A.O.	1,500	101	Tskhinvali
IX. *Azerbaydzhan S.S.R.*, including Mountainous	33,300	4,232	Baku
Karabakh A.O.	1,700	143	Stepanakert
Nakhichevan' A.S.S.R.	2,100	162	Nakhichevan'
X. *Armenian S.S.R.*	11,500	2,007	Yerevan
XI. *Kazakh S.S.R.*	1,044,300	11,270	Alma-Ata
Alma-Ata Oblast	87,500	1,734	Alma-Ata
East Kazakhstan Oblast	37,400	834	Ust'Kamenogorsk
Karaganda Oblast	151,800	1,369	Karaganda
Semipalatinsk Oblast	69,100	641	Semipalatinsk
South Kazakhstan Kray, including Chimkent	187,100	1,900	Chimkent
Oblast	46,400	898	Chimkent
Dzhambul Oblast	55,800	637	Dzhambul
Kzyl-Orda Oblast	84,800	365	Kzyl-Orda
Virgin Land Kray, including	230,800	3,535	Tselinograd
Kokchetev Oblast	30,400	612	Kokchetev
Kustanay Oblast	75,800	931	Kustanay
North Kazakhstan Oblast	15,800	556	Petropavlovsk
Pavlodar Oblast	49,000	605	Pavlodar
Tselinograd Oblast	59,800	831	Tselinograd
West Kazakhstan Kray, including	280,600	1,257	Aktyubinsk
Aktyubinsk Oblast	115,300	477	Aktyubinsk
Gur'yev Oblast	107,200	335	Gur'yev
Ural'sk Oblast	59,300	445	Ural'sk
XII. *Uzbek S.S.R.*	172,900	9,492	Tashkent
Andizhan Oblast	3,400	1,481	Andizhan
Bukhara Oblast	55,700	702	Bukhara
Fergana Oblast	3,700	1,138	Fergana
Kara-Kalpak A.S.S.R.	64,300	573	Nukus
Khorezm Oblast	1,700	433	Urgench
Samarkand Oblast	12,000	1,181	Samarkand
Surkhan-Dar'ya Oblast	17,200	1,073	Termez
Syr-Dar'ya Oblast	9,000	602	Yangiyer
Tashkent Oblast	6,000	2,309	Tashkent

Division	Area (sq. m.)	Population (thousands	Administrative Centre
XIII. *Kirgiz S.S.R.*,	76,300	2,379	Frunze
including Osh Oblast	24,600	986	Osh
XIV. *Tadzhik S.S.R.*,	55,000	2,967	Dushanbe
including Mountain-ous Badakhshan A.O.	24,600	83	Khorog
XV. *Turkmen S.S.R.*	187,700	1,744	Ashkhabad

Adyge, *see* CIRCASSIANS.

Adyge Autonomous Oblast, within Krasnodar Kray (Northern Caucasus), is situated on the left bank of the River Kuban' opposite Krasnodar and the adjacent foothills of the main Caucasian range. Area 1,700 sq. m.; population (1959) 286,000 (33 per cent urban), Russians, Ukrainians and Circassians (88,000 in 1939). Wheat, maize and sunflowers are cultivated, cattle and horses raised, and there are food and woodworking industries. Administrative centre: Maykop (since 1936). The Autonomous Oblast was established in 1922 with Krasnodar as its administrative centre. For history *see* CIRCASSIANS.

Adzhar Autonomous Republic, within Georgia, is situated in the south-west of Georgia adjacent to the Black Sea and the Turkish frontier; it is largely mountainous and the seashore has a humid sub-tropical climate. Area 1,100 sq. m.; population (1959) 242,000 (43 per cent urban), mostly Georgians (some of them Adzharis) and Russians. The republic is the principal producer of tea and citrus fruits in Russia (tea plantations were first started in the 1880's); there are also oil-refining and engineering industries. The Autonomous Republic was established in 1921; the capital is Batumi.

Aginskoye, village in the Chita Oblast of south-eastern Siberia, about 75 m. south-east of Chita, administrative centre of the Agin-skoye Buryat National Okrug. Population (1956) 4,000, mainly Russian. It was founded in 1811. The National Okrug (area 7,900 sq. m.) was established in 1937, and had in 1959 a population of 49,000, predominantly Buryat.

Agitator, name given to a person who participates either voluntarily or professionally in the ' political education ' of the people in the interests of the Communist Party. Among the activities of an agitator is 'canvassing' at the time of elections. *See* A. Inkeles, *Public Opinion in Soviet Russia,* Cambridge, Mass., 1950.

Agrarian Revolution, term used by Communists and Populists at the time of the Bolshevik coup in November 1917 to describe the nationalization of all land, privately or communally (*see* MIR) owned, and its subsequent distribution for use by the peasants on an egali-tarian basis. This reversed Stolypin's (q.v.) agrarian policy, replacing it by the traditional Populist policy known as 'black redistribution' rather than implementing the Marxist provisions of the Social-Democratic programme, to which the Bolsheviks had hitherto adhered. The agrarian revolution secured to the Bolsheviks the support of the Left Socialist Revolutionaries and of the majority of peasants, the latter being decisive during the civil war; but on the other hand it strengthened the element of private peasant economy which defeated the control of the authorities and was fundamentally incompatible with the long-term Bolshevik aims. Eventually it resulted in the decision to impose the collectivization of agriculture (q.v.), which is sometimes referred to as the second agrarian revolution.

Agricultural Procurement, i.e. State procurement of agricultural products, took until 1958 the following forms:

1. Obligatory deliveries by the collective farms (*see* KOLKHOZ), individual peasants, *kolkhoz* members (from their personal plots), members of other co-operatives and wage and salary earners living in rural localities of grain, potatoes, vegetables, oil seeds, hay, meat, milk, eggs, wool, etc. The amounts to be delivered were fixed by the authorities on the basis of the acreage of land used by the farm. Prices paid for delivered products were also arbitrarily fixed by the authorities and were as a rule very low, so that in fact obligatory deliveries amounted to a tax in kind. They were first introduced in 1933.

2. Payment in kind by the *kolkhozes* for the work performed for them by the M.T.S. (q.v.); the rates of payment were fixed by the authorities, until 1954 in relation to the gross yield of crops and thereafter according to regions.

3. Sale by contract between the State procurement organizations and *kolkhozes*, *kolkhoz* members or individual peasants, principally of industrial crops, fruits, grapes, tea, etc. This type of sale was in fact also obligatory, but was more profitable since prices were much fairer than those paid for obligatory deliveries and part of the price could be paid in kind, in scarce manufactured goods.

4. The free sale of any surplus agricultural products to the State procurement agencies for prices also fixed by the authorities but much nearer to the market price (*see* KOLKHOZ MARKET). Although such sales were in principle free, the authorities frequently resorted to compelling them.

In 1958 a single system of State procurement of agricultural products was introduced, with unified purchase prices. Ostensibly the sale by the *kolkhozes* is voluntary, but in fact quotas are allocated (according to acreage) and *kolkhoz* chairmen can ill afford not to fulfil their quotas. On the whole the new system has been of considerable benefit to the *kolkhozes*. *See* R. Schlesinger, 'The New Structure of Soviet Agriculture,' *Soviet Studies,* vol. x, No. 3, Jan. 1959.

Agricultural Tax, money tax levied on all persons with earnings from agriculture. It is (since 1953) a kind of property tax, since the tax base is the amount of land used by a household, i.e. the personal plot of *kolkhoz* members or the size of cultivable land held by individual peasants. Rates are calculated roughly on a proportional basis, with variations to suit local conditions, and there are allowances for weaker groups of the population. There is a sharp class discrimination, the rates for individual peasants being twice as high as those for *kolkhoz* members, while on the other hand 'specialists' and leading officials are exempt from the tax. Agricultural tax was introduced in 1923 and was at first the largest single tax, but its value as a source of revenue soon declined and it now accounts for less than 1 per cent of budget receipts. Its main function since the 1930's has been to encourage (as it does now) or discourage the cultivation of personal plots. *See also* TAXATION. *See* F. D. Holzman, *Soviet Taxation*, Cambridge, Mass., 1955.

Agriculture. There were the following types and numbers of farms and agricultural enterprises at the beginning of 1959: *sovkhozes* (q.v.), 6,002 (1,400 in 1927); small subsidiary State agricultural enterprises, over 100,000; Technical Repair Stations (*see* M.T.S.), 4,000; M.T.S., 345; *kolkhozes* (q.v.), 69,100 (14,800 in 1927); independent peasants' households, 60,000 (24·8 million in 1927, of which 1·1 million were classified as 'kulak,' q.v.). Total agricultural land amounted to 609·1 million hectares in 1958. Of this total, 321·3 million were used by *kolkhozes* (including 6·1 million under the personal plots of *kolkhoz* members), 178·0 million were used by *sovkhozes* and other State agricultural enterprises, 1·5 million by workers and employees for small-scale private cultivation, and 0·05 million by other groups of the population (mainly independent peasants). Arable land under cultivation totalled 220·2 million hectares, of which 154·5 were used by *kolkhozes* (including 5·5 personal plots), 62·3 by *sovkhozes*, etc., 1·1 by workers and employees, and 0·02 by other groups.

Total sown area in 1958 was 195·6 million hectares, of which 125·2 were under grain crops (q.v.)—37·2 winter crops and 88·0 summer—12·3 were under industrial crops (q.v.), 11·6 potatoes and vegetables, and 46·5 forage crops (except grain forage). The share of grain crops in the total sown area dropped from 88·5 per cent in 1913 (present-day frontiers) to 64·0 per cent in 1958, while that of industrial crops increased from 4·1 per cent to 6·3 per cent; potatoes and vegetables increased from 4·4 per cent to 6·0 per cent, and forage crops from 2·8 per cent to 23·7 per cent. In 1958 29·1 per cent of the total sown area was that of *sovkhozes* and other State agricultural enterprises, 67·2 per cent was that of *kolkhozes*, 2·8 per cent personal plots of *kolkhoz* members, 0·9 per cent personal plots of workers and employees, and 0·01 per cent individual peasants and other groups of the population.

The main areas of arable land under cultivation are the Ukraine, central Russia, Kazakhstan, Western Siberia, the Volga region, the Urals and the Northern Caucasus. Forty-two per cent of all gainfully occupied people were engaged in agriculture and forestry (including working on personal plots) in 1958 (75 per cent in 1913); of these, 35·5 per cent were *kolkhoz* members engaged in collective farming and work on personal plots and 3·7 per cent were members of workers' and employees' families working privately on personal plots. *See further under* AGRARIAN REVOLUTION; COLLECTIVIZATION OF AGRICULTURE; INVESTMENT; LAND; LIVESTOCK; PEASANTS; VIRGIN LAND CAMPAIGN. *See* N. Jasny, *The Socialized Agriculture of the U.S.S.R.*, Stanford, 1949; H. Chambre, *L'Aménagement du territoire en U.R.S.S.*, Paris and The Hague, 1959; R. E. F. Smith, *The Origins of Farming in Russia*, Paris, 1960; *The Soviet Seven Year Plan* (introduction by A. Nove), 1960.

Agro-towns, term used in 1949 when Khrushchëv advanced the idea that agricultural settlements should be transformed into a kind of towns. This idea encountered opposition within the party leadership and was soon dropped. It has been revived since 1957 and is being tried out in some places, particularly the Ukraine, but the term 'agro-town' is not now used.

Air Defence Forces (the warning systems, fighter aviation and anti-aircraft artillery, including rockets and missiles) are for operational purposes organized into a number of Air Defence Districts which overlap with Military Districts (*see* ARMY) and cover only the main defended areas. The commanders of the districts are subordinate to the commander-in-chief of Air Defence Forces, who heads a separate Chief Administration at the Ministry of Defence. Administratively the Air Defence Forces are included in the Military Districts in which they are stationed, while the responsibility for technical training and ordnance development of the aircraft and artillery components rests with the commanders-in-chief of the air forces and of artillery (qq.v.) respectively. *See* R. L. Garthoff, *How Russia Makes War*, 1954, and *Soviet Strategy in the Nuclear Age*, 1958.

Air Force was estimated in 1959 to number 700,000 personnel and over 25,000 operational aircraft, having at its disposal about 1,000 airfields on the territory of the U.S.S.R. The air force consists of five commands:

1. *The Long Range* (i.e. strategic) *Air Force*, estimated at 1,200 turbo-prop and jet bombers with a range of 4,000–6,000 miles, speed of 500–600 m.p.h., and bomb load of 4–20 tons. It is divided into three or four air armies, and has an independent command directly under the Minister of Defence.

2. *The Frontal Air Force*, i.e. tactical light bomber force whose purpose is to assist the ground forces. It is divided into air armies or smaller formations which are administratively subordinated to the respective commanders of ground forces (Military Districts, Army Groups), but operationally is under the direct control of the commander-in-chief of the air forces.

3. *The Fighter Air Force*, which is the aviation component of the Air Defence Forces (q.v.), is operationally subordinated to the commander-in-chief of the latter, and administratively to the Military Districts in which the fighter air armies are stationed.

4. *The Aviation of the Airborne Troops* (q.v.), operationally under the commander of these troops, and

5. *The Naval Aviation* (*see* NAVY), under the commander-in-chief of the navy.

The commander-in-chief of the air forces, in addition to direct command of the tactical bomber force, is responsible for all air force training and aircraft ordnance. *See* A. Lee, *The Soviet Air Force*, 1950; R. L. Garthoff, *How Russia Makes War*, 1954, and *Soviet Strategy in the Nuclear Age*, 1958; A. Lee (ed.), *The Soviet Air and Rocket Forces*, 1959.

Airborne Troops were in 1959 estimated to number about 100,000 men. They include their own air transport element believed to be capable of carrying 10 per cent of the force in a single operation. The airborne troops command has the status of a Chief Administration in the Ministry of Defence and is responsible for the preparation of tactical doctrine, technical training, organization and equipment. In matters of training and equipment its air transport units are subordinated to the commander-in-chief of the air forces. The Red Army was the first to conceive of the airborne troops as a separate arm. In its infancy this new arm enjoyed the special favour of Marshal Tukhachevskiy (q.v.). An airborne operation was first demonstrated to foreign observers at the manœuvres of 1936, but the Soviet command failed to make adequate use of airborne troops during the Second World War. *See* R. L. Garthoff, *How Russia Makes War*, 1954, and *Soviet Strategy in the Nuclear Age*, 1958; B. H. Liddell Hart (ed.), *The Soviet Army*, 1956; H. S. Dinerstein, *War and the Soviet Union*, Santa Monica, California, 1958; A. Lee (ed.), *The Soviet Air and Rocket Forces*, 1959.

Aircraft Industry. No current figures of aircraft production are available, nor do Soviet sources give information on the location of the industry, though it is known that plants exist in, e.g., Kazan', Chelyabinsk, Balashov, Khar'kov and Taganrog. The most outstanding aircraft designers have been Sikorskiy, Tupolev (qq.v.), S. V. Il'yushin, A. S. Yakovlev, M. I. Mikoyan and M. Mil'. *See also under* AIR FORCE; CIVIL AVIATION. *See* D. Gallik, V. I. Tsonev *et al.*, *The Soviet Aircraft Industry*, Chapel Hill, North Carolina, 1955.

Akhmatova (pseudonym, maiden name **Gorenko**), **Anna Andreyevna** (*b.* 1888), poetess of Ukrainian parentage, wife of Gumilёv (q.v.) and a member of his Acmeist group. She started publishing in 1912 and her lyrical poetry soon became extremely popular with the intelligentsia. Between 1921 and 1940 she scarcely published anything, though she undertook some translations. In 1946 she, together with Zoshchenko (q.v.), was the chief target for Zhdanov's attacks in his campaign to reimpose strict party control over cultural life, and she was expelled from the Writers' Union. However, in the resurgence of literary life that followed Stalin's death Akhmatova again became active and, among other things, published translations from the Yiddish of several poems of leading Jewish poets who were shot in 1952. *See* G. Ivanov, *Peterburgskiye zimy*, New York, 1952; M. Slonim, *Modern Russian Literature*, New York, 1953; J. Lindsay (trans.), *Russian Poetry, 1917–1955*, 1957; V. Zavalishin, *Early Soviet Writers*, New York, 1958.

Akkerman, *see* BELGOROD-DNESTROVSKIY.

Ak-Mechet', *see* KZYL-ORDA.

Akmolinsk: 1. Oblast in northern Kazakhstan traversed by the River Ishim and the Trans-Kazakhstan and Southern Siberian Railways; it is mostly a rolling plain, with coal, aluminium, gold and building materials deposits. Area 59,400 sq. m.; population (1959) 633,000 (40 per cent urban), mostly Russians (50 per cent) and Ukrainians, also Kazakhs, Tatars, Germans, Mordva, Chuvash, Belorussians, Estonians, etc. It is one of the main areas of the Virgin Land Campaign (q.v.), with extensive wheat and millet cultivation, and sheep and cattle breeding in the south. There are engineering, non-ferrous metallurgy, food and leather industries.

2. Administrative, economic and cultural centre of the oblast, situated on the River Ishim, an important railway junction on the crossing of the Trans-Kazakhstan and Southern Siberian Railways. Population (1959) 101,000 (1939, 32,000). It has engineering (agricultural machinery, chemical industry equipment, railway repairs), food and light (felt boots) industries. Akmolinsk was founded in 1824 as a Russian fort, and became a town in 1862. Before the 1930's it was an important commercial centre with a big annual fair which attracted merchants from Siberia, Central Asia and China. It became the administrative centre of the oblast in 1939, and its heavy industries date from the Second World War.

Aksakov, Ivan Sergeyevich (1823–86), brother of Konstantin's, brilliant orator and publicist, the publisher and editor of several newspapers which were suppressed by the Government. After his brother's death he became leader of the Slavophiles (q.v.), and reached the height of his influence in 1876–8 as spokesman of the widespread enthusiasm for the liberation of the Balkan Slavs. *See* R. Hare, *Pioneers of Russian Social Thought*, 1951; T. G. Masaryk, *The Spirit of Russia* (2nd ed.), vol. i, 1955; M. B. Petrovich, *The Emergence of Russian Pan-Slavism, 1856–1870*, New York, 1956.

Aksakov, Konstantin Sergeyevich (1817–60), son of Sergey Timofeyevich, historian, literary critic, playwright and publicist. He was leader of the younger Slavophiles (q.v.), and in his writings he exposed the worst aspects of conditions in Russia, advocating the emancipation with land of the serfs and the maintenance of the village commune. *See* R. Hare, *Pioneers of Russian Social Thought*, 1951; M. B. Petrovich, *The Emergence of Russian Pan-Slavism, 1856–1870*, New York, 1956.

Aksakov, Sergey Timofeyevich (1791–1859), writer. In his *Family Chronicle* (trans. *Chronicles of a Russian Family*) and its sequel, *The Years of Childhood of Bagrov the Grandson*, he portrayed realistically an 18th-century Russian squire's family (basing the picture upon his own family's history) and conditions in Bashkiria, then being colonized.

Aktyubinsk: 1. Oblast in north-west Kazakhstan, traversed by the Orenburg–Tashkent railway; it is mostly steppe (black earth in the north), but desert in the south, and has phosphorite, nickel, chromium, lignite and oil deposits. Area 115,700 sq. m.; population (1959) 404,000 (44 per cent urban), Kazakhs, Russians, Ukrainians and Tatars. It has metallurgical, chemical, engineering and food industries, wheat cultivation in the north, and beef cattle raising. The area belonged partly to the Middle Hundred and partly to the Junior Hundred of the Kazakhs, and was annexed to Russia in 1731–40.

2. Administrative, economic and cultural centre of the oblast, situated on the Orenburg–Tashkent railway about 120 m. south-east of Orenburg. Population (1959) 97,000 (1939, 49,000), mostly Russians, also Kazakhs and Tatars. It has metallurgical (ferro-alloys), chemical and food industries. Aktyubinsk was founded in 1869 as a Russian fort and became a town in 1893.

Alans, Iranian-speaking tribe which inhabited the steppe region between the Caucasus and the River Don in the first centuries A.D.

and was routed in the 5th century by the Visigoths. *See* M. Rostovt-zeff, *Iranians and Greeks in South Russia*, 1922; G. Vernadsky, *The Origins of Russia*, 1959.

Alaska. Following their advance through Siberia, Russians reached Alaska in 1732, and the whole territory was soon annexed to Russia. Its fur riches were exploited by the Russian-American Company. Alaska was sold to the United States in 1867 for the sum of eight million dollars, shortly before the discovery of gold there. *See* H. A. Shenitz, 'Vestiges of Old Russia in Alaska,' *Russian Review*, vol. xiv, No. 1, Jan. 1955.

Alchevsk, *see* VOROSHILOVSK.

Aldan: 1. Navigable right tributary of the River Lena in Eastern Siberia, 1,400 m. in length. It has many tributaries, some of which have rich gold deposits discovered in 1922.

2. (until 1939 **Nezametnyy**). Economic centre of the Aldan gold-mining area, connected with the Trans-Siberian Railway by a four-hundred-mile-long highway. It was founded in 1923 and became a town in 1939. Mica has been mined in the Aldan area since 1942 and rich iron-ore deposits were discovered in the 1950's.

Aleksandropol', *see* LENINAKAN.

Aleksandrov, Aleksandr Vasil'yevich (1883–1946), composer and conductor. He studied at the Imperial Chapel, St Petersburg, later at the conservatory under Lyadov and Glazunov and subsequently at Moscow Conservatory under Vasilenko (composition) and Mazetti (singing). Working for a time as teacher and choirmaster, he finally joined the Moscow Conservatory in 1918, becoming professor in 1922. An outstanding choral conductor, Aleksandrov concentrated his efforts from 1928 in creating the Red Army Ensemble of song and dance. Among his many songs and patriotic compositions was the *Cantata about Stalin. See* R. Moisenko, *Realist Music*, 1949.

Aleksandrov, Georgiy Fëdorovich (*b.* 1908), philosopher, a party member since 1928, trained at the Institute of Red Professorship (q.v.). He worked in the agitation and propaganda department of the Central Committee from 1934, and headed the department, 1939–47. He was made a member of the Academy of Sciences, and in 1947 director of its Institute of Philosophy. His chief work, *A History of West European Philosophy in the Nineteenth Century*, 1944, was chosen by Zhdanov (q.v.) as the object of attack when he launched in 1947 the campaign against 'objectivism' in philosophy and allied subjects; Aleksandrov was specifically accused of presenting Marxism as a continuation of the Western philosophical tradition rather than as a qualitatively new phenomenon. In 1950 he was given the task of being the main official commentator upon Stalin's articles on linguistics, pointing out their implications for the traditional Marxist distinction between basis and superstructure. He was Minister of Culture in 1954–5, and is now working in the Institute of Philosophy of the Belorussian Academy of Sciences in Minsk.

Aleksandrov, Ivan Gavrilovich (1875–1936), outstanding engineer and economist. Educated at the Moscow Higher Technical School and the School of Railway Engineering, he worked until 1918 as a practical engineer and consultant. He then played a leading part in working out the Goelro (q.v.) electrification plan; headed in 1921-4 the subcommission for economic regionalization within the Gosplan (q.v.), laying the theoretical foundations for the territorial aspect of all subsequent economic planning (q.v.); designed the Dneproges (q.v.) power-station and devised the ways of industrial development of the adjacent areas (see SOUTHERN INDUSTRIAL REGION) in 1921-7; worked on a scheme for the electrification of Central Asia from 1928; headed, 1930-6, the studies aimed at the utilization of the power resources of the River Angara in Siberia; worked, 1932-6, on plans for irrigation and economic reconstruction of the lower Volga area; and on a general scheme for the development of the railway network. He became a member of the Academy of Sciences in 1932, where he set up and headed a transportation section. He also headed the committee which prepared the creation of the Central Asian University in Tashkent. One of the main representatives of the technocratic trend among the old intelligentsia, Aleksandrov repeatedly came under criticism for his 'bourgeois' views. See H. Chambre, L'Aménagement du territoire en U.R.S.S., Paris and The Hague, 1959.

Aleksandrovsk, see ZAPOROZH'YE.

Aleksandrovskoye, village in the Irkutsk Oblast (southern Siberia), situated 47 m. north-west of Irkutsk. It is known for its hard labour prison (established 1873, political prisoners from 1904), which became a concentration camp in 1919. From the late 1930's until the mid fifties it was an 'isolator' (q.v.) for important political prisoners.

Aleksey Mikhaylovich (1629-76), Czar of Muscovy from 1645, the father of Peter the Great. A code of laws was compiled during his reign which remained in force until the 19th century (see ULO-ZHENIYE); one of its main provisions was the final establishment of serfdom (q.v.). Other events of his reign were the Church reforms of Patriarch Nikon (q.v.) which led to schism in the Russian Church; attempts to establish a postal service and to reorganize the army on Western European lines; the reunification of the Ukraine with Muscovy, 1654, and the extension of Russian possessions in Siberia; and the waging of successful wars against Poland. Several rebellions took place under Aleksey Mikhaylovich, including the great uprising led by Stepan Razin (q.v.)

Alekseyev, Mikhail Vasil'yevich (1857-1918), general. An accomplished administrator and strategist, he was appointed commander-in-chief on the western front in 1915, and soon Chief of Staff to Nicholas II (the supreme commander-in-chief). In May-June 1917 he was commander-in-chief of all Russian armies, and then once more Chief of Staff under the supreme commander-in-chief Kerenskiy. In 1918 Alekseyev took the initiative in organizing an anti-Bolshevik movement, and formed in the south the first volunteer anti-Bolshevik army, but he soon died of pneumonia. See F. A. Golder, Documents of Russian History, 1914-1917, 1927.

Alexander I (1777-1825), emperor, son of Paul I. He was well educated by a Swiss republican tutor, a follower of Rousseau. Succeeding to the throne in 1801, he brought about several reforms during the first half of his reign: the establishment of the Council of State (q.v.) and of ministries, the foundation of a State school system and of several universities, the liberation of serfs (without land) in the Baltic Provinces and the granting of permission to landlords elsewhere to free their serfs with land, the grant of a constitution to Poland, and the abolition of torture. Later, however, he became a mystical reactionary, and undid much of the good previously done. His foreign policy depended upon alternate alliances with England and Napoleon; he inspired the Holy Alliance, and acquired for Russia a large part of the Caucasus, Finland and Bessarabia. The outstanding event of his reign was the Patriotic War of 1812 against Napoleon. *See also* ARAKCHEYEV; DECEMBRISTS; KUTUZOV; SPERANSKIY.

Alexander II (1818–81), emperor, known as the Czar-Liberator for his emancipation of the serfs in 1861 and liberation of Bulgaria from the Turks in 1878. He received a good education under the poet Zhukov-skiy, and succeeded to the throne on the death of his father Nicholas I in 1855. His reign saw the transformation and modernization of social and political life, and is known as the period of Great Reforms (q.v.). Abroad he adhered to the principle of non-interference except in the case of the Turkish massacres of the Bulgarians. Other outstanding events of his reign were the Polish uprising of 1863, the final conquest of the North Caucasus (*see* SHAMIL') and the development of underground revolutionary activities by the Populists (*see* POPU-LISM). The latter culminated in acts of terror against leading representatives of the state, and several attempts were made upon Alexander's life. He was finally assassinated upon the very day when he had signed a decree approving the plan for a representative assembly. *See also* LORIS-MELIKOV. *See* W. E. Mosse, *Alexander II and the Modernization of Russia*, 1958.

Alexander III (1845–94), second son of Alexander II. He succeeded to the throne in 1881. His internal policy, under the influence of Pobedonostsev (q.v.), was entirely reactionary; it resulted in the destruction of many of his father's achievements, in increasing discrimination against Jews, and in the russification of national minorities. A protectionist economic policy, however, encouraged the rapid industrialization of the country, leading to a great increase in the number of industrial workers and the consequent spread of Marxist and Social-Democratic ideas. Abroad, Alexander III followed a policy of peace and non-interference, and towards the end of his reign the Franco-Russian *rapprochement* took place. *See also* BUNGE.

Alexander Nevskiy (1220–63), Grand Prince of Vladimir. As Prince of Novgorod in 1240 he vanquished the Swedes on the River Neva (hence his name), and he defeated the Teutonic Knights in 1242 at the famous battle on the ice of Lake Peipus. He successfully defended Russia against the Lithuanians and was confirmed as Grand Prince in 1252 by the Khan of the Golden Horde. He spent the remainder of his life trying to improve the lot of the Russians and alleviate the misery caused by the Tatar invasion. He was canonized by the Orthodox Church, and an order instituted in his name by Peter the Great, though abolished in 1917, was revived as a military decoration in 1942.

Alexandra Fëdorovna (1872–1918), last Empress of Russia, daughter of the Grand Duke of Hesse and grand-daughter of Queen Victoria. She was brought up partly in England, and married Czar Nicholas II in 1894. The delicacy of their son Aleksey, who suffered from haemophilia, enabled Rasputin (q.v.) to establish his sway over her. During the First World War the empress had an unfortunate influence upon Nicholas's policy, and was widely (though wrongly) suspected of German sympathies. On the fall of the empire she shared her husband's captivity, and on 17th July 1918 was executed with him by the Bolsheviks at Yekaterinburg. *See* biography by S. Buxhoeveden, 1928; F. A. Golder, *Documents of Russian History, 1914–1917*, 1927; S. P. Mel'gunov, *Legenda o separatnom mire*, Paris, 1957.

Alexis (Aleksiy; lay name **Simanskiy, Sergey Vladimirovich)** (*b.* 1877), Patriarch of Moscow and All Russia, head of the Russian Orthodox Church. Educated at Moscow University (where he read law) and the Moscow Theological Academy, he took monastic vows and was ordained priest in 1903, subsequently teaching for several years at theological seminaries. He was ordained bishop in 1913 and was vicar in the dioceses of Novgorod and Petrograd, becoming archbishop in 1929, Metropolitan of Novgorod in 1932 and of Leningrad in the following year. Very conservative in theological matters, he was prominent in the struggle against the Renovated Church schism, was twice arrested in the 1920's and spent three years in banishment in Semipalatinsk. From the mid 1920's he pursued the policy of co-operation with the Soviet Government. He took a prominent part in the establishment of a *modus vivendi* between the Orthodox Church and the Soviet authorities in 1943 (*see* RELIGION), became the locum tenens upon the death of Patriarch Sergius in 1944, and was elected patriarch in the following year. He has secured a considerable expansion of Church work at the cost of demonstrating loyalty to the Soviet Government and support for their policies.

Allied Intervention, *see* CIVIL WAR.

Alma-Ata: 1. Oblast in southern Kazakhstan, situated between Lake Balkhash in the north, the Tien-Shan mountain system in the south and the Chinese border in the east, traversed by the River Ili and the Turksib Railway. It is mountainous in the south-east with lead and zinc deposits and vertical vegetation zones, has a fertile strip in the foothills and desert plain in the north. Area 87,800 sq. m.; population (1959) 1,402,000 (47 per cent urban), including, besides Kazakhs, Russians and Ukrainians, Germans, Koreans (since 1937), Uygurs and Dungans (since 1885) and Tatars. Lead and zinc ores are mined, there is extensive fruit growing, viniculture, tobacco, beet-root, poppy, grain, sugar-beet and rice cultivation, and sheep, cattle, horses and pigs are raised; industry is confined to the town of Alma-Ata and its immediate surroundings. For history *see* SEMIRECH'YE.

2. (until 1921 **Vernyy**). Capital and cultural centre of Kazakhstan, administrative and economic centre of the Alma-Ata Oblast, situated in the foothills on the Turksib Railway. Population (1959) 455,000 (1939, 222,000), mostly Russians and Kazakhs. It has large and varied food industries, also textile, leather, engineering, printing and cinema industries. It is an important academic centre, with the Kazakh Academy of Sciences (founded as a branch of the U.S.S.R. Academy, transformed 1946), a geophysical observatory and many other research institutions, a university (founded 1934) and several other higher educational establishments. Alma-Ata is a well-planned modern city with tree-lined streets and many parks (said to be foremost in this respect among Union Republic capitals of the U.S.S.R.). Known as a town in the 13th–14th centuries, Alma-Ata was ruined in feudal wars, and by the 17th century did not exist. It was refounded as a Russian fortress in 1854, became a town and provincial centre in 1867, and capital of Kazakhstan in 1929.

Alphabet. The modern Russian alphabet consists of 32 letters:

Аа	a in 'bath'	Рр	r
Бб	b	Сс	s
Вв	v	Тт	t
Гг	g in 'get'	Уу	oo in 'boot'
Дд	d	Фф	f
⎰Ее	ye in 'yes'	Хх	ch in Scottish 'loch'
⎱Ёё	yo in 'yonder'	Цц	ts
Жж	g in Fr. 'gens'	Чч	ch in 'chap'
Зз	z	Шш	sh
Ии	i in Fr. 'livre'	Щщ	shch
Йй	y in 'boy'	Ъъ	'hard sign'
Кк	k	Ыы	near to i in 'ill'
Лл	l	Ьь	'soft sign'
Мм	m	Ээ	e in 'get'
Нн	n	Юю	yu in 'Yukon'
Оо	o in 'lot'	Яя	ya
Пп	p		

It was designed on Peter the Great's orders to simplify the traditional Cyrillic alphabet (based on Greek and used since the 9th century) and to approximate the shape of the letters as far as possible to modern Latin letters. Four obsolete letters were dropped with the spelling reform introduced by the Provisional Government in 1917. Most other languages of the U.S.S.R. use modified forms of the Russian alphabet; of these, the Ukrainian alphabet was created in the mid 19th century, and Belorussian, Chuvash, Komi, Mordva, Udmurt, Ossetian, Avar, Kumyk and Altay (qq.v.) in the late 19th or early 20th centuries. Other alphabets based on the Russian were imposed by the central government in the late 1930's, replacing modified Latin alphabets which had likewise been imposed in the 1920's. The Latin alphabet, which in the period of 'latinization' was introduced even for many languages where the Russian alphabet had previously been used, is now used only by Lithuanians and Latvians and Estonians, and by the German, Finnish, Polish and Hungarian minorities. Arabic was used by most Muslim peoples until it was replaced by Latin in the 1920's, as was the Mongol alphabet previously used by Buddhists (Buryats and Kalmyks). The ancient Georgian, Armenian (both since the 4th century A.D.) and Hebrew (for Yiddish) alphabets have been preserved unaffected by the Soviet linguistic policy. *See* W. Kolarz, *Russia and her Colonies*, 1952.

Altay, Turkic-speaking people living in the Mountainous-Altay Autonomous Oblast (southern Siberia) and numbering (1959) 45,000 (47,700 in 1939). They are mostly Orthodox Christians, but there is much paganism; a new religion, Burkhanism, emerged among the Altay in 1904 which was both anti-Russian and anti-pagan. They are principally animal breeders (including deer, bred for their antlers, which are cut off when young and exported to China where they are used to make medicine) and hunters, now collectivized. The Altay did not form a single people until the 1920's, and were known under the names of their different tribes. Between 1922 and 1948 they were called Oyrots: this name is historical, since until the 18th century they were under the Dzungarian state of the Oyrats (Kalmyks). *See* W. Kolarz, *The Peoples of the Soviet Far East*, 1954.

Altay: 1. Mountainous region in southern Siberia and Mongolia which stretches from the north-west to the south-east. Its highest ridges (highest mountain Belukha, 13,644 ft) are ice-covered and rocky; the eroded parts, of middle height, have rich non-ferrous metal deposits (especially in the north-west) and the valleys are fertile. The region is divided between the Altay Kray and East Kazakhstan Oblast in Russia, Mongolia and Sinkiang.

2. Kray of the R.S.F.S.R., comprising a part of the Altay Mountains in the south and most of the Kulunda steppe in the north-west, traversed by the River Ob'; it has deposits of gold, non-ferrous metals and salts. Area 102,200 sq. m.; population (1959) 2,685,000 (33 per cent urban), Russians (since the 17th century), Ukrainians, Germans (since 1941) and Altays. Wheat, sunflowers and sugar-beet are cultivated, and cattle raised; there are food, textile, engineering (tractors, railway carriages, etc.) and chemical industries. Principal towns: Barnaul (administrative centre), Biysk, Rubtsovsk. The area was annexed in the 18th century by Russia; the first smelting plant was built in 1726 and agricultural colonization took place in the 19th century. New impetus was given to economic development by the Second World War and the Virgin Land Campaign (q.v.). The Mountainous-Altay Autonomous Oblast is within the kray.

Ambartsumyan, Viktor Amazaspovich (*b.* 1908), Armenian astrophysicist. Educated at Leningrad University, he taught there till 1944, and since then has been professor at Yerevan University; he became a member of the U.S.S.R. Academy of Sciences in 1953 and president of the Armenian Academy of Sciences in the same year. Since 1948 Ambartsumyan has been a vice-president of the International Astronomical Union. He joined the party in 1940 and is now a member of the Armenian party central committee. He has developed the theory of radial equilibrium of planetary nebulae; demonstrated the role of ultra-violet radiation and the radiation of the lines of the Lyman series; explained physical composition of the atmosphere and the shells of meteorites; developed a new method for studying the dynamics of star systems; and discovered new star clusters of the 'O' and 'T' classes. *See* V. A. Ambartsumyan, *Theoretical Astrophysics*, 1958.

Amtorg (Russian abbreviation for 'American trade'), New York firm for trading with the U.S.S.R. formed in 1924 through the fusion of Arcos-America Inc. and the Products Exchange Corporation with Soviet financial participation. Until the transfer of Soviet foreign trade transactions from abroad to the U.S.S.R. in 1935 Amtorg handled the bulk of the Soviet trade with the U.S.A., but since then its role in Soviet-American trade has diminished.

Amu-Dar'ya (ancient **Oxus**), river of Central Asia, rising in the Pamirs and flowing through Tadzhikistan, Turkmenia and Uzbekistan into the Aral Sea; for 200 m. it forms the Soviet-Afghan frontier. Total length 1,577 m. The river is navigable as far as Termez.

Amur: 1. River of eastern Asia (Chinese Heilungkiang, 'Black Dragon River') which is formed by the confluence of the Shilka and the Argun' westward of the Khingan Mountains. Its length, excluding the headwaters, is about 1,700 m., the first 800 m. flowing in a south-easterly direction and forming the frontier between Russia and China; it then flows north-east through the Khingan Mountains into the Sea of Okhotsk at Nikolayevsk. Principal tributaries: Sungari, Ussuri, Zeya and Bureya. The chief towns on the river are Blagoveshchensk, Aygun', Khabarovsk and Komsomol'sk.

2. Oblast of the R.S.F.S.R., situated in the Russian Far East between the Amur River and the Stanovoy Range, largely forested, with rich deposits of gold, coal and non-ferrous metals; it has a monsoon climate. Area 140,400 sq. m.; population (1959) 717,000 (60 per cent urban), mostly Russians and Ukrainians (since 1850). Grain is cultivated and dairy farming carried on, and there are gold- and coal-mining, saw-milling and food industries. Principal towns: Blagoveshchensk (administrative centre) and Svobodnyy. For history *see* FAR EAST; FAR EASTERN REPUBLIC.

Anadyr': 1. Navigable river in the Magadan Oblast of north-eastern Siberia which flows east from the Kolyma Mountains into the Anadyr' Gulf of the Bering Sea. Length 730 m.

2. (until 1930's **Novo-Mariinsk**). Urban settlement at the mouth of the River Anadyr', administrative and cultural centre of the Chukchi National Okrug of the Magadan Oblast. Population (1956) 4,600, mainly Russian. It has a fishing industry.

Analogy, in Soviet criminal law, a principle applied until 1958 according to which acts not explicitly described as crimes in the statutes could nevertheless be regarded as criminal and punished if the court considered them 'socially dangerous.' This principle, later taken over by the Nazis in Germany, was resorted to particularly frequently in 'counter-revolutionary' cases and in support of specific political campaigns of the party, e.g. during the collectivization of agriculture (q.v.). The theoretical validity of the doctrine of analogy and its application were restricted in the 1930's, and it was altogether eliminated in the legal reform (q.v.) of 1958. *See* R. Schlesinger, *Soviet Legal Theory,* 1945; H. J. Berman, *Justice in Russia,* Cambridge, Mass., 1950; G. C. Guins, *Soviet Law and Soviet Society,* The Hague, 1954.

Anarchism played an important part in Russian politics in the

19th and early 20th centuries, and its chief theorists, Bakunin and Kropotkin (qq.v.), were Russians. Anarchist tendencies were strong in the Populist movement, and in the process of political differentiation purely Anarchist organizations emerged towards the end of the 19th century, divided into Individualists, Syndicalists and Communists. Anarchists took an active part in the revolution of 1905 (q.v.) and again in that of 1917, when a Federation of Anarchist Groups was established as a co-ordinating centre. They joined the Soviets (q.v.) and energetically assisted the Bolsheviks in undermining the authority of the Provisional Government and in the seizure of power. Subsequent co-operation proved difficult and during the civil war Anarchists alternated between supporting and opposing the Bolcheviks (*see* MAKHNO). Anarchist organizations were finally suppressed in 1921, following the Kronstadt uprising. *See* T. G. Masaryk, *The Spirit of Russia* (2nd ed.), vol. ii, 1955; E. Yaroslavsky, *History of Anarchism in Russia, s.a.*

Ancient Russia. The 9th–6th centuries B.C. witnessed the rise of the first states on the territory of present-day Russia: in Transcaucasia and in Central Asia (*see* KHOREZM; SOGDIANA). Despite continual threats from their neighbours, the Assyrians and the Persians, and periodical subjugation by them as well as by other conquerors (Alexander the Great, the Romans), these early states were successful in developing distinct cultural and political traditions, which were carried on by their successors in late antiquity and in the Middle Ages (*see also* GEORGIA; ARMENIA). The northern shores of the Black Sea were another early centre of political development, populated successively by Cimmerians and Scythians in loose tribal federations, and in the 7th–6th centuries B.C. by Greek colonists who later fell under the domination of Rome and Byzantium (*see also* CHERSONESUS; CRIMEA). The Black Sea steppes were invaded in the first centuries A.D. both by the Goths from the west, who established a large but ephemeral state, and by the Huns and the Avars from the east. *See* M. Rostovtzeff, *Iranians and Greeks in South Russia*, 1922; G. Vernadsky, *Ancient Russia*, New Haven, 5th printing, 1959, and *The Origins of Russia*, 1959.

Andizhan: 1. Oblast of Uzbekistan situated in the eastern part of the Fergana Valley, traversed by the Fergana circular railway and the Great and Southern Fergana Canals; there are deposits of oil and natural gas. Area (1959) 1,600 sq. m.; population (1959) 768,000 (the highest density of population in any oblast of the U.S.S.R.—480 people per square mile; 23 per cent urban), mostly Uzbeks. It is a major cotton-growing area, producing 40 per cent of all cotton in the Fergana Valley; there is also silk and fruit growing, oil and natural gas extraction, some engineering and varied textile and food industries. Principal towns: Andizhan, Namangan (since 1960). For history *see* FERGANA VALLEY; KOKAND KHANATE.

2. Administrative, economic and cultural centre of the oblast, a railway junction on the Fergana circular line. Population (1959) 129,000 (first in the Fergana Valley; 1939, 85,000). It has engineering and food industries.

Andreyev, Andrey Andreyevich (*b.* 1895), Communist. Born in a peasant family, he worked as a labourer, joined the party in 1914 and soon became a member of the Petrograd party committee. After the Bolshevik seizure of power in 1917 (*see* OCTOBER REVOLUTION) he acted as a party and trade union organizer in the Urals, the Ukraine and Moscow. He was elected to the Central Committee in 1920, was one of its secretaries in 1924–5 and 1935–46, candidate member of the Politburo, 1926–30, and full member, 1932–52, chairman of the Central Control Commission, 1930–1, and of its successor the Committee of Party Control (q.v.), 1939–52. As first secretary of the party committee in North Caucasus, 1927–30, he was responsible for the collectivization of agriculture (q.v.) there, and as chairman of the Council for Collective Farms (q.v.), 1946–53, for the rigorous restoration of the *kolkhoz* system that followed the war, while as Commissar for Agriculture in 1943–6 he implemented the somewhat liberal policy towards the peasants which the leadership had decided to adopt during the war. He was twice in charge of railway transport (1931–5 and 1941–2), both times unsuccessfully. He is now chairman of the Soviet-Chinese Friendship Society.

Andreyev, Leonid Nikolayevich (1871–1919), author. In his plays and stories, which are impressionistic and symbolistic, he deals with abnormal and extreme situations, with God, evil, fate, death, solitude and sex. His writings were widely popular before 1917. Politically he was sympathetic to the revolution of 1905 (q.v.), but was against the 1917 revolution; he died in Finland as an exile.

Andreyev, Nikolay Nikolayevich (*b.* 1880), physicist, member of the Academy of Sciences since 1953. Since 1940 he has been in charge of a laboratory at the Physics Institute of the Academy of Sciences. His many works are mostly concerned with vibration and acoustics, both pure and applied (including architecture and music).

Angara, right affluent of the River Yenisey in Siberia, flowing through Lake Baykal. Length 1,300 m. Large hydro-electric stations are under construction near Irkutsk and Bratsk, both of which are on the Angara.

Angarsk, town in the Irkutsk Oblast (southern Siberia), situated on the River Angara and the Trans-Siberian Railway about 20 m. north-west of Irkutsk. Population (1959) 134,000 (1956, 90,200). It has engineering, building materials, saw-milling and food industries. Angarsk was founded in 1948 and became a town in 1951.

Angren, town in the Tashkent Oblast (Uzbekistan) situated 74 m. east of Tashkent. Population (1959) 55,000. It is the largest centre of coal- (lignite) mining in Central Asia, developed since the Second World War.

Animals, *see* LIVESTOCK; SOIL, FLORA AND FAUNA.

Anti-Party Group, official name applied to the group of leading Communists who, after the death of Stalin, 1953, and the fall of Beria, opposed the concentration of power in Khrushchëv's hands and the policy of partial de-Stalinization advocated by him. The known members of the group were the members of the Central Committee's Presidium—Malenkov, Kaganovich, Molotov, Bulganin, Saburov and Pervukhin—and the candidate member Shepilov. As always during periods of intense struggle for power among the party leadership, protestations of unity were frequent until the 'anti-party group' decided to strike in June 1957. Khrushchëv was out-voted in the Presidium and his removal as first secretary of the party was decided upon. But, apparently with the help of Marshal Zhukov, he managed to convene an emergency plenary session of the Central Committee, to which he successfully appealed. By a 'unanimous' decision (Molotov alone abstaining), Malenkov, Kaganovich, Molotov and Shepilov were expelled from the Presidium and the Central Committee; Saburov was removed from the Presidium, and Pervu-khin demoted to candidate member; Bulganin was reprimanded, but forced to make a humiliating confession and removed from the Presidium in 1958. All members of the group also lost their govern-ment posts and were given minor appointments; the fact that they were not liquidated has been taken as a sign of a genuine break with the practice of the previous two decades, though it would be more appropriate to make a comparison with the treatment of Stalin's opponents during the 1920's and early thirties.

Anti-Religious Propaganda is an important aspect of the activities of the Communist Party and its subsidiary organizations, since the Marxist ideology is incompatible with religion. A special organization for anti-religious propaganda (*see* ATHEISTS, MILITANT) existed 1925-43. Then the establishment of a *modus vivendi* between the Soviet authorities and some of the main Churches and other religious bodies in Russia was followed by a virtual cessation of anti-religious propaganda, such attacks as did continue being political rather than anti-religious. It was again revived after Stalin's death in a rather mild and inoffensive manner, but since 1956 has become increasingly persistent and vicious; in 1959 a new anti-religious journal, entitled *Science and Religion*, was founded.

Anti-Semitism in Russia was not widespread before 1917, despite the general belief to the contrary. An exception were the former Polish provinces in the west and south of the country (the so-called Pale of Settlement), where there was a tradition of anti-Semitism both in the towns and (particularly in the Ukraine) in the countryside which went back to the Polish period. On the official level, however, Jews by religion were legally discriminated against in certain fields (e.g. place of residence, ownership of land, education, state service), and, especially during the generally reactionary periods such as the reigns of Nicholas I, Alexander III and Nicholas II (qq.v.) until the revolution of 1905 (q.v.), there was a strong tendency to divert popular discontent into anti-Semitic channels. This attitude was responsible for the repeated waves of pogroms in the Pale of Settle-ment from the early 1880's until the revolution of 1905, which scandalized the whole civilized world and led, among other things, to considerable Russian Jewish emigration, especially to America. The infamous forgery known as the Protocols of the Elders of Zion was perpetrated by semi-official Russian circles, and during the 1905 revolution proto-Fascist anti-Semitic organizations colloquially known as the Black Hundred (q.v.), which equated Jews with revolutionaries, were formed with the blessing of the court. The Beylis case of 1911-13, in which a Jewish workman was unjustly accused of ritual murder and barely acquitted, was the Russian equivalent of the French Dreyfus case. The general licence and lawlessness of the civil war led to the worst wave of pogroms on territories in the south held by the Whites, and especially by the forces of the Ukrainian Directory (q.v.) under Petlyura.

The Soviet Government has formally always considered anti-Semitism a relic of the past, and active anti-Semitism is treated as a crime. On the popular level an increase of anti-Semitism was noticeable towards the end of the 1920's because of the prevalence of Jews among the Communist officials. Anti-Semitism reappeared in official circles at the time of the Great Purge (q.v.), when practically all Jews disappeared from leading positions in the party and government apparatus, and from then onwards increased continuously until Stalin's death; it was aided in its impact on the popular mind by the Nazi propaganda in the occupied territories during the war. Yiddish language schools were closed in 1938. The campaign against 'rootless cosmopolitans' launched in 1949 was largely an anti-Semitic campaign, during which all prominent Jewish writers and many scholars were arrested and subsequently shot. The famous Jewish Theatre in Moscow, and all Yiddish newspapers but one, were suppressed. The anti-Semitic policy culminated in the so-called Doctors' Plot (q.v.) in 1952, when the situation was so tense that pogroms reappeared and there were strong rumours of the impending deportation to Siberia of all Jews. Stalin's death brought about a relaxation and Jewish intellectuals were posthumously rehabilitated, but both official and popular anti-Semitism still exist. *See also* Jews. *See* E. E. Cohen (ed.), *The New Red Anti-Semitism*, Boston, Mass., 1953; 'Jews in the Soviet Union,' *New Leader*, Sept. 1959; F. Fejtö, *Les Juifs et l'anti-semitisme dans les pays communistes*, Paris, 1960.

Anti-Soviet Bloc of Rightists and Trotskiyites, alleged conspiracy led by Bukharin and Rykov, inspired by Trotskiy from abroad, which was used as an excuse for the third Show Trial of the Great Purge (q.v.) which took place in March 1938. Among the accused were Bukharin, Rykov, Yagoda (qq.v.), Krestinskiy—former member of the Politburo and secretary of the party's Central Committee —and Rakovskiy, a prominent leader of the Comintern and former head of the Ukrainian Soviet Government. They were accused of innumerable crimes, including espionage for Germany and Japan, plans to assassinate Lenin in 1918 and Stalin in the 1930's, and the actual murder of Kirov, Kuybyshev and Gor'kiy; they all 'confessed,' although Krestinskiy took the unprecedented step of withdrawing in court his earlier 'confession,' while Bukharin admitted 'counter-revolutionary' activities but rejected charges of any criminal ones. It was at this trial that Vyshinskiy, as public prosecutor, sank to the lowest depths of slander. The majority of the accused were shot. In the process of de-Stalinization since the 20th party congress (q.v.) the criminal charges have been dropped, and the reputations of some of the accused completely rehabilitated. See *Report of the Court Proceedings* (Eng. ed.), Moscow, 1938.

Anti-Soviet Trotskiyite Centre, alleged conspiracy headed by Pyatakov, Radek and Sokol'nikov (qq.v.) and inspired by Trotskiy from abroad, which served as the excuse for the second Show Trial of the Great Purge (q.v.) which took place in January 1937. Most of the accused were shot, though Radek and Sokol'nikov received ten-year prison sentences. See *Report of the Court Proceedings* (Eng. ed.), Moscow, 1937.

Antonov-Ovseyenko, Vladimir Aleksandrovich (1884–1939), revolutionary who joined the Social-Democratic Labour Party in 1903, adhering to its Menshevik faction. He took an active part in organizing mutinies in army units during the 1905 revolution, and later emigrated. During the First World War he supported Trotskiy's centrist position and returned to Russia after the February 1917 revolution; he then joined the Mezhrayontsy (q.v.) group, and together with it the Bolshevik Party. Antonov-Ovseyenko was one of the chief organizers of the October coup, and personally conducted the seizure of the Winter Palace and the arrest of the Provisional Government. He joined the first Soviet Government as one of the three men responsible for military and naval affairs; during the civil war he commanded various army groups, and afterwards became the head of the Political Administration of the Red Army. As a leading Trotskiyite he was dismissed from this post after the defeat of Trotskiy in 1925, and became Soviet Ambassador in Czechoslovakia. He was the Soviet Government's representative in Spain during the Spanish Civil War, and on his return to Russia disappeared during the Great Purge (q.v.). His reputation was rehabilitated in 1956.

Antonov Uprising, anti-Communist peasant movement in the Tambov province, 1919–21. The leader, Antonov, had been a Socialist Revolutionary since 1905, and in 1917 returned from banishment and became chief of the district militia. The uprising was joined by 50,000 peasants and deserters from the Red Army. The Socialist Revolutionary party provided the political leadership through the Unions of Toiling Peasantry headed by the Provincial Committee, which exercised civil authority. Government troops under Tukhachevskiy (q.v.) defeated the movement several times, but its final breakdown was a result of the New Economic Policy (q.v.).

Antony (lay name **Khrapovitskiy, Aleksey Pavlovich**) (1864–1934), metropolitan of the Russian Orthodox Church, theologian and philosopher, member of the Council of State from 1906. He was a leading advocate of the restoration of the Patriarchate and a staunch conservative and monarchist in politics. He emigrated after the civil war and in the 1920's became the head of the Russian Church administration in exile. In philosophy he was one of the precursors of modern Personalism, and his work, *Psychological Data in Favour of the Freedom of Will and Moral Responsibility,* was a vigorous attack on determinism.

Anuchin, Dmitriy Nikolayevich (1843–1923), anthropologist, geographer and liberal publicist, professor at Moscow University. He organized in Moscow an anthropological exhibition in 1879, and an all-Russian geographical exhibition in 1892, converting them both into permanent museums. He founded, 1894, and edited the leading geographical journal in Russia, *Zemlevedeniye.* Most outstanding geographers of the next generation were Anuchin's pupils. He belonged to the group of Moscow professors which directed the liberal newspaper *Russkiye Vedemosti*, and himself frequently wrote in it. After 1917 he took a prominent part in the Local Studies movement, and from 1919 co-operated with the Soviet authorities.

Anzhero-Sudzhensk, town in the Kemerovo Oblast (southern Siberia), about 45 m. north of Kemerovo, on the northern edge of the Kuznetsk coal-mining basin and on the Trans-Siberian Railway. Population (1959) 116,000 (1913, 15,000; 1936, 100,000; 1939, 69,000). It is a major coal-mining centre and has mining equipment and pharmaceutical industries. Founded in 1896, it became a town in the 1930's.

'**Apparatchiki**,' colloquial term for officials in the party, government, trade union, etc., apparatus. In fact *apparatchiki* in any field belong to one huge apparatus operated by the party authorities, and all important posts are filled by the cadres (q.v.) departments of the party committees (*see also* NOMENCLATURE). The term has a somewhat contemptuous connotation. The *apparatchiki* have been vividly depicted in Soviet literature, especially since Stalin's death, e.g. by Dudintsev (q.v.) in *Not by Bread Alone*.

April Theses, policy statement made by Lenin upon his return to Russia in April 1917 with the intention of directing the Bolshevik Party towards the seizure of power. Earlier the party leadership (Kamenev and Stalin) had taken up a position of conditional support for the Provisional Government. With his theses Lenin carried the bulk of the party with him, although an important section, including Kamenev, Zinov'yev and Rykov, remained opposed both to a seizure of power and to a one-party government, believing that this would have little chance of survival. *See* L. Schapiro, *The Communist Party of the Soviet Union*, 1960.

Apsheron, peninsula in the Caspian Sea at the eastern end of the Caucasus Mountains. The city of Baku and the large Baku oilfields are situated here.

Arakcheyev, Count Aleksey Andreyevich (1769–1834), favourite of Alexander I. He became War Minister in 1808. His name has become the symbol of intolerable despotism as a result of his reactionary internal policy.

Aral Sea, second largest stretch of inland water (after the Caspian Sea) in Asia, situated partly in the north of Uzbekistan and partly in Kazakhstan. Length 270 m.; breadth 165 m.; greatest depth 220 ft. The rivers Amu-Dar'ya and Syr-Dar'ya flow into the sea, which has no outlet but loses much water through evaporation. There are a number of small islands, mostly towards the eastern shore. The Aral Sea is believed to have formed, at one time, part of the Caspian Sea.

Arbitration. The present system of State arbitration was introduced in 1931, replacing earlier arrangements of 1922. Organs of State arbitration are attached to councils of ministers of all levels and to executive committees of the oblast and kray soviets, and subordinated to them. Their function is to resolve disputes relating to goods and services between institutions, enterprises and organizations of the 'socialized sector' of the economy. However, disputes involving *kolkhozes* and disputes between units belonging to the same ministry or other central institution are outside the jurisdiction of the State arbitration; in the latter case departmental arbitration takes place. The guiding principle of arbitration is furthering the fulfilment of the State economic plans. There is also a Foreign Trade Arbitration Commission (established 1932) for resolving disputes between Soviet economic organizations and foreign firms, and a Marine Arbitration Commission (established 1930), both attached to the All-Union Chamber of Commerce. *See* V. Gsovski and K. Grzybowski (eds.), *Government, Law and Courts in the Soviet Union and Eastern Europe*, vol. i, 1959.

Arbuzov, Aleksandr Yerminingel'dovich (*b.* 1877), chemist. Educated at Kazan' University, he has been professor there since 1911, member of the Academy of Sciences since 1942 and member of its Presidium, and head of the Kazan' branch of the academy since its establishment in 1945. Arbuzov is the author of many works on organic phosphorus compounds, industrial chemistry and the history of chemistry, and is the present head of the Kazan' chemical school.

Archangel (Archangel'sk): 1. Oblast of the R.S.F.S.R. in the north of European Russia, adjacent to the White, Barents and Kara Seas of the Arctic Ocean and including the islands in these seas. Area 228,600 sq. m. It is predominantly lowland, covered by coniferous forests and traversed by the Northern Dvina and the Pechora rivers. Population (1959) 1,278,000 (53 per cent urban), Russian (since 11th century) and some Nenets in the Nenets National Okrug. There are lumbering, wood-processing and fishing industries, and dairy cattle are raised (Kholmogory breed). Principal towns: Archangel, Severodvinsk and Kotlas; the famous Solovetskiy Monastery is situated on islands in the White Sea. The territory belonged to Novgorod until 1478, then to Muscovy. The area has been one of banishment since the 17th century, and of concentration camps from the 1920's to the mid 1950's.

2. Administrative, economic and cultural centre of the oblast, situated in the Northern Dvina delta 30 m. from the White Sea, the largest saw-milling centre and timber port of the U.S.S.R.; the port is open to navigation from May to October. Population (1959) 256,000 (1897, 21,000; 1917, 48,000; 1939, 251,000). Archangel was built around a 12th-century monastery in 1583 following the establishment of Anglo-Muscovite trade, and until the building of St Petersburg it held the monopoly of Muscovite foreign trade. It was an administrative centre of the northern territories of European Russia from 1702. Allied troops, predominantly British, occupied Archangel in 1918–19, and it was the seat of an anti-Bolshevik Government that held out until February 1920. During both world wars it was a major supply port for allied goods.

Architecture. Since medieval Russia was essentially a theocentric society, a knowledge of ecclesiastical architecture (*see* next article) is essential for understanding the dominant architectural trends up to the end of the 17th century. The earliest examples of secular architecture in stone date from the 15th century (*see* KREMLIN). These, together with other examples of domestic buildings from the 16th and 17th centuries, are all derived from wooden forms which continued to predominate. These houses and palaces were of no regular shape and larger buildings in fact consisted of separate 'units' joined together by means of stairways and covered passages. The agglomeration of roofs of various shapes and sizes gave the desired effect of picturesque asymmetry. The 17th century saw the increased use of baroque motifs (*see under* KREMLIN). Under Peter I this type of building ceased, although the old traditions of wooden architecture lived on in the provinces. For many years building in stone was permitted only in the new capital, St Petersburg, where buildings of a purely Western character were erected. Although the architecture of the Russian Empire followed all the trends and fashions prevalent in the West, it cannot be dismissed as being wholly derivative since certain features clearly spring, if only subconsciously, from the older, native traditions. These can be summarized as follows: an acute sense of the dramatic; the 'sculptural' treatment of a building as a three-dimensional entity; an uncommon genius for creating architectural *ensembles*. The Russian monarchs up to and including Nicholas I were all avid builders, and their personal tastes are clearly reflected in the buildings erected under them. The reign of Elizabeth (q.v.) is marked by the exuberant rococo-baroque structures of Rastrelli (q.v.). The accession of Catherine II (q.v.) brought a sudden reaction in favour of a simpler, more majestic Palladian style. Although Catherine's favourite architects were all foreigners (Vallin de la Mothe, Velten, Rinaldi, Cameron and, above all, Quarenghi), the three great Russian architects of her reign, Bazhenov, Kazakov and Starov (qq.v.), exerted untold influence. The distinctively Russian classical style evolved by these architects attained a glorious climax under Alexander I (q.v.), who was an insatiable builder and in whose reign were completed the great *ensembles* that make St Petersburg one of the outstanding architectural treasure-houses of the world. The most notable architects of the Alexandrian epoch were Zakharov, de Thomon, Stasov and, above all, Rossi (qq.v.), and also, for the excellent reconstruction work carried out in Moscow after 1812, Beauvais and Giliardi. The reign of Nicholas I brought a visible decline in standards of architectural taste. The reconstruction of the Winter Palace and the work of Thon (*see* ARCHITECTURE, ECCLESIASTICAL; KREMLIN) testify to an ever-growing eclecticism. The second half of the 19th century brought an even further decline in architectural taste. The pseudo-Russian style (cf. the Gothic Revival in the West), being supported by the Slavophiles (q.v.), emerged triumphant and produced such monstrosities as the Historical Museum and the Trading Rows on the Red Square, Moscow. At the turn of the century some interesting houses in the 'art nouveau' style were built by Shekhtel' and Lidval'. At this period it is interesting to note the youthful works of Shchusev (q.v.), Shchuko, Gel'freykh, Fomin and others working in the traditions of Russian Classicism or the Italian Renaissance, for subsequently these architects were to become the approved exponents of architectural Socialist Realism (q.v.).

The events of 1917 brought with them a fever of revolutionary activity in the arts. Like Mayakovskiy and Meyerhold (qq.v.), progressive young architects hailed the Proletarian Revolution as 'their' revolution and went on to proclaim what shape and form architecture should take in the new socialist society, namely that it should be a 'constructivist' technique expressing the forms and functions of the Machine Age and that all forms deriving from the past should be cast aside. There was a marked enthusiasm for dynamic forms based on the circle and the spiral. Projects appeared for 'theatres like electric dynamos, clubs like water turbines.' Tatlin planned a building of the Communist International in the form of a gigantic diminishing steel spiral within which were to be three glass geometric figures—congress rooms—rotating once a year, once a week, once a day according to the different councils that were to meet there. It is regrettable that the various rival architects' organizations (ARU, ASNOVA, SASS, WOPRA) devoted so much time and energy to purely dogmatic squabbles, but nevertheless some extremely interesting work was done by them, notably the Zuyev Communes Club in Moscow (Melnikov, Ginsburg and Barshch) and the Urals Polytechnic at Sverdlovsk (Lubetkin and Berthold). By the end of the 1920's Moscow had become a world centre for the most progressive trends of 20th-century architecture. The international competition for the proposed Palace of the Soviets in 1930 (see next article) attracted projects from all over the world and included entries by Le Corbusier, Gropius and even a Fascist architect, Brazini. The most interesting of the Russian entries was by Blum, Lubetkin and Sigalin. The winning project by Iofan has never been realized. Meanwhile it had become increasingly obvious that Constructivism appealed to the tastes neither of the proletariat nor of the party leaders. The early thirties saw the gradual introduction of the doctrine of Socialist Realism, which meant the death of all 'formalistic, decadent' experimentation in art. A decree of the Central Committee of the party in 1934 abolished individual architects' organizations and instituted a unified Union of Soviet Architects (under party control), and also the Academy of Architecture of the U.S.S.R. It was prescribed that buildings should be 'national in form and socialist in content.' Russian classicism was proposed as a style particularly worthy of imitation. Nevertheless the contemporary 'Western' idiom died slowly. In the mid thirties it was still possible to erect such buildings as the theatre on Mayakovskiy Square, Moscow (Shchusev), and the theatre at Rostov-on-Don (Shchuko and Gel'freykh), which, though by no means constructivist, are still predominantly American in feeling. In 1935 the government and the Central Committee passed a resolution for the 'reconstruction' of Moscow, which has resulted in much of the city changing its character completely. The new widened streets are lined with tall buildings, soulless in character, often encrusted with meaningless ornaments of classical or 'national' derivation. The stations of the Moscow Metro are notorious examples of Socialist Realism. They are lavishly treated with bronze, marble and mosaic and repeat classical and 17th-century motifs. After the last war a number of skyscrapers (*vysotnyye zdaniya*) were erected in Moscow, evocative in their outline of the towers of the Kremlin. Of these the new university (Rudnev, Cherny-shev, Abrosimov and Khryakov) is the most notable. The towers and spires of these buildings are richly decorated, true to 17th-century traditions. Of the reconstruction work carried out since the war, that of Simbirtsev at Stalingrad is particularly impressive. In recent years there appears to have been a relaxation of the canons of Classicism and nationalism and the growing number of buildings of a simpler, more functional nature should be watched with interest (*see* VLASOV).

See 'The Russian Scene,' *Architectural Review*, April 1932; C. G. E. Bunt, *Russian Art: From Scyths to Soviets*, 1947; Tamara Talbot Rice, *Russian Art*, 1949; Academy of Sciences of U.S.S.R., *Istoriya russkogo iskusstva*, Moscow, 1953–9; G. H. Hamilton, *The Art and Architecture of Russia*, 1954; P. Willen, 'New Era in Soviet Architecture?', *Problems of Communism*, vol. v, No. 4, July–Aug. 1956.

Architecture, Ecclesiastical. The architecture of pagan Russia was entirely in wood. The art of building in stone and brick came to Russia, together with its religion, from Byzantium. The Russians first learnt the arts of bricklaying and stone-masonry from Greek church builders, and consequently for centuries these arts were reserved almost exclusively for church use. The earliest churches of Kiev were almost certainly built by Greek architects. The oldest of them, the Tithes Church (Desyatinnaya Tserkov'), was destroyed by the Tatars and survives only in its foundations which show us a typically Byzantine ground-plan. Yaroslav's Cathedral of St Sophia, 1037, still survives, although most of its exterior is obscured by additions and encrustations in a heavy, provincial baroque. This was the largest and finest of the churches of ancient Russia. In plan it is a Greek cross set within a square with arcaded galleries filling in the spaces between the arms of the cross. It can thus be considered as in the tradition of the Church of the Apostles at Constantinople and St Mark's, Venice. The large central dome was surrounded by eight smaller ones (eleven according to some authorities). The church is built of brick with much blind arcading and with layers of stone-work; it is clearly a purely Byzantine work, typical of the period. The church of the same name at Novgorod, 1045–52, is based on it, but is much simpler in plan, while its proportions are narrower and more massive. It is built entirely in stone and is almost certainly the work exclusively of Russian builders. Its fortress-like appearance, its plain, unadorned white stone walls with their small narrow windows, its tower-like domes, all mark the beginning of the great tradition of church building that flourished in Pskov and Novgorod. The vast majority of Russian medieval churches were built to a much simpler plan than the two churches described above. Basically they were square with four piers (rarely columns) supporting the dome and with three apses projecting from the east end. Usually there was only one dome. The most impressive examples of medieval Russian archi-tecture are to be found in the 12th-century churches in the town of Vladimir. They are notable for the grace of their proportions and for the wealth of sculptured ornamentation lavished on their exteriors. (It must, of course, be remembered that sculpture was strictly banned from church interiors by the canons of the Orthodox Church.) Of these churches the largest was the Cathedral of the Dormition (Uspenskiy Sobor), built as a single-domed church in 1158 and considerably enlarged in 1189 when four corner domes were added. This church with its classical five-domed scheme came to be held in great veneration and served as a model for many other churches, notably the cathedral of the same dedication in the Moscow Kremlin (q.v.). The Church of the Intercession on the River Nerl' and the Cathedral of St Dimitriy at Vladimir are two other superb examples of this school of church building, the latter being particularly notable for its relief sculptures. It will be noted that the medieval Russian towns each contained a number of small 'cathedrals' (*sobory*). This did not mean that there was a corresponding number of bishops. The institution of the cathedral chapter does not exist in the Orthodox Church, and in theory every church should contain a bishop's throne in the centre of the apse facing the congregation from behind the altar. The term *sobor* means a collegiate church rather than a cathedral.

Although the earliest surviving examples date back only to the 16th century, it can be presumed that the traditions of wooden church buildings are of great antiquity, since wood has always been the favourite building material in Russia. The wooden churches bear no resemblance at all to the buildings described above. They are, basically, towers with tall, tent-shaped roofs crowned with small, lantern-like domes. The height and outline of the building bear no relation to the shape of the interior, which is box-like with a comparatively low, flat ceiling. It was most probably in such churches that the tall, five-tiered iconostasis grew up, shutting the sanctuary off completely from the body of the church. The fashion for the tall iconostasis spread from Russia to the whole of the Orthodox world. Wooden churches of this type enjoyed an enormous popularity in medieval Russia, and, with the new impetus given to stone-masonry in 15th-century Moscow (*see* KREMLIN), it is not surprising to see their basic forms translated into stone. The first of these stone 'tower' churches is the startlingly magnificent Ascension at Kolomenskoye near Moscow, built in 1532 to mark the birth of the young prince later to be known as Ivan the Terrible. This votive church, together with the church of St John the Baptist in the neighbouring village of D'yakovo (commemorating Ivan's coronation in 1547), served as the precursor of the famous Cathedral of St Basil the Blessed—or to give its correct name, the Cathedral of the Intercession on the Moat—in Moscow's Red Square. This fantastic church, built to commemorate the fall of Kazan' in 1552, consists of eight small 'tower' churches, each crowned with a dome, arranged symmetrically round a larger, dominating 'tent-shaped' tower. The whole, as at Kolomenskoye, is raised on a podium. It was built in red brick with its wealth of ornamentation in white stone. The present gaudy colouring was added in the 17th century. This church gives us the key to the aesthetic ideals of 16th- and 17th-century Muscovy. Both churches and palaces followed basically the same idea, namely a number of separate units of different sizes and outlines joined together by means of passages, galleries and stairways. The desire was to create in each building a kremlin or a fortress-monastery in miniature. The Patriarch Nikon (q.v.), as part of his campaign for liturgical reform, decreed that this type of church building should cease and that churches should be built according to the classical five-domed pattern of the Cathedral of the Dormition. The free adaptation and colourful use of Renaissance and baroque decorative motifs in 17th-century Moscow is of great interest. This tendency culminated at the end of the century in the style known as the Muscovite or Naryshkin Baroque. The best example of the churches of early St Petersburg is the Cathedral of Sts Peter and Paul, burial place of the emperors, built by the Italian Trezzini between 1712 and 1733. This is a 'hall' church completely Western in form with a very tall, slender, needle-like spire. This church contains a most interesting iconostasis of carved wood, gilt, by Zarudnyy. This revolutionary work, with its sculptured figures and amazingly wide central opening, gives a vivid idea of Peter the Great's plans for 'westernizing' the Church. An impressive synthesis of Western forms and local traditions was achieved in the magnificent mid-18th century churches of Ukhtomskiy and Rastrelli (q.v.), especially in the latter's Smol'nyy Monastery. The classical churches of Kazakov and Bazhenov (q.v.) are also of great interest. Starov's (q.v.) Cathedral of the Trinity, 1778–90, in the St Alexander Nevskiy Monastery, Leningrad, is a very fine example of a typical 'Counter-Reformation' church, conceived in the classical idiom. Voronikhin's famous Kazan' Cathedral, 1801–11, in Leningrad (now a 'Museum of Religion and Atheism') is also completely Western and classical in conception, although the asymmetrical placing of its semicircular colonnade may be regarded as a Russian feature. The last of the great churches of this classical tradition is Monferrand's St Isaac's Cathedral, 1817–57, in Leningrad, a building reminiscent of Soufflot's Panthéon, sumptuously if somewhat tastelessly decorated. Under Nicholas I there was a revival of national forms and traditions, the chief exponent of which was the architect Thon (1794–1881), whose gigantic Church of Christ the Saviour, Moscow, was demolished in 1930 to make room for the proposed Palace of the Soviets. At the beginning of this century Shchusev (q.v.) built several interesting churches inspired by the traditions of Novgorod and Pskov.

See D. R. Buxton, *Medieval Russian Architecture*, 1934; C. G. E. Bunt, *Russian Art: From Scyths to Soviets*, 1947; Tamara Talbot Rice, *Russian Art*, 1949; S. H. Cross, *Medieval Russian Churches*, Cambridge, Mass., 1949; Academy of Sciences of U.S.S.R., *Istoriya russkogo iskusstva*, Moscow, 1953–9; G. H. Hamilton, *The Art and Architecture of Russia*, 1954; A. Voyce, *The Moscow Kremlin*, 1955.

Area and Boundaries. The total area of the U.S.S.R. is approximately 8·6 million square miles. In the south Russia reaches a latitude of 35° N., while its northernmost point, 80° N., is well within the Arctic circle. It extends from longitude 20° E. to 170° W. The country is bounded on the west by Norway, Finland, the Baltic, Poland, Czechoslovakia, Hungary and Rumania; on the south by the Black Sea, Turkey, Persia, Afghanistan, China and Mongolia; on the east by the Pacific Ocean; and on the north by the Arctic Ocean. In the north-east the Bering Straits (35 m. in width) separate Russia from Alaska.

Arenskiy, Antoniy Stepanovich (1861–1906), prolific composer. He studied, 1879–82, with Rimsky-Korsakov at the St Petersburg Conservatory and was appointed professor of harmony and counterpoint at Moscow Conservatory in 1882. In 1894 he was recommended by Balakirev for the directorship of the Imperial Chapel, St Petersburg. Works comprise three operas: *A Dream on the Volga*, produced 1890; *Raphael*, produced 1894; and *Nal and Damayanti*, 1899; the ballet *Egyptian Night*; two symphonies; piano concerto; violin concerto; choral music; chamber music, including a piano trio in D minor; much piano music and songs. Although Arenskiy took a keen interest in folk music, his compositions are not particularly nationalistic, and strongly resemble those of Tchaikovsky, whose work he admired and performed. *See* V. M. Belaiev, 'Arensky,' *Cobbett's Cyclopedic Survey of Chamber Music*, 1929.

Argun', river which rises in the Khingan Mountains (western Manchuria) and flows north-north-east; it constitutes the frontier between Russia and China, and joins the Shilka to form the Amur. Length 440 m.

Arkhangel'skiy, Andrey Dmitriyevich (1879–1940), geologist, professor of Moscow University, member of the Academy of Sciences from 1929 and director of its Geological Institute from 1934. His many works were chiefly concerned with the stratigraphy and tectonics of European Russia and Central Asia, and with the study of mineral deposits, including the Kursk Magnetic Anomaly.

Armavir, town in the Krasnodar Kray (Northern Caucasus), on the River Kuban'. Population (1959) 111,000 (1897, 6,000; 1914, 44,000; 1926, 75,000; 1939, 84,000). It is the second largest economic centre of the kray, with diverse food and engineering industries, and an important railway junction. Founded in 1848 as an Armenian colony, it became a town in 1915 and was an important trade centre until 1930.

Armed Forces were estimated in 1959 to number 3,900,000 (2·3 million in the army, 0·5 in the navy, 0·7 in the air force and 0·35 security, border and labour troops). Khrushchëv stated at the beginning of 1960 that the armed forces numbered 3,623,000 men (apparently omitting the security troops) and that over the next two years they were to be reduced by 1·2 million (the Soviet armed forces stood at just over 5 million at the end of the war in 1945, and at 5·7 million in 1955). All armed forces are administered by the Ministry of Defence (since 1953), but the structure of administration and command is rather complicated, combining three different principles: general administration tends to be territorial (through Military Districts, fleets, etc.); technical training and ordnance are dealt with by branches, e.g. artillery, tanks, aviation; while operational command is built according to specific purposes, e.g. air defence. The Ministry of Defence is divided into Chief Administrations (departments) of all three kinds; there is also a Political Administration, which functions as a department of the party's Central Committee and has its representatives in all formations and units (see COMMISSAR), and the Chief Administration of Counter-Intelligence whose main task is to guard against political disaffection among the troops: it functions as a department of the K.G.B. (q.v.).

Since the establishment of the Soviet regime the armed forces have as a rule been headed by politicians rather than professional servicemen: Trotskiy (1918–24), Frunze (1924–5), Voroshilov (1925–40), Stalin (1941–7), Bulganin (1947–9 and 1953–5). Professional soldiers appointed to head the armed forces, Marshals Timoshenko (1940–1), Vasilevskiy (1949–53)—neither having responsibility for the navy—Zhukov (1955–7) and Malinovskiy (since 1957), have so far held their offices for a short time and apparently had no political ambitions with the exception of Marshal Zhukov (q.v.). Both in the official and popular esteem, the armed forces have held a higher place since 1917 (first as the Red Army of the civil war, then as the victors of the Second World War) than at any time since the early 19th century. Their political role has usually been small, with two exceptions. During the Second World War the political atmosphere was relaxed under pressure from the armed forces; and after Stalin's death they played an important part in the downfall of Beria (q.v.), with its consequent reduction in the powers of the security organs (q.v.), and in the defeat of the 'anti-party group' (q.v.) in 1957, after which for a few months—until Zhukov's fall—they emerged as a possible contender for power in the country with the Communist Party apparatus. *See also* AIRBORNE TROOPS; AIR DEFENCE FORCES; AIR FORCE; ARMY; MILITARY SERVICE; NAVY; NUCLEAR WEAPONS; OFFICERS; ROCKETS. *See* R. L. Garthoff, *How Russia Makes War*, 1954, and *Soviet Strategy in the Nuclear Age*, 1958; Z. Brzezinski (ed.), *Political Controls in the Soviet Army*, New York, 1954; H. S. Dinerstein, *War and the Soviet Union*, Santa Monica, California, 1958.

Armenia (Armenian **Hayastan**): 1. In the wider sense that territory which formed the core of the Armenian state in the past and which was to a considerable extent inhabited by Armenians until the end of the 19th century. It comprises the Armenian Republic of the U.S.S.R. and adjacent parts of Soviet Azerbaydzhan (Karabakh, Nakhichevan'), the north-eastern provinces of Turkey and the western parts of Persian Azerbaydzhan.

2. In the narrower sense, a Union Republic of the U.S.S.R., a mountainous region with a dry continental climate which lies in the south of central Transcaucasia; there are large deposits of copper and various mineral building materials. Area 11,600 sq. m.; population (1959) 1,763,000 (50 per cent urban), mostly Armenians (88 per cent), also Azerbaydzhanis (6 per cent), Russians and Kurds. There are copper, chemical, engineering, food and textile industries; viniculture, horticulture and sericulture are carried on, cotton and wheat cultivated and dairy cattle raised. On the River Razdan (which flows from the mountain lake Sevan) a cascade of hydro-electric stations is being constructed. Principal towns: Yerevan (capital) and Leninakan.

In antiquity Armenia constituted part of the Urartu state, and was later conquered successively by the Assyrians, Medes, Persians and by Alexander the Great. In 189 B.C. it regained its independence and became a powerful Hellenistic state under the dynasty of Artashesids, but through a series of defeats in battle was forced to become a Roman (later joint Roman-Parthian) protectorate. Christianity was introduced as the religion of the state in 301 under a new dynasty of Arshakids (A.D. 63–428). Armenia was divided between Persia and Byzantium in 387; in 628 the whole country became a vassal of Byzantium and in 652 of the Arabs, who soon transformed it into a province. It regained independence and prosperity under the third dynasty, Bagratids (886–1045), but new conquests followed: by Byzantium, Seljuk Turks, Mongols and Timur (1386–1402) and other Turkic invaders. The country was the scene of struggle between the Ottoman Empire and Persia in the 17th–18th centuries, and its north-eastern part was ceded by Persia to Russia in 1828, becoming a Russian province. Following the Bolshevik seizure of power in 1917, Russian Armenia joined the anti-Bolshevik Transcaucasian Federation (q.v.). When this disintegrated an independent Armenia was established dominated by the Dashnaktsutyun (q.v.) party. But existence was precarious because of the difficult international situation (Turkish invasion, disputes and war with Georgia and Azerbaydzhan), and in 1920 it was occupied by the Red Army and transformed into a Soviet republic, which was included in the Transcaucasian Federal Republic and the U.S.S.R. in 1922. With the abolition in 1936 of the Transcaucasian Federal Republic Armenia became a Union Republic of the U.S.S.R. Anti-Bolshevik guerrilla warfare in Armenia did not cease until 1923, and in more recent years there have been frequent complaints by the authorities of 'nationalist deviations' in the republic. See J. de Morgan, *The History of the Armenian People*, New York, 1949; F. Kazemzadeh, *The Struggle for Transcaucasia*, New York, 1951; R. Pipes, *The Formation of the Soviet Union*, Cambridge, Mass., 1954; M. Shaginyan, *Journey Through Soviet Armenia*, Moscow, 1954.

Armenians (Armenian **Hay**) number approximately 3,600,000, of whom 1·6 million live in the Armenian Union Republic, 1·2 million in other parts of the U.S.S.R. (the largest colonies being in Moscow, Baku, Tiflis, Rostov-on-Don and Armavir) and the remainder in many countries of Asia, Europe and America. The Armenian language forms an independent branch of the Indo-European family. St Gregory the Illuminator christianized the Armenians in the 3rd century A.D.; the majority of them now adhere to the Armenian Gregorian Church (whose head resides in the monastery of Echmiadzin, q.v.), and a small minority to the Armenian Catholic and the Armenian Protestant Churches. The bulk of the Armenians lived in the north-east provinces of the Ottoman Empire until the end of the 19th century, but the massacres of 1894–1922—resulting in the loss of over a million lives—led to the present concentration of the Armenian population in Transcaucasia. Armenians have played an important part in the economic, political and cultural life of Russia during the 19th and 20th centuries (*see* LORIS-MELIKOV; MIKOYAN; ORBELI; SHAUMYAN). *See also* BAGRATIDS. See J. de Morgan, *The History of the Armenian People*, New York, 1949; *Armenian Review*, Boston, Mass., 1948 ff.

Army. The ground forces were estimated in 1959 to number about

2,350,000 men, not counting frontier, internal security and labour troops (which were estimated at 350,000). The Chief Administration of ground forces in the Ministry of Defence is headed by the commander-in-chief of ground forces (at present Marshal A. A. Grechko), who is *ex officio* a First Deputy Minister of Defence. He does not, however, exercise operational command over the field forces, but is responsible for training, the development of tactical doctrine, and ordnance of the infantry and other ground forces except artillery (q.v.) and the tank troops, which have Chief Administrations of their own. For administrative and operational purposes the ground forces stationed on the territory of the Soviet Union are organized into eighteen Military Districts whose commanders are directly subordinate to the Ministry of Defence. Soviet troops in Poland and Hungary are under the command of the commander-in-chief of the Warsaw Pact forces (*see* Konev), while Soviet troops in Germany form the group of forces in Germany under a separate command. Military Districts situated near the frontiers of the U.S.S.R. are in case of war transformed into Army Groups ('fronts'); together with the Moscow Military District they are kept permanently on the alert. The weapons and equipment of the Soviet ground forces are considered by Western experts as adequate and simple in operation and maintenance, though lacking in comfort.

The army, and especially the infantry, has traditionally been considered the senior branch of the armed forces. The modern Russian army was created by Peter the Great (with the help of foreign—especially British—experts such as the generals Bruce and Gordon), who was himself a notable military thinker. After destroying the military power of Sweden in the Great Northern War, the Russian Army was almost invariably victorious throughout the 18th century: against Turkey, Prussia (in the Seven Years War) and the armies of revolutionary France in Italy. The military doctrine and training were systematically improved, and a distinct Russian school of military thought and practice was developed by outstanding military leaders: Rumyantsev and the greatest Russian military genius Suvorov (q.v.), who is said never to have suffered a defeat in battle. After Suvorov's death, this 18th-century tradition, based on attention to the intellectual, moral and physical qualities of the individual soldier, was discarded and replaced by a mechanical adoption of the formalistic Prussian military doctrine and regulations. Suvorov's principles were to some extent revived and suitably adapted under the pressure of circumstances by Kutuzov (q.v.) during the Patriotic War against Napoleon in 1812, but later the lifeless drill all but killed the Russian Army, and caused Russia's defeat in the Crimean War (q.v.). A 'back to Suvorov' movement started, which at first produced a pseudo-Suvorov one-sided doctrine of mass bayonet attack, responsible for heavy losses in the Turkish war of 1877–8 and the Russo-Japanese War (q.v.). Gradually, however, the genuine Suvorov traditions were partially revived and were again in evidence during both world wars (q.v.) and the civil war. The Imperial Army was demoralized after the February revolution (q.v.) of 1917 and dissolved soon after the Bolshevik seizure of power, but almost

immediately revived in the shape of the Red Army on the one hand
and the various White armies on the other (*see* CIVIL WAR). After the
civil war there was close co-operation between the Red Army and the
German Reichswehr in matters of training and weapon equipment.
The Great Purge (q.v.) was a severe blow to the armed forces, the
majority of the higher-ranking officers being liquidated on charges of
treason; these charges have been admitted since Stalin's death to
have been false. The effects of the purge were one of the reasons for
the poor showing of the Red Army in the Soviet-Finnish war of
1940–1 and in the early part of the Second World War; another
reason was the general dissatisfaction on the part of the mobilized
soldiers with the regime, which resulted in a high percentage of
surrenders and the considerable numbers of those willing to fight on
the German side (*see* VLASOV). The Second World War produced a
number of outstanding military leaders—Zhukov, Rokossovskiy,
Konev (qq.v.), Vasilevskiy, etc.—but Stalin's jealousy led to their
personal roles being played down. Since Stalin's death the leading
role in war-time successes has been claimed for the Communist Party
as a whole, and this was one of the reasons for the clash between the
majority in the party leadership and Marshal Zhukov, who attempted
to weaken the party position in the armed forces. *See also* ARMED
FORCES. *See* E. Tarle, *Napoleon's Invasion of Russia, 1812*, 1942;
D. F. White, *The Growth of the Red Army*, 1944; R. L. Garthoff, *How
Russia Makes War*, 1954, and *Soviet Strategy in the Nuclear Age*,
1958; Z. Brzezinski (ed.), *Political Controls in the Soviet Army*, New
York, 1954; B. H. Liddell Hart (ed.), *The Soviet Army*, 1956.

Artel' (Russian 'team'), traditional form of industrial co-operative
which existed especially among workers in itinerant and seasonal
trades. It was considered by the Populists an equivalent in the
industrial field of the agricultural commune (*see* MIR), and they
believed it would facilitate the transition of Russia to socialism
without going through the capitalist stage (*see* BERVI-FLËROVSKIY).
The term is now used officially for artisans' co-operatives (qq.v.) and
for collective farms, though *kolkhoz* (q.v.) is the usual word for the
latter.

Artëm, town in the Maritime Kray (Far East), situated 29 m.
north-east of Vladivostok, the centre of a coal mining area. Population (1959) 55,000 (1939, 35,000). It has a large thermal power-
station. Artëm was founded in 1924 and became a town in 1938.

Artëmovsk (until 1920's Bakhmut), town in the Stalino Oblast of
eastern Ukraine, 40 m. north of Stalino, a local cultural centre and
the chief salt-mining centre of the U.S.S.R. Population (1959) 61,000
(1897, 19,000; 1939, 55,000). Known as a fort and salt works since
1571, Artëmovsk became a town in 1783 and from 1920 to 1924 was
the administrative centre of the Donets coal-mining industry.

Artillery occupies a rather more important position in the Soviet
armed forces than it does in other countries. There is a special Chief
Administration for artillery in the Ministry of Defence (not subordinated to the commander-in-chief of ground forces), which is in
the charge of the Head of Artillery and is responsible for the development of tactical doctrine, training and equipment of artillery units.

Artillery makes up a considerable part of the Soviet army's combat personnel, and large artillery formations up to corps strength have existed. Artillery officers have their own career ladder, culminating in the rank of Chief Marshal of the Artillery which is one grade below the highest rank of Marshal of the Soviet Union. Soviet artillery is well equipped with modern weapons of various types and purposes, including atomic guns and tactical rockets.

Russian artillery has traditionally been known for its excellence, and artillery played a very important part in the offensive operations during the Second World War. The traditional high level of ballistic studies in Russia was underlined by the establishment in 1946 of the Academy of Artillery Sciences as a specialized learned institution. This academy has played a leading role in the development of inter-mediate range and inter-continental ballistic missiles. *See further under* ROCKETS. *See* R. L. Garthoff, *How Russia Makes War*, 1954, and *Soviet Strategy in the Nuclear Age*, 1958; B. H. Liddell Hart (ed.), *The Soviet Army*, 1956.

Artisans are mainly engaged in (1) individual repair work (e.g. cobblers, piano tuners, etc.), (2) the manufacture of articles of domestic use, primarily out of industrial waste and (3) in such old crafts (q.v.) as have survived (e.g. carpet weaving, silverwork, icon painting). The majority of artisans work in co-operatives (q.v.) (also doing a good deal of private work on the side), though a certain number of stubborn individualists continue to work entirely privately. No detailed figures of the number of artisans are available, because the official statistics, in accordance with the theoretical class structure, generally group co-operated artisans with *kolkhoz* peasants, and independent artisans with individual peasants; co-operated artisans numbered 1·3 million in 1958 (all artisans in 1913 numbered 5·4 million). The social status of co-operated artisans is in fact somewhat similar to that of *kolkhoz* peasants, and there is a considerable amount of discrimination against independent artisans, e.g. in the fields of taxation (*see* INCOME TAX), education, party membership, etc.

Artobolevskiy, Ivan Ivanovich (*b.* 1905), engineer, specialist in the theory of engines, member of the Academy of Sciences. His works are mainly concerned with the methods of kinematic analysis of mechanisms and problems of automation.

Artsimovich, Lev Andreyevich (*b.* 1909), physicist of Belorussian parentage, member of the U.S.S.R. Academy of Sciences and of its Presidium. Educated at Minsk University, he has taught at Leningrad and Moscow universities and worked at various research institutions of the Academy of Sciences. His work is concerned with nuclear physics, particularly the study of properties of fast electrons and theoretical electronic optics; he developed the theory of chromatic aberrations in electronic optical systems. In recent years Artsimovich has done much work on thermo-nuclear reactions.

Arzamas, town in the Gor'kiy Oblast. Population (1956) 39,000. From 1953 to 1958 it was capital of an oblast now absorbed by Gor'kiy Oblast. From 1802 till 1862 it had a school of painting, the first provincial school of its kind in modern Russia.

Asaf'yev, Boris Vladimirovich (1884–1949), prolific composer, pianist, teacher and musicologist, who studied under Lyadov at the St Petersburg Conservatory. In 1921 he was appointed teacher at Leningrad Conservatory, becoming professor in 1925 and in 1943 professor at Moscow Conservatory. His works comprise ten operas, including *The Bronze Horseman*, 1942; twenty-seven ballets, including *The Fire of Paris or the Triumph of the Republic*, 1932; three symphonies; much theatrical music; chamber music; songs, etc.; and literary works, including *Russian Music from the Beginning of the Nineteenth Century* (Moscow-Leningrad, 1930). Asaf'yev is regarded in Russia as 'a musician of great erudition and breadth of vision, the foremost musical scholar and thinker of our time' (Keldysh). *See* R. Moisenko, *Realist Music*, 1949.

Asbest (formerly **Kudel'ka**), town in the Sverdlovsk Oblast (Urals), situated 40 m. north-east of Sverdlovsk. Population (1959) 60,000 (1939, 29,000). It is the main centre of asbestos quarrying and processing in the U.S.S.R.; asbestos was first found here in 1720, and a settlement for its extraction was established in the same year.

Ashkhabad, town in Central Asia, capital and cultural centre of Turkmenia, situated in the Akhal-Teke oasis in the foothills of the Kopet-Dag range, on the Trans-Caspian Railway. Population (1959) 170,000 (1939, 127,000), mostly Russians. It has varied industries—glass, food, textile, leather, printing, metal-working, cinema equipment—and carpet weaving and other crafts. The Turkmen Academy of Sciences (established as a branch of the U.S.S.R. Academy of Sciences in 1940, transformed in 1951), a university (founded 1931 as a Pedagogical Institute, transformed 1950) and several other educational and research institutions are situated here. The famous Chalcolith and Bronze Age site of Anau (excavated since 1904) and the ruins of the Parthian capital Nisa are near the town. Ashkhabad was founded by the Russians in 1881 on the site of a Turkmen village as the administrative centre of the Trans-Caspian Region. In 1948 the town was almost entirely destroyed by an earthquake, but it is now rebuilt. From 1939 to 1959 it was the administrative centre of the Ashkhabad Oblast within Turkmenia, now abolished.

Aspirant, term applied since 1925 to graduate students working for a candidate's degree (*see* DEGREES). The present system of graduate studies dates from 1939. An aspirant's course of study lasts three years, or four years if by correspondence, during which time he must pass an examination and prepare a thesis; he may work either at a higher educational establishment or a research institute authorized to accept graduate students. All full-time aspirants receive grants. In 1958 there were 23,000 aspirants in the U.S.S.R. (1955, 30,800).

Assembly of the Land, *see* ZEMSKIY SOBOR.

Assessors ('People's Assessors'), citizens 'lawfully elected' to participate in the hearing of both criminal and civil cases in Soviet courts of law (q.v.). Any person aged 25 or over is eligible for election. Assessors for People's Courts are elected by universal vote for two years, those for higher courts by the corresponding soviets for five years. The elections are largely fictitious, the candidates being selected under the direction of the appropriate party organs (*see*

CADRES). While on duty (up to two weeks in a year) assessors have equal rights with the judge in passing verdict and sentence. Employees receive their normal pay. During the discussion which preceded the legal reform (q.v.) of 1958 it was suggested by the more liberal lawyers that the number of assessors should be increased for the hearing of particularly important criminal cases, which would have been a step towards reintroduction of trial by jury, but this suggestion was rejected.

Astrakhan': 1. Oblast of the R.S.F.S.R., on the lower Volga, semi-desert lowland with an extreme continental climate. Area 17,400 sq. m.; population (1959) 702,000 (52 per cent urban), Russian and some Tatars and Kazakhs. There is a fishing industry, salt working (from Lake Baskunchak), cattle and sheep raising for meat and wool, and some agriculture (melons, vines and cotton).

2. Administrative centre of the oblast, in the Volga delta about 60 m. from the Caspian Sea, economic and cultural centre of the northern part of the Caspian Sea area. Population (1959) 294,000 (1863, 43,000; 1914, 151,000; 1920, 100,000). Astrakhan' is the leading fishing centre of the U.S.S.R., with large fish canneries, and one of the biggest seaports in the country. It was the capital of the Astrakhan' Khanate until its conquest by Ivan the Terrible in 1556, when it was transferred from the right bank of the Volga to its present site. It was a flourishing centre for trade with Persia, Khiva and Bukhara until 1917.

Astronomy was pursued in the Middle Ages in Central Asia, where Biruni (11th century), and especially Ulug-bek (15th century), greatly contributed to its advance. Ulug-bek, who was ruler of the Timurid Empire, founded an observatory in Samarkand at which a new catalogue indicating the position of over 1,000 stars was compiled. In Russia proper, research in astronomy began after the establishment of the Academy of Sciences in 1725. Lomonosov (q.v.) is credited with the discovery of Venus's atmosphere. In 1839 V. Ya. Struve (q.v.) founded the famous Pulkovo Observatory near St Petersburg, often called in the 19th century 'the astronomical capital of the world.' This has concentrated on the study of stars, which has remained the chief preoccupation of Russian astronomers. The study of comets, initiated by Bredikhin (q.v.), has also continued. The works of Ambartsumyan (q.v.) are outstanding in astrophysics and cosmology. Complete 'cover-to-cover' translations of the journals *Journal of Astronomy* and *Bulletin of the Academy of Sciences of the U.S.S.R.: Geophysical Series* exist in English.

Atheists, Militant, League of, was founded by the Communist Party in 1925 and headed by Yaroslavskiy (q.v.). Its aim was to carry out anti-religious propaganda; this it did in a violent manner, employing such methods as arranging for the destruction of many church buildings, interfering in religious services and denouncing priests to the G.P.U. It was abolished in 1943. *See further under* RELIGION. *See* R. Fülöp-Miller, *The Mind and Face of Bolshevism*, 1927.

Atomic Weapons, *see* NUCLEAR WEAPONS.

Aulie-Ata, *see* DZHAMBUL.

Autarky, economic self-sufficiency. A policy of autarky rather than making use of the advantages of international division of labour has been pursued by the Soviet Government since the introduction of State monopoly of foreign trade in 1918, though the term 'autarky' has been avoided. The reason officially advanced for this policy is the need for economic independence in the face of 'capitalist encirclement' (q.v.). Since the establishment of Communist regimes in a number of other countries after the Second World War there have been attempts at applying the policy of autarky to the whole Communist bloc, which were theoretically justified in 1952 by Stalin when he formulated the doctrine of two world markets, a capitalist and a socialist. The expansion of trade with non-Communist countries since Stalin's death has not seriously altered the basic policy of autarky. On the propaganda level two incompatible ideas are simultaneously advanced: the need of the country for economic independence and, on the other hand, the desirability of the maximum expansion of foreign trade.

Autocracy (*samoderzhaviye*), the supreme power of the Russian emperors. The title 'autocrat,' which originated with the Byzantine emperors, was assumed by the Grand Princes of Muscovy when they freed themselves from subjection to the Tatar khans. Originally the title signified independence from any other ruler, but it later acquired the meaning of absolute monarch. After the 1905 revolution the power of the emperor was limited in practice by the legislative power of the State Duma and State Council, though the title 'autocrat' was retained in the constitution.

Automation, in industry, has proceeded at a quick pace during the 1950's, and Russia does not now lag behind advanced Western countries in this respect. There exist fully automatic hydro-electric stations, chemical plants and automatic production lines in some branches of engineering. According to the official theory, automation is a typical feature of production in a Communist system; it is beneficial under socialism, but disadvantageous to the workers under capitalism since it leads to increased unemployment. In practice, however, automation in the Soviet Union also leads to redundancy, unemployment and go-slow tactics on the part of workers, as is shown in Panferov's (q.v.) *In the Name of the Young. See* G. Segal, 'Automation and its Prospects,' *Soviet Survey*, No. 31, Jan.–Mar. 1960. A complete 'cover-to-cover' translation of the journal *Automation and Telemechanics* exists in English.

Autonomous Oblast, administrative territorial unit, often forming part of a kray (q.v.). Autonomous Oblasts are supposed to represent territorial autonomy for peoples who are not sufficiently numerous for the creation of an Autonomous Republic (q.v.). Each Autonomous Oblast is represented in the Soviet of Nationalities of the U.S.S.R. Supreme Soviet by five deputies. Internal administration is similar to that of an ordinary oblast. There are now nine Autonomous Oblasts, six in the R.S.F.S.R. (Adyge, Jewish, Karachay-Circassian, Khakas, Mountainous-Altay and Tuva) and one each in Georgia (South Ossetian), Azerbaydzhan (Mountainous-Karabakh) and Tadzhikistan (Mountainous-Badakhshan). *See* ADMINISTRATIVE TERRITORIAL DIVISIONS.

Autonomous Republic, administrative territorial unit which is supposed to represent territorial autonomy for peoples which do not qualify for a Union Republic (q.v.) of their own. There are at present 19 Autonomous Republics; they have such external symbols of statehood as constitutions, Supreme Soviets and Councils of Ministers, but in fact their administration is on the oblast level. Each Autonomous Republic is represented by eleven deputies in the Soviet of Nationalities of the U.S.S.R. Supreme Soviet (q.v.). *See* ADMINISTRATIVE TERRITORIAL DIVISIONS.

Autonomy according to the U.S.S.R. constitution is secured to national minorities who do not qualify for a Union Republic. The autonomy is territorial, Autonomous Republics or Autonomous Oblasts (qq.v.) being established in accordance with the numerical strength of the people concerned. In fact this autonomy is almost completely fictitious, since real power is everywhere in the hands of the strictly centralized Communist Party. In Imperial Russia Finland had almost complete internal autonomy, and the Muslim peoples of Central Asia and the primitive peoples of Siberia had a large measure of autonomy based on the Muslim law or tribal customs. Autonomist tendencies were strong among the Regionalists (*see* REGIONALISM), and cultural autonomy irrespective of residence, rather than territorial autonomy, was advocated for national minorities by several parties of the Left before the Bolshevik seizure of power, especially by the Bund and the Socialist Revolutionaries (qq.v.). The Provisional Government after February 1917 recognized the autonomy of the Ukraine, and was preparing similar measures for the other main peoples of Russia; regional autonomy was in fact established in the Cossack areas and in Transcaucasia. At the time of the formation of the Soviet Union in the early 1920's, Stalin, as Commissar for Nationalities in the Soviet Government, advanced proposals for incorporating the Ukraine, Belorussia and the Transcaucasian Republics into the R.S.F.S.R. as Autonomous Republics, but Lenin insisted on the present quasi-federal structure. Apart from the ostensible national autonomy the Communist theory does not recognize the principle of autonomy in any other sphere (*see* TOTALITARIANISM), though a partial exception is made for religion, where the party does not claim authority in matters of dogma or ritual. *See* V. Gsovski and K. Grzybowski (eds.), *Government, Law and Courts in the Soviet Union and Eastern Europe,* vol. i, 1959.

Avars, Caucasian-speaking Muslim people inhabiting most of western Daghestan and numbering (1959) 268,000 (the most numerous people in Daghestan). The Avar language is used throughout western Daghestan in schools and as a lingua franca. It is in the Avar area that the village of Gunib is situated, where Shamil' (q.v.) made his last stand against the Russians in 1856.

Averbakh, Leopol'd Leonidovich (1903–?), literary critic of Jewish origin, the theorist of the 'On Guard' and later of the R.A.P.P. (q.v.) groups, brother-in-law of Yagoda (q.v.). A fanatical Communist, he and his circle were constantly fulminating against the 'fellow travellers' (q.v.) in literature. Supported until 1932 by the party authorities, Averbakh almost succeeded in establishing himself as a dictator in the literary field; however, with the development of Stalinism (q.v.) Averbakh and his school were ousted to make way for the obligatory doctrine of Socialist Realism (q.v.). He disappeared during the Great Purge (q.v.).

Avksent'yev, Nikolay Dmitriyevich (1878–1943), politician, leader of the right wing of the Socialist Revolutionaries. After the February revolution in 1917 he was chairman of the Soviet of Peasants' Deputies, then Minister of the Interior in the Provisional Government and chairman of the Pre-Parliament (q.v.). He was a member of the Ufa Directory (q.v.) in 1918, and later emigrated.

Azef, Yevno Fishelevich (1869–1918), most notorious police agent in the revolutionary movement. He was one of the founders of the party of Socialist Revolutionaries, and during 1903–8 the head of its fighting organization, which for security reasons was completely autonomous. Playing a double game he organized and directed a number of important terroristic acts, including the assassination of the Minister of the Interior, Pleve. He was unmasked by Burtsev (q.v.) in 1908 and subsequently lived under an assumed name in Berlin dealing on the stock exchange. The Socialist Revolutionary party never recovered from the shock of Azef's exposure. *See* B. I. Nicolaevsky, *Aseff, The Russian Judas*, 1934.

Azerbaydzhan, country comprising eastern Transcaucasia and north-western Persia. The Transcaucasian part is a Union Republic of the U.S.S.R. It is mountainous in the north and south, with the Kura river lowland in the centre and the Talysh lowland in the south-east, and has a dry continental climate; there are rich deposits of oil, also iron, copper, lead and zinc ores and salt deposits. Area 33,400 sq. m.; population (1959) 3,698,000 (48 per cent urban), chiefly Turkic-speaking Azerbaydzhanis (67 per cent of the population), Russians (since the 19th century, 14 per cent) and Armenians (12 per cent). Azerbaydzhan has the third largest oil industry of the U.S.S.R., and also engineering, textile and food industries; there is cotton growing, sericulture, horticulture and viniculture, and sheep, buffalo and horses are raised (local breeds); old crafts (silk, carpets) are still practised. Principal towns: Baku (capital), Kirovabad and Sumgait.

The area belonged successively to Rome, Persia, the Arabs, Mongols and Seljuk Turks, and once more to Persia. There were several khanates semi-independent from Persia in the 18th century— Shirvan, Karabakh, Gandzha, Baku, Talysh, Nakhichevan', Kuba and Sheki—which were either conquered in Russo-Persian wars or else submitted voluntarily to Russia between 1804 and 1828. The oil industry was rapidly developed from the 1870's and Azerbaydzhan was the world's largest oil producer by the end of the century. It joined the Transcaucasian Federation after the Bolshevik seizure of power, and when the federation disintegrated an independent Azerbaydzhan Republic was established in 1918 under the domination of the Mussavat Party. But its existence was precarious because of the difficult international situation (military intervention by friendly Turks and hostile British, war with Armenia) and the internal conditions (continual mutual massacres of Armenians and

Muslims, the activities of the Bolshevik underground in Baku), and the Red Army had no difficulty in conquering it in 1920. The Azerbaydzhan Soviet Republic was proclaimed, being included in the Transcaucasian Federal Republic and the U.S.S.R. in 1922. Upon the Federal Republic's abolition in 1936 Azerbaydzhan became a Union Republic of the U.S.S.R.; it includes the Nakhichevan' Autonomous Republic and the Mountainous-Karabakh Autonomous Oblast. *See* F. Kazemzadeh, *The Struggle for Transcaucasia*, New York, 1951; W. Kolarz, *Russia and her Colonies*, 1952; R. Pipes, *The Formation of the Soviet Union*, Cambridge, Mass., 1954.

Azerbaydzhanis, Turkic-speaking people living in Azerbaydzhan, Georgia, Armenia and Daghestan, and numbering (1959) 2·9 million. They are mostly Shiah Muslims, but there are also some Sunni Muslims and sectarians. Azerbaydzhanis are the product of a mixture of several ethnic elements: the original, probably Caucasian-speaking, inhabitants of the area became Iranianized under the Sasanids, partly through immigration from Persia. The great Persian poet of the 12th century, Nizami, lived in Azerbaydzhan and is now celebrated as the Azerbaydzhani national poet. The Seljuk conquest in the 11th century started the process of Turkicization which continued in the following centuries. By the time of the Russian conquest in the early 19th century the bulk of the population were Turkicized and had begun to develop a national consciousness of their own, though they still lacked a common name: they were known as Transcaucasian Tatars by the Russians, and after 1917 as Azerbaydzhani Turks, until in the 1920's the name of Azerbaydzhanis became established. *See* C. W. Hostler, *Turkism and the Soviets*, 1957; S. A. Zenkovsky, *Pan-Turkism and Islam in Russia*, Cambridge, Mass., 1960.

Azov (ancient **Tanais**), river port in the Rostov Oblast, near the mouth of the Don. Population (1956) 37,400. Azov was founded as a Greek colony in the 3rd century B.C., became a Genoese colony in the 13th century, was subject to Turkey from 1471 and became Russian in 1739.

Azov, Sea of, northern arm of the Black Sea, connected to it by the narrow Kerch' strait (known in antiquity as Bosporus Cimmerius). Area 14,000 sq. m.; greatest length 220 m.; average breadth 80 m.; maximum depth 45 ft. The water is very fresh and the sea is frozen for three or four months almost every year. The Don and Kuban' rivers flow into the sea; its chief ports are Zhdanov, Taganrog and Kerch'. The Sivash, or Putrid Sea—a series of salty lagoons and marshes—lies to the west of the Sea of Azov, separated from it only by the long, narrow, sandy Arabat Peninsula.

B

Babushkin (until 1938 **Losinoostrovskaya**), town in the Moscow Oblast, 7 m. north of Moscow, a residential and industrial suburb. Population (1959) 112,000 (1939, 70,000), the majority of whom work in the capital.

Bagratids, royal dynasty of Armenia and Georgia. They ruled from 885 to 1045 in Armenia, and then in Georgia until its annexation in 1800 by Russia.

Bagration, Prince Pëtr Ivanovich (1765–1812), Georgian general, descended from the Bagratids (q.v.). He served with distinction in the battles of Austerlitz, 1805, and Eylau and Friedland, 1807. On Napoleon's invasion of Russia, 1812, he commanded the Second Russian Army, and was defeated by Davout at Mogilëv, though he succeeded in rejoining Barclay de Tolly's (q.v.) main force. Bagration was mortally wounded at the Battle of Borodino.

Bakh, Aleksey Nikolayevich (1857–1946), chemist and revolutionary. Educated at Kiev University, Bakh joined in 1881 the Narodnaya Volya (q.v.) Party and was active in the revolutionary underground until he emigrated in 1885; he lived in Paris and Geneva, working in laboratories of his own, and joined the party of Socialist Revolutionaries. He returned to Russia after the February revolution (q.v.) in 1917, and in 1918 founded the Physico-Chemical Institute in Moscow and in 1935 the Biochemical Institute of the Academy of Sciences, heading both until his death. Member of the Academy of Sciences from 1929, he was secretary of its department of chemical sciences, 1939–45, and president of the Mendeleyev Chemical Society from 1935. Bakh's own research was concerned with photosynthesis, breathing and other oxidation processes, and the ferments.

Bakhchisaray, town in the Crimean Oblast, 20 m. south of Simferopol'. Population (1956) 10,000 (1914, 17,000), before 1945 mostly Tatar. The capital of the Crimean Khanate, it has a famous palace built in 1519 and many historic mosques.

Bulthmut, *see* ARTËMOVSK.

Bakst, Lev Samoylovich (1868–1924), painter and theatrical designer, studied at the Academy of Arts and in Paris. He was one of the leading members of Mir Iskusstva (q.v.). His best work was done outside Russia for Diaghilev's Ballets Russes: sets and costumes for *Sheherezade, L'Oiseau de Feu, Cleopatra*, etc. His style of *décor* is based on the use of large splashes of colour combined with the utmost intensity of tone and with rhythmical exploitation of space. Bakst was a supreme master of theatrical costume but showed an excessive inclination towards the exotic.

Baku (Azerbaydzhani **Bakkhi**), capital of the Azerbaydzhan Republic, and one of the chief economic centres of the U.S.S.R.

Situated on the desert-like Apsheron Peninsula (western shore of the Caspian Sea), it has a hot climate and strong north-westerly winds. Population, including industrial suburbs subordinated to the city council, (1959) 968,000 (fourth in the U.S.S.R.; 1863, 14,000; 1917 (city only), 300,000; 1926, 453,000; 1939, 809,000), mainly Russian, Azerbaydzhani and Armenian. It is the centre of Baku oilfields, with refineries and cracking plants and engineering (chiefly oil industry equipment), light and food industries. It is one of the largest ports in the U.S.S.R., and the starting-point of the oil pipeline to Batumi (on the Black Sea). The city has outstanding architectural monuments of the 11th–15th centuries, the Azerbaydzhani Academy of Sciences (founded 1945) and a university (founded 1919).

Known since the 8th century, Baku was under Arab rule and later belonged to Shirvan and Persia. It was subject to Russia, 1723–35, then returned to Persia, and finally annexed by Russia in 1806. It became centre of Baku Province in 1859, and belonged to the independent anti-Bolshevik Azerbaydzhani Republic from 1918 to 1920, when it was captured by the Red Army.

Bakunin, Mikhail Aleksandrovich (1814–76), revolutionary leader and theorist of Anarchism. Of noble birth, he studied at Moscow University where he belonged to the famous Stankevich (q.v.) circle. He played a prominent part in the 1848 revolution in Western Europe, was handed over to the Russian authorities, banished to Siberia, but escaped abroad and became Marx's rival in the First International, leading the Anarchist wing against the adherents of State Socialism. On his role in the Russian revolutionary movement, *see under* POPULISM. *See* his *Œuvres* (2 vols.), Paris, 1895; A. J. Sack, *The Birth of the Russian Democracy*, New York, 1918; E. H. Carr, *Michael Bakunin*, 1937; B.-P. Hepner, *Bakounine et le panslavisme révolutionnaire*, Paris, 1950; J. M. Meijer, *Knowledge and Revolution*, Assen, Netherlands, 1955; P. Scheibert, *Von Bakunin zu Lenin*, Leiden, 1956; E. Lampert, *Studies in Rebellion*, 1957; R. Hare, *Portraits of Russian Personalities between Reform and Revolution*, 1959.

Balakirev, Miliy Alekseyevich (1836–1910), composer and conductor who studied under Dubuque and Eiserich. In 1855 he was taken by his patron Ulybyshev to St Petersburg, where he met Glinka, Musorgskiy, Rimsky-Korsakov and Borodin, to whom he gave tuition. He played a leading part in founding the Free School of Music in 1862, an institution which did much to promote the works of his associates, the Kuchka (q.v.), and the music of Berlioz, Schumann and (at a later date) Liszt. From 1867 he edited and published Glinka's works. The middle period of Balakirev's life was marked by intense poverty, which may have had physical and psychological effects. He was appointed director of the Imperial Court Chapel in 1883, and in 1897 served as a member of the Imperial Geographical Society's commission for the publication of Russian folk-songs. His works comprise: two symphonies (No. 1 in C major, 1866–98; No. 2 in D minor, 1907–8); two piano concertos; choral and orchestral works, including the symphonic poem *Tamara*, 1867–82; chamber music; many piano solos, including the 'oriental fantasy'

Islamey, 1869; piano transcriptions and two sets of folk-songs, 1866 and 1900.

Though Balakirev's creative career was a long one, his music shows remarkable consistency of style. An ardent follower of Glinka, his individual harmony is a synthesis of 'Eastern melody and rhythm and Western harmony and technique' (Grove). His orchestral music is characterized by strong rhythms and brilliant orchestration. His piano music, which is often of extreme difficulty (owing much to Liszt), contains many oriental features. His importance in Russian music lies in his work as a formative influence on the young Russian national school, and as a disciple and developer of the artistic principles of Glinka, especially in his leanings to the orient. *See* G. Abraham, *Studies in Russian Music*, 1935, and *On Russian Music*, 1939; G. Abraham and M. D. Calvocoressi, *Masters of Russian Music*, 1936.

Balances, Method of, the use in economic planning of a system of indices which shows the existing resources on the one hand and the needs to be met on the other. There are material, financial and labour balances which are combined into the final balance of the national economy. The application of this method of balances was introduced by the Gosplan (q.v.) in the 1920's, was hampered in the post-war period by the obsession with secrecy and security, but since Stalin's death has been insisted upon at all levels of economic planning (q.v.). Partly because of the large number of calculations involved, the balances arrived at are only very rough approximations, but it is intended to remedy this by the use of modern computers.

Balanchine (real name **Balanchivadze**), **Georgiy Melitonovich** (*b.* 1896), choreographer of Georgian parentage. After studying the piano and composition at the St Petersburg Conservatory, Balanchine left the Soviet Union in 1924 and was engaged by Diaghilev as choreographer, in which capacity he worked until the impresario's death in 1929. Of his ten Diaghilev productions, most successful were *Apollon Musagètes* and *The Prodigal Son*. He subsequently worked with René Blum and Colonel de Basil and other companies, finally settling in the United States, where his most recent productions have included Stravinsky's *Orphée*, 1948, and *Agon*, 1958.

Balashikha, town in the Moscow Oblast, an industrial (textiles) and residential suburb 12 m. east of the capital. Population (1959) 58,000.

Balashov, town in the Saratov Oblast of the R.S.F.S.R., on a tributary of the Don, 125 m. west of Saratov. Population (1959) 64,000. It is a railway junction and local industrial centre, with an aircraft plant and extensive food industries. Balashov was founded in the 17th century, and from 1953 to 1958 was centre of an oblast now abolished.

Balkars, Turkic-speaking people, closely related to the Karachay. They live in the Kabarda-Balkar Autonomous Republic on the northern slopes of the main Caucasian range, east of El'brus, and number (1959) 42,000 (1939, 43,000). They were subject to Russia from the 1820's, in 1921 were included into the Mountain People's Autonomous Republic, and in 1922 in the Kabarda-Balkar Autonomous Oblast. For alleged collaboration with the Germans the

Balkars were deported to Asiatic Russia in 1943 and were officially ignored as a people until 1957, when they were 'rehabilitated' and permitted to return home. *See* W. Kolarz, *Russia and her Colonies*, 1952; R. Conquest, *The Soviet Deportation of Nationalities*, 1960.

Balkhash: 1. Lake in the Karaganda and Alma-Ata oblasts (Kazakhstan), the fourth largest inland sea in the country. Length 150 m.; breadth 75 m. It is frozen from November to May. Shipyards have been established at the mouths of the Karatal, Lepsa and Ili rivers, the principal rivers feeding the lake.

2. Town in the Karaganda Oblast situated on the northern shore of the lake, a major centre of tne copper industry. Population (1959) 53,000 (1939, 33,000). Apart from the copper-smelting plant, Balkhash has a molybdenum factory and food industries. The town consists of several scattered settlements. The copper deposits in the area have been known since 1901; the town and plant were built in 1937–8, largely by forced labour.

Ballet. Russian ballet is fundamentally connected with the dance elements of the folk theatre and folk music, especially that of the *skomorokhi* during the Middle Ages (*see* FOLK MUSIC). The rise of ballet in Russia, however, came about through the inspiration of foreign artists; a regular ballet troupe being founded in St Petersburg in 1736 as a result of the arrival in 1734 of the dancer Landé and an important Italian company. This was the beginning of a constant stream of foreign visitors to Russia which included such famous names as Hilferding, Angiolini, Le Pic and Poirot. At the same time the first Russian artists—Berilova and Ye. I. Kolosova—made their appearance. Great impetus was given to Russian ballet during the first decades of the 19th century by the ballet master Didelot (1767–1837), a pupil of Vestris and Noverre, who considerably improved the *décor*, costume, machinery and properties; under his guidance Russian ballet rose to be the finest in Europe, the lavishness and brilliance of *décor* and choreography being unequalled. Foreign visitors included Duport, Batiste, Johanson and Taglioni, while native artists included A. I. Istomina, M. Danilova, Ye. I. Andreyanova, etc. The years 1837–47 marked a lull and temporary decline, but with the arrival of Petipa (q.v.) in 1847 a new era began. Whereas Petipa sought to create dramas and a manœuvrable *corps de ballet*, his rival Saint-Léon favoured national dances, character and solo dances, a factor which illustrates the growing popularity of the prima ballerina. Famous dancers included the foreigners Grisi (from 1850 to 1853) and Cerrito and the Russians L. I. Ivanov (1834–1901), N. K. Bogdanova, Murav'ëva and Lebedeva. From 1855 onwards Petipa gradually displaced Perrot as leading ballet master, and for the next twenty years foreigners were virtually absent from the Russian stage. In 1887 a new era began with the appointment of Vsevolozhskiy as director and the arrival of the Italians Zucchi, Giuri and Del-Era. Hostile to mime and drama, the Italians favoured pirouettes, 'points' and rapid *fouettés*. During the 19th century Russian dancers had developed primarily on French lines. Russian ballet as such hardly existed, but with the appearance of the Italian school a new scheme began to evolve. An important innovation was made in 1890 by the employment of Tchaikovsky's music to *The Sleeping Beauty*. Before this, music had been primarily of foreign origin or written by Pugni, Minkus or Drigo, composers of meagre ability; the use of Tchaikovsky's music, however, led to the incorporation of works by native composers such as Glinka, Borodin, Rimsky-Korsakov, Glazunov (qq.v.), etc. Among the Russian dancers of the time the names of Kshesinskaya, S. P. Preobrazhenskaya and V. Trefilova are of great importance.

Vsevolozhskiy was succeeded in 1899 by Volkonskiy and in 1902 by Telyakovskiy. The 20th century marked the appearance of a new epoch which culminated in the achievements of Diaghilev (q.v.) and the Ballets Russes. The principal aim of the new regime was to bring about a closer connection between music and ballet. Since the 1850's male dancing had become increasingly suppressed by the rise of the prima ballerina, and the need for reform was generally felt. Diaghilev and his followers attempted to produce not only a perfect union between the *corps de ballet*, painting and music but also an end to the autonomy of the individual. Among the principal influences promoting this may be mentioned the Siamese hand ballet, 1900, and the personality and theories of Isadora Duncan (1878–1927), who endeavoured to re-create the modelling and movement of ancient Greece (*see* FOKINE). In 1909 Diaghilev presented his first season of Russian opera and ballet, and this was the beginning of an association with Bakst, Benois (qq.v.), K. Korovin, Golovin, Fokine (q.v.), Karsavina, Ida Rubinstein, Nijinsky and Pavlova (qq.v.), artists with most of whom he was to work in close conjunction over the next two decades. The year 1910 saw the Paris *première* of Stravinsky's *The Firebird*, and this was followed by his *Petrushka*, 1911, with scenario by Benois, the leading parts being played by Nijinsky and Karsavina. The third of these highly original and epoch-making ballets was *The Rite of Spring*, 1913, and it is not an exaggeration to say that from that date Western ballet proceeded on a new path. From 1911 (the first London season) Diaghilev's Ballets Russes became permanently resident abroad, and from this period the ballet became international in the fullest sense of the word. If up to 1912 the ballets had been nationalistic and iconoclastic, for the next twelve years they were modernistic, reflecting contemporary theories and ideas. The third epoch of the Russian ballet is from about 1925 until Diaghilev's death in 1929.

In 1932 the company was regrouped by René Blum and Colonel de Basil and included Massine, Balanchine, Woizikowsky, Danilova and other members of the former Diaghilev company together with new dancers. In 1936 René Blum resigned and founded his own group, the René Blum Ballets de Monte Carlo. Fokine produced a number of ballets for him besides reviving several former productions, but after a year he was succeeded as artistic director by Massine, the company now assuming the title of Ballet Russe de Monte Carlo. The chief event of these years was the famous London season at Drury Lane in June 1938. In the same year the Ballet Russe de Monte Carlo departed for America, where it remained until Massine formed his own company (Ballet Russe Highlights) in 1943. Massine's company was dissolved in 1946. The Ballet Russe de Monte Carlo is still active, though it has yielded much to American influence. It is now directed by Sergei Denham.

The Ballet Russe de Colonel de Basil was taken over in 1938 by Educational Ballets Ltd and assumed the name of Covent Garden Russian Ballet. At the end of 1939 Colonel de Basil was appointed chairman and managing director and the company was renamed the Original Ballet Russe. After tours of Australia, South America and the United States it returned to Europe in 1947. The company dispersed in Paris. Attempts were made to revive it in England, but after a short tour the company was finally dissolved in 1952.

The Ballets Russes were an international organization working in isolation from Russia, and Soviet ballet remained uninfluenced by their innovations, appearing from the point of view of technique simply as a continuation of 19th-century practice. Soviet ballet has concentrated on quality rather than quantity. A prolonged and detailed course of study is necessary before a pupil is ready to make her début, and this emphasis on technique has resulted in the appearance of a pleiad of ballerinas and male dancers of the highest order, among whom may be mentioned Ulanova, Plisetskaya, Lepeshinskaya (qq.v.), R. Struchkova, Yermolayev, Preobrazhenskiy, Kondratov and Farmanyants (q.v.). The home of Soviet ballet is the Bolshoi Theatre in Moscow, though the Leningrad company and the Moscow Stanislavskiy Theatre are both of high standard. The Bolshoi School is managed with characteristic thoroughness and supplies dancers for most of the country's ballet companies. Directed by Ye. Bocharnikova, the teachers include A. A. Gorskiy, V. D. Tikhomirov and M. V. Vasil'yeva. Pupils enter the school at the age of 7 and receive three years' general education before beginning their training. They are not allowed to wear point shoes till the end of the fourth year. During the first twelve months of training tuition is restricted to the 'five positions,' after which they are given their point shoes. With the boys no real training is attempted till the age of 14 or 15. All training for boys and girls during the early years is executed at half speed or slow tempo, and not till the five positions, centre practice and the *enchaînements* are mastered are they permitted to start dancing *a tempo*. The schooling is meticulously planned from year to year. Point work is of short duration in most classes and steps are never complicated, the main attention being paid to position and 'finish.' At the Leningrad school the same meticulous care and scientific approach are maintained throughout all the years of training, particular stress being laid on strict 'Italian' classicism and technical virtuosity.

One of the most striking points of dissimilarity from Western ballet is the accent placed on the libretto. Ballet, like other forms of Soviet art, frequently serves a political purpose, and for that reason must be completely comprehensible and free from obscurity. Subjects are frequently taken from everyday life, from revolutionary history and also from the best productions of classical and contemporary literature. The political importance of ballet, which is zealously fostered and heavily subsidized by the State, is attested by the fact that it has incurred the censure of the Communist Party on no less than three occasions—in 1936, 1946 and 1948—when it was accused of 'anti-folk formalism' and lack of Socialist Realism (q.v.). Soviet ballet is not limited in its *genres* and comprises children's ballet, comic ballet, folk ballet, and even ballet united with song and dance, the dance groups of Aleksandrov and Moiseyev (qq.v.) being particularly well known. Close connection with folk creation forms one of the bases for the development of modern Soviet ballet. Ballet has attracted the attention of all the major Soviet composers, but in recent years there has been an increasing emphasis on the new national schools of the Soviet republics. Outstanding in this respect are the Georgian composer A. M. Balanchivadze and the Armenian Aram Khachaturyan (q.v.), whose ballet music makes full use of folk-song and national dances. Indeed, as in other spheres of art, it is the Soviet republics that offer many possibilities for the future and a union of national folk music with the Bolshoi technique might well produce some interesting offshoots in years to come. *See* C. W. Beaumont, *A History of Ballet in Russia*, 1930, and *Complete Book of Ballets*, 1937; T. Tsytovich, 'Sovetskiy balet na novom etape' in *Sovetskaya muzyka na pod'ëme*, Moscow-Leningrad, 1950; S. Lifar, *A History of Russian Ballet* (trans. Haskell), 1954; H. Bellew, *Ballet in Moscow Today*, 1956.

Baltic Provinces, pre-revolutionary name for the three provinces of the Empire, Estland, Livland and Kurland. Before their annexation to Russia in the 18th century these provinces had belonged to the Teutonic Knights and subsequently to Sweden and Poland. Though the majority of the population were Estonians and Latvians, the political and much of the economic power, in addition to the cultural influence, was wielded by the German minority. The primary aim of the russification measures (which dated from the 1880's and included the use of the Russian language in the administration and at Dorpat University) was to undermine this ascendancy of the German upper classes. The independent states of Estonia and Latvia created in 1918–19 were largely formed from the Baltic Provinces. *See also* GERMANS.

Baltic States, the three independent states of Estonia, Latvia and Lithuania which were formed after the First World War out of territories belonging to the former Russian Empire. Their independence was recognized by the Soviet Government in peace treaties signed in 1920, but in 1939 they were compelled by the Soviet Government to concede important military bases to Soviet troops, and in 1940 they were completely occupied, annexed and transformed into Union Republics of the Soviet Union. Soviet-style elections were held and the new parliaments 'unanimously resolved' to ask for admission to the Soviet Union. Despite the traditional anti-German attitude of the Baltic peoples, the subsequent terror and deportations caused them to welcome German troops in 1941 as liberators. Under German occupation they were included together with Belorussia in the Reich Commissariat 'Ostland.' As the Soviet Army advanced in 1944 many of the people fled to Sweden and Germany. The incorporation of the Baltic States into the Soviet Union has not been recognized by several countries, including Britain, where their accredited diplomatic representatives still function. *See* Royal Institute of International Affairs, *The Baltic States*, 1938; F. W. Pick, *The Baltic Nations*, 1945; J. A. Swettenham, *The Tragedy of the Baltic States*, 1952; S. W. Page, *The Formation of the Baltic States*, Cambridge, Mass., 1959; V. Gsovski and K. Grzybowski (eds.), *Government, Law and Courts in the Soviet Union and Eastern Europe*, 2 vols., 1959.

Baltic-White Sea Canal, *see* WHITE SEA-BALTIC CANAL.

Bandera, Stepan (1909–59), leader of the Ukrainian National League—an extreme Ukrainian nationalist organization—in Galicia before and during the Second World War. In 1941, when the Germans had occupied L'vov, Bandera's group announced the formation of an independent Ukrainian state and established a government; they were, however, arrested by the Germans and deported to concentration camps. The name Banderovites was applied after the war to all active Ukrainian nationalists who engaged in guerrilla warfare against the Soviet authorities in the western Ukraine. Bandera's adherents form the leadership of the fascist *émigré* grouping A.B.N. (*see under* ÉMIGRÉS). The circumstances surrounding his death in Munich suggested that he was murdered.

Banking. Apart from the normal functions of money issue and credit operations, the banks in the Soviet Union also have the function of direct control over the use of credits (*see* CREDIT). The State Bank of the U.S.S.R. (whose chairman is an *ex officio* member of the Council of Ministers) is the bank of issue, the clearing centre, almost the only source of short-term credits, and the Government treasury. It has branches in all administrative divisions of the country and is said to have the biggest volume of business in the world. The Foreign Trade Bank is a subsidiary of the State Bank. The Building Bank and the Agricultural Bank are long-term investment banks which handle all investment (q.v.) funds and finance the building industry. The Agricultural Bank is also responsible for long-term credit to *kolkhozes*. Soon after the seizure of power by the Bolsheviks in 1917 (*see* OCTOBER REVOLUTION) private commercial banks were confiscated and fused with the State Bank, which was renamed People's Bank. The policy of War Communism (q.v.) made banks seem superfluous, and the People's Bank was abolished in 1920. With the transition to the New Economic Policy (q.v.), the State Bank was re-established in 1921; several specialized banks were formed in 1922–4. After a series of reorganizations in 1930–2 the present system was established. For savings-banks *see* SAVINGS. *See* M. V. Condoide, *The Soviet Financial System*, Ohio, 1951.

Baptists are a numerous and actively proselytizing sect and may be found all over Russia. In 1944 they combined with some similar sects to form the 'Union of Evangelical Christians—Baptists,' for the first time in Russian history establishing something like a Protestant Church in the country. They are officially recognized by the Soviet Government (*see* RELIGION) and sometimes affirm doctrinal affinity between Christianity and communism. Baptists first appeared in Russia with the German colonists in the 18th century, and have spread among the Russian and Ukrainian population since the 1860's.

Baraba, wooded steppe region in south-western Siberia situated between the rivers Irtysh and Ob', traversed by the Trans-Siberian Railway. It is one of the principal areas of dairy farming in Siberia, and is now included in the Virgin Land Campaign (q.v.). The region has been colonized since the 18th century by Russians and Ukrainians, and since 1941 by Volga Germans.

Barannikov, Aleksey Petrovich (b. 1890), orientalist, member of the Academy of Sciences. His many works are chiefly concerned with modern Indian languages and the history of Indian culture. He has translated *Ramayana* into Russian, 1948.

Baranovichi (Polish **Baranowicze**), town in the Brest Oblast of Belorussia, 90 m. south-west of Minsk. Population (1959) 58,000, before the war half Jewish. It is an important railway junction (six lines) and has varied industries. Baranovichi was founded as a railway station in 1870.

Barclay de Tolly, Mikhail Andreyevich (1761–1818), general of Scottish descent. He was commander in Finland, 1808–9, and is famous for his daring march across the ice of the Gulf of Bothnia and his capture of Umeo. He was Minister of War from 1810 to 1813 and commanded the army against Napoleon in 1812, but his strategy of retreat caused dissatisfaction in the country, and after the defeat at Smolensk he was replaced as commander by Kutuzov (q.v.). He took command again, however, at Dresden, Kulm and Leipzig, being created a field marshal in 1814 and a prince in 1815.

Bardin, Ivan Pavlovich (1883–1960), metallurgist. Educated at the Kiev Polytechnical Institute, he worked in 1910–11 at a metal works in the U.S.A. and upon his return to Russia in the Southern Industrial Region (q.v.). In 1929–36 he directed the construction and the first period of operation of the Kuznetsk iron and steel plant (*see* KUZNETSK BASIN; STALINSK), and from 1937 worked in leading positions in the Commissariat (from 1946 Ministry) of Ferrous Metallurgy, for some time as deputy commissar. A member of the Academy of Sciences from 1932 and its vice-president from 1942, Bardin was during the war in charge of the mobilization of industrial resources of the eastern parts of the country for the war effort, and later of the restoration of the iron and steel industry in formerly occupied territories. He headed the Academy of Science's Institute of Metallurgy and as vice-president of the academy was in charge of co-ordinating the activities of its branches. In 1957 he was appointed chairman of the Soviet inter-departmental committee for the International Geophysical Year.

Barnaul, administrative, economic and cultural centre of the Altay Kray (southern Siberia), situated on the River Ob'. Population (1959) 320,000 (1861, 12,000; 1926, 74,000; 1939, 148,000). It has big textile (cotton from Central Asia), engineering and food industries, and the oldest local museum in Siberia. Barnaul became a town in 1771, having been founded in 1738 as a silver-smelting plant, and for a century it was the administrative centre of the Altay mining district; it later became the chief trading centre of the largest agricultural region in Siberia. New impetus was given to its industrial development by the building of the Turksib Railway and the Second

World War. It was one of the centres of the Virgin Land Campaign (q.v.) in the mid 1950's, and is the prospective site of a large iron and steel plant.

Barshchina, corvée, the unpaid labour due from a serf to his landlord before the emancipation of serfs in 1861. The reintroduction of a kind of serfdom in the form of the collectivization of agriculture (q.v.) brought about a new type of *barshchina* whereby *kolkhoz* peasants are obliged to put in a certain number of days' work per year (the average minimum now being 200) for uncertain and usually very low remuneration. *See also* KOLKHOZ; WORK-DAY UNIT.

Baryatinskiy, Prince Aleksandr Ivanovich (1814–79), general who distinguished himself in campaigns in the Caucasus in the 1830's–1850's. He completed the Russian conquest of the North Caucasian mountain peoples by defeating and capturing Shamil' (q.v.) at Gunib in 1859.

Bashkiria, Autonomous Republic within the R.S.F.S.R., situated in the south of the Ural Mountains and the adjacent lowland to the west, traversed by the Belaya (a tributary of the Kama); there are rich oil, iron ore and non-ferrous metal deposits. Area 56,000 sq. m.; population (1959) 3,335,000 (38 per cent urban), chiefly Russians (since the 16th century), and Bashkirs and Tatars. There are engineering, oil, chemical, metallurgical, textile and food industries; grain is cultivated, market gardening carried on, and cattle, sheep and horses raised. Principal towns: Ufa (capital), Sterlitamak, Oktyabr'-skiy and Beloretsk. The area was annexed to Muscovy after the conquest of Kazan'. Industrial development (metallurgy) began in the 18th century; oil extraction dates from the 1930's, and the engineering industry developed after the Second World War. *See* B. Nolde, *La Formation de l'Empire Russe*, vol. i, Paris, 1953.

Bashkirs (own name **Bashkort**), Turkic-speaking people who live in the Bashkir Autonomous Republic (constituting a quarter of its population) and the surrounding areas, numbering (1959) 983,000, of whom 62 per cent consider Bashkir their mother tongue. They have been known since the 9th century, when they were nomadic and partly spoke an Ugrian language related to Hungarian, and have been Muslims since the 14th century. They recognized the overlordship of the Volga Bulgarians and the Golden Horde, then of the khanates of Kazan', Nogay and Siberia, and of Muscovy from 1557. Russian colonization during the 17th and 18th centuries led to several Bashkir revolts. In 1917 a Bashkir nationalist government was formed in Orenburg, but in 1919 it joined the Bolsheviks. The majority of Bashkirs are now collective farm members. *See* R. Pipes, *The Formation of the Soviet Union*, Cambridge, Mass., 1954; S. A. Zenkovsky, *Pan-Turkism and Islam in Russia*, Cambridge, Mass., 1960.

Basmachi, popular anti-Communist resistance movement in Turkestan in 1918–24. Originally the Basmachi were ordinary brigands. The anti-Bolshevik autonomous government in Kokand (*see* TURKESTAN) employed some of the Basmachi as their military force, and after the suppression of the government by the Bolsheviks many of its adherents, including the Prime Minister, M. Chokayev, fled to the Basmachi and organized them as guerrillas. The movement spread throughout Turkestan and at times reduced the Soviet authority to the main cities and railways. Starting as an anti-Bolshevik movement, it developed into an anti-Russian one, and any Europeans might be massacred. The Basmachi were suppressed by 1924 except in the mountainous areas, where they were intermittently active until the early 1930's and again during the Second World War. To prevent any re-emergence the authorities resorted to resettling mountain Tadzhiks on the plains after the war. *See* R. Pipes, *The Formation of the Soviet Union*, Cambridge, Mass., 1954; A. G. Park, *Bolshevism in Turkestan*, New York, 1957; 'Basmachis: the Central Asian Resistance Movement, 1918–24,' *Central Asian Review*, vol. vii, No. 3, 1959.

Batalov, Aleksey Nikolayevich (*b.* 1929), one of the leading young film actors. He had his first part at the age of 15 in the partisan film *Zoya*, 1944, played first lead in *The Rumyantsev Case*, 1956, and became internationally known for his part in the Cannes Festival prize film *The Cranes are Flying*, 1957, in which he took the male lead.

Batalpashinsk, *see* CHERKESSK.

Bataysk, town in the Rostov Oblast (southern Russia), situated on the left bank of the Don 7 m. south of Rostov. Population (1959) 52,000 (1926, 29,000; 1939, 48,000). It is an important railway junction. Bataysk, which was a village until the 1930's, had a considerable trade in grain and cattle before the collectivization of agriculture (q.v.). It saw much fighting in the civil war and in 1943.

Batu (often **Batyy**), Mongol-Tatar khan, grandson of Genghis Khan. In 1236–40 he conquered Russia; he defeated the Hungarians and Poles, but was routed by the Czechs and Austrians. He was the founder of the Golden Horde (q.v.).

Batumi (ancient **Bathys**), capital, economic and cultural centre of the Adzhar Autonomous Republic, a port in the south-eastern corner of the Black Sea. Population (1959) 82,000 (1939, 70,000). It exports oil products (received by pipeline from Baku), citrus fruits and tea. It is a picturesque town, with a famous botanical garden of subtropical plants founded in 1911.

Baudouin de Courtenay, Ivan (Jan) Aleksandrovich (1845–1929), Polish philologist, professor at Kazan', Yur'yev, Cracow and St Petersburg (1901–18) universities. From 1918 he lived in Poland. In his works on general and comparative linguistics he developed the psychological theory of language and created the theory of phonems and phonetic alternations (*Versuch einer Theorie phonetischer Alternationen*, Strasbourg, 1895). He was the founder of the Kazan' and St Petersburg linguistic schools. As a publicist he defended the interests of the ethnic minorities in Russia, Poland, Austro-Hungary, etc.

Baybakov, Nikolay Konstantinovich (*b.* 1911), industrial manager. He was born in Baku, the son of an oil worker, studied at the Azerbaydzhan Industrial Institute (graduating 1932) and made a rapid career as an oil engineer and manager in Baku and Kuybyshev. He became Deputy People's Commissar for the Oil Industry in 1940,

Commissar (later Minister) in 1944, was chairman of the U.S.S.R. State Planning Commission (*see* GOSPLAN) in 1956, demoted to a similar post in the R.S.F.S.R. in 1957, and since 1958 has been chairman of a regional economic council. The great expansion of the oil industry in the Volga-Urals area in the 1940's and fifties was to a considerable extent due to Baybakov's energy and vision.

Baykal (Mongolian **Dalai Nor**, 'The Holy Sea'), freshwater lake in a mountainous region of southern Siberia, stretching from south-west to north-east. Length 390 m.; breadth 20–50 m.; area 12,500 sq. m.; 1,513 ft above sea level. Many rivers flow into Lake Baykal, the chief being the Selenga, and it has only one outlet, the Angara; it is rich in fish and there are also seals. The lake is the deepest in the world, its greatest depth being 5,660 ft.

Baykalean Mountains, several ranges surrounding Lake Baykal in southern Siberia and stretching in a north-easterly direction. The highest peak, Shebetuy in the Barguzin range, is 8,380 ft. The mountains have gold, tin, mica and coal deposits.

Baykov, Aleksandr Aleksandrovich (1870–1946), metallurgist and chemist, professor at the St Petersburg Polytechnical Institute, where he founded a large school of metal research, member of the Academy of Sciences. He continued the work of D. K. Chernov and Kurnakov (qq.v.), mainly in the field of transformations in metals and in the theory of metallurgical processes. His collected works were published in 1948.

Bazhenov, Vasiliy Ivanovich (1737–99), architect of great genius, but ill-starred. The son of a Moscow sexton, he worked under Ukhtomskiy, studied at Moscow University and the Academy of Arts, St Petersburg, whence he was sent to Paris and Rome. His plans are notable for his use of curves and intersecting axes and for his lavish use of columns. After the failure of his plans for the Kremlin (q.v.) and Tsaritsyno he fell into Catherine II's disfavour, and much of his work in Moscow was carried out anonymously. A superb example of his work in Moscow is the Pashkov House, now the Old Building of the Lenin Library. He exerted a tremendous influence on his contemporaries, particularly Kazakov (q.v.). *See also* ARCHITECTURE. *See* Tamara Talbot Rice, *Russian Art*, 1949; V. Snegirëv, *V. I. Bazhenov*, Moscow, 1950; Academy of Sciences of U.S.S.R., *Neizvestnyye i Predpolagayemyye Postroiki V. I. Bazhenova*, Moscow, 1951; G. H. Hamilton, *The Art and Architecture of Russia*, 1954; A. Voyce, *The Moscow Kremlin*, 1955.

Bednyy, Dem'yan (real name **Pridvorov, Yefim Alekseyevich**) (1883–1945), Communist poet. During the civil war and the 1920's his simple verses enjoyed widespread popularity, and he was regarded as the chief proletariat poet. *See* J. Lindsay (trans.), *Russian Poetry, 1917–1955*, 1957.

Belaya Tserkov' (Ukrainian **Bila Tserkva**), town in the Kiev Oblast of the Ukraine, 60 m. south-west of Kiev. Population (1956) 43,500, before the war half Jewish. Known since 1155, it was a centre of the Ukrainian Cossacks during the 17th century; it became Russian in 1793. It has suffered several Jewish pogroms since the first in 1648.

Belgorod: 1. Oblast of the R.S.F.S.R., situated in the south of the central Russian upland, in the black earth belt. Area 10,500 sq. m.; population (1959) 1,227,000 (18 per cent urban), Russians and Ukrainians. Wheat, sugar-beet and sunflowers are grown and there are food and some engineering industries. The large iron ore deposits of the Kursk Magnetic Anomoly are now beginning to be worked.

2. Administrative centre of the oblast, 40 m. north of Khar'kov. Population (1959) 71,000. It has large chalk quarries and the biggest slate factory in the U.S.S.R. Known since the 13th century, Belgorod was the centre of the Muscovite southern defence line in the 17th century, and the scene of fierce fighting between the Germans and the Soviet Army in 1943.

Belgorod-Dnestrovskiy (Rumanian **Cetatea Alba**, Turkish **Akkerman**, ditto Russian, 1806–1944), town in the Odessa Oblast of the Ukraine, situated in southern Bessarabia at the Dniester estuary. Population (1956) 21,600 (1885, 41,000; 1920, 40,000), Ukrainians, Russians, Jews, Moldavians, Greeks and Armenians. Founded as the ancient Greek colony of Tyras, it belonged in the Middle Ages variously to Kiev, Galicia, Tatars, Genoese and Moldavians; it became Turkish in 1479, Russian in 1806 and was Rumanian 1918–1940, 1941–4.

Belinskiy, Vissarion Grigor'yevich (1811–48), first representative of the non-noble radical intelligentsia, a literary critic and one of the leaders of Westernism (q.v.). He originated the sociological school of literary criticism which prevailed until the end of the 19th century and which has been revived by the Communists. See his *Selected Philosophical Works*, Moscow, 1956. See R. Hare, *Pioneers of Russian Social Thought*, 1951; H. E. Bowman, *Vissarion Belinski, 1811–1848, a Study in the Origins of Social Criticism in Russia*, 1954; R. W. Mathewson, *The Positive Hero in Russian Literature*, New York, 1958.

Beloretsk, town in Bashkiria situated on the upper course of the River Belaya, about 45 m. north-west of Magnitogorsk. Population (1959) 59,000, mostly Russians. It has ironworks and metal-working industries. Beloretsk was founded in 1762 as an ironworks. In 1773–1774 it was a stronghold of Pugachëv (q.v.).

Belorussia ('White Russia,' Belorussian **Belarus'**), Union Republic of the U.S.S.R., adjacent to the Polish frontier; it is situated in the western part of the Russian plain and is traversed from south-west to north-east by the Belorussian moraine upland with lowlands in the north and north-west (the Western Dvina and Niemen valleys) and in the south (the Dnieper and Pripet lowland, see POLES'YE); about one-quarter of the area is covered by mixed forests, about 10 per cent by marshes. It has a moderate humid continental climate and large deposits of peat. Area 81,000 sq. m.; population (1959) 8,055,000 (31 per cent urban), chiefly Belorussians (about 80 per cent of the total), Russians (since the 16th century, 9 per cent) and Poles (7 per cent), before the Second World War also many Jews (since the 14th century, now 2 per cent). There are engineering, wood-processing, food and light industries, coarse grain, potato and flax cultivation, dairy farming and pig breeding. Principal towns: Minsk (capital), Gomel', Vitebsk, Mogilëv; the republic is divided into the six administrative oblasts of Brest, Gomel', Grodno, Minsk, Mogilëv and Vitebsk.

The inhabitants of the area in the 9th century were the Russian (East Slav) tribes of Krivichi, Dregovichi, Polochane, Radimichi and Buzhane, all of whom fell under the authority of the Kievan State, though Polotsk remained a strong local centre of authority; the decline of Kievan strength in the 12th century brought about the emergence of the new principalities of Turov-Pinsk, Smolensk and Volhynia, which were incorporated in the Grand Duchy of Lithuania in the 13th–14th centuries. The whole of Belorussia was annexed by Russia in the Polish partitions of 1772–95, but from 1920 to 1939 western Belorussia was once more Polish. The area saw fierce fighting and suffered severely in both world wars. Belorussia was affected by the Polish risings of 1830 and 1863, in which a section of the Belorussian peasantry, in addition to the Polish or polonized gentry, took part. Later in the 19th century the Populist, Social Democratic and Zionist movements were all strong in Belorussia.

Demands for territorial autonomy began to be voiced at the beginning of the 20th century by the Revolutionary (later Socialist) Hromada Party, but they failed to enlist wide support. After the Bolshevik seizure of power in Russia a struggle ensued between Bolshevik, Ukrainian, Polish and Belorussian organizations and units of the Russian western front; in 1918, under German occupation, an independent Belorussian Republic was proclaimed, and in 1920 the country was occupied by the Poles and suffered several Jewish pogroms. An attempt was made in 1919 to establish a united Lithu-anian-Belorussian Soviet Republic; in 1921 a small Belorussian Republic was set up by the Communists, and in 1922 this became a constituent republic of the U.S.S.R. In 1924–6 the republic's area was increased by the inclusion of neighbouring territories to the east, and in 1939 by the inclusion of western Belorussia. Together with the Baltic States, Belorussia formed the Reich Commissariat 'Ostland' during the German occupation of 1941–4. As in other national republics of the U.S.S.R., power in Belorussia during the 1920's was largely in the hands of National Communists; when Stalin's supremacy was established these were eliminated, but accusations of 'nationalist deviations' in Belorussia have continued. *See* W. Kolarz, *Russia and her Colonies*, 1952; R. Pipes, *The Formation of the Soviet Union*, Cambridge, Mass., 1954; V. Seduro, *The Byelorussian Theatre and Drama*, New York, 1955; N. P. Vakar, *Belorussia, the Making of a Nation*, Cambridge, Mass., 1956, and *A Bibliographical Guide to Belorussia*, Cambridge, Mass., 1956; A. Adamovich, *Opposition to Sovietization in Belorussian Literature (1917–1957)*, Munich, 1958.

Belorussians (or **White Russians**), East Slav (q.v.) people closely related to the Great Russians and Ukrainians who inhabit Belorussia and the adjacent areas, numbering (1959) 7·8 million, of whom 84 per cent regard Belorussian as their mother tongue. During the 13th and 14th centuries, when the whole area belonged to the Grand Duchy of Lithuania, the Belorussians first developed a distinct identity; the Lithuanians were heavily outnumbered by, and culturally inferior to, the Russian element, and until the Grand Duchy's union with Poland in 1569 Russian was its official language. The advance of Catholicism and the polonizing influences that resulted from the union were opposed by the Orthodox Church and the *bratstvos* (q.v.), and the majority of Belorussians remained Russian and Orthodox. In the late 19th and early 20th centuries, when a Belorussian literature and press appeared, a national consciousness of their own emerged.

Belovo, town in the Kemerovo Oblast (southern Siberia), about 60 m. south of Kemerovo. Population (1959) 107,000 (1939, 43,000). It has coal-mining, zinc and engineering (radio and cinema equipment) industries.

Bel'tsy (Rumanian **Bălţi**), town in the Moldavian Republic, the economic centre of northern Bessarabia. Population (1959) 67,000 (1939, 31,000). It has varied food industries.

Belyayev, Mitrofan Petrovich (1836–1904), music publisher and musical Maecenas, who in 1885 founded a publishing house in Leipzig for benefit of national composers. He sponsored concerts in St Petersburg, and was the patron of Russian music at the Paris Exhibition in 1889. The joint string quartet by Rimsky-Korsakov, Borodin, Glazunov and Lyadov based on the notes ' B '–' La '–' F' was written in his honour. *See* KUCHKA.

Belyy, Andrey (real name **Bugayev, Boris Nikolayevich**) (1880–1934), leader of the younger Symbolists, a poet, novelist and literary theorist. His poems and novels (*Petersburg*, 1913–16) are obscure and difficult, being full of linguistic innovations and experiments; these had much influence upon Russian literary forms. *See* J. Lindsay (trans.), *Russian Poetry, 1917–1955*, 1957.

Bendery (Rumanian **Tighina**, Turkish **Bender**), town of the Moldavian Republic, situated on the River Dniester in Bessarabia. Population (1956) 37,900 (1914, 60,000; 1930, 32,000). It is a river port, railway junction, and has varied food industries. Bendery was founded by the Genoese in the 12th century and was a strong Turkish fortress from 1558. For later history *see* BESSARABIA.

Benediktov, Ivan Aleksandrovich (*b.* 1902), agricultural manager and diplomat, a party member since 1930 and member of the central committee since 1939. The son of a village post-office clerk, he worked at the age of 15 as a labourer in a textile factory, studied at the Economics Faculty of the Moscow Agricultural Academy (graduating 1927) and worked in agricultural administration in Uzbekistan and Moscow Oblast. During the Great Purge (q.v.) Benediktov was rapidly promoted to Commissar for Agriculture, a post which he occupied with short intervals until 1955, when he became Minister of Sovkhozes; in 1957 he was demoted to R.S.F.S.R. Minister of Agriculture. For a few months in 1953 he was ambassador in India, and has held this post again since 1959.

Benois, Aleksandr Nikolayevich (1870–1960), painter, illustrator and theatrical designer, art historian and critic. He studied law at St Petersburg University and attended classes at the Academy of Arts from 1887. In 1898 he and Diaghilev founded the periodical *Mir Iskusstva* (q.v.). He played an important part in familiarizing the

Russian public with Western artistic trends and, later, in acquainting Western Europe with the achievements of Russian ballet and the fine arts. Eighteenth-century St Petersburg and Versailles were recurrent subjects of his paintings. In 1907 he collaborated with Diaghilev in producing *Le Pavillon d'Armide*, for which Benois wrote the book and designed the *décor* and costumes. In 1908 *Boris Godunov* was shown in Paris with sets and costumes by Benois (in collaboration with the Moscow painter Golovin). The most famous of the ballets for which Benois wrote the book and created sets and costumes is *Petrouchka*. In 1954 he executed drawings for the catalogue of the Diaghilev Exhibition in Edinburgh. See his *The Russian School of Painting*, New York, 1916, and *Memoirs*, 1960.

Berdichev, town in the Zhitomir Oblast of the Ukraine, 116 m. south-west of Kiev. Population (1959) 53,000 (1863, 53,200; 1914, 75,300), before the war mainly Jewish. It has engineering, light and food industries, and is the centre of a sugar-producing area. Berdichev has been known since the 14th century; in the 19th century it was the chief commercial town of the right-bank Ukraine and the centre of the Hassidic religious movement, often called 'the Jerusalem of Volhynia.'

Berdyansk (1939–58 **Osipenko**), port in the Zaporozh'ye Oblast of the Ukraine, on the Sea of Azov. Population (1959) 65,000 (1914, 38,000; 1926, 26,000). It has an engineering industry (agricultural machinery and aircraft) and a cracking plant, and is a mud and health resort. Berdyansk was founded in 1827.

Berdyayev, Nikolay Aleksandrovich (1874–1948), philosopher, one of the chief representatives of modern Personalism (q.v.). A Marxist and member of the early Social Democratic circles in his youth, Berdyayev, together with a number of other young Marxist intellectuals, turned to Idealism (*Subjectivism and Individualism in Social Philosophy*, 1901) and later to Orthodox Christianity. He continued to be sympathetic to the revolutionary movement (q.v.) until the revolution of 1905 (q.v.), when he became disillusioned; he took part in the Vekhi (q.v.) symposium in 1909. Although he considered the outcome of the 1917 revolution inevitable, and in the social sense just (having indeed forecast the victory of the Bolsheviks ten years before), he was irreconcilably opposed to the new regime because of its suppression of human freedom. Elected to the chair of philosophy at Moscow University, he became extremely popular with the students; in 1921 he, together with Frank (q.v.), was able to found a free Philosophical Academy where lectures were open to the public. The academy had a sensational success, but together with other leading intellectuals Berdyayev was expelled from Russia in 1922. He first settled in Berlin, where he founded the Russian Academy of Philosophy and Religion, but later had to leave Germany and spent the last years of his life in France.

The philosophic genius of Berdyayev, which had already manifested itself in his *Meaning of Creativeness*, 1916, now developed to its full extent, and he became a leading Christian philosopher, exercising considerable influence on contemporary thought. The central theme of his teaching was human freedom, and he explored this problem in all directions and elaborated the concept of the free creative human personality as the true meaning of the Christian doctrine of man as the image of God. Though his interpretation of Russian thought shows brilliant insights, his general view of Russian history as being a series of approximations to a totalitarian ideal is over-simplified and exaggerated. *See* his *The End of Our Time*, 1932, *Christianity and Class War*, 1933, *Dostoievsky*, 1934, *Freedom and the Spirit*, 2 vols., 1935, *The Meaning of History*, 1936, *The Destiny of Man*, 1937, *The Origin of Russian Communism*, 1937, *Solitude and Society*, 1938, *Spirit and Reality*, 1939, *Slavery and Freedom*, 1943, *The Russian Idea*, 1947, *Towards a New Epoch*, 1949. *See* E. Porret, *La Philosophie Chrétienne en Russie: Nicolas Berdiaeff*, Neuchatel, 1944; E. Lampert, *Nicolas Berdyaev and the New Middle Ages*, 1945; O. F. Clarke, *Introduction to Berdyaev*, 1950; D. A. Lowrie, *Rebellious Prophet*, New York, 1960; W. Herberg (ed.), *Four Existentialist Theologians*, 1960.

Berezina, right affluent of the Dnieper, in Belorussia. Length 280 m. The Berezina is historically famous for the disastrous passage of Napoleon's army on its retreat from Moscow in 1812; in 1941 it was the scene of the defeat of large Soviet forces by the Germans.

Berezniki, town in the Perm' Oblast, on the River Kama. Population (1959) 106,000 (1926, 16,000). It has a huge chemical combine and is one of the main industrial centres of the Urals. Berezniki was founded as a sodium plant in 1883, and later absorbed Usol'ye, which had been a saltworks since the 16th century.

Berëzovo, urban settlement in the Khanty-Mansi National Okrug of the Tyumen' Oblast (Western Siberia). Population (1956) 5,700, Russian. It is a local fishing and fur-trapping centre, and the starting-point for a prospective natural gas pipeline to Sverdlovsk. Berëzovo was founded as a fortified town and administrative centre of the lower Ob' area in 1593, and has been an area of banishment since the 18th century.

Berg, Lev Semënovich (1876–1950), zoologist and geographer of Jewish origin, whose work was concerned with ichthyology, the physical geography of Russia, the origin of the loess soils, etc. He attracted much attention with his anti-Darwinist theory of 'nomogenesis.' *See* his *Nomogenesis*, 1926, and *Natural Regions of the U.S.S.R.*, Washington, D.C., 1950.

Beria, Lavrentiy Pavlovich (1899–1953), Georgian Communist, one of the most sinister figures of the Communist regime. He joined the Bolshevik Party in 1917 and from 1921 to 1931 worked in important positions in the Cheka and G.P.U. (qq.v.) organs of Transcaucasia. He was first secretary of the Transcaucasian committee of the Communist Party, and virtual dictator of Transcaucasia between 1932 and 1938. From 1938 to 1945 he was Commissar for Internal Affairs, and in addition a deputy prime minister in charge of security from 1941 to 1953. He was created a Marshal of the Soviet Union in 1945. The Great Purge (q.v.) was ended by Beria, who liquidated his predecessor Yezhov and many N.K.V.D. officials; he organized all the subsequent terroristic measures, which included the deportation of hundreds of thousands from eastern Poland, the Baltic States and the territories occupied by the Germans during the war. He was also in charge of the security police of the satellite states. Beria was defeated, arrested and shot as an 'imperialist agent' during the struggle for power which followed Stalin's death. In 1935 he had initiated the Stalinocentric fictitious historiography which was dominant until the 20th Congress of the Communist Party in 1956. *See* his *On the History of the Bolshevik Organizations in Transcaucasia*, 1939.

Berman, Yakov Aleksandrovich (1868–?), jurist and philosopher. He became a Social Democrat in 1890 and took part in the uprising in Moscow in 1905 as a member of the Menshevik military organization, but in 1906 went over to the Bolsheviks. In the following years he played a prominent part in the Bogdanovist ideological movement (*see* BOGDANOVISM), concentrating on problems of epistemology and logic. In his works *Dialectics in the Light of the Modern Theory of Knowledge*, 1908, and *The Essence of Pragmatism, New Currents in the Science of Thought*, 1911, Berman rejected dialectics as a mystical and scholastic doctrine and aimed at a synthesis of Marxism and Pragmatism. In 1917 he belonged to the Social Democrats Internationalists, but after the Bolshevik seizure of power again joined the Bolsheviks and was in 1917–18 chairman of the Moscow revolutionary tribunal. Later he taught at the Sverdlov Communist University, Moscow University, the Institute of Soviet Law, the Institute of Scientific Philosophy, etc., and was a leading exponent of the Communist legal philosophy until the Great Purge (q.v.), when he disappeared as an 'enemy of the people.'

Bernshteyn, Sergey Natanovich (*b.* 1880), mathematician of Jewish origin. Educated at Paris and Göttingen, he has taught at Khar'kov, Leningrad and Moscow universities, and is a member of the U.S.S.R. (since 1929) and the Ukrainian (since 1925) Academies of Sciences and a corresponding member of Paris Academy (since 1928). He has written extensively on the theory of differential equations, the theory of approximating functions by polynomials and the theory of probabilities; has created the so-called constructive theory of functions, and applied the theory of probabilities to physical and statistical problems.

Bervi-Flërovskiy (real name **Bervi**), **Vasiliy Vasil'yevich** (1829–1918), economist and Populist publicist. His book *The Position of the Working Class in Russia*, 1869, besides being the first extensive work on the subject, made an important contribution to Populist theory by pointing out the *artel'* (q.v.) as the equivalent among industrial workers of the peasant commune (*see* MIR). *See* J. H. Billington, *Mikhailovsky and Russian Populism*, 1958.

Berzin, Jan (1881–1938), Latvian Communist. He spent many years in western Europe and the U.S.A. before 1917, and was afterwards active as a Soviet diplomat in Switzerland, Finland, Austria and Britain. He was one of the principal organizers of the forced labour camps in Russia, and headed the Dal'stroy (q.v.) industrial combine and camp system from 1932. He was shot during the Great Purge (q.v.).

Bessarabia, area in south-eastern Europe situated between the rivers Dniester and Prut, the Danube delta and the Black Sea. It shared the same fate as other territories north of the Black Sea in antiquity and in the Middle Ages: continual nomadic invasions, Greek colonization, Roman rule and Genoese colonization. It was annexed by the newly established principality of Moldavia in 1367, which was subjugated by Turkey in 1513. Bessarabia was ceded to Russia, becoming a province of New Russia (q.v.) in 1812; southern Bessarabia was surrendered by Russia in the Paris Treaty of 1856 (and included in the newly established Rumania in 1859), but became Russian once more under the Berlin Treaty of 1878. Following the Bolshevik seizure of power, the anti-Bolshevik Land Council of Bessarabia first proclaimed the formation of the Moldavian People's Republic as part of the Russian Federation, then its independence and finally its incorporation into Rumania; in 1920 Britain, France, Italy and Japan recognized the incorporation, but the Soviet Government did not, and in 1940 it forced Rumania by ultimatum to cede Bessarabia and northern Bukovina. The area belonged once more to Rumania 1941–4, but in the peace treaty of 1947 was finally ceded to the Soviet Union. The greater part of Bessarabia forms the Moldavian Republic, while the north and south (predominantly non-Rumanian in population) are included in the Ukraine (*see* CHERNOVTSY and ODESSA). *See* B. Nolde, *La Formation de l'Empire Russe*, vol. ii, Paris, 1952.

Bezhitsa (1935–43 Ordzhonikidzegrad), former town in the Bryansk Oblast, fused with Bryansk in 1956.

Bezobrazov, Vladimir Pavlovich (1828–89), economist, geographer and liberal publicist. He made a successful career in the Ministry of Finance (eventually becoming a senator), combining it with scholarly work. In 1873–80 he edited the *Collection of State Knowledge* in eight volumes with contributions by many outstanding economists, jurists and political scientists; this work played an important role in the development of liberal thought in Russia. He also organized monthly 'economic dinners' attended by business men and administrators. A collection of his articles appeared in 1882 under the title *State and Society. Government, Self-government and Judicial Power*. *See* his *Études sur l'économie nationale de la Russie*, 2 vols., St Petersburg, 1883, 1886.

'Biological Crop,' system of calculating the harvest before it has actually been gathered (i.e. while the crops are still standing), practised from 1933 (for grain, 1940 for all crops) till 1953. This system, which did not allow for damage before harvesting or for wastage, had two aims: the imposition of higher deliveries to the State (*see* AGRICULTURAL PROCUREMENT) and exaggerated figures for propaganda purposes. It was one of the worst aspects of Stalin's agricultural policy.

Biology has been actively pursued in Russia since the 18th century, when the Academy of Sciences (q.v.) organized a series of expeditions to various parts of the country. Apart from K. E. von Bär's and A. O. Kovalevskiy's (q.v.) embryological works, biological research in the 19th and early 20th centuries was mainly devoted to physiology (L. I. Mechnikov, Sechenov, Timiryazev, Pavlov, Vvedenskiy, qq.v.). During the last decades Pavlov's work has been continued by Orbeli (q.v.) and others, while Vvedenskiy's school has been chiefly represented by Ukhtomskiy (q.v.). Comparative morphology and embryology have been further advanced by A. N. Severtsov, Navashin (qq.v.), I. I. Shmal'gauzen, etc.; there are three distinct trends in morphological studies: evolutionary, functional and ecological. Genetics was flourishing in the 1920's and early thirties, largely thanks to N. I. Vavilov (q.v.). Biochemistry is now pursued with great stress, as well as biophysics, where Lazarev's (q.v.) work is continued. In microbiology there is an interesting geological trend, forming a part of the bio-geochemical studies initiated by Vernadskiy (q.v.). In the study of soils, pioneered in Russia by Dokuchayev, Vil'yams and Pryanishnikov (qq.v.) have headed two rival schools. Outstanding in descriptive and systematic biology are the works of the botanist Komarov and the helminthologist Pavlovskiy (qq.v.). Lysenko's (q.v.) obscurantist dictatorship, first in genetics (since the late 1930's) and from 1948 until after Stalin's death in the whole field of biology, caused considerable harm. *See* J. G. Crowther, *Soviet Science*, 1936; E. Ashby, *Scientist in Russia*, 1947; J. S. Huxley, *Soviet Genetics and World Science*, 1949; J. Langdon-Davies, *Russia puts the Clock Back*, 1949; G. H. Beale, 'Changing Trends in Soviet Attitudes to Biology,' *Soviet Studies*, vol. vii, No. 1, 1955; *Symposium on Radiobiology* (Moscow, 1955), New York, 1956; A. L. Kursanov *et al.* (eds.), *Summaries of Papers from the Second All-Union Conference on Photosynthesis* (1957), New York, 1957; A. I. Oparin, *The Origin of Life on the Earth*, 1957; K. M. Bykov (ed.), *Textbook of Physiology*, Moscow, 1958.

Complete cover-to-cover translations of the following journals exist in English: *Bulletin of Experimental Biology and Medicine*; *Journal of Microbiology, Epidemiology and Immunobiology*; *Journal of Abstracts: Biology*; *Entomological Review*; *Sechenov Physiological Journal of the U.S.S.R.*; *Microbiology*.

Birobidzhan, administrative centre of the Jewish Autonomous Oblast in the Khabarovsk Kray (Far East), on the Trans-Siberian Railway, 78 m. west of Khabarovsk. Population (1959) 41,000. It has light and woodworking industries, and became a town in 1928, having formerly been a small railway station, Tikhon'kaya.

Biysk, town in the Altay Kray (southern Siberia), the starting-point of a highway to Mongolia. Population (1959) 146,000 (1926, 46,000). It is the centre of an agricultural area, and has engineering, food and textile industries; its museum has a rich collection of exhibits on ethnography and the history of the Altay Mountains area. Biysk was founded as a fortress by the Russians in 1709.

Black Earth (*chernozëm*), belt of rich and fertile black soil, containing a proportion of humus, which stretches from the Carpathians and the Black Sea to the Altay Mountains, and is found in small patches farther east. Its normal depth is about 1 ft, but in some places it is over 3 ft deep.

Black Hundred, name applied by their adversaries to the extreme right-wing elements in Russia in the early 20th century. They supported anti-Semitism, absolutism and nationalism, and carried out pogroms against Jews and students. The Black Hundred set up organizations of a fascist kind (e.g. the Union of the Russian People) during the revolution of 1905 (q.v.).

Black Market, *see* SPECULATORS.

Black Sea (ancient **Pontus Euxinus**) is bounded on the north and east by the U.S.S.R., on the west by Rumania, Bulgaria and Turkey, and on the south by Turkey. Greatest length about 720 m.; greatest breadth about 380 m.; total area 170,000 sq. m.; greatest depth about 7,000 ft. It joins the Sea of Azov by Kerch' Strait, and the Mediterranean by the Bosphorus, the Sea of Marmora and the Dardanelles. The chief rivers emptying into the Black Sea are the Danube, Dniester, Bug, Dnieper, Rion; the principal Russian ports are Odessa, Nikolayev, Novorossiysk, Batumi and Poti. The Treaty of Paris in 1856 closed the Black Sea to all warships, but in 1871 this treaty was abrogated, and both Turkey and the Soviet Union have fleets in it. As a result of the armistice signed at Mudros on 30th October 1918, giving allied ships access through the Dardanelles and the Bosphorus, the British Navy was legally enabled to enter the Black Sea during the British intervention in the civil war. Soviet policy is that the Black Sea should be open only to the warships of nations bordering on it. See *The Black Sea Coast of the Soviet Union, a Short Guide,* Moscow, 1957.

Blagoveshchensk, administrative, economic and cultural centre of the Amur Oblast in the Far East, situated on the River Amur. Population (1959) 94,000 (1914, 76,500; 1939, 59,000). There are engineering (gold-mining equipment since 1893) and varied food industries. Blagoveshchensk was founded in 1653 and restored in 1856. At the time of the Boxer rising in China (1900) five thousand Chinese inhabitants were evicted and drowned by Russian troops.

'**Blat**' (slang word for 'string-pulling'). The practice of *blat* is very widespread, especially in the acquisition of scarce commodities, and is carried on not only by individuals in their personal interest but also by managers to get hold of goods which are needed for their enterprises but have not been allocated; in the latter case, *blat* frequently takes the form of mutually satisfactory barter. *See further under* TOLKACH. *See* J. S. Berliner, 'Blat is Higher than Stalin!,' *Problems of Communism,* Jan.–Feb. 1954, and *Factory and Manager in the U.S.S.R.,* Cambridge, Mass., 1957.

Blok, Aleksandr Aleksandrovich (1880–1921), leader of the younger Symbolists and their most outstanding poet. He had been deeply influenced by the ideas of Vladimir Solov'ëv (q.v.) and began his literary career in 1905 with *Poems of the Beautiful Lady,* which is devoted to worship of the ideal woman. By 1911, however, he had bitterly reacted against his earlier ideals, and the poems of *Nocturnal Hours* are concerned with the human misery of the city streets and restaurants. A further turn in his genius was brought about by the First World War, and his love for his country was manifested. He hailed the 1917 revolution, and, sympathetic to the Left Socialist Revolutionaries, co-operated with the Bolsheviks after their seizure of power, publishing in 1918 *The Twelve*—an apotheosis of the revolution—and *The Scythians,* an appeal to the West to support the new Russia. The Bolshevik dictatorship soon brought disillusionment, however, and when in 1921 he delivered an address on the anniversary of Pushkin's death he said: 'Peace and freedom are taken away . . . and the poet dies because he can no longer breathe; life has lost its meaning.' He died shortly afterwards. *See* his *The Twelve*, 1920; *The Spirit of Music*, 1946 (a selection of essays on art and politics). *See* G. Ivanov, *Peterburgskiye zimy*, New York, 1952; J. Lindsay (trans.), *Russian Poetry, 1917–1955*, 1957; R. Poggioli, *The Poets of Russia, 1890–1930*, Cambridge, Mass., 1960.

Blonskiy, Pavel Petrovich (1884–1941), psychologist and educational theorist, the father of 'pedology' (q.v.) in Russia, a former Socialist Revolutionary. His book *The Unified Labour School*, 1919, was the first attempt at creating a Communist education theory, and his views on 'free education' and polytechnic education—fitting in with the modernistic Bogdanovist (*see* BOGDANOVISM) views of the then Commissar of Education, Lunacharskiy—greatly influenced Soviet educational policy of the 1920's and early thirties. He disappeared during the Great Purge (q.v.), but his reputation has been rehabilitated since Stalin's death. *See* R. A. Bauer, *The New Man in Soviet Psychology*, Cambridge, Mass., 1952.

Blyukher Vasiliy Konstantinovich (1889–1938), Marshal of the Soviet Union. As an industrial worker he joined the Bolsheviks in 1916 and distinguished himself during the civil war as commander of Red Army units in the Urals and against General Wrangel; he was the first person to receive the decoration of the new Order of the Red Banner instituted by the Soviet Government. He commanded the special Far Eastern Army during the hostilities with the Chinese in 1929, and from then onwards was virtually the dictator of the Russian Far East, the only case when a military commander rather than the regional party secretary held the real power. He became a candidate member of the Central Committee in 1934, and a marshal in the following year. In 1937 he sat on the special military court which sentenced Tukhachevskiy (q.v.) and other leading Red Army commanders to death, but himself was soon caught up in the Great Purge (q.v.) and disappeared. His reputation was rehabilitated in 1957.

Boarding-schools are primary, incomplete secondary or secondary schools. There were over 500 boarding-schools in 1958, with 180,000 pupils; they are co-educational and may admit day pupils. Orphans and children of poor parents are maintained and educated free; for the rest, the fees are graded according to parents' means. Ninety per cent of the total costs are borne by the State. The curricula are the same as in other schools of corresponding grade, and the boarding-schools do not appear to offer better educational opportunities. Boarding-schools had been well known in Russia before the revolution, either as privileged schools (resembling English public schools) or as professional institutions (theological seminaries, military schools, etc.); they were revived on a small scale after the civil war to cater for the large number of orphans and homeless children; and in more recent years, in addition to the Suvorov and Nakhimov military schools, there were a few boarding-schools in regions and republics with a scattered population in the countryside. The idea of establishing boarding-schools on a large scale was first announced by Khrushchëv in his main report at the 20th party congress in 1956. They are sometimes referred to as the principal type of school in the future Communist society, and there was a plan to increase the number of pupils to over a million by 1960, but the general reform of education in 1958 drew attention away from boarding-schools. See S. V. Utechin, 'Educational Problems,' *The Soviet Cultural Scene, 1956–1957*, ed. by W. Z. Laqueur and G. Lichtheim, 1958.

Bobruysk, town in the Mogilëv Oblast of Belorussia, river port on the Berezina. Population (1959) 97,000 (1939, 84,000). It has woodworking (the largest in Belorussia), engineering (since 1898), food and light industries. Bobruysk has been known since the 16th century and became Russian in 1793; its fortress played an important role in the Patriotic War of 1812 and it was the scene of a major German defeat in 1944.

Bodaybo, town in the Irkutsk Oblast (south-eastern Siberia), situated on the River Vitim, 1,120 m. north-east of Irkutsk. Population (1956) 14,600. It is the centre of the rich Lena gold-mining area. Founded in 1863, it became a town in 1903. In 1912 a workers' strike procession near Bodaybo was fired upon by troops, with many casualties.

Bogdanov (real name **Malinovskiy**), **Aleksandr Aleksandrovich** (1873–1928), philosopher, sociologist, economist and politician. A Social Democrat since the 1890's, Bogdanov joined the Bolsheviks in 1903 and together with Lenin led the 'stone-hard' Bolsheviks and the whole Bolshevik faction between 1904 and 1909; he was then leader of the Left Bolshevik 'Vperëd' (q.v.) group. During the First World War he was a military surgeon. Though outside the Bolshevik Party after 1917, he was widely influential as a theorist of 'proletarian culture' (*see* PROLETKUL'T). From 1923 he confined himself to the problem of blood transfusion (founding the first institute in Russia devoted to the study of the subject), and he died as the result of an experiment upon himself. Bogdanov was much influenced by Mach and Avenarius, and his system of Empiriomonism (*Empiriomonism*, 3 parts, 1905–6) is an attempt at a synthesis of Marxism and Empirio-criticism; his Tectology, or 'universal organizational science' (*Tectology*, first complete ed., 1922), was an extension of Empiriomonism into the field of sociology. His textbooks (*A Short Course of Economic Science*, 1896, Eng. ed. 1923, and *A Course of Political Economy*, 1910) were for a long time standard works on Marxian economics in Russia. *See also* BOGDANOVISM. *See* L. Schapiro, *The Communist Party of the Soviet Union*, 1960.

Bogdanovism, modernistic trend in the Bolshevik ideology. It originated at the turn of the century, when some of the weaknesses of the Marxian theory were realized in Social Democratic circles, and aimed at upholding Marxism by supplementing it with modern ideas. This was effected by Bogdanov himself (q.v.) in the fields of epistemology and sociology; by Berman (q.v.) in logic; by S. Vol'skiy (q.v.) in ethics; by Shulyatikov in aesthetics; by Gor'kiy and Lunacharskiy (qq.v.) in religious theory; by Pokrovskiy (q.v.) in historiography; by

Blonskiy (q.v.) in the theory of education; by Gastev and Kerzhentsev (qq.v.) in the scientific organization of labour; and by Kollontay (q.v.) in the theory of sex relations and the family. All these theories, though strongly disapproved of by Lenin, were widely influential among Communists in Russia until they were suppressed by Stalin in the 1930's. *See* S. V. Utechin, 'Bolsheviks and their Allies after 1917: the Ideological Pattern,' *Soviet Studies*, Oct. 1958.

Bogomolets, Aleksandr Aleksandrovich (1881–1946), pathologist. Educated at the New Russia University (Odessa), he was professor at Saratov University from 1911 and at the 2nd Moscow University from 1925, a member of the Academy of Sciences. He adhered to the experimental physiological trend in pathology. His work was mainly concerned with internal secretion and was summed up in his *Crisis of Endocrinology*, 1927. He also suggested a new classification of constitutional types (*Introduction to the Doctrine of Constitutions and Diatheses*, 1926).

Bogoraz (also known under the pseudonym **Tan**), **Vladimir Germanovich** (1865–1936), ethnographer of Jewish origin. As a student he was a member of 'Narodnaya Volya' (q.v.) and was banished to Siberia, where he became interested and took part in the study of the Paleo-Asiatic (q.v.) and other indigenous peoples. He worked in the United States for several years and later became curator of the Ethnography Museum of the Academy of Sciences and professor at St Petersburg University. In the 1920's he actively co-operated with the Soviet regime, believing that it would preserve the way of life of the primitive peoples. He was the moving spirit behind the Committee of the North (q.v.), which, however, disappointed his hopes. *See* his *The Chukchee*, New York, 1904–10.

Bogucharskiy (real name **Yakovlev**), **Vasiliy Yakovlevich** (1861–1915), historian and politician. He belonged to the Legal Marxists (q.v.) and later became one of the few genuine Economists (*see* Economism). As a historian of the revolutionary movement, he was the author of the first important works on revolutionary Populism.

Bolm, Adolf (1884–1951), dancer and choreographer who studied at the Imperial School, St Petersburg, until 1904, becoming a soloist at the Mariinskiy Theatre. In 1908–9 he toured Scandinavia with Pavlova, becoming a member of Diaghilev's Ballets Russes in 1909. Settling in the United States in 1917, he organized the Ballet Intime, the first of many similar undertakings during his residence in America. As a dancer, particularly in *Prince Igor*, his energetic powers may be said to have done much to restore the male dancer to his rightful position. His work as a film choreographer has been of great importance. *See* F. Gadan and R. Maillard, *A Dictionary of Modern Ballet*, 1959.

Bolshevism (from Russian *bol'she*, more), that radical trend in Russian Social Democracy (*see* Russian Social Democratic Labour Party) which later developed into a system of totalitarian dictatorship, the first successful modern totalitarian movement. Lenin was the founder and main representative of Bolshevism, and his ideas and activities dominated it to such a degree that it is often regarded as identical with Leninism (q.v.), though there were in fact other trends in Bolshevism, the principal being Bogdanovism (q.v.).

The name Bolshevism derived from the majority obtained by Lenin at the end of the 2nd Congress of the R.S.D.L.P. in 1903, after several delegates had left. But the main principles of Bolshevism had already been worked out by Lenin since the 1890's in the struggle against the so-called 'Legal Marxists' and Economism (qq.v.), and had been implemented in the activities of the Iskra (q.v.) organiza-tion established by Lenin in 1900. Bolshevism existed after 1903 as a more or less organized faction (or a number of warring sub-factions) within the Social Democratic Party until 1912, when the Leninists broke from all other Social Democratic trends. The name 'Social Democratic Labour Party (Bolsheviks)' was retained until 1918, when it was replaced by the name of 'Communist Party (Bolsheviks),' and the word Bolsheviks was dropped in 1952. The term Bolshevism is now used in Russia only in the historical sense.

The Bolsheviks took an active part in the revolution of 1905 (q.v.), but their real chance came after the February revolution (q.v.) of 1917, when the successive democratically minded coalition govern-ments (*see* PROVISIONAL GOVERNMENT) proved unable to provide the leadership required for a democratic reorganization of the country in the midst of war. The Bolsheviks achieved a majority in a number of important soviets (q.v.) in the autumn, and with the assistance of the Red Guards (q.v.) were able to seize power on 7th November (*see* OCTOBER REVOLUTION and CONSTITUENT ASSEMBLY). For the further history of Bolshevism *see* COMMUNIST DICTATORSHIP. *See* B. Russell, *Practice and Theory of Bolshevism*, 1920; O. H. Gankin and H. H. Fisher, *The Bolsheviks and the World War*, 1940; L. H. Haim-son, *The Russian Marxists and the Origins of Bolshevism*, 1955; L. Schapiro, *The Origin of the Communist Autocracy*, 1955, and *The Communist Party of the Soviet Union*, 1960; D. Treadgold, *Lenin and his Rivals*, 1955.

Bondarchuk, Sergey Fëdorovich (*b.* 1920), Ukrainian film actor, perhaps the most outstanding of the younger generation of Soviet actors. His first film was *The Young Guard*, 1948, from the novel by Fadeyev (q.v.), in which he was a resistance worker who died in a Nazi prison, and among his other roles was the title part in *Taras Shevchenko*, 1951, the story of the Ukrainian national poet. In 1959 he both directed and took the lead in *A Man's Destiny*, which won first prize at the Moscow Festival in that year. He went to Rome in January 1960 to make the film *It was Night in Rome*, directed by Roberto Rossellini.

Bonuses play an important part in the remuneration of workers and employees. The bonus system is extensive and complicated. Bonuses can be roughly divided into those which accrue automatic-ally upon specified performances in respect of quantity, quality, economy in the use of materials, etc., and those which are paid as a reward for more intangible achievements, particularly those of whole brigades (q.v.), workshops, plants, etc. Bonuses of the former kind are paid out of the regular wages fund, while the latter come from the Director's Fund (q.v.). There is also an additional arrangement for awarding bonuses to managerial personnel by ministries or Economic Councils (q.v.). In the past (since the 1930's) bonuses have sometimes been very substantial, and current reform of the wage structure is partly designed to reduce their role. *See also* WAGES.

Books, *see* PRESS.

Borislav (Ukrainian **Boryslav,** Polish **Boryslaw**), town in the L'vov Oblast (western Ukraine), 45 m. south-west of L'vov. Population (1956) 29,600. It has ozokerite mines (since 1846), oil and gas wells, and produces oil-mining equipment.

Borisoglebsk, town in the Voronezh Oblast (central Russia), 120 m. east of Voronezh. Population (1959) 54,000. It has extensive food industries, and the famous Borisoglebsk oak forest is near by. Founded as a Muscovite outpost in the 17th century, the town was an important centre of the grain trade until the collectivization of agriculture (q.v.).

Borisov, town in the Minsk Oblast (Belorussia), situated on the Moscow–Minsk railway and the River Berezina, about 40 m. north-east of Minsk. Population (1959) 59,000. It has large woodworking and wood-processing industries, also musical instruments and hardware. Borisov has been known since 1127 and became a town in 1563. From the 14th century till 1795 it belonged to Lithuania-Poland and was a fortress. In 1812 the remnants of Napoleon's army made their disastrous crossing of the Berezina near Borisov.

Borodin, Aleksandr Porfir'yevich (1833–87), composer. Professionally he was a chemist, the author of many important works on organic chemistry. He was largely a self-taught musician, a decisive impulse being given to his musical creation by his meeting with Balakirev in 1862, and his subsequent association with the Kuchka (q.v.). A brilliant linguist, he travelled extensively and enjoyed the personal friendship of Liszt. His life was a continual struggle against time and ill health, the latter being exacerbated by the hypochondria of his wife. Works comprise one opera, *Prince Igor*, 1869–87 (unfinished, completed by Rimsky-Korsakov and Glazunov), produced in St Petersburg in 1890; three symphonies: No. 1 in E flat major, 1862–7, No. 2 in B minor, 1869–76, No. 3 in A minor, 1886–7 (unfinished); the 'musical picture' *In the Steppes of Central Asia*, 1880; chamber music, including two quartets: No. 1 in A major, 1875–9, No. 2 in D major, 1881–5; a quantity of piano music and songs. Borodin never considered himself a professional musician; nevertheless, considering the number of his non-musical commitments, his work is of the highest standard. A confirmed follower of Glinka, his music (much of which is programmatic) also shows the influence of Schumann, Berlioz and Liszt, though strongly flavoured with Russian folk music. *Prince Igor* clearly stems from Italian opera and Glinka's *Ruslan*, but its unique quality derives from the ingenious elaboration of folk-song, which is subtly interwoven into the musical fabric. As a symphonist Borodin is one of the greatest Russian masters. His harmony is bold and original, his orchestration lavish and effective. Borodin's songs, in particular, are representative of his total output in their mixture of epic-heroism, lyricism and good-natured humour. *See* G. Abraham, *Borodin, the Composer and his Music*, 1927, *Studies in Russian Music*, 1935, and *On Russian Music*, 1939; G. Abraham and M. D. Calvocoressi, *Masters of Russian Music*, 1936.

Borodin (real name **Gruzenberg**), **Mikhail Markovich** (1884–1952), Communist of Jewish origin. He spent many years before 1917 as an emigrant in America and there belonged to the American Socialist Party. He worked as an agent of the Communist International from 1918, was arrested in Glasgow in 1922 and after six months' imprisonment was expelled from Britain. He was invited to China by **Sun Yat** sen in 1923, and acted as high adviser to the Central Executive Committee of the Kuomintang until 1927. Borodin died in a concentration camp, but has been posthumously rehabilitated.

Borovikovskiy, **Vladimir Lukich** (1757–1825), portrait and icon painter. Born in the Ukraine, he studied at the Academy of Arts and with Levitskiy (q.v.). He painted an extensive series of portraits of members of Russian society: intimate (the sisters Gagarin, Bezborodko and his daughters) as well as formal (**Paul I, the Vice-Chancellor** Kurakin). Light purple tones predominating in many of his mature works produce a certain air of coldness and reserve. He created his own type of female portrait: often quite plain, coy and always individualized and original in spite of superficial similarity of their postures and gestures. His portraits, however, are lacking in the psychological characterization which distinguishes his contemporary and teacher Levitskiy. As an icon painter, Borovikovskiy was influenced by the Ukrainian school; his best work of this kind is the *Annunciation* in the Cathedral of the Virgin of Kazan' in Leningrad. He broke with the traditions of the 18th century, and was the forerunner of romanticism in Russian painting.

Borzhomi, health resort in Georgia, on the River Kura 93 m. west of Tiflis. Population (1956) 15,600. It has a fine climate, and its mineral waters are sold throughout Russia.

Botkin, **Sergey Petrovich** (1832–89), outstanding physician, specialist in internal diseases. Educated at Moscow University and abroad (where among his teachers were Virchow and Claude Bernard), Botkin became professor of the Medico-Surgical Academy in St Petersburg and was the first to introduce into Russia the ideas and practices of his foreign teachers, thus founding the physiological trend in Russian clinical medicine. He wrote the classical *Clinical Course of Internal Diseases*, 3 vols., 1867–75, *General Foundations of Clinical Medicine*, etc., as well as publishing and editing *Professor Botkin's Archive of the Clinic of Internal Diseases* (founded 1862) and the *Weekly Clinical Gazette* (founded 1881). In 1881–9, as a member of the St Petersburg City Duma, he was curator of the city's hospitals.

Bourgeoisie, in Marxist theory the exploiting class in capitalist society which lives by appropriating the surplus value of the labour of the proletariat (q.v.). It is supposed in fact to be controlling policy and the administration in 'capitalist' states whatever their apparent form of government. This rule of the bourgeoisie is destined to be overthrown through a proletarian revolution and replaced by a Dictatorship of the Proletariat (q.v.). This abstract theory was rigidly adhered to by Russian Marxists, especially the Bolsheviks. Thus in their view the Provisional Government (q.v.) in 1917 was bourgeois, although in fact it was ultimately made up almost entirely of socialists and radicals. Since the Bolshevik seizure of power (*see* OCTOBER REVOLUTION) any opposition, within or outside the party, to the leadership of the moment has been branded as inspired by and in the interests of the bourgeoisie, either internal or foreign (*see* CAPITALIST ENCIRCLEMENT).

Boyars, higher nobility until the time of Peter the Great; they headed the civil and military administration, and took part in the Boyars' Duma (Prince's, later Czar's, Council).

Boycottists, group of left-wing Bolsheviks, who in 1906–7 advocated a boycott by Social Democrats of the State Duma on the grounds that participation in parliamentary institutions would have an adverse effect upon the party's revolutionary work. They failed to carry with them the bulk of the Bolshevik faction, who followed Lenin's policy of 'utilizing legal institutions.' Most of the Boycottists later joined the Vperëd (q.v.) sub-faction. *See* J. L. H. Keep, 'Russian Social Democracy and the First State Duma,' *Slavonic and East European Review*, vol. xxxiv, No. 82, Dec. 1955; L. Schapiro, *The Communist Party of the Soviet Union*, 1960.

Bratsk, town in the Irkutsk Oblast (south-eastern Siberia), on the River Angara and the Tayshet–Lena railway. Population (1959) 51,000 (1956, 2,400). One of the largest hydro-electric stations in the world (planned capacity 3,600,000 kw.) is being built here (since 1955), and Bratsk is intended to become a major industrial centre with wood-processing and chemical plants. It was founded as a fort in 1631.

Bratstvo ('brotherhood'), name of Orthodox organizations which existed from the 16th to the 18th centuries in the towns of Belorussia and the Ukraine, when these territories belonged to the Polish-Lithuanian state. They were connected with a church, organized similarly to a guild, and had religious and charitable functions. Later they were the main channel for resistance to Catholic and polonizing influences. Bratstvos established printing-presses and schools, some of which reached a high level of scholarship. The most famous were in L'vov and Kiev.

Bredikhin, Fëdor Aleksandrovich (1831–1904), astronomer. Educated at Moscow University, he taught there, was director of Moscow Observatory, 1873–90, and Pulkovo Observatory, 1890–4, and a member of the Academy of Sciences from 1890. His work was chiefly concerned with the study of comets and meteor streams. In his *On Comets' Tails*, 1862, he developed a mechanical theory of comet forms.

Breshko-Breshkovskaya, Yekaterina Konstantinovna (1844–1934), revolutionary of noble Polish origin, nicknamed 'the Grandmother of the Russian Revolution.' She was a member of the Socialist Revolutionary Party, and spent many years in prison, banishment and underground work. She emigrated to Prague after the Bolshevik seizure of power. *See* her *Reminiscences and Letters* (ed. A. S. Blackwell), Boston, 1918, and *Hidden Springs of the Russian Revolution* (ed. L. Hutchinson), 1931; A. J. Sack, *The Birth of the Russian Democracy*, New York, 1918.

Brest: 1. Oblast in south-west Belorussia, situated mainly in the

Poles'ye with its typical mixed forests and marshes. Area 13,000 sq. m.; population 1,205,000 (23 per cent urban), mostly Belorussians, before the war also Jews and Poles. Lumbering, grain and potato growing and pig breeding are the main activities in the oblast. Principal towns: Brest, Baranovichi, Pinsk.

2. (formerly **Brest-Litovsk**, Polish **Brześć Nad Bugiem**). Administrative and an economic and cultural centre of the oblast, situated on the River Bug, a major transportation centre (the frontier station on the Moscow–Warsaw line, five railway lines, the Dnieper–Bug canal). Population (1956) 73,000 (1910, 53,000; 1931, 48,400). It has varied food and light industries. Brest has been known as a fortified town since 1017; it became Lithuanian in 1319, Polish in 1569, Russian in 1795 and again Polish 1919–39. In 1596 the council which established the Uniate Church met in Brest. As an important fortress it saw much fighting in both world wars; the peace treaty between Soviet Russia and Germany was signed here in 1918.

Brest-Litovsk, Treaty of, separate peace treaty between Russia and Germany which was signed on 3rd March 1918 in Brest, popularly known in Russia as 'the Indecent Peace.' By this treaty Russia gave up large territories in the west, including the Baltic Provinces and the Ukraine, and was obliged to demobilize the army. The value of the treaty to Germany, who had hoped to transfer large numbers of troops to the western front, was to a large extent nullified by the long-drawn-out negotiations, though their occupation of the Ukraine was a great economic gain. The treaty was unilaterally abrogated by the Soviet Government after Germany's defeat by the Western Allies.

The question of concluding the treaty caused a crisis among the Bolshevik leadership. Peace had been one of the main Bolshevik slogans when they seized power, and Lenin was therefore for concluding a treaty at any cost, even if the Allies would not participate. His position was challenged by two factions, headed by Trotskiy and Bukharin. Bukharin and the Left Communists (q.v.) considered peaceful relations with any bourgeois imperialist government to be inconceivable and were in favour of a revolutionary war even if that meant defeat and extinction for the Soviet power; the majority of the party's Central Committee took up Trotskiy's attitude of 'neither peace nor war,' in the expectation of a proletarian revolution in Germany. Both these factions were indirectly supported by the widespread revulsion in the country against a separate peace. Trotskiy, leading the Soviet delegation to Brest, informed the Germans that the Soviet Government would cease to fight but would not conclude a peace, whereupon the Germans began to advance. Simultaneously Lenin threatened his resignation, and under the combined influence of the German advance and Lenin's blackmail the Central Committee reversed its decision and supported Lenin by a small majority. From Stalin's time it has always been maintained in the official Soviet accounts that Trotskiy was acting against his instructions. *See* J. Wheeler Bennett, *Brest-Litovsk: the Forgotten Peace,* 1938; G. Freund, *The Unholy Alliance,* 1957; L. Schapiro, *The Communist Party of the Soviet Union,* 1960.

Brezhnev, Leonid Il'ich (*b.* 1906), Communist. Born in the Ukraine of a working-class family, he started work at the age of 15 and through part-time training became a land surveyor. Working as a surveyor in the Urals from 1927, he rose by 1930 to be the deputy head of the Urals Agricultural Administration. He joined the party in 1931, and until 1935 studied at the Metallurgical Institute in his home town Dneprodzerzhinsk, subsequently becoming an engineer in the iron and steel works there. During the Great Purge (q.v.) he advanced rapidly to the position of a secretary of the Dnepropetrovsk oblast party committee; his association with Khrushchëv dates from this period. A senior political officer during the war, he afterwards returned to party work, and from 1946 to 1952 was in turn first secretary of the Zaporozh'ye and Dnepropetrovsk oblast committees and of the Moldavian central committee. In 1952 he was elevated to membership of the Central Committee of the party and candidate membership of its Presidium, and became one of the secretaries of the Central Committee. Upon Stalin's death in 1953 he was dropped from the Presidium and appointed first deputy head of the Chief Political Administration of the armed forces. In 1954 he became first secretary of the Kazakhstan central committee and in this capacity took a leading part in the Virgin Land Campaign (q.v.). After the 20th party congress (q.v.) in 1956 he again became a candidate member of the Presidium of the Central Committee and one of its secretaries, and in 1957, after the expulsion of the 'anti-party group' (q.v.), a full member of the Presidium. He succeeded Voroshilov as chairman of the Presidium of the Supreme Soviet (i.e. titular head of state) in 1960.

Brigade, team, the usual form of the organization of labour both in industry and agriculture, whereby a group of workers or *kolkhoz* peasants are subordinated to a 'brigadier' (team leader) who is responsible for the distribution of work and the fulfilment of norms. Remuneration is sometimes calculated on the basis of the brigade's work. The so-called 'Socialist emulation' (q.v.) is frequently staged between brigades; exemplary brigades are awarded such titles as 'Shock Brigade,' 'Stakhanov Brigade' or (currently) 'Brigade of Communist Labour.'

Broadcasting, *see* RADIO; TELEVISION.

Brodskiy, Isaak Izrailevich (*b.* 1884), painter, who studied at the Odessa Art School and at the Academy of Arts in St Petersburg under Repin (q.v.); he was influenced by the Mir Iskusstva and by Serov (qq.v.). After the Bolshevik seizure of power he became one of the founders of Socialist Realism (q.v.) in painting. In the 1920's he painted such 'revolutionary' subjects as 'The Opening Ceremony of the 2nd Congress of Comintern in the Uritskiy Palace' and 'The Execution of the Twenty-six Commissars.' For a time he served as an official portraitist of Stalin. While Brodskiy's art is not devoid of strong points (his drawing is always precise, his palette effectively restricted and laconic), his inordinate success pointed out the way to many a mediocrity who, eager to climb on the band-wagon of Socialist Realism, disguised his lack of talent by the choice of ideologically acceptable subject-matter.

Brusilov, Aleksey Alekseyevich (1853–1925), general, the most successful Russian commander of the First World War, later a leading representative of National Bolshevism (q.v.). He was supreme commander-in-chief of the Russian forces in July and August 1917, under the Provisional Government (q.v.), but joined the Red Army after the Bolshevik seizure of power. During the Polish Soviet war of 1920 Brusilov appealed to all Russian officers to join the Red Army. *See* his *A Soldier's Notebook, 1914–18*, 1930.

Bryansk: 1. Oblast of the R.S.F.S.R., south-west of Moscow, situated in the Desna Poles'ye lowland with the fringes of the central Russian upland in the east. It has large peat deposits and is partly covered with mixed forests (the famous Bryansk Forests). Area 13,500 sq. m.; population (1959) 1,547,000 (35 per cent urban), mostly Russians (also Jews before the Second World War). The oblast has engineering, cement, glass, cloth, wood-processing and other industries; grain, potatoes and hemp are grown, and dairy cattle, pigs and bees kept. The industrial area of Bryansk has been important since the beginning of the 18th century. Principal towns: Bryansk, Klintsy.

2. Administrative, economic and cultural centre of the oblast, situated on the River Desna. Population (1959) 206,000 (1913, 31,000; 1939, 174,000). It is a major centre of industry and transportation (locomotives and rolling-stock—since the 1870's—other engineering, cement, clothing, meat processing, large peat-fed power-station; six railway lines), is on the gas pipeline from Dashava to Moscow, and an oil pipeline from Kuybyshev to Bryansk is being built. Known since 1146 as a fortress and capital of a principality, Bryansk became Lithuanian in the 14th century and Muscovite in the 16th. In 1956 it absorbed the neighbouring industrial town of Bezhitsa.

Bryullov, Karl Pavlovich (1799–1852), painter of historical compositions and portraits. He studied under his father, a wood-carver, and at the Academy of Arts, 1809–21. From 1822 to 1835 he worked in Rome, where his famous 'Last Days of Pompeii' was painted. Later in St Petersburg he painted a number of brilliant society portraits (N. Kukol'nik, Countess Samoylova, Princess Volkonskaya). Although the gigantic 'Last Days of Pompeii' was acclaimed in Italy and Russia, it was criticized when exhibited in Paris, 1834, as being twenty years behind the times. In it Bryullov shows himself an excellent designer and draughtsman, but an inferior colourist; he is at his best in portraits. His second large historical composition, 'The Siege of Pskov,' was a failure from the beginning and was not completed.

Bubnov, Andrey Sergeyevich (1883–1940), Bolshevik. He joined the party in 1903, took part in the revolution of 1905 (q.v.), and then until 1917 worked in the local party committees in Russia. He became prominent during 1917 and was elected to the first Politburo on the eve of the October coup. During the civil war he was a leading commissar on various fronts. Though he had joined the Left Communists (q.v.) in 1918, and later the Democratic Centralists (q.v.), and the Trotskiyites in 1923, he supported Stalin in the inner-party struggle after Lenin's death, and after Trotskiy's defeat was appointed head of the Political Administration in the Red Army (replacing the Trotskiyite Antonov-Ovseyenko, q.v.). In 1929 he replaced Lunacharskiy (q.v.) as Commissar of Education in the R.S.F.S.R., and carried out the school reforms of the 1930's, from 1932 under the direction of Zhdanov (q.v.). Bubnov was also well known as a party historian. He disappeared during the Great Purge (q.v.), but his reputation was rehabilitated after the 20th party congress (q.v.).

Budënnyy, Semën Mikhaylovich (*b.* 1883), Marshal of the Soviet Union (since 1935). As a non-commissioned officer in the cavalry he distinguished himself in the First World War. He joined the Bolsheviks in 1918 and during the civil war made a brilliant career, becoming commander of the First Cavalry Army, with Voroshilov as his political commissar. His military exploits, particularly the long march from the North Caucasus to Poland in 1920, earned him great fame, and he became a legendary figure in the Soviet Union. He was subsequently Inspector of Cavalry, an appointment that gradually diminished in importance. In 1937 he sat on the special military court which sentenced Tukhachevskiy (q.v.) and other leading Red Army commanders to death. After the German invasion in 1941 he was appointed commander of the south-western front, but his career there was short and disastrous and he was soon shifted to an unimportant position. He has for many years been a member of the Presidium of the Supreme Soviet, a purely decorative position. He continues to concern himself with horses and horse breeding. His memoirs were published in Russia in 1959.

Budget. The State budget is worked out by the Ministry of Finance and passed at the beginning of each calendar year by the Supreme Soviet (q.v.); a few unimportant alterations are usually made during the passing of the budget through the chambers of the Supreme Soviet, which normally takes two days. The function of the budget in the Soviet economic system is neither purely fiscal, as in *laissez-faire* states of the past, nor the chief means of economic policy, as in contemporary welfare states, but to serve as a subsidiary means of direct economic planning (q.v.). The budget accounts for about a half of the national income and expenditure, only those of the *kolkhozes* and other co-operatives, individual peasants, unco-operated artisans and independent professional people being left out.

On the revenue side, which in 1958 amounted to 672·3 milliard pre-1961 roubles, the main items are the turnover tax (q.v.; 304·5 milliard), deductions from profits (q.v.) of State enterprises (135·4 milliard), other taxes (*see* TAXATION; 68·5 milliard), and the Social Insurance Fund (33·1 milliard). The internal loans (*see* GOVERNMENT BONDS) accounted for only 10·6 milliard roubles in 1958, though in previous years the revenue from them had been considerably more important (44·3 milliard in 1956). On the expenditure side (total 642·7 milliard roubles in 1958), the largest item is the financing of the economy (290·3 milliard), closely followed by expenditure for 'social and cultural purposes' (214·2 milliard), including education (86·0), health (41·2) and other social services; next come defence (93·6 milliard) and administration (12·0 milliard). The defence expenditure shown includes only the actual expenditure of the Ministry of Defence, including the below-cost price paid for weapons, the balance being covered by the allocations for the national economy. *See* R. W. Davies, *The Development of the Soviet Budgetary System*, 1958.

Bug: 1. The *Southern Bug* (Ukrainian *Boh*), river which rises in Podolia and flows south-east into the Dnieper estuary of the Black Sea. Length 445 m.; principal port Nikolayev. In 1941–3 the river constituted the demarcation line between the German and the Rumanian zones of occupation.

2. The *Western Bug*, a right tributary of the Vistula, rising in Galicia, forming part of the Russo-Polish frontier, and joining the Vistula near Warsaw. Length 440 m.; principal port Brest.

Bugul'ma, town in the Tatar Autonomous Republic, 140 m. south-east of Kazan', one of the main centres of the Tatar-Bashkir oilfields. Population (1959) 61,000 (1926, 14,000). Apart from oil extraction, which started in the Bugul'ma area in 1949, it has varied food industries and is a local cultural centre. It was founded in 1741.

Building Industry. The following table shows the increase in production capacities in selected fields due to capital construction:

	1918–1928	1928–1932	1933–1937	1938–30.6.41	1.7.41–1945	1946–1950	1951–1955
Steel [1]	0·4	2·8	7·6	3·5	8·7	8·9	8·9
Coal-mining [1]	5·6	57·0	78·4	54·0	111·3	107·3	116·1
Power-stations [2]	0·7	2·8	3·6	2·8	4·7	8·4	17·6
Spindles [3]	0·6	1·0	0·7	1·2	0·8	2·2	1·9
Leather footwear [4]	11	25	44	20	50	76	58

The average number of employees in the building industry in 1957 was 5·5 million (0·7 in 1928, 2·5 in 1940); of these, 4·7 million were workers and 0·4 engineers and technicians. Building is progressively concentrated in the hands of building contractors, the percentage of work done by contracting organizations having risen from 10 per cent in 1918–28 to 85 per cent in 1956–7. The building industry was administered by various ministries until the reorganization of economic administration in general in 1957, when it was handed over to the Economic Councils (q.v.). During the first Five Year Plan period the main construction projects were carried out in co-operation with foreign firms of technical consultants. *See also* BUILDING MATERIALS; HOUSING; INVESTMENT.

Building Materials. The following table shows the production of building materials for selected years:

	1913 [10]	1928	1940	1955	1958
Cement [5]	1·5	1·8	5·7	22·5	33·3
Bricks [6]	2·9	2·8	7·5	20·8	28·3
Slate [7]	9	39	206	1,488	2,393
Window glass [8]	23·7	34·2	44·7	99·7	132·9
Reinforced concrete sections [9]	—	—	—	5·3	18·9

[1] Million tons p.a.   [2] Million kw.   [3] Millions.   [4] Million pairs p.a.
[5] Million tons.   [6] Milliards.   [7] Million standard pieces.
[8] Million square metres.   [9] Million cubic metres.   [10] Within inter-war frontiers.

The building materials industry is largely concentrated in central Russia and the Ukraine. A complete 'cover-to-cover' translation of the journal *Cement* exists in English.

Bukhara: 1. Oblast of Uzbekistan, comprising the western part of the Zeravshan oasis and the surrounding deserts; large natural gas deposits were discovered in the mid 1950's at Gazli (q.v.). Area 47,400 sq. m.; population (1959) 573,000 (22 per cent urban), mostly Uzbeks and Tadzhiks. Cotton, fruit and grapes are cultivated, sericulture practised and Astrakhan sheep bred; the industries of the area are concerned with processing the agricultural products. For history *see* SOGDIANA; TRANSOXANIA; BUKHARA KHANATE.

2. Administrative, economic and cultural centre of the oblast. Population (1959) 69,000 (1939, 50,000), Uzbeks and Tadzhiks; although the former prevail numerically, the Persian cultural tradition predominates and Tadzhik is principally used in the schools. It has light and food industries. There are many architectural monuments, including a pre-Islamic temple, the tomb of Ismail Samanid (9th century), and the Ulugbek (15th century) and Mir-Arab (16th century) *medressehs*. Bukhara is one of the oldest centres of civilization in Central Asia. In the 9th–10th centuries it was the capital of the Samanid state, from the 16th century till 1920 of the Bukhara Khanate, and then until 1924 of the Bukhara People's Republic. For many centuries it was a major centre of Islamic learning. Because of both its political and religious traditions, it has been unduly neglected during the Soviet period.

Bukhara Khanate, 16th–20th-century state in Central Asia. It was founded by the Uzbek Khan Sheybani, who in 1500–7 conquered the Timurid domains in Transoxania. In 1555 Abdullah Khan (q.v.) transferred the capital from Samarkand to Bukhara, hence the name Bukhara Khanate. Internal feuds weakened the state, it split up into a number of principalities and in 1740 was conquered by Nadir Shah of Persia. In 1753 Bukhara regained independence, but did not recover its supremacy over Khorezm, Merv, Badakhshan, Tashkent and the Fergana Valley. Its rulers, who now had the title of emir, had unlimited powers within the framework of Shariat and customary law. In the exercise of their power they could normally rely on the support of the Uzbek tribal chieftains and the Muslim clergy. Ethnically the population consisted largely of Uzbeks (who remained the politically dominant element), Sarts and Tadzhiks. From the 1840's Bukhara was the object of rivalry between Russian and British imperial interests. The Bukhara army suffered a crushing defeat from the Russians in 1866, and two years later a peace treaty ceded some of the best lands of Bukhara, including Samarkand, to Russia and established a Russian protectorate over the khanate. An end was put to the slavery and the wars which had hitherto been rife; apart from this the Russians did not interfere in the internal life of the khanate, although a Russian political agent resided in the new town of Kagan eight miles from the capital. For later history *see* BUKHARA PEOPLE'S SOVIET REPUBLIC. *See* S. A. Zenkovsky, *Pan-Turkism and Islam in Russia*, Cambridge, Mass., 1960.

Bukhara People's Soviet Republic, ephemeral regime which existed on the territory of the former Bukhara Khanate in 1920–4, being one of the first regimes of the type later known as 'people's democracies.' It was established by the Russian and local Communists with the help of the Red Army units which stormed the capital of the khanate and deposed the last emir, although he had taken a neutral position during the Russian Civil War. The resistance of the local population (*see* DASHNAKHI) was countered with ruthless repression. The 'pacification' cost the country half of its arable land and livestock (including 75 per cent of the horses); eight towns and hundreds of villages were destroyed or greatly damaged. By 1924 open rebellion was suppressed and Bukhara was proclaimed a Socialist Republic and 'received' into the U.S.S.R. A few months later it was dismembered in the process of the so-called National Delimitation of Central Asia (q.v.). *See* S. A. Zenkovsky, *Pan-Turkism and Islam in Russia*, Cambridge, Mass., 1960.

Bukharin, Nikolay Ivanovich (1888–1938), politician, a leading theorist of the Bolshevik Party, called by Lenin 'the darling of the party.' He joined the Bolsheviks in 1906, and was active during the First World War in attempts at organizing the internationalist elements among Russian *émigré* Social Democrats, as well as in Scandinavia and the U.S.A. He returned to Russia after the February revolution (q.v.) in 1917 and played a prominent part in the preparation for the seizure of power in the Moscow party organization. He headed the Left Communists (q.v.) in opposition to Lenin in 1918, but despite this remained on good personal terms with Lenin and, together with him was the chief author of the party programme adoped in 1919, becoming a candidate member of the Politburo. In the trade union discussion he sided against Lenin, allying himself with Trotskiy, but in the inner party struggle after Lenin's death, when he became a full member of the Politburo, he supported Stalin against Trotskiy and later Zinov'yev and Kamenev, and was the chief advocate of the continuation of the New Economic Policy (q.v.). He replaced Zinov'yev as head of the Comintern in 1925, but soon fell out with Stalin and led the Right Opposition (q.v.) against him in 1928–9, losing all his leading positions after his defeat. He remained, however, a member of the Central Committee until 1936, and took an active part in drawing up the Stalin Constitution (q.v.). He appeared as the chief defendant in a show trial during the Great Purge (q.v.) and was executed (*see* ANTI-SOVIET BLOC OF RIGHTISTS AND TROTSKIYITES). Bukharin was a notable Marxist theorist (*see* DIALECTICAL MATERIALISM) and was influenced to some extent by Bogdanov. Many of his ideas re-emerged among the revisionists (*see* REVISIONISM) after Stalin's death, particularly in Poland, Hungary and East Germany. *See* his *A B C of Communism*, 1922; J. Hecker, *Moscow Dialogues*, 1933; E. H. Carr, *A History of Soviet Russia* (6 vols.), 1950–9; L. Schapiro, *The Origin of the Communist Autocracy*, 1955, and *The Communist Party of the Soviet Union*, 1960; S. Heitman, *An Annotated Bibliography of N. I. Bukharin's Published Works*, 1958.

Bukovina ('Beech-tree country'; Ukrainian **Bukovyna**, Rumanian **Bucovina**, German **Buchenland**), historical name (since 1392) of the area in eastern Europe which is situated in the Carpathian foothills and the upper reaches of the Dniester, Prut and Seret rivers. It belonged to Roman Dacia, was devastated by the Huns, colonized from the 6th century by East Slavs and from the 12th century by Rumanians. It was the core of the Moldavian Principality (established in the 14th century) which fell under Turkish suzerainty in 1512. In 1775 Bukovina was ceded to Austria, in 1861 granted autonomy and in 1918 occupied by the Rumanians. Southern Bukovina fell to Rumania by the St Germain Peace Treaty of 1919, and the whole of Bukovina by the Sèvres Treaty of 1920. Northern Bukovina (which has a Ukrainian majority, see CHERNOVTSY) was ceded in 1940 to the U.S.S.R. following an ultimatum to Rumania, again belonged to Rumania 1941–4 and was ceded finally to the U.S.S.R. by the peace treaty of 1947.

Bulakhovskiy, Leonid Arsen'yevich (*b.* 1888), Ukrainian philologist, member of the Ukrainian Academy of Sciences and director of its Institute of Linguistics. His works are chiefly concerned with the history of the Russian and Ukrainian languages and with accents in Slav languages. He directed the work on the rules of Ukrainian spelling that have been in force since 1946.

Bulgakov, Sergey Nikolayevich (1871–1944), theologian, philosopher and economist. Beginning as a Legal Marxist (q.v.), he later became an Idealist (*see* IDEALISM) and in 1918 an Orthodox priest. As a Christian Socialist he was a Constitutional Democratic member of the 2nd Duma, and took part in the Vekhi (q.v.) symposium. In 1922 Bulgakov, together with other leading intellectuals, was expelled from Russia, and later became a professor at the Russian Theological Institute in Paris, where he further developed V. Solov'ëv's controversial doctrine of 'Sophia, the Wisdom of God.' Main works: *Capitalism and Agriculture* (2 vols.), 1900; *From Marxism to Idealism*, 1903; *Two Cities. Enquiries on the Nature of Social Ideals* (2 vols.), 1911; *Philosophy of Economics*, 1912; *The Light that Never Fades*, 1917; *Quiet Thoughts*, 1918; *On God-Manhood* (2 vols.), Paris, 1933–6; *Philosophy of the Name*, Paris, 1953. *See* his *Social Teaching in Modern Russian Orthodox Theology*, Evanston, Illinois, 1934; *The Orthodox Church*, 1935; *The Wisdom of God*, 1937; N. Lossky, *History of Russian Philosophy*, 1951; V. V. Zenkovsky, *A History of Russian Philosophy*, vol. ii, 1953; L. Zander, *Bog i mir. Mirosozertsaniye o. S. Bulgakova*, Paris.

Bulganin, Nikolay Aleksandrovich (*b.* 1895), Communist, who joined the Bolshevik Party in 1917. He worked in leading positions in the Cheka, 1918–22, and in the Supreme Council of National Economy, 1922–7. Thereafter he held the following posts: 1927–31 manager of the Moscow Electroworks; 1931–7 chairman of the Moscow City Council; 1937–8 chairman of the Council of People's Commissars (Prime Minister) of the R.S.F.S.R.; 1938–41 chairman of the board of the State Bank and deputy chairman of the U.S.S.R. Council of People's Commissars; 1941–3 a political officer on the western front (working for a time with Zhukov), also a member of the State Defence Committee (q.v.) and from 1944 deputy People's Commissar for Defence; 1947–9 and 1953–5 Defence Minister, and simultaneously 1947–55 a deputy prime minister. He became a member of the Central Committee of the party in 1934 and of its Presidium in 1948; he was created marshal at the end of the war. Bulganin played a secondary role in the new collective leadership after Stalin's death, but when Malenkov resigned in 1955 he was, on Khrushchëv's recommendation, appointed Prime Minister, and for a time appeared to be working in harmony with Khrushchëv. But in 1957 he joined the so-called 'anti-party group' (q.v.); when this was defeated he recanted and was reprimanded and gradually demoted (chairman of the board of the State Bank, then in 1958 chairman of the Stavropol' Economic Council). Not until the end of 1958 was he expelled from the Presidium of the Central Committee and his association with the 'anti-party group' made public. It was reported early in 1960 that he was living in retirement near Moscow. *See* W. Leonhard, *Kreml ohne Stalin*, Cologne, 1959.

Bulgar, or **Great Bulgar,** capital of the Volga Bulgarians and the economic centre of the Volga region from the 10th to 15th centuries; international fairs were held there. In 1431 it was destroyed by Muscovite troops, and its ruins were at the village of Bolgary, 60 m. south of Kazan', in the Tatar Republic, until it was flooded by the reservoir of the Volga hydro-electric station.

Bund, usual abbreviation of the official name of the Jewish Social Democratic Party in Russia and Poland. It was founded in 1897 and took a prominent part in the formation a year later of the Russian Social Democratic Labour Party (q.v.). It was then the strongest social democratic organization in the country, but, modelling itself on German social democracy, was opposed to Lenin's organizational and tactical principles, and left the Russian party in 1903; among the chief points of disagreement were the Bundists' demands to be recognized as the sole representatives of Jewish workers, and for internal autonomy within the R.S.D.L.P. In 1906 the Bund rejoined the R.S.D.L.P., and thereafter generally sided with the Mensheviks. It supported the Provisional Government in 1917; after the Bolshevik seizure of power the majority of the Bund, led by R. Abramovich, opposed the Bolsheviks, but a minority, led by M. Rafes, co-operated with them and finally joined the Communist Party. The activities of the Bund were suppressed in Russia during the 1920's, but continued in Poland until the Second World War, and remnants of the organization still exist in the U.S.A. *See* L. Schapiro, *The Communist Party of the Soviet Union*, 1960.

Bunge, Nikolay Khristianovich (1823–95), economist and statesman of German descent. He was professor and rector (by appointment and twice by election) of Kiev University, manager of the Kiev branch of the State Bank, Minister of Finance, 1881–6, and chairman of the Committee of Ministers, 1887–95. He reorganized and greatly improved the budgetary system, reduced the redemption payments (q.v.), abolished the poll-tax and was preparing the introduction of a general income-tax; he also established the Peasant Land Bank (q.v.) and the Nobility Land Bank, furthered industrialization of the country through a protectionist policy and extensive railway construction, and started modern labour legislation in Russia by establishing the office of factory inspectors, 1882. *See* his *Esquisses de littérature politico-économique*, Geneva, 1898.

Bunin, Ivan Alekseyevich (1870–1954), author who continued the traditions of the 19th-century Realistic school in Russian literature. As a young man he belonged to Gor'kiy's literary circle. His stories and novels (*The Life of Arsen'yev*, 1927, Eng. *The Well of Days*, 1946) portray with great brilliance love, death and the past. In 1920 he emigrated to Paris, and in 1933 was awarded the Nobel Prize for Literature, the only Russian writer to receive it until its award to Boris Pasternak (q.v.) in 1958. *See* his *Memories and Portraits*, 1952; R. Poggioli, *The Art of Ivan Bunin*, 1953.

Burdenko, Nikolay Nilovich (1876–1946), surgeon, professor at Yur'yev and Moscow universities, member of the Academy of Sciences from 1939, chief medical inspector of the Russian Army after the February revolution (q.v.) in 1917 and chief surgeon of the Red Army during the Second World War, chairman of the medical council at the Commissariat of Health (from 1937), founder and first president of the Academy of Medical Sciences, chairman of the All-Union Association of Surgeons (from 1935), Fellow of the Royal Society. He joined the Communist Party in 1939. Burdenko was one of the pioneers of neurosurgery; he opened in 1929 the neurosurgical clinic which has developed into the present large Institute of Neurosurgery of the Academy of Medical Sciences.

Bureau of the Majority Committees, non-statutory organization formed by Lenin in 1904 after his rift with the Bolshevik-dominated central committee (led by Krasin) of the Russian Social Democratic Labour Party (q.v.). It was headed in Russia by Bogdanov, who was able to attract a considerable number of Marxist left-wing intellectuals. The bureau usurped the functions of the central committee in relation to those local committees whose support it was able to gain; its principal aim was to call a third congress of the party, which was finally achieved after the beginning of the 1905 revolution in agreement with the remaining members of the central committee (the majority of which had been arrested). *See* L. Schapiro, *The Communist Party of the Soviet Union*, 1960.

Bureaucracy, in the sense of government through a multiplicity of offices and officials, is a typical characteristic of the Soviet system. This is owing to three principal factors: (*a*) the tradition of bureaucratic rule in Russia, which goes back to the Muscovite period; (*b*) the State ownership of most of the country's economy; (*c*) Lenin's organizational views, which were based upon the principle of integrating as many spheres of activity as possible in order to facilitate party control over them. The Communist theory only recognizes the first of these factors, maintaining that bureaucracy is a characteristic of bourgeois rule and that there is no ground for it in a socialist system. Throughout the Soviet period there have been frequent campaigns to combat bureaucracy (the most important recent one being the 'territorialization' of economic management, *see* ECONOMIC COUNCILS); but the refusal to recognize the causes of bureaucracy makes efforts to overcome it somewhat futile. The evils of bureaucracy are universally recognized, but the attitude towards it is generally fatalistic. *See* M. Fainsod, *How Russia is Ruled*, Cambridge, Mass., 1953; R. N. Carew Hunt, *A Guide to Communist Jargon*, 1957.

Burtsev, Vladimir L'vovich (1862–1936), politician, historian of the revolutionary movement. He lived mostly in emigration, but despite this became famous in Russia for his ability to unmask police agents within the revolutionary organizations. After the outbreak of the First World War he took up a patriotic standpoint and returned to Russia, where in 1917 he resumed publication of the journal *Byloye* (*The Past*) which he had previously published abroad. Emigrating once more in the early 1920's, he now concentrated on bringing to light the most disreputable sides of the Bolsheviks' activities.

Buryat Autonomous Republic (until 1958 **Buryat-Mongol Autonomous Republic**) lies in south-eastern Siberia, occupying the western part of Transbaykalia, traversed by the Trans-Siberian Railway; it is a mountainous area with an extreme continental dry climate, largely covered by coniferous forests and having deposits of rare metals, gold, brown coal, iron ore and graphite. Area 135,500 sq. m.; population (1959) 671,000 (41 per cent urban), chiefly Russians and Buryats. There are engineering (locomotives), mining, food (meat products, sugar), fishing and timber industries; sheep and cattle breeding are carried on. The capital is Ulan-Ude. The Autonomous Republic was established in 1923.

Buryats, Mongolian-speaking people who live in south-eastern Siberia around Lake Baykal in the Buryat Autonomous Republic, and in the Irkutsk and Chita oblasts, where there are respectively the Ust'-Orda Buryat National Okrug and the Aginskoye Buryat National Okrug. In 1959 they numbered 253,000. They are Buddhists or Christians by religion and mostly engage in agriculture, particularly animal raising. The Buryat people has been known since 1207. When Russians arrived in the area during the 17th century they found the Buryats divided into several clans headed by princelings. In the 19th century they had local self-government in the form of so-called Steppe Dumas. During the civil war an anti-Bolshevik theocratic Buryat state was proclaimed in Transbaykalia.

Buslayev, Fëdor Ivanovich (1818–97), philologist and historian of art, professor at Moscow University, member of the Academy of Sciences. In his works he dealt with the interdependence of language, folklore and art in the history of Russian culture (*On the Influence of Christianity on the Slavonic Language*, 1848; *Historical Grammar of the Russian Language*, 2 vols., 1858; *Historical Outlines of Russian Folklore and Art*, 2 vols., 1861; *General Concepts on Russian Icon Painting*, 1866; etc.).

Butlerov, Aleksandr Mikhaylovich (1828–86), chemist. Educated at Kazan' University, where he was a pupil of Zinin (q.v.), he worked for a time under Wurz in Paris, was professor and elected rector at Kazan' and later professor at St Petersburg University, a member of the Academy of Sciences and president of the Russian Chemical Society. His work was chiefly concerned with isomerism and the structure of chemical combinations. His theory of structure, first advanced in 1861 and developed in his fundamental *Introduction to the Full Study of Organic Chemistry* (1864–6, German trans. 1868), has since been universally accepted. Among his pupils in Kazan' was Markovnikov (q.v.). Butlerov was a protagonist of women's education and did much to further it in Russia.

Buzuluk, town in the Orenburg Oblast (Urals), situated on the Kuybyshev–Orenburg railway about 80 m. south-east of Kuybyshev. Population (1959) 55,000. It has an engineering industry (oil industry equipment, tractor spare parts, etc.) and is the centre of an agricultural area and a local cultural centre. Near by is the famous coniferous Buzuluk Forest. The engineering industry dates from the Second World War. Buzuluk was founded as a Russian fortress in 1736 and became a town in 1781. Before the 1930's it had a considerable grain trade.

C

Cadets, *see* CONSTITUTIONAL DEMOCRATS.

Cadres, in Communist terminology, personnel, particularly leading personnel. The selection and training of cadres has been in the forefront of the party leadership's attention at least since the Iskra (q.v.) period. Stalin coined the slogan 'Cadres decide everything' in 1935, and laid down that they should be selected according to their efficiency and loyalty to the party leadership. In fact appointments to senior positions in all spheres of life are either made or confirmed by the cadres departments of party committees (*see* NOMENCLATURE). *See* R. N. Carew Hunt, *A Guide to Communist Jargon*, 1957; J. A. Armstrong, *The Soviet Bureaucratic Élite*, New York, 1959.

Calendar. The Julian Calendar ('Old Style') was used in Russia until 1918 and is still used by the Russian Orthodox Church. The Gregorian Calendar ('New Style') was introduced by the Bolshevik Government, but during the 1920's and early thirties a new Era of the October Revolution (counting the years from 1917) was used semi-officially with the implication that it would be universally accepted after the world proletarian revolution. During the years of the first Five Year Plan weeks were abolished and replaced by five- (later six-) day periods; the names of days were dropped, and they were simply numbered. Weeks and day names were reintroduced, and Sunday again made a holiday, in 1940.

Canals, *see* INLAND WATERS; RIVER TRANSPORT.

Capital officially does not exist in the U.S.S.R., since according to the Marxist economic theory it is a category of the capitalist mode of production; instead of the term capital the expression 'financial resources' is used. Almost all the capital needed for financing the economy has come throughout the Soviet period from internal sources, that is by restricting consumption. The main sources of capital are the turnover tax (q.v.) and other taxes (*see* TAXATION), profits (q.v.) of State enterprises, State loans (*see* GOVERNMENT BONDS) and the Social Insurance Fund (*see* INSURANCE), as well as the profits of *kolkhozes* and other co-operatives (qq.v.).

Foreign capital has been of comparatively minor significance. During the 1920's there was a certain amount of investment by foreign concessionaries (*see* CONCESSIONS). With the annexation of eastern Poland, some Finnish territory, the Baltic States, Bessarabia, northern Bukovina, a part of East Prussia, Transcarpathian Ukraine, southern Sakhalin and the Kurile Islands in 1939–46, the capital available in these territories was taken over by the Soviet Government. Considerable capital was derived from the war-time lend-lease (q.v.) programme. Finally, war booty and reparations (q.v.) were also foreign sources of capital. *See further under* CREDIT; INVESTMENT.

Capital Goods, *see* CONSUMER GOODS; FOREIGN TRADE; INDUSTRY.

85

Capital Punishment is described in the Fundamentals of Criminal Legislation of 1958 as an exceptional measure of punishment. It may be applied (in peace-time) in the form of shooting for most political crimes (q.v.) as well as for banditry and for murder with aggravating circumstances; it may not be applied to persons under 18 or to pregnant women. Capital punishment was unknown in medieval Russia, but was introduced in Muscovy with the development of modern criminal law in the 15th–16th centuries. The Ulozheniye (q.v.) of 1649 provided the death penalty for almost all types of crime. Under the influence of the ideas of the Enlightenment, capital punishment was abolished by the Empress Elizabeth in 1754. It was reintroduced by Catherine II for State crimes and violation of quarantine regulations, but seldom applied. The Provisional Government in 1917 again abolished the death penalty, but soon restored it at the front. The Bolsheviks, who were theoretically opposed to it, proclaimed its abolition in 1918 and 1919, but in both cases it was soon restored, and the Criminal Code of 1922 provided (ostensibly temporarily) for death by shooting 'as the highest measure of social defence' for 'counter-revolutionary' acts and for corruption. In 1927 it was limited to 'counter-revolutionary' acts, but in 1932 theft of State property was added. In 1943 hanging was introduced for those sentenced to death for malicious treason. Capital punishment in peace-time was abolished once more in 1947, allegedly in accordance with the public wish and because of the 'solidity of the Soviet state and social order' and the 'immense loyalty of the Soviet people to their country and government.' However, it was restored in 1950, again allegedly on the demand of the public, for treason, espionage and sabotage; premeditated murder with aggravating circumstances was added in 1954. *See* R. Schlesinger, *Soviet Legal Theory*, 1945; H. J. Berman, *Justice in Russia*, Cambridge, Mass., 1950; G. C. Guins, *Soviet Law and Soviet Society*, The Hague, 1954; W. W. Kulski, *The Soviet Regime*, Syracuse, 1954; V. Gsovski and K. Grzybowski (eds.), *Government, Law and Courts in the Soviet Union and Eastern Europe*, vol. ii, 1959.

Capitalist Encirclement, that is, the fact that the Soviet Union was surrounded by 'capitalist' states, played an important part in the theoretical justification for all terroristic and oppressive measures against the people, and for the continued existence of the State as such after the liquidation of the 'exploiting classes' when, according to Marxian theory, it should have begun to 'wither away.' The establishment of Communist rule in many countries on the frontiers of the U.S.S.R. since the Second World War has removed the 'capitalist encirclement' in the old sense, although the defence organizations of the non-Communist world, such as N.A.T.O., etc., are represented in Soviet propaganda as an attempt to continue it. *See* R. N. Carew Hunt, *A Guide to Communist Jargon*, 1957.

Capitalist Survivals, in the official phraseology, a pejorative term for any characteristics or practices which are either inconsistent with the official ideology or deviate from the party line of the moment. Some characteristics thus described may in fact be attributable to the continuation of pre-1917 attitudes, while others are due to Soviet conditions or simply to normal human behaviour. In the past, for example, trade, the family and patriotism have at different times been condemned as capitalist survivals, and currently religion, nationalism, crime and drunkenness are still so regarded.

Car Industry. Total vehicle production in 1958 was 511,390 (840 in 1928, 145,000 in 1940, 74,700 in 1945, 362,900 in 1950). Of these there were 389,199 lorries and buses and 122,191 cars (50 in 1928, 5,500 in 1940, 5,000 in 1945, 107,800 in 1955, 97,800 in 1956). Car production is almost entirely concentrated in the R.S.F.S.R., the main works being situated in Moscow, Yaroslavl' and Gor'kiy (built in the 1920's and early thirties); during and immediately after the war new works were built in Miass in the Urals, in Ulyanovsk and Pavlovo (near Gor'kiy), as well as in Kutaisi (Georgia) and Minsk; in the late 1950's a bus plant was built in Kurgan (western Siberia) and small passenger car production started in Zaporozh'ye (Ukraine). Car models currently produced are the large saloons ZIL 111 (85 m.p.h.) and Chayka (8 cylinder, 180 h.p., 100 m.p.h.) and the small family cars, the Volga and the new Moskvich (65 m.p.h.); 35,000 cars were exported in 1957, and 2,000 imported. See *U.S.S.R. Today and Tomorrow*, Moscow, 1959.

Caspian Sea (ancient **Mare Caspium**, or **Mare Hyrcanium**), largest inland sea in the world, on the boundary between Europe and Asia, extending from 36° 40' to 47° 20' N. lat., and 46° 50' to 55° 10' E. long. Length (north–south) 680 m.; breadth between 130 and 270 m.; total area 170,000 sq. m.; greatest depth: north basin, 2,526 ft, south basin, 3,006 ft. The Caspian is mostly in Soviet territory, with Persia on the south. There are no tides, but fierce storms make navigation difficult. The principal rivers flowing into the sea are the Volga, Ural, Emba, Terek, Kura and Atrek; it is connected with the Black, Baltic and White seas by canals via the Volga River. The chief Russian ports are Astrakhan', Baku, Gur'yev, Makhachkala and Krasnovodsk. The sea abounds in fish (especially salmon and sturgeon).

Catherine II, often called 'the Great' (1729–96). The daughter of a Prussian field marshal, she married the future emperor Peter III in 1745 and succeeded to the throne in 1762 after his murder by her supporters in the Guards. Her many lovers included eminent soldiers and administrators such as Potëmkin (q.v.). Though immoral and unprincipled, Catherine was a highly intelligent woman, and throughout her reign corresponded with Voltaire, Diderot, etc. She was an outstanding diplomat and administrator, and a tireless worker. Many of her ideas were over-ambitious, such as reviving the Byzantine Empire or dislodging the British from India, but she was normally a realist.

In 1766 she called together a Great Commission of elected representatives of all social classes (with the exception of serfs) and all nationalities (with the exception of nomads) which was to prepare the foundations for a new legal code; the instructions to be followed by this commission were drawn up by Catherine herself and largely based upon Montesquieu. The evils of the administration and a widespread desire for greater efficiency and for the extension of local government were disclosed by the commission, but few reforms were actually achieved: two that were accomplished were the expansion of local self-government in the towns and the reorganization of the provincial administration. In 1785 Catherine promulgated the Charter to the Gentry, which greatly increased their privileges and aggravated the existing discontent in the country that had already, in 1773, resulted in a peasant revolt under Pugachëv (q.v.). Abroad the chief events of the reign were the three partitions of Poland, with great territorial gains for Russia, two successful wars with Turkey and a war with Sweden. For Catherine's policy towards the Ukraine see UKRAINIANS. See G. S. Thomson, *Catherine the Great and the Expansion of Russia*, 1947; D. Maroger (ed.), *The Memoirs of Catherine the Great*, New York, 1955.

Caucasians, term used in Russia in two senses. In the wider sense it is applied to all the native peoples of the Caucasus, including both North Caucasus and Transcaucasia. In the narrower sense it denotes only those peoples of the Caucasus whose languages belong to the Caucasian, or Japhetic (as Marr, q.v., called it), family. There are three branches of this family: the north-western, comprising Abkhazians, Abaza and Circassians; the north-eastern, comprising the Chechens, Ingushes and the peoples of Daghestan (Avars, Dargins, Lezgians and about two dozen small tribes); and the southern, or Kartvelian, branch, comprising the Georgians, with their many local subdivisions, and the west Kartvelian peoples: Megrelians, Svans and Chans. These Caucasian peoples are the indigenous population of the area.

Caucasus: 1. The great mountain range which stretches from the Taman Peninsula on the Black Sea to the Apsheron Peninsula on the Caspian. Length about 750 m.; greatest breadth about 150 m.; highest peaks El'brus (18,470 ft), Dykh-Tau, Koshtan-Tau and Kazbek; the twin-headed Ushba mountain (15,410 ft), one of the most famous peaks, is often called 'the Matterhorn of the Caucasus.' The mountains rise in terraces from the grassy and forested plateau to the north; the snow-line of the central ridge is at a height of 10,500 ft. The central spurs are either pure granite or granitic, but there are also mica- and talc-schists and other metamorphic rocks. Arborescent growths, aquatic plants and pines characterize the flora, and wolves, lynxes, panthers, jackals, wild boars and aurochs are found here. The principal rivers of the range are the Kuban' and the Rion, which flow into the Black Sea, and the Terek and the Kura which flow into the Caspian. Both the Terek and the Georgian Military Road (constructed with much difficulty at a height of 8,000 ft) run through the famous Dar'yal Gorge (q.v.), the principal pass of the mountain range. See A. F. Mummery, *My Climbs in the Alps and Caucasus*, 1895; D. W. Freshfield, *The Exploration of the Caucasus*, 1896; Sir John Hunt and C. Brasher, *The Red Snows*, 1960.

2. Name given to the whole region of the Caucasus mountain range, the Kuban', Kuma and Manych basins in the north (North Caucasus) and Transcaucasia (q.v.) in the south; this area includes the Krasnodar and Stavropol' krays and the Chechen-Ingush, Daghestan, Kabarda-Balkar and North Ossetian Autonomous

Republics of the R.S.F.S.R., and the Union Republics of Armenia, Azerbaydzhan and Georgia. Population (1959) about 18,000,000. The principal mineral resources of the area are oil (Baku, Groznyy, Maykop), natural gas (Stavropol'), manganese (Chiatura), copper (Armenia), lead and zinc (North Ossetia), coal (Georgia) and iron ore (Azerbaydzhan); the industries of the area are concerned with the extraction and processing of these minerals. At the beginning of the century the Caucasus led the world in the production of oil; engineering has chiefly been developed since the 1930's. Wheat and maize are cultivated, and horticulture and viniculture carried on. In addition sunflowers and tobacco are cultivated in North Caucasus, and cotton, tea, citrus fruits and silk in Transcaucasia.

The Caucasus has had a turbulent history since the earliest times, and the continual incursions of peoples from both the south and north have rendered its ethnical composition very complex. In antiquity parts of the region were conquered by the Scythians, Persians, Macedonians under Alexander the Great, Romans and Parthians, and later by the Arabs, Byzantium, Khazars, Cumans, Mongols and Turks. The Caucasus was a bone of contention between Turkey, Persia and Russia in the 18th century, but Russian rule was gradually extended over the whole area between the end of that century and the 1870's. Much fighting took place here during both the civil war and the Second World War, and much discord between the various peoples of the Caucasus. In 1943 the indigenous Chechens, Ingushes, Balkars, Karachays and Kalmyks were deported from North Caucasus to Central Asia for alleged collaboration with the Germans, and were only rehabilitated by the decree on deported peoples of 1957. *See further under* CIRCASSIA; COLCHIS; COSSACKS; SHAMIL'; TRANSCAUCASIA; and the names of the individual peoples and administrative units. *See* D. Tutaeff, *The Soviet Caucasus*, 1942; F. Kazemzadeh, *The Struggle for Transcaucasia*, 1951; B. Nolde, *La Formation de l'Empire Russe*, vol. ii, Paris, 1952; W. Kolarz, *Russia and her Colonies*, 1954; R. Pipes, *The Formation of the Soviet Union*, 1954; G. Jorré, *The Soviet Union, the Land and its People*, 3rd imp., 1955.

Cecchetti, Enrico (1850–1928), Italian teacher, dancer and ballet master. Though Italian by birth Cecchetti worked for the greater part of his life at the Imperial Theatre, St Petersburg, as a dancer and subsequently a teacher, his pupils including Nijinsky, Karsavina, Pavlova and, at a later date, Dolin, Lifar and Alicia Markova. His work with the Diaghilev company and his influence on modern dancing as a whole were of the greatest importance. *See also* BALLET; DIAGHILEV; and individual entries. *See* C. W. Beaumont and S. Idzikowski, *A Manual of the Theory and Practice of Classical Theatrical Dancing*, 1922.

Cells, Communist Party, until 1934 the official name of the primary organizations (q.v.) of the Communist Party.

Censorship of all printed matter and entertainment (down to the level of circuses and variety shows) is exercised by different departments of the Ministry of Culture on the basis of instructions from the Central Committee of the party. 'Internal censorship' is universally necessary, whereby authors, editors, etc., carefully assess what would be permissible in the eyes of the party at a particular moment; this phenomenon was admirably described in 1953 after Stalin's death by Tvardovskiy (q.v.) in his poem 'The Far Distances.' Also officially subject to censorship are telegrams (their text must be clear and unambiguous), and dispatches sent by foreign correspondents to their newspapers abroad. The privacy of correspondence, though formally guaranteed in the constitution, is in fact frequently and arbitrarily violated by the postal authorities.

The censorship regulations in Russia were always more severe than in the more liberal countries of Europe. Censorship was first officially introduced by Peter the Great for theological works, and the idea of a general censorship was first realized in 1803. The first comprehensive law on censorship was promulgated in 1826. In 1865 preventive censorship was abolished for newspapers and for bigger books, but the development of the revolutionary movement resulted in new restrictive measures. Censorship broke down during the revolution of 1905 (q.v.), and in 1905–6 laws were passed which considerably liberalized publication: preventive censorship was completely abolished, new periodical publications could be started without permission, and any question of breaking the law had to be heard in the courts instead of being dealt with by administrative measures; imported books, however, were subject to special regulations. All censorship of the press completely disappeared after the February revolution (q.v.) of 1917, but it was reintroduced in an extremely severe form after the Bolshevik seizure of power. The period of Stalin's rule witnessed the highest point of totalitarian control, in which all forms of censorship were one of the basic elements. Since Stalin's death censorship has been somewhat relaxed, but this does not satisfy the intellectual opposition (q.v.), which continues to press for further liberalization. *See* A. Inkeles, *Public Opinion in Soviet Russia*, Cambridge, Mass., 1950; M. Fainsod, 'Censorship in the U.S.S.R.—Documented Record,' *Problems of Communism*, March–April, 1956; L. Gruliow, 'How the Soviet Newspaper Operates,' *Problems of Communism*, vol. v, No. 2, 1956; M. Futtrell, 'Banned Books in the Lenin Library,' *Soviet Studies*, vol. x, No. 3, Jan. 1959; R. Conquest, *Common Sense on Russia*, 1960.

Central Asia, geographical and historical area comprising the Uzbek, Turkmen, Tadzhik and Kirgiz Union Republics (qq.v.) and the Alma-Ata, Dzhambul, South Kazakhstan and Kzyl-Orda oblasts of Kazakhstan (qq.v.). The term Central (Russian *srednyaya*) Asia replaced in the 1920's the previously more common Turkestan (q.v.); it is now normally used in the Soviet Union to denote only the four Union Republics and does not include southern Kazakhstan. Central Asia includes the Pamir and Tien-Shan mountain systems, and the Kopet-Dag range in the west, a fertile belt at the foot of the mountains, and deserts in the north. It borders the Caspian Sea in the west and the Aral Sea and Lake Balkhash in the north, and is traversed by the two great rivers Amu-Dar'ya and Syr-Dar'ya; other main rivers are the Murgab, Zeravshan, Chu and Ili. The rivers have been used since ancient times for irrigation, and important oases have thus been created—*see* FERGANA VALLEY; KHOREZM; MERV; ZERAVSHAN VALLEY—some of which have been the cradles of ancient civilizations. With a population of 13·7 million in 1959 (without southern Kazakhstan), of which the indigenous Muslims form the large majority, the economic importance of Central Asia is considerable, as it produces nearly all the cotton in the country. *See also* NATIONAL DELIMITATION OF CENTRAL ASIA. *See* the quarterly *Central Asian Review*, 1953 ff; G. Jorré, *The Soviet Union, the Land and its People*, 3rd imp., 1955; R. Loewenthal, *The Turkic Languages and Literature of Central Asia, a Bibliography*, The Hague, 1957.

Central Auditing Commission, one of the central organs of the Communist Party, elected at the party congresses. Its task is to supervise the finances of the party and the efficiency of the internal functioning of the party apparatus. It is a purely technical body, with no power or political significance.

Central Committee of the Communist Party is, according to the party statute, the highest organ of the party between congresses. Members and candidate members of the Central Committee are elected by the party congresses (133 and 122 respectively were elected at the 20th party congress in 1956). The Central Committee 'forms' its Presidium and secretariat, as well as the Committee of Party Control (qq.v.), and between the congresses directs all the activities of the party. Officially it 'guides' the Soviet Government and all the openly existing organizations in the country through party groups in these organizations. In fact the Central Committee as a corporate body has had a chequered career. It hardly functioned at all before the February revolution (q.v.) of 1917 because of factional strife within the party and Lenin's predilection for personal rule. From 1917 till 1934 it acted as a quasi-parliament for the party, with considerable freedom of discussion and opposition, and in moments of particularly acute factional struggle a majority in the Central Committee was decisive. To free himself from this dependence, Stalin, with the help of the N.K.V.D., liquidated 70 per cent of the Central Committee between the 17th and 18th party congresses (1934–9), and from then until Stalin's death it existed almost in name alone.

The Central Committee again acquired a position similar to that before 1934 during the period of 'collective leadership' after Stalin's death, when the warring factions among the leaders had to appeal to it for support. Its action in favour of Khrushchëv and against the 'anti-party group' (q.v.) in 1957 was decisive for the consolidation of Khrushchëv's power, and since 1958 the role of the Central Committee has again diminished, though not so far to the degree which it did under Stalin; in official propaganda it is still 'the collective wisdom of the Central Committee' rather than of Khrushchëv that is the basis upon which decisions are made. The apparatus of the Central Committee, working under the secretariat, has since the 1920's been the effective government of the country, since (1) its scope is wider than that of the Supreme Soviet and the Council of Ministers (qq.v.), including, most important, the party itself; (2) several government departments exist only on the republic level and the corresponding departments of the Central Committee are the only directing organs in the centre; and (3) in any question of doubt or disagreement, government departments are obliged to refer to the Central Committee. *See* J. Towster, *Political Power in the U.S.S.R.*, New York, 1948; M. Fainsod, *How Russia is Ruled*, 1953; M. Rush, *The Rise of Khrushchëv*, Washington, D.C., 1958; L. Schapiro, *The Communist Party of the Soviet Union*, 1960.

Central Executive Committee, executive organ of the Congresses of Soviets of Workers' and Soldiers' (from 1918 also Peasants') Deputies in 1917–36. The committee elected at the first Congress of Soviets in June 1917 had a Menshevik and Socialist Revolutionary majority, but from November 1917 onwards the Bolsheviks, having established their dictatorship in the country, manipulated membership of the committee according to the needs of the moment; for a few years some Left Socialist Revolutionaries and other non-Bolsheviks participated in the committee, but the practice was discontinued in the early 1920's. With the formation of the U.S.S.R. in 1922 there were both all-Union and republic Central Executive Committees, which had both legislative and administrative functions. The successive chairmen of the committee acted formally as the head of state: Kamenev immediately after the October coup, then Sverdlov until 1919, and Kalinin 1919–36. By the Stalin Constitution (q.v.) of 1936, the functions of the Central Executive Committee were transferred partly to the Supreme Soviet and partly to its Presidium.

Central Statistical Administration, government department subordinated directly to the U.S.S.R. Council of Ministers, its head having a seat in the council (since 1957). Its main task is to provide the Government with statistical data. It has the right to demand from all government departments, organizations, institutions and enterprises statistical material and accounts; to approve instructions and forms of accounting in enterprises and institutions of all government departments; to issue directives on accounting and statistical matters which are obligatory for all government departments; and to annul unauthorized accounting. The first statistical department was set up in Russia at the Police Ministry in 1811. A Central Statistical Committee was established in 1857 as a department of the Ministry of the Interior; this was re-formed and renamed the Central Statistical Administration in 1918, was raised to the position of a full commissariat in 1926, but was demoted again in 1930 and until 1948 was included in the State Planning Commission (*see* GOSPLAN). The status and functions of the administration were greatly increased in 1957 in connection with the reform of the economic management. *See also* ECONOMIC COUNCILS; INDUSTRIAL MANAGEMENT.

Cesis (formerly **Wenden**), town in Latvia situated 60 m. north-east of Riga. Population (1939) 9,000. The ruins of the castle (built 1210) where the Grand Masters of the Teutonic Knights resided 1237–1577 are here.

Chaadayev, Pëtr Yakovlevich (1793–1856), thinker who maintained in his 'Philosophic Letter' (published in 1836) that the Russian past and present had no meaning, and that her future could only lie in a reunion with the great body of European civilization and with the

Roman Catholic Church. He thus stimulated the great division between the Westernists and the Slavophiles (qq.v.) in Russian thought. He was declared insane by the authorities, but continued to play an active part in Moscow's social life. *See* N. Lossky, *History of Russian Philosophy*, 1951; R. Hare, *Pioneers of Russian Social Thought*, 1951; V. V. Zenkovsky, *A History of Russian Philosophy*, vol. i, 1953; I. G. Masaryk, *The Spirit of Russia* (2 vols.), 2nd ed., 1955.

Chaliapin, *see* SHALYAPIN.

Chapayev, Vasiliy Ivanovich (1887–1919), Red Army hero of the civil war, formerly a labourer. He commanded a division in the Urals. He has remained a popular figure thanks to a book devoted to him by his political commissar D. Furmanov (published in 1923) and the famous film *Chapayev* of 1934.

Chapayevsk (for some time in the 1920's **Trotsk**), town in the Kuybyshev Oblast (Volga region), 27 m. south-west of Kuybyshev. Population (1959) 83,000. There are varied industries, including agricultural machinery, building materials and food.

Chaplygin, Sergey Aleksandrovich (1869–1942), mathematician and physicist, professor at Moscow University, director of the Moscow Higher Women's Courses, member of the Academy of Sciences from 1929. From 1920 to 1930 he was the head of the Central Aero-Hydrodynamic Institute and later headed its general theoretical team. He did much pioneering work in the dynamics of gases, 1902, aerodynamics (study of the profiles of aircraft wings, 1910 ff.) and ballistics, as well as some work in general mechanics and pure mathematics.

Chardzhou (until 1940 **Chardzhuy**): 1. Oblast in Turkmenia, stretched along the middle course of the Amu-Dar'ya River, comprising the Amu-Dar'ya oasis and a part of the Kara-Kum desert; there are rich deposits of sulphur and salt. Area 36,100 sq. m.; population (1959) 320,000 (39 per cent urban), Turkmens, Uzbeks, Russians and Armenians. Cotton is cultivated, market gardening carried on (Chardzhou melons), Astrakhan sheep raised, and there are cotton and silk processing industries. Before 1924 the area belonged to Bukhara.

2. Administrative, economic and cultural centre of the oblast, situated on the River Amu-Dar'ya and the Trans-Caspian Railway. Population (1959) 66,000 (1939, 55,000). Its chief importance is as a transportation centre: goods are transferred here from river to rail and vice versa, and it is the starting-point of the Chardzhou–Kungrad railway which leads to the Khorezm oasis. There are also silk and cotton processing, Astrakhan fur and chemical (phosphate fertilizers) industries.

Chavchavadze, Prince Il'ya Grigor'yevich (1837–1907), Georgian poet and publicist. He and his literary and artistic circle were the main centre of Georgian cultural life; their outlook was progressive and pro-Russian.

Chaykovskiy, Nikolay Vasil'yevich (1850–1926), Populist politician. He played an outstanding role in the first revolutionary Populist organization, which was formed by M. Natanson in St Petersburg in 1869 and soon became known as the Chaykovskiy circle. The group was the main centre of revolutionary Populism until 1874 and among its members were many future leaders of the revolutionary movement in Russia, including Kropotkin, and in the provincial branches Zhelyabov (*see* NARODNAYA VOLYA) and P. B. Aksel'rod (*see* LIBERATION OF LABOUR GROUP). Becoming interested in religious problems, he left politics and tried to establish a religious commune in America; he later lived for many years in England. Returning to Russia during the revolution of 1905 (q.v.), he left the party of Socialist Revolutionaries and became a leading member of the more moderate Popular Socialist Party and of the co-operative movement. During the First World War he was active in defence work, and after the February revolution (q.v.) of 1917, together with the other old revolutionaries Kropotkin and Plekhanov, strongly opposed the Bolsheviks. After the Bolshevik seizure of power (*see* OCTOBER REVOLUTION) Chaykovskiy took the initiative in forming the Union for the Regeneration of Russia, an anti-Bolshevik conspiratorial organization of moderate socialists and liberals. During the civil war (q.v.) he headed the anti-Bolshevik government in the north of Russia, and was later a member of the Russian delegation (not officially recognized by the Allies) at the Paris Peace Conference. He remained abroad and died in England.

Chaykovskiy, P. I., *see* TCHAIKOVSKY.

Cheboksary, capital, economic and cultural centre of the Chuvash Autonomous Republic, situated on the Volga 85 m. west of Kazan'. Population (1959) 104,000 (1926, 9,000), Russian and Chuvash. It has electrical engineering, woodworking, food and textile industries. Cheboksary has been known since 1371.

Chebyshev, Pafnutiy L'vovich (1821–94), mathematician, member of the Royal Society of London. His chief works were on the theories of prime number, probabilities, integrals, quadratic forms, gearings, etc. He came near to devising a straight-line motion, but this was finally achieved by one of his pupils.

Chechen-Ingush Autonomous Republic, within the R.S.F.S.R., is situated in Northern Caucasus, comprising a part of the slopes of the main Caucasian range and the adjacent plain astride the River Terek; there are deposits of oil. Area 7,400 sq. m.; population (1959) 711,000 (41 per cent urban), chiefly Russians, Chechen and Ingush. There are oil extraction, engineering and food industries, maize and wheat are cultivated, market gardening carried on and cattle and pigs raised. The capital is Groznyy. In 1921 the area was included in the Mountain People's Republic; the Chechen Autonomous Oblast was singled out in 1922, the Ingush Autonomous Oblast in 1924, and in 1934 they were combined into the Chechen-Ingush Autonomous Oblast (raised to the status of Autonomous Republic in 1936). In 1943 the native population was deported for alleged collaboration with the Germans, and a year later the republic was abolished, the major part forming the core of Groznyy Oblast and the remainder being annexed to Georgia, North Ossetia and Daghestan. The republic was re-established after the 1957 decree on the rehabilitation of deported peoples.

Chechens, Caucasian-speaking people living in the Chechen-Ingush Autonomous Republic (North Caucasus) and numbering (1959)

418,000 (1939, 408,000); they are fanatical Sunni Muslims. In the low-lands and foothills they engage in agriculture, and in the mountain pastures in sheep raising. The Chechens have been known since the 17th century, and until the 19th century lived divided into many tribal and local groups with no political or social hierarchy. In the 19th century they put up determined resistance to Russian conquest and were the most fanatical followers of Shamil' (q.v.); after their defeat 39,000 (one-fifth of the total) left Russia for Turkey. During the civil war they fought both the Cossacks and the Bolsheviks, and continued anti-Communist guerrilla warfare in the mountains, which flared up especially fiercely during the collectivization of agriculture (q.v.). In 1943, when the German Army was approaching the Chechen territory, they began another anti-Communist uprising; in conse-quence they were all deported by the Soviet authorities to Kazakh-stan and western Siberia. They were 'rehabilitated' in 1957 and permitted to return. *See* W. Kolarz, *Russia and her Colonies*, 1952; R. Pipes, *The Formation of the Soviet Union*, Cambridge, Mass., 1954; R. Conquest, *The Soviet Deportation of Nationalities*, 1960.

Cheka (abbreviation for **Extraordinary Commission**), Soviet political police from 1917 to 1922. The 'All-Russian Extraordinary Commission for Fighting Counter-Revolution and Sabotage,' headed by Dzerzhinskiy, was responsible for the local, territorial and 'functional' (in the armed forces and the transport system) Chekas. The Bolshevik leadership considered a policy of Red Terror to be essential for the survival of the regime, and this was carried out by the Cheka. It established internal security troops and a system of concentration camps, effected the arrest and execution of arbitrarily selected persons or groups (including the shooting of hostages), and exercised censorship of the press. Members of the Soviet security organs are still referred to as chekists. *See further under* SECURITY ORGANS. *See* E. J. Scott, 'The Cheka,' in *St Antony's Papers*, No. 1, Soviet Affairs, 1956; E. H. Carr, 'The Origin and Status of the Cheka,' *Soviet Studies*, vol. x, No. 1, July 1958.

Chekhov, Anton Pavlovich (1860–1904), author, the son of a grocer and grandson of a serf. He succeeded in paying his way through university and qualifying as a doctor by tutoring and writing for humorous magazines. Having practised for a time, he decided to devote himself entirely to literature, but made much use of his medical training in his writings. He travelled to the penal colony of the Sakhalin Island in 1890, and on his return described it with sin-cerity and perception. He suffered for most of his life from tuber-culosis and this was the cause of his death. Chekhov wrote many short stories, several long stories (*The Steppe, A Dreary Story, Ward No. 6, Peasants*, etc.) and the following plays: *Ivanov*, 1887, *The Sea-gull*, 1896, *Uncle Vanya*, 1897, *The Three Sisters*, 1901, and *The Cherry Orchard*, 1903. His fame dated from the nineties, and the Moscow Art Theatre first made its reputation with his plays. In 1900 he was elected to the Academy of Sciences, but resigned in protest two years later when the Czar declined to permit the election of Maksim Gor'kiy. Chekhov was friendly with both Tolstoy and Gor'kiy, being influenced by the one and influencing the other. His writing mirrored the social life of the 1880's and nineties, and through his descriptions of ordinary provincial families he gave an original interpretation of human behaviour. His influence spread to Western Europe and America during the 1920's, and among authors clearly indebted to him were Katherine Mansfield, Virginia Woolf, Elizabeth Bowen and Ernest Hemingway. *See* W. A. Gerhardi, *Anton Chekhov, a Critical Study*, 1923; R. Hingley, *Chekhov, a Biographical and Critical Study*, 1950; D. Magarshack, *Chekhov, a Life* and *Chekhov the Dramatist*, 1952; W. H. Bruford, *Anton Chekhov*, 1957; M. P. Chekhova, *The Chekhov Museum in Yalta*, Moscow, 1958; V. Yermilov, *A. P. Chekhov*, Moscow; and the bibliography by A. Heifetz, *Chekhov in English*, 1949.

Chelpanov, Georgiy Ivanovich (1862–1936), psychologist, professor of philosophy and psychology at Kiev (1892–1906) and Moscow (1907–23) universities. An idealist in philosophy, Chelpanov was in psychology a follower of W. Wundt, and in 1911 founded the Institute of Experimental Psychology in Moscow which he directed until 1923. After 1917 he attempted to introduce elements of materialism into the explanation of psychic processes, but was strongly attacked by ostensibly Marxist psychologists (his former pupils Blonskiy and Kornilov, qq.v.) and lost his positions both at the university and in his institute. Among his chief works were: *Problems of Space Perception in Connection with the Doctrine of Apriorism and Inbornness* (2 parts), 1896–1904; *Brain and Soul*, 1900 (6th ed., 1918); *On Memory and Mnemonics*, 1900; *On Contemporary Philosophical Trends*, 1902; *Introduction to Philosophy*, 6th ed., 1916; *Textbook of Psychology*, 13th ed., 1916; *Introduction to Experimental Psychology*, 3rd ed., 1924; *Psychology and Marxism*, 2nd ed., 1925; *Objective Psychology in Russia and America*, 1925; *Psychology or Reflexology ?*, 1926; *Outlines of Psychology*, 1926.

Chelyabinsk: 1. Oblast of the R.S.F.S.R., situated on the eastern slopes of the southern Urals, with mixed forests in the north and steppe in the south. Area 34,300 sq. m.; population (1959) 2,982,000 (76 per cent urban), mostly Russian (since the 18th century) with some Bashkirs, Tatars and Kazakhs. The oblast has large deposits of high-grade iron ore, ferro-alloys, manganese, chromium, nickel, copper, zinc, gold, brown coal and building materials; it has the largest iron and steel industry of the Urals, together with engineering, non-ferrous metallurgy and chemical industries. Other activities are wheat growing and cattle raising. Principal towns: Chelyabinsk, Magnitogorsk, Kopeysk, Zlatoust, Korkino and Miass. The industrial development of the oblast began in the 18th century, when the first ironworks were built, but it has been particularly rapid since the early 1930's.

2. Administrative, economic and cultural centre of the oblast, the second most important industrial city of the Urals. Population (1959) 688,000 (thirteenth in the U.S.S.R., second in the Urals; 1897, 20,000; 1917, 47,000; 1931, 117,000; 1945, 400,000). The chief industries are engineering (tractors, aircraft, machine tools), electrical equipment and metallurgy (steel, ferro-alloys, zinc); there is also a large lignite-fed power-station. The city is a major transportation

centre (five railway lines, airport). Founded in 1648 on the site of a Tatar village, Chelyabinsk became a Cossack fortress in 1746, and until the end of the 19th century was an important trading point through which the mining towns of the southern Urals were supplied with agricultural products from Western Siberia. Its commercial importance was further heightened by the construction of the Trans-Siberian Railway in the 1890 s; the first industries also appeared at that time. Chelyabinsk replaced Tyumen' as the 'gateway to Siberia' for goods and settlers. The city was raised to its present industrial position by the pre-war Five Year Plans and the Second World War.

Chelyuskin, Cape, of the Taymyr Peninsula in northern Siberia; it is the northernmost point of the Asian continent (lat. 78° N.).

Chemical Industry. The output of basic products in recent years has been as follows: sulphuric acid (monohydrate) 4·8 million tons in 1958 (0·1 in 1913, 1·6 in 1940); calcium soda (95 per cent)1·6 million tons in 1957 (0·2 in 1913, 0·5 in 1940); caustic soda (92 per cent) 631,000 tons in 1956 (55,000 in 1913, 190,000 in 1940). The output of artificial and synthetic fibres reached 166,600 tons in 1958 (11,100 in 1940), and in addition 71,000 tons were imported (mostly from Western Europe). For chemical fertilizers *see* FERTILIZERS; for synthetic rubber *see* RUBBER INDUSTRY. The principal chemical works are situated in central Russia (Moscow, Yaroslavl', Dzerzhinsk), Leningrad, the Donets Basin and the Urals (Berezniki). See *U.S.S.R. Today and Tomorrow*, Moscow, 1959.

Chemistry dates in Russia from the middle of the 18th century, when Lomonosov first formulated the principle of the conservation of matter and put forward the idea of atomic structure of matter. In the 19th century the Kazan' chemical school headed by Zinin, Butlerov and Markovnikov (qq.v.) greatly contributed to the development of organic chemistry. Other schools of organic chemistry were those of Favorskiy and Zelinskiy (qq.v.). The greatest name in physical chemistry was Mendeleyev (q.v.), who in 1869 established the Periodic Law of atomic weights, marking an epoch in the history of science. Other notable works in physical chemistry were those of Bakh, Kablukov and Kurnakov (qq.v.), while Chugayev (q.v.) founded an important school in inorganic chemistry. In recent decades physical chemistry has been advanced by Semënov, Frumkin (qq.v.) and V. G. Khlopin (radiochemistry), and organic chemistry by Chichibabin, Namëtkin, Arbuzov, Nesmeyanov (qq.v.) and their schools. See J. G. Crowther, *Soviet Science*, 1936; N. A. Bakh (ed.), *Symposium on Radiation Chemistry*, New York, 1956; *General Questions on Electrochemical Kinetics and the Reaction Mechanics of Electrochemical Reductions: Reports of the Fourth Conference on Electrochemistry* (*Moscow, 1956*), New York, Consultants' Bureau, 1958; *All-Union Conference on the Application of Radioactive and Stable Isotopes and Radiation in the National Economy and Science* (*Moscow, 1957*), *Abstracts of Papers* (3 vols.), New York, 1957.

Complete 'cover-to-cover' translations of the following journals exist in English: *Biochemistry*; *Journal of Analytical Chemistry*; *Journal of Inorganic Chemistry*; *Journal of General Chemistry*; *Journal of Applied Chemistry*; *Colloid Journal*; *Journal of Abstracts*:

Chemistry; Bulletin of the Academy of Sciences of the U.S.S.R.: Section of Chemical Sciences.

Cheremisses, *see* MARI.

Cheremkhovo, town in the Irkutsk Oblast (south-eastern Siberia), situated on the Trans-Siberian Railway 80 m. north-west of Irkutsk. Population (1959) 123,000 (1926, 14,000; 1939, 56,000). The town is the second centre of the Irkutsk-Cheremkhovo industrial area, and the centre of the Cheremkhovo coal basin, which extends for 300 m. along the Trans-Siberian from Nizhneudinsk to Lake Baykal.

Cherepnin, Nikolay Nikolayevich (*b.* 1873), composer and conductor who studied under Rimsky-Korsakov at St Petersburg Conservatory. He conducted the Belyayev concerts, and worked with Diaghilev as conductor, 1909–14. He was the teacher of Prokofiev. His works comprise three operas, including *The Marriage Broker*; ballets, including *Le Pavillon d'Armide*, 1903; piano concerto, 1907; orchestral works; church music, including a religious cantata, *Pilgrimage and Passions of Virgin Mary* (based on medieval Russian chants); songs, etc. Cherepnin's music is primarily Russian, but shows traces of French Impressionism. *See* M. Montagu-Nathan, *Contemporary Russian Composers*, 1917.

Cherepovets, town in the Vologda Oblast (in the north of European Russia), situated at the northern tip of the Rybinsk Reservoir 72 m. west of Vologda. Population (1959) 92,000. It has an iron and steel plant (using ore from the Kola Peninsula and coal from the Pechora Basin) which is uneconomical unless the bulk of production is based on scrap; it is a crossing point of the Volga–Baltic waterway and the railway line from Leningrad to the east. Cherepovets was founded in 1780; the iron and steel plant was built after the Second World War.

Cherkasov, Nikolay Konstantinovich (*b.* 1903), one of the most famous of the older Soviet actors, a Communist Party member since 1940. He began as a stage mime, later becoming a comedy, vaudeville and dramatic actor in Leningrad, and has been in films since 1926. His main roles are Professor Polezhayev in *Baltic Deputy*, 1937, the Czarevich Aleksey in *Peter the First*, 1937 and 1939, and Maksim Gor'kiy in *Lenin in 1918*, 1939. He became internationally famous for his title roles in Eisenstein's *Alexander Nevsky*, 1938, and *Ivan the Terrible, Parts I and II*, 1944–5. *See* his *Notes of a Soviet Actor*, Moscow.

Cherkassy: 1. Oblast in central Ukraine, largely situated on the right bank of the Dnieper in the wooded steppe part of the black earth belt. Area 8,100 sq. m.; population (1959) 1,504,000 (23 per cent urban), almost entirely Ukrainian (before the war also Jewish). Wheat and sugar-beet are grown, cattle and pigs raised, and there are also food industries. Principal towns: Cherkassy, Uman' and Smela. The area belonged to the medieval Kievan state; it became Lithuanian in 1362, Polish in 1569 and Russian in 1793.

2. Capital and an economic and cultural centre of the oblast, situated 96 m. south-east of Kiev on the Dnieper. Population (1959) 83,000 (1897, 30,000). It has food and some engineering industries, and there are many rest-homes and sanatoria near the town. Cherkassy was probably founded at the end of the 13th century, and was the capital of the Ukrainian hetmans from 1386 to 1649.

Cherkessk (formerly **Batalpashinsk**, in the 1930's **Sulimov, Yezhovo-Cherkessk**), administrative, economic and cultural centre of the Karachay-Circassian Autonomous Oblast in the Stavropol' Kray (North Caucasus), situated on the River Kuban' 60 m. south of Stavropol'. Population (1959) 47,000, chiefly Russian and Ukrainian. It was founded in 1803 as a Cossack *stanitsa* (village) and became a town in 1880.

Cherkesy, *see* CIRCASSIANS.

Chernigov (Ukrainian **Chernihiv**): 1. Oblast in northern Ukraine, situated north-east of Kiev; its northern part is in the Poles'ye and the southern part in the wooded steppe, black earth belt. Area 12,500 sq. m.; population (1959) 1,553,000 (22 per cent urban), almost entirely Ukrainian (before the war also Jewish). Agriculture (grain, potatoes, hemp and sugar-beet, cattle and pigs) is the principal branch of the economy in the oblast; industries are mainly concerned with processing agricultural products. Principal towns: Chernigov, Priluki and Nezhin. The area belonged to the medieval Kievan state, later for some time to Lithuania-Poland, and since 1654 again to Russia.

2. Administrative, cultural and an economic centre of the oblast, situated 130 m. north-east of Kiev on the River Desna. Population (1959) 89,000. There are varied industries, including large wool-processing and textile factories. A university was opened in 1957 on the basis of the famous Historical-Philological Lycée which had existed in Nezhin since 1820. There are several 11th–12th-century churches and interesting buildings of the 17th century. Chernigov was the principal town of the Severyane tribe from the 7th century, and the capital of Chernigov Grand Principality from 1024 until 1239.

Chernogorsk, town in the Khakas Autonomous Oblast (southern Siberia), centre of the Minusinsk coal-mining basin, situated 10 m. north of Abakan. Population (1959) 51,000 (1932, 25,000; 1939, 17,000), mainly Russians. Chernogorsk was founded in 1907 as a mining settlement.

Chernov, Dmitriy Konstantinovich (1839–1921), metallurgist, professor at the Artillery Academy in St Petersburg. His works were mainly concerned with the structure of steel; he developed new methods of thermal treatment of steel which brought him international fame, and applied them in the production of steel cannons and missiles.

Chernov, Viktor Mikhaylovich (1873–1952), leader of the Socialist Revolutionaries. He was Minister of Agriculture in Kerenskiy's Provisional Government, and was elected chairman of the Constituent Assembly in 1918. In 1920 he emigrated, and he died in America. *See* his *The Great Russian Revolution*, New Haven, 1936, and *Pered burey*, New York, 1953.

Chernovtsy: 1. Oblast in western Ukraine comprising the northern parts of Bukovina and Bessarabia, situated in the Carpathian foothills, traversed by the River Prut and partly covered by oak and beech forests. Area 3,100 sq. m.; population (1959) 776,000 (26 per cent urban), mostly Ukrainians (those living in the Carpathian Mountains belong to the Hutsul tribe). Wheat and sunflowers are grown, sheep are raised, and there are lumbering, woodworking and food industries. For the history of the area *see* BUKOVINA; BESSARABIA.

2. (Ukrainian **Chernivtsi**, Rumanian **Cernauti**, German **Czernowitz**). Administrative, economic and cultural centre of the oblast, situated on the River Prut. Population (1959) 145,000 (1930, 111,000), Ukrainians and Jews. It has textile, engineering and food industries, and a university founded in 1875. Chernovtsy has been known since 1407, became a town in 1786 and the capital of Bukovina in 1849. During the late 19th and early 20th centuries it was a centre of the Ukrainian national movement.

Chernyakhovsk (until 1946 **Insterburg**), town in the Kaliningrad Oblast (former East Prussia) of the R.S.F.S.R., 57 m. east of Kaliningrad. Population (1959) under 50,000 (1939, 49,000). It has some industry and is an important railway junction. Founded by the Teutonic Knights in 1337 as a castle, it has been a town since 1583.

Chernyshevskiy, Nikolay Gavrilovich (1828–89), literary critic and publicist, leader of the radical intelligentsia during the 1850's and sixties, who subsequently spent nineteen years in banishment in Siberia. With his many articles from 1854 to 1864 in the radical journal the *Contemporary* (q.v.), his novel *What is to be Done?*, his *Notes on J. S. Mill's 'Political Economy'* and his dissertation *The Aesthetic Relations of Art and Reality* (setting forth a rigorously utilitarian view of art), Chernyshevskiy established the basis of revolutionary Populism (q.v.), prepared the ground for the spread of Marxism and provided an important element of the future Bolshevik ideology. *See* R. Hare, *Pioneers of Russian Social Thought*, 1951; T. G. Masaryk, *The Spirit of Russia* (2nd ed.), vol. ii, 1955; R. W. Mathewson, *The Positive Hero in Russian Literature*, New York, 1958; F. Venturi, *Roots of Revolution*, 1960.

Chërnyy Peredel ('Black Redistribution'), Populist revolutionary organization formed in 1879 as a result of the split of the Zemlya i Volya organization. It was led by Plekhanov and P. B. Aksel'rod, both of whom soon emigrated. Although the centre of the organization disintegrated, its local groups continued to exist for several years and were one of the elements which produced Russian social democracy. *See also* POPULISM; RUSSIAN SOCIAL DEMOCRATIC LABOUR PARTY.

Chersonesus (or **Chersonese**, Russian **Khersones**), ruins of an ancient Greek city in south-western Crimea, 2 m. west of Sevastopol'. Chersonesus was founded in the 5th century B.C., and until its decline in the 14th century it was the commercial and administrative centre of western Crimea. Excavations of the site have been undertaken since 1827.

Chervonets, monetary unit in 1922–47 equal to ten roubles. The issue of Chervonets bank-notes helped to combat the inflation of 1917–24 and was a part of the monetary reform of 1922–4.

Chiatura, town in Georgia situated 20 m. east of Kutaisi. Population (1956) 19,200. It is the centre of the Chiatura manganese-mining area which has been worked since 1879 and is one of the richest in the world.

Chicherin, Boris Nikolayevich (1828–1904), outstanding jurist, historian, philosopher and liberal politician, professor of Moscow University, Mayor of Moscow, 1882–3, later active in the Tambov province *zemstvo*. In philosophy (*Science and Religion*, 1879, 2nd ed., 1901; *Positive Philosophy and the Unity of Science*, 1892; *Foundations of Logic and Metaphysics*, 1894) he followed Hegel and opposed Positivism and Utilitarianism. His *Philosophy of Law*, 1900, is a masterpiece in which he derives law from freedom, the spiritual essence of man. As a historian (*Regional Institutions in Russia in the Seventeenth Century*, 1856; *Essays in the History of Russian Law*, 1858; *Sketches of England and France*, 1858) he was the recognized head of the 'étatist' school in Russian historiography; his view of the progressive 'enserfing' of the estates in 16th–17th-century Muscovy led him to the conclusion of the necessity for their emancipation in conditions of the modern state.

As a political theorist (*History of Political Doctrines*, 5 vols., 1869–1902; *Property and State*, 2 vols., 1882–3; *A Course in State Science*, 3 vols., 1894–8; *On Popular Representation*, 1899; *Problems of Politics*, 1903) Chicherin drew a clear distinction between society, consisting of manifold associations of persons bound by diverse interests, and the State, which is to him a union of free people bound by law and governed by the supreme power in the interests of the common good. The political ideal is a harmony of all four elements of the State, i.e. authority, law, freedom and the common good, and this harmony is most likely to be realized in constitutional monarchy. The most important and irreplaceable guarantee of freedom and law is the absolute independence of the courts. An ardent individualist and anti-socialist, Chicherin supported private property and freedom of contracts and opposed modern social legislation, which he considered an impermissible confusion of juridical law with moral law and of common good with charity. Rejecting both the 'night-watchman' view of the State and the subordination to it of all private activities, he saw much room for positive State action upon society, pointing to the beneficial reforms of Peter the Great and Alexander II (*see* GREAT REFORMS). Chicherin strongly argued against the established Church and State interference in religious matters; against the policy of assimilation of the national minorities and for respect for their rights and freedom; for freedom of thought and speech, autonomy of universities, etc. He envisaged progress in international relations through further complication of interdependent interests and the development of moral principles. His *Reminiscences* (4 vols., published 1929–34) are a valuable historical source.

Chicherin, Georgiy (or **Yuriy**) **Vasil'yevich** (1872–1936), diplomat who graduated from St Petersburg University and then worked in the Foreign Office. He joined the Social Democratic Labour Party, becoming a leading member of the Menshevik faction, in Berlin, where he had emigrated in 1904. He was active for many years in the labour movements of England, France and Germany. After the Bolshevik coup in 1917 Chicherin became a Bolshevik and was imprisoned in Brixton jail for having enemy associations. He was released in January 1918 and expelled from Britain in exchange for Sir George Buchanan. He returned to Russia, and as Commissar for Foreign Affairs negotiated and signed the treaty of Rapallo with Germany in 1922. Because of prolonged illness he resigned in 1930.

Chichibabin, Aleksey Yevgen'yevich (1871–1945), chemist. Educated at Moscow University, he was professor at the Moscow Higher Technical School from 1909 and member of the Academy of Sciences from 1928. He emigrated in 1930 and died abroad. His work in organic chemistry was devoted to the study of heterocyclic combinations (pyridine), and he greatly contributed to the development of the pharmaceutic industry in Russia.

Chief Administration, divisions within a ministry, corresponding to departments of a ministry in Britain; there are also Chief Administrations which do not belong to a ministry and are subordinated directly to the Council of Ministers.

Children are legally divided into legitimate and 'fatherless' (the term illegitimate is not used); the latter have no claims on the father (*see* MARRIAGE; INHERITANCE). This distinction did not exist between 1918 and 1944, when illegitimate children were treated legally in the same way as legitimate. Married mothers receive allowances for the fourth and subsequent children until the children reach the age of 5; unmarried mothers receive allowances beginning with the first child. There is an elaborate system of decorations for mothers who bring up large families, culminating in the title of Mother Heroine for ten children. Children are officially forbidden to be employed in industry before the age of 15 (since 1956, prior to that 14), but *kolkhoz* (q.v.) children have to work a certain number of days per year from the age of 12; young people between 15 and 17 employed in industry have shortened hours (since 1956), and those receiving part-time secondary education may be allowed time off from their jobs. Children can be held criminally responsible from the age of 16, and for particularly serious crimes from the age of 14 (from 1935 until the legal reform, q.v., of 1958, 14 and 12 respectively). The punishment of confinement to a 'corrective labour colony' may be applied to juveniles (*see* PENAL SYSTEM), but the death penalty is not applicable to those under the age of 18; no special juvenile courts exist (*see also* JUVENILE DELINQUENCY).

The responsibility of the upbringing of children is officially shared between the family and society at large, the latter acting through schools and the youth organizations (*see* OCTOBER CHILDREN; PIONEERS; KOMSOMOL); membership in the junior organizations is voluntary, but, especially for the child outstanding in any field, it is difficult to withstand the pressure to join the Komsomol. Great emphasis is laid by the party authorities on a uniform ideological upbringing for children, and if the family influence, religious or political, is deviant, the child is expected to side with society against his family, as for example in the case of Pavlik Morozov (q.v.). In the larger towns there are varied facilities for recreation and extra-curricular activities. *See* E. J. Simmons (ed.), *Through the Glass of Soviet Literature*, New York, 1953; V. Gsovski and K. Grzybowski (eds.), *Government, Law and Courts in the Soviet Union and Eastern*

1. Ukrainian landscape
(*Barnaby's Picture Library*)

2. Baku oilfields, 1957
(*Camera Press*)

3. Small town in the north-west, 1960

4. Bratsk hydro-electric station under construction, 1960

(*Associated Press*)

5   Kolkhoz market in European Russia, 1960

6. Moscow street scene, 1956
(*Barnaby's Picture Library*)

7. Moscow street scene, 1956
(*Barnaby's Picture Library*)

8. A primary school class, 1959
(*Camera Press*)

9. Old print of the Solovetskiy Monastery

(Radio Times Hulton Picture Library)

10. View of the Kremlin from the Moskva River

(Barnaby's Picture Library)

11. The Bell Tower of John the Great in the Moscow Kremlin
(*Barnaby's Picture Library*)

12. Minin arousing the citizens of Nizhniy Novgorod, from a painting by V. Ye. Makovskiy

(Radio Times Hulton Picture Library)

13. Eighteenth-century cartoon depicting an Old Believer resisting the cutting of beards enforced by Peter the Great

(*Radio Times Hulton Picture Library*)

14. Provincial town near Moscow, 1954
(Camera Press)

15. The Ukraina Hotel, Moscow
(*Barnaby's Picture Library*)

16. Peasant huts in Siberia, 1960

17. Generalissimo A. V. Suvorov
(Radio Times Hulton Picture Library)

18. Emperor Alexander II
(Radio Times Hulton Picture Library)

20. Professor S. A. Muromtsev
(Radio Times Hulton Picture Library)

19. Professor D. I. Mendeleyev
(Radio Times Hulton Picture Library)

21. P. A. Stolypin
(*Radio Times Hulton Picture Library*)

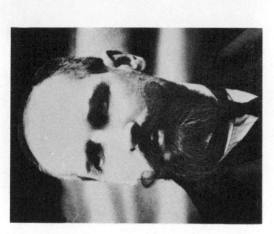

22. A. F. Kerenskiy
(*Radio Times Hulton Picture Library*)

23. Lenin presiding over a meeting of the Council of People's Commissars, October 1922
(Radio Times Hulton Picture Library)

25. N. I. Yezhov
(Planet News)

24. General L. G. Kornilov
(Radio Times Hulton Picture Library)

26. Marshal G. K. Zhukov
(*Camera Press*)

27. N. S. Khrushchëv
(Camera Press)

29. Academician I. V. Kurchatov
(Camera Press)

28. K. E. Tsiolkovskiy
(Planet News)

31. I. S. Turgenev
(*Radio Times Hulton Picture Library*)

30. A. S. Pushkin
(*Radio Times Hulton Picture Library*)

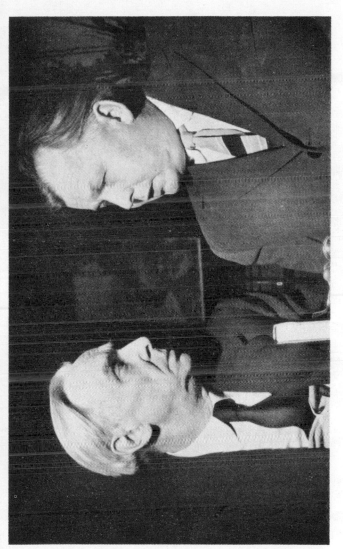

32. K. A. Fedin and A. T. Tvardovskiy in Britain, 1960

The Times)

33. Tamara Karsavina in 'The Firebird'
(*Radio Times Hulton Picture Library*)

34. The Bolshoi Theatre ballet rehearsing in London, 1956

(*Camera Press*)

35. F. I. Shalyapin
(Radio Times Hulton Picture Library)

36. S. M. Eisenstein
(*Radio Times Hulton Picture Library*)

37. Caucasian warrior (Shamil')
(*Radio Times Hulton Picture Library*)

38. Kazakh bard (Dzhambul Dzhabayev)
(*Radio Times Hulton Picture Library*)

Europe, vol. ii, 1959; A. Inkeles and R. A. Bauer, *The Soviet Citizen*, 1959; I. Mareuil, 'Extracurricular and Extrascholastic Activities for Soviet Schoolchildren' in G. Z. F. Bereday and J. Pennar, *The Politics of Soviet Education*, 1960.

Chimkent, town in Central Asia, administrative, economic and cultural centre of the South Kazakhstan Oblast, situated on the Turksib Railway about 70 m. north of Tashkent. Population (1959) 153,000 (1939, 74,000), Uzbeks, Kazakhs and Russians. It has a lead-smelting plant (the largest in the U.S.S.R.), a heavy engineering plant, a textile factory (the largest in Kazakhstan), a pharmaceutic factory (built 1885) and various food industries. Chimkent was founded in the 12th century, and before Russian annexation, 1864, was a Kokand fortress. It became a provincial centre in 1932.

Chinese in Russia numbered 26,000 in 1959, of whom 69 per cent regard Chinese as their mother tongue. They can be found in big cities throughout the country, many of them working as artisans or pedlars. They were much more numerous before the 1930's, particularly in the Far East, the southern portion of which was ceded by China to Russia in the 19th century. During the First World War many Chinese were recruited for work in Russia, and Chinese units played a noticeable part in the civil war on the Red side. Most Chinese in the Far East remained Chinese citizens and were expelled by the Soviet Government in the mid 1930's. *See* W. Kolarz, *The Peoples of the Soviet Far East*, 1954.

Chinese Eastern Railway, trunk line in Manchuria connecting Vladivostok with the Trans-Siberian Railway by a short route. A branch line from Harbin connects it with Dal'niy (Dairen) and Port Arthur. The Chinese Eastern Railway was built by the Russians in 1896–1903. After the Russo-Japanese War the southern line was ceded to Japan. During the Russian Civil War the Chinese Eastern Railway was controlled by the Whites and the Allies (Japan, U.S.A.). By a treaty with China in 1924 the Soviet Government recovered former Russian rights over the railway, though a dispute took place in 1929. It was sold by the U.S.S.R. to Japan in 1935.

Chirchik, town in the Tashkent Oblast (Uzbekistan), 20 m. northeast of Tashkent. Population (1959) 65,000 (1939, 15,000). It is an important industrial centre, with engineering (agricultural machinery, chemical industry equipment), chemical (nitrogen) and other industries, and a chain of hydro-electric stations.

Chistopol', town in the Tatar Autonomous Republic, situated 70 m. south-east of Kazan' on the River Kama. Population (1959) 51,000 (1901, 22,000; 1931, 15,500). It is the centre of the lower Kama agricultural area and has a large watch- and clock-making plant, evacuated there during the war. Chistopol' became a town in 1781, and before 1917 was the centre of a flourishing grain trade.

Chistyakovo, town in the Stalino Oblast (Ukraine), 47 m. east of Stalino. Population (1959) 92,000, mostly Russians. It is a major coal-mining centre (anthracite).

Chita: 1. Oblast of the R.S.F.S.R. in south-eastern Siberia, comprising the eastern part of Transbaykalia; it is a mountainous region largely covered with coniferous forests and having an extreme continental climate. Area 166,600 sq. m.; population (1959) 1,039,000 (55 per cent urban), mostly Russian (since the 17th century), also some Buryat and Evenki. There are large deposits of gold, tin, other non-ferrous metals, iron and coal; sheep and cattle breeding is carried on, spring grain grown, fur-trapping takes place in the north, and there are mining (since 1704), engineering and food industries. The area has been one of banishment since the early 19th century and of labour camps, 1930's–mid fifties.

2. Administrative, economic and cultural centre of the oblast, situated on the Trans-Siberian Railway. Population (1959) 171,000 (1917, 44,000; 1939, 121,000). It has locomotive works, saw-mills, and sheepskin and leather industries. In the 18th century Chita was a small Cossack fortified town; it became the seat of the Nerchinsk Gold-mining Administration during the 19th century, and the administrative centre of Transbaykalia in 1851. It was the head-quarters of Semënov's White Army (supported by the Japanese) from 1918 to 1920, and the capital of the Far Eastern Republic from 1920 to 1922.

Chkalov, Valeriy Pavlovich (1904–38), test pilot. He became famous in 1936 when he flew from Moscow over the North Pole to the United States in an ANT-25 plane designed by Tupolev (q.v.). He received much publicity and many honours, especially posthumously after he had crashed in 1938.

Chkalov, *see* ORENBURG.

Chudskoye, Lake (Estonian **Peipsi**), is situated between Estonia and the Pskov Oblast of north-western Russia. Length (north to south) 90 m.; width 32 m.; area 1,356 sq. m. Its southern arm forms the Pskov lake, and it is connected with the Gulf of Finland by the River Narova. The famous Ice Battle on the lake took place in 1224, when the Teutonic Knights were defeated by the Novgorodians.

Chugayev, Lev Aleksandrovich (1873–1922), chemist, pupil of Zelinskiy (q.v.), professor at the Moscow Higher Technical School, St Petersburg University and St Petersburg Technological Institute. His work was mostly devoted to the study of complex combinations, in which field he has had many pupils.

Chukchi, people who live in scattered groups in the north of the Russian Far East between the Bering Straits and the Kolyma River, speaking a Paleo-Asiatic language and numbering (1959) 12,000. They combine the physical features of American Indians and Mongols, and are divided into two groups: the sedentary coastal Chukchi who live by sea-animal hunting and fishing, and the semi-nomadic Reindeer Chukchi of the interior. They have been known since Russian Cossacks first reached the area in 1644, and fiercely resisted domination by Russia, being finally subdued only in the 1930's. *See* V. Bogoraz, *The Chukchee*, New York, 1904–10.

Chukchi National Okrug belongs to the Magadan Oblast. Area 274,500 sq. m.; population (1959) 47,000, mainly Russians, also Chukchi and Eskimoes. It has some coal-, lead- and zinc-mining, until the mid 1950's chiefly by forced labour. The okrug was formed in 1930; its administrative centre is Anadyr'.

Chul'man, settlement in southern Yakutia (Eastern Siberia), situated on the Amur–Yakutsk highway. It is the centre of the southern Yakutian coal-mining basin and is likely to become a centre of the iron and steel industry based upon large iron ore and coking coal deposits in the area.

Chuprov, Aleksandr Ivanovich (1842–1908), economist and liberal publicist. His research in agricultural economics had great influence upon contemporary thought in Russia, and laid the foundations for the future Neo-Populism (q.v.).

Chusovoy, town in the Perm' Oblast (Urals), 82 m. north-east of Perm'. Population (1959) 60,000. It has an iron and steel plant (founded 1879) producing high quality steel, and is an important railway junction.

Chuvash Autonomous Republic, within the R.S.F.S.R., is situated in the north of the Volga upland between Gor'kiy and Kazan', and consists of ravinous wooded steppe with mixed forests in the south-west and north; there are phosphorite and building materials deposits. Area 7,100 sq. m.; population (1959) 1,098,000 (24 per cent urban), mostly Chuvashes, also Russians and some Mordva and Tatars. Grain and potatoes are cultivated, cattle raised, and there are saw-milling, woodworking, chemical and food industries. A large hydro-electric station is planned for construction. Principal towns: Cheboksary (capital) and Alatyr'. The area was annexed to Russia with the conquest of Kazan' in 1552. In 1920 the Chuvash Autonomous Oblast was established, and in 1925 transformed into an Autonomous Republic.

Chuvashes, Turkic-speaking people numbering (1959) 1,470,000, who inhabit the Chuvash Autonomous Republic (forming three-quarters of its population) and also live in the surrounding areas of European Russia. They are probably descended from the medieval Volga Bulgarians, are Orthodox Christians and to a considerable degree russianized. Most Chuvashes are peasants working in collective farms. A Chuvash alphabet dates from 1872. *See* W. Kolarz, *Russia and her Colonies*, 1952.

Cinema. Under the Czarist regime a semi-official body called the Skobelev Committee, originally formed as an aristocratic philanthropic society, exercised a watching brief over the cinema industry. The Skobelev Committee also operated for a while under the Provisional Government. After the Bolshevik seizure of power supervision of films was handed over to the Commissariat of Education, and the department concerned with films was at first headed by Lenin's wife, N. Krupskaya. In 1918 the Moscow and Petrograd Cinema Committees were established and later merged into an All-Russian Cinema Committee (Kinokomitet), still under the Commissariat of Education. After nationalization this eventually became in 1922 the Central State Photo-Cinema Enterprise (Goskino), which also remained under the Commissariat of Education. But in 1929 an independent Cinema Committee, directly responsible to the Council of People's Commissars, took control of the industry. After many changes of name (including Soyuzkino) and organization, reflecting the disturbed political scene of the thirties, the Kinokomitet became a Ministry of the Cinema in 1946. In 1953 it was subordinated to the

Ministry of Culture, and is at present called the Chief Administration of the Cinema. It controls thirty-three film studios, each headed by a director and 'council.' The Moscow studio (Mosfilm), the largest in the country, was reorganized in 1960 into three 'councils.'

Regular film production began in Russia in 1907, and by 1917 no less than two thousand films had been made. A St Petersburg journalist and photographer, A. Drankov, was the first Russian to start feature film production in his country. He was soon followed by many others in Moscow. Russian films were, on the whole, no worse and no better than those of other countries. They borrowed heavily from the techniques of the early French and Scandinavian films. But in their turn they too made their contribution to the art, and even at that time had some influence on film-making in other countries. Pictorial composition, mobility and flexibility of the camera, skill in adapting Russian classics, dramatic realism and a certain exoticism were qualities in Russian film work much admired, and some of them were imitated by others.

The Russian cinema borrowed heavily not only from the classics of Russian literature but also from the theatre and ballet, and revealed the influence of such masters of those arts as Stanislavskiy (q.v.) and the ballet *décor* geniuses Bakst and Benois (qq.v.). One of the world's greatest stage producers, Vsevolod Meyerhold (q.v.), had three of his plays filmed. In the film world proper, among the outstanding names of the period were the directors Yakov Protazanov (q.v.), Nikolay Volkov, V. Turzhanskiy, Vladimir Gardin and Ivan Perestiani. Among the actors and actresses who won an international reputation were Vera Kholodnaya, V. Polonskiy and O. Runich. These were extremely photogenic and impressive figures, though their acting was somewhat primitive. On the other hand, the lovely and mysterious-looking Natalia Lysenko and the male lead V. Maksimov, as well as the director Perestiani, were also fine performers. The world-famous bass singer F. Shalyapin (q.v.) made some memorable appearances in the early Russian films, and the young tenor N. Kozlovskiy also gained valuable acting experience in films at that time. Undoubtedly the most remarkable figure was Ivan Mozdzhukhin, one of the pioneer actor-directors, who continued to make a great career for himself in exile in France in the early 1920's, eventually emigrating to America in 1926. Mozdzhukhin loved swashbuckling, adventurous, athletic roles in the Douglas Fairbanks style. Another personality of world stature was Vladislav Starevich, graphic artist, director and film cameraman. Soviet historians claim him as the inventor of the puppet, or cartoon, film, which he first started making in 1911. He certainly anticipated Walt Disney, but was long after Georges Méliès.

Among the more important pre-revolutionary films were Turzhanskiy's *Mozart and Salieri*, 1913, and *The Brothers Karamazov*; Protazanov's *Nikolay Stavrogin*, 1915, *Anna Karenina*, 1915, *Queen of Spades*, 1916, and *Father Sergius*, 1917, an adaptation of Lev Tolstoy's story of the same name; and Starevich's first feature cartoon film *The Grasshopper and the Ant*, 1913.

Many of the pre-revolutionary film-makers and actors, such as

Mozdzhukhin and Protazanov, emigrated to France and Germany, where they continued their work, and some eventually to the U.S.A. In France in particular, at Montreuil, the Russian *émigré* cinema flourished for a few years. It produced some famous films, in a distinctively Russian style: *Kean, Le Brasier Ardent, Casanova, Tales of the Arabian Nights, The Masked Woman* and many others.

A few of the *émigrés* (including Protazanov) returned to Russia and continued to produce films of the highest technical standard under the Soviet regime. Others of the pre-revolutionary leading lights in the film world had remained in Russia and did much to rebuild the broken and impoverished industry. Among these was Ivan Perestiani, the actor-director, who directed and partly wrote the first and most successful Soviet adventure film, *The Little Red Devils*, made in 1923 at the Georgian studios of the State cinema industry. Perestiani was 'purged' in the late 1920's, reinstated for a short time and then permanently relegated to obscurity; however, he lived on to the age of 90 and died only in 1959. Another pre-revolutionary director who made important films under the new regime was V. Gardin. In 1921, as director of the first State Cinema School (now the State Institute of Cinematography), he made, with the students of the school, the earliest Soviet full-length feature film on the revolution and the civil war, entitled *The Hammer and the Sickle*. He was largely responsible for organizing the local Ukrainian and Belorussian film industries. But he too became a victim of the political purges (q.v.): he was charged with 'bourgeois nationalism' and fell into disgrace when his film *Kastus' Kalinovskiy*, based on local material and written and directed by Gardin himself at the Belorussian studios in 1928, was banned. (The film has recently been 'rehabilitated.')

Thus the Soviet cinema took over a considerable heritage from the earlier Russian cinema. This included some of its faults as well as its achievements; among the former was its excessive theatricality and exaggerated histrionics, a fault from which the Soviet cinema still suffers.

The whole film industry, as well as the photographic materials industry, was nationalized on 27th August 1919 and put under the People's Commissariat of Education. By January 1922 Lenin felt the time had come to bring back formal and regular censorship (q.v.). He issued a directive which laid down much more specifically than hitherto the censorship duties of the Commissariat of Education over films. Lenin considered the cinema the most important of all arts, and envisaged three main tasks for it: it should be an informative but selective chronicle, rather like, as Lenin put it, 'the best of our Soviet newspapers'; secondly, films should be a kind of public lecture, covering, among other things, scientific and technological topics; and third, films should be entertaining and artistic. At the same time, however, this artistry should be devoted to 'propaganda for our ideas.' Films should present 'slices of life' and should be 'permeated with our ideas.'

The first Soviet films were little more than newsreels and documentaries, showing the battle fronts of the civil war, Lenin addressing the workers, or giving more direct messages such as urging peasants to

till or sow their fields or to join the Red Army. Even the few feature
films consisted of crude propaganda. The first Soviet film, made in
1918, was *Consolidation*, written by Lunacharskiy and directed by A.
Panteleyev, a pre-revolutionary director. It tells the story of an old
scientist who transfers his loyalty to 'the revolution.' An important
genre of early Soviet film was the anti-God or atheist production to
which considerable resources and effort were devoted for several
years, until atheist propaganda came to be generally discredited in
the middle to late twenties. Among the best known of this type of
film were Panteleyev's *Miracle-maker*, 1922, and Gardin's *Cross and
Mauser*, 1925.

The concept of art as the instrument of politics in the narrowest
sense was bound to lead to conflict. And the story of the Soviet
cinema is one of almost constant struggle between art and political
agitation. But to begin with there were many artists, writers, film
directors and others who themselves believed that art should really be
a kind of direct propaganda to the people. They were themselves
revolutionaries and wanted to overthrow the old canons of art. Many
of them identified the revolution with communism, and sincerely
regarded themselves, at first, as Communists. In the cinema this was
probably true not only of extreme *avant-gardists* but of the more
profound masters such as Dovzhenko, Pudovkin and Eisenstein
(qq.v.). This mood gave rise to all kinds of extremist experimentation. The various artistic groups influenced one another: the Left
Front in the Arts group (*see* FUTURISM) had its rough counterpart in
the cinema in FEKS—'the Factory of the Eccentric Actor'—set up
in 1922 by the directors Leonid Trauberg and Grigoriy Kozintsev,
later joined by Sergey Yutkevich. This group too rejected realism.
Their work was highly stylized and symbolic, making extensive use
of grotesque effects, including slapstick and music-hall and circus
techniques. Their manifesto declared that art should shock and be
'aimed at the nerves,' and that the art of the 20th century was
'eccentricism.' Another trend was that led by Dziga Vertov (q.v.),
which wanted to throw overboard the 'old' arts and to replace plots
and stories and actors playing parts by 'the art of facts.' Working on
the same lines as Vertov was Lev Kuleshov (q.v.), an assistant film
director in Czarist times and the first to make a proper study of the
theoretical principles of the cinema even before the revolution. At
first, during the relatively easy-going 'roaring twenties' of Soviet
artistic life, when the State was preoccupied with more immediate
and pressing problems, these revolutionary ideas and experiments
could be indulged fairly freely. Many of them died a natural death
because they were intrinsically worthless or stupid; others had a
considerable influence outside Russia, but inside the Soviet Union it
was inevitable that they should be suppressed. For these ideas became
increasingly preoccupied with their own subtlety, until their creators'
whole concern was not with *what* a film showed, but *how*. Such a
situation was clearly unacceptable to the authorities. Communist
Party officials were assigned to posts of administrative and ideological control in the film studios after a recommendation to that
effect by the 13th party congress in 1924. The number of studios was

drastically cut down and their administration centralized in order to intensify the party control.

Before the eclipse of the Soviet cinema as an art, it managed to develop and flourish for a while. The founding fathers of the modern Russian cinema were Vertov and Kuleshov. Pudovkin was a pupil of Kuleshov, and Eisenstein took many of his basic principles directly from Vertov. Outside Russia some of the world's leading exponents of the documentary film art, such as the American group of Robert Flaherty, Ernest Schoedsack and Merian Cooper, the German Walter Ruttmann and the Dutch Joris Ivens, both of whom made abstract or 'absolute' films, were considerably influenced by Vertov. Vertov adopted 'mounting,' that is, the technique of film editing which juxtaposes different series of film shots to achieve a special 'shock' effect on the audience, as the main and decisive key to film-making. In 1922 he launched his film magazine series *Kino-Pravda*, a predecessor of the American *March of Time* cine-magazine.

While Vertov became increasingly absorbed in the mechanical techniques of film-making, Kuleshov concentrated intensively on the psychological and emotional impact of these techniques upon audiences. His studio produced several outstanding Soviet directors, including Pudovkin. Kuleshov was the first to demonstrate academically what other directors, e.g. the American David Griffith, had already illustrated instinctively, namely that it is the juxtaposition of images that conveys the required emotion. His scientific reaffirmation of this principle had a considerable influence not only upon Pudovkin but also on Eisenstein and Dovzhenko.

Pudovkin developed Kuleshov's techniques to convey the whole breadth of human character as well as the plot or narrative. By cutting from a close-up of a person to a series of scenes or images illustrating character, not necessarily the immediate surroundings, he revealed personality and motive ever more profoundly with each cut. And by using such 'plastic material,' as he called it, he would convey the dynamic relationship between his characters and their whole social background. As most of Pudovkin's films were epics, the hero was often the personification of his background: in most cases the masses.

Dovzhenko employed a great deal of symbolism in his films. In his surrealistic symbols, such as the famous singing horses in *Arsenal*, he went much further than Eisenstein, but like Pudovkin he made the individual characters the centre of his plots and his heroes the personification of the masses.

Before entering films, Eisenstein had been influenced by Meyerhold (q.v.), with whom he worked in the Proletkul't (q.v.) theatre in the early twenties. In the theatre Eisenstein worked out techniques for using crowds in mass scenes, and he exploited this theatrical experience in his films. It was his preoccupation with crowds that led Eisenstein, in contrast to Pudovkin and Dovzhenko, to make the masses themselves the hero of most of his films. With his first film, *Strike*, 1925, he was using the cutting techniques of Vertov and Kuleshov. But he insisted even more upon what he called the 'shock attraction' of his juxtaposed cuts: the most famous example is the

Odessa Steps scene in his greatest film, *Battleship Potëmkin*. Eisenstein's most significant discovery was perhaps the difference between time on the screen and actual time. He used this fact to expand the most vital, yet brief, moments to emphasize their importance and also to eliminate inessential action or images which would be present in real life. Hence the paradox of Eisenstein, the protagonist of realism, relying increasingly not only on symbolic techniques but on imagery.

The impact of the internecine political struggle inside the country was first felt in its full force in 1927 and 1928, the key years of Stalin's initial success in eliminating his political opponents. Half of the 135 films made in those two years were suppressed, 13 of them being entirely banned and over one-third—including Eisenstein's *October*—restricted to limited audiences. At the same time the film studios were forced to get rid of some of their personnel on political grounds: Kuleshov was a victim and there were widespread dismissals in the Ukrainian, Belorussian and Georgian studios (the veteran Perestiani being involved in the purge of the latter). It was at this period that the so-called Komsomol group of film-makers tried to take the place of the established film personnel. But this group too was liquidated, since it represented the Komsomol (q.v.) as a vanguard acting independently of the party.

During the 1930's the first sound film (*The Road to Life*, from the book by Makarenko, q.v.) was produced, and also the first colour films, but otherwise little of value emerged from this period, with a few exceptions such as *Chapayev*, 1934, produced by the brothers Vasil'yev, and *Peter the First, Part I*, 1937. With the onset of the Great Purge (q.v.) many film workers were arrested (including some of those who had previously been 'purged' but reinstated); some were shot as 'enemies of the people,' and all signs of artistic independence were completely obliterated. After the signing of the Nazi-Soviet Pact (q.v.) in 1939 all anti-fascist and anti-German films (*Professor Mamlock, Soldiers of the Swamp, Alexander Nevskiy, The Oppenheim Family*) were withdrawn. From the Great Purge until 1956 Soviet films rarely rose above the propaganda sermon level, though during the Second World War propaganda extolling the party and Stalin was played down and the patriotic, nationalist theme, whether in an historical or contemporary context, became more sincere and was less inclined to violate artistic and historical integrity.

But in 1946, in the course of Zhdanov's (q.v.) campaign to re-establish ideological conformity, the Central Committee issued a decree which attacked a number of recent films, including Eisenstein's *Ivan the Terrible, Part II*, Pudovkin's *Admiral Nakhimov*, and *Simple People*, directed by Kozintsev and Trauberg. By 1949 the campaign against foreign influences in the arts had become a scarcely veiled form of anti-Semitism (q.v.), under the slogan of 'the struggle against cosmopolitanism.' The cinema industry, with its high proportion of Jewish personnel, was especially vulnerable. On 4th March 1949 the Minister of Cinematography launched the attack by denouncing in *Pravda* the director L. Trauberg as the 'ringleader of the cosmopolitans in the cinema.' Attacks on other Jewish film writers and critics followed: one of the accusations made against some was that they had praised Charlie Chaplin. As a result, both the quality and quantity of Soviet films degenerated catastrophically: in 1946 the output of feature films had dropped to 20, but by 1952, the year before Stalin's death, it had reached the record low of 5 (as against, e.g., India's 250 films in 1951, Japan's 215, the U.S.A.'s 432 and the post-1956 average annual output in the U.S.S.R. of about 100 films). In the period 1951-2 the party authorities decreed that the Soviet film industry should henceforth be allowed to produce 'only master-pieces'; production was to be restricted 'only to acknowledged masters of the art.' As a result no young or new producers were able to enter the industry. It was revealed after 1956 that this period was known in professional film circles as 'the time of few films.' A new type of film dominated such output as there was: the 'feature docu-mentary.' This differed from the true documentary in that authentic film records (newsreels, etc.) were not used, but real historical events re-enacted by professional actors and presented as virtually authentic historical records, thus giving the widest possible scope for the 're-writing of history' and the glorification of Stalin.

After 1956 this period of degradation of the Soviet cinema came under fire from Soviet film historians. The *Soviet Year-book of the Cinema* for 1957 described this era as 'a whole period which inflicted harm on our cinema.' The year-book also challenged Lenin's concept of the role of the cinema (though without mentioning Lenin's name): 'Such a conception turns art into something between a newspaper and a classroom . . . it leads to the absurd theory of art which postulates that there is only one "correct solution to every concrete artistic problem."'

In 1956 a whole crop of remarkable films appeared by young directors, most of them graduates of the State Institute of Cinemato-graphy; the chair of film direction here had been for long occupied by Eisenstein, and most of the lecturers (veterans of the cinema who had been compulsorily retired to the classroom during the purges) had kept alive their artistic traditions and integrity in the instruction studios of the institute. It was revealed in *Komsomolskaya Pravda* at the end of 1958 that some of the work done in these studios was far in advance of the normal run of 'party-line' films; much of it was influenced by the Italian post-war neo-realist school, but it also con-tained many original ideas which by Soviet standards were unorthodox. The press criticized this work and laid the blame at the door of the old professors in the film institute. For years the latter had apparently been teaching the rising generation of directors by a double standard: the students had been taught to produce one type of film for public exhibition, known as 'production films,' and another type in which they could indulge their artistic and creative talents, known as 'diploma films' (since students' examination results were assessed on the basis of this type of film).

The graduates of the film institute have applied a cunning com-bination of 'production' and 'diploma' film techniques to actual production, and by dint of skilful last-minute editing have managed to by-pass the censorship (q.v.). The result is that since 1956 films have again appeared by young directors which in some ways are worthy of the best period of the Soviet cinema. Like many films of that time they have a strong humanistic streak, but in contrast to those films of the 'heroic' period of the 1920's the post-1956 films lay a distinct emphasis on the individual as opposed to the collective or communal society. Among the best examples of these pioneering films by young directors are *Spring in Riverside Street*, 1956, directed by M. Khutsiev and F. Mironer of the Odessa studios; *Alien Relatives*, 1955, directed by M. Schweitzer; *The Forty-first*, 1956, directed by G. Chukhray; *Magdana's Little Donkey*, 1956, directed by the outstanding young Georgians R. Chkheidze and T. Abuladze; and *The Two Fēdors*, 1958, directed by M. Khutsiev. *The Cranes are Flying*, 1958, by the older director M. Kalatozov, though not quite in the same class, is still a remarkably sensitive film. But perhaps the most remarkable, if outwardly the least serious, film is the comedy *Carnival Night* directed by E. Ryazanov with a young cast; this is an extremely bold satire on bureaucratic authority, and in humorous fashion castigates many of the vices of official control of entertainment, and by implication of the arts in general, which have plagued the Soviet cinema and other spheres of cultural life since the late 1920's. Official reaction to most of these films has been hostile, and on occasion even reminiscent of the party's criticism of the cinema in the past.

In forming a picture and giving the flavour of modern Russia the Russian film has been to the rest of the world what the Russian novel was in the past. Its impact on the art of film-making everywhere has probably been even greater than that of the Russian novel on literature. Russian film directors and technicians, and those of other nationalities within the Soviet Union, have produced films that are acknowledged to be world masterpieces. At the Brussels World Exhibition in 1958 a jury from the International Bureau for the History of Cinematography included three Soviet films among the twelve best films of all time: they were Eisenstein's *Battleship Potēmkin*, 1925, Pudovkin's *Mother*, 1926, and Dovzhenko's *Earth*, 1930. *See* M. Bardiche and R. Brasillach, *The History of Motion Pictures* (trans. I. Barry), New York, 1938; P. Rotha, *The Film Till Now*, 1949; A. Inkeles, *Public Opinion in Soviet Russia*, Cambridge, Mass., 1950; M. Seton, *Eisenstein*, New York, 1952; D. Macdonald, 'Soviet Cinema,' *Problems of Communism*, No. 6, 1954, and No. 1, 1955; P. Babitsky and J. Rimburg, *The Soviet Film Industry*, New York, 1955; *Voprosy Kino-Isskustva*, 1957 year-book, Moscow, 1958; Z. ben Shlomo, 'The Soviet Cinema,' *Soviet Survey*, No. 29, 1959; H. Lunghi, 'The Changing Face of the Soviet Cinema,' *Listener*, 23rd July 1959; J. Leyda, *Kino: a History of the Russian and Soviet Film*, 1960.

Circassia, obsolete name for the area in North Caucasus inhabited by the Circassians in the early 19th century. It was sometimes wrongly applied to almost the whole of the Northern Caucasus.

Circassian Autonomous Oblast, *see* KARACHAY-CIRCASSIAN AUTONOMOUS OBLAST.

Circassians (Circassian **Adyge,** Russian **Cherkesy**), Caucasian-speaking people who live in the western part of North Caucasus, and exist in small groups in Syria and Jordan. They have been known since antiquity, and until the middle of the 19th century covered almost the whole area between the main Caucasian range, the River Kuban' and the Black Sea shore. They were christianized in the 6th century but adopted the Muslim religion in the 17th. Divided into several tribes, they were politically independent but under Turkish influence, and opposed the Russian advance (from the late 18th century) into their territory. An exodus of 500,000 Circassians to Turkey, half of them perishing *en route*, followed the final annexation by Russia in 1864. The Circassians are now officially treated as three peoples: the Kabarda (numbering 209,000 in 1959) in the Kabarda-Balkar Autonomous Republic; the Circassians (30,000 in 1959) in the Karachay-Circassian Autonomous Oblast; and the Adyge (80,000 in 1959) in the Adyge Autonomous Oblast. The term Circassian has sometimes been incorrectly applied to all the mountain peoples of the North Caucasus. *See* W. Kolarz, *Russia and her Colonies*, 1952.

Civil Aviation. Published statistics on civil aviation are deficient, no absolute figures being given. The length of internal civil air-lines increased 2·4 times by 1957 compared to 1940, freight traffic 15 times and passenger traffic 26 times. Moscow is the hub of the civil air-lines, from whence routes go out in all directions. The Eastern Direction includes the longest air route within the U.S.S.R., Moscow–Sverd-lovsk–Irkutsk–Khabarovsk–Vladivostok (4,700 miles); the Central Asia Direction includes lines to Kuybyshev–Tashkent; Baku Direction to Stalingrad–Astrakhan'–Baku; Caucasian Direction to Rostov and thence to Tiflis and the health resorts of the Black Sea coast and the Mineral Waters Group in Stavropol' Kray; Crimean Direction to Khar'kov–Crimea; South-western Direction to Kiev–Odessa; Western and North-western Direction to Minsk, to Riga and to Leningrad; and the Northern Direction to Archangel and to Vorkuta. By 1958 there were direct air services from Moscow to Copenhagen, Helsinki, London, Oslo, Paris, Stockholm, Vienna, Kabul, Delhi and the capitals of all Communist countries save North Vietnam. There were commercial co-operation agreements with B.E.A., K.L.M., Sabena, Swissair and Air India. The principal planes used by Soviet air-lines are the IL 12 and IL 14; the TU 104 jet and the TU 114 turbo-prop air-liners were introduced in 1956 and 1958 respectively on long distance internal and international routes. Regular civil aviation was begun in Russia in 1923, when the first air route Moscow–Nizhniy Novgorod was opened. *See also* AIRCRAFT INDUSTRY; TRANSPORT. See *U.S.S.R. Today and Tomorrow*, Moscow, 1959; A. Lee (ed.), *The Soviet Air and Rocket Forces*, 1959.

Civil Law. The system and main concepts of Soviet civil law are derived from the Roman law tradition. Its general part is concerned with subjects (citizens and juridical persons) and objects of rights (*see* CIVIL RIGHTS), while the special part consists of commodity (including property, q.v.) law, law of obligation (including contracts, q.v., and torts) and law of inheritance (q.v.). Labour law (q.v.), land law (*see* LAND), *kolkhoz* (q.v.) law and family law are treated as separate branches of law. The main purpose of Soviet civil law is not to safeguard private rights but to further the social and economic policy of the Communist Party (q.v.). Consequently there is a general clause in the Civil Code (Article 1) stating that civil rights are to be protected only if 'their exercise does not contradict their socio-economic purpose.' Civil procedure is also affected by this overall consideration, disputes between State enterprises or institutions being settled not in court but through arbitration (q.v.) and in such a way as to assist in fulfilling the State economic plans. Civil law was generally considered particularly 'bourgeois' by the Soviet legal theorists of the 1920's and early thirties (e.g. Pashukanis, q.v.), who contended that it would soon 'wither away' under socialism and should be replaced by a law of economic administration. *See also* JUDICIAL SYSTEM; LEGAL SYSTEM. *See* R. Schlesinger, *Soviet Legal Theory*, 1945; V. Gsovski, *Soviet Civil Law*, Ann Arbor, 1948; H. J. Berman, *Justice in Russia*, Cambridge, Mass., 1950; J. N. Hazard, *Law and Social Change in the U.S.S.R.*, 1953; G. C. Guins, *Soviet Law and Soviet Society*, The Hague, 1954; V. Gsovski and K. Grzybowski (eds.), *Government, Law and Courts in the Soviet Union and Eastern Europe*, vol. ii, 1959.

Civil Rights listed in Chapter 10 ('Fundamental Rights and Duties of Citizens') of the U.S.S.R. constitution (q.v.) include the right to work, to rest and leisure, to maintenance in old age and sickness, to education; equality between sexes, absence of discrimination by race or nationality, freedom of conscience, of speech, press, assembly, street processions and demonstrations, association; the inviolability of the person and the home, and the privacy of correspondence. In fact these rights are largely fictitious (*see* FICTION), since (1) most of them are not backed by legislation designed to make them enforceable through the courts; (2) there is in any case no independent judiciary to enforce them, and as a result the security organs (q.v.) are able to act extra-legally; and (3) most of the facilities necessary to the enjoyment of these rights are under the control of the party (e.g. the press, assembly halls, etc.). The Great Reforms (q.v.) of the 1860's created the framework for the protection of civil rights in Russia, but the development was slow, and by 1917 civil rights were not rooted sufficiently firmly either in the institutions or in the consciousness of the people to withstand the anarchy of the revolution and the determined onslaught of the Bolshevik dictatorship. *See* H. J. Berman, *Justice in Russia*, Cambridge, Mass., 1950; M. Fainsod, *How Russia is Ruled*, Cambridge, Mass., 1953; V. Gsovski and K. Grzybowski (eds.), *Government, Law and Courts in the Soviet Union and Eastern Europe*, vol. i, 1959.

Civil Service is not clearly identifiable in the U.S.S.R. because of the peculiarities of the Soviet economic system with its merging of the functions of governmental control and of practical management in the vast nationalized sector of the economy. Thus in the widest sense the civil service comprises the whole category of people who are classified in the official statistics as 'workers and employees' (except a small number of *kolkhoz* and artisans' co-operatives clerks, and domestic servants), who numbered 54·6 million in 1958. Narrower and more meaningful groupings which appear in Soviet statistics are the following: in 1958, 15·7 per cent of all those gainfully occupied (excluding the armed forces) were employed in the so-called 'unproductive' branches, of whom 10·0 per cent were in education and health services and 5·7 per cent in the apparatus of the government, party and other public organizations, municipal economy, passenger transport, credit and insurance institutions. In the government apparatus (including organs of economic administration) and the apparatus of the party and public and co-operative organizations there were 1,286,000 employees in 1958 (1,010,000 in 1928, 1,825,000 in 1940, 1,342,000 in 1956). The Soviet law distinguishes two particularly important groups among the State employees. One of these is 'official persons,' a group which roughly coincides (although it includes some persons who are not State employees, such as *kolkhoz* chairmen) with the statistical one of heads of enterprises, institutions and organizations, as well as of the main sections of such units, which numbered in 1956 2,240,000. The second group are the so-called 'representatives of authority,' comprising members of the U.S.S.R. and republic governments, officials of the courts of law and the procuracy (q.v.), officers of the armed services and officials of the Ministry of Internal Affairs (*see* M.V.D.) and of the Committee of State Security (*see* K.G.B.); deputies of the soviets of all levels are also officially regarded as 'representatives of authority.' Criminal law provides for higher penalties for any offences committed against members of this latter group. Ranks and corresponding uniforms were introduced for officials of a number of ministries and departments as well as for workers in transport and heavy industry from the mid 1930's until 1953, but they were abolished in 1954 except for the officials of the Ministry of Internal Affairs, the Committee of State Security, the procuracy, and rail, water and air transport.

State officialdom first emerged in the Muscovite period. It was replaced by a rigid system of civilian ranks by Peter the Great. The failure to modernize the civil service was one of the main deficiencies of Alexander II's Great Reforms (q.v.) and contributed to the inadequacy and instability of the imperial regime. The majority of civil servants either refused to collaborate with the new regime after the Bolsheviks had seized power, or else were 'purged' (*see* PURGES) during the 1920's and early thirties. The low educational level and inexperience of the new officials, who were appointed on the basis of political reliability and social origin, was felt until the Great Purge (q.v.), when again most of them disappeared. The present generation of officials are mostly products of Stalin's 'cultural revolution' (q.v.), and, having been accustomed to working under the constant terror of Stalin's rule, have been slow to adjust themselves to the somewhat more relaxed conditions of the post-Stalin era. *See also* 'APPARATCHIKI'; BUREAUCRACY.

Civil War, 1917–22, followed the Bolsheviks' seizure of power (*see* OCTOBER REVOLUTION) and the forcible dissolution of the Constituent Assembly (q.v.). The principal fronts of the war were the eastern, the southern, the northern and the north-western, the first two being the most important. In the winter of 1917–18 the Bolsheviks overthrew the Don Cossack regime under General Kaledin and engaged in minor operations against anti-Bolshevik elements round

Orenburg and on the Manchurian frontier. The two main fronts, the eastern and the southern, were constituted in the summer of 1918, following the Czechoslovak Legion's revolt along the Trans-Siberian line and Denikin's successes in the Northern Caucasus. In March 1919 the anti-Bolshevik forces under Admiral Kolchak again approached the Volga; thereafter they were continuously forced back until the capture of Kolchak in 1920. Following the voluntary incorporation of the Far Eastern Republic (q.v.) in 1922, Soviet rule once more extended to the Pacific. The southern front was consolidated by the early successes of General Denikin, and during the summer and autumn of 1919 his forces occupied most of southern Russia and the central black earth region, and they were advancing upon Moscow. But a series of defeats ensued and a retreat which, despite some successes in the southern Ukraine under the new commander General Wrangel, finally ended in 1920 with the evacuation of Sevastopol'. In the north the anti-Bolshevik forces were weak, and relied to a great extent upon the allied troops under British leadership which landed at Murmansk and Archangel in July–August 1918 and departed in the autumn of 1919. As a result of their departure the northern front was liquidated early in 1920. In the north-west the position was complicated by the emergence of the Baltic States (q.v.) and the presence of German troops under General von der Goltz. In the autumn of 1919 a White army under General Yudenich advanced from Estonia with the object of taking Petrograd, but by November this advance had been beaten off.

The most notable leader on the Bolshevik side was Trotskiy, who acted as War Commissar and chairman of the Revolutionary Military Council. Colonels Vatsetis and S. S. Kamenev were successively commanders-in-chief. Among the successful Bolshevik commanders in the field were former Imperial Army officers (e.g. Tukhachevskiy) and N.C.O.s (e.g. Budënnyy) and former professional revolutionaries (e.g. Antonov-Ovseyenko—though he had originally been an officer —Frunze, Voroshilov). The Council of Labour and Defence headed by Lenin and the Council for Army Supply headed by Krasin organized the Bolshevik war effort in the rear. The numbers taking part in the civil war were surprisingly small in the early stages, for the majority of the population remained passive. On the Red side, Bolsheviks apart, were the Left Socialist Revolutionaries, left and centre Social Democrats and the Anarchists; on the White side were the majority of Socialist Revolutionaries, those right-wing Social Democrats who did not accept the policy of the official Menshevik Party, and all parties standing to the right of them, the latter gradually increasing their influence. The two armies were almost identical in social composition: on both sides most of the officers were former professional officers and intelligentsia, and most of the rank and file were peasants; there was a larger proportion of workers in the Red armies than in the White. The causes of the Red victory were political—the failure of a unifying idea and a sense of common purpose to emerge among the Whites and the ineptitude of their handling of the peasants—and organizational, as well as the fact that no outstanding leader emerged on the White side.

The civil war was complicated by the half-hearted allied intervention in an attempt to re-establish the eastern front against the Central Powers, and also by the intervention of Germany, Japan, Finland, Poland, Turkey and Rumania, who all had territorial designs upon Russia (though the last two limited their intervention to occupying parts of Russian territory). Though the foreign intervention was sometimes important (e.g. the Austro-German occupation of the Ukraine, the Czechoslovak uprising along the Trans-Siberian Railway in 1918), the Allies lost interest in the civil war after their victory over Germany. Other complicating factors were the strong regionalist (*see* REGIONALISM) tendencies (the Cossacks, Siberia, the Far East) and the separatist movements on the fringes of the country, which resulted in the establishment of a number of independent states (Poland, the Baltic States, Transcaucasia) and of transitory nationalist governments (the Ukraine, Central Asia). Sporadic armed resistance to the Bolsheviks (the Kuban' region, Central Asia) lasted in some places until 1924 or even longer. *See* A. J. Sack, *The Birth of the Russian Democracy*, New York, 1918; B. Pares, *My Russian Memoirs*, 1931; G. Stewart, *The White Armies of Russia*, 1933; J. Bunyan, *Intervention, Civil War and Communism in Russia*, Baltimore, 1936; L. I. Strakhovsky, *The Origins of American Intervention in North Russia, 1918*, Princeton, 1937; A. G. Gordon, *The Russian Civil War*, 1937; A. Soutar, *With Ironside in North Russia*, 1940; W. H. Chamberlin, *The Russian Revolution* (2nd ed.), vol. ii, New York, 1954; R. Pipes, *The Formation of the Soviet Union*, Cambridge, Mass., 1954; L. Schapiro, *The Origin of the Communist Autocracy*, 1955; G. F. Kennan, *The Decision to Intervene*, 1958; C. J. Smith, Jr, *Finland and the Russian Revolution, 1917–22*, Athens, Georgia, 1958.

Classes, Social. Soviet society is theoretically divided into two friendly classes workers and peasants—and an intermediate stratum of the intelligentsia (q.v.) which originated from the two classes and serves their interests. The social structure is in fact a great deal more complex, and differences of income, prestige and power are considerable. There are the privileged classes of the party and State officials (including the security organs), the officers' corps, economic managers (*see* MANAGERIAL CLASS), the *élite* of the intelligentsia (scientists, higher technicians, writers, actors, etc.), the higher clergy of the recognized religious communities and the decorative *élite* of selected old Bolsheviks and 'exemplary' workers and peasants (*see* STAKHANOV MOVEMENT). The bulk of the intelligentsia, white-collar employees, manual workers and peasants can be classified together as the non-privileged classes, though between them as well as within each there are considerable differences. The majority of peasants (q.v.), indeed, can be regarded as belonging to the under-privileged classes, since they have certain legal disabilities (*see* KOLKHOZ; PASSPORT). Definitely under-privileged are the 'special settlers' (q.v.) and the inmates of 'corrective labour colonies' and camps (qq.v.). Upward social progress within a class is comparatively easy, but entry into a higher class is far more difficult. The privileged class as a whole is now largely self-perpetuating, although

Khrushchëv's educational reform of 1958 (*see* HIGHER EDUCATION; SECONDARY EDUCATION) has partly the same aims as Stalin's 'cultural revolution' (q.v.) in making it less easy for the children of the privileged classes and the ordinary intelligentsia to receive higher education, and on the other hand facilitating the entry of strictly selected people from among industrial workers and *kolkhoz* peasants into the category of 'specialists' (*see* INTELLIGENTSIA). *See* A. Inkeles, 'Social Stratification and Mobility in the Soviet Union, 1940–50,' *American Sociological Review*, vol. xv, 1950; S. V. Utechin, 'Social Stratification and Social Mobility in the U.S.S.R.,' *Transactions of the Second World Congress of Sociology*, vol. ii, 1954; K. Mehnert, *Der Sowjetmensch*, 5th ed., Stuttgart, 1959; A. Inkeles and R. A. Bauer, *The Soviet Citizen*, 1959; E. Helperin, 'The Metamorphosis of the New Class,' *Problems of Communism*, vol. viii, No. 4, July–Aug. 1959.

Climate. Russia lies within three climatic belts: the Arctic, the temperate and the subtropical. The Arctic belt stretches along the shores of the Arctic Ocean and has long, cold winters and short, cool summers with little precipitation. The temperate belt is divided into three regions: the Atlantic, from the western frontier to the River Yenisey, with a moderately continental climate; the East Siberian, between the Yenisey and the mountain ranges along the Pacific coast, with an extremely continental climate; and the Pacific, with a monsoon-type climate. The subtropical belt includes the southern shore of the Crimea, parts of Transcaucasia and Central Asia.

Coal Industry. Total coal extraction in 1958 amounted to 495·8 million tons (29·1 in 1913, 165·9 in 1940, 300·9 in 1952). Of the 1958 total, 181·7 million tons were produced in the Donets Basin, 75·3 in the Kuznetsk Basin, 61·0 in the coalfields of the Urals, 47·2 in the Moscow Lignite Basin, 36·1 in the Eastern Siberian fields, 24·3 in Karaganda, 20·0 in the fields of the Far East and 16·8 in the Pechora Basin (*see* VORKUTA). The average daily output of a pit in 1956 was 929 tons; out of the total of 1,002 pits, 335 were small, producing up to 500 tons daily, and 102 were large, producing over 2,000 tons daily. In 1958, 19·9 per cent of total production was by opencast mining, the average daily output of a mine in 1956 being 4,700 tons. Cutting, transport from the coal face and loading into the railway trucks is almost fully mechanized, but loading from the coal face was only mechanized to 40·1 per cent in 1958. Average productivity per man in 1958 was 40·0 tons per month: 33·2 in the pits (29·9 in 1940) and 227·7 in opencast mining (65·7 in 1940).

Codes of Law now in force are codes of the individual Union Republics, largely modelled on those of the R.S.F.S.R. which were promulgated in 1922–6. These are the Civil Code, Code of Civil Procedure, Criminal Code, Code of Criminal Procedure, Land Code, Labour Code and Family Code. Originating as they did in the conditions of the New Economic Policy (q.v.), their provisions are now often inapplicable because of changes in the policy of the party which the courts have to reflect and implement. On the other hand, much of the subsequent legislation, including some of the most important enactments, is not codified. New codes are in preparation, those of criminal law and procedure being based on principles laid down in the laws enacted in 1958 (*see* LEGAL REFORM).

The first Russian codes were the Russkaya Pravda (q.v.) of the Kievan period, and two Sudebniks and the Ulozheniye (qq.v.) of 15th–17th-century Muscovy. Then followed the Svod Zakonov (q.v.) of 1833. Modernized codes were prepared around the turn of the century, but there was a delay in putting them into force, and the Bolsheviks, after their seizure of power in 1917, immediately abolished the whole legal system. New leading Principles of Criminal Law, a Labour Code and a Family Code were, however, produced during the period of War Communism (q.v.), and the transition to the New Economic Policy necessitated the restoration of much of both the civil and criminal law. All-Union codes were in preparation for many years in accordance with the Stalin constitution of 1936, but the policy of decentralization embarked upon by the party leadership since 1956 has resulted in returning codification to the competence of individual republics. *See* H. J. Berman, *Justice in Russia*, Cambridge, Mass., 1950; V. Gsovski and K. Grzybowski (eds.), *Government, Law and Courts in the Soviet Union and Eastern Europe*, vol. i, 1959; L. B. Schapiro, 'Judicial Practice and Legal Reform,' *Soviet Survey*, No. 29, July–Sept. 1959.

Colchis (Russian **Kolkhida**), swampy lowland region, with a subtropical climate, situated in western Georgia along the lower Rioni River and the Black Sea shore. Citrus fruits and tea are cultivated.

Collective Agreements, agreements concluded yearly between the management of an industrial enterprise, building site or *sovkhoz* (q.v.) and the respective committee of the trade union. It restates the legal obligations of management and workers, and lays down some provisions for welfare measures. Collective agreements also formally commit the trade unions to work for raising productivity and for labour discipline. The draft agreements are discussed at meetings of employees; the purpose of these meetings is to give the employees some sense of participation in working out their conditions of work, but in fact there is much apathy since only minor points can be changed. The practice of collective bargaining and collective agreements had grown up in Russia with the growth of the trade unions after the revolution of 1905 (q.v.). It continued after the Bolshevik seizure of power, despite the difficulties arising from the fact that in most cases both managements and trade unions were acting under party control, until 1929, after which they soon lost all importance. The practice was discontinued in 1935, although the myth of collective bargaining was upheld vis-à-vis foreign trade unionists. The formality of collective agreements has again been adhered to since 1947. *See* H. J. Berman, *Justice in Russia*, Cambridge, Mass., 1950; S. M. Schwarz, *Labor in the Soviet Union*, New York, 1952; J. N. Hazard, *Law and Social Change in the U.S.S.R.*, 1953; M. Dewar, *Labour Policy in the Soviet Union, 1917–28*, 1956.

Collective Farms, *see* KOLKHOZ.

Collective Leadership, term frequently referred to as a basic principle of leadership in the Communist Party both after the death of Lenin and that of Stalin. In both cases the reaffirmation of this principle of oligarchy was aimed against potential claimants to the position of a single leader, and after Stalin's death it was also intended to mark a contrast between the new leadership and Stalin's personal despotism. With the rise to prominence of first Stalin and then Khrushchëv, the official insistence in the party propaganda on collective leadership gradually faded out. *See* E. H. Carr, *The Bolshevik Revolution*, vol. ii, 1954; R. N. Carew Hunt, *A Guide to Communist Jargon*, 1957; M. Rush, *The Rise of Khrushchëv*, Washington, D.C., 1958; M. Fainsod, 'What Happened to "Collective Leadership"?', *Problems of Communism*, vol. viii, No. 4, July–Aug. 1959.

Collectivization of Agriculture, process, begun in 1929, by which independent peasant holdings were amalgamated into collective farms (*kolkhozes*). The Communist Party launched this policy for a variety of reasons, ideological, political and economic; Stalin described the operation itself as a 'revolution from above.' Collectivization met with stiff resistance from the peasants, ranging from refusal to join the *kolkhozes* to armed uprisings, some of which were widespread and prolonged (e.g. in the Altay region of Siberia). The Communists attributed the opposition to the *kulaks* (q.v.), and it was overcome by a combination of administrative (confiscation of property, banishment, *see* SPECIAL SETTLERS), military and economic measures (including the artificial famine of 1932–3). By 1934, 71 per cent of all peasant holdings had been collectivized, by 1938 the figure was 93·5 per cent; 235,000 *kolkhozes* (1937) replaced the 26 million individual holdings of 1929. Collectivization achieved the final establishment of the power of the Communist Party in the countryside, and through it agriculture was integrated with the rest of the socialized economy; but its cost in terms of human suffering and material losses was extremely high. Millions of peasants died of starvation or were deported and sent to forced labour camps; the number of peasant households dropped by 7 million to 19 million in 1937; over half the total number of horses (18·5 million) and cattle (36·7 million), and an even greater proportion of other livestock, disappeared between 1928 and 1933; the output of agriculture fell by 30 per cent and did not recover until 1938. *See also* KOLKHOZ; M.T.S.; NEO-POPULISM; PEASANTS; TOZ. *See* W. H. Chamberlin, *Russia's Iron Age*, Boston, 1934; N. de Basily, *Russia under Soviet Rule*, 1938; N. Jasny, *The Socialized Agriculture of the U.S.S.R.*, Stanford, 1949; A. Baykov, *The Development of the Soviet Economic System*, 1950; D. Mitrany, *Marx Against the Peasant*, 1951; F. Belov, *History of a Soviet Collective Farm*, New York, 1955; M. Fainsod, *Smolensk under Soviet Rule*, 1959.

Collegium: 1. Advisory body attached to a ministry, composed partly of senior officials of that ministry and partly of outside experts, whose task is to consider major policy decisions.

2. Division of a higher court.

Combine (Russian *kombinat*), unit of economic management consisting of a number of enterprises which are connected by technological processes (e.g. the large metallurgical combines, iron and steel works) or belong to one branch of industry (e.g. oil extraction) or are small servicing enterprises in one locality (catering, hairdressers' saloons, etc.). A combine is managed by its director or manager on the 'single head' principle. The term combine has also sometimes been used to denote a number of enterprises connected by technological processes but not united under a single management, e.g. the Urals-Kuznetsk Combine (q.v.). *See* H. Chambre, *L'Aménagement du territoire en U.R.S.S.*, Paris and The Hague, 1959.

Cominform ('Communist Information Bureau'), co-ordinating organ of the Communist parties of the U.S.S.R., its European satellites, France and Italy, established in 1947 by Zhdanov and Malenkov. It was in some sense a successor of the Comintern (q.v.), but apart from its more limited membership it was also more restricted in its functions; in fact its most significant action was its condemnation of Tito and the Yugoslav Communist Party in 1948. The Cominform was dissolved in 1956.

Comintern (abbreviation for **Communist International**), association of Communist parties of the world established by Lenin in 1919. Other members of the Russian party who took a leading part in the Comintern were Zinov'yev, its first secretary-general, Trotskiy, Radek and Bukharin. Throughout its existence the Comintern was in fact little more than a tool in the hands of the Russian party leadership, who made use of it as they made use of the apparatus of the Soviet Government. Its internal life usually reflected the struggle in the Bolshevik leadership, Bukharin replacing Zinov'yev as secretary-general when the latter was defeated in Russia and himself later being replaced by Manuil'skiy. Most Comintern leaders, both Russian and foreign Communists living in exile in Russia, were liquidated during the Great Purge (q.v.), and the Comintern itself was dissolved in 1943. *See also* COMINFORM. *See* F. Borkenau, *The Communist International*, 1938; J. Degras (ed.), *The Communist International, 1919–43—Documents*, vol. i, 1956; C. M. Wilbur and J. Lien-ying How (eds.), *Documents on Communism, Nationalism and Soviet Advisers in China, 1918–27*, New York, 1956; C. B. McLane, *Soviet Policy and the Chinese Communists, 1931–46*, New York, 1958; W. Z. Laqueur, *The Soviet Union and the Middle East*, 1959.

'Commercial' Shops, State shops which existed during the period of rationing (q.v.) in retail trade, 1941–7, at which rationed goods could be bought freely for higher prices; in other words a kind of black market operated by the State. They were the equivalent of the Torgsin (q.v.) shops which existed in the 1930's.

Commissar, designation of various high ranking officials. The first commissars were appointed by the Provisional Government after the February 1917 revolution as the new regime's representatives at the headquarters of army groups on the front, and in the provinces where they replaced the former governors. The Bolsheviks made extensive use of the institution at the time of the seizure of power and in the first years of their rule, when there was a profusion of commissars of all kinds; the most important of these were the People's Commissars, who replaced the former ministers, and Military Commissars, who were party functionaries attached in a supervisory capacity to military commanders. People's Commissars were renamed ministers in 1946. The duties of Military Commissars varied at different times, ranging from complete equality of responsibility with the commander (including the purely military side) to responsibility only for the political education and reliability of the troops. Military Commissars were abolished in 1940 and replaced by Zampolits (i.e. Deputy Commanders for Political Affairs), reintroduced after the German invasion in 1941, but again replaced by Zampolits in 1942. Marshal Zhukov's dismissal as Minister of Defence in 1957 was partly due to his policy of undermining the position of the Zampolits. *See* M. Fainsod, *How Russia is Ruled*, Cambridge, Mass., 1953; Z. Brzezinski (ed.), *Political Controls in the Soviet Army*, New York, 1954.

Commissariat, name chiefly applied to (1) central government departments, corresponding to the former ministries, from 1917 to 1946; in 1946 these 'People's Commissariats' were renamed ministries; (2) local branches of the Ministry of Defence which are responsible for matters concerning registration for military service and the call-up.

Committee of Ministers, official name of the whole body of ministers between 1804 and 1906. Although one of the ministers had the title of Chairman of the Committee, it had no corporate responsibility and few specific duties. In the 1906 constitution the committee was replaced by a Council of Ministers (q.v.).

Committee of the North, committee formed in 1924 'to assist the small peoples of the far north.' It had been conceived by sympathetic ethnographers (V. G. Bogoraz, q.v., and L. Ya. Shternberg) as an organ for the protection of the small and primitive peoples against drastic interference from outside which would disrupt their traditional way of life, and at the same time for assisting them in cultural and economic development. In fact the committee, which was attached to the Central Executive Committee of the R.S.F.S.R., pursued a middle course, e.g. introducing in 1926–31 'clan soviets.' 'Cultural bases' set up by the committee in 1927–35 became in a number of cases the administrative centres of the National Okrugs (*see* OKRUG). The Committee of the North, which was motivated by an ideology similar to that of National Bolshevism (q.v.), was abolished in 1933. *See* W. Kolarz, *The Peoples of the Soviet Far East*, 1954.

Committee of Party Control, one of the highest organs of the Communist Party, set up by the Central Committee of the party; its task is to supervise party discipline, and it has its own representatives in all republics and oblasts who are independent of the local party organs. It was established in 1920 as the Central Control Commission (renamed in 1934), and has always been one of the main tools in the hands of those controlling the central party apparatus in their struggle against their opponents. *See* M. Fainsod, *How Russia is Ruled*, Cambridge, Mass., 1953; L. Schapiro, *The Communist Party of the Soviet Union*, 1960.

Committees of the Poor, auxiliary organizations of the Bolshevik Party which functioned in the countryside in the period of War Communism (q.v.). They were set up by local party organizations from among agricultural labourers and poor peasants, and often contained criminal elements. Their purpose was twofold: to assist the food-collecting detachments and to intensify the 'class struggle' in the villages through confiscation of property of well-to-do peasants and opponents of the Bolshevik regime. They were abolished with the introduction of the New Economic Policy (q.v.) in 1921.

Communes, in Communist theory the highest form of the organization of life and labour, whereby the members of the commune have no private property and hold even consumer goods in common. Many agricultural communes were set up during the period of War Communism (q.v.), usually in the houses of former local squires, and often by urban workers who had left the towns because of hunger, or by demobilized soldiers. These communes received much assistance from the authorities, but nevertheless were usually inefficient and soon disintegrated. The experiment was declared premature and the few remaining communes were transformed into collective farms at the time of the collectivization of agriculture (q.v.). Some monasteries during the 1920's were formally converted into communes by the monks in order to avoid persecution, but during the collectivization of agriculture such communes were declared to be bogus, and the monks were deported to forced labour camps. With regard to the Chinese experiment with communes in the late 1950's, Khrushchëv is reported to have said that in the Russian context the establishment of communes would be a reactionary venture. *See* M. Fainsod, *Smolensk under Soviet Rule,* 1959.

Communications, *see* POSTAL SERVICES; TRANSPORT.

Communism, state of society the achievement of which is the theoretical goal of the Communist Party (q.v.). Its basic features are supposed to be the absence of private property, of social classes and of the State, and adherence in economic and social life to the principle of 'from each according to his ability, to each according to his needs.' Since the seizure of power in Russia by the Bolsheviks Communism has been the official long-term goal of all policies of the Soviet Government, internal and external (see BOLSHEVISM, LENINISM). An attempt at a quick implementation of the few precepts contained in the *Communist Manifesto* of Marx and Engels and in the subsequent literature on the subject (including Lenin's *State and Revolution*), later called War Communism (q.v.) and ascribed to the necessities of the civil war, was succeeded by the New Economic Policy (q.v.), which was conceived as a temporary retreat in order to restore the economy and attract the peasants, and accompanied by Stalin's doctrine of building socialism in one country first. A new offensive was started in 1928–9 with the inauguration of the first Five Year Plan (q.v.) and the collectivization of agriculture (q.v.), and was accompanied by theoretical justification of practices apparently incompatible with the idea of communism and by the elaboration of the theory of socialism as the first stage of communism.

Socialism was declared in 1936 to have been essentially built, and the ensuing period was described as one of completing socialism and the transition to communism. No theoretical discussion of problems arising from this contention was permitted between 1938, when the *Short Course* of party history was published which summed up the classical Stalinist position (*see* STALINISM), and 1952, when Stalin came out with his *Economic Problems of Socialism in the U.S.S.R.* Only after the denunciation of Stalin at the 20th party congress (q.v.) in 1956 was the taboo definitely removed and the problem officially recognized to be in need of theoretical elucidation. The task became especially urgent after the declaration at the 21st party congress in 1959 that the U.S.S.R. was entering the stage of rapid construction of communism. However, there is still little evidence of genuine creative thought, though the exegesis of Khrushchëv's statements is often more elastic in form than the 'quotationism' of the Stalinist era. Khrushchëv's own ideas on the subject are so far confined to the following: decentralization of economic and general administration and gradual taking over of certain functions from the State by 'social' organizations—both representing a return from Stalin's *étatist* tendencies to the more basic Leninist conception of the role of the party; return to 'polytechnical education' (q.v.); and the gradual merger of *kolkhoz* (q.v.) and State property rather than the transformation of the former into the latter, a reversal of Stalin's 1952 position. *See* N. Buharin and E. Preobrazhensky, *A B C of Communism*, 1922; R. Schlesinger, *Marx, His Time and Ours*, 1950; E. H. Carr, *A History of Soviet Russia* (6 vols.), 1950–9; R. N. Carew Hunt, *Theory and Practice of Communism*, 1950, and (ed.), *Books on Communism*, 1960; J. Plamenatz, *German Marxism and Russian Communism*, 1954.

Communist Dictatorship was established in Russia by the Bolshevik Party in 1917. The Bolsheviks had originated as a radical wing of the Russian Social Democratic Labour Party (q.v.), and though they remained under this guise until after 1917 the founder and leader of the Bolshevik Party, Lenin, had early concentrated upon elaborating organizational and tactical principles of attaining and maintaining power, and on training his followers in the implementation of these devices (*see further under* BOLSHEVISM; ISKRA; LENIN; LENINISM). In the conditions of near anarchy that followed the February revolution (q.v.) of 1917, the Bolsheviks, led by Lenin and Trotskiy (with some financial help from the German authorities), established private armed detachments (*see* RED GUARDS), gradually neutralized the armed forces and the majority of the population by propaganda, and finally seized power in October (*see* OCTOBER REVOLUTION). The Bolshevik Government was at first called the Provisional Workers' and Peasants' Government, but upon their overwhelming defeat in the elections to the Constituent Assembly (q.v.) the Bolsheviks dispersed the Assembly and proclaimed a Dictatorship of the Proletariat (q.v.) which was to be exercized by the Communist Party (q.v.) through the soviets and the Cheka (qq.v.), as well as directly.

Civil war (q.v.) developed from armed resistance to the Communist dictatorship, and lasted from 1917 to 1922. Though the majority of the population remained passive, the Communists were able, through their skill in propaganda and organization, to muster greater support, especially among the peasants, which, together with the disunity in the anti-Communist camp, accounts for the Communist victory. Industry and agriculture were ruined, and the people grew weary of the economic policy of War Communism (q.v.); disaffection among those who had taken the Communist side during the civil war found expression in strikes and uprisings (*see* ANTONOV UPRISING; KRONSTADT). Lenin wisely decided upon a tactical retreat, and announced the New Economic Policy (q.v.) of concessions to peasants, private enterprise and consumers. The period of the N.E.P. (1921–7) was one of restoration of the economy, consolidation of the political monopoly of the Communist Party and, within the party, struggle for Lenin's succession and the gradual emergence of Stalin as the dominant figure.

His opponents ousted, Stalin embarked upon his policies of rapid expansion of heavy industry (*see* FIVE YEAR PLANS; PLANNING), enforced collectivization of agriculture (q.v.) and the so-called 'cultural revolution' (q.v.), and from 1934 he ruled as an absolute dictator. Opposition among his followers precipitated the assassination of Kirov (q.v.) and the Great Purge (q.v.) of 1937–8, which marked the highest point of the Communist terror (q.v.). The German invasion of Russia in 1941, coming as it did soon after the Great Purge, did not at first meet with universal resistance (for military aspects of the war *see* WORLD WAR II). The country was deeply divided in its attitude to the war, many visualizing Russia's defeat as a way of liberation from communism, and even being prepared to fight on the German side (*see* VLASOV). But German policy towards prisoners of war and in the occupied areas of Russia resulted in a swing of popular opinion, and the war became a second Patriotic War of the Russian people. After the war the presence of the Soviet Army facilitated the establishment of Communist regimes in central and south-eastern Europe, Manchuria and North Korea. Internally the post-war period until Stalin's death in 1953 was characterized by the suppression of the comparative freedom of the war years and the restoration of conformity (*see further under* COUNCIL FOR COLLECTIVE FARMS; SOCIALIST REALISM; ZHDANOV), by mass deportations, xenophobia, obscurantism and anti-Semitism (*see* STALINISM; DOCTORS' PLOT).

On Stalin's death in 1953, the 'collective leadership' (q.v.) of his closest collaborators succeeded, among whom Malenkov, Beria and Molotov at first held the leading positions. Despite continued affirmations of unity, a struggle for power at once set in. In 1953 Beria was defeated and executed, Malenkov was ousted from the premiership in 1955, and in 1957 Malenkov, Kaganovich and Molotov were expelled from the Central Committee as members of the 'anti-party group' (q.v.). The victors were Khrushchëv, Mikoyan and Zhukov, but a few months later this alliance was broken and Zhukov lost all his posts for undermining the party's influence in the armed forces. As first secretary of the Central Committee, Khrushchëv succeeded in packing the Presidium (q.v.) of the committee with his own nominees. The chief issue between the warring cliques was the scope and pace of de-Stalinization, which had begun immediately after Stalin's death out of the necessity for his successors to appear different from the late despot. Under the pressure of reviving public opinion and the need to make the administration and economic system more efficient, the process continued intermittently. As a result the security organs (q.v.) lost their preponderance in the state and much of their political power; most corrective labour camps were abolished and a legal reform (q.v.) undertaken; and some fictions (q.v.) of the Stalinist era were dropped. The situation in agriculture and the position of peasants improved (*see* AGRICULTURAL PROCUREMENT; KOLKHOZ; PEASANTS), as well as the manufacture and supply of industrial consumer goods; workers and employees were again allowed to change their place of work at will, working hours were reduced, wages of the lower-paid categories and pensions (q.v.) were raised and a serious effort made to tackle the housing (q.v.) situation. The reorganization of the economic administration (*see* ECONOMIC COUNCILS; INDUSTRIAL MANAGEMENT) gave somewhat greater scope to the manager, and a more liberal policy was pursued towards the intellectuals. While these and similar measures found opposition only among the die-hard Stalinists, the educational reform (*see* EDUCATION) aroused considerable controversy and widespread opposition. In general the policy of concessions has tended to whet the appetite, and a clearly discernible oppositional trend has emerged (*see* INTELLECTUAL OPPOSITION; REFORMISM; REVOLUTIONARY MOVEMENT) which has found its sharpest expression in the series of strikes and uprisings in the main concentration camp areas in 1953–5, and in the strikes and student unrest at the time of the Hungarian revolution in 1956. Since 1957 concessions have continued, though with diminished momentum, but there is no sign either that the critics are prepared to accept present conditions as satisfactory or that Khrushchëv and his associates are prepared to compromise on the basic issues, i.e. the political monopoly of the Communist Party and its claim to authority in all socially relevant fields. Tensions within the party leadership continue, as evidenced by the fall from power at the beginning of 1960 of Khrushchëv's own adherents in the Presidium, Kirichenko (q.v.) and Belyayev. *See also* FOREIGN POLICY. See S. and B. Webb, *Soviet Communism: a New Civilization?*, 1935; N. de Basily, *Russia under Soviet Rule*, 1938; H. Johnson, *The Socialist Sixth of the World*, 1941; N. Timasheff, *The Great Retreat*, New York, 1946; J. Towster, *Political Power in the U.S.S.R.*, 1948; E. H. Carr, *A History of Soviet Russia* (6 vols), 1950–9; D. J. Dallin, *The New Soviet Empire*, 1951; W. Gurian (ed.), *The Soviet Union*, Notre Dame, Indiana, 1951; F. Beck and W. Godin, *Russian Purge*, 1951; M. Fainsod, *How Russia is Ruled*, Cambridge, Mass., 1953, and *Smolensk Under Soviet Rule*, 1959; W. W. Rostow, *The Dynamics of Soviet Society*, 1953; R. Pipes, *The Formation of the Soviet Union*, Cambridge, Mass., 1954; L. Schapiro, *The Origin of the Communist Autocracy*, 1955, *The Communist Party of the Soviet Union*, 1960, and 'Has Russia Changed?,' *Foreign Affairs*, April 1960; R. A. Bauer *et al.*, *How the Soviet System Works*, Cambridge, Mass., 1956; J. N. Hazard, *The Soviet System of Government*, Chicago, 1957; F. L. Schuman, *Russia since 1917*, New York, 1957; D. J. R. Scott, *Russian Political Institutions*, 1958.

Communist Party of the Soviet Union, political party which has an absolute monopoly of power in the country. According to Article 126 of the Constitution, 'the most active and politically conscious citizens in the ranks of the working class, working peasants and working intelligentsia voluntarily unite in the Communist Party of the Soviet Union, which is the vanguard of the working people in their struggle to build communist society and constitute the core of all organizations of the working people, both public and State.' The party's monopoly of power in fact covers all spheres of economic life, social relations, political and cultural activities, artistic work and scientific theory; it is only in the doctrine and ritual of the Church that it does not claim authority. This dominating position was gradually achieved between 1917 and 1950 by the seizure of political power (*see* OCTOBER REVOLUTION), suppression of all other parties and non-Communist organizations, the nationalization of industry and trade, the collectivization of agriculture (q.v.), the elimination of foreign influences and the imposition by decree of specific views, doctrines and tastes (*see, e.g.,* LYSENKO, MARR; ZHDANOV). The party leadership is determined to maintain this monopoly of power, and its statements in this regard are most emphatic. Membership of the party at the time of the 20th congress in 1956 was 6·8 million full members and 0·4 million candidate members. The party works through a system of primary organizations (q.v.) and committees of various levels corresponding to the administrative divisions of the country which are headed by central committees in each Union Republic except the R.S.F.S.R. (for which there is a bureau of the all-Union Central Committee) and the Central Committee of the party as a whole. The lower party organizations are strictly subordinated to the higher ones (*see* DEMOCRATIC CENTRALISM).

The party first appeared in 1900 as a ginger group (*see* ISKRA) within the Russian Social Democratic Labour Party (q.v.), became in 1903 one of the latter's two factions (the Bolshevik faction) and in 1912 a separate party (changing its name to Communist Party in 1919 and finally dropping the word Bolsheviks in 1952). In 1921 inner-party factions were proscribed, and by 1930 all open oppositional groupings were suppressed. From 1934 to 1953 Stalin wielded absolute personal dictatorship within as well as outside the party. Supreme power is now concentrated in the Presidium (former Politburo) of the party's Central Committee (qq.v.), within which Khrushchëv has attained a dominant position. *See also* BOLSHEVISM; LENINISM; STALINISM. *See* N. Popov, *Outline History of the Communist Party of the Soviet Union* (2 vols.), New York, 1934; J. Towster, *Political Power in the U.S.S.R.*, New York, 1948; M. Fainsod, *How Russia is Ruled*, Cambridge, Mass., 1953; B. Meissner and J. S. Reshetar, *The Communist Party of the Soviet Union*, 1957; M. Fainsod, 'The Party in the Post-Stalin Era,' *Problems of Communism*, vol. vii, No. 1, Jan.–Feb. 1958; L. Schapiro, *The Communist Party of the Soviet Union*, 1960.

Communist Universities, establishments of quasi-higher education for Communist Party functionaries in the 1920's and thirties. The most important of them were the Sverdlov Communist University in Moscow (founded 1918), Zinoviev Communist University in Leningrad, Sun Yat Sen Communist University for Peoples of the East and

Marchlewski Communist University for Peoples of the West. There were 79 Communist universities in 1936 with over 40,000 students. They were abolished in 1938 when the system of party education was reorganized following the publication of the *Short Course of the History of the C.P.S.U.(B)*. *See* G. S. Counts, *The Challenge of Soviet Education*, New York, 1957.

Concentration Camps, *see* CORRECTIVE LABOUR CAMPS; CORRECTIVE LABOUR COLONIES.

Concerto. The distinction of writing the first Russian concerto in the modern sense of the word belongs to Rimsky-Korsakov, who, apart from a number of miscellaneous ventures, wrote one piano concerto, that in C$\sharp$ minor, 1882–3. His friend and contemporary, Balakirev, completed his first piano concerto in F$\sharp$ minor, *c.* 1885, and two movements of a second concerto in E$\flat$ major (completed by Lyapunov). By far the most important Russian composer of concertos in the 19th century is Tchaikovsky with his two piano concertos (No. 1 in B$\flat$ minor, 1874–5; No. 2 in G major, 1879–80) and the famous violin concerto in D major, 1878. Among the less important composers, Glazunov made several essays in this sphere, including two piano concertos, two violin concertos, a 'Concerto-Ballata' for cello and a concerto for saxophone, flute and strings. Skryabin wrote only one piano concerto, that in F$\sharp$ minor, *c.* 1894, while Medtner contributed three. Occupying rather an isolated position are the four piano concertos of Rakhmaninov, including the popular second concerto in C minor, 1901. Generally speaking, the accent in Russian concertos of the 19th century fell rather on the piano, perhaps because the majority of the Russian composers were excellent pianists (the piano in any case being the most accessible of instruments), and the Russians preferred the rich sonorities of the piano with its unlimited opportunities for virtuosity and colour.

Among the Soviet composers of the present generation, principal contributions to the concerto have come from Prokof'yev with his five piano concertos, two violin concertos and two cello concertos; Myaskovskiy with his violin concerto in D minor; Kabalevskiy with three piano concertos and a violin concerto; Khachaturyan with concertos for piano, 1936, violin, 1940, violin and cello, *c.* 1944, and cello, 1950; and Shostakovich with two concertos for piano, one for violin, and the famous work for piano, trumpet and strings, 1933. More in keeping with Western trends are the numerous efforts of Stravinsky which include the piano concerto, 1924, the violin concerto, 1931, the 'Dumbarton Oaks' concerto for sixteen wind instruments, 1938, the 'Ebony Concerto' for jazz band, 1944, and the Concerto for Strings, 1946—works which have done much to determine the course of West European music by their exploitation of new artistic concepts. *See also* ORCHESTRAL MUSIC and individual entries. *See* G. Abraham and M. D. Calvocoressi, *Masters of Russian Music*, 1936; A. Veinus, *The Concerto*, 1948.

Concessions to foreign firms were granted by the Soviet Government after 1920 in order to attract foreign capital. The concessions often went to firms which before the nationalization of industry had owned the enterprises concerned (e.g. the Lena Goldfields). Foreign business men were, however, mistrustful of offers of concessions, since they had already suffered confiscation without compensation by the Soviet authorities when industry was nationalized in 1918. There was also considerable disagreement among the Communist leadership over the question of concessions, Krasin (q.v.) being prominent in supporting them but more militant Bolsheviks opposing the very principle of granting concessions. Relations between the foreign concessionaries and the Soviet authorities were uneasy, and the latter resorted to various kinds of pressure, including deliberately engineered strikes, in order to embarrass them. Most foreign concessions were terminated with the end of the New Economic Policy (q.v.), though some functioned until the mid 1930's and the Japanese fishing concession until 1945.

Conciliators, pejorative term applied in Communist phraseology to (1) in general, those socialists who adopt a more conciliatory attitude towards non-socialists, and (2) specifically, Russian Social Democrats and Socialist Revolutionaries who adopted this attitude in 1917. The term was also used by Lenin and his associates for those Bolsheviks who were less inimical to the Mensheviks. *See* L. Schapiro, *The Communist Party of the Soviet Union*, 1960.

'Confessions,' statements during preliminary investigation or at the trial by persons accused of 'counter-revolutionary crimes' ostensibly acknowledging their guilt, usually imaginary. These statements, normally obtained by torture, were given a prominent place in the pseudo-judicial procedures which accompanied Stalin's terror, and have occasionally been resorted to since his death. However, Vyshinskiy's view that a confession was decisive proof of guilt in 'counter-revolutionary' cases has been repudiated since the 20th party congress in 1956. *See* H. J. Berman, *Justice in Russia*, Cambridge, Mass., 1950; F. Beck and W. Godin, *Russian Purge and the Extraction of Confessions*, New York, 1951; Z. K. Brzezinski, *The Permanent Purge*, Cambridge, Mass., 1956; B. D. Wolfe, *Khrushchëv and Stalin's Ghost*, New York, 1957; S. Wolin and R. M. Slusser (eds.), *The Soviet Secret Police*, New York, 1957.

Congresses of Soviets from the Bolshevik seizure of power in 1917 till 1936 were ostensibly the highest organs of State power in all the Union and Autonomous Republics and in the U.S.S.R. Between congresses, all-Union and republic Central Executive Committees, elected at the congresses, acted on their behalf. At the first Congress of Soviets, in June 1917, the Bolsheviks were in a minority. The 2nd congress, with which the October coup was timed to coincide, 'legitimized' the new regime and elected the first Council of People's Commissars. Until 1922 Congresses of Soviets included some non-Bolsheviks. In fact the congresses never had any real power and were merely used to rubber-stamp decisions of the party. The congresses were replaced in the Stalin constitution of 1936 by the Supreme Soviets (q.v.) of the U.S.S.R. and of the republics. *See* E. H. Carr, *The Bolshevik Revolution, 1917–23*, vols. i–iii, 1950–3, and *Socialism in One Country, 1924–6*, vol. ii, 1959.

Conscription, *see* MILITARY SERVICE.

Constituent Assembly, representative democratically elected assembly which met in Petrograd on 18th January 1918 and was forcibly dissolved by the Bolsheviks after only one session. All radical parties had demanded a Constituent Assembly that would establish a democratic system in the country, and the Provisional Government (q.v.) that followed the abdication of Nicholas II and his brother during the February revolution (q.v.) of 1917 was preparing elections to the Assembly, to which it intended to surrender power. The Bolsheviks accused the Government of procrastinating over the matter, and used this as one of the pretexts to seize power and establish their own government, which they also called 'provisional' at first.

Elections to the Assembly were held in most constituencies on 25th–27th November 1917 (though in several distant regions they were postponed, and in about a hundred constituencies not finally held at all) by secret ballot, universal, equal and direct franchise and proportional representation. The Bolsheviks lost the election: out of 41·7 million votes cast they received only 9·8 million, the Socialist Revolutionaries 17 million, the Mensheviks 1·4 million, the Constitutional Democrats 2 million, various non-Russian parties 7·6 million (of which 5 million went to Ukrainian parties), minor parties about 2 million, and the remainder of the votes cannot be identified. The 707 elected deputies were divided as follows: 370 Socialist Revolutionaries; 175 Bolsheviks; 40 Left Socialist Revolutionaries (pro-Bolshevik); 16 Mensheviks; 2 Popular Socialists; 17 Constitutional Democrats; 86 representatives of national parties; 1 cannot be identified.

Several leading Socialist Revolutionary and Constitutional Democratic deputies were arrested on their arrival in Petrograd, and before the Assembly met the Constitutional Democratic Party was outlawed; the leaders of the majority Socialist Revolutionary Party refused to take any protective measures. At the only session of the Assembly the elected chairman, V. M. Chernov, was unable to keep order, and the guards—sailors headed by an Anarchist—were openly hostile. The Bolsheviks demanded that the Assembly should recognize the Soviet Government and all its decrees; this demand was rejected, whereupon they walked out followed by the Left Socialist Revolutionaries. Those who remained hurriedly debated and approved a land law, a resolution on the state structure of Russia and an address to the allied powers; the Assembly was then dispersed by the guards on orders from the Bolshevik Government. In the civil war that followed the Socialist Revolutionaries based part of their appeal upon the idea of sustaining the authority of the Constituent Assembly, and in Samara in 1918 a committee of Assembly members set up a transitory anti-Bolshevik government. *See* A. J. Sack, *The Birth of the Russian Democracy*, New York, 1918; F. A. Golder, *Documents of Russian History, 1914–17*, 1927; O. H. Radkey, *The Election to the Russian Constituent Assembly of 1917*, Cambridge, Mass., 1950; W. H. Chamberlin, *The Russian Revolution*, 2nd ed., New York, 1954; L. Schapiro, *The Origin of the Communist Autocracy*, 1955.

Constitution. The present constitution (fundamental law) of the

U.S.S.R. was formally adopted by the 8th (extraordinary) Congress of Soviets of the U.S.S.R. on 5th December 1936. (This day, 'Constitution Day,' has since been held as a public holiday.) It consists of thirteen chapters.

Chapter 1, *The Social Structure*: Article 1 states that the U.S.S.R. is 'a socialist state of workers and peasants' (*see* CLASSES, SOCIAL); Articles 2 and 3 that ' the political foundation of the U.S.S.R. is the soviets . . . ,' 'all power in the U.S.S.R. belongs to the working people of town and country as represented by the soviets. . . .' The following articles are devoted to the economy: Article 4 states that 'the economic foundation of the U.S.S.R. is the socialist system of economy and the socialist ownership of the instruments and means of production . . .'; Articles 5–10 deal with property (*see* OWNERSHIP), while Article 11 states that 'the economic life of the U.S.S.R. is determined and directed by the State national economic plan . . .'; finally, Article 12 reads: 'Work in the U.S.S.R. is a duty and a matter of honour for every able-bodied citizen in accordance with the principle "He who does not work, neither shall he eat." The principle applied in the U.S.S.R. is that of socialism: "From each according to his ability, to each according to his work."'

Chapter 2, *The State Structure*, describes the quasi-federal structure of the state (*see* FEDERALISM) and the relations between the Union of Soviet Socialist Republics (q.v.) and the constituent Union Republics (q.v.), and lists the Autonomous Soviet Socialist Republics and Autonomous Oblasts (qq.v.) within each Union Republic. Chapters 3 and 4, *The Higher Organs of State Power in the U.S.S.R.* and *The Higher Organs of State Power in the Union Republics*, and Chapters 7 and 8, *The Higher Organs of State Power in the Autonomous Soviet Socialist Republics* and *The Local Organs of State Power*, are devoted to the Supreme Soviets (q.v.) and the local soviets (*see* LOCAL GOVERNMENT). Chapters 5 and 6, *The Organs of State Administration of the U.S.S.R.* and *The Organs of State Administration of the Union Republics*, deal with the Councils of Ministers and the individual ministries (qq.v.). Chapter 9, *The Courts and the Procurator's Office*, deals with the judicial system, courts of law and the procuracy (qq.v.).

Chapter 10, *Fundamental Rights and Duties of Citizens*: Articles 118–28 enumerate the civil rights (q.v.); Article 129 provides for the right of asylum for foreign citizens; Articles 130–3 deal with the citizens' duties, which include, apart from the ordinary duties of observing the laws and defending the country, the maintenance of labour discipline, respecting the rules of socialist intercourse and safeguarding and fortifying 'public, socialist property as the sacred and inviolable foundation of the Soviet system . . .'; persons violating the latter duty are 'enemies of the people.' Finally, there are Chapters 11, *The Electoral System* (*see* ELECTIONS), 12, *Arms, Flag, Capital*, and 13, *Procedure for Amending the Constitution*; the latter consists of a single Article, 146, requiring a two-thirds majority in both chambers of the Supreme Soviet. The key provision of the constitution is the second part of Article 126 (Chapter 10), which states that '. . . the most active and politically conscious citizens in the ranks of the working class, working peasants and working intelligentsia voluntarily unite in the Communist Party of the Soviet Union, which is the vanguard of the working people in their struggle to build communist society and constitutes the core of all organizations of the working people, both public and State.' This article, providing as it does for total monopoly of power by the Communist Party (q.v.), invalidates most of the rest of the constitution. Citizens' rights and democratic procedures are in fact either wholly fictitious (e.g. only one candidate standing for elections—*see also* FICTION) or else are respected and exercised just so far as may be expedient for the party. The ostensibly legislative, governing and judicial bodies are in practice the executors of party decisions, whose implementation the party authorities also direct and supervise. For early constitutional history of Russia *see* AUTOCRACY; BOYARS; COUNCIL OF STATE; HISTORY; LORIS-MELIKOV; SENATE; SPERANSKIY; VALUYEV; VECHE; ZEMSKIY SOBOR.

The modern constitutional movement began in Russia in the 18th century, and after a series of near successes (under Catherine II, Alexander I and Alexander II) and subsequent setbacks was successful during the revolution of 1905 (q.v.), and a constitution was promulgated in 1906 providing for a legislative Duma (q.v.). However, considerable powers remained vested in the emperor (the military, naval and court estimates, and full executive power), who continued to be officially referred to as an autocratic ruler, and the regime that existed from 1906 until 1917 is often called semi-constitutional. The February revolution (q.v.) of 1917 led to the formation of the Provisional Government (q.v.), whose principal task was to prepare for the convocation of a Constituent Assembly (q.v.). But the simultaneous setting up of the soviets brought about the state of 'dual power' (q.v.), which was replaced after the seizure of power by the Bolsheviks (*see* OCTOBER REVOLUTION) ostensibly by the Dictatorship of the Proletariat (q.v.) exercized through the soviets, and in fact by the dictatorship of the Communist Party. The Soviet constitutions of 1918 (of the R.S.F.S.R.), 1924 (of the U.S.S.R.) and the present one have merely described the formal framework, which has little resemblance to the actual structure of power. The constitution of 1936, prepared by a commission headed by Stalin and introduced by him at the Congress of Soviets, was until 1956 consistently referred to as the Stalin constitution. *See* E. H. Carr, *The Bolshevik Revolution*, vol. i, 1950; M. Fainsod, *How Russia is Ruled*, Cambridge, Mass, 1953; D. J. R. Scott, *Russian Political Institutions*, 1958.

Constitutional Democrats (abbreviation 'Cadets'), political party formed by left-wing liberals in 1905, whose most outstanding leader was Milyukov (q.v.). In the first State Duma in 1906 the Constitutional Democrats were the strongest party, dominating its proceedings, and in the succeeding Dumas they formed the chief opposition party. They entered the 'Progressive Bloc' which existed in the Duma in 1915–17 and united all parties except reactionaries and socialists with the intention of replacing the existing government by one which would command the trust of the country. Having failed in this, the Constitutional Democrats played an important part in the February

revolution (q.v.) in 1917 and in the Provisional Government; they
withdrew from the government in July, and the party was outlawed
by the Bolsheviks after their seizure of power. *See also* CON-
STITUENT ASSEMBLY; DUMA; PROVISIONAL GOVERNMENT. *See* A.
Tyrkova-Vil'yams, *Na putyakh k svobode*, New York, 1952; P. N.
Milyukov, *Vospominaniya 1859–1917* (ed. M. M. Karpovich and
B. I. Elkin, 2 vols.), New York, 1955; S. R. Tompkins, *Russian
Intelligentsia, Makers of the Revolutionary State*, Norman, Oklahoma,
1957.

Consumer Goods in the official Communist scale of values occupy a
lower place than capital goods. In accordance with this general view,
the rate of expansion of consumer goods production has consistently
been planned lower than that of capital goods production, and consumer goods industries are discriminated against in the allocation of
scarce materials. The resulting chronic shortage of consumer goods
has been one of the chief sources of dissatisfaction, and after Stalin's
death the 'collective leadership' headed by Malenkov made some
efforts, accompanied by much propaganda, to improve the situation.
Malenkov's contention that, heavy industry having already been
developed, the consumer goods industry could now be developed as
rapidly was utilized by his opponents as a 'deviation from the general
line of the party' in order to bring about his downfall in 1955.
Priority for heavy industry was again stressed in the propaganda, but
in recent years Khrushchev has once more revived Malenkov's line and
the supply of consumer goods (especially durables) has been considerably stepped up. The following table shows the sale of selected
consumer goods (factory-produced) in various years in thousands:

	1913	1928	1940	1950	1958
Clocks and watches	700	900	2,500	8,226	23,352
Sewing-machines	272	286	175	510	2,829
Bicycles and motor-cycles	29	34	207	797	3,309
Pianos	26	0·1	10	12	55[2]
Refrigerators	—	—	—	1·2	340
Washing machines	—	—	—	0·3	502
Vacuum cleaners	—	—	—	6·1	220
Leather footwear [1]	60	58	211	203	355·8
Rubber footwear [1][3]	27·9	36·3	69·7	110·8	158·7

Export of manufactured consumer goods formed 3·3 per cent of
total exports in 1957 (7 9 per cent in 1938), while in the same year
imports made up 11·4 per cent of total imports (1·0 per cent in 1938).
See also entries on car, food, light and textile industries, and FOREIGN
TRADE; HOUSING; RADIO; TELEVISION. See *The Soviet Seven Year
Plan* (introduction by A. Nove), 1960.

'Contemporary, The' (*Sovremennik*), journal founded in 1836 by
Pushkin. From 1847 to 1866, when it was owned and edited by
Nekrasov, it was the leading radical monthly and played an
important part in forming the views of the radical intelligentsia
(*see* CHERNYSHEVSKIY; DOBROLYUBOV).

Contracts figure prominently in the Soviet civil law. The main

Million pairs.   [2] 1957.   [3] Output.

types of contract which are subject to the provisions of the civil law are those concerning supply, rent of accommodation, building, transportation, credit and insurance. Labour contracts are regulated by the labour law (q.v.), while membership in *kolkhozes* and other co-operatives (qq.v.) is not treated as a contractual relationship. Since the bulk of material goods in the U.S.S.R. is owned by the State (*see* OWNERSHIP), the vast majority of contracts involve State institutions or enterprises, and the multiplicity of statutes and administrative rules leaves very little room for negotiated terms. However, a contractual form of relationships between State enterprises has been found expedient even when the relationships themselves are laid down in the economic plan. Disputes between State institutions or enterprises in respect of carrying out contracts are settled through arbitration (q.v.), as are the so-called 'pre-contract disputes' about terms which may arise between enterprises or institutions that are to enter into contracts according to the economic plan. A peculiar feature of the Soviet law of contracts is the provision that contracts which are legal in themselves and have a legal purpose, but are prejudicial to the interests of the State, are invalid. *See also* COPYRIGHT; HOUSING. *See* V. Gsovski, *Soviet Civil Law*, Ann Arbor, 1948; J. N. Hazard, *Law and Social Change in the U.S.S.R.*, 1953.

Co-operatives, according to the official theory, belong to the socialized sector of the economy (*see* OWNERSHIP). There are at present three types of co-operative: *kolkhozes* (q.v.), which are formally agricultural producers' co-operatives; producers' co-operatives of artisans (q.v.); and consumers' co-operatives, mainly in the countryside. There were in 1956 over 8,000 producers' co-operatives, and 20,000 consumers'. Workshops and other industrial enterprises belonging to producers' co-operatives numbered over 107,000 in 1955, and there were in addition about 28,000 workshops belonging to consumers' co-operatives. Co-operatives' (chiefly consumers') share in retail trade in 1957 was 29 per cent. In addition to ordinary retail trade, consumers' co-operatives also sell on a commission basis goods produced by individual peasants or by *kolkhoz* peasants on their personal plots. The co-operative system consists of individual consumers' and producers' co-operatives combined into unions corresponding to the administrative divisions of the country, the whole structure being headed by the Tsentrosoyuz (abbreviation for Central Council of Co-operative Unions), which for all practical purposes acts as a ministry; it is affiliated to the International Co-operative Alliance. The activities of the co-operatives are subject to State planning (q.v.). Members of producers' co-operatives are paid regular wages, and a part of any profits made is shared out between them; members are responsible for any losses made. *Kolkhozes*, though officially co-operative enterprises, are not part of the general co-operative structure, nor have they any unions of their own.

There was a traditional form of co-operative association in Russia, the *artel'* (q.v.), but the modern co-operative movement began only in the 1860's and seventies, when English, German and Swiss ideas on consumers, credit and agricultural co-operatives respectively found adherents in Russia. The movement grew particularly rapidly from the beginning of the 20th century, and by 1917 it was an important political and economic factor, to the extent that co-operative candidates were put up for election to the Constituent Assembly (q.v.). Co-operative activity continued after the Bolshevik seizure of power, though it was looked on with suspicion as it was largely led by Neo-Populists; during the 1920's it was gradually integrated into the Soviet system, with Communist nominees taking leading positions. In the late 1920's and early thirties housing co-operatives became prominent, and food rationing (q.v.) was administered by consumers' co-operatives. In 1935, however, both the housing co-operatives and the consumers' co-operatives in towns were taken over by the State without compensation. In 1946–9 consumers' co-operatives were again allowed to trade in the towns in agricultural products with the expressed purpose of creating competition for State shops. *See* E. M. Kayden and A. N. Antsiferov, *The Co-operative Movement in Russia during the War*, New Haven, 1929; S. and B. Webb, *Soviet Communism: a New Civilization?*, 1935; H. Schwartz, *Russia's Soviet Economy*, 2nd ed., 1954.

Copyright in literary and artistic works extends (since 1928) over the life of an author and the subsequent fifteen years, except in periodicals, encyclopaedias, photographs, cinema scenarios, films and choreographic productions, for which it is limited to ten years. There are also other limitations of copyright; e.g. the author has no copyright in a translation of his work; he can alienate it only to an officially recognized publishing house; the copyright can be appropriated by the State in the public interest (though royalties are payable in such a case). Foreign works are not protected unless there is a special treaty with the state concerned. *See* J. N. Hazard, *Law and Social Change in the U.S.S.R.*, 1953.

Corrective Labour Camps, official description of the forced labour or concentration camps. The first camps were set up in 1918 and the system expanded very considerably during the periods of the collectivization of agriculture and the Great Purge (qq.v.). The number of inmates was further increased by deportees from territories annexed by the Soviet Union 1939–40, prisoners of war, deportees from Russian areas that had previously been occupied by the Germans and deportees from eastern European countries occupied by the Soviet Army. After the Second World War over two hundred camps are known to have been in existence, spread all over the country, with small camps near most industrial towns and larger camps and camp groups situated in the distant mining and timber areas of the north and east. The total number of inmates has never been made known, but has been variously estimated at from three to fifteen million. All the chief construction undertakings of the 1930's to early 1950's, such as canals and hydro-electric stations, were largely carried out by forced labour. The regime in the camps was extremely harsh during the Great Purge and the war, but improved considerably after 1950. Various political groups existed in the camps after the war, and especially after the separation of political prisoners from ordinary criminals, and between 1953 and 1955 a series of strikes and revolts in the major camp areas (Karaganda, Noril'sk,

Vorkuta) took place which were a significant landmark in the development of the post-Stalin period. Since 1955 the Government has consistently been reducing the number and population of the camps; in 1956 many were transformed into 'corrective labour colonies' (q.v.), and the legal reform (q.v.) of 1958 abolished them as a separate category of penal institution. *See* D. J. Dallin and B. Nikolaevsky, *Forced Labour in Soviet Russia*, 1948; United Nations, *Report of the 'ad hoc' Committee on Forced Labour*, Geneva, 1953; M. Fainsod, *How Russia is Ruled*, Cambridge, Mass., 1954; W. W. Kulski, *The Soviet Regime*, Syracuse, 1954; D. J. Dallin, *The Changing World of Soviet Russia*, New Haven, 1956; S. Wolin and R. M. Slusser (eds.), *The Soviet Secret Police*, New York, 1957; H. J. Berman, 'Soviet Law Reform—Dateline Moscow 1957,' *Yale Law Journal*, vol. lxvi, No. 8, July 1957; B. Roeder, *Katorga: an Aspect of Modern Slavery*, 1958.

Corrective Labour Colonies, one of the main types of detention place since 1929. Inmates of the colonies are people sentenced to deprivation of liberty (until 1959 for up to three years only, those sentenced to longer terms being sent to 'corrective labour camps,' q.v.). Before 1956 they were usually situated near industrial centres, and their inmates worked in the local industrial enterprises. In 1956 many 'corrective labour camps' (about one-third according to Soviet sources) were transformed into 'corrective labour colonies.' The regime and conditions in general in the colonies are milder than in the camps. They are said to be since 1956 under the joint control of the Chief Administration of 'corrective labour colonies' of the Ministry of Internal Affairs and the local soviets, the latter acting through local supervisory commissions. *See* H. J. Berman, 'Soviet Law Reform—Dateline Moscow 1957,' *Yale Law Journal*, vol. lxvi, No. 8, July 1957.

Cossacks (Russian *kazaki*, Ukrainian *kozaky*), distinct section of the Russian population in the south of European Russia, southern Siberia and the Far East. The word, of Turkic origin, means 'free warriors.' The irregular frontier troops of the Crimean Khanate and the principality of Ryazan' during the 15th century were known as Cossacks, and in the following century large and vigorous Cossack communities arose along the banks of the middle and lower Dnieper and of the Don and its tributaries; they were established by people, chiefly peasants, who had fled from Poland-Lithuania and from Muscovy—from the one because of the national and religious oppression of the Orthodox Russian (Ukrainian) population, from the other because of political tyranny and heavy taxation, and in both cases because of the development of serfdom. For the further history of the Dnieper Cossacks *see* SICH; UKRAINE. Some Don Cossacks established themselves, also during the 16th century, on the rivers Ural and Terek, and there formed autonomous communities. Life in the Cossack territories had some resemblance to that in the American wild west. Apart from military raids, the occupations of the Cossacks were hunting, fishing and, from the 17th century, agriculture. Principles of direct democracy governed their internal organization, with elected *atamans* (*see* HETMAN). Relations between the Russian Government and the Cossacks were for a long time unstable, ranging from direct service, as in the conquest of Siberia (*see* STROGANOVS, YERMAK), to uneasy alliance vis-à-vis Turkey and to open rebellion (*see* PUGACHËV; RAZIN; TROUBLES, TIME OF). The Cossacks were gradually brought under the central authorities during the 18th and 19th centuries, retaining local self-government, and they became a prosperous, exclusive, hereditary estate of the realm. The Government created new Cossack communities (Astrakhan', Orenburg, Siberia, Transbaykalia, Kuban', Amur, Semirech'ye, Ussuri); some non-Russian peoples (Kalmyks, Bashkirs) were also made Cossacks. All Cossacks were obliged to serve in Cossack military units, which distinguished themselves in many wars, and they were also used for police purposes in the later 19th and early 20th centuries.

Following the February revolution of 1917 all Cossack communities transformed themselves into small republics with elected *atamans*, and the All-Russian Cossack Union was established, led by the Don *ataman* Kaledin; the South Eastern League (q.v.) was set up in October 1917 under Cossack leadership. Most Cossacks were hostile to the Bolshevik seizure of power, taking an active part in the civil war, and in, for example, the Kuban region continuing guerrilla war fare until 1924. All Cossack institutions were abolished by the Soviet Government in 1920, and Cossack service in the Red Army was restricted. A new wave of Cossack armed resistance was provoked by the collectivization of agriculture (q.v.), especially fierce in the Kuban' region in 1932–3. The Cossacks were officially 'forgiven' in 1936, and some cavalry units were renamed Cossack, although they were staffed by recruits from the Don and the North Caucasus irrespective of their origin. Cossack units during the Second World War fought in both the Soviet and the German armies; those of the latter who had taken part in the Italian campaign were compulsorily repatriated by the British in 1945. Despite the vicissitudes of the last four decades, Cossack self-awareness, traditions, peculiarities of dress (adapted from the Caucasian natives) and customs (horsemanship) have survived. *See* W. P. Cresson, *The Cossacks, their History and Country,* New York, 1919.

Cotton, *see* TEXTILE INDUSTRY.

Council for the Affairs of the Orthodox Church, government department attached to the Council of Ministers with supervisory and liaison functions. It was set up in 1943 when a *modus vivendi* was established between the Church and the Soviet authorities, and has pleni-potentiaries on republic and oblast levels. A similar Council for the Affairs of Religious Cults, dealing with non-Orthodox religious bodies, was set up in the following year.

Council for Collective Farms, extra-constitutional body established in 1946 under the chairmanship of A. A. Andreyev (q.v.) for the restoration of a rigid system of collective farming (*see* COLLECTIVIZA-TION OF AGRICULTURE), which had been somewhat relaxed during the war partly as a result of general war-time disorganization and partly in order to stimulate among the peasants hopes for the abolition of the system after the war. The council had its own hierarchy of officials who operated independently of all ordinary administrative bodies. It was abolished in 1953. *See* M. Fainsod, *How Russia is Ruled*, Cambridge, Mass., 1953.

Council of Ministers: 1. Name since 1946 of the governments of the U.S.S.R. and the Union and Autonomous Republics. Since 1958 the U.S.S.R. Council of Ministers has consisted of the chairman, his first deputies and deputies, ministers, chairmen of State committees of ministerial rank and chairmen of Councils of Ministers of the fifteen Union Republics. *See* M. Fainsod, *How Russia is Ruled*, Cambridge, Mass., 1953.

2. From 1804 to 1906 the meetings of ministers presided over by the emperor; such councils were sometimes called to discuss matters of extreme importance.

3. From 1906 to 1917 the name of the Russian Government, headed by a prime minister and resembling in function the British Cabinet. It was the successor of the Committee of Ministers (q.v.).

Council of People's Commissars, name of the Soviet Government and of the governments of individual republics after the Bolshevik seizure of power in 1917. It was changed to Council of Ministers (q.v.) in 1946.

Council of the Republic, *see* PRE-PARLIAMENT.

Council of State, in Imperial Russia, consultative body established by Alexander I consisting of senior officials appointed by the emperor for life whose task it was to deliberate on legislative proposals originating in government departments and make recommendations to the emperor. The 1906 constitution reformed the Council of State by making it partially elected and converting it into the second chamber of the legislature. *See further under* DUMA. *See* M. Paleologue, *An Ambassador's Memoirs* (3 vols.), New York, *s.a.*

Courland, *see* KURLAND.

Courts of Honour, Officers', in the Soviet Army, 'for guarding the dignity and honour of the rank of officer,' are elected annually by secret ballot of the officers' assembly of a regiment. Officers may not be judged by those of a lower rank. Officers' Courts of Honour were abolished after the Bolshevik seizure of power in 1917 (though they were retained in the White armies during the civil war), but re-instituted in 1940. *See* H. J. Berman and M. Kerner, *Soviet Military Law and Administration*, Cambridge, Mass., 1955, and *Documents on Soviet Military Law and Administration*, Cambridge, Mass., 1955.

Courts of Law are the supreme courts (q.v.) of the U.S.S.R. and the Union and Autonomous Republics, provincial (i.e. oblast, kray, Autonomous Oblast or okrug) courts, People's Courts (q.v.) and military tribunals (q.v.). All courts consist of both judges and assessors (qq.v.), who, except for the People's Courts and the military tribunals, are formally elected by the soviets (q.v.) of the corresponding level for five years. Provincial and supreme courts act as courts of appeal, and as first instance courts where this is provided for by the codes of procedure; higher courts generally supervise the work of the lower ones and have the right to reopen cases the handling of which is found unsatisfactory, whether on procedural or substantive grounds. The hearing is generally public, and the parties to a civil case and the accused in a criminal case may be represented by counsel (*see* LAW-YERS), while the prosecution is represented by the procurator (*see* PROCURACY). Trials are conducted in one of the official languages of the respective Union or Autonomous Republic, those unfamiliar with this language being guaranteed an interpretation and the right to use their own language. According to the constitution, courts are inde-pendent and subject only to the law, but this provision is officially interpreted in the purely technical sense of non-interference by out-side bodies in the court procedure. The courts are not independent of the party (*see* COMMUNIST PARTY OF THE SOVIET UNION) and are obliged actively to further its policy. In cases involving political offences even the procedural independence of the courts may be violated, but when no political interests of the party are involved the courts of law generally function satisfactorily. For irregular courts *see* JUDICIAL SYSTEM.

The system of lawcourts abolished after the Bolshevik seizure of power in 1917 had been established in the main by the judicial reform of 1864 (*see* GREAT REFORMS) and consisted of the peasant parish (*volost'*) courts (for petty cases involving peasants), the justices of the peace (q.v.), the circuit courts in each province, Chambers of Justice for groups of provinces, and the Senate (q.v.). Circuit courts were first instance courts for most cases, and the Chambers of Justice ordinary courts of appeal. Criminal (but not civil) cases were tried by jury. Cases involving armed resistance to the authorities were (from 1878) tried by military courts. Courts were genuinely independent and held in high esteem, except by those (Marxists and Anarchists on the one hand, reactionaries on the other) who were generally opposed to the rule of law.

Crafts. The principal old crafts which have survived in Russia are woodwork (spoons, tuns, sieves, baskets, ornamental boxes), chiefly in the northern part of central Russia; metalwork—cutlery and locks (mostly in Pavlovo and its neighbourhood) and black silverwork (Velikiy Ustyug); earthenware (Ukraine, Moscow area, Kirov Oblast); leatherwork (Kalinin Oblast); carpet weaving (Central Asia, Transcaucasia, Ukraine); lacework (Vologda Oblast); toys (Moscow area, Kirov Oblast); stone-carving (the Urals); bone-carving (Khol-mogory in the Archangel Oblast, also by the native peoples of northern Siberia); and icon and ornamental painting (Palekh in Ivanovo Oblast). The majority of craftsmen are artisans (q.v.), either co-operated or individual.

Credit plays an important part in the Soviet economy. Though the bulk of the investment (q.v.) and a part of the working capital of State enterprises are allocated through the budget as non-returnable grants free of interest, a considerable part of the working capital has to be obtained as short-term credits from the State Bank (*see* BANK-ING). Trade enterprises derive the bulk of their working capital from this source. Since practically all economic activities are planned, credit facilities are also planned, and each State enterprise has its own credit plan which specifies the purpose to which the money is to be put. The bank controls the use of credits and in order to ensure such control commercial credits between enterprises were forbidden as early as 1930. Long-term credits are far less important; they are granted to *kolkhozes* and other co-operatives (q.v.), to individual persons for building or acquiring houses (until 1960), and to a very small extent to State enterprises. Short-term credits amounted at the end of 1957 to 276·0 milliard pre-1961 roubles, including 110·1 to industry, 92·8 to trade, 31·7 to supply agencies, 25·5 to agriculture, 12·3 to building enterprises and 2·3 to transport and communications. Long-term credits totalled 36·5 milliard roubles, including 20·1 to *kolkhozes*, 8·8 to other enterprises and organizations, and 7·5 to individuals; other credits = 0·1. For foreign credits *see* ECONOMIC AID; FOREIGN DEBTS. *See* H. Schwartz, *Russia's Soviet Economy*, 2nd ed., 1954; D. Granick, *Management of the Industrial Firm in the U.S.S.R.*, New York, 1955; R. W. Davies, *The Development of the Soviet Budgetary System*, 1958.

'Credo,' name by which a statement of the policy of the genuine Economists (*see* ECONOMISM) among Russian Social Democrats came to be known. It was written by Kuskova in 1897, and provoked fierce attacks from Lenin and the 'Liberation of Labour' Group.

Crime is considered in the official theory a 'capitalist survival' (q.v.), with no roots in the Soviet social system. The incidence of crime is difficult to assess, since criminal statistics have not been published since the late 1920's. The available evidence shows that during the Soviet period it rose rapidly at the time of War Communism and of the collectivization of agriculture (qq.v.), immediately after the Second World War and following the amnesty after Stalin's death in 1953. Apart from crimes in the ordinary sense, such acts as expression of political dissent, private trading or (until 1956) absenteeism from work are treated as crimes in the U.S.S.R. *See further under* CRIMINAL LAW; LABOUR DISCIPLINE; POLITICAL CRIMES. *See* S. Timasheff, *The Great Retreat*, New York, 1946; G. C. Guins, *Soviet Law and Soviet Society*, The Hague, 1954; W. W. Kulski, *The Soviet Regime*, Syracuse, 1954.

Crimea (Tatar and Russian **Krym**), oblast of the Ukrainian Republic, comprising the Crimean Peninsula (ancient Taurica Chersonesus), almost entirely surrounded by the Black Sea and the Sea of Azov and connected with the mainland by the narrow Perekop isthmus. In the north it consists of lowland steppe, with the Crimean Mountains (highest peak Roman-Kosh, 1,545 ft) along the southern coast, which has a Mediterranean climate; there are deposits of iron ore and salt. Area 9,900 sq. m.; population (1959) 1,202,000 (64 per cent urban), Russians and Ukrainians (before the 1940's also Tatars, Jews, Germans, Greeks and Bulgarians). Wheat and tobacco are cultivated and viniculture, horticulture and sheep breeding carried on; there are iron-ore mining, chemical, engineering, building-stone quarrying and various food industries. The Crimea has many health and holiday resorts, receiving over 200,000 patients and tourists yearly. Principal towns: Simferopol' (administrative centre), Sevastopol', Kerch', Yevpatoriya, Feodosiya and Yalta.

In antiquity Crimea was inhabited by Cimmerians, Taurians and Scythians. Southern Crimea was colonized from the 7th century B.C. by Greeks, belonging later to Rome and Byzantium, and from the 13th century to Venice and Genoa; northern Crimea was subject from the 3rd century to continuous invasions by Goths (who survived there until the 16th century), Huns, Avars, Khazars, Pechenegs, Cumans and, in 1239, Tatars (*see* GOLDEN HORDE). Southern Crimea was conquered by the Turks in 1475, who established a suzerainty over the Crimean Khanate three years later which continued until 1774. Crimea was annexed to Russia and included in New Russia (q.v.) in 1783, the majority of Tatars emigrating to Turkey. The Allies landed in the Crimea during the Crimean War (q.v.) and took Sevastopol'. Several Tatar nationalist and Russian Communist and anti-Communist governments existed in Crimea in 1917–20; it was under German occupation in 1918, and witnessed many battles of the civil war. The Crimean (Tatar) Autonomous Republic within the Russian Federal Republic was established in 1921. In 1941–3 the Crimea was again occupied by the Germans and it was the scene of much fierce fighting (Sevastopol', Kerch', Perekop). In 1945, following the deportation of the Tatar population to Asiatic Russia, the Crimean Autonomous Republic was dissolved and the area transformed into an oblast, which in 1954 was transferred to the Ukraine. The Crimean Tatars were not included in the 1957 decree on the rehabilitation of deported peoples. *See* W. Kolarz, *Russia and her Colonies*, 1952; B. Nolde, *La Formation de l'Empire Russe*, vol. ii, Paris, 1952; R. Pipes, *The Formation of the Soviet Union*, Cambridge, Mass., 1954.

   Crimean War, 1853–6, between Russia on the one hand and Britain, France, Turkey and Austria on the other, had its roots in the conflict of British and Russian interests in Asia; in the long-standing problem of the control of the Dardanelles; and in the Russian policy of championing the Slav subjects of the Austrian Empire. The precipitating cause was the dispute over the Holy Places in Palestine: Napoleon III forced the Sultan of Turkey to grant certain privileges over the Holy Places to Roman Catholics, whereupon Nicholas I demanded a Russian protectorate over all Orthodox subjects of the Ottoman Empire. Attempts by Russia and Turkey to reach an agreement failed. France and Britain—strongly opposed to such an extension of Russian influence—supported Turkey, and in October 1853 Turkey declared war on Russia, being joined by France and Britain in March 1854; later Sardinia joined the Allies, and Austria took their side but did not take part in the fighting.

   Militarily the war proved disastrous for Russia, with heroic fighting by the troops (especially in the year-long defence of Sevastopol') but little distinction and many blunders among the commanders (except in the Caucasus against the Turks and the destruction of the Turkish fleet at Sinop, *see* NAKHIMOV). Defeats in the field, the death of Nicholas I (1855) and an Austrian ultimatum that she would take active part in the war persuaded the emperor, Alexander II, to accept the peace terms of the victorious Allies, which were finally confirmed in the Treaty of Paris, March 1856. By this treaty Russia was forbidden to rebuild her Black Sea fleet and the fortress at Sevastopol', she was obliged to cede southern Bessarabia and the mouths of the Danube, give up her protectorate over Moldavia and Wallachia and surrender any claim to a protectorate over the Orthodox subjects of

Turkey; the Dardanelles was closed to warships of all nations. The Black Sea clause of the treaty was unilaterally abrogated by Russia during the Franco-Prussian War. *See* L. Tolstoy, *Sevastopol*, 1863–87; H. W. V. Temperley, *England and the Near East*, vol. i, *The Crimea*, 1936; A. Lobanov-Rostovsky, *Russia and Europe, 1825–78*, Ann Arbor, 1954; P. Gibbs, *Crimean Blunder, the Story of War with Russia a Hundred Years Ago*, 1960.

Criminal Law. The new Fundamentals of Criminal Legislation of the U.S.S.R. and the Union Republics adopted in 1958 state that the U.S.S.R. legislation consists only of the Fundamentals themselves, the laws on state and military crimes, and if necessary on other crimes directed against the interests of the U.S.S.R.; the Criminal Codes (*see* CODES) remain, as before, republican. The Fundamentals deal with general problems of crime and responsibility, but do not contain a classification or list of crimes. The Criminal Code of the R.S.F.S.R., besides the state and military crimes, distinguishes 'other crimes against the system of administration'; official crimes; violation of rules about separation of Church from State; 'economic crimes'; crimes against life, health, freedom and dignity of person; property crimes; violation of rules protecting people's health, public security and order; and 'crimes constituting survivals of clan life.' A peculiar feature of Soviet criminal law is the category of 'economic crimes,' which includes violation of laws about nationalization of land, refusal to perform obligatory labour (*see* FORCED LABOUR), 'speculation' (*see* SPECULATORS) and output of sub-standard products. 'Survivals of clan life' are in fact mostly survivals of Islamic law and the customs of Islamic peoples, chiefly in relation to marriage (q.v.) and the position of women generally. *See further under* JUDICIAL SYSTEM; LABOUR DISCIPLINE; LAWYERS; LEGAL REFORM; LEGAL SYSTEM; PENAL SYSTEM; POLITICAL CRIMES; PROCURACY.

Criticism and Self-criticism, procedure by which people ostensibly denounce publicly shortcomings in their own or others' work. In 1948 Zhdanov stated that 'criticism and self-criticism' played in the socialist society the role which is played in class societies by class antagonisms, that is, it is the main driving force of social development. In fact 'criticism and self-criticism' is a fiction (q.v.) designed to show the ability of the party to force people either to vilify others or to denigrate themselves, and thus to demonstrate the power of the party leadership. This is one of the principal features of Stalinism (q.v.) that has been retained in the post-Stalin period. However, genuine criticism, which has developed in recent years, can sometimes be camouflaged under the guise of 'criticism and self-criticism.' *See* A. Inkeles, *Public Opinion in Soviet Russia*, Cambridge, Mass., 1950; R. N. Carew Hunt, *A Guide to Communist Jargon*, 1957.

Cui, César Antonovich (1835–1918), amateur musician who received some musical instruction from Moniuszko but was mostly self-taught. An authority on fortifications, he held the rank of lieutenant-general in the Engineers and taught at the School of Military Engineering; he was also president of the Imperial Russian Musical Society. His association with Balakirev began in 1857. Works comprise eleven operas (including *The Captive in the Caucasus*, Acts

I and II, 1857, Act III, 1881–2; *William Ratcliffe*, 1869; *Mademoiselle Fifi*, 1903); choral works; orchestral works; chamber music; piano music; songs, duets and quartets. Whereas the remainder of the Kuchka (q.v.) were at ease in dealing with the larger choral and orchestral forms, Cui was more successful as a miniaturist. His works suffer from a certain effeminacy and lack of virility, though by no means devoid of charm. Although a supporter of the national school, the folk element plays little part in his work, and his main service to Russian music lies in his role as music critic and propagandist of Balakirev and his followers. *See* G. Abraham and M. D. Calvocoressi, *Master of Russian Music*, 1936.

Cultural Revolution, official designation of a series of measures carried out in the later 1920's and early thirties aimed at creating a new educated class of proletarian and peasant origin and Communist convictions. The principal measures were (1) a policy of admission to secondary and higher education involving the total exclusion of children of the 'former exploiting classes,' including the clergy, restrictions on the admission of children of the intelligentsia, preferential treatment for industrial workers and compulsory recruitment for education among Communist Party and Komsomol members; (2) rapid expansion of Workers' Faculties and Technicums (qq.v.); (3) narrow specialization in higher educational establishments and the shortening of the duration of courses of study. The aims of the Cultural Revolution were to some extent achieved, though at the cost of a drastic lowering of the cultural level of the intelligentsia. The policy was abandoned in the mid 1930's in pursuance of Zhdanov's 'restoration' policy in education. Khrushchëv's educational reform of 1958 (*see* HIGHER EDUCATION; SECONDARY EDUCATION) has partly the same aims as the Cultural Revolution. *See also* CLASSES, SOCIAL; INTELLIGENTSIA.

Cumans (own name **Kypchak**, Russian **Polovtsy**), warlike Turkic-speaking people of the Middle Ages who appeared in the southern Russian steppes in 1054 and frequently raided the Kievan State and Byzantium. In 1238 they were conquered by the Mongols and became an ethnically dominant element in the Golden Horde (q.v.). They are the ancestors of a number of present-day Turkic-speaking peoples (*see* TURKS).

Currency. The chief monetary unit is the rouble, which is divided into 100 kopeks. The currency in circulation consists of bank-notes in denominations of 100, 50, 25 and 10, treasury notes of 5, 3 and 1 roubles and nickel and bronze coins of 20, 15, 10, 5, 3, 2 and 1 kopeks. Theoretically since 1950 the rouble has been based on a gold standard, the gold content of the rouble until 1960 being 0·222168 grams. This gold standard, however, is purely fictitious, since the actual price for gold when it is paid for in roubles (i.e. for gold sold in alloys for industrial purposes) is many times higher than warranted by the official parity. The foreign exchange rates are fixed by the Soviet Government unilaterally; until 1960 this was done on the basis of an arbitrarily fixed rate of 4 roubles to the American dollar (e.g. 11·2 to the £ sterling). These exchange rates grossly overvalue the rouble in relation to its internal purchasing power. This does not affect foreign trade, except with the Communist countries, since both prices and payments are normally in foreign currencies. In 1957 a special tourist rate of 10 roubles to the dollar was introduced. Currency operations, including dealings in gold and other precious metals, foreign currency, foreign bills, etc., are a State monopoly, being considered a part of the monopoly of foreign trade.

Two currency reforms were carried out by the Soviet Government, in 1924 (introducing the Chervonets, q.v.) and in 1947, both times in order to combat inflation. The 1947 reform provided for cash exchange of one new rouble for ten old, and devalued private bank accounts according to a sliding scale (more favourable than the cash exchange) and the accounts of *kolkhozes* and other co-operatives by one-fifth.

A third reform is to be put into force from 1st January 1961, introducing a 'heavy' rouble equal to ten former roubles. It is stated that during a period of three months it will be possible to exchange old notes and coins for new ones without any limit on the amount. At the same time all prices, taxes, wages, salaries, bank accounts, pensions, etc., will be reduced to one-tenth of their former nominal value. The reason for the reform is said to be administrative expediency.

Cybernetics has had a mixed reception in the U.S.S.R. While it was taken up by mathematicians working on the problems of mathematical logic, the theory of probabilities and linear programming (Kolmogorov, Sobolev, L. V. Kantorovich, qq.v., A. Ya. Khinchin) and utilized in designing electronic computers, etc., this had to be done cryptically until after Stalin's death in 1953, since the official ideologists condemned it as a 'bourgeois idealistic pseudo-science.' Only in 1955 was cybernetics publicly recognized as valid. Its application to human society is still opposed by the more conservative ideologists, but there are also enthusiasts for such application, especially among the younger philosophers (e.g. E. Arab-Ogly). *See also* OPERATIONS RESEARCH; SCIENTIFIC ORGANIZATION OF LABOUR.

Czar, title of the rulers of Muscovy from the 15th century until Peter the Great assumed the title Emperor of All Russia. Throughout the imperial period, however, the title czar was widely used. Though deriving from the Latin *Caesar* it lost its imperial rank (cf. German *Kaiser*) and became equivalent to king.

D

Daghestan ('Mountainous Country'), Autonomous Republic within the R.S.F.S.R., situated largely on the north-eastern slopes of the main Caucasian range and including the Nogay steppe lowland in the north, traversed by the lower course of the River Terek; it has deposits of oil and natural gas. Area 19,400 sq. m.; population (1959) 1,063,000 (30 per cent urban), mostly Caucasian-speaking Avars, Dargins, Lezgians and many smaller tribes, also Russians, Kumyks, Azerbaydzhanis and some Nogays. Cattle and sheep are raised, grain is cultivated, horticulture and viniculture carried on, and there are oil and gas extraction, food and metal-working industries; old crafts (carpets) are still carried on. Principal towns: Makhachkala (capital) and Derbent. The area was gradually annexed to Russia in the 18th and 19th centuries, the final stage being completed in 1859 with the defeat of Shamil' (q.v.). The Autonomous Republic was formed in 1920. *See* W. Kolarz, *Russia and her Colonies*, 1952, B. Nolde, *La Formation de l'Empire Russe*, vol. ii, Paris, 1952.

Dal'stroy (Russian abbreviation for Far Eastern Construction Trust), large State enterprise in the Magadan Oblast and north-eastern Yakutia (Far East), founded in 1930; gold and other precious metals and tin are mined there. Until 1953 it was subordinated to the Chief Administration of corrective labour camps (*see* GULAG). With the disbanding of most corrective labour camps (q.v.) that began in 1955 the activities of Dal'stroy shrank, and the trust itself was abolished with the establishment of the Economic Councils (q.v.) in 1957. After 1955 many young people were sent to Magadan Oblast to replace the former forced labourers. *See also* BERZIN; KOLYMA. *See* H. A. Wallace, *Soviet Asia Mission*, New York, 1946; V. Petrov, *It Happens in Russia*, 1951.

Daniel'son, Nikolay Frantsevich (1844–1918), economist, a Liberal Populist. He translated Marx's *Capital* into Russian and accepted much of the Marxian theory of capitalism, but saw no future for capitalism in Russia since he believed that foreign markets were necessary to capitalist development and they were already taken up by more advanced countries.

Danilevskiy, Nikolay Yakovlevich (1822–85), thinker and scientist, an anti-Darwinist and extreme Pan-Slavist. He was the first to expound a philosophy of history as a series of distinct civilizations (*Russia and Europe*, 1871). *See* E. J. Simmons (ed.), *Continuity and Change in Russian and Soviet Thought*, Cambridge, Mass., 1955; T. G. Masaryk, *The Spirit of Russia*, vol. i, 2nd ed., 1955; M. B. Petrovich, *The Emergence of Russian Pan-Slavism*, 1856–70, New York, 1956.

Danilova, Aleksandra (*b.* 1904), dancer who, after working at the Mariinskiy Theatre in Leningrad, left the Soviet Union, 1924, together with Balanchine, Yefimov and Gevergeva, joining Diaghilev and the Ballets Russes in the same year. Her most important roles included *Le Pas d'Acier*, *Apollon Musagètes* and *The Gods go a'Begging*. From 1932 she was a member of Colonel de Basil's company, but joined Massine's Ballet Russe de Monte Carlo in 1938. Her work with both Massine and Balanchine has become almost legendary, outstanding being her interpretations of *Le Beau Danube*, *La Boutique Fantasque*, *Danses Concertantes*, 1944, and *Swan Lake* and *Coppelia*. In 1953 she formed her own company. *See* F. Gadan and R. Maillard, *A Dictionary of Modern Ballet*, 1959.

Dargins, Caucasian-speaking Muslim people inhabiting the central part of eastern Daghestan and numbering in 1959 about 158,000. A tiny Darginian tribe, living in only one village, Kubachi, is famous for its metal-engraving craft.

Dargomyzhskiy, Aleksandr Sergeyevich (1813–69), composer and performer, largely self-trained. He held a post in the civil service at St Petersburg and travelled widely. He was acquainted with Balakirev and his followers, whom to some extent he influenced. Works comprise six operas (*Esmeralda*, *première* 1847; *The Mermaid*, 1856; *The Triumph of Bacchus*, 1867; *Rogdana*, unfinished; *Mazeppa*, unfinished; *The Stone Guest*, 1872); orchestral works, including *Kazachok*, *Baba Yaga*, *Fantasy on Finnish Themes*; vocal music, etc., including many songs. Dargomyzhskiy is chiefly known for his attempts (which in some ways anticipate Wagner) at reproducing natural speech inflections in music by means of melodic recitative. His nationalist feelings are reflected in his choice of folklore subjects, particularly in the opera *The Mermaid*. His songs are of especial interest, in their unusual harmonies, their wit and humour and their occasional employment of oriental material. *See* Rosa Newmarch, *The Russian Opera*, 1914; G. Abraham, *On Russian Music*, 1935, and *Studies in Russian Music*, 1939; G. Abraham and M. D. Calvocoressi, *Masters of Russian Music*, 1936.

Dar'yal, famous gorge, the main pass in the Caucasus Mountains, situated in the central part of the range; the River Terek flows through it. The pass has been fortified since very early times, and the ruins of ancient fortifications still exist. The Georgian Military Road runs through Dar'yal from Odzhonikidze to Tiflis.

Dashava, settlement in the L'vov Oblast (western Ukraine), the centre of a rich natural gas field (exploited since 1924) and the starting-point of a gas pipeline to Kiev and Moscow built after the Second World War.

Dashnaktsutyun, national revolutionary party founded in Armenia in 1890 with the intention of liberating Turkish Armenia by terrorizing Turkish officials, inciting reprisals, and thus drawing world attention to the Armenian question. The revolutionary character of the party, which was supported by the mass of the Armenian population, induced the Russian Government to adopt a series of anti-Armenian measures in Transcaucasia; the Dashnaktsutyun successfully carried out a policy of civil disobedience in Russia in 1903–5, and the Government was obliged to cancel these measures. The party remained Russophil until the Bolshevik seizure of power, when it became the chief party in the independent Armenian Republic of 1918–20. The party still exists, chiefly among Armenian *émigrés* abroad, continuing to advocate independence for Armenia.

Datov, Sarym (dates unknown), leader of an anti-Russian uprising of the Kazakhs of the Junior Hundred in 1783–97.

Daugava, *see* DVINA.

Daugavpils (until 1893 **Dünaburg,** then **Dvinsk** until 1920), town in Latvia situated on the Western Dvina, an important transportation centre (five railway lines). Population (1959) 65,000 (1860, 25,000; 1913, 130,000; 1925, 41,000), mostly Latvians (Latgals) and Russians. It has a railway repair works and other industries. Daugavpils was founded by the Livonian Knights in 1278 and belonged variously to Poland and Sweden; it became a Russian fortress in 1772 and saw much fighting in 1915. It was a flourishing commercial centre before the First World War, and capital of the Latgale province in independent Latvia, 1918–49.

Dauria, *see* TRANSBAYKALIA.

Deborin (real name **Ioffe**), **Abram Moiseyevich** (*b.* 1881), philosopher, educated at Berne University. He was a Bolshevik from 1903, but went over to the Mensheviks in 1907 and did not join the Communist Party until 1928. Deborin was deputy director of the Marx-Engels Institute under Ryazanov (q.v.), editor of the chief Marxist philosophical journal *Under the Banner of Marxism*, 1926–30, was made a member of the Academy of Sciences (q.v.) in 1929, and after the Communist Academy was fused with the Academy of Sciences became a member of the latter's presidium and secretary of the department for history and philosophy, 1935–45. In his works he advanced against the proponents of Mechanical Materialism (q.v.) an interpretation of Marxism which was condemned by Stalin in 1930 as 'menshevikizing idealism.' Main works: *Introduction to the Philosophy of Dialectical Materialism*, 1916; *Philosophy and Marxism*, 1926; *Dictatorship of the Proletariat and the Theory of Marxism*, 1927; *Hegel and Dialectical Materialism*, 1929; *Dialectics and Natural Science*, 1929; *Contemporary Problems of the Philosophy of Marxism*, 1929; *Lenin and the Crisis of Modern Physics*, 1930. See further under DIALECTICAL MATERIALISM; MARXISM. See J. Hecker, *Moscow Dialogues*, 1933; G. A. Wetter, *Dialectical Materialism*, 1958.

Decembrists, first revolutionary movement of the 19th century, formed after the Napoleonic wars. The movement chiefly comprised aristocratic officers—some of them republicans—and aimed at abolishing serfdom and introducing a liberal constitution. On the accession to the throne of Nicholas I (December 1825) the Decembrists carried out a badly organized and conducted revolt in St Petersburg, which led to five of them being hanged and several others banished to Siberia. *See* G. Mazour, *The First Russian Revolution, 1825*, Berkeley, California, 1937; M. Zetlin, *The Decembrists* (trans. G. Panin), New York, 1958.

Degrees, Academic. Academic degrees were abolished immediately after the October revolution (q.v.), but reintroduced in 1934. There are now two degrees in the U.S.S.R.: Candidate of . . . Sciences and Doctor of . . . Sciences. There is no degree corresponding to a B.A.

(those completing the full course of a higher educational establishment receive a diploma). The candidate's degree is approximately equivalent to a first research degree in Britain, and is normally taken after three years of post-graduate study (*see* ASPIRANT). The doctor's degree is conferred upon a person who has either a candidate's degree or the title of professor for a dissertation which makes a substantial contribution to scholarship; it is normally taken by people already well established in academic careers. Universities and certain other higher educational establishments are authorized to confer degrees, subject to subsequent approval by the All-Union Attesting Commission. In the period 1951–5 an average of 8,727 candidates' degrees and 577 doctors' degrees were conferred each year.

Democracy, theoretically the principle underlying the Soviet Government. In fact the soviets (q.v.) are little more than ceremonial gatherings, and the theory of Soviet democracy is a fiction (q.v.) designed to prevent the reappearance of genuine democratic tendencies.

Democratic tradition in Russian public life, though not strong, has asserted itself in one form or another almost continuously, from the *veche* (q.v.) of the Kievan period through the northern republics of the Middle Ages (Novgorod, Pskov, Vyatka), the Cossack communities in the south and the peasant commune (*see* MIR) to the local self-government (*see* ZEMSTVO) of the post-reform (*see* GREAT REFORMS) period, the State Duma after 1905 and the Constituent Assembly of 1918. Democracy did not figure prominently in the programmes of Russian political movements of the 19th century. The Decembrists had a democratic wing, but later the spread of socialist ideas among the radicals made them indifferent to political democracy (*see* POPULISM). There was a democratic trend among the liberal reformers of the 1860's and seventies, and towards the end of the century the democratic tendency reappeared among the revolutionaries in the short-lived People's Right Party, 1894–5. It gathered momentum in the Liberation (constitutional) movement of the early 1900's and was later chiefly represented by the Constitutional Democratic Party.

The so-called Revolutionary Democracy of 1917 which found its expression in the soviets was in fact a combination of Socialist (except their genuinely democratic moderate groups) and Anarchist elements. After the seizure of power by the Bolsheviks (*see* OCTOBER REVOLUTION) the soviets were transformed into organs of the Dictatorship of the Proletariat (q.v.), and for twenty years democracy was a pejorative term in Communist propaganda, being associated with the idea of a disguised bourgeois rule. However, with the introduction of the Stalin constitution (q.v.) of 1936, described as 'the most democratic constitution in the world,' the concept of Soviet democracy was invented, which played an important role in the ideology of Stalinism (q.v.). The post-Stalin measures of administrative decentralization are officially described as 'further democratization' of the Soviet regime. At the same time the radical elements among the intellectual opposition (q.v.) are aiming at a genuine democratic transformation of Russia.

Democratic Centralism, theoretically the main organizational principle of the Communist Party, defined as combining the formation of all leading party organs through election by party members or delegates from lower organs with strict hierarchical subordination. In fact only the second part of the formula has been rigorously and consistently implemented in all Leninist organizations whereas elections, if held at all, have usually been manipulated so as to ensure a majority for those in effective control of the central party apparatus. *See* M. Fainsod, *How Russia is Ruled*, Cambridge, Mass., 1953; R. N. Carew Hunt, *A Guide to Communist Jargon*, 1957; L. Schapiro, *The Communist Party of the Soviet Union*, 1960.

Democratic Centralists, opposition group among the upper ranks of the Communist Party in 1919–22, headed by the former Left Communists (q.v.) Sapronov, Osinskiy (real name Prince V. V. Obolenskiy) and Bubnov. They opposed Lenin's interpretation of the principle of Democratic Centralism (q.v.) and his policy of strictly centralized administration, and were in favour of a more liberal regime within the party. They advocated a dominant position within the soviets (q.v.) for deputies who were party members, but a certain autonomy for deputies from the local party committees; a relaxation of press censorship was also among their demands, and they opposed the one-man management in industry. Most of the Democratic Centralists later joined either the Trotskiyites or the Right Opposition (q.v.) and disappeared during the Great Purge (q.v.). *See* L. Schapiro, *The Origin of the Communist Autocracy*, 1955.

Denikin, Anton Ivanovich (1872–1947), general of humble birth who joined the army in 1887 and became a divisional commander in the Southern Army at the beginning of the First World War. Together with Kornilov (q.v.) he joined General Alekseyev's volunteer army in the Caucasus after the Bolshevik seizure of power, and on Kornilov's death in March 1918 became the commander of the anti-Bolshevik forces in southern Russia. A good soldier but no politician, he consistently adhered to the slogan of 'Russia united and indivisible.' In the area under his control he tried to restore to the landlords the land which the peasants had taken; his political position was thus undermined, and by November 1919 he had been completely defeated by the Bolsheviks. Denikin fled to Istanbul, was offered refuge in England, but chose to go to Belgium, later France and finally America, where he died. *See further under* CIVIL WAR. *See* his *The Russian Turmoil*, 1922, *The White Army*, 1924, and *Put' russkogo ofitsera*, New York, 1953.

Deputies, members of soviets (q.v.) of all levels. There are over one and a half million deputies and they form one of the main sections of the body of activists (q.v.). Since the soviets, especially on the higher levels, are little more than ceremonial gatherings, there is not much scope for the deputies to influence policy, but they are expected to do 'constituency work' among their electors, dealing with individual or local needs, and many deputies do in fact do this.

Derbent, town in the Daghestan Autonomous Republic, situated 150 m. north-west of Baku on the western shore of the Caspian Sea. Population (1956) 41,800 (1914, 33,000; 1926, 23,000). Horticulture is carried on, and there are fishing and wool-weaving industries; it has an ancient citadel and mosques. Derbent was founded by the Persians in the 5th century and became Russian in 1806.

Derpt, *see* TARTU.

Derzhavin, Gavriil Romanovich (1743–1816), poet, Minister of Justice, 1802–5. His most outstanding work is the philosophical ode *God*, and his poetry, marked by nobility and vigour of thought and expression, is the most distinguished achievement of the Classicist school in Russia.

Desna, navigable left tributary of the Dnieper which rises near Smolensk and joins the Dnieper near Kiev. Length 740 m. It is principally used for floating timber.

Detskoye Selo, *see* PUSHKIN.

Deviation, in Communist terminology, any departure from the official line laid down by the party, often referred to as the 'general line,' or from what the party leadership may maintain that its line has been in the past. The difference between deviation and opposition is that the latter is an organized group while the former is a trend. Both deviations and oppositions have normally been classified as either 'Left' or 'Right' though this is not always the case, e.g. nationalist deviation. *See also* LEFT OPPOSITION; RIGHT OPPOSITION. *See* R. N. Carew Hunt, *A Guide to Communist Jargon*, 1957.

Deyneka, Aleksandr Aleksandrovich (*b.* 1899), painter and graphic artist, studied in the Khar'kov Art School and the Moscow Art and Technical Workshops (Vkhutemas), 1921–5. In the 1920's he belonged to the leftist art societies Ost and October and was influenced by the less extreme Western movements, never going further than mild forms of expressionism and cubism. After the imposition of Socialist Realism (q.v.) upon art he managed to preserve some of his earlier formal achievements in his paintings, which were as a rule acceptable to the Stalinist critics from the point of view of subject-matter—sports, industry and military episodes. He was nevertheless criticized for his lack of conformism. Deyneka's best paintings ('The Defence of Petrograd,' 1927, 'Stage Runners,' 1947, and 'Doubles,' 1947) are sufficiently original not to be pictorial propaganda and sufficiently 'Soviet' in content to have ensured the survival (if not the popularity) of the painter under Stalinism (q.v.).

Dezhnëv, Semën Ivanovich (*c.* 1605–*c.* 1672), seafarer. In 1640–60 he made several combined river and sea journeys in north-east Siberia, passing in 1648 through the Bering Strait and thus discovering it eighty years before V. Bering.

Diaghilev, Sergey Pavlovich (1872–1929), impresario. Originally a law student at St Petersburg University, from 1897 he devoted himself to art and journalism, the fruits of his friendship with Benois, Nouvel and Filosofov being the founding of *Mir Iskusstva* (*The World of Art*), a journal which did much to raise the standards of typography and artistic appreciation. In 1899 Diaghilev was appointed special assistant to Prince Volkonskiy, the new Director of the Imperial Theatres, his main task being the editing of the theatre year-book. The following years saw the first of a series of his exhibitions of Russian and European art which culminated in the great

Paris exhibition in 1906. Inspired by the enthusiastic reception of the Paris public, Diaghilev determined to continue his propaganda for Russian works, 1907 seeing the performance of concerts of Russian orchestral music and 1908 productions of Russian opera, the highlight of the season being Shalyapin in Musorgskiy's *Boris Godunov*. The year 1909 marked the *première* of the Ballets Russes which met with unanimous applause, and this was the commencement of a series of sensational triumphs: *The Firebird* and *Sheherazade*, 1910, *Petrushka* and *Le Spectre de la Rose*, 1911, *L'Après-midi d'un Faune*, 1912, *The Rite of Spring*, 1913. The success of these early productions was due to the co-operation of such great artists as the painters Bakst, Benois and Golovine, the brilliant choreography of Fokine, the unsurpassed dancing of Nijinsky, Karsavina and Bolm, the employment of music by composers of the highest order—Borodin, Rimsky-Korsakov, Glazunov and Stravinsky (whom Diaghilev 'discovered')—and lastly to the overwhelming influence of Diaghilev himself, whose exacting standards would allow only of the best. In 1912 Diaghilev met Cocteau and from this time onwards gradually became estranged from his former collaborators, Bakst, Benois and Fokine. The advent of the First World War isolated him from Russia, but in 1916 and 1917 he undertook two tours in America, which, with the signing of peace, were followed by performances in London, 1918, and Paris, 1919. In this next period Diaghilev strove to keep up to date with contemporary movements, and his associates included Cecchetti, Massine, Larionov, Goncharova, Cocteau and Picasso. Centred primarily in Paris, he was attracted by the work of the École de Paris and the music of 'Les Six.' The final years of Diaghilev's life are marked by endless travel and feverish activity in an almost pathetic desire to satisfy the whims of a largely undiscriminating public. An outstanding success, however, was Stravinsky's *Les Noces* in 1923. Principal artists at this period were Lifar, Dolin, Danilova, Balanchine and Alicia Markova. Exhausted by his efforts on behalf of the Russian ballet, fatigued by the endless search for financial assistance and suffering from acute diabetes, Diaghilev died in Venice, a tired and disillusioned man.

It is difficult to assess Diaghilev's part in the evolution of the ballet. It is significant, however, that when severed from his ubiquitous influence a ballet was never the same. As an impresario he was unsurpassed in his powers of discrimination and his uncanny instinct for discerning talent and developing it. Among the leading names of today, in the fields both of ballet and music, many of the greatest have been associated with Diaghilev. With Diaghilev there could be no opposition. To argue with him was a question of stamina. His greatest fear was to be regarded as outmoded. He hated repetition. Diaghilev's personal achievement, his magnetic personality and his inflexible will-power have given him an immortal place in the annals of musical history. *See also* BALLET; FOKINE; MASSINE; and individual entries. *See* A. I. Haskell, *Diaghileff*, 1955.

Dialectical Materialism, official philosophy of the Communist Party, based on a combination of materialism with Hegelian dialectics. Originally worked out by Engels and Marx, it was further developed chiefly by Plekhanov and Lenin. Aggressiveness and intolerance typical of their philosophical writings have often been mistaken (especially by sympathetic but unsophisticated readers) for cogency and precision, which in fact they lack. Lenin's main philosophical work, *Materialism and Empiriocriticism* (directed against Bog-danovism, q.v., the chief rival of dialectical materialism as the Bolshevik philosophy), is a particularly poor piece of philosophizing, full of misnomers, paralogisms and inconsistencies. There has been little further development of dialectical materialism since Lenin, but in the 1920's two main schools of exegesis developed, headed by Bukharin and A. M. Deborin (qq.v.). Both were condemned in 1930 by Stalin, who used their arguments against each other, labelling Bukharin's school 'Mechanicism' and Deborin's 'Menshevikizing Idealism.' Stalin's own version, published in 1938 in the *History of the C.P.S.U. (Short Course)* and treated ostensibly as a gospel during his lifetime, is still apparently the main guide in the current official exegesis. Although dialectical materialism theoretically underlies the whole of Communist ideology (q.v.), the latter is in fact highly eclectic and contains many elements incompatible with its basic tenets. *See* J. Hecker, *Moscow Dialogues*, 1933; J. M. Somerville, *Soviet Philosophy*, New York, 1946; I. M. Bochenski, *Der Sowjet-russische Dialektische Materialismus*, Berne, 1950; G. A. Wetter, *Dialectical Materialism*, 1958.

Dictatorship of the Proletariat, according to Marxist theory the State power during the period of transition from capitalism to socialism. The Communist rule in Russia since 1917 has been theoretically a Dictatorship of the Proletariat and still is, although officially socialism has already been built and the present stage is one of transition to communism (q.v.). *See also* GOVERNMENT. *See* E. H. Carr, *A History of Soviet Russia* (6 vols.), 1950–9.

Dikiy, Aleksey Denisovich (*b.* 1889), theatre producer and stage and film actor. With Gelovani (q.v.) he specialized in portraying Stalin on stage and screen. His films include the 'feature documentaries' *The Thrust*, 1948, and *Battle for Stalingrad*, 1949, in both of which he played Stalin.

Dikson, seaport at the mouth of the Yenisey estuary, on the Northern Sea Route 1,246 m. from Archangel.

Director's Fund (renamed the Fund of the Enterprise in 1955), special fund established in 1936 which is at the disposal of the management of an industrial enterprise, made up of 1–6 per cent of the planned profits and 20–50 per cent of any profits above the plan figure; it is used for welfare measures and the payment of bonuses (q.v.), as well as for additional investment. The Director's Fund provides a measure of manœuvrability in the finances of enterprises, but on the other hand its calculation on the basis of planned profits is inequitable as between enterprises. *See further under* PROFITS. *See* D. Granick, *Management of the Industrial Firm in the U.S.S.R.*, New York, 1955; F. D. Holzman, *Soviet Taxation*, Cambridge, Mass., 1955.

Divorce has been difficult since 1944, and proceedings are complicated and costly. The function of the People's Court (q.v.) in divorce cases is limited to attempts at reconciliation. A higher court can grant divorce if the family is irreparably broken. No reasons are specified in the law and the court has full discretion; in practice divorce is denied if the break-up of the family is the fault of the party seeking divorce. The procedure is simplified in a few cases, notably if one of the spouses is under sentence of imprisonment for over three years, since 'it would be against the principles of Communist morality to force a Soviet citizen to continue marital union with a person who has committed a serious crime against the socialist society.' If divorce is granted the court simultaneously regulates all legal matters arising from this decision, again largely at its own discretion. The care of children is usually awarded to the mother. The law of 1944 effected a complete reversal of previous Communist legislation. In December 1917 divorce was permitted at the request of one or both parties without regard to reasons. In 1926 even the registration of divorce became unnecessary. Only in 1936 did registration again become obligatory, in the presence of both parties (though the request of one party for the divorce was still sufficient). *See* J. N. Hazard, *Law and Social Change in the U.S.S.R.*, 1953; W. W. Kulski, *The Soviet Regime*, Syracuse, 1954.

Dmitriy Donskoy (1350–89), Grand Prince of Moscow from 1363. His fame derives from his victory on the Don (thus Donskoy) over the Tatars in 1380, the first success against the Tatars since their conquest of Russia. Fire-arms were introduced into the Russian Army by Dmitriy.

Dmitriyevsk, *see* MAKEYEVKA.

Dneprodzerzhinsk (until 1936 **Kamenskoye**), town in the Dnepropetrovsk Oblast (Ukraine), a river port on the Dnieper 22 m. above Dnepropetrovsk. Population (1959) 194,000 (1926, 34,000; 1939, 148,000), Ukrainians and Russians. It is a major centre of industry, producing iron and steel (since the 1880's), chemicals, railway carriages and cement; a hydro-electric station is being built near by. Dneprodzerzhinsk was founded in the 18th century as a village and became a town in 1917.

Dneproges (Russian abbreviation for 'Dnieper Hydro-electric Station'), first of the large hydro-electric stations to be built in Russia, situated near Zaporozh'ye. Capacity 558,000 kw. The research and design work for the project were begun in 1905, the construction in 1927. Several foreign firms acted as consultants, and most of the equipment was supplied by the General Electric Company. The completion of the station in 1932 was acclaimed one of the first triumphs of 'socialist construction.'

Dnepropetrovsk (Ukrainian **Dnipropetrovs'ke**): 1. Oblast in south-eastern Ukraine, consisting largely of ravined but fertile lowland steppe traversed by the Dnieper. Area 12,400 sq. m.; population (1959) 2,708,000 (70 per cent urban), Ukrainians and Russians (before the Second World War also Jews and Germans). There are rich deposits of high-quality iron ore, manganese and lignite. The oblast has mining, metallurgical, chemical, engineering and food industries; wheat and sunflower growing and market gardening are carried on. Principal towns: Dnepropetrovsk, Krivoy Rog, Dneprodzerzhinsk and Nikopol'. The Ukrainian Cossacks were the first non-nomadic population to settle in the area on the Dnieper in the 16th century, and mass colonization took place during the 18th century (*see* NEW RUSSIA).

2. (until 1926 **Yekaterinoslav**). Administrative, an economic and cultural centre of the oblast, on the Dnieper, one of the chief industrial cities of the U.S.S.R. Population (1959) 658,000 (fifth in the Ukraine, fifteenth in the U.S.S.R.; 1897, 113,000; 1917, 217,000; 1923, 129,900; 1939, 527,000). It has large iron and steel, chemical and engineering industries, also light and food industries; a large tyre plant is being built, the equipment for which is being supplied by a group of British firms. The city is also an important transportation centre, having a river port, four railway lines and an airport. The university was founded as university courses for women in 1916, and given full status in 1918; there is a mining institute founded in 1899. Dnepropetrovsk was founded by Potëmkin in 1778 and became a provincial capital in 1783. A local commercial centre until the 1880's, it then developed rapidly as a centre of the iron and steel industry; the development of the engineering and chemical industries dates from the 1930's. The Second World War and the German occupation, 1941–3, inflicted much suffering and damage upon the city.

Dnieper (Ukrainian **Dnipro**, Russian **Dnepr**, ancient **Borysthenes**), third largest (after the Volga and the Danube) river of Europe, rising west of Moscow in the Valday upland and flowing west to Orsha, south to Kiev, south-east to Dnepropetrovsk, south to Zaporozh'ye and south-west into the Dnieper liman (estuary) of the Black Sea east of Odessa. Length 1,430 m.; drainage area 200,000 sq. m.; chief tributaries: Berezina and Pripet (on the right), Sozh and Desna (on the left); principal ports: Kiev, Dnepropetrovsk, Zaporozh'ye and Kherson. The Dnieper is largely a lowland river with a wide valley, quiet flow and high spring floods; from December to March–April it is ice-bound. The famous rapids between Dnepropetrovsk and Zaporozh'ye have been submerged by the construction of the Dneproges (q.v.). In the north the river traverses the forested regions of Smolensk Oblast and Belorussia (*see* POLES'YE), with peat and phosphate deposits, flax and potato cultivation and dairy farming; in the south it crosses the Ukrainian wooded steppe and steppe zones with their large iron and manganese ore deposits and wheat, sugar-beet and cotton cultivation. It is navigable for nearly 1,300 miles (from Dorogobuzh), the chief goods transported being mineral building materials and timber downstream and grain, oil products and coal upstream. The large hydro-electric stations of Dneproges and Kakhovka are on the Dnieper, and new ones are being built at Dneprodzerzhinsk and Kremenchug.

The river was part of the famous trade route from Scandinavia to Byzantium in the Middle Ages, and it played an important part in the history of Kievan Russia; the banks and islands of the middle and lower courses were colonized by Ukrainian Cossacks (*see* COSSACKS; SICH) in the 16th–18th centuries. Intensive development of navigation began in 1823. The battle for the Dnieper in August–December 1943 was one of the major operations on the eastern front during the Second World War. The Dnieper is the celebrated national river of the Ukrainians.

Dniester (Dnestr, ancient **Tyras**), navigable river which rises in the Carpathians and flows south-east into the Black Sea 30 m. south-west of Odessa. Length 880 m. It separates Bessarabia from Podolia (Ukraine), and from 1918 to 1940 the river was the frontier between the U.S.S.R. and Rumania.

Dobrolyubov, Nikolay Aleksandrovich (1836–61), famous literary critic of the *Contemporary* (q.v.), a protégé and friend of Chernyshevskiy (q.v.). A revolutionary socialist in politics, he was, together with Chernyshevskiy, the founder of the utilitarian Critical Realism school which prevailed in Russia until the end of the 19th century. *See* his *Selected Philosophical Essays*, Moscow, 1956. *See* M. Karpovich, 'The Historical Background of Soviet Thought Control' in W. Gurian (ed.), *The Soviet Union*, Notre Dame, Indiana, 1951; T. G. Masaryk, *The Spirit of Russia* (2nd ed.), vol. ii, 1955; F. Venturi, *Roots of Revolution*, 1960.

Doctors' Plot, alleged conspiracy among leading Moscow doctors (most of them Jewish) to murder prominent figures of the Soviet regime, including party leaders and marshals of the army. Though the accusations were only made public in December 1952, the doctors were said to have murdered Zhdanov in 1948, and the organs of state security were attacked for 'lack of vigilance.' The doctors were arrested and confessions extorted from them by torture (on Stalin's detailed orders), but no public trial was held. Immediately after Stalin's death in March 1953 those who survived were released, and the plot was declared to have been faked. The Doctors' Plot was a part of the anti-Semitic policy which characterized the last years of Stalin's rule (*see* ANTI-SEMITISM), and was also apparently a first move in an attempt to unleash a new wave of terror similar to the Great Purge (q.v.) of the 1930's. *See* M. Rush, *The Rise of Khrushchëv*, Washington, D.C., 1958.

Dokuchayev, Vasiliy Vasil'yevich (1846–1903), geologist and soil specialist, professor at St Petersburg University, later director of the New Alexandria Agricultural Institute in Poland. Dokuchayev was the pioneer of soil science in Russia and the founder of the evolutionary trend in this science. He gave the first satisfactory classification of soils and advanced the idea of soil zones which forms the foundation of soil geography. His view of soil as a natural body has greatly influenced subsequent thinking of Russian naturalists (*see* BERG; SUKACHËV; VERNADSKIY; WILLIAMS).

Don (ancient **Tanais**), navigable river rising in the central Russian upland and flowing south-east towards the Volga (with which it is connected by the Volga–Don Canal) near Stalingrad, then turning south-west to empty into the Sea of Azov. Length 1,230 m.; basin 162,000 sq. m. The principal tributaries of the Don are the Voronezh, Khopër, Medveditsa and Severeskiy Donets; the chief port is Rostov-on-Don. Cossacks colonized the banks of the Don and its tributaries from the 16th century, and the Don area was their main centre until the civil war.

Don Cossacks, *see* COSSACKS.

Donets Basin (usual abbreviation **Donbas**), principal coal-mining basin in Russia, the core of the Southern Industrial Region (q.v.). It lies in the Stalino and Lugansk oblasts of the Ukraine and the Rostov Oblast of the R.S.F.S.R., on the slightly inundated plain of the Donets Plateau; length (east–west) 240 m., width (north–south) 90 m., total area approximately 9,000 sq. m. There are rich deposits (about 70 milliard tons) of first-class anthracite and steam coal, in comparatively thin seams (usually under 3 ft), and also deposits of mercury, salt and mineral building materials; coal deposits have been shown by recent surveys to extend far beyond the old boundaries to the east, north and west. A large coal-mining industry has existed here since 1722, iron and steel since 1795, chemical since 1889 and heavy engineering since 1895; the first powerful thermo-electric stations were built in 1910. The main industrial centres of the Donets Basin are the Stalino-Makeyevka and Kadiyevka-Voroshilovsk conurbations, Lugansk, Gorlovka, Shakhty and Kramatorsk.

Coal was first discovered in 1721 and mining began at once; the 1870's were a period of rapid industrial development and the Donets Basin soon became Russia's main centre of heavy industry. Twice ruined, during the civil war and the Second World War, the industries were restored and further expanded on both occasions. The Donets Basin was a stronghold of the Bolshevik Party both before 1917 and during the civil war and the 1920's, and the Shockworkers' and Stakhanov movements (qq.v.) originated here; on the other hand, the anti-Communist Industrial Party (q.v.) was alleged to have many adherents among the technical intelligentsia of the Donbas.

Dorpat, *see* TARTU.

D.O.S.A.A.F. (Russian abbreviation for 'Voluntary Society for Assisting the Army, Air Force and Navy'), organization for the military training of civilians formed in 1951 through the fusion of separate societies for each arm of the services. *See also* OSOAVIAKHIM.

Dostoyevskiy, Fëdor Mikhaylovich (1822–81), author and thinker, one of the most celebrated figures in world literature. He was born in Moscow, the son of a doctor. His two great handicaps, lifelong epilepsy and a passion for gambling, are brilliantly described in *The Idiot* and *The Gambler*, 1864. He attended the St Petersburg engineering school but chose to write rather than become an army officer. His first work, *Poor Folk*, was published in 1846 and immediately acclaimed by the radical critics. He was arrested in 1849 for allegedly associating with a secret revolutionary socialist society, and was sentenced to death; after enduring a fearful moment of actually waiting to be shot (described in *The Idiot*) he received a last-minute reprieve and was imprisoned in Siberia. His experiences there furnished the material for his *Notes from the Dead House*, 1861–2. The first truly 'Dostoyevskian' work was the *Letters from the Underground*, 1864. During the late 1860's and the seventies—the period of his great novels *Crime and Punishment*, 1866, *The Idiot*, 1868, *The Possessed*, 1871–2, and *The Brothers Karamazov*, 1880—Dostoyevskiy was contending with almost continuous poverty. He propagated an original 'soil-bound' trend—national, democratic and Christian— his mediums being his own magazines *Time* and *Epoch*, 1861–5, the Conservative weekly the *Citizen*, 1873–4, and his *The Diary of a Writer*, published in separate volumes between 1876 and 1881. He spent several years in Western Europe, and the results of his observations, published in *The Diary of a Writer*, are a blend of Russian nationalism and Messianism and a deep appreciation of the treasures of European civilization. At the opening of Pushkin's monument in Moscow a few months before his death, Dostoyevskiy delivered a famous speech on the destiny of Russia and of the intelligentsia.

Dostoyevskiy's works have greatly influenced modern thought and the development of literature both in Russia and abroad. As a psychologist, his chief interests were the Russian national character and extreme conditions and situations, but his most profound contribution is in the field of social and religious thought. Here, apart from the special subject of the working of the Russian popular mind, he concentrated upon the problems of freedom and the destiny of man. He was the greatest opponent of atheistic humanism, and the inspirer on the one hand of existentialism and on the other of Christian personalism and solidarism. *See* his novels, trans. by Constance Garnett (12 vols.), 1912–20. Among the vast literature on Dostoyevskiy are: A. Gide, *Dostoyevsky* (Eng. trans.), 1925; J. Lavrin, *Dostoyevsky, a Study*, 1943; E. J. Simmons, *Dostoyevsky, the Making of a Novelist*, 1950; V. Seduro, *Dostoyevski in Russian Literary Criticism, 1846–1956*, New York, 1957; R. L. Jackson, *Dostoyevsky's Underground Men in Russian Literature*, The Hague, 1958; G. Steiner, *Tolstoy or Dostoyevsky, an Essay in Contrast*, 1960; V. Yermilov, *F. M. Dostoyevsky*, Moscow. *See also* H. de Lubac, *The Drama of Atheist Humanism*, 1949.

Dovzhenko, Aleksandr Petrovich (1894–1956), film director, of a Cossack family. He was a schoolmaster, a painter and a diplomat (in Berlin) before entering films at the age of 32. His films are full of poetic imagery and surrealistic symbols (*see further under* CINEMA). His world-famous *Earth*, 1930, was denounced by official critics as 'counter-revolutionary,' 'defeatist' and 'too realistic' in its picture of the peasantry. He redeemed himself with *Shchors*, 1939, a falsified portrayal of a Ukrainian Red Army hero of the civil war. Among his other films were the colour film *Michurin*, 1949, and *Poem of the Sea*, on which he was working at the time of his death.

Dragomanov, Mikhail Petrovich (1841–95), Ukrainian historian and politician, who lived in emigration from 1876. He was the leader of a Ukrainian national democratic movement which favoured a reorganization of the Russian state along federal and democratic lines. *See* FEDERALISM; REGIONALISM.

Drogobych, town in the L'vov Oblast of the Ukraine, situated 40 m. south-west of L'vov. Population (1959) 42,000, mostly Ukrainians (before the war chiefly Jews and Poles). It has been the centre of the Ukrainian oil industry since 1900, and is a railway junction. Drogobych has been known since the Kievan period; from 1939 to 1959 it was the administrative centre of Drogobych Oblast, now absorbed by L'vov.

Drought is a common danger in the most important grain-producing belt which stretches from the southern Ukraine and North Caucasus in the west across the Volga to the Altay area in the east. This belt has all the other conditions required for good grain growing (black earth soil, sufficient warmth), but frequently suffers from lack of rain and also, in the west, from dry hot winds originating in Central Asia. Since this is the principal grain-producing area, harvests vary considerably, and particularly severe droughts result in famine (notably 1891, 1921, 1946). Extensive afforestation projects were undertaken during the last years of Stalin's life, accompanied by great propaganda about 'changing nature,' but they were carried out so badly, chiefly by the unpaid labour of *kolkhoz* peasants (*see* FORCED LABOUR), that most of the trees did not take root and little was achieved. In part of the area, near big rivers (the Volga, Don, Kuban', Dnieper), artificial irrigation is gradually being developed.

Drunkenness is generally considered a national failing in Russia. Tradition ascribes to St Vladimir (q.v.) the words: 'It is Russia's joy to drink: we cannot do without it.' It has always been attributed to the unhappiness of life in Russia. Both because it impairs efficiency and because it contradicts the official fiction of the happy and prosperous life in the Soviet Union, the prevalence of drunkenness is embarrassing to the authorities, and frequent attacks are made on it, especially in the press. In recent years Khrushchëv himself has spoken out against the habit. The price of vodka was raised by 30 per cent in 1957, but consumption did not drop. *See* M. G. Field, 'Drink and Delinquency in the U.S.S.R.,' *Problems of Communism*, May–June 1955.

Dual Power, power structure that resulted from the February revolution (q.v.) in 1917, whereby the authority of the Provisional Government was constantly undermined by the rival influence of the soviets (q.v.) thus facilitating the Bolshevik seizure of power (*see* OCTOBER REVOLUTION). *See* O. Anweiler, *Die Rätebewegung in Russland, 1905–21*, Leiden, 1958; V. Gsovski and Grzybowski (eds.), *Government, Law and Courts in the Soviet Union and Eastern Europe*, vol. i, 1959.

Dual Subordination, principle of Soviet administration according to which each specialized part of the administrative apparatus is subordinated to the general territorial authority of the same level and to the relevant functional authority on a higher level; e.g. a rayon education department is subordinated both to the executive committee of the rayon soviet and to the oblast educational administration. This principle extends to all spheres, including the party, the economy, etc. *See* V. Gsovski and Grzybowski (eds.), *Government, Law and Courts in the Soviet Union and Eastern Europe*, vol. i, 1959.

Dudinka, capital of the Taymyr National Okrug in the Krasnoyarsk Kray (Siberia), a river port accessible to sea vessels, situated on the Yenisey 250 m. from its mouth. Population (1956) 17,000. It serves as the port of the Noril'sk industrial area, with which it is connected by a railway 79 m. in length.

Dudintsev, Vladimir Dmitriyevich (*b.* 1918), author. He received legal training, fought in the Second World War, was severely wounded and then worked as public prosecutor in a military court and as an industrial correspondent of a newspaper. In his first literary efforts he was influenced by Proust and Joyce. Between 1950 and 1955 he wrote the novel *Not by Bread Alone* (Eng. trans. E. Bone, 1957), a frank description of the Soviet social and political system and a hint to the 'Idealists,' shown to be struggling against the system in various spheres, to band together and concentrate upon the political side. The intellectual opponents of the regime (*see* INTELLECTUAL OPPOSITION) enthusiastically welcomed the novel's publication in 1956 as the first sign of a revival of Critical Realism, and it was an important factor in the widespread student unrest at the end of 1956. Dudintsev's surrealistic *New Year's Fable* (trans. M. Hayward, *Encounter*, June 1960) forcefully continues the theme of *Not by Bread Alone*.

Duma ('deliberation'), name of the representative assemblies that existed in pre-Soviet Russia, e.g. the State Duma, the Town Dumas and the Boyars' Duma. The constitution of 1906 established the State Duma as a lower chamber of the legislature (the upper was the Council of State, q.v., established in the early 19th century). All tax-payers and property-owners were enfranchised; elections were in-direct (save in the five largest cities) through electoral colleges based on social status. Though Duma members could question ministers, the latter were not responsible to the Duma. Legislation could be introduced by the Duma, and laws had to be passed by it and the State Council and signed by the emperor. Between 1906 and 1917 there were four Dumas, with large radical anti-government majorities in the first two—which were quickly dissolved—and assured right-wing majorities in the next two owing to a change in the electoral law (*see* STOLYPIN). Towards the end of this decade the Duma was developing into a properly functioning parliamentary institution, though it left much to be desired from the point of view of effective-ness and democratic requirements. Upon the abdication of the Czar in 1917 a provisional committee set up by the Duma entrusted Prince L'vov with the formation of a provisional government (q.v.). *See* B. Pares, *Russia and Reform*, 1907; S. N. Harper, *The New Electoral Law for the Russian Duma*, Chicago, 1908; W. F. Dodd, *Modern Constitutions*, vol. ii, 1909; A. J. Sack, *The Birth of the Russian Democracy*, New York, 1918; *Memoirs of Count Witte* (trans. A. Yarmolinsky), New York, 1921; F. A. Golder, *Documents of Russian History, 1914–17*, 1927; A. Levin, *The Second Duma*, New Haven, 1940; J. L. H. Keep, 'Russian Social Democracy and the First State Duma,' *Slavonic and East European Review*, vol. xxxiv, No. 82, Dec. 1955; S. R. Tompkins, *Russian Intelligentsia The Makers of the Revolutionary State*, Norman, Oklahoma, 1957.

Dumping was resorted to by the Soviet Government in its foreign trade operations in the late 1920's and early thirties, mostly in timber and grain. At the time it was widely believed abroad that this was done in order to disrupt the world market. Although the dis-rupting effect was doubtless not unwelcome to the Soviet leadership, the primary reason appears to have been the desire to obtain foreign currency quickly in order to pay for large imports of machinery for the needs of the first Five Year Plan (q.v.). Although there have been cases of dumping in recent years, on the whole Soviet trade agencies have held to market prices.

Düna, *see* DVINA.

Dünaburg, *see* DAUGAVPILS.

Dunayevskiy, Isaak Osipovich (1900–55), composer, violinist and conductor. He studied at Khar'kov Conservatory under Bogatyrëv and during the 1920's and thirties supervised and conducted the music of Moscow and Leningrad theatres; from 1938 to 1948 he was director of the Song and Dance Ensemble of the Central House of Culture of Railway-workers. A prolific vocal composer, he has written much music for films, including *Gay Fellows*, 1934, *The Kuban' Cossacks*, 1949, etc.; the former, with its melodiousness, liveliness and rhythmic vitality, began a new era in Soviet song. His *Song of the Gay Wind*, 1936, and *Song of Our Native Land*, 1936, were extremely popular. *See* R. Moisenko, *Realist Music*, 1949.

Dvina, two Russian rivers. The Northern Dvina is formed by the confluence of the rivers Sukhona and Yug, and flows north-west into the Dvina gulf of the White Sea. Length (with Sukhona) 820 m.; drainage area 138,000 sq. m. Its principal tributaries are the Vychegda and the Pinega; the chief ports are Archangel and Kotlas. The Northern Dvina was the main route of Muscovite foreign trade in the 16th and 17th centuries; it is now mostly used for floating timber. The Western Dvina (Latvian Daugava, German Düna) rises in the Valday upland near the source of the Volga and flows west into the Gulf of Riga. Length 637 m.; basin 33,000 sq. m. The principal ports are Riga, Daugavpils and Vitebsk. Navigation is limited by shallows. During the Middle Ages the Western Dvina was an important part of the trade route from Scandinavia to Byzantium. In 1915–16 it was an effective barrier against German offensives.

Dvinsk, *see* DAUGAVPILS.

Dykh-Tau, third highest mountain of the main Caucasian range, 17,190 ft.

Dyushambe, *see* STALINABAD.

Dzaudzhikau, *see* ORDZHONIKIDZE.

Dzerzhinsk (before 1917 Chernorech'ye, then Rastyapino until 1929), town in the Gor'kiy Oblast (central Russia), situated on the River Oka 20 m. west of Gor'kiy. Population (1959) 163,000 (1926, 10,000; 1939, 103,000). It is one of the principal centres of the chemical industry, producing synthetic ammoniac, fertilizers and explosives. Dzerzhinsk was originally a holiday resort, and became a town in 1929; industrial development began before 1917 and was particularly rapid during the 1930's.

Dzerzhinskiy (Polish Dzierzynski), Feliks Edmundovich (1877–1926), Communist, of Polish gentry by birth. He joined the Social Democratic Party of Poland and Lithuania (which later developed Bolshevik tendencies) in 1895, was imprisoned and banished to Siberia several times, and released from prison by the February revolution of 1917 (q.v.). Dzerzhinskiy then became a member of the Bolshevik Party's central committee, took active part in the seizure of power, and immediately thereafter established the Cheka (q.v.). He was chairman of the Cheka, and later the G.P.U., until his death, being simultaneously Commissar of Transport from 1921 and chairman of the Supreme Council of National Economy from 1924; in that year he also became candidate member of the Politburo. He supported Stalin in the inner-party struggle that followed Lenin's death, although he had belonged to the Left Communists (q.v.) in 1918.

Dzerzhinskiy, Ivan Ivanovich (*b.* 1909), composer who studied at Gnesin School in Moscow and Leningrad Conservatory, working under Asaf'yev from 1933. Works comprise several operas, including *Quiet Don*, 1935, and *The Storm*, 1940–55; orchestral works; vocal works; music for plays and films. *Quiet Don* achieved great success by its patriotism and simplicity. *See* R. Moisenko, *Realist Music*, 1949.

Dzhalal-Abad, town in the Fergana Valley belonging to the Osh Oblast of Kirgizia. Population (1956) 27,300, Uzbeks and Kirgiz. It has food, shoemaking and cotton-processing industries, and there are mineral springs in the vicinity. From 1939 to 1958 it was the centre of Dzhalal-Abad Oblast, now fused with Osh Oblast.

Dzhambul: 1. Oblast in southern Kazakhstan, situated west of Alma-Ata, traversed by the Turksib Railway, with the Tien-Shan foothills in the south and desert in the north; there are large deposits of phosphorite. Area 56,100 sq. m.; population (1959) 562,000 (36 per cent urban), mainly Kazakhs and Uzbeks, also Russians, Ukrainians, Tatars, Koreans and Dungans. There is irrigated agriculture in the foothills (sugar-beet, cotton, grain crops, market gardening); sheep are raised in the desert and in the mountains; and there are phosphorite extraction, chemical (phosphorite fertilizers) and food industries.

2. (until 1938 **Aulie-Ata,** then for a few months **Mirzoyan**). Administrative, economic and cultural centre of the oblast, situated on the River Talas and the Turksib Railway. Population (1959) 67,000 (1939, 38,000), Russians, Uzbeks and Kazakhs. It has food and chemical industries. Dzhambul was founded in the first centuries A.D., when it was known as Taraz; it was situated on the trade route to China. In 751 a decisive battle took place here between the Chinese and the Arabs, the Arab victory resulting in the establishment of Islam throughout Central Asia. It was later the capital of the Karakhanid state, but in the 13th century was razed by Genghis Khan's hordes. It was refounded at the end of the 18th century as a Kokand fortress; in 1864 it was taken by the Russians and a new Russian town was built side by side with the old; both parts of the town are still distinguishable.

Dzhezkazgan, town in the Karaganda Oblast (central Kazakhstan), situated on a branch of the Trans-Kazakhstan Railway about 280 m. south-west of Karaganda. Population (1956) 29,100, mainly Russians and other Europeans (former labour camp inmates). It is the main centre of the Dzhezkazgan industrial area (total population about 80,000 in 1956) which has the largest copper deposits in the U.S.S.R. (known since 1771); there are copper and manganese mining and copper smelting (since 1928) industries. The first copper-mines were built by a British firm in 1909. From the 1930's to the mid 1950's the area belonged to the Karaganda forced labour camp system, and an important camp uprising of the period 1953–5 took place here.

E

East Kazakhstan Oblast lies in southern Siberia, comprising the Oriferous Altay and the upper Irtysh valley, bordering on China; it has vast deposits of non-ferrous and rare metals—lead, zinc, silver, tin, copper, gold, wolfram, tungsten, cadmium and others—as well as sulphur. Area 37,600 sq. m.; population (1959) 732,000 (54 per cent urban), mainly Russian (over 70 per cent in 1939), also Kazakhs (over 20 per cent in 1939), Ukrainians, Tatars, Belorussians, Mordva and some Uzbeks. It is a major region of non-ferrous metallurgy; there are three big hydro-electric stations. Sheep, cattle and pigs are raised, wheat and oats cultivated. Principal towns: Ust'-Kameno-gorsk (administrative centre), Leninogorsk and Zyryanovsk. The area has attracted settlers since the earliest times, and there are many traces of prehistoric mining. From the early 15th century it belonged to the Kalmyk Dzungarian khanate; routed by the Chinese in 1758, the Kalmyks migrated to the Volga, and the area was gradually occupied by the Kazakhs of the Middle Hundred. Russian penetration and colonization had already begun in the 1720's, and the annexation of the region to Russia was completed in 1864 when the Chinese ceded their remaining territory in the area. The Russian mining industry in the Oriferous Altay dates from 1784.

East Slavs, branch of the Slav family of peoples, sometimes simply called the Russian branch, which consists of the three closely related peoples, Great Russians, Ukrainians and Belorussians (qq.v.). The East Slav tribes from which the present East Slav peoples are descended were united in the Kievan state (*see* KIEVAN RUSSIA) in the Middle Ages. The Mongol conquest and the absorption of the western and southern parts of the former Kievan Russia by Lithu-ania and Poland led to political and cultural isolation among the East Slavs, resulting in the development of the three distinct peoples. Consciousness of belonging to the same family was nevertheless strong among them all, and a rivalry developed in the 14th–16th centuries between Muscovy and the Grand Duchy of Lithuania, with its predominantly Belorussian and Ukrainian population, for 'gather-ing the Russian lands.' All three peoples shared in the formation of the empire and the development of the common Russian culture during the 18th and 19th centuries, and there was until the 1920's considerable uncertainty as to whether they were in fact distinct peoples.

Ecclesiastical Architecture, *see* ARCHITECTURE, ECCLESIASTICAL.

Echmiadzin, famous Armenian monastery, the religious centre of the Armenian Gregorian Church, situated 10 m. west of Yerevan. It has been the seat of the Armenian Patriarch ('Catholicos') since 1441.

162

The principal cathedral was founded by St Gregory, the Illuminator of the Armenians, in the year 303.

Economic Accountability, *see* KHOZRASCHËT.

Economic Aid to under-developed countries has been economically insignificant compared to aid from the non-Communist countries, though its propaganda value may, for various reasons, be disproportionately great. In 1957 aid from the Communist bloc (of which it is estimated that the U.S.S.R. contributed about three-quarters) equalled 160–200 million U.S. dollars (of which credits were 140–180, grants were 20, and contribution to the U.N. technical assistance programme was 1·4). In the same year the non-Communist countries gave aid totalling 4,800–4,900 million dollars (including U.S. and other governments, U.S. and other private investment, U.S. contribution to the U.N. technical assistance programme, and the International Bank for Reconstruction), of which U.S. Government grants alone amounted to 1,342 million dollars.

Unlike Western countries, the Soviet Union prefers to give credits rather than grants, though the interest charged is only 2–2½ per cent compared with the 4–5 per cent of the U.S. Government and the International Bank. During the period 1953–7 the Soviet bloc signed non-military credit agreements with under-developed countries to the value of 1,581 million dollars (of which the U.S.S.R. was the source of 1,227 million); among the principal recipients were Yugoslavia (28 per cent), India (23 per cent), Egypt (14 per cent), Syria (12 per cent), Afghanistan (7 per cent) and Indonesia (7 per cent). During the period 1945–57 the U.S. Government actually disbursed, in credits and grants, 2,597 million dollars' worth of aid.

A more important, though lesser known, part of Soviet economic aid is that given to other Communist countries; in the period 1946–57 such aid from the U.S.S.R. amounted to about 3,313·5 million dollars, of which Poland received about 26 per cent and China about 30 per cent. *See* J. S. Berliner, *Soviet Economic Aid*, New York, 1958; E. Bock, 'Soviet Economic Expansionism,' *Problems of Communism*, vol. vii, No. 4, July–Aug 1958; N. B. Scott, 'Soviet Economic Relations with Under-developed Countries,' *Soviet Studies*, vol. x, No. 1, July 1958; F. L. Pryor, 'Forms of Economic Co-operation in the European Communist Bloc,' *Soviet Studies*, vol. xi, No. 2, Oct. 1959.

Economic Councils, territorial units of economic administration set up in 1957. They are subordinated directly to the Councils of Ministers of the Union Republics, and are responsible for the administration of industry and building (except that of purely local relevance). The jurisdiction of most of the councils extends over one oblast, kray or Autonomous Republic, but some, especially outside the R.S.F.S.R., cover a group of oblasts. The smaller Union Republics have only one Economic Council each. The establishment of the councils was aimed at overcoming the evils of centralization inherent in the previous system of administering industry by branches through ministries. On the whole the reform has been beneficial to the economy, but there is now the opposite danger of 'localism,' i.e. that councils tend to put local interests first, although the strictly centralized party organizations are supposed to guard against this, and an effort to combat it was made by the establishment in 1960 of republican councils of national economy in the R.S.F.S.R. and the Ukraine. *See* P. J. D. Wiles, 'La Territorialisation de l'Économie Sovietique,' *L'Économie Sovietique en 1957*, Brussels; F. Brandel *et al.* (eds.), *Les Régions économiques en U.R.S.S.*, Paris, 1959.

Economic Materialism, term sometimes used for the sociological and historical aspects of Marxism. It is particularly associated with the historical theories of Pokrovskiy (q.v.) and N. A. Rozhkov (who themselves used it), but is rejected by Lenin and the Leninist school of thought, who prefer the term 'historical materialism' (q.v.). Pokrovskiy's 'economic materialism' is in fact an application of the Bogdanovist approach to history (*see* BOGDANOVISM).

Economic Theory has not on the whole been very original in Russia. Though there has been much theorizing, most of it reflected in turn the schools prevalent abroad (mercantilist, classical, historical, marginalist, Marxist, etc.). Only Populism produced a truly Russian trend in economic thought, from which, in its Neo-Populist phase (*see* NEO-POPULISM), emerged the important work of Kondrat'yev on business cycles. Other notable work of the 1920's was that of the Bogdanovist (*see* BOGDANOVISM) Bazarov on economic growth; the beginnings of input-output analysis were also made by W. Leontief in Russia in the 1920's. Virtually all economic research ceased during Stalin's rule and many leading economists (including Kondrat'yev, Bazarov and Groman) disappeared; the place of economic theory was taken by exercises in exegesis of Stalin's pronouncements on economic problems. Since Stalin's death there has been a revival of economic studies in general and considerable interest in contemporary economic theory and techniques of economic analysis. Of the surviving older economists, S. G. Strumilin (q.v.) is prominent in reviving the Marxist trend, while V. S. Nemchinov (q.v.) is encouraging the study of contemporary trends. *See* E. J. Simmons (ed.), *Continuity and Change in Russian and Soviet Thought*, Cambridge, Mass., 1955; R. L. Meek, 'The Teaching of Economics in the U.S.S.R. and Poland,' *Soviet Studies*, vol. x, No. 4, April 1959; H. S. Levine, 'Conversations with Planners,' *Soviet Survey*, No. 30, Oct.–Dec. 1959; W. Leontief, 'The Decline and Rise of Soviet Economic Science,' *Foreign Affairs*, vol. xxxviii, No. 2, Jan. 1960; G. Grossman (ed.), *Value and Plan*, Berkeley, California, 1960.

Economism, name given to the less dogmatic trend in Russian social democracy in the 1890's and 1900's by its opponents. In fact two different tendencies were described by this name: the genuine Economists (Kuskova, Bogucharskiy, Prokopovich, qq.v.) maintained that a separate social democratic party in Russia was premature and that Russian Marxists should participate in the constitutional movement of the liberal bourgeoisie while assisting the workers in their efforts to improve their economic position; the second trend affirmed the need for a social democratic party but asserted that its policy should be directed by the workers. The latter group was later influential in the Menshevik faction. *See also* CREDO. *See* L. Schapiro, *The Communist Party of the Soviet Union*, 1960.

Education. Since the educational reform of 1958 the main features of the educational system are the following (for pre-school education *see* KINDERGARTENS). Compulsory education begins at the age of 7 and extends over eight years. It is given in eight-year schools described as 'incomplete secondary,' with a uniform curriculum throughout the country. The first four classes often exist separately as primary schools. Fifty-nine languages are used as a medium of instruction in eight-year schools (some of them for only the first two or four years), the parents choosing the language for their children; in areas with considerable non-Russian population provision is made for Russian to be taken as an optional subject in non-Russian schools and vice versa. Most primary and eight-year schools are day-schools, but the number of boarding-schools (q.v.) has grown since 1956. Although eight-year education is officially compulsory, it has not yet in fact become universal. Having completed the eight-year school, those who want to receive further education have a choice of three ways. First there are the Vocational Technical Schools (*see* LABOUR RESERVES) which train apprentices for skilled manual work in one- to three-year courses; fees are payable in these schools, but the pupils receive normal apprentices' wages. Secondly there are general secondary schools (*see* SECONDARY EDUCATION), day-, boarding-, evening or correspondence, with three-year courses (four years in evening and correspondence schools) which prepare for higher education but also give training in a manual trade. Secondary education is provided in seventeen languages, and there are the same arrangements for optional learning of languages as in the eight-year schools. Thirdly there are professional secondary schools (including Technicums, q.v.) which train in three- to four-year courses intermediate technical personnel of all kinds: primary school-teachers, nurses, factory technicians, junior agronomists, etc. For higher education *see* this heading.

The State system of education was first set up in Russia in the late 18th century after the Austrian model. There was also a parallel system of Church schools (particularly favoured in the late 19th century by Pobedonostsev, q.v.) and there were many private schools. During the 19th century a number of outstanding pedagogues (*see* RACHINSKIY; L. N. TOLSTOY; USHINSKIY) raised the Russian educational theory and practice, particularly that of the primary schools, to a high level. Great advances were made in expanding primary education by the *zemstvos* (q.v.) after the Great Reforms (q.v.) of the 1860's. Plans for introducing universal compulsory education by 1922 were set in motion by the State Duma before the world war, but the war, revolution and civil war retarded the progress. Universal primary education was finally decreed in 1930 and extended to seven years in 1949 and to eight years in 1958; plans (proclaimed in 1952) to introduce universal ten-year education by 1960 were dropped in 1958. The school system and the content and methods of education have undergone several drastic changes since 1917. The first period (1917–32) was one of constant experimentation, at first, till 1929, under the influence of modernistic educational theories (*see* BLONSKIY; BOGDANOVISM; LABOUR SCHOOL; LUNACHARSKIY; POKROVSKIY; SHATSKIY) and the Marxist idea of 'polytechnical' education (q.v.), then under Bubnov (q.v.) as Commissar for Education with the aim of extending to education the methods adopted in other spheres of life at the time of Stalin's 'revolution from above.' The resulting chaos led to the adoption of a policy of restoration which was pursued for two decades under the general supervision of Zhdanov (q.v.). This greatly raised the efficiency of the schools, but educational theory during this period (see MAKARENKO; MEDYNSKIY) was almost sterile. An important feature of Zhdanov's policy was the permeation of the whole educational process with the Leninist 'party spirit' (see PARTYNESS). The years 1952–8 witnessed a partial reversal of the previous trend and a return to the idea of polytechnical education, while the reform of 1958, introduced on the initiative of Khrushchëv and according to his proposals, reveals his preference for the practices of the first Five Year Plan era. The following table gives some statistics of education in Russia (in thousands):

	1914 [4]	1940	1956	1958
Pupils in primary and secondary schools [1]	9,656	34,784	28,186	29,657
Including classes 8–10 [1]	152	2,370	5,047	3,396
Pupils in professional secondary schools [2]	54	787	1,407	1,125
Students in higher educational establishments [2]	127	558	1,177	1,180
Graduates from higher educational establishments [3]	12	126	260	291

See R. A. Bauer, *The New Man in Soviet Psychology*, Cambridge, Mass, 1952; N. DeWitt, *Soviet Professional Manpower*, Washington, D.C., 1955; G. S. Counts, *The Challenge of Soviet Education*, New York, 1957; G. S. Kline (ed.), *Soviet Education*, 1957; A. G. Korol, *Soviet Education for Science and Technology*, 1958; S. V. Utechin, 'Education in the U.S.S.R.,' *Political Quarterly*, vol. xxix, Oct.–Dec. 1958, and 'Khrushchëv's Educational Reform,' *Soviet Survey*, No. 28, April–June 1959; G. Z. F. Bereday and J. Pennar (eds.), *The Politics of Soviet Education*, 1960; E. Koutaissoff, 'Fifteen to Eighteen in Soviet Russia,' *Educational Review*, vol. xii, No. 3, June 1960.

Ehrenburg, Il'ya Grigor'yevich (*b.* 1891), writer of Jewish origin. Both before and after the revolution he lived much abroad, chiefly in Paris. He began his literary career as a Symbolist poet and has always shown a deep appreciation of art, but he soon turned to prose and has written in all *genres*, from novels to journalism. He has always been skilful in portraying the dominant mood of his milieu at a given moment: the gloom of patriots at Russia's agony under the rule of Bolshevik barbarians (*A Prayer for Russia*), the acceptance of

---

[1] Excluding adult schools.
[2] Excluding evening or correspondence pupils and students.
[3] Including evening and correspondence students.
[4] Present-day frontiers.

revolution by the National Bolsheviks (*Meditations*, 1921), the repugnance felt by many intellectuals for both capitalism and regimented communism (*Julio Jurenito*, 1922, trans. A. Bostock, 1958), the complex emotions that resulted from rapid industrialization (*The Second Day*, 1933), the hatred of Germans (*The War*, 1943), the anti-Western party line of the immediate post-war years (*The Storm*, 1948) and the 'thaw' that developed with the death of Stalin (*The Thaw*, 1954–6). He has taken part in the intellectual opposition (q.v.), his articles 'Lessons of Stendhal,' 1957, and 'Rereading Chekhov' being at odds with the official ideology; at the same time he is prominent in the Soviet 'peace' campaign. *See* J. Lindsay (trans.), *Russian Poetry, 1917–55*, 1957.

Eisenstein, Sergey Mikhaylovich (1898–1948), greatest Soviet film director. The son of a prosperous civil engineer from Riga, he studied architecture and engineering in Petrograd, enlisted in the Red Army in 1918 and in 1920 joined the Proletkul't (q.v.) Theatre in Moscow as designer and producer, where he came under the influence of Meyerhold (q.v.). His first film, *Strike*, 1925, was unpopular in Russia but won a prize in Paris. His most famous film, *Battleship Potëmkin*, 1925, was 'recognized' in Russia only after an initial success in Berlin. Production of *The General Line*, dealing with the collectivization of agriculture (q.v.), was suspended on government orders. *October*, 1927, was censored in those scenes depicting Trotskiy, and eventually denounced as 'formalistic' and banned. In 1928, together with Pudovkin (q.v.) and his assistant G. Aleksandrov, Eisenstein issued a manifesto condemning the advent of realistic sound and speech in films on the grounds that it would destroy the montage; they advocated using sound asynchronically, as a counterpoint to the visual image. In 1929 *Old and New*, a remake of *The General Line*, was criticized as 'unrealistic.'

In the same year Eisenstein left the Soviet Union, together with his cameraman Eduard Tisse and Aleksandrov, and toured Europe, arriving in the U.S.A. in 1930. In Mexico they made the film *Que Viva Mexico*, which proved too long for commercial showing. He returned to the Soviet Union in 1932, and was severely criticized at the 1935 Film Conference. He was more or less in forced retirement until his death, teaching at the Moscow State Film Institute and writing books on the theory of film-making. During the last seventeen years of his life he made only four films; *Bezhin Meadow*, 1937, was banned for 'exaggerating the destructive aspects of the revolution' (a reference to scenes of peasant misery during the collectivization of agriculture); *Alexander Nevskiy*, 1938, was made according to the new party teaching on national history and won a Stalin Prize; Part I of *Ivan the Terrible*, 1944, an allegory on Stalin, depicted Ivan as a benevolent tyrant and won Eisenstein another Stalin Prize; Part II, 1945, in which Ivan was consciously depicted as a neurotic and cruel despot, was denounced in the party Decree on the Cinema of September 1946. Eisenstein, who had already suffered a heart attack early in that year, did no more work before his death. *See also* CINEMA.

Ekibastuz, town in the Pavlodar Oblast (Kazakhstan), situated

about 75 m. south-west of Pavlodar, the centre of a rapidly developing mining area (opencast coal-mining, gold and rare metals).
Population (1956) over 15,000. Coal-mining was started here at the
end of the 19th century, but has only been properly developed since
1953.

El'brus, highest mountain in the main Caucasian range, its western
peak being 18,470 ft high; the other summit, first reached by D. W.
Freshfield in 1868, is 18,347 ft high. El'brus is an extinct volcano
whose glaciers cover 46 sq. m.; the Baksan glacier reaches down to
7,350 ft above sea level. *See* R. L. G. Irving, *Ten Great Mountains*,
1940.

Elections, procedure prescribed by law for constituting all soviets
(q.v.) and their executive bodies, as well as judges and assessors. The
law provides for universal, equal and direct election, with secret
ballot (since 1936), and formally this is strictly adhered to. However,
the elections are wholly fictitious, the fiction (q.v.) serving the double
purpose of making it more difficult to advocate true democratic
procedures, since ostensibly they exist, and also discrediting democratic institutions as such by making them appear worthless. In fact
there is always only one candidate on the ballot paper, chosen by the
relevant cadres department of the party. Elections are also prescribed
by statute for all the leading party organs and other organizations
such as the Komsomol, trade unions, etc.; such elections differ from
those for soviets in that there are normally more candidates than
places to be filled, thus offering some choice of individuals. *See* M.
Fainsod, *How Russia is Ruled*, Cambridge, Mass., 1953, and *Smolensk under Soviet Rule*, 1959; G. B. Carson, *Electoral Practices in the
U.S.S.R.*, 1956.

Electric Power. The total capacity of electric power-stations in
1958 was 53·4 million kw. (1·1 in 1913, 1·9 in 1928, 11·2 in 1940, 11·1
in 1945, 43·5 in 1956). Of this total the capacity of hydro-electric
stations was 10·9 million kw. (0·02 in 1913, 0·1 in 1928, 1·6 in 1940,
1·3 in 1945, 8·5 in 1956). The output of electric power was 233·4
milliard kwh. in 1958 (1·9 in 1913, 5·0 in 1928, 48·3 in 1940, 43·3 in
1945, 191·7 in 1956). Of the total output of electric power in 1957,
3·4 per cent was produced by small stations of up to 500 kw., 7·7 per
cent by stations with capacity from 500 to 9,999 kw., 25·0 per cent by
medium stations of 10,000–99,999 kw. and 63·9 per cent by large
stations of 100,000 kw. and over (of which there were 109). By 1950
the Soviet Union had taken second place in the world in the output of
electric power. Power-stations are principally concentrated in central
Russia, the Southern Industrial Region (q.v.) and the Urals, in all of
which places they are combined into regional grids. The main hydro-
electric stations are those on the Volga—near Kuybyshev, and at
Stalingrad (both with a full capacity of 2·3 million kw.)—and on the
Dnieper (*see* DNEPROGES). A station with 3·6 million kw. capacity is
under construction near Bratsk on the River Angara in eastern
Siberia. Out of the total electric power of 209·7 milliard kwh.
produced in 1957, industry consumed 138·3, transport 7·7 and agriculture 5·8 milliard kwh. In 1956, 62·9 per cent of the electric
power consumed by industry was used for moving power, and

26·2 per cent for technical purposes. By 1958 all Machine Tractor Stations, 96 per cent of *sovkhozes* and 49 per cent of *kolkhozes* had electricity.

Large-scale electrification started in Russia at the beginning of the 20th century, and received great impetus with the adoption of the Goelro (q.v.) plan in 1920. During Stalin's rule particular emphasis was laid upon the construction of hydro-electric stations, which were built without due regard to other, e.g. agricultural or fishing, interests. This policy was changed in 1958, several large-scale projects being abandoned, and priority is now given to the construction of thermal stations. The three main regional grid systems are being linked together by high voltage transmission lines to each of them from the Volga hydro-electric stations. A central Siberian grid from Novosibirsk through the Kuznetsk Basin to Irkutsk is also under construction. See J. P. Hardt, *Economics of the Soviet Electric Power Industry*, Montgomery, Alabama, 1955.

Elektrostal' (till 1938 **Zatish'ye**), town in the Moscow Oblast, 36 m. east of the capital. Population (1959) 97,000. It has steel and engineering industries, dating from the First and Second World Wars respectively.

Elista (1943–57 **Stepnoy**), capital of the Kalmyk Autonomous Republic, situated 150 m. south of Stalingrad. Population (1959) 22,000, Russians and Kalmyks. It has some food industries, and a koumiss sanatorium near by. Elista was founded in 1927 as administrative centre of the Kalmyk Autonomous Oblast, and during the period 1943–57, when Kalmyk autonomy was abolished, it belonged to Stavropol' Kray.

Elizabeth Petrovna (1709–62), daughter of Peter the Great, acceded to the throne in 1741, having overthrown the infant emperor Ivan VI with the assistance of the Guards. She took the duties of government seriously and attempted to carry on the policies of her father. She abolished the death penalty and was one of the founders of Moscow University.

Emancipation of the Serfs, *see* GREAT REFORMS; PEASANT LAND BANK; REDEMPTION PAYMENTS; SERFDOM.

Émigrés. There has been a continuous tradition of political emigration from Russia since the 1840's, and individual cases occurred much earlier. Most revolutionary organizations and leaders have at one time or another functioned in emigration; theoretical study and the publication of revolutionary literature were the most usual forms of work to be undertaken abroad (Herzen, three of the main theorists of Populism—Bakunin, Lavrov and Tkachëv (qq.v.)—the Ukrainophile Dragomanov, the Marxist Liberation of Labour Group, P. B. Struve with his journal *Liberation*, qq.v.). The executive committee of the Narodnaya Volya (q.v.) after the assassination of Alexander II, and the leadership of the Iskra (q.v.) organization headed by Lenin, were the main examples of leadership from abroad before the revolution of 1905 (q.v.). The political importance of the emigration declined during the constitutional period, although both Lenin and the official leadership of the Socialist Revolutionary Party again went abroad.

Political emigration on a large scale occurred after the Bolshevik seizure of power (*see* OCTOBER REVOLUTION) and again after the Second World War. Among the first emigration the whole range of political opinion was represented, and most of the political parties that were suppressed in Russia re-established their organizations abroad; there was also General Wrangel's army evacuated from the Crimea which became the nucleus of the Russian Military League, and a variety of cultural institutions, including two Russian universities (in Prague and Harbin), were established. United in their opposition to the Communist dictatorship (q.v.), the *émigrés* were disunited among themselves as to political aims and methods, and all efforts at co-ordination failed. New ideological and political trends emerged, partly in response to new conditions in Russia and partly under contemporary foreign influences: the Neo-Populist (q.v.) Peasant Russia organization, the 'Eurasians,' the N.T.S. (qq.v.) and the semi-fascist (*see* FASCISTS) Young Russians. The Soviet authorities were very sensitive to the activities of the *émigrés*, using all possible means to fight them, and at all the show trials of the 1920's and thirties the accused were said to have been inspired and guided by Russian *émigrés*.

During the Second World War the emigration split into three main groups: the defencists, who collaborated with the Soviet Government, the defeatists, who collaborated with the Germans, and those who remained both anti-Communist and anti-Nazi. The main features of the post-Second World War emigration were the virtual disappearance of all pre-war political organizations (except the Mensheviks and the N.T.S.) and the far more practical attitude towards Soviet reality and its problems as a result of the arrival in emigration of people with experience of life under Soviet conditions. The prevalent political stand has been revolutionary, although the emergence of reformism (q.v.) in Russia since Stalin's death has met with general sympathy and support among *émigrés*, and a programme of practical reforms was drawn up at a conference at The Hague in 1957, some of which have actually been implemented since in Russia (e.g. the abolition of the M.T.S.). There exist at present three main groupings in the emigration: an unofficial coalition of centre and moderate right organizations (the N.T.S., the Central League of Political Émigrés, the Russian National League and several federalist groups of national minorities); the so-called Paris Bloc of separatist national minority groups and certain left-wing Russian elements; and the fascist A.B.N. ('Anti-Bolshevik Bloc of Nations') led by western Ukrainians (*see* BANDERA). *See* G. Fischer, *Russian Émigré Politics*, New York, 1951; W. H. Chamberlin, 'Émigré Anti-Soviet Enterprises and Splits,' *Russian Review*, April 1954.

Engel's (until 1930's **Pokrovsk**), town in the Saratov Oblast, situated on the Volga opposite Saratov, of which economically it forms a part. Population (1959) 90,000, Russian and Ukrainian, until 1941 also German. It has meat-packing, engineering and textile industries. Engel's was founded by the Ukrainian Cossacks in the 18th century; from 1922 to 1941 it was the capital, economic and cultural centre of the Volga German Autonomous Republic.

Engineering Industry. The following table shows the output of selected products of the industry.

	1913[1]	1928	1940	1945	1950	1953	1958
Metal-cutting lathes[2]	1·8	2·0	58·4	38·4	70·6	91·8	138·6
Forging and pressing machines[2]	—	—	4·7	—	7·7	11·2	25·0
Metallurgical equipment[3]	—	—	23·7	—	111·2	172·1 [4]	172·7
Oil equipment[3]	—	—	15·5	1·0	47·9	48·8 [4]	72·7
Chemical equipment[3]	—	—	—	—	42·9	111·2 [4]	
Turbines ('000 kw.)	5·9	44·1	1,179	230	2,696	4,755	6,631
Locomotives	477	479	928	8	1,212	916	1,056
Rolling-stock ('000s)	11·0	8·7	31·0	—	52·0	27·0	43·0
Tractors[5] ('000s)	—	1·3	31·6	7·7	108·8	111·3	219·7
Grain combine harvesters[6] ('000s)	—	—	12·8	0·3	46·3	43·1	65·0
Looms ('000s)	4·6	3·7	1·8	0·01	8·7	10·2	14·4

The engineering industry is chiefly concentrated in central Russia, the Southern Industrial Region (q.v.), the Urals, the Volga region and western Siberia. The principal centres are Moscow and Leningrad, Gor'kiy, Yaroslavl', Minsk, Kiev, Khar'kov, Sverdlovsk, Chelyabinsk, Perm' Kuybyshev, Novosibirsk and Krasnoyarsk. Heavy engineering tends to concentrate in the proximity of the large iron and steel plants (the Donbas, the Urals, the Kuznetsk Basin); at the opposite extreme are such branches as electrical equipment, precision instruments, etc., which are found where skilled labour is easily available, e.g. Leningrad, Riga. *See also* CAR INDUSTRY; CONSUMER GOODS.

Enterprise, official Soviet term for a State-owned or co-operative firm, including State farms (*see* SOVKHOZ) but not *kolkhozes*. As a unit of production or trade a Soviet enterprise is essentially similar to firms of other countries, with the same diversity of size and vertical and horizontal forms of integration. In 1955 there were 206,000 industrial enterprises belonging to the State (producing 92 per cent of total industrial output), 135,000 co operative industrial enterprises (7 per cent of total output) and 350,000 small industrial enterprises belonging to *kolkhozes*. In 1956, 86·5 per cent of all manufacturing enterprises (except the smallest) employed up to five hundred men (91·6 per cent in 1913) and together they employed 26·3 per cent of all workers (41·1 per cent in 1913); enterprises with over a thousand workers made up 6·9 per cent in 1956 (3·9 per cent in 1913), employing together 60·7 per cent of all workers (43·7 per cent

---

[1] Present-day frontiers. [2] Thousands. [3] Thousand tons. [4] 1955.
[5] The peak output of tractors before the war was 112,900 in 1936.
[6] 43,900 grain combine harvesters were produced in 1937, and 131,500 in 1957.

in 1913). *See also* INDUSTRIAL MANAGEMENT and for trade enter-prises RETAIL TRADE. *See* J. S. Berliner, *Factory and Manager in the U.S.S.R.*, Cambridge, Mass., 1957.

Equality. Theoretically there exists in the Soviet Union basic social and political equality, since all citizens share the ownership of the means of production held by the State, and in the Marxist view it is private ownership of the means of production that is the foundation of all inequality. However, two important sources of inequality are not only sanctioned by the constitution (q.v.) but in fact form the very basis of the present social and political order: the principle of distribution (officially considered socialist) 'to each according to his work,' and the political monopoly of the Communist Party (q.v.). The former results in a range of incomes and other material benefits which is not less than in other societies, since official evaluation of an individual's work varies greatly and material incentives are ex-tensively used to raise the productivity of work and readiness to comply with other requirements of the authorities. The taxation system (*see* INCOME-TAX) and the inheritance (q.v.) law work in the same direction. The political monopoly of the Communist Party, with its highly *élitist* ideology and strictly hierarchical structure, leads to the establishment of hierarchies in all the other fields of activity which are controlled by the party (*see* CADRES; NOMENCLATURE). Equality of opportunity (through education, party membership, etc.), though frequently declared, is constantly violated by the policy of preferential treatment for various categories of people, and is in fact little more than a myth (q.v.). Egalitarian tendencies in material and social spheres were strong in the party until the early 1930's (*see* MAKHAYEVISM), though they were never particularly effective. Stalin in 1931 denounced egalitarianism as a 'petty bourgeois absurdity,' and in the following years created an elaborate system of inequalities of income and rank which permeated the whole society. Since his death some half-hearted attempts have been made to narrow the income range; official ranks have been abolished in several civilian ministries, and a reform of the inheritance law is being canvassed which would make it impossible to live on the interest from inherited capital. *See also* CLASSES. *See* N. S. Timasheff, *The Great Retreat*, New York, 1946; B. Moore, Jr, *Soviet Politics, the Dilemma of Power*, Cambridge, Mass., 1950; R. N. Carew Hunt, *A Guide to Communist Jargon*, 1957.

Erivan', *see* YEREVAN.

Esenin, *see* YESENIN.

Estland, most northerly of the Baltic Provinces, now forming part of Estonia. The area was subjugated and christianized by the Livonian Knights, 1211–27, and was ceded in 1238 to Denmark as the Duchy of Estland. It became Livonian once more in 1346, Swedish in 1561 and Russian in 1721.

Estonia (Estonian **Eesti** or **Eestimaa**), Union Republic of the U.S.S.R., bordering on the Gulf of Finland in the north, Latvia in the south, the Baltic Sea in the west and Lake Chudskoye in the east; it is mainly lowland plain, partially forested, with many lakes and marshes and a soft, almost maritime climate; there are large deposits of oil-shale. Area 17,800 sq. m.; population (1959) 1,197,000 (56 per cent urban), mostly Estonians (73 per cent), also Russians (22 per cent), before the war also Germans. There are oil-shale extraction and processing, electrical engineering, textile, wood-processing and food (bacon and butter) industries; dairy farming and pig raising are carried on, and grain, potatoes, vegetables and flax cultivated. Principal towns: Tallinn (capital), Tartu, Pärnu, Narva, Kohtla-Järve. For history *see* BALTIC PROVINCES; BALTIC STATES; EST-LAND. During the period of Estonian independence (1919–40) the country's industry declined, being cut off from the Russian market, but agriculture flourished with the export of butter and bacon to Britain and Germany. At first independent Estonia was a democratic republic, but in 1934 a dictatorship was established under President Päts, the leader of the most influential Agrarian Party, though this was later modified and a kind of representative assembly with limited powers was introduced. A Communist uprising in Tallinn was suppressed in 1924. *See* J. H. Jackson, *Estonia*, 1948; A. Oras, *Baltic Eclipse*, 1948; V. Druzhinin, *Soviet Estonia, a Survey*, Moscow, 1953; V. Rand, *Estonia*, 1953.

Estonians, Finnish-speaking people inhabiting Estonia, and living also in considerable numbers in Siberia as a result of colonization before 1917 and deportations since 1940. They are Lutheran Protestants (with an Orthodox minority of about 10 per cent) and number (1959) 969,000. The Estonians are the indigenous inhabitants of the area, but have always been under the influence and domination of Scandinavians, Germans or Russians; only in the 19th century did an Estonian national consciousness and movement develop. For history *see* BALTIC PROVINCES; BALTIC STATES.

Eupatoria, *see* YEVPATORIYA.

Eurasians ('*Yevraziytsy*'), ideological and political movement which existed during the 1920's and thirties among Russian *émigrés*; they emphasized the Asiatic factors in the making of Russia and the Asiatic elements in Russian culture (e.g. the philologist Prince N. S. Trubetskoy, the economist and geographer P. N. Savitskiy and the historian G. Vernadsky). Some prominent Eurasians, e.g. Prince D. S. Svyatopolk-Mirsky, ultimately came to regard Soviet Russia as the true expression of the 'Eurasian' nature of Russia.

Evenki (old name **Tungus**), Tungus-speaking people who live scattered over a huge area in Siberia, from the River Yenisey to the Sea of Okhotsk, numbering (1959) 24,000 (38,000 in 1939). They have been known since the 14th century, and subjected to Russia since the 17th. The Evenki are semi-nomadic and engage in fur-trapping, fishing and reindeer breeding; their pagan religious practices are known as Shamanism.

Evenki National Okrug lies within the Krasnoyarsk Kray. Area 287,600 sq. m.; population (1959) 10,000 (20 per cent urban), mainly Russians, some Evenki. There are large mineral resources (Tungus coal basin) scarcely yet exploited. The National Okrug was established in 1930; its administrative centre is Tura. *See* W. Kolarz, *Russia and her Colonies*, 1952.

Eykhenbaum, *see* FORMALISM.

F

Fadeyev (real name **Bulyga**), **Aleksandr Aleksandrovich** (1901–56), outstanding representative of the group of proletarian writers, much influenced by L. Tolstoy. His best novels are *The Rout*, 1927, dealing with Siberian Red guerrillas during the civil war, and *The Young Guard*, 1945, about a young patriots' guerrilla group in the Donets Basin behind the German lines (*see* YOUNG GUARD). Fadeyev, a member of the Communist Party since 1918 and a member of its Central Committee, exercised much influence upon the development of Soviet literature, and was general secretary of the Writers' Union from 1946 to 1955. He played a leading part in Zhdanov's post-war campaign for Socialist Realism (q.v.) against any trace of freedom or realism in literature, but in 1947 was himself charged with failing to give sufficient prominence to the role of the party in *The Young Guard* and was compelled to produce a new version in 1951. In his latter years Fadeyev became an alcoholic, and finally committed suicide after Khrushchëv's denunciation of Stalin at the 20th party congress (q.v.).

Family, as in other modern societies, normally consists of two generations, parents and children. However, traditionally the Russian family, especially among peasants, has included also the grandparents, and this is still frequently the case. This fact is recognized in Soviet law, which has no provision for the inheritance of a peasant household (q.v.) since it passes naturally from one generation to the next. Among the Muslim peoples polygamy can still be found, though officially it is illegal (*see further under* CRIMINAL LAW). In Marxist theory the family of the future Communist society was to be simply a free association of individuals, ungoverned by any contract or tradition and not responsible for the upbringing of children, who should be in the care of the community. In the 1920's and early thirties energetic attempts were made by the Communists to bring about such a state of affairs and to undermine the family as an institution. However, resistance was strong, and Stalin's general policy of the restoration of traditional social forms that began in the mid thirties put an end to these efforts. It is officially regarded as part of the family's duty to bring up children with correct ideological and political attitudes, though in fact it is generally realized that the influence of the family is likely to contribute to heterodox views. *See also* CHILDREN; MARRIAGE; WOMEN. *See* W. Petersen, 'The Evolution of Soviet Family Policy,' *Problems of Communism*, vol. v, No. 5, Sept.–Oct. 1956; F. E. Moseley, 'The Russian Family: Old Style and New,' in R. N. Anshen's (ed.) *The Family: its Function and Destiny*, revised ed., New York, 1959.

Famines have periodically occurred in Russia because of drought (q.v.). In earlier times they frequently caused peasant unrest and rioting in the towns. The severe famine of 1891–2, following the comparatively calm 1880's, aroused renewed social and political activity on the part of the opposition. It is memorable for the relief work led by L. Tolstoy, and the sharp clash it caused between Populists and Marxists headed by Plekhanov, the latter considering the impoverishment of the peasantry advantageous for the development of capitalism and thus ultimately for the cause of proletarian revolution. The famine of 1921, adding as it did to the already great misery caused by the civil war and the policy of War Communism, gave great impetus to the New Economic Policy (qq.v.); internal relief work was headed by Gor'kiy and other non-Communist intellectuals (e.g. Kuskova), most of whom were thereupon expelled from Russia, and foreign relief work was chiefly undertaken by American and British missions, many of them Quakers. The next famine, that of 1932–3, was created artificially by the authorities as a means of breaking the resistance of the peasants to the collectivization of agriculture (q.v.); the harvests in those years were adequate (and indeed grain was exported), but the grain was removed from the countryside by armed detachments chiefly composed of internal security troops and Komsomol members; many towns in the areas principally affected (the Ukraine, North Caucasus, the Volga region, and Kazakhstan) also suffered.

The last famine, in 1946–7, was partly caused by a drought, but partly, especially in the areas unaffected by the drought (such as central Russia), by the peasants' resistance to the rigorous restoration of the collective farm system which had been somewhat relaxed in the war years (*see* COUNCIL FOR COLLECTIVE FARMS). One result of this famine was the delay, compared to other countries, of the postwar upward trend in the birth-rate. At the time the Soviet Government denied the existence of the famine and refused all offers of help from abroad.

Far East, Russian, comprises the Maritime and Khabarovsk krays and the Amur, Magadan, Kamchatka and Sakhalin oblasts of the R.S.F.S.R.; the Chita Oblast is sometimes also regarded as belonging to the Far East. The area was gradually annexed by Russia between 1649 and 1875; a part of Sakhalin and the Kurile Islands were subsequently lost temporarily to Japan, but restored to Russia in 1945. Area 1,243,500 sq. m.; population (1959, without Chita Oblast) 4,508,000, chiefly Russian and Ukrainian colonists, the indigenous Tungus and Paleo-Asiatic peoples being almost extinct or assimilated (before 1938–45 there was also a large Japanese, Korean and Chinese population, now expelled or deported). The colonists of the area developed strong regional tendencies in the early 20th century, and these were partially expressed in the creation of the Far Eastern Republic and the somewhat special position of the Far Eastern Kray 1926–38. It has been a place of banishment and forced labour camps. *See also* DAL'STROY. *See* W. Kolarz, *The Peoples of the Soviet Far East*, 1954; E. Thiel, *The Soviet Far East*, 1957; A. Malozemoff, *Russian Far Eastern Policy, 1881–1904*, Berkeley and Los Angeles, 1958.

Far Eastern Republic, transitory buffer state between Soviet Russia and Japan which existed 1920–2 in the Russian Far East. It was formally an independent democratic republic, but in fact one of the first 'people's democracies,' dominated by Communists. It was annexed to Russia after the Japanese departure from Vladivostok.

Farmanyants, Georgiy (*b.* 1922), dancer. After entering the Bolshoi Theatre School, Moscow, he graduated in 1940, becoming principal male dancer. A recipient of many honours and awards, he is reckoned one of the finest character dancers in present-day Russia.

Fascists have not played an important role in Russian political development, although proto-fascist organizations (*see* BLACK HUNDRED) were active during the revolution of 1905 (q.v.). Fascist groups existed among Russian *émigrés* in the 1920's and thirties, but they were small in numbers and insignificant. Fascist traits were predominant in the organization of the Young Russians (who became Soviet patriots immediately after the Second World War, many of them, including their leader Kazembek, returning to Russia) and a certain influence of the early Italian fascism was felt in the N.T.S. (q.v.). However, during the Great Purge (q.v.) the term fascist was used indiscriminately for all real or imaginary opponents of Stalinism (q.v.), and the alleged prevalence of fascist conspiracies served as a justification for the purge itself. A fascist grouping exists in the post-Second World War emigration (*see* ÉMIGRÉS).

Favorskiy, Aleksey Yevgrafovich (1860–1945), chemist. Educated at St Petersburg University (under Mendeleyev and Butlerov, qq.v.), he was professor there from 1896, member of the Academy of Sciences from 1929 and founder and director of its Institute of Organic Chemistry, 1934–8. He was among the pioneers in the chemistry of non-saturated organic combinations, and for many years worked on acetylene and synthetic rubber. Among his many pupils was Ipat'yev (q.v.).

February Revolution, 1917, downfall of the monarchy and the establishment of the 'dual power' (q.v.) of the Provisional Government and the Soviets of Workers' and Soldiers' Deputies (qq.v.). From 1915 the leaders of the liberal groupings in the Duma (*see* CONSTITUTIONAL DEMOCRATS) and in the country (*see* UNION OF ZEMSTVOS) had been engaged in a semi-conspiracy aimed at replacing the bureaucratic government by one which would enjoy the confidence of the country. Such was the loss of trust in Nicholas II and his government that disorders in the capital were sufficient to persuade him to abdicate. Throughout Russia the change-over came about peacefully and was welcomed. But in the midst of war the Provisional Government and the country at large proved unequal to the immense task of democratic reconstruction (especially the urgent need for land reform), and they failed to face successfully the appearance of a new phenomenon—the emergence on the political scene of a totalitarian power, the Bolsheviks. *See further under* CONSTITUENT ASSEMBLY; KERENSKIY; OCTOBER REVOLUTION. See A. J. Sack, *The Birth of the Russian Democracy*, New York, 1918; F. A. Golder, *Documents of Russian History, 1914–17*, 1927; A. F. Kerensky, *The Catastrophe*, 1927; C. E. Vulliamy (ed.), *From the Red Archives*, 1929;

B. Pares, *My Russian Memoirs*, 1931; M. T. Florinsky, *The End of the Russian Empire*, New Haven, 1931; L. Trotsky, *The History of the Russian Revolution* (3 vols.), 1932–3; B. Pares, *The Fall of the Russian Monarchy*, 1939; W. H. Chamberlin, *The Russian Revolution*, vol. i, New York, 1954; N. Sukhanov, *The Russian Revolution*, 1955; S. P. Mel'gunov, *Legenda o separatnom mire*, Paris, 1957; O. Anweiler, *Die Rätebewegung in Russland, 1905–21*, Leiden, 1958; M. Paleologue, *An Ambassador's Memoirs* (3 vols.), New York, s.a.

Federalism, ostensibly a principle on which the government of the Soviet Union is based. In fact the country is ruled by the strictly centralized Communist Party (q.v.) and the federal nature of the U.S.S.R. is largely a fiction (q.v.) designed to prevent the re-emergence of genuine federalist or separatist trends. Federalist tendencies have in fact deep roots in Russian history. In modern times a federal reorganization of Russia was advocated by the Decembrists, Populists, Regionalists and the party of Socialist Revolutionaries (qq.v.). After the February revolution (q.v.) of 1917 it was proclaimed by all the main non-Great Russian political movements (the Central Rada in the Ukraine, the All-Russian Muslim Union, etc.), and the Provisional Government (q.v.) took the first practical steps towards its implementation. The concept of federalism was rejected by the Bolsheviks before 1917, but in the years following their seizure of power (*see* OCTOBER REVOLUTION) Lenin adopted it as a useful stratagem, and insisted on a quasi-federal structure of the Soviet state as against Stalin's concept of autonomism. *See also* AUTONOMY; NATIONALITIES POLICY; UNION REPUBLIC. *See* J. Towster, *Political Power in the U.S.S.R., 1917–47*, New York, 1948; E. H. Carr, *A History of Soviet Russia: the Bolshevik Revolution*, vol. i, 1950; W. Kolarz, *Russia and her Colonies*, 1952; M. Fainsod, *How Russia is Ruled*, Cambridge, Mass., 1953; R. Pipes, *The Formation of the Soviet Union*, Cambridge, Mass., 1954; R. Schlesinger (ed.), *The Nationalities Problem and Soviet Administration*, 1956; J. N. Hazard, *The Soviet System of Government*, Chicago, 1957; D. J. R. Scott, *Russian Political Institutions*, 1958.

Fedin, Konstantin Aleksandrovich (*b.* 1892), novelist, a fellow traveller (q.v.). With his *Cities and Years*, 1924, he revived in post-revolutionary Russia the realistic novel. His chief themes are the revolution and civil war and the impact of revolutionary Russia upon Europe (*The Brothers*, 1928, *The Abduction of Europe*, 1934–5, *First Joys*, 1945, *An Extraordinary Summer*, 1948). He became head of the Moscow writers' organization after Stalin's death, and in 1959 he replaced Surkov (q.v.) as the Secretary-General of the Writers' Union (q.v.). He is widely respected for his moderate stand in matters of literary policy. *See* E. J. Simmons, *Russian Fiction and Soviet Ideology*, New York, 1958.

Fëdorov, Ivan Fëdorovich (*d.* 1583), first printer in Russia, producing the first printed book in Moscow in 1563. He continued his work in Lithuania and Poland, where he fled from Muscovy.

Fëdorov, Nikolay Fëdorovich (1828–1903), thinker who worked for twenty-five years as librarian in the Rumyantsev Museum (now the Lenin Library) in Moscow. He believed that the ideal society of the future—classless and universal—would be founded upon the conquest of the forces of nature and would concentrate all its energies upon the paramount task of resurrecting the dead (*The Philosophy of the Common Cause*, 1906). Many of Fëdorov's ideas have been widely popular during the Soviet period; they have influenced scientific research, technical development (e.g. towards the utilization of solar energy and interplanetary travel), various organizations (the Local Studies Movement) and even government policy (e.g. the establishment of labour armies in 1920). *See* N. Lossky, *History of Russian Philosophy*, 1951; V. V. Zenkovsky, *A History of Russian Philosophy*, vol. ii, 1953; S. V. Utechin, 'Bolsheviks and their Allies after 1917: the Ideological Pattern,' *Soviet Studies*, vol. x, No. 2, Oct. 1958; R. Hare, *Portraits of Russian Personalities between Reform and Revolution*, 1959.

Fëdorov, Yevgraf Stepanovich (1853–1919), mineralogist, professor of the Moscow Agricultural Institute, in 1905–10 elected director of the St Petersburg Mining Institute. In his classical work *Symmetry of the Regular Systems of Figures*, 1890, Fëdorov described all the 230 possible groups of symmetry in space, determining the location of elementary particles in crystal systems. He invented the two-circle goniometer (or theodolite-goniometer) and a universal optical table named after him.

Fedotov, Pavel Andreyevich (1815–52), *genre* painter, largely self-taught. In his small well-painted canvases Fedotov satirized the everyday life and morals of the newly rich merchants and the impoverished nobility. Often called 'the Russian Hogarth,' he was free of bitterness towards the subjects of his satire and his work was denounced as deficient in social criticism by the radical members of the Peredvizhniki (q.v.), for whose advent in the 1860's Fedotov's art prepared the ground.

Fellow Traveller, name applied by Russian Communists in the 1920's to those intellectuals, especially writers, who were not Communists but were prepared to accept the Soviet regime. *See further under* NATIONAL BOLSHEVISM; R.A.P.P.

Feodosiya (ancient **Theodosia**, then **Kaffa** until 1804), Black Sea port in south-eastern Crimea. Population (1956) 42,600, mostly Russians. It has tobacco and hosiery industries, and a pleasant sand beach. There are the ruins of medieval walls, and the town has an archaeological museum, 1811, and a gallery of the paintings of Ayvazovskiy. Feodosiya was founded in the 6th century B.C. by the Greeks, and was a flourishing centre of the Black Sea Genoese colonies from 1260 to 1475, when it became Turkish; it has been Russian since 1774. There was much fighting in the area 1941–2.

Feofan Grek (Theophanes 'the Greek'), painter of Greek origin who was active in Russia in the late 14th century and died between 1405 and 1419. His frescoes were discovered during the restoration of the Church of the Transfiguration, Novgorod, in 1918. Evidently brought up in the Constantinople of the first Paleologos, Feofan adjusted his Byzantine Renaissance style to the simpler, less sophisticated Russian requirements. His frescoes are full of energy and dynamism; the holy images possess deep psychological penetration but are painted in free and laconic brush strokes with perfect precision of the mass and of the white linear highlights.

Fergana: 1. Oblast in Uzbekistan situated in the central part of the Fergana Valley, traversed by the Fergana circular railway and the Great Fergana Canal. Area (1959) 2,700 sq. m.; population 938,000 (32 per cent urban), mostly Uzbeks and Tadzhiks. Cotton growing, sericulture and horticulture are highly developed; there are textile and food industries, oil extraction and processing; fertilizers and building materials are also produced. Principal towns: Kokand, Fergana, Margelan. For history *see* FERGANA VALLEY; KOKAND KHANATE.

2. (formerly **Novyy Margelan,** then **Skobelev**). Administrative and an economic and cultural centre of the oblast. Population (1959) 80,000 (1939, 36,000). It has textile (cotton and silk) and food industries, and there is coal and oil extraction in the vicinity. Fergana was founded in 1865 by the Russians as the administrative centre of the Fergana Valley.

Fergana Valley, region in Central Asia north of Pamir, enclosed by mountain ranges of the Tien-Shan system and traversed by the middle course of the River Syr-Dar'ya, about 8,000 sq. m. in area; it is flat desert in the centre, which is surrounded by the largest, most densely populated (about 3½ million) and highly developed oasis in Central Asia. There are oil, coal, rare metals and other deposits, but the region's main economic importance is as the principal cotton-growing area in the U.S.S.R. All the main centres of the oasis are connected by a circular railway, and there are many irrigation canals, including the Great Fergana Canal (170 m. long), which was built in six weeks in 1939 by compulsory labour of all the peasants in the area. For administrative purposes the region is divided between the Uzbek, Tadzhik and Kirgiz republics: the Uzbek part, in the centre of the valley, is divided into the Andizhan and Fergana oblasts; the Tadzhik portion, in the west, forms part of Leninabad Oblast; and the Kirgiz part comprises the mountain slopes in the north, east and south, and forms the Osh Oblast.

From ancient times Fergana was one of the principal centres of population, crafts and commerce in Central Asia; politically weaker than the other two main centres, Khorezm and the Zeravshan Valley, it was frequently subordinated to the latter. However, in the 18th century a powerful khanate of Kokand arose, whose core was the Fergana Valley. The khanate was conquered and annexed by Russia in 1864, and the valley was included as an oblast in Russian Turkestan. During the civil war the Fergana Valley formed the nucleus of the anti-Bolshevik Autonomous Turkestan Government, with Kokand as its capital. After the defeat of this government the valley was one of the main centres of the Basmachi (q.v.) guerrilla movement until well into the 1930's. The so-called 'national delimitation of Central Asia' (q.v.) in 1924, and subsequent changes in administrative divisions, were partly aimed at splitting up the historical, cultural and political unity of the Fergana Valley.

Fersman, Aleksandr Yevgen'yevich (1883–1945), geologist. Educated at Odessa, Moscow, Paris and Heidelberg universities, he taught in Moscow and St Petersburg and was elected a member of the Academy of Sciences in 1919, concentrating thereafter on work in the academy. A pupil of Vernadskiy (q.v.), Fersman developed and continued his work in mineralogy and geochemistry (*Geochemistry*, 4 vols., 1933–9), studying mineral deposits not only in Russia (apatites in the Kola Peninsula, radium ores in Fergana, etc.) but also in a number of western European countries. He laid the foundations of regional geochemistry and gave a geochemical description of European Russia.

Fertilizers. The production of mineral fertilizers amounted to 12·4 million tons in 1958 (0·07 in 1913, 0·1 in 1928, 3·2 in 1940, 5·5 in 1950, 9·6 in 1955). Mineral fertilizer production is mainly concentrated in the chemical plants of the Ukraine, the Moscow area, the Urals, Leningrad and the Tashkent Oblast in Central Asia. Until the late 1920's mineral fertilizers played an insignificant role in agriculture, manure being the principal fertilizer used. With the halving of livestock during the collectivization of agriculture (q.v.) and the very small production of mineral fertilizers, the soil was starved over a long period, and only since Stalin's death in 1953 have efforts been made to improve the situation.

Fet (real name **Shenshin**), **Afanasiy Afanas'yevich** (1820–92), impressionist, lyric and mystic poet (*Evening Lights*, 4 vols., 1883–1891), a leading representative of the 'art for art's sake' school. He was also an eminent translator of Shakespeare, the classical Latin poets, Goethe and Schopenhauer.

Fictions constitute a very important element in the Communist power system. In Bentham's definition, 'A fictitious entity is an entity to which, though by the grammatical form of the discourse employed in speaking of it existence is ascribed, yet in truth and reality existence is not meant to be ascribed. . . . The fiction . . . is the mode of representation by which the fictitious entities thus created . . . are dressed up in the garb, and placed upon the level, of real ones.' Much of the official Communist ideology, propaganda and agitation (qq.v.) is fictitious, the function of these official fictions being not to convince but to ensure ostensibly conformist behaviour. Thus fictions are different from myths (q.v.), which are believed by a part of the population, though some myths gradually degenerate into fictions, and what is a fiction in Russia may be a myth abroad. The majority of fictions now in use relate to the internal life of the country, and have been deliberately created as fictions, i.e. they are not meant to be believed in Russia. Indeed to take fictions at their face value might be very dangerous. When no longer convenient, fictions are either quietly dropped and not mentioned thereafter, or else condemned as deviations or distortions of the correct interpretation of the relevant basic doctrine (e.g. the discarding of the fiction of Stalin as the incarnation of absolute wisdom and benevolence). Some of the main fictions are: the fictionalized history, particularly of the party itself; the 'moral and political unity of the Soviet people'; the 'most democratic constitution in the world'; the principle of distribution 'to each according to his work'; the 'happy and prosperous life'; 'socialist humanism'; the 'freedom of learning and art'; the 'people's love for the Soviet state, the Communist Party and its leaders'; the 'labour enthusiasm of the Soviet people'; 'vigilance'; the 'people's wrath' (against foreign 'imperialists' or internal 'enemies of the people'); and 'criticism and self-criticism' (q.v.). The effectiveness of fictions is conditional upon sanctions for noncon-formism, and the period of the greatest flourishing of fictions (which the Bolsheviks had begun to use already before 1917) was that of Stalin's terror (*see* STALINISM), when universal dissembling was perhaps the most obvious feature of the mode of life. The relaxation of terror after Stalin's death resulted in the demonstration by the intellectual opposition (q.v.) of the true nature of most fictions, and they have lost some of their coercive force. The role of fictions in Communist theory and Soviet life has been systematically studied by the 'axiological' school of Sovietology (q.v.). *See* J. Bentham, *Theory of Fictions* (ed. C. K. Ogden), 1932; R. Redlich (ed.), *Ocherki bol'-shevizmovedeniya*, Frankfurt-on-Main, 1956.

Filatov, Vladimir Petrovich (1875–1956), ophthalmologist and surgeon, taught at Moscow and Odessa universities. He became famous for his work on transplantation of the cornea and tissue therapy.

Finance, *see* BUDGET; CREDIT; INVESTMENT.

Finns, group of peoples of northern and eastern Europe, belonging racially to three sub-races of the White or Europeoid race—the Nordic, the Baltic and the Ural—and speaking languages of the Finnish family, which is related to the Ugrian. They are divided into four sub-groups: (1) the Baltic, including the Finns proper of Finland, the Karelians, the Estonians and a number of smaller peoples (largely russianized), e.g. the Ingrians; (2) the Lapps; (3) the Volga Finns—the Mordva and the Mari; and (4) the Permian Finns—the Udmurts and the Komi. Since ancient times they have lived in their present areas, exposed to the pressure of powerful neighbours—Scandinavians, Germans and Russians—and usually under their rule. A number of Finnish tribes which inhabited what is now the centre and north of European Russia were assimilated by the Russians, and the Great Russians are largely the result of this process. Christianized by their neighbours, the Finns fell under their cultural influence, and the use of Finnish languages for writing started comparatively late—Komi in the 14th century, Finnish and Estonian in the 16th and others in the 19th–20th centuries.

First International, usual name for the International Workmen's Association founded by Marx in 1864 which existed until 1873. The leaders of Russian revolutionary Populism, Bakunin and Lavrov (qq.v.), joined it while in emigration, and a Russian section of the International formed by followers of Chernyshevskiy (q.v.) existed in Geneva in 1870–2. The Russian section sided with Marx against Bakunin in the struggle between State socialists and anarchists. Some of its members took an active part in the Paris Commune; others later participated in the first social democratic organizations in St Petersburg.

Fishing Industry. In 1958 the fish catch (including sea animals) amounted to 2,931,000 tons (1,018,000 in 1913; 840,000 in 1928;

2,849,000 in 1956). The principal fishing grounds are the Barents and White seas (30 per cent in 1956), the Far East (24 per cent), the Caspian Sea (17 per cent) and the Baltic Sea (10 per cent); part of the northern and Baltic fishing fleet makes its catch in the Atlantic (about 8 per cent of the total). There is a special whaling fleet operating in the Antarctic and whales make up 5·6 per cent of the total catch; the catch of crabs is concentrated along the shores of Kamchatka. The River Volga and its tributaries, and the Sea of Azov, have had their rich fish resources decimated by pollution and haphazard fishing over the last twenty years. The largest and most modern fish processing plants are in Murmansk and Astrakhan'.

Five Year Plans, plans for the development of the country's economy. The first Five Year Plan covered the years 1928–32, the second 1933–7, the third 1938–42 (implementation interrupted by the war), the fourth 1946–50, the fifth 1951–5, and the sixth was intended to cover the years 1956–60. However, this last plan was scrapped in 1957, and its two last years have been included in the current Seven Year Plan (q.v.). *See further under* GOSPLAN; PLANNING. *See* M. Dobb, *Soviet Economic Development since 1917*, 1948; H. Schwartz, *Russia's Soviet Economy*, 2nd ed., 1951; H. Chambre, *L'Aménagement du territoire en U.R.S.S.*, Paris and The Hague, 1959; *The Soviet Seven Year Plan* (introduction by A. Nove), 1960.

Florenskiy, Pavel Aleksandrovich (1882–?), Orthodox priest, philosopher, theologian, physicist and universal erudite. As a student he was one of the founders of the Union of Christian Struggle, which advocated a radical renovation of social life on the basis of the Christian faith. As a lecturer of the Moscow Theological Academy he published in 1914 his main work, *The Pillar and Foundation of Truth*, an attempt at an Orthodox theodicy with the help of a philosophy of All-Unity (*see* SOLOV'ËV, V. S.). Shortly after the Bolshevik seizure of power he was banished to Central Asia, but soon returned and for some time worked at the Academy of Sciences in the field of advanced physics. However, in the 1920's he was deported to the Solovetskiy concentration camp, and the last thing known of him is that he was transferred from there to a camp in Siberia. Florenskiy's ideas have considerably stimulated subsequent Russian philosophical and theological thought; Losev (q.v.) in particular, especially his cosmological views and his philosophy of the name, appears to have been much influenced by him. *See* N. Lossky, *History of Russian Philosophy*, 1952; V. V. Zenkovsky, *A History of Russian Philosophy*, vol. ii, 1953.

Florovskiy, Georgiy Vasil'yevich (*b.* 1893), theologian and philosopher, Orthodox priest, professor at the Russian Theological Institute in Paris and subsequently at the St Vladimir Theological Seminary in New York. His *magnum opus*, *The Ways of Russian Theology* (Paris, 1937), broke new ground in its interpretation of the history of Russian thought.

Fok, Vladimir Aleksandrovich (*b.* 1898), outstanding physicist and mathematician. Educated at Petrograd University, he has been professor there since 1932 and member of the Academy of Sciences since 1939. He has made important contributions to quantum mechanics, quantum electrodynamics, the theory of light diffraction, the general theory of relativity and many fields of mathematics and mathematical physics. He has always stood up for the rights of physicists, and in 1953, shortly before Stalin's death, published an article in *Voprosy Filosofii* (q.v.) entitled 'Against Ignorant Criticism of Present-Day Physical Theories.' See J. G. Crowther, *Soviet Science*, 1936.

Fokin, M. D., leader of a transitional semi-Populist, semi-Marxist underground organization which existed under different names (Populist Socialists, Marxists, etc.) in 1884–1903. Sharing with the Narodnaya Volya (q.v.) Tkachëv's 'Jacobin' view of a seizure of power by a revolutionary minority as a prerequisite for a socialist reconstruction of society, but disappointed with the tactics of Narodnaya Volya, Fokin and his associates devoted themselves to the selection and training of personnel needed for this task; at the same time they were striving to create among workers and intellectuals an atmosphere favourable to the idea of such a revolution. They thus anticipated Lenin's strategy. Lenin himself joined one of Fokin's circles in Kazan' in 1887. Russian social democracy in the Volga area and in Khar'kov sprang directly from Fokin's organization.

Fokine, Mikhail Mikhaylovich (1880–1942), dancer and choreographer. A pupil of Karsavin, Gerdt and Legat at the Imperial Ballet School of the Mariinskiy Theatre, he was later engaged there as a soloist, 1898. Though outstanding as a dancer, he studied choreography with Johansson, at the same time favouring the ideas propagated in Diaghilev's *Mir Iskusstva*. Two further influences in the forming of his artistic credo were the performances of the Siamese hand ballet and the theories of Isadora Duncan, whose dancing furnished him with many new ideas. His first ballets, in 1905, were *Acis and Galatea* and *The Dying Swan*, the role immortalized by Pavlova, and these were followed by numerous works, most successful being *Le Pavillon d'Armide*, 1907, and *Une Nuit d'Égypte*, 1908. In the latter year he was introduced, through Benois, to Diaghilev, with the result that he was invited to act as choreographer for the first season of the Ballets Russes at Paris the next year. Fokine's contributions were *Le Pavillon d'Armide*, *Les Sylphides*, *Cléopâtre* and, most of all, the 'Polovtsian Dances' from *Prince Igor*, which achieved unprecedented success. The year 1910 saw the production of *Carnaval*, *Shoboranado* and *The Fire Bird*, in which he danced with Karsavina. In 1911 Fokine was engaged only as choreographer as Nijinsky wished to have no opposition. Nevertheless he created four new ballets, *Le Spectre de la Rose*, *Narcisse*, *Sadko* and *Petrushka*. In the final year of Fokine's collaboration with Diaghilev, 1912, his ballets included *Le Train Bleu* and *Thamar*. Following the ill-fated performance of *Daphnis and Chloë* Fokine returned to Russia, but two years later was persuaded to rejoin Diaghilev as dancer and choreographer. With the outbreak of war he again returned to Russia but was unable to settle down. Leaving his native land in 1918 he worked in Europe and America, but it was not till he joined René Blum and the Ballets de Monte Carlo that he was able to recapture his former genius. After a short period with Colonel de Basil in 1937 he spent his last years in America, his final production being the ballet *Russian Soldier* (Ballet Theatre, 1941) based on Prokof'yev's suite *Lieutenant Kizhe*. He died in New York.

Fokine's contribution to ballet was the exact counterpart of the efforts of Bakst, Benois and Diaghilev. Independent geniuses, united in their beliefs that music, costume and painting were 'equal partners with the dance,' that ballet should represent a co-ordination of the arts, they saw that progress could only be achieved through a break in the established traditions. Fokine's innovations are numberless, but among his reforms may be mentioned the greater freedom given to the *corps de ballet*, the emancipation of the male dancer and the increase in dramatic action, a process which was given its final formulation by Massine. *See also* BALLET; DIAGHILEV; MASSINE; and individual entries. *See* P. Lieven, *The Birth of Ballets-Russes*, 1936.

Folk Music in Russia developed with the culture of the Eastern Slavs, whose music took the form of songs intimately connected with natural forces and human emotions. The ritual songs fall into three categories, the funeral lamentations, the wedding rituals and the so-called 'calendar songs.' The official adoption of Christianity in the year 988 had at first little or no effect on folk music, which continued to flourish and thus preserved unconsciously, even to the present day, many of the old pagan rites. The principal form of folk-song, apart from the ritual songs, to survive from the Kievan and Novgorod periods is the *bylina*, or epic ballad; there were also numerous comic, humorous and satirical songs played and sung by the *skomorokhi* (jesters and buffoons). Russian folk-song reflects the life and experiences of the Russian people, and in later periods lyrical, satirical and historical songs were written, embodying in musical forms occurrences of political or domestic importance. The most recent form of folk-song is the so-called *chastushka*, or popular song of the day, which is sometimes of a satirical or humorous nature.

The late 18th century saw the appearance of the first collections of folk-songs, the most famous being those of Trutovskiy, Lvov-Prach and Kirsha Danilov. These served as a constant source of inspiration for Russian composers, although subsequent generations tended to regard their content as unscientific. Later collections were made by the Russian nationalist composers (Balakirev, Rimsky-Korsakov, Tchaikovsky, qq.v., etc.). Russian folk-song is distinguished by its diversity and irregularity, much of it being written in the natural major and minor scales. The ritual and comic songs are often of a simple chant-like nature, while the protracted lyrical, historical and wedding songs are characterized by their melodic wealth; the latter are frequently sung polyphonically.

Folk instrumental music is in most cases directly connected with folk-song. Ancient chronicles frequently refer to the presence of string, wind and percussion instruments. The most common stringed instruments of the Eastern Slavs were the *gusli* and the *gudok*. Of later origin were the *domra* and the balalaika, the former being the favourite instrument of the *skomorokhi*. Wind instruments are equally varied, including shepherds' pipes (*rozhki*), trumpets (*truby*), natural horns (*roga*) and primitive whistles and flutes (*dudki, svirelki,* etc.). Of particular interest are the *kuvichki,* a Russian form of ' Pan-pipes.' Folk instrumental *ensembles* often consist of groups of instruments, the *khorovods,* or round-dances, in the province of Kursk, for example, being accompanied by several *dudki* and *kuvichki.* The most common instrument of the present era is the accordion, which plays an important role as both a solo and an accompanying instrument.

Food Industry. The following table shows the production of selected foodstuffs for various years (factory produced).

	1913	1928	1940	1945	1950	1958
Meat [1]	1,042	678	1,501	663	1,556	3,364
Butter and other milk products [2]	2·3	1·9	6·5	2·9	8·5	20·4 [4]
Granulated sugar [1]	1,347	1,283	2,165	465	2,523	5,434
Vegetable oil [1]	471	448	798	—	819	1,446 [4]
Tinned goods [3]	95	125	1,113	558	1,535	4,055
Confectionery goods [1]	109	99	790	212	993	1,673

The main branch of the food industry is flour-milling, which is chiefly concentrated in the principal grain growing areas (Ukraine, North Caucasus, Volga region and the southern, black earth part of central Russia). The sugar industry is largely concentrated in the Ukraine (which in 1955 produced 71 per cent of all sugar) and the black earth region of central Russia. The meat industry is more evenly spread, in the Ukraine, central Russia, North Caucasus, the Urals, Western Siberia, Kazakhstan and the Volga area; in each of these regions, however, there are only a few large meat-processing factories, and animals consequently have to be driven over long distances. The main concentrations of the tinned goods industry are in the fruit and vegetable growing areas, the Ukraine, North Caucasus and Moldavia. The main vegetable oils produced are from sunflower and cotton seeds, and the industry is chiefly concentrated in Central Asia, North Caucasus and the Ukraine.

Before the Second World War food products made up 9–13 per cent of total Soviet imports, the main items being cocoa beans, coffee, tea, rice and fruits; since the war, however, particularly in recent years, the emphasis has been shifted to meat, vegetable oil, rice and sugar, and food imports have been increased to about 15 per cent of total imports. In 1955 imported meat was equivalent to over 9 per cent of internal meat production, vegetable oil to over 17 per cent (both chiefly imported from China), sugar to about 16 per cent and salted herrings to over 20 per cent, but since then imports have dropped.

Before the Five Year Plans (q.v.) era a high proportion of foods was produced in peasant households and sold either directly or through co-operatives without any factory processing. With the collectivization of agriculture (q.v.), the suppression of private

---

[1] Thousand tons.   [2] Million tons, in terms of milk.
[3] Million standard tins.   [4] 1957.

trade, and the neglect of consumer goods (q.v.) production throughout the period of Stalin's rule, there developed severe shortages of
most necessary foods. Production of foodstuffs has been considerably
expanded since Stalin's death, but even with the increase in imports
the supply of most food items per head of population is still inadequate and far behind that in economically advanced countries.

Forced Labour exists in the Soviet Union in peace-time and in
civilian life in the following forms: (1) Labour is extracted from the
inmates of 'corrective labour colonies' (q.v.). (2) An offender may be
sentenced to 'corrective labour without deprivation of liberty'; its
duration is up to one year, and the court decides whether the sentence
is to be served at the offender's place of work (with a reduction of
wages of up to 20 per cent) or elsewhere (but not in a 'corrective
labour colony,' which is a place of detention). (3) Under the so-called
'popular building method,' local peasants and townspeople are compelled to work on building new roads, railways or irrigation canals;
this work is ostensibly voluntary, which is a fiction (q.v.). In 1936–58
peasants, whether *kolkhoz* members or not, were obliged to work for
six days yearly (men from 18 to 45 years of age, women 18 to 40),
without remuneration, on road construction. (4) There is a similar
quasi-voluntary participation of townspeople in the harvest in
sovkhozes and *kolkhozes*. (5) Young specialists (*see* INTELLIGENTSIA),
upon finishing higher or professional secondary education, are (since
1933) obliged to accept a job assigned to them by the authorities for
three years; the same applies to young skilled workers upon finishing
their apprenticeship at a Vocational Technical School (*see* LABOUR
RESERVE). (6) The rules of the so-called 'organized recruitment of
labour for industry and construction' compel the *kolkhoz* administration to provide when required a specified number of men for employment, usually in a remote locality, for at least one year (or one season
if the work is seasonal). (7) The 'special settlers' (q.v.), i.e. people
deported from their previous place of residence, have no choice but to
take up employment available in the places of forced residence. (8)
The quasi-voluntary migration of young people to areas of new
development in the east of the country (including the Virgin Land
Campaign, q.v.) is a milder form of (7) devoid of the stigma of
political and social inferiority. (9) Membership in a *kolkhoz* is hereditary, and it is very difficult to obtain permission to leave the
kolkhoz; consequently a considerable proportion of the agricultural
labour may be regarded as forced. *See* D. Dallin and B. Nikolaevsky,
Forced Labour in Soviet Russia, 1948; N. Jasny, *The Socialized
Agriculture of the U.S.S.R.*, Stanford, 1949; S. Schwarz, *Labour in
the Soviet Union*, New York, 1952; W. W. Kulski, *The Soviet Regime*,
Syracuse, 1954; B. Moore, *Terror and Progress*, Cambridge, Mass.,
1954.

Foreign Debts of the Soviet Government are difficult to assess. The
two biggest outstanding items are the value of foreign property in
Russia confiscated in the course of the nationalization of industry
(q.v.) and the debt arising from the war-time supplies under the
American Lend-Lease and the British and Canadian Mutual Aid
programmes (*see* LEND-LEASE). The Soviet Government has refused

to pay either of these debts, although as early as 1922 it recognized the principle of settling the former by negotiation; in the same way it had agreed to negotiate upon the foreign debts of the Imperial and Provisional governments. The only important foreign loan has been an American loan made immediately after the war, which amounted to roughly a quarter of a million dollars. In the matter of short-term commercial credits from trading partners the Soviet Union has a good record as a prompt payer.

Foreign Policy. For Russian foreign policy before 1917 *see* cross-references under HISTORY.

The Communist Party leaders have always regarded foreign policy not as a field where different principles apply from those which govern internal policy, but rather as an extension of the latter, having essentially the same aims though requiring the use of somewhat different methods. While taking advantage of the Soviet Union's status as a sovereign state, and since the Second World War as a great power, the party leadership employs all normal methods of diplomacy and war, but also considers it natural to employ more questionable methods in order to influence internal developments in foreign countries, e.g. manipulating foreign Communist parties either directly or through special bodies such as the Comintern or Cominform (qq.v.), 'peace' committees, students' organizations, etc.

The Bolsheviks' seizure of power (*see* OCTOBER REVOLUTION) in the middle of the world war, and their declared intention to stop fighting, delayed the recognition of the Soviet Government by the Allies, and the signing of a separate peace treaty with Germany (*see* BREST-LITOVSK) led to a complete boycott of the new regime by the allied powers. In the ensuing civil war (q.v.) the Allies intervened on the anti-Bolshevik side, originally with the intention of re-establishing the eastern front, and only when the civil war was substantially over did the question of recognition really arise. Between 1920 and 1925 all major powers save the United States (which delayed until 1933) recognized the Soviet Government. In 1922 the Treaty of Rapallo was concluded with Germany, thus ending the isolation of Soviet Russia. Apart from Germany, Soviet diplomacy in the early 1920's was chiefly active in Asia. In 1922 treaties of friendship were signed with Turkey, Persia and Afghanistan, and increasing Soviet influence in this area, and interference in China (where the Soviet Government supported the Kuomintang), combined with Soviet financial contributions to the British miners' trade union in 1926, resulted in increasingly strained relations with Great Britain, which finally severed diplomatic relations in 1927 (re-establishing them two years later with the advent of the Labour Government). However, this did not prevent the Soviet Union from participating in the international disarmament negotiations in Switzerland in 1927–8, though she was not among the original signatories of the Kellogg Pact.

In the 1930's Soviet foreign policy was marked by demands for collective security and a 'united front' against fascism, by pacts of non-aggression with Poland, Latvia, Lithuania, Estonia and Finland, and by military pacts with France and Czechoslovakia; the U.S.S.R. joined the League of Nations in 1934. During the Spanish Civil War military aid in the form of tanks, planes and technical personnel was sent to the Republicans, and efforts were made to achieve complete Communist domination of the anti-Franco forces.

As a result of the Munich Pact of September 1938, the Soviet Government regarded itself as absolved from its obligations to France and Czechoslovakia (though it has recently been claimed in the U.S.S.R. that a secret offer of direct assistance should they request it was made to the Czechs), and an abrupt change of front came about with the signing of the Nazi-Soviet Pact (q.v.) in August 1939; Soviet troops crossed the Polish frontier in September and the partition of Poland between Germany and the U.S.S.R. followed. In November the Soviet Union attacked Finland, and despite gallant resistance on the Finnish side and a poor showing by the Soviet army, a peace treaty was enforced upon Finland in March 1940 whereby the Soviet Union acquired a part of western Karelia with Vyborg, and the military base of Hanko. The annexation of the Baltic States (q.v.) was completed by the summer of 1940, and Rumania was forced to cede Bessarabia and northern Bukovina to the U.S.S.R. In April 1941 the Soviet Union signed a treaty of non-aggression with Japan; thus when the German invasion began in June she was saved from having to fight the war on two fronts. (For military action on the Russian front see WORLD WAR II.) Soviet treaties with various allied governments followed the outbreak of war on the Russian front, and an agreement with the Polish Government in exile was reached which abrogated the territorial changes resulting from the Nazi-Soviet Pact and provided for the release of many Poles from Soviet concentration camps. But continuing disagreement over the frontier question, together with the Polish exiled government's demand for an investigation on the basis of evidence produced by the Germans that large numbers of Polish officers had been massacred in Russia, led to relations between the Soviet and Polish governments being broken off in 1943. The conferences of Yalta (February 1945) and of Potsdam (July–August 1945) (qq.v.) between the U.S.A., Great Britain and the U.S.S.R. brought considerable gains to the last-named, the Potsdam Agreement assigning the northern part of East Prussia (see KALININGRAD) to the Soviet Union. The Czechoslovak Government ceded Sub-Carpathian Russia (see TRANSCARPATHIA) to the Soviet Union in 1945, and in 1946 a new frontier was drawn with Poland, roughly along the line which the Western Allies had thought acceptable at the time of the peace conference in 1919, which left in Soviet hands most of the territory already annexed in 1939.

The immediate post-war years were characterized by the consolidation of Soviet domination in the countries of Eastern Europe (treaties with Czechoslovakia in 1943, Yugoslavia, 1946, Albania, 1947, Poland, Rumania, Hungary and Bulgaria, 1948) and by the intransigent attitude of the Soviet Government towards its war-time allies, including the failure to meet its obligations under the war-time Lend-Lease (q.v.), or to agree upon conventional and atomic disarmament or upon peace treaties with Austria and Germany (though peace treaties were signed in 1947 with Rumania, Hungary and

Bulgaria, and with Finland). This attitude culminated in the unsuccessful Soviet attempt to dislodge the Western Allies from Berlin by the blockade of 1948. Friction between the Soviet authorities and Marshal Tito of Yugoslavia resulted in an open breach in mid 1948, when the Yugoslav treaty was denounced by the Soviet Union and the Yugoslav Communist Party expelled from the Cominform; relations between the two countries remained hostile until a formal declaration of friendship was signed in 1955, but were again openly exacerbated by Soviet action in Hungary in 1956, and the position of Yugoslavia vis-à-vis the Soviet Union remains equivocal. From 1948 Soviet relations with the West were dominated by hostility to Western rearmament and to all defensive agreements between the countries of the West; a meeting between the deputies of American, British, French and Soviet Foreign Ministers in Paris in the spring of 1951 failed to reach agreement on any outstanding issues.

In the Far East the Soviet Union's brief participation in the war against Japan resulted in the annexation of southern Sakhalin and the Kurile Islands and the establishment of a Communist regime in North Korea. In October 1949 the Soviet Government broke off relations with the Kuomintang Government in China (with which a treaty of co-operation had been signed in 1945) and recognized Mao Tse-Tung's Communist government in Peking. It supported North Korea in its attack upon South Korea in June 1950, alleging that it was the South Koreans who, with American connivance, had first crossed the frontier, and approved Chinese intervention in the following year, giving considerable assistance in weapons and technical specialists.

During 1954 and 1955 various East-West meetings took place in order to try to solve outstanding issues and bring about a reduction in tension (January 1954, Foreign Ministers' meeting in Berlin on Germany and Austria; April, Geneva Conference on Korea and Indo-China; July 1955, heads of governments' conference in Geneva; October, meeting of Foreign Ministers). The only concrete result of this series of meetings was the unexpected declaration in April 1955 that the Soviet Government was willing to sign an Austrian treaty, which was in fact signed in Vienna on 15th May. In the same month the Eastern Security Treaty (Warsaw Pact) was signed between the Soviet Union and her satellites, Albania, Bulgaria, Czechoslovakia, Hungary, Poland and Rumania. The dissolution of the Cominform early in 1956 and the visits to Britain of Malenkov (March) and of Bulganin and Khrushchëv (April) appeared to be signs on the part of the post-Stalin leadership of a desire for somewhat improved formal relations with the West, but any progress in such a direction was violently reversed by the Soviet intervention to suppress the Hungarian anti-Communist revolution of October–November 1956, and the Soviet Government remains in defiance of the United Nations, which has frequently called upon it to withdraw its troops from Hungary and to admit U.N. observers.

At the end of 1957 Khrushchëv suggested another meeting of heads of governments, and in November 1958 issued his so-called 'ultimatum' to the Western powers over the status of Berlin, threatening that if no agreement was reached within six months the Soviet Union would sign a separate peace treaty with East Germany and hand over her occupation rights in Berlin (and control of communications with the city) to the East German Government. However, this 'ultimatum' was not followed up by any concrete steps, and though a meeting of the four Foreign Ministers (with 'observers' from West and East Germany) took place in May 1959 to discuss the subject, no practical conclusions were reached. Throughout 1959 Khrushchëv reiterated his view that outstanding problems should be discussed at a 'summit' meeting, and such a meeting was agreed upon for 1960. Khrushchëv visited the United States in September 1959, and an ostensible lessening of tension in Soviet-American relations ensued, which, however, was abruptly reversed following the shooting down of an American reconnaissance plane over Soviet territory in May 1960 and Khrushchëv's violent refusal to continue with the 'summit' meeting in June, though he travelled to Paris to attend it. On the question of the banning of atomic tests, protracted negotiations have been taking place between representatives of the U.S., Britain and the U.S.S.R. since October 1958, and though some progress has been made any conclusive agreement is still held up by Soviet obstruction over a really effective control and inspection system. It was agreed in 1959 that negotiations on the general question of controlled disarmament should be reopened in 1960; however, when these negotiations began in March of that year, the Soviet delegation walked out a few weeks later, saying that the Western powers were being obstructive and insincere.

The state of Sino-Soviet relations is difficult to assess. Despite continual protestations of the closest friendship, there have been signs that Soviet and Chinese leaders do not co-operate in complete harmony; particularly noticeable have been the lack of obvious Soviet support (either in the internal press or in official statements) for the Chinese suppression of the revolt in Tibet in the spring and summer of 1959, and the studied neutrality over Chinese actions in India's frontier areas in the autumn of that year. Serious ideological differences, especially over the Chinese Communists' insistence upon the inevitability of war with 'capitalist' states, also became apparent during 1960.

Important aspects of Soviet foreign policy in recent years would seem to be the following: exclusion of a general atomic war as an instrument of policy; the deliberate creation of artificial crises with no other aim than to keep the West in a state of nervousness (e.g. threats and accusations against Persia and Turkey, the Berlin 'ultimatum'); determination not to permit any political or economic independence to the satellite countries, even at the cost of a serious setback in prestige among foreign Communists and the 'uncommitted' countries; the desire to reduce the isolationism and hysterical xenophobia that characterized the last years of Stalin's rule, chiefly through wider cultural contacts and personal visits of political leaders from East to West and vice versa; and the desire to increase Soviet political influence in under-developed and 'uncommitted' countries, through economic aid (q.v.) and personal visits of political leaders. On the last point, to judge from the way in which Soviet-Egyptian and Soviet-Indian relations have developed in recent years, it seems doubtful if the Soviet methods are likely to achieve their aim.

See L. Fischer, *The Soviets in World Affairs* (2 vols.), 1930; F. R. Dalles, *The Road to Teheran. The Story of Russia and America, 1781–1943*, Princeton, N.J., 1944; M. Beloff, *Foreign Policy of the Soviet Union, 1929 41* (2 vols.), 1947–8, and *Soviet Policy in the Far East, 1944–51*, 1953; Royal Institute of International Affairs, *The Soviet-Yugoslav Dispute*, 1948; D. G. Bishop, *Soviet Foreign Relations, Documents and Readings*, Syracuse, 1950; L. Schapiro, *Soviet Treaty Series* (3 vols.), Washington, 1950–5; J. Degras, *Soviet Documents on Foreign Policy, 1917–39* (3 vols.), 1951–3; E. H. Carr, *The Interregnum, 1923–4*, 1954; C. M. Wilbur and J. Lien-ying How (eds.), *Documents on Communism, Nationalism and Soviet Advisers in China, 1918–27*, New York, 1956; H. L. Boorman *et al.*, *Moscow-Peking Axis*, New York, 1957; G. Freund, *Unholy Alliance*, 1957; C. B. McLane, *Soviet Policy and the Chinese Communists, 1931–46*, New York, 1958; *Stalin's Correspondence with Churchill, Attlee, Roosevelt and Truman, 1941–5*, 1958; L. Spektor, *The Soviet Union and the Muslim World, 1917–58*, Seattle, 1959; W. Z. Laqueur, *The Soviet Union and the Middle East*, 1959; R. M. Slusser and J. R. Triska, *A Calendar of Soviet Treaties, 1917–57*, Stanford, California, 1959; A. Dallin, *Soviet Conduct in World Affairs*, New York, 1960; H. Seton-Watson, *Neither War Nor Peace*, 1960; P. E. Mosely, *The Kremlin and World Politics*, New York, 1960.

Foreign Trade. In respect of foreign trade the Soviet Union took sixth place in the world in 1957 (sixteenth in 1938). Of total foreign trade in 1957, 74 per cent was carried on with Communist countries (55 per cent in 1946, 81 per cent in 1950). The first place in Soviet foreign trade is taken by Eastern Germany (19·5 per cent), followed by China (15·4 per cent); among non-Communist countries Finland takes first place, followed by Britain, Western Germany and France. The following table shows the structure of imports and exports for selected years (in percentage of the total):

	1913	1928	1938	1950	1955	1958
Exports						
Machinery and equipment	0·3	0·1	5·0	16·3	24·3	18·5
Fuel and raw materials	42·8	63·1	57·7	50·7	57·9	65·9
Grain and consumer goods	56·9	36·8	37·3	33·0	18·5	15·6
Imports						
Machinery and equipment	15·9	23·9	34·5	27·1	35·3	24·5
Fuel and raw materials	63·4	67·8	60·7	56·6	44·6	51·6
Grain and consumer goods	20·7	8·3	4·8	16·3	20·1	23·9

In the export of machinery and equipment the Soviet Union took fifth place in 1957, first in manganese ore, fourth in iron ore, third in sawn timber, second in cotton. In the same year it took second place in the import of machinery and equipment and shared third place in rubber; imported consumer goods made up over 10 per cent of total retail trade in 1957.

Foreign trade has been a State monopoly since 1918, and is carried on by the Ministry of Foreign Trade through twenty-four foreign trade agencies specializing in different categories of goods and through permanent trade delegations attached to Soviet embassies abroad. The Soviet Government prefers bilateral trade agreements with foreign countries to any general or multilateral agreements such as G.A.T.T., and in 1958 had commercial treaties and agreements with forty-seven foreign governments. Soviet foreign trade is always subordinated to the general political aims of the party leadership, and has mostly been directed towards achieving the greatest possible degree of self-sufficiency (*see* AUTARKY), though in recent years there has been considerable stress on expanding foreign economic relations. The Soviet Union has a good record as a prompt payer for imports, though trade relations on the whole are difficult for the foreign partners because of excessive centralization of the Soviet foreign trade apparatus. *See also* ECONOMIC AID; FOREIGN DEBTS; LEND-LEASE. *See* H. Schwartz, *Russia's Soviet Economy*, 2nd ed., 1954; R. L. Allen, 'A Note on Soviet Foreign Trade Statistics,' *Soviet Studies*, vol. x, No. 4, April 1959; A. Zauberman, 'Economic Integration,' *Problems of Communism*, vol. viii, No. 4, July–Aug. 1959; A. Nove and D. Donnelly, *Trade with Communist Countries*, 1960.

Formalism, school of literary criticism and theory in Russia which emerged during the First World War. The Formalists (V. Shklovskiy, B. Eykhenbaum, R. Jakobson, etc.) rejected both the sociological and metaphysical approaches to literary analysis, and considered art primarily as techniques and devices. From this standpoint they analysed both classical and contemporary Russian literature, and through their theoretical works on prosody influenced the development of the literary language. Since Formalism was incompatible with what the party demanded from literary criticism, the school was suppressed in 1930, despite attempts on the part of some of its adherents to compromise with the official Marxist ideology. Charges of Formalism were made by the party spokesmen both during the campaign of 1936–7 against experimentation in the arts (e.g. against Shostakovich and Meyerhold), and during the post-war period of Zhdanov's dictatorship in cultural life and the subsequent campaign of 1949 against 'cosmopolitanism' in scholarship and the arts. *See* V. Erlich, *Russian Formalism*, The Hague, 1955.

Foynitskiy, Ivan Yakovlevich (1847–1913), jurist of Belorussian parentage, son of a serf. Educated at St Petersburg University, he taught there from 1871 until his death, simultaneously serving in the Senate (q.v.) and becoming a senator in 1900. His special fields were criminology, where he was a founder of the sociological school, penology (particularly the study of penitentiary institutions) and criminal procedure. A convinced opponent of banishment Foynitskiy did much to eliminate it in Russia. He took an active part (1882–1901) in the commission which drafted a new criminal code (*see* CODES OF LAW). Chief works: *Course of Criminal Procedure* (2 vols.), 1887–98, *The Doctrine of Punishment*, 1889, *Course of Criminal Law. Special part—Crimes against Person and Property*, 1890, *Factors of Criminality*, 1893.

Frank, Semën Lyudvigovich (1877–1950), philosopher of Jewish parentage, a leading representative of the early twentieth-century religious and philosophical renaissance in Russia. A Marxist and Social Democrat in his youth, Frank, together with a number of Legal Marxists (q.v.), turned to Idealism and later to Orthodox Christianity, taking part in the symposium *Vekhi* (q.v.) in 1909. From 1912 to 1922 he taught at St Petersburg, Saratov and Moscow universities, but in 1922 was expelled from Russia together with other leading intellectuals, and lived thereafter in Berlin, Paris and London. Frank's system of philosophy based on the idea of All-Unity was developed in his works *Philosophy and Life*, 1910, *The Object of Knowledge*, 1915, *Man's Soul*, 1917, *Spiritual Foundations of Society*, 1930, *The Imperceptible. An Ontological Introduction into the Philosophy of Religion*, 1939, *Light in Darkness. An Attempt at Christian Ethics and Sociology*, 1949. See his *God with Us*, 1946, and his talks on V. Solov'ëv on the B.B.C. Third Programme, *The Listener*, 1949; N. Lossky, *History of Russian Philosophy*, 1951; V. V. Zenkovsky, *A History of Russian Philosophy*, 1953, and (ed.) *Sbornik pamyati S. L. Franka*, Munich, 1954.

Frumkin, Aleksandr Naumovich (*b.* 1895), chemist of Jewish origin, member of the Academy of Sciences. Educated at Strasbourg and Bern, he taught at the New Russia University in Odessa, since 1922 has worked at the Physical Chemistry Institute in Moscow and since 1930 has been professor at Moscow University. In 1928–9 he was visiting professor of colloid chemistry at the university of Wisconsin. His work is mainly concerned with kinetics and the mechanisms of electrochemical reactions, electrocapillary phenomena, etc.; he established the connection between Lippman's Equation and Gibbs's general theory of absorption. *See* J. G. Crowther, *Soviet Science*, 1936.

Frunze (until 1926 **Pishpek**), city in Central Asia, capital, economic and cultural centre of Kirgizia, situated in the valley of the River Chu on a branch of the Turksib Railway about 120 m. west of Alma-Ata. Population (1959) 217,000 (1939, 93,000), mostly Russians. It has varied food (including a big meat-packing plant), textile and engineering (agricultural machinery, food industry equipment, machine tools, etc.) industries. The Kirgiz Academy of Sciences (established in 1943 as a branch of the U.S.S.R. Academy of Sciences, transformed in 1954) and a university (founded in 1932 as a Pedagogical Institute, transformed in 1951) are situated here. Frunze was founded in 1846 as a Kokand fortress and was captured by the Russians in 1864. It became administrative centre of the Kirgiz Autonomous Oblast in 1924; from 1939 to 1959 it was the administrative centre of the Frunze Oblast within Kirgizia, now abolished.

Frunze, Mikhail Vasil'yevich (1885–1925), Bolshevik military leader, formerly a professional revolutionary, the son of a Moldavian settler in Turkestan. He was active during the revolution of 1905 (q.v.) in Ivanovo-Voznesensk and in the uprising in Moscow. During the civil war he defeated Admiral Kolchak in 1919 and General Wrangel in 1920. Frunze took Stalin's side in the inner-party struggle and replaced Trotskiy as People's Commissar (Minister) for Military and Naval Affairs in January 1925.

Fuel. The following table shows the consumption of the principal fuels in percentages of total fuel consumed.

	1913	1955	1958
Coal	50·3	64·8	59·6
Oil	28·8	21·1	25·7
Natural gas	—	2·4	5·4
Other fuels	20·9 [1]	11·7	9·3

During the current Seven Year Plan (q.v.) period, it is intended to increase the percentage of oil and natural gas to 51 in order to improve the fuel balance, since the cost of production and conveyance is much lower than that of coal. *See* entries on coal, gas and oil industries.

Futurism, literary and artistic trend in Russia (approximately 1910–30). Its name and its principal idea—the abandonment of the past and the creation of a new art consonant with the machine age— were derived from Italy and France, but most Russian Futurists were far more uncompromising in their attitude to contemporary society. There were several organized groups of Futurists, the most important, the Cubo-Futurists, being also the most radical in both the artistic and the political sense. Their leader and theorist was V. Khlebnikov (1885–1922), and the most outstanding of all Futurists, Mayakovskiy (q.v.), also belonged to this group; they regarded the Bolshevik seizure of power as in keeping with their own extremism and in the first years of the Bolshevik regime, when the cultural policy of the Government was under Bogdanovist influence (*see* BOGDANOVISM; LUNACHARSKIY), they assumed a quasi-official position, establishing the organization Left Front in the Arts (among whose younger members were Pasternak, Kirsanov, qq.v., and N. Aseyev). Most of them became disillusioned with the regime, and the organization itself was dissolved in 1930. Despite their exaggerations, which sometimes went beyond the limits of comprehension, the Futurists had an important influence upon Russian poetry through their linguistic innovations. *See also* FORMALISM. *See* G. Ivanov, *Peterburgskiye zimy*, New York, 1952; M. Slonim, *Modern Russian Literature*, New York, 1953; V. Zavalishin, *Early Soviet Writers*, New York, 1958.

[1] Largely firewood.

G

Gabovich, Mikhail Markovich (*b.* 1905), dancer. After studying at the Bolshoi School, Moscow, he entered the Conservatoire in 1924, becoming principal dancer. He was appointed director of the Moscow Technicum in 1938 and has received many prizes and awards.

Gagauz, Turkic-speaking people who live mostly in Dobruja, but form a sizable minority in southern Bessarabia and live also in small groups in the Zaporozh'ye Oblast of the Ukraine, in the North Caucasus and in Kazakhstan; their total number in the U.S.S.R. is (1959) 124,000. They are Orthodox Christians, and for this reason have always been quite distinct from the Turks. Their origin is not clear. Those Gagauz who live in the U.S.S.R. migrated to Russia in the late 18th and early 19th centuries as a result of the Russo-Turkish wars and the Turkish oppression of Christians.

Galich (Ukrainian **Halych,** Polish **Halicz**), small town in the Stanislav Oblast (Galicia), situated 70 m. south-east of L'vov. Population (1921) 3,400. It has the ruins of a castle and several medieval churches. It was capital of Galich principality, and later of the Kingdom of Galicia and Volhynia, during the 11th–13th centuries; it became Polish in 1340 and Austrian in 1772. Galich was the scene of bitter fighting in 1914. From 1919 to 1939 it was Polish.

Galicia, area in western Ukraine comprising the L'vov, Stanislav and Ternopol' oblasts, embracing the northern slopes of the Carpathian Mountains in the south and a part of the Volhynia-Podolia upland in the north. It belonged to the Kievan state (*see* KIEVAN RUSSIA), became an independent principality in 1152, was fused with Volhynia, 1199–1340 (*see* GALICIA AND VOLHYNIA, KINGDOM OF), and became Polish in 1349; it was an Austrian crown land, 1772–1918 (when it included a part of Little Poland around Cracow), then Polish again and was annexed by the U.S.S.R. in 1939. It was occupied by the Germans 1941–4 and included in the Government General (i.e. Poland).

Galicia and Volhynia, Kingdom of, medieval state composed of the principalities of Galicia and Volhynia. In 1199 these were fused into one principality whose prince received from the Pope the title of king in 1254. Volhynia became Lithuanian in 1340, Galicia Polish in 1349. From 1772 to 1918 the Kingdom of Galicia and Volhynia (Lodomeria) was also the official name of Galicia as an Austrian crownland.

Gandzha, *see* KIROVABAD.

Gapon, Georgiy Apollonovich (1870–1906), Orthodox priest and active promoter of Police Socialism (q.v.). He founded the Assembly of Russian Workers in St Petersburg in 1903, which soon became penetrated by Social Democratic agitators. The procession of workers led by Gapon on 9th January 1905 ('Bloody Sunday') with the intention of presenting a rather provocative petition to the Czar was fired upon by the police, and this was the start of the revolution of

1905 (q.v.). Gapon issued revolutionary appeals to the country and tried to establish himself as the leader of the movement, but, distrusted by revolutionary parties, he was murdered by a Socialist Revolutionary. *See* his *The Story of my Life*, 1905.

Garm, former oblast (1939–50) of Tadzhikistan which included the mountainous country in the central part of the republic.

Gas Industry. In 1958, 29·9 milliard cubic metres of gas were produced (28·1 natural gas). The main areas of natural gas extraction are the Volga-Urals Oil Area, the North Caucasus, the Ukraine and Central Asia. The principal gas pipelines run from Saratov, Dashava and Stavropol' to Moscow; new pipelines are under construction from Dashava and Stavropol' to Leningrad, from Shebelinka to Dnepropetrovsk and Odessa, from the Tatar-Bashkir oilfields to Gor'kiy and Perm' and from Gazli in the Bukhara Oblast to Chelyabinsk and Sverdlovsk. The extraction of natural gas has been rapidly developing since the Second World War, but the gas-processing industry is in its infancy, and much oil gas is burnt up.

Gasprinskiy (Gaspirali), Ismail Bey (1851–1914), Crimean Tatar Pan-Turkist publicist and modernist reformer. From 1883 he published in Bakhchisaray the newspaper *The Interpreter* (using a ' common Turkic ' language based on the Ottoman Turkish) which was the main organ of the Pan-Turkist movement in Russia. In 1884 he founded a reformed Muslim school which served as a model throughout the country until the establishment of the Soviet regime. *See* C. W. Hostler, *Turkism and the Soviets*, 1957; S. A. Zenkovsky, *Pan-Turkism and Islam in Russia*, Cambridge, Mass., 1960.

Gastev, Aleksey Kapitonovich (1882–1939), poet and theorist of the organization of labour. An industrial worker and Social Democrat, Gastev, under the influence of Bogdanov and Lunacharskiy (qq.v.), devoted himself to the idea of creating a new proletarian culture instead of the existing bourgeois one, and to active membership of the Proletkul't (q.v.). At first this expressed itself in a kind of industrial poetry. But from the early 1920's he concentrated on working out and popularizing a theory of the scientific organization of labour (q.v.) which, he believed, through integrating the entire social experience of the worker around his work movements, would form the essential basis for a true proletarian culture; for this purpose he set up the Central Institute of Labour which he directed until he disappeared during the Great Purge (q.v.). *See* V. Zavalishin, *Early Soviet Writers*, New York, 1958; S. V. Utechin, ' Bolsheviks and their Allies after 1917: the Ideological Pattern,' *Soviet Studies*, Oct. 1958.

Gatchina (after 1924 **Trotsk**, then **Krasnogvardeysk** until 1944), town in the Leningrad Oblast, 28 m. south-west of Leningrad. Population (1956) 33,300 (1936, 42,000). There are several 18th-century buildings and parks. During the 19th century Gatchina was a favourite residence of the emperors; the famous Gatchina palace (built 1766) suffered great damage during 1941–4.

Gazli, rich natural gasfield in the Bukhara Oblast (Uzbekistan) about 60 m. north-west of Bukhara. It was discovered in the mid 1950's; gas extraction will be rapidly developed during the current Seven Year Plan and pipelines will be built to Tashkent and Chelyabinsk.

Gelovani, Mikhail Georgiyevich (*b.* 1892), Georgian theatre and film actor who specialized, with Dikiy (q.v.), in portraying Stalin on stage and screen. His films include the 'feature documentaries' *The Siberians*, 1940, *Valeriy Chkalov*, 1941, *The Defence of Tsaritsyn*, 1942, *The Vow*, 1946, and *The Fall of Berlin*, 1949, in all of which he played Stalin.

Geography as an academic study dates in Russia from the travelogues of Daniel the Pilgrim, who visited the Holy Land in 1106–8, and the Tver' merchant A. Nikitin, who travelled to India in 1466–72. The 16th and 17th centuries were marked by the compilation of the first general map of Muscovy, with an extensive explanatory text, and the discovery and description of Eastern Siberia. Throughout the 18th and 19th centuries the Academy of Sciences (q.v.) organized expeditions for a systematic study of Russia and adjacent countries and seas (e.g. Potanin, q.v.). Voyeykov's works were important in climatology and hydrology. The study of the Arctic Ocean (*see* PAPANIN; SCHMIDT; VIZE) acquired particular importance in connection with the establishment of the Northern Sea Route (q.v.). The problems of glaciology and of permanently frozen subsoils have been intensively investigated. In theoretical physical geography Berg's (q.v.) school studies the geographical *milieu* as a whole and individual 'landscapes.' Anuchin (q.v.) established a geographical school at Moscow University which treats physical and human geography as one discipline. Economic geography, vigorously pursued since the 18th century, has generally adopted a regional approach (e.g. Bezobrazov, Mendeleyev, I. G. Aleksandrov, qq.v.). *See* L. S. Berg, *Natural Regions of the U.S.S.R.*, New York, 1950; T. Shabad, *Geography of the U.S.S.R.*, New York, 1951; N. N. Baransky, *Economic Geography of the U.S.S.R.*, Moscow, 1956; W. A. D. Jackson, 'Geography' in H. H. Fisher's (ed.) *American Research on Russia*, Bloomington, Indiana, 1959.

Geology as an academic discipline dates in Russia from the mid 19th century. Russian geology acquired international repute through the works of Karpinskiy and Obruchev (qq.v.) in stratigraphy and tectonics, Ye. S. Fedorov (q.v.) in mineralogy and V. O. Kovalevskiy (q.v.) in palaeontology, while Dokuchayev (q.v.) was the founder of soil science and Vernadskiy (q.v.) of geochemistry. The latter's work has been continued by Fersman (q.v.) and others. Arkhangel'skiy (q.v.) contributed to many branches of geological science. Gubkin (q.v.) was most outstanding in the study of mineral deposits and in directing prospecting work in recent decades. A Geological Committee was founded in Russia in 1882 as a government department in charge of prospecting, which, after several reorganizations during the Soviet period, is now the Ministry of Geology and Preservation of Mineral Deposits. *See* J. G. Crowther, *Soviet Science*, 1936. A complete cover-to-cover translation of the journal *Prospecting and Preservation of Natural Resources* exists in English.

Georgia (Georgian **Sakartvelo**), Union Republic of the U.S.S.R., situated in western Transcaucasia adjacent to the Black Sea and the Turkish frontier; it is a largely mountainous region, with the main Caucasian range in the north, the Lesser Caucasus in the south, elevated plains in the east and the Colchis lowland in the west. Western Georgia (*see* ABKHAZIA; ADZHAR AUTONOMOUS REPUBLIC; IMERETIA; MINGRELIA) has a humid Mediterranean climate and subtropical vegetation; eastern Georgia (*see* KAKHETIA; SOUTH OSSETIAN AUTONOMOUS OBLAST) has a dry continental climate. The main rivers of Georgia are the Kura and the Rioni; there are large deposits of manganese, also coal, oil, peat and mineral waters. Area 26,900 sq. m.; population (1959) 4,044,000 (42 per cent urban), mostly Georgians (63 per cent), also Armenians (11 per cent), Russians (11 per cent), Azerbaydzhanis (4 per cent), Abkhazians (2 per cent) and Ossetians (3·5 per cent). Maize, wheat, tobacco, tea and citrus fruits are cultivated, viniculture and sericulture carried on, sheep, pigs and poultry raised, and there are varied food, light, engineering, metallurgical, coal- and manganese-mining and oil extraction and refining industries. Principal towns: Tiflis (capital), Kutaisi, Batumi, Sukhumi, Rustavi, Chiatura, Poti, Mtskheta, Telavi.

Georgia was well known in antiquity, and a Georgian kingdom in Iberia is known to have existed in the 3rd century B.C. Sometimes united and sometimes divided into two or three kingdoms and several principalities, Georgia endured conquest and domination by Romans, Persians, Byzantium, Arabs, Seljuk Turks, Mongols, the Ottoman Empire and again Persia. The most famous Georgian rulers were King David IV, the Builder (1089–1125), and Queen Tamara (1184–1213), both of the House of Bagratids. Georgia and its vassal territories included the whole of Transcaucasia and neighbouring areas during the rule of Tamara, and it was to her that the famous poem *The Knight in Panther's Skin* was dedicated by the contemporary Georgian poet Rustaveli. Prior to 1774 western Georgia was under Turkish suzerainty and eastern Georgia under Persian. The king of eastern Georgia was granted Russian protection in 1783, and the last east Georgian king, threatened by Persia, ceded his country to Russia in 1800; most west Georgian princes followed suit in 1803–4, though it was not until 1858 that the mountainous Svanetia was annexed.

The 19th and early 20th centuries witnessed a rapid growth of population and economic and cultural progress in Georgia. The Mensheviks and the Georgian Socialist Federalists (a Populist party advocating a Transcaucasian Federation within a federal Russia) predominated in Georgian politics. After the October Revolution (q.v.) a Transcaucasian Federation (q.v.) was in fact established under Menshevik leadership, but it soon disintegrated. From 1918 to 1921 Georgia was a democratic republic with a Menshevik government, at first independent, subsequently under British occupation, and mostly at war with Armenia and Azerbaydzhan; it was conquered without difficulty in 1921 by the Red Army assisted by local Communists, and was transformed into a Soviet republic, belonging 1922–36 to the Transcaucasian Soviet Federal Republic. A large-scale anti-Communist uprising in Georgia was suppressed in 1924, as were riots in Tiflis in 1956. *See* W. E. D. Allen, *A History of the Georgian People*, 1932; B. Nolde, *La Formation de l'Empire Russe*, vol. ii, Paris, 1952; D. M. Lang, *The Last Years of the Georgian Monarchy, 1658–1832*, 1957.

Georgians, Caucasian-speaking people inhabiting most of Georgia who number (1959) 2·65 million. The Georgians are not a homogeneous people; there are still considerable differences between those living in different geographical and historical areas of Georgia, and the various groups still use their own historical names, some of which go back to antiquity. They have been predominantly Orthodox Christians since the year 318, though there are some groups of Sunni Muslims, notably the Adzhars. The West Kartvelian peoples, notably the Megrelians (q.v.), are officially treated as Georgians, though they have not yet been assimilated. For history *see* GEORGIA. Georgians have played an important part in all spheres of Russian life both before and after 1917, e.g. General Bagration (q.v.), the leading Menshevik politician, I. G. Tsereteli (1882–1959), Stalin, Ordzhonikidze and Beria (qq.v.).

Gerasimov, Aleksandr Mikhaylovich (*b.* 1881), painter, studied in the Moscow Art School, 1903–15. A conservative plodder who has never been in sympathy with modern experimentation in art, he assured himself an extraordinary success in the years of Stalin's rule by painting heavily monumental and pompous portraits of Politburo members; he has also painted landscapes and still life which show no signs of modern influence, but that of Peredvizhniki and at best of Repin (qq.v.). Gerasimov's work was in line with Stalin's personal artistic taste, to the extent that in the course of less than ten years he was four times awarded the Stalin Prize.

German Volga Republic, *see* GERMANS; VOLGA GERMAN REPUBLIC.

Germans in Russia live scattered throughout the country, being mainly concentrated in Western Siberia and northern Kazakhstan, and number (1959) 1·6 million, 75 per cent considering German their mother-tongue. Germans first settled on the territory of the present-day U.S.S.R. in the late 12th–early 13th century, when the Teutonic Order conquered the Baltic Provinces (q.v.). Until the late 19th century, as landlords and the majority of the townspeople, they were the politically, economically and culturally dominant element of the population in the area. Their proximity to the capital (St Petersburg) and their cultural level, combined with the 18th-century policy of westernization in Russia, resulted in a considerable number of these Baltic Germans being drawn into the imperial administration and the army. Their political and cultural role in the Baltic Provinces diminished when the Russian Government adopted an anti-German policy in the 1880's and nineties, and the governments of independent Latvia and Estonia carried out land reforms in the 1920's which deprived the German landlords of their economic position. The majority of Baltic Germans were repatriated to Germany in 1940–1 by agreement between the German and Soviet governments. Another category of Germans in Russia was the colonists who first settled on the lower Volga and in the south (Volhynia and New Russia, q.v.) in the late 18th and early 19th centuries. These were mostly farmers, who received certain privileges from the Russian Government in the early period of settlement and soon became very prosperous, owning a high proportion of land and thus causing resentment among the Russian population. After the Bolshevik seizure of power a Volga

German Republic (q.v.) was established, but both there and in the south many Germans suffered as *kulaks* (q.v.) during the collectivization of agriculture (q.v.). All Germans not living in Nazi-occupied territories by September 1941 were deported to Western Siberia, where they were treated as 'special settlers' (q.v.). Those in Nazi-occupied territory were transported to Germany or to western Poland (at that time annexed by Germany). The third category of Germans in Russia was professional and commercial people who immigrated at various times and lived throughout Russia, mostly in the towns; to a greater or lesser extent these became assimilated. Many of these were also deported to Siberia in 1941. From 1941 until after Stalin's death Germans were officially non-existent in Russia. In 1957, when several deported peoples were rehabilitated, Germans ceased to be treated as 'special settlers' and were recognized as an ethnic group, though they were not permitted to return to their former homes. *See* W. Kolarz, *Russia and her Colonies*, 1954; R. Conquest, *The Soviet Deportation of Nationalities*, 1960.

Gershenzon, Mikhail Osipovich (1869–1925), historian and publicist of Jewish origin. His works—*P. Ya. Chaadayev*, 1908, *History of Young Russia*, 1908, *Historical Sketches*, 1910, *Images of the Past*, 1911, etc.—are mostly concerned with the history of ideas in 19th-century Russia. Gershenzon belonged to the Vekhi (q.v.) group and took an active part in the development of a Solidarist social philosophy (*see* SOLIDARISM).

Gihel's, Emil' Grigor'yevich (*b.* 1916), brilliant pianist, the winner of many prizes and diplomas, who studied with Reinwald at Odessa and at Moscow under Neuhaus. His playing is manly, and is characterized by sharp dynamic contrasts, sensitivity to rhythm and exceptional virtuosity. He is an outstanding representative of the new school of Russian pianists.

Gilyaks (now officially called by their own name **Nivkhi**), Paleo-Asiatic people, numbering 4,000 in 1959, who live near the mouth of the Amur and on the Sakhalin Island. Until the 20th century they retained a form of group marriage. The Gilyaks are mostly fishermen, now collectivized.

Gipsies in Russia numbered 132,000 according to the 1959 census, but it is clear that because of difficulties in registering them this cannot be an exact figure. They are usually bilingual (though 59 per cent regard Romany as their mother-tongue), officially Orthodox Christians, and still mostly lead a nomadic life. They arrived in Bessarabia in the 15th century, and gradually spread northwards and eastwards, reaching central and northern Russia by the 18th century. Unlike those in western Europe, Russian gipsies were never actively oppressed, though continual attempts were made to settle them, both before and after 1917, and in 1955 a government decree was issued providing for their deportation if they refused to engage in 'productive work.' On the other hand, a Gipsy Theatre (founded 1931) still exists in Moscow. Gipsies in Russia have been immortalized by Pushkin in his poem *Tsygany*.

Glavk, Russian abbreviation for Chief Committee, later also for Chief Administration (q.v.).

Glazov, town in the Udmurt Autonomous Republic (Urals), situated on the Perm'–Kirov railway about 130 m. west of Perm'. Population (1959) 59,000 (1939, 16,000), Russians and Udmurts. It has saw-milling and metal-working industries and is a local cultural centre. Before the establishment of the Udmurt Autonomous Oblast (later Republic), with Izhevsk as capital, Glazov was considered the chief centre of the Udmurt people. Formerly an Udmurt village, Glazov became a town in 1780.

Glazunov, Aleksandr Konstantinovich (1865–1936), composer and conductor, who studied, on the advice of Balakirev (whom he met in 1879), with Rimsky-Korsakov, and was the possessor of a remarkable musical memory. He was appointed professor of music at the St Petersburg Conservatory, 1899, becoming director in 1909. He left Russia in 1928. Works comprise three ballets, *Raymonda, Les Ruses d'Amour* and *The Seasons*; incidental music; choral music; eight symphonies, orchestral works, including the tone-poems *Sten'ka Razin* and *The Forest,* two *Overtures on Greek Themes* and *Fantasia on Finnish Themes*; two violin concertos; two piano concertos; and much chamber, vocal and instrumental music. A prolific and highly skilled musician, Glazunov early became attracted to the Kuchka (q.v.). His music is colourful and sensitively orchestrated, though seldom transgressing the bounds of orthodoxy. Writing at a period when the tendencies inaugurated by Glinka were becoming commonplace, he grew increasingly concerned with considerations of form and purely abstract music, though still writing music of great charm and sympathy. Like Balakirev he was never attracted to opera, despite his love of picturesque subjects. His contribution to ballet music was of considerable importance (*see* BALLET). *See* G. Abraham, *On Russian Music,* 1929; G. Abraham and M. D. Calvocoressi, *Masters of Russian Music,* 1936.

Glebov, Igor', pseudonym of Asaf'yev, B. V. (q.v.)

Glière, Reinhold Moritsevich (1875–1956), prolific composer of Belgian descent, also a conductor and teacher. He studied the violin and composition at Kiev, and under Arenskiy, Taneyev and Ippolitov-Ivanov at Moscow Conservatory. From 1913 to 1920 he was director of the Kiev Conservatory, and from 1920 to 1941 professor at Moscow Conservatory. His pupils include Prokof'yev, Myaskovskiy, Knipper, Mosolov, Khachaturyan, etc. Works comprise five operas, including *Shah Senem,* 1923–5, and *Rachel,* 1942–3; many ballets, including *The Red Poppy,* 1926–7, and *Taras Bul'ba,* 1951–2; a cantata, *Glory to the Soviet Army,* 1953; three symphonies, No. 1 in E flat major, 1899–1900, No. 2 in C minor, *c.* 1907, and No. 3 in B minor, the programme symphony *Il'ya Muromets,* 1909–11; orchestral works, including *The Sirens,* 1908, and *Zapovit,* 1939–41; a cello concerto, 1945–6; a horn concerto, 1951; chamber works, etc.; songs; and music for plays and films. Glière is a composer who spans two eras, though remaining primarily an adherent of the classical traditions of Russian music. Keenly interested in folklore, his opera *Shah Senem* was based on Azerbaydzhanian subjects and folk music, and did much to stimulate the native growth of operatic art in that republic. Glière's orchestral music is well written and lavishly orchestrated, but suffers from lack of a clearly pronounced personal idiom. *See* L. Sabaneev, *Modern Russian Composers*, 1929.

Glinka, Mikhail Ivanovich (1804–57), composer, usually but erroneously termed 'the founder of Russian opera' (*see* OPERA). An excellent linguist and mathematician, he was brought up amidst the atmosphere of folk music, and studied under John Field and Carl Meyer in St Petersburg and Dehn in Berlin. He travelled widely, both in Russia and abroad, enjoyed the friendship of Griboyedov, Pushkin, Zhukovskiy (qq.v.) and Mickiewicz, and was acquainted with Donizetti, Bellini, Mendelssohn, Liszt and Berlioz. His works comprise two operas, *A Life for the Tsar*, 1836, now renamed *Ivan Susanin*, and *Ruslan and Lyudmila*, 1842; incidental music to *Prince Kholmskiy*, 1840; church music; secular choral works; many orchestral works, including *Jota Aragonesa* (Spanish Overture No. 1), 1845, *Summer Night in Madrid* (Spanish Overture No. 2), 1848, and *Kamarinskaya*, 1848; chamber music; much piano music and many songs. After his death his works were edited and published by Balakirev (q.v.). Glinka effected a subtle compromise between the forms of French grand opera, Italian vocal technique, German counterpoint and Russian folk-song. His employment of oriental material, the brilliance of his orchestration and his inspired treatment of folk-song had immense effect upon his successors. His harmonic innovations alone anticipate later procedure by several decades. *See* G. Abraham, *On Russian Music*, 1929; G. Abraham and M. D. Calvocoressi, *Masters of Russian Music*, 1936.

Gmyrya, Boris Romanovich (*b.* 1903), deep bass. After studying till 1935 at the Constructional Engineering Institute at Kharkov, he entered the Conservatory where he worked under Golubev till 1939. In the same year he was accepted at the Shevchenko Theatre, Kiev, where he has since taken the leading bass roles. A Ukrainian by origin, he has distinguished himself as a performer of Ukrainian vocal music.

Gnesin, Mikhail Fabianovich (1883–1957), composer, teacher and musicologist, who studied at St Petersburg Conservatory under Rimsky-Korsakov and Lyadov until 1909. He helped to found the Don Conservatory, becoming director in 1920; he was a professor at Moscow Conservatory, 1925–30, and at Leningrad, 1935–44. His pupils include Khachaturyan and Khrennikov. Works comprise an opera-poem *The Youth of Abraham*, 1921–3; works for chorus and orchestra, including *Symphonic Monument, 1905–17*, 1925; orchestral works; choral and chamber works; incidental music and folk-song arrangements. He is the author of several theoretical works on music. Gnesin's compositions owe much to his study of folk music, especially Jewish. *See* R. Moisenko, *Realist Music*, 1949.

Godunov, Boris Fëdorovich (1552–1605), boyar of Tatar origin who rose to become Czar of Muscovy. He became powerful during the latter part of Ivan the Terrible's reign, and practically ruled the country during the reign of Ivan's son Fëdor. On the latter's death in 1598 the Zemskiy Sobor (q.v.) elected Godunov czar. However, he was very unpopular, being regarded as a usurper, and was believed to have been concerned in bringing about the death of the rightful heir,

Prince Dmitriy; he died during the advance on Moscow of a false claimant to the throne. *See* TROUBLES, TIME OF.

Goelro (Russian abbreviation for 'State Plan for the Electrification of Russia'), plan worked out in 1920 for building a number of regional power-stations in order to increase the output of electricity within ten to fifteen years to 8·8 milliard kwh. (compared to 1·9 in 1913); an output of 8·4 was reached by 1930, by which time the original plan had been superseded by the first Five Year Plan. The Goelro plan was based on the preparatory work carried out during the First World War by technocratically minded experts (*see* ALEKSANDROV; GRINEVETSKIY). Krzhizhanovskiy drew Lenin's attention to the preliminary work and was put in charge of the Commission to prepare the final draft. Lenin immediately seized upon the plan, primarily for propaganda purposes, and coined the slogan 'Communism is Soviet power plus electrification of the whole country.' Present-day propaganda ascribes the initiative for the plan to Lenin. *See* H. Chambre, *L'Aménagement du territoire en U.R.S.S.*, Paris and The Hague, 1959.

Gogol', Nikolay Vasil'yevich (1809–52), writer, Ukrainian by origin. He lived abroad, mainly in Rome, from 1836 to 1846. Traditionally Gogol' is regarded as the father of the Realist school in Russian literature, though Pushkin had already laid its foundations. Among his chief works are two series of stories and sketches depicting life in the Ukraine (*Evenings on a Farm near Dikan'ka* and *Mirgorod*); the historical story *Taras Bul'ba*, an exciting portrait of the Zaporozh'ye Cossacks; *The Government Inspector*, 1836, a comedy of the failings of provincial administrative officials; and *Dead Souls*, 1837, a novel portraying different types of serf-owning provincial gentry. Most of Gogol's work is permeated by what he himself called 'the laughter through tears invisible to the world'; it combines social criticism with the mysticism and political conservatism that alienated him from the majority of his generation of writers but made him the precursor of much subsequent religious thought in Russia. *See* J. Lavrin, *Nikolai Gogol, 1809–52*, 1951; D. Magarshack, *Gogol, a Life*, 1957; N. V. Riasanovsky, *Nicholas I and Official Nationality in Russia, 1825–55*, Berkeley and Los Angeles, 1959.

Gold. Recent data on gold production are not available, though it is believed to be considerable. The main areas where gold is found are Kolyma in the Far East, Aldan and Bodaybo in Eastern Siberia, the Ural Mountains, and Krasnoyarsk Kray and Kemerovo Oblast in central Siberia. Until the disbanding of the main concentration camps (*see* CORRECTIVE LABOUR CAMPS) in the mid 1950's gold was largely mined by forced labour. The Soviet Government has shown reluctance to use its gold reserves to pay for imports. Ostensibly the Soviet currency (q.v.) is based on a gold standard. *See* J. D. Littlepage and D. Bess, *In Search of Soviet Gold*, 1939.

Golden Horde, medieval Mongol-Tatar state formed in 1236 by Batu, a grandson of Genghis Khan. It comprised most of the present European Russia and Western Siberia, with Saray on the lower Volga as its capital. The majority of the Russian principalities were conquered by the Mongols in 1237–40 and the princes became vassals of the Golden Horde khans (*see* MONGOL CONQUEST). Under Khan Uzbek in the 14th century Islam became the dominant religion of the state. The Golden Horde suffered defeats from Dmitriy Donskoy (q.v.) and Timur towards the end of the 14th century, and in the middle of the 15th century the state broke up into the khanates of Kazan', Astrakhan', Crimea and Siberia. *See also* CUMANS; MONGOLS; TATARS; TURKS; UZBEKS.

Golden Horn Bay, inlet of the Peter the Great Gulf of the Sea of Japan, upon which stands the port of Vladivostok.

Golovnin, Vasiliy Mikhaylovich (1776–1831), vice-admiral and famous navigator, who explored the coasts of Kamchatka and Alaska. He served as a volunteer in the British Navy, 1801–6. He was a prisoner of the Japanese, 1811–13, and circumnavigated the world, 1817–19. In 1823 he became intendant-general of the Russian Navy, and was responsible for the construction of more than two hundred warships, including the first ten Russian steamships. *See* his *Journey Round the World*, 1822, and *Narrative of My Captivity in Japan*, Eng. ed. (3 vols.), 1824.

Gol'tsev, Viktor Aleksandrovich (1850–1906), jurist and publicist. For many years he was the editor of the liberal journal *Russkaya Mysl'*, and he was the author of a number of books on the history of Russian law and education.

Gomel': 1. Oblast in south-eastern Belorussia, situated largely in the Poles'ye, traversed by the Dnieper and its right tributary the Pripet, largely covered with coniferous forests and marshes. Area 15,800 sq. m.; population (1959) 1,355,000 (29 per cent urban), Belorussian and Russian, before the war also Jewish. There are large deposits of peat; rye, potatoes, flax and hemp are grown, there is dairy farming and pig breeding, and food, light, lumbering, wood-processing and engineering industries. Principal towns: Gomel' and Mozyr'.

2. Administrative, economic and cultural centre of the oblast, an important railway junction (five lines). Population (1959) 166,000 (1897, 37,000; 1939, 139,000), before the war half Jewish. It has engineering (agricultural machinery), chemical and clothing industries. The famous palace of Prince Paskevich was built in the 18th century. Gomel' has been known since 1142, became Lithuanian in 1537 and again Russian in 1772; it was included in Belorussia in 1926. The town was largely destroyed during the Second World War and is now being restored.

Goncharov, Ivan Aleksandrovich (1814–91), novelist, at one time editor of an official newspaper, and censor, 1856–73. In the psychological study which made him famous, *Oblomov*, 1859, he portrayed the character of a completely indolent and slothful gentleman; the hero became a symbol of the agreeable laziness which is held to be a typical Russian characteristic. In *The Frigate 'Pallada,'* 1858, he describes his journey to Japan, and in *The Precipice*, 1869, confronts an ordinary family of gentry with a Nihilist. *See* J. Lavrin, *Goncharov*, 1954.

Gori, town in Georgia, 47 m. north-west of Tiflis. Population (1956) 33,100. It has been known since the 17th century and is the birthplace of Stalin; the house where he was born is now a museum.

Gor'kiy (until 1932 **Nizhniy Novgorod**): 1. Oblast of the R.S.F.S.R., situated in European Russia astride the Volga near its confluence with the Oka; the northern part of the oblast is lowland largely covered with coniferous forests, and the southern part, on the right bank of the Volga, includes the northern part of the Volga upland and lies in the wooded steppe zone. Area 28,200 sq. m.; population (1959) 3,500,000 (52 per cent urban), mostly Russians (since the 13th century), also some Mordva, Chuvash and Mari. There are engineering, chemical and metal-working industries in the highly industrialized centre and in the south-west of the oblast, and lumbering in the north; there is also grain, flax, potato and dairy farming, and a large hydro-electric station. Principal towns: Gor'kiy, Dzerzhinsk, Pavlovo, Kulebaki and Arzamas.

2. Administrative, economic and cultural centre of the oblast, the largest city in Russia east of Moscow, situated on the right bank of the Volga at the mouth of the Oka. Population (1959) 942,000 (third in the R.S.F.S.R., fifth in the U.S.S.R.; 1897, 96,000; 1917, 148,000; 1920, 88,000; 1939, 644,000). It is one of the most important industrial centres of the U.S.S.R., with a large engineering industry, including a vast automobile plant (built 1930–2) and the Sormovo transport engineering plant; there are also Diesel motor, machine-tool, etc., works, oil-processing, glass, woodworking and various light and food industries. Gor'kiy is a major transportation centre, with the largest river port in the country, five railway lines and an airport. The city has a university (established 1918, abolished 1930, re-established 1931), a polytechnical institute (formed in 1898 in Warsaw, evacuated during the war and reopened in Gor'kiy in 1916) and several other higher educational establishments. The drama theatre, established in 1798, is one of the oldest in Russia; there is a kremlin (built 1374–1511) and there are interesting churches and other buildings of the 17th–19th centuries.

The Grand Prince of Vladimir founded Gor'kiy in 1221 on the site of a Bulgarian settlement as a frontier fortress against the Volga Bulgarians and the Mordva, and it played a similar role in the long struggle against the Tatars. In 1350 it became the capital of Suzdal'-Nizhniy Novgorod principality and rivalled the growing influence of Moscow; it was annexed by Muscovy in 1392 and was its base for the conquest of Kazan' in 1552. During the Time of Troubles (see TROUBLES, TIME OF) Gor'kiy was one of the centres of the patriotic forces: here, in 1611, K. Minin launched the movement for the liberation of Moscow from the Poles. The annual fair, founded in 1525 in nearby Makar'yev (transferred to Gor'kiy in 1817) to assist in the economic struggle against Kazan', was the biggest in Russia, and made the city the country's chief commercial centre; it was abolished in 1930. The industrial development of Gor'kiy began early in the 19th century (flour mills); its heavy industry dates from 1849 (Sormovo works), and several factories were evacuated there from Riga during the First World War. Development was greatly speeded up from 1930, and within five years the city attained its present industrial eminence. Gor'kiy was a provincial capital from 1719, and from 1929 to 1934 was the capital of Gor'kiy Territory, which comprised the present Gor'kiy and Kirov oblasts and the Udmurt, Mari and Chuvash Autonomous Republics. It was one of the principal Bolshevik strongholds during the civil war and the 1920's.

Gor'kiy, Maksim (real name **Peshkov, Aleksey Maksimovich**) (1868–1936), writer and publicist, born of an artisan family and early orphaned. He lacked any formal education, and in his youth wandered about Russia and had many different jobs (described in *Childhood*, 1913, *My Apprenticeship*, 1918, and *My Universities*, 1923). Gor'kiy started writing in 1892, achieving fame in Russia by 1898 with his collected tales and abroad in 1902 with his play *The Lower Depths*. His early writings were romantic stories of tramps and gipsies; he turned then to Chekhovian stories and plays of depressing lives and futile intellectuals, and later to exposing capitalist society in a Marxist fashion (*Mother*, 1907, *The Artamonov Business*, 1925, *Klim Samgin*, 1927–36). He supported the Bolsheviks and, together with Krasin (q.v.), was their main source of income before and during the revolution of 1905. He lived as an *émigré* on Capri from 1906 to 1913 and with Bogdanov established the anti-Leninist Left-wing Bolshevik sub-faction Forward in 1909 (*see* VPERĕD). In collaboration with Lunacharskiy (q.v.) he developed the ideology of 'God-building,' an attempt to supplement Marxism with a new religion for the future collectivized working man (*Confession*, 1908). After the February revolution of 1917 he set up a non-Bolshevik Left Social Democratic group called New Life (after its paper, which he published). Though he opposed the Bolshevik seizure of power, he co-operated with the regime from 1919 and was instrumental in saving many intellectuals from terror and starvation. He again emigrated to Italy for the years 1921–8, first attacking the Soviet regime, then becoming its apologist and finally returning to the U.S.S.R. He headed the Writers' Union (q.v.) which was set up in 1932 by the party to replace all literary associations (which were dissolved), and was declared founder of the Socialist Realism (q.v.) school. Gor'kiy, who during the last years of his life was a close friend of Stalin, was pre-eminent in extolling all aspects of Stalinism, including the forced labour camp system (*White Sea Canal*, 1934). He had always suffered from tuberculosis, and probably died naturally, but at the Bukharin show trial of 1938 was stated to have been a victim of the Anti-Soviet Bloc of Rightists and Trotskiyites (q.v.). *See* A. S. Kaun, *Maxim Gorky and his Russia*, 1932.

Gorlovka, city in the Stalino Oblast of the Ukraine, situated 20 m. north-east of Stalino. Population (1959) 293,000 (fourth in Donbas; 1897, 2,000; 1926, 23,000; 1939, 181,000). It is one of the important and rapidly growing industrial centres of the Donets Basin, with large coal-mining, engineering (mining machinery), chemical and other industries; in the northern suburb of Nikitovka there are mercury-mines. It is connected by an oil pipeline with the Groznyy oilfields of the North Caucasus. The mining school in the city was founded in 1876 and was one of the first in Russia. Gorlovka was founded in 1867 as a mining settlement and became a town in 1930.

Gorno-Altay Autonomous Oblast, *see* MOUNTAINOUS-ALTAY AUTONOMOUS OBLAST.

Gorno-Altaysk (formerly **Ulala**, 1932–48 **Oyrot Tura**), administrative, economic and cultural centre of the Mountainous-Altay Autonomous Oblast (southern Siberia), situated 60 m. south-east of Biysk near the Chuya highway to Mongolia. Population (1959) 27,000, mostly Russians. Gorno-Altaysk was founded as a village, and became a town in 1928.

Gosplan (Russian abbreviation for 'State Planning Commission'), government departments on the all-Union and Union Republic level for the planning and co-ordination of economic activities. They produce both the annual and the long-term economic plans, supervise the allocation of resources and the distribution of products, etc. The internal structure of Gosplan comprises three types of departments and sections, according to branches of the economy, regions and specific functions such as supply of raw materials, labour, etc. Gosplan was founded in 1921 under the chairmanship of Krzhizhanovskiy, and during the 1920's was largely run by ex-Menshevik enthusiasts for economic planning, e.g. Groman, and technocratically minded engineers, e.g. Aleksandrov; but the first Five Year Plan, devised by them so as not to disorganize the economy as a whole, was found by the party leadership to be insufficient, and this served as a pretext for a wave of terror against the technical intelligentsia and Social Democrats (*see* INDUSTRIAL PARTY; MENSHEVIKS; SHAKHTY). Since then Gosplan has usually been directed by people belonging to the party leadership (*see* KOSYGIN; SABUROV; VOZNESENSKIY). There have been several reorganizations of Gosplan; the latest, in connection with the reform of the economic administration in 1957 (*see* ECONOMIC COUNCILS), resulted in Gosplan taking over part of the many co-ordinating functions of the former ministries; several leading officials of Gosplan are in consequence now members of the Council of Ministers (q.v.) and have the title of minister. In 1960 responsibility for the long-term economic planning for the whole U.S.S.R. was transferred from Gosplan to the State Scientific Economic Council (Gosekonomsovet). *See* H. Schwartz, *Russia's Soviet Economy*, 2nd ed., 1954; H. Chambre, *L'Aménagement du territoire en U.R.S.S.*, Paris and The Hague, 1959.

Government: 1. As the chief executive organ of the country, *see* COUNCIL OF MINISTERS.

2. As the structure of political power, the Government is officially a Dictatorship of the Proletariat (q.v.) exercised since 1936 in democratic forms (*see* CONSTITUTION). In fact it is a totalitarian dictatorship of the Communist Party (q.v.), exercised through the party apparatus, the security organs, the soviets, ministries, trade unions, Komsomol (qq.v.), the economic administration and many other organizations and institutions. For an account of the historical development of government in Russia *see* cross-references under HISTORY. *See also* BOLSHEVISM; LENINISM; STALINISM; TOTALITARIANISM. *See* M. Fainsod, *How Russia is Ruled*, Cambridge, Mass., 1953; J. N. Hazard, *The Soviet System of Government*, Chicago, 1957; D. J. R. Scott, *Russian Political Institutions*, 1958.

Government Bonds have existed from the 1920's in two categories: 1. Bonds issued annually until 1958, to which subscription was in practice compulsory, though the fiction of voluntary subscription was maintained; annual subscriptions amounted to roughly three to four weeks' earnings, and were deducted automatically from wages and salaries. They took the form either of interest-yielding bonds or of lotteries, the latter becoming increasingly predominant. They were not ordinarily negotiable except by special permission in case of severe illness, etc., in which case the State would pay one-third of the face value. They were twice converted, in the late 1930's and in 1947, new bonds at a lower rate of interest being issued in return for old ones due to be repaid in the near future. The issue of these bonds was discontinued in 1958; repayment of the debt to bond-holders was postponed for 'twenty or twenty-five years,' and interest and prize money were frozen.

2. Interest-bearing bonds that are freely bought and sold from the Savings Bank, which in its turn buys up the total issue of bonds.

The total budget revenue from government bonds was 44·3 milliard pre-1961 roubles in 1956 (31·0 in 1950), of which 32·8 milliard roubles were subscription bonds (26·4 in 1950) and 10·0 milliard roubles negotiable bonds (3·1 in 1950). Government expenditure on repayment, interest and administrative costs totalled 16·3 milliard roubles in 1956 (5·1 in 1950). In 1958 total revenue was 10·6 milliard roubles, of which 3·2 milliard were subscription bonds and 6·5 milliard negotiable bonds; government expenditure amounted to 3·7 milliard roubles. *See* F. D. Holzman, *Soviet Taxation*, Cambridge, Mass., 1955.

G.P.U. (abbreviation for 'State Political Administration'), Soviet security service from 1922 to 1934. In functions and powers it resembled its predecessor, the Cheka (q.v.). Its operations were directed against the Church, 'socially alien' elements and former members of opposition parties during the N.E.P. period, and against private *entrepreneurs* and traders, the old intelligentsia and *kulaks* during the following years of the first Five Year Plan and the collectivization of agriculture. The internal party conflict was also an increasing concern of the G.P.U. Its name was changed to N.K.V.D. (q.v.) in 1934. *See further under* SECURITY ORGANS.

Grain Crops. The sown area under grain crops has fluctuated considerably during the Soviet period, as is shown in the following table (totals in million hectares, selected individual crops in percentage of the total).

	1913 [1]	1928	1940	1945	1953	1958
Total	104·6	92·2	110·5	85·3	106·7	125·2
Wheat	31·6	30·1	36·4	29·2	45·3	53·2
Rye	27·8	26·7	21·1	24·0	19·1	14·2
Oats	18·3	18·7	18·3	16·9	14·4	11·8
Barley	12·7	7·9	10·2	12·2	9·0	6·8
Maize	2·1	4·8	3·3	4·9	3·3	6·4

The principal grain-growing areas are northern Kazakhstan, central Russia, the Ukraine, Western Siberia, the Urals, the Volga region and the North Caucasus. The barn crop harvest in 1958

[1] Present-day frontiers.

amounted to 141·2 million tons (86·0 in 1913, 73·3 in 1928, 95·5 in 1940, 82·3 in 1955), an all-time record for Russia. Grain production as a whole is still insufficient, and especially forage crops. Average total grain production 1954–5 was 566 kilogrammes per head of population, of which only 30 per cent was forage grain (36 per cent in 1913). Yields are low, the average for all grain crops having fluctuated, 1953–8, between 7·7 and 11·3 metric hundredweights per hectare (8·2 in 1913). The average yield of summer wheat in the same period fluctuated between 5·3 and 10·7 (7·3 in 1913).

Grain is a traditional object of Russian export: 5·1 million tons of grain were exported in 1958, making up 8·3 per cent of total Soviet exports (33·3 per cent in 1913, 3·3 per cent in 1928, 21·3 per cent in 1938, 18·5 per cent in 1950); in 1913 the Russian grain export formed 30·4 per cent of the world total. *See also* AGRICULTURE; VIRGIN LAND CAMPAIGN.

Grave, Dmitriy Aleksandrovich (1863–1939), mathematician, a pupil of Chebyshev (q.v.), professor at Kiev University, honorary member of the Academy of Sciences, 1929. His many works were concerned with higher algebra, theory of numbers, theory of groups, as well as the mathematical aspects of cartography, etc. He was one of the first scientists to co-operate with the Soviet regime. Among his pupils was O. Yu. Schmidt (q.v.).

Great Purge, wave of terror which convulsed the country in 1936–8 (known in Russia as the *yezhovshchina*, from the then head of the N.K.V.D., Yezhov). Kirov's assassination in 1934 was used as an excuse for the arrest of former oppositionists, but the range widened until by mid 1936 arrests became arbitrary and almost indiscriminate, though higher officials and some national minorities suffered more than the remainder of the population. The majority of the Central Committee (including many faithful Stalinists), Yagoda (Yezhov's predecessor as head of the N.K.V.D.), and even Politburo members, were among the arrested, and all were accused of sabotage, treason, preparation of terroristic acts, espionage, etc., and were proclaimed 'enemies of the people.' They were summarily sentenced to death or to long imprisonment in 'corrective labour camps' by special N.K.V.D. three-man committees (*see* TROYKA), the sole proof of their guilt being 'confessions' extracted by torture. Only a few cases were presented at the Zinov'yev, Pyatakov and Bukharin show trials.

The number of victims of the Great Purge cannot be ascertained, but estimates of eight or ten million are probably not exaggerations. When Beria replaced Yezhov as N.K.V.D. chief the purge ended. An ideological justification for it was given by Stalin, who declared that as a country progresses towards full socialism the class struggle intensifies. The consequences of the Great Purge were the complete victory of Stalin's dictatorial rule through his personal secretariat and the security organs, the promotion of the latter above the party, and the appearance of that atmosphere of insincerity and fictitiousness (*see* FICTION) which characterized Soviet public life until the post-Stalin 'thaw.' *See* F. Beck and W. Godin, *Russian Purge and the Extraction of Confessions*, 1951; A. Weissberg, *Conspiracy of Silence,*

1952; H. Dewar, *The Modern Inquisition*, 1953; B. D. Wolfe, *Khrushchëv and Stalin's Ghost*, 1957.

Great Reforms, radical changes in the social and political life of Russia effected by the reforms of Alexander II, of which the following were the most important: emancipation of the serfs with land (*see* SERFDOM) in 1861, and reform of their self-government system (*see* MIR); local government reform—provincial, 1864 (*see* ZEMSTVO), municipal, 1870; establishment of the autonomy of the universities, 1863, and the introduction of universal military service, 1874; and a judicial reform, introducing among other things trial by jury in criminal cases, 1864. With the support both of the emperor and of progressive public opinion, these reforms were carried out by liberal ministers and officials in the face of opposition (and sometimes sabotage) from both conservatives and revolutionaries. A representative assembly with consultative functions was to be set up to 'crown the edifice' of the reforms in 1881, but on the very day of the signing of the decree Alexander II was assassinated. The police and the civil service remained unreformed, with serious consequences for future developments. *See* H. Seton-Watson, *The Decline of Imperial Russia*, 1952; G. Fischer, *Russian Liberalism. From Gentry to Intelligentsia*, Cambridge, Mass., 1958; W. E. Mosse, *Alexander II and the Modernization of Russia*, 1958.

Great Russians, name used for the most numerous people of Russia to distinguish them from Belorussians and Ukrainians, together with whom they constitute the Russian or Eastern branch of the Slav family. They number (1959) 114,600,000, and form 83 per cent of the population in the R.S.F.S.R. as well as considerable minorities in all other republics of the U.S.S.R. The Great Russians are largely the product of the mixture of the northern and eastern Russian tribes of the early Middle Ages with the neighbouring Finnish tribes.

Grechaninov, Aleksandr Tikhonovich (1864–1956), composer, who studied under Rimsky-Korsakov at St Petersburg Conservatory and with Safonov at Moscow Conservatory. In 1922 he left his native country and finally settled in the U.S.A., acquiring American citizenship in 1946. Works comprise operas, including *Dobrynya Nikitich*, 1902, and *Sister Beatrice*, 1912; five symphonies; chamber music; church music; piano pieces; songs and folk-songs, etc. Though outmoded in his musical thought Grechaninov's music is of considerable interest, especially the children's pieces. *See* M. Montague-Nathan, *Contemporary Russian Composers*, 1917; L. Sabaneev, 'Grechaninov,' in the journal *Dominant*, 1928; A. T. Grechaninov, *My Life* (trans. N. Slonimsky), New York, 1952.

Greeks in Russia numbered 310,000 in 1959, of whom 42 per cent regarded Greek as their mother-tongue. They are divided into two distinct groups: (1) Those who live mostly along the north and north-eastern shores of the Black Sea (the former New Russia, q.v.), particularly in and around the town of Mariupol' (now Zhdanov), are the descendants of 18th- and 19th-century immigrants from Greece, speaking modern Greek; some Greeks of this group were deported to Central Asia at the beginning of the Second World War, and some were repatriated to Greece during the German occupation. (2) Those living in Transcaucasia and some parts of the Northern Caucasus (now numbering about 150,000) are the descendants of immigrants from Asiatic Turkey, many of them Turkic-speaking; some of these came to Russia in the 19th century to settle in the territories vacated by Circassians and Abkhazians who had emigrated to Turkey. *See* W. Kolarz, *Russia and her Colonies*, 1952.

Grekov, Boris Dmitriyevich (1882–1953), historian, pupil of Klyuchevskiy. His main field of research was medieval Russian history (*Kievan Russia*, 1939, *Peasants in Russia from the Earliest Times to the Seventeenth Century*, 1946, *The Golden Horde and its Fall*, 1950). Grekov's National Bolshevik (*see* NATIONAL BOLSHEVISM) school of historiography superseded Pokrovskiy's school as the officially recognized one from the middle 1930's. *See* STALINISM; ZHDANOV. *See* his *The Culture of Kiev Rus* (Eng. ed.), Moscow, 1949; C. E. Black (ed.), *Rewriting Russian History*, New York, 1956.

Griboyedov, Aleksandr Sergeyevich (1798–1829), author, famous for his one great play, *Woe from Wit*, 1823, a satirical comedy upon Russian high society not published until 1833 because of rejection by the censor. He became minister-plenipotentiary to Persia in 1828 and was murdered there during anti-Russian riots.

Grigor'yev, Apollon Aleksandrovich (1822–64), literary critic, the chief representative of the 'soil-bound' school of literary criticism. In his writings he emphasized the organic character and the original roots of Russian popular life, in this resembling the Slavophiles but not taking up their anti-Western position. *See* V. V. Zenkovsky, *A History of Russian Philosophy*, vol. i, 1953; T. G. Masaryk, *The Spirit of Russia* (2nd ed.), vol. i, 1955.

Grigor'yev, Sergey (*b.* 1883), ballet master, dancer and *régisseur*. After studying until 1900 at the Imperial School, St Petersburg, Grigor'yev was employed by Diaghilev as *régisseur* for the first Paris season of the Ballets Russes in 1909, remaining permanently with Diaghilev until the impresario's death in 1929. From 1932 he worked with Colonel de Basil in the Ballets Russes de Monte Carlo and its successor in Australia, the Original Ballet Russe. Since then he has been attached to the Royal Ballet. He is the possessor of a remarkable memory. *See* S. Grigoriev, *The Diaghilev Ballet, 1909–29*, 1953.

Grinevetskiy, Vasiliy Ignat'yevich (1871–1919), engineer and economist, professor (later director) of the Moscow Higher Technical School. He was a prominent figure among the Russian technical intelligentsia, supported the Whites during the civil war, and died in Yekaterinodar. In *The Post-war Prospects of Russian Industry* (Khar'kov, 1919; 2nd ed., Moscow, 1922) Grinevetskiy described the principal problems of Russia's economic development and suggested the most appropriate methods of solving them. The book had much influence upon Russian economic thought of the 1920's and early thirties, and the Five Year Plans largely incorporated the aims outlined in it, though in fact compulsion rather than economic incentives was resorted to.

Grodno: 1. Oblast in west Belorussia, situated largely on the moraine hills of the Belorussian upland, and traversed by the River Niemen. Area (1959) 7,600 sq. m.; population (1959) 897,000 (25 per cent urban), Belorussians, some Russians, Jews and Lithuanians (before the war also Poles). There is grain, potato and flax growing, and pigs and cattle are raised; the industries of the oblast are food, saw-milling and woodworking. Principal towns: Grodno, Novogrudok.

2. Administrative, economic and cultural centre of the oblast, situated on the Niemen 80 m. south-west of Vilnius. Population (1959) 72,000 (1888, 45,000; 1910, 65,500; 1939, 49,000). It has fine cloth, tobacco and wood-processing industries, and is an important transportation centre; there are many architectural monuments of the 12th–18th centuries. Grodno has been known since 1128, when it was the capital of a principality; it became Lithuanian in 1398 (and was the second capital of Lithuania), Russian in 1795, and was Polish 1919–39.

Groman, Vladimir Gustavovich (1875–?), economist and politician of half-German parentage. He joined the Social Democratic Party in 1900, its Menshevik faction in 1905, and was prominent in propaganda work during and after the revolution of 1905 (q.v.). He became a 'liquidationist' (q.v.) after 1905 and a 'defencist' during the First World War, working in one of the Government's war-time economic organizations. After the February revolution (q.v.) in 1917 he was responsible for the food supply of the capital. He left the Menshevik Party in order to take an active part in the economic planning (q.v.), and from 1923 to 1928 was the leading figure in the Gosplan (q.v.), as a member of its Presidium and main inspirer of its work; in particular he developed the balances (q.v.) method. However, he was dismissed in 1928 for refusing to revise the first version of the first Five Year Plan in line with Stalin's views on forced industrialization and collectivization of agriculture. Even after his dismissal he continued to argue publicly his point of view, was arrested in 1930 and figured as the chief defendant at the Menshevik trial in 1931, where he 'confessed' to wrecking activities. His reputation has not been rehabilitated since Stalin's death. *See* N. Jasny, 'A Soviet Planner—V. G. Groman,' *Russian Review*, Jan. 1954; S. V. Utechin, 'Bolsheviks and their Allies after 1917: the Ideological Pattern,' *Soviet Studies*, Oct. 1958.

Gromyko, Andrey Andreyevich (*b.* 1909), diplomat of Belorussian parentage. An economist by education, and a party member since 1931, Gromyko was transferred to diplomatic work in 1939 after the Great Purge (q.v.), which had depleted the foreign service. He became counsellor at the Soviet Embassy in Washington in 1939, succeeded Litvinov as ambassador to the U.S.A. in 1943, was permanent representative of the U.S.S.R. in the Security Council of the United Nations, 1946–8, deputy Foreign Minister, 1947–52 and again 1953–7, ambassador to Great Britain, 1952–3, and succeeded Shepilov as Foreign Minister in 1957. He is the first career diplomat to occupy this latter post in the Soviet Government, and his role seems to be purely technical.

Groznyy, capital, economic and cultural centre of the Chechen-Ingush Autonomous Republic (North Caucasus), situated on a tributary of the River Terek, the largest town of the Caucasian foothills and the centre of the Groznyy oilfields. Population (1959) 240,000 (1897, 16,000; 1926, 97,000; 1939, 172,000), chiefly Russians. It has cracking plants and refineries, an engineering industry (oil industry equipment), and is the starting-point of oil pipelines to Makhachkala, Tuapse and Gorlovka. Groznyy was founded in 1818 by General A. P. Yermolov, became a town in 1870 and a centre of the oil industry in 1893. From 1944 to 1957 it was capital of the Groznyy Oblast.

Gubkin, Ivan Mikhaylovich (1871–1939), geologist, professor and rector of the Moscow Mining Academy, founder and director of the Academy of Sciences' Institute of Mineral Fuels, member of the academy from 1929, chairman of its council for the study of productive forces, 1930–6, and vice-president from 1936. He joined the Communist Party in 1921. From 1910 Gubkin took an active part in directing practical prospecting work, first on behalf of the Geological Committee and from 1918 as the head of the geological service in the country. A leading oil specialist, he personally directed the study of the Volga-Urals Oil Area (q.v.).

Guchkov, Aleksandr Ivanovich (1862–1936), chairman of the Octobrist Party and President of the 3rd State Duma. In the First World War he was chairman of the Duma Committee on Military and Naval Affairs, and subsequently chairman of the non-governmental Central War Industries Committee. He became Minister for War and Navy in the Provisional Government that followed the February 1917 revolution but resigned in May.

Guided Missiles, *see* ROCKETS.

Gulag (Russian abbreviation for 'Chief Administration of Camps'), department of the Ministry (former Commissariat) of Internal Affairs in charge of 'corrective labour camps' and colonies (qq.v.) which existed 1934–60. Besides being responsible for the camps themselves, Gulag was also a vast economic administration for the supply of food, etc., to camp inmates and staff and for the many industrial undertakings (mining, timber-felling) and construction projects in which forced labour was used. Plan targets were assigned to it in the same way as to industrial ministries in the Five Year Plans, and some of the most important enterprises, such as the Noril'sk uranium-mines, were run by Gulag. The fate of Gulag after the abolition of the all-Union M.V.D. (q.v.) in 1960 is unknown.

Gumilëv, Nikolay Stepanovich (1886–1921), poet and monarchist who was shot by the Bolsheviks, the husband of Anna Akhmatova (q.v.). A disciple of the Symbolist school, he later rejected its tenets and formed his own 'Acmeist' group devoted to a kind of dynamic neo-Classicism. His verses, in some sense reminiscent of Kipling, are concerned with adventure, struggle and heroism. *See* G. Struve, *Soviet Russian Literature, 1917–50*, Norman, Oklahoma, 1951; G. Ivanov, *Peterburgskiye zimy*, New York, 1952; M. Slonim, *Modern Russian Literature*, New York, 1953.

Gunib, fortress and village in the centre of the Daghestan Mountains, 50 m. south-west of Makhachkala, situated on an almost inaccessible conic mountain. Population (1926) 387. Gunib was the last refuge of Shamil', the chief of the mountain tribes, who surrendered here to Russia in 1859.

Gur'yev: 1. Oblast in western Kazakhstan adjacent to the Caspian Sea, traversed by the lower course of the River Ural, the River Emba and the Gur'yev-Orsk railway; there are oil deposits in the lower Emba area. Area 107,300 sq. m.; population (1959) 288,000 (56 per cent urban), mainly Kazakhs, also Russians and Koreans. There is oil extraction and processing, sheep raising, and fishing. The north of the oblast formed part of the traditional 'gateway to Europe' for the nomadic peoples of Asia. In the 13th–15th centuries the area belonged to the Golden Horde (and one of its capitals was situated here), then to the Nogay khanate. In the 16th century Russian Cossacks from the Volga began to settle on the banks of the Ural. The Kazakh Junior Hundred was formed east of the Ural in the 17th century, and in the following century, pressed by the Kalmyks and the Turkmens, sought Russian protection. Oil extraction began in 1911.

2. Administrative, economic and cultural centre of the oblast, situated at the mouth of the Ural. Population (1959) 78,000 (1939, 41,000), mainly Russians. It has oil-processing, fishing and metal-working industries, and is the starting-point of an oil pipeline to Orsk. There is a branch of the Kazakh Academy of Sciences. Gur'yev was founded in the early 17th century by Russian fishermen, and remained simply a centre of the fishing settlements until the 1930's.

Gus'-Khrustal'nyy, town in the Vladimir Oblast (central Russia), situated 40 m. south of Vladimir. Population (1959) 53,000. It is an important centre of the glass industry (including crystal glass and glass fibres), with several factories and a unique crystal glass museum. Glass-working in the area dates from 1756, when the crystal glass factory was founded by Mal'tsev.

Gutsuls, *see* HUTSULS.

H

Hague Conference, peace conference called by Nicholas II in 1899 with a view to 'a possible reduction of the excessive armaments which weigh upon all nations' which was to be effected by 'putting a limit to the progressive development of the present armaments.' Little was achieved either at this conference or at its successor in 1907, though a permanent court was constituted, with an international office at The Hague.

Health Services. All medical treatment is free (with the exception of prescriptions which must be paid for), though better facilities are often available on payment. In 1958 there were 362,000 doctors (1913, 23,000), i.e. 17 doctors per 10,000 population (1 in 1913). All doctors are employed in hospitals or clinics, but they may have a private practice in addition to their employment. The number of hospital beds has risen from 207,000 in 1912 to 1,533,000 in 1958, i.e. from 13 beds to 73 per 10,000 population. There were in 1958 305,000 beds in sanatoria and 161,000 in rest-homes; in 1957 over three million wage and salary earners were enabled to spend some time in sanatoria or rest-homes either free or paying 30 per cent of the cost. *See* H. E. Sigerist, *Socialized Medicine in the Soviet Union*, 1937; M. G. Field, 'The Soviet Doctor's Dilemma,' *Problems of Communism*, vol. vi, No. 1, Jan.–Feb. 1957; G. S. Poudoev, *Notes of a Soviet Doctor*, 1959; A. Nove, 'Towards a "Communist Welfare State"?,' *Problems of Communism*, vol. ix, No. 1, Jan–Feb. 1960.

Heavy Industry, *see* entries on coal, engineering, iron and steel, and oil industries, and NON-FERROUS METALS.

Herzen (Russian **Gertsen**), **Aleksandr Ivanovich** (1812–70), thinker and publicist, a founder of Populism (q.v.). Living in emigration (chiefly in London) from 1847, he set up the Free Russian Press and published *The Bell*, the first Russian *émigré* paper, which had much influence inside Russia. As a liberal socialist Herzen repudiated the notion that human beings could or should be sacrificed for the sake of any abstract principle. *See* his *My Past and Thoughts*, 1924, *From the Other Shore*, 1956, and *Selected Philosophical Works*, Moscow, 1956. *See* E. H. Carr, *The Romantic Exiles*, 1932; R. Hare, *Pioneers of Russian Social Thought*, Oxford, 1951; T. G. Masaryk, *The Spirit of Russia*, vol. ii, 2nd ed., 1955; P. Scheibert, *Von Bakunin zu Lenin*, Leiden, 1956; E. Lampert, *Studies in Rebellion*, 1957; M. Partridge, 'A. Herzen and the English Press,' *Slavonic Review*, vol. xxxvi, No. 87, June 1958; F. Venturi, *Roots of Revolution*, 1960.

Hetman, title of the highest officer of the Zaporozh'ye Cossacks from the late 16th century and of the head of the Cossack state, 1648–1764. The title was revived during the German occupation of the Ukraine in 1918, and for seven months General P. Skoropads'kyy ruled the country as hetman.

Higher Education, as understood in Russia, is that which follows full secondary education (q.v.), either general or professional. It is more vocational in character than in most countries. There are a great number of higher educational establishments, divided into universities (q.v.), which enjoy a higher prestige, and others, usually called institutes. Some of the latter, usually called polytechnical institutes, are a kind of technical university; the rest are more or less narrowly specialized. Courses normally take four to six years. Since the 1958 educational reform (*see* EDUCATION) evening or correspondence study combined with regular employment is compulsory for students of many higher educational establishments in their first two or three years. Applicants are admitted to entrance examinations if they can produce a satisfactory certificate of 'worthiness' from a party, Komsomol or trade-union committee, from the management of their place of work or at least from their headmaster, stressing the politically relevant aspects of their character. Preferential treatment is accorded to applicants with at least two years of regular employment and to those discharged from military service, and special preparatory courses are organized for them. Enterprises, institutions and collective farms are encouraged to second deserving and politically reliable young people to higher educational establishments and to maintain them during their course of study provided they return to the same place of work. Other students receive State grants according to need and performance. No fees have been payable since 1956. Syllabuses are laid down and textbooks prescribed by the government departments in charge of the particular branch of study, while the Ministry of Higher and Professional Secondary Education supervises the teaching methods, and the teachers or individual institutions have little scope for manœuvre. About four hundred hours of lectures and seminars during the course of study in all establishments of higher education are taken up by political subjects —'dialectical and historical materialism,' political economy and history of the Communist Party. On completion of their course the best students are given a chance of graduate work (*see* ASPIRANT), while the rest are assigned to work at the discretion of special placing commissions. People with higher education occupy a definite place in the social hierarchy; they make up the upper ranks of 'specialists' (*see* INTELLIGENTSIA) and as such enjoy certain economic and social privileges.

The first establishments of higher education in Russia were theological academies. Universities and specialized institutes followed in the 18th and 19th centuries, moulded chiefly after the German pattern. The first higher women's courses were set up as private bodies in the 1860's and after the 1905 revolution women were allowed to attend universities as external students. Several attempts before 1905 to restrict the admission of applicants from the 'lower orders' did not prevent the increasing democratization of the student body. Since 1917 higher education has had a chequered development. During the 1920's and thirties there was a dual system of higher education, the authorities favouring Communist universities, Red Professorship Institutes (qq.v.) and similar new foundations at the expense of the traditional establishments. The latter suffered from shortage of funds, low academic level of entrants (resulting from the disorganization of secondary education and from political and social discrimination between applicants), arbitrary 'purges' of the teaching staff and continuous reorganizations resulting in ever narrower specialization. The policy of stabilization pursued by the authorities for two decades, from the mid 1930's till the mid 1950's, brought about the disappearance of duality in higher education (most of the post-revolutionary Communist foundations were abolished) and the restoration of the prestige of traditional institutions at the price of ideological integration, freedom from social discrimination between applicants, tuition fees, grants according to performance instead of need and privileges for people with higher education. All these factors combined resulted in greatly raising the standards of achievement, but at the same time largely confined higher education to the children of the intelligentsia. The rapid expansion of secondary education in 1950–6 was not accompanied by a corresponding expansion of higher education, and the entrance examinations became highly competitive, further increasing the share of students coming from educated families. Students played an active part in the intellectual opposition (q.v.) which developed after Stalin's death (as they did before 1917), and this was one of the reasons for Khrushchëv's reform of higher education in 1958, which signified a partial return to the conditions of the 1920's and thirties. The following table illustrates the problem of school-leavers (in thousands).

	1950	1953	1955	1956	1957	1958
Completed secondary school	315	500	1,100	1,300	1,500	1,600
Admission to higher educational establishments:						
Full-time	228·4	265·1	257·2	231·2	219·7	213·9
Evening and correspondence	120·7	165·7	204·2	227·5	218·6	239·4

The following table shows graduates (including evening and correspondence) from higher educational establishments according to subjects of study (in thousands):

	1958
Industry, building, transport and communications	93·6
Agriculture	30·9
Economics and law	24·0
Medicine, physical culture and sport	26·0
Education (i.e. all university students, plus Pedagogical and Library Institute students)	113·6
Art (including music and drama)	2·6

The following table gives a comparison between the U.S.S.R. and the U.S.A. (in thousands):

	1955	
	U.S.S.R.	U.S.A.
Persons completing higher education	245·8	292·9
Per million of population	1·2	1·8
Technological graduates [1]	66	23
Per cent of total graduates	27	8

[1] In 1957, 83 and 31 respectively.

Hiiumaa (Russian **Khiuma,** Swedish **Dagö**), island belonging to Estonia, situated in the Moonsund Archipelago off the eastern shore of the Baltic Sea, north of Saaremaa Island. Area 367 sq. m.

Historical Materialism, official designation of the sociological and historical doctrine of Marxism. *See also* DIALECTICAL MATERIALISM; ECONOMIC MATERIALISM; MATERIALISM.

Historiography. There have been three principal trends in modern Russian historiography. Historians belonging to the Westernist (q.v.) trend maintain or imply the essential similarity of Russia's historical development to that of Western Europe, and emphasize actual similarities and Western influences. Opposed to them have been the Slavophiles (q.v.), postulating the essential originality of Russian history and institutions and stressing their differences from those of Western Europe. Finally, the Eurasians (q.v.) have interpreted Russian history in terms of the peculiarities of the country's geographical and cultural position between Europe and Asia, and especially emphasized oriental influences. The conservative monarchist school of Tatishchev and Karamzin (qq.v.) developed the first logical scheme of Russian history, as passing through the stages of monarchy, particularization (12th–15th centuries) and new monarchy. It was superseded by the 'historical' school led by S. M. Solov'ëv (q.v.), with its organic view of Russia's historical development in common with Western Europe, and the *étatist* school of B. N. Chicherin (q.v.), which regarded the State as the direct creator of history and concentrated upon the study of State institutions. An extreme westernist position was taken by the Marxists (*see* LEGAL MARXISTS; LENIN; PLEKHANOV), who studied the development of capitalism in Russia, and by Pokrovskiy (q.v.) and his school, who concentrated upon the history of the class struggle and the revolutionary movement. Slavophile historiography has been chiefly interested in the conditions of everyday life and the culture and spirit of the people, especially the peasants; the romantic school of Slavophiles proper contrasted communal and paternalistic tendencies shown in Russian history with the individualism and legalism of the West. They were succeeded by the Populists (*see* POPULISM), who saw in the peasant commune (*see* MIR) a distinguishing feature of Russian society which determined a different historical course for the country. Berdyayev's (q.v.) neo-Slavophile theory equates traditional Russian communalism and paternalism with totalitarianism.

Most contemporary schools tend to take up intermediate positions, combining various features of the main trends. Thus the Eurasian school assimilated several points of the *étatists* and the Slavophiles. The liberal historian Klyuchevskiy (q.v.), author of the first 'economist' theory of Russian history as that of 'a country in the process of being colonized,' continued some traditions of the historical and the *étatist* schools. Milyukov's and Platonov's (qq.v.) views were similar. The National Bolshevik school (*see* NATIONAL BOLSHEVISM) headed by Grekov (q.v.) combined Marxist, *étatist* and Eurasian trends. Beria (q.v.) initiated a largely fictitious (*see* FICTIONS) Stalinocentric historiography which found its best expression in the *Short Course* of party history published in 1938. This school has been officially condemned since Stalin's death. The currently approved trend represents a mixture between Lenin, Pokrovskiy and Grekov. *See* R. J. Kerner, *The Urge to the Sea. The Course of Russian History*, Berkeley, California, 1946; K. Mehnert, *Weltrevolution durch Weltgeschichte. Die Geschichtslehre des Stalinismus*, Kitzingen-on-Main, 1950; P. B. Struve, *Sotsialnaya i ekonomicheskaya istoriya Rossii*, Paris, 1952, T. G. Masaryk, *The Spirit of Russia* (2 vols.), 2nd ed., 1955; C. E. Black (ed.), *Rewriting Russian History*, New York, 1956; S. V. Utechin, 'Soviet Historians and Historiography Today,' *Occidente*, vol. xii, No. 1, Jan.–Feb. 1956, and 'The Year 1917: New Publications on Party History,' *Soviet Survey*, No. 21, Nov.–Dec. 1957; L. Labedz, 'Soviet Historiography between the Thaw and the Freeze,' *Soviet Survey*, No. 15, May 1957; A. G. Mazour, *Modern Russian Historiography*, Princeton, N.J., 1958; L. Schapiro, 'A New History—A New Mythology,' *Problems of Communism*, vol. ix, No. 1, Jan.–Feb. 1960.

History, *see* ANCIENT RUSSIA; KIEVAN RUSSIA; MONGOL CONQUEST; MUSCOVY; IMPERIAL RUSSIA; FEBRUARY REVOLUTION; COMMUNIST DICTATORSHIP; FOREIGN POLICY.

General Bibliography: A. Leroy-Beaulieu, *The Empire of the Tsars and the Russians* (3 vols.), New York, 1898; V. O. Klyuchevsky, *History of Russia* (5 vols., trans. C. J. Hogarth), New York, 1911–13; G. Vernadsky, *Political and Diplomatic History of Russia*, Boston, 1936, and *A History of Russia* (4th ed.), New Haven, 1954; S. R. Tompkins, *Russia through the Ages*, New York, 1940; P. N. Milyukov, *Outlines of Russian Culture* (3 vols., ed. M. M. Karpovich), Philadelphia, 1941; P. Grierson, *Books on Soviet Russia, 1917–42*, 1943; W. B. Walsh, *Russia under Tsars and Commissars: a Reader's Guide*, Syracuse, 1946; N. Berdyayev, *The Russian Idea*, 1947; B. H. Sumner, *Survey of Russian History*, 2nd ed., 1948; A. G. Mazour, *Russia Past and Present*, New York, 1951; W. Weidlé, *Russia Absent and Present*, New York, 1952; M. T. Florinsky, *Russia, a History and an Interpretation* (2 vols.), New York, 1953; Sir B. Pares, *A History of Russia*, 3rd ed., 1955; E. J. Simmons (ed.), *Continuity and Change in Russian and Soviet Thought*, Cambridge, Mass., 1955; R. D. Charques, *Short History of Russia*, 1956; W. B. Walsh, *Russia and the Soviet Union*, Ann Arbor, 1958; R. N. Carew Hunt, *Books on Communism*, 1959; J. S. Curtiss, 'History' in H. H. Fisher's (ed.) *American Research on Russia*, Bloomington, Indiana, 1959.

Periodicals: Slavonic and Eastern European Review, London; *Russian Review*, New York; *American Slavic and East European Review*, Manasha; *Soviet Studies*, Oxford; *Soviet Survey*, London; *St Antony's Papers*, London; *Problems of Communism*, Washington; *Bulletin, Institute for the Study of the U.S.S.R.*, Munich.

Holy Synod, consultative and administrative body under the Patriarch (q.v.) of Moscow and All Russia. In Imperial Russia the Most Holy Synod (1721–1917) was the highest administrative organ of the Russian Orthodox Church, having been established by Peter the Great on the Lutheran model to replace the Patriarchate.

Homel, *see* GOMEL'.

Hooliganism has in recent years appeared officially as a serious problem. As in other modern industrial societies, an important form of hooliganism is gang warfare, apparently motiveless, among working-class youths. In 1957–8 special armed teams of civilians were formed in many towns to assist the militia in combating hooliganism. A definite political element in current hooliganism can be deduced from the facts that membership of the armed teams must be on party or Komsomol recommendation and that the teams themselves are directly attached to the local party committees, as well as from the fact that they are reported in the press as, among other things, dispersing even small and apparently harmless street gatherings. There have been several cases reported of attempts on the lives of team members. *See* R. S., 'Voluntary Militia and Courts,' *Soviet Studies*, vol. xi, No. 2, Oct. 1959.

Hotin, *see* KHOTIN.

Housing. According to the constitution, the bulk of the housing in the towns is State-owned; such State-owned houses and flats are administered either by the town soviets or by enterprises, institutions, etc. Apart from State-owned housing there are a comparatively small number of houses and blocks of flats belonging to the co-operatives, and the rest are owned privately. Out of the total of 781 million square metres of urban housing space at the end of 1958 (180 in 1913, 216 in 1926, 421 in 1940), 257 million square metres were privately owned; the proportion of privately owned housing has not decreased during the 1950's. The minimum floor space officially considered necessary is 9 square metres per person (living space, 12–13 square metres of total floor space), but actual conditions fall short of this requirement; the average was 7·8 (total floor space) in 1959 (7·2 in 1913, 8·3 in 1926, 7·1 in 1940, 7·7 in 1956). The situation varies in different towns: thus Moscow had 8·7 square metres per person in 1959 (8·2 in 1926, 6·9 in 1940, 7·4 in 1956), but Kuybyshev had 6·9, Minsk 6·8 and Tashkent 5·1; on the other hand, Riga had 12·1 square metres per person.

The right of individual persons to buy or build a private house was affirmed in 1948 and loans were granted for this purpose until 1960. The housing shortage, caused by rapid industrialization both before 1913 and since the beginning of the Five Year Plans period, and further aggravated by the Second World War, has been one of the main sources of dissatisfaction, and considerable efforts are being made to overcome it: 46·7 million square metres of housing space were built by the State and co-operatives (excluding *kolkhozes*) in 1958, compared to 29·5 in 1956 and 17·8 in 1950; 24·5 million were built privately by townspeople and employees of State agricultural enterprises.

In rural areas the overwhelming majority of houses are privately owned, either by peasant families (*see* PEASANT HOUSEHOLD) or by individuals. *Kolkhoz* members and the rural intelligentsia built for themselves 2·7 million houses in 1946–50, 2·3 million in 1951–5 and 2 million in 1956–8.

Rents in State-owned houses and flats are generally low and are graded according to income, being normally 5–10 per cent of the income; large families receive reductions of up to 15 per cent. There are official limits to the rents that private owners may charge for houses, flats or rooms, but they are not strictly enforced. *See* T. Sosnovy, *The Housing Problem in the Soviet Union*, New York, 1954, and 'The Soviet Housing Situation Today,' *Soviet Studies*, vol. xi, No. 1, July 1950; *The Soviet Seven Year Plan* (introduction by A. Nove), 1960.

Hrushevs'kyy, Mykhaylo Serhiyovych (1866 1934), Ukrainian historian and politician, educated at Kiev University; he became professor at L'vov University in 1894 and president of the Shevchenko Scientific Society there (which at that time was the chief centre of Ukrainian intellectual activity) in 1897. He joined the party of Ukrainian Socialist Revolutionaries after the February 1917 revolution and was president of the Ukrainian Central Rada (*see* UKRAINE, *History*). In 1918 he emigrated, but returned to Kiev in 1924 and became a member of the Ukrainian Academy of Sciences, and in 1929 of the U.S.S.R. Academy of Sciences. He was arrested and deported from Kiev in 1930, and died at Kislovodsk.

Hrushevs'kyy founded the nationalist school of Ukrainian historiography based upon the idea that Kievan Russia was a uniquely Ukrainian state, not common Russian. Main works: *History of the Ukraine-Russia* (10 vols.), 1898–1936, *Outline History of the Ukrainian People*, 1904, *History of Ukrainian Literature* (5 vols.), 1923–6.

Hughesovka, *see* STALINO.

Hutsuls, ethnic group of the Ukrainian people who live in the Carpathian Mountains (Stanislav, Transcarpathia and Chernovtsy oblasts). They engage chiefly in cattle breeding. The origin of the Hutsuls is unknown; having lived for centuries in comparative isolation in the mountains they have preserved many archaic traits in their material culture and their customs.

Hyperborean Mountains, ancient name of the Ural Mountains (q.v.).

I

Iberia, ancient name for eastern Georgia.

Icon and Church Fresco Painting. From the conversion of Kievan Russia (988) till the reforms of Peter the Great Russian pictorial art served almost exclusively the interests of the Christian religion and of the Church. Painters and craftsmen came to Kiev together with Greek priests and monks from Byzantium; Greek icons were imported. Russian craftsmen soon assimilated the Byzantine tradition and in the course of several generations achieved an astonishing degree of mastery. The first Christian churches in Kiev—Desyatinnaya, Sancta Sophia, St Michael, Holy Trinity (in the St Cyril Monastery), the Cathedral of Dormition (in the Pecherskaya Lavra) —were lavishly decorated with frescoes and mosaics according to the principles of the Byzantine iconography. In the 12th and 13th centuries local icon- and fresco-painting schools appeared in Novgorod, Pskov, Vladimir, Galich and Polotsk. Mural painting dominated in Novgorod and Vladimir. In the Church of the Saviour at Nereditsa there were most original and well-preserved (until the Second World War, when the church was completely destroyed) examples of early Novgorod frescoes. Of the earliest icons very few have survived. The venerated 12th-century Virgin of Vladimir is of beautiful workmanship but was probably brought from Constantinople; it served as the prototype for innumerable icons. Of a little later date is the large panel of Annunciations, probably executed by Russian masters under Greek supervision. Within 150 or 200 years there developed a typically Russian style, characterized by two-dimensional, ornamental and colouristic treatment as opposed to the three dimensions, modelling and subdued tonality of the Hellenistic style. The Pskov icon of the Four Saints is a striking example of this development. The expression of the eyes is another pointer: Russian masters developed a subjective anti-illusionist way of painting the eyes—they look inwards and beyond, and gaze vaguely through the spectator. The backgrounds were more and more often covered with gold-leaf. The treatment tended to become graphic rather than pictorial. The technique of *ozhivki*, or white linear highlights, was used instead of chiaroscuro for modelling the faces and hands. In the 14th century this process met with resistance from renewed Byzantine influence. But the greatest of the Greeks who came at this time to Russia, Feofan Grek (q.v.), adopted some of the Russian formal findings, notably *ozhivki*, which he used to achieve a bold, dramatic effect. Early in the 15th century the Moscow school reached its height in the art of Andrey Rublëv (q.v.), who, adopting the innovations of Byzantium, charged his icons with deeply felt rhythm and movement expressed through self-contained composition and continuous flowing contours.

Throughout the 15th century the Novgorod school continued to adhere to the traditional schematic and strictly two-dimensional style, and developed larger narrative icons made up of four, twelve or more scenes painted on the same panel. The first icons treating historical or contemporary events were produced by masters of Novgorod. One of these icons is the famous 'Battle between Novgorod and Suzdal'' which recounts the miracles that occurred when Novgorod was besieged by the armies of Suzdal' in 1169. The heritage of Feofan Grek and Rublëv served as a point of departure for the personal and mystical art of the Moscow master Dionisius (late 15th century), who was much admired for his delicate colours.

In the 16th century religious painting lost most of the classic inspiration present in the preceding age and acquired decorative features together with a closer observation of nature. At the same time icon-painters began to exercise greater freedom in the choice of iconographical subjects, and the dogmas of medieval tradition were losing their power. After the great fire of 1547, which devastated Moscow, icon-painters were brought in large numbers from Novgorod and Pskov to take part in the work of restoration. They were organized in the government workshops, which were in effect the first State art schools in Russia. Becoming thus the servants of the czar rather than of the Church, they turned out in increasing numbers didactic paintings and scenes from Russian history, glorifying the deeds of the Kievan princes. In contrast to the State-organized icon industry, there existed in the late 16th and early 17th centuries a remarkable phenomenon — icon-painting for the private requirements of the powerful Stroganov family (see STROGANOV SCHOOL).

The last great Russian icon-painter was Simon Ushakov (1626–86), who worked in the czar's workshops. He was influenced by Western art, which at that time had begun to penetrate into Russia. His icons were a competent but not wholly convincing attempt to adapt the traditional iconography to the new forms. After the westernizing reforms of Peter the Great secular painting began to play the predominant role in Russian art, and icon-painting soon degenerated into mannerisms and empty repetitions of the old themes devoid of their medieval spirituality and sincerity. See also PAINTING. See N. P. Kondakov, The Russian Icon, 1927; C. G. E. Bunt, Russian Art: From Scyths to Soviets, 1946; G. H. Hamilton, Art and Architecture of Russia, 1954.

Idealism, as an epistemological and ontological trend in the Russian philosophical tradition, is chiefly represented by the Stankevich (q.v.) circle in their period of enthusiasm for the German Idealism, and by the Neo-Leibnizians and Neo-Kantians of the late 19th–early 20th centuries. The Neo-Kantian phase was important in the philosophical development of the former Legal Marxists (q.v.) Berdyayev, Bulgakov, Frank and Struve (qq.v.) at the turn of the century (see also NOVGORODTSEV). Moral idealism has been very strong, and most influential thinkers of the 19th and early 20th centuries were Idealists in their ethical views. From the official Marxist point of view, any non-materialist position is described as Idealist. See B.-P. Hepner, Bakounine et le panslavisme révolutionnaire, Paris,

1950; N. Lossky, *History of Russian Philosophy*, 1951; V. V. Zenkovsky, *A History of Russian Philosophy*, 1953.

Ideology, according to Marxian theory, is a set of ideas typical of a social class and originating in its material interests and position in society. Marxism itself is regarded as the ideology of the proletariat, since allegedly it reflects and serves the interests of that class. At the same time it is said to be the only objective and scientific ideology, since there is no need for the proletariat to distort and misrepresent the truth as do the exploiting classes. Marxism-Leninism (which ostensibly is orthodox Marxism further developed by Lenin in accordance with its spirit and the new requirements of the time) is the official ideology of the Communist Party, and is held to be the only legitimate ideology in the U.S.S.R., since in the absence of classes with interests contrary to those of the working class there is no social basis for any other ideology.

This dogmatic view of ideology, which is partly of a mythical (*see* MYTHS) and partly of a fictitious (*see* FICTIONS) nature, has little in common with the reality. Official ideology has always been manipulated, by Lenin, Stalin and Khrushchëv alike, according to their political needs of the moment, and regardless of truth, orthodoxy, consistency or the interests of any particular social class (*see further under* BOLSHEVISM; COMMUNISM; LENINISM; STALINISM). Besides the currently accepted version of the official ideology, the authorities have always, except in the years 1935–43, for reasons of expediency tolerated other, more or less alien, sets of ideas. At first these were Bogdanovism (q.v.), Social Democratism (*see* MENSHEVIKS; PLEKHANOV; POTRESOV), Makhayevism, Syndicalism, Anarchism (qq.v.), radical Populism (*see* POPULISM), Neo-Populism, Technocratism (qq.v.), Fëdorovism (*see* FËDOROV) and National Bolshevism (q.v.)— all of which were suppressed by 1935. Since 1943–4 religious beliefs of officially recognized religious communities have been tolerated as rival ideologies, though they are treated in propaganda as relics of the past. The re-emergence of active political opposition since Stalin's death has not so far resulted in any striking new ideological developments. The reformist trend (*see* REFORMISM) has evolved a vague ideology of Progressivism, a kind of liberal Communism. The known ideologies current among the revolutionary elements (*see* REVOLUTIONARY MOVEMENT) are the so-called True Leninism (a mixture of Social Democratic and Syndicalist ideas), Popular Capitalism (encouraged by foreign, particularly American, broadcasts) and Solidarism (q.v.). *See* E. J. Simmons (ed)., *Through the Glass of Soviet Literature*, New York, 1953; R. N. Carew Hunt *et al.*, 'Ideology and Power Politics: A Symposium,' *Problems of Communism*, vol. vii, March–April 1958; A. Inkeles and R. A. Bauer, *The Soviet Citizen*, 1959; H. H. Fisher (ed.), *American Research on Russia*, Bloomington, Indiana, 1959.

Igarka, town in the Krasnoyarsk Kray (central Siberia), a river port accessible to sea vessels, situated 425 m. from the mouth of the Yenisey. Population (1956) 15,200 (1932, 12,000). It has a major saw-milling industry (for export) and a graphite plant, and is a local cultural centre. Igarka was founded in 1928 and developed largely by forced labour; with the release of many political prisoners in the mid 1950's the population declined drastically.

Ignat'yev, Semën Denisovich (*b.* 1903), Communist. He joined the party in 1926 and made a career during the Great Purge (q.v.), becoming first secretary of the party committee in Buryat-Mongolia in 1938; later he occupied the same position in Bashkiria (1944–7 and 1954–7) and Tataria (1957–60), and in 1947–9 was second secretary of the Belorussian party central committee. He was Minister of State Security (*see* M.G.B.) in 1951–3, member of the Presidium (q.v.) of the party's Central Committee, 1952–3, and a secretary of the Central Committee for a short time in 1953. He was relieved of the latter post allegedly for 'political blindness and slackness' as Minister of State Security in connection with the 'Doctors' Plot' (q.v.), but at the 20th party congress in 1956 Khrushchëv said that Ignat'yev had acted on Stalin's orders.

Il'in, Ivan Aleksandrovich (1882–1956), philosopher and publicist, professor at Moscow University, who was expelled from Russia in 1922, together with other leading intellectuals. Thereafter he worked in the Russian Academy of Religion and Philosophy in Berlin and later at the Russian Institute of Berlin University; expelled from Germany in 1936, he lived in Switzerland. Il'in's main works are *Hegel's Philosophy as a Doctrine of Concreteness of God and Man* (2 vols.), Moscow, 1918, *On Resistance to Evil by Force*, Belgrade, 1926, and *Axioms of Religious Experience*, Zürich, 1955.

Il'inskiy, Igor' Vladimirovich (*b.* 1901), stage and film actor. From 1920 he worked mostly with Meyerhold (q.v.) until the latter's theatre was closed in 1938, and since then he has worked in the Malyy Theatre. His comic and satirical roles, on both stage and screen, have enjoyed great popularity.

Illiteracy. Until the second half of the 19th century the overwhelming majority of people in Russia were illiterate. The educational efforts after the Great Reforms (q.v.) considerably improved the situation, and by 1917 about 40 per cent of the population over 10 years old was literate. The civil war retarded progress, but it was resumed as soon as conditions permitted. A special campaign for 'liquidating illiteracy' among adults was carried out in 1920–35. By 1939 over 80 per cent of the population was literate, but the Second World War again brought about an increase in illiteracy. The ideal of universal education is still not achieved in the Soviet Union, and even now illiterate young adults can be met.

Literacy, in percentage of population aged 9–49:

	Total Population	Urban Population	Rural Population	Men	Women
1897: Census	26	56	22	39	14
1926: Census	57	81	51	72	43
1939: Census	89	94	86	95	83
1959: Census	98	99	98	99	98

See N. S. Timasheff, 'Overcoming Illiteracy,' *Russian Review*, autumn 1942.

Il'men', lake in the Novgorod Oblast whose outlet is the River Volkhov which flows north into Lake Ladoga. Length, east to west, 30 m.; greatest breadth 24 m. The Il'men' was on the trade route from Scandinavia to Byzantium during the Middle Ages, and the surrounding area formed the core of the Novgorod Republic.

Il'minskiy, Nikolay Ivanovich (1822–91), director of a Tatar teachers' training seminary in Kazan'. He did much to develop modern education among the non-Russian peoples of the Volga-Urals area, and designed an educational system for national minorities based on the use of native languages. Despite his fine achievements in the educational field, his reputation was marred by his endeavours to convert the Tatars to Christianity.

Imanov, Amangel'dy (1873–1919), leader of the 1916 anti-Russian uprising in the Kazakh steppe. He soon joined the Bolshevik Party and during the civil war commanded a Bolshevik unit which fought against the Cossacks and the Kazakh units on the White side.

Imeretia, area of western Georgia (Transcaucasia) in the upper part of the Rioni basin around Kutaisi, noted for its silk and wine, manganese (Chiatura) and coal-mining. It was an independent kingdom from the 16th to 18th centuries, and in 1804 was annexed by Russia.

Imperial Russia. The reign of Peter the Great (1672–1725, q.v.) witnessed the transformation of the Muscovite state into a westernized empire. Imperial Russia played an active part in the concert of the Great Powers of Europe throughout the 18th century, and through conquests from Sweden and Turkey and the partitions of Poland further extended its territory in the west and south to include the Baltic provinces (q.v.), Belorussia, Lithuania, the Ukraine west of the Dnieper, and the Black Sea shores (*see* NEW RUSSIA). Internally the century was one of the growth of manufactures, education and learning (Moscow University founded 1755), increasing influence of the westernized gentry, frequent palace revolutions, and the emergence of modern literature and of social criticism (*see* RADISHCHEV). *See further under* the individual sovereigns, Elizabeth Petrovna, Peter III, Catherine II.

In many ways the first half of the 19th century was a continuation of the 18th, with Peter the Great and Catherine II, the philosophy of the Enlightenment, Lomonosov (q.v.) and Radishchev as the main sources of inspiration in administration (*see further under* ALEXANDER I; NICHOLAS I; SPERANSKIY) and intellectual life, and with further territorial acquisitions (Finland, Poland, Bessarabia and the Caucasus). The influence of the French Revolution and the experience of the Napoleonic wars were new elements of importance. Increasing contact with Western Europe, and the sense of the strength of the people that came with the victorious Patriotic War of 1812, produced the first revolutionary movement (*see* DECEMBRISTS). Nicholas I's resultant conservative policy, and growing bureaucratization, were popularly blamed for Russia's defeat in the Crimean War (q.v.).

The desire for the modernization of the country's social and political life and for widespread reforms was strong, and the reign of Alexander II (q.v., 'the Czar Liberator') was a period of Great Reforms (q.v.), beginning with the emancipation of the serfs in 1861. Simultaneously a new force appeared upon the political scene, the intelligentsia, partly liberal and reformist, partly radical and revolutionary. The liberals, despite their division (see SLAVOPHILES; WESTERNISM), were active participants in the introduction and implementation of the reforms, while the radicals, chiefly Populists (q.v.), eventually adopted the tactics of terror; their assassination of the Czar Liberator upon the very day when he was to 'crown the edifice of the reforms' by the establishment of a representative assembly was largely responsible for the reactionary policies of Alexander III (q.v.). Henceforward revolution was to be a constant theme in Russian history.

The last decades of the 19th century saw rapid industrial development behind protective tariffs, the growth of the industrial working class and the beginnings of the labour movement (see STRIKES; TRADE UNIONS) and of modern factory legislation (see BUNGE; WITTE). Splendid work, especially in education and the field of medical services, was achieved by the local government bodies (see ZEMSTVO). Yet the central government remained in the hands of a bureaucracy which was hostile to the very ideas of political freedom and popular representation, and which relied upon the police to maintain the existing order; religious and linguistic minorities were particularly harshly treated. Thus the early political parties were necessarily semi-conspiratorial, illegal organizations, whether their aims were all-Russian (see RUSSIAN SOCIAL DEMOCRATIC LABOUR PARTY; SOCIALIST REVOLUTIONARIES) or national (see BUND; DASHNAKTSUTYUN). The repression of Alexander III was on the whole successful, but the weak and vacillating policy of his son Nicholas II (q.v.) enabled both the revolutionary and the constitutional movements (the latter depending principally on the zemstvos and professional associations) to gather momentum, and this, together with the defeat in the Russo-Japanese War (q.v.) of 1904, brought about the revolution of 1905 (q.v.).

The end of the revolution in 1907 saw Russia with a constitution that was far from perfect but that left much to ordinary current legislation, with a legislative Duma (q.v.) elected by popular vote, with legal parties (see CONSTITUTIONAL DEMOCRATS; OCTOBRISTS) and with trade unions. Reform to establish the responsibility of the Government to the Duma seemed only a matter of time. With the appearance of the Vekhi (q.v.) movement among the liberal intelligentsia and of 'liquidationism' (q.v., see also MENSHEVIKS) in social democracy, it seemed that a responsible and undogmatic liberal opposition was about to appear. The Government itself inaugurated sensible agrarian reforms (see STOLYPIN), and industry was booming. But the First World War brought all these healthy developments to an end. Russia had taken an active part in the imperialist exploits of the Great Powers, and for long had been Britain's main rival in Asia. Turkey and the Caucasus were the earlier areas of mutual suspicion, followed by Central Asia, most of which was conquered by Russia under Alexander II, and the Far East, where Britain sympathized with Japan against Russia (*see* RUSSO-JAPANESE WAR). Alexander III's 'alliance of three emperors,' which he believed essential for stabilizing peace in Europe, was weakened by the emergence of Germany as a strong imperialist power, and by antagonism between Russia and Austria-Hungary in the Balkans, where Russia consistently followed a pro-Slav policy. The Franco-Russian treaty, 1891, reversed the previous alignment of powers. Nicholas II took the initiative in calling The Hague Conference (q.v.) in 1899, continuing his father's policy of peace in Europe, but he could not retard the drift towards catastrophe. Inside Russia the First World War resulted in a further deterioration of the relations between, on the one hand, the public, now organized in the Union of Zemstvos (q.v.), the Municipal League, the War Industries Committee and the Progressive Bloc in the Duma (*see* CONSTITUTIONAL DEMOCRATS), and, on the other, the Court and the Government (*see* ALEXANDRA FËDOROVNA; RASPUTIN). The bloodless February revolution (q.v.) of 1917 was almost universally welcomed. *See also* WORLD WAR I. *See* R. N. Bain, *The Pupils of Peter the Great, 1697–1740*, 1897; D. Mackenzie Wallace, *Russia*, 2nd ed., 1905; E. J. Dillon, *The Eclipse of Russia*, 1918; J. F. Baddeley, *Russia in the Eighties*, 1921; S. Yu. Witte, *Vospominaniya* (2 vols.), Berlin, 1922 (Fr. trans., Paris, 1921); M. de Taube, *La Politique Russe d'avant-guerre et la Fin de l'Empire des Tsars (1904–1917)*, Paris, 1928; B. Pares, *My Russian Memoirs*, 1931; M. M. Karpovich, *Imperial Russia, 1801–1917*, 1932; A. Kornilov, *Modern Russian History*, New York, 1943; D. Footman, *Red Prelude*, 1944; B. H. Sumner, *Peter the Great and the Emergence of Russia*, 1950; G. S. Thompson, *Catherine the Great and the Expansion of Russia*, New York, 1950; H. Seton-Watson, *The Decline of Imperial Russia, 1855–1914*, 1952; B. Nolde, *La Formation de l'Empire Russe* (2 vols.), Paris, 1952–3; C. de Grunwald, *Tsar Nicholas I* (trans. B. Patmore), 1954; A. Lobanov-Rostovsky, *Russia and Europe, 1825–78*, Ann Arbor, 1954; D. Maroger (ed.), *The Memoirs of Catherine the Great*, New York, 1955; T. G. Masaryk, *The Spirit of Russia* (2 vols.), New York, 1955; P. Scheibert, *Von Bakunin zu Lenin*, Leiden, 1956; H. Jablonowski, 'Die russischen Rechtsparteien, 1905–17,' in *Russland-Studien. Gedenkschrift für O. Hoetzsch*, Stuttgart, 1957; C. Jelavich, *Tsarist Russia and Balkan Nationalism*, Berkeley, California, 1958; R. Charques, *The Twilight of Imperial Russia: the Reign of Tsar Nicholas II*, 1958; M. S. Anderson, *Britain's Discovery of Russia, 1535–1815*, 1958; A. Malozemoff, *Russian Far Eastern Policy, 1881–1904*, Berkeley and Los Angeles, 1958.

Imperialism, in Leninist theory the highest and last stage in the development of capitalism, another term for 'monopolistic capitalism,' stressing a different aspect of the same phenomenon. Lenin adopted the economic theory of imperialism from J. H. Hobson, grafting it on to the traditional Marxist historical scheme. Imperialism creates conditions for a socialist revolution and the dictatorship of the proletariat (q.v.) as a transitional phase towards socialism. History is bound to take this course, and any other view is in the last resort a rationalization of the desire to delay the inevitable. This theory of imperialism provided a justification for the seizure of power by the Bolsheviks and for suppressing all opposition. The notion that any opponent of Stalin was an 'agent of imperialism' was one of the chief fictions (q.v.) of Stalinism (q.v.). The contention that 'world imperialism' must try through its agents to undermine the Soviet regime was used as a theoretical justification for the Great Purge (q.v.) and the Stalinist terror in general, and is still often resorted to in dealing with the revolutionary underground. All relations between the Communist-ruled countries and the outside world are analysed in terms of the struggle between two systems, imperialism and socialism, in which the latter is bound to win and replace the former. National liberation movements in colonial territories are seen as undermining the very foundations of imperialism and hastening the victory of socialism. A 'socialist' country is by definition incapable of being 'imperialist,' and therefore accusations of imperialism against the Soviet Union or Communist China are treated as imperialist propaganda. *See* J. A. Hobson, *Imperialism*, 3rd ed., 1938; V. I. Lenin, *Imperialism: the Latest Stage in the Development of Capitalism*, 1924; N. I. Bukharin, *Imperialism and the World Economy*, 1930; R. Schlesinger, *Marx, His Time and Ours*, 1950; R. N. Carew Hunt, *A Guide to Communist Jargon*, 1957.

Incentives, in the Soviet economy, include both compulsion (*see* FORCED LABOUR; LABOUR DISCIPLINE; LABOUR LAW) and encouragement. The latter includes material interest and persuasion. Material interest is by far the more important of the two in its practical effect. The chief forms of its application are the big differentiation in wages (q.v.) and salaries according to qualifications and proficiency, the work-day unit (q.v.) system of remuneration in the *kolkhozes*, the manipulation of prices for agricultural products and a highly complex system of bonuses (q.v.). The element of persuasion consists of the general Communist propaganda and agitation (q.v.) and of special devices aimed at increasing productivity of labour, such as 'Socialist emulation' and 'Stakhanovism' (qq.v.; *see also* BRIGADE), which are semi-fictitious (*see* FICTION) and of little economic significance. Traditional Marxist theory envisaged only the incentive of zeal for work in a socialist society, considering non-economic compulsion as pre-capitalist and material interest as a characteristic incentive under capitalism. Attempts at equalization and even total abolition of money payments were made during the period of War Communism (q.v.), but very soon both material incentives in the form of high salaries for 'bourgeois specialists' and forced labour (at first for 'socially alien elements') were introduced. In 1930 Stalin finally declared that the principle of equal wages was a 'petit bourgeois' deviation, and throughout his rule compulsion and material interest were increasingly applied as incentives. Since Stalin's death, however, the element of compulsion has considerably decreased, and attempts have been made somewhat to narrow the differentiation in wages and salaries, though the principle of material interest is strongly affirmed. *See* S. M. Schwarz, *Labor in the Soviet Union*, New York, 1952; M. Fainsod, *How Russia is Ruled*, Cambridge, Mass., 1953; H. Schwartz, *Russia's Soviet Economy*, New York, 2nd ed.,

1954; G. R. Barker, *Incentives and Labour Productivity in Soviet Industry, s.a.*

Income-tax is levied on the incomes of all those who are not primarily engaged in agriculture (*see* AGRICULTURAL TAX). For purposes of assessment taxpayers are divided into five classes: (1) workers, salaried employees, students and advocates; (2) artisans in co-operatives; (3) artists and writers; (4) other independent professional people; (5) independent artisans and other persons whose income is not derived from State or co-operative employment, e.g. the clergy. Rates are only slightly progressive for the first two categories (the second paying 10 per cent more), rising from 5·5 per cent at Rs. 1800 per annum to 13 per cent at Rs. 12,000 per annum. They are, however, much more progressive for the other three groups, rising to 23 per cent at Rs. 70,000 per annum and 55 per cent at Rs. 300,000 per annum for artists and writers, and to 55 per cent and 65 per cent at Rs. 70,000 per annum for categories 4 and 5 respectively (all figures relate to the year 1953). The exemption levels also differ for each category. Invalids, inventors and people who have received certain decorations have high exemption limits, and among those completely exempt from income-tax are national servicemen, pensioners, prospectors for gold and other rare metals and winners of Lenin Prizes. Any taxpayer with three or more dependants (not including a wife if she is capable of working) has 30 per cent deducted from the amount of tax for which he is assessed. Income-tax was introduced in 1922. Its fiscal role is small; it has brought in about 7 per cent of total revenue in recent years, and it is intended to abolish it altogether. Even the present rates are favourable to higher income groups compared to Welfare State practice in other countries, and abolition, if carried through, will be a retrograde step. A tax amounting to about one-tenth of their gross money income levied on *kolkhozes* is also called income-tax. *See further under* TAXATION. *See* F. D. Holzman, *Soviet Taxation*, Cambridge, Mass., 1955.

Indigirka, river in north-eastern Siberia which rises in the Oymyakon plateau and flows north into the East Siberian Sea. Length 1,100 m.; basin 140,000 sq. m.

Industrial Crops. In 1958 the sown area under industrial crops was 12·3 million hectares (4·9 in 1913,[1] 8·6 in 1928, 11·8 in 1940, 13·1 in 1956), i.e. 6·3 per cent of the total sown area. Of the four main industrial crops, cotton is grown in Central Asia and Transcaucasia, flax mainly in the northern part of central Russia and in Belorussia, sunflowers and sugar-beet in the Ukraine, Moldavia, North Caucasus, the southern (black earth) part of central Russia, and the lower Volga area. *See also* FOOD INDUSTRY; TEXTILE INDUSTRY.

Industrial Management is an important branch of State administration in the Soviet Union, since most of the industry is State-owned (*see* NATIONALIZATION OF INDUSTRY; OWNERSHIP). Three principles of industrial management have competed with one another during the Soviet period: management by branches, 'functional' management and territorial management. The principle of branch management

---

[1] Present-day frontiers.

asserted itself most strongly towards the end of Stalin's rule, but since his death, and particularly since the establishment of the regional Economic Councils (q.v.) in 1957, the territorial principle has acquired greater weight. It is not, however, the only one. All three principles are supposed to be taken into account in economic planning (q.v.). Several ministries for particular branches of industry still exist, and within the Economic Councils there are departments for different branches of industry. The functional element appears in the strict control of the financial side of management by the State Bank (*see* CREDIT) and in the activities of the State committees on labour and wages, on new technology, etc.

On the enterprise (q.v.) level there has been a similar conflict between the principle of 'single-head' and collegiate management. The collegiate principle was more favoured by the authorities in the 1920's, particularly in the form of a 'triangle' consisting of the manager, the secretary of the party committee and the chairman of the factory's trade union committee. 'Single-head' management was affirmed in 1929, but, though it eliminated trade union participation in management, interference from the party apparatus continued. During the latter years of Stalin's life the party organizations lost much of their direct influence in industrial management, while the role of the heads of enterprises, backed by the ministries, increased. The organization of industrial management played an important role in the struggle between Stalin's successors, Malenkov seeking to perpetuate the predominance of the branch and 'single-head' systems, while Khrushchëv resorted to territorialization and increased power for the party apparatus. Special party commissions have now been formed in industrial enterprises to supervise the activities of the management. *See also* INDUSTRY; MANAGERIAL CLASS. *See* G. Bienstock *et al.*, *Management in Russian Industry and Agriculture*, 1944; D. Granick, *Management of the Industrial Firm in the U.S.S.R.*, New York, 1954; M. Dewar, *Labour Policy in the Soviet Union, 1917–28*, 1956; J. S. Berliner, *Factory and Manager in the U.S.S.R.*, Cambridge, Mass., 1957.

Industrial Party, organization made up of leading technicians which is alleged to have existed in the late 1920's with the object of undermining the Soviet regime by industrial sabotage. The 1930 show trial of Industrial Party members in Moscow (including its alleged leader Professor Ramzin) marked an important point in the persecution of the technical intelligentsia. *See also* RAL'CHINSKIY; PURGES.

Industrialization of Russia, in the sense of the expansion of modern industries, essentially began under Peter the Great. Strong impetus was given to the process by the emancipation of the serfs in 1861 (*see* GREAT REFORMS; SERFDOM) and by the Five Year Plans (q.v.) which began in 1928. In the first and third periods of rapid industrialization the prevailing motives were somewhat similar—the desire on the part of the Government to strengthen and modernize the country in deliberate competition with other countries; in the second period the industrialization was largely due to private enterprise, although the role of the Government was not inconsiderable, particularly through protective tariffs and large-scale railway building (see, e.g., BUNGE; WITTE). By 1913 Russia held fifth place in the world in total industrial output, and fourth place in engineering. By 1937 she had taken second place in the world. The process of industrialization has been reflected in the progressive urbanization of the country: urban population was estimated at 6 per cent in 1860, was 18 per cent in 1913 and 48 per cent in 1959. See O. Hoeffding, 'State Planning and Forced Industrialization,' *Problems of Communism*, vol. viii, No. 6, Nov.–Dec. 1959.

Industry. Of the total industrial output in 1958, about 94 per cent was produced by State-owned industrial enterprises (6·4 per cent in 1928, 90·3 per cent in 1937, 91·8 per cent in 1950), about 6 per cent by co-operative enterprises (13 per cent in 1928, 9·5 per cent in 1937, 8·2 per cent in 1950) and an insignificant amount by unco-operated artisans (q.v.). In 1928 the output of private industry amounted to 17·6 per cent of total output (0·2 per cent in 1937). 6 per cent of the total output in 1958 was by enterprises subordinated directly to the all-Union Government (69 per cent in 1953), and 94 per cent by those subordinated to Union Republic governments (31 per cent in 1953); 71 per cent of the total was by enterprises administered by the regional Economic Councils (q.v.). The total industrial personnel (excluding members of producers' co-operatives, people working in the industrial enterprises of *kolkhozes* and in some small subsidiary enterprises) averaged 19·6 million in 1958 (8 million in 1932, 11 million in 1940, 14·1 million in 1950); of this total 16·2 million were workers, 354,000 apprentices, 1·7 million technical personnel and 0·8 million employees (from charwomen to directors). The average annual number of hired workers in 1913 was about 3·5 million. *See further* entries on food, heavy, light and local industries, and CONSUMER GOODS; ENTERPRISE; INDUSTRIAL MANAGEMENT; INDUSTRIALIZATION; NATIONALIZATION OF INDUSTRY; PRODUCTIVITY OF LABOUR. See *Comparisons of the U.S. and Soviet Economies* (Joint Economic Committee, 8th Congress, 1st Session), Washington, D.C., 1959; A. Nove, *Communist Economic Strategy: Soviet Growth and Capabilities*, Washington, D.C., 1959; H. Chambre, *L'Aménagement du territoire en U.R.S.S.*, Paris and The Hague, 1959; *The Soviet Seven Year Plan* (introduction by A. Nove), 1960.

Ingrians (sometimes called 'Leningrad Finns'), Finns living in Leningrad and its environs who are the direct descendants of the original inhabitants of the area; they numbered (1959) 93,000 (115,000 in 1926). They engage chiefly in market gardening and crafts.

Ingush, Caucasian-speaking people, closely related to the Chechens, who live in the Chechen-Ingush Autonomous Republic (North Caucasus) and number (1959) 102,000. They are Sunni Muslims. In the lowlands and foothills they engage in agriculture, and in the mountains in sheep raising. The Ingush have been known since the 17th century, and for a long time were not distinguished from the Chechens; unlike the Chechens, the Ingush did not take part in the resistance to Russian conquest in the 19th century (see SHAMIL'). They did, however, participate in the anti-Communist guerrilla warfare, and in 1943, together with the Chechens, were deported to Kazakhstan. They were 'rehabilitated' in 1957 and permitted to return. *See* W. Kolarz, *Russia and her Colonies*, 1952; R. Pipes, *The Formation of the Soviet Union*, Cambridge, Mass., 1954; R. Conquest, *The Soviet Deportation of Nationalities*, 1960.

Inheritance. The present law on inheritance is based mainly on decrees of 1943 and 1945. There is no limit on the size of the inheritance, and no inheritance tax, only a registration fee of up to 10 per cent of the estate. Heirs by law are divided into three classes: (1) children (in the case of the father, only legitimate children), spouse, disabled parents and disabled dependants; (2) able-bodied parents; (3) brothers and sisters. In the absence of a will, members of the first class share equally in the estate (after the surviving spouse's half of the property acquired by both during the marriage has been deducted); if there are no heirs of the first class, those of the second class are called, and if neither of them is alive those of the third class. The testator is free in his bequests within the circle of his legal heirs, except that he cannot disinherit his minor children or other dependants incapable of work. He may leave his property to a State agency or a public organization (except the Church or other religious body). In the absence of legal heirs he may leave it to other persons; bank deposits can be left to other persons in any case. The Bolsheviks abolished inheritance in 1918, but it was reintroduced with the beginning of the New Economic Policy (q.v.). Many of the restrictions originally imposed have been removed in subsequent legislation. *See* J. N. Hazard, *Law and Social Change in the U.S.S.R.*, 1953; G. C. Guins, *Soviet Law and Soviet Society*, The Hague, 1954; V. Gsovski and K. Grzybowski (eds.), *Government, Law and Courts in the Soviet Union and Eastern Europe*, vol. ii, 1959.

Inland Waters. The chief rivers of European Russia have their sources comparatively near one another in the Central Russian up land. Some flow south—the Volga into the Caspian Sea, the Don into the Sea of Azov and the Dnieper into the Black Sea; others flow north—the Northern Dvina into the White Sea—and north-west —the Western Dvina into the Baltic. Other important rivers of European Russia are the Pechora in the north-east, flowing into the Barents Sea, the Neva in the north-west, connecting Lake Ladoga and the Gulf of Finland, the Niemen in the west, flowing into the Baltic Sea, the Dniester and the delta part of the Danube in the south, flowing into the Black Sea, the Kuban' flowing into the Sea of Azov, and the River Ural (traditionally regarded as the frontier between Europe and Asia) in the south-east, flowing into the Caspian.

In Asiatic Russia the principal rivers have their sources in the mountains of the south; they flow north into the Arctic Ocean (the Ob', Yenisey and Lena), east (the Amur, flowing into the Sea of Okhotsk) and north-west (the Amu-Dar'ya and Syr-Dar'ya, flowing into the inland Aral Sea). Other important rivers flowing north are the Khatanga and the Olenëk between the Yenisey and the Lena, and the Yana, Indigirka and Kolyma to the east of the Lena. In the south-west there are the Ili, flowing into Lake Balkhash, the Murgab, whose water is entirely used up for irrigation, and the Kura in Trans-caucasia, flowing into the Caspian Sea.

The largest lakes are the Caspian and the Aral seas; other big lakes are Ladoga and Onega, in the north-west of European Russia, and Baykal (the deepest lake in the world, 4,500 ft), Balkhash and Issyk-Kul' in the south of Asiatic Russia.

Most of the chief rivers of European Russia are connected with one another by artificial waterways, of which the principal are the Volga-Neva system, the White Sea-Baltic system and the Volga-Don and Moscow-Volga canals. Artificial reservoirs are in most cases connected with large hydro-electric power-stations: the Rybinsk, Kuybyshev and Stalingrad reservoirs on the Volga, the Tsymlyanskiy on the Don and the Kakhovka on the Dnieper.

Insterburg, see CHERNYAKHOVSK.

Insurance is the monopoly of the Central State Insurance Department (Gosstrakh), which is directed by the all-Union Ministry of Finance. Obligatory insurance covers collective farm (see KOLKHOZ) property, buildings, livestock and crops; the housing estates of the majority of industrial enterprises; and the insurance of passengers on all public transport save suburban trains. The principal forms of voluntary insurance are life and accident insurance, insurance against fire and other acts of God, insurance of co-operative and trade union property and insurance of cargoes. Extra insurance of cattle and crops may be undertaken in addition to the obligatory insurance. The Foreign Insurance Department (Ingosstrakh) of the Ministry of Finance undertakes the insurance of property belonging to foreign companies or citizens, chiefly in regard to foreign trade transactions and merchant marine shipments. Apart from the commercial insurance, there is also a Social Insurance Fund (administered by the trade unions) which is made up of contributions by employers, and is used for paying sickness benefits and financing health resorts.

Intellectual Opposition to the regime and its policies has been a traditional feature of Russian society since the appearance of the intelligentsia (q.v.) in the 19th century. Its two traditional forms have been the constitutional movement (see CONSTITUTIONAL DEMOCRATS; GREAT REFORMS; OCTOBRISTS; PROGRESSIVE PARTY; ZEMSTVO) and the revolutionary movement (q.v.); after the Bol-shevik seizure of power (see OCTOBER REVOLUTION) a third form developed in the so-called 'internal emigration,' i.e. withdrawal from active life into pure science, pure art, etc. In the 1920's a certain degree of opposition on the part of the Mensheviks, Neo-Populists and technocrats was tolerated. Stalinism (q.v.) left no room for any overt opposition, but immediately after Stalin's death it revived. It first manifested itself in the exposure of many Soviet fictions (q.v.) and then in the emergence of a reformist trend (see REFORMISM), the more radical elements of which advocate the restriction of party influence in intellectual and social life. Existing institutions (such as the editorial boards of literary and learned periodicals, the jury for awarding Lenin Prizes, q.v., Komsomol organizations, etc.) have been used for oppositional purposes, as well as newly created organs, e.g.

the almanac *Literary Moscow* and handwritten students' journals; and works which censorship prevents being published in Russia (e.g. Pasternak's *Dr Zhivago*, or *The Trial Begins*, which appeared under the pseudonym Abram Tertz) have been published abroad. A strikingly successful means was the demonstrative silence and non-co-operation of most prominent writers during the tenure of office of Surkov (q.v.) as secretary of the Writers' Union. The post-Stalin opposition has been most determined and vocal among the writers, particularly in the Moscow writers' organization (*see* LITERATURE; WRITERS' UNION). In 1954-7 the party authorities generally took repressive measures against the intellectual opposition, including the dismissal of editors and expulsion from the Writers' Union, but from 1958 a more conciliatory policy was adopted, the principal gestures being the reinstatement of Tvardovskiy and Panfërov (qq.v.) and the dismissal of Surkov. The officially proclaimed policy of 'consolidation' (which demands the basic acceptance by the opposition of the party ideology and policies) has had little success, although a certain *modus vivendi* appears to have been reached in a number of fields. *See* 'Soviet Literature; the Conspiracy of Silence,' *Soviet Survey*, No. 19, Sept. 1957; T. Scriven, 'The "Literary Opposition,"' *Problems of Communism*, vol. vii, No. 1, Jan.–Feb. 1958; R. Conquest, *Common Sense about Russia*, 1960.

Intelligentsia, term which originated in Russia but is not used there in its general meaning of 'the part of a nation that aspires to independent thinking.' In the official Soviet terminology the intelligentsia is a stratum (not a class) of Soviet society which includes non-manual employees above the clerical level, independent professional people and students. In 1956 the intelligentsia (excluding their families) numbered 15·5 million. For income-tax (q.v.) purposes the intelligentsia is divided into employees and independent professional people: the latter include authors, artists, doctors in private practice, etc., mostly organized in professional associations. Another official distinction is between specialists (numbering 7·5 million in 1958, as against 190,000 in 1913), who are people with higher or professional secondary education, and the rest, the former enjoying certain privileges, e.g. in employment and salary and exemption from agricultural tax (q.v.).

Before 1917 the meaning of the term intelligentsia was not professional: it was that part of educated society which held radical left-wing views. From the 1860's the intelligentsia developed a strong self-consciousness which transcended ideological and political differences. In the Populist (*see* POPULISM) view, the intelligentsia, the peasants and the industrial workers were 'the people' whose interests the Populists had at heart. Marxists regarded the intelligentsia with suspicion or hostility, except that part of it which in their view was serving the interests of the proletariat; the latter point was interpreted by Lenin as requiring support for his own faction. Finally, Makhayevists (*see* MAKHAYEVISM) regarded the intelligentsia as a separate and exploiting class. In the 19th and early 20th centuries a large part of the membership, and in all cases the leadership, of the radical parties was formed by the intelligentsia.

After the Bolshevik seizure of power the term acquired a pejorative meaning, being applied to all educated people, and although people of diverse views (*see* IDEOLOGY) were co-operating with the regime, the Leninist and Makhayevist views on the intelligentsia predominated in the party. The intelligentsia and their children were during the 1920's and early thirties discriminated against in party membership, employment, education, and even in the courts. Stalin's 'cultural revolution' (q.v.) was aimed at replacing this unreliable old intelligentsia with a new one. It was Stalin who in 1936 gave the term its current official meaning and put an end to the baiting of intellectuals. From then onwards the official prestige and social status of the intelligentsia steadily grew, until in the short period of Malenkov's power specialists, who by then had to a considerable extent become a self-perpetuating class (*see* HIGHER EDUCATION), were treated as virtually the only people worthy of holding important positions. Since 1956, when large sections showed themselves to be not altogether reliable (*see* INTELLECTUAL OPPOSITION), Khrushchëv has in this field, as in many others, revived some of the attitudes and practices of the late twenties and early thirties, especially in the fields of education and admission to the party. *See* S. R. Tompkins, *The Russian Intelligentsia, Makers of the Revolutionary State*, Norman, Oklahoma, 1957; W. Markert, 'Zur gesch. Bedeutung der russischen "Intelligenzia" in *Russland-Studien. Gedenkschrift für O. Hoetzsch*, Stuttgart, 1957; G. Fischer, *Russian Liberalism, from Gentry to Intelligentsia*, Cambridge, Mass., 1958; special numbers on Russian intelligentsia of *Soviet Survey*, No. 29, July–Sept. 1959, and *Daedalus*, summer 1960.

Internationalism is officially one of the principles of Communist ideology and practice. Theoretically it is a fellow feeling between the 'toilers' (particularly the proletariat) of all nations based on the essential identity of their class interests. In fact the interpretation and application of this principle have varied according to general changes in the policy of the party leadership. In relation to the party itself, Lenin refused to recognize the authority of the 2nd (Socialist) International, and set up the Comintern (q.v.) as an agency subordinate to his own party, although the latter was formally a section of the larger whole; his successors have adhered to this policy, changing from time to time the forms (*see* COMINFORM). The Soviet state was at first widely regarded, particularly by the Left Communists (q.v.), as an instrument of world revolution, but since 1924, when Stalin's idea of first building socialism in one country prevailed, internationalism has been held to be identical with the interests of the U.S.S.R.; the latter, in fact, has throughout its existence appeared in the double role of a national state and a force used for installing and maintaining in power wherever possible Communist minorities obedient to the Moscow leadership. The composition of the party and the State apparatus was cosmopolitan until the Great Purge (q.v.), 1936–8, which eliminated the foreigners. In 1946–53 Stalin pursued a policy of strict isolation from the outside world, accompanied by official xenophobia and Great Russian chauvinism: a mere interest, real or imputed, in things foreign was enough for an accusation of 'servility before the bourgeois West' and 'cosmopolitanism,' which in many cases led to arrest and execution. *See further under* ANTI-SEMITISM; NATIONALISM; NATIONALITIES POLICY; PATRIOTISM.

Intuitivism is a strong trend in Russian epistemology, beginning with H. S. Skovoroda (q.v.). It was one of the central points in the philosophy of the early Slavophiles (q.v.) and received a systematic treatment by N. O. Losskiy (q.v.). The importance of Intuitivism is played down in the official Soviet works on the history of Russian philosophy. *See* N. Lossky, *The Intuitive Basis of Knowledge*, 1919, and *History of Russian Philosophy*, 1951; V. V. Zenkovsky, *A History of Russian Philosophy* (2 vols.), 1953.

Inventions are theoretically protected since 1931 in two ways, by patents and by 'authors' certificates.' According to the Soviet legal authorities only foreigners now claim patents, while Soviet citizens receive certificates. These bring them an income which is calculated as a percentage of the savings effected by the State industry through the application of the invention, and may be considerable. *See* J. N. Hazard, *Law and Social Change in the U.S.S.R.*, 1953.

Investment. Since almost all the means of production must by the constitution be State-owned, and almost all the rest are owned by *kolkhozes* and other co-operative organizations (*see* OWNERSHIP), the only forms of investment open to private citizens are house property (*see* HOUSING) and Government Bonds (q.v.). Of the gross State and co-operative (excluding *kolkhoz*) fixed investment ('capital invest-ment' in Soviet terminology) during the period 1918–58, 48·0 per cent went into industry (42·4 per cent into producers' goods in-dustries and 5·6 per cent into consumer goods industries), 8·7 per cent into agriculture, 12·8 per cent into transport and communica-tions, 14·8 per cent into housing and 15·7 per cent into trade, educa-tion, health services, etc. In 1958 the distribution was 46·1 per cent industry (40·0 per cent and 6·1 per cent respectively), 9·3 per cent agriculture, 8·9 per cent transport and communications, 19·9 per cent housing and 15·8 per cent the remainder; including private housing, the percentage of overall capital investment that went into housing in 1958 was 25 per cent. Capital investment by *kolkhozes* (excluding payments for machinery formerly belonging to the M.T.S., q.v.) totalled 28·2 milliard pre-1961 roubles in 1958 compared to 22·2 milliard invested by the State in agriculture, and this has been a typical relationship during the post-war period.

Interest on capital cannot serve as a guide to investment in the Soviet Union, since this is officially considered a characteristic of a capitalist economy, but similar though less satisfactory devices are in fact used in calculations. Investment decisions are made on the basis of the prospective output targets. As a result of the decentraliza-tion of the economic administration (*see* ECONOMIC COUNCILS) the share of capital investment in enterprises and organizations directly subordinated to the central government fell from 91 per cent in 1956 to 24 per cent in 1958, while that invested in enterprises subordinated to Union Republic governments increased correspondingly. The bulk of State investment is made by budgetary allocation and the money is made available free of interest through the Bank of the National

Economy (*see* BANKING); a small part of the money for investment in an enterprise comes from the Director's Fund (q.v.). *See also* NATIONAL INCOME. *See* F. Brandel and F. Perroux (eds.), *Critères des choix de l'investissement en U.R.S.S.*, Paris, 1959; *The Soviet Seven Year Plan* (introduction by A. Nove), 1960; G. Grossman (ed.), *Value and Plan*, Berkeley, California, 1960.

Ioffe, Abram Fëdorovich (1880–1960), physicist of Jewish origin. Educated at St Petersburg Technological Institute, he worked under Röntgen in Munich in 1902–6, and later taught in St Petersburg (from 1915 at the university). Elected member of the Academy of Sciences in 1920, he was later director of its Physico-Technical Institute in Leningrad. His many published works are chiefly concerned with the quantum theory of light, mechanical properties of crystals, and dielectrics and semi-conductors. *See* his *Semiconductor Thermoelements and Thermoelectric Cooling*, 1957; J. G. Crowther, *Soviet Science*, 1936.

Ipat'yev, Vladimir Nikolayevich (1867–1952), chemist. Educated at the Artillery Academy in St Petersburg, he was professor there from 1900, and member of the Academy of Sciences, 1916–36. In 1927 he did not return from a business trip abroad, and from 1930 worked in Chicago (with the Universal Oil Products Company) and as professor at North-western University, Illinois. His work on catalytic reactions greatly contributed to the development of industrial catalysis.

Ippolitov-Ivanov, Mikhail Mikhaylovich (1859–1936), composer and conductor who studied under Rimsky-Korsakov at St Petersburg Conservatory and was a friend of Borodin and Balakirev and their associates. In 1894 he was appointed professor of the Moscow Conservatory, of which he was director from 1906 to 1922. Works comprise six operas; choral works; orchestral works, including *Caucasian Sketches*, 1894; *Musical Pictures of Uzbekistan*; chamber works; vocal works, etc. He also completed Musorgskiy's opera *The Marriage* and is the author of several literary works. Though essentially a follower of the traditions of the Kuchka (q.v.), the influence of Tchaikovsky may also be detected in his compositions. His best-known work, *Caucasian Sketches*, was the result of his personal study of Cossack folk music. His efforts as teacher and composer have been of considerable importance in the musical life of the Soviet Union. *See* his 'Fifty Years of Russian Music in my Memories,' *Musical Mercury*, New York, 1937.

Iranians. The main Iranian-speaking people in the U.S.S.R. are the Tadzhiks of Central Asia whose language belongs to the western branch of the Iranian group; to the same branch belong the Baluchi, the Persians (who can be found in both Central Asia and Trans-caucasia, where together they numbered 29,000 in 1959) and the Talysh (q.v.), Kurds and Tats of Transcaucasia. The Kurds, who numbered 59,000 in 1959, live mostly on the Karabakh plateau (south-west Azerbaydzhan and eastern Armenia); they are chiefly Sunni or Shiah Muslims, although the Yezids, who numbered 15,000 in 1926, have a syncretic religion of their own which involves the worship of Satan. The Tats, who live mostly in north-east

Azerbaydzhan and southern Daghestan, numbered 70,000 in 1926, of whom over 30,000 were Shiah Muslims (11,000 in 1959) and 26,000 Jews (commonly known in Russia as Mountain Jews). To the east Iranian branch belong the small Pamir tribes in the Mountainous Badakhshan Autonomous Oblast, and to the north Iranian branch the Ossetians (q.v.) of the Caucasus. Until the 9th–11th centuries the Iranians were the dominant ethnic element in Central Asia (Khorezmians, Sogdians and Bactrians) and in the south of European Russia (Scythians, Sarmats and Alans). In Central Asia, however, they underwent a gradual process of Turkicization, although Persian remained the official and literary language in the Bukhara and Kokand khanates, and in the cities of Bukhara and Samarkand Persian (though called Tadzhik) still takes precedence over Uzbek. In European Russia the Iranian element contributed to the formation of the East Slav culture. *See* M. Rostovtzeff, *Iranians and Greeks in South Russia*, 1922.

Irbit, town in the Sverdlovsk Oblast (Urals), situated 125 m. north-east of Sverdlovsk. Population (1956) 41,200 (1897, 20,000; 1926, 12,000). It has motor-cycle and other engineering factories, and woodworking and pharmaceutical industries. Irbit was founded in 1633 and ten years later its famous annual fair, the second largest in Russia, was established, which for a long time was the focus for Russian trade with Siberia, Central Asia and China; the fair continued to exist until 1930.

Irkutsk: 1. Oblast of the R.S.F.S.R., in south-eastern Siberia north and west of Lake Baykal, situated on the central Siberian plateau and largely covered with coniferous forests. Area 296,500 sq. m.; population (1959) 1,979,000 (62 per cent urban), chiefly Russian (since the 17th century), also Buryat and Evenki. There are large deposits of coal, iron ore, gold, salt and mica, and huge resources of water power. The oblast has coal, iron ore and gold-mining, lumbering, engineering and chemical industries; and grain growing, cattle breeding, fur-trapping and fishing (Lake Baykal) are carried on. A large hydro electric station has been built near Irkutsk and another is under construction at Bratsk. Principal towns: Irkutsk, Cheremkhovo, Angarsk and Bratsk. The area has been one of banishment and labour camps. The Ust'-Ordynskiy Buryat National Okrug lies within the oblast.

2. Administrative centre of the oblast and chief cultural centre of Eastern Siberia, situated on the River Angara and the Trans-Siberian Railway near Lake Baykal. Population (1959), 365,000 (1892, 51,000; 1917, 90,000; 1939, 250,000). It has heavy engineering, wood-processing, light and food industries, and is the chief transportation centre of Eastern Siberia. There is a branch of the U.S.S.R. Academy of Sciences in the city, and a university established in 1918. Irkutsk was founded as a Cossack fort in 1652, became a town in 1686 and the capital of Eastern Siberia in 1822; industrial development dates from the 1930's. The town has been a place of banishment since the 18th century; some of the Decembrists (q.v.) were banished there and played an important part in the development of the town, as later did banished participants in the Polish uprisings.

Iron and Steel Industry. The following table shows the expansion of the industry's output (million tons).

	1913	1920	1928	1936	1940	1945	1950	1958
Pig-iron	4·2	0·1	3·3	14·4	14·9	8·8	19·2	39·6
Steel	4·3	0·2	4·3	16·4	18·3	12·3	27·3	54·9
Rolled metal	3·6	—	3·4	12·5	13·1	8·5	20·9	42·9
Iron ore	9·2	—	6·1	27·8 [1]	29·9	—	39·7	88·8

Blast-furnace efficiency per nominal period of operation (cubic metres of useful furnace volume necessary for the production of one ton of pig-iron) was 2·3 in 1913, 1·9 in 1928, 1·2 in 1940, 1·0 in 1950 and 0·8 in 1958. The average daily production of steel per square metre of hearth in open-hearth furnaces per calendar period of operation amounted to 2·1 tons in 1928, 4·2 in 1940 and 7·2 in 1958. Over 90 per cent of pig-iron is produced in blast-furnaces with automatic regulation of draught; automation of other processes is being introduced, particularly of rolling plant, but complete automation of the entire production process has not yet been achieved in any branch of the industry. The average number of workers employed in the industry in 1957 was 637,000 (274,000 in 1913, 332,000 in 1940).

The iron and steel industry is largely concentrated in the Southern Industrial Region (q.v.) and the Urals, with the Kuznetsk Basin and central Russia as other important centres. The largest iron and steel plants are those of Magnitogorsk, Stalinsk, Nizhniy Tagil and Zaporozh'ye, which together produced about 40 per cent of all pig-iron in 1957; plants of similar size are in the process of construction near Karaganda and a second one at Stalinsk. A considerable proportion of iron ore mined in the Soviet Union is now exported—10·8 million tons in 1957—exclusively to the Communist countries of Europe, and the U.S.S.R. takes fourth place in the world as an exporter of iron ore. In the same year 1·3 million tons of pig-iron and 1·9 of rolled metal were exported; apart from the Communist countries, pig-iron is chiefly exported to Britain, and rolled metal to India, Argentina and Finland. Comparatively small quantities of pig-iron and rolled metal are imported.

Ironworking on a considerable scale first developed in the 17th century in central Russia and Karelia in the north-west. The Urals industry dates from Peter the Great's time and developed so rapidly that by the end of the 18th century Russia was the leading producer of pig-iron in the world, much of it being exported to Britain. During the 19th century Russia at first fell behind the more advanced countries of Western Europe, but the development from the 1870's of the Southern Industrial Region laid the foundations for large-scale expansion, which has since been continuous except for the periods of the civil war, the Great Purge and the Second World War. By 1940 the output of the iron and steel industry in the U.S.S.R. was the second largest in the world. *See* M. G. Clark, *The Economics of Soviet Steel*, 1956; L. Roitburd, *Soviet Iron and Steel Industry: Development and Prospects*, Moscow, 1956.

[1] 1937.

Irtysh, river in Western Siberia, the principal tributary of the Ob'. It rises in the Altay Mountains in Sinkiang, flows north-west through Lake Zaysan to Tobol'sk, then north and joins the Ob' from the left. Length 2,760 m.; major tributaries: Tobol and Ishim; chief ports: Omsk, Semipalatinsk, Pavlodar, Ust'-Kamenogorsk and Tobol'sk. The Irtysh flows through regions with rich deposits of non-ferrous metals (Altay), coal (Ekibastuz) and salt, fertile steppes (Baraba, Kulunda) and forests. Navigation began in the 17th century and the river is almost wholly navigable; the principal goods shipped are timber, grain and coal.

Ishim, river in south-western Siberia, left tributary of the Irtysh, which rises in the Kazakh hills and flows through fertile land which is now rapidly being cultivated. Length 1,400 m.

Ishimbay, town in the Bashkir Autonomous Republic (Urals), situated on the River Belaya south of Sterlitamak. Population (1956) 44,400. It is the centre of the Ishimbay oilfields, the first to be exploited in the Volga-Urals Oil Area.

Iskra ('Spark'), unofficial organization established in 1900 by Lenin, Martov and Potresov within the Russian Social Democratic Labour Party (q.v.) to unite the more orthodox Marxist and politically minded party members against economism and reformism (qq.v.). All three leaders of the organization went abroad, where they collaborated with the Liberation of Labour Group (q.v.) to publish the newspaper *Iskra*. Having virtually achieved control of the party's local committees in Russia, Iskra convened a packed 2nd congress of the party during which they themselves split, the Bolshevik faction being created by the 'hard' Iskraists. Lenin's organizational and tactical principles were first shaped and put into practice during the Iskra period. *See* L. H. Haimson, *The Russian Marxists and the Origins of Bolshevism*, Cambridge, Mass., 1955; B. D. Wolfe, *Three who made a Revolution*, 1956; L. Schapiro, *The Communist Party of the Soviet Union*, 1960.

Islam, *see* MUSLIMS.

Isolators, special prisons administered by the Committee of State Security (*see* K.G.B.) for particularly important political prisoners who are kept incommunicado, usually for life. The best-known isolators were those of Vladimir, Verkhneural'sk and Aleksandrovskoye near Irkutsk; the latter is known to have been closed in the mid 1950's, others may still exist. *See* A. Weissberg, *Conspiracy of Silence*, 1952; W. Claudius, 'In a Soviet Isolator,' *Soviet Affairs*, No. 1 (St Antony's Papers, No. 1), 1956; S. Wolin and R. M. Slusser (eds.), *The Soviet Political Police*, New York, 1957.

Issyk-Kul': 1. Salt lake in Kirgizia (Central Asia), situated 5,000 ft above sea level. Area 2,300 sq. m. It is fed by many streams, and has large quantities of fish.

2. Former oblast of Kirgizia which included a part of the Tien-Shan mountainous country around the lake Issyk-kul'.

Itil', capital of the medieval Khazar Khanate; its site was on the lower Volga near the present-day Astrakhan'.

Ivan I (1301–40) became Prince of Muscovy, 1305, Grand Prince, 1328, nicknamed 'Kalita' ('Money-bag'). Crafty and economical, he began the consolidation of Russian territories. Moscow replaced Vladimir as the metropolitan see of the Russian Church during his reign.

Ivan III (1440–1505), Grand Prince of Muscovy from 1462, sometimes called 'the Great.' He greatly enlarged the Muscovite territory, annexing the Novgorod Republic, Tver' and several other principalities. Russia was finally liberated from the Tatar yoke when Ivan ceased in 1480 to pay token tribute to the Kazan' Khanate; he subsequently claimed the title of czar. In 1497 a legal code was introduced (*see* SUDEBNIK). Ivan was married to a Byzantine princess.

Ivan IV (1530–84), Czar of Moscow and 'all Russia,' called 'the Terrible.' He was crowned at the age of 17, having acceded to the throne in 1533, and was married seven times. For thirteen years he ruled with a group of good advisers from the clergy and the boyars (the so-called 'Selected Council') and with the Zemskiy Sobor (q.v.); during this period he introduced a new code of law, 1550 (*see* SUDEBNIK), conquered Kazan' and Astrakhan' and established diplomatic and commercial relations with England. From 1560, however, to the end of his life he was almost deranged; losing all trust in the boyars and the clergy, he withdrew from the ordinary business of government and devoted himself to eradicating subversion wherever he saw it through a special body of police who were outside the law and responsible only to himself; during this time great cruelties were perpetrated. The conquest of Siberia was begun in 1581. The latter phase of Ivan's rule is considered 'progressive' by official Soviet historiography because it was directed against feudal survivals.

Ivanov, Aleksandr Andreyevich (1806–58), painter, studied at the Academy of Arts, worked in Italy, 1830–57. He spent over twenty years on his *magnum opus* 'The Appearance of the Messiah to the People,' in which he attempted to fuse realism of expression with mystical religious feeling. It proved a noble failure, but in the course of his work on it Ivanov produced a large number of interesting and often brilliant studies (especially of nudes) which appear almost impressionist. He paid close attention to the reconstruction of historical detail. Towards the end of his life he conceived a series of religious scenes and executed over 250 preparatory drawings. Striving towards spirituality he exhibits a knowledge of Byzantine art unique for his times.

Ivanov, Aleksey Petrovich (*b.* 1904), baritone. He studied at Leningrad Conservatory till 1932, becoming a soloist at the Bolshoi Theatre, Moscow, in 1938. A winner of many prizes, his work is held in great esteem, being outstanding in its realism.

Ivanovo: 1. Oblast of the R.S.F.S.R., north-east of Moscow, on the Volga; it is a lowland plain partly covered by mixed forests and having peat deposits. Area 9,300 sq. m.; population (1959) 1,306,000 (66 per cent urban). It has an extensive textile industry, with engineering and chemical industries chiefly serving it; old handicrafts are carried on, including the famous Palekh miniatures. Agriculture specializes in dairy and vegetable produce for the towns and in flax and potatoes for industrial needs. Principal towns: Ivanovo, Kineshma, Shuya and Vichuga.

2. (1871–1932 **Ivanovo-Voznesensk**). Administrative, economic and cultural centre of the oblast, situated 145 m. north-east of Moscow. Population (1959) 332,000 (1897, 18,000; 1914, 168,000; 1926, 111,500; 1939, 285,000). It is the largest centre of the textile industry after Moscow, and has engineering (textile and peat-working machines) and food industries; there are two peat-fed power-stations. Ivanovo has been known since the 14th century, and though it remained a village until 1871 it became a commercial and manufacturing centre as early as the beginning of the 17th century. Before the emancipation of serfs in 1861 most of the workers and factory owners of Ivanovo were serfs. The town was a centre of the labour movement from the 1880's, and one of the first Soviets of Workers' Deputies existed there in 1905; both before 1917 and during the 1920's it was an important stronghold of the Bolsheviks.

Izhevsk, capital, economic and cultural centre of the Udmurt Autonomous Republic, about 170 m. north-east of Kazan'. Population (1959) 283,000 (1920, 45,000; 1939, 176,000). It is an important centre of the engineering (motor-cycles, small arms) and metal-working industries. Izhevsk was founded as an iron foundry in 1760, destroyed by Pugachëv in 1774, and became a town in 1918. In August 1918 workers overthrew the Communists in the town and formed the 'Izhevsk Division' which fought on the side of the Whites during the civil war.

Izmail, town in the Odessa Oblast (Ukraine), situated in southern Bessarabia on the Danube. Population (1956) 43,400 (1892, 31,000). There are various food industries, and it is the seat of the Soviet Danube Shipping Administration. Izmail has been known since the 16th century; it was a Turkish fortress and was stormed by Suvorov in 1790. For further history *see* BESSARABIA.

'**Izvestiya**' ('News'), daily newspaper published by the Presidium of the Supreme Soviet of the U.S.S.R. which was founded after the February 1917 revolution as the mouthpiece of the Petrograd Soviet. It was published jointly by the Central Executive Committee of Soviets and the Petrograd Soviet from August 1917, becoming editorially a duplicate of *Pravda* after the Bolshevik seizure of power, and being transferred to Moscow in 1918. The average daily circulation in 1957 was 1·55 million. In 1960 *Izvestiya* became an evening paper.

J

Jakobson, R. O., *see* FORMALISM.

Japhetic Languages, *see* CAUCASIANS.

Jehovah's Witnesses have only appeared in Russia since the Second World War, as a result of contacts with members of the sect in the annexed areas of eastern Poland and the Baltic States, as well as with foreign members of the sect in concentration camps in Germany during the war. They are extremely active in proselytizing, and because of their defiance of all temporal authority are the most harshly persecuted religious community in the Soviet Union. During the great strikes in the main forced labour camp areas in 1953–5, Jehovah's Witnesses played a prominent, though in accordance with their principles non-violent, part. In the Soviet press they are continuously represented as 'agents of foreign imperialism.' An old sect of ' Jehovists' which has existed in Russia since the 19th century is distinct from the Jehovah's Witnesses.

Jelgava (formerly German **Mitau**, Russian **Mitava**), town in Latvia, 25 m. south-west of Riga, an important railway junction. Population (1956) 31,600 (1935, 34,000). It has textile and sugar industries. Jelgava was founded by the Livonian Knights in 1226, and became capital of Kurland in 1561; it was Russian from 1795 to 1920. The future King Louis XVIII lived in Jelgava Palace as an *émigré* at the time of the French Revolution.

Jewish Autonomous Oblast, situated in the Khabarovsk Kray (Russian Far East), in the Amur bend west of Khabarovsk, partly forested and having rich mineral resources. Area 13,900 sq. m.; population (1959) 163,000, mostly Russians and Ukrainians, also Jews. There are gold-mining and timber industries, grain cultivation and dairy farming. Administrative centre Birobidzhan. The area was first colonized by Russians in 1852, and by Jews in 1928; the Autonomous Oblast was established in 1934. *See* W. Kolarz, *The Peoples of the Soviet Far East*, 1954.

Jews in Russia number, according to the 1959 census, 2,268,000 (3 million in 1939 and over 5 million after the annexations of 1939–40), the Soviet Union thus having the second largest concentration of Jews in the world. They live throughout the country, mostly in the towns, and can be found in all occupations, although practically none are left in the higher ranks of the party and government apparatus. The so-called Jewish Autonomous Oblast (q.v.) in the Far East has a very small Jewish population. The vast majority of Jews in the Soviet Union are Ashkenazim, and 21 per cent of all Jews gave Yiddish as their mother tongue in 1959. Apart from these there are four small Jewish ethnic groups: Crimean Jews (or Krymchaks), who speak Crimean Tatar; Mountain Jews in Daghestan and Azerbaydzhan, who numbered 26,000 in 1926 and speak the Tat language (*see*

IRANIANS); the Georgian Jews, speaking Georgian (about 20,000 in 1926); and Bukharan Jews in Central Asia (also about 20,000), who speak Tadzhik or Uzbek. All these small communities descend from Jewish immigrants of ancient or medieval times from the Near East.

There were very few Jews in Russia until the partitions of Poland in the late 18th century. The attitude of the Russian authorities was basically hostile, though it fluctuated with the general political atmosphere. The authority of the Jewish communal organizations (*kahal*) was officially recognized and not interfered with; no direct attempts were made to convert the Jews except in the time of Nicholas I, when about 100,000 Jewish youths were made to serve in the army and came under very strong pressure to be baptized. Russia was the home of the largest number of Jews in the 19th century, and all the main cultural and political developments in Jewish life took place there—the rise of Hassidism, the development of modern literature in both Hebrew and Yiddish, the spread of Zionism and the growth of the Jewish socialist movement (*see* BUND). Jews played an active part in the general cultural and political life of the country, being prominent from the late 19th century in both the liberal and the revolutionary movements. Many former restrictions were removed after the revolution of 1905 (q.v.), and after the February revolution (q.v.) of 1917 the Provisional Government established complete legal equality for Jews.

The Communist attitude towards the Jews was at first ambivalent; on the one hand they suppressed all Jewish autonomous communities and organizations as well as all cultural activities in Hebrew: the Jewish religion, like others, was persecuted; on the other hand, as with other national minorities, the Soviet authorities tried to win the co-operation of Jews, considered not as a religious but as an ethnic group (*see* NATIONALITIES POLICY), through the wide use of Yiddish in schools, the press, the theatre, etc. The Yiddish Theatre in Moscow, directed by Mikhoels, was until its closure in 1949 among the best theatres in the country. Efforts were made to encourage Jewish agricultural settlement in the Ukraine, Crimea and the Far East, but had little success. Many Jews were prominent in the leadership of the Communist Party (Trotskiy, Zinov'yev, Kamenev, Kaganovich, etc.) and among the local officials until the time of the Great Purge (q.v.); since then their numbers have steadily declined. At the beginning of the Second World War no special efforts were made to evacuate Jews from the western territories, and as a result about three million perished under the Nazi occupation. All references to the special sufferings of the Jews during the war were suppressed until after Stalin's death. The Soviet Government's attitude towards the partition of Palestine and the establishment of the state of Israel in 1947 was for a brief period favourable (since they were regarded as 'anti-imperialist' moves), but soon became hostile because of the welcome from Russian Jews. A policy of persecution of the Jews was followed until 1953, with the aim of eradicating them as an ethnic minority who might have loyalties outside the Soviet Union; all remnants of Jewish culture and religion were suppressed except for a few synagogues and one weekly Yiddish newspaper with a circulation of about 1,000 published in Birobidzhan. Since Stalin's death direct persecution has ceased, though various unofficial forms of discrimination exist, and there are still no Yiddish schools. *See also* ANTI-SEMITISM. *See* S. M. Schwarz, *The Jews in the Soviet Union*, Syracuse, 1951; W. Kolarz, *Russia and her Colonies*, 1952; E. J. Simmons (ed.), *Through the Glass of Soviet Literature*, New York, 1953; 'Soviet Jewry after Stalin,' *Soviet Survey*, No. 18, Aug. 1957; S. Federbush (ed.), *World Jewry Today*, 1959; A. A. Greenbaum, *Jewish Scholarship in Soviet Russia, 1918–41*, Boston, Mass., 1959.

Journals, *see* PRESS.

Judges are theoretically independent and subject only to law. Peope's Court (q.v.) judges are ostensibly elected for five years by adult vote, those of higher courts by corresponding soviets for the same period. Candidates must be 25 years old. No legal training is necessary; in 1958 55·4 per cent of all judges in People's Courts had higher education, and 37·1 per cent specialized secondary education. In fact judges are selected by the cadres (q.v.) departments of territorial party organizations in conjunction with the Ministries of Justice, and in their work they have to implement the policy of the party. Apart from party discipline they are under the jurisdiction of disciplinary divisions of superior courts and can be 'recalled' before the end of their term of office. Before 1917 all judges in the general courts established by the judicial reform of 1864 were qualified jurists, and they were genuinely independent and irremovable. *See also* ASSESSORS; COURTS OF LAW. *See* D. M. Wallace, *Russia*, 2nd ed., 1905; H. J. Berman, *Justice in Russia*, Cambridge, Mass., 1950; G. C. Guins, *Soviet Law and Soviet Society*, The Hague, 1954; W. W. Kulski, *The Soviet Regime*, Syracuse, 1954; M. Fainsod, *Smolensk under Soviet Rule*, 1959.

Judicial System. According to the constitution, justice is administered in the U.S.S.R. exclusively by the regular courts of law (q.v.). However, decrees passed in several Union Republics in 1956–7 introduced a system of trial for 'parasitic existence'—i.e. refusing to take up employment approved of by the authorities (which is not a criminal offence)—by 'meetings of citizens' living in the neighbourhood. Such meetings can punish 'parasites' by banishment, and are in fact a formal cover for administrative decisions. Another form of irregular court is the so-called 'comradely court' which existed in the late 1920's and early thirties and is now to be resuscitated. Its jurisdiction is to extend to petty offences and cases of 'antisocial behaviour' which are not officially criminal offences, and it is to act under the supervision of trade unions in the towns and of local soviets (q.v.) in the countryside. Of far greater importance for the perversion of justice and the undermining of all respect for the judicial system were the notorious *troykas* (q.v.) of the security organs. The present judicial system has developed gradually since 1917, when, after the Bolshevik seizure of power, the well-functioning system of lawcourts established by the judicial reform of 1864 (*see* GREAT REFORMS) was abolished. *See* V. Gsovski and K. Grzybowski (eds.), *Government, Law and Courts in the Soviet Union and Eastern Europe*, vol. i, 1959; R. S., 'Voluntary Militia and Courts,' *Soviet*

Studies, vol. xi, No. 2, Oct. 1959; R. Schlesinger, 'Social Law,' *Soviet Studies*, vol. xii, No. 1, July 1960.

Justice, Ministries of, exist in the Union Republics (with the exception of Tadzhikistan, which abolished its Ministry of Justice in 1958) and Autonomous Republics for the purposes of juridical administration: administrative and financial aspects of the courts, the system of public notaries, supervision of the advocates' colleges, legal training and codification of the laws. A Ministry of Justice was first established in Russia in 1804. After the Bolshevik seizure of power in 1917 (*see* OCTOBER REVOLUTION) it was replaced by a People's Commissariat of Justice with very wide functions, including investigation and prosecution in criminal cases, supervising the courts' activities and issuing directives to them, administration of places of detention, etc., some of which have since been transferred to other bodies. The Procuracy (q.v.) was constituted as a separate service under the Procurator General in 1933. Administration of places of detention was transferred to the Commissariat for Internal Affairs in 1934, apparently transferred back to the Ministry of Justice after Beria's fall in 1953, but returned to the Ministry of the Interior in 1956. Supervision of the courts was finally transferred to the supreme courts of the Union Republics in 1958. A U.S.S.R. Ministry of Justice was set up in 1938, but it was abolished in 1956 and a juridical commission formed instead for codification. *See* V. Gsovski and K. Grzybowski (eds.), *Government, Law and Courts in the Soviet Union and Eastern Europe*, vol. i, 1959.

Justices of the Peace were introduced by the judicial reform of 1864 to try petty cases, both civil and criminal. They were elected by uyezd *zemstvo* assemblies and Town Dumas for three years. There were certain property, education and experience qualifications; Jews were ineligible. In 1889 justices of the peace were abolished in thirty-five provinces and replaced by Land Captains. The institution was gradually restored between 1912 and 1917, but 'suspended' by the Bolshevik Government in November 1917 and never in fact revived. *See* D. M. Wallace, *Russia* (2nd ed.), vol. ii, 1905.

Juvenile Delinquency. No statistics on juvenile delinquency have been published since the late 1920's. According to the available information it rose rapidly at the time of the collectivization of agriculture (e.g. by 100 per cent in Moscow between 1931 and 1934) and in the years following the Second World War, in both cases as a result of the great increase in the numbers of homeless children. Other causes of the increase of juvenile delinquency in the early 1930's were the limitation of the authority of parents which played a prominent part in the Communist educational policy until the mid 1930's (*see* FAMILY), the free sale of alcohol to juveniles and the influence of the cinema. Progressive ideas about re-educating juvenile delinquents were popular until the mid 1930's. In 1918 all persons under 17 were exempt from criminal responsibility, and special commissions were set up to deal with juvenile delinquents. A number of reformatories were set up in the 1920's, some of which achieved outstanding successes (*see* MAKARENKO). The official attitude changed sharply in 1935, when the age of criminal responsibility was lowered to 14 and even to 12 for particularly serious crimes (though few children between 12 and 14 were in fact charged). No consideration was to be given to age in the application of penalties provided for by the Criminal Code. Special corrective colonies for juveniles were formed by the Ministry of the Interior, but in fact minors have frequently been sent to ordinary places of confinement. Since Stalin's death it has again become possible to advocate special consideration for juvenile delinquents, and the legal reform (q.v.) of 1958 raised the age of criminal responsibility to 16 (14 for serious crimes). *See also* CHILDREN; HOOLIGANISM; PENAL SYSTEM. *See* S. Timasheff, *The Great Retreat*, New York, 1946; J. N. Hazard, *Law and Social Change in the U.S.S.R.,* 1953; W. W. Kulski, *The Soviet Regime*, Syracuse, 1954; V. Gsovski and K. Grzybowski (eds.), *Government, Law and Courts in the Soviet Union and Eastern Europe*, vol. ii, 1959; R. Beermann, 'Criminology and Juvenile Delinquency Reconsidered,' *Soviet Studies*, vol. xi, No. 4, April 1960.

K

Kabalevskiy, Dmitriy Borisovich (*b.* 1904), composer, conductor and musicologist who studied at Moscow Conservatory under Myaskovskiy, 1929, teaching there from 1932 and becoming professor in 1939. He is an excellent conductor. His works comprise operas, including *Colas Brugnon*, 1938, *Sem'ya Tarasa*, 1950, and *Nikita Vershinin*, 1955; four symphonies; three piano concertos; violin concerto; cello concerto; orchestral works; two string quartets; many choruses, songs, piano works, transcriptions; music to plays and films, and literary works. Like Prokof'yev's, which in some ways it resembles, Kabalevskiy's music is often filled with quiet, sardonic humour. His work, though not highly individual, is of the finest craftsmanship. *See* G. Abraham, *Eight Soviet Composers*, 1943.

Kabarda, *see* CIRCASSIANS.

Kabarda-Balkar Autonomous Republic, within the R.S.F.S.R., is situated on the northern slopes of the main Caucasian range and the adjacent lowland, chiefly west of the River Terek bend; there are rich deposits of non ferrous metals (molybdenum, tungsten, zinc, lead, etc.) and gold and platinum, also iron ore, arsenic, coal and building materials. Area 4,800 sq. m.; population (1959) 420,000 (38 per cent urban), Circassians, Balkars, Russians, Ukrainians, Ossetians, Georgians and Tatars. There are non-ferrous metallurgical, engineering (developed since 1928, specializing in oil industry equipment) and various food industries; wheat, maize and sunflowers are cultivated, and cattle, sheep and horses (Kabarda breed) raised. The capital is Nal'chik. The area became a Muscovite protectorate in 1552, was contested by Russia, Crimea and Turkey in the 17th and 18th centuries and finally became Russian in 1825. In 1917–18 it belonged to the anti-Bolshevik South-Eastern League (q.v.) and in 1921 to the Mountain People's Autonomous Republic (q.v.). The Kabarda Autonomous Oblast was established in 1921 and Balkar added to the name in the following year; in 1936 it was raised to the status of an Autonomous Republic. The Balkars were deported to Central Asia in 1948 for alleged collaboration with the Germans, and their name was deleted from the republic; with their rehabilitation in 1957 the name Kabarda-Balkar was restored. *See* B. Nolde, *La Formation de l'Empire Russe*, vol. ii, Paris, 1952.

Kablukov, Ivan Alekseyevich (1857–1942), chemist, a pupil of Markovnikov, Butlerov (qq.v.) and Arrenius, professor of the Moscow Agricultural Institute and from 1903 at Moscow University, honorary member of the Academy of Sciences (from 1932). He did much to develop physical chemistry in Russia, his own work being mainly concerned with electro-chemistry of non-water solutions. His textbooks were widely popular (*Basic Principles of Inorganic Chemistry*, 1900, 13th ed., 1936).

Kadiyevka, town in the Lugansk Oblast (eastern Ukraine), 28 m. west of Lugansk. Population (1959) 180,000 (sixth in Donbas; 1926, 17,000; 1936, 78,000; 1939, 135,000). It is one of the principal industrial centres of the Donets Basin and the largest coal producer in the Lugansk Oblast; there are coking, chemical and iron and steel plants. Kadiyevka was founded as a mining settlement in the 1840's and became a town in the 1930's; its industrial development dates from the late 19th century and has been especially rapid since the 1930's. The Stakhanov movement (q.v.) originated in nearby Irmino in 1935.

Kaganovich, Lazar' Moiseyevich (*b.* 1893), Communist of Jewish origin who began life as a leather-worker and after joining the Bolshevik Party in 1911 was active in the leather-workers' union. He led the Bolshevik seizure of power in Gomel' and then specialized in party organizational work, advancing rapidly. He has held the following posts: member of the Central Committee from 1924; 1925–1928 head of the party organization in the Ukraine; 1928–39 secretary of the Central Committee; from 1930 member of the Politburo (later Presidium) of the Central Committee; 1930–5 secretary also of the Moscow party committee; 1929–34 in charge of the collectivization of agriculture, and 1933–4 of the party purge; 1935–44 People's Commissar for Transport, simultaneously directing other ministries; a deputy prime minister from 1938; during the Second World War member of the State Defence Committee (q.v.) and high political officer in the Caucasus; 1946–7 again headed the party organization in the Ukraine. Kaganovich was one of Stalin's chief lieutenants, but his influence declined in the last years of Stalin's life. He became more prominent after Stalin's death in 1953, but in 1957, as a member of the 'anti-party group' (q.v.), was expelled from the Central Committee and its Presidium and dismissed from the post of a first deputy prime minister. For a time he was then reportedly manager of an asbestos plant in Asbest in the Urals, but early in 1960 was believed to be living in retirement near Moscow.

Kairov, Ivan Andreyevich (*b.* 1893), professor of education. He succeeded Potëmkin (q.v.) as Minister of Education of the R.S.F.S.R. and President of the Pedagogical Academy in 1946, and after Zhdanov's death in 1948 began the process of reversing the Zhdanov-Potëmkin educational policy. His main measures were the rapid expansion of full secondary education with the aim of making it compulsory by 1960, and reintroducing the idea of polytechnical education (q.v.). He was replaced as Minister of Education by Afanasenko in 1957 but has remained President of the Pedagogical Academy.

Kakhetia, area of eastern Georgia (Transcaucasia) in the valley of the Alazani, a tributary of the Kura. The chief town is Telavi, and the area is well known for its wine. From the 8th century it was an independent kingdom, from 1010 part of the Georgian kingdom, independent again, 1468–1762, and then part of the East Georgian kingdom which joined Russia in 1801.

Kakhovka, town in the Kherson Oblast (southern Ukraine), a river port situated on the Dnieper 45 m. above Kherson. Population (1956

19,200. An important hydro-electric station (capacity 336,000 kw.) was built near Kakhovka in the 1950's, and a small town, Novaya Kakhovka, has developed from the settlement established at the site of the power-station. Kakhovka was a lively trade centre before 1917, and saw fierce fighting in 1920 during the civil war.

Kaledin, Aleksey Maksimovich (1861–1918), general, elected ataman (i.e. 'headman') of the Cossack armies in July 1917. He headed the anti-Bolshevik Don Cossack government after the Bolshevik seizure of power (*see* OCTOBER REVOLUTION), but committed suicide on being defeated by the Bolsheviks.

Kalinin (until 1931 **Tver'**): 1. Oblast of the R.S.F.S.R., north-west of Moscow, astride the River Volga (which rises here), situated on the Valday moraine upland; it has many lakes and is partly covered with mixed forests. Area 32,100 sq. m.; population (1959) 1,802,000 (44 per cent urban), mostly Russian, partly also Karelian (since 16th–17th centuries). There are peat and lignite deposits; the industries of the oblast are textiles, engineering, saw-milling, tanning and shoe-making, and old handicrafts are also practised. Flax and potatoes are grown, and dairy cattle raised. Principal towns: Kalinin, Vyshniy Volochëk and Rzhev. Tver' province was famous during the 19th century for its liberal-minded local government.

2. Administrative, economic and cultural centre of the oblast, situated on the Volga and the Moscow–Leningrad railway. Population (1959) 261,000 (1914, 66,000; 1920, 166,000; 1939, 216,000). It has large textile (cotton and flax) and engineering (rolling stock, textile and peat-working machinery) industries; a large printing plant was built during the 1950's. There is a 16th-century church and there are many interesting buildings of the 18th–19th centuries. Kalinin has been known since 1209 and soon became the capital of Tver' Principality (later Grand Principality); after a long rivalry with Muscovy it was absorbed by the latter in 1485. In the 14th and 15th centuries it was an important centre of crafts and commerce. The Tver' merchant Nikitin travelled to India between 1466 and 1472, and left a description of his journey.

Kalinin, Mikhail Ivanovich (1875–1946), Communist, for many years titular head of the Soviet state. Of peasant origin, and a metal-worker until 1917, he joined the Social Democratic movement in 1897 and, although always of fairly moderate views, its Leninist wing (*see* ISKRA) in 1902. He was opposed to Lenin's defeatist policy during the First World War, and to the aim of a Bolshevik seizure of power after the February revolution (q.v.) of 1917. He became a Central Committee member in 1919, Politburo member, 1926, was chairman of the Central Executive Committee of the Soviets of the R.S.F.S.R., 1919–1937, and of the U.S.S.R. Central Executive Committee (q.v.) from 1922, and chairman of the Presidium of the U.S.S.R. Supreme Soviet, 1937–46. Kalinin supported Stalin in the party struggle following Lenin's death. Though not very influential, he was likable and easily approached, often trying to alleviate hardship in individual cases.

Kaliningrad: 1. Oblast of the R.S.F.S.R., bordering on the Baltic Sea in the west, Lithuania in the north and east and Poland in the south; it is hilly lowland partially covered with well-kept mixed forests. Area 5,800 sq. m.; population (1959) 610,000 (64 per cent urban), chiefly settlers from central Russia. There are varied engineering, woodworking and food industries, and there is intensive agriculture. Principal towns: Kaliningrad (administrative centre) and Sovetsk. The area, originally populated by the Lithuanian tribe of Prusses, was conquered by the Teutonic Knights in the 13th century, and formed part of the territory of the Order until 1525, when it became part of the Duchy of Prussia; from 1618 to 1945 it was part of the German province of East Prussia. The area has been under Soviet administration since 1945 pending a German peace treaty; the German population fled, or was deported or expelled, and the Kaliningrad Oblast was formed in 1946.

2. (until 1946 **Königsberg**). Administrative, economic and cultural centre of the oblast, an important ice-free port on the Vistula Bay in the Baltic Sea. Population (1959) 202,000 (1939, 372,000). It has shipbuilding, engineering, chemical, woodworking and food industries. The town grew up around a castle of the Teutonic Knights, and in 1457 became the residence of the High Master of the Order; from 1525 to 1618 it was the residence of the dukes of Prussia, and from 1618 to 1945 the capital of East Prussia. The inner part of the city was ruined during the siege of 1945. Königsberg University, founded in 1544, was abolished in 1945.

Kalinovskiy, Konstantin Semёnovich (1836–64), leader in Belorussia of the Polish uprising of 1863. He was less concerned with Polish national aims than with the grievances of the peasants.

Kalmyk Autonomous Republic lies in the south-east of European Russia, west of the lower Volga and adjacent to the Caspian Sea; it is a dry steppe and semi-desert lowland with a continental climate. Area 29,600 sq. m.; population (1959) 183,000 (21 per cent urban), Kalmyks and Russians. There is extensive sheep breeding and the area is used for winter grazing for sheep from many parts of eastern Caucasus; grain and melons are cultivated, and there is a fishing industry. The capital is Elista. For history see KALMYKS. The Kalmyk Autonomous Oblast was established (within Stavropol' Kray) in 1957, and it was raised to the status of an Autonomous Republic in 1958.

Kalmyks, semi-nomadic Mongol-speaking Buddhist people who lived in East Turkestan until the 17th century. They then moved west and, forcing the Nogays to retreat to the south-west, occupied the territory astride the lower Volga, between the rivers Don and Ural. The majority (about 300,000) returned to their original home in 1771 but most of them perished en route in fighting the Kazakhs; a minority (about 50,000) remained west of the Volga and later many of them became Cossacks. The Kalmyks belonged to the anti-Bolshevik South-Eastern League (q.v.) after the October 1917 revolution; in 1920 a Kalmyk Autonomous Oblast was established and in 1933 it was transformed into an Autonomous Republic. In 1939 the population of the republic was 200,000, including 134,000 Kalmyks. It was partly occupied by the Germans in 1942, and abolished by the Soviet Government in 1943, when all Kalmyks were deported to Central Asia. The decree on the rehabilitation of deported peoples issued in 1957 provided for the return of the Kalmyks. According to the 1959 census there were 106,000 Kalmyks in the U.S.S.R. *See* W. Kolarz, *Russia and her Colonies*, 1952; R. Conquest, *The Soviet Deportation of Nationalities*, 1960.

Kaluga: 1. Oblast of the R.S.F.S.R. south-west of Moscow, situated in the north-west of the Central Russian upland and partly covered with mixed forests; there are deposits of lignite, peat and building materials. Area 11,500 sq. m.; population (1959) 936,000 (37 per cent urban). Agriculture in the oblast produces coarse grains, potatoes and hemp, and dairy cattle, pigs and poultry (Kaluga geese) are raised. The chief industries are engineering, woodworking, glass, paper (since 1720), textile and food. The first atomic power-station in the world was built in Obninsk in Kaluga Oblast in 1957.

2. Administrative, economic and cultural centre of the oblast, situated on the River Oka. Population (1959) 133,000 (1914, 55,000; 1920, 41,000; 1939, 89,500). It has transport and electrical engineering, chemical, woodworking and food industries. There are interesting buildings of the 18th–19th centuries, a drama theatre which was founded in 1777, and the Tsiolkovskiy (q.v.) Museum. Kaluga has been known since 1389 as a Muscovite outpost, and during the 17th–19th centuries was an important centre of the grain trade. It was occupied by the Germans for a brief period in 1941.

Kamchatka: 1. Peninsula in the Russian Far East, situated between the Sea of Okhotsk, the Pacific and the Bering Sea. It is mountainous, with twenty-two functioning volcanoes, including Klyuchevskaya Sopka (1,479 ft), and many hot springs and geysers. There are coal and sulphur deposits.

2. Oblast of the R.S.F.S.R., comprising the peninsula and the adjacent mainland. Area 182,400 sq. m.; population (1959) 220,000, chiefly Russians (since the 17th century), also some Koryaks and other small tribes. There are fishing, fish-processing, woodworking and fur-trapping industries, and the beginnings of agriculture (potatoes) and animal husbandry. The administrative centre is Petropavlovsk-Kamchatskiy. The area has been one of banishment (since the 18th century) and labour camps.

Kamenets Podolskiy (Ukrainian **Kam'yanets' Podil's'kyy**), cultural centre of the Khmel'nitskiy Oblast (Ukraine), situated 40 m. north-east of Chernovtsy. Population (1956) 33,000 (1914, 50,000). It has some food industries. There are the remains of a 14th-century fortress, and churches of the 15th–18th centuries. Kamenets-Podolskiy has been known since 1196, and was a provincial capital during the 19th and early 20th centuries.

Kamenev (real name **Rozenfel'd**), **Lev Borisovich** (1883–1936), Communist of Jewish origin, joined the Social Democratic Party in 1901. A supporter of Lenin from the first, he directed the Bolshevik organization from abroad with him and Zinov'yev between 1909 and 1914; he then returned to Russia to undertake responsibility for the newspaper *Pravda* and for the Bolshevik members of the Duma. He was banished to Siberia on the outbreak of war, but returned after the February revolution (q.v.) of 1917 to lead the Bolshevik Party until Lenin's arrival from abroad; he opposed Lenin's intention to seize power and advocated the establishment of a coalition of all socialist parties. After the October revolution (q.v.) he became chairman of the Central Executive Committee of the Soviets and chairman of the Moscow Soviet; later deputy chairman of the Council of People's Commissars (i.e. deputy prime minister), and a Politburo member, 1919–25; he was ambassador to Italy, 1926–7. Kamenev sided with Stalin against Trotskiy after Lenin's death, but later, with Zinov'yev and Trotskiy, headed the opposition to Stalin (*see* LEFT OPPOSITION). Twice expelled from the party but both times readmitted, he was again expelled and sentenced to five years' imprisonment in 1935, retried the following year (*see* GREAT PURGE) and sentenced to death. *See* E. H. Carr, *The Interregnum, 1923–4,* 1954, and *Socialism in One Country, 1924–6,* vol. i, 1958; L. Schapiro, *The Communist Party of the Soviet Union,* 1960.

Kamensk-Shakhtinskiy (formerly **Kamenskaya**), town in the Rostov Oblast, situated on the Severskiy Donets (a tributary of the Don) 120 m. north of Rostov-on-Don. Population (1959) 58,500 (1897, 24,000). It has coal-mining, engineering and artificial fibre industries. Kamensk-Shakhtinskiy was founded in 1817 and until the 1930's was a prosperous Cossack *stanitsa* (village).

Kamensk-Ural'skiy, town in the Sverdlovsk Oblast, situated 87 m. south-east of Sverdlovsk. Population (1959) 141,000 (1926, 5,000; 1939, 51,000). It is a rapidly growing industrial centre (large aluminium plant, pipe foundry and a large power-station). Kamensk-Ural'skiy was founded in 1682 as an iron-smelting works, the first in the Urals.

Kamenskoye, *see* DNEPRODZERZHINSK.

Kamyshin, town in the Stalingrad Oblast, a river port on the Volga half way between Stalingrad and Saratov. Population (1959) 55,000 (1939, 24,000). It has textile (since the mid 1950's) and flour-milling industries, is an important transportation centre (transfer of grain, salt and oil from water to rail) and a centre of a market-gardening area (melons). Kamyshin was founded in 1668.

Kandinskiy, Vasiliy Vasil'yevich (1866–1944), painter. After taking a degree in law and economics at Moscow University he studied art in Munich from 1896; he became a co-founder, with Franz Mark, of the 'Blaue Reiter' group. He was the first Russian painter to produce purely abstract works. His first abstractions were in the expressionist manner; he later introduced into his work the geometrical elements of Malevich (q.v.), and was also influenced by Paul Klee, his colleague in the Bauhaus. Kandinskiy's abstract forms were of astonishing variety. He emigrated from Russia in 1921 and lived first in Germany and then, until his death, in France. He published important theoretical works on abstract art. *See* his *Point and Line to Plane,* New York, 1947; W. Grohmann, *Wassily Kandinsky,* 1959.

Kansk, town in the Krasnoyarsk Kray (central Siberia), situated on the Trans-Siberian Railway 135 m. east of Krasnoyarsk. Population (1959) 74,000. It has woodworking, textile, wood-processing and food industries, and is the centre of a rapidly developing industrial area (coal-, mica- and salt-mining). Kansk was founded in 1640 as a Russian fort. Coal-mining in the area began in 1904.

Kantorovich, Leonid Vital'yevich (*b.* 1912), mathematician.

Educated at Leningrad University (graduating in 1930), he has been professor there since 1934 and a corresponding member of the Academy of Sciences since 1958. His main works are devoted to the theory of functions of a real variable, approximate methods of analysis, electronic computers (particularly programming) and operations research (*Mathematical Methods of Organization and Planning of Production*, Leningrad, 1939). In recent years Kantorovich, together with V. V. Novozhilov, took the initiative in reviving the marginalist trend in economic thought (*Economic Calculation of the Optimum Utilization of Resources*, Moscow, 1959). *See* J. M. Montias, 'Planning and Efficiency—A Note on L. V. Kantorovich,' *Problems of Communism*, May–June 1960; A. Zauberman, 'New Winds in Soviet Planning,' *Soviet Studies*, vol. xii, No. 1, July 1960.

Kapitsa, Pëtr Leonidovich (*b.* 1894), physicist, member of the Academy of Sciences since 1939, Fellow of the Royal Society. Educated at the Petrograd Polytechnic Institute, he worked under Ioffe (q.v.) until his emigration in 1921 to England, where he worked under Rutherford, from 1924 as deputy head of the Cavendish Magnetic Research Laboratory at Cambridge. Induced to visit the U.S.S.R. in 1934, he was not permitted to return to England, and he finally agreed to work after refusing to do so for several months. His English laboratory was bought and set up in Moscow as the Institute of Physical Problems, which he has headed 1936–46 and again since Stalin's death, having in the meantime reportedly suffered imprisonment for refusing to work on the military uses of nuclear energy. He is believed to be so engaged now. His main theoretical works are concerned with the study of low temperatures, and he discovered, 1938, the phenomenon of superfluidity in liquid helium. *See* A. Kramish, *Atomic Energy in the Soviet Union*, 1960.

Kara Sea, part of the Arctic Ocean off the shores of Western Siberia between Novaya Zemlya and Severnaya Zemlya. The Northern Sea Route passes through the Kara Sea, whose chief port is Dikson. The principal rivers which flow into the sea are the Ob' and the Yenisey, both of which form long estuaries.

Karachay, Turkic-speaking people who live in the Karachay-Circassian Autonomous Oblast on the northern slopes of the main Caucasian range, west of El'brus, on the upper Kuban' River, and number (1959) 81,000 (76,000 in 1939), of whom 74 per cent regard Karachay as their mother tongue. Known since the 16th century, they were under the suzerainty of the Kabarda, from 1733 of Turkey, and were conquered by the Russians in 1828. They made up four-fifths of the population in the Karachay Autonomous Oblast which existed from 1926 until 1943. The Karachay were deported to Asiatic Russia in 1943 for alleged collaboration with the Germans. The decree on the rehabilitation of deported peoples in 1957 provided for their return to their homeland. *See* W. Kolarz, *Russia and her Colonies*, 1952; R. Conquest, *The Soviet Deportation of Nationalities*, 1960.

Karachay-Circassian Autonomous Oblast lies within the Stavropol' Kray (North Caucasus) along the upper Kuban' River, consisting of lowland steppe in the north and embracing the Caucasian foothills in the south. Area 5,500 sq. m.; population (1959) 277,000 (24 per cent urban), mostly Russians (since the 19th century), Circassians and Karachay, also Abaza and Nogay. Grain is cultivated and market gardening and livestock breeding carried on. Principal towns: Cherkessk (administrative centre) and Karachayevsk. The area was included in the Mountain People's Republic in 1921; the Karachay-Circassian Autonomous Oblast was formed in 1922 and in 1926 divided into a Karachay Autonomous Oblast and a Circassian National Okrug, the latter being raised to the status of Autonomous Oblast two years later. In 1943 the Karachay were deported to Asiatic Russia and their Autonomous Oblast abolished; after the 1957 decree on the rehabilitation of deported peoples the Karachay-Circassian Autonomous Oblast was re-established.

Karachayevsk (until 1943 **Mikoyan-Shakhar**, then **Klukhori** until 1957), town in the Karachay-Circassian Autonomous Oblast of the Stavropol' Kray (North Caucasus), situated on the River Kuban' and the Sukhumi Military Road 90 m. south of Stavropol'. Population (1933) 3,400. It has some industry (woodworking and food). Karachayevsk was founded in 1927 as capital of the Karachay Autonomous Oblast; this was abolished in 1943 and the town and the surrounding area belonged to Georgia until 1955.

Karaganda: 1. Oblast in Kazakhstan lying in the central part of the republic in the Kazakh hills; it is largely semi-desert and desert, with large deposits of coal, copper, iron ore and manganese. Area 152,700 sq. m.; population (1959) 1,022,000 (78 per cent urban), Russians, Kazakhs, Ukrainians, Belorussians, Tatars, Koreans, Germans, etc. There is coal- and copper-mining, non-ferrous metal-lurgy (copper, tungsten), chemical, engineering (mining equipment), building materials and food industries; sheep and camels are kept and wheat and millet cultivated. Principal towns: Karaganda, Temir-Tau, Balkhash and Dzhezkazgan. The area belonged to the Kazakh Middle Hundred and was annexed to Russia in the early 19th century. The metallurgical industry dates from the 1830's, coal-mining from 1857 and agricultural Russian and Ukrainian coloniza-tion from the late 19th century. Since 1931 it has been an area of very rapid industrial development, until the mid 1950's based almost entirely on the forced labour of concentration camp inmates and people in banishment. The Karaganda system of forced labour camps, embracing almost the whole oblast and some adjacent areas, was one of the most important in the U.S.S.R., and some of the camps may still exist. Successive categories of people to be banished to the region were peasants who resisted collectivization, engineers banished in connection with the Shakhty and Industrial Party trials, Koreans banished from the Far East in 1937, and Volga Germans, Crimean Tatars, etc., deported during and after the Second World War. During the current Seven Year Plan a new iron and steel plant, one of the largest in the U.S.S.R., is being built in Temir-Tau.

2. Administrative, economic and cultural centre of the oblast, the main industrial centre in Kazakhstan, situated in the centre of the oblast on the Trans-Kazakhstan Railway, consisting of a number of urban settlements scattered over an area of 270 sq. m. Population

(1959) 398,000 (1939, 156,000). It has coal-mining, engineering and food industries. Karaganda was founded as a mining settlement in 1857, became a town in 1931 and provincial centre in 1934. The Karaganda *sovkhoz* near the city, the former agricultural base of the forced labour camp system, is an important agricultural research centre.

Karaim, Turkic-speaking people living mostly in the Crimea (particularly Yevpatoriya) and Lithuania (in the Trakai area), numbering (1959) 5,900, almost completely assimilated. Their religion is similar to Judaism but they do not recognize the Talmud. According to recent research they are probably descendants of the Khazars (q.v.). For a long time their main centre was Chufut-Kale.

Kara-Kalpak Autonomous Republic, within Uzbekistan, comprises the northern part of the Khorezm oasis and the adjacent deserts to the west and south-east of the Aral Sea. Area 60,100 sq. m.; population (1959) 510,000 (27 per cent urban), mostly Kara-Kalpaks and Uzbeks, also some Kazakhs and Russians. Cotton, rice and lucerne are cultivated, Astrakhan sheep bred, and there are cotton- and lucerne-processing and fishing industries. Capital Nukus. For early history *see* KHIVA; KHOREZM. The Kara-Kalpak Autonomous Oblast was formed in 1925 within the Kazakh Autonomous Republic; it was raised to the status of Autonomous Republic in 1932 and transferred from the R.S.F.S.R. to Uzbekistan in 1936.

Kara-Kalpaks ('Black caps'), Turkic-speaking people living in Central Asia, mostly in the delta of the Amu-Dar'ya River (Kara-Kalpak Autonomous Republic), but also near Samarkand and in the Fergana Valley. In 1959 they numbered 173,000. They are Muslims, mostly engaged in agriculture and fishing. They have been known since the 16th century, when they lived along the lower and middle courses of the Syr-Dar'ya. They were later partly subjected to the Kazakhs, and in the 18th century, pressed by the Kazakhs, migrated to their present habitation.

Kara-Kum, sandy desert in Central Asia between the Caspian Sea in the west and the Amu-Dar'ya in the east, the Kopet Dag range in the south and the Ust'-Urt plateau in the north, with a total area of about 140,000 sq. m. It is sparsely populated by Turkmens, and used as pasture for sheep (including Astrakhan breed) and camels. Water is supplied by artificial wells of up to two hundred yards in depth. The Kara-Kum canal which is now under construction will bring Amu-Dar'ya water for the irrigation of the south-eastern part of the desert. There are sulphur deposits in the central part of Kara-Kum which have been exploited since the 1930's.

Karamzin, Nikolay Mikhaylovich (1766–1826), historian and belletrist, author of *The History of the Russian State* (12 vols.). Politically a conservative, Karamzin led the new Sentimental school in literature, and contributed much to the formation of the modern Russian literary language. See *Letters of a Russian Traveller, 1789–90* (trans. F. Jonas), 1958; R. Pipes, *Karamzin's Memoir on Ancient and Modern Russia. A Translation and Analysis*, Cambridge, Mass., 1959.

Karelia, Autonomous Republic within the R.S.F.S.R., situated in north-west Russia adjacent to the Finnish border, a forested hilly plain with many lakes and a comparatively mild climate; there are large deposits of granite, marble and other building stones, and mica. Area 66,600 sq. m.; population (1959) 649,000 (63 per cent urban), Russians (since the 11th century) and Karelians. There are timber, wood-processing and quarrying industries, dairy farming and fishing. Capital Petrozavodsk. The area belonged to the Novgorod Republic from the 12th century; south-western Karelia (now forming part of Leningrad Oblast) was contested by Swedes and Russians until the 18th century, and by Finns and Russians in the 20th century (*see* VYBORG). The Karelian Labour Commune was established in 1920, renamed the Karelian Autonomous Republic in 1923, became in 1940 the Karelo-Finnish Union Republic, but since 1956 has once more been an Autonomous Republic. *See* W. Kolarz, *Russia and her Colonies* 1952.

Karelians, Finnish-speaking people living in Finland and in the U.S.S.R.; their total number in the U.S.S.R. was 167,000 in 1959 (253,000 in 1939), of whom less than half live in the Karelian Autonomous Republic and the rest in the Kalinin Oblast (central Russia); 71 per cent consider Karelian their mother tongue. In the Karelian Autonomous Republic they make up less than a quarter of the population, although they are in the majority in some northern and western districts. Karelians have been known since the 9th century. Those now living in Russia have been under strong Russian influence since the 12th century and were gradually included in the Novgorodian Republic, being christianized by Russians; they are thus Orthodox, unlike the Finnish Karelians who are Lutherans. By a Muscovite-Swedish peace treaty in 1617 many Russian Karelians came under Swedish rule, but, ill at ease in a Protestant country, considerable numbers of them fled to Russia and were settled in what is now Kalinin Oblast. Karelian folklore is very rich, and the famous Finnish national epic *Kalevala* was written down in Russian Karelia in the 19th century. During the 1920's and thirties the linguistic affinity between Russian Karelians and Finns was minimized in official policy, and a separate Karelian literary language was being developed, but this policy was abandoned in 1940 and since then standard Finnish has been used in the Karelian Republic. A Karelian National Okrug existed in the Kalinin Oblast in the 1930's.

Kareyev, Nikolai Ivanovich (1850–1934), historian and sociologist, professor at St Petersburg University. His many works dealt with the modern history of Western Europe and the philosophy of history and sociological theory, where he was one of the main exponents of Mikhaylovskiy's 'subjective method.'

Karpinskiy, Aleksandr Petrovich (1847–1936), famous geologist. Educated at the St Petersburg Mining Institute, he was professor there, 1869–97, took an active part in setting up the Geological Committee and was its director, 1885–1903, president of the Russian Mineralogical Society, member of the Academy of Sciences from 1886 and its president from 1916 until his death. Karpinskiy's work enriched all branches of geological science; he studied the stratigraphy and tectonics of the Ural Mountains and the Russian plain and the mineral resources of these regions, and also made important contributions to palaeontology, mineralogy and petrography. After the seizure of power by the Bolsheviks Karpinskiy preserved the autonomy of the Academy of Sciences until 1929 (*see further under* ACADEMY OF SCIENCES).

Karsavin, Lev Platonovich (1882–1952), philosopher and historian. Expelled from Russia in 1922, together with other leading intellectuals, he first lived in Berlin, taking part in Berdyayev's Russian Academy of Religion and Philosophy, but soon became professor of history at Kaunas University (Lithuania) and joined the Eurasian (q.v.) movement. He was arrested in 1948 in connection with the 'anti-cosmopolitanism' campaign, and died in a concentration camp. In his works he developed Vl. Solov'ëv's doctrine of All-Unity and claimed that philosophy must be the servant of theology (*Noctes Petropolitanae*, Petrograd, 1922; *Philosophy of History*, Berlin, 1923, etc.).

Karsavina, Tamara Platonovna (*b.* 1885), prima ballerina, sister of Lev. After studying at the Imperial Ballet School under Johansson, Gerdt, Sokolova and Cecchetti she made her debut in 1902, joining Diaghilev for the first season of the Ballets Russes in 1909. Her most famous roles over the succeeding years included *Lo Spectre de la Rose*, which she danced with Nijinsky, *The Fire Bird* and *Giselle*. Karsavina has devoted her whole life to ballet and has been received with acclaim all over the world. Her diversity, her sensitivity, her supreme artistry, her charming personality and above all her radiant beauty have made her one of the greatest and most lovable artists of our time. *See* her *Theatre Street* and *Ballet Technique*, 1956.

Karshi, town in Uzbekistan, was administrative, economic and cultural centre of the Kashka-Dar'ya Oblast, situated in the Karshi oasis. Population (1959) 19,000, Uzbeks and Tadzhiks. There is some food and light industry. Karshi has been known since the 14th century as a centre of crafts.

Karskiy, Yevfimiy Fëdorovich (1861–1931), Belorussian philologist. Educated at the Institute of History and Philology in Nezhin, he was professor at Warsaw University from 1884 and a member of the Academy of Sciences from 1916. He was the founder of Belorussian linguistics and philology in general, and his works in this field (including his fundamental work *Belorussians*, 3 vols., 1903–22) were decisive in establishing Belorussian as a separate East Slav language and not merely a group of Russian dialects.

Kashka-Dar'ya, former oblast in Uzbekistan, situated south of the Zeravshan Valley, traversed by the Bukhara–Stalinabad railway. Area 11,300 sq. m.; population (1959) 510,000 (13 per cent urban), mostly Uzbeks and Tadzhiks. Cotton, grain, fruit and grapes are cultivated, Astrakhan and Gissar sheep and Karabair horses bred, and there are cotton-processing, silk and food industries. Principal towns: Karshi (administrative centre) and Shakhrisyabz. For history *see* BUKHARA KHANATE; SOGDIANA; TRANSOXANIA; TURKESTAN. In 1960 it was abolished and the area absorbed by the Surkhan-Dar'ya Oblast.

Katkov, Mikhail Nikiforovich (1818–87), conservative publicist. From 1845 to 1850 he was professor of philosophy at Moscow

University, and then until his death editor and publisher of the daily paper *Moskovskiye Vedomosti* (*Moscow Record*) and of the monthly journal *Russkiy Vestnik* (*Russian Herald*): both became very influential as the main organs of conservative opinion. At first Katkov was a great admirer of British institutions, but after the Polish uprising of 1863 he became the leader of nationalist sentiment, opposed the Great Reforms (q.v.) and advocated a return to pre-reform conditions. *See* M. Raeff, 'A Reactionary Liberal: M. N. Katkov,' *Russian Review*, vol. xi, No. 3, July 1952; T. G. Masaryk, *The Spirit of Russia* (2 vols.), 2nd ed., 1955.

Kaufman, Konstantin Petrovich (1818–82), general. He was appointed military governor of Turkestan in 1867 and in the following year took Samarkand (*see* BUKHARA KHANATE). He commanded an expedition against Khiva in 1873 and three years later completed the conquest of the Kokand Khanate (q.v.).

Kaunas (formerly Russian **Kovno**), town in Lithuania, situated on the River Niemen, an economic and cultural centre of the republic. Population (1959) 214,000 (1914, 88,000; 1939, 152,000), before 1939 many Jews. It has engineering, woodworking and food industries, and is an important railway junction and a river port; a large hydroelectric station is under construction. There are many architectural monuments of the 14th–18th centuries. Kaunas has been known since the 13th century and became Lithuanian in 1404; during the 15th–17th centuries it was a centre of flourishing Lithuanian-Polish trade with Russia and Western Europe. It became Russian in 1795 and a provincial capital in 1842. In 1915–18 and 1941–4 the town was occupied by the Germans, and it was the *de facto* capital of independent Lithuania, 1918–40. The university, established in 1922, was abolished in 1951.

Kavelin, Konstantin Dmitriyevich (1818–85), jurist, historian, philosopher and liberal publicist, one of the leading Westernists (*see* WESTERNISM), professor at Moscow and St Petersburg universities, later at the Military Juridical Academy. Kavelin originated the *étatist* school of Russian historiography; in philosophy he was a representative of Ideal-Realism, which he defended against the Materialism of Sechenov and the metaphysics of Samarin in a polemic on problems of psychology which attracted much attention. Historical development was for him a process of the emancipation of human personality, and he advocated emancipation of the serfs with land, full legal equality of women, vigorous local government, etc. His collected works were published in four volumes in 1897–1900. *See* A. G. Mazour, *Modern Russian Historiography*, 2nd ed., 1958.

Kaverin (real name **Zil'ber**), **Veniamin Aleksandrovich** (*b.* 1902), prominent writer of Jewish origin, who consistently asserts the need for freedom in artistic creation, a former member of the 'Serapion Brothers' group (*see* ZAMYATIN). His stories and novels include *Nine Tenths of Fate*, 1926, *The Ruffian*, 1928, *Artist Unknown*, 1931, *The Fulfilment of Desires*, 1935–6, *Two Captains*, 1940–5, *The Open Book*, 1950, *Searchings and Hopes*, 1957. At the 2nd Writers' Congress in 1955 he outlined a kind of 'bill of rights' for writers.

Kazakhs (the same name as 'Cossacks,' q.v.), Turkic-speaking people (formerly called Kirgiz by the Russians) living in Kazakhstan and numbering (1959) 3·6 million. They are Sunni Muslims, but Islam has not taken such deep roots among them as among, for example, the Uzbeks. Until the collectivization of agriculture (q.v.) in the early 1930's they were a nomadic pastoral people, and they are still predominantly engaged in animal husbandry—sheep, horses, camels—though since the 19th century there had been some agriculture, and many Kazakhs now work in industry. Ethnically and linguistically the Kazakhs are a very homogeneous people, although remnants still exist of their complicated clan system. The clan names reveal that various Turkic, Mongol and Iranian elements went into the formation of the Kazakh people; the predominant strain was the Kypchak (see CUMANS). The Kazakhs broke off from the Golden Horde (q.v.) in 1456 and part of them moved east and south-east to occupy the whole of present-day Kazakhstan. During the following century three primitive states gradually developed among them: the Junior Hundred, the most numerous, in the original Kazakh territory of present north-west Kazakhstan; the Middle Hundred, in the present northern and central Kazakhstan; and the Senior Hundred in south-east Kazakhstan (see SEMIRECH'YE). In 1723 the strong Dzungarian (Kalmyk) state attacked the Kazakhs, and conquered large parts of their territory, but rather than submit the Senior Hundred withdrew to the west, returning later after the rout of the Kalmyks by the Chinese. Faced with the Kalmyk threat, the Junior and Middle Hundreds asked for Russian protection in the 1730's, but Russian rule did not become a reality until the 19th century, while the Senior Hundred, situated between the advancing Russians and the expansionist Kokand Khanate (q.v.), chose to submit to the Russians in 1846. Russian rule was indirect and had little impact until the beginnings of Russian colonization of the fertile northern Kazakhstan and Semirech'ye in the late 19th and early 20th centuries. Russian-Kazakh relations deteriorated, and in 1916 the anti-Russian uprising in Turkestan spread to the Kazakhs, where it was led by Imanov (q.v.). During the civil war an autonomous anti-Bolshevik Kazakh government was set up by the local intelligentsia, which co-operated with the Whites. Outstanding national figures of the past have been the leaders of anti-Russian uprisings, K. Kasimov and S. Datov, the orientalist and explorer Ch. Valikhanov (1837–65), and Abay Kunanbayev (1845–1904), the founder of modern Kazakh literature; the venerable folk-singer Dzhambul Dzhabayev (1846–1945) was used by the Communist authorities in the 1930's as a leading propagandist of the Stalin cult. Nationalist tendencies are strong among the Kazakhs, and especially manifested themselves during the collectivization of agriculture and the Virgin Land Campaign (qq.v.). See further under KAZAKHSTAN. See T. G. Winner, The Oral Art and Literature of the Kazakhs of Russian Central Asia, Durham, N.C., 1958; R. A. Pierce, Russian Central Asia, 1867–1917, Berkeley and Los Angeles, 1960; S. A. Zenkovsky, Pan-Turkism and Islam in Russia, Cambridge, Mass., 1960.

Kazakhstan, Union Republic of the U.S.S.R., lying between the lower course of the Volga and the Caspian Sea in the west and the Altay Mountains in the east, comprising the north of Central Asia and the south of West Siberia. It is the second largest of the Union Republics (area 1,064,100 sq. m.) after the R.S.F.S.R., and is third in population after the R.S.F.S.R. and the Ukraine. It is largely lowland in the north and west (West Siberian, Caspian and Turan lowlands), hilly in the centre (Kazakh hills) and mountainous in the south and east (Tien-Shan and Altay mountains). Kazakhstan is extremely rich in mineral deposits: coal (Karaganda, Ekibastuz), oil (Emba), iron ore (Kustanay and Karaganda oblasts), copper (Dzhezkazgan, Balkhash), other non-ferrous metals (Oriferous Altay and South Kazakhstan Oblast), gold (in the central and northern parts), etc. The climate is continental and mostly very dry. The chief rivers are the Irtysh and its tributaries the Ishim and the Tobol in the north, the Ural and the Emba in the west (both flowing into the Caspian Sea), the Syr-Dar'ya in the south (flowing into the Aral Sea), the Ili (into Lake Balkhash) and the Chu (which dries up in the desert). There are steppes in the north, with black earth and chestnut soils, semi-deserts and deserts further south and vertical vegetation zones in the Tien-Shan and Altay mountains. Forests cover less than 5 per cent of the area.

Population (1959) 9,310,000 (44 per cent urban; 1939, 6,094,000). The ethnical composition is very complex, with no single nationality forming an absolute majority. The biggest group are the Russian (43 per cent) and Ukrainian (8 per cent) settlers who live throughout the republic in the towns and form an absolute majority in the north and east; Kazakhs themselves come next (30 per cent), forming an absolute majority in the west; there are also many Tatars (2 per cent) and Uzbeks (1·5 per cent) and some Uygurs and Dungans (immigrants from China), Koreans (deported from the Far East in 1937 and settled mainly in southern and central Kazakhstan), Germans, Chechens and Karachays (deported during the Second World War, many of whom have now left Kazakhstan); finally there are numerous representatives of other European Russian nationalities (Belorussians, Mordva, Moldavians, Poles, Bulgarians, Tatars, etc.) who arrived principally in three waves: first in the colonization of the 19th and early 20th centuries, then as forced labourers in the 1930's and forties, and lastly during the Virgin Land Campaign (q.v.), 1953–6.

The principal towns (population over 100,000) are Alma-Ata (capital), Karaganda, Semipalatinsk, Chimkent, Petropavlovsk, Ust'-Kamenogorsk, Ural'sk and Akmolinsk. There are coal-mining (since 1856), oil extraction and processing, iron and steel and non-ferrous metallurgical, engineering (since the Second World War), chemical, food (especially meat) and light industries. Agriculture is mostly concentrated in the north, where it is of the west Siberian type with wheat cultivation and cattle breeding, and in the south, where it follows the typical Central Asian pattern (cotton, rice, fruit and melons on irrigated land). The chief means of transportation are railways—three trunk-lines running from north to south (Orenburg–Tashkent, Trans-Kazakhstan, Turksib) and one from east to west (Southern Siberian). The republic is divided into fifteen oblasts: five in the north (Kustanay, North Kazakhstan, Kokchetav, Akmolinsk and Pavlodar), two in the east (Semipalatinsk and East Kazakhstan), four in the south (Alma-Ata, Dzhambul, South Kazakhstan and Kzyl-Orda), three in the west (West Kazakhstan, Aktyubinsk and Gur'yev) and one in the centre (Karaganda). For early history *see* KAZAKHS. A Kirgiz Autonomous Republic was set up within the R.S.F.S.R. in 1920, as a result of the National Delimitation of Central Asia (q.v.) southern Kazakhstan, which until then had belonged to the Turkestan Autonomous Republic, was fused with the Kirgiz Autonomous Republic in 1925, which was renamed Kazakh at the same time and raised to Union Republic status in 1936. *See* P. Alampiev, *Soviet Kazakhstan*, Moscow, 1958; J. A. Newth, 'State Farms in the Kazakh S.S.R.,' *Soviet Studies*, vol. x, No. 3, Jan. 1959.

Kazakov, Matvey Fëdorovich (1738–1813), architect, a master of the classical style and greatly influenced by Bazhenov (q.v.). His work centred on Moscow, the most notable examples being the Columned Hall of the Club de la Noblesse (now 'House of the Unions'), the Golitsyn Hospital, the Moscow University and the Senate House in the Kremlin (q.v.). *See also* ARCHITECTURE. *See* G. H. Hamilton, *The Art and Architecture of Russia*, 1954.

Kazan', capital and economic centre of the Tatar Autonomous Republic, one of the chief centres of Russian and the centre of Tatar culture; it is situated on the Volga, 51 m. above the mouth of the Kama. Population (1959) 643,000 (third on the Volga, sixteenth in the U.S.S.R.; 1917, 193,000; 1920, 146,000; 1939, 398,000), Russians and Tatars. It has large engineering (aircraft, agricultural and transportation machinery, typewriters, shipyards in nearby Zelenodol'sk), chemical (explosives, synthetic rubber, soap, photographic films), leather, fur (half the Russian output) and other industries. It is a major transportation centre, with a river port, airport (seven regular passenger lines) and an important railway junction near by. There is a branch of the U.S.S.R. Academy of Sciences (1945), a university (1804), several theatres (one founded in the 18th century) and many architectural monuments of the 16th–19th centuries.

Kazan' was founded in the mid 13th century by the Tatars and became capital of the independent Kazan' Khanate in 1445; it was destroyed by Ivan the Terrible in 1552. It was capital of the Volga region from 1708, was seized and burnt by Pugachëv in 1774, and became a provincial capital in 1781. The Caspian fleet for Peter the Great's Persian campaign was built here. Light and food industries developed during the 18th century, and heavy industry during the 1930's. In 1758 the first Russian provincial lay secondary school was established in Kazan', and in 1811 the first provincial newspaper was produced there. The Theological Academy (founded as the Slavonic-Latin Academy in 1723) was abolished after 1917. The city's former status as the intellectual capital of eastern Russia has much diminished since 1917. *See* B. Nolde, *La Formation de l'Empire Russe*, vol. i, Paris, 1952.

Kazbek, one of the highest mountains in the main Caucasian range (16,546 ft).

Keldysh, Yuriy Vsevolodovich (*b.* 1907), distinguished musicologist, professor of the Moscow State Conservatory. He is the author of the three-volume *History of Russian Music* and a large number of works and articles on Russian classical and Soviet music.

Kemerovo: 1. Oblast of the R.S.F.S.R., situated in southern Siberia largely in the Kuznetsk Basin; it has large and varied deposits of coal, also iron ore, zinc, manganese and gold. Area 37,300 sq. m.; population (1959) 2,788,000 (77 per cent urban), mostly Russians (since the 17th century), also Shorians; it is the most densely populated oblast in Siberia. There are coal-mining, iron and steel (since 1771), non-ferrous metallurgical, chemical and engineering industries. Agriculture specializes in dairy farming and potatoes and other vegetables for town consumption. Principal towns: Kemerovo, Stalinsk, Prokop'yevsk, Leninsk-Kuznetskiy, Anzhero-Sudzhensk, Kiselëvsk and Belovo. It is an area of rapidly expanding industry, and was one of labour camps until the mid 1950's.

2. (until 1932 **Shcheglovsk**). Administrative and one of the economic and cultural centres of the oblast, situated on the River Tom' (a tributary of the Ob'). Population (1959) 277,000 (third in the Kuznetsk Basin; 1926, 22,000; 1939, 133,000). It has chemical (since 1916), engineering and coal-mining industries. Kemerovo was founded in 1918 through the fusion of two villages—Shcheglova (founded 1720) and Kemerovo (founded 1836)—and has grown continuously in industrial importance since 1929.

Kerch' (ancient **Panticapaeum**), town in the Crimean Oblast, situated on the Kerch' Peninsula. Population (1959) 99,000 (1926, 36,000; 1939, 104,000). It is an important centre of industry and transport, having iron and steel (since 1846) and shipbuilding industries and fisheries; it is a seaport, with a train ferry to the Caucasus. There are many ancient ruins and an archaeological museum founded in 1826. Kerch' was established as a Greek colony in the 6th century B.C., and was capital of the Bosporan Kingdom from the 5th century B.C. to the 4th century A.D.; then it became in turn Roman, Byzantine, Tatar and Turkish. It became Russian in 1774 and was destroyed in the Crimean War and in 1941–3.

Kerenskiy, Aleksandr Fëdorovich (*b.* 1881), politician, born in Simbirsk, the son of a headmaster. After reading law at St Petersburg University he practised as a barrister and became popular for his powerful defence in political cases. He was elected to the 4th Duma in 1912 and there led the Labour group of moderately socialist peasant members (*see* TRUDOVIKS); he later joined the Socialist Revolutionaries. At the beginning of the February 1917 revolution he became deputy chairman of the St Petersburg Soviet of Workers' Deputies and Minister of Justice in the Provisional Government (q.v.), in May Minister of War and the Navy, in July Prime Minister, and in September, following the Kornilov (q.v.) affair, also supreme commander-in-chief. The policy of the democratically minded provisional coalition governments which Kerenskiy headed was to carry on the war and postpone fundamental reforms until a Constituent Assembly (q.v.) could be convoked. The Bolsheviks, in co-operation with their allies the Anarchists and the Left Socialist Revolutionaries, were thus enabled to utilize the war weariness and the impatience of the politically immature Russian masses in order to seize power (*see* OCTOBER REVOLUTION). Kerenskiy emigrated to Paris in 1918, where he published a left-wing paper *Dni* (*The Days*); he has lived in the U.S.A. since 1940. *See* his *The Crucifixion of Liberty*, 1933, and *The Road to Tragedy*, 1935; F. A. Golder, *Documents of Russian History, 1914–17*, 1927; W. H. Chamberlin, *The Russian Revolution*, vol. i, New York, 1935.

Kerzhentsev (real name Lebedev), **Platon Mikhaylovich** (1881–1940), Communist. He joined the Bolsheviks in 1904, and his bibliographical pamphlet *Library of a Social Democrat* was extensively used in propaganda during the revolution of 1905 (q.v.). After the revolution he worked underground, then emigrated, continuing to write for the Bolshevik press, including *Pravda*. Returning to Russia after the February revolution (q.v.) of 1917, he joined M. Gor'kiy's anti-Leninist Left Social Democratic paper *New Life*. After the Bolshevik seizure of power (*see* OCTOBER REVOLUTION) he was deputy editor of *Izvestiya* and manager of the Russian Telegraphic Agency, and ambassador to Sweden, 1921–3, and Italy, 1925–6. An active participant in the Proletkul't (q.v.), he applied his moderately Bogdanovist (*see* BOGDANOVISM) approach to the problem of the 'scientific organization of labour' (q.v.) and was, 1923–4, chairman of the Council for Scientific Labour Organization attached to the Commissariat of Worker-Peasant Inspection (q.v.) and organizer of the Time League. Later he was deputy manager of the Central Statistical Administration (q.v.), deputy head of the Agitprop, deputy chairman of the Communist Academy and director of its Institute of Literature, Art and Language. In 1933–6 he was chairman of the All-Union Radio Committee, and in 1936–8 of the Arts Committee of the Council of People's Commissars. *See* S. V. Utechin, 'Bolsheviks and their Allies after 1917: the Ideological Pattern,' *Soviet Studies*, Oct. 1958.

Kesh, *see* SHAKHRISYABZ.

K.G.B. (Russian abbreviation for 'Committee of State Security') name of the Soviet security service since 1953. Its functions and methods resemble those of its predecessors the M.G.B. and M.V.D. (though it employs terror to a far lesser extent), but it holds a lesser position in the state and is subordinated to control by the party. The party leaders are apparently concerned that the security service should not become a tool in the hands of any one person. *See further under* SECURITY ORGANS. *See* V. Gsovski and K. Grzybowski (eds.), *Government, Law and Courts in the Soviet Union and Eastern Europe*, vol. i, 1959.

Khabarovsk: 1. Kray of the R.S.F.S.R., situated in the Far East on the lower Amur River and along the Okhotsk littoral; it is mostly mountainous with a cold monsoon climate, and is largely covered with forests; there are rich deposits of gold, coal and iron ore. Area 318,400 sq. m.; population (1959) 1,143,000 (74 per cent urban), chiefly Russians and Ukrainians, also Jews (since 1928) and small Paleo-Asiatic tribes (until 1937 also Koreans and Chinese). The kray has mining and metallurgical industries, lumbering and fisheries; agriculture is carried on in the south. Principal towns: Khabarovsk,

Komsomol'sk, Sovetskaya Gavan' and Nikolayevsk-on-Amur. Russians first reached the area in 1649–53, and it finally became Russian 1858–60. The Jewish Autonomous Oblast was established within the kray in 1934.

2. Administrative centre of the kray, situated on the Amur and the Trans-Siberian Railway; it is the largest city, the main transportation and political centre and the second cultural centre of the Russian Far East. Population (1959) 322,000 (1913, 55,000; 1923, 34,000; 1939, 207,000). It has engineering, oil-refining and other industries. Khabarovsk was established as a military post in 1858, and in 1880 replaced Nikolayevsk-on-Amur as capital of the Maritime Province. It was mainly held by the Whites between 1918 and 1922, and was capital of the whole Soviet Far East, 1926–38.

Khachaturyan, Aram Il'ich (*b.* 1903), Armenian composer and conductor, who studied at Moscow Conservatory until 1934 under Myaskovskiy, becoming professor there in 1951. His works comprise ballets, including *Gayane*, 1942, and *Spartak*, 1952–4; the choral and orchestral *Poem about Stalin*, 1938; two symphonies; piano concerto, 1936; violin concerto, 1940; orchestral works; solo instrumental works for violin and for piano; incidental music to plays and films; folk-song arrangements; and literary works. Khachaturyan has assimilated many musical features of his native Armenia into his compositions, though his work is essentially Russian in subject-matter and outlook. His use of exotic folk-music of widely differing cultures, and of unusual rhythms and timbres, gives his work distinctive colouring. *See* G. Abraham, *Eight Soviet Composers*, 1943; R. Moisenko, *Realist Music*, 1949; G. Shneerson, *A. Khachaturyan*, Moscow, 1959.

Khakas, Turkic-speaking Orthodox people living in the Khakas Autonomous Oblast (southern Siberia) and numbering (1959) 57,000. They are mostly animal breeders and hunters, now collectivized. The Khakas, who are partly Turkicized Samoyeds (q.v.), did not form a single people until the 1920's, and were known under the names of their different tribes or under the geographical names of Minusinsk or Abakan Tatars. The name Khakas has been adopted as a revival of the medieval name of the Kirgiz who then inhabited the Minusinsk Basin. *See* W. Kolarz, *The Peoples of the Soviet Far East*, 1954.

Khakas Autonomous Oblast, in the Krasnoyarsk Kray, is situated in the extreme south of the kray in the Minusinsk Basin west of the River Yenisey. There are deposits of coal, iron ore, gold and copper. Area 23,900 sq. m.; population (1959) 414,000 (54 per cent urban), Russians (since the 18th century) and Khakas. There is coal, gold and iron ore mining; there is lumbering and food industries and cattle and sheep raising. The administrative centre is Abakan.

Khanty (formerly Russian **Ostyaks**), Ugrian-speaking people who live scattered in the Khanty-Mansi National Okrug and the surrounding areas, numbering 19,000 in 1959. They were conquered by the Siberian Tatars, and stubbornly opposed Russian conquest and rule in the 16th–18th centuries. The Khanty are mostly fishers and hunters, now collectivized.

Khanty-Mansi National Okrug, in the Tyumen' Oblast (Western

Siberia), lies astride the middle course of the River Ob'; it consists of swampy forested lowland and has natural gas deposits. Area 212,600 sq. m.; population (1959) 125,000 (27 per cent urban), chiefly Russian, also Khanty and Mansi. The chief activities are fishing, fur-trapping and grain and potato growing. Principal towns: Khanty-Mansiysk and Berëzovo. The area formed part of the Siberian Khanate and was annexed by Russia in the 16th century; the National Okrug was formed in 1930.

Khanty-Mansiysk (until 1940 **Ostyako-Vogul'sk**), administrative centre of the Khanty-Mansi National Okrug, situated on the River Irtysh near its confluence with the Ob'. Population (1956) 19,000, mostly Russians. It has a fishing industry. Khanty-Mansiysk was built in the 1930's.

Khar'kov (Ukrainian **Kharkiv**): 1. Oblast in north-eastern Ukraine, situated in the south-west of the Central Russian upland, in the black earth belt, traversed by the Severskiy Donets (a tributary of the Don). Area 12,200 sq. m.; population (1959) 2,517,000 (62 per cent urban), Ukrainians, Russians and Jews. There are large engineering, food and natural gas extraction industries; wheat, sugar-beet, sunflowers, vegetables and tobacco are grown, and there is dairy farming and pig breeding. It was the eastern border area of the Kievan State and then of the Pereyaslav Principality, and was absorbed by Lithuania in 1362; it became Muscovite in 1503 and was largely colonized by Cossack refugees from Polish-held Ukraine.

2. Administrative centre of the oblast, one of the chief economic and cultural centres of the Ukraine and of the whole Soviet Union. Population (1959) 930,000 (second in the Ukraine, sixth in the U.S.S.R.; 1917, 288,000; 1920, 230,000; 1926, 417,000; 1939, 833,000), Ukrainians, Russians and Jews. It is the largest industrial centre of the Ukraine, with a huge engineering industry (locomotives, tractors, aircraft, turbines, electrical and mining equipment, machine tools, agricultural machinery, bicycles, etc.) and varied light industries. Khar'kov is the third transportation centre of the country (after Moscow and Leningrad), with eight railway lines and eight regular airlines. It has a university and other higher educational and research establishments, and notable buildings of the 17th–20th centuries.

The city was founded by immigrants from the right bank of the Ukraine in 1654, and was an important frontier fortress and the headquarters of a Cossack regiment until 1765; it then became a provincial capital. It was the intellectual centre of southern Russia from the 18th century (Khar'kov College, founded in 1721 in Belgorod and transferred to Khar'kov in 1726; university, founded in 1805), and during the 19th century it was a centre of the Ukrainian literary and national movement. Economically its importance dates from the second half of the 18th century, when it became a commercial town with large fairs; Khar'kov was the gateway to the Donets Basin, and the banking and business centre of the Southern Industrial Region (q.v.), from the 1870's; its own heavy industry dates from the same period (agricultural machinery plant in 1879, locomotive plant in 1897). During the First World War several large factories were evacuated to the city from Riga, and many new ones were built during the 1930's. Both before 1917 and in the 1920's Khar'kov was an important Bolshevik stronghold; from 1919 to 1934 it was capital of the Ukrainian Soviet Republic. The city was a key point of several important operations between 1941 and 1943, changing hands five times and being largely ruined.

Khatanga, river in northern Siberia, rising in the central Siberian plateau and flowing north-east into the Khatanga Bay of the Laptev Sea. Length 940 m.; basin 130,000 sq. m.

Khazars, Turkic-speaking people unknown since the 12th century, who lived astride the lower Volga in the early Middle Ages. From the 7th century the Khazar state embraced a huge area from the Urals to beyond the Dnieper and from the Caucasus to the rivers Oka and Kama; it declined after the Khazars' defeat in 966 by the Kievan prince Svyatoslav. The Khazars were culturally under the influence of the Central Asian peoples, especially of Khorezm; the Jewish religion predominated among them, but others were tolerated. *See* G. Vernadsky, *Ancient Russia,* New Haven, 5th printing, 1959.

Kherson: 1. Oblast in southern Ukraine, north of the Crimea, a region of flat, dry steppe traversed by the Dnieper. Area 10,500 sq. m.; population (1959) 827,000 (40 per cent urban), Ukrainians and Russians. Agriculture is the main activity of the oblast, with wheat and sunflower cultivation and cattle, pig (Ukrainian steppe breed) and sheep (Askania breed) raising. There are also engineering, food and textile industries, and a large hydro-electric station; a vast irrigation system is being constructed. Principal towns: Kherson and Kakhovka. The famous Askania-Nova nature reservation is in the oblast. The area was annexed by Russia, 1774–83, having previously been virtually unpopulated.

2. Administrative, economic and cultural centre of the oblast, a port on the Dnieper situated 15 m. from its mouth. Population (1959) 157,000 (1914, 81,000; 1923, 41,000; 1939, 97,000). It has shipbuilding, textile, agricultural engineering and food-canning industries; the chief import is oil from Batumi, and grain and manganese ore are exported abroad. Kherson was founded in 1778 by Potëmkin as a seaport and naval base, and became a provincial capital in 1803.

Khersones, *see* CHERSONESUS.

Khiva, town in the Khorezm Oblast (Uzbekistan), former capital of the Khiva Khanate. Population (1933) 23,700. It has some cotton-processing and silk industry, and old crafts (embroidery and wood-carving) are carried on. There are many architectural monuments, including the Islam-Khodzha minaret, the tomb of the Kungrad khans, the palace (now a museum) of the khans, etc.

Khlebnikov, *see* FUTURISM.

Khmel'nitskiy (Ukrainian **Khmel'nyts'kyy**): 1. (until 1954 **Kamenets-Podol'skiy**). Oblast in the Ukraine situated between the rivers Dniester and Southern Bug on the Volhynia-Podolia upland in the black earth wooded steppe belt. Area 8,100 sq. m.; population (1959)

1,609,000 (19 per cent urban), mostly Ukrainians (before the war also Jews and Poles). It is an important agricultural area, with sugar-beet and wheat cultivation, horticulture, and cattle and pig breeding; there are also food, metal-working and light industries. Principal towns: Khmel'nitskiy and Kamenets-Podol'skiy. The region belonged to Volhynia, became Lithuanian in 1363, Polish in 1430 and Russian in 1793.

2 (until 1954 **Proskurov**). Administrative centre of the oblast since 1940, an important railway junction situated on the Southern Bug. Population (1959) 62,000 (1914, 41,000), before the war almost half Jewish. It has engineering (machine tools), textile and food industries. Khmel'nitskiy has been known since the 15th century.

Khmel'nyts'kyy, Zinoviy Bohdan (1593–1657), Ukrainian hetman who roused the Ukrainian Cossacks against Polish rule in 1648 and gained several victories with the aid of the Crimean Tatars. He obtained protection from Muscovy and became a vassal of the Czar Aleksey Mikhaylovich in 1654. *See* G. Vernadsky, *Bohdan, Hetman of Ukraine*, New Haven, 1941.

Khodskiy, Leonid Vladimirovich (1854–1919), economist and radical publicist, professor of St Petersburg University. His chief works were *The Land and its Tiller* (2 vols.), 1891, and textbooks of political economy, finance and statistics. He published and edited the monthly journal *Narodnoye khozyaystvo* (*National Economy*), 1900–5, and the daily paper *Nasha zhizn'* (*Our Life*), 1904–6, after suppression renamed *Tovarishch* (*Comrade*), *Stolichnaya pochta* (*Metropolitan Mail*) and finally *Nasha gazeta* (*Our Paper*), all of them serving as periodical organs of Russian Bernsteinians (*see* ECONOMISM; KUSKOVA; PROKOPOVICH) and the Labour group of Duma deputies.

Khodzhent, *see* LENINABAD.

Kholmogory, village in the Archangel Oblast, situated on the Northern Dvina 52 m. south-east of Archangel. Population (1926) 1,000. It is the centre of a dairy-farming area (Kholmogory breed). Kholmogory has been known since 1355 and was the capital of the Russian North under Novgorod and Moscow until 1700; it was a lively trade centre in the 15th–16th centuries. Lomonosov (q.v.) was born here.

Khomyakov, Aleksey Stepanovich (1804–60), lay theologian and philosopher, the most outstanding thinker among the older Slavophiles (q.v.). His concept of *sobornost'* (q.v.) has greatly influenced Russian religious and social philosophy. *See* his *The Church is One*, 1948. *See* N. M. Zernov, *Three Russian Prophets*, 1944; N. A. Berdyaev, *The Russian Idea*, 1947; N. Lossky, *History of Russian Philosophy*, 1951; V. V. Zenkovsky, *A History of Russian Philosophy*, vol. i, 1953; E. J. Simmons (ed.), *Continuity and Change in Russian and Soviet Thought*, Cambridge, Mass., 1955; M. B. Petrovich, *The Emergence of Russian Panslavism, 1856–70*, New York, 1956.

Khorezm: 1. One of the main oases of Central Asia, situated along the lower course and in the delta of the Amu-Dar'ya. It is now divided between the Khorezm Oblast and the Kara-Kalpak Autonomous Republic of Uzbekistan, and the Tashauz Oblast of Turk-

menia, though geographically, historically and economically it forms
one compact whole. The total population is about 1,200,000, mostly
Uzbeks (who form an absolute majority), Turkmens and Kara-
Kalpaks, also Russians, Koreans (since 1937), Kazakhs and some
Persians (descendants of former slaves). Irrigated agriculture is the
main occupation of the inhabitants (cotton, lucerne, rice); there is
also sheep (Astrakhan) and horse (Yomud) breeding, and there are
fishing and cotton-processing industries. The construction in the
1950's of a railway from Khorezm to Chardzhou linked the oasis with
the railway net of the country and greatly improved its economic
prospects.

Khorezm is one of the oldest centres of civilization in Central Asia,
and throughout recorded history displayed considerable state-
building tendencies. It is first mentioned in the Avesta and in
Darius' Behistun inscription (c. 520 B.C.), when it belonged to the
Achaemenid Empire. In the 4th century B.C. it appears as an independent state which in the following century extended its influence
from the Caspian Sea to the Fergana Valley. In the 1st and 2nd
centuries A.D. it belonged to the Kushan state, but then regained
independence under the rulers of the Afrigid dynasty. It was then
inhabited by Iranian-speaking people who adhered to Zoroastrianism
and used Aramaic letters, and whose art shows Hellenistic and
Buddhist influences as well as characteristic local features. The
capital was Kyat, on the right bank of the Amu-Dar'ya (now the
urban settlement Shabbaz in the Kara-Kalpak Autonomous Republic). Khorezm was conquered by the Arabs in 712. In 995 the
country was united under the emirs of northern Khorezm, whose
capital Urgench (now the urban settlement Kunya-Urgench in the
Tashauz Oblast) became a major seat of Arabic learning (Al-Biruni
and Avicenna worked there). Later the country fell under the suzerainty of the Gaznevid and the Seljuk sultans. But the local rulers,
who assumed the title of Great Khorezmshahs, not only in fact regained independence but formed a great empire, which at the height
of its power under Muhammed II (1200–20) included the whole of
Central Asia and Iran. However, in 1220 it was conquered and laid
waste by Genghis Khan. Khorezm was included in the Golden Horde
(q.v.), and Urgench, being an important point on the route to Europe,
was restored and experienced a new period of prosperity until it was
taken and destroyed again by Timur in 1388. By this time the population of Khorezm had already been Turkicized. A century of struggle
between Timurids and the Golden Horde for Khorezm was followed
by the Uzbek conquest in 1505. Soon Khorezm became an independent Uzbek state which was known in Russia and Western
Europe as the Khiva Khanate after Khiva had become its capital.
Internal feuds, raids by Turkmen, Kazakh and Kalmyk tribesmen
and wars with Bukhara weakened the state, and in 1740 it was
conquered by Nadir Shah of Persia. Persian rule lasted only a few
years, but it was not until the beginning of the 19th century that
Khorezm again rose to power and prosperity. Its khans subjected
most of the Turkmen tribes, but their attempts to extend their rule
to Kazakhs, who were Russian subjects, and their attacks on Russian

merchants led to hostilities with Russia. The first Russian expedition of 1839–40 was unsuccessful, but the second, in 1873, led to the surrender of the khan, who ceded the territory on the right bank of the Amu-Dar'ya and recognized Russian suzerainty. The Russians released 15,000 slaves, mostly Persians, and took over foreign relations, but otherwise did not interfere in the life of Khorezm, and the oasis did not participate in the rapid economic advance of Russian Turkestan. In 1920 Khorezm was occupied by Red Army units, the khan deposed and Khorezm declared a People's Soviet Republic, one of the first of the type later to be known as 'people's democracies.' In 1923 it was renamed a Socialist Republic and 'received' into the U.S.S.R., and a year later was dismembered in the process of the so-called National Delimitation of Central Asia (q.v.). *See* V. V. Barthold, *Four Studies on the History of Central Asia*, vol. i, Leiden, 1956; M. Holdsworth, *Turkestan in the Nineteenth Century*, 1959; S. A. Zenkovsky, *Pan-Turkism and Islam in Russia*, Cambridge, Mass., 1960.

2. Oblast of Uzbekistan, occupying the south-western part of the Khorezm oasis on the left bank of the Amy-Dar'ya. Area 1,800 sq. m.; population (1959) 380,000 (17 per cent urban), nine-tenths Uzbek. Principal towns: Urgench (administrative centre) and Khiva.

Khorog, town in Tadzhikistan, administrative and cultural centre of the Mountainous Badakhshan Autonomous Oblast, situated in south-west Pamir near the River Pyandzh. Population (1959) 8,000, Russians (since the 1930's) and Tadzhiks. The Pamir Botanical Garden of the Tadzhik Academy of Sciences is situated near by. Khorog, formerly a village, became a town in the 1930's.

Khotin (Rumanian **Hotin**), town in the Chernovtsy Oblast (Ukraine), situated in northern Bessarabia on the Dniester. Population (1937) 34,000 (1922, 32,000; 1930, 15,000), mostly Ukrainian. It has ruins of 13th-century Genoese and 18th-century Turkish fortresses. Khotin was variously held by Moldavians, Poles and Turks; it became Russian in 1812 and was Rumanian from 1918 to 1940 and from 1941 to 1944.

'**Khozraschët**' (Russian abbreviation for 'economic calculation'), principle upon which most economic enterprises which belong to the State operate. It implies strict accounting, and in particular calculation of costs per unit of output, and is in some sense a substitute for the profit principle in private economy. *See* A. Baykov, *The Development of the Soviet Economic System*, 1950; F. D. Holzman, *Soviet Taxation*, Cambridge, Mass., 1955.

Khrennikov, Tikhon Nikolaeyevich (*b.* 1913), composer who studied at Moscow Conservatory until 1936 under Shebalin. Works comprise operas, including *Into the Storm*, 1936–9, and *Frol Skobeyev*, 1946–9; two symphonies; piano concerto, 1932–3; piano works; many songs; music to plays and films; and literary works. Like most of the younger Soviet composers, Khrennikov draws inspiration from folk-song and people's choruses. He possesses considerable powers of lyricism and drama. *See* R. Moisenko, *Realist Music*, 1949.

Khrushchëv, Nikita Sergeyevich (*b.* 1894), Communist, since 1953 first secretary of the Central Committee of the party. Of a peasant family, he received little education, and joined the Communist Party in 1918 while working as a locksmith in the Donets Basin; during the civil war he was a minor commissar in Budënnyy's First Cavalry Army. He soon began to specialize in party organizational work, and, having attracted the attention of Kaganovich, became second secretary of the Moscow party organization in 1934, first secretary in 1935 and first secretary of the Ukrainian party organization in 1938. He was active in carrying out the Great Purge (q.v.), both in Moscow and in the Ukraine. He became a member of the Politburo in 1939, and was a high-ranking political officer with the armed forces during the war. For some time during Stalin's last years he was the party's chief agricultural expert, but his first ambitious project in this sphere—to combine groups of collective farms into 'rural cities' (*see* AGRO-TOWNS)—was a fiasco and had to be abandoned. The inner-party struggle that followed Stalin's death resulted in Khrushchëv replacing Malenkov as the first secretary of the Central Committee, and he emerged as the most powerful member of the 'collective leadership' (q.v.) after Malenkov's resignation in 1955. He ousted his chief rivals, Malenkov, Kaganovich, Molotov (*see* ANTI-PARTY GROUP) and Zhukov, from the party leadership in 1957, and in the following year replaced Bulganin as chairman of the Council of Ministers (i.e. Prime Minister), while retaining the leadership of the party.

In his rise to power Khrushchëv closely followed the technique employed by Stalin before 1934. His policy is generally one of de-Stalinization in the sense of removing some of the worst aspects of Stalinism (q.v.): preventive terror, neglect of agriculture, extreme centralization in economic and general administration, disregard for economic considerations, ossification of society, rigorous application of Socialist Realism (q.v.) in the arts, fictionalization of public life (*see* FICTIONS), extreme chauvinism and xenophobia, and isolationism and aggressiveness in foreign policy (q.v.). However, he firmly adheres to the Leninist principles of the political monopoly of the party, of party organization and 'partyness' (q.v.) as the criterion of correct behaviour in all spheres of life, and hitherto he has retained such distinctive Stalinist policies as the collectivization of agriculture and preference for heavy industry in economic development, and is repeating Stalin's so-called 'cultural revolution' (q.v.), that is, attempting to change the social composition of the intelligentsia. Although Khrushchëv's policies have undoubtedly brought considerable improvements in the life of the people, he has not achieved any great popularity in Russia. He made a considerable impression as a shrewd politician upon foreign statesmen, especially in connection with his visit to the U.S.A. in 1959, but this has been to some extent dissipated by his subsequent handling of relations with foreign governments and the United Nations Organization. *See also* TWENTIETH PARTY CONGRESS. *See* his *For Victory in Peaceful Competition with Capitalism*, 1960. *See* B. D. Wolfe, *Khrushchëv and Stalin's Ghost*, 1957; M. Rush, *The Rise of Khrushchëv*, Washington, D.C., 1958; W. K. Medlin, 'Khrushchëv: a Political Profile,' *Russian Review*, vol. xvii, No. 4, Oct. 1958, and vol. xviii, Nos. 1 and 2, Jan.

and April 1959; *Let us Live in Peace and Friendship. The Visit of N. S. Khrushchëv to the U.S.A.* (*sine loco*), 1959; 'Khrushchëv at the Helm,' *Problems of Communism*, vol. viii, Nos. 1–6, 1959; G. Paloczi-Horvath, *Khrushchëv: the Road to Power*, 1960.

Khutor, Russian word for an individual farm or a small group of farms outside the village. The agricultural policy of Stolypin (q.v.) was aimed at enabling peasants to leave the village community (*see* MIR) and establish themselves in *khutors*: between 1907 and 1916 over two million peasant households left the community, and another four million applied to do so. All *khutor* land was compulsorily returned to the village communities after the Bolshevik seizure of power. The *khutor* peasants were automatically regarded as *kulaks*, and during the collectivization of agriculture (q.v.) were either sent to 'corrective labour camps' or deported as 'special settlers' (qq.v.). In the Baltic States during their independence *khutors* became the main form of rural settlement, and many have remained, although the policy of abolishing them is being pursued by the Soviet authorities. *See* G. T. Robinson, *Rural Russia under the Old Regime*, 2nd ed., New York, 1949.

Kiev (Ukrainian **Kyyiv,** Russian **Kiyev**): 1. Oblast of the Ukraine, situated largely on the right bank of the Dnieper, lowland in the north (*see* POLES'YE) and east, upland in the south-west; there are large deposits of peat. Area 11,100 sq. m.; population (1959) 2,821,000 (55 per cent urban), mostly Ukrainians (before the war also many Jews). There are food, light and engineering industries; coarse grain, flax and potatoes are cultivated in the north, wheat and sugar-beet in the south and vegetables in the Kiev metropolitan area. Principal towns: Kiev and Belaya Tserkov'. The area formed the heart of the medieval Kievan Principality and of the Kievan state; it became Lithuanian in 1362, Polish in 1569 and Russian partly in 1667 and partly in 1793.

2. Administrative centre of the oblast, capital of the Ukrainian Republic, directly subordinated to the government of the republic; it is one of the oldest and most beautiful Russian cities (described in the chronicles as 'mother of the Russian towns'), and a major economic and cultural centre of the U.S.S.R.; it is situated on the high right bank of the middle course of the Dnieper. Population (1959) 1,102,000 (first in the Ukraine, third in the U.S.S.R.; 1897, 248,000; 1917, 576,000; 1920, 366,000; 1926, 514,000; 1939, 847,000; 1956, 991,000), Ukrainians, Russians and Jews. It has large and varied engineering industries (equipment for food, woodworking and light industries, for printing establishments, shops, offices, hospitals, laboratories, etc.; also river vessels, wagons, motor-cycles, chemical and electro-technical equipment, machine tools), and also light, food, printing and polygraphic industries; a natural gas pipeline runs from Dashava. The city is an important centre of transportation, with four railway trunk-lines, a river port and an airport. Among its many academic institutions are the Ukrainian Academy of Sciences (founded in 1918 under Hetman Skoropads'kyy), a university (founded in 1805 as a Polish lyceum in Kremenets in Volhynia, transferred to Kiev as a university in 1834, abolished in 1920,

re-established in 1933), a polytechnical institute, 1898, and a conservatoire (founded in 1868 as a musical school, transformed in 1913). There are also an opera and ballet theatre (founded in 1867, Ukrainian since 1926), a Russian drama theatre, 1891, and many museums, among them the famous Kiev Cave Monastery (transformed into a museum in 1926, partly reopened as monastery 1941).

Kiev is a treasury of medieval Russian and of Ukrainian architecture: the most outstanding 10th–12th-century buildings are the Tithes Church (foundations), the cathedral of St Sophia (with many mosaics and frescoes), the ruins of the Golden Gate, and the Kiev Cave Monastery; the most outstanding buildings of the 17th–18th centuries, in the Ukrainian baroque style, are the cathedral of St Nicholas and several buildings in the Cave Monastery, and in the rococo style there is the bell-tower of the St Sophia Cathedral, St Andrew's Church and the former Theological Academy. The Grave of Askol'd is in the 19th-century Empire style, the university classical, and the cathedral of St Vladimir is an example of pseudo-Byzantine architecture. Modern vandalism has destroyed some of the most precious architectural monuments: the 12th-century monastery of the Archangel Michael was ruined by the Bolsheviks during the period of 'militant atheism' and the 11th-century cathedral of the Assumption during the German occupation in 1941.

The city's continuous existence can be traced from the 8th century; it became capital of the Polyane tribe and of the Kievan state in the 9th century, was ruined in 1240 by the Tatars and became Lithuanian in 1362, Polish in 1569 and Muscovite in 1654. It was a provincial administrative centre from 1797 and the seat of the governor-general of the south-western region, in 1917–19 the seat of various transitory Ukrainian nationalist governments (see UKRAINE, History), and has been the capital of the Ukrainian Soviet Republic since 1934. Kiev was occupied by the Germans in 1918 and 1941–3, by the Poles in 1920, changed hands several times during the civil war and saw bitter fighting in 1941 and 1943. Lying on the trade route from Scandinavia to Byzantium, Kiev was a major commercial centre in the 10th–12th centuries. It recovered in the 14th century from Tatar devastation, and received municipal autonomy under the Magdeburg Law in 1499 (abolished 1833). Its commercial importance developed steadily (especially after the transfer of the Annual Contract Fair from Dubno to Kiev in 1797) and during the 19th century it was one of Russia's principal centres of commerce (chiefly agricultural produce, particularly sugar); there was little industry, however, until the 1930's. The first tramway in Russia was built in Kiev in 1898. The city is the historical centre of Russian and Ukrainian culture. Christianization of Russia began with the people of Kiev in 988, until 1299 it was the centre of the Russian Orthodox Church, and during the 14th–17th centuries it was the religious and cultural centre of the Russian (Ukrainian and Belorussian) inhabitants of Lithuania and Poland (Kiev College founded in 1615, transformed into an academy in 1689, into a theological academy in 1810, abolished after 1917). During the 19th century it was a centre of the Ukrainian literary and national movement, of Populism and later of

Social Democracy. See *Guide Book and Directory* (in English), Kiev, 1956.

Kievan Russia, 9th–13th-century state, ruled by princes (later Grand Princes) of the House of Rurikids (q.v.). It comprised the territories inhabited by all East Slav tribes (who by the 6th century had spread over the forested country north of the steppes, the Dnieper Basin and the land to the north of it, and beyond the Western Bug) and some adjacent Finnish tribes (who inhabited the north between the Gulf of Finland and the upper Volga); in the west it bordered upon the West Slavs, in the north-west on the ancestors of the present Lithuanians and Latvians (who lived on the Niemen and the Western Dvina), and in the east on two Turkic-speaking peoples who had established powerful states on the middle and lower Volga (*see* KHAZARS; VOLGA BULGARIANS). Outstanding rulers of Kievan Russia were: Princess Olga (q.v.), who became a Christian and was canonized; Svyatoslav, who vanquished the Khazars; St Vladimir (q.v.), who introduced Christianity into Russia, 998; Yaroslav the Wise (1019–54), who introduced the first legal code (*see* RUSSKAYA PRAVDA); and Vladimir Monomakh (1113–25), who for a brief period checked the feuds among the descendants of Yaroslav's sons, among whom the country had been divided.

The continuation of these feuds after the death of Vladimir Monomakh contributed to the disintegration of Kievan Russia and the rise of regionalism (*see* GALICIA AND VOLHYNIA; NOVGOROD; VLADIMIR), but there were also economic and political causes. The Crusades changed the pattern of world trade, and the international economic ties of Kievan Russia, which was situated on the great trade routes from Scandinavia to Byzantium and from Western Europe to Central Asia, were seriously weakened. Different social and political developments in the chief regions (increased power of the prince in Vladimir, of the *veche*, q.v., in Novgorod and of the *boyars* in Galicia) hastened the process, and the state was finally destroyed with the Mongol conquest (q.v.) of 1237–40. The 'gathering of Russian lands'—that is, of lands which had belonged to Kievan Russia—was a significant element in the policies of the czars of Muscovy, the Imperial and even the Soviet governments, and was not finally achieved until the 1940's. *See* G. Vernadsky, *Kievan Russia*, New Haven, 1948; H. Paszkiewicz, *The Origin of Russia*, 1954; B. Grekov, *Kiev Rus*, Moscow, 1959; M. Tikhomirov, *The Towns of Ancient Rus*, Moscow, 1959.

Kindergartens. There were 36,800 kindergartens in the U.S.S.R. in 1958, with 2·4 million children aged 3 to 7. The number of kindergartens is very inadequate. They are mostly to be found in urban locations (0·4 million children in rural localities), but even there only children of working mothers with no one at home to look after them can as a rule be admitted. Fees are graded according to the parents' income. Some formal instruction is given to the six-to-seven-year-old children, and a strong political element is obligatory. Kindergartens were in their infancy in Russia before 1917, but a number of outstanding pedagogues, such as M. Kh. Sventitskaya (1855–1932), L. K. Shleger (1863–1942) and Ye. I. Tikheyeva (1886–1944), had devoted themselves to pre-school education and laid the foundations on which the present system has been built. *See* A. P. Pinkevitch, *The New Education in the Soviet Republic*, New York, 1929; N. DeWitt, *Soviet Professional Manpower*, Washington, D.C., 1955; G. L. Kline (ed.), *Soviet Education*, 1957.

Kineshma, town in the Ivanovo Oblast, situated on the right bank of the Volga. Population (1959) 84,000 (1926, 34,000; 1939, 75,000). It has an old textile industry, and serves as the river port for the Ivanovo industrial area (importing cotton, oil, timber, etc.). Kineshma has been known since the 15th century.

Kireyevskiy, Ivan Vasil'yevich (1806–56), Slavophile philosopher. In his works *On the Character of European Enlightenment in its Relation to the Enlightenment of Russia*, 1852, and *On the Possibility and Necessity of New Principles in Philosophy*, 1856, he formulated the main epistemological and historiographical views of the Slavophiles (q.v.). *See* R. Hare, *Pioneers of Russian Social Thought*, 1951; N. O. Lossky, *History of Russian Philosophy*, 1951; V. V. Zenkovsky, *A History of Russian Philosophy*, vol. i, 1953; T. G. Masaryk, *The Spirit of Russia* (revised ed.), New York, 1955.

Kirgiz, Turkic-speaking people living in the Kirgiz Republic and numbering (1959) 974,000 (884,000 in 1939). They are Muslims and are still mostly pastoral people. The Kirgiz are of a clearly Mongoloid racial type, and are probably the product of a mixture between Mongol tribes which invaded Semirech'ye (q.v.) in the 12th and 13th centuries and the Turkic-speaking Kirgiz who in the 7th–17th centuries lived in the upper Yenisey area and some of whom came with the Mongol invaders.

Kirgizia, Union Republic of the U.S.S.R. lying in Central Asia and bordering upon China, predominantly in the Tien-Shan mountain system but including a part of the Fergana Valley in the south-west and the upper parts of the Chu and Talas river valleys in the north. It is traversed by the River Naryn, a headstream of the Syr-Dar'ya, and the lake Issyk-Kul' lies in the north-east. Kirgizia has the richest pastures in Central Asia, and varied mineral deposits (coal, oil, ozokerite, antimony, mercury, lead, sulphur, arsenic and building materials). Area 76,600 sq. m.; population (1959) 2,066,000 (34 per cent urban; 1939, 1,458,000), Kirgiz (about 40·5 per cent in 1959), Russians (30 per cent) and Ukrainians (7 per cent) in the north, Uzbeks (11 per cent) and Tadzhiks in the Fergana Valley, also some Uygurs and Dungans. Animal husbandry is the main agricultural pursuit (sheep, goats, cattle, horses, bees); over a half of the cultivated area is irrigated, and cotton, sugar-beet, tobacco, fruit and grapes are grown and sericulture carried on, while grain crops (wheat, oats, barley, maize) are cultivated in the unirrigated regions. There are metal-working and engineering (agricultural machinery, food industry equipment) industries, largely confined to the capital of the republic, and also varied food, textile and mining industries. While the north of the republic and the Fergana Valley are served by railways, the mountainous areas are traversed by the Frunze-Naryn-Kashgar (in China), the Pamir (Osh-Khorog) and the new Frunze-Osh highways. The capital of the republic is Frunze. and there are two oblasts, Osh, comprising the Kirgiz part of the Fergana Valley, and Tien-Shan. In the 1940's and 1950's there were also Frunze, Talas, Issyk-Kul' and Dzhalal-Abad oblasts. For early history *see* KOKAND KHANATE; SEMIRECH'YE.

The area was gradually annexed by Russia in 1855–76. Russian and Ukrainian agricultural colonization was resented by the indigenous population, and in 1916 the Kirgiz took part in the uprising prompted by the mobilization of native peoples (hitherto exempt from military service) for labour battalions. As a result of the 'National Delimitation of Central Asia' (q.v.) in 1924, the Kirgiz (then called Kara-Kirgiz) Autonomous Oblast was established within the R.S.F.S.R., which in 1926 was raised to the status of Autonomous Republic and in 1936 to Union Republic.

Kirichenko, Aleksey Illarionovich (*b.* 1908), Communist. The son of a Ukrainian soldier, he received little education. For some years he headed the party organization in Odessa, and in 1953 became first secretary of the party in the Ukraine. As one of Khrushchëv's closest associates he rose to membership of the Presidium (q.v.) of the party's Central Committee in 1955, and in 1957 moved to Moscow as a secretary of the Central Committee. He appeared to be Khrushchëv's general deputy in directing the party, with special responsibility for senior party appointments and for the security organs (q.v.). At the beginning of 1960 he was unexpectedly demoted to the position of first secretary of the party in Rostov Oblast, possibly because it was considered that he was concentrating excessive power in his hands; he also lost his position as member of the Presidium of the Central Committee.

Kirov: 1. Oblast of the R.S.F.S.R., in the north-east of European Russia astride the River Vyatka; it is a rolling plain partly covered with forests and marshes, and having deposits of peat, iron ore and phosphorite. Area 47,300 sq. m.; population (1959) 1,919,000 (37 per cent urban), mostly Russian (since the 12th century). There are engineering, iron and steel (since the 18th century), lumbering, woodworking, leather and chemical industries, and old handicrafts are practised (furniture, toys); agriculture specializes in dairy cattle raising and the cultivation of flax. The area formed the independent Vyatka Republic in the 12th–15th centuries, and was absorbed by Muscovy in 1489. Prior to 1917 it was well known for vigorous local government (*see* ZEMSTVO).

2. (before 1780 **Khlynov,** then until 1934 **Vyatka**). Administrative, economic and cultural centre of the above, on the River Vyatka. Population (1959) 252,000 (1913, 44,000; 1939, 144,000). It has engineering, chemical, woodworking and leather industries, and school equipment is produced. There is a large public library founded by Herzen. Kirov has been known since 1174 when it was founded by colonists from Novgorod; it was the centre of Russian colonization of the area and the capital of Vyatka Republic.

Kirov (real name **Kostrikov**), **Sergey Mironovich** (1886–1934), joined the Bolsheviks in 1905 and took part in the establishment of Soviet power in the Caucasus after the October revolution (q.v.) in 1917. From 1921 he headed the party in Azerbaydzhan and from

1926 in Leningrad, becoming a Politburo member in 1930. Kirov supported Stalin against his rivals, but is believed to have led the opposition within the Central Committee to Stalin's personal rule after the 17th party congress, 1934. His assassination in December 1934, in circumstances which indicate Stalin's complicity, began the wave of terror that developed into the Great Purge (q.v.). See B. D. Wolfe, *Khrushchëv and Stalin's Ghost*, 1957; L. Schapiro, *The Communist Party of the Soviet Union*, 1960.

Kirovabad (before 1804 and 1918–35 **Gandzha;** 1804–1918 **Yelisavetpol'**), town in Azerbaydzhan, the second economic and cultural centre of the republic. Population (1959) 116,000 (1914, 60,000; 1925, 55,500; 1939, 99,000). It has textile, food and agricultural engineering industries; there is iron ore mining in nearby Dashkesan. The town is surrounded by fruit gardens and vineyards, and sericulture is carried on; it has many architectural monuments, and the tomb of the famous medieval poet Nizami is here. Kirovabad was founded in the 5th or 6th century, and became an important medieval centre of commerce and culture; it was annexed to Russia in 1804, together with the khanate of which it was the capital.

Kirovograd: 1. Oblast in southern Ukraine, situated on the right bank of the Dnieper, largely on the Dnieper upland; it consists of black earth steppe with a few remaining oak forests, and has deposits of lignite. Area 9,200 sq. m.; population (1959) 1,218,000 (31 per cent urban), mostly Ukrainians. Wheat, sunflowers and sugar-beet are grown, and cattle are raised; there are food, chemical, agricultural engineering and coal-mining industries. Colonization began in the 1740's, the area having previously been virtually unpopulated.

2. (until 1924 **Yelisavetgrad**, then **Zinov'yevsk** till 1936, and **Kirovo** till 1939). Administrative, economic and cultural centre of the oblast, situated 120 m. west of Dnepropetrovsk. Population (1950) 127,000 (1914, 76,000; 1926, 66,000; 1939, 100,000), Ukrainians and Russians (before the war also Jews). It has engineering (agricultural machinery) and food industries. Kirovograd was founded as a fortress in 1754 and soon became the administrative centre of New Serbia; it was an important commercial town before 1917. The first Jewish pogroms in Russia took place in Kirovograd in 1881.

Kirsanov, Semën Isaakovich (*b.* 1906), poet. He was a disciple of Mayakovskiy (q.v.) and a member of the latter's 'communist-futurist' group Left Front in the Arts until it was dissolved in 1930. Apart from many propagandistic poems he has written delightful lyrical verse (*Cinderella*, 1935; *Four Notebooks*, 1940). At the height of the intellectual ferment in 1956 Kirsanov published *Seven Days of the Week*, a symbolic poem on the efforts of the intellectuals to save Russia from her critical condition (Russia being symbolized by a dangerously ill friend who needs a 'new heart'). Under pressure he recanted. See J. Lindsay (trans.), *Russian Poetry, 1917–55*, 1957; E. Stillman (ed.), *Bitter Harvest*, New York, 1959.

Kiselëvsk, town in the Kemerovo Oblast (southern Siberia), in the Stalinsk conurbation 35 m. north-west of Stalinsk, bordering on Prokop'yevsk. Population (1959) 130,000 (1939, 44,000). It is a major coal-mining and engineering (mining equipment) centre in the

Kuznetsk Basin, founded as a mining settlement within Prokop'-yevsk in the 1930's, becoming a town in 1936.

Kishinëv (Rumanian **Chisinau**), capital, economic and cultural centre of the Moldavian Republic, situated in the centre of Bessarabia. Population (1959) 214,000 (1918, 133,000; 1939, 112,000), Jews, Moldavians and Russians. It has extensive food (wine, tinned fruit) and tobacco industries, varied light industries and agricultural engineering. The city has the Moldavian branch of the U.S.S.R. Academy of Sciences, 1949, and a university, 1945. Kishinëv has been known since 1420, was Turkish in the 16th century, became Russian in 1812 (capital of Bessarabia) and was Rumanian 1918–40 and 1941–4. It was a centre of trade in agricultural products during the 19th century; the School of Horticulture and Viniculture was established in 1842 and had importance for the whole of southern Russia. In 1903 a Jewish pogrom took place and there were several hundred victims.

Kislovodsk, health resort in the Mineral Waters group of spas in Stavropol' Kray (North Caucasus). Population (1959) 79,000. Its mineral water *narzan* is sold all over Russia for nervous and heart troubles. There are forty-four sanatoria and rest-homes in the town, which is visited by approximately 125,000 patients each year. The healing properties of the springs have been known since the late 17th century, and Kislovodsk was founded in 1803.

Kizel, town in the Perm' Oblast (Urals), 125 m. north-east of Perm', the centre of the Kizel coal-mining basin which stretches north-south along the Kizel–Chusovoy railway. Population (1959) 60,000 (including Kospash, which was fused with Kizel in 1957). Mining equipment is manufactured and there is a large power-station supplying energy for the Kizel and Berezniki industrial area. Kizel was founded in 1765.

Klaipeda (German **Memel**), town in Lithuania, an ice-free port on the Baltic Sea. Population (1959) 89,000 (1939, 41,000), Lithuanians and Russians (before 1945 mostly Germans). It has wood-processing and textile industries, also fisheries. Klaipeda was founded by the Livonian Knights in 1253, and was an important centre of trade from the 16th century. The town and the surrounding area belonged to East Prussia, but, having a sizable Lithuanian minority, were assigned to Lithuania by the Treaty of Versailles. In 1939 the Lithuanian Government yielded to an ultimatum from Nazi Germany and ceded the area; at the end of the Second World War it was again included in Lithuania, which had already been annexed to the Soviet Union in 1940. From 1950 to 1953 the town was the administrative centre of Klaipeda Oblast, now abolished.

Klin, town in the Moscow Oblast, situated on the Moscow–Leningrad railway, 45 m. from the capital. Population (1959) 53,000 (1949, 28,000). It has glass and textile industries. Klin has been known since 1234 and until 1482 belonged to Tver' Principality. It was occupied by the Germans for a short time in 1941.

Klintsy, town in the Bryansk Oblast (central Russia), 100 m. south-west of Bryansk. Population (1956) 39,000. It has been an important centre of light industry since the early 19th century, and its chief product is woollen fabrics. Klintsy was founded in the 17th century as a refuge of the Old Believers (q.v.).

Klukhori, see KARACHAYEVSK.

Klyuchevskiy, Vasiliy Osipovich (1841–1911), historian, disciple of S. M. Solov'ëv and his successor as professor at Moscow University, where he became famous as a lecturer. He participated in the constitutional movement of the *zemstvo* liberals and in evolving the electoral law for the 1st Duma. His works have widely influenced historians of Russia, both native and foreign. Among his main works are: *Foreigners' Reports on the Muscovite State,* 1866–7, *Boyars' Duma in Ancient Russia,* 1882, *The Origin of Serfdom in Russia,* 1885, *History of Social Estates in Russia,* 1886–7, and *Course of Russian History,* 1904–10 (Eng. trans. *A History of Russia,* 5 vols., New York, 1911–13).

Knipper, Lev Konstantinovich (*b.* 1898), composer, conductor and folk-music specialist, a pupil of Glière. He has done much work with the Red Army. His works comprise operas, including *North Wind,* 1929–30; ballets, including the 'opera-ballet' *Candide,* 1926–7; cantatas; fourteen symphonies; violin concerto; orchestral works; chamber works; many songs; arrangements, etc. Several of Knipper's symphonies (No. 3, 1932; No. 4, 1933) employ a chorus, purely instrumental sections alternating with vocal episodes. The song *Polyushko* from the Fourth Symphony acquired international renown. *See* G. Abraham, *Eight Soviet Composers,* 1943.

Kogan, Leonid Borisovich (*b.* 1924), violinist who studied under Yampol'skiy at Moscow Conservatory until 1948. The winner of many awards, he is one of the most talented representatives of the younger generation of Russian violinists.

Kokand, town in the Fergana Oblast (Uzbekistan), situated in the centre of the Fergana Valley at the beginning of the Fergana circular railway. Population (1959) 105,000 (1939, 85,000). It has various light and food industries, and a chemical plant producing fertilizers. Kokand was the capital of the Kokand Khanate (q.v.) and in 1917–1918 of the short-lived anti-Bolshevik autonomous government of Turkestan. From 1875, when it was annexed to Russia, until 1917 it was an important banking and business centre. Kokand was largely destroyed when stormed by the Red Army in 1918, and because of its past political associations was consistently neglected during the Soviet period until in 1957 it became the seat of the Economic Council (q.v.) for the Uzbek part of the Fergana Valley.

Kokand Khanate, 18th–19th-century state in Central Asia. Its nucleus was the Fergana Valley (q.v.), which became independent from the Bukhara Khanate (q.v.) in the middle of the 18th century and for a short time around 1760 recognized Chinese suzerainty. At the height of its power in the 1820's and thirties, the Kokand Khanate included the whole course of the River Syr-Dar'ya in the north-west, Semirech'ye (q.v.) to the River Ili in the north-east, Darvaz, Kara-tegin, Kulyab and the West Pamir in the south. The capital of the state was Kokand, the main commercial centre Tashkent. Internal dissension (especially the interminable strife between the sedentary Sarts and the semi-nomadic Uzbek tribesmen of the Kypchak clan) and continuous wars with Bukhara greatly weakened the khanate, and it fell an easy victim to the Russians, whose gradual advance since 1850, provoked by Kokand raids on Russia's Kazakh subjects, finally resulted in the annexation of the whole territory of the khanate by 1876. *See* M. Holdsworth, *Turkestan in the Nineteenth Century*, 1959.

Kokchetav: 1. Oblast in northern Kazakhstan, situated on the border of the West Siberian lowland and the Kazakh hills, largely in the Ishim steppe, traversed by the Trans-Kazakhstan and Middle Siberian Railway trunk-lines; there are deposits of gold. Area 30,500 sq. m.; population (1959) 491,000 (25 per cent urban), mostly Russians and Ukrainians, also Kazakhs, Tatars and Germans. There is wheat cultivation, cattle and sheep breeding, gold-mining and butter production. The health resort of Borovoye is in the oblast.

2. Administrative and economic centre of the oblast, situated at the junction of the two railways, about 280 m. north-west of Karaganda. Population (1959) 40,000 (1939, 17,000), chiefly Russians and Ukrainians, also Tatars and Kazakhs. It has food (meat and flour) and metal-working (scales, spare parts for agricultural machinery) industries, and is a local cultural centre. Kokchetav was founded at the beginning of the 19th century as a Cossack village, and became a town in 1824.

Kola, peninsula in north-western Russia, between the Barents Sea and the White Sea. It forms, together with the adjacent mainland, the Murmansk Oblast.

Kolchak, Aleksandr Vasil'yevich (1870–1920), Crimean Tatar by birth, admiral and Arctic explorer; he commanded the Baltic, and subsequently the Black Sea, fleet during the First World War. He led the anti-Bolshevik struggle in Siberia, 1918–19, overthrew the Ufa Directory (q.v.) and was recognized by anti-Bolshevik organizations as the Supreme Ruler of Russia. A long retreat followed his early successes; he was finally taken prisoner and shot at Irkutsk.

Kol'chugino, *see* LENINSK-KUZNETSKIY.

Kolguyev, island in the Barents Sea, off the coast of the Archangel Oblast; it is covered with tundra and has few inhabitants. Area 1,350 sq. m.

Kolkhida, *see* COLCHIS.

Kolkhoz (Russian abbreviation for 'collective economy'), main form of agricultural organization in the U.S.S.R. Statutorily a *kolkhor* is a co-operative undertaking of a number of peasants (embracing a village or a number of small neighbouring villages) who pool their land and other means of production and are paid in kind and money according to the amount of work they put in (*see* WORK-DAY UNIT). In fact *kolkhozes* are managed by the party and the Government through *kolkhoz* chairmen who, though ostensibly elected, are actually appointed by the cadres departments of the party organizations (*see* CADRES; NOMENCLATURE). The abolition of the M.T.S. (q.v.) in 1958 and the sale of their agricultural machinery to the *kolkhozes* has made the latter more independent economically. But the system of obligatory (in fact) sales of agricultural products at fixed prices to the State (*see* AGRICULTURAL PROCUREMENT) and

the very narrow limits for decisions on farm policy by the *kolkhozes*
themselves make it impossible for the majority of *kolkhozes* to achieve
an adequate income.

Membership in a *kolkhoz* is automatic for those born into it, and it
is difficult for a member to leave. The *kolkhoz* system does not
normally provide sufficient material incentives for the peasants to
take an interest in their work, and their general standard of living is
still probably lower than before the collectivization of agriculture
(q.v.), despite some improvement since 1953. A remedy is seen by
more enterprising chairmen in a gradual transition to monthly money
payments to the members; some economists, e.g. Strumilin (q.v.),
suggest that the *kolkhozes* should be permitted to form larger co-
operative associations in order to pool their resources, and the
introduction of a form of ground rent, the absence of which now puts
those *kolkhozes* with poor natural resources at a disadvantage. The
number of *kolkhozes* has been steadily decreasing recently, as a result
of amalgamations and the transformation of the weaker ones into
sovkhozes (q.v.): in 1958 there were 69,100 *kolkhozes* averaging 245
peasant households each. *See further under* COLLECTIVIZATION OF
AGRICULTURE; PEASANTS. *See* F. Belov, *History of a Soviet Collective
Farm*, New York, 1955; R. D. Laird, *Collective Farming in Russia.
A Political Study of the Soviet Kolkhozy*, Lawrence, Kansas, 1958;
V. Gsovski and K. Grzybowski (eds.), *Government, Law and Courts in
the Soviet Union and Eastern Europe*, vol. ii, 1959; R. Schlesinger,
'The New Structure of Soviet Agriculture,' *Soviet Studies*, vol. x,
No. 3, Jan. 1959; L. Volin, 'Reform in Agriculture,' *Problems of
Communism*, vol. viii, No. 1, Jan.–Feb. 1959; A. Nove, 'The Incomes
of Soviet Peasants,' *Slavonic and East European Review*, vol. xxxviii,
No. 91, June 1960.

Kolkhoz Market, form of retail trade for the sale of agricultural
produce. It is used by *kolkhozes* for the sale of any surplus after their
sales to the State (*see* AGRICULTURAL PROCUREMENT), by *kolkhoz*
peasants for the sale of produce from their personal plots and by any
other person who may have agricultural produce for sale. Kolkhoz
market accounted in 1958 for 5·7 per cent of total retail trade (17 per
cent in 1932, 14 per cent in 1940, 46 per cent in 1945); of total retail
trade in food it accounted for 9·4 per cent (26 per cent in 1932, 20 per
cent in 1940, 51 per cent in 1945). Prices are not fixed and are determined by supply and demand. *See* H. H. Ware, 'The Collective Farm
Peasant Market,' *Journal of Farm Economics*, vol. xxxii, No. 2,
1950; J. T. Whitman, 'The Kolkhoz Market,' *Soviet Studies*, vol. vii,
No. 4, July 1956.

Kollontay, Aleksandra Mikhaylovna (1872–1952), politician and
theorist of 'free love.' She joined the revolutionary movement in the
1890's, was a Bolshevik in 1904–5 but later became a Menshevik
'liquidationist' (q.v.). From 1908 she lived in emigration, taking an
active part in social democratic work in several Western European
countries and the U.S.A., and was a member of the International
Bureau of Women Socialists. During the First World War she took
up an internationalist position and from 1915 assisted Lenin in his
efforts to build up an international Leninist faction (the 'Zimmerwald

Left'). Returning to Russia after the February revolution (q.v.) in 1917, she became a member of the Bolshevik Central Committee. After the Bolshevik seizure of power (*see* OCTOBER REVOLUTION) she was Commissar for Social Security in the first Soviet government, but left it over the Brest-Litovsk treaty (q.v.) which she opposed (*see* LEFT COMMUNISTS). In 1920–1 she was the head of the women's department of the Central Committee and one of the leaders of the Workers' Opposition (q.v.), and in 1921 2 secretary of the International Women's Secretariat of the Comintern. From 1923 she was a diplomat, representing the U.S.S.R. in Norway, 1923–6 and 1927–1930, Mexico, 1926–7, and Sweden, 1930–45. A participant in the Proletkul't (q.v.), Kollontay applied the Bogdanovist (*see* BOG-DANOVISM) approach to the problem of sex relations and advanced the 'winged Eros' theory according to which individuals should in a socialist society be free to associate with different persons of the opposite sex for different purposes. This theory, though disapproved of by Lenin in common with most other modernist views, was widely popularized, since it helped to weaken family ties by making the traditional family appear 'old-fashioned.' *See* her *The Workers' Opposition in Russia*, 1923, and *Free Love* (trans. C. J. Hogarth), 1932.

Kolmogorov, Andrey Nikolayevich (*b.* 1903), outstanding mathematician, educated at Moscow University and professor there since 1931, member of the Academy of Sciences since 1939. He is a leading authority of international repute on the theory of probabilities (where he is the author of the currently most popular axiomatic theory) and mathematical logic, and in recent years he has shown much interest in cybernetics (q.v.). In 1958 Kolmogorov defended the existing system of higher education (q.v.) against Khrushchëv's reform proposals, and in 1960 supported the revived marginalist trend in economic thought.

Kolomna, town in the Moscow Oblast, situated on the Moskva River near its confluence with the Oka, 72 m. south-east of Moscow. Population (1959) 100,000 (1939, 75,000). It has been an important centre of the engineering industry since 1863, producing locomotives and machine tools; there are towers of a 16th-century fortress, and interesting buildings of the 14th–18th centuries. Kolomna has been known since 1177 and became a Muscovite outpost in 1300.

Kol'tsov, Aleksey Vasil'yevich (1808–42), poet, a peasant's son who received no education. His poetry, popular in Russia, deals with nature and peasant life, and his verses resemble folk poetry in style and form.

Kolyma, river in north-eastern Siberia which rises in the plateau between the Verkhoyansk and the Cherskiy ridges and flows northeast into the East Siberian Sea. Length 1,600 m.; basin 250,000 sq. m. In recent years a large gold-mining industry has been developed in the upper Kolyma region (*see* MAGADAN), which was notorious for its forced labour camps.

Komarov, Vladimir Leont'yevich (1869–1945), botanist and geographer, professor at St Petersburg University, member (from 1920), vice-president, 1930–6, and president, 1936–45, (after Karpinskiy's (q.v.) death) of the Academy of Sciences. His fundamental works are devoted to the flora of Manchuria, China, Mongolia, the Russian Far East and Siberia. He singled out the Manchurian floristic region, and introduced the concept of series of genetically related species.

Komi, Finnish-speaking people who live in the north-east of European Russia and number (1959) 431,000. Orthodox Christians since the 14th century (*see* STEPHEN OF PERM'), they are the most civilized of the 'northern peoples' of Russia. The Komi are mostly peasants, now collectivized. There are two branches of the Komi people, traditionally known as Zyryans (now officially called simply Komi, making up about 60 per cent of the total) and Permyaks (now called Komi-Permyaks); the former live in the Komi Autonomous Republic and the latter in the Komi-Permyak National Okrug. *See* W. Kolarz, *Russia and her Colonies*, 1952.

Komi Autonomous Republic, of the R.S.F.S.R., is situated in the north-east of European Russia, comprising the basins of the Pechora and Vychegda rivers; it is largely forested lowland and has rich deposits of coal (Pechora basin) and oil. Area 158,900 sq. m.; population (1959) 804,000 (59 per cent urban), mostly Russians and Komi. There are timber, coal-mining (since the 1930's) and oil extraction (since 1745) industries; dairy farming and grain cultivation are carried on. Principal towns: Syktyvkar (capital) and Vorkuta. The area belonged to the Novgorod Republic from the 13th century; the Komi Autonomous Oblast was established in 1921 and was transformed into a republic in 1936. It has been an area of banishment and labour camps.

Komi-Permyak National Okrug lies within Perm' Oblast. Area 8,600 sq. m.; population (1959) 220,000 (23 per cent urban), Komi-Permyaks and Russians. There is grain and dairy farming and a timber industry. The National Okrug was established in 1929; its administrative centre is Kudymkar.

Komsomol (Russian abbreviation for 'Young Communist League'), youth organization set up in 1918 to assist the Communist Party; membership is for young people between 14 and 26 years of age, and in 1956 stood at 18·5 million. The Komsomol played an active role in carrying out the collectivization of agriculture (q.v.). The open expression of deviating views has sometimes emerged in the Komsomol, particularly in the post-Stalin period (*see* INTELLECTUAL OPPOSITION). *See* S. I. Ploss, 'From Youthful Zeal to Middle Age,' *Problems of Communism*, vol. vii, No. 5, Sept.–Oct. 1958, and A. Kassoff, 'Afflictions of the Youth League,' ibid.; R. T. Fisher, *Pattern for Soviet Youth: a Study of the Congresses of the Komsomol, 1918–54*, New York, 1959.

Komsomol'sk-on-Amur (until 1932 **Permskoye**), town in the Khabarovsk Kray (Far East), situated on the Amur 230 m. north-east of Khabarovsk. Population (1959) 177,000 (1932, 160; 1939, 71,000). It is an important industrial centre of the Russian Far East (iron and steel, shipbuilding, saw-milling, engineering). Komsomol'sk was founded as a village in 1858, and has been a town since 1932, partly built and populated by members of the Komsomol.

'Kommunist,' main theoretical journal of the Communist Party of the Soviet Union, published by the Central Committee (fifteen issues a year). It was founded in 1924 and was called *Bol'shevik* until 1952. Circulation (1956) 700,000.

Komsorg (Russian abbreviation for 'Komsomol organizer'), official in charge of a primary organization (q.v.) of the Komsomol which for one reason or another is considered particularly important, e.g. at a major building site. A Komsorg is appointed by a superior committee of the Komsomol, though he may frequently be also 'elected' as secretary of the primary organization.

Konev, Ivan Stepanovich (*b.* 1897), Marshal of the Soviet Union, the son of a peasant, who joined the Red Army and the Communist Party in 1918. During the Second World War he distinguished himself as the commander of army groups which won several important battles, including those which resulted in the liberation of Khar'kov, 1943, and of Kirovograd, 1944. He was the Soviet representative on the Allied Control Commission in Vienna after the war. From 1946 to 1955 he was Commander-in-Chief Land Forces and Chief Inspector Land Forces, and from 1955 was First Deputy Minister of Defence and the commander-in-chief of the Warsaw Pact forces, retiring from this post in 1960 on grounds of ill health. Konev was chairman of the special court which sentenced Beria (q.v.) in 1953.

Koni, Anatoliy Fëdorovich (1844–1927), lawyer. He made a brilliant career as a procurator and judge, was finally a senator in charge of the criminal cassation department of the Senate, and after 1906 a member by appointment of the State Council. He first attracted public attention in 1878 when V. I. Zasulich was acquitted by jury with Koni as the presiding judge. Later his pleas and summings-up earned him great fame as an orator, and they are still studied by lawyers in Russia.

Konotop, town in the Sumy Oblast (northern Ukraine), an important railway junction on the Moscow–Kiev line, about 125 m. north-east of Kiev. Population (1959) 53,000, mostly Ukrainians. It has engineering and metal-working industries, mainly connected with railway maintenance, and is a local cultural centre. Konotop was founded in 1640 as a Polish fortress.

Konstantinovka, town in the Stalino Oblast (Ukraine). Population (1959) 89,000 (1926, 25,000; 1939, 96,000). It is an important centre of the chemical, glass and metallurgical industries, and of transportation. The town was largely destroyed during the Second World War.

Kopek (*kopeyka*), monetary unit, one-hundredth of a rouble.

Kopeysk, town in the Chelyabinsk Oblast (Urals), situated in the Chelyabinsk conurbation 8 m. south-east of Chelyabinsk. Population (1959) 160,000 (1936, 65,000; 1939, 60,000). It is the chief centre of lignite-mining in the Chelyabinsk area, and has an engineering industry producing agricultural and mining equipment. Kopeysk was founded as a mining settlement before 1917, and has been a town since the 1930's.

Korin, Pavel Dmitriyevich (*b.* 1892), painter who studied in the icon-painters' workshop in Palekh and in the Moscow School of Painting, 1912–16; he was influenced by Nesterov (q.v.). He has produced an extensive series of portraits of the artistic *élite* of the Soviet Union. With comparative boldness, Korin emphasizes the qualities of mind and will of his sitters by distorting their physical appearance, making them appear gaunter and fiercer.

Korkino, town in the Chelyabinsk Oblast (Urals), 22 m. south of Chelyabinsk. Population (1959) 85,000 (1939, 12,000). It has a large opencast coal-mining industry (since 1934), and is the main centre of coal-mining in the Chelyabinsk Basin.

Korkunov, Nikolay Mikhaylovich (1853–1904), jurist and political theorist, professor at St Petersburg University. In his theory he combined the empirical and the psychological approaches, and he was the founder of the St Petersburg psychological school of Russian jurisprudence whose most extreme exponent was Petrazhitskiy (q.v.). Korkunov defined law as the delimitation of interests, and considered the State a juridical relation between individuals, the object of which is the State power, the latter being not a will but a force springing from the people's consciousness of their dependence on the State. Proceeding from this, Korkunov generalized Montesquieu's doctrine of the division of powers into a theory of shared power. *See* his *General Theory of Law*, Boston, Mass., 1909.

Kornilov, Konstantin Nikolayevich (1879–1957), psychologist, professor at various higher educational establishments in Moscow, including the university. Studying human reactions with the help of a 'dynamoscope' designed by himself, he developed a 'reactological' theory of psychology which he considered to be Marxist. In 1923 Kornilov took the lead in denouncing (together with Blonskiy, q.v.) the psychological views of his former teacher Chelpanov (q.v.) as idealistic, and in the same year replaced him as director of the Moscow Institute of Experimental Psychology. He held this position until 1930 (being also editor of the journal *Psychology* from 1928), when he was himself dismissed after his views had been denounced as both 'mechanistic' and 'idealistic.' He recanted in 1931. Kornilov's main works are *Doctrine of Human Reactions*, 1921, and *Textbook of Psychology*, 1926. *See also* his 'Psychology in the Light of Dialectical Materialism' in C. Murchison's (ed.) *Psychologies of 1930*, Worcester, Mass., 1930.

Kornilov, Lavr Georgiyevich (1870–1918), general of half Kirgiz birth who commanded a brigade in 1915, was captured by the Germans but escaped. As the Petrograd Military District commander in 1917 he arrested Nicholas II and his family. He became commander-in-chief of all Russian forces in August 1917, realized the danger of a Bolshevik coup and, believing the Provisional Government (q.v.) incapable of meeting it, was prepared to suppress the soviets (q.v.), if necessary against the will of the Government. Believing that the Prime Minister, Kerenskiy, was in fact in favour of such a step, Kornilov started a troop movement towards Petrograd from his headquarters at the front, but was stopped and arrested on Kerenskiy's orders. This 'Kornilov affair' resulted in a further weakening of the Government and strengthening of the Bolsheviks, the latter appearing as allies of the democratic forces in laying the ghost of a right-wing dictatorship. Kornilov escaped in December and formed, with General Alekseyev, the first anti-Bolskevik volunteer units; he was killed in an early battle of the civil war. *See* A. J. Sack, *The Birth of the Russian Democracy*, New York, 1918; A. F. Kerensky, *Prelude to Bolshevism, the Kornilov Rising*, New York, 1919; F. A. Golder, *Documents of Russian History, 1914–17*, 1927; A. Ascher, 'The Kornilov Affair,' *Russian Review*, vol. xii, No. 4, Oct. 1953; L. I. Strakhovsky, 'Was there a Kornilov Rebellion?—a Reappraisal of the Evidence,' *Slavonic and East European Review*, vol. xxxiii, No. 81, June 1955.

Korolenko, Vladimir Galaktionovich (1853–1921), writer of Ukrainian-Polish birth, a leader of the Liberal Populists and co-editor of *The Russian Wealth*, their main journal; he was banished to Siberia for six years. Humanitarianism and optimism pervade his writings (e.g. the novel *The Blind Musician*, 1886), which deal mainly with 'the wronged and the humiliated.' He died of exhaustion and starvation in the famine of 1921. *See* R. F. Christian, 'V. G. Korolenko (1853–1921): a Centennial Appreciation,' *Slavonic and East European Review*, vol. xxxii, No. 79, June 1954.

Korosten', town in the Zhitomir Oblast (Ukraine), 93 m. northwest of Kiev. Population (1956) 34,000, before the war half Jewish. It has metal-working, china and quarrying industries. Korosten' was capital of the Drevlyane tribe in the 9th–10th centuries.

Korsakov (1905–45 **Otomari**), town in the south of Sakhalin Oblast (Far East), the most important seaport of the island, situated 25 m. south of Yuzhno-Sakhalinsk. Population (1956) 32,000 (1897, 300; 1934, 46,000). It has some fishing and saw-milling industries. Korsakov was founded in 1876 as a Russian fortress; it was Japanese, 1905–45.

Koryak National Okrug lies within Kamchatka Oblast. Area 116,400 sq. m.; population (1959) 28,000 (22 per cent urban). There are oil and coal deposits, and fishing and coal-mining (for local use) industries. The National Okrug was established in 1930, and its administrative centre is the village of Palana.

Koryaks, Paleo-Asiatic people who live in the Koryak National Okrug of Kamchatka Oblast (Russian Far East); in 1959 they numbered 6,000. They have been known since the 17th century and are mostly fishers and reindeer breeders, now collectivized. *See* W. Kolarz, *The Peoples of the Soviet Far East*, 1954.

Kostomarov, Nikolay Petrovich (1817–85), Ukrainian historian, one of the main representatives of the regionalist school in Russian historical and political thought (*see* REGIONALISM). He was professor of history at St Petersburg University.

Kostroma: 1. Oblast of the R.S.F.S.R., north-east of Moscow, chiefly north of the Volga, largely forested lowland. Area 23,200 sq. m.; population (1959) 919,000 (39 per cent urban). There are textile, lumbering and wood-processing industries, old crafts are carried on, and there is flax growing and dairy farming (Kostroma breed).

2. Administrative, economic and cultural centre of the oblast, situated on the Volga. Population (1959) 171,000 (1914, 67,000; 1920, 50,000; 1939, 121,000). It has linen-milling, engineering and food

industries, and many interesting churches and other buildings of the 16th–19th centuries. Kostroma was founded in 1152, and in the 13th and 14th centuries was the capital of a principality. It was conquered by the Muscovites in 1364, and then became an important commercial and manufacturing centre. A university was founded in 1919 but later abolished.

Kosygin, Aleksey Nikolayevich (*b.* 1904), Communist. Born in St Petersburg in a working-class family, he volunteered for the Red Army in 1919, received training as a co-operative organizer and until 1929 worked in the co-operatives in Siberia, joining the party in 1927. Then until 1935 he studied at a textile institute and became a textile engineer at a factory in Leningrad. There he attracted Zhdanov's attention and made a spectacular career during the Great Purge (q.v.), becoming chairman of the Leningrad City Soviet in 1938 and U.S.S.R. Commissar for the Textile Industry in 1939. From 1940 until the death of Stalin in 1953 he was deputy chairman of the U.S.S.R. Council of People's Commissars (Council of Ministers from 1946) and simultaneously chairman of the Council of Ministers of the R.S.F.S.R., 1943–6, U.S.S.R. Minister of Finance in 1948 and Minister of Light Industry, 1948–53. He had become a Central Committee member in 1939, candidate member of the Politburo in 1946 and a full member in 1948. He escaped the fate of many other Zhdanovites (*see* LENINGRAD CASE) after Zhdanov's death, but was not included even in the enlarged Presidium of the Central Committee after the 19th party congress in 1952. Minister for the Consumer Goods Industry from 1953, he began to rise again with the diminution of Malenkov's influence, becoming a candidate member of the Central Committee's Presidium after the fall of the 'anti-party group' (q.v.) in 1957, and chairman of Gosplan (q.v.) in 1958. In 1960 he became a first deputy prime minister and again a full member of the Central Committee's Presidium.

Kotlas, town in the Archangel Oblast (northern Russia), situated at the confluence of the Northern Dvina and the Vychegda. Population (1956) 37,000 (1936, 21,000). It has wood-processing and ship-repairing industries, and is an important transportation centre (river port, three railway lines). Kotlas became a town in 1917; in the 1930's–1950's it was the receiving point for the forced labour camps along the Kotlas–Vorkuta railway.

Kovalevskaya, Sof'ya Vasil'yevna (1850–91), mathematician of remarkable ability. She studied at Heidelberg, Berlin and Moscow universities, and in 1884 was appointed lecturer in Stockholm, becoming professor there five years later. She achieved distinction with her work on the rotation of a solid body about a fixed axis, which won her the Prix Bordin of the Academy of Paris, 1888.

Kovalevskiy Aleksandr Onufriyevich (1840–1901), zoologist, one of the founders of comparative embryology, professor at Odessa and St Petersburg universities. His chief works dealt with the embryology of invertebrates, and he prepared the way for the Gastraea theory of Haeckel; he was one of the chief exponents of Darwinism in Russia. While professor in Odessa Kovalevskiy belonged to a scientific circle that included Mechnikov and Sechenov (qq.v.).

Kovalevskiy, Maksim Maksimovich (1851–1916), historian, sociologist and liberal politician (*see* PROGRESSIVE PARTY), professor at Moscow, St Petersburg and a number of foreign universities, and founder of the Russian High School in Paris (a kind of free university). Among his many works were *Communal Landownership*, 1879, *The Social Structure of England at the End of the Middle Ages*, 1880, *Primitive Law*, 1886, *Law and Custom in the Caucasus* (2 vols.), 1890, *The Origin of Modern Democracy* (4 vols.), 1895–9, and *Sociology* (2 vols.), 1910. He was one of the leading exponents of the comparative method in sociology.

Kovno, *see* KAUNAS.

Kovrov, town in the Vladimir Oblast (central Russia). Population (1959) 100,000. It is an important centre of industry (engineering, textile and food) and transportation (four railway lines, port on the River Klyaz'ma). Kovrov was a medieval village in Suzdal' Principality, and became a town in 1778; its commercial and industrial importance dates from the 19th century.

Kozlov, *see* MICHURINSK.

Kozlov, Frol Romanovich (*b.* 1908), Communist. Born a peasant, he began work at 15, joined the party in 1926 and received technical education. He made a rapid career during and after the Great Purge (q.v.) in the party apparatus, and from 1949 in Leningrad. He became a member of the Central Committee, 1952, of its Presidium, 1957, chairman of the R.S.F.S.R. Council of Ministers in the same year and a first deputy chairman of the U.S.S.R. Council of Ministers, 1958. After Kirichenko's fall in 1960 Kozlov became a secretary of the Central Committee and now apparently ranks second in the party hierarchy after Khrushchëv.

Krachkovskiy, Ignatiy Yulianovich (1883–1951), outstanding orientalist. Educated at St Petersburg University, he was professor there from 1918 and a member of the Academy of Sciences from 1921. His many works on Arabic and Amharic philology (especially modern and classical Arab literature, including Christian and Spanish) brought him international repute. In 1923 he was elected member of the Arab Academy in Damascus.

Kramatorsk, town in the Stalino Oblast (eastern Ukraine), situated about 50 m. north of Stalino. Population (1959) 115,000 (1926, 12,000; 1935, 142,000; 1939, 94,000), Russians and Ukrainians. It is the largest centre of heavy engineering (metallurgical, coal-mining and other equipment) in the Donets Basin, and an important railway junction. Kramatorsk was founded as a railway station in the late 19th century, and has been a town since the early 1930's.

Kramskoy, Ivan Nikolayevich (1837–87), painter. He studied from 1857 at the Academy of Arts but left in 1863 with a group of other students in protest against the prescribed subject in the competition for a gold medal. He became one of the founders of the Peredvizhniki (q.v.). Kramskoy was a competent draughtsman but had little feeling for colour. His paintings (including the famous 'Christ in the Wilderness') are executed in a dry, naturalistic style.

Krasin, Leonid Borisovich (1870–1926), Communist. As a student in 1890 he joined one of the earliest Social Democratic organizations in Russia, becoming in 1900–3, while working as an engineer, a leading member of Iskra (q.v.) and of the Bolshevik faction. He opposed Lenin's dictatorial methods within the party, 1904–5, and had him expelled from the Central Committee, but in company with Lenin and Bogdanov led the Bolshevik faction in the 1905 revolution. In 1909 he broke once more with Lenin, and worked in the Siemens-Schuckert Company, first in Berlin then as managing director of the St Petersburg branch. From 1918 he was chairman of the Council for Army Supply and People's Commissar for Trade and Industry and for Transportation in the Soviet Government. He was a member of the Presidium of the Supreme Council of National Economy and later Commissar for Foreign Trade; between 1922 and 1926 he was twice ambassador to Britain and once to France. Krasin's immense business and technical skill enabled him to play a leading part in organizing the Soviet economy, and his example persuaded many technical specialists to work for the Soviet Government. *See* life by his wife, 1929; L. Schapiro, *The Communist Party of the Soviet Union*, 1960.

Krasnodar: 1. Kray of the R.S.F.S.R., situated in the North Caucasus adjacent to the Black Sea and the Sea of Azov, traversed by the River Kuban'; the northern part of the kray is black earth lowland, and in the south it includes the north-western part of the main Caucasian range, almost wholly forested. There are deposits of oil, gas and cement marl. Area 32,700 sq. m.; population (1959) 3,766,000 (39 per cent urban), Russians, Ukrainians, some Armenians and Circassians. The kray is a major agricultural region, with wheat, sunflower, rice and tobacco cultivation, extensive horticulture and viniculture and livestock breeding. There are also food industries, oil extraction and refining, cement production and agricultural engineering. Principal towns: Krasnodar, Armavir, Sochi, Novorossiysk, Maykop, Yeysk. The area north of the Kuban' belonged to the Crimean Khanate and was annexed by Russia in 1783; in 1829 the Black Sea littoral was annexed from Turkey, and by 1864 the Circassians south of the Kuban' had been conquered, many of them emigrating to Turkey. Don and Zaporozh'ye Cossacks were the first Russian and Ukrainian colonists. The Kuban' region was a stronghold of anti-Bolshevik resistance in 1918–20 and 1929–33 (*see* COLLECTIVIZATION OF AGRICULTURE); it saw much fighting in 1942–3.

2. (until 1920 **Yekaterinodar**). Administrative, economic and cultural centre of the kray, situated on the River Kuban'. Population (1959) 312,000 (1914, 100,000; 1939, 193,000). It has varied food and light industries, metal-working and oil refining, and is an important railway junction. Krasnodar was founded by Cossack colonists from Zaporozh'ye in 1749, and in 1860 became capital of the Kuban' Cossack region. It was a centre of anti-Bolshevik resistance in the civil war, and was occupied by the Germans in 1942–3. In 1919 a university was founded, but soon abolished.

Krasnogvardeysk, *see* GATCHINA.

Krasnokamsk, town in the Perm' Oblast (Urals), situated on the River Kama 25 m. west of Perm'. Population (1959) 54,000. It is a major centre of the paper industry, with the largest paper mill in the country; in the surrounding area there is oil extraction (since 1934). Krasnokamsk was founded as a workers' settlement when the building of the paper mill was started in 1930.

Krasnotur'insk (till 1944 **Tur'inskiye Rudniki**), town in the Sverdlovsk Oblast (Urals), situated in the Serov industrial area about 6 m. north-west of Serov. Population (1959) 62,000 (1939, 10,000). It is an important centre of the aluminium industry, and there is coal-mining in the area. Krasnotur'insk was founded in 1760 as a copper- and iron-mining settlement; it became a town in 1944.

Krasnovodsk, town in Turkmenia, a port on the Caspian Sea (oil and cotton export to European Russia) and starting-point of the Trans-Caspian Railway. Population (1956) 38,000, mainly Russians. Krasnovodsk was founded by the Russians in 1869. In the 1940's and 1950's it was for some time the administrative centre of Krasnovodsk Oblast, which was twice formed and abolished.

Krasnoyarsk: 1. Kray of the R.S.F.S.R., situated in central Siberia along the whole course of the River Yenisey, comprising parts of the Western Siberian lowland on the left bank and of the Central Siberian plateau on the right bank; it is mostly covered with coniferous forests but has tundra in the north and fertile steppe 'oases' in the south; there are large deposits of coal-graphite, iron ore, gold, non-ferrous metals (copper, nickel, aluminium) and uranium. Area 927,200 sq. m.; population (1959) 2,614,000 (50 per cent urban), Russians (since the 17th century), also Khakas and some Evenki, Yakuts and Nenets. There are mining, engineering, timber and food industries, grain cultivation, cattle and reindeer breeding and fur-trapping. Principal towns: Krasnoyarsk, Noril'sk, Kansk, Abakan. The Khakas Autonomous Oblast and the Taymyr and Evenki National Okrugs lie within the kray. It has been an area of banishment and labour camps, and is now one of the most rapidly developing regions of Siberia.

2. Administrative, economic and cultural centre of the oblast, situated on the River Yenisey and the Trans-Siberian Railway. Population (1959) 409,000 (third in Siberia; 1897, 27,000; 1914, 80,000; 1926, 72,000; 1939, 190,000; 1956, 328,000). It has heavy engineering (cranes and other building industry equipment, locomotives, rolling stock, agricultural machinery, shipbuilding), light and food industries. Krasnoyarsk was founded as a Russian fort in 1628, became a provincial administrative centre in 1823 and expanded rapidly as the commercial centre of a gold-mining area. Industrial development dates from the building of the Trans-Siberian Railway and especially from the Second World War.

Krasnyy Luch (formerly **Krindachevka**), town in the Lugansk Oblast (eastern Ukraine). Population (1959) 94,000 (1926, 12,500; 1939, 59,000). It is a major coal-mining (chiefly anthracite) centre of the Donets Basin, and the large Shterovka power-station is near by. Krasnyy Luch was founded as a workers' settlement and became a town in 1929.

Kravchinskiy, *see* STEPNYAK.

Kray, territorial administrative unit, similar to an oblast but usually containing an Autonomous Oblast within its boundaries.

Kremenchug (Ukrainian **Kremenchuk**), town in the Poltava Oblast (central Ukraine), situated on the Dnieper. Population (1959) 86,000 (1914, 100,000; 1926, 59,000; 1939, 90,000). It has transport, engineering and textile industries, and is the transfer point of timber from water to rail for Khar'kov; a big hydro-electric station is under construction, and iron ore deposits have recently been discovered in the vicinity. Kremenchug was founded as a fortress in 1571 and was capital of New Russia (q.v.), 1765–89. It suffered greatly in the civil war and the Second World War.

Kremlin ('Kreml''), citadel within a town, originally medieval fortresses but in their present form mostly dating from the 16th–17th centuries. The most famous is the Moscow Kremlin, built to a triangular plan on a low hill at the confluence of the Moskva and the Neglinnaya rivers (the latter below street level since the early 19th century). The present rampart and towers in red brick were built by a number of Italian architects under Ivan III. The fanciful spires and tent-shaped roofs were added to the towers in the 17th century when the fortifications began to lose their purely defensive significance. Being the administrative centre of both Church and State, the Kremlin contained many palaces, churches, monasteries and government offices. In the centre are the three most important *sobory* (*see* ARCHITECTURE, ECCLESIASTICAL). The oldest and largest of them is the Cathedral of the Dormition (Uspenskiy Sobor), scene of the imperial coronations, built in 1475–9 by the Italian Aristotele Fioravante, who was ordered to copy the church of the same dedication at Vladimir; he was also strongly influenced by the monumental simplicity of the churches of Novgorod and Pskov. Apart from giving a new impetus to the art of stone-masonry in Moscow, this church was for generations to serve as a canon for truly 'orthodox' church building.

The Cathedral of the Archangel Michael (Arkhangel'skiy Sobor), the burial place of the rulers of Moscow until the time of Peter I, was built 1505–9 by Alevisio the 'New' of Milan, and marks the first appearance in Russian architecture of decorative motifs of the Italian Renaissance which were to become a feature of the 17th-century Muscovite 'baroque.' The Cathedral of the Annunciation (Blagoveshchenskiy Sobor), 1484–9, was the work of architects from Pskov. Its picturesque complexity foreshadows the churches of the 16th and 17th centuries. The bell-tower of Ivan the Great, begun in 1505 and completed in 1600 under Boris Godunov (q.v.), is 270 feet high, and, since for centuries it was the highest point in Moscow, served as a look-out in times of war. The Palace of the Facets (Granovitaya Palata), built 1487–91 by Ruffo and Solario, derives its name from the decorative treatment of its façade. It contains a large square hall with an enormous vault resting on a single squat pier in the centre. Behind it rises the Terem Palace, 1635–6, built in the 'pyramid' style that has figured persistently in Russian architecture, i.e. with a terrace surrounding each successively smaller storey. Both interior and exterior are richly encrusted with carved stone decorations that show a fusion of native and baroque elements. Its small rooms with their low vaults, though largely 'restored' in the 19th century, still evoke the daily life of the 17th-century Muscovy czars. The palaces and other secular buildings of the medieval Kremlin were in fact an agglomeration of comparatively small structures (*palaty*) linked together by means of covered galleries and stairways. This type of picturesque asymmetry was particularly prized by the Muscovites.

In 1701 a disastrous fire destroyed all the wooden buildings of the Kremlin and seriously damaged the stone palaces and churches. Under Peter the ruined Kremlin lay largely neglected. He did, however, build a fine stone arsenal in its north corner. Kazakov, an assistant of Bazhenov (qq.v.), built the severely classical Senate House, 1776–89, with its famous rotunda. The Kremlin suffered greatly from the fire and the French occupation of 1812. The present Great Kremlin Palace was built 1839–49 by Thon, an exponent of the official 'Russo-Byzantine' style. The massive proportions of this tasteless building dwarf the neighbouring cathedrals. The interior, though sumptuous, testified to a pathetic decline of imperial taste. Here the Supreme Soviet now holds its sessions. Since the revolution some excellent restoration work has been carried out in the three cathedrals and in other Kremlin churches, making it all the more difficult to understand the senseless destruction of the Chudov and Voznesenskiy monasteries, both so rich in historical associations. *See* D. R. Buxton, *Medieval Russian Architecture*, 1934; C. G. E. Bunt, *Russian Art: From Scyths to Soviets*, 1946; T. T. Rice, *Russian Art*, 1949; S. H. Cross, *Medieval Russian Churches*, Cambridge, Mass., 1949; G. H. Hamilton, *The Art and Architecture of Russia*, 1954; A. Voyce, *The Moscow Kremlin. Its History, Architecture and Art Treasures*, Berkeley, California, 1954.

Krivoy Rog (Ukrainian **Kryvyy Rih**), city in Dnepropetrovsk Oblast (southern Ukraine), situated 85 m. south-west of Dnepropetrovsk. Population (1959) 386,000 (1914, 18,000; 1926, 36,000; 1939, 189,000), Ukrainians and Russians (before the war also Jews). It is the centre of the Krivoy Rog iron-ore area—one of the richest in the world—and has large iron and steel, chemical and engineering (mining equipment) industries; it is also a local cultural centre. Krivoy Rog was founded by Zaporozh'ye Cossacks in the 17th century; its recent growth is due in part to the fusion of mining settlements which stretched for forty miles from north to south. The Scythians mined iron ore here several centuries B.C.; modern industrial development dates from 1881 and is still continuing rapidly. The town suffered much during the civil war and the Second World War.

'Krokodil,' humorous weekly magazine issued by the publishing house of *Pravda*. Although it is obliged to follow the political line of the party, its cartoons and jokes are frequently penetrating, and sometimes even double-edged. Circulation (1957) one million.

Kronstadt (Russian **Kronshtadt**), town and naval fortress in the Leningrad Oblast, subordinated to the Leningrad City Council, situated on Kotlin Island in the Gulf of Finland, 18 m. west of Leningrad. Population (1956) under 50,000 (1897, 60,000; 1926, 31,000). It was founded in 1703 by Peter the Great as a naval base and until the 1880's was the commercial harbour of St Petersburg. The Kronstadt sailors supported the Bolsheviks enthusiastically in 1917, but in 1921 rose against the Communist dictatorship in the famous Kronstadt Rising. *See* G. Katkov, 'The Kronstadt Rising,' *St Antony's Papers*, No. 6, Soviet Affairs, No. 2, 1959.

Kropotkin (until 1926 Romanovskiy Khutor), town in the Krasnodar Kray (North Caucasus), situated on the River Kuban' and the North Caucasus Railway. Population (1959) 54,000. It is an important centre of food industries (vegetable oil, fruit and vegetable canning, meat and dairy products) and a railway junction. Kropotkin grew up near the railway station Kavkazskaya which was built in 1875, and it became a town in 1926.

Kropotkin, Prince Pëtr Alekseyevich (1842–1921), geographer and revolutionary, a leading theorist of Anarchism. Having travelled widely in Manchuria and Eastern Siberia studying the orography of the area, he proved that the main structural lines of Asia run from south-west to north-east, and later compiled the Russian section for E. Reclus's *Universal Geography*. In 1872 he joined the International Working Men's Association in Switzerland, and sided with Bakunin against Marx. He was imprisoned in Russia, 1874–6, and France, 1883–6, and expelled from Switzerland, 1881, for revolutionary propaganda. He returned to Russia from England (where he had lived since 1886) after the February 1917 revolution. Kropotkin developed the theory of Communist Anarchism based upon the idea of mutual aid; he opposed all State power, and advocated the abolition of states, and of private property, and the transformation of mankind into a federation of mutual-aid communities. His chief following was in France. *See* his *The State, its Part in History*, 1898, 1943; *Fields, Factories and Workshops*, 1899, 1919; *Memoirs of a Revolutionist* (2 vols.), 1899, 1906; *Mutual Aid, a Factor of Evolution*, 1902, 1939; *Modern Science and Anarchism*, 1903, 1943; *The Orography of Asia*, 1904; *Russian Literature*, 1905, 1916; *Ethics: Origin and Development*, 1924; and his article 'Anarchism' in *Encyclopaedia Britannica*. *See also* A. J. Sack, *The Birth of the Russian Democracy*, New York, 1918; R. N. Baldwin (ed.), *Kropotkin's Revolutionary Pamphlets*, 1927; H. Read (ed.), *Kropotkin, Selections from his Writings*, 1942; T. G. Masaryk, *The Spirit of Russia*, vol. ii, 2nd ed., 1955; R. Hare, *Portraits of Russian Personalities between Reform and Revolution*, 1959; F. Venturi, *Roots of Revolution*, 1960.

Kryashin ('baptized'), Orthodox Christian Tatars who in 1926 numbered about 101,000. They are the descendants of Tatars who were compulsorily baptized partly in the 16th century (so-called 'Old Kryashins') and partly in the 18th century ('New Kryashins'). The majority of the New Kryashins returned to the Muslim faith in the mid 19th century.

Krylenko, Nikolay Vasil'yevich (1885–1940), active Bolshevik during the revolution of 1905 (q.v.), then an Anarcho-Syndicalist (*In Search of Orthodoxy*); he later rejoined the Bolshevik Party. During the Bolshevik seizure of power (*see* OCTOBER REVOLUTION) he played an active role, and was a Commissar for War in the first Bolshevik government. A warrant-officer at the time of the coup, he was soon afterwards appointed commander-in-chief of the Russian forces. In 1918 he became public prosecutor in the revolutionary tribunals, and in 1922 Deputy Commissar (later Commissar) of Justice of the R.S.F.S.R. and chief public prosecutor at the Supreme Court, taking part in the earlier show trials. He was appointed Commissar of Justice for the U.S.S.R. in 1936, but was arrested during the Great Purge (q.v.) in 1937 and probably died in an isolator (q.v.).

Krylov, Aleksey Nikolayevich (1863–1945), scientist, professor at the Naval Academy in St Petersburg, member of the Academy of Sciences from 1916, chairman of its group for physics and mathematics, 1929–34. His chief works, which brought him an international reputation, are concerned with the theory of the ship (calculations of stability, buoyancy, etc.); he also worked on the general theory of vibration and on approximate integration of differential equations with application to ballistics. He built the first calculating machine in Russia, an apparatus for integrating differential equations.

Krymskiy, Agafangel Yefimovich (1871–1941), outstanding Ukrainian philologist. Educated at the Lazarev Institute of Oriental Languages in Moscow and at Moscow University, he was professor at the Lazarev Institute 1898–1918, and member of the Ukrainian Academy of Sciences and head of its philology section from 1918 until the 1930's when he was dismissed and arrested as a 'bourgeois nationalist.' He published many works on the history and literature of Islamic peoples (including *History of Arabs and Arabic Literature, Lay and Ecclesiastical*, 2 vols., 1911–12; *History of Turkey and of its Literature*, 2 vols., 1910–16), as well as works on Slavonic philology and Ukrainian history.

Kuba, khanate in north-eastern Azerbaydzhan, semi-independent from Persia, established in the 18th century, later annexed by Russia and abolished in 1806.

Kuban' (ancient **Hypanis**), navigable river which rises at a height of 14,000 ft in Mt El'brus of the main Caucasian range and flows north-west, then west into the Sea of Azov, entering it through many arms which form an extensive delta. Length 600 m.; chief port Krasnodar. The Kuban' area has been largely populated by Cossacks since the 18th century.

Kuchka (Moguchaya Kuchka, Russian for 'The mighty handful,' sometimes known as 'the Five'). This term, arising from a eulogistic article by Stasov in 1867, was the name given to the group of nationalist composers Balakirev, Borodin, Cui, Musorgskiy and Rimsky-Korsakov, qq.v., who, professing their allegiance to Glinka, sought to create Russian music free from German academic traditions. In so doing they incurred the hostility of the brothers Rubinshteyn (q.v.), who, as ardent admirers of Western music, sought to propagate international art. Whereas the Rubinshteyns had received a thorough training in harmony and counterpoint, the Kuchka group were largely amateurs, Rimsky-Korsakov alone acquiring complete mastery of his art by unceasing effort. It was through Rimsky-Korsakov's work as a composer and a reviser of his associates' music (much of which was left incomplete) that Russian national music in the 19th century was able to make a valuable contribution to musical history. Tchaikovsky may be considered to occupy an intermediary position between the Kuchka and the 'Westerners.' The rise of 19th-century nationalism in music was brought about almost entirely by literary and political considerations, and the interest of composers in folklore and the historical past was neglected in their choice of patriotic and national themes. The 'mighty handful' were by no means unanimous in their artistic and musical outlook—a factor which makes their association all the more remarkable. *See* G. Abraham, *Studies in Russian Music*, 1935, and *On Russian Music*, 1939; G. Abraham and M. D. Calvocoressi, *Masters of Russian Music*, 1936.

Kudymkar, capital of the Komi-Permyak National Okrug in the Perm' Oblast (Urals), situated 90 m. north-west of Perm'. Population (1956) 20,000. It is a local cultural centre. Kudymkar was founded in the 16th century, became capital of the National Okrug in 1929 and a town in 1938.

Kulak ('fist'), epithet applied before 1917 to miserly merchants or to peasants who gained a hold over their fellows, e.g. village usurers. It was used in Communist propaganda after the 1917 revolution for all comparatively prosperous peasants, who were disfranchised and subjected to heavy taxation. *Kulak* became a word of abuse during the collectivization of agriculture (q.v.) for those who declined to join the collective farms, and the policy of 'liquidating the *kulaks* as a class' resulted in the disappearance of over 5,000,000 peasant households, the peasants being deported either to 'corrective labour camps' or as 'special settlers' (qq.v.).

Kuleshov, Lev Vladimirovich (*b.* 1899), film director, worked as assistant director before 1917. He filmed newsreels of the Red Army during the civil war, and formed a film production group devoted to the analysis of recognized film classics, from which he worked out new techniques of editing (*see further under* CINEMA). He taught at the Moscow Film Institute, 1921–30. His films include *Extraordinary Adventures of Mr West in the Land of the Bolsheviks*, 1924, and an adaptation of Jack London's story *By the Law*, 1926. Kuleshov's theories (e.g. that an actor should lose his identity and become an instrument of the director's will) were often carried to extremes, and in the late 1920's he was reprimanded by the authorities for 'formalism' (q.v.). He redeemed himself with *The Siberians*, 1940, depicting Stalin.

Kulibin, Ivan Petrovich (1735–1818), self-taught mechanic and inventor. Few of his many inventions found practical application, and he died destitute. All his life Kulibin endeavoured to build a *perpetuum mobile*.

Kulunda, steppe area in south-western Siberia, between the rivers Irtysh and Ob', the Altay Mountains and Baraba; it consists of about 35,000 sq. m. divided between the Altay Kray and the Kazakh Republic (Pavlodar Oblast). It is one of the chief agricultural regions of Western Siberia, with wheat growing and sheep and cattle breeding, and is now included in the Virgin Land Campaign (q.v.).

Kulyab, town in south-western Tadzhikistan, a local economic (cotton processing) and cultural centre. Population (1956) 20,000. It was the administrative centre of Kulyab Oblast, now abolished, from 1939 to 1950.

Kumyks, Turkic-speaking people, descended from the Cumans, who live in the Daghestan Autonomous Republic of Northern Caucasus. They inhabit the lowland along the Caspian shore and number (1959) 135,000. From the 15th century the Kumyks had an independent state named after its capital Tarki (near Makhachkala); they came under Russian suzerainty in 1559 and were finally annexed in 1784. Kumyk literature dates from the 19th century. See W. Kolarz, *Russia and her Colonies*, 1952.

Kungur, town in the Perm' Oblast (Urals), situated on the Perm'–Sverdlovsk railway 55 m. south-east of Perm'. Population (1959) 65,000. It has engineering (oil industry equipment), leather and saw-milling industries, and is the centre of an agricultural area; near by is a famous stalactite cave. Kungur was founded as a fortress in 1648 and has long been known as a centre of the leather industry. One of its technical schools was founded in 1877.

Kuntsevo, town 7 m. west of Moscow, absorbed into the city area in 1960. Population (1959) 128,000 (1939, 61,000). It has been known since the 15th century, and is now an industrial (aircraft and woollen industries) and residential suburb of the capital.

Kurchatov, Igor' Vasil'yevich (1903–60), physicist, professor at Leningrad University and the Physico-Technical Institute there; member of the Academy of Sciences and of its presidium and director of its Institute of Atomic Energy; a party member since 1948. He was educated at the Tauric University in Simferopol' and taught at Baku and Leningrad. From the 1930's he studied nuclear chain reactions under neutron bombardment and artificial radioactivity; he developed a theory of nuclear isomerism. Kurchatov was a leading figure in the field of nuclear physics and directed the utilization of nuclear energy for both military and peaceful purposes. See J. G. Crowther, *Soviet Science*, 1936; A. Kramish, *Atomic Energy in the Soviet Union*, 1960.

Kurds, see IRANIANS.

Kurgan: 1. Oblast of the R.S.F.S.R., situated in the south of the West Siberian lowland, traversed by the River Tobol; it is a region of wooded steppe with black earth soil and a continental climate. Area 27,400 sq. m.; population (1959) 1,002,000 (33 per cent urban), Russians (since the 17th century) and some Tatars. The oblast has wheat cultivation, dairy farming, sheep raising and extensive food and varied engineering industries.

2. Administrative, economic and cultural centre of the oblast, situated on the River Tobol, the Trans-Siberian Railway and the oil pipeline from Bashkiria. Population (1959) 145,000 (1914, 25,000; 1939, 53,000). It has flour-milling, butter (since 1893), meat and engineering (agricultural machinery) industries, and is an important railway junction. Kurgan was founded in 1653 and became a town in 1782; until 1917 it was a major centre for trade in cattle and butter.

Kuriles (Japanese **Chishima**), chain of thirty-six islands in the North Pacific between Kamchatka and Hokkaido, belonging to the Sakhalin Oblast. Total area 5,700 sq. m.; population about 15,000,

Russians and some Ainu (before 1945 Japanese), who engage in fishing and sea-animal hunting. The chief settlement is Kuril'sk on Iturup Island. From the 18th century the Kuriles were Russian, from 1875 Japanese, and Russian once more since 1945 in accordance with the agreement reached at the Yalta Conference.

Kurisches Haff, bay of the Baltic Sea off the coast of the Kaliningrad Oblast (former East Prussia) and Lithuania. It extends along the coast south of Klaipeda for more than fifty miles and is separated from the open sea by the Kurische Nehrung, a narrow sandy ridge. It opens into the sea in the north by a narrow channel.

Kurland, historical name of the part of Latvia which lies south of the Western Dvina. The area belonged to the Livonian Knights, from 1561 was a duchy under Polish suzerainty, and was Russian, 1795–1918.

Kurnakov, Nikolay Semënovich (1860–1941), chemist, professor at the Mining, Electrotechnical and Polytechnical institutes in St Petersburg, member of the Academy of Sciences from 1913. During the First World War Kurnakov took an active part in the setting up and work of the Commission for the Study of Russia's Natural Resources. In 1918–22 he founded several research centres which were combined in 1934 into the Institute of General and Inorganic Chemistry of the Academy of Sciences, which he headed until his death. Kurnakov's own work was concerned with the study of complex combinations—alloys and solutions—and he was a pioneer of physico-chemical analysis (*Introduction to Physico-Chemical Analysis*, 4th ed., 1940). He also studied salt resources and discovered the Solikamsk (q.v.) potassium salt deposits.

Kuropatkin, Aleksey Nikolayevich (1848–1925), general who joined the army in 1864. He was chief of staff to Skobelev (q.v.) in the Russo-Turkish war of 1877. In 1897 he became commander-in-chief in the Caucasus and in the following year Minister of War. He was commander-in-chief in Manchuria on the outbreak of the Russo-Japanese war (q.v.) and met with a series of defeats which culminated in the disaster of Mukden, whereupon he resigned and was replaced by General Linevich. He commanded the northern front in the First World War until his appointment in 1916 as Governor of Turkestan. Kuropatkin published several works on the Balkan and Central Asian campaigns, and a history of the Russo-Japanese war in which he admitted his own mistakes (*The Russian Army and the Japanese War*, 1909). See *Memoirs of Count Witte* (trans. A. Yarmolinsky), New York, 1921.

Kursk: 1. Oblast of the R.S.F.S.R., situated on the Central Russian upland in the black earth belt; there are large deposits of iron ore (known as the Kursk Magnetic Anomaly) and phosphorite. Area 11,500 sq. m.; population (1959) 1,481,000 (20 per cent urban), Russians and some Ukrainians. Wheat, sugar-beet, hemp and sunflowers are cultivated, dairy farming, pig and poultry raising and beekeeping are carried on, and there are extensive food and some engineering industries. Kursk belonged to the principality of Chernigov in the Middle Ages, and later to Novgorod-Severskiy; it became Lithuanian in 1362 and Muscovite in 1503. In 1941–3 it was occupied by the Germans, and it was the scene of an important battle in 1943.

2. Administrative, economic and cultural centre of the oblast, the oldest town in the central black earth region, situated 125 m. west of Voronezh. Population (1959) 203,000 (1914, 83,000; 1926, 82,000; 1939, 120,000). It has engineering, chemical, food, clothing and shoe industries, and is an important railway junction. Kursk has been known since 1095, became the capital of a small principality in the 12th century, was destroyed by the Tatars in 1240, ro ootablished as part of the Muscovite southern defence line in the 16th century, and became a provincial capital in 1797. Its industrial development dates from the 1930's; before then it was an important commercial centre.

Kusevitskiy, Sergey Aleksandrovich (1874–1959), double-bass virtuoso, conductor and composer who made his début as conductor in 1907 and founded a music-publishing firm with his wife in 1909, profits from which went to help Russian composers. Between 1910 and 1918 he established the Kusevitskiy Symphony Orchestra in Russia, which toured extensively. In 1917 he was appointed director of State symphony orchestras and next year director of the Moscow Bolshoi Theatre. From 1920 to 1924 he conducted in Britain and Europe, and from 1921 till 1928 organized and conducted the Concerts Koussevitzky in Paris. He was conductor of the Boston Symphony Orchestra, 1924–49. Among his many services to music, Kusevitskiy did much to bring about the recognition of Skryabin. As a conductor his work achieved international renown, and his programmes often included contemporary music. He was also the publisher of Stravinsky.

Kuskova, Yekaterina Dmitriyevna (1869–1959), publicist and social worker. She was one of the few genuine Economists (*see* ECONOMISM) and the author of their 'Credo' (q.v.). In 1905 she took a leading part in the formation of the Union of Unions an association of professional bodies from which the Constitutional Democratic Party sprang—but she soon left active politics and devoted herself mainly to the co-operative movement. In 1921 she was one of the moving spirits in Maksim Gor'kiy's famine relief committee, whose appeals to the world public resulted in the Nansen and Hoover relief missions. She was expelled from Russia in 1922, together with a large group of leading intellectuals, and lived in Prague and after the Second World War in Geneva. Until her last days she was active as a journalist, advocating a peaceful and gradual evolution of the Soviet regime.

Kuskovo, former town, a suburb of Moscow, which was fused with Perovo in the 1930's and absorbed into the Moscow city area in 1960. From the early 16th century it was an estate of the Cheremetev family, and has an 18th-century summer residence (now a museum) with a palatial manor-house, a park and a church.

Kustanay: 1. Oblast of Kazakhstan, situated in the west of northern Kazakhstan bordering on the southern Urals, traversed by the River Tobol and the South and Middle Siberian Railways; it is mostly black earth steppe with large iron ore and lignite deposits. Area 75,400 sq. m.; population (1959) 705,000 (27 per cent urban), mostly Russians and Ukrainians (two-thirds of the population), also Kazakhs and some Tatars, Mordva, Germans and Koreans. It is one of the main areas of the Virgin Land Campaign (q.v.), with wheat cultivation, cattle raising and food industries. A large iron ore mining and dressing plant is under construction. The area, which was inhabited by the Kazakhs of the Middle Hundred, was annexed to Russia in 1740.

2. Administrative, economic and cultural centre of the oblast, situated on the River Tobol and the new Middle Siberian Railway. Population (1959) 86,000 (1939, 34,000), mostly Russians. It has varied food and light industries, and is an important transportation centre. Kustanay was founded in 1879 by Russians.

Kutaisi, town in Transcaucasia, the industrial and cultural centre of western Georgia, situated on the River Rioni. Population (1959) 128,000 (1914, 57,000; 1926, 48,000; 1939, 78,000), mostly Georgians. It has engineering (mining equipment, lorries), silk, woollen, wine and tobacco industries; in the vicinity there is a hydro-electric station and coal- and barite-mining. The town has a theatre (founded 1861) and medieval architectural monuments. Kutaisi was founded in antiquity, and since the 8th century has been almost continuously the capital of western Georgia (*see* ABKHAZIA; IMERETIA), frequently destroyed by invaders. It became Russian in 1810, and was the administrative centre of Kutaisi province.

Kutuzov, Mikhail Illarionovich (1745–1813), field marshal, commanded the Russian forces in the Russo-Turkish war in 1811 and the Patriotic War against Napoleon, 1812–13, surrendering Moscow but subsequently driving Napoleon from Russia. He was widely popular among the people, but disliked by Alexander I.

Kuybyshev (until 1935 **Samara**): 1. Oblast of the R.S.F.S.R., situated on the middle Volga, largely on its left bank, in the black earth belt; there are large deposits of oil, natural gas, oil shale, phosphorite and sulphur. Area 21,000 sq. m.; population (1959) 2,257,000 (62 per cent urban), chiefly Russians (since the 16th century), also Tatars. There are engineering, oil extraction and processing, saw-milling and varied food industries; wheat and sunflowers are cultivated, and cattle and pigs raised. A hydro-electric station (2,100,000 kw., the largest in Europe) was constructed here, 1950–6. Principal towns: Kuybyshev, Syzran', Chapayevsk, Novo-kuybyshevsk. The area was annexed by Muscovy as part of the Kazan' Khanate in 1552.

2. Administrative, economic and cultural centre of the oblast, one of the main industrial centres of the U.S.S.R., situated on the Volga and the main Moscow–Siberia railway. Population (1959) 806,000 (second on the Volga, eighth in the U.S.S.R.; 1914, 146,000; 1926, 176,000; 1939, 390,000). It has large engineering industries (machine tools, automobile and tractor parts, boilers, cables, precision instruments, equipment for food, light, chemical and shipbuilding industries), as well as oil-processing, saw-milling, food and light industries. It has several higher educational establishments, and an old-established theatre (1851).

Kuybyshev was founded as a fortress in 1586, became a town in 1688, provincial administrative centre in 1851 and the seat of the anti-Bolshevik Committee of Members of the Constituent Assembly in 1918; many Soviet government departments and foreign diplomatic missions had their headquarters here during the Second World

War. Industrial development began in the late 19th century, when the town became an important centre of the flour-milling and grain trade; the metal-working industry dates from the First World War. Industry expanded rapidly during the 1930's, and especially during the Second World War with the evacuation to Kuybyshev of many factories from western parts of the country, and its industrial position was further raised by the construction of the Volga hydro-electric station. A university was founded in 1918 but abolished in 1927.

Kuybyshev, Valerian Vladimirovich (1888–1935), Communist. The son of an army officer, he was educated at an army cadet school, joined the Bolsheviks in 1904 and from 1906 was a professional revolutionary. Periods of underground work, mostly in Siberia, alternated with prison and banishment. After the February revolution (q.v.) in 1917 he headed the Bolshevik organization in Samara and organized the Bolshevik seizure of power there. A Left Communist (q.v.) in 1918, he spent the civil war as a high-ranking political commissar in the Red Army, taking a leading part in 1919 in the re-establishment of Soviet power in Turkestan. In 1920 he was transferred to trade union work, then to economic, and in 1922 to party management (member and secretary of the Central Committee). From 1923 until his death Kuybyshev was deputy chairman of the Council of People's Commissars, simultaneously heading the united Central Control Commission (*see* COMMITTEE OF PARTY CONTROL) and the Commissariat of Worker-Peasant Inspection (q.v.), 1923–6, succeeding Dzerzhinskiy as chairman of the Supreme Council of National Economy in 1926, and Krzhizhanovskiy as chairman of Gosplan (q.v.) in 1930. Kuybyshev took Stalin's side in the inner-party struggle after Lenin's death, and from 1927 was a member of the Politburo. At the show trial of the 'Anti-Soviet Bloc of Rightists and Trotskiyites' (q.v.) in 1938 the defendants were accused of having murdered Kuybyshev, but this contention was quietly dropped in 1958. *See* L. Schapiro, *The Communist Party of the Soviet Union*, 1960; R. W. Davies, 'Some Soviet Economic Controllers, iii: Kuibyshev,' *Soviet Studies*, vol. xii, No. 1, July 1960.

Kuznetsk, town in the Penza Oblast (central Russia), on the Penza–Kuybyshev railway about 60 m. east of Penza. Population (1959) 57,000. It is a major centre of the sheepskin clothing industry, has some engineering (textile machinery) and is a local cultural centre. Kuznetsk has been known since the 17th century and became a town in 1780.

Kuznetsk Basin (abbreviation **Kuzbas**), largest coal-mining basin in the U.S.S.R., and one of the largest in the world, situated in the Kemerovo Oblast (southern Siberia) between the two ranges which branch off north and north-west from the highlands of the North Altay—the Kuznetsk Alatau in the east and the Salair range in the west; it is traversed by the River Tom'. The area of the coal-bearing deposits is 10,000 sq. m., and the whole industrial area of the basin is 27,000 sq. m.; the deposits of coal are estimated at 450,000,000,000 tons, and there are also deposits of iron ore in Shoria and of non-ferrous metals in the Salair range.

Local tribes had known the art of ironworking since prehistoric

times; the first Russian iron-smelting works was built in 1697, and
lead and silver smelting began in the 1780's. Coal deposits were discovered in 1721 and first used for iron smelting in 1827; industrial
coal-mining began in 1851 and expanded with the building of the
Trans-Siberian Railway and the First World War. Great industrial
development began in 1930 when the Kuznetsk Basin became a part
of the Ural-Kuznetsk combine; during the 1930's large iron and steel,
zinc, and chemical plants and power-stations were built, and the
Kuznetsk Basin became the country's second coal-supplier after
Donbas; after the Urals it was the chief industrial base of the
country's war effort during the Second World War, old industries
being much expanded and new ones (aluminium, engineering) being
developed. Since the war industrial expansion has continued; the
iron and steel industry was gradually converted to the use of the
Shorian and nearby Khakas ores instead of those from the Urals, but
since these deposits are not large further expansion of the industry
is to be based upon ores from eastern Siberia. *See also* KEMEROVO.

Kyakhta, town in the Buryat Autonomous Republic (south-
eastern Siberia), situated 144 m. south of Ulan-Ude close to the
Mongolian frontier. Population (1956) 10,000 (1936, 12,000), Russians.
Kyakhta was founded in 1728 as a suburb of Troitskosavsk, which
was also later named Kyakhta. Until the 1860's it was the centre of
the Russo-Chinese tea trade.

Kypchaks, *see* CUMANS.

Kyzyl (formerly **Belotsarsk**, then **Kem-Bel'der**), administrative,
economic and cultural centre of the Tuva Autonomous Oblast
(southern Siberia), situated on the Yenisey and connected by a highway with Minusinsk. Population (1959) 34,000 (1939, 10,000), mainly
Russians. Processing the agricultural products of the area provides
some industry. Kyzyl was founded by Russians in 1914.

Kzyl-Orda: 1. Oblast in southern Kazakhstan astride the lower
course of the Syr-Dar'ya River, adjacent to the Aral Sea, traversed by
the Orenburg–Tashkent railway; apart from the Syr-Dar'ya oasis it is
desert. Area 89,600 sq. m.; population (1959) 329,000 (47 per cent
urban), Kazakhs (since the 17th century), Russians (since 1847),
Koreans (since 1929), also some Ukrainians, Tatars and Uzbeks. Rice,
cotton and melons are cultivated, sheep and camels kept, and there is
fishing in the Aral Sea; there are salt works in the region. The lower
Syr-Dar'ya area was one of the oldest centres of civilization in
Central Asia, but was destroyed by Genghis Khan's hordes. From the
early 19th century the area belonged to the Kokand Khanate and it
was annexed to Russia in 1864.

2. (**Ak-mechet'** till 1853, **Perovsk** till 1917, then again **Ak-Mechet'**
till 1926). Administrative, economic and cultural centre of the oblast,
situated on the Syr-Dar'ya and the Orenburg–Tashkent railway.
Population (1959) 66,000 (1939, 47,000), Russians, Kazakhs and
Koreans. It has food industries (rice and meat processing). Kzyl-
Orda was founded in the early 19th century as a Kokand fortress,
was captured by the Russians in 1853, was capital of the Kazakh
Autonomous Republic, 1926–9, and has been provincial centre since
1938.

L

Labour Book, introduced in 1938, is required for every worker or employee applying for a new job. It contains a full record of his previous employment filled in by the management. On appointment the labour book must be surrendered to the new management and is kept in the office. In fact scarcity of labour often prompts managers to disregard the regulations concerning labour books. *See* H. Schwartz, *Russia's Soviet Economy*, New York, 2nd ed., 1954; W. W. Kulski, *The Soviet Regime*, Syracuse, 1954.

Labour Day, *see* WORK-DAY UNIT.

Labour Discipline is regulated in each enterprise by rules which are principally based upon decisions of the party and Government taken in 1938–41. Infringement of the rules can be punished by reprimands, transfer to lower-paid work or dismissal, while failings that result in material loss to the enterprise (e.g. producing sub-standard work, wasting scarce materials) are punishable by fines. The worker has the right to appeal against such punishments, either to the Labour Disputes Commission (*see* LABOUR DISPUTES) or to the courts. Between 1940 and 1955 absenteeism and lateness were treated as crimes which were punished by up to three months' forced labour at the place of employment.

Labour Disputes are in most cases settled either by conciliation or through the courts. Conciliation is effected by the Commission of Labour Disputes, composed of equal numbers of representatives of management and of trade unions; it is bound to consider a dispute within five days. If the worker or employee is dissatisfied with the Commission's decision (or if it is unable to reach a decision) he takes his case to the trade union committee, and if the latter's decision is unsatisfactory to either management or worker the case may then go to the courts. If the management side is dissatisfied with the Commission's decision the case may go straight to the courts. Outside the competence of this whole procedure are questions of appointments, dismissals and disciplinary measures concerning higher-level employees, salary and wage scales, policy decisions on redundancy, calculation of seniority for pension and other rights, allocation of living space, etc.; all these are dealt with administratively. *See also* LABOUR DISCIPLINE; STRIKES; TRADE UNIONS. *See* V. Gsovski and K. Grzybowski (eds.), *Government, Law and Courts in the Soviet Union and Eastern Europe*, vol. ii, 1959.

Labour Law is treated as a separate branch of law, regulating the employment of wage and salary earners and labour relations of members of producers' co-operatives. The provisions of the labour law cover procedures of appointment, its termination, collective contracts (*see* COLLECTIVE AGREEMENTS), working hours and holidays, wages (q.v.), safety measures, labour discipline (q.v.), procedures for solving conflicts (*see* LABOUR DISPUTES) and social insurance (*see* SOCIAL SERVICES). Although the law treats employment primarily as a contractual relationship, the multiplicity of normative provisions in fact leaves very little room for negotiated terms of the labour contract. Freedom to enter into or terminate a labour contract is restricted (*see* FORCED LABOUR), and several forms of forced labour (including the labour relations of *kolkhoz* members) fall altogether outside the labour law. Restrictions on the employment of women and children (qq.v.) are frequently disregarded.

Modern labour legislation started in Russia in the 1880's, when employment of women and children was regulated and factory inspectors were introduced. The working day was limited to 11½ hours in 1897. Trade unions were legalized early in the 20th century, and obligatory insurance was introduced in 1912. A Ministry of Labour was set up after the February revolution (q.v.) of 1917. An eight-hour day was decreed immediately after the October revolution (q.v.) and in 1918 the first Code of Labour Laws was adopted, mainly concerned with the protection of workers in private employment. It was replaced in 1922 by a new code which is still in force, though many of its provisions have been superseded by later legislation. A seven-hour day (six in hazardous occupations) and thirty-five-hour week (with one free day in six) were introduced in 1928, after a brief experiment with a 'continuous working week' with one free day in five. The Commissariat of Labour was abolished in 1933 and some if its functions handed over to the trade unions. Throughout the 1930's legislation was increasingly directed towards tightening labour discipline and the elimination of all vestiges of employees' influence on the conditions of their work. This process culminated in the decree of 1940 which reverted to the eight-hour day and forty-eight-hour week, and made leaving a job without permission, absenteeism and late-coming criminal offences punishable by forced labour at the place of work. This harsh decree remained in force (except for the war years, with an eleven-hour day and almost complete militarization of labour) until 1956, when employees were, as a general rule, allowed to leave their jobs with a fortnight's notice and the working week was shortened by two hours. Further reduction of working hours is in progress. The draft of the new all-Union Fundamentals of Labour Legislation, instead of the obsolescent Labour Code, was published in 1959. *See* V. Gsovski, *Soviet Civil Law*, Ann Arbor, 1948; S. M. Schwarz, *Labor in the Soviet Union*, New York, 1952; V. Gsovski and K. Grzybowski (eds.), *Government, Law and Courts in the Soviet Union and Eastern Europe*, vol. ii, 1959.

Labour Reserves, system of vocational training (q.v.) of skilled workers which was introduced in 1940 on the basis of the compulsory call-up of boys (1947 also girls) for apprenticeships in trade schools and other vocational schools of different levels. The compulsory call-up was abolished in 1955. Training and uniform (and in the case of boarders also board and lodging) were free, but after completing their training the young workers had no choice of work and were often directed to jobs in outlying parts of the country. The schools of the

Labour Reserves system were converted into (fee-paying) vocational technical schools after the educational reform of 1958. *See* S. M. Schwarz, *Labor in the Soviet Union*, New York, 1952; N. De Witt, *Soviet Professional Manpower*, Washington, D.C., 1955; A. G. Korol, *Soviet Education for Science and Technology*, New York, 1957.

Labour School, name given to all schools of general education during the 1920's. The concept of the 'Unified Labour School' involved a departure from the traditional differentiation between elementary and secondary schools (held to have reflected the division of society into exploiting and exploited classes) and the implementation of the 'labour principle,' that is, polytechnical education (q.v.) and the combining of instruction with productive work. The idea was abandoned in the 1930's, but has been revived in a modified form since 1952, though the term Labour School is not now used. *See also* BLONSKIY; EDUCATION; SHATSKIY.

Ladoga, Lake, largest lake in Europe, with the exception of the Caspian Sea, situated in north-western Russia, lat. 59° 56′ to 61° 46′ N., long. 29° 53′ to 32° 50′ E., bordering upon the Leningrad Oblast and the Karelian Autonomous Republic. Area 7,230 sq. m.; maximum depth 780 ft. The chief inflowing rivers are the Volkhov, the Svir' and the Vuoksa, and the outlet is by way of the Neva into the Gulf of Finland. Lake Ladoga is subject to violent storms, and a chain of navigable canals has therefore been constructed round the southern shores. There is a famous monastery on the Valaam Island. In 1939–1940, and again in 1944, there was much fighting for the lake between Russia and Finland.

Lakes, *see* INLAND WATERS.

Land. According to the constitution all land is State-owned (*see* AGRARIAN REVOLUTION). It is used by the State directly or allocated for use to *kolkhozes* and other co-operatives (qq.v.) or to individuals: to individual peasants (*see* PEASANTS), for private houses (*see* HOUSING) or for personal cultivation on a small scale by workers and employees in some enterprises. Ground rent is officially considered inapplicable in a socialist society, as according to the Marxist theory it is a category of the feudal and capitalist modes of production. However, the absence of rent grossly distorts all economic calculations, and since Stalin's death some economists have suggested its reintroduction in a disguised form.

Of the total land area of 2,233·3 million hectares in 1958, 763·0 were used by the *kolkhozes* (including 6·6 million for the personal plots of *kolkhoz* members), 267·3 million by *sovkhozes* and other State-owned agricultural enterprises, 1·7 million hectares were used by the small cultivation of workers and employees, 0·1 million by other groups (chiefly individual peasants); the State Land Fund comprised 261·5 million hectares and the Forest Fund 887·3 million; all other users of land (industry, towns, etc.) took up 52·4 million hectares. Of the total land area, 60·1 million hectares was agricultural land. *See also* AGRICULTURE; COLLECTIVIZATION OF AGRICULTURE; PEASANTS; TIMBER INDUSTRY.

Landau, Lev Davidovich (*b.* 1908), physicist, member of the Academy of Sciences. Educated at Leningrad University, he has been working in theoretical physics at the Academy of Sciences' Institute of Physical Problems in Moscow since 1937. He developed a thermodynamic theory of so-called phase transitions of second order in solid bodies, showing their connection with qualitative changes in symmetry of the body during transition; and a macroscopic theory of superfluidity phenomenon of liquid helium, predicting the possibility of sound wave diffusion in liquid helium at two different speeds. *See* J. G. Crowther, *Soviet Science*, 1936; L. D. Landau and E. M. Lifshitz, *Quantum Mechanics: Non-Relativistic Theory*, 1958, and *Statistical Physics*, 1958.

Lappo-Danilevskiy, Aleksandr Sergeyevich (1863–1919), historian and philosopher. Educated at St Petersburg University, he taught there from 1890 and became a member of the Academy of Sciences in 1899. His range of scholarship was very wide (*Scythian Antiquities*, 1887; *The Organization of Direct Taxation in Muscovy in the 17th Century*, 1890; *Researches in the History of Peasant Bondage*, 1901), but his main achievement was in methodology, particularly in the theory of the treatment of sources (*Methodology of History*, 2 vols., 1910–13; 2nd ed., 1923). He took part in the revival of critical idealism (q.v.) at the beginning of the century and contributed to the symposium *Problems of Idealism*, 1902. He died as a result of the privations of War Communism (q.v.). *See* his 'The Development of Science and Learning in Russia' in J. D. Duff's (ed.) *Russian Realities and Problems*, 1917; A. G. Mazour, *Modern Russian Historiography*, 2nd ed., 1958.

Lapps in Russia live in Murmansk Oblast. They make up only about 5 per cent of the whole Lapp people, numbering in 1959 about 1,800. Their chief occupation is reindeer keeping. Russian Lapps have been Christians since the 16th century, when the Pechenga monastery was founded for their conversion.

Latgalians, distinct branch of the Latvian people inhabiting the eastern part of Latvia, speaking a dialect of their own, and numbering about 300,000. They differ from Latvians proper in that for several centuries they were under Polish rule and are therefore Catholics and not Lutherans; Russian influence is also noticeable in Latgalia. The official policy, both in independent Latvia and since its incorporation into the Soviet Union, has been to assimilate Latgalians with Latvians proper, though in recent years some latitude has been allowed in Latgalian folklore, etc.

Latvia (Latvian **Latvija**), Union Republic of the U.S.S.R., situated in the north-west adjacent to the Riga Gulf of the Baltic Sea, traversed by the Western Dvina; it is mostly lowland, with many lakes and marshes and partially covered with mixed forests. Area 24,800 sq. m.; population (1959) 2,093,000 (56 per cent urban), mostly Latvians (62 per cent) and Russians (27 per cent); before the war also Germans and Jews. There are diverse engineering, food, light and timber industries; grain, flax and potatoes are cultivated, and dairy farming and pig breeding carried on. Principal towns: Riga (capital), Liepaja, Daugavpils, Jelgava. (For history *see* BALTIC PROVINCES; BALTIC STATES). During Latvia's independence, 1918–40, its heavy industries and seaports declined owing to the loss of the Russian market, but agriculture flourished with the export of butter and bacon to Britain and Germany. Independent Latvia was first a parliamentary republic with many parties, but in 1934 the Prime Minister Ulmanis set up a dictatorial nationalist regime after a coup. *See* A. Spekke, *Latvia and the Baltic Problem*, 1955; V. Gsovski and K. Grzybowski (eds.), *Government, Law and Courts in the Soviet Union and Eastern Europe*, vol. i, 1959.

Latvians, Baltic-speaking people inhabiting Latvia, and living also in various parts of Russia, particularly Siberia, as a result of colonization before 1917 and deportations since 1940. They are mostly Lutheran Protestants, though the Latgalian (q.v.) minority are Catholics, and number (1959) 1·4 million. The Latvians are the indigenous inhabitants of the area, but have always been under the influence and domination of Germans, Scandinavians or Russians, and only in the 19th century did a Latvian national consciousness and movement develop; the latter was directed primarily against the German landowners, and during the 1905 revolution Latvia was one of the main areas of peasant uprisings. The Bolshevik Party had a comparatively strong following among the Latvians, and many Latvian Communists were prominent in Russia after 1917. *See* W. K. Matthews, *A Century of Latvian Poetry, an Anthology*, 1957.

Lavrent'yev, Mikhail Alekseyevich (*b.* 1900), mathematician, member of the U.S.S.R. (since 1946) and Ukrainian (since 1939) Academies of Sciences; he has taught at Moscow and headed various mathematical research institutions (including the Institute of Precision Mechanics and Calculation Techniques of the Academy of Sciences, 1950-3); he joined the party in 1952. In 1957 Lavrent'yev suggested the establishment and became chairman of the Siberian division of the U.S.S.R. Academy of Sciences. He has made a new geometric approach to the theory of functions of complex variables, advancing his own principles—the 'Adherence Principle,' a metric study of the correspondence of boundaries in a conformal mapping; properties of functions represented by convergent series of polynominals, etc. He also developed the theory of quasi-conform mappings which leads to geometric methods for solutions of many problems in mathematics and mathematical physics, worked on the mathematics of continuous media, etc.

Lavrov, Pëtr Lavrovich (1823–1900), professor of mathematics, thinker and revolutionary, a leader of the Populists. His special interests were ethics and the history of thought; he contributed to liberal journals on sociology, philosophy and anthropology and edited the *Encyclopaedic Dictionary*, 1861–4. Banished in 1866 he emigrated in 1870, edited the revolutionary journal *Forward* until 1872, and joined the First International. Lavrov developed the philosophy of history (*Historical Letters*, 1868–9) which predominated in later Populist thought. See *Lettres historiques*, Paris, 1903. *See also* A. J. Sack, *The Birth of the Russian Democracy*, New York, 1918; J. M. Meijer, *Knowledge and Revolution*, Assen, Netherlands, 1955; T. G. Masaryk, *The Spirit of Russia*, (2nd ed.), vol. ii, 1955; R. Hare, *Portraits of Russian Personalities between Reform and Revolution*, 1959; F. Venturi, *Roots of Revolution*, 1960.

Law, *see* LEGAL SYSTEM, and entries on separate branches of law.

Lawyers are divided into 'advocates' who advise and represent individual clients in civil and criminal cases, and 'juridical consultants' who advise and represent State enterprises and institutions. Advocates, of whom there are about 18,000, are considered as practising a liberal profession and are organized into colleges on a territorial basis, supervised by the Ministries of Justice and by party organizations within the colleges. Their remuneration is based on fees graded according to a fixed scale. Juridical consultants, whose number is estimated at about 50,000, are State employees, but otherwise they are not very different from advocates specializing in civil cases (*see* ARBITRATION). Lawyers are a modern creation in Russia, brought to life by the judicial reform of 1864 (*see* GREAT REFORMS), replacing the traditional solicitors. Like the whole new legal system of which it was a part, the profession was remarkably successful and soon developed high standards and a corporate consciousness. Its outstanding representatives (Koni, Maklakov, Muromtsev, Spaso-vich, qq.v., K. K. Arsen'yev, F. N. Plevako, etc.) enjoyed great respect as national figures. The prevalence of the theory of the 'withering away of law' in the period of the 'Dictatorship of the Proletariat' (q.v.) and the obvious incompatibility of Stalin's terror with respect for the law combined to produce the attitude of scarcely concealed hostility towards lawyers on the part of the authorities. Their income and social standing are low in comparison with the pre-1917 situation and with the position of other professional groups, except school-teachers. Nevertheless they try to uphold the traditions of the profession, and in cases which are not considered political by the authorities the advocates can and do genuinely act in the interests of their clients. *See* V. Gsovski, *Soviet Civil Law*, Ann Arbor, 1948; V. Gsovski and K. Grzybowski (eds.), *Government, Law and Courts in the Soviet Union and Eastern Europe*, vol. i, 1959.

Lazarev, Pëtr Petrovich (1878–1942), physicist, professor at the Moscow Higher Technical School, member of the Academy of Sciences. He worked in molecular physics and photochemistry, developed the ionic theory of nervous irritation and guided the study of the Kursk Magnetic Anomaly. He is regarded as the father of bio-physics in Russia.

Lebedev, Pëtr Nikolayevich (1866–1912), physicist. Educated at the Moscow Higher Technical School and at Strasbourg and Berlin universities (at both of which he was a pupil of Kundt), he was professor at Moscow University from 1900, founding the first big physical school in Russia. His own research was connected with Maxwell's electromagnetic theory, and his main achievement was a brilliant experimental proof of the pressure of light on solids (1901) and gases (1910).

Left Communists, participants in the Left Opposition (q.v.) of 1918 led by Bukharin and including Dzerzhinskiy, Bubnov, Kuybyshev and other leading figures. They started by opposing the conclusion of a peace treaty with Germany, but went on to criticize many aspects of Lenin's policy. They failed to carry the Bolshevik Central Committee with them, and the onset of the civil war temporarily put an end to factional strife among the Bolsheviks. *See* L. Schapiro, *The Origin of the Communist Autocracy*, 1955, and *The Communist Party of the Soviet Union*, 1960.

Left Opposition, or **Left Deviation,** generally, in Communist parties and in the Communist International, that more radical trend which opposes the policy of the dominant group and emphasizes revolutionary principles or the proletarian nature of the party. In Russia the principal Left Oppositions were those led by Bukharin in 1918 (*see* LEFT COMMUNISTS), by Trotskiy in 1923, by Zinov'yev and Kamenev in 1925, and the 'combined opposition' of 1927. *See* F. Borkenau, *The Communist International*, 1938; L. Schapiro, *The Origin of the Communist Autocracy*, 1955, and *The Communist Party of the Soviet Union*, 1960.

Legal Marxists, that group of economists and sociologists which during the 1890's advocated and developed Marxist views in the legal (as opposed to underground) press. It included P. B. Struve, Tugan-Baranovskiy, Bulgakov and Berdyayev. They, as well as Plekhanov and Lenin, popularized Marxism in Russia and largely succeeded in converting the socialist intelligentsia from Populism. *See* D. W. Treadgold, *Lenin and his Rivals*, 1955.

Legal Reform, of December 1958, introduced new Fundamentals of Criminal Legislation, Law on Criminal Responsibility for State Crimes, Law on Criminal Responsibility for Military Crimes, new Judiciary Acts (*see* COURTS OF LAW) and new Fundamentals of Criminal Procedure. The very unsatisfactory state of the legislation (*see* CODES), much of which was obsolete, had already in the 1930's led to preliminary work on a reform. However, the Great Purge (q.v.), the war and the political conditions of the last years of Stalin's rule prevented early completion of this work. After Stalin's death an additional reason for reform was the official desire to dissociate the new regime from the abuses of the Stalin era (*see* SOCIALIST LEGALITY). The 1958 reform eliminated the institution of analogy (q.v.); laid down the exclusive jurisdiction of regular courts in criminal cases, eliminating the special courts of the security organs (*see* TROYKA); stressed that *corpus delicti* must be proved for conviction; narrowed the concept of complicity, raised the age of criminal responsibility (*see* CHILDREN; JUVENILE DELINQUENCY) and shortened the maximum terms of imprisonment (*see* PENAL SYSTEM); redefined the concept of proof, only the factual data obtained by the court by various means being now termed proofs and not the means of obtaining them (such as the statements of the defendant) as well; legalized the status of a suspect in criminal procedure; slightly extended the rights of the accused (counsel may now be brought in after the completion of preliminary investigation, and not after the committal for trial as before); and reintroduced the institution of lay prosecutors and lay 'defence counsel' abolished in the late 1930's. During the discussion which preceded the reform the more liberal-minded jurists (e.g. Strogovich, q.v.) suggested more radical steps, and in particular the reintroduction of trial by jury, of the competitive trial instead of the inquisitorial, as well as a clear statement of presumption of innocence (i.e. in fact habeas corpus), but these suggestions were explicitly rejected as 'bourgeois.' Dealing with State crimes, the reform abolished special responsibility of a traitor's or defector's family (even family members ignorant of the act had previously been liable to banishment to 'remote parts of Siberia'), narrowed the definition of a terroristic act, and limited responsibility for betrayal of State secrets to officials and members of the armed forces. But at the same time it introduced a number of new 'crimes' such as refusal to return from abroad or spreading 'slanderous inventions vilifying the Soviet state and social system' with the aim of undermining or weakening the Soviet regime (*see* POLITICAL CRIMES). Work on the reform of other branches of Soviet law is continuing. *See* L. Schapiro, 'Judicial Practice and Legal Reform,' *Soviet Survey*, No. 29, July–Sept. 1959.

Legal System of the U.S.S.R. is dominated by the fact that the law is officially considered an instrument for carrying out the policy of the Communist Party. The basic structure and the main concepts of Soviet law are derived from the Russian version of the Roman law tradition (there are also elements of Russian customary law in the present *kolkhoz* law). In theory the sole legislators are the Supreme Soviets (q.v.) of the U.S.S.R. and of the Union and Autonomous Republics (*see* LEGISLATION). In practice all the major decisions in the field of law, as in all other socially relevant fields, are taken by the party leadership (*see* PRESIDIUM). The latter has adopted, according to what it thought expedient, the following courses in relation to the law: (1) allowing it to develop autonomously through court decisions based on interpretation, custom or tradition, in such fields as are considered to be of comparatively little consequence for the main policies pursued at the time (e.g. in 1918–22 when old statutory law had been declared invalid and few new laws promulgated); (2) embodying its decisions in regularly passed laws which are properly applied by the administration and courts (e.g. the disfranchisement of 'socially alien elements' before 1936); (3) securing an interpretation of existing laws inconsistent with their spirit; (4) announcing its decisions in a non-legal form, but later translating them into laws (e.g. the long-term economic plans—*see* PLANNING—are usually announced as decisions of party congresses, but are later, at least in part, reflected in the budget); (5) ignoring the existing law but carrying out its illegal decisions openly and later incorporating their results into the law (e.g. the collectivization of agriculture, which resulted in the development of a new branch of law—the *kolkhoz* law —and the quasi-compulsory settlement of the Virgin Land areas in 1954–6); (6) acting illegally without acknowledging at the time or subsequently legalizing such acts (e.g. torture of prisoners in Stalin's time, and hiring out of concentration camp inmates to State farms); (7) promulgating fictitious laws (*see* FICTION) which are not meant to be applied save in a ceremonial way (e.g. the largely fictitious constitution which is ostensibly in force now).

The existence of a large body of fictitious law of recent making and of institutionalized arbitrariness on the part of the policy-makers are the two outstanding distinguishing features of the Soviet legal system. *See further under* CIVIL LAW; CLASSES; CODES OF LAW;

CONSTITUTION; CRIMINAL LAW; JUDICIAL SYSTEM; KOLKHOZ; LABOUR LAW; LAND; MARRIAGE; SOCIALIST LEGALITY; for the history of Russian law *see also* GREAT REFORMS; LEGAL REFORM; REVOLUTIONARY LEGALITY; RUSSKAYA PRAVDA; SUDEBNIK; SVOD ZAKONOV; ULOZHENIYE. *See* V. Gsovski and K. Grzybowski (eds.), *Government, Law and Courts in the Soviet Union and Eastern Europe*, vol. i, 1959.

Legal Theory, *see* CHICHERIN; KAVELIN; KORKUNOV; MUROMTSEV; PASHUKANIS; PETRAZHITSKIY; REYSNER; VYSHINSKIY; FICTION; IDEOLOGY; LEGAL SYSTEM; REVOLUTIONARY LEGALITY; SOCIALIST LEGALITY; and entries on branches of law. *See* R. Schlesinger, *Soviet Legal Theory*, 1945; J. N. Hazard (ed.), *Soviet Legal Philosophy*, Cambridge, Mass., 1951; H. Kelsen, *The Communist Theory of Law*, 1955.

Legislation, according to the Stalin constitution of 1936, is the prerogative of the Supreme Soviets of the U.S.S.R. and the Union Republics. However, even formally, this is consistently applied only in the case of budgets. Many important laws, even involving constitutional changes, are issued as *ukases* (q.v.) of the Supreme Soviets' presidia, with subsequent rubber-stamping by the soviets. Moreover, the Council of Ministers, alone or together with the Central Committee of the party, frequently makes decisions of great importance, ostensibly in pursuance of the law, and also sometimes amounting to changing the constitution. Legislation is in a chaotic state: many obsolete laws remain unrepealed, there was till 1958 no uniform system of publication of new laws, and there are secret laws not published at all (this practice, which had been discontinued in 1906, was officially reintroduced in 1924). *See also* CODES OF LAW; LEGAL REFORM. *See* V. Gsovski, *Soviet Civil Law*, Ann Arbor, 1948; H. J. Berman, *Justice in Russia*, Cambridge, Mass., 1950, and 'Soviet Law Reform —Dateline Moscow 1957,' *Yale Law Journal*, vol. lxvi, No. 8, July 1957.

Lemberg, *see* L'vov.

Lemeshev, Sergey Yakovlevich (*b.* 1902), tenor. After entering a military school in 1920 he appeared in concerts and on account of his outstanding abilities was sent to Moscow Conservatory, where he studied under Rainskiy till 1925. After working with Stanislavsky at the Bolshoi Theatre for several years, he became a soloist there in 1931. Popular as a concert artist, he has done much to foster interest in Soviet music and folk-song. *See* M. L'vov, *S. Y. Lemeshev*, Moscow-Leningrad, 1947.

Lena, one of the longest rivers of Siberia, rising in the Baykalean Mountains west of Lake Baykal and flowing north-east to Yakutsk, then north into the Laptev Sea of the Arctic Ocean, forming a large delta (over 10,000 sq. m.). Length 2,670 m.; drainage area 943,000 sq. m.). The Lena is navigable almost throughout its course for four or five months a year; its chief tributaries are the Vitim, Olëkma and Aldan on the right, and the Vilyuy on the left. Principal ports: Osetrovo and Yakutsk. It flows through mountainous country in its upper and middle reaches, and through the central Yakutian lowland in its lower reaches; most of its basin is covered by coniferous forests, with perpetually frozen subsoil. Vitim (*see* BODAYBO) and Aldan are gold-mining areas, and near Yakutsk coal-mining is carried on. The principal goods exported from the Lena Basin are timber, furs and gold; industrial products and food are imported.

Lend-Lease. War-time aid given to the Soviet Union under the United States Lend-Lease Programme and the British and Canadian Mutual Aid programmes consisted of supplies on generous credit terms amounting to almost 13 milliard dollars' worth (of which about 11·2 milliards came from the United States). About half of the lend-lease supplies were military equipment, and the rest food, leather footwear, motor vehicles, various metals, textiles, etc. The Soviet Government has consistently refused to make even the token repayment asked for by the United States, except for the return of some obsolete ships. *See* R. H. Dawson, *The Decision to Aid Russia, 1941,* North Carolina, 1959.

Lenin (real name Ul'yanov), **Vladimir Il'ich** (1870–1924), founder and leader of the Communist Party and the Communist International, founder of the Soviet state and first head of the Soviet Government. Born at Simbirsk, the son of an inspector of schools, the young Lenin was much influenced, even while a schoolboy, by the revolutionary and socialist literature of Populism (q.v.), and by the execution in 1887 of his elder brother for the attempted assassination of Alexander III. For taking part in students' riots Lenin was expelled from Kazan' University, but later graduated in law (with a gold medal) as an external student of St Petersburg University. He belonged to Fokin's organization (q.v.) and to the first Marxist circles in Kazan' and Samara in 1887–93, moving to St Petersburg in the latter year and joining its main Marxist circle, of which he soon became the leader, in attacks upon Populism and Legal Marxism (q.v.). Two years later, together with Martov, he set up the St Petersburg Union for the Struggle for the Liberation of the Working Class with the purpose of substituting practical agitation among workers for theoretical propaganda among students. He was arrested in the same year and in 1897 banished to southern Siberia, where he continued his journalistic and underground activities. Upon his release in 1900 he emigrated to Western Europe.

Meanwhile the Russian Social Democratic Labour Party (q.v.) had been formed in 1898, and Lenin, already concentrated on the problems of seizing and maintaining power, set out to capture the party. He established the unstatutory organization Iskra (q.v.) in 1900, and 'packed' the 2nd party congress of 1903, at which, however, the Iskra organization itself split, Lenin's supporters forming the Bolshevik faction. He soon lost control over the party, and even over his own Bolshevik faction, and in 1905 was expelled from the largely Bolshevik Central Committee (headed by Krasin) for disorganizing the work of the party. However, he had already formed a rival 'stone-hard' Bolshevik sub-faction (Bogdanov, Lunacharskiy, Litvinov, Rykov), and attacked the Central Committee until they were prepared to make peace. Returning to Russia in October 1905, Lenin, together with Bogdanov and Krasin, led the Bolshevik faction through the last stages of the revolution of 1905 (q.v.) and then emigrated once more. Petty *émigré* strife and intrigues took up the following years, during which Lenin once more lost control over the ostensibly reunited Social Democratic Party and over his own faction, breaking with the Bogdanovists and the 'party-minded' Bolsheviks Rykov and Sokol'nikov; Zinov'yev and Kamenev were now his chief lieutenants. A group of a dozen hand-picked Leninists elected in Prague in 1912 a 'central committee of the Social Democratic Party,' and in advance 'expelled' from the party all those who refused to obey this committee. Having thus broken with everyone else, Lenin concentrated on guiding his followers' attempts to widen their influence in the growing Russian labour movement by gaining control in trade unions, co-operatives, educational associations, etc., as well as through the daily newspaper *Pravda* and the Bolshevik members of the Duma. During the First World War he lived in Switzerland with Zinov'yev, advocating a defeatist attitude for Russian workers and organizing international anti-war conferences of left-wing Social Democrats.

Lenin returned to Russia through Germany after the February revolution (q.v.) in 1917, and from this time until the assassination of the German ambassador in Russia in 1918 the Bolsheviks received financial support from the German Government, of which Lenin was apparently aware. From the time of his return Lenin was planning an armed uprising against the Provisional Government (q.v.), thereby alienating Kamenev and Zinov'yev but gaining the support of his erstwhile bitter opponent Trotskiy, who became his chief supporter in organizing and conducting the October revolution (q.v.) and in setting up the Soviet (q.v.) Government. Lenin became chairman of the Council of People's Commissars (Prime Minister), holding this post until his death.

The first actions of his government were the nationalization of the land, the establishment of the Cheka (q.v.), the suppression of non-socialist parties, the dispersal of the Constituent Assembly (q.v.) and the conclusion of the Brest-Litovsk peace treaty (q.v.) with Germany. Then followed the civil war (q.v.), with the policy of War Communism (q.v.), and thereafter the period of the New Economic Policy (q.v.). After the treaty of Brest-Litovsk, Sverdlov and Stalin were Lenin's closest collaborators, and from 1919 he was assisted in leading the party and Government by the Politburo (q.v.), of which most prominent Bolsheviks were members. Within the party there was almost constant opposition to Lenin's policies (*see* DEMOCRATIC CENTRALISTS; LEFT COMMUNISTS; WORKERS' OPPOSITION) until the packed 10th party congress of 1921 formally condemned all internal party factions (*see* COMMUNIST PARTY). An attempt on Lenin's life in which he was wounded was made by Left Socialist Revolutionaries in 1918, and from 1922 he suffered from the brain disease which finally killed him. His mummy is displayed in the mausoleum on the Red Square in Moscow.

Lenin had a powerful charismatic quality, and a genius for organization and tactics, intrigue and demagogy; his writings on these topics are among the classics of political theory (e.g. *What is to be Done?*, 1902, *The Infantile Disease of 'Leftism' in Communism*,

1918). But his philosophical efforts are miserable (*Materialism and Empiriocriticism*, 1909) and little originality can be found in his writings on economics (*Imperialism as the Highest Stage of Capitalism*, written 1916). He was a realist who took a highly utilitarian and opportunist attitude towards Marxian theory, paying it much lip-service but in fact using the works of Marx and Engels as useful sources for suitable quotations. In private life modest, in his personal relationships gentle and kind, Lenin was without moral scruples in politics. *See also* LENINISM. See his *Selected Works* in 12 vols., 1936–1938; memoirs by his wife Krupskaya, 1932, and by Gor'kiy, 1932; R. Fülöp-Miller, *Ulyanov*, 1927; C. Hollis, *Lenin*, 1938; C. Hill, *Lenin and the Russian Revolution*, 1947; D. Shub, *Lenin, a Biography*, New York, 1948; B. D. Wolfe, *Three who made a Revolution*, 1956; S. W. Page, *Lenin and World Revolution*, New York, 1959; L. Schapiro, *The Communist Party of the Soviet Union*, 1960.

Lenin Prizes are awarded yearly for outstanding achievements in science, technology, literature or the arts by government-appointed committees of experts. There is also an International Lenin Peace Prize awarded for services to the Communist-sponsored 'peace campaign.' The award of a Lenin Prize carries a substantial sum of money and the title of 'Laureate of the Lenin Prize.' Lenin Prizes were originally established after Lenin's death but gradually petered out; Stalin Prizes were introduced in 1939 but renamed Lenin Prizes in 1956. The award of the prizes normally reflects the official party line, but in recent years the committee for prizes in literature and the arts have joined the intellectual opposition (q.v.) by refusing to honour party favourites; in 1960 this was countered by the authorities, who changed the composition and procedure of the committee.

Leninabad: 1. Oblast of Tadzhikistan, comprising the western part of the Fergana Valley and the upper part of the Zeravshan Valley; there are deposits of coal, oil and non-ferrous metals. Area 9,900 sq. m.; population (1959) 666,000 (37 per cent urban), mostly Tadzhiks and Uzbeks. It is a major cotton-, food-, wine- and silk-producing area; there are varied mining, textile and food industries. For history *see* FERGANA VALLEY; SOGDIANA; TRANSOXANIA.

2. (until 1936 **Khodzhent**). Administrative, economic and cultural centre of the oblast, situated on the Syr-Dar'ya at the entrance to the Fergana Valley. Population (1959) 77,000 (1939, 46,000). It has varied textile and food industries. Leninabad is one of the most ancient cities of Central Asia. It was stormed by Alexander the Great, who then founded here a new fortress called Alexandria Eskhata ('the Outermost Alexandria'). Ten centuries later, in 711, it was stormed and plundered by the Arabs. In 1220 the town was razed and the entire population slain by Genghis Khan. In the early 19th century it was included in the Kokand Khanate and in 1866 was annexed by Russia. The town and surrounding area belonged to Uzbekistan, 1924–9. A big hydro-electric station on the Syr-Dar'ya has recently been completed.

Leninakan (until 1924 **Aleksandropol'**), town in Armenia, situated 55 m. north-west of Yerevan. Population (1959) 108,000 (1914, 49,000; 1926, 42,000). It has been an important industrial centre since the late 19th century (textile, metal-working and food industries), and old crafts (carpets and cloth) are practised. Pumicestone and tufa are quarried in the vicinity. Leninakan was founded in 1834 by the Russians on the site of an ancient fortress.

Leningrad: 1. Oblast of the R.S.F.S.R., adjacent to the Gulf of Finland and lakes Ladoga and Onega; it is half-forested lowland, with deposits of bauxite, oil-shale and peat. Area 33,200 sq. m.; population (1959) 4,561,000 (86 per cent urban), principally Russians, also Finns, Estonians, Karelians and some small Finnish peoples. The supplying of Leningrad city is the principal object of the oblast's economy; there is peat and oil-shale extraction, timber, aluminium, building materials, food and light industries, while agriculture concentrates upon the cultivation of vegetables, potatoes and coarse grain, and upon dairy farming and fishing. Principal towns: Leningrad, Vyborg, Volkhov, Gatchina. The area, except the territory west of the Karelian Isthmus, belonged to Novgorod, during the 16th–17th centuries was sometimes partly held by Sweden, and in 1721 finally became Russian. The Karelian Isthmus, together with Vyborg, belonged to Finland from 1809 to 1940 and from 1941 to 1944. The greater part of the oblast was occupied by the Germans during the Second World War and was the scene of much fierce fighting.

2. (until 1914 St Petersburg, then Petrograd until 1924). Second largest city of the U.S.S.R., second only to Moscow as an economic and cultural centre, directly subordinated to the government of the R.S.F.S.R. It is situated at the head of the Gulf of Finland on both banks of the River Neva and the islands of its delta. Population (1959) 2,888,000 (with suburbs, 3,300,000). It has large engineering works (shipbuilding, precision instruments), and also electrical, chemical, woodworking, food and light industries. The hydroelectric stations of the oblast supply electricity to the city, coal comes from Vorkuta and Poland, and gas from Estonia by pipeline (a new pipeline to convey natural gas from Stavropol' is now under construction). Twelve railway lines radiate from Leningrad. Its seaport, frozen from January to April, is one of the largest in the world, but because the U.S.S.R. volume of foreign trade is small it handles comparatively little traffic; the river port, one of the most important in the country, stands at the end of two artificial waterways, the Volga-Baltic and the White Sea-Baltic. In 1953 Leningrad had 47 higher educational establishments—including the university, founded in 1804 with 100,000 students (1910, 23 establishments with 12,000 students). Among the 40 museums are the Hermitage (founded by Catherine the Great), with its splendid collection of European paintings, and the Russian Museum of native art (founded 1895). The 1,700 libraries include the Saltykov-Shchedrin Public Library, 1795, with 10 million volumes, and the Academy of Sciences Library with 8 million volumes. There are 16 theatres, including the opera and ballet theatre (founded 1783) and the drama theatre (founded 1832).

Leningrad is among the best-planned and most beautiful cities in the world. The principal part stands on the left bank of the Neva, and the central point is the Admiralty which is surrounded by the lovely

Alexander Garden. Three long and broad boulevards radiate from this point: the Nevskiy Prospekt to the east, the Voznesenskiy Prospekt to the south and the Gorokhovaya Ulitsa to the south-east. The oldest building in the city is the Peter and Paul fortress, 1703. Among the baroque buildings of the early 18th century are the Alexander Nevskiy monastery, 1710, the cathedral of Sts Peter and Paul, 1733, the university, 1742, the Winter Palace, 1762, and the Smol'nyy convent, 1764; the neo-classical buildings of the late 18th and early 19th centuries include the Academy of Arts, 1772, the Marble Palace, 1785, the Taurida Palace, 1788, Michael Castle, 1800, the cathedral of the Virgin of Kazan', 1811, the Exchange, 1816, the rebuilt Admiralty, 1823, the Michael Palace, 1825 (now the Russian Museum), the *ensembles* of the Palace Square, 1829, the Senate Square, 1834, and the drama theatre, 1832, and St Isaak Cathedral, 1858. The famous Bronze Horseman monument to Peter the Great, which stands in the Decembrists' Square (former Senate Square), was constructed on the orders of Catherine the Great. Little has been added to the beauty of the city by the buildings of the late 19th and the 20th centuries, though the stadium, 1950, and the underground, 1956, are worth noting.

Leningrad was founded in 1703 by Peter the Great, and was the capital of Russia from 1712 until 1918; even since 1918 it has retained the unofficial status of second capital of the Soviet Union. It was the chief seaport of the country (replacing Archangel) from its foundation, and from the second half of the 18th century also the principal industrial centre—at first shipbuilding and engineering, later textiles. From its first years the city was an important place of higher education and learning, the naval academy being founded in 1715, the engineering school in 1719, the artillery school in 1721 and the Academy of Sciences in 1725 (transferred to Moscow in 1934). The radical and revolutionary movements of the 19th century were based upon Leningrad, and the labour movement and social democracy flourished there. From the revolution of 1905 the Bolsheviks were strong in St Petersburg, and although the Leningrad party organization, led by Zinov'yev, was in opposition to the central leadership during the mid 1920's, the city was a Bolshevik stronghold during the civil war and afterwards until the early 1930's. Kirov's assassination in Leningrad in 1934 set in motion the wave of terror throughout the country which reached its peak in the Great Purge (q.v.). Leningrad was besieged during the Second World War for two years, and earned the title of ' Hero City.' *See* N. Porfiridov *et al.*, *The Russian Museum, a Short Guide*, Moscow, 1955; P. Kann, *Leningrad*, Moscow, 1959.

Leningrad Case, name by which the action is known which was taken against prominent members of Zhdanov's faction after the latter's death in 1948, instigated by Zhdanov's rival Malenkov. The senior Zhdanovite, Politburo member Voznesenskiy (q.v.), and all leading officials in Leningrad—Zhdanov's province for many years— were arrested and shot. The action was not made public until Khrushchëv's secret speech at the 20th party congress (q.v.) in 1956; it was one of the chief accusations made against the 'anti-party group' (q.v.) in the following year.

Leninism, main form of Bolshevism (q.v.), the theory and practice of the seizure and maintenance of power evolved and applied by Lenin within the Russian Social Democratic Labour Party (q.v.), the Russian state and the world Communist movement. Ostensibly Leninism is but a further development of Marxism. In 1920 Stalin described Leninists as that group of Marxists which switches the centre of gravity of the problem from the outward recognition of Marxism to its implementation: 'designing ways and means of realizing Marxism which correspond to circumstances, changing these ways and means when circumstances change—that is what this group primarily pays attention to.' The main theoretical sources of Leninism, in addition to Marxism, were the teaching of Chernyshevskiy (q.v.) on the role of the peasantry in a Russian social revolution, and the views of the ' Jacobin' wing of Russian Populism (q.v.) that a revolutionary minority was necessary for the seizure of State power and the implementation of radical reforms through the State machine; the organizational tenets of Leninism are based on Ogarëv's (q.v.) theory of revolutionary organization.

Starting from basic Marxist principles, Leninism maintains that the proletariat cannot spontaneously evolve either a socialist ideology or organizational forms necessary for bringing about a socialist revolution. The correct socialist ideology must be inculcated into the proletariat by the radical intelligentsia, who provide also the initial cadres of professional revolutionaries and train workers suitable for this role. The problems of organization and tactics of the party built around a core of professional revolutionaries, and of the mass organizations led by the party, occupy a central place in the theory of Leninism, and the manner in which these problems are dealt with is its main contribution to political theory. The problems of the Dictatorship of the Proletariat (q.v.) and the role of the soviets (q.v.) and the trade unions (q.v.) were solved in accordance with the basic view on the role of the party. A further extension of the Marxist theory was the adaptation and reinterpretation by Lenin of J. A. Hobson's theory of imperialism; according to Lenin, Russia had reached the imperialist stage, which was the last stage in the development of capitalism, and was thus ready for a socialist revolution. After Lenin's death Stalin further developed the theory of Bolshevism, combining Leninism with National Bolshevism (q.v.). *See further under* COMMUNISM; IDEOLOGY; STALINISM. *See* J. Stalin, *Leninism,* 1940; R. N. Carew Hunt, *Theory and Practice of Communism,* 1950; J. Plamenatz, *German Marxism and Russian Communism,* 1954; L. H. Haimson, *The Russian Marxists and the Origins of Bolshevism,* 1955; L. Schapiro, *The Origin of the Communist Autocracy,* 1955; D. Treadgold, *Lenin and his Rivals,* 1955; A. G. Meyer, *Leninism,* Cambridge, Mass., 1957; S. W. Page, *Lenin and World Revolution,* New York, 1959; A. B. Ulam, *The Unfinished Revolution,* New York, 1960.

Leninogorsk (until 1939 **Ridder**), town in the East Kazakhstan Oblast, the main mining centre of the Oriferous Altay. Population (1959) 67,000 (1939, 50,000). It has lead, zinc, silver, copper, gold and rare metals mining (since 1784), and lead and rare metals are smelted.

Leninsk-Kuznetskiy (until 1925 **Kol'chugino**), town in the Kemerovo Oblast (southern Siberia), situated 47 m. south of Kemerovo. Population (1959) 132,000 (1917, 2,000; 1926, 20,000; 1939, 83,000). It is a major centre of coal-mining in the Kuznetsk Basin. Leninsk-Kuznetskiy was founded as a coal-mining settlement in 1864.

Lenkoran', town in Azerbaydzhan, a port on the Caspian Sea situated 160 m. south of Baku. Population (1956) 30,800, mostly Talysh. It is the centre of a subtropical region where rice, citrus fruits and tea are grown. Lenkoran' has been known since the 17th century, was the capital of Talysh Khanate under Persia in the 18th century and became Russian in 1813.

Leonov, Leonid Maksimovich (*b.* 1899), writer, fellow traveller (q.v.), the leading representative in present-day Russian literature of the Dostoyevskian tradition. Novels: *The Badgers*, 1925; *The Thief*, 1927; *Sot'*, 1930; *Skutarevskiy*, 1932; *The Road to the Ocean*, 1935; *The Russian Forest*, 1953. Plays: *The Orchards of Polovchansk*, 1936–1938; *The Wolf*, 1938; *Invasion*, 1942; *Lenushka*, 1943; *The Golden Carriage*, 1954; and stories: *The End of a Petty Man*, 1924. See R. Hingley, 'Leonid Leonov,' *Soviet Survey*, No. 25, July–Sept. 1958; E. J. Simmons, *Russian Fiction and Soviet Ideology*, New York, 1958.

Leont'yev, Konstantin Nikolayevich (1831–91), thinker and publicist of extreme anti-liberal and anti-democratic views, a brilliant literary critic. He denounced the 'levelling bourgeois progress' of Europe, but repudiated the ideas of the Slavophiles (q.v.) and advocated Byzantine asceticism. To some extent Leont'yev was a forerunner of Nietzsche. See N. A. Berdyaev, *Leontiev* (trans. G. Reavey), 1940; R. Hare, *Pioneers of Russian Social Thought*, 1951; T. G. Masaryk, *The Spirit of Russia* (2nd ed.), vol. ii, 1955.

Lepeshinskaya, Olga Vasil'yevna (*b.* 1916), ballerina. A pupil of the Bolshoi School until 1933, Lepeshinskaya ranks with Ulanova and Plisetskaya (qq.v.) as one of the greatest Soviet dancers of the present era. She is distinguished by her masculine strength and virtuosity. See H. Bellew, *Ballet in Moscow Today*, 1956.

Lermontov, Mikhail Yur'yevich (1814–41), poet and novelist of Scottish ancestry. A Guards officer, he was twice sent on active service in the Caucasus as a punishment for his poem on the death of Pushkin in 1837 attacking the court, and for taking part in a duel. He was killed in another duel in the Caucasus. He carried on, in his novel *A Hero of our Time*, 1840, the 'superfluous man' theme begun by Pushkin. The truest Romantic of all Russian poets, Byronic in both his character and his work, Lermontov created a brilliant supernatural portrait in his poem of demoniac love, *Demon*, 1856. See A. Heifetz, *Lermonotov in English*, 1942 (a bibliography).

Lesevich, Vladimir Viktorovich (1837–1905), philosopher and psychologist, the chief representative in Russian philosophy of Neo-Positivism. Under the influence of Lavrov and Avenarius he expounded the doctrine of 'critical positivism' and the 'subjective method' (q.v.) in sociology. His collected works were published in 1915.

Leskov, Nikolay Semënovich (1831–95), writer and masterly stylist. His novels (*Cathedral Folk*, 1872) and stories (*The Enchanted Wanderer*,

1873; *The Sealed Angel*, 1873, etc.) are chiefly concerned with the Church and clergy and with popular beliefs and superstitions; his prose excels in richness and colourfulness. Though firmly anti-radical (*No Way Out*, 1864), Leskov was mistrusted by the conservatives for his denouncement of ecclesiastical bureaucracy. He was either ignored or attacked from both sides politically, and real esteem for him came only after his death.

Letts, *see* LATVIANS.

Levitan, Isaak Il'ich (1860–1900), landscape painter, studied at the Moscow Art School, 1873–85; he became a member of the Peredvizhniki (q.v.). His understanding of and his power to express the lyrical beauty of the central Russian countryside have never been equalled.

Levitskiy, Dmitry Grigor'yevich (1735–1822), portrait painter, studied in Kiev and St Petersburg. From 1771 he directed the portrait-painting class at the Academy of Arts. One of the greatest Russian masters of the psychological portrait, Levitskiy also surpassed all his predecessors in technical brilliance. He was susceptible to the contemporary Western trends and quickly adapted them for his own use. Thus his first creative period, up to the mid 1780's, shows signs of French influence ('Architect Kokorinov,' 'Prince A. M. Golitsyn,' etc.), whereas later he derived inspiration mainly from English painting. Levitskiy never failed to reveal the essential personality of the sitter, and created the character and style of St Petersburg society, not unlike van Dyck who earlier had done the same for the English aristocracy.

Lezgians (formerly also called **Kyurins**), best known of the Caucasian-speaking peoples of Daghestan; they also live in north Azerbaydzhan. They number (1959) 223,000 (134,000 in 1926), and are Sunni Muslims, mostly peasants, now collectivized. Their cultural centre is Derbent. In the 18th century the Lezgians formed several khanates which were at first semi-independent from Persia but came under Russian rule between 1800 and 1830. In the past the name Lezgian was frequently applied to all the mountain peoples of Daghestan.

Libau, *see* LIEPAJA.

Liberation of Labour Group, one of the earliest Russian Marxist organizations, established in 1883 by the former Populists Plekhanov and P. B. Akselrod while living in emigration in Western Europe, influential in popularizing Marxism in Russia. They associated with Lenin against reformism and economism (*see* ISKRA) in 1900, and dissolved in 1903.

Liepaja (formerly Russian **Libava**, German **Libau**), town in the Latvian Republic, an ice-free port situated on the Baltic Sea. Population (1959) 71,000 (1914, about 100,000; 1935, 57,000), Latvians and Russians (until 1940 also Germans). It has engineering, woodworking, fishing and fish-canning industries, and is an important centre of transportation (five railway lines). Liepaja has been known since 1263 and became a town in 1625 (for history *see* KURLAND). Before 1914 it had a flourishing export trade which declined when Latvia became independent.

Lifar, Serge (*b.* 1905), dancer and choreographer. He studied at the State Central Studio until 1922, joining Diaghilev and the Ballets Russes in 1923. After a course with Cecchetti (q.v.) his dancing began to attract great attention and he featured in most of the principal ballets together with Massine, Karsavina, Spesivtseva, etc. After Diaghilev's death in 1929 he occupied several posts, finally joining the Paris Opera ballet in 1931, where he remained for many years creating new ballets, infusing new life and instituting many necessary reforms. Lifar's work is marked by his dramatic powers, his distaste for realism and his *penchant* for neo-classicism. In his rehabilitation of the male role, his vision, his powers of organization and his great vitality, he has been of immense service in the revival of French ballet. *See* his *Manifeste du chorégraphe*, Paris, 1935, and *A History of Russian Ballet*, 1954.

Light Industry, official Soviet term for the textile, leather and allied industries, chiefly producing consumer goods. *See* CONSUMER GOODS; RETAIL TRADE; TEXTILE INDUSTRY.

Likhachëv, Ivan Alekseyevich (1896–1957), industrial manager, Communist Party member from 1917. The son of a peasant, he was active in the Cheka, 1917–21, and in the trade unions, 1921–6, studying at the same time at the Mining Academy and the Institute of Electromechanics. He was manager of the Moscow car works, which are now named after him, 1926–39 and 1940–50; from 1950 to 1953 he was manager of an aircraft engineering works. Likhachëv was U.S.S.R. People's Commissar for Engineering, 1939–40, and Minister of Road Transport, 1953–7.

Lipetsk: 1. Oblast of the R.S.F.S.R., its western part situated on the Central Russian upland and its eastern part in the Oka-Don lowland, traversed by the upper course of the Don; it lies in the black earth belt, is partly covered with forests and has deposits of iron ore. Area 9,300 sq. m.; population (1959) 1,144,000 (30 per cent urban). The oblast has grain and potato cultivation, dairy cattle and pig breeding, and engineering, iron and steel, and food industries. Principal towns: Lipetsk and Yelets.

2. Administrative and economic centre of the oblast, situated 70 m. north of Voronezh. Population (1959) 156,000 (1926, 21,000; 1939, 67,000). It has an iron and steel industry (intermittently since the 17th century), engineering (tractors) and other industries, and a mud spa (since 1805). Lipetsk was founded in the 13th century, became capital of Lipetsk Principality and was destroyed by the Tatars in 1284. It was refounded by Peter the Great as an ironworks, and became a town in 1779.

Liquidationism, pejorative name applied by Bolsheviks and 'party-minded' Mensheviks in 1910–14 to that trend within Russian social democracy (led by Potresov) which laid the main emphasis on work in the State Duma, trade unions, co-operatives, workers' educational associations and other legal institutions, and was averse to reviving the old conspiratorial party apparatus which had largely disappeared in 1908–9. After the outbreak of the First World War liquidationism became 'defencism.' Later the term acquired a wider meaning in Communist parlance, and denoted all attempts (real or imaginary) to weaken the influence of the party apparatus. *See* L. Schapiro, *The Communist Party of the Soviet Union*, 1960.

'Literary Gazette,' bi-weekly newspaper published since 1929, since 1932 on behalf of the Soviet Writers' Union (q.v.). From 1946 until Stalin's death in 1953 it was the voice of extreme 'partyness' (q.v.). Since then, however, it has intermittently followed a more liberal and critical line.

Literature. Although some of the legends of medieval Russia are based upon pagan mythology, the real beginnings of Russian literature date from the conversion of the country to Christianity. Religious texts and legends or chronicles make up this early literature, and until the 20th century folk literature took its themes from these, varying the characters in different regions and centuries so that the same plot might at different times have Vladimir I, Ivan the Terrible, Peter the Great, etc., as the central figure. Not until the 19th century, when its merits were first truly recognized, were any systematic collections of folk literature made, and the *Byliny*—epic songs of popular poetry—were not collected in bulk until the early 20th century.

In the Kievan period (*see* KIEVAN RUSSIA) the principal original literary works were the *vita* of St Theodosius, *c.* 1080, the *Pilgrimage of Abbot Daniel to the Holy Land*, *c.* 1108, the *Testament* of Prince Vladimir Monomakh and the famous *Lay of Igor's Raid* (soon after 1185). The period of feudal particularism produced, among other notable works, the *Journey Beyond the Three Seas*, a description of his travels to India in 1466–72 by the Tver' merchant A. Nikitin. The Muscovite period (*see* MUSCOVY) was richer in literature, but the principal achievements were in the fields of autobiography (*The Archpriest Avvakum's Life Written by Himself*, 1672–3) and political journalism (the correspondence between Ivan the Terrible and Prince Kurbskiy). During the late 17th century Ukrainian clerics from Kiev, who through their contact with Poles were acquainted with medieval western literature, exercised a strong influence upon the intellectual and literary life of Muscovy.

The 18th century witnessed the emergence of modern Russian literature, when the French Classical standards were adopted by the Classicist school (Prince A. Kantemir, 1708–44; V. K. Trediakovskiy, 1703–69; M. V. Lomonosov, 1711–65; A. P. Sumarokov, 1718–77). The most notable playwrights of this school were D. I. Fonvizin (1745–92; author of *The Minor*) and A. S. Griboyedov (q.v.) and its greatest poet was G. R. Derzhavin (q.v.); to the Classicist school also belong the famous fables of I. A. Krylov (1769–1844). Two new literary trends in Russia, partly overlapping with the later Classicism, resulted from successive western influences: the Sentimental school headed by N. M. Karamzin (q.v.), and the Romantic, headed by V. A. Zhukovskiy (q.v.). Russia's greatest poets, A. S. Pushkin and M. Yu. Lermontov (qq.v.), can be regarded as partly Romantics.

The apprenticeship of Russian literature was concluded, and maturity achieved, with Pushkin. He was influenced in his formative years by the Classicist, Sentimental and Romantic schools, and acknowledged his debt to Derzhavin, Karamzin and Zhukovskiy, as well as to Voltaire and Byron. An important phase in his development produced Romantic poems, but his greatest achievements in both verse (*Eugen Onegin*) and prose initiated the new Realistic trend which was to predominate in subsequent literature.

The Golden Age of Russian literature was inaugurated by Pushkin, and though his younger contemporaries Lermontov and Gogol' both had strong Romantic traits (the former, indeed, is the most truly Romantic of Russian poets), they both followed Pushkin in turning to Realism; the only great writer of the period to escape this turn was the poet Tyutchev (q.v.). With the advent of Realism, prose replaced poetry as the chief literary form (N. V. Gogol', S. T. Aksakov, qq.v.). Gogol's path of Critical Realism was followed by their successors, rather than Aksakov's sympathetic recollection of the life around him, and with the Critical Realists the novel emerged as the principal *genre*. The great novelists of the time were I. S. Turgenev and I. A. Goncharov (qq.v.), and among the lesser ones M. Ye. Saltykov (q.v., pseudonym N. Shchedrin) is notable for his social and political satire. The dramatic *genre* was also highly suitable to the requirements of Critical Realism (Gogol' and A. N. Ostrovskiy, q.v.), and fiction in this school received much encouragement from the two contemporary factions of literary critics and publicists, the Westernists (*see* WEST-ERNISM) and the Slavophiles (q.v.); the only notable poet of the school was N. A. Nekrasov (q.v.)

However, Critical Realism did not hold complete sway, and its tenets were challenged by several writers of outstanding talent who rebelled against its stylistic austerity and comparative narrowness of social criticism. United on these points alone, the rebels each went their own highly individual ways and each established a new tradition. N. S. Leskov (q.v.), with his incomparable richness of language, concentrated upon positive types in a strongly anti-radical manner. L. N. Tolstoy (q.v.), transcending the limits of social realism and confronting his heroes not only with their environments but with themselves, became the father of Psychological Realism. F. M. Dostoyevskiy (q.v.) went even further, confronting man with spiritual problems and realities, and his art might be termed Pneumatological (i.e. Spiritual) Realism. Finally, in a time of prose and the social utility of art, pure poetry was championed by A. A. Fet (q.v.). Benefiting to some extent from the new influence was A. P. Chekhov (q.v.), who combined in his work most of the traditions of the past.

The reaction against Critical Realism developed on the eve of the 20th century into a frontal attack from the modernists. The Symbolists, most of them poets, were the chief modernist school, led first by D. S. Merezhkovskiy (q.v.) and then by A. Blok (q.v.); A. Belyy (q.v.), a leading Symbolist, began experimenting with prose style, in this to some extent following Leskov's example. During and after the revolution of 1905 M. Gor'kiy (q.v.) led a Critical Realist come-back (*see also* ANDREYEV; BUNIN). The popularity of this rather naturalistic school was brief, and already before the First World War it was beginning to yield place to another trend, the Neo-Realists (*see* PRISHVIN; A. N. TOLSTOY), who combined realistic content with the stylistic innovations of A. Belyy and their own leader A. Remizov

(1877–1957). In poetry the Symbolists were soon opposed by two new and hostile trends, the Acmeists, led by N. Gumilev and his wife, A. Akhmatova (qq.v.), and the Futurists (*see* FUTURISM), of whom V. Mayakovskiy (q.v.) was the most outstanding.

This was the literary scene at the time of the Bolshevik seizure of power in 1917. Many writers emigrated during the civil war (Gor'kiy, Bunin, Andreyev, Merezhkovskiy, A. Tolstoy, Ehrenburg, q.v., etc.), while in Russia the Futurists and the young proletarian poets of the Proletkul't (q.v.) dominated literature, each group vying for recognition as the true representatives of the new regime. The relaxation of the regime during the New Economic Policy period witnessed the revival of old groups and the appearance of new ones. Outspoken critics of the regime continued to be silenced, while the rest of the writers could loosely be grouped as 'proletarian writers' holding Communist views and 'fellow travellers' (q.v.) who supported the revolution for other reasons; both groups were split into various antagonistic associations based on ideological or artistic differences. Among the fellow travellers the most outstanding were B. Pil'nyak (1894–?1937), I. Babel', L. M. Leonov (q.v.), Yu. Olësha (*b.* 1899), the 'Serapion Brothers' group (including K. A. Fedin, V. A. Kaverin, M. Zoshchenko, qq.v.) who followed Zamyatin (q.v.) and Neo-Realism, and the peasant poet S. Yesenin (q.v.). The most talented and productive of the proletarian writers were A. A. Fadeyev and M. A. Sholokhov (qq.v.). While poetry had characterized the civil war period, prose was now predominant again, and has on the whole remained so. Again the novel was the main *genre*; Tolstoy's Psychological Realism was revived by Fadeyev and Sholokhov, and the Dostoyevskian tradition by Leonov.

During Stalin's 'revolution from above' of the first Five Year Plan and the collectivization of agriculture (qq.v.), a quasi-dictatorial position in the literary field was assumed by the Association of Proletarian Writers (*see* R.A.P.P.), but this was abolished in 1932, together with all other literary associations, and the Union of Soviet Writers (*see* WRITERS' UNION) was set up, whose members were soon committed to the official conformity of Socialist Realism (q.v.). Gor'kiy, returned from emigration, was proclaimed a model of this method, while A. A. Zhdanov (q.v.) maintained overall supervision on behalf of the party in literature as in other ideological fields.

During the Second World War the atmosphere was again somewhat relaxed, but in 1946 party control was re-established by Zhdanov in an even more rigorous form, and the years 1946–53 were almost sterile in literature; the main features of the period were lifeless idealization of the regime, idolization of Stalin and extreme xenophobia.

Almost immediately after Stalin's death a 'thaw' occurred, and lively artistic and political controversy has developed and continued ever since despite various setbacks (*see* INTELLECTUAL OPPOSITION; WRITERS' UNION). The most interesting trends that have emerged are the revived Critical Realism and what might be called Critical Symbolism. The former is chiefly concerned with exposing the fictions (q.v.) of Soviet life, and among its principal representatives are Dudintsev, Yashin and, of the older generation, to some extent Panfërov (qq.v.). A recognized school within this trend, led by V. V. Ovechkin and V. F. Tendryakov, devotes itself to village life, while others (e.g. D. Granin, and to some extent Yevtushenko, q.v.) reflect the life and moods of the post-Stalin young generation. A special place is occupied by writers who, while adopting the forms of Critical Realism, have little in common with it in spirit, e.g. G. Ye. Nikolayeva, whose stand is similar to that of Khrushchëv in denouncing Stalin (*The Battle on the Way*), and V. Kochetov, who is almost unique in using Critical Realism from the standpoint of Stalinist reaction. Critical Symbolism in its purest form is represented in Kirsanov's (q.v.) work, but Leonov's *Russian Forest*, Tvardovskiy's (q.v.) poem *Far Distances*, much of Yevtushenko's poetry and the most outstanding work of the period, Pasternak's (q.v.) *Dr Zhivago*, all belong essentially to this trend. The post-Stalin period has also been characterized by a fresh flowering of lyric poetry and lyrical short stories, as well as the appearance of genuine literary criticism. *See* P. Kropotkin, *Russian Literature*, 1905; B. G. Guerney (ed.), *Treasury of Russian Literature*, New York, 1943; M. Baring (ed.), *The Oxford Book of Russian Verse*, 2nd ed., 1948; J. Lavrin, *Pushkin to Mayakovsky*, 1948; G. Struve, *Soviet Russian Literature*, *1917–50*, Norman, Oklahoma, 1951; E. J. Simmons (ed.), *Through the Glass of Soviet Literature*, New York, 1953; M. Slonim, *Modern Russian Literature*, New York, 1953; C. Donning, *Russian Tales and Legends*, 1956; W. E. Harkins, *Dictionary of Russian Literature*, 1957; J. Lindsay (trans.), *Russian Poetry, 1917–55*, 1957; R. Conquest (ed.), *Back to Life*, 1958; V. Zavalishin, *Early Soviet Writers*, New York, 1958; D. S. Mirsky, *A History of Russian Literature* (ed. F. J. Whitfield), New York, 1958; E. Stillman (ed.), *Bitter Harvest*, New York, 1959; R. Poggioli, *The Poets of Russia, 1890–1930*, Cambridge, Mass., 1960; Maurice Baring, *Landmarks in Russian Literature*, 2nd ed., 1960.

Lithuania (Lithuanian **Lietuva**), Union Republic of the U.S.S.R., situated in the north-west adjacent to the Baltic Sea, traversed in the south by the River Niemen, an undulating lowland plain with many small lakes and marshes, partially covered with mixed forests. Area 25,200 sq. m.; population (1959) 2,711,000 (39 per cent urban), mostly Lithuanians (79 per cent), also Russians (8·5 per cent) and Poles (8·5 per cent) (before the war many Jews). Grain, potatoes and flax are cultivated, dairy farming and pig breeding carried on, and there are diverse food and light industries, also newly developing engineering and electro-technical industries; many old crafts are still practised. Principal towns: Vilnius (capital), Kaunas, Klaipeda, Siauliai.

Lithuanian statehood dates from the 13th century; the chief preoccupations of its dukes (later Grand Dukes) were resistance to the Teutonic Knights in the west and territorial expansion to the east and south, where Lithuania became a successor state to Kievan Russia. The Grand Duchy of Lithuania stretched almost to Moscow in the east and reached the Black Sea in the south by 1430, the vast majority of its population being Orthodox Russians and Russian being the official language. The most important dukes of the period were Gediminas (1316–41) and Algirdas (1345–77). The Grand Duke Jagaila (Polish Jagiello) was elected King of Poland in 1385, a personal union being established between the two states which in 1569 were united in the Polish Commonwealth. Most of the present area of the country was acquired by Russia in the third partition of Poland, 1795; following the Polish uprising of 1863, which spread to Lithuania, the Lithuanian language was forbidden to appear in print, and between 1864 and 1904 all Lithuanian literature was smuggled from Germany. A strong national and a Social Democratic movement (the latter especially among Jewish artisans) grew up during the late 19th and early 20th centuries. Lithuania was occupied 1915–18 and 1941–4 by the Germans and suffered severely during the Second World War. During its period of independence (1919–40) Lithuania was at first a democratic republic, but became a dictatorship under President A. Smetana in 1926. (For recent history see BALTIC STATES; VILNIUS.) The Hungarian and Polish events of 1956 were strongly echoed in Lithuania, particularly among students. See K. Pelekis, *Genocide: Lithuania's Threefold Tragedy*, 1949; G. Metelsky, *Lithuania*, Moscow, 1959; A. E. Senn, *The Emergence of Modern Lithuania*, New York, 1959; V. Gsovski and K. Grzybowski (eds.), *Government, Law and Courts in the Soviet Union and Eastern Europe*, vol. i, 1959.

Lithuanians, Baltic-speaking people inhabiting Lithuania and numbering (1959) 2·3 million. Lithuanian is one of the most archaic of the living Indo-European languages. Samogitians (*see* SAMOGITIA) and the inhabitants of the Klaipeda area form distinct minorities; the latter are Lutherans, while the predominant religion is Roman Catholicism. Unlike Latvians and Estonians, Lithuanians have a long tradition of statehood (*see* LITHUANIA). After the fusion with Poland, the polonized Lithuanian aristocracy played an important part in the affairs of the Polish Commonwealth. Following a land reform in 1922 the majority of Lithuanian peasants chose to live on separate farmsteads instead of in the traditional villages, and although they were collectivized in the late 1940's the building of new *kolkhoz* settlements is proceeding slowly.

Little Russia, Little Russians, obsolete names for the Ukraine, Ukrainians (qq.v.).

Litvinov (real name **Vallakh**), **Maksim Maksimovich** (1876–1951), politician and diplomat of middle-class Jewish birth who joined the Social Democratic Labour Party in 1898 and its Leninist faction (*see* ISKRA) in 1901. He participated actively in the revolution of 1905 (q.v.), procuring arms from abroad. Working as a clerk in London from 1907, he continued his political activities and was appointed representative of the Soviet Government in Britain after the Bolshevik seizure of power in 1917, but was soon arrested in retaliation for the arrest of Sir R. Bruce Lockhart and subsequently exchanged for him. Appointed Deputy People's Commissar for Foreign Affairs in 1921, Commissar in 1930, he was a frequent representative of the U.S.S.R. at international conferences and after 1934 at the League of Nations, where he was eloquent in advocating disarmament. He was removed from office in May 1939, prior to the pact with Hitler (*see*

NAZI-SOVIET PACT), but reappointed as Deputy Commissar for Foreign Affairs, 1941–6, and was also ambassador to the U.S.A., 1941–3.

Livadiya, seaside resort on the southern coast of the Crimea, 2 m. south-west of Yalta. Before 1917 it was an imperial estate, and there are two palaces, in one of which the Yalta Conference (q.v.) took place in 1945.

Livestock. The number of domestic animals (in millions, 1st January each year) is shown in the following table for selected years (present-day frontiers apply for 1916):

	1916	1928	1934	1941	1946	1953	1959
Cattle	58·4	60·1	33·5	54·5	47·6	56·6	70·8
including cows	28·8	29·3	19·0	27·8	22·9	24·3	33·3
Pigs	23·0	22·0	11·5	27·5	10·6	28·5	48·7
Sheep and goats	96·3	107·0	36·5	91·6	70·0	109·9	139·2
Horses	38·2	36·1	15·4	21·0	10·7	15·3	11·5

Of the total number of cows in 1959, 9·8 per cent were owned by *sovkhozes* and other State enterprises, 34·6 per cent by *kolkhozes*, 38·2 per cent by *kolkhoz* members, 17·3 per cent by workers and employees and 0·1 per cent by individual peasants and others.

The principal local breeds of dairy cattle are Kholmogory and Yaroslavl'; Friesians are the main foreign breed. Local breeds of beef cattle include the Ukrainian Grey, Kalmyk (now called Astrakhan') and Kazakh, while British breeds are imported for improving stock. Among pigs, English Large White and several local cross-breeds from them predominate. There are several local coarse fleece and mutton breeds of sheep (including the 'Astrakhan' in Central Asia), and a few fine fleece local breeds have been developed by crossing with the foreign Rambouillet and Precos merinos. The old Russian cart-horses, e.g. Bityug, are extinct, or nearly so, but there are a number of good new lines of cross-breeds from Belgian and British stock. The most famous harness horse is the Russian Trotter. Several good old local riding breeds exist in Central Asia, of which the Turkmen ones (Teke and Yomud) are the best known; the most widely used, particularly in Cossack units of the army, is the Anglo-Don cross-breed.

Per thousand of population, domestic animals in selected years numbered:

	1928	1956	1959
Cattle	440	294	339
including cows	218	138	159
Pigs	182	170	274
Sheep and goats	754	581	668
Horses	238	64	60

Total output of meat in 1958 was 7·7 million tons; in addition 0·2 million tons were imported, mainly from China. Milk output in 1958 was 58·8 million tons (average yield per cow in *kolkhozes* and *sovkhozes* being 2·0 tons).

Livland (Livonia), one of the former Baltic Provinces (q.v.) of

Russia, which was divided in 1918 between Estonia and Latvia. It belonged to the Teutonic Knights from the 13th century to 1561, then to Poland, to Sweden from 1629 and to Russia from 1721.

Lobachevskiy, Nikolay Ivanovich (1793–1856), famous mathematician. He became professor at Kazan' University in 1816 and was its rector, 1827–46, when the university flourished under his aegis. He was a pioneer of the modern non-Euclidian geometry. Among his chief works are *Principles of Geometry*, 1829–30, *Imaginary Geometry*, 1835, *New Principles of Geometry*, 1835–8, and *Pan-géométrie* (Fr. trans. 1902). *See* F. Engel, *N. I. Lobatchewsky*, 1899; H. E. Wolfe, *Introduction to Non-Euclidean Geometry*, New York, 1945.

Local Government, in the true sense, does not exist in the U.S.S.R., its place being taken by what the constitution terms 'local organs of State power,' that is, soviets (q.v.) and their executive organs. The departments of executive committees of the provincial and local soviets (e.g. health, education, etc.) work under the system of dual subordination (q.v.) usual in the U.S.S.R. administrative apparatus. *Kolkhozes* are under the supervision of the agricultural departments of the local soviets, while only a very small part of industry, of purely local character, is administered by the soviets, the bulk of industry being in the care of the Economic Councils (q.v.), which are directly subordinated to the Councils of Ministers (q.v.) of the Union Republics. Since the death of Stalin local soviets have in practice had slightly more scope for manœuvre than previously. Local government in the modern sense was established in Russia during the Great Reforms (q.v.; *see also* ZEMSTVO) of the 1860's, except at the parish council level where it was introduced immediately after the February revolution (q.v.) of 1917. The principle of local government being incompatible with the Leninist idea of a thoroughly integrated and centralized administrative system, all local government institutions were abolished in the first months after the Bolshevik seizure of power (*see* OCTOBER REVOLUTION) and their functions taken over by the soviets. *See* P. Vinogradoff, *Local Government in Russia*, 1915; P. P. Gronsky and N. J. Astrov, *The War and the Russian Government*, New Haven, Conn., 1929; T. J. Polner, *Russian Local Government During the War and the Union of Zemstvos*, 1930; L. G. Churchwood, 'The Agricultural Reorganization and the Rural District Soviets,' *Soviet Studies*, vol. x, No. 1, July 1958; D. J. R. Scott, *Russian Political Institutions*, 1958.

Local Industry, official term for industries whose products are primarily intended for local consumption and which are based upon local raw materials and fuel. Local industry is administered by the provincial and local soviets, and not by the Economic Councils (q.v.).

Lodygin, Aleksandr Nikolayevich (1847–1923), electrical engineer. He invented in 1872 and patented in 1874 the first incandescent lamp, which, though it did not find practical use, apparently influenced Edison's work (who invented his carbon thread vacuum incandescent lamp in 1879). From the early 1880's Lodygin lived mostly abroad, and died in the U.S.A.

Lomonosov, Mikhail Vasil'yevich (1711–65), great scientist and poet, the son of an Archangel fisherman. He ran away to Moscow at the age of 17, and was educated at a State school, later at St Petersburg and Freiburg universities. He worked at the Academy of Sciences in St Petersburg and made many contributions to scientific research, among them the enunciation of the principle of the conservation of matter and the partial anticipation of the atomic theory of the structure of matter later developed by Lavoisier and Dalton. He was energetic in working for the spread of education in Russia and was largely responsible for the foundation of Moscow University. As a poet Lomonosov belonged to the Classicist school. He has ever since been venerated in Russia as a symbol of Russian creative genius, and an area of the 'dark side of the moon' was named after him when a Soviet rocket photographed the moon in 1959.

Lopatin, Lev Mikhaylovich (1855–1920), philosopher and psychologist, chairman of the Moscow Psychological Society from 1899 until it ceased to exist after 1917; he died of general debility as a result of conditions prevailing during the civil war. Lopatin belonged to the philosophical tradition of Leibnitz, and developed a doctrine of creativity as the basis of philosophical anthropology and ethics. His concept of 'creative causality' to some extent anticipated ideas developed by Henri Bergson.

Loris-Melikov, Count Mikhail Tarielovich (1825–88), statesman of Armenian birth who headed the Supreme Commission nominated to investigate the causes of and to suppress terrorism after a series of Populist attempts upon the life of Alexander II. Loris-Melikov used the dictatorial powers of the Commission to conciliate liberal opinion, and the period of his rule was known as 'the dictatorship of the heart.' He became Minister of the Interior when, after six months, the Commission ceased to operate, and evolved a plan for a representative assembly with consultative functions and a system of cabinet government; however, Alexander II's assassination in 1881 enabled Pobedonostsev (q.v.) to prevail upon Alexander III to reject it, whereupon Loris-Melikov resigned. *See also* GREAT REFORMS.

Losev, A. F. (1892–?), philosopher of great learning and promise whose biography and fate are unknown. In his books (published in Russia) he applied dialectics to the data of phenomenological analysis (*Antique Cosmos and Modern Science, The Philosophy of Name, Dialectics of Artistic Form, Music as a Subject of Logic*—all 1927—*Outlines of the Antique Symbolism and Mythology*, vol. i, 1930).

Losinoostrovskaya, *see* BABUSHKIN.

Losskiy, Nikolay Onufriyevich (*b.* 1870), philosopher, one of the founders of modern intuitivism and personalism (qq.v.). He became a professor at Petrograd University in 1916 and was expelled from Russia in 1922 together with other leading intellectuals. He lived first in Czechoslovakia, subsequently in the U.S.A. Among his works are *The Intuitive Basis of Knowledge*, 1919; *The World as an Organic Whole*, 1928; *Freedom of Will*, 1932; *Value and Existence*, 1935; *History of Russian Philosophy*, 1951.

Luck, *see* LUTSK.

Lugansk (until 1958 **Voroshilovgrad**): 1. Oblast of the Ukraine, situated in the central part of the Donets Basin, a ravined area on the left bank of the Severskiy Donets in the black earth steppe belt;

there are large deposits of coal (half anthracite). Area 10,300 sq. m.; population (1959) 2,457,000 (79 per cent urban), Ukrainians and Russians. There are iron and steel, engineering, chemical, food and light industries, wheat and sunflower cultivation, market gardening, and cattle and pig raising. Principal towns: Lugansk, Kadiyevka, Voroshilovsk, Krasnyy Luch. Until its annexation and colonization by Russia in 1753 (*see* NEW RUSSIA) the area was virtually unpopulated; the first colonists were Serbian immigrants. Industrial development dates from the late 18th century. The Stakhanov Movement originated here. During the German occupation (1941–3) heroic deeds were performed in the town of Krasnodon by the underground youth organization Young Guard (q.v.).

2. (1935–58 **Voroshilovgrad**). Administrative, economic and cultural centre of the oblast, the oldest industrial centre of the Donets Basin. Population (1959) 274,000 (fifth in the Donets Basin; 1917, 60,000; 1939, 215,000). It has large engineering and metallurgical industries (locomotives, mining equipment, machine tools, automobile parts, building industry equipment, pipes). Lugansk has been known since the mid 18th century, becoming a town in 1882 and provincial centre in 1938. In 1796 a cannon foundry was built; the first experiments in Russia in the smelting of iron with coke took place in the following year. A large locomotive plant was constructed in 1900, and the pace of industrial development increased during the 1930's.

Lunacharskiy, Anatoliy Vasil'yevich (1873–1933), literary critic and politician who participated in Marxist circles as a youth and later joined the Bolshevik faction of the Social Democratic Labour Party. He supported Lenin against the Central Committee in 1904–5, but in 1909 broke with him and formed, with Bogdanov and Gor'kiy, the left-wing Bolshevik sub-faction 'Forward' (*see* VPERĒD). He was an internationalist during the First World War, returned to Russia after the February 1917 revolution (q.v.) and soon rejoined the Bolsheviks. From the October revolution (q.v.) till 1929 he was People's Commissar for Education in the R.S.F.S.R. Lunacharskiy supported the flourishing of Bogdanovism (q.v.) during the 1920's; modernistic experiments in education ceased with his removal from the ministry. Appointed ambassador to Spain in 1933, he died in Paris while on his way.

Lutsk (Ukrainian **Luts'ke**, Polish **Luck**), administrative, economic and cultural centre of the Volhynia Oblast (western Ukraine). Population (1959) 49,000 (1931, 36,000), mostly Ukrainians (before the war also Jews and Poles). It has varied industries (food, agricultural machinery, etc.). Lutsk has been known since 1085, belonged to Volhynia, became Lithuanian in 1336, Polish in 1569, Russian in 1791 and again Polish, 1919–39. It was the scene of much fighting in 1916.

Luzin, Nikolay Nikolayevich (1883–1950), mathematician, head of the Moscow mathematical school, professor at Moscow University from 1917, member of the Academy of Sciences from 1929. His works were mainly concerned with the theory of functions of a real variable (*Integral and Trigonometric Series*, 1915; *Lectures on Analytical Sets and their Applications*, 1930). Luzin's pupils (who include Lavrent'yev and Kolmogorov, qq.v.) have applied methods developed by him to many fields of mathematics.

L'vov (Ukrainian **L'viv**, Polish **Lwów**, German **Lemberg**): 1. Oblast of the Ukraine, situated in Galicia adjacent to the Polish frontier on the northern slopes of the Carpathian Mountains and the Volhynia-Podolia upland, traversed by the upper Western Bug and the Dniester, partially covered by mixed forests. Area 4,700 sq. m.; population (1959) 2,115,000 (38 per cent urban), chiefly Ukrainians, before the war many Poles and Jews. Deposits of oil, natural gas, ozokerite and salt are worked, and there are engineering, coal-mining, chemical, woodworking and diverse light and food industries; grain and potatoes are cultivated and cattle and pigs raised. Principal towns: L'vov, Drogobych, Borislav. For history *see* GALICIA.

2. Administrative centre of the oblast, and principal economic and cultural centre of the western Ukraine. Population (1959) 410,000 (seventh in the Ukraine; 1931, 316,000; 1939, 340,000), chiefly Ukrainians, before the war mostly Poles and Jews. It has large metallurgical (engineering, electro-technical), food and textile industries, and is an important centre of transportation (nine railway lines, airport). A branch of the Ukrainian Academy of Sciences is situated here (founded in 1873 as the Shevchenko Society), and among its higher educational institutions are a university (1661, before 1862 Latin and German, then Polish and partly Ukrainian, now Ukrainian), polytechnical (1844) and veterinary (1897) institutes, and a conservatoire, 1904. There are many interesting buildings of the 13th–18th centuries. L'vov was founded about 1250 and soon afterwards became the capital of Galicia; in 1340 it became Polish, and in 1356 received Magdeburg Law. The city was an important centre of the Russian (Ukrainian) Orthodox religious and cultural movement, and also of crafts and commerce (Armenian, later also Jewish, merchants). It became the chief centre of the Ukrainian national movement after 1848. There was severe fighting here in 1914–15, 1920 (Soviet-Polish war) and 1944.

L'vov, Aleksey Fëdorovich (1798–1870), violinist, conductor and composer, director of the Imperial Chapel, 1836. His works comprise three operas, including *Bianco e Gualtiero* and *Undine*; a violin concerto; chamber music, etc., and church music. L'vov is best known as the composer of the Imperial Russian National Anthem *God Save the Tsar*. *See* M. Montagu-Nathan, *A History of Russian Music*, 1914.

L'vov, Prince Georgiy Yevgen'yevich (1861–1925), Constitutional Democrat, active in the *zemstvo* movement and chairman of the All-Russian Union of Zemstvos. He was empowered to form a provisional government (q.v.) by the Provisional Committee of the State Duma after Nicholas II's abdication in February 1917, and was Prime Minister until Kerenskiy replaced him in July. He emigrated to France after the Bolshevik seizure of power.

Lyadov, Anatoliy Konstantinovich (1855–1914), composer and teacher, who studied under Rimsky-Korsakov at the St Petersburg Conservatory, becoming a professor there in 1878. He assisted Balakirev and Lyapunov in their researches into folk music on behalf of the Imperial Geographical Society. His works comprise a ballet, *Leila and Adelai* (unfinished); choral works; orchestral works, including *Eight Russian Folk-songs*; the symphonic poems *Baba Yaga*, *The Enchanted Lake*, *Kikimora*, etc.; much piano music; songs and folk-song collections. Lyadov is primarily a miniaturist and his short piano and orchestral pieces are charmingly and imaginatively written. There is a child-like freshness and naïveté about many of his works, in particular the children's songs (op. 14 and 18), which show a wonderful insight into the realm of youth and fantasy. *See* G. Abraham and M. D. Calvocoressi, *Masters of Russian Music*, 1936; M. Montagu-Nathan, 'A. K. Lyadov, a Man of Letters,' *Musical Opinion*, April, May 1940.

Lyapunov, Aleksandr Mikhaylovich (1857–1918), mathematician. Educated at St Petersburg University, he was professor at Khar'kov from 1892 and a member of the Academy of Sciences from 1901. His works were concerned with the problems of stability of movement, the theory of potential, equilibrium figures of liquid rotating mass and the theory of probabilities. In all these fields he achieved outstanding results.

Lyapunov, Sergey Mikhaylovich (1859–1924), pianist, composer and teacher, who attended classes of the Imperial Musical Society at Nizhniy-Novgorod and studied at Moscow Conservatory under Klindworth, Tchaikovsky and Taneyev. From 1884 to 1902 he was assistant musical director of the Court Chapel in St Petersburg, in 1893 a member of the Imperial Geographical Society's commission to study folk music, and in 1910 was appointed professor at St Petersburg Conservatory. He emigrated to Paris in 1918. His works comprise two symphonies; two piano concertos; a *Ukrainian Rhapsody for Piano and Orchestra*; orchestral works, including the symphonic poem *Zhelyazova Volya*; many piano solos, including *Études d'exécution transcendante (à la mèmoire de François Liszt)*; and numerous songs and folk-song arrangements. Lyapunov is essentially a follower of the Russian national school (*see* KUCHKA), and his music is distinguished by great charm and brilliance. His piano music is often of immense difficulty, with subtle rhythmical complexities. Many of his works are based on folk music. *See* G. Abraham and M. D. Calvocoressi, *Masters of Russian Music*, 1936.

Lyashchenko, Pëtr Ivanovich (1876–1955), economist and economic historian. He studied science and economics at St Petersburg University, teaching there and at Tomsk and Rostov universities. He was later a Senior Research Officer at the Economics Institute of the U.S.S.R. Academy of Sciences, and from 1943 was a corresponding member of the academy. His *History of the National Economy of Russia to the 1917 Revolution* (Eng. ed., New York, 1949) is a standard textbook.

Lysenko, Trofim Denisovich (*b.* 1898), agronomist and biologist, of Ukrainian origin. He followed Michurin in practical plant breeding, and came to reject the chromosome theory of heredity generally accepted by modern geneticists. Against this he advances the essentially Lamarckist view that heritable changes can be brought about in plants by environmental influences, such as subjecting wheat to extremes of temperature, and by grafting. Claiming that his views correspond to Marxism, he succeeded in enlisting the support of the party authorities, and became in 1938 President of the Academy of Agricultural Sciences. He instituted a rule of terror in the academy, vilifying especially the founder of the academy, N. I. Vavilov (q.v.). In 1948 Lysenko precipitated an international scandal in the world of science by claiming the authority of the Central Committee of the Communist Party for his views, and from then until Stalin's death he was in the position of a dictator in the whole field of biology. He was criticized in 1953 by Khrushchëv, who made him responsible for the backward state of Soviet agricultural science, and was dismissed as President of the Academy of Agricultural Sciences in 1954, though he remained in the presidium of the U.S.S.R. Academy of Sciences. In subsequent years it was shown in the specialist journals in Russia that Lysenko had falsified the results of his experiments. But he again succeeded in winning the confidence of Khrushchëv, who in 1958 publicly praised him and attacked his critics; as a result his chief opponents in the Academy of Sciences have again been dismissed. However, Lysenko's 'Michurinist biology' has not regained its former dominant position. *See* his *Soviet Biology*, 1948, and *Essays in Agrobiology* (Eng. ed.), Moscow, 1954; E. A. Ashby, *Scientist in Russia*, 1947; J. S. Huxley, *Soviet Genetics and World Science, Lysenko and the Meaning of Heredity*, 1949; J. Langdon-Davies, *Russia Puts the Clock Back*, 1949.

Lys'va, town in the Perm' Oblast (Urals), situated 83 m. east of Perm'. Population (1959) 73,000. It has been an important centre of the iron and steel industry since the late 18th century.

Lyubertsy, town in the Moscow 'green belt,' an industrial suburb on the Moscow–Kazan' railway, south-east of the capital. Population (1959) 93,000. It is an important centre of agricultural engineering.

Lyublino, rapidly growing suburb south of Moscow, absorbed by the capital in 1960. Population (1959) 86,000. It has engineering (transport machinery) and woodworking industries.

M

Magadan: 1. Oblast of the R.S.F.S.R., situated in the north of the Russian Far East between the Sea of Okhotsk and the Bering Straits; it is a largely mountainous area, with coniferous forests in the south-west and tundra in the north-east, and rich deposits of gold, tin and rare metals. Area 472,700 sq. m.; population (1959) 235,000 (81 per cent urban), Russians and other European settlers (mostly ex-prisoners), also some Chukchi (the Chukchi National Okrug is in the oblast). The industries are gold- and tin-mining, fishing and reindeer raising; food and consumer goods are almost all imported. From the 1930's to the mid 1950's it was one of the most notorious areas of forced labour camps (*see* DAL'STROY; KOLYMA), and some camps still exist. The mining industry was built up entirely on forced labour. The release of the majority of prisoners and the departure of many of them in the 1950's resulted in an acute shortage of labour, and efforts are being made to fill the gap by attracting voluntary settlers to the region and by semi-compulsory colonization.

2. Administrative, economic and cultural centre of the oblast, a port on the Sea of Okhotsk and the starting-point of a highway to the gold-mining area on the upper Kolyma. Population (1959) 62,000 (1939, 27,000; 1956, 55,000; 1958, 24,000). There is some industry, including a motor repair works. Magadan was founded in 1933 and became a town in 1939, absorbing the fishing village of Nagayevo.

Magnitogorsk, city and local cultural centre in the Chelyabinsk Oblast (Urals), situated on the River Ural. Population (1959) 311,000 (1939, 146,000). It is one of the principal industrial centres of the country, with a huge iron and steel plant (the largest in Russia) based upon local ore deposits which have been worked since the 18th century and on coal from the Kuznetsk Basin and Karaganda; subsidiary industries include chemicals and engineering. The city is the terminus of the oil pipeline from Shkapovo in Bashkiria. Magnitogorsk was founded in 1929 to accommodate the builders and workers of the iron and steel plant, which was built 1929–33 by forced labourers (peasants who had refused to join the *kolkhoz*) and some young enthusiasts of 'Socialist construction,' with technical assistance from American experts; since then it has constantly expanded. *See* J. Scott, *Behind the Urals*, 1942.

Makarenko, Anton Semënovich (1888–1935), schoolmaster who distinguished himself in the 1920's as the head of two special schools for homeless children and juvenile delinquents. His main principles in the handling of these children were the value of collective, useful work and the need to treat each child with trust and respect. His experience is interesting and valuable, but its importance for general educational theory has been unduly exaggerated in the Soviet Union. *See* his *A Book for Parents* (Eng. ed.), Moscow, 1954, and *The Road to Life* (Eng. ed.), Moscow, 1955; W. L. Goodman, *A. S. Makarenko*,

333

Russian Teacher, 1949; I. Lezine, *A. S. Makarenko, pédagogue soviétique*, Paris, 1954.

Makarova, Tamara Fëdorovna (*b.* 1907), one of the best-known older Soviet film actresses who has created the archetype of the 'new Soviet woman,' a party member since 1943. She has worked in films since 1927, including *Seven Brave Ones*, 1935, *Komsomol'sk*, 1937, *Teacher*, 1939, *The Vow*, 1946 (one of the most notorious Stalin cult films), *The Young Guard*, 1948, and *Village Doctor*, 1952.

Makeyevka (until early 1930's **Dmitriyevsk**), city in the Stalino Oblast (Ukraine), situated 8 m. east of Stalino and forming part of its conurbation. Population (1959) 358,000 (second in the Donets Basin; 1926, 51,000; 1939, 242,000). It is a major centre of industry in the Donets Basin (iron and steel, chemical, coal-mining, heavy engineering). Makeyevka was founded in 1899 to provide accommodation for the builders and workers of the iron and steel plant which was constructed 1898–1900 and has since expanded constantly except during the civil war, the German occupation, 1941–3, and the subsequent periods of restoration. The rapid growth of the city during the 1930's was partly the result of the absorption of neighbouring settlements.

Makhachkala (until 1921 **Petrovsk-Port**), capital, economic and cultural centre of the Daghestan Autonomous Republic (North Caucasus), a port on the Caspian Sea. Population (1959) 119,000 (1926, 34,000; 1939, 87,000), mostly Russians and Kumyks. It has engineering (aircraft), oil-refining (pipeline from Groznyy), textile, shoe and fish-canning industries. The Daghestan branch of the U.S.S.R. Academy of Sciences is situated here. Makhachkala was founded in 1844 as a Russian fort, and became a town in 1857; it was made capital of Daghestan in 1921.

Makhayevism, trend in Russian social and political thought, akin to Syndicalism (q.v.), which was given a systematic expression in 1898–1900 by Makhayskiy (J. W. Machajski), a former Polish Social Democrat. In his main work, *The Brain Worker* (published 1905), he argued that knowledge was a means of production and that consequently the intelligentsia was an exploiting class. Social Democracy, according to Makhayskiy, is the class ideology of the intelligentsia. The task of the working class is not merely to assist the intelligentsia in socializing the material means of production belonging to the bourgeoisie, but to socialize knowledge as well (by confiscating private libraries, abolishing inheritance, throwing all educational establishments open to anyone, etc.). Makhayevist tendencies were strong in the Bolshevik Party until the early 1930's, and many measures taken after the seizure of power in 1917 were influenced by Makhayevist ideas. *See* S. V. Utechin, 'Bolsheviks and their Allies after 1917: the Ideological Pattern,' *Soviet Studies*, Oct. 1958.

Makhno, Nestor Ivanovich (1889–1935), Ukrainian anarchist leader. Imprisoned for a terroristic act in 1907, he was released after the February revolution (q.v.) of 1917. He organized a gang in the southern Ukraine during the civil war, composed of peasants who disliked both the Red and the White sides; his raids involved great violence, and, although he condemned anti-Semitism, pogroms and great brutality. He was temporarily allied with the Red Army in 1919 and 1920 and his movement operated legally in Soviet territory, but discord soon developed between his band and the Red Army; he was defeated, and emigrated. *See* D. Footman, 'Nestor Makhno,' *St Antony's Papers*, No. 6, Soviet Affairs, No. 2, 1959.

Maklakov, Vasiliy Aleksandrovich (1870–1957), lawyer and liberal politician, member of the 2nd, 3rd and 4th Dumas. A leading Moscow advocate, Maklakov acquired great popularity as a counsel for the defence in political cases during the revolution of 1905 (q.v.). As a politician, he represented the more moderate liberal wing of the Constitutional Democratic Party. Appointed ambassador to France by the Provisional Government (q.v.) in 1917, he was regarded until his death as unofficial head of the Russian *émigré* colony in Paris. His memoirs (*Iz Vospominanii*, New York, 1954) are important for the understanding of political developments in the Duma period. *See* M. Karpovich, 'Two Types of Russian Liberalism; Miliukov and Maklakov' in E. J. Simmons's (ed.) *Continuity and Change in Russian and Soviet Thought*, Cambridge, Mass., 1955.

Malenkov, Georgiy Maksimilianovich (*b.* 1902), Communist, of a middle class background. He became a minor commissar in the Red Army in 1919 and in 1920 joined the Communist Party. He studied at a Moscow technical institute, 1921–5, and then worked in the apparatus of the party's Central Committee and in the Moscow committee of the party under Kaganovich. From 1934 to 1939 he headed the Central Committee department for leading party personnel and as such was one of the chief perpetrators of the Great Purge (q.v.). He became member and secretary of the Central Committee in 1939 and head of its administration of cadres. In 1941 he became a candidate member of the Central Committee's Politburo and from 1941 to 1945 was the member of the State Defence Committee (q.v.) responsible for the technical equipment of the army and air force, also a high-ranking political officer on various fronts. He became chairman of the Committee for Rehabilitation of former occupied territories in 1943, secretary of the Central Committee and a deputy prime minister after the war, and a member of the Central Committee's Politburo in 1946. He presented the Central Committee's report at the 19th party congress in 1952. Malenkov became Prime Minister and the most prominent member of the 'collective leadership' (q.v.) after Stalin's death in 1953, and took the lead in denouncing Beria (q.v.). In 1955 he was obliged to make a humiliating confession of failure, and resigned the premiership; during his two years in office he had advocated the policy of equal development of capital goods and consumer goods (q.v.) industries, which policy was officially discarded after his resignation. Malenkov was expelled from the Central Committee in 1957 as a member of the 'anti-party group' (q.v.) and appointed manager of the Ust'-Kamenogorsk hydro-electric station in East Kazakhstan. *See* M. Ebon, *Malenkov*, 1953.

Malevich, Kazimir Serafimovich (1878–1935), painter of Polish origin, studied in Kiev and at the Moscow Art School. Starting as a follower of the impressionists, Malevich progressed through phases of Cézanne and Van Gogh influences, expressionism, fauvism, cubism, etc., to the creation of a style of his own, which he called Suprematism. His first Suprematist paintings were exhibited in 1915 in Petrograd; they were formal arrangements of geometrical elements, notably a black square on a white ground. In 1918 he showed his famous 'white on white' series. Malevich attempted to re-create the two-dimensional spirituality of icons through the medium of abstract painting. After the 1917 revolution and the Bolshevik seizure of power, when many painters proclaimed utilitarian social functions of art as the only true ones, Malevich continued to insist on the primarily spiritual values of abstract paintings. Unlike Kandinskiy (q.v.), Chagall and many others he remained in Russia, and in the last years of his life was forced by the obligatory doctrine of Socialist Realism (q.v.) to cease his original creative work, and painted only a few intimate portraits in a stiff 'realist' manner. See *Kasimir Malevich. Catalogue of Exhibition at Whitechapel Gallery*, 1959.

Malinovskiy, Rodion Yakovlevich (*b.* 1898), Marshal of the Soviet Union. He took part in the civil war, joined the party in 1926 and graduated in 1930 from the M.V. Frunze Military Academy. During the Second World War he commanded an army in the Stalingrad offensive, 1942, the south-western army group, 1943, and the 2nd Ukrainian army group, 1944; the latter, under his command, occupied Rumania and Hungary. In 1945 Malinovskiy commanded the Transbaykalian army group in the war against Japan, and in 1945–6 the Soviet forces in Manchuria. After the war he commanded a military district in Russia until 1957, when he succeeded Marshal Zhukov (q.v.) as Minister of Defence. He has been a candidate member of the party's Central Committee since 1952.

Managerial Class does not officially exist as a distinct social class, people in managerial positions in the economy being treated as belonging to the Soviet intelligentsia (q.v.). It is indeed difficult to draw the dividing line between the economy managers and other groups comprising the political and intellectual *élite*, since they are all in the Nomenclature (q.v.) and can be, and frequently are, transferred by the cadres (q.v.) departments of the party committees to leading work outside the economic field. There is, however, a distinct core of technical and economic managers with a well-developed self-consciousness.

The managerial class emerged in Russia towards the end of the 19th century; many of its members were organized in various industrialists' associations, headed by the Council of the Congresses of Industry and Commerce, as well as in various voluntary societies for the promotion of industry and trade. They soon developed somewhat technocratic tendencies. Many of them collaborated with the Bolshevik regime from its inception, in spite of such practices as workers' control (q.v.), the 'triangle' system of factory management (*see* INDUSTRIAL MANAGEMENT), etc., in the 1920's, but they were nevertheless treated with suspicion by the Communist authorities and, as members of the old intelligentsia, subject to various discriminations. The 'cultural revolution' (q.v.) was to a considerable extent directed against the old managerial class, and the first wave of terror in the Stalin era (*see* PURGES) was aimed at the technical intelligentsia.

Most remaining members of the old managerial class disappeared during the Great Purge (q.v.), and the present managers are largely the products of Stalin's cultural revolution and the subsequent period of Zhdanov's educational policy. They are of mixed social origin, practically all are party members, and most are 'specialists' (*see* INTELLIGENTSIA). They form an important pressure group and to some extent share power with the party apparatus, but suggestions that either the Communist dictatorship is a form of managerial rule or that the managers are going to establish their rule by replacing the party apparatus and thus putting an end to the Communist system seem exaggerated. *See* J. Burnham, *The Managerial Revolution*, 1943; G. Bienstock *et al.*, *Management in Russian Industry and Agriculture*, 1944; H. Achminow, *Die Macht im Hintergrund*, Grenchen, 1950; D. Granick, *Management of the Industrial Firm in the U.S.S.R.*, New York, 1954; J. S. Berliner, *Factory and Manager in the U.S.S.R.*, Cambridge, Mass., 1957; G. Gibian, 'The Factory Manager in Soviet Fiction,' *Problems of Communism*, No. 2, March–April 1959; J. F. Hough, 'The Technical Elite versus the Party,' *Problems of Communism*, vol. viii, No. 5, Sept.–Oct. 1959; D. Granick, *The Red Executive*, 1960.

Mandel'shtam, Leonid Isaakovich (1879–1944), outstanding physicist of Jewish origin. Educated at New Russia (Odessa) and Strasbourg universities, he was professor at the Odessa Polytechnical Institute from 1918 and at Moscow University from 1925. His works were mainly concerned with optics, theory of vibration and radio. In 1928 (together with G. S. Landsberg) he discovered—simultaneously with C. V. Raman—the combinational dispersion of light (known in Russia as the Mandel'shtam-Raman effect). His collected works were published in 1947–50. Mandel'shtam's philosophical position in lectures on the theory of relativity and quantum mechanics was criticized by protagonists of the official ideology. *See* J. G. Crowther, *Soviet Science*, 1936.

Mansi (formerly Russian **Yugra**, then **Voguls**), Ugrian-speaking people of Western Siberia who live in the west of the Khanty Mansi National Okrug (Tyumen' Oblast) and number (1959) 6,000. They are hunters, reindeer breeders and labourers, partly russified. They have been known since the 11th century, and stubbornly resisted Muscovite rule in the 15th–16th centuries.

Margelan, town in the Fergana Oblast (Uzbekistan), situated 10 m. north of Fergana. Population (1959) 68,000 (1939, 46,000). It is an important centre of the silk- and cotton-processing industries. Margelan is an ancient town with many historic buildings; according to local legend Alexander the Great died here.

Margiana, ancient name of the Merv (q.v.) oasis. It was one of the oldest centres of civilization in Central Asia, known since the 6th century B.C. when it was inhabited by sedentary agricultural Iranian-speaking people. It was conquered by Persia in 512 B.C., by Alexander the Great, *c.* 328 B.C., and later belonged to the Seleucids, the Graeco-Bactrian kingdom, Parthia, the Kushan kingdom and again Persia. In the 3rd century B.C. the whole oasis was surrounded by a wall almost 150 m. long. For later history *see* MARY; MERV.

Mari (formerly known as **Cheremises**), people of the Finnish family who live in the Mari Autonomous Republic and adjacent areas, numbering (1959) 504,000. Orthodox Christians since the 16th century, they are mostly peasants, now collectivized. In the 8th century the Mari lived under Khazar rule, from the 9th to the 13th centuries under the Volga Bulgarians, from 1236 to 1552 under the Tatars, and finally under the Russians. *See* W. Kolarz, *Russia and her Colonies*, 1952.

Mari Autonomous Republic lies on the left bank of the Volga between Gor'kiy and Kazan'; it is largely forested lowland. Area 8,900 sq. m.; population (1959) 647,000 (28 per cent urban), mostly Mari (47 per cent in 1939) and Russians (since the 16th century). The industries are timber, wood-processing, metal-working (agricultural implements) and food; grain and flax cultivation and dairy farming are carried on. Capital Yoshkar-Ola.

Mariinskiy Waterway, *see* VOLGA-BALTIC WATERWAY.

Maritime (Russian **Primorskiy**) **Kray,** of the R.S.F.S.R., is situated in the southern part of the Russian Far East between the Manchurian frontier and the Sea of Japan; it is largely mountainous and forested, and has rich deposits of coal, tin, lead, zinc and gold. Area 64,100 sq. m.; population (1959) 1,379,000 (67 per cent urban), mostly Russians and Ukrainians (since the mid 19th century), also before the 1930's Koreans and Chinese. The industries of the kray are fishing, coal-mining, non-ferrous metallurgy and shipbuilding. Soya, wheat and rice are cultivated, and dairy farming is carried on. Principal towns: Vladivostok, Ussuriysk, Nakhodka, Artëm. The area was ceded to Russia in 1858 by China. *See* W. Kolarz, *The Peoples of the Soviet Far East*, 1954.

Mariupol', *see* ZHDANOV.

Markov, Andrey Andreyevich (1856–1922), mathematician. Educated at St Petersburg University, he was professor there from 1886 and a member of the Academy of Sciences from 1896. His studies were concerned with the theory of numbers and the theory of probabilities, where he continued the work of his teacher Chebyshev (q.v.) and laid the theoretical foundations for statistical physics and for many of the modern developments in the theory of probabilities.

Markovnikov, Vladimir Vasil'yevich (1838–1904), chemist, a pupil of Butlerov (q.v.), professor at Kazan', New Russia (Odessa) and Moscow universities. His work was mainly concerned with the further development of Butlerov's theory of the structure of chemical combinations, and with the study of Caucasian oil. Among his pupils was Kablukov (q.v.).

Marr, Nikolay Yakovlevich (1864–1934), philologist of Scottish-Georgian origin. A specialist in the Caucasian languages, to which he gave the name Japhetic, Marr proceeded to develop a 'Japhetic' theory according to which the Indo-European and Semitic languages represented a later stage in the development of Caucasian languages; finally he came to a general theory of the origins of language and thought, claiming that this was an extension of Marxism into the field of linguistics. Although this theory was almost completely lacking in any factual basis, it was supported by the party authorities until Stalin rejected it as 'anti-Marxist and unscientific' in 1950. Thereafter 'Marrism' became a term of official abuse. *See* J. Ellis and R. W. Davies, 'The Crisis of Soviet Linguistics,' *Soviet Studies*, vol. ii, No. 3, Jan. 1951; W. K. Matthews, 'Developments in Soviet Linguistics since the Crisis of 1950,' *Slavonic and East European Review*, vol. xxxiv, No. 82, Dec. 1955.

Marriage, as a legal institution, is basically regulated by the R.S.F.S.R. Code of Laws on Marriage, Family and Guardianship of 1926 and the corresponding codes of the other republics. The marriageable age is 18 in the R.S.F.S.R., Belorussia and the republics where the R.S.F.S.R. codes are in force, though local authorities may in exceptional circumstances reduce it for women by one year. In the Ukraine, Moldavia, the Transcaucasian and the Central Asian republics the marriageable age is 16 for women; in the Ukraine and Moldavia the authorities may reduce the required age by six months for residents in rural localities. Marriage is forbidden between relatives in the direct line of descent and between brothers and sisters or half-brothers and half-sisters. In 1947 marriage was forbidden between Soviet citizens and foreigners, but this restriction was removed in 1954. Bigamy is forbidden, but is not a punishable offence, except in cases when it can be considered a survival of tribal custom or Muslim law. Marriage by religious ceremony alone is invalid. According to the 1926 code *de facto* marriage had the same legal status as registered marriage, but an all-Union law of 1944 made registration with the Civil Status Registry the sole form of contracting a legally valid marriage, thus reverting to the provision of the 1918 code. Children born out of wedlock are officially treated as 'fatherless,' though the term 'illegitimate' is not used.

Before 1917 marriage was treated as an essentially religious institution and governed by the canon law of various denominations. Religious marriage was obligatory for all but the pagans. Marriages between Orthodox or Roman Catholics and non-Christians, as well as between Protestants and pagans, were forbidden. Then until the mid thirties the officially accepted view was the traditional Marxist one that the family would 'wither away' as a legal institution under communism. Marriage and the family were further undermined by a kind of 'free love' theory championed by Kollontay (q.v.). The policy of the restoration of old social norms embarked upon in the mid 1930's reversed this trend. *See* R. Schlesinger, *Soviet Legal Theory*, 1945; V. Gsovski, *Soviet Civil Law*, Ann Arbor, 1948; H. J. Berman, *Justice in Russia*, Cambridge, Mass., 1950; J. N. Hazard, *Law and Social Change in the U.S.S.R.*, 1953; G. C. Guins, *Soviet Law and Soviet Society*, The Hague, 1954; W. Petersen, 'The Evolution of Soviet Family Policy,' *Problems of Communism*, vol. v, No. 5, Sept.–Oct. 1956.

Martens, Fëdor (Friedrich) Fëdorovich (1845–1909), jurist of Baltic-German origin, the most outstanding Russian expert in international law. He was professor at St Petersburg University, member of the Council of the Ministry of Foreign Affairs, a leading member of the Institut de Droit International, Russian representative at many international conferences, and permanent member of the Court of

Arbitration at The Hague. He prepared the programmes of the Brussels Conference of 1874 (on the codification of the law of war) and of the first Hague Conference of 1899. His (and D. A. Milyutin's, q.v.) project of 'Laws and Customs of War,' submitted to the Brussels Conference, was incorporated into the *règlement* adopted at The Hague, and he received the Nobel Peace Prize in 1902. Martens held that the degree of personal freedom accorded to the citizens of a state is the right criterion of that state's participation in international relations; hence only states recognizing the rights of individuals can be members of a properly organized international community. *See* his *Recueil des traités et conventions conclus par la Russie avec les puissances étrangères*, 15 vols., St Petersburg, 1874–1909; *Russia and England in Central Asia*, 1879; *Modern International Law of Civilized Peoples* (2 vols.), St Petersburg, 1882–3 (5th ed., 1904–5), trans. into French, German, etc.

Martov (real name **Tsederbaum**), **Yuliy Osipovich** (1873–1923), leader of the Mensheviks, a Social Democrat since 1892. He broke with Lenin in 1903, having previously collaborated with him in the Union for the Struggle for the Liberation of the Working Class and in the Iskra (q.v.) organization. Unlike the majority of Mensheviks he took an internationalist stand against their 'revolutionary defencism' after the February revolution (q.v.) of 1917, but became official leader of the Menshevik Party after the Bolshevik seizure of power (*see* OCTOBER REVOLUTION). In 1920 he headed a Menshevik delegation abroad, and remained in Berlin where he edited the monthly *Socialist Courier. See* L. H. Haimson, *The Russian Marxists and the Origins of Bolshevism*, Cambridge, Mass., 1955; L. Schapiro, *The Communist Party of the Soviet Union*, 1960.

Marxism. Already in the 1840's Marx's early writings were known in the philosophical circles of Stankevich and Herzen (qq.v.), where the developments of Hegelianism were closely followed. During the 1860's the *Communist Manifesto* and the *Statute of the International Working Men's Association* were published in Russian abroad and were discussed in Russia in the legal press. The first volume of *Capital* was published legally in 1872 (second and third volumes in 1885 and 1896 respectively). The first academic economist in Russia to become a Marxist was N. I. Ziber (1844–88), who taught in Kiev University. By the 1890's most economic theorists had accepted Marx's theory of surplus value. At the same time Marxism was gaining influence in revolutionary circles (*see* REVOLUTIONARY MOVEMENT). Populists (*see* POPULISM) generally accepted Marx's views on capitalism, though they denied their relevance for Russia. A specifically Marxist trend in the revolutionary movement developed from 1883, when simultaneously the Liberation of Labour Group (q.v.) headed by G. Plekhanov was formed abroad and the so-called Blagoyev Group in St Petersburg. An important role in the process of transition to Marxism was played in the 1880's and nineties by the conspiratorial organization founded by Fokin (q.v.) from which emerged a number of revolutionary Marxists, including Lenin. A heated controversy between Liberal Populists and a group of the then orthodox Marxists (*see* LEGAL MARXISTS) in the 1890's was inconclusive, but did much to attract interest to revolutionary Marxism.

The Russian Social Democratic Labour Party (q.v.), founded in 1898, officially adhered to the Marxist ideology. In the following years most of the Legal Marxists realized the weakness and inadequacy of the Marxist position and, through the intermediate stage of neo-Kantian Idealism, came to Personalism and Solidarism in philosophy, and through Liberalism to Liberal Conservatism or Christian Socialism in politics. Another group of Marxists, following Bernstein, went the way of Economism (q.v.). More important than the latter from the theoretical point of view were those young Marxists, headed by A. A. Bogdanov, who embarked upon the task of supplementing Marxism with modernist ideas (see BOGDANOVISM). Lenin's theoretical interests were centred upon grafting Marxism on to the traditional stock of ' Jacobin' organizational and tactical ideas in order to adapt them to capitalist conditions (see LENINISM). Plekhanov and the majority of Menshevik (q.v.) theorists remained orthodox (and rather sterile) Marxists, while the so-called Liquidationists (q.v.), headed by A. N. Potresov (q.v.), after the revolution of 1905 (q.v.) largely abandoned the revolutionary attitude for a reformist one.

After the seizure of power by the Bolsheviks (see OCTOBER REVOLUTION) in 1917, Leninism and Bogdanovism were the two prevalent trends in Russian Marxism, while others were to some extent tolerated during the 1920's. The activities of the outstanding Marxologist D. B. Ryazanov (q.v.) largely belong to this period. The establishment of Stalin's personal rule was followed by the imposition of his blend of heterogeneous ideas (see STALINISM) which he claimed to be further developments of orthodox Marxism-Leninism. The position has essentially remained the same in the post-Stalin period. No serious work on Marxist theory has appeared in Russia since the 1920's. See R. Schlesinger, Marx, His Time and Ours, 1950; R. N. Carew Hunt, Marxism Past and Present, 1954; J. Plamenatz, German Marxism and Russian Communism, 1954; L. T. Haimson, The Russian Marxists and the Origins of Bolshevism, Cambridge, Mass., 1955; H. Marcuse, Soviet Marxism: Critical Analysis, New York, 1958; A. B. Ulam, The Unfinished Revolution, New York, 1960; K. A. Wittfogel, 'The Marxist View of Russian Society and Revolution,' World Politics, vol. xii, No. 4, July 1960.

Marxism-Leninism, Institute of, chief institution of research into the theory and history of communism. It was formed as the Marx-Engels-Lenin Institute in 1931 through a fusion of the Marx-Engels Institute (founded by Ryazanov, q.v., in 1924) and the Lenin Institute (founded by Kamenev, q.v., in 1923); the latter had already absorbed the Commission on Party History (Istpart). Before the fusion both institutes and the Commission had done much valuable work, including the publication of collected works of Marx and Engels and of Lenin. After the fusion the institute was principally used as a tool for the glorification of Stalin. Stalin's name was added to the designation of the institute after his death, but since the 20th party congress in 1956 it has been known under its present name.

From 1953 to 1957 the principal ideological pronouncements of the party leadership ostensibly came from the institute.

Mary (formerly **Merv**): 1. Oblast in Turkmenia comprising the basins of the rivers Murgab and (since 1959) Tedzhen. Area (without the Tedzhen basin) 34,600 sq. m.; population (1959, without the Tedzhen basin) 354,000 (34 per cent urban), Turkmens and some Russians. It is the main cotton-growing area in Turkmenia and the principal producer of fine fibre cotton in the U.S.S.R.; Astrakhan sheep are raised. There are cotton and silk processing industries (the latter since the 5th century), and the old craft of carpet weaving is carried on. The southernmost point of the U.S.S.R., Kushka, is in the oblast. The area was annexed by Russia in 1884–5.

2. Administrative, economic and cultural centre of the oblast, situated on the River Murgab and the Trans-Caspian Railway. Population (1959) 48,000. Mary was founded in the 3rd century B.C. 18 miles east of its present site. (For history *see* MERV, 2.) It was destroyed by Bukhara in 1787 and the new town was built by the Russians in 1885.

Massine, Léonide (*b.* 1894), choreographer and dancer. After studying acting and dancing at the Imperial School, Moscow, in 1913 he met Diaghilev, who had just quarrelled with Nijinsky. After being placed in the hands of Cecchetti, in 1914 he appeared in Fokine's *Légende de Joseph*. His first appearance as choreographer was in 1915, and between that date and 1924 his works included *Les Femmes de bonne humeur, Parade, Contes Russes, La Boutique Fantasque, Le Tricorne, Pulcinella* and a new version of *Le Sacre du Printemps*. From 1921 to 1924 he undertook independent work as a dancer and teacher in London and Paris, but in 1924 rejoined Diaghilev, with whom he remained till 1928. From 1932 to 1936 he worked with Colonel de Basil's company, producing ballets and dance arrangements of classical symphonies, and from 1937 with René Blum. Since then he has resided mostly in America. Massine is the legitimate successor to the reforms of Fokine which he has appropriated and developed in his own highly personal manner. In his work, which is of the greatest variety, mime and dancing are fused and there is complete co-ordination between music and the individual.

Materialism is the official designation of the basic ontological and sociological positions of Marxism, and the Marxist philosophy is commonly referred to in the Soviet Union as Dialectical and Historical Materialism. Materialism as interpreted by Lenin is essentially a naïve realism. Materialism in this sense is obligatory in the treatment of any philosophically relevant subject, except by authorized spokesmen of officially recognized religious bodies (*see* IDEOLOGY). Before the spread of Marxism, Materialism was represented in Russia by Bakunin, Chernyshevskiy, Pisarev and to some extent by scientists such as Sechenov (qq.v.). In recent works on the history of Russian philosophy published in the Soviet Union, the importance of Materialism in the Russian philosophical tradition is grossly exaggerated, and often naturalism or positivism are presented as Materialism. *See also* DIALECTICAL, ECONOMIC, HISTORICAL and MECHANICAL MATERIALISM. *See* N. Lossky, *History of Russian*

Philosophy, 1951; V. V. Zenkovsky, *A History of Russian Philosophy*, 2 vols., 1953; G. A. Wetter, *Dialectical Materialism*, 1958.

Mathematics made its first successes in the present territory of the U.S.S.R. in the works of the great medieval scholars al-Khorezmi (9th century) and al-Biruni (10th–11th centuries), who lived in Central Asia and wrote in Arabic; their tradition was continued in Central Asia until the 15th century. In Russia mathematics began to develop with the establishment of the Academy of Sciences, and the first outstanding mathematician was L. Euler, who lived in St Petersburg 1726–44. A native mathematical genius was Lobachevskiy (q.v.), one of the creators of the non-Euclidian geometry. The St Petersburg mathematical school (Ostrogradskiy, Chebyshev, Markov, Kovalevskaya, Lyapunov, Steklov, qq.v.) made considerable advances in the 19th and early 20th centuries in mathematical analysis, theory of numbers, probabilities theory and mathematical physics. Among the more important recent work is that of Lavrent'yev (q.v.) on the theory of analytical functions, of Petrovskiy, Sobolev Kantorovich (qq.v.), and others on functional analysis, of Bernshteyn, Kolmogorov (qq.v.) and A. Ya. Khinchin on the theory of probabilities, of Grave, Schmidt (qq.v.), etc., on algebra, and of Luzin (q.v.) on differential geometry. *See also* CYBERNETICS. See *American Mathematical Society Translations*, Series 2, vols. i–vi, Providence, 1955–7; S. G. Mikhlin, *Integral Equations and their Applications to Certain Problems in Mechanics, Mathematical Physics and Technology*, 1957; A. Vucinich, 'Mathematics in Russian Culture,' *Journal of the History of Ideas*, vol. xxi, No. 2, April–June 1960. A complete 'cover-to-cover' translation of the journal *Applied Mathematics and Mechanics* exists in English.

Maverannakhr, *see* MĀWĀRA'NNAHR.

Māwāra'nnahr (Arabic 'beyond the river'), medieval (10th–16th centuries) Arabic name of the region in Central Asia between the rivers Amu-Dar'ya and Syr-Dar'ya (ancient Sogdiana) and the adjacent area east of the middle course of the Syr-Dar'ya. *See* TRANSOXANIA.

Maximalists, radical Populist (*see* POPULISM) group which split off from the Socialist Revolutionaries in 1904. They took an active part in the 1905 revolution, resorting—both during the revolution and afterwards—like the Bolsheviks to so-called 'expropriations,' i.e. robbery. They co-operated with the Bolsheviks after the latter's seizure of power in 1917 and were represented in the Central Executive Committee (q v.) The group disintegrated in 1920, and the majority joined the Bolshevik Party.

Mayakovskiy, Vladimir Vladimirovich (1893–1930), poet, the leading Russian representative of the Futurist school; he joined the Bolshevik faction of the Russian Social Democratic Labour Party for a short time in 1908. His early poems were published in the Futurist collection *A Slap in the Face to Public Taste*, 1912. Mayakovskiy put his talent to work for the Communist Party after the Bolshevik seizure of power, and played an active role in all propaganda campaigns, but his political poems (*Left March*, 1919, *150,000,000*, 1920, *V. I. Lenin*, 1924, *Good!*, 1927, *Verses on the Soviet Passport*, 1930) and plays (*Mystery-Buff*, 1918, *The Bed Bug*, 1929, *The Bath House*,

1930) were marked by a lively presentation of the orthodox themes. Misfortune in love and disillusionment with the party drove him to suicide. Mayakovskiy's poetic novelties had much effect upon contemporary and subsequent Russian poetry and in 1935 he was declared by Stalin to be 'the best, most talented poet of the Soviet epoch'; since then he has been officially regarded as a model of Socialist Realism (q.v.). *See further under* FUTURISM. See *Mayakovsky and his Poetry*, compiled by H. Marshall, Bombay, 1942; 3rd ed., 1955; J. Lindsay (trans.), *Russian Poetry, 1917–55*, 1957; R. Poggioli, *The Poets of Russia, 1890–1930*, Cambridge, Mass., 1960; P. Blake (ed.), *The Bedbug and Selected Poetry* (trans. M. Hayward and G. Reavey), New York, 1960.

Maykop, administrative centre (since 1936) of the Adyge Autonomous Oblast, in the Krasnodar Kray (North Caucasus). Population (1959) 82,000, mostly Russians. It has woodworking and food industries, and important oilfields near by; there is a famous Bronze Age barrow in the vicinity. Maykop was founded in 1857, and was occupied by the Germans 1942–3.

Mazepa, Ivan Stepanovych (1645–1709), Ukrainian hetman, elected in 1687. He built many churches and endeavoured to spread education, but his attempts to consolidate the privileged position of the Cossack upper stratum caused discontent among the peasants and rank-and-file Cossacks. He negotiated with the Polish king, Stanislaw Leszczynski in 1705, and later with Charles XII of Sweden, with the object of throwing off the sovereignty of the Muscovite czar. Peter the Great, however, trusted him and did not believe information about his treasonable activities; when in 1708 Charles XII invaded the Ukraine, Mazepa, with the support of the Zaporozh'ye Cossacks (*see* SICH), joined him, but they were defeated in the battle of Poltava, 1709, and fled to Turkey.

Mechanical Materialism, or 'Mechanicism,' term used by Deborin and later by Stalin to describe the interpretation of Marxist philosophy represented by Bukharin. It was alleged to be, and to some extent was in fact, influenced by Bogdanovist ideas (*see* BOGDANOVISM). *See also* DIALECTICAL MATERIALISM; MATERIALISM.

Mechanics. The semi-literate 18th-century craftsman Kulibin (q.v.) is reputed to have been the first remarkable Russian mechanic, but the flowering of this science in Russia dates from the late 19th century (Lyapunov, q.v.). In the early 20th century N. Ye. Zhukovskiy and Chaplygin (qq.v.) were pioneers in aerodynamics, Tsiolkovskiy (q.v.) in rocketry, A. N. Krylov (q.v.) in the theory of ships. Aero-hydromechanics has continued to attract the principal attention in recent decades, outstanding results being achieved by, among others, Sedov and Lavrent'yev (qq.v.). *See also* AIRCRAFT; MATHEMATICS; ROCKETS. See J. G. Crowther, *Soviet Science*, 1936. Complete 'cover-to-cover' translations of the following journals exist in English: *Automation and Telemechanics*; *Applied Mathematics and Mechanics*; *Journal of Abstracts: Mechanics*.

Mechnikov, Il'ya Il'ich (1845–1916), biologist. He graduated from Khar'kov University at 19, and then studied at Giessen, Göttingen, Munich and Naples. He was professor of zoology and comparative anatomy at Odessa University, 1873–82, and in 1888 became the head of a bacteriological laboratory at the École Normale in Paris under Pasteur. He worked together with A. Kovalevskiy (q.v.) on the embryology of invertebrates, discovered the white corpuscles of the blood (*Intra-Cellular Digestion*, 1882), originated the theory of phagocytes, 1884, showed the curative nature of inflammation (*The Comparative Pathology of Inflammation*, 1892) and investigated the problem of ageing (*The Nature of Man*, 1903, Eng. trans. 1938; *Optimistic Essays*, 1907; *The Prolongation of Human Life*, 1910). In 1908 he shared the Nobel Prize for Medicine. *See* O. Mechnikov, *Life of Elie Metchnikoff, 1845–1916*, 1921.

Mechnikov, Lev Il'ich (1838–88), sociologist and geographer, brother of Il'ya, professor at the Neuchâtel Academy in Switzerland. In his chief work, *Civilization and the Great River Systems*, 1889, he argued that the influence of geographical conditions is decisive in determining the course of historical development.

Medicine made its first important advances in Russia in the middle of the 19th century, when Botkin (q.v.) introduced the ideas of Virchow and Claude Bernard into Russian medical theory and practice, and Pirogov (q.v.) achieved outstanding successes in surgery and laid the foundations of military surgery. The physiological trend originated by Botkin continued to predominate in recent decades (e.g. A. D. Speranskiy, A. A. Bogomolets, qq.v., and their schools), though pathological anatomy has also been intensively studied (e.g. by Abrikosov, q.v.); Vishnevskiy, Burdenko, Filatov, Bakulev (qq.v.) and others have continued the Pirogov tradition in surgery. *See also* BIOLOGY; HEALTH SERVICES. *See* J. G. Crowther, *Soviet Science*, 1936; H. E. Sigerist, *Socialized Medicine in the Soviet Union*, 1937; *Scientific Session on the Physiological Teaching of I. P. Pavlov*, Moscow, 1951; M. G. Field, 'The Soviet Doctor's Dilemma,' *Problems of Communism*, vol. vi, No. 1, Jan.–Feb. 1957; F. G. Korotkov *et al.* (eds.), *Soviet Research on Remote Consequences of Injuries caused by the Action of Ionizing Radiation*, New York, 1957; G. S. Pondoev, *Notes of a Soviet Doctor*, 1959; *Soviet Pharmaceutical Research* (3 vols.), Consultants Bureau, New York. Complete ' cover-to-cover' translations of the following journals exist in English: *Bulletin of Experimental Biology and Medicine*; *Journal of Microbiology, Epidemiology and Immunobiology*; *Pharmacology and Toxicology*.

Medtner, Nikolay Karlovich (1879–1951), composer and pianist of German parentage, who studied at Moscow Conservatory under Arenskiy, Taneyev and Safonov, later becoming professor there; he emigrated in 1921. His works comprise three piano concertos; violin sonatas; piano sonatas; songs. Medtner owes little to Russian music, being rather an adherent of the 19th-century German tradition of Schumann and Brahms. His music, however, is always cheerful and often programmatic. *See* L. Sabaneev, 'Nikolay Medtner,' *Modern Russian Composers*, 1929.

Medynskiy, Yevgeniy Nikolayevich (1885–1957), well-known exponent of the official Soviet educational theory of the 1930's and forties. *See* his *Education in the U.S.S.R.*, 1953.

Megrelians, or **Mingrelians,** West Kartvelian people inhabiting Mingrelia (in western Georgia) who numbered about 240,000 in 1939. Despite the official policy of assimilation with the Georgians, they still retain their own language and to some extent a separate national consciousness, and accusations of Megrelian nationalism are sometimes made against local Communist officials.

Melekess, town in the Ul'yanovsk Oblast, situated on the Kuybyshev reservoir and the railway line Ul'yanovsk–Ufa, 56 m. east of Ul'yanovsk. Population (1959) 51,000 (1939, 32,000). It has food and textile industries and is a local cultural centre. Melekess was founded in 1626; it was an industrial (pig-iron, potash, candles, leather) and commercial village, and became a town in the 19th century.

Melitopol', town in the Zaporozh'ye Oblast (southern Ukraine), situated in Tauria 65 m. south of Zaporozh'ye. Population (1959) 95,000 (1926, 25,000). It has varied engineering (since 1912) and food industries, and is a local cultural centre; the town is the centre of a rich fruit-growing area (cherries, apricots, etc.). Melitopol' became a town in 1841 and saw much fighting in 1943.

Memel, see KLAIPEDA.

Mendeleyev, Dmitriy Ivanovich (1834–1907), great scientist and business man. Born in Tobol'sk, son of the headmaster of the local secondary school, he was educated at the St Petersburg Pedagogical Institute, did post-graduate work at Heidelberg (with Bunsen, Kirchhoff and Kopp) and taught at St Petersburg University from 1857 (professor from 1861) until his resignation as a result of disagreement with the Minister of Education in 1890. After resigning, besides attending to his own business in the Urals, he headed the Chamber of Measures and Weights from 1893 until his death, was a member of the commission for preparing a new customs tariff, etc. Mendeleyev's greatest service to science was his periodic system of elements (*Foundations of Chemistry*, 2 parts, 1869–71, Eng. trans. 1892) which summed up the achievements of classical chemistry, but he also did important work in crystallography, organic chemistry (petroleum), theory of solutions, physical properties of gases and liquids, meteorology, etc.

Himself a successful industrialist, Mendeleyev was a determined protagonist of a rapid industrial development for Russia through utilization of her rich mineral resources (coal of the Donets, Kuznetsk and Karaganda basins, Baku oil and metals of the Urals), advanced technology, protectionist tariffs and the spread of education (*The Tariff Explained*, 1892, *Thoughts on the Development of Agriculture*, 1899). He was a recognized spokesman of the new managerial class (q.v.) in Russia, and in his later works developed a political ideology of the Russian brand of Technocratism which he called 'gradualism' (*Cherished Thoughts*, 1903–5, *On Knowing Russia*, 1906, *Thoughts on the Theory of Knowledge*, 1909). His philosophical position Mendeleyev defined as Realism and he opposed both Idealism and Materialism (qq.v.).

Mensheviks (from *men'she*, fewer), political party set up in August 1917 at a unification congress of several Social Democratic groups. Prior to 1917 the word had been used to denote the non-Leninist faction of the Russian Social Democratic Labour Party (q.v.). After the latter had split in 1903, all the recognized party leaders save Lenin were on the Menshevik side (which consisted of the 'soft' Iskraists and 'Economists,' *see* ISKRA; ECONOMISM), which soon secured control of the party's main newspaper and most of the local committees. The Mensheviks advocated a broad proletarian party and collaboration with liberals against autocracy and for a democratic constitution. They co-operated locally with the Bolsheviks during the 1905 revolution, and formally reunited with them in 1906, but relations remained strained because the Bolsheviks continued their attempts to dominate the party completely, despite its predominantly Menshevik character at the time. The emergence of several different trends among the Mensheviks themselves served to complicate the situation further; these trends were the 'liquidationists' (q.v.) (so named by their opponents) led by Potresov (q.v.), who doubted that with the granting of the constitution in 1906 a conspiratorial underground was still needed; the 'party-minded Mensheviks,' led by Plekhanov (q.v.), who believed that it was; the centre, under Martov (q.v.) and Aksel'rod, who wished to maintain the unity of all Mensheviks; and Trotskiy's supporters, who wanted to unify all Social Democrats. A new regrouping took place with the First World War: the internationalists under Martov and Trotskiy, and the defencists under Potresov and Plekhanov (now reconciled). Several organized groups of Mensheviks existed after the February 1917 revolution, the chief one—led by F. I. Dan—maintaining the policy of revolutionary defencism, i.e. defence of the new revolutionary Russia. Most soviets had a majority of Mensheviks, who supported and later took part in the Provisional Government. After the Bolshevik seizure of power the official Menshevik Party, led by Martov, attempted to adopt tactics of legal opposition to the Bolsheviks. In 1922 the party was suppressed, though many former Mensheviks continued working in Soviet institutions. In 1931 a show trial of Mensheviks took place in Moscow, though actually only one of the accused was a Menshevik. In 1920 a delegation of Mensheviks left Russia, and still exists in the U.S.A., issuing the monthly *Socialist Courier* in New York; its present leader is R. A. Abramovich. See L. H. Haimson, *The Russian Marxists and the Origins of Bolshevism*, 1955; L. Schapiro, *The Communist Party of the Soviet Union*, 1960.

Menshikov, Aleksandr Danilovich (1673–1729), statesman and field marshal who rose from a poor Moscow family to be Peter the Great's most powerful collaborator in his reforms. After Peter's death Menshikov ruled the country during the reign of Catherine I and the minority of Peter II, but was ousted by court intrigue and banished to Siberia where he died.

Menshikov, Aleksandr Sergeyevich (1787–1869), general and admiral, great-grandson of Aleksandr Danilovich, who unsuccessfully commanded the Russian forces during the Crimean War at Alma, Inkerman and around Sevastopol'.

Merezhkovskiy, Dmitriy Sergeyevich (1865–1941), literary critic, writer, a leader of the older Symbolists who was influential in the religious revival among Russian intellectuals in the early 1900's. His first poems, 1888, and his essay *On the Causes of Decline of Contemporary Russian Literature*, 1892–3, were the harbingers of Russian Symbolism and of the discarding of the traditional sociological school in literary criticism. From 1906 to 1912, and after 1917, he lived in France. Among his works are the trilogy *Christ and Anti-Christ*, 1893–1902, the essay *Tolstoy and Dostoyevskiy*, 1901, and the anti-collectivist treatise *The Coming Hamite*, 1906.

Merv: 1. One of the chief oases of Central Asia, situated around the lower course of the River Murgab; it is now the main part of the Mary Oblast of Turkmenia. Merv, known in antiquity as Margiana (q.v.), belonged in the early Middle Ages to the Sasanid Empire. It was conquered by the Arabs in 651, who ruled there until the 10th century. Since then it has had a very turbulent history, belonging variously to its stronger neighbours Persia, Khorezm and the states centred on the Zeravshan Valley (*see* BUKHARA KHANATE; TRANS-OXANIA; TURKESTAN), and suffering invasions of nomadic Turkmens. However, the greatest disasters were the break through the Sultan-bend dam of the River Murgab in 1163 and the conquest by Genghis Khan's Mongols in 1221–2, when according to tradition up to 1,300,000 men, women and children perished. During the 16th–18th centuries the oasis was gradually occupied by Turkmen tribesmen, some of whom became sedentary or semi-sedentary. In 1884 the Merv oasis voluntarily submitted to Russia and was annexed.

2. Ruins of a former city which was the centre of the oasis, situated near the present town of Bayram-Ali 18 m. east of Mary. The city, known in antiquity as Antiochia Margiana, was founded in the 3rd century B.C. on the site of an earlier settlement. Its periods of greatness were 651–821, when it was the seat of the Arab rulers of Khorasan and Transoxania and one of the main centres of Islamic learning, and 1118–57, when it was the capital of the Seljuk Empire under its last sultan, Sandzhar. Several mausoleums, mosques and castles of the 11th–12th centuries survived and are among the best monuments of Muslim art in Central Asia. The city was destroyed by the Mongols in 1221–2 and never fully recovered. It was finally abandoned after the Bukharan raid of 1787, when the Sultanbend dam was again destroyed and the inhabitants dispersed. Study and excavations on the site have been going on intermittently since 1890.

3. *See* MARY, 2.

Meshchëra, lowland area lying in the Moscow, Ryazan' and Vladimir oblasts between the Oka and its tributaries the Moskva and the Klyaz'ma. There are many lakes and peat marshes, pine and spruce forests, rich alluvial grazing lands, and phosphorite deposits. In the Middle Ages the area was inhabited by the Finnish tribe Meshchëra, who were assimilated by the Russians in the 16th century, and the present-day Russians inhabiting this area are known as Meshchëra. Meshchëra was included in the Virgin and Idle Land Campaign (q.v.).

Meshcherskiy, Prince Vladimir Petrovich (1839–1914), reactionary publicist, editor and publisher of the weekly *Grazhdanin* (*The Citizen*), subsidized by the Government, in which he advocated a return to the conditions that prevailed before the Great Reforms (q.v.). After the 1880's he was influential in government and court circles.

Messerer, Asaf Mikhaylovich (*b.* 1903), dancer, choreographer and teacher. After studying at the Leningrad School until 1921 he acted as choreographer of many ballets, finally becoming ballet master at the Bolshoi Theatre, Moscow. He is generally reckoned one of the greatest male dancers and teachers in Russia today and has received many decorations and awards.

Meyerhold, Vsevolod Emil'yevich (1874–1942), outstanding actor and director. A pupil of V. I. Nemirovich-Danchenko and Stanislavskiy (q.v.), he worked in the Moscow Art Theatre, 1898–1902, and various provincial, Moscow and St Petersburg (1906–17) theatres. He joined the Communist Party in 1918 and for a time was in charge of all the Moscow theatres on behalf of the Commissariat of Education (then headed by Lunacharskiy, q.v.). In 1920 Meyerhold founded his own theatre in Moscow, and from 1923 he also produced plays in the Theatre of the Revolution. Meyerhold was probably the most gifted and extreme of all the modernistic innovators in the theatrical world, and he found a most congenial playwright in Mayakovskiy (q.v.). Following repeated accusations of Formalism (q.v.) in the thirties, Meyerhold's theatre was closed down in 1938. He worked for a year at the Stanislavskiy Moscow Opera Theatre, but was arrested in 1939 and disappeared. His reputation has been partially rehabilitated since Stalin's death. *See further under* THEATRE. *See* J. Jelagin, *Taming the Arts*, New York, 1951; M. Bradshaw (ed.), *Soviet Theatres, 1917–41*, New York, 1954; T. Cole and H. K. Chinoy (eds.), *Actors on Acting*, 1960.

Mezen', river which rises in the Timan ridge (northern Russia) and flows north-west into the Mezen' Bay of the White Sea. Length 545 m.

Mezhdunarodnaya Kniga (Russian for 'International Book'), State foreign trade agency. It exports and imports books and other printed matter, gramophone records and postage stamps (for collectors); it also arranges for the publication abroad of Soviet books and music.

Mezhdurechensk, town in the Kemerovo Oblast (southern Siberia), situated on the River Tom' and the South Siberian Railway. Population (1959) 55,000. It is a new coal-mining centre of the Kuznetsk Basin, founded in the early 1950's.

Mezhrayontsy, colloquial name for a Social Democratic group headed by K. K. Yurenev which was formed in St Petersburg in 1913 by people not belonging to either the Bolshevik or the Menshevik factions, mostly adherents of Trotskiy and Plekhanov. They took up a defeatist position during the First World War and conducted anti-war propaganda in the forces. The group acquired great significance after the February 1917 revolution, when many prominent left-wing Social Democrats, including Trotskiy himself and Lunacharskiy, joined it upon return from emigration or banishment. The group immediately started close co-operation with the Bolsheviks, and joined them *in corpore* at the 6th congress of the party in July 1917. *See* L. Schapiro, *The Communist Party of the Soviet Union*, 1960.

M.G.B. (Russian abbreviation for 'Ministry of State Security'), name of the Soviet security service, 1946–53, successor of the N.K.V.D. and N.K.G.B., essentially similar to them in functions and methods, and like them under the direct orders of Stalin. Its chief operations were those against the 'cosmopolitans' (mainly Jewish intellectuals) in 1949, and against the erstwhile supporters of Zhdanov (*see* LENINGRAD CASE). These initiated the new wave of terror, resembling the Great Purge (q.v.), that culminated in the discovery of the alleged 'Doctors' Plot' (q.v.) in 1952 but ended with the death of Stalin. *See further under* SECURITY ORGANS.

Miass, town in the Chelyabinsk Oblast (Urals), situated 56 m. south-west of Chelyabinsk. Population (1956) 35,000. It is the centre of a gold-mining area and has produced cars since 1944. The Il'men nature reservation—a 'mineralogical paradise'—is in the neighbourhood. Miass was founded as a copper-smelting works in 1773.

Michael (1596–1645), first of the house of Romanov (q.v.), elected czar of Muscovy and Russia in 1613 by the Assembly of the Land after the Time of Troubles (*see* TROUBLES, TIME OF). A feeble and commonplace person, he was faced with the difficult job of re-establishing order internally and defending the country externally against Poland and Sweden; in this task he depended upon his father, Patriarch Philaret of Moscow, several favourites, and the Assembly of the Land, which met sixteen times during his reign.

Michurin, Ivan Vladimirovich (1855–1935), plant breeder who through skilful crossing created a number of varieties of fruit trees suitable for the climate of central Russia. He believed in the Lamarckian theory of inheritance of acquired characteristics, and, like his American counterpart L. Burbank, built spurious scientific theories, ignoring modern genetics. These theories have been inflated by Lysenko (q.v.) into a complete 'progressive Michurinist biology' which is favoured by the Communist Party authorities. *See* E. Simmons (ed.), *Continuity and Change in Russian and Soviet Thought*, Cambridge, Mass., 1955.

Michurinsk (until 1932 **Kozlov**), town in the Tambov Oblast (central Russia), 45 m. north-west of Tambov. Population (1959) 80,000 (1914, 50,000). It has engineering, food and textile industries, and is a major railway junction; there are several horticultural research institutes. Michurinsk was founded as a fortified town in the Muscovite southern defence line in 1636.

Mikhaylov, Nikolay Aleksandrovich (*b.* 1906), Communist. Born in Moscow, he was a manual worker, joined the party in 1930 and was an insignificant party propagandist until the Great Purge (q.v.), when he rose spectacularly and became first secretary of the Komsomol's central committee in 1938, having actively contributed to the downfall and arrest of his predecessor, A. V. Kosarev; he remained in this position till 1952. He became a member of the party's Central Committee in 1939, one of its secretaries in 1952, and after Stalin's death succeeded Khrushchëv as first secretary of the Moscow party committee; but in 1954 he was appointed ambassador to Poland, and in 1955 became Minister of Culture, a position of secondary importance, from which he was relieved in 1960, and appointed U.S.S.R. ambassador to Indonesia.

Mikhaylovskiy, Nikolay Konstantinovich (1842–1904), literary critic, sociologist, publicist and chief theorist of Populism (q.v.). *See* T. G. Masaryk, *The Spirit of Russia*, vol. ii, 2nd ed., 1955; J. H. Billington, *Mikhailovsky and Russian Populism*, 1958; R. Hare, *Portraits of Russian Personalities between Reform and Revolution*, 1959.

Mikhoels (real name **Vovsi**), **Solomon Mikhaylovich** (1890–1948), outstanding Jewish actor and director. Having studied law at Petrograd University, he joined the Yiddish theatrical studio in Petrograd in 1919, which in 1921 was transformed into the State Yiddish Theatre (Moscow), where he became artistic director in 1929. His productions cover both Yiddish (Sholom-Aleykhem, Mendele-Moykher-Sforim) and world classics (e.g. Shakespeare's *King Lear*). Mikhoels died in mysterious circumstances and a few months later, in 1949, his theatre was closed during the campaign against 'cosmopolitanism' (*see* ZHDANOV).

Mikoyan, Anastas Ivanovich (*b.* 1895), Armenian Communist, educated at a theological seminary. He joined the Bolshevik Party in 1915, and first worked in Tiflis and Baku. He has held the following positions: in 1921 head of the party organization in Nizhniy-Novgorod, and 1922–6 in the North Caucasus; since 1926 in charge of foreign and internal trade, and since 1930 also of food industries; member of the Central Committee since 1923; candidate member of the Politburo in 1926, full member since 1935; deputy prime minister since 1937. After Stalin's death Mikoyan appears to have consistently supported Khrushchёv, and as the latter's power was consolidated Mikoyan has become one of the most influential figures in the party leadership. His visit to the U.S.A. in 1958 was a considerable personal success. Mikoyan has the reputation of being a rather more reasonable person than most Communist leaders.

Mikoyan-Shakhar, *see* KARACHAYEVSK.

Military Service is listed in the constitution of 1936 as one of the fundamental duties of citizens. The present regulations date from 1939, and provide for call-up for active service for a period of two to five years (according to the arm). The call-up begins at the age of 19 except for those who complete secondary education at 17 or 18, when it is effective immediately. Other ranks remain on the reserve until the age of 50, officers from 50 to 60 according to rank, and generals and admirals till 65. The reserve consists of men who have done military service, men who have been certified as fit but have not actually served, and women between the ages of 19 and 50 who have had medical, veterinary or special technical training. Young reservists are liable for call-up for short-term training periods. Before the Great Reforms (q.v.) of Alexander II's reign only peasants and burghers were liable for military service (the gentry having been released from compulsory State service in 1762); recruitment was haphazard, and those who had the misfortune to be recruited had to serve for twenty-five years. The duration of military service was reduced to sixteen years in 1861, and Milyutin's military reforms of 1874 introduced the principle of universal military service for all men of 20 years for a period of six years, with reductions according to educational stand-ards (university graduates serving for six months). The Bolsheviks abolished conscription in January 1918 but reintroduced it a few months later.

Military Tribunals, special courts with a hierarchy of their own, but subordinated to the Military Division of the U.S.S.R. Supreme Court (q.v.). There are Military Tribunals in the army, navy and organs of State security (*see* SECURITY ORGANS), having jurisdiction over all crimes committed by military and security personnel and all cases of espionage. Until the legal reform (q.v.) of 1958 they also had juris-diction over crimes of a military character committed by certain classes of civilians, and over all 'State crimes'; in the past Military Tribunals formed part of the terror apparatus, e.g. the show trials of the Great Purge (q.v.) were conducted before the Military Division of the Supreme Court. *See* H. J. Berman and M. Kerner, *Soviet Military Law and Administration,* Cambridge, Mass., 1955.

Militia, name adopted after the February revolution (q.v.) of 1917 for the police. It was retained by the Bolsheviks, though the militia was gradually transformed from a rather haphazard organization into a regular police force. The militia was centrally organized under the Ministry of Internal Affairs (*see* M.V.D.) from 1934 until 1960; with the abolition of the central ministry in 1960 it has once again become the responsibility of the Union Republic governments. Under Yezhov and Beria it was not responsible to the local authorities, but it is now subject to the usual principle of dual subordination (q.v.). The militia discharges ordinary police duties and does not normally take part in the activities of the security organs (q.v.).

Milyukov, Pavel Nikolayevich (1859–1943), historian and leader of the Constitutional Democratic Party, member of the Duma, 1907–17. He was Foreign Minister in the Provisional Government (q.v.) that followed the February revolution (q.v.) of 1917, lived later in Paris and died in London. *See* his *Russia and its Crisis,* Chicago, 1906; *Outlines of Russian Culture* (ed. M. M. Karpovich, 3 vols.), Phila-delphia, 1941; *Vospomimaniya, 1859–1917* (ed. by M. M. Karpovich and B. I. Elkin, 2 vols.), New York, 1955; S. R. Tompkins, *Russian Intelligentsia, Makers of the Revolutionary State,* Norman, Oklahoma, 1957; G. Fischer, *Russian Liberalism. From Gentry to Intelligentsia,* Cambridge, Mass., 1958.

Milyutin, Count Dmitriy Alekseyevich (1816–1912), Minister of War, 1861–81, who introduced universal military service, 1874, and re-organized the military administration; he resigned with Loris-Melikov (q.v.).

Milyutin, Nikolay Alekseyevich (1818–72), brother of Dmitriy, deputy Minister of the Interior, and active in the Great Reforms (q.v.), especially in preparing the emancipation of the serfs. He carried out a similar reform, in particularly liberal vein, when appointed state secretary in Poland after the 1863 uprising.

Mingrelia, historical name of the area in western Georgia north of the River Rioni adjacent to the Black Sea which is inhabited by Megrelians (q.v.). In 1952 an alleged Megrelian nationalist organiza-tion, which included the leading local party officials, was liquidated.

Minin, Kuz'ma (*d.* 1616), butcher from Nizhniy-Novgorod who organized the army which, commanded by Prince Pozharskiy, ejected the Poles from Moscow in 1612 (*see* TROUBLES, TIME OF).

Minister, head of a ministry; since 1957 high-ranking officials of the State Planning Committee can also be given the title of minister. From 1917 to 1946 the name People's Commissar was used instead of minister. *See also* COMMISSAR; COMMITTEE OF MINISTERS; COUNCIL OF MINISTERS.

Ministry, important government departments in the U.S.S.R. and the Union and Autonomous republics. There are three categories of ministries: those which exist only on the all-Union level, only on the republic level (e.g. Ministries of Education), and those which exist at both levels (e.g. Ministries of Finance). During Stalin's rule there was a marked preference for ministries of the first and third categories, but the decentralization policy since Stalin's death has favoured instead the second and third categories. The total number of ministries on the all-Union level, which in the last years of Stalin's life was over fifty, has greatly diminished since his death. Most of the economic ministries were abolished in 1957 in connection with the territorialization of economic administration; several others have been transformed into State Committees, though retaining their ministerial rank. Ministries were originally established in Russia in 1804, replacing Peter the Great's 'colleges'; from 1917 to 1946 they were called People's Commissariats. *See* M. Fainsod, *How Russia is Ruled*, Cambridge, Mass., 1953; V. Gsovski and K. Grzybowski (eds.), *Government, Law and Courts in the Soviet Union and Eastern Europe*, vol. i, 1959.

Minorities occupy an ambiguous position in Communist theory. On the one hand, in so far as communism is derived from the earlier theories of totalitarian democracy, minorities tend to be disregarded, but on the other, Lenin assigned to one particular political minority, the Communist Party, the role of the organizer of a socialist revolution, leader of the proletariat, and sole repository of political power in the system of the Dictatorship of the Proletariat. In present-day theory the party is described as 'the guiding and directing force' in Soviet society. Minorities play yet another part in Leninist theory: the party can and must make use of minorities within any group or organization for the purpose of extending its influence. For ethnic minorities in Russia *see* NATIONALITIES POLICY and entries on individual peoples; for religious minorities *see* RELIGION.

Minsk (Belorussian **Mensk**): 1. Oblast in central Belorussia, hilly in the north-west, but largely lowland and partly covered with pine and birch forests; there are large deposits of peat. Area (1959) 13,500 sq. m.; population (1959) 1,728,000 (43 per cent urban), mostly Belorussians (before the war many Jews). The oblast has engineering, woodworking, food and leather industries; coarse grains and potatoes are cultivated, and pigs and cattle raised. Principal towns: Minsk, Borisov and Molodechno.

2. Capital, economic and cultural centre of the Belorussian Republic and of the oblast. Population (1959) 509,000 (1910, 105,000; 1917, 153,000; 1920, 104,000; 1939, 237,000; 1948, 231,000; 1956,

412,000), mostly Belorussians and Russians (before the war half Jewish). It has large and varied engineering (lorries, tractors, bicycles, machine tools, instruments), textile, leather and food industries, and is an important transportation centre on the Moscow–Warsaw and Khar'kov–Liepaja railways. There are several higher educational establishments, including a university (founded 1921) and the Belorussian Academy of Sciences (founded in 1922 as the Institute of Belorussian Culture, transformed 1929), in the city. Minsk has been known since 1067, and belonged to the Polotsk Principality; it became capital of Minsk Principality in 1101, and Lithuanian in 1326. Magdeburg Law was introduced in the local government of the city in 1499. It was an important commercial and cultural centre of Lithuania, became Russian in 1793 (provincial capital) and capital of Belorussia in 1918. Minsk was occupied by the Germans in 1918 and 1941–4, by the Poles in 1920, and was largely destroyed in the Second World War. Its industrial development began in the 1870's, and received new impetus in the 1930's and after 1945.

Minusinsk, town in the Krasnoyarsk Kray (central Siberia), 328 m. south of Krasnoyarsk, a river port on the Yenisey and centre of an important agricultural area. Population (1926) 20,000. It has saw-milling and food industries, and a rich local museum (founded 1877). Minusinsk was founded in the mid 18th century and became a town in 1822; Lenin spent three years of banishment in the nearby village of Shushenskoye.

Minusinsk Basin, area in the Krasnoyarsk Kray (central Siberia), south of Krasnoyarsk, surrounded by the Kuznetsk Alatau and Sayan ranges and traversed by the Yenisey. It is a steppe region, partly wooded, with an extreme continental climate. The inhabitants are Russian (since the 18th century) and Khakas. The Minusinsk Basin is the principal agricultural area of central and eastern Siberia (grain, cattle, sheep, horses), and parts of it have been included in the Virgin Land Campaign (q.v.); there is also gold- and coal-mining in the basin. It is one of the oldest centres of population in Siberia, and has many ancient barrows, some of which have recently been excavated.

Mir, one of the names for the village communities before 1917. The Mir existed from at least the 16th century, and was a form of peasant self-government with considerable powers over the individual peasant households, such as collecting taxes and redistributing the land. The Slavophiles and Populists regarded the Mir as a uniquely Russian institution and wished to perpetuate it; but it hindered the development of agriculture, and Stolypin's (q.v.) reform which enabled peasants to leave the Mir was a great boon. *See further under* PEASANTS.

Mir Iskusstva ('World of Art'), movement in Russian art at the end of the 19th century and beginning of the 20th centuries. The name is that of a periodical founded by Diaghilev, Benois (qq.v.) and others in 1898, which appeared until 1904 and became the centre of the artistically most advanced Russian painters and critics. The magazine printed important articles on the latest trends in West European painting and on evaluations of ancient Russian art. Mir Iskusstva organized exhibitions in which almost all the outstanding painters of the time took part, notably Vrubel', Serov and Levitan (qq.v.). It was the first artistic society in Russia which opposed the utilitarian interpretation of art and proclaimed the slogan 'art for art's sake.' The best representatives of Mir Iskusstva, including Benois, Bakst (qq.v.), Roerich, Larionov and Dobuzhinskiy, emigrated to Western Europe after the Bolshevik seizure of power, and some of them collaborated with great success with Diaghilev's ballet company.

Mirzoyan, see DZHAMBUL.

Mishars, distinct group of the Tatar people, numbering in 1926 about 242,000; they are probably Tatarized descendants of the Finnish tribe of Meshchëra (q.v.).

Mitau, see JELGAVA.

Mochalov, Pavel Stepanovich (1800–48), great actor of the Malyy Theatre in Moscow, from 1817 until his death. His main roles were Hamlet, Othello, Romeo, Richard III, King Lear and Coriolanus in Shakespeare, Don Carlos, Karl Moor and Ferdinand in Schiller, and Chatskiy in Griboyedov's (q.v.) *Woe from Wit.* His Hamlet, 1834, set the canon for this role in Russia for nearly a century.

Mogila, Pëtr (*c.* 1596–1647), Orthodox priest, of a noble Wallachian family, who became Metropolitan of Kiev in 1632. He drew up a *Catechism,* 1645, and the *Confession of Faith,* 1643, which were accepted by the Synod of Jerusalem in 1672. *See* H. F. Graham, 'Peter Mogila, Metropolitan of Kiev,' *Russian Review,* vol. xiv, No. 4, Oct. 1955.

Mogilëv (Belorussian **Mohilëv**): 1. Oblast in eastern Belorussia, situated in the Dnieper lowland, partly covered with mixed forests and traversed by the Dnieper; there are large deposits of peat. Area 10,600 sq. m.; population (1959) 1,130,000 (32 per cent urban), mostly Belorussians (before the war many Jews). Grain, potatoes and flax are cultivated, pigs and cattle are raised; there are engineering, chemical, woodworking, food and leather industries. Principal towns: Mogilëv and Bobruysk.

2. Administrative and an economic and cultural centre of the oblast, situated on the Dnieper. Population (1959) 121,000 (1914, 54,000; 1926, 50,000; 1939, 99,000). It is an important centre of industry (engineering, chemical, light and food). There is a cathedral, 1780, and a local museum, 1867. Mogilëv was founded as a castle *c.* 1267, and by 1341 was Lithuanian. It was made a town in 1526, became Polish in 1569 and Russian in 1772 (provincial capital in 1778). It was a well-known commercial centre from the 14th century. In 1914–17 Mogilëv was the site of the Russian Supreme H.Q., and much fighting took place in 1943–4.

Moiseyev, Igor' Aleksandrovich (*b.* 1906), folklore specialist and choreographer. He studied at the Bolshoi Ballet School in Moscow, making his début in 1924. On becoming ballet master he began to take an interest in the folk-dances of the Soviet republics. Collecting dancers from different regions of the U.S.S.R., he founded a school in Moscow whereby he hoped to create a national folk ballet, at the same time providing a stimulus to classical ballet. The fruits of his work have appeared in the form of the *Football Dance, Sailors' Dance,*

Poem from Moscow, etc. Moiseyev's dancers have toured extensively in the Soviet Union and abroad and have achieved great popularity by their colour and vitality. In addition to the new repertoire they still perform the traditional dances. *See* F. Bowers, *Entertainment in Russia. Theatre, Ballet and Entertainment in Russia Today*, New York, 1959.

Moldavian Republic, Union Republic of the U.S.S.R. established in 1940, comprising the central part of Bessarabia and a strip along the left bank of the Dniester; it is largely hilly with black earth soil. Area 13,000 sq. m.; population (1959) 2,885,000 (22 per cent urban), Moldavians (65 per cent), Ukrainians (15 per cent), Russians (10 per cent) and Jews and Gagauz (3·3 per cent each). Wheat, maize and sunflowers are grown, and there is viniculture and horticulture; the republic has food and light industries. Principal towns: Kishinëv (capital), Bel'tsy, Tiraspol', Bendery. For history *see* BESSARABIA. A Moldavian Autonomous Republic was created within the Ukraine in 1921.

Moldavians, branch of the Rumanian people inhabiting the northern part of Rumania, and living also in the Moldavian Republic of the U.S.S.R. and the adjacent parts of Bessarabia where they number (1959) 2·2 million. They are the only Romance-speaking people in the U.S.S.R., though 40–50 per cent of their vocabulary is of Slav (Ukrainian) origin. They are mostly peasants, since 1947 collectivized, and practise Orthodox Christianity. The origin of the Moldavian people is still not entirely clear, though they are doubtless the product of a mixture between the Romanized original Thracian inhabitants of the area and the Slavs. Their culture developed under Byzantine and Slav influences, and until the 17th century Church Slavonic was their literary and official language; the first documents and books in Moldavian (using the Cyrillic alphabet) appeared in the 16th century. Some Moldavians played an important part in Russian public and cultural (e.g. A. Kantemir) life during the 18th century. *See also* BESSARABIA.

Molodechno: 1. (until 1945 **Vileyka**). Oblast from 1940 to 1960 in north-western Belorussia, a moraine area with many lakes and partly covered with mixed forests; there are deposits of peat. Area (1959) 9,400 sq. m.; population (1959) 810,000 (15 per cent urban), mostly Belorussians. It had grain, flax and potato growing, pig and dairy cattle raising, and food, linen-milling and woodworking industries. The area was Lithuanian by 1263, Russian 1793/5–1919, and again Polish 1919–39. In 1960 the oblast was abolished and the territory divided between Vitebsk, Minsk and Grodno oblasts.

2. (Polish **Molodeczno**). Administrative centre of the oblast until its abolition. Population (1959) 26,000. It has some industry and is a railway junction. Molodechno has been known since the 16th century; it was the scene of much fighting in 1915–20, and was almost completely destroyed during the Second World War (occupied by the Germans 1941–4). Since 1960 it belongs to Minsk oblast.

Molotov, *see* PERM'.

Molotov (real name **Skryabin**), **Vyacheslav Mikhaylovich** (*b.* 1890), Communist who joined the Bolsheviks in 1906. As a member of the

Russian Bureau of the party's Central Committee he was irreconcilably opposed to the Provisional Government (q.v.) immediately
after the February 1917 revolution, unlike Kamenev and Stalin, thus
anticipating Lenin's position. He specialized in party organizational
work after the Bolshevik seizure of power, and has held the following
positions: 1920–5, head of the party organization in the Ukraine;
1921–30, second secretary (after Stalin) of the party's Central Committee; from 1926 member of the Politburo and of the Presidium of the
Executive Committee of the Comintern; 1930–40, chairman of the
Council of People's Commissars (Prime Minister), subsequently
deputy chairman till 1957; 1941–5, deputy chairman of the State
Defence Committee (q.v.); 1939–49 and 1953–6, Commissar (from
1946 Minister) for Foreign Affairs. Molotov was a faithful lieutenant
of Stalin from the early 1920's and his position in the party was
second only to Stalin's; after the latter's death his influence declined.
In 1957, as a member of the 'anti-party group' (q.v.), he was expelled from the Central Committee and its Presidium and dismissed
from his posts as first deputy prime minister and Minister of State
Control; he was appointed ambassador to the Mongolian People's
Republic. In 1960 he was appointed the U.S.S.R.'s permanent
delegate to the International Atomic Energy Agency. As a diplomat
Molotov earned a reputation for extreme stubbornness, and was
frequently successful because of this quality. *See* B. Bromage,
Molotov, the Story of an Era, 1956.

Mongol Conquest. The Mongol armies appeared on the Volga in
1236, having in the previous three decades conquered China, Central
Asia, Iran and Transcaucasia and established several semi-independent
states. Batu Khan (q.v.), who already ruled the steppes to the north
of the Aral Sea and Lake Balkhash, began to penetrate further west,
and within four years had conquered the Volga Bulgarians (q.v.) and
the disunited Russian principalities (*see* KIEVAN RUSSIA) with the
exception of Novgorod. The Golden Horde (q.v.), Batu's state, thus
established its suzerainty over the Russian princes. A century later
the grip of the Horde over its vassal territories began to weaken, and
during the 14th century most western and southern Russian principalities came under the new power of the Grand Duchy of Lithuania,
which had been founded in the mid 13th century. Within the territory still held by the Horde, the small principality of Moscow absorbed many of its neighbours until it felt strong enough to challenge
the Horde, and in 1380 Dmitriy Donskoy (q.v.) led a coalition of
Russian princes to defeat the Tatars. However, it was not until
another hundred years had passed that Moscow ceased to pay
tribute to the Tatars. During the 15th century the Golden Horde
disintegrated into a number of khanates (Astrakhan', Crimea,
Kazan' and Siberian). *See* G. Vernadsky, *Mongols and Russia*, New
Haven, 1953; V. V. Barthold, *Four Studies on the History of Central
Asia*, vol. i, Leyden, 1956.

Mongols. There are two Mongol-speaking peoples in the U.S.S.R.,
the Buryats (q.v.) of south-eastern Siberia, who belong to the eastern
Mongols, and the Kalmyks (q.v.) of the lower Volga area, who belong
to the western Mongol branch. Almost the whole territory of the

present U.S.S.R. (except western Ukraine, Belorussia and the Baltic Republics) was conquered by the Mongols under Genghis Khan and his successors in the early 13th century (*see* GOLDEN HORDE; TRANS-OXANIA). But the Mongols were only a small ruling minority in the conquering hordes, soon assimilated by the majority which consisted of various Turkic tribes, and the main ethnic result of the conquest was to facilitate the Turkicization of Central Asia and to a lesser extent of European Russia and the Caucasus. *See also* TATARS. *See* V. V. Barthold, *Four Studies on the History of Central Asia*, vol. i, Leyden, 1956.

Mordva, people of the Finnish family (speaking two similar languages, Erzya and Moksha) who live in small groups scattered among the Russian population in the area between Gor'kiy and Ryazan' in the west and the Urals in the east. They numbered (1959) 1,285,000 (1,450,000 in 1939). They have been known since the 6th century, were christianized in the 18th century, and are russianized to a considerable extent. *See* W. Kolarz, *Russia and her Colonies*, 1952.

Mordva Autonomous Republic, formed 1930, lies in central Russia south-east of Moscow, in the Volga upland in the east and the Oka-Don lowland in the west, partly covered by oak forests. Area 10,100 sq. m.; population (1959) 999,000 (18 per cent urban) Russians (since the 12th century), Mordva (37 per cent in 1939) and Tatars. Grain, hemp and potatoes are cultivated, dairy cattle and bees are kept, and there are saw-milling and food industries. Principal town Saransk (capital). The famous former monastery of Sarov is situated in the republic, as was the Pot'ma concentration camp until the mid 1950's.

Morozov, Pavlik (Pavel Trofimovich) (1918–32), member of the Young Pioneer organization who was murdered by his relatives because he betrayed his parents to the Soviet authorities for trying to assist banished *kulaks* (q.v.). This was the period of fierce peasant resistance to the collectivization of agriculture, and Morozov's action has been held up in the official propaganda as a glorious example to other children, to such an extent that a statue was erected to him in his home village, and various children's clubs were named after him.

Moscow (Russian **Moskva**): 1. Oblast of the R.S.F.S.R., situated between the upper Volga and the Oka, on the Smolensk-Moscow upland in the north and west and the Meshchëra lowland in the south-east; it is partly forested, with a moderately continental climate, and has deposits of phosphorite and peat. Area 18,100 sq. m.; population (1959) 10,938,000 (78 per cent urban), almost exclusively Russian outside the city. The principal features of the oblast's economy (excluding Moscow city) are a large engineering industry (locomotives and rolling stock, machine tools, agricultural machinery), textile and chemical industries; grain, vegetable, potato and flax cultivation, and dairy farming. There is a dense rail and road network, and the Moscow–Volga Canal. Principal towns: Moscow, Perovo, Kuntsevo, Podol'sk, Babushkin, Orekhovo-Zuyevo, Serpukhov, Kolomna, Mytishchi, Elektrostal', Lyubertsy, Noginsk, Tushino, Lyublino. The famous St Sergius Trinity monastery (*see* TROITSE-SERGIYEVA LAVRA) is situated in the oblast.

The area belonged to the Kievan state, and then was divided between the Rostov-Suzdal' (later Vladimir), Ryazan' and Smolensk principalities. From 1283 a separate Moscow principality existed, and this became the core of Muscovy and of modern Russia. In 1812 the battle of Borodino took place here; in 1941–2 almost half the oblast was occupied by the Germans, and it suffered greatly from fierce and extensive fighting. In 1960 Moscow city absorbed several suburbs (including Babushkin, Kuntsevo, Lyublino, Perovo and Tushino), and the administration of the green belt around the capital was transferred from the oblast to the city.

2. Capital of the oblast, of the Russian Federal Republic (to whose government it is directly subordinated) and of the U.S.S.R., situated on both banks of the River Moskva. It is the largest city and chief economic, political and cultural centre of the country. Population (1959, without suburbs) 5,032,000; it was about 100,000 in the 16th century; 1790, 175,000; 1830, 305,000; 1871, 602,000; 1897, 1,039,000; 1912, 1,618,000; 1917, 1,701,000; 1920, 1,028,000; 1926, 2,020,000; 1939, 4,183,000. The city has large engineering, textile, electrical, chemical and food industries. Electricity is supplied (apart from local power-stations) by a direct high-voltage line from the Kuybyshev hydro-electric station, and natural gas by pipelines from Saratov and Stavropol'. Moscow is the hub of the country's railway network, with eleven trunk-lines (connected inside the city by a circular line) and nine passenger stations; there are three river ports (passenger services to Gor'kiy, Ufa and Rostov-on-Don via the Moskva and Oka rivers or the Moscow-Volga Canal) and three passenger airports (Central, Vnukovo, Bykovo).

The U.S.S.R. Academy of Sciences (founded 1725 in St Petersburg, transferred in 1934) is here, the Academy of Arts, and many other research institutes and specialized academies. In 1954 the city had 93 higher educational establishments (including correspondence, but excluding military) with 168,000 students (excluding correspondence), as against 20 establishments with 34,000 students in 1915; among the most notable are the university, 1755 (the oldest Russian university), the Higher Technical School, 1832, the Agricultural Academy, 1865, the Railway Transport Institute, 1896, the Institute of Chemical Technology, 1898, the Conservatoire, 1866, and the Institute of Architecture (founded as an architectural school in 1789). There are 116 museums and permanent exhibitions, including the Tret'yakov Gallery of Russian Art (opened to the public in the 1880's), the Museum of Visual Arts, Museum of Oriental Cultures, 1918, the State Historical Museum, 1873, the Polytechnic Museum, the Lenin Museum and the Agricultural Exhibition. Among the 3,200 libraries is the Lenin Library (founded in 1862 as the Rumyantsev Museum) with 19 million volumes. The city has 34 theatres, including the Bolshoi Theatre of Opera and Ballet, 1780, the Malyy Theatre of Drama, 1806, and the Art Theatre, 1898. Moscow is the seat of the Patriarch and the spiritual centre of the Russian Orthodox Church; its Theological Academy (founded 1685, abolished after the revolution, re-established after the Second World War) is in the Troitse-Sergiyeva Lavra.

The Kremlin (q.v.), on the north bank of the river, is the centre of the city, and extending around it on the north side of the river, with a radius of about a mile, is a line of boulevards; outside this line, and concentric with it, is a second line of boulevards, with a radius of about 1½ miles; and beyond this, forming a girdle around the older part of the city, is an outer rampart with a circumference of 26 miles; on the outskirts lies the Circular Railway. Few of Moscow's old buildings have been preserved, since, being built of wood, they were destroyed in the many fires the city has suffered. Apart from the Kremlin the chief architectural monuments are the Cathedral of the New Convent of the Virgin, 1525, the Intercession Cathedral (Vasiliy Blazhennyy Church) in the Red Square, 1560, the Nativity Church in Putinki (17th century) and the old Printing House, 1679; 18th- and early 19th-century buildings in neo-classical style include the Assembly of the Nobility, 1771 (now the House of Unions), the old building of the Lenin Library, 1786, the old university building, 1793, and the Bolshoi Theatre, 1824. Late 19th- and early 20th-century buildings of interest include the Town Hall, 1892 (now the Lenin Museum), the Polytechnic Museum, the Historical Museum, 1874, the Museum of Visual Arts, 1912, and the Kazan' railway station (begun in 1914). 'Constructivism' dominated Moscow architecture in the 1920's and early thirties, while the new 'Soviet Classicism' has developed since the 1930's; among pre-war examples are the Moskva Hotel, Gor'kiy Street and the underground stations, while post-war examples are the 'tall buildings,' including the new university building. During the 1930's some of the city's architectural monuments were destroyed, including the famous Chapel of the Iberian Virgin, 1669—one of the most revered churches in Russia— and the Church of the Redeemer, built in 1839–83 to commemorate the Patriotic War of 1812.

History. Moscow is first mentioned in the chronicles in 1147 as a settlement near the southern border of the Rostov-Suzdal' Principality. It became the capital of a separate principality in the 13th century, of the Grand Principality of Vladimir in the 14th century, and later of Muscovy. It was the seat of the Metropolitans (later Patriarchs) of the Russian Orthodox Church from the early 14th century. In 1712 the capital was transferred to St Petersburg by Peter the Great, but throughout the imperial period Moscow retained the status of a second capital of the country, and became the official capital once more in 1918. It has been an important commercial centre since the Middle Ages, and the centre of many crafts, attracting a large artisan population, since the 16th century. Large manufactures developed from the mid 17th century, and modern industry (textiles and metal-working at first) from the 1830's. The first Moscow waterworks were built 1779–1805, the sewage system 1874–98, electric light was introduced in 1883, tramways in 1899, and construction of the underground began in 1932. During the 19th and early 20th centuries Moscow was the centre of the Slavophile, Zemstvo and co-operative movements (qq.v.), and one of the principal centres of the labour movement and social democracy; the Bolsheviks' influence on the Moscow workers was limited. The city was

Paris Commune. 1971

$10.00

Viking

—

—

Price of Glory

Verdun, 1916   1962

5.95   St. Martin

often the centre of inner-party opposition to the official leadership during the 1920's, and since Stalin's death has been the centre of intellectual opposition (especially the Moscow Writers' Union) and of student unrest (November–December 1956). See *Moscow*, Foreign Languages Publishing House, Moscow, 1955; S. P. Druzhinin, *The Tretyakov Gallery, a Short Guide*, Moscow, 1955; M. Fekhner *et al.*, *State Historical Museum, a Short Guide*, Moscow, 1958; O. Constantien and H. Hubmann, *Moscow*, Munich, 1958.

Moscow Lignite Basin, large deposits of lignite which stretch in an arch-shaped strip through Ryazan', Tula, Kaluga, Smolensk, Kalinin, Novgorod and Leningrad oblasts. The discovery of lignite here was made in 1722 and it has been mined since the 1850's. A great expansion of the mining industry has taken place since the 1930's, and in 1957 the Moscow Lignite Basin took third place in the country, after the Donets and Kuznetsk basins. The chief industrial towns of the area are Tula and Stalinogorsk.

Moscow-Volga Canal, artificial waterway which connects the River Moskva with the upper Volga; total length 80 m. It was built, largely by forced labour, between 1932 and 1937.

Mountain People's (Russian **Gorskaya**) **Autonomous Republic,** transitory administrative-political division in North Caucasus (1921–1924) with Vladikavkaz as capital; it was gradually broken up into separate national units.

Mountain-Altay Autonomous Oblast (until 1948 **Oyrot Autonomous Oblast**), in the Altay Kray, situated in the centre of the Altay mountainous area, traversed by the highway to Mongolia which starts at Biysk. Area 35,700 sq. m.; population (1959) 159,000 (19 per cent urban), Russians (over 70 per cent) and Altays. Cattle, sheep and deer are bred (the latter for their antlers, which are exported to China for making medicine), and fishing, hunting and bee-keeping practised; there are food (cheese, butter), timber and mining (mercury, gold) industries. The district is very beautiful and healthy, and there is some tourism. The administrative centre is Gorno-Altaysk. For history *see* ALTAYS. The Autonomous Oblast was formed in 1922.

Mountainous Badakhshan, Autonomous Oblast of Tadzhikistan comprising the whole of the Pamir. Area 24,600 sq. m.; population (1959) 73,000 (11 per cent urban), Tadzhiks in the west and Kirgiz in the east. The main occupation of the inhabitants is goat, sheep and yak keeping. The oblast is connected by highways with Stalinabad and the Fergana Valley. Administrative centre Khorog. Before 1924 West Pamir belonged to Bukhara; East Pamir became Russian in 1895. The Autonomous Oblast was created in 1925.

Mountainous- (Russian **Nagorno-**) **Karabakh Autonomous Oblast,** formed in 1923, in Azerbaydzhan on the eastern slopes of the Lesser Caucasus, partly covered with oak and beech forests. Area 1,700 sq. m.; population (1959) 131,000 (21 per cent urban), mostly Armenians. Sericulture and viniculture are carried on, and sheep, cattle and horses raised. Principal towns: Stepanakert (administrative centre) and Shusha. About one-fifth of the population was massacred or killed in the war between Armenia and Azerbaydzhan in 1818–20; in

1920–1 there was anti-Bolshevik guerrilla warfare by Armenian nationalists.

Moussorgsky, see MUSORGSKIY.

Mozhaysk, town in the Moscow Oblast 69 m. west of Moscow. Population (1956) 12,600. Mozhaysk has been known since 1231 and became a Muscovite western frontier fortress in 1303. The battle of Borodino took place six miles west of the town in 1812, and it saw much fighting in the winter of 1941–2.

M.T.S. (Russian abbreviation for 'Machine and Tractor Station'), State enterprises which until 1958 carried out all machine work in the *kolkhozes* (q.v.) and generally supervised them. During the collectivization of agriculture (q.v.) political departments of the M.T.S. were the party's strongholds in the countryside. In 1957 there were 7,900 M.T.S.; in the following year most of them were transformed into Technical Repair Stations and their machinery sold to the *kolkhozes*. By the end of 1958 there remained only 345 M.T.S., while 4,000 Technical Repair Stations had been formed. Besides carrying out repairs, the repair stations sell machinery, fuel and fertilizers to the *kolkhozes*. See J. Miller, 'The Reorganization of the M.T.S.' *Soviet Studies*, vol. x, No. 1, July 1958; W. K., 'A Review of Soviet Agricultural Policy,' *Soviet Survey*, No. 26, Oct.–Dec. 1958; L. Volin, 'Reform in Agriculture,' *Problems of Communism*, vol. viii, No. 1, Jan.–Feb. 1959; R. D. Laird *et al.*, *The Rise and Fall of the M.T.S. as an Instrument of Soviet Rule*, Lawrence, Kansas, 1960.

Mtskheta, town in Georgia, 13 m. north of Tiflis. Population (1956) 5,100. Mtskheta has been known since the early 4th century, and was capital of Iberia (eastern Georgia) until superseded by Tiflis in the mid 6th century; it remained the religious centre of Georgia. It is a treasury of Georgian architecture of the 6th–11th centuries, and ruins of even older buildings (from the 4th century B.C.) have been excavated near by.

Mukachevo (Hungarian **Muncács,** Czech **Mukačevo**), town in the Transcarpathian Oblast (Ukraine). Population (1956) 44,000, Ukrainians, Jews and Hungarians. It has food, tobacco, woodworking (furniture) and textile industries, and is the main industrial centre of Transcarpathia; there is a 14th-century castle. Mukachevo has been known since the 12th century and became a town in 1445.

Municipal Services, see TOWNS.

Murav'ëv, Count Mikhail Nikolayevich (1796–1866), governorgeneral in Vilna in 1863–5 who crushed with great cruelty the Polish uprising of 1863; he was a bitter opponent of Alexander II's reforms (*see* GREAT REFORMS).

Murgab, river in Central Asia, rising in Afghanistan and petering out in the sands of the Kara-Kum Desert in Turkmenia. Length about 800 m. Most of its water is used up for irrigation in the Merv (q.v.) oasis situated in its lower reaches.

Murmansk: 1. Oblast of the R.S.F.S.R., situated in the extreme north-west of Russia, comprising the Kola Peninsula and the adjacent mainland; it has tundra along the northern coast and coniferous forests farther south, and has a cool maritime climate; there are rich deposits of aluminium, nickel, copper, iron, rare metals and phosphate. Area 55,900 sq. m.; population (1959) 567,000 (92 per cent urban), Russians, some Lapps. Principal towns: Murmansk, Kandalaksha, Kirovsk.

2. Administrative, economic and cultural centre of the oblast, an ice-free port on the Barents Sea. Population (1959) 226,000 (1926, 9,000; 1939, 119,000). It has a large fishing and a shipbuilding industry, and is an important port, being the terminus of the Northern Sea Route. Murmansk was founded in 1915 (the nearby settlement of Kola in 1264) and became provincial capital in 1938. It was used for allied supplies in both world wars, and suffered greatly from German bombing in 1941.

Murom, town in the Vladimir Oblast (central Russia), situated on the River Oka. Population (1959) 73,000. It has engineering, textile and woodworking industries, and also market gardening (Murom cucumbers). There are many interesting buildings of the 16th–19th centuries. Murom has been known since 862, became capital of Murom Principality in the 12th century, and Muscovite in 1393.

Muromtsev, Sergey Andreyevich (1850–1910), jurist and liberal politician. He was professor at Moscow University, editor of *Yuridecheskiy Vestnik* and chairman of the Moscow Juridical Society. An authority on civil law, he was a follower of Ihering and the chief exponent in Russia of the positivist school in jurisprudence. He advocated the adoption in Russia of some features of English legal practice, such as a greater freedom of the judge in relation to the written law and the extension of trial by jury to civil cases. As a politician he was active in local government, prominent in the constitutional movement, and was a member of the central committee of the Constitutional Democratic Party. Muromtsev was unanimously elected chairman of the 1st State Duma, held this post with dignity and great concern for the rights of the Duma, and after its dissolution presided over the meetings of Duma members in Vyborg and signed the Vyborg appeal.

Muscovy, 14th–18th-century state. The first princes of Moscow were vassals of the Grand Princes of Vladimir in the 13th century after the Mongol-Tatar conquest (*see* GOLDEN HORDE; MONGOL CONQUEST), but during the following century Moscow gradually gained ascendancy over adjacent principalities (facilitated by its advantageous position in the centre of the then north-east of Russia, where it was sheltered from Tatar raids and well placed for commercial development), and eventually it replaced Vladimir as capital of the Grand Principality. The principal rulers of this period were Ivan I and Dmitriy Donskoy (qq.v.). Ivan III (q.v., 'the Great') greatly enlarged the territory of Muscovy, absorbing the republic of Novgorod in 1478, and it was during his reign that the tribute paid to the Tatars was finally abolished (1480). By the time of Ivan IV (q.v., 'the Terrible') Muscovy had absorbed all Russian lands (including the republics of Vyatka, 1489, Pskov, 1510, and the Grand Principalities of Tver', 1485, and Ryazan', 1521), and in 1547 he took the title Czar of All Russia; during his rule Muscovy became a multinational state through the conquest of the Tatar khanates of Kazan', Astrakhan' and Siberia.

The House of Rurikids (q.v.) soon died out, and the Time of Troubles (*see* TROUBLES, TIME OF) followed, a period of near anarchy. However, in 1613 the House of Romanov (q.v.) was established, which carried on the policies of its forerunners by conquering the remainder of Siberia and incorporating the Ukraine (under Aleksey Mikhaylovich, q.v.). The origins of the latter move lay in the rivalry for hegemony in Russia between Muscovy and Poland that went back to 1569 (when Lithuania became united with Poland). Catholic Poland was at a disadvantage in the struggle for the Orthodox population of Belorussia and the Ukraine, and when the Ukrainian Cossacks under Khmel'nyt'skyy (q.v.) had liberated their country from the Poles they sought union with Muscovy in 1654 (*see further under* UKRAINE, *History*; UKRAINIANS). However, half of the Ukraine was soon lost again to Poland, and not regained until the partitions of Poland of the late 18th century. The last Czar of Muscovy and the first Russian emperor (from 1721), Peter the Great (q.v.), opened a new chapter in Russian history.

Muscovy was the cradle of the Great Russian people. Its legal system was developed through the codes of 1479 and 1550 (*see* SUDEBNIK) and of 1649 (*see* ULOZHENIYE); politically it was an auto-cracy limited by the Boyars' Duma and the Zemskiy Sobor (q.v.). Muscovy was culturally isolated from the rest of Europe, originally by Tatar domination, then by the enmity between the Orthodox and the Roman Catholic Churches that followed the Florentine Union, 1439, and the fall of Constantinople, 1453. Its political ideology was based upon the conceptions of 'gathering the Russian land' (*see* KIEVAN RUSSIA) and 'Moscow—the third Rome.' *See* R. N. Bain, *The First Romanovs*, 1905; B. Alexeyev, 'The Restoration of Order and the First Romanovs,' *Slavonic and East European Review*, No. 2, 1923; B. Nolde, *La Formation de l'Empire Russe*, vol. i, Paris, 1952; M. S. Anderson, *Britain's Discovery of Russia, 1535–1815*, 1958; G. Vernadsky, *Russia at the Dawn of the Modern Age*, New Haven, 1960.

Music, *see* entries on BALLET; CONCERTO; FOLK MUSIC; OPERA; ORCHESTRAL MUSIC; SONG; SYMPHONY; and individual composers and performers. *See* A. Olkhovsky, *Music under the Soviets*, New York, 1955.

Muslims. The Muslim peoples of the Soviet Union are most of the Turkic- and Iranian-speaking peoples (*see* IRANIANS; TURKS), as well as the Caucasian-speaking mountain peoples of North Caucasus (*see* CAUCASIANS) and the Adzhars (q.v.) of Georgia. They are all Sunni Muslims except the Azerbaydzhanis, the Talysh and the Tats, who are Shiah Muslims, and a part of the Tadzhiks, who are Ismailites. There are four separate Muslim administrations: one for the European part of the U.S.S.R. and Siberia, headed by the Mufti resident in Ufa; one for Central Asia and Kazakhstan with the seat of the Mufti in Tash-kent; one for North Caucasus and Daghestan, with the Mufti in Buynaksk; and one for Transcaucasia headed by the Sheikh-ul-Islam in Baku. Only one Muslim theological seminary exists, in Bukhara.

Islam was introduced in the present territory of the U.S.S.R. with the Arab conquests in Transcaucasia and Central Asia of the 7th–8th centuries. It took deep roots in these parts, and extended to the Turkic people of European Russia at the time of the Golden Horde (q.v.). There were attempts at forcible baptism of the Tatars immediately after the Russian conquest of the Kazan' khanate and again in the 18th century, and at the time of the Caucasian wars of the mid 19th century (*see* SHAMIL') and during the uprising in Central Asia in 1916 holy wars were proclaimed against the Russian infidels; but on the whole the relationships between the Muslims and the Russian authorities were good. A modernist movement among Muslims in Russia, largely led by Tatars (*see* GASPRINSKIY; SULTAN-GALIYEV), developed in the late 19th and early 20th centuries. During the revolution of 1905 the modernists formed an All-Russian Muslim Union which urged regional autonomy, and they subsequently dominated the Muslim faction in the Duma, which associated itself with the Constitutional Democratic Party. There were also a number of regional Muslim parties of a more radical character, the most important of which was the Mussavat (q.v.) in Azerbaydzhan. The Council of the Muslim Union supported the Provisional Government in 1917; it was suppressed when the Bolsheviks seized power. A Russian Party of Communist Muslims, formed in 1918, was soon merged with the All-Russian Communist Party. During the 1920's the Communist policy towards Islam, largely influenced by Muslim Communists (e.g. Sultan-Galiyev), was much more restrained than towards other religions. There was a strong religious element behind the Basmachi (q.v.) guerrilla movement in Central Asia. Since 1943-4 Islam, like the other main religions, has been officially tolerated by the authorities. *See* W. Kolarz, *Russia and her Colonies*, 1953; R. Pipes, *The Formation of the Soviet Union*, Cambridge, Mass., 1954; I. Spektor, *The Soviet Union and the Muslim World, 1917-58*, Seattle, 1959; G. Wheeler, *Racial Problems in Soviet Muslim Asia*, 1960; S. A. Zenkovsky, *Pan-Turkism and Islam in Russia*, Cambridge, Mass., 1960.

Musorgskiy, Modest Petrovich (1839-81), one of the most original and far sighted of all Russian composers. He received piano lessons from Anton Herke, studied church music, was influenced by contemporary liberal thinkers and lived in close contact with the Kuchka (q.v.). His declining years were marked by unsuccessful struggle against dipsomania. Works comprise numerous operatic projects, including *Boris Godunov* (first version 1868-9, second version 1871-2, *see* RIMSKY-KORSAKOV), *Khovanshchina* (1872-80; *see* RIMSKY-KORSAKOV), *Sorochintsy Fair* (1874-80, unfinished, completed by Cui in 1915); several choral works, including *The Destruction of Sennacherib* for chorus and orchestra (first version 1867, second version 1874); orchestral works, including *St John's Night on the Bare Mountain*, 1867; piano works, including the suite *Pictures from an Exhibition*, 1874; and many songs, including the cycles *The Nursery*, 1868-72, *Sunless*, 1874, and *Songs and Dances of Death*, 1875-7. Essentially national in outlook, his music runs the entire gamut of emotion. In his desire for realism he may be compared with Kramskoy, Surikov, Gay and Repin. Musically his style stems from the works of Glinka, Schumann, Balakirev, Liszt and

Meyerbeer, but much of his harmony refuses to fit into any established category save that of folk music. Steeped in folk-song from his earliest days, Musorgskiy reproduces human inflection with remarkable fidelity. *See further under* OPERA; SONG. *See* M. D. Calvocoressi, *Mussorgsky* (completed by G. Abraham), 1946.

Mussavat, democratic Muslim party formed in 1911–12 in Baku by a group of young intellectuals, many of whom had collaborated during the revolution of 1905 with local Bolshevik organizations. It was originally pan-Islamic, advancing no uniquely Azerbaydzhani demands, and as a pro-Turkish party had to suspend open activity during the First World War. It was the principal party among Muslims in Transcaucasia, and later in the Azerbaydzhan Republic, after the February 1917 revolution. *See* F. Kazemzadeh, *The Struggle for Transcaucasia*, New York, 1951; S. A. Zenkovsky, *Pan-Turkism and Islam in Russia*, Cambridge, Mass., 1960.

M.V.D., Russian abbreviation for 'Ministry of Internal Affairs.' This ministry played an important role for a short time in 1953 when it was fused, following Stalin's death, with the Ministry of State Security (*see* M.G.B.). Beria, the head of the M.V.D., used its apparatus to consolidate his own position during the struggle among Stalin's successors. The security service was once more separated from the M.V.D. after Beria's downfall, and placed under the K.G.B. (q.v.). At the beginning of 1960 the all-Union ministry was abolished, and its functions taken over by the governments of the Union Republics. *See further under* SECURITY ORGANS.

Myaskovskiy, Nikolay Yakovlevich (1881–1950), composer and teacher who studied under Glière and later at the St Petersburg Conservatory with Lyadov and Rimsky-Korsakov. He served at the front as a military engineer, 1914–18. In 1921 he was appointed professor at Moscow Conservatory, where his pupils included Kabalevskiy, Khachaturyan, Shebalin, etc. His works comprise twenty-seven symphonies; two cantatas; orchestral works; violin concerto; cello concerto; thirteen string quartets; songs, piano pieces; and numerous literary works. Myaskovskiy is undoubtedly one of the most prolific of all modern symphonic writers; his works are essentially Soviet. He is avowedly a follower of the formal principles of Beethoven and Tchaikovsky and of classical traditions, though not indifferent to contemporary ideas. *See* G. Abraham, *Eight Soviet Composers*, 1943; A. Ikonnikov, *Myaskovsky: His Life and Work*, 1946; R. Moisenko, *Realist Music*, 1949.

Myths, in the modern sense of '. . . not descriptions of things, but expressions of a determination to act' (Sorel), have played an important role in the ideology (q.v.) of the Communist Party, and have provided the foundations for much of its propaganda and agitation (qq.v.), both before the seizure of power (*see* OCTOBER REVOLUTION) and since (*see* BOLSHEVISM; LENINISM; STALINISM). Myths are to be distinguished from fictions (q.v.), since the former are believed by a part of the population in Russia, while the latter are not; though some myths gradually degenerate into fictions, and what is a fiction inside Russia may be a myth abroad. Most myths are consciously operated by the party leadership and ideologists, irrespective of whether they themselves believe them. Communist myths are of diverse origin: some of them were originally rational theoretical propositions, but later lost their rational character (e.g. the myths about the scientific character of the Communist doctrine, about 'capitalist encirclement,' about the inevitability of war with the 'capitalist' states), while others were deliberately created as myths (e.g. the myths about the realization of socialism in the U.S.S.R., about the U.S.S.R. as the most progressive country in the world, about 'enemies of the people'); still others originated spontaneously among the people but have been utilized in the official propaganda (e.g. the myth about the liberal evolution of the Soviet regime which was several times used during Stalin's rule, and the myth about Lenin as a benevolent figure). *See* A. Koestler, *The Yogi and the Commissar,* 1945; G. Sorel, *Reflections on Violence,* Eng. trans., 1950; W. Gurian, *Bolshevism: a Study of Soviet Communism,* 1952; S. V. Utcchin, 'New Myths for Old,' *Twentieth Century,* Jan. 1954; *Ocherki bol'shevizmovedeniya* (*Essays in Bolshevismology*), ed. R. N. Redlich, Frankfurt-on-Main, 1956.

Mytishchi, town in the Moscow 'green belt,' an industrial and residential suburb north of the capital. Population (1959) 99,000 (1926, 17,000). It has a large and varied engineering industry (lorries, underground coaches, laboratory equipment), and the earliest Moscow waterworks (built 1779) are here.

N

Nadezhdinsk, see SEROV.

Nagorno-Karabakh Autonomous Oblast, see MOUNTAINOUS-KARA-
BAKH AUTONOMOUS OBLAST.

Nakhichevan': 1. Autonomous Republic in Azerbaydzhan, established 1924, situated between the Persian frontier and Armenia; it is
dry mountainous country with large deposits of salt. Area 2,100 sq.
m.; population (1959) 142,000 (27 per cent urban), mostly Azerbaydzhanis, some Armenians. The chief occupations are irrigated
agriculture (cotton, tobacco, grain), horticulture, sheep raising, salt-
mining, stone quarrying, cotton ginning, silk spinning and fruit
canning.

2. Capital and cultural centre of the republic. Population (1959)
25,000. It has food and wine industries, and there are salt-mines in
the vicinity; two 12th-century mausoleums have been preserved.
According to an Armenian legend, Nakhichevan' was founded by
Noah, whose grave is alleged to be here; it was an important commercial centre in the Middle Ages, and became Russian in 1828.

Nakhichevan'-on-Don, former town, now merged with Rostov-on-
Don. Population (1914) 71,000. It was founded by Armenian colonists
from the Crimea in 1780 and became a lively commercial centre
during the 19th century.

Nakhimov, Pavel Stepanovich (1803–55), admiral. During the
Crimean War (q.v.) he commanded the Russian Navy in the Black
Sea, and in 1853 destroyed the Turkish flotilla at Sinop. He was
mortally wounded during the siege of Sevastopol'. A naval decoration, the Nakhimov Order, was instituted in 1944, and naval cadet
schools bearing his name were established.

Nakhodka, town in the Maritime Kray (Far East), a port on the Sea
of Japan, about 45 m. east of Vladivostok. Population (1959) 63,000.
It is a new town built in the 1950's; in 1958 it replaced Vladivostok as
the port of call for foreign ships.

Namangan: 1. Former oblast in Uzbekistan situated in the north of
the Fergana Valley, traversed by the Syr-Dar'ya River, the Northern
Fergana Canal and the Fergana circular railway; it has deposits of
oil. Area 2,700 sq. m.; population (1959) 594,000 (26 per cent urban),
mostly Uzbeks. Cotton, fruit and grapes are cultivated, and sericulture is carried on; there are light and food industries. For history
see FERGANA VALLEY; KOKAND KHANATE. In 1960 the oblast was
abolished and the area divided between Andizhan and Fergana
oblasts.

2. Town in the Andizhan oblast, formerly centre of the Namangan
Oblast, situated on the Fergana circular railway. Population (1959)
122,000 (1939, 80,000). It has textile, leather and varied food
industries.

Namëtkin, Sergey Semënovich (1876–1950), chemist. Educated at Moscow University, he taught there and at other higher educational establishments in Moscow, was in 1919–24 rector of the 2nd Moscow University, member of the Academy of Sciences from 1939 and director of its Institute of Mineral Fuels, 1939–48, and of the Institute of Petroleum, 1948–50. His works in organic chemistry were chiefly concerned with the general theory of carbohydrates, 1900–24, and the chemistry and technology of oil, 1925–50.

Narodnaya Volya ('People's Freedom,' or 'People's Will'), Populist revolutionary organization which was formed in 1879 after the split of the Zemlya i Volya organization. It adhered to the 'Jacobin' idea of a seizure of power, and in practice concentrated on the assassination of government representatives. It murdered Alexander II in 1881, and although most of its leading members were arrested before or soon after the assassination (and several, including the leader Zhelyabov, executed), what was left of the organization continued to exist in small groups, both in Russia and in emigration. In 1887 the St Petersburg group, led by A. Ul'yanov (Lenin's older brother), attempted the assassination of Alexander III. Some of the younger Narodnaya Volya members carried their tradition into Russian social democracy, later becoming Bolsheviks, but the majority remained Populist and combined with other groups to form in 1902 the party of Socialist Revolutionaries (q.v.). *See further under* POPULISM. *See* D. Footman, *Red Prelude*, 1944; S. R. Tomkins, *Russian Intelligentsia. The Makers of the Revolutionary State*, Norman, Oklahoma, 1957; F. Venturi, *Roots of Revolution*, 1960.

Narodnik, Russian for 'Populist,' *see* POPULISM.

Narva, river port in Estonia, half way along the Tallinn–Leningrad railway. Population (1956) 21,000. It has a large textile industry (since the 19th century) and a big hydro-electric station is near by; there are many interesting buildings of the 14th–19th centuries. Narva was founded in 1223 by the Danes, and became Livonian in 1347, Swedish in 1581 and Russian in 1704; it was an important centre of commerce from the 14th century. In 1700 Charles XII defeated the Russians near Narva; the town was occupied by the Germans in 1918 and 1941–4.

Nar'yan-Mar, administrative centre of the Nenets National Okrug (Archangel Oblast), a seaport situated at the mouth of the River Pechora. Population (1956) 11,000, mostly Russian. It has sawmilling and fishing industries.

Narym, swampy forested region in the north of Tomsk Oblast (Western Siberia), traversed by the River Ob'; iron ore deposits have recently been discovered. Area about 100,000 sq. m.; population (1935) 145,000, mostly Russians, also some Khanty. The inhabitants engage in lumbering, hunting and fishing. Narym has been a place of banishment since the 1860's.

Naryn, town in Kirgizia, administrative and cultural centre of the Tien-Shan Oblast, situated on the River Naryn 220 m. southwest of Frunze, with which it is connected by a motorway. Population (1959) 15,000, Russian and Kirgiz. There is some industry. Naryn was founded by the Russians in 1868 as a fortified post on the path from Kashgaria to the Chu River valley, and had some commercial significance.

National Bolshevism, post-1917 political trend whose supporters, though not Communists, believed the Bolsheviks to be the only party competent to govern Russia effectively and to defend Russian national interests. During the 1920's the trend found expression through the 'Change of Landmarks' movement, both in Russia and among Russian *émigrés*. It subsequently became an important element in Stalinism (q.v.) and was especially vigorous during the Second World War. Among the principal representatives of National Bolshevism were General Brusilov, the writer A. N. Tolstoy and the historian B. D. Grekov. *See* S. V. Utechin, 'Bolsheviks and their Allies after 1917: the Ideological Pattern,' *Soviet Studies*, Oct. 1958.

National Delimitation of Central Asia, official name of the administrative and territorial reorganization of Central Asia in 1924. At the end of the civil war there existed in Central Asia the Autonomous Republic of Turkestan (which belonged to Russia) and the People's Republics (ostensibly independent) of Bukhara and Khorezm. The two latter were in 1923 transformed into Soviet republics and in 1924 were 'received' into the Soviet Union. The National Delimitation was immediately undertaken, and resulted in the establishment of the Union Republics of Turkmenia and Uzbekistan, the Tadzhik Autonomous Republic (within Uzbekistan) and two Autonomous Oblasts, Kara-Kirgiz (now Kirgizia), within the R.S.F.S.R., and Kara-Kalpak, which was included in the already existing Kirgiz Autonomous Republic (now Kazakhstan); the Kirgiz Autonomous Republic itself (also belonging to the R.S.F.S.R.) was enlarged by the territory which is now known as southern Kazakhstan. All these units still exist, although there have been several boundary changes and most of them have been raised to a higher administrative status.

The ostensible reason for the reorganization was to make administrative units correspond to the nationality of the inhabitants—nationality being understood as comprising people of one vernacular language. But another important reason obviously was to prevent the establishment of any one large and strong unit in Central Asia. The situation which has resulted from the National Delimitation and subsequent changes lends itself to strong criticism on two grounds. Firstly, the 'nationality' principle has not in fact been consistently carried out—clearly in order to prevent the existence of a powerful Uzbekistan; several areas adjacent to the present frontiers of that republic, with Uzbek-speaking majorities, have been included in Tadzhikistan, Kirgizia, Kazakhstan, Turkmenia and the Kara-Kalpak Autonomous Republic, without any historical, geographical, economic or other justification. Secondly, the very principle of vernacular language as a basis for territorial delimitation is scarcely appropriate to Central Asian conditions. The great majority of Uzbeks and Tadzhiks living in the oases are culturally and historically one people (originally Iranian-speaking but Turkicized in varying degrees), and before 1924 were called Sarts as distinct from the semi-nomadic Uzbeks and mountain Tadzhiks. In these conditions the criterion of vernacular language is almost irrelevant. The application of the language principle in dividing Central Asia also runs against almost all geographical, historical and economic factors: on the one hand, clearly defined units in all these senses, such as the Khorezm oasis or the Fergana Valley, are parcelled out arbitrarily between different administrative units, and on the other, areas which have practically nothing in common except a section of the population speaking the same language have been combined into one unit. *See* A. G. Park, *Bolshevism in Turkestan*, New York, 1957; G. Wheeler, *Racial Problems in Soviet Muslim Asia*, 1960.

National Democratic Parties existed in Georgia and Belorussia. During the 1920's Belorussian National Democrats, though suppressed as an organized party, were able to exercise a considerable influence, particularly in the cultural sphere, where they co-operated with the Bolsheviks in carrying out the policy of 'Belorussianization.' Most of them were purged in 1933.

National District, *see* OKRUG.

National Income is defined by Soviet economists so as to include only the net product of industry, agriculture, building, transport and communications services directly involved in material production, and trade, while non-material services such as education, health service, administration, the armed forces and passenger transport are omitted. In this sense (that is, roughly, value added in material production net of amortization) the national income amounted in 1958 to about 1,250 milliard roubles in current prices, or about a half of gross output. Of the total, industry accounted for 54 per cent, agriculture for 23 per cent and building for 8 per cent in 1955; in the same year almost three-quarters of the total was produced in the State enterprises, 15 per cent in *kolkhozes* and other co-operatives, and the rest, amounting to more than one-tenth, privately, i.e. from the personal plots of *kolkhoz* members, personal plots and spare-time work of workers and employees, by individual peasants and uncooperated artisans. Such a high figure of private income is explained by the fact that in conditions of scarcity goods privately produced and realized command high prices.

The main items of income produced in the State enterprises were wages (q.v.) and salaries, turnover tax and profits (qq.v.). About a quarter of the total national income is used for 'accumulation,' that is, net capital formation (of which gross fixed investment, q.v., makes up about 80 per cent); material consumption takes up the remaining three-quarters (95 per cent being the consumption of the population). *See* A. Bergson, *Soviet National Income and Product in 1937*, New York, 1953; A. Bergson and H. Heymann, *Soviet National Income and Product, 1940–8*, New York, 1954; A. Nove and A. Zauberman, 'A Soviet Disclosure of Ruble National Income,' *Soviet Studies*, vol. xi, No. 2, Oct. 1959.

Nationalism is regarded in Communist ideology as an attribute of a bourgeois society, and expressions of it in the Soviet Union, when unwelcome to the authorities, are invariably attacked as 'bourgeois nationalism.' The one exception to this rule is Great Russian nationalism, which until the mid 1930's was always officially referred to as

'Great Power chauvinism,' but which since then has not been specifically condemned. In fact the party leadership has frequently made use of nationalist sentiments (*see* NATIONALITIES POLICY). During the war a genuine national patriotic feeling flared up as a result of the early experience of prisoners of war and of civilians under German occupation; the chauvinism of Stalin's last years was a deliberate policy of exploiting this war-time nationalism for the purpose of isolating the country from the outside world, and it met with considerable success among the war generation; it appears that the present young generation, lacking experience either of the war or of Stalin's last years, are on the whole free from the extremes of nationalist feeling. *See* N. Timasheff, *The Great Retreat*, New York, 1946; W. Kolarz, *Russia and her Colonies*, 1952; F. C. Barghoorn, *Soviet Russian Nationalism*, 1956.

Nationalities Policy, of the Communist Party and the Soviet Government, has undergone several drastic changes. At first the Bolsheviks denied the need for a special nationalities policy, believing the national problem to be relevant only in conditions of a 'bourgeois' state. However, after the 1905 revolution Lenin realized the potential importance of nationalist tendencies among the non-Russian peoples of the empire in the struggle against the established order. He therefore adopted the slogan of 'self-determination,' including secession, and defended it against those romantic inter-nationalists Rosa Luxemburg and Bukharin who clung to Lenin's former view. Yet Lenin consistently rejected the idea of organizing the party on national lines. The contradiction between the slogan of self-determination and the reality of a centralistic party was 'solved' through a quasi-federal structure of the Soviet state and the fiction (q.v.) of territorial autonomy for smaller peoples. Throughout the 1920's the policy of the party leadership was distinctly anti-Russian and one of encouragement for non-Russian nationalists provided they collaborated with the Communists. However, from the mid 1930's the opposite course was taken, and Russian patriotism was fostered, particularly during the war, at the expense of local nationalisms. In the last years of Stalin's life this assumed the proportions of obscurantist chauvinism and anti-Semitism (q.v.). Since Stalin's death there has been considerable uncertainty and wavering, but on the whole policy has been better balanced between Great Russian and other nationalisms, though the former still predominates. *See further under* AUTONOMY; FEDERALISM; NATIONAL DELIMITATION OF CENTRAL ASIA. *See* W. Kolarz, *Russia and her Colonies*, 1952, and 'The Nationalities under Khrushchëv,' *Soviet Survey*, No. 24, April–June 1958; R. Pipes, *The Formation of the Soviet Union*, Cambridge, Mass., 1954; F. C. Barghoorn, *Soviet Russian Nationalism*, 1956; R. Schlesinger (ed.), *The Nationalities Problem and Soviet Administration*, 1956; R. Conquest, *The Soviet Deportation of Nationalities*, 1960; G. Wheeler, *Racial Problems in Soviet Muslim Asia*, 1960.

Nationalization of Industry, through confiscation, was carried out by the Soviet Government during the period of War Communism (q.v.) except for the smallest enterprises (employing fewer than ten men, or fewer than five if there was any kind of mechanical power).

Private enterprise was again permitted to expand in industry during the period of the New Economic Policy (q.v.), but all private firms were confiscated, except for some foreign concessions (q.v.), in 1930. *See* V. Gsovski and K. Grzybowski (eds.), *Government, Law and Courts in the Soviet Union and Eastern Europe*, vol. ii, 1959.

Navashin, Sergey Gavrilovich (1857–1930), biologist, member of the Academy of Sciences. He taught at Kiev and Tiflis universities and headed the Biological Institute in Moscow. His work was devoted to cytology and embryology of plants, and his discovery in 1898 of double fertilization in Angiospermae was the starting point of fruitful research in cytogenetic problems by himself and his followers.

Navy, Soviet, was estimated (1959) to consist of 37 cruisers, 230 destroyers, 500–600 large and medium submarines and many smaller ships (but no aircraft carriers), with a total tonnage of 1,600,000 (600,000 in 1940) and 500,000 men. The main offensive weapon is the submarine, while the surface vessels are intended primarily for defence and combined land and sea operations. In design and equipment the ships are comparable to the corresponding American and British models, some submarines and cruisers being fitted with guided or ballistic missiles. The Soviet Navy is subordinated to the Ministry of Defence, and the Commander-in-Chief of the Navy (at present Admiral S. G. Gorshkov) is a First Deputy Minister of Defence. The navy is divided into four fleets: Baltic (main bases Tallinn, Kronstadt, Riga, Kaliningrad and Baltiysk), Black Sea (main base Sevastopol'), Pacific (formed 1932, main base Vladivostok) and Northern (formed 1933, main base Polyarnyy near Murmansk). Each fleet includes, besides naval forces, coastal defence (artillery and infantry) units and a land-based naval air formation, the total strength of the naval air arm being estimated at 4,000 aircraft. There are also four flotillas of smaller ships on the Danube, Dnieper, the Amur and the Caspian. Political control is exercized by the head of Naval Political Administration (subordinated to the Chief Political Administration of the Armed Forces) through political officers (*see* ZAMPOLIT) and the network of party organizations.

A modern Russian navy was first built by Peter the Great. Close relations were maintained throughout the 18th and early 19th centuries with the British Navy, many Britons serving in the Russian Navy and many Russian naval officers receiving their training in the British Navy. From the late 18th century until the Russo-Japanese War (q.v.) of 1904–5 Russia ranked third in naval strength after Britain and France. However, the navy was always considered to be of secondary importance to the army. The Russians scored a number of important naval victories, mainly over the Turks, the chief ones being those of Tchesme, 1770, and Sinop, 1853; the most outstanding naval commanders were Samuel Greig, F. F. Ushakov (1743–1818) and Nakhimov (q.v.). In 1905 the Russian fleet was routed by the Japanese at Tsushima, and Russia sank to sixth place as a naval power. The First World War caught Russia in the middle of a programme of rebuilding her navy, and the latter's only notable contributions were skilful mine-laying operations in the Baltic and the Black Sea.

Already during the revolution of 1905 (q.v.) several mutinies occurred in the navy, and after the February revolution (q.v.) of 1917 the sailors, particularly of the Baltic fleet, fell completely under the influence of the Bolsheviks and Anarchists. They played a decisive part in the seizure of power by the Bolsheviks (*see* OCTOBER REVOLUTION) and the dispersal of the Constituent Assembly (q.v.). During the civil war Baltic sailors appeared on all fronts as fanatical Bolsheviks, while the Black Sea fleet, formerly commanded by Admiral Kolchak (q.v.), was neutral or supported the White side. The revolutionary fervour of the Baltic sailors turned after the end of the civil war against the Communist dictatorship, and the Kronstadt rising, 1921, made history as the first large-scale anti-Communist revolutionary action. Restoration and expansion of the navy proceeded throughout the late 1920's and the thirties with the main emphasis on submarines, so that by the beginning of the Second World War the Soviet Union had the greatest number of submarines in the world. But the naval officers' corps was decimated by the Great Purge (q.v.) and the performance of the navy during the war was even more disappointing than in the First World War. However, since the end of the war a great programme of modernization and expansion has been carried out (at first with the help of German experts and using German and allied models), and now the Soviet Navy is the second largest in the world. Much credit for this achievement goes to Admiral N. G. Kuznetsov, who was Commander-in-Chief of the Soviet Navy almost continuously from 1939 until 1953. *See also* ARMED FORCES. *See* M. Mitchell, *The Maritime History of Russia*, 1949; R. L. Garthoff, *How Russia Makes War*, 1954, and *Soviet Strategy in the Nuclear Age*, 1958; R. Hough, *The Fleet that had to Die*, 1958; M. G. Saunders (ed.), *The Soviet Navy*, 1958.

Nazi-Soviet Pact, colloquial name for the treaty of non-aggression, followed by one on 'friendship and boundary,' which were concluded between the Soviet Union and Germany on 23rd August and 28th September 1939 respectively; the non-aggression treaty contained a secret protocol on the division of Poland and the Baltic States (q.v.). Stalin's change of front which resulted in these treaties precipitated the outbreak of the Second World War. Until Germany invaded Russia in June 1941 the Soviet Government co-operated with the Nazis in diplomacy, propaganda and the supply of war materials, especially oil. The treaties have never been publicly denounced in the Soviet Union, and as late as 1959 were defended as expedient by Khrushchëv. *See* M. Beloff, *The Foreign Policy of Soviet Russia*, vol. ii, 1949; A. Rossi, *The Russo-German Alliance*, 1950.

Nebit-Dag (until late 1930's **Nefte-Dag**), town in Turkmenia on the Trans-Caspian Railway, 95 m. south-east of Krasnovodsk. Population (1956) 30,400. It is the centre of an oil- and ozokerite-producing area, and was built in the 1930's.

Nekrasov, Nikolay Alekseyevich (1821–77), poet whose main topic was the misery of the lower classes, and who did much to focus the attention of educated society upon it. He owned and edited the radical journals *The Contemporary* (q.v.) and *The Notes of the Fatherland*. Chief poems: *Who Lives Well in Russia?*, *The Railway*, *Peasant*

Children and *Russian Women*. He was the favourite poet of the radical intelligentsia.

Nemchinov, Vasiliy Sergeyevich (*b.* 1894), economist and statistician, Communist Party member since 1940. He was educated at the Moscow Commercial Institute (graduating 1917), was head of the Department of Statistics of the Moscow Agricultural Academy, 1928–48, and its director 1940–8. Since 1947 Nemchinov has been a professor at the Academy of Social Sciences attached to the Communist Party Central Committee; since 1946 a member of the U.S.S.R. Academy of Sciences; since 1949 chairman of its Council for the Study of Productive Forces; and since 1953 a member of its presidium. In 1953–9 he was the head of the academy's department for economics, philosophy and law. In the conditions of official obscurantism characteristic of the last years of Stalin's life Nemchinov upheld the integrity of scholarship (e.g. in the Lysenko, q.v., scandal in 1948, and against the official line in the controversy on statistics in 1950). Since Stalin's death he has played a leading role in the revival of economic studies, particularly in relation to regional and welfare planning and to the use of mathematical methods. *See* V. S. Nemchinov (ed.), *Primeneniye matematiki v ekonomicheskikh issledovaniyakh*, Moscow, 1959; A. Zauberman, 'New Wind in Soviet Planning,' *Soviet Studies*, vol. xii, No. 1, July 1960.

Nenets National Okrug lies within the Archangel Oblast. Area 70,100 sq. m.; population (1959) 45,000 (56 per cent urban), Russians and Nenets (*see* SAMOYEDS). There is reindeer raising, fishing, hunting and coal-mining. The National Okrug was established in 1929; its administrative centre is Nar'yan-Mar. The area has been one of banishment (since the 17th century) and labour camps.

Neo-Populism, ideological trend during the 1920's, led by N. D. Kondrat'yev, its senior theorist being Professor A. N. Chelintsev. It was a development of Liberal Populism and, on the basis of field studies, claimed that Marxist theory was not relevant to the peasant economy, and that agricultural policy should support individual peasant farming and encourage peasant co-operatives. Neo-Populism was regarded by the Communists as a *kulak* (q.v.) ideology, and the trend was suppressed and its leaders imprisoned with the onset of the collectivization of agriculture (q.v.). *See also* PEASANT HOUSEHOLD. *See* S. V. Utechin, 'Bolsheviks and their Allies after 1917: the Ideological Pattern,' *Soviet Studies*, Oct. 1958.

'N.E.P. Men,' pejorative term for people who took advantage of the opportunities for private enterprise in trade and industry which were afforded by the New Economic Policy (q.v.) in the 1930's. Although they greatly helped in restoring the country's economy, they were subject to social and legal disadvantages (e.g. discrimination against their children in education, disfranchisement, discrimination in the courts, etc.). With the end of the N.E.P. and the transition to 'Socialist reconstruction' the property of 'N.E.P. men' was confiscated and many of them were deported to forced labour camps; during the Great Purge (q.v.) it was often an incriminating circumstance to have had a 'N.E.P. man' relative.

Nerchinsk, town in the Chita Oblast (south-eastern Siberia), situated 130 m. east of Chita. Population (1956) 11,600 (1937, 15,000). Gold, non-ferrous and rare metals are mined in the Nerchinsk area, in the past (since the 19th century) largely by forced labour. Nerchinsk was founded in 1653; a Russo-Chinese treaty was signed here in 1689.

Nesmelov, Viktor Ivanovich (1863–1920), Christian philosopher, professor of Kazan' Theological Academy. In his works (*The Science of Man*, vol. i, 3rd ed., 1905; vol. ii, 2nd ed., 1907; *Faith and Knowledge*, 1913) he appears as a precursor of the modern Christian Existentialism. *See* V. V. Zenkovsky, *A History of Russian Philosophy*, vol. ii, 1953.

Nesmeyanov, Aleksandr Nikolayevich (*b.* 1899), chemist. Educated at Moscow University, he has taught there since 1922 and was its rector in 1948–51. He has been a member of the Academy of Sciences since 1943 and succeeded S. I. Vavilov as president of the academy in 1951. He joined the party in 1944. His research work is concerned with the chemistry of metallo-organic compounds, and he has developed methods of obtaining element-organic compounds of various metals. In 1958 Nesmeyanov opposed Khrushchëv's plan for educational reform (*see* EDUCATION).

Nesterov, Mikhail Vasil'yevich (1862–1942), painter, studied at the Moscow School of Art and at the Academy of Arts. He began as one of the Peredvizhniki (q.v.) with paintings in the vein of sentimental realism; he ended as an honorary 'socialist realist' (*see* SOCIALIST REALISM) and the laureate of the Stalin Prize, awarded to him for one of his fine portraits. But Nesterov was above all a religious painter; he fused the figures of his monks, holy old men and saintly youths, serenely placed in the foreground, with an idyllically placid Russian landscape, realized as a flat background plane, and achieved a highly artistic expression of the peaceful, gentle and unworldly character of the Russian medieval faith.

Neva, river flowing west out of Lake Ladoga (north-west Russia) into the Gulf of Finland. Although its length is only 46 miles it is very full, since it is the only outlet of Lake Ladoga. The whole area of the Neva is dominated by Leningrad, which is situated in and around its delta. The Neva forms part of the inner waterways connecting the Baltic Sea with the Volga and the White Sea.

New Economic Policy (abbreviation N.E.P.), economic policy practised by the Bolshevik Government, 1921–8, with the aims of restoring the economy by making concessions to private enterprise in agriculture, trade and industry, and of neutralizing the peasants politically. The policy was successful, and by 1927 the production level of 1913 had again been reached. *See also* FIVE YEAR PLANS; WAR COMMUNISM. *See* M. Dobb, *Soviet Economic Development since 1917*, 1948; E. H. Carr, *The Bolshevik Revolution, 1917–23*, vol. ii, 1952, *The Interregnum, 1923–4*, 1954, and *Socialism in One Country, 1924–6*, vol. i, 1958; H. Schwartz, *Russia's Soviet Economy*, 2nd ed., 1954.

New Russia, obsolete name for the steppe area north of the Black Sea and the Sea of Azov which was acquired by Russia (chiefly conquered from Turkey) in the 18th and early 19th centuries, and was colonized from various parts of Russia as well as from the Balkans and Germany. It comprised the present Moldavian Republic, the oblasts of Odessa, Nikolayev, Kherson, Kirovograd, Crimea, Dnepropetrovsk, Zaporozh'ye, Stalino and Voroshilovgrad of the Ukraine, and parts of the Rostov Oblast and Krasnodar Kray of the Russian Federal Republic. *See* B. Nolde, *La Formation de l'Empire Russe*, vol. ii, Paris, 1953; N. D. Polons'ka-Vasylenko, *The Settlement of the Southern Ukraine (1750–75)*, New York, 1955.

New Serbia, 18th-century name of that part of New Russia which lay west of the Dnieper, populated partly by Serbian colonists, 1752–1753, who are now completely assimilated. It was made up of the present Kirovograd and part of Dnepropetrovsk oblasts, with Novomirgorod as capital.

Newspapers, *see* PRESS.

Nicholas I (1796–1855), emperor, third son of Paul I. His accession in 1825 was followed by the Decembrists' (q.v.) uprising. He was badly educated, but honest and with a strong sense of duty. The chief events of his reign were: the codification of existing laws (*see* SPERANSKIY), the banning of the sale of serfs without their families, and a considerable improvement in the position of Crown peasants; successful wars with Persia, 1826–8, and Turkey, 1827–9, the Polish uprising of 1830–1, and the Crimean War (q.v.), during which Nicholas died. *See* C. de Grunwald, *Tsar Nicholas I* (trans. B. Patmore), 1954; N. V. Riasanovsky, *Nicholas I and Official Nationality in Russia, 1825–55*, Berkeley and Los Angeles, 1959.

Nicholas II (1868–1918), son of Alexander III, first cousin of King George V, the last Emperor of Russia, acceding to the throne in 1894. Intelligent, charming and patriotic, he was nevertheless reactionary in outlook and vacillating and weak in character. He declared his resolve to preserve the principle of autocracy in a reply to the Tver' Zemstvo's address on his accession, but was obliged by the revolution of 1905 (q.v.) to grant a constitution providing for a legislative assembly (*see* DUMA). Externally the chief events of his reign were the consolidating of the Franco-Russian alliance, the convening by Nicholas of the Hague Conference (q.v.) in 1899, the occupation of Port Arthur (q.v.) in 1896 and of Manchuria, 1900, and the Russo-Japanese War (q.v.). Shortly after the outbreak of World War I (q.v.) he took over as commander-in-chief of the armed forces, and left the government of the country to his wife (*see* ALEXANDRA FËDOROVNA) —effectively, to Rasputin (q.v.). At the outset of the February revolution (q.v.) of 1917 he at once accepted the advice to abdicate tendered by the Duma leaders and the military commanders; at first confined to the palace at Tsarskoye Selo, he was then banished to Siberia. He was brought with his family to Yekaterinburg after the Bolshevik seizure of power (*see* OCTOBER REVOLUTION), and all were shot by the Cheka on Lenin's orders. *See* E. J. Dillon, *The Eclipse of Russia*, 1918; *Memoirs of Count Witte* (trans. A. Yarmolinsky), New York, 1921; C. E. Vulliamy (ed.), *Letters of the Tsar to the Tsaritsa, 1914–17*, 1929; V. N. Kokovtsov, *Out of My Past*, 1935; E. J. Bing (ed.), *Letters of Tsar Nicholas and Empress Marie*, 1937; Sir B. Pares, *The Fall of the Russian Monarchy*, 1939; V. I. Gurko, *Features and*

Figures of the Past. Government and Opinion in the Reign of Nicholas II, 1939; S. P. Mel'gunov, *Sud'ba imp. Nikolaya II posle otrecheniya*, Paris, 1951, and *Legenda o separatnom mire*, Paris, 1957; R. Charques, *Twilight of Imperial Russia: the Reign of Tsar Nicholas II*, 1958; P. M. Bykov, *The Last Days of Tsardom*, s.a.; M. Paleologue, *An Ambassador's Memoirs* (3 vols.), New York, s.a.

Niemen (Russian **Neman**, Lithuanian **Nemunas**, German **Memel**), navigable river in Belorussia and Lithuania which rises near Minsk and flows north-west into the Kurisches Haff of the Baltic Sea. Length 590 m.; chief port Kaunas.

Nijinska, Bronislava (*b.* 1890), dancer, choreographer and teacher, sister of Vatslav Nijinsky. After studying at the Imperial Theatre School, St Petersburg, until 1908, she appeared with Nijinsky in the first season of the Ballets Russes. 'La Nijinska' (the title given her by Diaghilev) enjoys the distinction of being the first woman choreographer, the most outstanding ballets in her varied and brilliant career being *Les Noces*, 1923, *Les Comédiens jaloux*, 1932, and *Pictures from an Exhibition*, 1944. Her work as a teacher has been of the greatest significance. *See also* DIAGHILEV.

Nijinsky, Vatslav Fomich (1890–1950), dancer and choreographer of Polish birth. A pupil of Legat and Gerdt, he studied at the Imperial Ballet School, St Petersburg, from 1900. He attracted attention by his performance in Fokine's *Le Pavillon d'Armide*, 1907, but continued his studies with Cecchetti. In 1908 he met Diaghilev and was immediately enrolled to dance with the Ballets Russes, 1909 seeing him feature in *Cléopâtre*, *Le Pavillon d'Armide*, *Le Festin* and *Les Sylphides*. In 1910 he appeared in *Le Carnaval*, *Sheherazade* and *Giselle*, each role being received with great acclaim. In 1911, as the result of 'the Nijinsky incident,' he left the Imperial Theatres and was permanently engaged by Diaghilev. Each programme from then on centred round Nijinsky, *Le Spectre de la Rose* and *Petrushka* being great successes. Under Diaghilev's guidance he appeared as choreographer and dancer in *L'Après-midi d'un Faune*, but owing to the inordinate time spent on rehearsals, this estranged him from Fokine. The year 1913 saw Nijinsky's productions of *Jeux* and *Le Sacre du Printemps*, the latter of which, by its extreme barbarity and originality, caused a furore. In the same year the Ballets Russes went to South America without Diaghilev, and on their arrival Nijinsky unexpectedly married a dancer, Romola de Pulska, which gave Diaghilev much displeasure. Refusing to dance on one occasion, Nijinsky was dismissed, and this was the commencement of his rapid decline. Already a victim of mental disease and lacking Diaghilev's business acumen, he experienced a series of disasters. His last appearance was in 1917, only ten years after his début. He spent the remainder of his life in an asylum. Though a brilliant dancer and choreographer, Nijinsky was incapable of communicating his thoughts to others. Nevertheless his unique powers of dancing and mime, his physical agility and his wonderful insight into widely differing roles rightly gained for him the title of 'le dieu de la danse.' *See* S. Lifar, *A History of Russian Ballet*, 1954.

Nikanor (lay name **Brovkovich, Aleksandr Ivanovich**) (1826–90), archbishop of Kherson, Christian philosopher and conservative political thinker, of Belorussian parentage. In his main philosophical work (*Positive Philosophy and Supersensual Being*, 3 vols., 1875–88) he to some extent anticipates Husserl's phenomenological constructions. He took a leading part in the polemics against L. N. Tolstoy's views on Church and State. *See* V. V. Zenkovsky, *A History of Russian Philosophy*, vol. ii, 1953.

Nikolayev (Ukrainian **Mykolayiv**): 1. Oblast in southern Ukraine, black earth lowland steppe adjacent to the Black Sea, traversed by the Southern Bug. Area 9,600 sq. m.; population (1959) 1,015,000 (39 per cent urban), Ukrainians and Russians (before the war also Jews and Germans). Wheat and sunflowers are cultivated, market gardening is carried on and there are large engineering and food industries. The area was virtually unpopulated until its annexation by Russia from Turkey, 1774–91.

2. Administrative, economic and cultural centre of the oblast, situated at the estuary of the Southern Bug. Population (1959) 224,000 (1914, 120,000; 1923, 81,000; 1939, 169,000), Russians and Ukrainians. It is a major centre of industry (large shipyards, agricultural engineering, food and light industries) and a seaport. Nikolayev was founded by Potëmkin in 1788 as a shipbuilding and naval base; it became a provincial capital in 1802, a commercial port in 1862, and has had large-scale industry since 1895.

Nikolayevsk-on-Amur, seaport in the Khabarovsk Kray (Far East), situated on the Amur 37 m. from its mouth. Population (1956) 34,600 (1914, 16,500; 1926, 7,400). It is the centre of an important fishing and gold-mining region; there is a school of navigation (since the 1850's) and a teachers' training school for the peoples of the Russian Far East. Nikolayevsk-on-Amur was founded as a naval base in 1850 and for the next thirty years was capital of the Russian Pacific territories; from 1934 to 1956 it was capital of the Lower Amur Oblast within the Far Eastern and then the Khabarovsk Kray.

Nikol'sk-Ussuriyskiy, *see* Ussuriysk.

Nikon (1605–81), Patriarch of Moscow, 1652–8, by birth a Mordvin. The schism which developed in the Russian Church resulted from the rejection by a section of the clergy and of laymen (the Old Ritualists, or Old Believers, q.v.) of various reforms which Nikon introduced: the unification of the ritual, the correction of books used in church services, etc. Nikon's attempt to raise the authority of the Church above that of the State led to a conflict with the czar Aleksey Mikhaylovich; the Patriarch was defeated, condemned by the Church Council in 1666–7, and confined to a monastery.

Nikopol', town in the Dnepropetrovsk Oblast (Ukraine), situated on the Dnieper 70 m. south-west of Dnepropetrovsk. Population (1959) 81,000. It is an important centre of metallurgy (pipe-rolling mill) and engineering, the centre of a rich manganese-mining area, and a river port. Nikopol' was founded in the 18th century on the site of the destroyed Zaporozh'ye Sich, and became a town in 1782.

Nivkhi, *see* GILYAKS.

Nizhniy Novgorod, *see* GOR'KIY.

Nizhniy Tagil, city in the Sverdlovsk Oblast (Urals), situated 75 m.

north of Sverdlovsk. Population (1959) 338,000 (fifth in the Urals; 1914, 45,000; 1926, 39,000; 1939, 160,000). It is one of the principal metallurgical and engineering centres of the Urals, with a vast iron and steel works, a railway-car plant (the biggest in Russia) and coking and chemical plants. Iron and copper ores and gold are mined in the Nizhniy Tagil area, and the city is surrounded by a number of smaller iron- and copper-producing towns. It was founded as an iron-works in 1725; the first experimental railway in Russia was built here is 1834. Industrial development has been especially rapid since the 1930's.

N.K.G.B. (Russian abbreviation for 'People's Commissariat of State Security'), Soviet security service, 1943–6, with essentially similar functions to its predecessor the N.K.V.D. Its main operations were concerned with 'unreliable elements' in territories previously occupied by the Germans and with prisoners of war and civilian deportees returning from Germany. Many of these were deported to Asiatic Russia or sentenced to terms in 'corrective labour camps' (q.v.); certain entire native peoples of southern Russia suffered the former treatment, i.e. Balkars, Chechens, Ingush, Crimean Tatars, Kalmyks and Karachays (qq.v.). The N.K.G.B. was renamed M.G.B. (q v.) in 1946. *See further under* SECURITY ORGANS.

N.K.V.D. (Russian abbreviation for 'People's Commissariat of Internal Affairs'), Soviet security service, 1934–43, essentially resembling its predecessors the Cheka and G.P.U. (qq.v.) but having the further responsibility for all places of detention (including 'corrective labour camps,' q.v.), the ordinary police and civil registry offices. It was successively headed by Yagoda, Yezhov (1936–8) and Beria, and effected the Great Purge (q.v.), thus becoming the most powerful organ in the state and the chief tool of Stalin's dictatorship. After the Great Purge one of its main operations was to deport all 'unreliable elements' from the border and the newly annexed territories of the Baltic States, eastern Poland, Bessarabia and northern Bukovina. It was split in 1943 into two commissariats, the N.K.V.D. and the N.K.G.B., the latter having responsibility for State security. *See further under* SECURITY ORGANS.

Nogay, Turkic-speaking people who live in the north of Daghestan and in the Karachay-Circassian Autonomous Oblast (North Caucasus), numbering (1959) 41,000. They are Sunni Muslims, and mostly peasants (now collectivized) especially engaged in sheep rearing. They made up part of the Golden Horde, but in the 14th century established a separate Nogay Horde which later disintegrated. Between the 16th and 18th centuries they submitted voluntarily to Russia.

Noginsk (formerly **Bogorodsk**), town in the Moscow Oblast, 42 m. east of Moscow. Population (1959) 93,000 (1926, 38,000; 1939, 81,000). There are varied textile (since the 19th century) and some metal-working industries. Known as a village since the 16th century, Noginsk became a town in 1781.

Nomenclature, lists of the more important posts in various fields and of people who are considered suitable to fill these posts, which are kept by the cadres (q.v.) departments of the party committees from the rayon committees upwards. Appointments to such posts are in fact either made or confirmed by the cadres departments irrespective of the formal procedure of appointment. To be in a nomenclature is an indication of membership of the ruling class. *See* M. Fainsod, *Smolensk Under Soviet Rule*, 1959.

Non-Ferrous Metals. No absolute figures on the production of non-ferrous metals are given in Soviet statistics. The main deposits of copper ores are in central Kazakhstan, the Urals and Armenia; zinc and lead are normally found together in polymetallic ores in the Oriferous Altay, southern Kazakhstan, North Ossetia, the Kuznetsk Basin, and the Maritime Kray in the Far East; aluminium in the form of bauxite is found in the Leningrad Oblast, the Urals and northern Kazakhstan; deposits of tin exist in Transbaykalia and north-eastern Yakutia, and of nickel in Pechenga (Murmansk Oblast) and Noril'sk in northern Siberia. The non-ferrous metal industry is concentrated near the deposits, or in the case of aluminium near big electric power-stations. The main centres are the Oriferous Altay (East Kazakhstan Oblast)—the oldest centre of the non-ferrous metal industry in Russia—the Urals, Karaganda Oblast in Kazakhstan and Transcaucasia. Before the Second World War non-ferrous metals were not exported; after the war they were exported to the Communist countries, and since 1955 also to other countries. Imports have been considerably smaller since the war than before, the largest item being tin from China.

Non-Party Bolsheviks, propaganda term used in the 1930's and forties for those activists (q.v.) who were not formally party members. The concept was used to sustain the fictions (q.v.) of the 'moral and political unity of the Soviet people' and the 'Bloc of Communists and Non-Party People' at elections.

Noril'sk, town in the Krasnoyarsk Kray (central Siberia), situated near the lower course of the Yenisey, 69° N., surrounded by but not a part of the Taymyr National Okrug; it is the northernmost town in Russia. Population (1959) 108,000. It is an important industrial centre (coal-mining, uranium, nickel, copper and platinum works). It is connected by a 79-mile-long railway with the port of Dudinka on the Yenisey. Noril'sk was founded in 1935 and became a town in 1953. Until the mid 1950's it was one of the principal concentration camp areas, and the town and its industries were built entirely by forced labour; a large-scale strike of camp inmates took place in 1953.

Norms, term used in the Soviet economy in several senses, including: (1) the amount of work an industrial worker or a peasant is supposed to carry out during a workshift; the fulfilment of the norm is an important factor in the calculation of remuneration, though the relationship between the two varies. In practice there are two conflicting tendencies: on the one hand, to raise the norms either to a 'scientific' level (by time and motion study and similar devices) or else by using the performance of 'shock-workers' (q.v., *see also* STAKHANOV MOVEMENT) as a pretext; and on the other hand, the desire of managements to adjust norms so that the workers receive a wage consistent with the current level; *see also* WAGES; (2) the amount of raw materials, fuel, etc., which is supposed to be used for a unit of output; (3) the amount of agricultural produce to be sold to the State. *See* D. Granick, *Management of the Industrial Firm in the U.S.S.R.*, New York, 1955; J. S. Berliner, *Factory and Manager in the U.S.S.R.*, Cambridge, Mass., 1957.

North Kazakhstan Oblast is situated in south-western Siberia, traversed by the River Ishim and the Trans-Siberian and Trans-Kazakhstan railways. Area 15,800 sq. m.; population (1959) 454,000 (34 per cent urban), mostly Russians and Ukrainians, also Tatars, Mordva, Germans and Kazakhs. Wheat and other grain crops and sunflowers are cultivated (greatly expanded during the Virgin Land Campaign), cattle and sheep bred, and there are metal-working, food (meat, flour, butter), leather and felt industries, chiefly concentrated in the administrative centre of the oblast, Petropavlovsk. The territory was inhabited by the Kazakh Middle Hundred and was annexed to Russia in the early 18th century.

North Ossetian Autonomous Republic, of the R.S.F.S.R., lies on the northern slopes of the central part of the main Caucasus range and the adjacent lowland, traversed by the River Terek; there are deposits of lead, zinc, silver and oil. Area 3,100 sq. m.; population (1959) 449,000 (53 per cent urban), mostly Ossetians and Russians. Wheat and maize growing, horticulture and sheep and cattle raising are carried on; the industries are non-ferrous metallurgy, oil extraction and food (including cheese). The capital is Ordzhonikidze. The area was included in the Mountain People's Autonomous Republic in 1920, the North Ossetian Autonomous Oblast was formed in 1924, and the republic in 1936. It was largely occupied by the Germans in 1942, and saw bitter fighting. *See* W. Kolarz, *Russia and her Colonies*, 1952.

Northern Sea Route, system of shipping lanes which traverses the coastal waters north of Siberia from the Bering Straits in the east to the straits between the Barents and the Kara seas in the west. It has been principally developed by the Glavsevmorput' (Chief Administration of the Northern Sea Route), whose first director, 1932–9, was O. Yu. Schmidt (q.v.). During the 1930's the whole economic development of northern Siberia was the responsibility of the administration. Both politically and economically the route is of considerable importance. *See* T. E. Armstrong, *The Northern Sea Route*, 1952; C. Krypton, *The North Sea Route*, New York, 1953, and *The Northern Sea Route and the Economy of the Soviet Union*, 1956; J. Lied, *Siberian Arctic*, 1960.

Novaya Zemlya ('New Land'), Arctic archipelago consisting of two large and several small islands off the coast of European Russia. The Northern Sea Route passes through the Strait of Matochkin Shar between the two main islands, and through Yugorskiy Shar south of the southern island. The archipelago is very sparsely inhabited by Samoyeds who engage in reindeer raising, trapping, and the collection of eider down, and by Russians working on the meteorological stations. Novgorodians are said to have visited the islands in the 11th century.

Novgorod: 1. Oblast of the R.S.F.S.R., situated in north-western Russia, with lowland around Lake Il'men in the west and the Valday upland in the east, partly covered with mixed forests; there are deposits of lignite, peat and high-quality clays. Area 20,600 sq. m.; population (1959) 740,000 (38 per cent urban). There are lumbering, wood-processing, peat extraction and linen-milling industries; old crafts are practised, and flax cultivation and dairy farming carried on. Principal towns: Novgorod, Borovichi and Staraya Russa (a mineral water spa). The area was the heart of the vast northern Russian territories which were dominated by Novgorod city in the Middle Ages.

2. Administrative and cultural centre of the oblast, one of the oldest Russian towns, traditionally considered the cradle of Russian statehood, situated 119 m. south-east of Leningrad. Population (1959) 61,000 (in the 14th century allegedly 400,000). It has woodworking, china and food industries. The town is a treasury of Russian architecture of the 11th–19th centuries (a kremlin, the St Sophia Cathedral), and since 1929 extensive excavations have been made by A. V. Artsikhovskiy, culminating in the discovery of 11th–16th-century birch-bark scrolls. According to the Russian chronicles, the Varangian (Scandinavian) prince Rurik arrived in Novgorod, by invitation of the inhabitants, in 862, and this year is traditionally regarded as marking the foundation of the Russian state. The capital was transferred to Kiev by Oleg in 882, but Novgorod remained the chief centre of foreign trade, obtaining self-government in 997 from Yaroslav the Wise and achieving independence in 1136. The Novgorod Republic (officially styled 'Sovereign Great Novgorod') embraced the whole of northern Russia to the Urals, and was governed by the assembly of townspeople (see VECHE); as military commanders, princes from other Russian centres were invited. Novgorod was captured by Ivan III and annexed to Muscovy in 1478, but retained its commercial position until St Petersburg was built; it became a provincial capital in 1727. The town suffered much during the Second World War, being occupied 1941–4.

Novgorodtsev, Pavel Ivanovich (1866–1924), jurist and philosopher, professor at Moscow University, 1903–18, and founder and dean of the Russian Juridical Faculty in Prague, 1922–4, one of the leading ideologists of the Constitutional Democrats. He advocated the revival of the doctrine of natural law, and emphasized the independent validity of the moral evaluation of political and social events. Novgorodtsev was editor of the symposium *Problems of Idealism*, 1903, a landmark in the history of Russian thought (*see further under* VEKHI). His principal works are *The Historical School of Jurists*, 1897, *Kant's and Hegel's Teachings on Law and State*, 1902, *The Crisis of Contemporary Legal Consciousness*, 1909, *The Political Ideals of the Ancient and Modern World*, 1910, and *On the Social Ideal*, 1917.

Novikov, Nikolay Ivanovich (1744–1818), journalist and publisher, a freemason. He edited and published several periodicals and *The Library of Old Russian Authors* in thirty volumes. He endeavoured to spread education and to ameliorate social conditions, and was imprisoned during the last years of Catherine II's reign.

Novocherkassk, town in the Rostov Oblast (southern Russia), situated 33 m. north-east of Rostov-on-Don. Population (1959) 94,000 (1914, 67,000; 1926, 62,000). It has an engineering industry (locomotives, machine tools, mining equipment) and is an important academic centre (Polytechnical Institute, 1907; Zootechnical and Veterinary Institute, founded in Warsaw in 1840 and evacuated to Novocherkassk in 1916; the Don Cossacks Historical Museum). Novocherkassk was founded as capital of the Don Cossack Region in 1805; it was one of the chief centres of the anti-Bolshevik movement and the White armies in 1917–20, and was capital of the transitory Don state and South-eastern League (q.v.).

Novokuybyshevsk, town in the Kuybyshev Oblast (Volga region), an industrial suburb 10 m. south-west of Kuybyshev. Population (1959) 63,000. It has a large oil-processing plant. Novokuybyshevsk grew up as a workers' settlement around the plant, and became a town in 1950.

Novo-Mariinsk, see ANADYR'.

Novonikolayevsk, see NOVOSIBIRSK.

Novorossiysk, town in the Krasnodar Kray (North Caucasus), port on the Black Sea. Population (1959) 93,000 (1926, 68,000; 1939, 95,000). It is the most important centre of cement industry in the country and has also metal-working, food and light industries. Novorossiysk was founded in 1838 as a Russian fort; industrial development dates from 1881 when the first cement factory was built. Before 1914 the port of Novorossiysk (built in 1888) was second only to Odessa as a grain-exporting port. Novorossiysk was partly occupied by the Germans in 1942–3 and greatly suffered from fighting.

Novoshakhtinsk, town in the Rostov Oblast (southern Russia), situated on the Rostov–Khar'kov highway about 12 m. north-west of Shakhty. Population (1959) 104,000 (1939, 48,000). It has coal-mining and chemical industries.

Novosibirsk: 1. Oblast of the R.S.F.S.R., situated in Western Siberia along the Trans-Siberian Railway, traversed by the River Ob', largely lowland with coniferous forests in the north, and steppe (see BARABA and KULUNDA) in the south. Area 68,400 sq. m.; population (1959) 2,299,000 (55 per cent urban), mostly Russians, also Ukrainians, Germans and some Tatars. There are engineering, light and food industries, a big hydro-electric station and wheat and dairy farming. Russia gradually annexed the area in the 16th–early 18th centuries.

2. (until 1925 **Novonikolayevsk**). Administrative centre of the oblast, the largest city and chief industrial and cultural centre of Siberia, situated on the River Ob' and the Trans-Siberian Railway. Population (1959) 887,000 (eighth in the U.S.S.R.; 1917, 69,000; 1926, 120,000; 1939, 404,000; 1956, 731,000). It has engineering (mining and electrical equipment, tools, agricultural machinery) and varied light and food industries; it is also a major centre of transportation (railway junction, river port, airport with five regular passenger services). A branch of the U.S.S.R. Academy of Sciences was established in 1933, and transformed into the Siberian division of the academy in 1956, with all branches in Siberia and the Far East subordinated to it; it concentrates upon the natural sciences. A new type of university, attached to the division, is being set up to train research workers; there are also several other higher educational establishments. Novosibirsk was founded in connection with the construction of a railway bridge over the Ob' in 1893. It was developing as a commercial centre of the surrounding agricultural area until 1930; industrial development dates from the first Five Year Plan period, and especially from the Second World War. The city was the administrative centre of Siberia, 1925–30, and of Western Siberia, 1930–7.

Novosibirskiye Islands ('New Siberian Islands'), group of islands in the Arctic Ocean north-east of the Lena Delta, forming a part of Yakutia. Area 9,650 sq. m. The islands include Kotel'nyy, Fadeyevskiy, New Siberia and Lyakhov; apart from being visited by hunters they are mostly uninhabited. There are many furred animals, and the bones of mammoths and other extinct animals have been found. The islands were discovered by Ivan Lyakhov in 1770. Since 1928 several Soviet weather stations have been established here.

Novo-Troitsk, town in the Orenburg Oblast (Urals), situated on the River Ural in the Orsk industrial area 11 m. south-west of Orsk. Population (1959) 57,000 (1939, 3,000). It has a large cement factory, and a new iron and steel plant is under construction.

Novyy Margelan, see FERGANA.

'Novyy Mir' ('*New World*'), literary journal, an organ of the Writers' Union (q.v.), founded in 1925; circulation (1959) 140,000. It acquired a particular prominence after the death of Stalin in 1953, when its editorial board, headed by Tvardovskiy (q.v.) and including Sholokov, Leonov and Fedin (qq.v.), embarked upon a policy of exposing Stalinist fictions (q.v.) and advocating freedom of literary expression. The first head-on clash with the party authorities came after the publication in December 1953 of V. Pomerantsev's article 'On Sincerity in Literature'; six months later Tvardovskiy was dismissed and the editorial board reconstituted, but under the new editor, K. Simonov, the journal again slipped into nonconformism and in 1956 was one of the chief mouthpieces of the intellectual opposition (q.v.), again incurring official disfavour. However, Simonov was still compromised in the eyes of the literary public for having allowed himself to be used to replace Tvardovskiy, and the latter's reappointment as editor was finally achieved in 1958.

N.T.S. (Russian abbreviation for 'Popular Labour Alliance,' also known as 'Russian Solidarists'), revolutionary organization advocating the overthrow of the Soviet regime and the establishment of a democratic system combining adult suffrage with the representation (in a separate chamber) of professional, regional, etc., bodies. Its philosophy is based upon the tenets of Solidarism (q.v.). The organization was founded in 1930 by *émigré* students who were to some extent influenced by the corporativist ideas of early Italian fascism. During the Second World War many N.T.S. members worked underground in the German-occupied territories of Russia and in the Vlasov (q.v.) movement. Since the war the N.T.S., with its headquarters abroad, has been the only organized revolutionary body apart from some non-Russian separatist groups. The N.T.S. tactics, which before Stalin's death were based upon building up a 'molecular' organization in Russia, have in the post-Stalin period included co-operation with the radical reformists (*see* REFORMISM). The N.T.S. publishes a number of periodicals, including the weekly *Possev* (founded 1945), and has its own radio station 'Free Russia'; it is now headed by V. D. Poremskiy. The Soviet Government has appeared in recent years to be concerned over the activities of the N.T.S. (perhaps overestimating their effect); it has protested to foreign governments and at the United Nations against their countenancing of N.T.S. work abroad, particularly in Berlin, and has several times resorted to the kidnapping, as well as the attempted assassination, of leading members of the organization. *See also* ÉMIGRÉS; REVOLUTIONARY MOVEMENT. *See* N. Khokhlov, *In the Name of Conscience*, 1960; Y. A. Trushnovich, *The Peaceful Offensive of Freedom and the Free World Public*, Frankfurt-on-Main, 1960.

Nuclear Weapons. By the end of the Second World War the Soviet Union was far behind the Western Allies and Germany in the development of atomic weapons. In the immediate post-war years the work in this field was intensified, and use was made of material and specialists from Germany as well as of information obtained from America and Britain through espionage and defectors. The first atom bomb was exploded in 1949 and the first hydrogen bomb in August 1953. In the following years various types of atomic weapons have been developed for strategic and tactical use, and at the beginning of 1960 it was stated that rockets (q.v.) with nuclear warheads (q.v.) were the principal weapons of the Soviet armed forces (q.v.). *See* R. L. Garthoff, *Soviet Strategy in the Nuclear Age*, 1958; A. Kramish, *Atomic Energy in the Soviet Union*, 1960.

Nukus, capital, economic and cultural centre of the Kara-Kalpak Autonomous Republic (Central Asia), situated in Khorezm oasis on the right bank of the Amu-Dar'ya River at the beginning of its delta. Population (1959) 39,000 (1939, 10,000). It has some industry and fisheries.

O

Ob', river in Western Siberia which rises in the Altay Mountains and flows north-west, then north into the Ob' Bay (500-mile-long estuary) of the Kara Sea. Length from confluence of the two head-streams, 2,300 m., from the source of its chief tributary, the Irtysh, 3,500 m.; drainage area over 1,100,000 sq. m. Apart from the further-most upper reaches, the Ob' is a typical plain river, wide and slow with many arms and islands. It flows chiefly through a marshy forested area (*see* NARYM). Besides the Irtysh, the principal tributaries are the Chulym and the Tom', and the principal ports are Novosibirsk and Barnaul. The river is navigable throughout, and is mainly used for carrying timber, grain and coal. The hydro-electric station built at Novosibirsk in 1954–7 is the first to exploit the resources of the Ob'. It was first visited by the Novgorodians in the 11th century, and the region was colonized by Russians from the 16th century. The basin of the Ob' has been an area of banishment (since the 17th century), labour camps and rapid economic development.

Obdorsk, *see* SALEKHARD.

Oblast, territorial administrative unit, corresponding to a province. *See also* AUTONOMOUS OBLAST.

Obligatory Deliveries, of agricultural products, *see* AGRICULTURAL PROCUREMENT.

Obninsk, town in the Kaluga Oblast (central Russia), situated on the Moscow–Kiev railway, 60 m. south-west of Moscow. The first atomic power-station was built here in 1954, and Obninsk was made a town in 1956. *See* A. Kramish, *Atomic Energy in the Soviet Union,* 1960.

Obraztsov, Vladimir Nikolayevich (1874–1949), engineer, professor at the Moscow Institute of Railway Engineers, 1935–40 head of the Railway Research Institute, member of the Academy of Sciences and of its presidium from 1939. Author of many works on the design, construction and exploitation of railways, he also acted as consultant to various institutions and organizations dealing with transportation problems (e.g. the Moscow underground).

Obruchev, Vladimir Afanas'yevich (1863–1956), geologist and geographer, professor of the Tomsk Technological Institute, 1901–12, the Tauric University at Simferopol', 1919–20, and the Moscow Mining Academy, 1921–9, member of the Academy of Sciences from 1929 and chairman of its committee (from 1939 director of the institute) for the study of permanently frozen subsoil, honorary president of the U.S.S.R. Geographical Society from 1947. He studied the geology and geography of Turkestan, Mongolia, northern China, Sinkiang and Siberia (*Geology of Siberia*, 1935–9) and the gold deposits of Siberia and the Russian Far East.

Obukhova, Nadezhda Andreyevna (*b.* 1886), mezzo-soprano. She studied under Mazetti at Moscow Conservatory until 1912, appearing for the next four years as a concert artist. From 1916 to 1943 she was a soloist of the Bolshoi Theatre, making her début as Polina in *The Queen of Spades*. Of wide tastes and abilities, she is also a distinguished solo performer.

October Children, Communist organization for children aged 6 to 9, founded in 1925.

October Revolution, seizure of power on 7th November (25th October Old Style) 1917 by the Bolshevik Party. Kerenskiy's Provisional Government (q.v.) was overthrown by the Petrograd Soviet's Military Revolutionary Committee (made up of Bolsheviks, Left Socialist Revolutionaries and Anarchists) with the aid of the Red Guards (q.v.), and a new 'Provisional Workers' and Peasants' Government' (Council of People's Commissars) was established with Lenin at the head. *See also* CONSTITUENT ASSEMBLY. *See* A. J. Sack, *The Birth of the Russian Democracy*, New York, 1918; F. A. Golder, *Documents of Russian History, 1914–17*, 1927; W. H. Chamberlin, *The Russian Revolution*, New York, 1935; E. H. Carr, *The Bolshevik Revolution*, vol. i, 1950; S. P. Mel'gunov, *Kak bol'sheviki zakhvatili vlast'*, Paris, 1953; O. Anweiler, *Die Rätebewegung in Russland, 1905–21*, Leyden, 1958.

Octobrists, political party of right-wing liberals who drew their support from the right wing of the *zemstvo* movement, liberal civil servants and business men, so named after the Imperial Manifesto of 17th October 1905 granting the constitution. Led by A. I. Guchkov (q.v.) and M. V. Rodzyanko, they were the majority party in the 3rd and 4th Dumas, and took part in the 'progressive bloc' (*see* CONSTITUTIONAL DEMOCRATS) during the First World War and in the 1917 Provisional Government (q.v.).

Odessa (Ukrainian **Odesa**): 1. Oblast in south-western Ukraine, adjacent to the Black Sea and including southern Bessarabia; it is largely fertile black earth lowland with some oak forests in the hilly north. Area 12,800 sq. m.; population (1959) 2,028,000 (47 per cent urban), mostly Ukrainians and Russians. There are food, metal-working and light industries; it is a rich agricultural area (wheat, maize, sunflowers, viniculture, cattle, pigs, fishing). Principal towns: Odessa, Izmail, Belgorod-Dnestrovskiy. The area east of the Dniester was annexed by Russia from Turkey in 1791 and formed a part of New Russia (q.v.). For the history of southern Bessarabia *see* BESS-ARABIA.

2. (before 1794 **Khadzhibey**). Administrative centre of the oblast, an important economic and cultural centre of the U.S.S.R., situated on the Odessa Bay of the Black Sea. Population (1959) 667,000 (fourth in the Ukraine, fourteenth in the U.S.S.R.; 1897, 404,000; 1914, 630,000; 1923, 317,000; 1939, 602,000), Russians, Ukrainians and Jews. It has large engineering industries (machine tools, ships, agricultural machinery, food industry equipment, cranes, mining equipment, etc.), also food, textile, chemical (the largest fertilizer plant in the Ukraine) and film industries; it is a major centre of transportation (second largest seaport, after Baku, in the country, three railway

lines, airport). There are several beach and mud health resorts. Odessa is generally considered the headquarters of the criminal underworld in the country. The university, established in 1817 as the Richelieu Lyceum, was transformed into the university of New Russia in 1865, abolished in 1920, but re-established in 1933; there is a Conservatoire, 1913, and there are many other higher educational establishments, a municipal library, 1830, an opera and ballet theatre, 1809, an historical museum, 1825, and a picture-gallery, 1898. Odessa is among the best-planned Russian cities, and there are several notable buildings of the 19th century in the classical style.

Known since the 14th century, Odessa belonged to Lithuania, then to the Crimean Tatars, and became Turkish in 1764; it was stormed by the Russians in 1789 and annexed in 1791, becoming the residence of the Viceroy of New Russia in 1805. As a result of the *porto-franco* regime, 1819–49, Odessa quickly became the second largest (after St Petersburg) foreign trade port in the country (grain export); its industrial development dates from the second half of the 19th century, with food and light industries appearing first. The city was a centre of *émigré* Greek and Bulgarian patriots, and also of the Ukrainian cultural and national movement, of Jewish culture, of the labour movement and of social democracy. In 1854 it was bombarded by the Allies, and it suffered several Jewish pogroms. Odessa was occupied by the Austrians in 1918, changed hands several times during the civil war and after a gallant defence was occupied by the Rumanians 1941–4, becoming the capital of Transnistria (q.v.).

Odnodvorets ('owner of one farmstead'), name by which the descendants are known of the colonists from northern and central Russia who in the 16th–17th centuries were settled in the then southern border provinces of Muscovy (present-day Ryazan', Voronezh, Lipetsk, Kursk and Orël oblasts) and in return for the grant of a farmstead were liable for military service against the Crimean Tatars. Until the emancipation of the serfs, 1861, their social position was equivocal, in that they did not belong either to the nobility or to the peasants. They still retain many characteristics of the northern Great Russians, and a sense of their historical origins. See J. Mavor, *An Economic History of Russia* (2 vols.), 1914.

Oesel, *see* SAAREMAA.

Officers, of the armed forces, are estimated to number between 595,800 and 650,000. Since an officer's career is in many respects very attractive, the problem of recruitment is not a difficult one. The formal requirements are physical fitness and complete secondary education. Successful applicants are given two or three years' training in military schools before they are commissioned. A special category of recruits are those who have already passed through the Suvorov schools (army) and the Nakhimov schools (navy)—boarding-schools for boys, principally sons of officers, which give a preliminary military training in addition to ordinary secondary education. Intensive training continues after commission. Aspiring and promising officers are recommended for full-time study at military academies (of which there are about twenty), most of which give training for battalion up to divisional duties; the Frunze General Staff Academy and the Voroshilov Higher Military Academy give training for corps and the highest command and staff duties.

Taken together as a class, officers belong to the privileged classes of Soviet society (see CLASSES); generals and marshals belong to the ruling stratum and are highly privileged. Officers are more highly paid than most of their civilian counterparts; their pay is not taxed and they are normally given free accommodation. They also have the right to buy scarce goods at low prices in special military shops. The authority of officers over their subordinates is generally greater than in most other countries. There are separate officers' clubs, and *esprit de corps* is enhanced by the Courts of Honour (q.v.). On the other hand, the burden of work and standards of discipline are very exacting. In addition to their normal military duties, all officers must undergo and participate in political schooling, and are under the constant supervision of political officers (see ZAMPOLIT), the party organizations in the units (most officers are party members) and the security organs (q.v.), which are represented in every unit.

The term 'officer' and all ranks were abolished after the Bolshevik seizure of power. Ranks were restored in the 1930's and the term 'officer' was officially reintroduced in 1943 as part of the policy of restoring traditional symbols characteristic of Stalinism (q.v.). *See* B. H. Liddell Hart (ed.), *The Soviet Army*, 1956.

Ogarëv, Nikolay Platonovich (1813–77), publicist and revolutionary, a life-long friend of Herzen (q.v.). In 1857–63 he developed a theory of revolutionary organization, strategy and tactics which dominated the Russian revolutionary movement (q.v.) in the 1860's and later formed the basis of Lenin's organizational and tactical views (see LENINISM). *See* E. H. Carr, *The Romantic Exiles*, 1933; S. V. Utechin, 'Who taught Lenin,' *Twentieth Century*, July 1960.

Oil Industry. Oil production in 1958 amounted to 113·2 million tons (11·6 in 1901, 9·2 in 1913, 31·1 in 1940, 19·4 in 1945, 59·3 in 1954, 70·8 in 1955, 83·8 in 1956). In 1913 almost the whole oil production was concentrated in the Caucasus (Baku and Groznyy). From the 1930's oil extraction began in the Volga-Urals Oil Area (q.v.), where it has risen rapidly since 1944 when the rich Devon deposits were discovered. By 1957 the oilfields in the east of the country were producing three-quarters of the total output. A certain over-production of oil occurred in the late 1950's. The principal oil pipelines run from Baku to Batumi (built 1906), Groznyy to Tuapse, 1928, Armavir to Donbas, Gur'yev to Orsk, and Tuymazy to Omsk, 1955; many pipelines are under construction, among them Ufa-Irkutsk, Tatar oilfields to Moscow and Yaroslavl' via Gor-kiy, Kuybyshev-Bryansk and Saratov-Voronezh. The main oil-processing plants are in Baku and Groznyy and there are new ones in Kuybyshev and Omsk. Oil has been a traditional Russian export, though the quantities exported have varied greatly: 18·1 million tons of oil and oil products were exported in 1958 (5·2 in 1931, 1·4 in 1938, 0·5 in 1946, 1·1 in 1950). Of the 1957 total, 7·7 million tons were exported to the countries of the Communist bloc, and of the remainder 55 per cent went to Western Europe and 20 per cent to Finland. At the same time the Soviet Union imported oil and oil products—4·3 million tons in 1958, mostly from Rumania and Austria. *See also* FUEL INDUSTRY. *See* H. Hassmann, *Oil in the Soviet Union*, Princeton, 1954.

Oistrakh, David Fëdorovich (*b.* 1908), outstanding violinist and teacher. Until 1926 he studied under Stolyarskiy at Odessa, and from 1934 was a professor at Moscow Conservatoire. He has travelled widely and is the holder of many prizes and awards. His repertoire, which is vast, includes all the most important classical and modern works. A possessor of phenomenal technique, he is equally successful in solo and *ensemble* work. His pupils include his son, O. M. Parkhomenko, V. A. Pikaizen, etc.

Oistrakh, Igor' Davidovich (*b.* 1931), son of David, also a violinist who studied under Stolyarskiy. He won first prize in the Wieniawski Competition in Warsaw in 1949, and has performed and recorded much with his father.

Oka, navigable river, a right tributary of the Volga, which rises in the central Russian upland and flows north-east to join the Volga at Gor'kiy. Length 940 m.; chief ports: Gor'kiy, Ryazan', Dzerzhinsk and Kaluga.

Okhlopkov, Nikolay Pavlovich (*b.* 1900), actor and director. He has been on the stage since 1918, first in Irkutsk and since 1922 in Moscow. He headed the Realistic Theatre in 1931–6, worked in Tairov's (q.v.) Kamernyy Theatre and the Vakhtangov (q.v.) Theatre, and since 1943 has headed the Moscow Drama Theatre (named after Mayakovskiy in 1954). Since Stalin's death he has been active in reviving the theatre, and himself produced *Hamlet* in 1954 and revived Mayakovskiy's *The Bed Bug* in the true Meyerhold (q.v.) tradition.

Okhotsk, Sea of, inlet of the North Pacific in the Russian Far East, divided from the ocean by the Kamchatka Peninsula and the Kurile Islands, and from the Sea of Japan by Sakhalin and Hokkaido islands. Its main tributary is the River Amur; chief ports: Magadan and Korsakov.

Okhrana ('Defence'), colloquial name of the security police before 1917. Liberal opinion, in both Russia and Western Europe, regarded its activities as vicious, and indeed its employment of *agents provocateurs*, though on a modest scale, cannot but be condemned. However, experience of both Communist and Fascist security police in the 20th century makes the activities of the Okhrana, which worked within strict legal norms, appear extremely mild. It was abolished by the Provisional Government after the February revolution of 1917. *See* A. T. Vasilev, *The Ochrana*, New York, 1930.

Okrug, name of an administrative territorial unit forming part of an oblast or an Autonomous Republic. There are no okrugs in the U.S.S.R. at present except National Okrugs. There are now nine of these, all for the peoples of Siberia and the far north (Nenets, Yamal-Nenets, Khanty-Mansi, Taymyr, Evenki, Ust'-Ordynskiy Buryat, Aginskoye Buryat, Chukchi and Koryak), formed between 1929 and 1937. They are mostly sparsely populated, with the natives in a minority. National Okrugs have each one representative in the Soviet of Nationalities (q.v.) of the U.S.S.R. Supreme Soviet. Originally conceived by sympathetic ethnographers (*see* BOGORAZ) of the Committee of the North (q.v.) as a kind of reservation, the National Okrugs have in fact become an instrument for integrating the lives of the natives into the Soviet system. In 1932–8 the economy of most of the National Okrugs was in the hands of the Northern Sea Route (q.v.) administration, and afterwards, until 1953, largely formed a part of the economic system of the forced labour camps, some of which were situated in the National Okrugs.

Oktyabr'skiy, town in Bashkiria, situated 90 m. west of Ufa, one of the main centres of the Tatar-Bashkir oilfields, the starting-point of a pipeline to Ufa. Population (1959) 65,000, mostly Russian, also Tatars and Bashkirs. Oktyabr'skiy was founded in 1940 and became a town in 1946.

Old Believers, large sect which in the 17th century separated itself from the Russian Orthodox Church; they took the name of 'Old Believers' or 'Old Ritualists' because they refused to recognize the service books as edited and corrected by Patriarch Nikon (q.v.). They later divided into the moderates, or Priestists, and the extremists, or Priestless, the latter rejecting the priesthood and all sacraments save baptism and confession, and regarding all other Christians as in the grip of antichrist. Since 1800 many of the Priestists have been reincorporated into the Church, though they retain their own rites. Until the middle of the 19th century all Old Believers were persecuted by the State. Some local groups who have kept to this day many 17th-century features in their everyday life and language exist in the forested area north of the Volga (Kostroma and Gor'kiy oblasts), in the Altay and in Transbaykalia. *See* P. Pascal, *Avvakum et les débuts du Raskol*, 1938; S. Bolshakoff, *Russian Nonconformity*, 1950; W. Kolarz, *Religion in the Soviet Union*, 1961.

Ol'denburg, Sergey Fëdorovich (1863–1934), orientalist, member of the Academy of Sciences from 1901 and its permanent secretary, 1904–29, Minister of Education in the Provisional Government in 1917. His many works were devoted to the comparative study of the folklore, ethnography and art of various peoples of Russia, Western Europe and South-east Asia, the history of Buddhism, Indian literature, etc. From 1897 until his death he directed the publication of a fundamental *Collection of Buddhist Texts*.

Olga, St (*c.* 879–969), wife of Prince Igor of Kiev, who ruled as regent after his death in 945. She was baptized in 958 and canonized by the Greek Orthodox Church after her death; her commemoration day is 11th July. She attempted unsuccessfully to introduce Christianity into Russia.

Omsk: 1. Oblast of the R.S.F.S.R., situated in Western Siberia, lowland traversed by the River Irtysh with mixed forests in the north and steppe in the south. Area 53,900 sq. m.; population (1959) 1,646,000 (43 per cent urban), mostly Russians, also Ukrainians and some Tatars. There is wheat growing and dairy farming, and there are engineering, lumbering, woodworking, chemical, food and light industries. The area was gradually annexed by Russia in the 16th–early 18th centuries; it developed extensive dairy farming and butter production in the late 19th century.

2. Administrative, economic and cultural centre of the oblast,

situated on the River Irtysh and the Trans-Siberian Railway. Population (1959) 579,000 (second in Siberia; 1914, 128,000; 1926, 162,000; 1939, 289,000). It has engineering (agricultural and other machinery, electrical equipment), oil-refining (pipeline from Tuymazy in Bashkiria) and varied light and food industries. Omsk was founded as a Russian fortress in the southern defence line of Western Siberia in 1716, becoming a town in 1804, provincial capital in 1822, administrative centre of Western Siberia in 1838, and of the Steppe territory (now central and east Kazakhstan) in 1882. When it was reached by the Trans-Siberian Railway it became the commercial centre of Western Siberia and the largest Siberian town. In 1918 the Bolsheviks were overthrown in Omsk and for more than a year it was the centre of anti-Bolshevism in Siberia and the seat of Kolchak's government. In 1919–22 it was the seat of the Bolshevik Siberian Revolutionary Committee. Industrial development has been especially rapid since the Second World War.

Onega, second largest lake in Europe, in north-western Russia. It is connected by the River Svir' with Lake Ladoga and the Baltic, and by artificial waterways (White Sea-Baltic Canal, Volga-Baltic Waterway) with the White Sea and the Volga. Area 3,800 sq. m.

Opera, in Russia, first arose in the last decades of the 18th century following the visit to Russia of a number of Italian musicians, chief among whom were Araja, Galuppi, Traetta, Cimarosa and Paisiello. The first real Russian opera did not appear, however, until 1779. This was *The Miller Magician, Deceiver and Matchmaker* by Sokolovskiy and Ablesimov. Based on folk tunes, *The Miller* enjoyed such great success that in a short while it was followed by numerous other operatic projects which led to the founding of a school of Russian opera composers (the majority of whom were serfs), including V. A. Pashkevich, Matinskiy, Ye. I. Fomin and D. S. Bortnyanskiy. The rise of Russian opera was connected with the growth of cultural and musical life, not only in the capital but throughout the country, wealthy landowners vying with one another to procure trained musicians, many of whom were sent to study abroad, usually in Italy. It is significant that from almost non-existent beginnings Russian opera rose to remarkable heights in the space of only two decades, culminating in the achievements of Fomin (with *The Coachmen*, 1787) and Bortnyanskiy (*Le Fils Rival*, 1787). Despite the foreign influences at court the new opera remained essentially Russian in character, making use of folk-songs and so developing them that by the end of the century composers were able to write freely in the folk idiom, thus anticipating the procedures of Glinka by almost fifty years.

With the dawn of the 19th century, however, a new set of values came into being, and Russian opera fell under the influence of German Romantic opera as exemplified by Weber. The Russian composers Cavos, Davydov and Verstovskiy still employed folksongs in their operas, but there was a general expansion of forms and ideas which brought Russian opera into line with the leading European compositions. The most decisive figure of the 19th century was Glinka, who raised Russian opera to unprecedented heights; his works *A Life for the Czar (Ivan Susanin)*, 1836, and *Ruslan and Lyudmila*, 1842, determined the course of Russian opera for the remainder of the century. Whereas *A Life for the Czar* was essentially Russian, *Ruslan* was more Italian and oriental—a surprisingly effective combination. Its influence may be seen especially in Borodin's *Prince Igor*.

Following the pattern of Glinka, though gradually striking independent paths, are Rimsky-Korsakov's fifteen operas, principal among which are *The Snow Maiden*, 1880–1, *Sadko*, 1894–6, and *The Golden Cockerel*, 1906–7, a unique mixture of folk music, fantasy and lyricism. An original place is occupied by Dargomyzhskiy in his operas *Rusalka*, 1856, and *The Stone Guèst*, 1872, whereby he sought to reproduce speech inflections and intonations in musical form. Of similar intention are the operas of Musorgskiy, *Boris Godunov*, 1871–1872, and *Khovanshchina*, which, together with *Ruslan* and *Prince Igor*, constitute the high-water mark of Russian operatic creation. *Boris Godunov* in particular is unequalled in its emotional and dramatic impact, its stark realism and its amazing originality. In complete contrast are the operas of Tchaikovsky, which tend to sacrifice drama to sentiment, besides refraining from fierce nationalism; of principal importance are *Eugen Onegin*, 1878, and *The Queen of Spades*, 1890.

The 20th century is best illustrated by the works of Stravinsky, Shostakovich and Prokof'yev. Chief among Stravinsky's operas are *The Soldier's Tale*, 1918, *Mavra*, 1922, and *The Rake's Progress*, 1951, his more recent works being more international in content and subject-matter. Shostakovich has made several ventures into this field, including *The Nose*, 1929, and *Lady Macbeth of Mtsensk*, 1935, and into comic opera. Prokof'yev's works comprise *The Love for Three Oranges*, 1921, *The Flaming Angel*, 1925, and *War and Peace*, 1942, the latter a work of mammoth proportions. Of importance also is Shaporin's *The Decembrists*, 1953. As in other spheres of Russian art, the present tendency is towards conservatism and comprehensibility, the standard subjects being either those of contemporary life or pages from Russia's stormy past. *See also* entries on individual composers. *See* R. Newmarch, *The Russian Opera*, 1914; M. Grinberg, *Sovetskaya opera*, Moscow, 1953.

Operations Research. Russians were among the pioneers of operations research (L. V. Kantorovich, *Mathematical Methods of Organization and Planning of Production*, 1939), but the official obscurantism of the post-war period (*see* STALINISM; ZHDANOV) prevented its application outside the field of technology. However, since the late 1950's the importance of operations research for economic planning (q.v.) has been officially recognized, and measures are being taken to ensure its wider appreciation and application. A leading part has been played in this by Nemchinov (q.v.). *See also* CYBERNETICS; SCIENTIFIC ORGANIZATION OF LABOUR.

Optina Pustyn', famous former monastery situated in the Kaluga Oblast of central Russia. It was founded in the 15th century, and during the 19th century was a centre of the activities of the Startsy (*see* STARETS).

Orbeli, Leon Abgarovich (1882–1959), physiologist of Armenian origin, until 1950 professor and head of the Military Medical Academy and Colonel-General of the Army Medical Service, member (since 1935) and vice-president, 1942–6, of the Academy of Sciences, secretary of its department of biological sciences till 1948 and director of the academy's Institute of Physiology. Continuing the work of his teacher Pavlov, Orbeli studied the adaptational-trophical functions of the sympathetic nervous system and worked on many other problems of general and evolutionary physiology. In 1950 he was dismissed from all his leading positions for allegedly misinterpreting Pavlov's teachings. Orbeli had in fact stressed the importance of the subjective element in the study of higher nervous activity and the functioning of the perceptive organs. See *Scientific Session on the Physiological Teaching of I. P. Pavlov*, Moscow, 1951.

Orchestral Music. The influence of Berlioz, Schumann and (at a later date) Liszt, together with the innovation of Glinka, cannot be underestimated in determining the evolution of Russian music in the 19th century. The whole of Russian orchestral music, however, is characterized by certain tendencies and formulae which constantly recur; for example, the use of folk themes and folk subjects, the love of programmes, the world of fantasy seen through the eyes of a child, power to depict scenes of natural beauty or elemental fury, the gift of colourful and effective orchestration. The first real attempts at orchestral music comparable with Western achievements were made by Glinka. Outstanding are his two Spanish overtures, his incidental music to *Prince Kholmsky*, 1840, and his fantasy *Kamarinskaya*, 1848, which established a method of treating folk music which was faithfully observed by his followers until well into the 20th century (*see* KUCHKA). Balakirev's main works are the symphonic poem *Tamara*, 1867–82, a magnificent evocation of tempestuous passion and oriental voluptuousness, and the overture and incidental music for Shakespeare's *King Lear*, 1858–61, which looks back rather to Schumann and Berlioz. Borodin made only one essay in this sphere, the 'musical picture' *In the Steppes of Central Asia*, 1880. Like much of Rimsky-Korsakov's work, this conjures up a wonderful atmosphere of space and desolation and has a unique nostalgia and charm. Rimsky-Korsakov's contributions include a number of picturesque and colourful compositions, outstanding among which are the symphonic suite *Sheherazade*, 1888, and the *Spanish Capriccio*, 1887. Of a rather different category is Musorgskiy's *St John's Night on the Bare Mountain*, 1867, which in its suggestion of primitive and orgiastic rites did much to influence the subsequent course of European music (particularly Stravinsky and Prokof'yev). The heights of lyrical emotion are reached by Tchaikovsky in his overture-fantasy *Romeo and Juliet*, 1870, while his fantasy *Francesca da Rimini*, 1876, is unique among his compositions (with the possible exception of *Manfred*) in its depiction of wilderness and vacuity. Among the later nationalist composers may be mentioned Glazunov with his dramatic tone-poem *Sten'ka Razin*, 1885, Lyadov, composer of several short and charming orchestral pieces (*Kikimora, Baba Yaga, The Enchanted Lake*) and Ippolitov-Ivanov's *Caucasian Sketches*, 1894. Rachmaninov's *Isle of the Dead*, 1907, and Lyapunov's *Zhelyazova Volya* are also of merit. A class apart is occupied by Skryabin in his *Poem and Ecstasy*, 1908, and *Prometheus: the Poem of Fire*, 1909–10, which in a sense parallels Diaghilev's aims in seeking to effect a union of all the arts. In the present era the works of Prokof'yev and Stravinsky are outstanding. From the primitivism of the *Scythian Suite* Prokof'yev has run the whole gamut of musical experience culminating in such achievements as *Romeo and Juliet*, *Cinderella*, etc., while Stravinsky's contribution to, and place in, modern music are unequalled. In the Soviet Union there is at present a renewed interest in the folk music of the union republics, a field which offers great prospects for future development. *See also* BALLET; CONCERTO; OPERA; SYMPHONY; and entries on composers.

Ordzhonikidze: 1. (until 1939 **Vladikavkaz**, 1944–54 **Dzaudzhikau**). Capital, economic and cultural centre of the North Ossetian Autonomous Republic (North Caucasus), situated on the River Terek. Population (1959) 164,000 (1897, 44,000; 1939, 131,000), mostly Russians. It has lead and zinc works and food industries. Ordzhonikidze was founded as a Russian fortress in 1783, and became capital of Terek Oblast in 1863; it was capital of the Mountain People's Autonomous Republic, 1921–4.

2. *See* YENAKIYEVO.

Ordzhonikidze, Grigoriy Konstantinovich (1886–1937), Georgian Communist who joined the Bolsheviks in 1903 and became a Central Committee member in 1912, spending several years in prison and banishment. He was Extraordinary Commissar of the Soviet Government in southern Russia after the October Revolution (q.v.) in 1917, directed the party in the Caucasus in 1920 and in Transcaucasia in 1921–6. He became deputy head of the Government and chairman of the party's Central Control Commission (*see* COMMITTEE OF PARTY CONTROL) in 1926, a Politburo member and chairman of the Supreme Council of National Economy in 1930, and Commissar for Heavy Industry in 1932. Ordzhonikidze was one of Stalin's leading supporters, but died in obscure circumstances during the Great Purge (q.v.), and was alleged by Khrushchëv at the 20th party congress (q.v.) to have been forced to commit suicide by Stalin. *See* L. Schapiro, *The Communist Party of the Soviet Union*, 1960; R. W. Davies, 'Some Soviet Economic Controllers, iii: Ordzhonikidze,' *Soviet Studies*, vol. xii, No. 1, July 1960.

Ordzhonikidzegrad, *see* BEZHITSA.

Orekhovo-Zuyevo, town in the Moscow Oblast, 57 m. east of the capital. Population (1959) 108,000 (1926, 63,000; 1939, 99,000). It has a large textile industry, mostly cotton. Orekhovo-Zuyevo was founded in 1917 by the fusion of several industrial villages, the chief ones being Orekhovo and Zuyevo. It is an old centre of silk weaving, the first factory having been started in 1797 by the serf-industrialist Morozov. Modern labour legislation in Russia was in part the result of the famous strike in Orekhovo-Zuyevo in 1885.

Orël: 1. Oblast of the R.S.F.S.R., a ravinous area situated south of Moscow on the central Russian upland largely in the black earth belt. Area 9,500 sq. m.; population (1959) 926,000 (24 per cent urban). Grain, hemp, potatoes and tobacco are cultivated, dairy farming and pig breeding carried on, and there are food and metal-working industries. In the Middle Ages the area belonged to the principalities of Chernigov and then Novgorod-Severskiy, was intermittently Lithuanian from 1356 and finally Muscovite in 1503. It was occupied by the Germans in 1941–3.

2. Administrative, economic and cultural centre of the oblast, situated on the River Oka. Population (1959) 152,000 (1914, 91,000; 1920, 64,000; 1939, 111,000). It is an industrial and transportation centre (agricultural and textile machinery, leather and food industries; railway junction). Orël was founded as a fortified town in the Muscovite southern defence line against the Crimean Tatars in 1564, and became a provincial capital in 1779; it was a commercial (grain trade) centre in the 18th–19th centuries. In 1943 it was the scene of much fighting and was largely destroyed.

Orenburg (1938–58 **Chkalov**): 1. Oblast of the R.S.F.S.R., situated south of the Urals, largely fertile level steppe, including in the east the southernmost part of the Ural Mountains; there are deposits of iron ore, chrome, nickel, copper, sulphur, oil, phosphorite and coal. Area 47,800 sq. m.; population (1959) 1,831,000 (45 per cent urban). Spring wheat is cultivated and cattle and sheep are raised; there are engineering, mining, metallurgical, oil-refining, food and other industries; a shawl-weaving craft is carried on. Principal towns: Orenburg, Orsk, Buzuluk.

2. Administrative, cultural and an economic centre of the oblast, situated on the River Ural. Population (1959) 260,000 (1897, 73,000; 1939, 172,000). It has extensive engineering (rolling stock), flour, meat, leather and silk industries, and is an important centre of transportation. Orenburg was founded as a fortress in the Orenburg Fortified Line along the River Ural in 1735, and was manned by Cossacks. It became the administrative centre of the southern Urals and the adjoining steppe area in 1744, and was the main point of an extensive barter trade with the Kazakhs and the base of the Russian advance into Central Asia. It was a centre of anti-Bolshevism, 1918–19, and capital of the Kirgiz (Kazakh) Autonomous Republic, 1920–4.

Orgburo, from 1919 to 1952 one of the central organs of the Communist Party, 'formed' by the Central Committee from among its members. It was concerned with organizational matters and was headed by Stalin after he became Secretary-General (q.v.) of the Central Committee in 1922.

Orlova, Lyubov' Petrovna (b. 1902), most famous Soviet comedy actress. She studied at the Moscow Musical Conservatoire and the Moscow Ballet School, and acted in the Moscow Musical Theatre of Nemirovich-Danchenko (q.v.). She has appeared in films since 1926, and played in most of the highly popular comedies of the thirties (*The Jolly Fellows*, 1934; *Volga-Volga*, 1938; *The Bright Way*, 1940), and also in *Circus*, 1936, as the American actress Marion Dixon; *Spring*, 1947; *Meeting on the Elbe*, 1949, as an American spy; and *Glinka*, 1952.

Orography. The relief of Russia varies greatly. A vast plain, transected by the Ural Mountains (greatest height 6,200 ft), lies between

the western frontier and the River Yenisey; to the west of the Urals
it is known as the Russian or East European plain, and to the east as
the West Siberian lowland. About one quarter of the whole area of the
country is taken up by the Russian plain, parts of which such as the
Central Russian and Volga uplands, the Donets and Timan ridges,
rise to between 650 ft and 1,100 ft, while other parts (the Black Sea,
Caspian Sea and other lowlands) are below 650 ft and occasionally
even below sea level. To the south of the Russian plain rise the
Caucasian, Crimean and Carpathian mountains. To the south of the
West Siberian lowland lie the Kazakh hills, farther south the Turan
lowland, and in the extreme south rise the mountain chains of Tien-
Chan (Victory Peak, 24,187 ft), Pamir-Alay (Stalin Peak, 24,598 ft,
the highest point in Russia) and Kopet-Dag.

Almost a half of the country, to the east of the Yenisey, is mountainous, with a few lowlands and depressions. The Central Siberian
plateau (average height 1,500–2,000 ft) lies between the rivers
Yenisey and Lena; in the south it is bordered by the Altay (highest
peak 13,644 ft) and Sayan mountains and by those of the Lake
Baykal system, and in the east by a complex system of mountains the
easternmost of which are long ridges stretching along the Pacific
shore, including, in the Kamchatka Peninsula, several volcanoes. *See*
G. Jorré, *The Soviet Union, the Land and its People*, 3rd imp., 1955.

Orsha, town in the Vitebsk Oblast (Belorussia), situated on the
Dnieper and the Moscow–Minsk railway. Population (1959) 64,000. It
has linen, metal-working (since 1873) and food industries, and there
is a big peat-fed power-station near by. It is an important railway
junction (six lines) and the starting-point of shipping on the Dnieper.
Orsha has been known since 1067, became Lithuanian in the 13th
century and Russian in 1772. In the 16th–18th centuries it was an
important Polish fortress near the Russian frontier, and was frequently fought over. It was also an outpost of Catholicism and had
eight Catholic monasteries.

Orsk, town in the Orenburg Oblast (southern Urals), situated on the
River Ural 112 m. south-east of Orenburg. Population (1959) 176,000
(1926, 14,000; 1939, 66,000). It is the centre of the rapidly growing
Orsk-Khalilovo industrial area (iron and steel, non-ferrous metallurgy), and the town itself has heavy engineering, oil-cracking (pipeline from Gur'yev in the Emba oilfields) and meat-packing industries.
Orsk was founded as a fortress in 1735, and until the 1930's had a
cattle trade.

Orthodox Church is the main religious community in Russia. There
are two autocephalous Orthodox Churches in the country, the
Russian and the Georgian. The Russian Orthodox Church is headed
by the Patriarch (q.v.) of Moscow and All Russia (since 1945 Alexis,
q.v.), who ranks fifth among the Orthodox Patriarchs and administers the Church affairs together with the Holy Synod (q.v.).
There are (1959) 73 dioceses and over 20,000 parishes. Of the bishops,
five, those of Moscow, Leningrad, Kiev, Minsk and Novosibirsk, have
the title of Metropolitan, and several of archbishop; the Metropolitan
of Kiev and Galicia is officially described as Exarch of the Ukraine.
There are several dozen monasteries and convents, with 5,000 monks

and nuns; among the functioning monasteries are two of the most revered, the Kiev Cave Monastery and the St Sergius Trinity Monastery near Moscow (*see* TROITSE-SERGIYEVA LAVRA), the latter serving as the residence of the Patriarch. There are two theological academies, in Moscow and Leningrad, and eight seminaries for the training of priests. The Russian Orthodox Church outside Russia is divided between four jurisdictions, those of the Moscow Patriarchate, the oecumenical Patriarchate of Constantinople (both having an Exarch in Paris), the so-called Russian Church Abroad, headed by Metropolitan Anastasius, and the autocephalous American Orthodox Church, which mostly consists of Russians by origin.

The Orthodox Church has played a fundamental role in the history of Russia since Kievan times (*see* KIEVAN RUSSIA), in its culture (*see* LITERATURE), and in the shaping of the Russian national character; in the popular mind it has always been closely linked with the image of the Russian people. Especially in times of struggle against foreigners (e.g. under the Tatar yoke, during the Time of Troubles and the Second World War) it played an important part in upholding the national spirit. The most revered saints of the Russian Church are Sts Sergius of Radonezh, Theodosius, Stephen of Perm' and Seraphim of Sarov (qq.v.), and among the most outstanding Church leaders, apart from the Patriarchs, have been the Metropolitans Alexis (14th century), Philip (16th century, who publicly denounced Ivan the Terrible and was martyred), Peter Mogila (q.v.), Philaret (q.v.) and Antony (q.v.), and Archbishop Theophan Prokopovich (q.v.). *See also* RELIGION. *See* W. H. Frere, *Links in the Chain of Russian Church History*, 1918; J. S. Curtiss, *The Russian Church and the Soviet State*, Boston, Mass., 1953; M. Spinka, *The Church in Soviet Russia*, New York, 1956; A. V. Kartashev, *Ocherki po istorii russkoy tserkvi*, vol. i, Paris, 1959; C. de Grunwald, *Saints of Russia*, 1960; W. Kolarz, *Religion in the Soviet Union*, 1961.

Osh: 1. Oblast of Kirgizia comprising that part of the Fergana Valley which belongs to Kirgizia; there are deposits of brown coal, antimony, mercury, oil and sulphur. Area 28,500 sq. m.; population (1959) 871,000 (32 per cent urban), mostly Uzbeks and Kirgiz, also Russians and some Uygurs. Cotton, silk, fruit and grapes are cultivated, and cattle and sheep raised; there are cotton and silk processing, mining and food industries. Principal towns: Osh and Dzhalal-Abad. For history *see* FERGANA VALLEY; KOKAND KHANATE.

2. Administrative, economic and cultural centre of the oblast, situated in the south-east corner of the Fergana Valley. Population (1959) 65,000 (1939, 33,000). It has silk and food industries, and is the starting-point of a highway to Pamir.

Osinniki, town in the Kemerovo Oblast (southern Siberia), situated in the Stalinsk conurbation 15 m. south-east of Stalinsk. Population (1959) 68,000. It is a new centre of coal-mining, and there is a large thermal power-station (the Southern Kuzbas) near by.

Osipenko, *see* BERDYANSK.

Osoaviakhim (Russian abbreviation for 'Society for Furthering Defence, Aviation and Chemical Warfare') was established in 1927 for the military training of civilians. By 1939 it had more than twelve million members. The chairman of its central council, R. P. Eideman, was one of the leading Red Army commanders sentenced to death with Tukhachevskiy (q.v.) in 1937. *See also* DOSAAF.

Ossetians, Iranian-speaking people who inhabit the northern and southern slopes of the central part of the main Caucasus range, numbering (1959) 410,000. They are mostly Orthodox Christians, but some are Sunni Muslims. The Ossetians are descended from the medieval Alans; during the 17th century the northern Ossetians were subject to Kabarda princelings. From the 18th century they came under strong Russian influence, and between 1801 and 1806 all Ossetians were annexed to Russia. *See* W. Kolarz, *Russia and her Colonies*, 1952.

Ostrog (Ukrainian **Ostroh**), town in the Rovno Oblast (western Ukraine), situated 120 m. north-east of L'vov. Population (1931) 13,000. Known since 1100, Ostrog was an important centre of Russian (Ukrainian) Orthodox culture in the 16th century, and had an academy (theological school) which was founded in the 1570's. The first Church Slavonic Bible was printed here by Ivan Fëdorov in 1581.

Ostrogradskiy, Mikhail Vasil'yevich (1801–61), mathematician, one of the founders of Russian mathematics. Educated at Khar'kov University and the Sorbonne (where he was the pupil of Cauchy, Laplace, Fourier and Ampère), he taught at various higher educational establishments in St Petersburg and became a member of the Academy of Sciences in 1831. His studies were concerned with various fields of mathematical analysis and its applications.

Ostrovskiy, Aleksandr Nikolayevich (1823–86), playwright of Gogol's school of Critical Realism who had a predominant influence upon play-writing in Russia during the second half of the 19th century and is regarded as the true founder of Russian dramaturgy. His plays were concerned with the evils of contemporary Russian society, especially those of the merchant class, and are still extremely popular; many of their titles have become proverbs.

Ostyako-Vogul'sk, *see* KHANTY-MANSIYSK.

Ostyaks, *see* KHANTY.

Ownership is defined in Soviet law in the conventional way as the right to hold, to use and to dispose. According to Marxist theory, ownership is the basic social relationship. Private ownership of the means of production underlies the division of society into exploiting and exploited classes, which in turn gives rise to the class struggle and the development of State and law. Abolition of private ownership of the means of production is the main function of a socialist revolution and the chief prerequisite for the construction of a socialist society. These principles are embodied in the U.S.S.R. constitution, which postulates the dominant position of 'socialist' property in two forms—State property and co-operative property. All the main means of production, including land and other natural resources, most industrial buildings and equipment, the chief means of transportation, etc., as well as most trading organizations, all credit institutions, the bulk of housing in towns and almost all educational and health establishments, are State property. *Kolkhoz* property (agricultural equipment, animals, etc.) makes up the bulk of co-operative property. There exists, further, 'personal' property of citizens—houses, consumer goods, domestic animals, bank deposits, State bonds, etc., which is theoretically considered to be derivative of 'socialist' property, since it is based mainly on earnings in the socialized sector of the economy. And finally there is the private property of the remaining individual peasants and non-co-operated artisans. The amount of private and of some items of 'personal' property (e.g. houses) owned by one person is severely restricted. A key article of the Civil Code which regulates property relations postulates that its provisions apply in so far as they do not contradict the interests of the State, but in fact since the mid 1930's property rights have on the whole been protected by the courts. Confiscation of personal property plays perhaps a greater role in the Soviet penal system than is otherwise usual.

Before 1917 private property was prevalent in Russia, though a large part of arable land was owned by peasant communes (*see* Mir) and there was considerable State (land, railways, ordnance factories, etc.), municipal, *zemstvo* (q.v.), Church, co-operative, etc., property. For the developments after 1917 *see* COLLECTIVIZATION OF AGRI-CULTURE; NATIONALIZATION OF INDUSTRY; NEW ECONOMIC POLICY; WAR COMMUNISM. The existence of two forms of 'socialist' property, and consequently of two classes, workers and peasants, was held by Stalin to be the main distinguishing feature of the present 'socialist,' as opposed to the future 'communist,' society, and he envisaged eventual absorption of co-operative property by the State (this was in fact already started in the 1930's). Inferior status is no longer attached to the co-operative property since the abolition of the M.T.S. (q.v.) and the sale of agricultural machinery to the *kolkhozes* in 1957, both forms of 'socialist' property now being officially expected to fuse, with the transition to communism, into 'communistic' property. *See also* ARBITRATION; COPYRIGHT; INHERITANCE; TAXATION. *See* H. J. Berman, *Justice in Russia*, Cambridge, Mass., 1950; J. N. Hazard, *Law and Social Change in the U.S.S.R.*, 1953; V. Gsovski and K. Grzybowski (eds.), *Government, Law and Courts in the Soviet Union and Eastern Europe*, vol. 2, 1959.

Oyrots, *see* ALTAY.

P

Painting. Modern art was introduced into Russia during the reforms of Peter the Great (for the history of pre-Petrine painting *see* ICON AND CHURCH PAINTING). The country, which until then had been highly suspicious of anything coming from the outside world, was now wide open to European influences. This meant nothing less than a revolution in artistic tastes and attitudes. The assimilation of the new art was achieved by means of a two-way traffic: Western artists came to Russia to work and to instruct and gifted young Russians were sent to European countries to study. The Academy of Fine Arts was officially founded in St Petersburg in 1757 and organized on a permanent basis in 1764. Portraiture and the art of interior decoration were the first to develop, since they were best suited to the requirements of the court and of the westernized noblemen—the only group appreciative of the new art in the beginning. Only about two generations were necessary to achieve the accumulation of technical knowledge and taste that would ensure continuity and progress, and already by the 1760's the Russian portraitists Levitskiy and Borovikovskiy (qq.v.) were second to none in Europe, while A. P. Losenko (1731–73) was attempting in his 'St Vladimir and Rogneda' the most difficult task of creating from scratch a Russian historical painting in the grand manner.

The ensuing development of Russian art should not be judged by modern Western standards with their emphasis on originality and stylistic and technical innovations. Russian art had been subservient to the Church and the faith for an inordinately long time, and even after its secularization it continued to be 'iconological'—in other words, concerning itself with meaning rather than with the means of its communication. This approach is helpful in evaluating Russian art throughout the 19th century, and in its light the problem of Western influence acquires a special coherence and significance. It is important to remember that every sensitive Russian artist in the early 19th century had to assimilate not only the contemporary European styles but also all those that the Russian pictorial tradition did not include, especially Classicism and baroque. Thus the brilliant portraits of O. Kiprenskiy (1773–1836) show signs of baroque influence as well as of the French Romanticism, and he began as an academic Neo-Classicist. But from the iconological point of view the subjects of his portraits are primarily treated as individuals, whereas his immediate predecessor, Borovikovskiy saw men and women chiefly as types and representatives of a class. Bryullov (q.v.), Bruni (1800–75) and A. Ivanov (q.v.) tried without much success to create monumental historical and religious works on an eclectic basis. Their task was impossible, but Ivanov nevertheless foreshadowed the movement towards Realism and beyond In the 1830's and forties the first

Russian *genre* painters appeared, among them the original, if techni-
cally somewhat naïve, artist Venetsianov (q.v.). The prophet of things
to come was Fedotov (q.v.), who, having studied the Dutch masters
and Hogarth's prints, applied his satirical brush to the manners of
Russian society; from him to the founder of 'ideological realism,'
Perov (q.v.), was only a step.

In 1863 the first open rebellion against academism took place in St
Petersburg. A group of students of the academy, competing for the
annual gold medal, refused to paint the prescribed historical subject,
'The Banquet of the Gods in Valhalla.' They insisted on their right to
paint a contemporary *genre* scene. This again illustrates the Russian
painters' preoccupation with content rather than form in art. Such
an approach was in line with a theory of aesthetics formulated by
Chernyshevskiy (q.v.) in 1855. Thirteen painters and one sculptor
resigned from the academy in protest, and formed an Artists' Co-
operative Society which was reorganized in 1870 into the 'Society for
Travelling Art Exhibitions,' known as the Peredvizhniki (q.v.). This
movement, asserting the utilitarian social function of art, remained
predominant for over twenty years, although most of its followers
still received their formal training at the academy. A different
approach to art grew slowly and less conspicuously, that of the
nationalist Slavic revival which had been gathering momentum with
the progress of serious scholarly research in the fields of Russian
history and archaeology. In painting the outstanding figures of the
Slavic revival were V. M. Vasnetsov and the much more important
master Nesterov (q.v.), who began experimenting with new modes
of expression on the lines of the French post-impressionists. A
position all his own belongs to M. Vrubel' (q.v.), the greatest imaginative painter of the end of the 19th century. A decisive blow to
the Peredvizhniki was delivered by the formation of an aesthetical
movement known as Mir Iskusstva (q.v.). After 1900 it was the
'purpose painters' of all kinds who were on the defensive, and
Russian painting for the first time in its history not only ceased to be
'backward' from the formal point of view, but was often in the
avant-garde of European art. In 1911 Kandinskiy (q.v.) produced the
first truly abstract paintings, and the styles of Suprematism (*see*
MALEVICH) and Rayonism (or 'Luchism') were originated by Russian
painters. The epigones of Mir Iskusstva demonstrated to the sophisticated public of Western Europe their superiority and exquisite
taste in the art of theatrical décor (*see* BALET; DYAGILEV).

But these triumphs were short-lived. After the seizure of power in
October 1917, the Bolsheviks soon proceeded to establish their
dictatorship in art. In 1921 some of the best *avant-garde* painters—
Kandinskiy, Chagall, Gabo, Pevsner—left Russia, never to return.
In the 1920's there existed a certain freedom of formal research and
of discussion between numerous artistic groups, all claiming to be
'proletarian.' But in 1932 the party directive 'On the reorganization
of all existing literary and artistic groups and the formation of a
single Union of Soviet Artists' was published in *Pravda*. The style
known as Socialist Realism (q.v.) began to be enforced. Russian art
was once more subservient, this time to the personal 'artistic taste'

and political objective of one man (*see* BRODSKIY; DEYNEKA; GERASIMOV; KORIN; SAR'YAN). Towards the end of the Second World War there were hopes that the position in the arts (as in other fields) would change for the better. In 1947 an old Russian artist who had just returned from emigration was applauded at a meeting of the Moscow Union of Artists when he said 'Art must be free.' But these hopes were answered by Zhdanov's (q.v.) campaign against 'cosmopolitanism.' Since Stalin's death in 1953 the situation has slightly improved. There are greater opportunities for seeing the paintings of modern Western masters. The young Russian painters openly prefer non-political *genre*, landscape and intimate portraiture to the subject-matter approved by the party; and there is evidence that some of them experiment in private with modern styles. But the experience of non-iconological painting has been interrupted for at least one whole generation, and as yet there is no single new name that holds promise for Russian art. For the present the tradition of imposed iconology continues. *See* A. Benois, *The Russian School of Painting*, New York, 1916; G. K. Lukomski, *History of Modern Russian Painting*, 1945; C. G. E. Bunt, *Russian Art: From Scyths to Soviets*, 1946; M. Alpatov, *Russian Impact on Art*, New York, 1950; C. Gray, 'The Genesis of Socialist-Realist Painting,' *Soviet Survey*, No. 27, Jan.–Mar 1959.

Pal'chinskiy, Pëtr Ioakimovich (*d.* 1929), engineer and politician who was influential in technocratically minded industrial circles prior to the First World War; a leading member of the Central War Industries Committee during the war, he became after the February revolution (q.v.) of 1917 Deputy Minister of Trade and Industry in the Provisional Government (q.v.). He defended the Winter Palace (the seat of the Government) against the Bolsheviks in the October revolution (q.v.). Pal'chinskiy remained an opponent of the Communist regime, but worked in the State Planning Commission (*see* GOSPLAN) as a leading technical expert. At the beginning of the campaign against the old intelligentsia (*see* PURGES) he was accused of sabotage and shot, and at the Industrial Party (q.v.) trial in 1930 was said to have established an underground 'League of Engineering Organizations' which subsequently developed into the Industrial Party. *See* M. J. Larsons, *An Expert in the Service of the Soviets*, 1929.

Palekh, urban settlement, former village, in the Ivanovo Oblast (central Russia), situated 35 m. south-east of Ivanovo. Population (1956) 3,300. It has been the centre of the craft of Russian icon painting since the 16th century; when this became difficult the craftsmen took up, since 1922, the painting of papier mâché boxes. Artists from Palekh have been engaged in restoring the frescoes of the Moscow Kremlin cathedrals in the 1940's and 1950's.

Paleo-Asiatics, group of small peoples living in the Russian Far East, each of them numbering a few thousand or even a few hundred. The more numerous of them are the Chukchi and Koryaks (qq.v.), who live in their National Okrugs, and the Gilyaks (q.v.), who live on the mouth of the Amur and Sakhalin Island. The others are the Yukagirs (about 400 in 1959), living in two groups in the Kolyma river basin: when the Russians arrived in the 17th century they were inhabiting the whole area from the lower Lena in the west to the

Anadyr' in the east, and put up a heroic though hopeless resistance
to the Cossacks; the Itelmens (1,100 in 1959—4,000 in 1926—of
whom all but 300 spoke only Russian) along the western shore of the
Kamchatka Peninsula: they too were more numerous in the 18th
century but a number of anti-Russian uprisings, cruelly suppressed,
and epidemics decimated them; and finally there are a few settlements of Eskimoes on the Bering Straits and Wrangel Island,
numbering about 1,100, and Aleutians who were settled in about
1825 by the Russian-American Company on the Commander Islands
near Kamchatka, now numbering about 400. Paleo-Asiatics are the
oldest inhabitants of north-east Asia, and are an intermediate group
between the other Asiatic peoples of the Mongoloid race and the
American Indians. Their languages do not belong to any of the main
linguistic families, and their relationship to one another is obscure;
their pagan religious practices, like those of other small Siberian
tribes, are known as Shamanism. *See* W. Kolarz, *The Peoples of the
Russian Far East*, 1954.

Panfërov, Fëdor Ivanovich (1896–1960), author. He first became
widely known in 1928 for his novel *Bruski*. In 1953 he excited lively
controversy with his novel *The Mother River Volga*, one of the first
critical works in the post-Stalin era, which dealt with the life of
provincial party officials. This incurred the displeasure of Surkov
(q.v.), then the secretary of the party organization of the Writers'
Union (q.v.), and Panfërov was dismissed from the editorship of the
literary journal *Oktyabr'* and expelled from the Union, ostensibly for
drunkenness. He was, however, reinstated in 1958 and appointed a
member of the board of the presidium of the Union. *In the Name of
Youth* (1960) is revealing on contemporary conditions in Russia,
though it includes a travesty of the author's own experiences on a
visit to England.

Papanin, Ivan Dmitriyevich (*b.* 1894), Communist official, a party
member since 1919. He took part in Polar expeditions from 1931, and
in 1937 was put in charge of the North Polar Drift Expedition in
which four men drifted on ice floes from the North Pole to the
northern Atlantic; this was the first of such Soviet expeditions, and
Papanin received much publicity and praise. In 1938 he succeeded
O. Yu. Schmidt as head of the Northern Sea Route (q.v.) administration, retiring in 1946. *See* his *Life on an Icefloe*, 1947; T. E. Armstrong,
Northern Sea Route, 1952, and *Russians in the Arctic, Soviet Exploration, 1937–57*, 1958.

Parnu (formerly German **Pernau**, Russian **Pernov**), seaport in
Estonia situated on the Gulf of Riga. Population (1956) 33,600 (1914,
25,000). It is a health and holiday resort, and has some fish-canning
and other industries. Pärnu was founded in 1255, and belonged
variously to the Teutonic Knights, Poland and Sweden; it was
Russian, 1710–1918. In 1952–3 it was the administrative centre of
Pärnu Oblast within the Estonian Republic.

'Partiynaya Zhizn'' ('*Party Life*'), fortnightly journal of the Central
Committee, chiefly concerned with the internal life of the party
organizations, on which it is rather informative. Circulation (1957)
500,000.

Partorg (Russian abbreviation for 'Party Organizer'), party official in charge of a primary organization (q.v.) which for one or another reason is considered particularly important (e.g. in large plants, major building sites, etc.). He is appointed by a superior party committee or the Central Committee itself.

'Partyness' (Russian *partiynost'*), principle of placing the interests of the party (identified with the interests of the party leadership at a given moment) above any other interests in all spheres of activity. This demand was advanced by Lenin for party members in 1905, but since the pronouncement of the fiction (q.v.) of the 'moral and political unity of the Soviet people' by Molotov in 1936 it has been extended in principle to everyone. Zhdanov's (q.v.) cultural policy in 1946–8 enforced the implementation of 'partyness' even in such fields as music and biology. The intellectual opposition (q.v) since 1956 is to a considerable extent directed precisely against 'partyness.' But the redefinition of Socialist Realism (q.v.) in 1959 explicitly equated the latter with 'partyness.' *See* R. N. Carew Hunt, *A Guide to Communist Jargon*, 1957; G. A. Wetter, *Dialectical Materialism*, 1958.

Pashukanis, Yevgeniy Bronislavovich (1891–1937), jurist, the most prominent Soviet legal theorist. He studied at St Petersburg University, where he belonged to a Bolshevik youth organization, and later joined the party. In his main work, *General Theory of Law and Marxism*, 1924, Pashukanis tried to construct a Marxist theory of law by reducing legal phenomena to social relationships based on a market economy. Hence all law, in his view, is private and bourgeois; as such it is incompatible with socialism and destined to 'wither away' in a socialist society. This theory gained ascendancy in the 1920's, and Pashukanis himself became vice-President of the Communist Academy and director of its Institute of Soviet Construction and Law. Pashukanis's theory was clearly incompatible with Stalin's intentions, and from 1930 he was made to recant, but continued to teach, took part in the preparation of the 1936 constitution, and became Deputy Commissar of Justice in that year. But the following year he was vilified as an 'enemy of the people' and disappeared (*see* GREAT PURGE). His reputation was rehabilitated in 1957. See *Soviet Legal Philosophy*, Cambridge, Mass., 1951; H. Kelsen, *The Communist Theory of Law*, 1955; J. N. Hazard, 'Pashukanis is No Traitor,' *American Journal of International Law*, vol. li, No. 2, 1957.

Passport, internal, is described by the Soviet legal authorities as 'a most important means of protecting public order and State security.' Since 1932 Soviet citizens of 16 years of age and over residing in towns, urban settlements, rayon (q.v.) centres, frontier areas and certain other localities, as well as those working on building sites, water or railway transport or State farms, are obliged to possess a passport. Changes of place of residence, employment and marital status are entered in the passport by the authorities for purposes of supervision and regulation. Particulars of passports are noted in 'house books' where all occupants have to be registered within twenty-four hours of arrival. Employees in defence industries, coal-mining, transport and banks surrender their passports to the managements for the duration of employment. Peasants as a general rule have no passports and are consequently severely restricted in their choice of occupation and movement (they are allowed to spend up to five days in a town of the oblast in which they live). There are a few other exceptions, notably members of the armed forces on active service, 'special settlers' (q.v.) and people held in places of detention and 'corrective labour colonies' (q.v.). *See* W. W. Kulski, *The Soviet Regime*, Syracuse, 1954.

Pasternak, Boris Leonidovich (1890–1960), most outstanding contemporary poet and novelist, of Jewish origin. He studied music and philosophy at Moscow and Marburg, and joined the Futurist (q.v.) literary movement as a young man. He wrote lyrical poems (*A Twin in Clouds*, 1914; *Over the Barriers*, 1917; *My Sister Life*, 1922; *Themes and Variations*, 1923; *The Second Birth*, 1932; *On Early Trains*, 1943; *The Terrestrial Expanse*, 1945), as well as autobiographical (*Spektorskiy*, 1926) and historical (*Lieutenant Schmidt*, 1926; *The Year 1905*, 1927) poems and some prose works (reminiscences, *The Safe Conduct*, 1931).

Pasternak led the life of an 'internal *émigré*' from the late 1920's; unable to publish original works, he made brilliant translations of Shakespeare's tragedies, Goethe's *Faust*, Petőfi and Georgian poets. His novel *Dr Zhivago* (first published abroad in 1957, its publication having been forbidden in the Soviet Union) is an effective condemnation of the Bolshevik revolution as a spiritual reaction. In 1958 he was awarded the Nobel Prize for Literature, but was forced to withdraw his first acceptance of it. Vilified by official speakers, and expelled from the Writers' Union (q.v.) on party orders, he remained quite uncowed and continued his work. The official campaign against him diminished during 1959. He was widely considered the spiritual leader of that section of the intellectual opposition (q.v.) which rejected Marxism. *See* his *Selected Poems* (trans. J. M. Cohen), 1946, *Dr Zhivago* (trans. H. M. Hayward and M. Harari), 1958, and *An Essay in Autobiography*, 1959; J. Lindsay (trans.), *Russian Poetry, 1917–55*, 1957; V. Erlich, 'A Testimony and a Challenge—Pasternak's "Dr Zhivago",' *Problems of Communism*, Nov.–Dec. 1958; H. M. Hayward, '"Dr Zhivago" and the Soviet Intelligentsia,' *Soviet Survey*, No. 24, April–June 1958; R. Poggioli, *The Poets of Russia, 1890–1930*, Cambridge, Mass., 1960.

Patriarch, of Moscow and All Russia, title of the head of the Russian Orthodox Church. In administering Church affairs he is assisted by the Holy Synod (q.v.). The Russian Church belonged to the Patriarchate of Constantinople until 1589, when a separate see of Moscow and All Russia was established. Outstanding Patriarchs in the 17th century were Philaret (the father of the first czar of the House of Romanov, Michael Fëdorovich, q.v.) and Nikon (q.v.). Both regarded their office as equal to, or higher than, that of the czar in dignity, and the office was abolished by Peter the Great, who in 1721 established the Most Holy Synod as the highest organ of the Church. After the fall of the monarchy in 1917 (*see* FEBRUARY REVOLUTION) a Church Council met in Moscow to re-establish the Patriarchate, and Tikhon was elected Patriarch. From Tikhon's death in 1925 the Soviet authorities refused to permit the election of a new Patriarch until 1943, when the locum tenens, Metropolitan Sergius, was elected; he died the following year, and in 1945 the present Patriarch, Alexis (q.v.), was elected.

Patriotism was until the 1930's treated in Communist ideology as a reactionary concept used by the bourgeoisie for its class interests, though in fact the Bolsheviks did not hesitate to appeal to patriotic sentiment during the civil war (*see* NATIONAL BOLSHEVISM). Since 1934 a new concept of 'Soviet patriotism' has been developed, appealing to pride in actual or fictitious achievements of the Soviet regime; but when faced with a severe test during the Second World War the Communist leadership found it necessary to revert to appeals to traditional Russian patriotism, and especially to that of the major ethnic groups, the Great Russians and Ukrainians. 'Soviet patriotism,' restored in name after the war, in fact amounted to extreme Great Russian chauvinism during the last years of Stalin's life. Under Khrushchëv's rule an attempt is being made to revive the original pre-war interpretation of 'Soviet patriotism.' *See* W. W. Rostow, *The Dynamics of Soviet Society*, 1953; F. C. Barghoorn, *Soviet Russian Nationalism*, New York, 1956.

Pavlodar: 1. Oblast in northern Kazakhstan situated largely in the West Siberian lowland and partly in the Kazakh hills, traversed by the River Irtysh and the Southern Siberian Railway; it is mainly fertile steppe and has deposits of coal, copper, gold and iron ore. Area 53,300 sq. m.; population (1959) 485,000 (27 per cent urban), Kazakhs (40 per cent), Russians (35 per cent), also Ukrainians, Germans, Belorussians, Bulgarians, Mordva, Chuvashes, Tatars, etc. Wheat, millet and melons are cultivated (greatly expanded during the Virgin Land Campaign), sheep and cattle raised, there is salt-panning and there are varied food industries; coal and gold are beginning to be mined.

2. Administrative and economic centre of the oblast, on the Irtysh and the Southern Siberian Railway. Population (1959) 90,000 (1939, 29,000), Russians, Ukrainians, Tatars and Kazakhs. Most of the manufacturing industries of the oblast are concentrated here. Pavlodar was founded in 1720 as a Russian fort, was later a village, became a town in 1861 and provincial centre in 1938. It is one of the main centres of new industrial development during the current Seven Year Plan (a combine harvester and Diesel motor plant—the largest in the U.S.S.R.—an aluminium and an oil-processing plant).

Pavlov, Ivan Petrovich (1849–1936), famous physiologist, the son of a village priest. He was educated at a theological seminary, St Petersburg University and the Military Medical Academy. He became director of the physiological department of the Institute of Experimental Medicine in 1891, professor of physiology at the Military Medical Academy in 1897 and an academician in 1907. He worked on the physiology of circulation, and then on digestion; it was in the course of the latter work that he developed the theory of conditioned reflexes which he later applied to the study of human psychology. He was awarded the Nobel Prize for Medicine in 1904 and the Copley Medal of the Royal Society in 1915. Although Pavlov remained a strong churchman, and was openly critical of the Soviet regime, the Soviet Government supported his work because his theory of conditioned reflexes was regarded as a prop for the materialist ideology. In the last years of Stalin's life Pavlov's teaching was officially made the obligatory basis of all medical theory. *See* his *Experimental Psychology and Other Essays*, New York, 1957; B. P. Babkin, *Pavlov, a Biography*, 1951.

Pavlov, Mikhail Aleksandrovich (1863–1958), metallurgist, professor at the Yekaterinoslav Higher Mining School and St Petersburg Polytechnical Institute, member of the Academy of Sciences since 1932. His blueprints for the design of the blast furnace and open hearth equipment (published in 1902 and 1904 respectively) were widely used both in Russia and abroad. He was also the author of many textbooks.

Pavlova, Anna Pavlovna (1881–1931), prima ballerina and teacher. A pupil of Johansson and Gerdt at the Imperial Theatre School, St Petersburg, she made her début at the Mariinskiy Theatre in 1899, becoming prima ballerina in 1906. After several international tours she joined Diaghilev's Ballets Russes in 1909, featuring in *Les Sylphides*. Valuing her independence, however, she left Diaghilev in 1911, visiting her native land for the last time in 1914. Establishing permanent residence in London, she formed a small company which toured all over the world. Pavlova's powers have been described as 'finished technique subordinated to poetical inspiration.' A fervent disciple of her art, a severe self-critic, a romantic and, above all, a superb artist, Pavlova will always be remembered as the prima ballerina *par excellence*. *See* A. H. Franks, *Pavlova, a Biography*, 1956; H. Algeranoff, *My Years with Pavlova*, 1957.

Pavlovo, town in the Gor'kiy Oblast (central Russia), situated on the River Oka 40 m. south-west of Gor'kiy. Population (1956) 42,600. It has varied metal-working industries (buses, tools, cutlery, hardware), and has been known for its metal-working crafts since the 17th century.

Pavlovskiy, Yevgeniy Nikanorovich (*b.* 1884), zoologist and parasitologist, member of the Academy of Sciences (since 1939) and of the Academy of Medical Sciences, Lieutenant-General of the Army Medical Service, president of the U.S.S.R. Geographical Society (since 1952). Educated at the Military Medical Academy in St Petersburg, he has been professor there since 1921, simultaneously working in the Institute of Experimental Medicine, 1933–44; since 1942 he has been director of the Academy of Sciences' Zoological Institute. He joined the party in 1940. Pavlovskiy organized over 160 expeditions to Central Asia, Transcaucasia, etc., for the study of vermin and infectious diseases. He is a co-founder of the oecological trend in parasitology.

Pavlovskiy Posad (until 1844 **Vokhna**), town in the Moscow Oblast, situated on the Moscow–Gor'kiy railway, about 40 m. east of the capital. Population (1959) 55,000. It is a centre of textile industries (cotton, silk, woollen) and has a visual aids factory (built late 1940's). It was well known in the 18th century for its silk fabrics, and became a town in 1844.

Peasant Household is treated as a legal entity for several purposes. The ownership of the house, domestic animals and the simple agricultural implements permitted to peasants (whether *kolkhoz* members or not) is vested in the household as a whole and not in any particular individual. Consequently this peasant property is not inherited, but passes naturally from one generation to another. Plots of land for personal use of *kolkhoz* members are allotted to the household, and agricultural tax (q.v.) is also levied on the household. Before the collectivization of agriculture (q.v.) the peasant household was the main economic unit in the countryside. The Neo-Populist (*see* NEO-POPULISM) concept of the 'peasant labour economy' was based on the peasant household. *See* V. Gsovski and K. Grzybowski (eds.), *Government, Law and Courts in the Soviet Union and Eastern Europe*, vol. ii, 1959.

Peasant Land Bank, State-owned bank established in 1883 by the Minister of Finance, Bunge (q.v.), for assisting peasants in the purchase of land. This was done by making loans on favourable terms, and greatly facilitated the transfer into the hands of the peasants of lands left to the nobility at the time of the emancipation of serfs in 1861. By 1905 nearly one-third of such lands had been bought by the peasants through the Bank. *See* G. T. Robinson, *Rural Russia under the Old Regime* (2nd ed.), New York, 1949.

Peasant Union, organization set up during the revolution of 1905 (q.v.) on the initiative of Populist intellectuals. Two congresses were held in 1905, attended by peasant delegates from many provinces. The Union demanded nationalization of the land and its use only by those who tilled it (*see* AGRARIAN REVOLUTION), but there were differences between adherents of peaceful and of violent methods of achieving this. The Union disintegrated in 1906 but its aims were later represented in the Duma by the Trudoviks (q.v.).

Peasants, according to the official theory, are one of the two classes (q.v.) in Soviet society. Current Soviet statistics make it difficult to estimate the total number of peasants. *Kolkhoz* (q.v.) peasants are usually grouped together with co-operated artisans (q.v.), since both are regarded as participating in co-operative ownership of their respective means of production (*see* OWNERSHIP); in 1956 they together made up 40·0 per cent of the population (2·0 per cent in 1928, 57·9 per cent in 1937). Similarly, individual peasants are grouped together with unco-operated artisans, making together 0·5 per cent of the population in 1956 (66·7 per cent in 1913, 74·9 per cent in 1928, 5·9 per cent in 1937; the figures for 1913 and 1928 do not include the so-called *kulaks*, q.v.); households of individual peasants numbered about 60,000 in 1959. The third category of peasants, those working in *sovkhozes* and other State agricultural enterprises and until 1958 in the M.T.S. (q.v.; now Technical Repair Stations), are not officially regarded as peasants but as workers, since they are wage-earners; they numbered in 1958 (without family members) 5·9 million. With the abolition of the M.T.S. most of their 2 million workers became *kolkhoz* members.

The legal position of these various categories of peasants differs. *Sovkhoz* workers are in a comparatively privileged position, since they have guaranteed minimum wages, benefit from all social services (q.v.), are not tied to their jobs, and many of them have internal passports (q.v.), being thus enabled to travel outside their own province. Within the *kolkhozes*, former M.T.S. workers are privileged vis-à-vis the ordinary *kolkhoz* members, since they have retained rights similar to those of *sovkhoz* workers save that they cannot leave the *kolkhoz*; their earnings and social service benefits are guaranteed from *kolkhoz* funds and not from the State. *Kolkhoz* peasants are legally obliged to put in a certain minimum amount of work in the *kolkhoz* per year (since its establishment in 1939 it has twice been raised, and now takes up most of the year). This obligation begins at the age of 12, and covers all able-bodied members of a household. They are not permitted to own draught animals or agricultural machinery, but have the right to the use of plots of land from one-half to one and a quarter acres in size, and to own a cow (several in semi-nomadic areas) and small animals and poultry for their personal use. They are subject to agricultural tax (q.v.) and until 1958 had to make compulsory deliveries to the State of milk, meat, wool, eggs and some other agricultural products for token payments. Although they have little time to devote to their personal plots, earnings from them, especially in the economically backward majority of *kolkhozes*, form the principal part of their income, since they have no regular income (*see* WORK-DAY UNIT).

Individual peasants, who together with unco-operated artisans still number about 1 million (1956), in addition to the disabilities of *kolkhoz* peasants (save that they are not tied to the land), are subject to severe limitations of the size of their farms and the number of draught animals they may own (one horse or two oxen) and to heavy taxation (*see* AGRICULTURAL TAX); unlike *kolkhoz* peasants they have not been freed from the obligatory deliveries to the State. These discriminations against individual peasants are expressly aimed at squeezing them out of existence. For history of peasants *see* AGRARIAN REVOLUTION; COLLECTIVIZATION OF AGRICULTURE; GREAT REFORMS; MIR; PEASANT LAND BANK; REDEMPTION PAYMENTS; SERFDOM; STOLYPIN.

Peasant rebellions have been one of the traditional features of Russian history, the most important ones being those led by Razin and Pugachëv (qq.v.). Agrarian disorders (seizures of landlords' estates by the peasants) were an important element in the revolution of 1905 (q.v.) and in 1917. After the Bolshevik seizure of power, peasants were on the one hand decisive in ensuring the Red victory in the civil war (q.v.), and on the other they provided the most important element in the anti-Communist uprisings both in the early years (e.g. the Antonov uprising, q.v.) and during the collectivization of agriculture. The interests of the peasants were paramount with the Populists (*see* NEO-POPULISM; POPULISM; SOCIALIST REVOLUTIONARIES) and were represented in the Duma by the Trudoviks (q.v.). Marxism in all its variations is essentially hostile to peasants, and according to the official theory they are to disappear as a class with the attainment of full communism. *See* G. T. Robinson, *Rural Russia under the Old Regime* (2nd ed.), New York, 1949; N. Jasny, *The*

Socialized Agriculture of the U.S.S.R., Stanford, 1949; D. Mitrany, *Marx Against the Peasant*, 1951; D. W. Treadgold, *The Great Siberian Migration*, Princeton, N.J., 1957; T. Scriven, 'Literature and the Peasant,' *Problems of Communism*, vol. viii, No. 6, Nov.–Dec. 1959; A. Inkeles and R. A. Bauer, *The Soviet Citizen*, 1959; V. Gsovski and K. Grzybowski (eds.), *Government, Law and Courts in the Soviet Union and Eastern Europe*, vol. ii, 1959; R. D. Laird *et al.*, *The Rise and Fall of the M.T.S. as an Instrument of Soviet Rule*, Lawrence, Kansas, 1960; A. Nove, 'The Incomes of Soviet Peasants,' *Slavonic and East European Review*, vol. xxxviii, No. 91, June 1960.

Pechenga (1920–45 **Petsamo**), urban settlement in the Murmansk Oblast, an ice-free port on the Barents Sea 75 m. north-west of Murmansk. Population (1939) 500. Important deposits of nickel and uranium are worked near by. Pechenga was founded in 1533 as a monastery, and was a Muscovite foreign trade port during the 16th century. It belonged to Finland, 1920–45.

Pechora, navigable river which rises in the Ural Mountains and flows north, south-west and north again into the Barents Sea. Length 1,100 m.; basin 126,000 sq. m.; chief ports: Pechora and Nar'yan-Mar. The basin is the coldest region of Europe and has the thickest snow cover; there are large coal deposits (*see* VORKUTA).

Pechory (Estonian **Petseri**), town in the Pskov Oblast (north-western Russia), situated 25 m. west of Pskov. Population (1938) 5,000, half Estonian. It is well known for the Pskov-Pechory cave monastery, founded in 1473. Pechory was a frontier fortress until the 18th century, and belonged to Estonia, 1920–45.

Pedology, subsidiary pedagogical discipline widely practised in Russia in the 1920's and early thirties. It was considered to be a science of child development, using experimental and observational techniques and taking into account both hereditary and environmental factors. In a special decree of the party's Central Committee in 1936 it was declared to be a pseudo-science, its teaching and practice were abolished, and its chief exponents disappeared during the Great Purge (q.v.). *See* A. P. Pinkevich, *The New Education in the Soviet Republic*, New York, 1929; G. S. Counts, *The Challenge of Soviet Education*, New York, 1957.

Peipus, *see* CHUDSKOYE.

Penal System. The 'Fundamentals of Criminal Legislation' adopted in 1958 state that the purpose of punishment is not only to penalize the offender for the crime but also to correct and re-educate him, as well as to prevent the repetition of crimes by the same person or others. Basic punishments are: (1) confinement to a 'corrective labour colony' or prison (qq.v.) for up to 10 years (up to 15 years for particularly serious crimes); confinement to a labour colony for juveniles for up to 10 years if the offender is under 18; (2) banishment for up to 10 years (not applicable to juveniles, pregnant women or women with children under 1 year of age); (3) corrective labour without deprivation of freedom (*see* FORCED LABOUR) for up to' 1 year; (4) deprivation of the right to occupy certain positions or pursue certain activities for up to 5 years; (5) fine (without option of imprisonment, or vice versa); (6) public censure. Categories (2), (4) and (5) can also be applied as additional punishments, while confiscation of property and deprivation of military or other ranks and titles can only be inflicted as additional punishments. Service in a corrective battalion for up to 2 years can be substituted for imprisonment or applied as a basic punishment when the offender is a conscript; for all servicemen up to 2 months in the guard-house are substituted for corrective labour without deprivation of freedom. Capital punishment (q.v.) by shooting exists for certain exceptional offences. Deprivation of electoral rights as a criminal punishment was abolished in 1958. Minimum as well as maximum penalties for specific offences are laid down by the Criminal Code and by the new Law on Criminal Responsibility for State Crimes, but the court can apply milder punishments. There are the usual provisions for mitigating or aggravating circumstances as well as for cumulative and conditional sentences.

The theories of 'class justice' and 'withering away of the law' current in official circles in the 1920's and early thirties led in the court practice to discrimination according to the social status and 'social origin' of the defendant (the 'socially alien elements' receiving much heavier penalties) and to comparatively mild sentences except for offences which were considered political; emphasis was laid, at least in theory, on the re-educative function of the penal system. All this was thrown overboard from the mid 1930's, and increasingly harsh punishments were introduced even for minor offences such as petty theft. The maximum length of imprisonment was raised from 10 to 25 years, and hard labour reintroduced as a special kind of punishment (even though the forced labour in ordinary concentration camps was hard by any comparison), as well as death by hanging. However, since Stalin's death the penal policy has become milder, concentration camps (see CORRECTIVE LABOUR CAMPS) have officially been abolished, and the legal reform (q.v.) of 1958 introduced a more humane system of penalties, except for political offences (see POLITICAL CRIMES). See V. Gsovski and K. Grzybowski (eds.), *Government, Law and Courts in the Soviet Union and Eastern Europe*, vol. ii, 1959; K. Grzybowski, 'Soviet Reform of Criminal Law of 1958,' *Osteuropa-Recht*, 6. Jahrg., Nos. 2–3, 1960.

Pensions. Old-age pensions are paid to male wage and salary earners at the age of 60 provided they have worked for not less than 25 years (women at 55 having worked for 20 years); pensionable age is reduced for those who have worked in especially dangerous or difficult conditions. Pensions vary from 100 per cent to 50 per cent of previous monthly earnings, but in any case are not less than Rs. 30 per month or more than Rs. 120 (new roubles). Disability pensions are granted in cases of loss of working capacity from injury at work or occupational disease. 'Loss of bread-winner' pensions may be granted to close relatives who had been dependent upon a deceased person's earnings. Service pensions exist for men retired from the armed forces or their widows. All pensions are non-contributory, but are reduced if the pensioner continues to work. *Kolkhoz* peasants are not entitled to any pensions, but some *kolkhozes* run their own insurance schemes. The present scheme of State pensions has been in existence since 1956;

before then pension laws were much less favourable. There is also a special category of 'personal pensions' which may be granted either to old revolutionaries or to individuals (or their relatives) for exceptional services. At the beginning of 1959, 18·2 million people were receiving State pensions of one kind or another. *See also* SOCIAL SERVICES. *See* A. Nove, 'Towards a "Communist Welfare State"?', *Problems of Communism*, vol. ix, No. 1, Jan.–Feb. 1960.

Penza: 1. Oblast of the R.S.F.S.R., situated south-east of Moscow largely on the Volga upland in the black earth belt, partly covered by oak forests. Area 16,900 sq. m.; population (1959) 1,510,000 (33 per cent urban), chiefly Russians (since the 17th century), also Mordva and Tatars. Grain, vegetables, sunflowers and hemp are cultivated, and cattle, pigs and horses kept; there are engineering, food, woodworking and textile industries. The area belonged to the Kazan' Khanate, and became Russian in 1552.

2. Administrative, economic and cultural centre of the oblast, situated on the River Sura (a tributary of the Volga). Population (1959) 254,000 (1914, 80,000; 1939, 160,000). It has varied engineering (bicycles, watches, etc.), food and wood-processing industries. Penza was founded as a military and administrative centre in 1666, and is an old cultural centre of the black earth belt, with a School of Horticulture, 1822, and a School of Painting, 1897.

People's Courts, lower courts with jurisdiction usually covering one rayon (q.v.) or a small town. They are first instance courts for all civil and criminal cases, except when a higher court decides otherwise. Both judges and assessors (qq.v.) of a People's Court are formally elected by the inhabitants of its area of jurisdiction, on the basis of adult suffrage, but in fact they are selected by the cadres (q.v.) departments of the party committees. People's Courts were established soon after the Bolshevik seizure of power in 1917 to replace the justices of the peace (q.v.), the peasant parish (*volost'*) courts and in part the Circuit Courts. *See also* COURTS OF LAW.

'People's Freedom, The,' *see* NARODNAYA VOLYA.

'People's Will, The,' alternative translation of the name Narodnaya Volya (q.v.).

Peredvizhniki (i.e. 'travellers' or 'wanderers'), movement in Russian art of the 19th century. Its name is derived from Tovarishchestvo peredvizhnykh khudozhestvennykh vystavok ('Society for Travelling Art Exhibitions'), formed in 1870. The Peredvizhniki pursued the aim of providing for the members of the society the facilities for exhibiting and selling their work; it played the leading role in Russian art for over twenty years and attracted contributions from all the important contemporary painters. Arranging exhibitions in the provinces, the Peredvizhniki was able to reach a wide public and to acquaint it with the paintings of contemporary interest, which often implied or openly propounded a criticism of the social order in Russia. The first leader of the movement was Kramskoy (q.v.), one of the 'thirteen contestants' who resigned from the Academy of Arts in 1863 in protest against painting for a competition on a prescribed subject. In 1890 the Peredvizhniki became outmoded by the new artistic movement, Mir Iskusstva (q.v.). It soon lost all its influence, although nominally the society existed until the 1920's. *See also* PEROV; REPIN.

Perekop (ancient Greek **Taphros**), village (town until 1925) on the Perekop isthmus between the Crimea and the mainland. Traces of Greek fortifications still exist. Perekop was a Tatar fortress from the 15th century, and became Russian in 1783. Heavy fighting took place during the civil war, in 1941 and in 1943–4.

Pereyaslav-Khmel'nitskiy (until 1953 **Pereyaslav**), town in the Kiev Oblast (Ukraine), situated 42 m. south-east of Kiev. Population (1956) 9,000 (1935, 17,000). Pereyaslav-Khmel'nitskiy has been known since 907, and was capital of the Pereyaslav Principality, 1054–1239. In 1654 the supremacy of the Czar of Muscovy was acknowledged here by the Ukrainian Cossack Assembly.

Perm' (1940–57 **Molotov**): 1. Oblast of the R.S.F.S.R., situated on the western slopes of the Ural Mountains and the adjacent plain, traversed by the River Kama and half covered with coniferous forests; there are large salt and some coal, oil and chromium deposits. Area 62,800 sq. m.; population (1959) 2,998,000 (59 per cent urban), mostly Russians (since the 14th century), also some Tatars and Permyaks (the Komi-Permyak National Okrug lies within the oblast). There are large engineering, metallurgical, chemical, coal-mining and wood-processing industries, and large power-stations, including the Kama hydro-electric station; grain and flax are cultivated and dairy farming is carried on. Principal towns: Perm', Berezniki, Kizel, Lys'va, Kungur, Chusovoy, Solikamsk. Salt works have existed here since 1430 and copper works since 1574 (*see* STROGANOV); the area was annexed by Muscovy in 1472.

2. Administrative, economic and cultural centre of the oblast, situated on the River Kama. Population (1959) 628,000 (third in the Urals, seventeenth in Russia; 1914, 62,000; 1926, 120,000; 1939, 306,000). It is one of the chief industrial centres of the Urals, with heavy engineering (ships, mining and oil industry equipment, etc.), chemical, woodworking and leather industries. It is the transportation centre of the north-western Urals (river and air ports, three railway lines); there is a university (founded in 1916 as a branch of Petrograd University) and an opera and ballet theatre, 1871. Perm' was founded in 1568 as a village, becoming a town and administrative centre of the northern Urals in 1781; it had a copper works from 1723, and later developed as an important centre of commerce. Industrial development was especially rapid in the 1930's and after the Second World War.

Perov, Vasiliy Grigor'yevich (1833–82), painter of *genre* and portraits, studied at Arzamas and at the Moscow Art School, 1853–61. He was a founder member of the Peredvizhniki (q.v.). Perov was the leading exponent of social criticism in art; his paintings, exposing the cruelty, corruption and inefficiency of the police, clergy and other servants of the State, played a not insignificant part in the radical movement against the autocracy. At times Perov's sentimentality in treating the hardships and sorrows of the poor becomes too concentrated, as is indicated by the following titles: 'The Village Burial,' 'The Drowned Girl,' 'Aged Parents at their Son's Grave.' Artistically his works were not in the least original, and they are now of value only as social documents.

Perovo, industrial suburb south-east of Moscow. Population (1959) 143,000 (1926, 24,000; 1939, 63,000). It has engineering (agricultural and road-building equipment) and chemical industries, and several agricultural research institutes. In the 1930's Perovo absorbed the neighbouring suburb of Kuskovo, and in 1960 was itself absorbed by Moscow city.

Perovsk, *see* KZYL-ORDA.

Personalism, in Russia, developed as a distinct philosophical trend in the late 19th–early 20th centuries, largely under the inspiration of Leibnitz in ontology, and the older Slavophiles (q.v.) and Dostoyevskiy in ethics and social philosophy. Its chief representatives were N. O. Losskiy (q.v.) and the thinkers of the Vekhi (q.v.) group (especially N. A. Berdyayev). In the wider sense of being particularly interested in and attaching great value to the problems of human personality, Personalism is characteristic of many Russian thinkers, including Herzen, Lavrov, Mikhaylovskiy, Chicherin and Lopatin (qq.v.). *See* N. Lossky, *History of Russian Philosophy*, 1951; V. V. Zenkovsky, *A History of Russian Philosophy* (2 vols.), 1953.

Pervoural'sk, town in the Sverdlovsk Oblast situated on the Sverdlovsk–Perm' railway, 31 m. west of Sverdlovsk. Population (1959) 90,000. It is an important centre of the metallurgical industry (pipe-rolling mill). Pervoural'sk was founded by Demidov in 1732 as an ironworks.

Pervukhin, Mikhail Georgiyevich (*b.* 1904), Communist. Born of a working-class family in the Urals, he joined the party in 1919, studied in Moscow, 1922–9, and became an electrical engineer. His career took a spectacular turn during the Great Purge (q.v.), when within one year (1937–8) he rose from manager of a power-station to First Deputy Commissar (Minister) for Heavy Industry. He was later Minister of Power Stations and Electrical Industry (1939–40, 1953–1955), of Chemical Industry (1942–50), a deputy prime minister (1940–4, 1950–5) and a first deputy prime minister (1955–7) and chairman of the State Planning Committee (1956–7). In 1939 he became a member of the Central Committee, and in 1952 a member of its Presidium. During the period of 'collective leadership' after Stalin's death, Pervukhin was usually considered as belonging to the 'managerial' faction headed by Malenkov. He joined the so-called 'anti-party group' (q.v.) in its struggle against Khrushchëv in 1957, but recanted upon its defeat, was demoted to candidate member of the party Presidium and after a short period as chairman of the State Committee for Foreign Economic Relations was appointed ambassador to East Germany.

Peter I, the Great (1672–1725), first Russian emperor, youngest son of Czar Aleksey Mikhaylovich. On the death of his half-brother, Fëdor III, in 1682, the Patriarch of Moscow and the leading boyars decided that Peter should reign rather than his older but incompetent half-brother Ivan. However, Ivan's older sister Sophia organized a palace coup, as a result of which Peter and Ivan were jointly crowned and Sophia appointed regent. During the next seven years Peter, though receiving little formal education, acquired a mass of knowledge and technical skills, chiefly from foreigners in Russian service (among them the Swiss Lefort, the Scotsman Patrick Gordon and the Dutchman Timmerman).

In 1689 Peter forced Sophia to resign, and assumed the government of the country himself, though leaving formal precedence to Ivan. Among his first achievements were the creation of a disciplined army (in which he was assisted by Gordon and Lefort) and the beginnings of a navy and merchant fleet. Anxious to acquire a part of the Black Sea, he declared war on Turkey and after a long siege took the fortress of Azov in 1696. Early in the following year, eager for more knowledge, he left Russia and visited the three Baltic provinces, Prussia, Hanover and Amsterdam (where he worked as a shipwright for some time); he visited England for three months on the invitation of William III, and when he left took with him a number of British engineers, artificers, surgeons, artisans, etc. During these travels he acquired much valuable information, studying astronomy, natural philosophy, geography, anatomy and surgery. He returned to Russia early in 1698 on receiving news of a military rebellion, though before he arrived it had already been suppressed by General Gordon; Peter's wife, however, was suspected of complicity, and he divorced her and had her confined to a convent. In 1700 Peter allied himself with the kings of Poland and Denmark against Sweden, and soon he conquered a part of Swedish territory (Ingria) where he laid the foundations of the new capital of Russia, St Petersburg. The Russians were several times defeated during the long struggle with Sweden, but were finally victorious at the Battle of Poltava on 8th July 1709. Peter then made war upon Turkey, and lost the port of Azov and its surrounding territory. In 1712 he married his mistress (who became Catherine I on his death) and in 1716–17 made another tour of Europe with her. Suspecting his son Aleksey of treason, he ordered his execution, but Aleksey died before sentence could be carried out. In 1722 he once more embarked upon war, this time with Persia, and took three Caspian provinces, together with the towns of Derbent and Baku.

Though personally cruel, Peter was a great monarch who transformed Russia and set her on the path to becoming a great European power. Among the most important of his reforms were the abolition of the Moscow Patriarchy (see PATRIARCH) and its replacement by a synod subordinated to the czar; the reform of the central government (with the establishment of specialized government departments —'colleges') and of provincial administration (with the appointment of provincial governors); the introduction of a well-organized military and civil service, open to any suitably qualified person without regard to his origins; financial reforms (including the introduction of a poll-tax); the development of trade and industry; and the encouragement of scholarship. In 1721 Peter was proclaimed Emperor of All Russia, and in the following year he promulgated a new law whereby each monarch was to nominate his own successor. See E. Schuyler, *Peter the Great, Emperor of Russia* (2 vols.), New York, 1890; B. H. Sumner, *Peter the Great and the Emergence of Russia*, 1950; V. Klyuchevsky, *Peter the Great* (trans. L. Archibald), 1958.

Peter III (1728–62), emperor, Duke of Holstein, born at Kiel, succeeding his aunt Elizabeth on the throne in 1762 and immediately returning to Frederick the Great those Prussian provinces conquered by Russia during the Seven Years War. Ineffective and weak-minded, he followed good advice in proclaiming the famous edict which released the gentry from compulsory state service. He was overthrown by a Guards' plot in favour of his wife, Catherine II, and is believed to have been killed by her lover Orlov.

Peter the Great Gulf, wide inlet of the Sea of Japan on the coast of the Russian Far East, stretching from the Tumen River (Korean frontier) to Cape Povorotnyy. Vladivostok is its chief port.

Petergof, *see* PETRODVORETS.

Petipa, Marius (1822–1910), French choreographer and teacher who came to St Petersburg in 1847 and remained there for the rest of his life. Becoming ballet master in 1858, he achieved his first major success with *La Fille du Pharaon,* 1862, and for the next forty years held an unrivalled position. Petipa's influence on the course of Russian ballet cannot be sufficiently stressed, his principal innovations being the introduction of new steps, the employment of music of the highest quality (Tchaikovsky's *The Sleeping Beauty,* 1890; *The Nutcracker,* 1892; *Swan Lake,* 1895), and finally the successful coalescence of French classical ballet with the Italian acrobatics as exemplified by Zucchi, Legnani and Cecchetti. His pupils included Fokine, Legat and Gorsky. *See also* BALLET. *See* his *Russian Ballet Master* (trans. H. Whittaker), 1958.

Petrazhitskiy (Petrazycki), Lev Iosifovich (1867–1931), jurist of Polish parentage, professor at St Petersburg University till 1918, when he emigrated, later professor at Warsaw University; a Constitutional Democratic member of the 1st Duma in 1906. Apart from several works on civil law (*The Doctrine of Income,* German (2 vols.), 1893–5; *The Limited Company,* 1898) he wrote *Outlines of a Philosophy of Law,* 1900, *On Motives of Human Actions,* 1904, *Foundations of Emotional Psychology,* 1906, *Theory of State and Law in Connection with the Theory of Morals* (2 vols.), 1907, etc., in which he expounded an original psychological theory of law. Instead of the traditional division of law into private and public he advocated a division into a 'law of centralization' motivated by modern considerations of social service, and a 'law of decentralization' free from such considerations. Petrazhitskiy's views to some extent influenced early Soviet legal theory. See *Law and Morality: L. Petrazycki,* Cambridge, Mass., 1955 (a selection from his principal writings with an introduction by N. Timasheff); A. Meyendorff, 'L. Petrazycki' in *Modern Theories of Law,* 1933; F. S. C. Northrop, 'Petrazycki's Psychological Jurisprudence,' *University of Pennsylvania Law Review,* vol. civ, No. 5, 1956, reprinted in his *The Complexity of Legal and Ethical Experiences,* Boston and Toronto, 1959.

Petrodvorets (until 1944 **Petergof**), town in the Leningrad Oblast (subordinated to the Leningrad City Council), situated on the southern shore of the Gulf of Finland. Population (1956) 20,000. It grew up around a palace built in 1711, and is famous for its 18th–19th-century imperial palaces and parks, with magnificent fountains and cascades. During the German occupation of 1941–3 it was ruined, but has been partially rebuilt. *See* N. Fyodorova and A. Raskin, *Petrodvorets*, Moscow, 1956.

Petrograd, *see* LENINGRAD.

Petrokrepost' (until 1611 **Oreshek,** then **Nöteborg,** 1702–1944 **Shlissel'burg),** town in the Leningrad Oblast, situated on Lake Ladoga at the start of the River Neva. Population (1956) 6,400. It has an old fortress which was used from the 18th century until February 1917 as a prison for important political offenders. Petrokrepost' was founded by Novgorodians in 1323, and was Swedish, 1611–1702. It was occupied by the Germans, 1941–3.

Petropavlovsk: 1. Administrative, economic and cultural centre of the Kamchatka Oblast (Russian Far East), situated on the eastern shore of the Kamchatka Peninsula. Population (1959) 86,000 (1934, 7,500; 1956, 58,000). It is an important fishing port. Petropavlovsk was founded by Bering as an administrative, naval and trading base in 1740; in 1854 it was bombarded by the Allies.

2. Town in south-western Siberia, administrative, economic and cultural centre of the North Kazakhstan Oblast, situated on the River Ishim and the Trans-Siberian Railway at the junction of the Trans-Kazakhstan Railway. Population (1959) 131,000 (1939, 92,000), mostly Russians, also Tatars, Kazakhs, Germans, etc. It has a large meat-packing plant (built in 1929 and handling cattle from northern Kazakhstan and the adjacent oblasts of Western Siberia) and other food industries, also leather, clothing and some engineering industries. Petropavlovsk was founded as a Russian fortress in 1752, became a town in 1807 and a provincial centre in 1932. Industrial development dates from the late 19th century; engineering and metalworking from the Second World War.

Petrovsk-Port, *see* MAKHACHKALA.

Petrovskiy, Ivan Georgiyevich (*b.* 1901), mathematician. Educated at Moscow University, he became professor there in 1933 and rector in 1951; he is a member of the Academy of Sciences. His works are mainly concerned with the theory of differential equations, algebraic geometry and the theory of probability.

Petrozavodsk, capital, economic and cultural centre of the Karelian Autonomous Republic, situated on the Onega Lake 190 m. northeast of Leningrad. Population (1959) 135,000 (1926, 27,000; 1939, 70,000). It has engineering works (timber industry equipment). There is a university (established in 1940) and a branch of the U.S.S.R. Academy of Sciences. Petrozavodsk was founded as a cannon foundry in 1703 and became a town in 1777.

Petsamo, SEE PECHENGA.

Philaret (lay name **Drozdov, Vasiliy Mikhaylovich**) (1783–1867), preacher and theologian, Metropolitan of Moscow from 1826. He wrote two catechisms, and started work upon a translation of the New Testament into Russian. *See* his *Select Sermons* (Eng. trans., 1873); R. W. Blackmore, *The Doctrine of the Russian Church,* 1845.

Physics, as an academic discipline, was first introduced into Russia after the foundation of the Academy of Sciences in 1725. The main field of physical research in Russia throughout the 18th and 19th centuries was electricity, the most outstanding achievement being the independent invention of radio by Popov (q.v.). Important work was done in the study of the photo-effect by Stoletov (q.v.) and the pressure of light by Lebedev (q.v.). In recent decades the work of Fok, Tamm and Landau (qq.v.) has been prominent in theoretical physics; of Tamm, Kurchatov, Artsimovich (qq.v.), V. I. Veksler and others in nuclear physics and the study of cosmic rays; of Rozhdestvenskiy, S. I. Vavilov, Mandel'shtam, Tamm (qq.v.) and others in optics; of Mandel'shtam and N. D. Papaleksi in the theory of oscillation; of Kapitsa (q.v.) and Landau in the study of low temperatures; of Ioffe (q.v.) in the study of solid bodies, dielectrics and semiconductors; Landau in the study of magnetism; N. N. Andreyev (q.v.) in acoustics, etc. See J. G. Crowther, *Soviet Science*, 1936; *Soviet Research in Physics*, Physics Collection Nos. 1–7, New York, Consultants Bureau, 1955–6; A. I. Akhiezer and V. B. Berestetsky, *Quantum Electrodynamics*, New York, 1957; *Conference on the Physics of Nuclear Fission*, Moscow, 1957; *Physics of Nuclear Fission*, 1958. Complete 'cover to-cover' translations of the following journals exist in English: *Journal of Acoustics*; *Biophysics*; *Technical Physics*; *Experimental and Theoretical Physics*; *Crystallography*; *Physics of Metals and Metallurgy*; *Journal of Abstracts: Physics*; *Bulletin of the Academy of Sciences of the U.S.S.R.: Physical Series*.

Pinsk, town in the Brest Oblast (Belorussia), situated on the River Pripet. Population (1956) 36,500 (1914, 37,000; 1939, 25,000). It has woodworking industries. Pinsk has been known since 1097, was the capital of Pinsk Principality in the 13th century, became Lithuanian in 1320, was Polish, 1569–1793 and 1920–39, Russian, 1793–1920 and since 1939. It was the capital of Pinsk Oblast, 1939–54, now absorbed by Brest Oblast.

Pioneers, Communist organization for children aged 9 to 14. It was founded in 1922 as an adjunct of the Komsomol movement, and took over many of the outward aspects of the Scout movement which was suppressed. Membership is not officially compulsory but is in fact almost universal. From the late 1930's until after Stalin's death the Pioneer organization, though formally in existence, was almost moribund; since then, however, efforts have been made to infuse new life into it, mainly by reviving some of the Scout activities. A council for Pioneer organization, with advisory functions, has recently been set up by the central committee of the Komsomol.

Pirogov, Nikolay Ivanovich (1810–81), famous surgeon, educationalist and liberal publicist, professor of Dorpat University and of the Medico-Surgical Academy at St Petersburg, 1856–61 curator of the Odessa educational district. Besides being the author of classical works on surgical anatomy and clinical surgery, Pirogov pioneered the use of ether narcosis and inflexible gypsum bandages, and was the founder of military surgery (*Foundations of General Military Field Surgery*, 1865–6, based on his experiences during the defence of Sevastopol' in 1854). A materialist in his youth, Pirogov later became a vitalist and a believer. The Pirogov Society, named in his honour, was founded in 1883 and was the chief Russian medical society (*see* SOCIETIES); its congresses (known as Pirogov congresses) attracted much public attention. In 1894–1905 it was dominated by radical elements, but later became predominantly liberal and was suppressed by the Bolsheviks in 1922.

Pisarev, Dmitriy Ivanovich (1841–68), literary critic and thinker, the chief representative of Nihilism in Russia. He wrote in several radical journals, including Nekrasov's *Notes of the Fatherland.* Pisarev exercised a strong influence on the young people of the 1860's, directing their attention away from the traditional artistic and social values towards the study of the natural sciences. *See* his *Selected Philosophical, Social and Political Essays* (Eng. ed.), Moscow, 1958; N. Lossky, *History of Russian Philosophy*, 1951; M. Karpovich, 'Historical Background of Soviet Thought Control' in W. Gurian's (ed.) *The Soviet Union*, Indiana, 1951; V. V. Zenkovsky, *A History of Russian Philosophy*, vol. i, 1953; T. G. Masaryk, *The Spirit of Russia* (2nd ed.), vol. ii, 1955.

Pishpek, *see* FRUNZE.

Planning. All spheres of public activity in the U.S.S.R. are officially planned, planning being considered a distinguishing feature of the socialist society. Of particular importance is economic planning, which encompasses almost the whole economic life of the country (exceptions being the activities of individual peasants, unco-operated artisans, 'speculators' and the *kolkhoz* market, qq.v.). There are two types of plan—long-term (Five Year Plans, Seven Year Plan, qq.v.— or even longer, so called 'perspective' plans), and current plans (yearly, quarterly, etc.). Both long-term and current plans are drawn up by the central planning organs (*see* GOSPLAN) on the basis of directions from the highest party authorities in conjunction with the ministries concerned and (since 1957) the regional Economic Councils (q.v.). Draft plans are sent down to the enterprises concerned and discussed at meetings of the employees, the fiction (q.v.) being maintained that the plans actually emanate from the enterprises. The plans are drawn up in both physical (requirements of raw materials, output, number of people employed) and monetary (costs, prices, profits) terms, and balances (q.v.) are calculated wherever considered appropriate. The plans ostensibly have the force of law. In fact they are practically never carried out as such, some targets being surpassed, others not reached. One of the chief reasons for this is the party's insistence upon 'over-fulfilment' with the help of such practices as 'Socialist emulation', 'Stakhanovism' (qq.v.), etc. Considerable changes in the plan by the authorities during the plan period are also frequent. In order to offset these difficulties the managements resort to string-pulling, unofficial dealings, etc. (*see* BLAT; TOLKACH). Thus the plans do not eliminate disproportions and waste (sometimes they actually cause them), but they are useful in providing landmarks by which managements and the public at large orientate themselves.

The first attempt by the State to regulate the main branches of the economy was made during the First World War, and from this developed the ideas of many technocratically minded experts (e.g. Grinevetskiy, Aleksandrov, Pal'chinskiy, qq.v.) on long-term economic planning which in fact laid the foundations for the economic plans of the Soviet period. Another theoretical root was the traditional Social Democratic views on planned economy. The early Soviet plans—Goelro (q.v.) and the first Five Year Plan—were largely drawn up by technocrats and ex-Menshevik economists (e.g. Groman, Larin, Strumilin, qq.v.); the few Bolsheviks active in early economic planning (e.g. Krzhizhanovskiy) were valuable as intermediaries between the technical experts and the Communist authorities. Up to and including the first version of the first Five Year Plan the tasks laid down and targets envisaged were economically justifiable, but with the establishment of Stalin's rule these were declared to be insufficient and due to deliberate sabotage (see PURGES), and subsequent plans were subordinated to Stalin's personal preferences, which resulted in planned disproportions and in particular in the neglect of agriculture and consumer goods (qq.v.). Since Stalin's death in 1953 various changes have been made in the machinery of planning. Since the elimination of the 'anti-party group' (q.v.) in 1957 economic planning has been characterized by a certain degree of decentralization on the one hand and greater regard for sound economics on the other. See M. Dobb, Soviet Economic Development since 1917, 1948; A. Baykov, The Development of the Soviet Economic System, 1950; H. Schwartz, Russia's Soviet Economy, 2nd ed., 1954; C. Bobrowski, Formation du Système Soviétique de Planification, Paris and The Hague, 1956; F. Brandel and F. Perroux (eds.), Les Méthodes actuelles Soviétiques de planification, Paris, 1959; H. Chambre, L'Aménagement du territoire en U.R.S.S., Paris and The Hague, 1959; H. S. Levine, 'Conversations with Planners,' Soviet Survey, No. 30, Oct.–Dec. 1959; The Soviet Seven Year Plan (introduction by A. Nove), 1960; G. Grossman (ed.), Value and Plan, Berkeley, California, 1960; A. Zauberman, 'New Winds in Soviet Planning,' Soviet Studies, July 1960.

Platonov, Sergey Fëdorovich (1860–1933), professor at St Petersburg University, a historian whose main field of research was the 17th-century Time of Troubles (see TROUBLES, TIME OF). His Lectures on Russian History (10th ed., 1917; Eng., History of Russia, 1925) was a widely used textbook. A leading opponent in the intellectual field to the Communist regime, protesting strongly at the Communist falsification of history, he was dismissed from the Academy of Sciences, arrested, and died in banishment.

Plekhanov, Georgiy Valentinovich (1857–1918), politician, a member in early youth of the Populist revolutionary organization Land and Freedom, and after its split the leader of its non-terroristic successor Chërnyy Peredel (q.v.). He emigrated to western Europe in 1880 and there became converted to Marxism. In 1883 he founded the Liberation of Labour Group (q.v.), which played an important role in spreading Marxism in Russia and in opposing the rival ideology of Populism (q.v.). On the foundation of the Russian Social Democratic Labour Party, 1898, Plekhanov supported its more politically minded and orthodox Marxist wing (see ECONOMISM; ISKRA) and collaborated with Lenin; he supported the Bolsheviks at and immediately after the 2nd party congress in 1903, but soon joined the Mensheviks. He split with the majority of Mensheviks in 1910 on the question of 'liquidationism' (q.v.) and set up a sub-faction of 'party-minded' Mensheviks, once more co-operating with Lenin for a period. He advocated an allied victory during the First World War as a means of advancing socialism. He returned to Russia after the February revolution (q.v.) of 1917 and set up a bitterly anti-Bolshevik right-wing social democratic organization 'Unity,' but died soon after the Bolshevik seizure of power. Plekhanov is known as 'the father of Russian social democracy'; for many years he represented it in the Socialist International and was one of the latter's leaders; he was a rigidly orthodox Marxist, sharply opposing any revisionist trends. *See* A. J. Sack, *The Birth of the Russian Democracy*, New York, 1918; L. H. Haimson, *The Russian Marxists and the Origins of Bolshevism*, Cambridge, Mass., 1955.

Plisetskaya, Maya (*b.* 1928), ballerina. A pupil of the Bolshoi School until 1944, Plisetskaya is one of the outstanding contemporary dancers, her work being distinguished by its essential femininity and sensitivity. Her greatest role is that of Odette-Odile in *Swan Lake*. She is now one of the principal ballerinas of the Moscow Bolshoi Theatre. *See* H. Bellew, *Ballet in Moscow Today*, 1956.

Pobedonostsev, Konstantin Petrovich (1827–1907), statesman and jurist, senator, 1868, member of the State Council, 1872, and Procurator of the Holy Synod of the Russian Orthodox Church, 1880. The reactionary policies of Alexander III were inspired by Pobedonostsev. *See* his *Reflections of a Russian Statesman* (trans. R. C. Lang), 1898; T. G. Masaryk, *The Spirit of Russia*, 2nd ed., 1955; R. Hare, *Portraits of Russian Personalities between Reform and Revolution*, 1959.

Podolia (Ukrainian **Podillya**), area in western Ukraine, comprising north-eastern Galicia (Ternopol' Oblast) and Khmel'nitskiy and Vinnitsa oblasts; it lies largely between the rivers Dniester and Southern Bug, on the Volhynia-Podolia upland. Podolia belonged to the Kievan State, then to the Kingdom of Galicia and Volhynia, Lithuania and Poland; eastern Podolia has been Russian since 1793, western Podolia became Austrian in 1772 and was again Polish, 1918–39.

Podol'sk, town in the Moscow Oblast, 25 m. south of the capital. Population (1959) 124,000 (1926, 20,000; 1939, 72,000). It is a centre of engineering and cement industries. Podol'sk was founded as a village and became a town in 1764; industrial development dates from the late 19th century.

Podvoyskiy, Nikolay Il'ich (1880–1948), Communist who joined the Social Democratic Labour Party in 1901 and subsequently its Bolshevik faction. After the 1905 revolution he owned a publishing house for social democratic literature. During the First World War he ceased active party work and was engaged in work connected with the economic war effort, but immediately after the February revolution (q.v.) of 1917 he became a member of the first legal Bolshevik St Petersburg Committee and of its executive; he then became chairman of the Military Commission of the party's Central Committee and editor of the Bolshevik newspaper for soldiers. At the time of the seizure of power he was chairman of the Military Revolutionary

Committee of the Petrograd Soviet. He entered the first Soviet Government as one of the three men responsible for military and naval affairs, and was one of the principal organizers of the Red Army and a high-ranking commissar during the civil war. Later, however, his position declined, and from the 1930's he was on the staff of the Marx-Engels-Lenin Institute. His death passed unnoticed, but since the death of Stalin his memory has been revived.

Pogroms, see ANTI-SEMITISM.

Pokrovskiy, Mikhail Nikolayevich (1868–1932), historian and politician, a pupil of Klyuchevskiy, member of the Bolshevik faction of the Social Democratic Labour Party from 1905, and of the left-wing Bolshevik sub-faction 'Forward' (*see* VPERËD) in 1909. He became chairman of the Moscow Soviet after the Bolshevik seizure of power in 1917, and was Deputy Commissar of Education from 1918 to 1932. In 1918 he was a Left Communist (q.v.). He established and headed many of the organizations and institutions which implemented Communist Party control in the field of learning (Communist Academy, Institute of Red Professorship, Society of Marxist Historians, etc.). Pokrovskiy's theory that history is 'politics turned to the past' still characterizes Soviet historiography, though in 1934–6 his historical school was officially declared to be mistaken, and was superseded by Grekov's National Bolshevik school. *See* his *Brief History of Russia*, 1933; C. E. Black (ed.), *Rewriting Russian History*, New York, 1956.

Polekhs, ethnic group of the Great Russian people who inhabit the eastern Poles'ye (parts of Bryansk, Kaluga and Orël oblasts). They are probably direct descendants of the Russian inhabitants of the area in the Kievan period (*see* KIEVAN RUSSIA) who, protected by the forests, were able to remain there throughout the period of the 13th–15th centuries when the wooded steppe and steppe regions to the south and east suffered from Tatar devastation and became largely deserted.

Poles, in the U.S.S.R., live mostly in the Ukraine west of the Dnieper, Belorussia and Lithuania, that is, territories which until the late 18th century belonged to the Polish-Lithuanian Commonwealth. However, during the 19th and 20th centuries many Poles migrated further east, or were banished, so that now people of Polish origin can be met throughout the country. They numbered nearly 800,000 in 1926 according to the census, though the Poles themselves claimed that there were about 1½ million. The 1939 census, taken at a time when Poles in the border areas were under acute persecution, gave the number at about 630,000. As a result of the Nazi-Soviet Pact (q.v.) the Soviet Union annexed in October 1939 territories with over 4½ million Polish inhabitants, but parts of this territory around Bialystok and Przemysl were returned to Poland in 1944, and all but a few hundred thousand of the Poles from the newly annexed territories were soon repatriated. The present number of Poles in Russia is (1959) 1·4 million, of whom 45 per cent regard Polish as their mother tongue. The history of Russo-Polish relations throughout the Muscovite period was one of rivalry for the inheritance of Kievan Russia and the Grand Duchy of Lithuania. An attempt by Poland during the Time of Troubles (see TROUBLES, TIME OF) in the 17th century to absorb Muscovy was followed by the gradual absorption of Polish territory by Russia until the divisions of Poland in the late 18th century. Since then Poles have played an important part both in the revolutionary movements in Russia and in the State apparatus, both before 1917 and after (e.g. the first two heads of the security organs, Dzerzhinskiy and Menzhinskiy).

Poles'ye: 1. Swampy lowland area in western Russia, comprising the Pripet Basin and the adjacent part of the Dnieper lowland in the east, about 60,000 sq. m., partly covered with pine and oak forests. The area has large deposits of salt, potash and peat; there is lumbering and some agriculture.

2. Former oblast in southern Belorussia, 1938–54, with Mozyr' as capital. It is now included in Gomel' Oblast.

Police, see MILITIA; SECURITY ORGANS.

Police Socialism, attempt to prevent workers from being influenced by revolutionary socialism through the establishment of a legal workers' movement largely controlled by police agents. Such attempts were made in Russia between 1900 and 1905. See GAPON; ZUBATOV.

Politburo, chief policy-making organ of the Communist Party until 1952. Lenin had always had a group of policy-makers around him, and the first Politburo was formed on the eve of the Bolshevik seizure of power in 1917; it was given a permanent position in 1919, when it consisted of five members. The institution was rendered impotent towards the end of Stalin's life, finally abolished in 1952, and replaced by the Presidium (q.v.) of the Central Committee. See M. Fainsod, *How Russia is Ruled*, Cambridge, Mass., 1953; L. Schapiro, *The Communist Party of the Soviet Union*, 1960.

Political Commissars, incorrect designation, sometimes used abroad, for Military Commissars (see COMMISSAR).

Political Crimes. The new Law on Criminal Responsibility for State Crimes adopted in 1958 deals in its first part with 'particularly dangerous State crimes.' This part of the 1958 law replaced the first part of Chapter I of the R.S.F.S.R. Criminal Code, on 'counter-revolutionary crimes,' and covers substantially the same field. The offences and penalties for them are the following: (1) treason to the motherland, defined as a conscious act aimed at harming the independence, territorial inviolability or military strength of the U.S.S.R., going over to the enemy side, espionage, delivering State or military secrets to a foreign state, flight abroad or refusal to return from abroad, assisting a foreign state in hostile activities against the U.S.S.R., as well as a conspiracy aimed at seizing power—deprivation of liberty for 10–15 years, or death; (2) espionage by foreigners—7–15 years or death; (3) terroristic acts, defined as assassination of, or serious bodily injury caused to, a statesman, public figure or representative of authority, and committed in connection with his State or public activities with intent to undermine or weaken the Soviet regime—imprisonment for 10–15 years or death for assassination, and imprisonment for 8–15 years for injury; (4) terroristic acts against a representative of a foreign state, with intent of provoking a war or international complications—the same penalty; (5) diversion, defined as ruining or damaging State or social property, causing mass poisoning, epidemics or epizootics, with intent to weaken the Soviet State—imprisonment for 8–15 years or death; (6) wrecking, defined as action or omission aimed at undermining any branch of the national economy or the functioning of the State organs or public organizations with intent to weaken the Soviet state (if committed through utilizing State or public institutions, enterprises, organizations, or by way of hindering their normal work)—imprisonment for 8–15 years; (7) anti-Soviet agitation and propaganda, defined as agitation or propaganda with intent to undermine or weaken the Soviet regime or to commit other particularly dangerous State crimes, spreading with the same intent slanderous inventions, vilifying the Soviet state and social system, as well as disseminating, fabricating or keeping, with the same intent, literature of the same content—deprivation of freedom for 6 months to 2 years or banishment to a specified place for 2 to 5 years; but if committed by a person who had previously been convicted for particularly dangerous State crimes, or committed in time of war, deprivation of freedom for 3–10 years; (8) war propaganda in any form—deprivation of freedom for 3–8 years; (9) organizational activities aimed at preparing or committing particularly dangerous State crimes, at forming an organization with intent to commit such crimes, as well as participation in an anti-Soviet organization—punished according to articles 1–8 above; (10) particularly dangerous crimes committed against another toilers' state (i.e. one ruled by a Communist Party)—punished according to articles 1–9 above. Crimes listed in articles 1–5 carry in all cases, as an additional punishment, confiscation of property.

These provisions serve as a legal basis for terroristic measures by the Communist Government against their political opponents (*see* TERROR). The situation was especially aggravated during Stalin's rule by frequent convictions (by irregular courts, *see* TROYKA) for alleged political crimes on false evidence. *See also* CRIMINAL LAW; LEGAL REFORM; PENAL SYSTEM.

Political Theory in Russia begins in the Kievan period (*see* KIEVAN RUSSIA) with the *Original Chronicle* and Vladimir Monomakh's *Charge* to his sons. Their main theme of Russian unity found continuation in the political philosophy of the *Word of Igor's Campaign* (*see* LITERATURE) and the Muscovite doctrine of 'gathering the Russian lands.' Another medieval Muscovite (*see* MUSCOVY) doctrine was that of 'Moscow, the third Rome,' while republican Novgorod (q.v.) evolved a theory of limited princely power (chiefly military) derived from the will of the citizens. In the political correspondence of Ivan the Terrible (q.v.) with Prince Kurbskiy in the 16th century, the opposing standpoints of early absolutism and feudal liberties were eloquently formulated. The following century saw an attempt by Patriarch Nikon (q.v.) to argue the supremacy of spiritual power over the temporal. In the 18th century the doctrines of Enlightened Absolutism (Peter the Great, Tatishchev, Lomonosov, qq.v.) and of Constitutionalism (Pososhkov, q.v., Ya. P. Kozel'skiy) were widely adhered to, and towards the end of the century the first expression of revolutionary radicalism was given by Radishchev (q.v.).

The first quarter of the 19th century saw these trends further developed—constitutionalism by Speranskiy (q.v.) and the revolutionary trend in the writings of the Decembrists (q.v.). It was during the reign of Nicholas I (1825–55) that the doctrine of enlightened absolutism gave way to the doctrine of 'orthodony, autocracy and nationality,' formulated by the Minister of Education, Count A. S. Uvarov, which remained the official ideology until the end of the autocratic regime (*see* AUTOCRACY). At the same time the two main ideological and political schools of 19th-century Russia emerged: the Westernist and the Slavophile (*see* WESTERNISM, SLAVOPHILES). From the mid 19th century until after the revolution of 1905 (q.v.) the development consisted mainly of further differentiation and transformation within both schools, with occasional overlapping and mutual borrowing.

The Slavophiles were on the whole more conservative, the main trends among them being the liberal Slavophilism of the period of the Great Reforms (q.v., *see also* SAMARIN), the democratic, conservative 'soil-bound' trend (*see* DOSTOYEVSKIY, A. GRIGOR'YEV) and the Panslavist trend (*see* DANILEVSKIY). Two highly original conservative thinkers, Leont'yev and Rozanov (qq.v.), shared with the Slavophiles their rejection of Western ways. The divisions among the Westernists were much clearer cut and understandably bore a greater resemblance to contemporary thought in Western Europe. Outstanding among the conservatives were Katkov, Pobedonostsev and Tikhomirov (qq.v.), the liberal Westernists were represented by, for example, B. N. Chicherin, Kavelin, Gol'tsev and Klyuchevskiy (qq.v.), while the radical thought soon embraced socialism and the dominant radical trend was Populism (q.v.). Social Democracy (*see* RUSSIAN SOCIAL DEMOCRATIC LABOUR PARTY) diverged from the main Populist stream in the 1880's, and at the turn of the century Leninism (q.v.) emerged as a combination of the Russian version of Jacobinism and Marxism (q.v.). Other important offshoots of Populism were Anarchism and Regionalism (qq.v.).

The experience and the outcome of the 1905 revolution strengthened reformist tendencies (*see* REFORMISM), and two trends that had not been particularly significant hitherto became prominent —Technocratism (*see* MENDELEYEV, PAL'CHINSKIY, RYABUSHINSKIY) and Solidarism (q.v.). The new political doctrines which have developed since the 1917 revolution are National Bolshevism (q.v.), Eurasianism (*see* EURASIANS) and Stalinism (q.v.). *See also* IDEOLOGY, REVOLUTIONARY MOVEMENT. *See* P. I. Novgorodtsev, *Ob obshchestvennom ideale*, Moscow, 1917; J. D. Duff (ed.), *Russian Realities and Problems*, 1917; T. G. Masaryk, *The Spirit of Russia* (2 vols.), 1919; 2nd ed., 1955; R. Fülöp-Miller, *The Mind and Face of Bolshevism*, 1927; D. S. Mirsky, 'The Eurasian Movement,' *Slavonic Review*, Dec. 1927; J. F. Hecker, *Russian Sociology*, 2nd ed., 1934; N. Berdyaev, *The Origin of Russian Communism*, 1937, and *The Russian Idea*, 1947; M. Karpovich, 'A Forerunner of Lenin: P. N. Tkachev,' *Review of Politics*, vol. vi, July 1944; D. Hecht, *Russian Radicals Look to*

America, 1825–1894, Cambridge, Mass., 1947; N. Lossky, *History of Russian Philosophy*, 1951; R. Hare, *Pioneers of Russian Social Thought*, 1951; N. V. Riasanovsky, *Russia and the West in the Teachings of the Slavophiles*, Cambridge, Mass., 1952, and *Nicholas I and Official Nationality in Russia*, Berkeley and Los Angeles, 1959; V. V. Zenkovsky, *A History of Russian Philosophy* (2 vols.), 1953; E. J. Simmons (ed.), *Continuity and Change in Russian and Soviet Thought*, Cambridge, Mass., 1955; L. H. Haimson, *The Russian Marxists and the Origins of Bolshevism*, Cambridge, Mass., 1955; D. W. Treadgold, *Lenin and his Rivals*, New York, 1955; L. Schapiro, *The Origin of the Communist Autocracy*, 1955, and 'The Vekhi Group and the Mystique of Revolution,' *Slavonic and East European Review*, vol. xxxiv, No. 82, Dec. 1955; P. Scheibert, *Von Bakunin zu Lenin*, Leiden, 1956; M. B. Petrovich, *The Emergence of Russian Panslavism*, New York, 1956; H. McLean *et al.* (eds.), *Russian Thought and Politics*, Cambridge, Mass., 1957; V. Leontovitsch, *Geschichte des Liberalismus in Russland*, Frankfurt-am-Main, 1957; E. Lampert, *Studies in Rebellion*, 1957; A. Yarmolinsky, *Road to Revolution*, 1957; A. G. Mazour, *Modern Russian Historiography*, 2nd ed., 1958; G. Fischer, *Russian Liberalism*, Cambridge, Mass., 1958; J. H. Billington, *Mikhailovsky and Russian Populism*, 1958; S. V. Utechin, 'Bolsheviks and their Allies after 1917: the Ideological Pattern,' *Soviet Studies*, Oct. 1958, and 'Who Taught Lenin?', *Twentieth Century*, July 1960; F. Venturi, *Roots of Revolution*, 1960.

Politruk (Russian abbreviation for 'Political Leader'), party official responsible for the political education and reliability of troops at company level; at this level he is the equivalent of the Military Commissar (*see* COMMISSAR). Politruks were abolished by Marshal Zhukov in 1957, but reintroduced after his dismissal. *See* Z. Brzezinski (ed.), *Political Controls in the Soviet Army*, New York, 1954.

Polotsk, town in the Vitebsk Oblast (Belorussia), situated on the Western Dvina. Population (1956) 38,100 (16th century, over 100,000; 1914, 31,000; 1933, 25,000). It has varied food and light industries and there are a number of 11th– and 12th–century churches (including the Cathedral of St Sophia, built 1044–66, the third oldest in Russia). Polotsk has been known since 862, and from the 10th century was capital of Polotsk Principality, which maintained independence from Kiev but came under Lithuanian suzerainty in 1307 and was abolished in 1385. In 1772 Polotsk became Russian. In 1941–4 the town was occupied by the Germans and suffered severely from bitter fighting. It was the capital of Polotsk Oblast (now abolished), 1944–54.

Poltava: 1. Oblast in central Ukraine, situated on the left bank of the Dnieper, lowland wooded steppe with chiefly black earth soil. Area 11,200 sq. m.; population (1959) 1,630,000 (30 per cent urban), Ukrainians, before the war also Jews. Wheat, maize, sugar-beet and sunflowers are cultivated, horticulture carried on, cattle and pigs (Mirgorod breed) raised, and there are varied food, metal-working and light industries. Principal towns: Poltava and Kremenchug. The area belonged to Pereyaslavl' Principality, became Lithuanian in 1362, Polish in 1569 and Muscovite in 1667.

2. Administrative, economic and cultural centre of the oblast, situated 70 m. south-west of Khar'kov. Population (1959) 141,000 (1939, 128,000). It has food, textile and engineering industries, and there are interesting buildings of the 17th–19th centuries. Poltava has been known since 1174, during the 17th century was a centre of the Ukrainian Cossacks, and became provincial capital in 1802. It was a flourishing commercial centre in the 18th–19th centuries, and one of the principal centres of the Ukrainian literary and national movement during the 19th century. In 1709 Peter I defeated Charles XII of Sweden and Mazepa (q.v.) in the famous battle of Poltava.

Polytechnical Education, basic concept of the Communist educational theory. According to Marx there should be 'technical instruction which acquaints with the basic principles of all production processes, and at the same time gives to the child or adolescent skill in handling the simplest tools of all branches of industry.' Earlier attempts to introduce polytechnical education in Russia were abandoned in 1937. However, the policy of 'polytechnicalization' was revived in 1952, and the new (1959) curricula of the primary and secondary schools seek to implement the principle of polytechnical education, though obligatory apprenticeship in one particular trade would seem to contradict it. One-third of all school time in the three upper forms (9th–11th) of the general secondary schools is reserved for 'polytechnic' subjects and trade apprenticeship. *See* M. J. Shore, *Soviet Education: its Psychology and Philosophy,* New York, 1947; N. DeWitt, *Soviet Professional Manpower,* Washington, D.C., 1955; A. G. Korol, *Soviet Education for Science and Technology,* 1957; S. V. Utechin, 'Current Problems of Soviet Secondary Education,' *Soviet Survey,* No. 12, Feb. 1957, and 'Khrushchëv's Educational Reform,' ibid., No. 28, April–June 1959; G. Z. F. Bereday and J. Pennar (eds.), *The Politics of Soviet Education,* 1960.

Polzunov, Ivan Ivanovich (1730–66), mechanic who in 1763–6 designed and built the first steam engine in Russia, improving on the Newcomen model. He died shortly before his engine was put into operation; after functioning for two months the engine was damaged and later forgotten.

Pomors ('seashore dwellers'), ethnic group of the Great Russians, living on the shores of the White and Barents seas and the lower courses of the Northern Dvina and Pechora rivers, who are the descendants of medieval Russian colonists (from the 12th century onwards), chiefly from Novgorod. They are seafarers and fishermen. Lomonosov was a Pomor, as also is the well-known Soviet polar navigator V. I. Voronin.

Popov, Aleksandr Stepanovich (1859–1905), physicist and electrotechnician who independently and before Marconi invented radiotelegraphy, demonstrating a receiver in 1895 and a successful transmission in March 1896. Popov's priority was disputed, particularly after his death, but finally established by a special commission in 1908. *See* E. Ashby, *A Scientist in Russia,* 1947.

Population. The total population of the U.S.S.R. was officially estimated at the beginning of 1960 to be 212 million. The following table shows the increase of population since 1913:

		Millions
1913:	present-day frontiers	159·2
	inter-war frontiers	139·3
1926:	census of 17 Dec.	147·0
1939:	census of 15 Jan.	170·6
	estimate including	
	annexations in 1939–40	190·7
1959:	census of 15 Jan.	208·8

Males made up 45 per cent of the population in 1959, as compared to 48 per cent in both 1926 and 1939; in the 31 and under age group they formed 50 per cent, and of the population aged over 31, 37·5 per cent. Birth, death, natural increase (per thousand of population) and infant mortality rates are shown in the following table:

	1913	1940	1950	1958
Births	47·0	31·3	26·7	25·3
Deaths	30·2	18·1	9·7	7·2
Natural increase	16·8	13·2	17·0	18·1
Deaths of infants under 1 year per 1,000 live births	273	184	81	41

The average expectation of life for men has risen from 31 years in 1896–7 to 63 in 1955–6, and for women from 33 years to 69. In 1958 marriages per thousand of population numbered 12·5 and divorces 0·9. The following table shows the change in the age structure of the population between 1939 and 1959:

Age Group	Percentage of Total Population	
	1939	1959
0–9	22·8	22·2
10–15	14·9	8·2
16–19	6·8	7·0
20–24	8·3	9·7
25–29	9·7	8·7
30–34	8·2	9·1
35–39	6·8	5·6
40–44	5·0	5·0
45–49	4·1	5·9
50–59	6·6	9·2
60–69	4·5	5·6
70 and over	2·3	3·8

Urban population formed 48 per cent of the total in 1959, as compared to 18 per cent in 1913 and 1926, and 33 per cent in 1939 (see further under Towns). The average density of the population is 9·4 per square kilometre. The distribution of the population is very uneven. Vast areas in the north of European Russia, in Siberia and Central Asia have less than 1 person per square kilometre, whereas the areas with the densest population have over 150 inhabitants per square kilometre (e.g. Moscow Oblast 232·7, Stalino Oblast in the Donets Basin 160·9, Andizhan Oblast in the Fergana Valley 182·9). Seventy per cent of the total population lives in the European part of the country (excluding the Urals); the great mass is concentrated within the area bounded by the western frontier and a line from Leningrad to the upper Volga, along the Volga to Stalingrad and thence along the Don to the Sea of Azov. Outside this area there are considerable clusters of population only in parts of the Caucasus, the main oases of Central Asia, the industrial areas of the Urals and the Kuznetsk Basin, and along the Trans-Siberian Railway.

The following table shows the distribution by occupation of all occupied persons except students and military personnel (in percentages of the total number of occupied persons):

	1913	1928	1937	1958
Industry and building	9	8	24	31
Agriculture and forestry	75	80	56	42
Transport and communications	2	2	5	7
Trade, catering and supply	9	3	4	5
Education and health services	1	2	5	10
Others	4	5	6	5

Ethnically the population is very diverse, consisting of several dozens of peoples and ethnic groups. They all belong to two of the main races of mankind, the European and the Mongol. The most convenient classification is that based upon language. The majority of the population belongs to the Indo-European family (*see* ARMENIANS; EAST SLAVS; GERMANS; GIPSIES; GREEKS; IRANIANS; LATVIANS; LITHUANIANS; MOLDAVIANS; SLAVS). The next largest linguistic group are the Turkic-speaking peoples (*see* TURKS), followed by the Finns and Caucasians (qq.v.). Smaller linguistic groups are the Mongols, Koreans, Chinese, Tungus, Ugrians, Paleo-Asiatics and Semites (qq.v.). A numerous people who do not fit into the linguistic classification are the Jews (q.v.). The following peoples numbered at least a million in 1959:

Great Russians	114·6 m.	Moldavians	2·2 m.
Ukrainians	37·0 m.	Germans	1·6 m.
Belorussians	7·9 m.	Chuvashes	1·5 m.
Uzbeks	6·0 m.	Latvians	1·4 m.
Tatars	5·0 m.	Tadzhiks	1·4 m.
Kazakhs	3·6 m.	Poles	1·4 m.
Azerbaydzhanis	2·9 m.	Mordva	1·3 m.
Armenians	2·8 m.	Turkmens	1·0 m.
Georgians	2·6 m.	Bashkirs	1·0 m.
Lithuanians	2·3 m.	Kirgiz	1·0 m.
Jews	2·3 m.	Estonians	1·0 m.

See further under ADMINISTRATIVE TERRITORIAL DIVISIONS; CLASSES; RELIGION. *See* F. Lorimer, *The Population of the Soviet Union*, Geneva, 1946; E. M. Kulischer, *Europe on the Move. War and Population Changes, 1917–47*, New York, 1948; G. Jorré, *The Soviet Union, the Land and its People*, 3rd imp., 1955; 'L'U.R.S.S. et sa Population,' *Population*, Paris, June 1958; J. A. Newth, 'The First Press Release on the 1959 Census,' *Soviet Studies*, vol. xi, No. 1, July 1959, 'The Soviet Labour Force in the Fifties,' ibid., No. 4, April 1960, and 'Nationality and Language in the U.S.S.R., 1959,' ibid.; M. K. Roof,

'The Russian Population Enigma Reconsidered,' *Population Studies*, vol. xiv, No. 1, July 1960; G. V. Selegin, 'The First Report on the Recent Population Census in the Soviet Union,' ibid.

Populism (*narodnichestvo*), ideological and political movement which emerged among the radical intelligentsia during the 1860's; its harbingers were Herzen and Chernyshevskiy (qq.v.), who believed that with its peasant communes (*see* MIR) Russia could attain socialism by means of a peasant revolution, escaping the capitalist stage. During the 1870's revolutionary Populism was especially strong, and over a thousand students went to the countryside ('into the people'—hence the name) as propagandists. The majority of them were adherents of Bakunin's view that the peasants were ready to rise against the State and the landlords, though some (e.g. Chaykovskiy, q.v.) followed Lavrov in holding that an adequate number of peasant leaders must first be trained. In 1876 a predominantly Bakuninist underground organization Land and Freedom was founded, but it had little success and in 1879 split into the Narodnaya Volya (q.v.), accepting P. N. Tkachëv's 'Jacobin' views on the seizure of State power by a revolutionary minority, and the Chërnyy Peredel (q.v.) (i.e. universal distribution of the land), which remained Bakuninist and was led by Plekhanov. Alexander II was assassinated by the former organization (led by A. Zhelyabov), whereupon it was broken up by the police, though scattered and unconnected groups existed throughout the 1880's and early nineties. The Chërnyy Peredel, in collaboration with some Lavrovist groups, gave birth to the Russian social democratic movement.

The predominating trend during the 1880's and nineties was Liberal Populism, whose leader, Mikhaylovskiy, emphasized the humanitarian and evolutionary elements in the teachings of Herzen and Lavrov, and whose followers in local government (*see* ZEMSTVO) did splendid practical work among the peasants. The liberal and the revived revolutionary trends combined in 1902 in the party of Socialist Revolutionaries (q.v.), but both tendencies continued, resulting in several splits and the formation of minor parties (moderate Popular Socialists and Maximalists in 1905, Left Socialist Revolutionaries in 1917). Lenin was much influenced by the Tkachëv tradition, which became an integral part of Leninism (q.v.), while the Neo-Populists (q.v.) carried on the Liberal Populist tradition. *See* T. G. Masaryk, *The Spirit of Russia* (2 vols.), 2nd ed., 1955; J. H. Billington, *Mikhailovsky and Russian Populism*, 1958; F. Venturi, *The Roots of Revolution*, 1960.

Port Arthur, town, ice-free port and an important naval base in Manchuria, at the southern end of Liaotung Peninsula. Russian naval base from 1898, Port Arthur fell to the Japanese during the Russo-Japanese War (q.v.), causing a serious loss of prestige to the Russian Government. It was ceded to Japan, but in 1945 again occupied by Russians. The Soviet Government secured the renewal of concession in 1945 and 1950, but was obliged to return the base to the Chinese in 1955.

Positivism is a strong trend in Russian epistemology, greatly influenced by Comte, Buckle, Mill and Spencer. It began with Herzen,

Chernyshevskiy and Pisarev, and was later represented by Lavrov, Mikhaylovskiy and Lesevich (qq.v.). Many outstanding Russian scientists (e.g. I. I. Mechnikov, V. I. Vernadskiy, qq.v.) also adhered to Positivism. In official Soviet works on the history of Russian philosophy Positivism is often represented as Materialism (q.v.). *See* N. Lossky, *History of Russian Philosophy*, 1951; V. V. Zenkovsky, *A History of Russian Philosophy* (2 vols.), 1953.

Pososhkov, Ivan Tikhonovich (1652–1726), economist, a peasant by birth who became a rich factory owner. In his *Book on Scarcity and Wealth* (written 1724) he put forward plans for economic reforms based upon the teaching of the Mercantilist school. He also advocated judicial reform and representative government. After the death of Peter the Great Pososhkov was arrested and died a prisoner.

Pospelov, Pëtr Nikolayevich (*b.* 1898), Communist Party official. He joined the party in 1916 and worked in various provincial party organizations until 1924, when he was transferred to Moscow. There he worked in the apparatus of the Central Committee, studying Marxism-Leninism at courses attached to the Communist Academy and at the Red Professorship Institute; he later became a member of the editorial boards of *Pravda* and *Bolshevik*, and in 1934 a member of the Committee of Party Control (q.v.). During the Great Purge (q.v.) in 1937 he became deputy head of the Agitation and Propaganda Department of the Central Committee, in 1939 a member of the Central Committee, in 1940 editor of *Pravda* and in 1949 Director of the Institute of Marxism-Leninism. After Stalin's death in 1953 Pospelov became a secretary of the Central Committee and in 1957 a candidate member of its Presidium. He was made a member of the U.S.S.R. Academy of Sciences in 1953.

Postal Services are administered by the U.S.S.R. Ministry of Communications. In 1958 there were 60,000 post and telegraph offices and telephone exchanges (including 47,000 in rural localities). There were 2·4 million telephones (0·3 in rural areas). In the same year 3,985 million letters were sent, 88 million parcels, and 223 million telegrams. The beginnings of a State postal system, by horse courier, were introduced in Russia in the 13th century following the Mongol conquest, and it was properly organized by the mid 17th century. In 1874 Russia joined the International Postal Union.

Potanin, Grigoriy Nikolayevich (1835–1920), traveller, geographer and politician, one of the main representatives of Siberian Regionalism (q.v.). He was included on a respected figure in the anti-Bolshevik Siberian Government in 1918.

Potebnya, Aleksandr Afanas'yevich (1835–91), outstanding Ukrainian philologist. Educated at Khar'kov University, he was professor there from 1875 and a corresponding member of the Academy of Sciences from 1877. Potebnya was the founder of the psychological school in Russian linguistics, and published many works on general linguistics (*Thought and Language*, 1862; 5th ed., 1926), historical syntax, semantics, etymology, phonetics, dialects and folklore.

Potëmkin, Prince Grigoriy Aleksandrovich (1739–91), statesman and favourite of Catherine II, of obscure origin. He was Viceroy of New

Russia (q.v.) from 1774, field marshal and president of the War Department from 1784. He persuaded the Crimean Khan to abdicate in Catherine's favour in 1783, and the Crimea was annexed to Russia. The expression 'Potëmkin villages' originated from Catherine's visit to New Russia in 1787, when Potëmkin erected fake villages in order to make the area appear more populated than in fact it was. *See* G. Soloveytchik, *Potëmkin, a Picture of Catherine's Russia*, 2nd ed., New York, 1949.

Poti (ancient **Phasis**), seaport in Georgia, on the Black Sea at the mouth of the River Rioni, the centre of Colchis. Population (1956) 42,500 (1939, 16,000). It has food and engineering industries, and since the 1880's has been the port for exporting manganese from Chiatura. Poti has been known since the 5th century B.C., when it was a Greek colony; it was a Turkish fortress until captured by the Russians in 1828.

Potresov, Aleksandr Nikolayevich (1869–1934), Social Democrat who collaborated with Lenin in the Iskra (q.v.) organization but was soon repelled by his opportunism and lack of moral principles in politics. He became leader of the right-wing Mensheviks (*see* LIQUIDATIONISM) after the revolution of 1905 (q.v.), but refused to join the Menshevik Party after the October revolution of 1917 because he held that its policy of opposing the Bolsheviks only by legal means was too circumscribed. In 1927 he emigrated and continued active opposition to the Bolshevik system.

Potsdam Conference, held at Potsdam 16th July–1st August 1945 between Churchill and Attlee (Britain), Truman (U.S.A.) and Stalin (U.S.S.R.) in order to determine the future of Germany after her unconditional surrender on 7th May 1945. The agreement arising from the conference provided: (1) that a committee of foreign ministers of Britain, France, the U.S.A., China and the U.S.S.R. should be set up to work out peace treaties with Germany's allies; (2) that the commanders-in-chief of Britain, France, the U.S.A. and the U.S.S.R. should exercise supreme authority in their respective zones of Germany, and should act jointly in the control council on matters affecting all Germany; (3) that Germany should be disarmed and demilitarized, that Nazism should be wiped out and the German people re-educated on democratic lines, and that no central German government should for the moment be set up; (4) that a part of East Prussia with Königsberg should be transferred to the U.S.S.R., and the Oder-Neisse line be made the provisional western frontier of Poland; (5) that war criminals should be brought to trial.

Prague Conference, of 1912, *see* LENIN.

'Pravda' (*Truth*), daily newspaper, chief organ of the Communist Party. It has been issued since 1912, save for the years 1914–1917 when war-time censorship banned it because of its defeatist policy. Among its chief editors have been Stalin, Bukharin and Shepilov. *Pravda* editorials normally serve in Russia as a guide to the current 'party line,' and the rest of the press is obliged to follow its editorial policy, though since the post-Stalin 'thaw' some newspapers and journals have shown a certain degree of independence. Present circulation (1957) 5·5 million.

Pre-Parliament, colloquial name for the Temporary Council of the Republic which was established by the Democratic Conference prior to the Bolshevik seizure of power in 1917. It acted as a consultative body to the Provisional Government (q.v.) and was entitled to question ministers. *See* A. J. Sack, *The Birth of the Russian Democracy,* New York, 1918; F. A. Golder, *Documents of Russian History, 1914–17,* 1927; W. H. Chamberlin, *The Russian Revolution,* vol. i, 1935.

Presidium: 1. Of the Communist Party's **Central Committee:** the chief policy-making body in the U.S.S.R. It replaced the Politburo (q.v.), which Stalin abolished in 1952. At first there was an inner Bureau of the Presidium, which was in fact the equivalent of the former Politburo, but immediately after Stalin's death this was abolished, and the Presidium itself, reduced in numbers, took its place. Since then the history of the Presidium has been one of struggle between rival cliques and individuals (the downfall of Beria in 1953, the ousting of Malenkov as Premier in 1955, the expulsion of the 'anti-party group,' q.v., and of Marshal Zhukov in 1957–8, and of Kirichenko and Belyayev in 1960), and of the gradual consolidation of Khrushchëv's power. However, the Presidium clearly plays a more active role than did the Politburo under Stalin after 1934. It now consists of 15 members: Voroshilov, since 1926, Mikoyan, 1935, Khrushchëv, 1939, Suslov, 1955, also 1952–3, Shvernik, 1957, also 1952–3, Aristov, 1957, also 1952–3, Kuusinen, 1957, also 1952–3, Brezhnev, 1957, Ignatov, 1957, Furtseva, 1957, Kozlov, 1957, Mukhitdinov, 1957, Kosygin, 1960, also 1948–52, Podgornyy, 1960, and Polyanskiy, 1960; and of 6 candidate members: Korotchenko, since 1957, Kalnberzin, 1957, Kirilenko, 1957, Mazurov, 1957, Mzhavanadze, 1957, and Pospelov, 1957. Nearly all of these are professional party officials, whereas Malenkov's policy during his ascendance was to shift the balance in favour of economic administrators. *See* M. Rush, *The Rise of Khrushchëv,* Washington, D.C., 1958; M. Fainsod, 'What Happened to "Collective Leadership"?', *Problems of Communism,* vol. viii, No. 4, July–Aug. 1959.

2. Of the Supreme Soviet of the U.S.S.R.: a body which since the adoption of the Stalin constitution in 1936 has played the constitutional role of head of state, replacing the earlier Central Executive Committee (q.v.). The Presidium is formally elected at a joint meeting of both chambers of the Supreme Soviet. Between the sessions of the Supreme Soviet the Presidium issues ordinances (*see* Ukaze), often on important matters, thus playing a major role in legislation. Ceremonial functions are performed by the Chairman of the Presidium (1936–45 Kalinin, 1945–53 Shvernik, 1953–60 Voroshilov, since 1960 Brezhnev). There are also presidiums of the Supreme Soviets of the Union and Autonomous Republics.

Press: *Books.* The number of book titles published in Russia in 1913 was 26,912 (within present-day frontiers; 26,174 within the inter-war frontiers); it fell to 14,825 in 1923, rose to 54,646 in 1931, fell to 37,647 in 1937, rose to 45,830 in 1940, fell to 18,353 in 1945; from 1948 to 1953 it oscillated between 40,000 and 43,000, and thereafter rose rapidly, reaching 64,000 in 1958. The total number of copies published rose from 89 million in 1913 to 867 million in 1930, fell to 463 million in 1935, reached another pre-war maximum of 715 million in 1939, fell sharply in 1940 to 462 million, and has risen almost consistently in the post-war period from 298 million in 1945 to 1,103 million in 1958. Of the total number of titles published in 1955 slightly over 10 per cent were fiction, but of total copies 28 per cent were fiction. In 1956 books were published in 122 languages, including 36 foreign languages. The following table shows a comparison of the number of titles published in 1913 and 1958 in some of the main languages of Russia.

	1913	*1958*
Russian	23,805	45,312
Tatar	340	317
Armenian	257	951
Georgian	232	1,432
Ukrainian	228	3,980
Azerbaydzhani	91	780
Chuvash	56	205
Kazakh	40	640
Uzbek	37	810
Belorussian	2	481

Periodicals. The following tables show the number and circulation of newspapers and of journals and magazines in selected years.

Newspapers:	*1913* [1]	*1934*	*1937*	*1950*	*1958*
Titles	1,055	10,668	8,521	7,831	10,463
Circulation [2]	3·3 m.	34·7 m.	36·2 m.	36·0 m.	59·0 m.

Journals and Magazines:	*1913* [1]	*1932*	*1939*	*1954*	*1958*
Titles	1,472	2,144	1,592	1,718	3,824
Circulation [3]	—	318 m.	254 m.	306 m.	637 m.

Newspapers, journals and magazines are published in over 50 languages (against 14 in 1913). Newspapers and other periodicals are published by the Communist Party, the Komsomol, trade unions, governmental bodies, professional associations and learned institutions. The leading daily newspapers are *Pravda* and *Izvestiya* (qq.v.); other important newspapers are *Trud* (the organ of the trade unions), *Komsomol'skaya Pravda* (published by the Komsomol, q.v.), the *Literary Gazette* (q.v.) and the *Red Star* (published by the Ministry of Defence). The main journals are *Kommunist* (q.v.), the literary monthly *Novyy Mir* (q.v.), the illustrated weekly magazine *Ogonëk* (circulation, 1955, 1 million), the humorous magazine *Krokodil* (q.v.) and the women's magazine *Rabotnitsa* (circulation, 1955, 1·2 million).

Printing began in Russia in 1563 (*see* FËDOROV, I. F.). The first newspaper was started in 1702 and the first mass circulation popular daily in 1876. Serious and humorous journals began to appear in the 1760's. Clandestine and *émigré* publications existed from the 1840's, exercising a considerable influence. Most newspapers before the

---

[1] Present-day frontiers.   [2] Per issue.   [3] Per annum.

Bolshevik seizure of power were privately owned, and usually represented a more or less definite political trend; all of them except the Bolshevik *Pravda* (founded 1912) were suppressed after the October revolution (q.v.); most journals were also suppressed, but a few scientific ones were permitted to continue. Lenin considered the press one of the chief tools of the party and all aspects of publishing are under strict party control, editors being in fact appointed by the cadres (q.v.) departments of the party committees. Most contemporary *émigré* (q.v.) political groups publish their own newspapers and journals, some of which reach readers in the U.S.S.R. *See also* CENSORSHIP. *See* A. Inkeles, *Public Opinion in Soviet Russia*, Cambridge, Mass., 1950; L. Gruliow, 'How the Soviet Newspaper Operates,' *Problems of Communism*, vol. v, No. 2, 1956; International Press Institute, *The Press in Authoritarian Countries*, Zürich-New York, 1959; B. I. Gorokhoff, *Publishing in the U.S.S.R.*, Bloomington, Indiana, 1959; Yu. Saltanov, 'Publication in the Humanities' in D. Grant's (ed.) *The Humanities in Soviet Higher Education*, Toronto, 1960.

Pressure Groups play an important role in the political life of the U.S.S.R., since, because of the political monopoly of the Communist Party, different interests cannot organize themselves into separate political parties, and such interests as do receive consideration achieve this through informal pressure. It is often possible to identify representatives of special interests within such seats of power as the Central Committee of the party and its Presidium (qq.v.), and such ceremonial gatherings as the party congresses and the Supreme Soviet (q.v.). In most cases pressure groups are based on and operate through existing parts of the power apparatus. The main pressure groups at present are the party apparatus, the economic management (*see* MANAGERIAL CLASS), the armed forces, the security organs, scientists and the 'intellectual opposition' (q.v.), while the government apparatus, the trade union bureaucracy, the leadership of the Komsomol and the religious bodies play a less important role. Nationalist tendencies find their expression through any or all of these organized pressure groups. Since Stalin's death pressure groups have had greater scope than previously for evolving and expressing their views. *See* R. Bauer, A. Inkeles and C. Kluckhohn, *How the Soviet System Works*, Cambridge, Mass., 1956.

Prices. The price system in the Soviet Union is very complex, and only the principal types of price can be dealt with. For most capital goods there are unified State wholesale prices which are charged to State enterprises and institutions. These so-called 'branch' prices are not necessarily identical with those paid to producers, the latter in some branches to some extent varying according to cost of production. A small rate of profit is included in the price, and for a few commodities, such as oil, also the turnover tax (q.v.). Such capital goods as go into retail trade, e.g. some building materials, paints, etc., are treated for pricing purposes like manufactured consumer goods (q.v.). There are two kinds of State wholesale prices for most manufactured consumer goods: those paid to the producer by the wholesale trading organizations and those paid to the latter by retail trade organizations, the difference being due to the turnover tax and discount. State retail prices for these goods are calculated as the price paid by retail organization plus fixed gross profit. The majority of these retail prices are determined by the central government, but since the mid 1950's an increasing number have been fixed by the governments of the Union Republics. Prices of some goods produced by local industry (q.v.) or by producers' co-operatives (q.v.) are fixed either by the local authorities or by the co-operative unions.

There are three kinds of State wholesale prices for agricultural products: (1) purchase price paid to the *kolkhozes*; (2) delivery price paid to the *sovkhozes*; (3) unified prices paid by State enterprises to the State, which include the gross profit of the procurement organizations (*see* AGRICULTURAL PROCUREMENT). Prices of goods sold in the *kolkhoz* market (q.v.) are not regulated by the State and depend upon supply and demand, but they are influenced by the available supply of goods in State and co-operative shops.

Since the present system of wholesale prices was introduced in 1928, two upward price revisions have taken place, in 1936 and 1949, on both occasions following the establishment of new retail prices after the end of rationing (q.v.). Since 1949 the policy has been one of systematic lowering of retail prices rather than of increasing wages (q.v.). For the index of retail prices *see* RETAIL TRADE. *See* H. Schwartz, *Russia's Soviet Economy*, 2nd ed., 1954.

Primary Organization, official name of the party organizations at the lowest level. They are formed at enterprises, institutions and organizations, and not on the territorial principle, but are subordinated to the rayon (q.v.) party committee. At least three party members are necessary to form a Primary Organization, and those with more than ten members have an elected bureau (very large organizations have a committee). Party guidance and control over the life of the country is largely exercised through the Primary Organizations.

Pripet (Russian **Pripyat'**, Belorussian and Polish **Prypec**), navigable river in southern Belorussia and north-western Ukraine, a right tributary of the Dnieper which it joins near Kiev. Length 500 m. The Pripet flows through a marshy area (the Pripet Marshes, *see* POLES'YE) which saw much fighting in both world wars.

Prishvin, Mikhail Mikhaylovich (1873–1954), writer, naturalist and ethnographer. He unites in his works brilliant descriptions of nature and life with a subtle message of the ethics of love and creativeness. Main works: *In the Land of Unfrightened Birds*, 1907; *The Calendar of Nature*, 1923, *The Springs of Berendey*, 1925, *Root of Life*, 1932, *Tree Drippings*, 1940, *The Larder of the Sun*, 1943, and the autobiographical novel *The Chain of Kashchey*, 1930.

Prisons in the Soviet penal system (q.v.) are considered places of detention for those sentenced to deprivation of freedom for 'particularly dangerous crimes.' They have been administered by the Ministry (former Commissariat) of Internal Affairs (*see* M.V.D.) since 1934 with a short interval after the fall of Beria in 1953 when they were transferred to the Ministries of Justice (q.v.); before 1934 they had also been administered by the Commissariat of Justice.

Statistics of prisoners have not been published for many years, but available evidence suggests that prisons are often overcrowded; during the collectivization of agriculture and the Great Purge (qq.v.) the overcrowding reached fantastic degrees. A separate category are 'prisons of special purpose' (*see* ISOLATOR) administered by the Committee of State Security (*see* K.G.B.). *See* W. W. Kulski, *The Soviet Regime*, Syracuse, 1954; S. Wolin and R. M. Slusser (eds.), *The Soviet Secret Police*, New York, 1957.

Private Enterprise, *see* ARTISANS; CONCESSIONS; NATIONALIZATION OF INDUSTRY; NEW ECONOMIC POLICY; PEASANTS; SPECULATORS.

Procuracy, State agency (created in 1922 within the Commissariats of Justice of the Union Republics) with comprehensive functions of supervising the legality of actions of all organs exercising public authority, including the courts and places of confinement, and of prosecuting in criminal cases. Since 1936 the procuracy has been organized on a strictly centralized pattern, all republic and local procurators being appointed by and subordinated to the Procurator-General of the U.S.S.R., who is appointed by the Presidium of the Supreme Soviet. Like all other State organs, the procuracy is controlled by the Communist Party at all levels. The procuracy has failed to protect the rights of individuals against the State, the procurators themselves being subject to party discipline and the terror of the organs of State security, while Vyshinskiy, as Procurator-General, took an active part in perfecting the system of terror. A new (1955) statute on the procuracy is designed to strengthen its position, especially in relation to the security organs, whose actions it is meant to supervise. Procuracy was first introduced in Russia by Peter the Great with the functions of general supervision. The judicial reform of 1864 transformed it into an organ of criminal prosecution. It was abolished in 1918 but re-established in 1922 with both functions. *See* J. Towster, *Political Power in the U.S.S.R., 1917-47*, New York, 1948; H. J. Berman, *Justice in Russia*, Cambridge, Mass., 1950; M. Fainsod, *How Russia is Ruled*, Cambridge, Mass., 1953, and *Smolensk under Soviet Rule*, 1959; W. W. Kulski, *The Soviet Regime*, Syracuse, 1954; J. N. Hazard, *The Soviet System of Government*, Chicago, 1957; D. A. Loeber, 'The Soviet Procuracy and the Rights of the Individual against the State,' *Journal of the International Commission of Jurists*, vol. i, No. 1, The Hague, autumn 1957; N. S. Timasheff, 'The Procurators' Office in the U.S.S.R.,' *Law in Eastern Europe*, No. 1, Leyden, 1958; G. G. Morgan, 'The Procuracy's "General Supervision" Function,' *Soviet Studies*, vol. xi, No. 2, Oct. 1959.

Productivity of Labour in the most efficient industrial enterprises is comparable to that in similar enterprises of the advanced countries in the West. At the other end of the scale is productivity of labour in agriculture, which is usually very low by standards of modern agriculture. The output of pig-iron per worker in blast-furnace shops was 2,518 tons in 1958, that of steel per worker in the open-hearth shops was 1,133 tons and that of rolled metal per worker in rolling shops was 391 tons. The average (pit and opencast mining) monthly extraction of coal per worker in the coal industry was 40 tons. The average productivity of labour in mining and manufacturing industries as a whole in 1958 was about ten times that of 1913, and had increased by 721 per cent over that of 1928, by 140 per cent over 1940 and by 74 per cent over 1950; in building the corresponding figures were 477 per cent over 1928, 130 per cent over 1940 and 88 per cent over 1950; on the railways it was 435 per cent, 99 per cent and 81 per cent. The yearly rate of increase in the mining and manufacturing industries as a whole has been 6–8 per cent during the 1950's. The productivity of labour in the *kolkhozes* (excluding work on personal plots of members) was in 1958 70 per cent above that in 1940, 72 per cent above 1950 and 48 per cent above 1953; in *sovkhozes* and other State agricultural enterprises it was 43 per cent higher than in 1940, 56 per cent higher than in 1950 and 35 per cent higher than in 1953. See *Comparisons of the U.S. and Soviet Economies* (Joint Economic Committee, 86th Congress, 1st Session), Washington, D.C., 1959.

Professional Associations exist in the U.S.S.R. in order to integrate into the system of party control (*see* COMMUNIST PARTY) professional people, particularly those who are not employees and therefore do not belong to the trade unions (q.v.). Like the trade unions, the professional associations have the double function of caring for the interests of their members and ensuring their conformity. The most important is the Writers' Union (q.v.); others are the unions of Composers, of Artists, of Architects and of Journalists, and the All-Russian Theatrical Society (and similar societies in the other Union Republics). There are no professional associations for doctors or lawyers. *See also* SOCIETIES.

Profits. Apart from the profits of *kolkhozes* and other co-operatives, which are residual, profits, like all other economic categories, are planned, a small rate of profit being included in the State wholesale and retail prices. Profits in excess of the planned profits may be made by lowering costs. A part of the profits may be retained for the Director's Fund (q.v.), and the rest is taken by the State and is in fact a profits tax. The main purpose of operating with profits in State enterprises is to allow a margin of safety in the enterprises' finances and to give an incentive (*see* INCENTIVES) to management and employees. *See* D. Granick, *Management of the Industrial Firm in the U.S.S.R.*, New York, 1955.

Progressive Party, political party formed in 1912 through the fusion of the Party of Peaceful Renovation and the Party of Democratic Reforms. Before the fusion deputies of both parties had formed one parliamentary group in the 3rd Duma; the party had 36 deputies in the 3rd Duma and about 50 in the 4th; among its leaders were P. P. Ryabushinskiy, M. M. Kovalevskiy (qq.v.) and A. I. Konovalov. Its members were mainly progressive business men and liberal intellectuals, and the party occupied a position between the Constitutional Democrats and the Octobrists (qq.v.), aiming at the fusion of all three into one liberal party capable of forming a strong government backed by a solid majority in the Duma. During the First World War the Progressive Party joined the Progressive Bloc (*see* CONSTITUTIONAL DEMOCRATS); many of its supporters took an active part in the War Industries Committees. After the February revolution (q.v.) in 1917 several leaders of the Progressive Party entered the Provisional Government (q.v.). The party was suppressed by the Bolsheviks in 1918.

Prokof'yev, Sergey Sergeyevich (1891–1953), brilliant pianist and prolific composer, who studied under Rimsky-Korsakov, Lyadov, Cherepnin, Glazunov and Glière at the St Petersburg Conservatory, 1904–15. In 1918 he undertook a world tour, appearing as conductor-performer of his own works, and finally returned to Russia in 1933. His compositions, numbering more than a hundred, include eight operas (among them *The Love for Three Oranges*, 1919; *The Fiery Angel*, 1927; *War and Peace*, 1942); seven ballets (e.g. *Chout*, 1915–20; *Le Pas d'Acier*, 1925; *The Prodigal Son*, 1928; *Romeo and Juliet*, 1936); seven symphonies; five piano concertos; two violin concertos; two cello concertos; numerous works for soloists, chorus and orchestra (including *Seven, They are Seven*, 1917, and *Alexander Nevsky*, 1938—the latter first appearing as the incidental music to the film of the same name); chamber works; piano works; sonatas for different instruments; songs; choruses; orchestral works (*Scythian Suite*, 1915, originally the ballet suite *Ala and Lolly*; *Lieutenant Kizhe*, 1934, originally film music); music for plays (*Boris Godunov*, 1936; *Eugene Onegin*, 1936; *Hamlet*, 1938); film music (*The Queen of Spades*, 1936; *Ivan the Terrible*, two parts, 1942–5; *Lermontov*, 1943).

Prokof'yev has divided the elements of his style into five categories: classicism, innovation, the 'motor-element,' lyricism and grotesqueness (or good-natured irony). A diverse yet original composer, his music shows remarkable consistency. He values form as one of the great essentials of music. His early works are iconoclastic, the later mellowed with experience. Together with Shostakovich he is regarded as one of the leading Soviet composers. The ballet *Romeo and Juliet* introduced a new psychological force into that *genre*, so that even when divorced from its context the music nevertheless suggests the action by its intense emotional power. *See* his *Autobiography, Articles and Reminiscences*, Moscow, s.a.

Prokopovich, Sergey Nikolayevich (1871–1955), economist and politician. A Marxist and Social Democrat in the 1890's, Prokopovich, with his wife Kuskova (q.v.), later, under the influence of Bernstein's ideas, headed the genuine Economist (*see* ECONOMISM) trend in Russian social democracy. In 1905 he took an active part in the formation of the Constitutional Democratic Party and was a member of its central committee, but soon left the party and took up a position between it and the socialist parties. He was one of the founders of the trade unions (q.v.) and also active in the co-operative movement. Though not a Duma member, Prokopovich and his circle exercised a strong influence upon the Labour Group (*see* TRUDOVIKS). In 1917 he became Minister of Food in Kerenskiy's government, being at the time a member of the Popular Socialist Party. Though he was against the Bolshevik seizure of power (*see* OCTOBER REVOLUTION), he disapproved of violent methods, and during the civil war devoted himself entirely to the co-operative movement. Expelled from Russia in 1922 together with other leading intellectuals, he confined himself thereafter to the academic study of the Soviet economy, and during the inter-war period his institute in Prague was the leading institution in this field. *See* his *Histoire économique de l'U.R.S.S.* (trans. M. Body), Paris, 1952.

Prokopovich, Theophan (1681–1736), Ukrainian theologian and Church dignitary. Having completed his education in Rome he taught at the theological academy in Kiev and became its rector. In 1716 he was called by Peter the Great to St Petersburg and, as Archbishop of Pskov, being an enthusiastic supporter of the Petrine idea of the Russian Empire, took an active part in Peter's reforms, both within the Church (*see* HOLY SYNOD) and in the civil administration.

Prokop'yevsk, city in the Kemerovo Oblast (southern Siberia), situated in the Stalinsk conurbation. Population (1959) 282,000 (second in the Kuznetsk Basin; 1926, 11,000; 1939, 107,000). It is the largest coal-mining centre in the Kuznetsk Basin (high-grade coking coal), and has engineering (mining equipment) and various food and light industries. Prokop'yevsk was founded as a coal-mining settlement in 1918 and became a town in 1931; its growth is partly the result of the fusion of neighbouring settlements, and it now stretches along the railway for a distance of 15 miles.

Proletariat, in Marxist theory, is the exploited class of capitalist society which lives by the sale of its labour. A proletarian revolution is supposed to overthrow the rule of the bourgeoisie (q.v.) and to establish a Dictatorship of the Proletariat (q.v.) as a transitory stage to the establishment of full communism. Lenin added to this doctrine the theory that a necessary condition for the proletariat carrying out its role was the existence of a highly centralized revolutionary party to organize and lead the proletarian masses; in his view the proletariat was itself unable to build such a party or to evolve the necessary theory, and left to itself the proletariat was only capable of producing trade unionism. These general notions on the proletariat and its historical role obscured for Russian Marxists and Leninists the actual conditions and aspirations of the working class, and led to the paradoxical situation of the Communist dictatorship being a dictatorship over the working as well as other classes in the name of the proletariat. *See* R. N. Carew Hunt, *A Guide to Communist Jargon*, 1957.

Proletkul't (Russian abbreviation for 'Proletarian Cultural and Educational Organizations'), organization established after the February revolution of 1917 by Bogdanovists (*see* BOGDANOVISM) with the intention of producing a proletarian culture as an indispensable basis for a socialist revolution. It became widely influential after the October revolution, and until 1919 remained independent of the Soviet Government and the Communist Party; it was then subordinated to the Commissariat of Education, transferred to the trade unions in 1925, and eventually abolished in 1932. *See* G. Struve, *Soviet Russian Literature, 1917–50*, Norman, Oklahoma, 1951; M. Slonim, *Modern Russian Literature*, 1953.

Propaganda, in Communist theory, is distinguished from agitation in that the latter is concerned with arousing the emotions necessary for a desired course of action, whereas propaganda aims at conveying the more abstract ideas and theories. Communist propaganda is devoted to the elucidation and propagation of the Marxist-Leninist theory in its current interpretation (*see* IDEOLOGY), which in fact means the spreading of the myths and fictions (qq.v.) considered useful by the party leadership at a given time. All cultural and educational activities, except the religious, are supposed to be the vehicles of Communist propaganda in the Soviet Union (*see* COMMUNIST PARTY; TOTALITARIANISM), and the entire propaganda effort is directed by special departments of the party committees on all levels. Propaganda work is generally considered second in importance only to cadres (q.v.) work. *See* A. Inkeles, *Public Opinion in Soviet Russia*, Cambridge, Mass., 1950; M. Fainsod, *How Russia is Ruled*, Cambridge, Mass., 1953; A. Inkeles and R. A. Bauer, *The Soviet Citizen*, 1959; H. McClosky and J. E. Turner, *The Soviet Dictatorship*, 1960.

Property, *see* OWNERSHIP.

Prosecutor, *see* PROCURACY.

Proskurov, *see* KHMEL'NITSKIY.

Protazanov, Yakov Aleksandrovich (1881–1945), one of the greatest pre-revolutionary film directors. Starting his career in 1910, he had made eighty films by 1918, including *War and Peace*, 1915, *The Queen of Spades*, 1916, and *Father Sergius*, 1917–18. He emigrated in 1918 but returned to Russia in 1922, and under the Soviet regime made fifteen films, including *His Call*, 1925, about party enrolment, the satire *The Three Millions*, 1926, *The Forty-First*, 1926, *Don Diego and Pelagea*, 1928, and the anti-religious *Feast of St Jorgen*, 1930. Protazanov encouraged many stage actors to enter films. From 1936 until his death he worked in the Yerevan studios in Armenia.

Provisional Government was established after the abdication of Nicholas II and his brother in March 1917, headed first by Prince L'vov, then by Kerenskiy (qq.v.). Made up of liberals and moderate socialists, the government attempted to achieve its main tasks of carrying on the war and convening a Constituent Assembly (q.v.); it was hampered from the left by the soviets and from the right (*see* KORNILOV), underrated the dangers of a Bolshevik coup and was unable to face them adequately, and was overthrown on 7th November. *See* A. J. Sack, *The Birth of the Russian Democracy*, 1918; F. A. Golder, *Documents of Russian History, 1914–17*, 1927; P. N. Milyukov, *Vospominaniya, 1859–1917* (eds. M. M. Karpovich and B. I. Elkin) (2 vols.), New York, 1955.

Prut, left tributary of the Danube, rising in the Carpathian Mountains and flowing south-east to join the Danube near Galati, forming the frontier between Rumania and the U.S.S.R. Length 590 m. In 1944 it was the scene of much fighting.

Pryanishnikov, Dmitriy Nikolayevich (1865–1948), agrochemist and agrobiologist, professor of Moscow University and Moscow Agricultural Academy, member of the Academy of Sciences. His works were mainly concerned with problems of plant feeding and the use of artificial fertilizers. He is chiefly known for his study of nitrogen circulation in plants.

Przheval'skiy (Przewalski), Nikolay Mikhaylovich (1839–88), traveller and geographer of Polish origin. A regular officer in the Russian Army (he passed through the Military Academy in St

Petersburg and rose to the rank of major-general), Przheval'skiy was greatly influenced by Semënov-Tyan-Shanskiy (q.v.), who inspired and organized Przheval'skiy's five expeditions—one to the Ussuri area in the Russian Far East, 1867–9, and four to Mongolia, Sinkiang and Tibet, 1870–85. He studied the orography (e.g. establishing the predominantly latitudinal direction of the mountain ranges), climate, flora and fauna (discovering the wild horse named after him) of these regions, and brought back large botanical and zoological collections. He was elected an honorary member of the Academy of Sciences in 1878.

Pskov: 1. Oblast of the R.S.F.S.R., situated south-west of Leningrad adjacent to Lake Chudskoye, lowland with many lakes and swamps and partly covered by mixed forests. Area 22,500 sq. m.; population (1959) 954,000 (27 per cent urban), Russians, some Estonians and Latvians. Flax is cultivated and dairy farming carried on. Principal towns: Pskov, Velikiye Luki, Pechory. The area formed part of the Novgorod Republic in the 11th–14th centuries, becoming independent in 1348 and being absorbed by Muscovy in 1510.

2. Administrative, cultural and an economic centre of the oblast. Population (1959) 81,000. It has linen-milling, agricultural and textile engineering, and food industries, and is an important railway junction. There are many notable architectural monuments of the 12th–17th centuries. Pskov was known from 903 as an outpost of Novgorod, was capital of the Pskov Republic, 1348–1510, and then a Muscovite fortress. It was the leading centre of trade with Western Europe until the building of St Petersburg. The town was occupied and largely destroyed, 1941–4.

Psychology. See BLONSKIY; CHELPANOV; KAVELIN; KORKUNOV; KORNILOV, K. N.; LESEVICH; LOPATIN; ORBELI; PAVLOV, I. P.; PETRAZHITSKIY; REYSNER; SECHENOV; UKHTOMSKIY; VYSHESLAVTSEV. See C. Murchison (ed.), *Psychologies of 1930*, Worcester, Mass., 1930; V. M. Bechterev, *General Principles of Human Reflexology*, 1933; H. J. Berman and D. H. Hunt, 'Criminal Law and Psychiatry: The Soviet Solution,' *Stanford Law Review*, vol. ii, No. 4, July 1950; I. D. London, 'Psychology in the U.S.S.R.,' *American Journal of Psychology*, vol. lxiv, 1951; J. Wortis, *Soviet Psychiatry*, Baltimore, 1950; R. A. Bauer, *The New Man in Soviet Psychology*, Cambridge, Mass., 1952; B. Simon (ed.), *Psychology in the Soviet Union*, 1957.

Publishing, see PRESS.

Pudovkin, Vsevolod Illarionovich (1893–1953), film director. Before the First World War he studied chemistry at Moscow University, then served in the army and was a prisoner of war in Germany. He was a pupil of Kuleshov (q.v.) in the Moscow State Film Institute. His most famous films are *Mother*, 1926, *The End of St Petersburg*, 1927, and *Descendant of Genghis Khan*, 1929. In *Life is Beautiful*, 1930, he tried to put into practice the manifesto issued jointly with Eisenstein (q.v.) on using sound as counterpoint, but without success. He made several more films before the Second World War, including *Suvorov*, 1940. His first post-war production, *Admiral Nakhimov*, 1946, was severely criticized in the party decree on the cinema.

Pudovkin wrote several works on the theory of the cinema in which he insisted, among other things, that 'films should be produced by living people as a free development of creative individuality and not as the execution of an order.' *See* his *Film Technique and Film Acting*, 1958. *See also* CINEMA.

Pugachëv, Yemel'yan Ivanovich (1726–75), Cossack leader of a popular revolt during the reign of Catherine II. In 1773 he declared himself Emperor Peter III and published a 'manifesto' promising the liberation of the serfs. Many peasants, Cossacks and nomadic Bashkirs and Kazakhs participated in the revolt, which covered the Volga area and the Urals; after it had been crushed Pugachëv was quartered. *See* A. Gaissinovitch, *La Revolte de Pougatchev*, Paris, 1938.

Purges, in the 1920's and thirties, periodical campaigns undertaken by the authorities to 'cleanse' the party, the administrative apparatus, trade unions, etc., of 'socially alien' or otherwise unreliable elements. The term has acquired abroad a different meaning, and is applied to the waves of terror which have shaken the country at different times during the Soviet regime. The most important of these were the terror against the old intelligentsia, 1928–31 (*see* INDUSTRIAL PARTY; MENSHEVIKS; NEO-POPULISM; SHAKHTY; UNION FOR THE LIBERATION OF THE UKRAINE); the universal terror of 1936–8, known in Russia as the *yezhovshchina* and abroad as the Great Purge (q.v.); the operations in the annexed territories of eastern Poland, the Baltic States, Bessarabia and northern Bukovina in 1939–41; the 'purging' which took place in 1944–6 in the formerly enemy-occupied territories and among returned prisoners of war and civilian deportees; and the 'anti-cosmopolitan'—essentially anti-Semitic—campaign of 1949–53, culminating in the so-called 'Doctor's Case' (*see* DOCTORS' PLOT), which appeared to be the first move in a new wave of universal terror that was only avoided by Stalin's death. There have been no purges in the second sense since Stalin's death. *See* Z. K. Brzezinski, *The Permanent Purge*, Cambridge, Mass., 1956.

Pushkin (before 1917 Tsarskoye Selo, 1917–37 Detskoye Selo), town in the Leningrad Oblast, 15 m. south of Leningrad and subordinated to its city council. Population (1956) 38,200. It has the famous 18th-century baroque palace built by Rastrelli, and some beautiful 18th-century parks; the Pushkin Memorial Museum is here (formerly the *lycée* where the poet was educated). Pushkin was founded in 1718, and the first railway in Russia was built between St Petersburg and Pushkin in 1837.

Pushkin, Aleksandr Sergeyevich (1799–1837), one of the great figures of world literature, universally regarded by Russians as their most illustrious national genius. Descended from an old noble family, and maternally from General A. Gannibal, an Ethiopian, he received a first-class education and held sinecures at the Foreign Office, 1817–1824, and at the court from 1834. He grew up on the ideas of the Enlightenment and the French Revolution, and as a young man was personally friendly with, and politically sympathetic to, the Decembrists (q.v.). He was twice banished, once to New Russia (q.v.) in 1820 and once to a family estate in 1824, for atheistic and revolutionary pronouncements, but he later became a liberal. Though on good terms with Nicholas I (who freed him from the ordinary censorship, undertaking this task himself), he was too proud and independent for the court cliques, who were continuously intriguing against him and finally involved him in a duel in which he was fatally wounded.

Pushkin's first poem was published when he was 15; his early lyrics were influenced by Voltaire, Parny, Anacreon, and by the Russian Classicists (Derzhavin) and Romantics (Zhukovskiy). He was much swayed by Byron during the 1820's, but then deserted Romanticism and set the stage for Realism in Russian literature. His masterpiece is the 'novel in verse' *Eugene Onegin*, 1823–31, often called an encyclopaedia of contemporary Russian life. Other works: *Ruslan and Lyudmila*, 1819, *Caucasian Prisoner*, 1821, *Fountain of Bakhchisaray*, 1822, *Gipsies*, 1824 (all long poems in the romantic or Byronic vein); the historical poem *Poltava*, 1828, and the philosophical *The Bronze Horseman*, 1833; the play *Boris Godunov*, 1825; the short and long stories *Belkin's Tales*, 1830; *The Queen of Spades*, 1834, *Dubrovskiy*, 1834, *The Captain's Daughter*, 1836; fairy tales in verse, etc. See E. J. Simmons, *Pushkin*, 1937; J. Lavrin, *Pushkin and Russian Literature*, 1947.

Putrid Sea, *see* AZOV, SEA OF.

Pyatakov, Grigoriy Leonidovich (1890–1937), Communist. In his youth he adhered to Anarchist views, but in 1910 joined the Bolsheviks. In 1915, while abroad, he supported Bukharin against Lenin on the issues of the nationalities policy (q.v.) and the role of the State. In 1917, as chairman of the Kiev Soviet, he took a leading part in the Bolshevik coup there. Subsequently he headed the leftist faction in the Ukrainian Communist Party and in 1918 the Soviet government of the Ukraine. In the following years he played an important part in directing the Soviet economy as a member of the presidium of the Supreme Council of the National Economy. A Left Communist (q.v.) in 1918, Pyatakov was from 1920 onwards a consistent adherent of Trotskiy on the issues over which the latter opposed Lenin, and later in the struggle against Stalin. Nevertheless he retained his position in the economic administration, and in the 1930's was Ordzhonikidze's deputy at the Commissariat for Heavy Industry. During the Great Purge (q.v.) he was accused of heading a 'Trotskiyite centre' and was chief defendant at the second show trial in 1937 (*see* ANTI-SOVIET TROTSKIYITE CENTRE), when he was condemned to death. See R. Pipes, *The Formation of the Soviet Union*, Cambridge, Mass., 1954; I. Deutscher, *The Prophet Unarmed: Trotsky, 1921–9*, 1959; L. Schapiro, *The Communist Party of the Soviet Union*, 1960.

Pyatigorsk, town in the Stavropol' Kray (Northern Caucasus), situated 90 m. south-east of Stavropol', the main centre of the Mineral Waters group of spas. Population (1959) 69,900. It is a large health resort (a spa since 1803), and also a local cultural centre. Pyatigorsk was founded in 1780; the poet Lermontov was killed here in a duel in 1841.

Pyatnitskiy Choir, *see* ZAKHAROV.

R

Rabfak, Russian abbreviation for 'Workers' Faculty' (q.v.).

Rachinskiy, Sergey Aleksandrovich (1833–1902), professor of botany at Moscow University who gave up academic life in order to devote himself to village primary education. He was a friend of Pobedonostsev and an enthusiast of Church schools.

Rachmaninov, *see* RAKHMANINOV.

Rada (Ukrainian 'council'). For the Ukrainian Central Rada of 1917–18 *see* UKRAINE, *History*.

Radek (real name **Sobelsohn**), **Karl** (1885–1939), cosmopolitan revolutionary of Jewish origin, born at L'vov (then in Austria-Hungary). He was active as a leading publicist of the left wing of the German Social Democratic Party before the First World War, and during the war in international anti-militarist circles, simultaneously being in touch with representatives of the German Government. He was a Bolshevik agent in Sweden after the February 1917 revolution, worked among the Spartacists in Germany in 1918 and was imprisoned there. He settled in Russia in 1922, becoming a leading functionary of the Communist International and in 1926 rector of the Sun Yat-Sen Communist University established in Moscow for Chinese and other Far Eastern students. As a leading member of the Trotskiyite opposition Radek was expelled from the party in 1927 and in 1928 banished to the Urals. He was reinstated in 1930 and became the chief foreign affairs commentator in the Moscow newspapers, but again expelled in 1936. At one of the big show trials of the Great Purge in 1937 (*see* ANTI-SOVIET TROTSKIYITE CENTRE) he was tried together with Pyatakov (q.v.) and sentenced to ten years' imprisonment. He must have died in an isolator (q.v.). *See* his *Portraits and Pamphlets*, 1935.

Radio. The total output of sound broadcasting was in 1957 nearly 600 hours per day on domestic and external services, in over 90 languages; Moscow Radio's broadcasts made up 180 hours, and it has three programmes for home audiences. In 1957 there were 8,348,000 radio receivers (1,767,000 in 1950) and 24,773,000 earphones or loudspeakers for receiving programmes by wire from radio relay centres (9,686,000 in 1950). Wireless telegraphy was invented in Russia in 1896 by A. S. Popov (q.v.) simultaneously with, and independently of, Marconi. Sound broadcasting began in 1922 from a transmitter in Moscow. Two years later there were three more transmitters, in Leningrad, Kiev and Nizhniy Novgorod, and by 1937 there were ninety transmitters. The number and power of transmitters have been rapidly increasing since the war, the power being doubled between 1950 and 1957. In recent years V.H.F. broadcasting has been introduced in some of the densely populated industrial areas. Political control over radio programmes is exercised by the Ministry

of Culture under the direction and supervision of the party committees. An unusual feature of radio in the U.S.S.R. is its task of
jamming foreign broadcasts in Russian and in many other languages,
not only those of the U.S.S.R. but also of several countries of central
and eastern Europe; a large number of transmitters are engaged in
this task; jamming of the Voice of America and B.B.C. broadcasts in
Russian was discontinued in 1959–60, but selective jamming was
introduced a few months later. See A. Inkeles, *Public Opinion in
Soviet Russia*, Cambridge, Mass., 1950; A. Inkeles and R. A. Bauer,
The Soviet Citizen, 1959.

Radishchev, Aleksandr Nikolayevich (1749–1802), writer and
thinker, generally regarded as the founder of the revolutionary
tradition in Russia. In his *Journey from St Petersburg to Moscow*, 1790
(Eng. ed. Cambridge, Mass., 1958), he forcefully portrayed the
inhumanity of serfdom, and called for a revolution. As a result he
was charged with high treason and sentenced to death, but this was
commuted to ten years' banishment in Siberia. He continued to
write while in banishment and after the death of Catherine the Great
in 1796 he was allowed to return. In 1801 he was made a member of a
commission for the codification of laws, but despairing of his efforts
on behalf of the serfs he committed suicide in the following year. His
Journey and his tragic life made a strong impression upon Russian
progressive thought in the 19th century. See V. V. Zenkovsky, *A
History of Russian Philosophy*, vol. i, 1953; E. J. Simmons (ed.),
Continuity and Change in Russian and Soviet Thought, Cambridge,
Mass., 1955; D. M. Lang, *The First Russian Radical*, 1959.

Railways. In 1958 the total length of railways was 122·8 thousand
kilometres (71·7 in 1913—present-day frontiers—116·9 in 1950), of
which 9·5 thousand kilometres were electrified; that is, there were
5·5 kilometres of railways per thousand square kilometres of territory.
Railways are largely concentrated in European Russia, the densest
networks being in the Donets Basin, the Moscow industrial area and
the western Ukraine. In 1958, 73·5 per cent of traction for freight
traffic was by steam engines, 15·1 per cent electric and 11·4 per cent
Diesel. Freight traffic by railway was 1,302·0 milliard ton-kilometres,
and passenger traffic 158·4 milliard passenger-kilometres. Of 1,616·9
million tons of goods transported by rail, coal and coke accounted for
478·8 million tons, mineral building materials for 324·2 million tons,
timber for 121·5 million tons, oil and oil products for 112·5 million
tons, ores for 108·1 million tons, iron and steel (including scrap) for
88·3 million tons, and grain and grain products for 71·5 million tons.
The railways are intensively exploited: 10·7 million tons of goods per
kilometre were carried in 1958.

The first railway line was opened in Russia in 1837; the St Petersburg–Moscow line was finished in 1851. The basic railway network
was largely constructed in the 1860's–1870's and in the 1890's; railway construction continued very rapidly, especially during the First
World War when 10·9 thousand kilometres were built. Most of the
railway construction between the two world wars was based upon
plans already made before 1917. The present network is very insufficient, but the main efforts are now directed towards improving

technical efficiency rather than building new lines. *See also* CHINESE EASTERN RAILWAY; TRANSPORT; TRANS-SIBERIAN RAILWAY; TURKSIB.

Rakhmaninov, Sergey Vasil'yevich (1873–1943), precocious pianist and composer who studied at St Petersburg Conservatory and subsequently at Moscow Conservatory under Ziloti, Zverev, Taneyev and Arenskiy. He travelled extensively, appeared in London in 1899, and left Russia in 1917. Works comprise three operas; choral works, including *The Bells*, 1910; two symphonies; four piano concertos; symphonic poem *The Isle of the Dead*, 1907; *Rhapsody on a Theme by Paganini* for piano and orchestra, 1934; some chamber music; much piano music; many songs. Though not essentially national in style, Rakhmaninov's music is harmonically individual. Generally speaking, however, his skill is best seen in his smaller works, particularly the songs, which in their way are occasionally of the highest order. His piano music owes much to Liszt and Chopin. *See* A. Gronowicz, *Sergei Rachmaninov*, New York, 1946; J. Culshaw, *Sergei Rachmaninov*, 1949; V. I. Serov, *Rachmaninoff*, 1952.

Ramzin, Leonid Konstantinovich (1887–1948), engineer, a leading specialist in boiler-making. Educated at the Moscow Higher Technical School, he was professor there from 1920, organized the Thermotechnical Institute and was its director in 1921–30. At the Industrial Party (q.v.) trial in 1930 he was alleged and confessed to have headed (together with Pal'chinskiy, q.v., and after the latter's arrest) this organization of technocratically minded engineers. He was sentenced to death, but the sentence was commuted to ten years' imprisonment with confiscation of property. While serving his sentence Ramzin was allowed to continue work on the development of a new water tube boiler which he had designed in 1930, and was frequently used as a consultant. He received a Stalin Prize in 1943 and in the following year became professor at the Moscow Institute of Energy and scientific head of his old Thermotechnical Institute.

R.A.P.P. (Russian abbreviation for 'Russian Association of Proletarian Writers'), organization of Communist writers (Averbakh, Fadeyev, qq.v., Gladkov, Libedinskiy, etc.), mostly of non-proletarian origin, which advocated a reorganization of literary work on industrial lines under strict party control, and took up an uncompromising attitude towards 'fellow travellers' (q.v.) and less intransigent Communists. During the first Five Year Plan era the R.A.P.P. was allowed by the authorities to terrorize its literary adversaries and to denounce them as 'class enemies.' However, since the R.A.P.P. members were genuine in their fanaticism for communism their organization did not fit into Stalin's scheme for eliminating all genuine factions and establishing total personal domination; in 1932 R.A.P.P., together with other literary organizations, was dissolved by a decision of the Central Committee of the party and a single Union of Soviet Writers established. *See* E. J. Brown, *The Proletarian Episode in Russian Literature, 1928–32*, New York, 1953; R. W. Mathewson, *The Positive Hero in Russian Literature*, New York, 1958.

Raskol'niki, *see* OLD BELIEVERS.

Rasputin, Grigoriy Yefimovich (1872–1916), mystic and mounte-bank who had a pernicious and deadly influence upon the course of affairs during the last years of the empire. By birth a Siberian peasant, he was uneducated and had no occupation. Those who met him believed that he wielded hypnotic and clairvoyant powers, and when he was brought to the imperial court in 1905 he appeared to save the life of the heir to the throne (who suffered from haemophilia) on several occasions. He thus acquired a limitless influence over the empress, and during Nicholas II's absence at the front during the First World War Rasputin secured the dismissal of all liberal minis-ters and virtually ruled Russia through ministers appointed on his advice. The public was horrified, and when all attempts to dislodge Rasputin had failed he was murdered by two relatives of the emperor and the leading right-wing Duma member Purishkevich. *See* M. V. Rodzianko, *The Reign of Rasputin*, 1927; C. E. Vulliamy (ed.), *From the Red Archives*, 1929; Sir B. Pares, *The Fall of the Russian Mon-archy*, 1939; S. P. Mel'gunov, *Legenda o separatnom mire*, Paris, 1957.

Rastrelli, Count Varfolomey Varfolomeyevich (1700–71), architect. He studied in Europe, but was also influenced by 17th-century Muscovite architecture. His style was basically baroque, but with rococo elements; his plans are completely cubic and rectilinear with a marked absence of curves, and he is notable for his lavish use of decoration (grouped columns, mouldings), colour and gilding. His magnificent interior enfilades were much copied. As court architect to Elizabeth his principal works were the palaces of Petergof and Tsarskoye Selo, the Winter Palace and the Smol'nyy Monastery, St Petersburg, in which he achieved a remarkable fusion of rococo and native elements. *See also* ARCHITECTURE; ARCHITECTURE, ECCLESIASTICAL.

Rastyapino, *see* DZERZHINSK.

Rationing, of consumer goods, existed on a small scale in the period of War Communism (q.v.), and on a much larger scale in 1931–4 and 1941–7. There were different systems of rationing for different localities of the country (more comprehensive for the larger towns and main industrial areas; the majority of the agricultural population received no rations and had to fend for themselves). Even in the regions where the system was most comprehensive, only the main foodstuffs were rationed; other scarce goods were distributed outside the general rationing system. Ration scales differed for (1) workers doing heavy work, (2) ordinary workers, (3) white-collar workers, officials, students, etc., (4) dependants, (5) children. 'Responsible officials' in the party, government, economic, etc., apparatus re-ceived heavy workers' or workers' rations. Various closed shops existed for particular privileged categories, such as the military, security personnel and foreigners, where scarce goods could be bought at low prices. There were also so-called 'commercial shops' (q.v.) during the third rationing period, where scarce goods were available to anyone for higher prices.

Rayon, administrative territorial unit, corresponding to a rural district in England, forming part of an oblast or kray, and itself sub-divided into village soviets (corresponding to parish councils). In

Union Republics which are not divided into oblasts the rayons are directly subordinated to the republican governments. Larger towns are also subdivided for administrative purposes into a number of rayons. All local government functions and other activities within the rayon are controlled by the rayon party committee.

Razin, Stepan (diminutive **Sten'ka**) **Timofeyevich** (*d.* 1671), Don Cossack who led a peasant revolt in 1670, seizing large territories in the south-east of European Russia and all towns on the Volga from Astrakhan' to Samara. He was finally defeated, and broken on the wheel in Moscow. Razin is a popular hero of Russian folklore.

Raznochintsy ('people from various ranks'), semi-official term used in the 19th century for that part of the Russian intelligentsia which was of non-noble origin.

Realism, *see* LITERATURE; SOCIALIST REALISM.

Rebikov, Vladimir Ivanovich (1866–1920), composer who studied at Moscow Conservatory, and with Müller in Berlin. His works comprise six operas, including *In the Storm*, 1894; church music; orchestral works; piano pieces, etc. Although influenced at first by Tchaikovsky, Rebikov's later work shows independent thought, some of his music being of a highly experimental order. He also introduced a kind of pantomime called 'melo-mimic.' *See* A. Rowley, 'Rebikov,' *Music Review*, vol. iv, No. 2, 1943.

Red Army ('Worker-Peasant Red Army'), official name from 1918 till 1946 of the Soviet Army (q.v.).

Red Guards, armed units made up mostly of factory workers, which were employed by the Bolsheviks to seize power in 1917. *See* OCTOBER REVOLUTION.

Red Professorship, Institute of, institution which existed 1921–30 to prepare teachers of philosophy, political economy and party history, and to provide personnel for higher positions in the party apparatus; all the leading theoreticians of the party taught in it. In 1930 it was split into several separate institutes, which were all abolished in 1939. Its successor is the Academy of Social Sciences (q.v.).

Redemption Payments, fixed annual sums paid by those peasants who were ex-serfs to the Government for the land they received out of the landlords' estates at the time of the emancipation of the serfs in 1861. The nobility had been immediately compensated by the Government at prices in most areas higher than the current value of the land. The redemption payments were originally intended to be spread over 49 years, but because of heavy arrears the Government several times reduced the total amount of the debt. In 1896 the payments were postponed and in 1906 they were remitted altogether. *See* G. T. Robinson, *Rural Russia under the Old Regime*, New York, 2nd ed., 1949.

Reformism, political strategy aimed at changing the existing conditions through the machinery of the established regime. Reformism played a very important part in the development of 19th-century Russia (*see* GREAT REFORMS). After the 1905 revolution there was the moderate reformism of the Stolypin Government and the Octobrist Party, aimed at strengthening the semi-constitutional system through social reforms; and the radical reformism of the Constitutional Democrats and the right-wing socialist groups (*see* LIQUIDATIONISM; POPULISM; TRUDOVIKS). There was a variety of reformist trends in the 1920's, most of which (*see* MENSHEVIKS; NEO-POPULISM) were suppressed by 1930; but National Bolshevism (q.v.) had some success and became one of the main elements in the official ideology of Stalinism (q.v.). Reformist tendencies re-emerged after Stalin's death. Khrushchëv's policy of concessions is moderate reformism, somewhat similar to that of Stolypin, while radical reformism manifests itself on the one hand in efforts to restrict party interference in, and to assert the autonomy of, cultural life, economic management, etc., and on the other in attempts to democratize the party itself. *See also* INTELLECTUAL OPPOSITION; REVISIONISM. *See* H. Seton-Watson, *The Decline of Imperial Russia*, 1952; L. Schapiro, *The Origin of the Communist Autocracy*, 1955; S. V. Utechin, 'Bolsheviks and their Allies after 1917; the Ideological Pattern,' *Soviet Studies*, Oct. 1958.

Refugees, term frequently applied to *émigrés* from Russia, (*a*) at the time of the civil war, and (*b*) after the Second World War. The large numbers of people who had left Russia in 1919–20 posed a new and unexpected problem for the League of Nations, which set up a committee under F. Nansen to deal with them; one of the committee's actions was to issue to the refugees international travel documents popularly known as Nansen passports. At the end of the Second World War the Western Allies found large numbers of Soviet citizens (forced labourers, prisoners of war who escaped from repatriation camps, Vlasovites, etc.) throughout western Europe, whom in accordance with the terms of the Yalta Agreement they were to repatriate speedily to the Soviet Union. This agreement was officially interpreted by the Allies as referring to all those who had been Soviet citizens resident in the U.S.S.R. at the beginning of September 1939 (i.e. excluding former residents of territories subsequently annexed by the U.S.S.R.). As a result, until the United Nations decision of 1947 that only war criminals could be compulsorily repatriated, many Russian refugees who did not wish to return to the Soviet Union had to disguise themselves as western Ukrainians, Latvians, etc.; and until 1947 there were cases in the American and French zones of Germany of forcible repatriation of Russian civilians who either could not or would not 'assume' another nationality. The Soviet authorities accused the Western Allies of holding Soviet citizens against their will and of encouraging among them anti-Soviet political activities; in fact strong efforts were made to suppress all political activity among Russian refugees in the displaced persons' camps for some years, and every assistance was given to those who wished to return to the Soviet Union. The majority of able-bodied Russian refugees had by the early 1950's been enabled to emigrate overseas, principally to the U.S.A., Australia, Britain, Canada and South America. *See also* ÉMIGRÉS. *See* A. Inkeles and R. A. Bauer, *The Soviet Citizen*, 1959.

Regionalism, political trend advocating the reorganization of Russia into a number of more or less autonomous regions. Regionalist tendencies appeared almost as soon as the centralized Muscovite state was consolidated, having their roots in the old principalities which were absorbed by Muscovy (q.v.). Modern regionalism emerged in the 19th century. Some protagonists visualized a federal structure for Russia (*see* DRAGOMANOV; FEDERALISM), while others, e.g. the Siberian Regionalists (*see* YADRINTSEV), were primarily concerned with advocating a kind of dominion status for one or another particular region of the country. Regionalist tendencies were strongly manifested after the fall of the monarchy in 1917 (*see* FEBRUARY REVOLUTION); under the Provisional Government (q.v.) such regionalist bodies as the Ukrainian Central Rada and the Cossack Union sprang up, and after the Bolshevik seizure of power, apart from the Ukraine, the South-eastern League, the Transcaucasian Federation, Turkestan and Siberia (qq.v.) were established by anti-Bolsheviks as independent regions with governments of their own, intended to become parts of a future democratic federal Russian state. At the same time on the Bolshevik side strong regional bodies existed in Moscow (for central Russia) and in Petrograd (for the north-west). Regional tendencies in the Russian Far East were made use of by both the Bolsheviks and the Japanese in 1920 in order to establish the buffer state of the Far Eastern Republic (q.v.). However, in general the Communist leadership followed the policy of splitting up historical regions administratively on ethnical or linguistic lines (*see*, for example, NATIONAL DELIMITATION OF CENTRAL ASIA). During the 1920's the administration of the R.S.F.S.R. was reorganized on regional lines, but the new arrangement was scrapped in the mid 1930's, partly at any rate because of Stalin's dislike of the increasing power of the regional party or military leaders. Khrushchëv's reorganization of the economic administration in 1957 has, unintentionally, given renewed encouragement to regionalist tendencies. *See* W. Kolarz, *The People of the Soviet Far East*, 1954; R. Pipes, *The Formation of the Soviet Union*, Cambridge, Mass., 1954.

Regionalization, of Economic Management, *see* ECONOMIC COUNCILS; INDUSTRIAL MANAGEMENT.

Reisner, *see* REYSNER.

Reizen, Mark Osipovich (*b.* 1895), bass. From 1917 to 1919 he studied singing at the Khar'kov Conservatory under Bugamelli, making his début in 1921. From 1925 to 1930 he featured as soloist of the Leningrad State Academic Theatre of Opera and Ballet, and from 1930 of the Bolshoi Theatre, Moscow. A distinguished exponent of the principal bass roles, he has travelled widely, appearing as both an operatic and solo artist.

Religion. The majority of believers in Russia are Christians and belong to the Russian Orthodox Church; another autocephalous Orthodox Church is the Georgian. There are also a considerable number of so-called Old Believers (q.v.). The Protestant denominations are the Lutheran in Latvia, Estonia and among the German population, and the Baptist (q.v.) throughout the country; there are also various smaller sects, among which the Jehovah's Witnesses (q.v.) have lately become particularly active. Lithuanians, Latgalians, western Belorussians and the Polish population belong to the Roman Catholic Church (q.v.), a part of the western Ukrainians are

Catholics of the Greek Rite (see UNIATES), and most Armenians belong to the Armenian Gregorian Church. The next biggest religious groups are the Muslims (q.v.), followed by the Jews (q.v.) and the Buddhists (among the Buryats and the Kalmyks). The pagan Shamanism is practised among small Siberian tribes (see PALEO-ASIATICS, TUNGUS).

The imperial authorities before 1917 regarded themselves as the protectors of all non-pagan religions in their non-sectarian forms. The Marxist ideology regards all religion as essentially a tool in the hands of the exploiting classes and expects it to wither away in the socialist society. Its continued existence in the Soviet Union is officially explained as a 'survival of the feudal and capitalist past.' While affirming the incompatibility of religion with Marxism, the Communist authorities have in practice adopted varying policies at different times and towards different religions. Generally speaking, anti-religious measures increased in severity until they culminated in the wholesale arrest of priests of all denominations during the Great Purge (q.v.). As part of the war-time policy of relaxation in almost all spheres, a *modus vivendi* was arrived at in 1943–4 between the Soviet authorities and the Orthodox, Armenian, Lutheran and Baptist Churches, the Muslims and the Buddhists (see COUNCIL FOR THE AFFAIRS OF THE ORTHODOX CHURCH), while relations with the Roman Catholic Church and the Jewish communities have remained hostile, and the Uniates are suppressed. In return for this concession, representatives of all the chief religions take part in the Soviet Government's 'peace' propaganda. Anti-religious propaganda (q.v.) has again been revived since 1956. *See* N. S. Timasheff, *Religion in Soviet Russia*, 1942; W. Gurian (ed.), *The Soviet Union*, Notre Dame, Indiana, 1951; W. Kolarz, 'Recent Soviet Attitudes towards Religion,' *Soviet Survey*, No. 13, Mar. 1957, and *Religion in the Soviet Union*, 1961.

Rent, *see* HOUSING; LAND.

Reparations received by the Soviet Union after the Second World War cannot be assessed with any certainty. Enormous amounts of war booty, including capital and consumer goods, food and various services in Soviet-occupied countries, were appropriated until 1950. In East Germany and Manchuria it was estimated to amount to at least 4 milliard dollars' worth. After 1950 the payment of reparations was regulated with those countries with whom the Soviet Union signed peace treaties. Receipts from reparations in the widest sense played a very important part in Soviet post-war reconstruction (*see* CAPITAL). *See also* LEND-LEASE. *See* H. Schwartz, *Russia's Soviet Economy*, 2nd ed., 1954.

Repin, Il'ya Yefimovich (1844–1930), painter who was born in the Ukraine and worked as a youth with icon painters. In 1863 he studied at the Society for the Encouragement of Art, and 1864–71 at the Academy of Arts; he became a member of the Peredvizhniki (q.v.). The most accomplished of the 19th-century realists, Repin was also the most prolific and versatile of Russian artists. He painted with equal facility portraits, historical and religious compositions, *genre* scenes, landscapes, etc. All his works are done with an obvious gusto and a fine sense of colour; his brilliant portraits of Musorgskiy and

Mendeleyev deserve special mention. In his important historical and contemporary *genre* canvases he was rather prone to the story-telling and sentimental moralizing characteristic of the Peredvizhniki. But some of these works have redeeming features: well-expressed character and situation, and a masterly exploitation of drama. Repin's best-known paintings are 'The Bargemen' (or 'The Volga Boatmen'), 'The Religious Procession in Kursk Province,' 'Ivan the Terrible with the Body of his Son,' and 'Zaporozh'ye Cossacks Drafting a Reply to the Turkish Sultan.' Repin lived the last years of his life in Finland and worked chiefly on religious paintings.

Republics, *see* AUTONOMOUS REPUBLIC; UNION REPUBLIC.

Retail Trade is carried out through State shops, co-operative shops and the *kolkhoz* market (q.v.). Of the 1958 total of retail trade, 65·2 per cent was carried out by State shops (30 per cent in 1932, 63 per cent in 1940, 42 per cent in 1945), 29·1 per cent by co-operative shops (53 per cent in 1932, 23 per cent in 1940, 12 per cent in 1945) and 5·7 per cent in the *kolkhoz* market (17 per cent in 1932, 14 per cent in 1940, 46 per cent in 1945). The value of State and co-operative retail trade (including eating places—restaurants, canteens, etc.) in milliard roubles in current prices was 677·2 in 1958 (12 in 1928, 40 in 1932, 175 in 1940, 360 in 1950, 502 in 1955). Of the total, 26 per cent was rural trade. Ten per cent of the total in 1958 was made up by eating places. Food accounted for 54·6 per cent of total State and co-operative retail trade, and fabrics, clothing and footwear for 25·5 per cent. The index of retail prices (1940=100) was 181 in 1950 (197 for food, 161 for other goods) and 138 in 1958 (145 for food, 130 for other goods). In 1958 there were 519,300 State and co-operative shops, kiosks, etc. (155,000 in 1928, 407,000 in 1940, 245,000 in 1945, 416,000 in 1950); in the same year there were 130,900 eating places (15,000 in 1928, 88,000 in 1940, 73,000 in 1945, 95,000 in 1950). In 1958, 52 per cent of shops were in rural areas, and 2·8 million people were employed in shops and eating places; both the number and distribution of shops and eating places, and the number of people employed in them, are very insufficient.

After the suppression in principle of all private trade during the period of War Communism (q.v.), private retail trade was again permitted under the New Economic Policy (q.v.), and in 1924 88 per cent of all shops were privately owned, with 53 per cent of the total turnover in retail trade. However, in the following years discrimination against private trade increased, and in 1930 only 6 per cent of the shops and turnover was accounted for by private traders. There has been no open private trading, except in the *kolkhoz* market, since 1931. *See also* SPECULATORS; TRADE.

Revda, town in the Sverdlovsk Oblast (Urals), situated on the Sverdlovsk-Kazan' railway 29 m. west of Sverdlovsk. Population (1959) 55,000. It has iron, copper and chemical industries. Revda was founded by Demidov in 1732 as a copper and iron works.

Revel', *see* TALLINN.

Revisionism, in Marxist parties, a tendency to revise the officially accepted interpretation of Marxism in a way detrimental to the prospects of revolution or the Dictatorship of the Proletariat (q.v.).

The official requirement is that the theory should be further developed in accordance with its spirit, neither sticking to the letter ('dogmatism') nor violating the spirit ('revisionism'). The chief examples of revisionism in the past were Bernsteinism, with its Russian variety Economism (q.v.), and in Russia Legal Marxism (q.v.) and Bogdanovism (q.v.). Suppressed in the Communist Party by Lenin and Stalin, revisionism re-emerged after Stalin's death in both the Bernsteinian and the Bogdanovist forms, the former revising the official view of contemporary capitalism and the latter advocating the freedom of cultural activities from control by the party bureaucracy. Although revisionism has been declared a greater danger than dogmatism at the moment, it is still to some extent tolerated in Russia (and to a far greater extent in Poland). The practical consequences of revisionism, particularly after the 20th party congress (q.v.), in undermining the established regime, have been considerable, since a theoretically ideocratic regime, such as the Communist, can ill afford heterodoxy; it is all the more important because the trend finds most of its adherents among young people. *See further under* INTELLECTUAL OPPOSITION; REFORMISM. *See* L. Labedz, 'The Shadow of Revisionism,' *Soviet Survey*, No. 20, Oct. 1957; D. S. Zagoria, 'The Spectre of Revisionism,' *Problems of Communism*, vol. viii, No. 4, July–Aug. 1958; W. Z. Laqueur and G. Lichtheim (eds.), *The Soviet Cultural Scene, 1956–7*, 1958.

Revolution of 1917, *see* FEBRUARY REVOLUTION; OCTOBER REVOLUTION.

Revolution of 1905 was caused by a combination of two movements: the constitutional movement of the *zemstvos* and the liberal intelligentsia, and the revolutionary movement of the illegal parties, mainly the Russian Social Democratic Labour Party and the Socialist Revolutionaries (qq.v.). The revolution opened with a workers' demonstration being fired upon in St Petersburg on 'Bloody Sunday' in January 1905 (*see* GAPON). Nation-wide disturbances ensued: the soviets (q.v.) appeared on the scene; political strikes (including the general strike of October 1905), mutinies in the armed forces (e.g. the battleship *Potëmkin*), the seizure of landlords' estates by the peasants, and armed uprisings (including one in Moscow) took place; authority virtually collapsed in some parts of the country, in places for a period of several weeks. Widespread unrest continued until the summer of 1907. The revolution resulted in the setting up (by the Imperial Manifesto of October 1905) of a constitutional regime with a legislative Duma (q.v.), and in the legalization of political parties and trade unions; in the initiation of Stolypin's (q.v.) agrarian reforms; and in disillusioning the progressive part of the intelligentsia with revolutionism (*see* VEKHI). *See* A. J. Sack, *The Birth of the Russian Democracy*, New York, 1918; *Memoirs of Count Witte* (trans. A. Yarmolinsky), New York, 1921; B. Pares, *My Russian Memoirs*, 1931; V. I. Gurko, *Features and Figures of the Past. Government and Opinion in the Reign of Nicholas II*, 1939; G. T. Robinson, *Rural Russia under the Old Regime*, 2nd ed., New York, 1949; H. Seton-Watson, *The Decline of Imperial Russia*, 1952; O. Anweiler, *Die Rätebewegung in Russland, 1905–21*, Leyden, 1958.

Revolutionary Legality, term used in Soviet legal theory to describe the use of the law to further the ends of the party leadership. Its more precise meaning has undergone two changes. It was first used to explain the flexibility of Bolshevik judicial practice, with its reliance on the 'revolutionary conscience'; after the introduction of the Stalin constitution in 1936 it stressed, on the contrary, the new elements of stability (*see* SOCIALIST LEGALITY); and since Stalin's death it has been used as a euphemism for the elimination of the worst excesses of Stalinism (q.v.). *See also* LEGAL SYSTEM. *See* R. Schlesinger, *Soviet Legal Theory*, 1945; H. J. Berman, *Justice in Russia*, Cambridge, Mass., 1950; G. C. Guins, *Soviet Law and Soviet Society*, The Hague, 1954; H. Kelsen, *The Communist Theory of Law*, 1955; S. Wolin and R. M. Slusser (eds.), *The Soviet Secret Police*, New York, 1957.

Revolutionary Movement, in Russia, dates from the early 19th century, and may be divided into three phases—up to 1918, between the two world wars, and since the Second World War.

The first revolutionary organizations were those of the Decembrists (q.v.), followed by several secret societies of the 1830's–1860's, when the movement acquired a radical and socialist political outlook, largely under the influence of Herzen and Chernyshevskiy (qq.v.). A comprehensive theory of revolutionary organization and tactics was developed by Ogarëv (q.v.). The dominant ideology within the revolutionary movement in the 1870's and eighties was Populism (q.v.), with the 'Jacobin' trend represented by Tkachëv and the Narodnaya Volya (qq.v.). The first Marxist revolutionary organizations appeared in the 1880's (*see* LIBERATION OF LABOUR GROUP), and the Russian Social Democratic Labour Party (q.v.) gradually developed in the 1890's. An important role was played during the late eighties and early nineties by a transitional organization, little known to historians, which was headed by Fokin (q.v.) and combined 'Jacobinism' with increasing Marxist influence, thus laying the foundations for Leninism (q.v.), which resuscitated Ogarëv's organizational and tactical plans. The revolutionary movement culminated in the revolution of 1905 and the February revolution of 1917 (qq.v.); the latter was primarily carried out by a semi-conspiracy of the leaders of the liberal Progressive Bloc (*see* CONSTITUTIONAL DEMOCRATS) and the Union of Zemstvos (q.v.) and less by the revolutionary parties. The seizure of power by the Bolsheviks (*see* OCTOBER REVOLUTION) represented a triumph of the 'Jacobin' trend.

Revolutionary activities against the Bolshevik regime from 1918 until the 1930's (*see* ANTONOV UPRISING; BASMACHI; COLLECTIVIZATION OF AGRICULTURE; KRONSTADT; MAKHNO) were mostly led by Socialist Revolutionaries, ex-Socialist Revolutionaries, Anarchists, or by nationalist organizations of the non-Russian minorities.

The most important acts of open resistance of the post-Second World War period were the great strikes and revolts in the main concentration camp areas (*see* CORRECTIVE LABOUR CAMPS), which were led by coalitions of Marxists ('True Leninists' and Trotskiyites), 'Vlasovites' (*see* VLASOV) and national minority groups. Revolutionary tendencies have been strong among active *émigrés* from the

Soviet regime since the 1920's, and at present the N.T.S. (q.v.) and several non-Russian nationalist organizations operate both abroad and in Russia (*see further under* ÉMIGRÉS). *See* A. J. Sack, *The Birth of the Russian Democracy*, New York, 1918; E. E. Kluge, *Die russische revolutionäre Presse, 1855–1905*, Zürich, 1948; J. M. Meijer, *Knowledge and Revolution*, Assen, Netherlands, 1955; F. Venturi, *Roots of Revolution*, 1960; S. V. Utechin, 'Who Taught Lenin?', *Twentieth Century*, July 1960.

Revolutionary Tribunals, special courts established by the Bolsheviks immediately after their seizure of power in 1917 to fight 'counter revolution' in the widest sense, including the black market. They were to be guided exclusively by the circumstances of the case and the demands of 'revolutionary consciousness' (*see* REVOLUTIONARY LEGALITY), and not by any written law. *See* R. Schlesinger, *Soviet Legal Theory*, 1945; J. N. Hazard, *The Soviet System of Government*, Chicago, 1957.

Reysner (Reussner), Mikhail Andreyevich (1868–1928), jurist of half-German origin. He taught law at Tomsk and later (having spent several years in emigration where he joined the Bolshevik wing of the Social Democratic Party in 1905) at St Petersburg University. After the Bolshevik seizure of power in 1917 he became a departmental head in the Commissariat of Justice. In his works (*The Theory of Petrazhitskiy, Marxism and Social Ideology*, 1908; *The State*, 1911; *The Fundamentals of the Soviet Constitution*, 1918; *The State and the Church*, 1919; *The State of the Bourgeoisie and the R.S.F.S.R.*, 1923; *Law, Our Law, Foreign Law, General Law*, 1925; *The History of Political Doctrines*, 1929) Reysner tried in a Bogdanovist fashion (*see* BOGDANOVISM) to supplement Marxism with a modern legal theory, reintroducing Petrazhitskiy's (q.v.) doctrine in Marxist terms. Reysner's views served for a time as a theoretical justification for the concept of 'revolutionary legal consciousness' (*see* REVOLUTIONARY LEGALITY), but were later discarded. *See* J. N. Hazard (ed.), *Soviet Legal Philosophy*, Cambridge, Mass., 1951; H. Kelsen, *The Communist Theory of Law*, 1955.

Richter, Svyatoslav Teofilovich (*b.* 1914), pianist. He first studied the piano with his father, and from 1933 to 1937 was chorus master of the Odessa Theatre of Opera and Ballet. He studied at the Moscow Conservatory under Neuhaus till 1947. Richter is the winner of many prizes and awards, his playing being distinguiished by its range and sympathy. He is outstanding in his interpretations of Bach and Beethoven. *See* Y. Milstein, 'Svyatoslav Richter' in *Sovetskaya Muzyka*, No. 10, 1948.

Ridder, *see* LENINOGORSK.

Riga, capital, economic and cultural centre of Latvia, an important industrial and cultural centre of the U.S.S.R., situated near the mouth of the Western Dvina. Population (1959) 605,000 (eighteenth in the Soviet Union; 1914, 530,000; 1935, 385,000; 1939, 355,000), chiefly Latvians and Russians (before 1940 Latvians and Germans). It has diverse engineering (electrical, transport, agricultural equipment), chemical, light, food and woodworking industries. The city is an important centre of transportation (a port on the Baltic Sea, six railway lines and an airport). There is the Latvian Academy of Sciences (founded 1946, library founded 1524), a university, 1919 (founded in 1861 as the Polytechnical Institute), and an historical museum, 1834. In the Old Town there are many 13th–19th-century churches and other buildings of historical interest. It has the famous Rigas Jurmala seaside resort area.

Riga was founded in 1201 by Bishop Albert, the founder of the Order of Brothers of the Sword; it enjoyed considerable autonomy under the Livonian Order, and was a member of the Hanseatic League from 1282. It became an independent city-republic after the disintegration of Livonia in 1561, was Polish from 1582 and Swedish from 1621. In 1710 it was conquered by Peter the Great and it was ceded to Russia in the peace treaty of Nystad, 1721. The city was the capital of the province of Livland, of independent Latvia, 1918–40, and the administrative centre of Riga Oblast in the Latvian Republic, 1952–3, now abolished. Peace treaties between Soviet Russia and Latvia, 1920, and Soviet Russia and Poland, 1921, were signed in Riga, which was occupied by the Germans, 1917–18 and 1941–3.

Riga, Gulf of, in the east coast of the Baltic Sea south of the Gulf of Finland, separated from the sea by Saaremaa Island. Length 100 m.; greatest width 60 m.; greatest depth 22 fathoms. The river Western Dvina flows into the Gulf past the port of Riga; it is frozen for about 120 days in the year.

Right Opposition, or Right Deviation, in Communist parties and in the Communist International, opposition to the policy of the dominant group by the more moderate elements who stress the need for co-operation and compromise with non-Communists. The principal Right Opposition in Russia, 1928–9, was led by Bukharin, Rykov and Tomskiy, who advocated a policy of greater conciliation towards the peasants. *See* F. Borkenau, *The Communist International*, 1938; I. Deutscher, *Stalin*, 1949; L. Schapiro, *The Communist Party of the Soviet Union*, 1960.

Rimsky-Korsakov, Nikolay Andreyevich (1844–1908), composer, conductor and unrivalled teacher. He received partial instruction from Ulich and Canille, met Balakirev in 1861, and voyaged abroad, 1862–5. He was appointed professor of composition and instrumentation in St Petersburg Conservatory in 1871, until 1884 was Inspector of Naval Bands, was conductor of the Free Music School concerts, 1874–8, and of the Russian Symphony Concerts (inaugurated by Belyayev) 1886–1900. His many distinguished pupils include Lyadov, Ippolitov-Ivanov, Grechaninov, Glazunov, Stravinsky, Prokof'yev and, through Shteynberg, Shostakovich. His works comprise: fourteen operas, including *The Snow Maiden*, 1880–1, *Sadko*, 1894–6, *Czar Saltan*, 1898–1900, *The Golden Cockerel*, 1906–7; numerous choral works; many orchestral works, including *Antar*, 1868, *Spanish Capriccio*, 1887, *Sheherazade*, 1888; chamber music; vocal works; piano works; many songs; folk-songs (forty-nine folk-songs, collected by T. I. Filippov and harmonized by Rimsky-Korsakov, 1875; *Collection of Russian Folk-songs*, 1875–6). He revised and completed Musorgskiy's *Boris Godunov* and *Khovanshchina*, and Borodin's *Prince Igor*.

Rimsky-Korsakov's works are characterized by their elegance and charm, freshness and exuberance, but suffer from repetition and certain clichés which are barely compensated for by sparkling orchestration. Most of his operas are based on national subjects and abound in folk music. Musically he is heir to Glinka, but owes much to his study of ecclesiastical and oriental music. His work is of the finest craftsmanship. *See further under* BALLET; KUCHKA; OPERA; ORCHESTRAL MUSIC; SONG. *See* his *My Musical Life*, 1942; G. Abraham and M. D. Calvocoressi, *Masters of Russian Music*, 1936.

Rioni (ancient **Phasis**), river in Transcaucasia, rising in the southern slopes of the Caucasus and flowing to Poti on the Black Sea. Length 200 m. Its link with the voyage of the Argonauts gave it fame in antiquity.

River Transport. The total length of navigable rivers is over 520,000 kilometres; inland waterways (including canals) amounted to 133,100 kilometres in 1958 (59,400 in 1913). In 1958 freight traffic by inland waterways amounted to 85·5 milliard ton-kilometres (28·5 in 1913), and passenger traffic to 4·0 milliard passenger-kilometres (1·4 in 1913). The principal goods transported by water are timber and firewood and mineral building materials. The main inland waterway is the Volga, which, together with its tributary the Kama, carries more than a half of all goods and passengers. Canals of importance are the Volga-Don, White Sea-Baltic, Moscow-Volga and the Volga-Baltic Waterway (qq.v.). Intensive canal construction in Russia began under Peter the Great in the late 17th–early 18th centuries, and before the advent of the railways they were of great importance, connecting the main river systems. Official enthusiasm for canals revived under Stalin, when large numbers of forced labourers were used in their construction. *See also* TRANSPORT.

Rivers, *see* INLAND WATERS.

Road Transport. In 1958 the total length of all registered roads (including tracks) was 1,442,600 kilometres, of which hard-surface roads covered 235,900 kilometres (24,300 in 1913, 225,700 in 1957). Most roads are very bad, scarcely passable in spring and autumn. There are a few modern motorways, chiefly connecting Moscow with Minsk, Kiev, Khar'kov and the Crimea, Yaroslavl', Gor'kiy, Ryazan' and Leningrad. Even the main roads are ill serviced by petrol stations, garages and cafés. Freight traffic by motor transport amounted to 76·8 milliard ton-kilometres in 1958, and passenger traffic by public buses to 42·6 milliard passengers-kilometres. Bus services exist in nearly 900 towns, and there are 5,085 inter-town bus and coach routes with a total length of 525,300 kilometres (1958). *See also* TRANSPORT.

Rockets. The Soviet Union is ahead of other countries in the development of rockets, both for military use and for cosmic research. This is partly due to long traditions in Russia of first-class work in ballistics and of the study of rocketry and the problems of cosmic travel (*see* TSIOLKOVSKIY). The Soviet Union was the first to use rockets in war—batteries of rocket-launchers firing short-distance rockets were already in use in 1942. Work was intensified after the war, with the assistance of plans and specialists from Germany, and short, intermediate and long-range (inter-continental) guided and ballistic missiles were developed for carrying nuclear warheads. The stage reached by the Soviet Union in rocketry became evident with the launching in October 1957 of the first artificial earth satellite (see SPUTNIK). Two more earth satellites followed, and in 1959 three rockets were fired towards the moon, of which the first travelled past the moon to become a satellite of the sun, the second hit the moon's surface, and the third was fitted with equipment which successfully photographed 'the dark side of the moon.' See L. V. Berkner (ed.), *Manual on Rockets and Satellites*, 1958; A. Lee (ed.), *The Soviet Air and Rocket Forces*, 1959; U.S.S.R. Academy of Sciences, *The Other Side of the Moon* (trans. J. B. Sykes), 1960.

Rokossovskiy, (Rokossowski), Konstantin Konstantinovich (*b.* 1896), Marshal of the Soviet Union. Born in Warsaw as the son of a Polish engine-driver, he took part in the First World War and in 1919 joined the Red Army and the Bolshevik Party. Rokossovskiy was one of the most outstanding Soviet commanders during the Second World War: commanding first an army and then various army groups, he distinguished himself in the battles of Moscow, 1941–2, Stalingrad, 1942–3, Kursk, 1943, and in Belorussia, East Prussia, Pomerania and in the battle for Berlin in 1944–5. He was twice awarded the title Hero of the Soviet Union and in 1944 became a marshal. After the war Rokossovskiy commanded the Soviet forces in Poland and in 1949 was officially transferred to the Polish Army, becoming Minister of Defence, commander-in-chief, Deputy Prime Minister of Poland and a member of the Politburo of the Polish Communist Party; he held these posts until November 1956, when the popular anti-Communist and anti-Russian feeling forced the new regime headed by Gromulka to dismiss him. Since 1956 he has been a deputy Minister of Defence of the U.S.S.R.

Roman Catholics. In the U.S.S.R. the majority of Lithuanian believers, as well as large minorities in Latvia (see LATGALIANS) and in Belorussia, are Roman Catholics. The Soviet Government is thus forced to recognize the existence of the Church, but remains hostile to it and does not permit normal contacts with the Vatican. See W. Kolarz, *Religion in the Soviet Union*, 1961.

Romanov, House of, ruling house of Russia from 1613 to the February 1917 revolution. The first czar of the House, Michael Fëdorovich, was elected by a specially summoned Zemskiy Sobor at the end of the Time of Troubles (see TROUBLES, TIME OF). Male primogeniture ordered the succession until the time of Peter the Great, who introduced the principle of the choice of a successor by the reigning monarch; this principle was followed until Paul I restored the previous system. From Peter the Great's time the Romanovs bore the title of emperor. The male line died with Peter II (1730), and the emperors from Peter III (1762) onwards belonged to the family of Holstein Gottorp (related through Peter the Great's daughter to the Romanovs), though they assumed the name of Romanov.

Rossi, Karl Ivanovich (1775–1849), architect of Italian origin, Russian by upbringing. As the chief architect of Alexander I he played a very great part in creating the great architectural *ensembles* of St Petersburg. He was responsible for the Palace Square (in front of the Winter Palace) with the adjoining Admiralty and Senate squares, for the *ensembles* of the Michael Palace (now the Russian Museum) and of the Aleksandra (now Pushkin) Theatre. Behind the latter runs the famous Theatre Street (now the Street of the Architect Rossi) which is one of the finest creations of its kind in the world. *See also* ARCHITECTURE. *See* Tamara Talbót Rice, *Russian Art*, 1949; G. H. Hamilton, *The Art and Architecture of Russia*, 1954.

Rostov: 1. Town in the Yaroslavl' Oblast situated 35 m. south-west of Yaroslavl', probably the oldest town in central Russia. Population (1956) 29,200. It has some linen-weaving and food industries; an old enamel-painting craft is still practised. There is a kremlin and there are many notable churches of the 13th–17th centuries. Rostov has been known since 862, becoming capital of central Russia in the 11th century and of Rostov Principality in 1207. It was annexed in 1474 by Muscovy, became the seat of an Orthodox Metropolitan in 1587, and during the 16th–19th centuries was an important centre of commerce.

2. Oblast of the R.S.F.S.R., situated in the south of European Russia adjacent to the Sea of Azov, traversed by the lower course of the Don and including the eastern part of the Donets Coal Basin. Area 38,900 sq. m.; population (1959) 3,314,000 (57 per cent urban), Russians, many of them Cossacks (since the 16th century). There are large engineering (agricultural machinery, locomotives, machine tools, boilers), coal-mining, food and shoemaking industries; wheat, sunflowers and vegetables are cultivated, and cattle, sheep and horses (Don breed) raised. Principal towns: Rostov-on-Don, Taganrog, Shakhty, Novoshakhtinsk, Novocherkassk, Kamensk-Shakhtinsky. For history *see* COSSACKS. The development of heavy industry dates from the 1860's.

3. **Rostov-on-Don,** administrative, economic and cultural centre of the oblast, situated 25 m. from the mouth of the Don. Population (1959) 597,000 (1914, 200,000; 1920, 177,000; 1926, 308,000; 1939, 510,000), Russians and Armenians. It is one of the principal centres of the engineering industry in the country (agricultural machinery since 1898, aircraft, shipbuilding, etc.), and also has tobacco, food, shoemaking and textile industries. It is an important centre of trans-portation—transfer from seagoing and river ships to railway and vice versa, the 'gateway to the Caucasus.' The city is the most important cultural centre of the North Caucasus and neighbouring regions (university, founded in 1869 in Warsaw, transferred to Rostov in 1917). Founded in 1761 as a fortress, it became a town in 1797 and absorbed the port of Temernik (founded 1749). In 1888 it was included in the Don Cossack Region, in the early 1920's absorbed Nakhichevan'-on-Don, and was the administrative centre of North Caucasus, 1923–34. It has been a commercial centre (export) since the early 19th century, and industrial development dates from 1846. Rostov was held by the Whites, 1918–20, and was occupied by the Germans in 1918, 1941 and 1942–3.

Rostovtsev, Mikhail Ivanovich (1870–1952), historian and archae-ologist, professor at St Petersburg University, 1901–18, at the university of Wisconsin, 1920–4, and at Yale from 1925. His works on ancient history have had much influence upon modern thought on the subject. *See* his *Iranians and Greeks in South Russia*, 1922, *The Social and Economic History of the Roman Empire*, 1926, *A History of the Ancient World* (2 vols.), 1926–7, and *The Social and Economic History of the Hellenistic World* (3 vols.), 1941.

Rostropovich, Mstislav Leopol'dovich (*b.* 1927), cellist. Receiving his first lessons from his father, he subsequently studied at Moscow Conservatory, where his teachers were Kozolupov (playing) and Shebalin (composition). Since 1947 he has taught at the Conservatory, being appointed lecturer in 1953. Held in high esteem within the Soviet Union, he has travelled widely and is renowned for his participation with Gilel's and Richter.

Rouble (*rubl'*), monetary unit. The official rate of exchange prior to the 1960–1 monetary reform was 11·40 roubles to the £, but the actual purchasing power of the rouble on the internal Russian market was about 6*d*. There are 100 kopeks in 1 rouble. *See also* CURRENCY.

Rovno (Ukrainian **Rivne**, Polish **Rowne**): 1. Oblast in western Ukraine, lying in the Poles'ye lowland in the north and the Volhynia-Podolia upland in the south, partly covered with pine and oak forests. Area 7,800 sq. m.; population (1959) 927,000 (17 per cent urban), chiefly Ukrainians, before the war also Jews, Poles and Germans. Grain, potatoes and sugar-beet are cultivated, cattle and pigs raised, and there are food and woodworking industries. The area belonged to Volhynia, became Lithuanian in the 14th century, Polish in 1569, Russian in the Polish partitions of 1793 and 1795, and again Polish, 1920–39. It was occupied by the Germans in 1918 and 1941–4.

2. Administrative centre of the oblast and a local cultural centre, situated 110 m. north-east of L'vov. Population (1959) 57,000. It has flour milling and some food and metal-working industries. Rovno has been known as a commercial town on the Kiev–Poland route since 1282; it was a Russian fortress in the First World War, seeing much fighting in both world wars and in the Soviet-Polish war in 1920. It became a provincial capital in 1939, and was the residence of the German Reichskommissar for the Ukraine, 1941–4.

Rozanov, Vasiliy Vasil'yevich (1856–1919), philosopher and publicist, the author of numerous brilliant and paradoxical essays which criticized contemporary theories of knowledge, morals, education, the philosophy of history, and aesthetics from a point of view similar to Nietzsche's. Rozanov was the first to use the simile of the 'Iron Curtain,' later taken up by Sir Winston Churchill. *See* his *Fallen Leaves*, 1920, and *Solitaria*, 1927; G. Ivask (ed.), *Vasili Rozanov, Selected Works*, New York, 1956; R. Hare, *Portraits of Russian Personalities between Reform and Revolution*, 1959.

Rozhdestvenskiy, Dmitriy Sergeyevich (1876–1940), physicist. Educated at St Petersburg University, he did post-graduate work in Germany and France, was professor at Petrograd University from 1914, director of its Physical Institute, organizer and director, 1918–1932, of the State Optical Institute, member of the Academy of Sciences. His work in experimental physics was concerned with anomalous dispersion in the vapours of base metals, and with the theory of spectral series. He was one of the first scientists to co-operate with the Soviet regime and did much to organize the production of optical glass in the U.S.S.R. *See* J. G. Crowther, *Soviet Science*, 1936.

R.S.F.S.R., *see* RUSSIAN SOVIET FEDERATIVE SOCIALIST REPUBLIC.

Rubakin, Nikolay Aleksandrovich (1862–1945), bibliographer and a promoter of adult correspondence courses in Russia, a radical Populist in politics. His encyclopaedic work *Among Books* (3 vols.), 1906, is an invaluable guide to the Russian literature of the period. He lived chiefly in Switzerland and died there, leaving his very rich library to the Soviet Government.

Rubber Industry is chiefly concerned with the production of synthetic rubber, which was started in the U.S.S.R. in 1932 (the first country in the world) and is now chiefly concentrated in central Russia (Yaroslavl', Voronezh and Yefremov in Tula Oblast), where it is based on ethyl alcohol from potatoes; there is also a plant in Kazan' working on oil, and in Yerevan on calcium carbide. The domestic output of synthetic rubber is insufficient, and some is imported from East Germany. Natural rubber is also imported, chiefly from Malaya and Indonesia; in 1957 the U.S.S.R. imported 146,000 tons of natural rubber, sharing with Japan third place as an importer (after the U.S.A. and Great Britain). In 1958, 14·4 million tyres were produced (0·1 million in 1928, 3·0 in 1940, 1·4 in 1945). For rubber footwear *see* CONSUMER GOODS.

Rubinshteyn, Anton Grigor'yevich (1830–94), pianist, prolific composer, and teacher who studied under Villoing in Moscow and later under Dehn in Berlin. He founded the St Petersburg Conservatory in 1862, and toured extensively. His works comprise twenty operas, including *The Demon* (*première* 1875); six symphonies; five piano concertos; two cello concertos; violin concerto; orchestral works, including the symphonic poem *Russia*, 1882; chamber and piano works; songs, vocal music, etc. Rubinshteyn was fundamentally a brilliant pianist, with a technique modelled on that of Liszt. His compositions suffer from over-facility and lack of individuality, and though sometimes employing Russian themes are alien to them in spirit. His smaller works are of some merit. A confirmed supporter of Teutonicism, he was hostile to the aims of Kuchka (q.v.). *See* G. Abraham, 'Anton Rubinstein: Russian Composer,' *Musical Times*, Dec. 1945.

Rubinshteyn, M. M. (1880–?), philosopher and educationalist whose fate is unknown. Originally a follower of Rickert, Rubinshteyn analyses in his main work (*On the Meaning of Life*, 2 vols., 1927) the problem of man and his creative capacity on the lines of modern Existentialism. *See* V. V. Zenkovsky, *A History of Russian Philosophy*, vol. ii, 1953.

Rubinshteyn, Nikolay Grigor'yevich (1835–81), pianist and teacher, brother of Anton, who studied under Kullak and Dehn in Berlin. In 1859 he founded the Russian Musical Society in Moscow, and in 1864 the Moscow Conservatory. He travelled widely, and was akin to his brother in outlook. His pupils include Taneyev and Ziloti. His compositions are of little importance. *See* C. S. D. Bowen,

Free Artist: the Story of Anton and Nicholas Rubinstein, New York, 1939.

Rubinstein, Ida (1885–1960), dancer and impresario. A pupil of Fokine, she appeared in the first seasons of Diaghilev's Ballets Russes, her main roles being the title roles in *Sheherazade* and *Cléopâtre*. Possessing private means, she formed her own company in 1912, wherein she made use of the leading artists of the day, including Bakst, Benois, Massine, Fokine, Stravinsky, Ravel, etc. Outstanding among her productions of the 1928 season was Debussy's *Le Martyre de Saint-Sebastien*, in which she featured as actress and dancer. Subsequent undertakings included Stravinsky's *Perséphone*, 1934, and Ravel's *La Valse*. Though of great talent and personal beauty, Rubinstein was handicapped by an underdeveloped technique. *See* F. Gadan and R. Maillard, *A Dictionary of Modern Ballet*, 1959.

Rublëv, Andrey (*c.* 1360–1430), icon painter, active in Moscow and Vladimir. Adopting the innovations of Paleologos painting which had been brought from Constantinople to Russia by Feofan Grek (q.v.), with whom he probably worked in his youth, Rublëv achieved a most effective synthesis of iconographic contents with aesthetical values of rhythm and line. He combined a subtle and sensitive understanding of late Greek art with a very personal draughtsmanship and a genius for composition. His serene Trinity in the Troitse-Sergiyeva Lavra monastery (q.v.) is widely known in reproductions; this painting has never been surpassed in expression of exalted emotion emphasized by minute but significant elements of observed nature.

Rubtsovsk, town in the Altay Kray (southern Siberia), 165 m. south-west of Barnaul. Population (1959) 111,000 (1939, 38,000). Since the Second World War it has become a major centre of agricultural engineering (including tractors) and of various food industries.

Rudnyy, new town in the process of construction in the Kustanay Oblast (Kazakhstan), 30 m. south-west of Kustanay. Population (1958) about 40,000. It is the site of the building of a large iron-ore mining and dressing plant which will supply Magnitogorsk.

Rurik (Ryurik) (*d.* 879), semi-legendary founder of the ruling house of Rurikids, a leader of a Varangian (q.v.) group of warriors who sat as a prince in Novgorod from 862. He is sometimes identified by scholars as the Viking Hrörekr of Denmark, who raided western Europe up to 860. The origin of Russian statehood is traditionally dated from the year 862. The great Kievan state (*see* KIEVAN RUSSIA) was founded by Rurik's successor Oleg.

Rurikids, ruling house established by Rurik, to which the princes and grand princes of Kiev, the grand princes of Vladimir and the grand princes and czars of Muscovy belonged until 1598.

Russian Social Democratic Labour Party. In the late 1870's the first small underground Social Democratic groups had appeared in Russia; during the 1880's and early nineties the Liberation of Labour Group (q.v.) and several organizations for spreading Marxism among industrial workers were established, chiefly by former Populists, and from 1894 or 1895 many of these were engaged in agitation among the workers aimed at stirring up economic struggle. The Social Democratic

Labour Party, founded in 1898, united orthodox Marxists and revisionists (*see* LEGAL MARXISTS), trade unionist (*see* ECONOMISM) and more politically minded people, but the latter, led by Lenin, at once set out to take control of the party (*see* ISKRA). The party split into the two factions of Bolsheviks and Mensheviks at its second congress in 1903, and though it was formally reunited, 1906–12 (and sporadically until 1917), both factions continued to exist, breaking up further into various sub-factions after the revolution of 1905 (q.v.). In 1919 the Bolsheviks ceased to use the name Russian Social Democratic Labour Party, but the Mensheviks retained it. *See also* BOLSHEVISM; LENINISM; LIQUIDATIONISM.

Russian Soviet Federative Socialist Republic (abbreviation R.S.F.S.R.), official name of the largest, most populous and economically most important Union Republic of the U.S.S.R. It comprises most of the territory with predominantly Great Russian population —the larger part of European Russia, Siberia and the Far East. Area 6,593,400 sq. m. (nearly three-quarters of the U.S.S.R. total); population (1959) 117,534,000 (56 per cent of the total), of which 52 per cent is urban: Great Russians 83 per cent, Tatars 3·5 per cent, Ukrainians 3 per cent, etc. The name Soviet Federative Socialist Republic was adopted in 1918, and is misleading because the administrative structure is not even formally federal but centralized. Its fourteen Autonomous Republics take up only about one-quarter of its territory, the rest consisting of ordinary administrative units— oblasts and krays. In many ways the R.S.F.S.R. is less of a separate entity than the smaller Union Republics, its institutions being either identical with or overshadowed by those of the U.S.S.R.; for example, it has no separate Communist Party organization. Since Stalin's death, however, its identity has become somewhat more pronounced. *See* E. H. Carr, *The Bolshevik Revolution*, vol. i, 1950; T. Fitzsimmons (ed.), *R.S.F.S.R.*, 2 vols., New Haven, 1957; V. Gsovski and K. Grzybowski (eds.), *Government, Law and Courts in the Soviet Union and Eastern Europe*, vol. i, 1959.

Russians. The word is used in English in three senses: (1) to describe all inhabitants of Russia (Russian *rossiyane*), the equivalent of the use of 'British'; the Russian word *rossiyane* is now seldom used in Russia and has been replaced officially by 'Soviet people'; (2) to describe the people belonging to the East Slav (q.v.), or Russian, branch of the Slav family—the Great Russians, Ukrainians and Belorussians; the Russian term for this is *russkiye*, and is used frequently but not officially; (3) to describe the Great Russian people alone; the Russian word *russkiye* is now most commonly used in this sense, the expression 'Great Russian' being purely literary.

Russkaya Pravda ('Russian Truth'), first collection of Russian laws, a kind of 'lex Russica' compiled according to tradition under Yaroslav the Wise (1019–54). It is mainly a list of penalties to be paid in money to the injured person. *See* G. Vernadsky, *Medieval Russian Laws*, New York, 1947; H. J. Berman, *Justice in Russia*, Cambridge, Mass., 1950.

Russo-Japanese War, 1904–5, resulted from the conflict of Russian and Japanese interests in Asia, and the inept handling of affairs by

the Russian Government and the emperor, Nicholas II, who was
strongly under the influence of the adventurer Bezobrazov, against
the advice of the Foreign Minister Count Lamsdorf and the Prime
Minister Witte (q.v.)—the latter having been dismissed as Minister of
Finance in 1903 largely because of his dissent over the emperor's Far
Eastern policy. The immediate causes of the war were Russia's
refusal to withdraw completely from Manchuria (as she was pledged
to do under an agreement of 1902) and her expressed intention to
acquire further concessions in Korea. Bezobrazov's 'East Asiatic
Company for the Exploitation of Timber in Korea and Manchuria'
began operations on the Korean side of the Yalu River, and on 6th
February 1904 the Japanese attacked the Russian fleet at Port
Arthur (q.v.). The war proved disastrous for the Russian forces, and
found little support in the country at large. The decisive battle took
place at Tsushima in May 1905, when the Baltic fleet was almost
annihilated by the Japanese. Britain, who had given moral support to
Japan, suggested American mediation, and this offer was accepted by
both sides. A peace treaty was signed at Portsmouth (U.S.A.) in
September 1905 by which Russia ceded to Japan the southern half
of Sakhalin Island (q.v.), Port Arthur and the southern line of the
Chinese Eastern Railway (q.v.). *See* C. A. Court-Repington (*The
Times* correspondent), *War in the Far East*, 1904–5; K. I. Asakawa,
Russo-Japanese Conflict, 1905; A. N. Kuropatkin, *The Russian Army
and the Japanese War*, 1909; *Memoirs of Count Witte* (trans. A.
Yarmolinsky), New York, 1921; V. N. Kokovtsov, *Out of my Past*,
1935; R. Hough, *The Fleet that had to Die*, 1958; A. Malozemoff,
Russian Far Eastern Policy, 1881–1904, Los Angeles, 1958.

Rustavi, town in Georgia, situated on the River Kura 30 m. south-
east of Tiflis. Population (1959) 62,000. It is a centre of the iron and
steel industry in Transcaucasia and was founded in 1948 in connection with the construction, 1941–50, of the metallurgical plant.

Ruthenia, latinized form of the name 'Russia,' sometimes used to
denote the area inhabited by those Ukrainians who by religion are
Catholics of the Eastern Rite (Uniates); it is made up of Galicia
and Transcarpathia, the last especially being frequently called by
this name.

Ryabushinskiy, Pavel Pavlovich (*b.* 1871), business man and liberal
politician. After the death of his father in 1894 he became the head of
a vast family business (textiles, banking, land) which he further
developed with great success; in 1916 the Ryabushinskiy concern
built the first Russian automobile works in Moscow. He took a
leading part in the organizations of business people: in 1913 he was
elected chairman of the Society of Cotton Industrialists, in 1915 he
advanced the idea of War Industries Committees and became a
member of the Central War Industries Committee and chairman of
the Moscow committee. He was a leader of the Progressive Party
(q.v.) and publisher of its newspaper *Utro Rossii* ('*The Dawn of
Russia*.')

Ryazan': 1. Oblast of the R.S.F.S.R., situated south-east of
Moscow, lying in the Oka Basin and taking up part of the Meshchëra
in the north and the Oka-Don lowland in the south, in the north

largely covered with mixed forests; there are deposits of lignite (part of the Moscow Lignite Basin). Area 15,300 sq. m.; population (1959) 1,444,000 (30 per cent urban), Russians and some Tatars. Grain and potatoes are cultivated, horticulture and dairy farming practised, and there are food, engineering, coal-mining and woodworking industries. The area formed part of the Chernigov and later of the Murom-Ryazan' principalities, became independent in the mid 12th century, and in 1521 was absorbed by Muscovy.

2. (until 1778 **Pereyaslavl'-Ryazanskiy**). Administrative, economic and cultural centre of the oblast, situated on the River Oka. Population (1959) 213,000 (1897, 46,000; 1939, 95,000; 1956, 136,000). It has engineering (machine tools, agricultural and transport equipment), food and shoe industries. Ryazan' has been known since 1095, and was capital of the Ryazan' Principality from the early 14th century until 1521.

Ryazanov (real name **Gol'dendakh**), **David Borisovich** (1870–1938), Communist theorist. He became a Marxist in 1889 and in the following years set up the early Social Democratic circles in Odessa. After five years of imprisonment and three of police supervision he emigrated, and during the Iskra (q.v.) period headed the splinter group 'Bor'ba' ('Struggle'), trying to reconcile the Iskraists with the 'Economists' (see ECONOMISM). After the split at the 2nd party congress in 1903 he remained a 'non-factional' Social Democrat, and during the revolution of 1905 took a leading part in establishing trade unions in Odessa and St Petersburg, then emigrated once more. During the First World War he took up an internationalist position, but rejected Lenin's idea of defeat for one's own country. After the February revolution of 1917 Ryazanov became chairman of the Central Bureau of the St Petersburg trade unions, and joined the Bolsheviks. He later established himself as the most outstanding Communist marxologist, editing the complete works of Marx and Engels, Plekhanov's works, founding the Marx-Engels Institute and heading it until 1930, when he was dismissed and (1931) expelled from the party in connection with the Menshevik trial. He disappeared during the Great Purge (q.v.). See L. Schapiro, *The Communist Party of the Soviet Union*, 1960.

Rybakov, Boris Aleksandrovich (*b.* 1908), historian and archaeologist, member of the Academy of Sciences since 1958 and director of its Institute of Archaeology. Educated at Moscow University, he has taught there since 1939. Since 1932 he has conducted excavations in a number of old Russian towns, including Moscow and Chernigov. In his monumental *Handicrafts of Ancient Russia* (1948) and other works he stresses the indigenous character of much of the material culture of Kievan Russia. See review article by N. Andreyev, *Slavonic Review*, vol. xxviii, No. 70, Nov. 1949.

Rybinsk (1946–58 **Shcherbakov**), town in the Yaroslavl' Oblast (central Russia), situated at the Rybinsk Reservoir on the Volga. Population (1959) 181,000 (1926, 56,000; 1939, 144,000). It has engineering (printing machinery, road-building equipment), shipbuilding (since the 16th century), food (flour mills) and saw-milling industries; there is also a powerful hydro-electric station. Rybinsk has been known since 1137, and became a town in 1777. Its commercial development dates from the 16th century, and prior to 1917 it was a flourishing centre of the grain and flour trade in the Volga Basin, visited by tens of thousands of merchants during the summer.

Rybinsk Reservoir, artificial reservoir created by a dam on the Volga above Rybinsk, and bordering on Kalinin, Vologda and Yaroslavl' oblasts. Length from north-west to south-east 60 m., width 25 m., area 1,800 sq. m. The reservoir forms part of the Volga-Baltic Waterway (q.v.).

Rykov, Aleksey Ivanovich (1881–1938), politician who joined the militant wing (*see* ISKRA) of the Social Democratic Labour Party in 1901, and later the Bolshevik faction. As an underground agent in Russia he disliked Lenin's dictatorial orders from abroad, finally breaking with him in 1910 and becoming a leader of the 'Party-minded' Bolsheviks (a sub-faction which took a conciliatory line towards the Mensheviks). He held to this conciliatory attitude after the February 1917 revolution, and after the Bolshevik seizure of power in October advocated a coalition government of all socialist parties. In 1918–20 and 1923–4 he was chairman of the Supreme Council of National Economy, in 1921–4 deputy chairman of the Council of People's Commissars, and followed Lenin as chairman, 1924–30; he was also a member of the Politburo. He supported Stalin against Trotskiy and Zinov'yev during the inner-party conflict which followed Lenin's death, but became one of the most prominent leaders of the Right Opposition (q.v.) against the compulsory collectivization of agriculture. He was made Commissar for Posts and Telegraphs after the defeat of the opposition, but was sentenced to death in 1938 in the final show trial of the Great Purge (q.v.). *See* ANTI-SOVIET BLOC OF RIGHTISTS AND TROTSKIYITES. *See* L. Schapiro, *The Communist Party of the Soviet Union,* 1960.

Rykovo, *see* YENAKIYEVO.

Rzhev, town in the Kalinin Oblast (central Russia), situated on the Volga 70 m. south-west of Kalinin. Population (1956) 42,000 (1939, 54,000). It is the centre of a flax-growing area, and has a linen-milling industry; it is an important railway junction. Rzhev has been known since 1216; it saw much fighting in 1942–3.

S

Saaremaa (German **Oesel**), island in the Baltic Sea at the entry to the Gulf of Riga. Area 1,000 sq. m. It belongs to Estonia.

Saburov, Maksim Zakharovich (*b.* 1900), Communist. Born of a working-class family in the Donbas, he started work at 13. He joined the party in 1920 and volunteered for a 'special purpose detachment' for suppressing armed resistance to the regime. From 1921 to 1928 he worked in the party apparatus and propaganda, studying at the Sverdlov Communist University, 1923–6. Later he studied engineering in Moscow and made a successful professional career, advancing rapidly during the Great Purge (q.v.). From 1938 he worked in the Gosplan (q.v.), was its chairman, 1941–4, and again 1949–55, and chairman of the State Economic Commission for current planning in 1955–6. Simultaneously he was a deputy prime minister in 1941–4 and 1947–55 and a first deputy prime minister in 1955–7. Saburov became a member of the Central Committee and of its Presidium in 1952, and during the period of 'collective leadership' (q.v.) after Stalin's death was usually considered as belonging to the 'managerial' faction headed by Malenkov. He joined the so-called 'anti-party group' (q.v.) in its struggle against Khrushchëv in 1957, but recanted upon its defeat and was removed from the party Presidium and the Government. After working for a time as deputy chairman of the Committee for Economic Co-operation of the Soviet bloc countries he was in 1958 appointed the manager of a factory in Syzran'.

Sadovskiy, Prov Mikhaylovich (1818–72), famous actor. He received little education and started acting in provincial troupes at the age of 13. Noticed by Shchepkin (q.v.), he was in 1839 invited to the Malyy Theatre in Moscow, where he continued Shchepkin's realistic tradition. His repertoire included Shakespeare (Fool in *King Lear*), Molière, Gogol' (q.v.), and especially A. N. Ostrovskiy (q.v.). Sadovskiy was the main contemporary interpreter of Ostrovskiy's plays, and set the tradition of their performance at the Malyy Theatre. His son, Mikhail Provovich (1847–1910), grandson, Prov Mikhaylovich (1874–1947), and great-grandson, Mikhail Provovich, have also been leading actors of the Malyy Theatre.

St Petersburg, *see* LENINGRAD.

Sakhalin: 1. Island in the Russian Far East, over 600 m. long and between 16 and 125 m. broad, between the Sea of Okhotsk and the Sea of Japan, separated from the mainland by Tatar Strait and from Hokkaido Island (Japan) by La Perouse Strait. It has deposits of coal, oil and gold. Sakhalin was under a Russo-Japanese condominium from 1855 and became Russian in 1875; the southern part of the island, to 50° N., was ceded to Japan in 1905. By the Yalta Agreement the Soviet Government was conceded the right to retake the southern half.

2. Oblast of the R.S.F.S.R., comprising the island of Sakhalin and the Kurile Islands. Area 33,600 sq. m.; population (1959) 651,000 (75 per cent urban), Russians (until 1945 over 400,000 Japanese). There are fishing, oil, coal-mining and wood-processing industries; potato, vegetable and dairy farming. Principal towns: Yuzhno-Sakhalinsk (administrative centre) and Korsakov. The northern part of the oblast formed from 1932 an oblast within the Far Eastern (later Khabarovsk) Kray, while the southern part, annexed from Japan, became the Southern Sakhalin Oblast in 1946; in 1947 the two were fused.

Salavat, town in Bashkiria (Urals), situated on the River Belaya about 90 m. south of Ufa. Population (1959) 60,000, Russians, Tatars, Bashkirs. It was founded after the Second World War as the centre of an important oilfield, and became a town in 1954.

Salekhard (until 1933 **Obdorsk**; Nenets **Salehard**), administrative, economic and cultural centre of the Yamal-Nenets National Okrug, in the Tyumen' Oblast (Western Siberia), situated on the lower Ob'. Population (1956) 16,000, mainly Russian. It has fish canneries and is connected with Vorkuta by railway. Salekhard was founded in 1595.

Saltykov, Mikhail Yevgrafovich (pseud. **N. Shchedrin**) (1826–1889), satirical writer who was in government service, was banished, and retired in 1868 as vice-governor of a province to devote himself to literature. He was co-editor of *The Contemporary* (q.v.) and edited its successor as the leading radical journal, *The Notes of the Fatherland*. He developed to a high degree the art of social and political satire, his many sketches, novels and stories being concerned with the exposure of traditional and contemporary conditions in Russia (e.g. *Provincial Sketches*, 1856). *See* K. Sanine, *Saltykov-Chtchedrine: sa vie et ses œuvres*, Paris, 1955.

Samanids, native (Iranian) dynasty of the rulers of Transoxania (q.v.) in Central Asia from the year 875 to 999, nominally under the suzerainty of the caliphs. At the height of their power the Samanids ruled over a vast territory comprising almost the whole of Central Asia (except Semirech'ye) as well as large areas of Persia and Afghanistan. The capital of their domains, Bukhara, Samarkand and other principal towns were great centres of Islamic learning (Avicenna, Al-Khorezmi, Al-Biruni). The Samanids favoured the use of Persian as opposed to Arabic, and Persian poetry flourished during their rule (Firdousi, Rudaki).

Samara, *see* KUYBYSHEV.

Samarin, Yuriy Fedorovich (1819–76), Slavophile publicist and politician. He was an enthusiastic supporter of the Great Reforms (q.v.) and himself took an active part in the preparation of the emancipation of the serfs; it was partly due to his influence that the ownership of land after emancipation was transferred to the peasant communes (*see* MIR) rather than to individual peasants. *See* R. Hare, *Pioneers of Russian Social Thought*, 1951; T. G. Masaryk, *The Spirit of Russia*, vol. i, 2nd ed., 1955; M. B. Petrovich, *The Emergence of Russian Panslavism, 1856–70*, New York, 1956.

Samarkand: 1. Oblast of Uzbekistan comprising the middle part of the Zeravshan Valley and the mountainous areas to the north and south. Area 14,600 sq. m.; population (1959) 1,151,000 (27 per cent urban), Uzbeks and Tadzhiks. Cotton, lucerne, rice, grapes and fruit (Samarkand cherries) are cultivated, Astrakhan sheep and Karabair horses bred, and there is sericulture. Industries of the oblast are cotton processing, food, building materials and some engineering. For history see BUKHARA KHANATE; SOGDIANA; TRANSOXANIA. The area was annexed to Russia in 1868.

2. (ancient **Marakanda**). Administrative, economic and cultural centre of the oblast. Population (1959) 195,000 (1939, 136,000), Uzbeks and Tadzhiks. It has engineering (tractor parts, cinema equipment), food, cotton-processing and silk industries. The Uzbek State University (founded 1927 as a Pedagogical Institute, transformed 1933) is here, also several other higher educational establishments and several research institutes, including the Astrakhan Sheep Institute, the Institute of Tropical Medicine and the Museum of Uzbek Culture. The town is a treasury of Islamic architecture, with the Gur-Emir Mausoleum where Timur and his successors are buried, the Bibi-Khanum mosque, the Ulugbek *medresseh*, etc. All these are situated in the old town, whereas the industries and the administrative and chief educational institutions are in the Russian-built new town. Samarkand is the oldest city in Central Asia, dating from the 4th or 3rd millennium B.C. It was the main centre of Sogdiana, and in the 14th century A.D. Timur made it the capital of his empire. For many centuries Samarkand was an important centre of Islamic learning. From 1924 until 1930 it was the capital of Uzbekistan.

3. *See* TEMIR-TAU.

Samogitia (Lithuanian **Zamaitis**, Russian **Zhmud'**), historical name for north-western Lithuania, inhabited by people (Zhmuds) whose language and customs differ somewhat from those of the Lithuanians proper. Samogitia belonged to the Teutonic Knights from the 13th to early 15th centuries, and then passed to Lithuania, remaining a semi-autonomous area until the mid 16th century.

Samoyeds, group of peoples inhabiting the shores of the Polar Ocean from the White Sea in the west to the River Khatanga in the east, speaking languages akin to the Finno-Ugrian family, and numbering (1959) 29,000. They are semi-nomadic reindeer keepers in the north, and sedentary fishers in the south (Tomsk Oblast), both now collectivized. Known since the 11th century, they were vassals of Muscovy from the 16th century, but throughout the 16th and 17th centuries they carried on the struggle for independence. Three Samoyed National Okrugs were established in 1929–30 (*see* NENETS; TAYMYR; YAMAL).

Samoylova, Tat'yana Yevgen'yevna (*b.* 1935), female lead in *The Cranes are Flying*, her first film. Daughter of a stage actor, she learnt ballet dancing as a child, and on leaving school entered Vakhtangov Theatre Studio. Her film *Unposted Letter*—the story of diamond prospectors in Yakutia—was severely censured by *Pravda* in February 1960. Together with Inna Makarova, Iya Arepina, Izol'da Izvitskaya and Klara Luchko, Samoylova is one of the most promising of the younger Soviet actresses.

Saransk, capital, economic and cultural centre of the Mordva Autonomous Republic, situated 145 m. south-east of Gor'kiy. Population (1959) 90,000, mainly Russians. It has varied industries, including electrical equipment, and there is a university established in 1957. Saransk was founded as a fort in 1680, and became a town in 1780.

Sarapul, town in the Udmurt Autonomous Republic (Urals), situated on the River Kama and the Kazan'-Sverdlovsk railway, 30 m. south-east of Izhevsk. Population (1959) 68,000, Russian. It has engineering (oil and timber industry equipment, wireless sets), leather and woodworking industries and is a local cultural centre. Sarapul has been known since 1596, became a town in 1780 and has long been famous for its leatherwork and shoes.

Saratov: 1. Oblast of the R.S.F.S.R., situated on both banks of the lower Volga, an area of dry steppe with black earth and chestnut soils; there are large deposits of natural gas, oil and building materials. Area 38,700 sq. m.; population (1959) 2,167,000 (54 per cent urban), mostly Russians and Ukrainians (before the war also Germans). Wheat, sunflowers, tobacco and mustard are cultivated (often endangered by droughts), cattle are raised, and there are food, engineering, gas- and oil-extraction, textile and cement industries. Construction of a large hydro-electric station was begun in 1956, but stopped in 1958 owing to a change in economic policy; the first pipe-line to supply gas to Moscow has its starting-point in the oblast. Principal towns: Saratov, Engel's, Vol'sk, Balashov. The area was annexed by Muscovy in the mid 16th century, having previously been almost unpopulated, and was gradually colonized, especially after the late 18th century.

2. Administrative and economic centre of the oblast, cultural centre of the whole lower Volga region, situated on the right bank of the Volga. Population (1959) 581,000 (1897, 137,000; 1914, 218,000; 1923, 187,000; 1939, 372,000). It is an important centre of industry and transport—varied engineering, gas and oil, and printing industries, transfer of Baku oil to railway for central Russia. There are some interesting buildings of the 19th century, a university, 1909, conservatoire, 1912, arts museum, 1885, the Radishchev and Cherny-shevskiy museums and many scientific institutions.

Saratov was founded as a fortified town in 1590 on the site of a Tatar settlement on the left bank, and was transferred to the right bank in 1674. It was an important centre of trade in fish and salt from the mid 17th century; from the mid 19th century till the 1920's it was the largest city on the Volga and the principal centre of flour milling and the grain trade in the country. Heavy industry has developed since the 1930's, especially during and after the war. Saratov became a provincial capital in 1780, and was one of the best-administered cities in Russia; it was capital of the Lower Volga Region, 1928-31.

Saray, capital of the Golden Horde on the left bank of the lower Volga; it was founded in the 13th century and destroyed in 1460 by the Russians.

Sarov, former famous monastery in the Mordva Autonomous

Republic, founded in 1679. It was venerated as the abode of St Seraphim of Sarov and the resting-place of his bones.

Sart, name applied until the 1920's to the majority of the urban and rural sedentary population in the oases of Central Asia to distinguish them from the nomadic or semi-nomadic Uzbeks who had retained the tribal system and from the Tadzhiks of the mountains. They were the descendants of the original Iranian inhabitants of the area, but from the 6th century a process of Turkicization took place as a result of conquests by many Turkic-speaking tribes, and by the 20th century only a minority of Sarts spoke Tadzhik alone, while the majority spoke a Turkic language (so-called Chagatay) in everyday life but used Persian as a literary language. Since the National Delimitation of Central Asia (q.v.) in 1924 the Tadzhik-speaking Sarts have been counted as Tadzhiks, while the bilingual or Chaga-tay-speaking Sarts have been officially regarded as Uzbeks, and the contemporary Uzbek literary language is based on Chagatay.

Sar'yan, Martiros Sergeyevich (b. 1880), Armenian landscape painter, studied at the Moscow School of Art, 1897–1903. He worked in Yerevan (Armenia) and in Moscow, and was associated with the Mir Iskusstva movement (q.v.) and its successor Zolotoye Runo ('The Golden Fleece'). Saryan's distinctive style was formed under the influence of Cézanne and other French post-impressionists; it is distinguished by the bold use of strong, fresh, freely applied and contrasting colours. This style is unique among Soviet landscapists, who since the triumph of Socialist Realism (q.v.) have as a rule worked in the vein of timid and monotonous illusionism. In his paintings Saryan invariably depicts the typical features of his native Caucasian mountains.

Savings, private, can be deposited in the Savings Bank, of which in 1958 there were 58,584 branches (41,359 rural). Savings accounts numbered 47·0 million in 1958 (3·5 in 1927–8, 17·3 in 1940, 14·3 in 1950), of which 34·4 million were in towns. The average savings account in 1958 amounted to 1850 roubles (1250 in 1950)—1996 roubles in urban areas (1516 in 1950) and 1454 roubles in rural areas (531 in 1950) (figures in pre-1961 roubles). Interest is paid upon savings accounts.

Sayan Mountains, in southern Siberia, consist of two ranges, East Sayan and West Sayan, separated by the Minusinsk Basin. Average height 6,000 ft; Munku-Sardyk Mountain is over 11,400 ft.

Schmidt, Otto Yul'yevich (1891–1956), mathematician and polar explorer. As a young man he was a Social Democrat Internationalist, but joined the Bolsheviks soon after their seizure of power. During the 1920's he took part in expeditions to Central Asia, in 1930 became director of the Arctic Institute in Leningrad, and from 1932 to 1938 was the head of the Northern Sea Route (q.v.) administration. He became famous for his polar expeditions, notably on the *Sibiryakov*, 1932, the first ship to navigate the whole Northern Sea Route in one season, on the *Chelyuskin*, 1933–4, and for his leadership of the expedition which established the first floating station at the North Pole (*see* PAPANIN). The *Chelyuskin* expedition met with disaster when the ship was crushed in the ice, and the rescue of its members by air made a great popular impact (the title of 'Hero of the Soviet Union' was first established for the pilot rescuers). Schmidt's activities bore the mark of being strongly influenced by N. F. Fëdorov (q.v.). Dismissed in the course of the Great Purge, he continued academic work as professor of mathematics in Moscow University. *See* T. E. Armstrong, *Russians in the Arctic, Soviet Exploration 1937–57*, 1958.

Scientific Organization of Labour, term used especially until the mid 1930's for methods of raising efficiency. The study of the subject in Russia was greatly influenced by contemporary foreign examples, such as the Ford and Taylor systems, though both were formally condemned on ideological grounds. Special importance was ascribed to this matter by some representatives of the Bogdanovist (*see* BOGDANOVISM) ideological trend (*see* GASTEV; KERZHENTSEV), for whom the construction of socialism was largely synonymous with the scientific organization of labour. All these studies were suppressed by Stalin, since in fact they were incompatible with the bogus methods of the 'Stakhanov movement' (q.v.), and though practical improvements in working methods continued to be made all theorizing ceased. In recent years efforts have been made to revive work in this field. *See* R. A. Bauer, *The New Man in Soviet Psychology*, Cambridge, Mass., 1952.

Scriabin, *see* SKRYABIN.

Sculpture as an art has been on the whole rather alien to Russia. The Russian Orthodox Church explicitly forbade the embellishment of churches with three-dimensional images: only two interesting examples of early ornamental relief work are extant—in the Church of St Demetrius, Vladimir, *c.* 1195–1200, and the Church of St George, Yur'yev-Pol'skiy, 1229–34. Sculpture was introduced in Russia as a Western art form only at the time of the westernizing reforms of Peter the Great. The imported marbles were mostly of second-rate quality and so were many of the sculptors who agreed to come to Russia to work and to instruct. The first two Russian sculptors of note were F. I. Shubin (1740–1805), who made competent portrait busts, and M. I. Kozlovskiy (1753–1802), who carved caryatids for the throne room of the Pavlovsk Palace. I. P. Martos (1745–1835) was the author of the famous, if incongruous, group 'Minin and Pozharskiy' which stands in the Red Square, Moscow. In St Petersburg P. K. Klodt (1805–67) created a more fortunate landmark for the city—the four horse-tamers on the Anichkov Bridge. M. M. Antokol'skiy (1843–1902) is known for his realistic reconstructions of historical figures—'Ivan the Terrible,' 'Peter the Great'—but his reputation in Europe was based on his sardonic crouched 'Mephistopheles.' With the ascendance of the Mir Iskusstva movement (q.v.) the quality of sculptures improved; Prince P. Trubetskoy produced a number of bold dynamic portraits, and the painters Somov and Vrubel' (q.v.) dabbled with considerable success in designing decorative majolica and porcelain figurines. After the period of fierce experimentation sculpture as well as painting became the victim of Socialist Realism (q.v.); the works of Shadr, Mukhina, Andreyev and Konenkov (after his return from America in 1946) show that the style of 'monumental idealism' (which is what Socialist Realism amounts to in the case of this art form) has contributed scarcely anything to the development of Russian sculpture. *See* C. G. E. Bunt, *Russian Art: From Scyths to Soviets*, 1946; C. H. Hamilton, *Art and Architecture of Russia*, 1954.

Sebastopol, *see* SEVASTOPOL'.

Sechenov, Ivan Mikhaylovich (1829–1905), 'the father of Russian physiology,' professor at St Petersburg and Moscow universities. A follower of Darwin and Chernyshevskiy, Sechenov advanced a materialist conception of psychic and spiritual phenomena, both in his special works (*Reflexes of the Brain*, 1863; *Physiology of the Nervous System*, 1866, etc.) and in his psychological and epistemological writings (*Object Thought and Reality*, 1892; *Impressions and Reality*). *See* V. V. Zenkovsky, *A History of Russian Philosophy* (2 vols.), 1953.

Secondary Education has in Russia traditionally meant the kind of post-primary education which prepares for higher education of university level. Since 1918 the first stage of secondary education has been combined with primary education in comprehensive schools of one kind or another. Since the educational reform of 1958 it is the eight-year incomplete secondary school which is compulsory for children of 7–15 years of age. The four upper classes of this school form the first stage of secondary education, which is thus uniform. The second stage has been divided since the 1930's into two main branches—general and professional (for the latter *see* EDUCATION). General secondary education is now received either in three-year secondary or comprehensive schools, or else in four-year evening, seasonal or correspondence secondary schools. The curricula of all these types of general secondary school are essentially identical, aimed at a balance between the humanities, theoretical sciences and 'polytechnical' (*see* POLYTECHNICAL EDUCATION) subjects, each group being allotted about one-third of the total time. All pupils will in future be required to undergo training in a trade and to pass a qualifying examination while at school. Two school hours a week are reserved for optional subjects, and this may to some extent ameliorate the lack of differentiation in general secondary education. Such differentiation had existed before 1917 (when there were three types of general secondary schools—classical gymnasia, real schools and commercial schools), but it was not reintroduced when secondary education was restored in the 1930's, and its promoters (among whom was the Academy of Pedagogical Sciences) were unsuccessful in 1958. Secondary education has suffered most from government educational policy, both before 1917 and after.

A State system of secondary education was established in the late 18th century for able and deserving children from all classes, but repeated attempts were made (especially in the 1880's) to exclude children from the 'lower orders.' The total number of secondary school pupils was small and the number of free places limited. In the 1920's the class principle of admission was revived and retained until 1935, those discriminated against being children from the former privileged classes and children of disfranchised parents, e.g. peasants who refused to join the collective farms and were classified as *kulaks*.

This, together with ceaseless experimentation with school forms and the content and methods of instruction, disorganized secondary education. General secondary education was abolished altogether in 1930, but gradually restored in the following years. From 1936 until 1958 the main form of secondary education was the ten-year comprehensive secondary school which until 1953 aimed exclusively at preparing for higher education. The scholarly attainment compared not unfavourably with secondary education elsewhere, except for the absence of classical languages and the generally poor teaching of foreign languages. The number of pupils in the three upper forms, which had risen sharply in the 1930's, was kept down after the war by the fees (*see* TUITION FEES) and the virtual absence of free places. Expansion began in 1949, and in 1952 the aim was set to achieve universal compulsory secondary education by 1960. This aim was vigorously pursued till 1956, but there was no corresponding expansion of higher education, and the resulting juvenile unemployment contributed to the reversal of the policy of expansion.

The 1958 reform limited compulsory schooling to eight years. Only about one-third of all the ten-year secondary schools which existed in 1958 have been transformed into new three-year day-schools, though many others continue as evening schools. The gradual shift since 1952 towards 'polytechnical education,' though it has undoubtedly done something to prepare the young people for manual jobs, has resulted in lower standards particularly in the humanities; other contributing factors have been the abolition of promotional examinations in 1957, reduced opportunities for higher education, and probably the great numerical expansion itself. The latter, at least, will no longer operate now, and the possibility of a more intensive concentration on selected optional subjects may again improve standards. *See further under* EDUCATION. *See* N. DeWitt, *Soviet Professional Manpower*, Washington, D.C., 1955; A. G. Korol, *Soviet Education for Science and Technology*, 1957; S. V. Utechin, 'Current Problems of Soviet Secondary Education,' *Soviet Survey*, No. 12, Feb. 1957, 'Education in the U.S.S.R.,' *Political Quarterly*, vol. xxix, No. 4, Oct.–Dec. 1958, and 'Khrushchëv's Educational Reform,' *Soviet Survey*, No. 28, April–June 1959.

Secretariat of the Central Committee, one of the chief seats of power in the U.S.S.R., directing the apparatus of the party's Central Committee. It consists of several secretaries elected by the Central Committee, each of them in charge of one or more departments. The first secretary (formerly Secretary-General, q.v.) is the highest ranking party official and is always a member of the Presidium (formerly Politburo, qq.v.) of the Central Committee. Some of the other secretaries are also usually members or candidate members of the Presidium, and those who are not rank immediately after. *See* M. Fainsod, *How Russia is Ruled*, Cambridge, Mass., 1953; L. Schapiro, *The Communist Party of the Soviet Union*, 1960.

Secretary-General of the Central Committee, official designation, 1922–34, of the post held by Stalin in the party hierarchy. This unique position at the head of the party apparatus enabled him to manipulate appointments, and indeed all organizational affairs, and greatly facilitated his rise to personal dictatorship. The abolition of the title of Secretary-General after the 17th party congress appears to have been one of the measures in the attempt to curb Stalin's power which precipitated the Great Purge (q.v.). Thereafter there was no special designation to distinguish Stalin from other Central Committee secretaries, but in September 1953 Khrushchëv was officially elected first secretary. He has since used this position in a way similar to Stalin. *See* E. H. Carr, *The Bolshevik Revolution*, vol. i, 1950; M. Rush, *The Rise of Khrushchëv*, Washington, D.C., 1958; L. Schapiro, *The Communist Party of the Soviet Union*, 1960.

Security Organs, of the Soviet regime, have developed out of the 'fighting teams' which were set up by the Bolsheviks in accordance with Lenin's organizational plan during the revolution of 1905 (q.v.) and were re-established as the Red Guards after the February revolution of 1917. Following the October coup the Red Guards were used for fighting 'counter-revolution,' and this has remained the main function of the security organs, which have been known under different names at different periods (*see* CHEKA; G.P.U.; K.G.B.; M.G.B.; M.V.D.; N.K.G.B.; N.K.V.D.). At first subordinate to the party, the security organs grew in importance when Stalin began to use them against his opponents within the party, until at the time of the Great Purge (q.v.) they assumed the highest position in the apparatus of power, above the party itself and subordinate only to Stalin personally. During this process the command of the security organs passed successively from a revolutionary fanatic, Dzerzhinskiy, first to obedient party officials, Menzhinskiy and Yagoda, and then to the degenerate sadist Yezhov. During Beria's long tenure of command, 1938–53, the vast apparatus of the security organs consolidated its position as the most powerful, privileged and irresponsible section of society; in such a situation it was only natural that immediately after Stalin's death Beria should have attempted to seize supreme power in the state, and his failure was followed by a drastic curtailment of the powers of the security organs, their subordination once again to the party control, and the appointment of a professional policeman, Serov, to the command. The emergence of an active political opposition, especially since 1956, has brought about on the one hand renewed emphasis on the importance of the security organs, and on the other the appointment (in 1958) of a politician, Shelepin, to head them. *See* M. Fainsod, *How Russia is Ruled*, Cambridge, Mass., 1953; S. Wolin and R. M. Slusser (eds.), *The Soviet Secret Police*, New York, 1957; V. Gsovski and K. Grzybowski (eds.), *Government, Law and Courts in the Soviet Union and Eastern Europe*, vol. i, 1959; H. McClosky and J. E. Turner, *The Soviet Dictatorship*, 1960; A. Kramish, *Atomic Energy in the Soviet Union*, 1960.

Sedov, Leonid Ivanovich (*b*. 1907), scientist. Educated at Moscow University, and professor there since 1937, he worked at the Central Aero-Hydrodynamic Institute from 1931 and at the Central Institute of Aircraft Engine Building from 1947, member of the Academy of Sciences since 1953. He continued the work of N. Ye. Zhukovskiy and Chaplygin (qq.v.) on the theory of wings and the dynamics of gases, finding new mathematical methods and applying them to other fields of theoretical mechanics. He has also done some work in astrophysics, and in recent years has been closely associated with the design and launching of artificial earth satellites (*see* SPUTNIK).

Selenga, navigable river in Asia, rising in the Khangay Mountains in Mongolia and flowing north-east into Lake Baykal. Length 920 m. Its principal port is Ulan-Ude.

Semënov, Nikolay Nikolayevich (*b.* 1896), physicist and chemist, member of the Academy of Sciences. Educated at Petrograd University, he has taught in Leningrad and (since 1944) in Moscow. He joined the party in 1947. His works are mainly concerned with the theory of chain reactions, and he shared the Nobel Prize for Chemistry in 1956. In a much-discussed article published in 1959 Semënov condemned the bureaucratic planning of academic research as practised in the U.S.S.R., and asserted that science, unlike technology, developed according to the logic of scientific inquiry and not according to the needs of industrial production. *See* J. G. Crowther, *Soviet Science*, 1936.

Semënov-Tyan-Shanskiy, Pëtr Petrovich (1827–1914), outstanding geographer and statistician. Educated at St Petersburg and Berlin universities, he made extensive travels in Turkestan, studying the orography of Tien Shan (and proving that it is not of volcanic origin) and collecting much mineralogical, botanical, entomological and ethnographic material. As a leading figure in the Russian Geographical Society (vice-president and virtual head from 1873) he organized and inspired many expeditions to Central Asia, including those of Przheval'skiy, Potanin, Kropotkin and Komarov (qq.v.). Semënov took an active part as an expert member in the commissions for preparing the emancipation of the serfs, 1861, and the military reforms, 1874 (*see* GREAT REFORMS). He was director of the Central Statistical Committee, 1864–75 (organizing the first Russian statistical congress in 1870, which laid the foundations of the *zemstvo*, q.v., statistics), and chairman of the Statistical Council in 1875–97 (directing the first Russian population census in 1897). He became an honorary member of the Academy of Sciences in 1873 and member of the Council of State (q.v.) in 1897. He published the *Geographical and Statistical Dictionary of the Russian Empire* (5 vols.), 1863–85, edited (together with V. I. Lamanskiy) *Russia. Full Geographical Description of our Fatherland* (19 vols.), 1899–1914, etc. An ardent collector of Flemish and Dutch art (*Essays in the History of Netherlands Painting*, 2 parts, 1885–90), he gave his rich collection to the Hermitage Museum in St Petersburg.

Semevskiy, Vasiliy Ivanovich (1848–1916), historian and publicist, professor at St Petersburg University. His works, mainly dealing with the history of peasants in Russia in the 18th and 19th centuries, established the Populist (*see* POPULISM) school of Russian social history.

Semipalatinsk: 1. Oblast in eastern Kazakhstan, situated largely in the Kazakh hills south of the River Irtysh, traversed by the Turksib Railway. Area 65,600 sq. m.; population (1959) 487,000 (47 per cent urban), mostly Russians, also Kazakhs, Ukrainians, Mordva, Germans, Bulgarians and Tatars. Wheat is cultivated (and was expanded greatly during the Virgin Land Campaign of 1954–6) in the north, and sheep and cattle are raised in the south; industry is almost entirely confined to the town of Semipalatinsk.

2. Administrative, economic and cultural centre of the oblast, situated on the Irtysh and the Turksib Railway. Population (1959) 155,000 (1939, 110,000), mostly Russians, also Kazakhs (about 20 per cent) and Tatars (about 7 per cent). It has a large meat-packing plant (the second in the U.S.S.R.) and various other food industries, and a wool-processing and other textile factories. There are several higher educational establishments and two museums, one of which, the Local Studies Museum (founded 1883), is the oldest in Kazakhstan. The house where Dostoyevskiy lived in banishment is here. Semipalatinsk was founded in 1718 as a Russian fortress, became a town in 1783, and provincial centre in 1854.

Semirech'ye (Russian translation of Turkic 'Dzhety-su'—'Seven rivers'), geographical and historical region in Central Asia, between Lake Balkhash and the upper course of the River Naryn, comprising a lowland desert in the north and the central part of the Tien-Shan Mountains in the south, with a narrow fertile belt at the foothills. It is now divided between Kazakhstan (Alma-Ata Oblast) and Kirgizia. In the last centuries B.C. and the first centuries A.D. it was inhabited, like the rest of Central Asia, by Iranians. In the 6th–8th centuries it belonged to the West Turkic kaganate which had its centre here; later there were ephemeral local Turkic states until one of them, the Karakhanid state (10th–12th centuries), extended its power over Kashgaria and Transoxania. During this period Arabic Muslim culture made considerable progress in the area, while Turkic literature also developed. The population seems to have been completely Turkicized by this time. In the 12th century Kara-Kitay, defeated by the Chinese, migrated westwards and established a new state on the territory previously belonging to the Karakhanids, with Balasagun in Semirech'ye as their capital. In 1219–21 Semirech'ye was conquered by Genghis Khan's Mongols, the towns destroyed and the agricultural population dispersed. Semirech'ye was included in the Chagatay domain and after the latter split up Semirech'ye, where a Mongol nomadic horde established itself, was known as Mogolistan (14th–17th centuries).

In the 15th century Kazakhs (q.v.), having broken off the Uzbek Khanate, arrived in Semirech'ye from the north-west and established their own khanate there. When this broke up in the following century Semirech'ye remained the home of the Senior Hundred. At the same time the mixed Turkic-Mongol tribes in the Tien-Shan Mountains began to identify themselves as Kirgiz (q.v.). In the late 17th century both Kazakhs and Kirgiz were partly driven out and partly conquered by the Kalmyks (q.v.) of Dzungaria, who occupied Semirech'ye. After the rout of the Kalmyks by the Manchu-Chinese army in 1758 the Kazakhs and Kirgiz returned to Semirech'ye. In the 1830's the area was conquered by the Kokand Khanate (q.v.), but in 1846 the Kazakh Senior Hundred exchanged Kokand for Russian suzerainty. In 1864 the rest of Semirech'ye was conquered by the Russians and in the following year Semirech'ye Oblast was formed within Turkestan (q.v.). *See* V. V. Barthold, *Four Studies on the History of Central Asia*, vol. i, London, 1956; M. Holdsworth, *Turkestan in the Nineteenth Century*, 1959; R. A. Pierce, *Russian Central Asia, 1867–1917*, Berkeley and Los Angeles, 1960.

Semites. There are two peoples in the Soviet Union speaking Semitic languages, the Assyrians and the Arabs. The former, who number in the U.S.S.R. (1959) 22,000, live in small groups scattered mostly in Transcaucasia; they are Christians of various denominations, and speak Syriac (using the Russian alphabet for writing). They are chiefly peasants or unskilled labourers. According to their own tradition they are the descendants of the ancient Assyrians, and this may well be the case. They fled to Russia from Turkey during and immediately after the First World War. The Arabs, who numbered 8,000 in 1959 (22,000 in 1939), live mostly in several villages in Uzbekistan, where they came from Afghanistan in the 17th and 18th centuries, although according to their own tradition they are the descendants of the Arab conquerors of the 8th century. They are largely assimilated and mostly speak Uzbek or Tadzhik. Jews, (q.v.) in Russia, though of Semitic origin, cannot be regarded as belonging to the Semitic linguistic family, since they either have no knowledge of Hebrew at all or else use it solely as the language of their religion; modern cultural life in Hebrew was suppressed after the Bolshevik seizure of power.

Senate, one of the highest government bodies in Imperial Russia. It was established by Peter the Great in 1711 as the highest administrative, legislative and judicial organ, subordinated directly and exclusively to the emperor. As time went on its functions diminished, and from the judicial reform of 1864 (*see* GREAT REFORMS) until the Bolshevik seizure of power it acted only as the supreme Court of Appeal; it also had the right of interpretation of the laws. Senators were appointed by the emperor from among members of the upper three ranks in the civil and military services.

Separation of Powers does not exist in the U.S.S.R. and is rejected by the Communists generally and by Lenin in his *State and Revolution*, 1917, as a fiction of the bourgeois political theory designed to mislead the masses. The distribution of government functions between various institutions is not meant to constitute a separation of powers, since they are all organs of the Dictatorship of the Proletariat (q.v.) and have to implement the policy of the Communist Party (q.v.). *See* A. Y. Vyshinsky (ed.), *The Law of the Soviet State*, New York, 1948; J. Towster, *Political Power in the U.S.S.R., 1917–47*, New York, 1948; M. Fainsod, *How Russia is Ruled*, Cambridge, Mass., 1953; J. N. Hazard, *The Soviet System of Government*, Chicago, 1957; V. Gsovski and K. Grzybowski (eds.), *Government, Law and Courts in the Soviet Union and Eastern Europe*, vol. i, 1959.

Seraphim of Sarov, Saint (1759–1833), monk of the Sarov monastery, the first known Starets (q.v.) and a saint of the Orthodox Church (canonized in 1903). He spent sixteen years as a hermit, and fifteen as a recluse. *See* A. F. Dobbie-Bateman, *St Seraphim of Sarov*, 1936; G. P. Fedotov, *A Treasury of Russian Spirituality*, 1950.

Serfdom in Russia grew from two roots: one was the slavery which had existed from the earliest times, the other the diverse economic obligations of the peasants towards the landlords, the most common being voluntary serfdom in return for a loan. After the promulgation in Muscovy of the legal code of 1649 (*see* ULOZHENIYE) serfdom became a State institution rather than a private relationship. The distinction between serfs and slaves gradually disappeared, and under Catherine II both categories were fused under the name of serfs, though in fact their position was much nearer to that of slaves. In 1783 serfdom was extended to the Ukraine, and to New Russia (q.v.) in 1797, but it never existed in the north of European Russia or Siberia. Masters had almost complete power over their serfs, though they were under general obligations to maintain them in famine, to provide seed in case of crop failure and to refrain from 'ruining or dealing cruelly' with them. Serfs, like other peasants in Great Russia, had a measure of self-government in the village communes (*see* MIR), though the landlords had extensive powers of supervision over these. Various projects for the emancipation of the serfs were considered by the Government from the time of Catherine II, but it was not finally achieved until 1861 (*see* GREAT REFORMS). The existence of serfdom was a serious obstacle to economic and social development, and an offence to the sentiments of the educated society (*see*, e.g., RADISH-CHEV); the memory of it contributed much to the development of radical political trends among the intelligentsia and the peasants (*see* POPULISM). *See* D. Mackenzie Wallace, *Russia*, 2nd ed., 1905; G. T. Robinson, *Rural Russia under the Old Regime*, 2nd ed., New York, 1949.

Sergeyevich, Vasiliy Ivanovich (1835–1911), jurist and historian, professor and for some time rector of St Petersburg University, after 1905 member by appointment of the State Council. He was head of the conservative Positivist school of the history of Russian law, and held that the development of Russian institutions was analogous to that of Western Europe, and in particular that the Zemskiy Sobor (q.v.) should be regarded as an early type of representative assembly.

Sergius of Radonezh, Saint (1314–92), founder of the famous monastery of the Holy Trinity (Troitse-Sergiyeva Lavra, q.v.), and a saint of the Orthodox Church. Before the battle of Kulikovo against the Tatars in 1380 he blessed Prince Dmitriy Donskoy and foretold his victory. St Sergius is the most popular saint in Russia and is regarded as patron of the country. *See* N. M. Zernov, *St Sergius— Builder of Russia*, 1939.

Serov (before 1939 **Nadezhdinsk**, except a few years in the mid 1930's when it was **Kabakovsk**), town in the Sverdlovsk Oblast (Urals), situated 200 m. north of Sverdlovsk. Population (1959) 98,000 (1926, 33,000; 1939, 65,000). It is a major industrial centre (high quality iron and steel on charcoal), and was founded as an iron-works in 1894 to supply rails for the construction of the Trans-Siberian Railway.

Serov, Aleksandr Nikolayevich (1820–71), composer and critic who was educated at the School of Jurisprudence, St Petersburg, where he met Stasov, later to be his staunch literary opponent; in 1842 he met Glinka. He studied with Hunke at St Petersburg. At first hostile to Wagner, he became his firm supporter after a visit to him in Lucerne in 1858. Works comprise three operas, *Judith*, 1862, *Rogneda*, 1865, and *The Power of Evil*, 1867–71 (completed by Solov'ëv); orchestral works; sacred music, etc. Although he was an adherent of western music, the national element plays a certain part in Serov's compositions; his style is influenced more by Spontini and Meyerbeer than by Glinka. *See* G. Abraham and M. D. Calvocoressi, *Masters of Russian Music*, 1936.

Serov, Ivan Aleksandrovich (*b.* 1905), prominent security official. Born in a village in the Vologda Oblast, Serov as a young man in the early 1920's was chairman of a village soviet, and joined the party in 1926. He then received training at a military school and served as an artillery officer. Having studied at a military academy, he was in 1939 transferred to security work. From 1939 to 1941 he was Commissar for Internal Affairs in the Ukraine, working under Khrushchëv who was the party boss there, and being directly responsible for terror and deportations in the newly annexed western Ukraine, northern Bukovina and southern Bessarabia. From 1941 he was First Deputy Commissar for State Security, Deputy and First Deputy Commissar for Internal Affairs of the U.S.S.R. (*see* M.G.B.; M.V.D.), and in this capacity organized the deportations from the Baltic States (q.v.) in 1941 and the deportations of whole peoples (Balkars, Chechens, Crimean Tatars, Ingushes, Kalmyks, Karachays, Volga Germans, qq.v.) during the war. In 1944–5 he was deputy commander of an army group, and in 1945–7 deputy Supreme Commander of the Soviet forces in Germany, being in fact the head of Smersh (q.v.) and in charge of all security measures there. In 1954–1958 he was chairman of the Committee of State Security (*see* K.G.B.). He came to England in 1956 to prepare for the forthcoming visit of Bulganin and Khrushchëv, whom he was intended to accompany, but violent press reaction in Britain resulted in his removal from their party. For his activities Serov has received the rank of army general, the title of Hero of the Soviet Union, six orders of Lenin, four orders of the Red Banner, an order of Suvorov (1st class), two orders of Kutuzov (1st class), etc. *See also* SECURITY ORGANS. *See* S. Wolin and R. M. Slusser (eds.), *The Soviet Secret Police*, New York, 1957.

Serov, Valentin Aleksandrovich (1865–1911), son of A. N., painter, studied under Repin (q.v.) privately and at the Academy of Arts, 1880–4. He specialized in portraiture of the Russian aristocracy and upper middle class. His style is distinguished by elegance and subdued silvery grey shades. His best paintings are the intimate portraits, especially those of children, and his 'Girl with Peaches' is a masterpiece of Russian art.

Serpukhov, town in the Moscow Oblast, situated on the River Oka 60 m. south of Moscow. Population (1959) 105,000 (1939, 91,000). It has textile and engineering industries; there are interesting churches of the 16th–17th centuries. Serpukhov has been known since 1339, and was capital of a principality in the 14th and 15th centuries. Its industrial development dates from the 19th century.

Servants are privately employed as domestic help (both resident and daily), chauffeurs and gardeners. No figures on the number of servants are published, but the practice of employing servants is widespread in the social strata which can afford them. Conditions of employment are settled privately, although theoretically the general provisions on minimum wages apply. There is no trade union for servants.

Sevan, or **Gokcha,** largest lake in the Caucasus, lying in the Armenian plateau in Transcaucasia 6,400 ft above sea level. Area 336 sq. m. The River Razdan, which flows into the River Aras from Lake Sevan, has a chain of electric power-stations.

Sevastopol', town in the Crimean Oblast, a major naval station and seaside resort on the Black Sea, directly subordinated to the government of the Ukrainian Republic. Population (1959) 148,000 (1914, 77,000; 1923, 64,000; 1939, 114,000). There is a naval museum, 1869, a biological station of the Academy of Sciences, 1871, an archaeological museum, 1892, and a 'Defence of Sevastopol'' panorama, 1905. The town was founded in 1783 near the site of ancient Chersonesus and was almost completely ruined during the sieges of 1854–5 (*see* CRIMEAN WAR) and 1941–2, falling after heroic defence on both occasions.

Seven Year Plan, for the years 1959–65, was introduced to replace the two last years of the sixth Five Year Plan (q.v.) and the full period of what was to be the seventh Five Year Plan. The scrapping of the sixth plan was officially attributed to the need to take into account new discoveries of natural resources. However, in the past such discoveries—no less important than the present ones—did not affect the plans, adjustments being made in the process of carrying them out. It is more likely therefore that the main reason for the decision (which was made in 1957) was to avoid embarrassment for the new leadership headed by Khrushchëv over the likely failure to achieve a number of important plan targets, especially in agriculture. The main targets for the year 1965 (apart from such indices as the increase of the national income, total industrial output or real incomes of the population, the calculation of which by Soviet statisticians and planners is methodologically wrong and therefore of little value) are as follows (percentage increases compared to 1958 in brackets):

Pig-iron, million tons, 65–70 (77 per cent).

Steel, million tons, 86–91 (66 per cent).

Coal, million tons, 600–612 (23 per cent).

Oil, million tons, 230–240 (112 per cent).

Gas, milliard cubic metres, 150 (403 per cent).

Electric power, milliard kwh., 500–520 (123 per cent).

Metal-cutting lathes, thousands, 190–200 (45 per cent).

Cars and lorries, thousands, 750–856 (68 per cent).

Cement, million tons, 75–81 (143 per cent).

Cotton fabrics, milliard metres, 7·7–8·0 (38 per cent).

Leather footwear, million pairs, 515 (45 per cent).

Grain, million tons, 160–176 (29 per cent).

Meat and fat, million tons slaughter-weight, 16 (103 per cent).

Milk, million tons, 100–105 (80 per cent).

The rates of growth envisaged for most items of the industrial output are lower than in the previous plans, and are deliberately so calculated in order to make it easier to 'over-fulfil' the plan. Where the planned growth is particularly fast, as, for example, in gas extraction, it is due to the fact that the industry is still in its infancy in the Soviet Union. It is likely, on the basis of the experience of the first two years, that the industrial targets will mostly be achieved; the prospect for agriculture is much more doubtful, as, for example, the targets for animal products would require far more fodder than is conceivable with the planned production of fertilizers.

The advertised overall aim of the Seven Year Plan is to surpass the United States output of 1958 by 1965 in a number of major items. This can certainly be achieved, but such an achievement would have little relevance beyond superficial propaganda, since the economic policy of the United States is not guided by the principle of maximum output. *See also* PLANNING. *See* A. W. Haslett (ed.), *The Soviet Seven Year Plan, 1959–65,* 1959; L. H. Herman, 'The Seven-Year Haul,' *Problems of Communism,* No. 2, Mar.–April 1959; *The Soviet Seven Year Plan* (introduction by A. Nove), 1960.

Severodvinsk (until 1958 **Molotovsk**), town in the Archangel Oblast, a port on the Dvina Bay of the White Sea about 30 m. west of Archangel. Population (1959) 79,000 (1939, 21,000). It has metal-working, building materials and food (dairy products and meat) industries.

Severtsov, Aleksey Nikolayevich (1866–1936), biologist, professor at Yur'yev, Kiev and Moscow universities, member of the Academy of Sciences. His works were concerned with evolutionary morphology of vertebrates (he developed, for example, the now accepted theory of the origin of the latter's extremities) and the general theory of evolution. In his main theoretical work, *Morphological Regularities of Evolution* (which first appeared in German abroad in 1931, Russian ed. 1939), Severtsov advanced a new theory on the relation of individual and historical development of organisms (which he called the theory of phylembryogenesis), including a classification of the main directions of biological progress.

Shadrinsk, town in the Kurgan Oblast (Western Siberia), situated on the Sverdlovsk–Kurgan railway, 160 m. south-east of Sverdlovsk. Population (1959) 52,000 (1931, 31,000). It has engineering (car parts, printing presses), food and light industries, and is a local cultural centre; there is an agricultural experimental station near by, headed by T. S. Mal'tsev. Shadrinsk was founded in 1662, became a town in 1712, and during the 19th and early 20th centuries it had, in addition to industry, a considerable trade in grain, lard, butter and cattle.

Shakhmatov, Aleksey Aleksandrovich (1864–1920), outstanding philologist. Educated at Moscow University, he taught there from 1890, became a member of the Academy of Sciences in 1894, and chairman of its section for Russian language and literature in 1906. His many works on the history of the Russian language and early Russian literature (especially the chronicles) gained him international fame.

Shakhrisyabz (ancient **Kesh**), town in the Surkhan-Dar'ya Oblast (Uzbekistan), situated on a branch line of the Bukhara–Stalinabad railway about 40 m. south of Samarkand. Population (1932) 14,200, Uzbeks and Tadzhiks. It is the centre of the Shakhrisyabz oasis; there are varied textile and food industries and a famous embroidery craft is carried on. Shakhrisyabz is one of the oldest towns in Central Asia; it was the centre of the anti-Arab religious and social movement led by Mukanna in the 8th century and the birth-place of Timur, whose palace still stands. In 1959 the nearby urban settlement of Kitab (population 8,600 in 1933) was fused with Shakhrisyabz.

Shakhty (formerly **Aleksandrovsk-Grushevsk**), town in the Rostov Oblast, situated in the Donets Basin, 50 m. north-east of Rostov-on-Don. Population (1959) 196,000 (1926, 41,000; 1939, 135,000). It is a centre of coal-mining (anthracite), electricity production and pig-iron smelting in the eastern Donbas, and was founded in 1829 as a coal-mining settlement. In 1928 the 'Shakhty case'—a show trial of 'wreckers' from Shakhty—was staged, initiating a wave of terror against the technical intelligentsia (*see further under* PURGES). In 1954–8 it was capital of the Kamensk Oblast, now abolished.

Shalyapin, Fëdor Ivanovich (1873–1938), celebrated bass and actor. He began his career in 1896 in Mamontov's private opera company in Moscow, where he featured in the roles of Boris, Ivan the Terrible, and the Miller in Dargomyzhskiy's *Rusalka*. In 1901 he went to Milan, in 1908–9 worked with Diaghilev in Paris, and in 1913 appeared at Drury Lane at the Russian Opera season organized by Sir Thomas Beecham. During the First World War and afterwards he remained in Russia helping to organize theatrical productions, but finally emigrated in 1921. He visited America in 1908 and again 1922–5. Although he continued to perform, his last years were overshadowed by ill health. Shalyapin's genius lay in his remarkable musical and dramatic insight into the operatic role, his sense of stagecraft, and the wide range of his voice. *See* his *Pages from my Life*, New York, 1927, and *Man and Mask*, 1932.

Shamil' (1797–1871), religious and political leader of the North Caucasian Muslim mountain peoples in their resistance to Russian conquest. He surrendered to the Russians at Gunib in 1859 and was taken to central Russia. He died in Mecca. In the last years of Stalin's life Shamil' was treated in the official historiography as a Turkish and British agent, having previously been extolled by Pokrovskiy's school.

Shantar Islands, archipelago in the Sea of Okhotsk in the Russian Far East.

Shaporin, Yuriy Aleksandrovich (*b.* 1887), composer and teacher. He studied at the St Petersburg Conservatory until 1918 under Sokolov, Shteynberg and Cherepnin, and was greatly influenced by Gor'kiy, Blok and A. Tolstoy. He supervised the musical department of the Pushkin Theatre in Leningrad, 1928–34. In 1939 he was appointed professor at Moscow Conservatory. Works comprise operas, including *The Decembrists*, 1947–53; the symphony-cantata *On the Field of Kulikovo*, 1939; the oratorio *The Lay of the Battle for the Russian Land*, 1943–4; songs; arrangements; and music for films, including *Kutuzov*. Shaporin's major works are distinguished by their gigantic proportions, their melodiousness and their employment of popular songs. *See* R. Moisenko, *Realistic Music*, 1949.

Shatskiy, Stanislav Teofilovich (1878–1934), pioneer of education through labour in Russia. He started experiments in introducing productive labour as an essential element in the educational process before the First World War, and was particularly influential during the 1920's. *See* LABOUR SCHOOL.

Shaumyan, Stepan Georgiyevich (1878–1918), Armenian Communist who joined the Social Democratic Labour Party in 1901 and later its Bolshevik faction. After the 1905 revolution he took an active part in upholding Leninist orthodoxy against ideological 'revisionists.' He became chairman of the Baku Soviet after the February 1917 revolution, and at the 6th congress (1917) was elected to the Central Committee of the party. At the time of the seizure of power he became chairman of the Military Revolutionary Committee in Baku, in 1918 plenipotentiary of the party's Central Committee and of the Soviet Government in the Caucasus, chairman of the Baku Council of People's Commissars and Commissar for Foreign Affairs. He was one of the 'twenty-six commissars' who were shot by the anti-Bolshevik authorities in Transcaspia.

Shchepkin, Mikhail Semёnovich (1788–1863), famous actor, one of the founders of realism on the Russian stage. Born as a serf, he received little formal education, and joined a travelling theatrical troupe in 1805; he did not receive his freedom until 1821 (a public subscription was launched in 1818 to buy it). From 1823 he worked in the Malyy Theatre in Moscow. His repertoire included Shakespeare (Polonius in *Hamlet*), Molière, Schiller, Griboyedov and Gogol', but he did not understand A. N. Ostrovskiy (q.v.) and opposed the staging of his plays. Shchepkin was prominent in the Moscow intellectual circles of the 1840's and fifties, maintaining close relations with both Westernists and Slavophiles (qq.v.), as well as with the Ukrainian poet Shevchenko (q.v.).

Shcherbakov, *see* RYBINSK.

Shchukin, Boris Vasil'yevich (1894–1939), theatre and film actor. With Shtraukh (q.v.) he specialized in stage and screen portrayals of Lenin—*Lenin in October*, 1937, and *Lenin in 1918*, 1939.

Shchusev, Aleksey Viktorovich (1873–1949), architect. He studied at the St Petersburg Academy of Arts of which he became academician in 1910. He became a member of the U.S.S.R. Academy of Architecture in 1939, and an academician of the Academy of Sciences in 1943. His early work was based on Novgorod-Pskov traditions (*see* ARCHITECTURE, ECCLESIASTICAL). Outstanding examples of his work are Kazan' railway station, Moscow, in 17th-century style, 1913–26; Lenin Mausoleum, Moscow, recalling Muscovite 'ziggurat' forms, 1925–30; and the Marx-Engels-Lenin Institute, Tiflis, combining classical and Georgian features (Stalin Prize, 1941). Other notable works in Moscow include the theatre on Mayakovskiy Square, the Hotel Moskva and the 'Komsomol'skaya Kol'tsevaya' Metro station. He was an approved exponent of Socialist Realism (q.v.). *See also* ARCHITECTURE.

Shebalin, Vissarion Yakovlevich (*b.* 1902), composer who studied with Myaskovskiy at Moscow Conservatory until 1928, remaining there as teacher, becoming professor in 1935 and director, 1942–8. His works comprise the opera *The Taming of the Shrew*, 1955; two cantatas; four symphonies; symphonic suites and overtures; violin concerto; choral and orchestral works; chamber music, including seven string quartets; songs; piano music, etc.; music to films, including *Pugachëv*, 1937, *Glinka*, 1945, and *Sadko*, 1953; he completed Musorgskiy's opera *Sorochintsy Fair*. Shebalin's contribution to chamber music is considerable, combining national characteristics with the classical traditions. He owes much to Taneyev. *See* G. Abraham, *Eight Soviet Composers*, 1943.

Shebelinka, natural gas fields near Khar'kov in the Ukraine. Pipelines are under construction to Khar'kov-Bryansk and Dnepropetrovsk-Odessa.

Sheki, 18th-century khanate in northern Azerbaydzhan, with Nukha as its capital, which was semi-independent from Persia. It became Russian in 1805 and was abolished about 1820.

Shelepin, Aleksandr Nikolayevich (*b*. 1918), Communist, chairman of the Committee of State Security (*see* K.G.B.) since 1958, succeeding Serov. Born in Voronezh in a middle-class family, he studied at the Moscow Institute of History, Philosophy and Literature in 1936–9. He joined the party in 1940 and until 1958 worked in the Komsomol apparatus, succeeding Mikhaylov (q.v.) as first secretary of its central committee in 1952. At the same time he became a member of the party Central Committee. The choice of Shelepin as the security chief seems to indicate the importance of opposition among the young people and the need for new methods in dealing with this opposition.

Shemakha, town in Azerbaydzhan, situated 80 m. west of Baku, the main centre of earthquakes in Transcaucasia. Population (1955) 9,800 (1914, 23,000; 1932, 5,000). It has viniculture and wine production. Ruins of the tomb of the Shirvan shahs have been preserved, and there is a local museum. Shemakha was known to Ptolemy, and was later the capital of Shirvan and a famous centre of silk weaving; it became Russian in 1805.

Shepilov, Dmitriy Trofimovich (*b*. 1905), politician of whose early life little is known. He became head of the propaganda department of the Central Committee in 1948, chief editor of *Pravda* in 1952, was a secretary of the Central Committee in 1955–6 and again in 1957, succeeded Molotov as Foreign Minister in 1956 and became a candidate member of the Presidium of the Central Committee. In the struggle among the party leaders he at first supported Khrushchëv, but changed sides and joined the 'anti-party group' (q.v.) in 1957. After the defeat of the group he was expelled from the Central Committee and is reportedly teaching political economy at an institute in Frunze. As Foreign Minister Shepilov initiated the active Soviet policy in the Middle East. *See* W. Z. Laqueur, *The Soviet Union and the Middle East*, 1959.

Shershenevich, Gabriel' Feliksovich (1863–1912), jurist of Polish origin, professor at Kazan' and Moscow universities, Constitutional Democratic deputy of the 1st Duma. A leading authority on civil law, Shershenevich adhered to the normativist school and strongly criticized the concept of natural law, at the same time trying to find connections between legal phenomena on the one hand and economic and political factors on the other. Chief works: *System of Commercial Actions*, 1888; *Copyright in Literary Works*, 1891; *Course of Civil Law*, 1901; *History of Philosophy and Law*, 2nd ed., 1907; *General Doctrine of Law and State*, 1908; *Course of Commercial Law* (4 vols.), 1908; *Textbook of Russian Civil Law* (2 vols.), 2nd ed., 1914; *Textbook of Commercial Law*, 9th ed., 1919.

Shestov (real name **Shvartsman**), **Lev Isaakovich** (1866–1938), religious philosopher, of Jewish parentage, expelled from Russia in 1922, together with other leading intellectuals. His works are mainly devoted to a critique of rationalism (including ethical rationalism) and secularism (*Good in the Teaching of Tolstoy and Nietzsche*; *Philosophy of Tragedy—Dostoyevskiy and Nietzsche. Apotheosis of Groundlessness*, 1905; *Kierkegaard and Existentialist Philosophy*; *Athen und Jerusalem*, 1938, etc.). See V. V. Zenkovsky, *A History of Russian Philosophy*, vol. ii, 1953.

Shevchenko, Taras Hryhorovych (1814–61), most renowned Ukrainian poet, bought out of serfdom by a group of Russian and Ukrainian intellectuals. In 1847 he was banished to Orenburg for ten years, and forbidden to write or paint, on account of his participation in a secret Pan-Slavic society, the Brotherhood of Sts Cyril and Methodius. He lived subsequently in St Petersburg. Shevchenko had a profound influence upon Ukrainian literature and the Ukrainian national movement. His chief poems, written in a popular romantic vein, are found in the collection *Kobzar*, 1840. See his *Selected Poems* (trans. C. A. Manning), 1945; W. K. Matthews, *Taras Ševčenko: the Man and The Symbol*, 1951.

Shilka, navigable river in south-eastern Siberia which rises in Mongolia and flows north-east through eastern Transbaykalia to form, with the River Argun', the River Amur. Length 850 m. Its basin is a rich gold-bearing area.

Shipov, Dmitriy Nikolayevich (1851–1920), liberal politician. He was for many years chairman of the Moscow Zemstvo and became widely known for his work there. He organized unofficial congresses of *zemstvo* representatives in the 1890's and early 1900's which played an important part in the constitutional movement. In 1905 he became one of the founders and leaders of the Octobrist Party, and in 1906 of the small Party of Peaceful Renovation. See G. Fischer, *Russian Liberalism, From Gentry to Intelligentsia*, Cambridge, Mass., 1958.

Shipping. Total cargo traffic (by ships under the administration of the Ministry of Merchant Navy) was 57·4 milliard ton-miles in 1958 (10·7 in 1913, 5·0 in 1928, 12·8 in 1940, 44·5 in 1956). Total passenger traffic was 0·7 milliard passenger-miles in the same year (0·6 in 1913, 0·2 in 1928, 0·9 in 1955). Export accounts for 11 per cent of total cargo carriage. The principal goods carried by shipping are oil, coal, ores, mineral building materials and timber. In 1958, 44,500 people were employed in the Merchant Navy. The greatest amount of cargo carriage is to and from the ports of the Black Sea and the Sea of Azov basin (Odessa, the second largest port in the country, Novorossiysk,

Zhdanov, Poti, Batumi, etc.); next come the ports of the Caspian Sea (Baku, the largest port in the country, Astrakhan', Makhachkala, Krasnovodsk); then the ports of the Far Eastern basin, all comparatively small (Vladivostok, Nakhodka, etc.); then the ports of the northern basin, again small (Murmansk, Archangel and the chief ports on the Northern Sea Route, q.v.); finally the ports of the Baltic Sea (Leningrad, Riga, Tallinn, etc.). Before 1913 Leningrad was the largest port of the country, and Riga the third largest, but both have declined. The only Soviet international passenger line is Leningrad–London via Helsinki, Stockholm and Copenhagen. *See also* TRANSPORT.

Shirvan, area in north-eastern Azerbaydzhan north of the River Kura. From the first centuries A.D. it was a separate khanate (with Shemakha as capital), usually under foreign suzerainty (Persian, Arab, Turkish, Mongol, again Persian, from 1805 Russian); it was annexed by Russia in 1820.

Shklovskiy, *see* FORMALISM.

Shlissel'burg, *see* PETROKREPOST'.

Shlyapnikov, Aleksandr Gavrilovich (1883–1943), Bolshevik, a metalworker by trade. He joined the party in 1903 and after the revolution of 1905 spent several years in France, taking part in the labour movement there. In 1915 he was entrusted by Lenin with setting up the Russian Bureau of the Central Committee to direct the party work inside Russia, where Molotov was one of his lieutenants. After the February revolution in 1917 Shlyapnikov and the Russian Bureau anticipated Lenin's position by taking up an intransigent attitude towards the Provisional Government, against the more conciliatory line of Kamenev and Stalin. Shlyapnikov took an active part in the preparation of the October coup, mainly in the trade unions, and became Commissar for Labour in the first Soviet government. He was the leader of the Workers' Opposition (q.v.) in 1920–1, was dismissed from the Government, and expelled from the Central Committee in 1922 and from the party in 1933. He occupied minor positions until the Great Purge (q.v.), when he disappeared. He must have died in an isolator (q.v.). Shlyapnikov's reminiscences, *On the Eve of 1917* and *The Year 1917*, are an important source of party history of the period. *See* L. Schapiro, *The Origin of the Communist Autocracy*, 1955, and *The Communist Party of the Soviet Union*, 1960.

Shock-workers' Movement, movement that existed from 1927 to 1935 among industrial and building workers, chiefly the young ones, with the object of speeding up work processes. It was inspired and directed by the Communist Party but was largely genuine; the movement later gave way to the Stakhanov movement (q.v.).

Sholokhov, Mikhail Aleksandrovich (*b.* 1905), outstanding novelist. Sholokhov has spent most of his life in the Don Cossack region, where he was born. He was not active in the civil war but joined the Communist Party in the early 1920's. His first writings, begun in 1924, were stories of the Don Cossacks, and he achieved fame in 1928 with the publication of the first volume of *The Quiet Don* (4 vols., 1928–40; Eng. trans. *And Quiet Flows the Don*, 1934, *The Don*

Flows Home to the Sea, 1940). This is, up to the present, the most popular single work by a Soviet writer, a kind of Cossack *War and Peace* which depicts the life of the Don Cossacks on the eve of and during the First World War and during the revolution and the civil war. His second important work, *Virgin Soil Upturned* (vol. i, 1931, trans. 1935; vol. ii finished in 1959), is concerned with the Cossacks' opposition to the forced collectivization of agriculture in their region. *See also* NOVYY MIR. *See* E. J. Simmons, *Russian Fiction and Soviet Ideology*, New York, 1958.

Shorians, Turkic-speaking people who live in the south of the Kuznetsk Basin (Kemerovo Oblast) in southern Siberia, numbering (1959) 15,000. Their chief occupations are hunting and cedar-nut collecting. The Shorians now form a small minority in Shoria, where large iron ore deposits are being exploited. From 1929 to 1939 a Shorian National Okrug existed.

Shostakovich, Dmitriy Dmitriyevich (*b.* 1906), prolific composer, brilliant pianist and teacher; he studied under Nikolayev and Shteynberg at the Leningrad Conservatory. From 1939 to 1948 he was a professor at Leningrad, and subsequently at Moscow, Conservatory. In 1936–7, and again in 1948, he was accused by party critics (the second time in a resolution of the Central Committee) of Formalism (q.v.). Early in 1960 he became secretary of the R.S.F.S.R. Union of Composers. His works comprise: operas, including *The Nose*, 1927–8, and *Lady Macbeth of Mtsensk*, 1930–2; ballets, including *The Golden Age*, 1929–30; choral works, including *Poem of our Country*, 1947; the oratorio *Song of the Forests*, 1949; eleven symphonies; a violin concerto; two piano concertos; six string quartets; miscellaneous chamber works; the song cycle *From Jewish Folk Poetry* (for soprano, contralto, tenor and piano), 1948; music for plays (*Hamlet*, 1932; *King Lear*, 1940) and films, including the Gor'kiy cycle, 1935–7; and many other musical and literary compositions. Shostakovich is one of the most individual of modern Russian composers, ranking with Prokof'yev. His music, which is always of the highest craftsmanship and eminently playable, is often dignified and austere, yet sometimes hovers on the borders of garishness. *See* I. Martynov, *Shostakovich: the Man and his Work*, New York, 1947; R. Moisenko, *Realist Music*, 1949; A. Werth, *Musical Uproar in Moscow*, 1949; D. Rabinovich, *Dmitry Shostakovich*, 1960.

Shteynberg, Maksimilian Oseyevich (1883–1946), composer who studied under Lyadov, Rimsky-Korsakov and Glazunov at St Petersburg Conservatory, where he remained as teacher and was appointed professor in 1915. His pupils include Shaporin and Shostakovich. Works comprise operas; ballets, including *Metamorphoses*, 1913; works for soloists, chorus and orchestra, including *Cantata to the Memory of Pushkin*, 1937; five symphonies, including the 5th Symphony ('Symphony-rhapsody on Uzbek theme'), 1942; violin concerto, 1946; orchestral works; chamber music; songs; folk-song arrangements, transcriptions, etc.; and theoretical works. Much of his music is based on the folk music of the Soviet republics. *See* R. Moisenko, *Realist Music*, 1949.

Shtraukh, Maksim Maksimovich (*b.* 1900), theatre and film actor.

With Shchukin (q.v.) he specialized in stage and screen Lenin roles; he played Lenin in the films *Man with the Gun*, 1938, *The Vyborg Side*, 1939, and *Yakov Sverdlov*, 1940.

'Shturmovshchina' (Russian, the habit of 'storming'), pejorative term describing the widespread practice of uneven production in an enterprise, with fits of 'storming' towards the end of a plan period alternating with slackness.

Shul'gin, Vasiliy Vital'yevich (*b.* 1878), reactionary publicist and politician of Ukrainian parentage, member of the 2nd, 3rd and 4th Dumas. As an *émigré* in the early 1920's he was deceived by G.P.U. *provocateurs* (*see* 'TRUST') into believing that they were acting on behalf of a strong monarchist underground in Russia; they organized an ostensibly illegal visit for Shul'gin to Moscow, Leningrad and Kiev, where he met G.P.U. agents masquerading as underground monarchists. Shul'gin was arrested by the Soviet authorities in Prague in 1945 and spent several years in forced labour camps, but was released in 1956 and now lives in the Soviet Union.

Shusha, town in the Mountainous-Karabakh Autonomous Oblast (Azerbaydzhan), a mineral water spa. Population (1956) 5,700 (1914, 43,000; 1932, 6,000), mostly Armenians. There are ruins of a former fortress. Shusha was founded in 1752 and until 1823 was capital of the Karabakh Khanate. It had the biggest carpet industry in the Caucasus until 1918.

Shuya, town in the Ivanovo Oblast (central Russia), 19 m. southeast of Ivanovo. Population (1959) 64,000. It has a large textile industry (cotton) and textile industry machinery is produced; the old craft of making sheepskin coats is carried on. Shuya was founded in the late 14th century, and had a lively trade with the Volga towns and, via Yaroslavl', with England; the first textile manufactory dates from 1775.

Shvernik, Nikolay Mikhaylovich (*b.* 1888), Communist. Born in St Petersburg of a working-class family, and himself a worker, Shvernik joined the party in 1905 and was active in the underground work in various parts of the country. After the Bolshevik coup he was chairman of the Samara Soviet, a commissar in the Red Army during the civil war, and then for some time active in trade union work. In 1923–8 he was in the party apparatus, as a member of the presidium of the Central Control Commission (*see* COMMITTEE OF PARTY CONTROL), secretary of the Leningrad regional committee, of the Central Committee and of the Urals regional committee. In 1928 he was transferred to trade union work to fight the Right Opposition there, and in 1930 replaced Tomskiy as secretary of the Trade Union Central Council. He became First Deputy Chairman of the Presidium of the U.S.S.R. Supreme Soviet in 1944 and succeeded Kalinin as chairman (i.e. as ceremonial head of state) in 1945. After Stalin's death he was shifted back into his old job as the head of the trade union apparatus, but in 1956 was made chairman of the Committee of Party Control. Shvernik has been a member of the Central Committee since 1925, was a member of its Organizational Bureau from 1930, candidate member of the Politburo from 1939, and of the Central Committee's Presidium from 1953, becoming a full member of the latter in 1957. He has never had any political weight during his career.

Siauliai (Russian **Shyaulyay**, formerly **Shavli**), town in Lithuania, 115 m. north-west of Vilnius. Population (1959) 60,000 (1939, 31,000). It has food industries and is an important railway junction. The town witnessed much fighting in 1915; it was capital of Siauliai Oblast, 1950 3.

Siberia, area comprising the Asiatic part of Russia with the exception of Central Asia. The term is not a very specific one: in physical geography it is taken to denote the whole territory between the Ural Mountains and the Pacific Ocean, reaching in the south-west to the Kazakh hills; but in economic and political geography the Urals region, the Russian Far East and northern Kazakhstan are usually excluded. The chief natural regions of the area are the West Siberian lowland between the Ural Mountains and the Yenisey, the Central Siberian plateau between the Yenisey and the Lena, and the mountainous regions in the south (*see* ALTAY; BAYKALEAN MOUNTAINS; SAYAN MOUNTAINS) and north-east. The climate is continental throughout, the degree of continentality increasing from west to east, with very cold winters, especially in the north-east (where the 'cold pole' lies, *see* VERKHOYANSK), and a monsoon climate in the southern part of the Far East. The subsoil is permanently frozen in large parts of Siberia. Of the chief rivers, the Lena, Ob' and Yenisey flow meridionally from the mountains in the south to the Arctic Ocean, while the Amur flows from west to east into the Sea of Okhotsk. In West Siberia there are many lakes, but the largest is Lake Baykal in the south-east. Vegetation is in latitudinal zones, with tundra along the Arctic coast, coniferous forest (most characteristic of the Siberian landscape), wooded steppe (*see* BARABA), and steppe in the extreme south (*see* ISHIM; KULUNDA; TOBOL). There are vertical vegetation zones in the mountainous regions.

Siberia (in the narrower sense) is very sparsely populated; in 1959 it had 18,228,000 inhabitants, with only 10–15 persons per square mile in the most densely populated areas (the wooded steppe in West Siberia) and less than one person per square mile in vast territories of the north. Just over a half of the population is urban, the main concentration being in the south, especially in Kemerovo Oblast. The chief cities (over 200,000 in 1959) are Novosibirsk, Omsk, Krasnoyarsk, Stalinsk, Irkutsk, Barnaul, Prokop'yevsk, Kemerovo and Tomsk. Russian and other settlers from European Russia (who have colonized Siberia since the 16th century) form an overwhelming majority, the indigenous population numbering less than one million and nowhere making up a majority. The most numerous is the Turkic-speaking group, with Tatars in the west, Yakuts in the north-east, and the peoples of the southern mountains (*see* ALTAY; KHAKAS; SHORIANS; TUVA), followed by the Buryats in the south-east (who belong to the Mongol group), the Finno-Ugrian group in the north-west (*see* KHANTY; MANSI; SAMOYEDS) and the Tungus group which is scattered throughout Eastern Siberia.

Siberia has great natural resources: coal (*see* CHEREMKHOVO; CHUL'MAN; KUZNETSK BASIN), iron ore (*see* ALDAN; ANGARA;

MINUSINSK BASIN; NARYM), non-ferrous metals (*see* ALTAY;
NORIL'SK; TRANSBAYKALIA), gold (*see* ALDAN; BODAYBO; KEMER-
OVO; TOMSK) and diamonds (*see* YAKUTIA). There are also great
timber resources, fertile black earth soil in the south-west and the
water power of the great rivers. Exploitation of these resources
followed the Russian conquest of Siberia, which began in the 1580's
(*see* MANGAZEYA; YERMAK) and was completed with the annexation
of the West Siberian steppes in the early 19th century. Fur was at
first the prime attraction; metallurgy began in the 18th century, and
gold-mining in the 19th. The First World War saw the beginnings of
modern industrial development, which has been especially intensive
since the 1930's (*see* FIVE YEAR PLANS; URAL-KUZNETSK COMBINE).
The construction of the Trans-Siberian Railway and the agrarian
reforms of Stolypin (q.v.) greatly facilitated agricultural colonization.
A prosperous farming community was built up in Siberia (which never
suffered serfdom), which at the beginning of the 20th century
specialized in dairy products and exported much to Britain, but was
ruined by the collectivization of agriculture (q.v.). The Virgin Land
Campaign of 1953–6 was aimed at expanding Siberian grain production. Siberian Regionalism (q.v.)—a political trend advocating a
kind of dominion status for Siberia within Russia—developed in the
late 19th–early 20th centuries, and in 1918 a short-lived Siberian
Government was established (*see* CIVIL WAR). All Siberia, in the
narrower sense, now belongs to the R.S.F.S.R., and is divided into the
Altay and Krasnoyarsk krays, the Kurgan, Tyumen', Omsk, Novosibirsk, Kemerovo, Tomsk, Irkutsk and Chita oblasts, the Buryat and
Yakut Autonomous Republics and the Tuva Autonomous Oblast.
Siberia has been a place of banishment for criminal and political
prisoners since the 18th century, and from the 1930's until the mid
1950's was the main region of 'corrective labour camps,' some of
which may still exist. It is now the main area of new industrial
development during the current Seven Year Plan. A new impetus to
scientific research on a large scale has been given by the setting up in
1956 in Novosibirsk of the Siberian division of the U.S.S.R. Academy
of Sciences. *See also* under the cities and administrative divisions
listed above. *See* G. Kennan, *Siberia and the Exile System* (2 vols.),
New York, 1891; V. Zenzinov, *The Road to Oblivion*, 1932; G. Jorré,
The Soviet Union, the Land and its People, 3rd imp., 1955; D. W.
Treadgold, *The Great Siberian Migration*, Princeton, N.J., 1957; J.
Lied, *Siberian Arctic*, 1960.

Siberian Khanate, 15th-century Tatar state established in Western
Siberia following the disintegration of the Golden Horde (q.v.). It was
annexed to Muscovy in 1582 after its conquest by Cossacks under
Yermak. *See* B. Nolde, *La Formation de l'Empire Russe*, vol. i, Paris,
1952.

Siberians, common name for the Russian inhabitants of Siberia.
They arrived there in three main waves. The first colonists, chiefly
from northern Russia, came gradually in the 16th–early 19th
centuries (including towards the end of the period many deported
criminals), and their descendants are known as Old Inhabitants. As
time went on they developed certain peculiarities in their way of life

and character, and, though they continued to regard themselves as Russians, by the end of the 19th century a definite Siberian regionalist trend had developed (*see* SIBERIA; YADRINTSEV). However, some small groups of Old Inhabitants in north-eastern Siberia have almost lost their Russian identity; e.g. in Yakutia they have adopted the Yakut language, while others were known under different geographical names and now generally refer to themselves simply as 'Local Russians.' The second wave of colonists came in the late 19th and early 20th centuries as a result of organized peasant colonization, mostly from the over-populated southern Great Russian and Ukrainian provinces; these were officially called New Settlers, but were nicknamed 'people from Russia' by the Old Inhabitants. The third wave, that of the 1930's, forties and fifties, was mainly made up of (*a*) people deported as a result of the collectivization of agriculture and the Great Purge, (*b*) war-time evacuees and deportees and (*c*) semi-compulsorily recruited workers for the Virgin Land Campaign, 1953–6, and the new industrial projects in Siberia. *See* D. W. Treadgold, *The Great Siberian Migration*, Princeton, N.J., 1957.

Sich (Russian **Sech'**), fortified camp on the lower Dnieper which was the centre of the Ukrainian Cossacks during the 16th, 17th and 18th centuries. In a broader sense the name is used for the whole Cossack territory on both banks of the lower Dnieper, north of the Crimean Khanate, and for the Cossack military organization in that area; the latter was abolished in 1775. *See* B. Nolde, *La Formation de l'Empire Russe*, vol. ii, Paris, 1952.

Sikorsky, Igor' Ivanovich (*b.* 1889), aircraft designer, educated at the St Petersburg Naval Academy and the Polytechnical Institute in Kiev. In 1913 he built and flew the first successful four-engined aeroplane, and during the First World War designed four-engined bombers for the Russian Army. He emigrated to America in 1919 and became an American citizen in 1928. Since the 1930's he has been the leading designer of helicopters, now directing his own company.

Simbirsk, *see* UL'YANOVSK.

Simferopol' (ancient Greek **Neapolis**), administrative and cultural centre of the Crimean Oblast (Ukraine). Population (1959) 189,000 (1897, 49,000; 1926, 87,000; 1939, 143,000), Russians and Ukrainians. It has varied food and engineering industries, and the Crimean branch of the Ukrainian Academy of Sciences. Prehistoric and Scythian settlements have been excavated here. Simferopol' was founded as capital of Tauria province in 1784 on the site of an ancient settlement; in 1918 it was capital of the Crimean Tatar nationalist government, in 1920 of General Wrangel's White government, and 1921–46 of the Crimean Autonomous Republic. In 1918 a university was established, but abolished seven years later.

Sivash, *see* AZOV, SEA OF.

Skobelev, *see* FERGANA.

Skobelev, Mikhail Dmitriyevich (1843–82), general who distinguished himself in the Russian campaigns in Turkestan (the conquest of Kokand, 1875–6, and of Turkmenia, 1881) and in the

Russo-Turkish war of 1877–8. His military ability and personal bravery brought him great popularity in the army. *See* F. Maclean, *A Person from England and Other Travellers*, 1958.

Skovoroda, Hryhoriy Savych (1722–94), Ukrainian philosopher who passed most of his life as an itinerant teacher of morals. The Slavophiles (q.v.) later adopted his epistemological views, which became one of the chief sources of modern Russian Intuitivism (q.v.).

Skryabin, Aleksandr Nikolayevich (1872–1915), composer and fine pianist who studied at Moscow Conservatory under Taneyev and Safonov, travelled abroad, and came in contact with the mystic philosophy of Merezhkovskiy (q.v.) and Vyacheslav Ivanov. Works comprise three symphonies; piano concerto, *c.* 1894; orchestral works, including *The Poem of Ecstasy*, 1908, and *Prometheus: the Poem of Fire*, 1909–10; and many piano works, including the 24 preludes. Skryabin is one of the few Russian composers to evince that mystical vein so common in Russian literature. His work, which though not employing the folk idiom is nevertheless Russian in spirit, shows a gradual transition from simplicity to amazing complexity. Skrayabin aspired to a complete synthesis of all the arts, which was to culminate in a masterpiece which would transform the world; for this purpose he devised a 'mystic' chord, which formed the basis of much of his composition. His music is occasionally overpowering in its emotional force. *See* Eaglefield Hull, *Scriabin*, 1916; L. Sabaneev, *Skryabin*, Moscow, 1923; G. Abraham and M. D. Calvocoressi, *Masters of Russian Music*, 1936.

Slavophiles, 19th-century philosophical and political movement which emphasized the national individuality of Russia, idealized the Russian past and opposed westernization (*see* WESTERNISM); Slavophiles proper were liberal but not democratic, and they gave strong support to the peasant communes (*see* MIR). The reforms of Alexander II achieved parts of their programme. The leaders of the Slavophiles were Khomyakov, Kireyevskiy, the Aksakovs and Samarin (qq.v.). The movement largely merged with Panslavism from the 1860's. *See* A. Gratieux, *A. S. Khomiakov et le mouvement Slavophile* (2 vols.), Paris, 1939, and *Le Mouvement Slavophile à la veille de la révolution*, Paris, 1953; R. Hare, *Pioneers of Russian Social Thought*, 1951; V. V. Zenkovsky, *A History of Russian Philosophy*, vol. i, 1953; T. G. Masaryk, *The Spirit of Russia* (2nd ed.), vol. i, 1955; P. Scheibert, *Von Bakunin zu Lenin*, 1956.

Slavs. Of the three branches of the Slav family, the East Slavs (q.v.) live entirely in Russia. Of the West Slavs, the Poles (q.v.) are numerous in Russia and there were many Czech colonists in the Ukraine and North Caucasus until the Second World War, after which they were mostly repatriated by agreement between the Soviet and Czechoslovak governments, 25,000 remaining in 1959, as well as 15,000 Slovaks. There were also many Bulgarian settlers in the Ukraine (in the former New Russia, q.v.) who, being Orthodox, emigrated from Turkish rule in the 18th and 19th centuries; they number (1959) 324,000 (114,000 in 1939); many were repatriated to Bulgaria during the German occupation, but many more migrated to the U.S.S.R. after the war. Another South Slav people, the Serbians, had also taken part in the colonization of New Russia (*see* NEW SERBIA), but they are now completely assimilated.

Slavyansk (until 1798 **Tor**), town in the Stalino Oblast (Ukraine), situated in the Donets Basin 110 m. south-east of Khar'kov. Population (1959) 83,000. It has salt-mines (since the 17th century), soda works and an engineering industry, a big thermal power-station, and also saline and mud baths. Slavyansk was founded as a fortified town in 1676.

Slogans, device often resorted to in party propaganda. Before the Bolshevik seizure of power, and in the first years of the Soviet regime, their function was to appeal for popular support for the party's policy; since the full development of the totalitarian system in the 1930's they have served to inform party functionaries of shifts in the party line. *See* D. N. Jacobs, 'Slogans and Soviet Politics,' *American Slavic and East European Review*, vol. xvi, No. 3, 1957.

Smersh (Russian abbreviation for 'Death to the Spies'), special division of the Soviet security organs, 1942–6, headed by Abakumov and Serov (qq.v.), which had the task of eliminating real or potential opponents of the Soviet regime among Soviet citizens who had for a greater or lesser time been outside the control of the Soviet authorities during the Second World War: those who had lived in German-occupied territories, who had been prisoners of war, civilian deportees or refugees. The methods employed were mass arrests, summary executions or deportation to camps or specified areas in Siberia or Central Asia. In the immediate post-war period Smersh was also active among Russian occupation troops abroad. *See* S. Wolin and R. M. Slusser (eds.), *The Soviet Secret Police*, New York, 1957.

Smolensk: 1. Oblast of the R.S.F.S.R., situated west of Moscow on the Smolensk-Moscow upland, traversed by the upper Dnieper, partly covered with mixed forests; there are deposits of peat and lignite. Area 19,200 sq. m.; population (1959) 1,140,000 (32 per cent urban). There are flax cultivation and dairy farming, food, textile, woodworking and engineering industries. Principal towns: Smolensk and Vyaz'ma. The area belonged to the Kievan state, became an independent principality in 1127, Lithuanian in 1404 and Muscovite in 1514.

2. Administrative, economic and cultural centre of the oblast, situated on the Dnieper. Population (1959) 146,000 (1914, 71,000; 1920, 57,000; 1939, 157,000). It has textile (linen), woodworking, food and engineering industries, and is an important centre of transportation. There are many notable churches and other buildings of the 12th–19th centuries. Known since 865, Smolensk was the capital of the Krivichi tribe and of Smolensk Principality; from 1404 to 1514 it was Lithuanian and then a key Muscovite western fortress and important centre of commerce and administration. It was the scene of bitter fighting in 1812 and 1941, being largely destroyed in the battles of 1941–3. In 1919 a university was set up but abolished eleven years later. *See* M. Fainsod, *Smolensk under Soviet Rule*, 1959.

Sobolev, Leonid Sergeyevich (*b.* 1898), novelist. He acquired notoriety in 1957 when he accused oppositional writers of following the call of Russian *émigrés* for a 'heroic feat of silence' in face of party

demands that they should recant. This drew a favourable comment
from Khrushchëv; and Sobolev, though not formally a party member,
was appointed to the chairmanship of the newly founded Union of
Writers of the R.S.F.S.R. *See* 'Soviet Literature: the Conspiracy of
Silence,' *Soviet Survey*, No. 19, Sept. 1957.

Sobolev, Sergey L'vovich (*b.* 1908), mathematician. Educated at
Leningrad University, he has been professor of Moscow University
since 1935, member of the Academy of Sciences since 1939; he joined
the party in 1940. He has worked on the dynamics of elastic bodies,
developing the theory of plane waves in elastic half-space with stress-
free boundary; developed a method of integrating linear and non-
linear equations with partial derivatives of hyperbolic type in the
given initial conditions; and has worked on the theory of generalized
functions. In recent years Sobolev took the initiative in openly
advocating the use of cybernetics, which had been considered
contrary to Marxism and therefore a bourgeois 'pseudo-science.'

Sobornost' ('conciliarism'), principle of unity in multiplicity, free
unity in the service of common higher values. This concept, developed
by Khomyakov as the basis of the Orthodox Church consciousness,
has been applied to other fields as well, particularly to that of social
philosophy. The Slavophiles saw in the Russian peasant commune
(*see* MIR) the embodiment of the principle of *sobornost'* in social life.
S. L. Frank used the term as an equivalent to Tönnies' *Gemeinschaft*
(community) as opposed to *Gesellschaft* (society). The principle of
sobornost' lies at the basis of contemporary Russian Solidarism (q.v.).
The Stalinist (*see* STALINISM) fiction of the 'moral and political unity
of the Soviet people' was a perversion of the doctrine of *sobornost'*.
See V. V. Zenkovsky, *A History of Russian Philosophy* (2 vols.), 1953.

Sochi, town in the Krasnodar Kray (North Caucasus), situated
on the Black Sea at the foot of the main Caucasian range. Population
(1959) 95,000. It is one of the finest health resorts in the country, with
a subtropical climate and sulphur springs; there are 58 sanatoria, and
in 1955 there were over 160,000 patients and visitors. Sochi was
established as a spa in 1910 and has developed particularly rapidly
since 1933.

Social Democracy, *see* MARXISM; RUSSIAN SOCIAL DEMOCRATIC
LABOUR PARTY.

Social Services. The most important social services are education,
the health service and pensions (qq.v.). Wage and salary earners are
entitled to annual paid leave of from 12 to 24 working days (according to the nature of the work) per year; those employed in especially
dangerous occupations may receive up to 48 days; school-teachers,
teachers in higher education establishments and certain categories of
scientists receive 48 working days' leave. Employed women receive
112 days' paid maternity leave. The amount of sickness benefit
payable to an employee depends upon the length of employment of
the recipient in the particular enterprise or establishment. (Unlike
other social services, sickness benefit is paid out of the Social Insurance Fund, which is made up of contributions from employers.)
For children's allowances *see* CHILDREN. No unemployment benefit is
payable, since officially unemployment (q.v.) does not exist in the

U.S.S.R. Rents in State-owned houses and flats are low and are graded according to income. *Kolkhoz* peasants do not benefit from any of these services but health and education (*see* KOLKHOZ; PEASANTS); other categories who are not wage or salary earners (artisans, q.v., and independent professional people) benefit only from the health and education services and the graded rents. However, some *kolkhozes* and artisans' co-operatives have their own insurance schemes. Professional associations (q.v.) administer charitable funds for sickness or other need among their members. Social insurance was first introduced in Russia by a law of 1912 which provided for contributory benefits in cases of sickness, disability or death for 2·5 million wage and salary earners in the mining and manufacturing industries. The present system of benefits is non-contributory. *See* A. Nove, 'Towards a "Communist Welfare State"?,' *Problems of Communism*, vol. ix, No. 1, Jan.–Feb. 1960.

Socialist Emulation, device first introduced during the first Five Year Plan period for raising the productivity of labour, whereby factories, collective farms, brigades (q.v.), workers, or entire regions and republics compete with one another in achieving specific targets. It is the duty of party branches, trade unions and managements to organize Socialist emulation and to control the fulfilment of the obligations undertaken. Socialist emulation often exists only on paper; the shock-workers', Stakhanovite and (currently) Communist Labour Brigades' movements are connected with Socialist emulation. In the 1930's the device was extended to virtually all fields of work, but after the war some of the most absurd instances (e.g. school-teachers engaging in 'Socialist emulation' for the smallest number of bad pupils) were dropped, though in accordance with Khrushchëv's general tendency to revive practices of the first Five Year Plan period they are again being urged.

Socialist Legality, term used in Soviet legal theory in the 1930's and forties for practices aimed at stabilizing the social and political conditions of Stalinism (q.v.). Like revolutionary legality (q.v.) it has been used since Stalin's death as a euphemism for the elimination of the worst excesses of Stalinism (q.v.). *See* R. Schlesinger, *Soviet Legal Theory*, 1945; J. N. Hazard (ed.), *Soviet Legal Philosophy*, Cambridge, Mass., 1951; H. Kelsen, *The Communist Theory of Law*, 1955; I. Lapenna, 'Socialist Legality,' *Soviet Survey*, No. 25, July–Sept. 1958.

Socialist Realism, 'basic method' of literature and art, conceived by Stalin, Zhdanov and Gor'kiy as a further development of Lenin's requirement of 'partyness of literature.' It is defined as the 'truthful, historically concrete presentation of reality in its revolutionary development' which 'must be combined with the task of the ideological remaking and education of toilers in the spirit of socialism.' Socialist Realism first became compulsory for writers in 1932 with the dissolution of all existing writers' associations by the Communist Party and their replacement by the Soviet Writers' Union (q.v.). In practice the conflicting requirements contained in the official definition of the method could seldom be satisfied, and it was in fact the artistic aspect of Stalinism (q.v.). Artistic life was practically extinguished by the enforcement of Socialist Realism, especially after the party decrees on literature and art of 1946–8. The growing struggle for freedom of creative work that followed Stalin's death often takes the form of attacks upon the method. The concept of Socialist Realism was redefined in 1959 at the 3rd Writers' Congress, and explicitly equated with 'partyness' (q.v.). *See also* FADEYEV; GOR'KIY; ZHDANOV. *See* G. Struve, *Soviet Russian Literature, 1917–1950*, Norman, Oklahoma, 1951; R. Hingley, 'The Soviet Writers' Congress,' *Soviet Survey*, No. 29, July–Sept. 1959; G. Zekulin, 'Socialist Realism,' *Soviet Studies*, vol. xi, No. 4, April 1960.

Socialist Revolutionaries, political party established in 1902 by supporters of revolutionary Populism (q.v.), among whose leaders were Chernov and Avksent'yev (qq.v.). A federal structure for the Russian state, self-determination for non-Russian peoples and socialization of the land, in addition to the common radical demands, were the main features of the party's programme. Its tactics included assassination of leading government personalities, and this was undertaken by an autonomous 'fighting organization,' led for many years by the police agent Azef (q.v.). A section of the party, the Left Socialist Revolutionaries, supported the Bolshevik seizure of power in 1917 and took part in the Bolshevik Government until the Brest-Litovsk treaty in 1918. The Socialist Revolutionaries formed the majority in the Constituent Assembly (q.v.) which was dispersed by the Bolsheviks. In 1922 the party was suppressed. *See* A. J. Sack, *The Birth of the Russian Democracy*, New York, 1918; B. Savinkov, *Memoirs of a Terrorist*, New York, 1931; V. Zenzinov, *Perezhitoye*, New York, 1953; D. W. Treadgold, *Lenin and his Rivals*, 1955; L. Schapiro, *The Origin of the Communist Autocracy*, 1955; T. G. Masaryk, *The Spirit of Russia* (2nd ed.), vol. ii, 1955; O. H. Radkey, *The Agrarian Foes of Bolshevism*, New York, 1958.

Societies. According to Article 126 of the Soviet constitution, citizens have the right to 'combine in public organizations: trade unions, co-operative associations, youth organizations, sport and defence organizations, cultural, technical and scientific societies.' This right is qualified by the provision in the same article that the Communist Party 'constitutes the core of all organizations of the working people.' There are in fact many societies, which can be roughly divided into three categories: (1) those which exist purely for purposes of representation abroad, such as the Soviet Peace Committee (founded 1949), the Committee of Soviet Youth Organizations (founded 1941), the Soviet Committee for Solidarity of the Asian Countries (founded 1956), the United Nations Association (founded 1956), etc., which do not in fact function as societies proper within Russia; (2) societies which, like the first category, are aimed exclusively at furthering the interests of the party, but which do function within the country as mass organizations, e.g. the Komsomol, the Pioneers (qq.v.), the Society for the Dissemination of Political and Scientific Knowledge (founded 1947); (3) genuine societies, representing learned, cultural, sporting, etc., interests (some of which date from before 1917), which are only subject to party control to ensure conformity; examples in this category are the

Red Cross Society (founded 1867), the Geographical Society (founded 1845), the Moscow Naturalists' Society (founded 1805), sports societies such as the Dynamo and Spartak, the para-military society Dosaaf (q.v.) and the various societies known as 'scientific-technical' which exist in many branches of industry.

Societies appeared in Russia in the 18th century (the Imperial Free Economic Society, 1765), and the first secret societies also began to function then (the freemasons). The proliferation of societies was continuous throughout the 19th and early 20th centuries, embracing all fields of interest. They sometimes had difficulties with the authorities, chiefly because on occasions they were used as tools or mouthpieces by revolutionary organizations; geographical societies were also made use of by local nationalists. After the Bolshevik seizure of power most societies were suppressed, including the most eminent (such as the Free Economic Society and the medical Pirogov Society); others were gradually integrated into the system of party control. Two kinds of society which existed in the early Soviet period were later suppressed by Stalin: Communist-dominated societies such as the Society of Old Bolsheviks, the Society of Former Political Hard Labour Prisoners and Exiles (both suppressed in 1935) and the League of Militant Atheists (suppressed in 1943); and societies which had been tolerated though not formally recognized, such as the Political Red Cross which helped left-wing political prisoners. Small secret societies, usually short-lived, have existed throughout the Soviet period. During the general student unrest of 1956–7 there were attempts in Leningrad and several other cities to set up youth societies without party or Komsomol tutelage.

Sogd, or **Sogdiana**, ancient name of the region in Central Asia which comprises the basins of the Zeravshan and Kashka-Dar'ya, now divided between the Samarkand, Bukhara and Surkhan-Dar'ya oblasts of Uzbekistan and the Leninabad Oblast of Tadzhikistan. Inhabited by Iranian-speaking people, Sogdiana was one of the earliest centres of civilization in Central Asia. It is first mentioned in Darius' Behistun inscription, when it belonged to the Achaemenid kingdom. It was later conquered by Alexander the Great after strong resistance, and belonged successively to the Seleucids, the Graeco-Bactrian kingdom, Kushans, Ephtalites and Turks until it was conquered by the Arabs in 672–709. For later history *see* BUKHARA KHANATE; TRANSOXANIA; TURKESTAN. The Sogdian alphabet (a form of Aramaic) provided the basis for the Uygur alphabet, which in turn served as a basis for the Mongol and Manchu alphabets. The fusion of native and Greek elements in the Hellenistic culture of Sogdiana was of great importance for the future cultural development of Central Asia. Samarkand, the chief centre of Sogdiana, was among the great cities of the ancient world. *See* V. V. Barthold, *Four Studies on the History of Central Asia*, vol. i, Leyden, 1956.

Soil, Climate, Flora and Fauna. Four zones, each with its own characteristic combination of soils, vegetation and animals, run right across Russia from the west to the east. The tundra zone, roughly coinciding with the Arctic climatic belt, has poor, marshy soil, scarce vegetation in the form of grasses, scrubs, mosses and lichens, and there are few animals—reindeer, Arctic foxes and lemmings; among the birds which live permanently in the tundra are ptarmigan and Arctic owls, though many migrants—geese, ducks, snipe, etc.—live in this zone in the summer.

South of the tundra, in the temperate climatic belt, lies the forest zone, which takes up approximately half the total area of the country and reaches as far south as Kiev-Kaluga-Ryazan'-Gor'kiy-Kazan'-Ufa in European Russia and Tyumen'-Tomsk in Western Siberia. In East Siberia and in the Russian Far East the forest zone extends to the slopes of the southern mountains (*see* OROGRAPHY) and the Mongolian and Chinese frontier. In the forest zone the soils are of the grey, *podzol* type, and there are many marshes. In vegetation it is divided into two subzones: the taiga with coniferous forests (spruce and pine in European Russia, larch, fir, spruce, pine and cedar in Siberia); and the mixed forests subzone with predominantly deciduous species (chiefly oak in the west and linden in the east, also elm, maple, ash, beech, birch, aspen and alder), with an admixture of pine. The borderline between these two subzones of vegetation runs from Leningrad to Yaroslavl' and Gor'kiy, east of which the mixed forests form a very narrow belt along the southern edge of the forest zone as far as the Yenisey. They reappear in the monsoon area along the Amur and on the Pacific coast north of Vladivostok, where there is an admixture of subtropical species. Animals typical of the forest zone are the elk, brown bear, glutton, fox, marten, squirrel and hare; in Siberia there are also the reindeer, lynx and sable, and in the mixed forests of European Russia the roebuck. Typical birds of the taiga are the capercailzie, hazel hen, nuthatch and crossbill; of the mixed forests, titmice, thrushes, goldfinches, etc. The fauna of the Far East mixed forests is very rich; in addition to typical taiga species there are also deer, wild boars, tigers, leopards and pheasants.

To the south of the forest zone lies the steppe zone, subdivided into the forested steppes, steppes proper and semi-deserts. The forested steppes stretch in a narrow belt between the mixed forests and proper steppes, the semi-deserts similarly between the steppes and the deserts, both being transitional subzones with mixed characteristics. The steppe zone has fertile black earth (*chernozëm*) and chestnut soils. Natural vegetation—mixed grasses in the north and feather grass with fescue in the south—has almost disappeared in European Russia, where the steppes are almost completely cultivated, but it is still preserved in Western Siberia. Rodents are the most typical animals of this zone—hamsters, suskils, field-mice and marmots, as well as wolves and foxes; among birds there are larks, cranes, partridges, eagles, ducks and geese. Reptiles are much more numerous in the steppe than in the forests—lizards, snakes (adders), etc.; insects include the migrating locust.

The desert zone lies between the steppes in the north and the mountains in the south, and is confined to Central Asia from the lower Volga to the Altay Mountains, and to eastern Transcaucasia. The northern deserts are still within the temperate climatic belt, with cold winters, while the southern deserts have a dry subtropical climate. The desert soils are sandy, stony or clayey, according to the subsoil. Vegetation is sparse and consists of wormwood, various halophytes, and saxaul shrubs. Desert animals include the wild ass, gazelle, jerboa and a variety of reptiles, including the giant monitor lizard. In the natural oases there are thickets of poplar, willow, bamboo and wild sugarcane, and here the fauna is also rich—tigers, wild cats, jackals, deer, pheasants, ibis and storks.

There are also small areas of subtropical vegetation in Russia, namely the Colchis and Talysh in Transcaucasia, and the southern coast of the Crimea. The mountainous areas have vertical vegetation zones which correspond roughly to the latitudinal zones of the plains.

Sokol'nikov (real name **Brilliant**), **Grigoriy Yakovlevich** (1888–1939), politician of Jewish birth who in 1905 joined the Bolshevik faction of the Social Democratic Labour Party. As a 'party-minded Bolshevik' in 1910 he opposed Lenin's intolerance towards the Mensheviks. He became a member of the Bolshevik central committee after the February 1917 revolution, a member of the first Politburo on the eve of the seizure of power, and afterwards was responsible for the nationalization of the banks. As chairman of the third Soviet delegation he signed the peace treaty of Brest-Litovsk (q.v.) in 1918. He was a high-ranking commissar in the Red Army during the civil war, and People's Commissar of Finance, 1921–6. He took part in the 'new opposition' (*see* LEFT OPPOSITION), was in charge of the oil industry, 1928–9, and ambassador to Britain, 1929–32. Sokol'nikov was sentenced to ten years' imprisonment in 1937 at the second show trial (*see* ANTI-SOVIET TROTSKIYITE CENTRE) of the Great Purge (q.v.); he must have died in an isolator (q.v.).

Solidarism, as a trend in modern Russian social thought, gradually developed during the 19th and early 20th centuries. Its basic concept —that of free unity in multiplicity (*see* SOBORNOST')—was first stated by A. S. Khomyakov (q.v.) as an ecclesiological principle. Further inspiration came from Dostoyevskiy, Kropotkin's theory of mutual aid, and from the West European co-operative and Christian Socialist movements. Politically the representatives of Solidarism ranged from conservatism (Dostoyevskiy) through liberalism (V. S. Solov'ëv and the Vekhi group) to moderate socialism (I. I. Yanzhul and the Popular Socialist Party). The term Solidarism was first adopted by Professor G. C. Guins, who formulated the idea of a Solidarist system of law. At present Solidarism is the official social theory of the N.T.S. (q.v.). *See* V. Arsen'yev (ed.), *O solidarizme,* Frankfurt-on-Main, 1955.

Solikamsk, town in the Perm' Oblast (Urals), situated on the River Kama 110 m. north of Perm'. Population (1956) 41,200 (1945, 47,000). It has large potash-mines, and fertilizers and paper are produced. Solikamsk was founded as a saltworks in 1430, and was probably the first permanent Russian settlement in the Urals.

Solovetskiy Monastery, former Orthodox monastery situated on the Solevetskiy Islands of the White Sea, founded in 1429. It was an important religious, cultural and economic centre of the Russian North for many years, and a fortress and place of banishment for religious and political offenders from the late 16th century. The monastery challenged the authority of the Patriarch and the czar from 1667 until 1676, when it was captured by Muscovite troops. It was shelled by British warships during the Crimean War. In 1920 the monastery was abolished and transformed into a concentration camp for political offenders.

Solov'ěv, Sergey Mikhaylovich (1820–79), historian, professor and rector of Moscow University, author of *The History of Russia from the Earliest Times* (covering the period up to 1774, 29 vols.), the most outstanding representative of the 'organic' view of the historical process in Russian historiography (q.v.).

Solov'ěv, Vladimir Sergeyevich (1853–1900), philosopher and poet, son of S.M. He evolved the first comprehensive philosophical system in the history of Russian thought, the philosophy of 'All-Unity.' Through personal religious intuition and the study of philosophy, Solov'ěv discarded his early atheistic materialism and accepted Christianity, holding that the ideal essence of the world existed in the mind of God and naming this essence Sophia—conceiving of it as a feminine entity—of whom he experienced three visions. He revived the Christian humanism of such thinkers as Erasmus, Thomas More and St Francis de Sales, gave it a philosophic and theological justification, and advocated the introduction of the principle of holiness into every sphere of social life. He sought for a synthesis of the Orthodox and Roman Catholic Churches, believing their reconciliation to be of paramount importance for Europe, and his work was very influential in the movement for the reunion of the Churches. Influenced by Dostoyevskiy and the Startsy (*see* STARETS), Solov'ěv in his turn had a far-reaching influence upon the Russian religious philosophers of the early 20th century and the poets of the Symbolist school, especially Blok. He foreshadows in his writings many of the ideas of such writers as Péguy and Maritain. *See* his *War, Progress and the End of History*, 1915, *The Justification of the Good*, 1918, *God, Man and the Church*, 1938, *The Meaning of Love*, 1946, *Lectures on God-manhood*, 1948, *Russia and the Universal Church*, 1948; L. M. Lopatin, 'The Philosophy of Vladimir Solov'ěv,' *Mind*, vol. xxv, N.S., No. 100, Aberdeen, 1916; N. B. Zernov, *Three Russian Prophets*, 1944; *A Solov'ěv Anthology* (ed. S. L. Frank), 1950; N. Lossky, *History of Russian Philosophy*, 1952; V. V. Zenkovsky, *A History of Russian Philosophy*, vol. ii, 1953; R. Hare, *Portraits of Russian Personalities between Reform and Revolution*, 1959.

Sol'vychegodsk, town in the Archangel Oblast, situated on the River Vychegda near Kotlas. Population (1956) 3,600. It has many outstanding architectural monuments of the 16th–17th centuries. Sol'vychegodsk has been known for its saltworks since the 14th century (*see* STROGANOVS), and was a flourishing commercial centre in the 16th–17th centuries.

Song. It is a peculiarity of Russian music that writers invariably seem to be ill at ease in dealing with the larger forms, with the result that instead of consisting of one logical growth an opera or symphony tends to be made up of a series of scenes only loosely connected with the basic idea. However, in the smaller forms, particularly in song, Russian music may claim a leading place in world culture. The origins of Russian song may be found partly in folk music, of both the town and village *genres* (*see* FOLK MUSIC), and partly in the *kanty* (short two- or three-part instrumental, later vocal, laudatory odes first written for ceremonial purposes) at the time of Peter the Great. The 18th and early 19th centuries saw the rise of a number of composers of Russian song such as Titov, Alyab'yev and Varlamov, culminating in the achievements of Glinka and Dargomyzhskiy. Glinka wrote more than eighty-five songs which are distinguished by their lyricism and feeling, while Dargomyzhskiy may be considered the first to introduce satirical features into Russian song, an essentially Russian characteristic. Elements of exoticism and harmonic peculiarities also appear in his work. Balakirev was a prolific song writer, his music reflecting (and in some way determining) the artistic trends of his associates (*see* KUCHKA). Borodin's songs are highly original and, though often only of short duration, most effective in their use of colour and expressive dissonance. Some of the harmonies anticipate later procedures by almost fifty years. Unique among the writers of song, not only in Russia but throughout the world, is Musorgskiy, whose songs run the full range of both musical characterization and emotion. Many of his songs are miniature music dramas, some (such as *The Nursery* cycle) see the world through the naïve, innocent eyes of a child, while others are unequalled in their laconic revelation of human passions and weaknesses. Rimsky-Korsakov wrote more than eighty songs of great charm and quality. Tchaikovsky's songs suffer from repetitiveness, but among them are some outstanding examples of effusions of deep emotion. Mention must also be made of the contributions of Rakhmaninov (many of them highly dramatic), A. G. Rubinshteyn, Arenskiy, Medtner, Lyadov and Glazunov—composers whose songs, charming and effective in their way, deserve to be better known.

The element of childhood has always figured strongly in Russian song, and this, together with folk-song, has been continued by Soviet composers such as Gnesin, Shaporin, Knipper and Prokof'yev. *See* G. Abraham, *Studies in Russian Music*, 1935, and *On Russian Music*, 1939; G. Abraham and M. D. Calvocoressi, *Masters of Russian Music*, 1936, C. Stief, *Studies in the Russian Historical Song*, Copenhagen, 1953.

Sormovo, industrial suburb 6 m. west of Gor'kiy, on the Volga. The Sormovo works, built 1849–50, are one of the largest engineering plants in the country, producing ships, railway cars (since 1873), locomotives (since 1899) and tanks (since 1919). A large part of Soviet submarine building is concentrated in Sormovo, and the extensive programme of canal construction (*see* INLAND WATERWAYS) in the 1940's and fifties was aimed at facilitating their access to the seas. From the 1880's Sormovo was an important centre of labour movement.

South-eastern League, regional organization of Cossacks, Caucasian mountain peoples and the nomadic peoples of North Caucasus which was formed in October 1917. After the Bolshevik seizure of power it proclaimed itself an independent republic, but soon disintegrated.

South Kazakhstan Oblast is situated astride the middle course of the River Syr-Dar'ya, traversed by the Orenburg-Tashkent railway;

it is largely desert, with ranges of the Tien-Shan mountain system in the south which have rich deposits of zinc, lead, lignite and rare metals. Area 57,900 sq. m.; population (1959) 924,000 (36 per cent urban), mainly Kazakhs (about 50 per cent), Russians (about 33 per cent) and Uzbeks, also Koreans. Cotton, grain and sugar-beet are cultivated, fruit grown and sheep and goats raised; there are non-ferrous metallurgy, engineering, cotton-processing, food (sugar, meat) and pharmaceutic industries. Principal towns: Chimkent (administrative centre) and Turkestan. For history *see* KOKAND KHANATE; TRANSOXANIA; TURKESTAN.

South Ossetian Autonomous Oblast, in Georgia, lies on the southern slopes of the central part of the main Caucasian range. Area 1,500 sq. m.; population (1959) 96,000 (25 per cent urban), Ossetians (since the 14th century) and Georgians. The main occupation is goat and sheep raising. The oblast was formed in 1922 and the administrative centre is Staliniri.

Southern Industrial Region comprises the Donets Basin (q.v.), the Dnepropetrovsk and Zaporozh'ye oblasts of the Ukraine, and the Kerch' Peninsula of the Crimea. It includes the Donets coalfields, the iron-ore deposits of Krivoy Rog and Kerch', and the iron and steel and engineering industries based upon them. In the wider sense the region also includes the machine-building centres of Khar'kov, Rostov-on-Don and Taganrog. Modern industrial development began in the Southern Industrial Region in the 1870's, and by 1895 it had overtaken the Urals as Russia's main centre of heavy industry. Until the 1930's Khar'kov was the region's principal commercial centre. Prior to the Bolshevik seizure of power the industrialists of the region played a prominent part in economic circles, and wielded considerable influence upon the Government's economic policy. As a result of destruction during the civil war and the Second World War (when it was occupied by the Germans), and extensive industrial development in the eastern parts of the country since the 1930's, the Southern Industrial Region no longer holds its former dominant position, but it has remained in the first place among the centres of heavy industry.

Sovetsk (until 1946 **Tilsit**), town in the Kaliningrad Oblast (former East Prussia), situated on the Niemen 55 m. north-east of Kaliningrad. Population (1956) 34,100 (1939, 59,000), chiefly settlers from central Russia (before the war wholly German). It has timber and paper industries. The town was founded as a castle by the Teutonic Knights in 1288, and became a town in 1552. The emperors Alexander I and Napoleon I met here in 1807 and concluded a peace treaty between France and Russia. For recent history *see* KALININGRAD.

Soviet of Nationalities, one of the two chambers of the U.S.S.R. Supreme Soviet. It is elected on the basis of twenty-five deputies from each Union Republic, eleven from each Autonomous Republic, five from each Autonomous Oblast and one from each National Okrug; but the deputies are not required to be, and very often are not, of the nationality they are supposed to represent. The Soviet of Nationalities has the same structure and functions as the other chamber, the Soviet of the Union (q.v.), except that since 1957 it has an additional standing committee on economic planning. It is the successor of the Soviet of Nationalities within the Central Executive Committee (q.v.) which existed 1918–36. *See further under* SUPREME SOVIET. *See* M. Fainsod, *How Russia is Ruled*, Cambridge, Mass., 1953.

Soviet of the Union, one of the two chambers of the U.S.S.R. Supreme Soviet. It is elected on the basis of one deputy for 300,000 people. It is the successor of the Soviet of the Union which existed before 1936 within the Central Executive Committee (q.v.). *See further under* SUPREME SOVIET.

Soviet Union, *see* UNION OF SOVIET SOCIALIST REPUBLICS.

Sovietology, academic study of Soviet Russia and of such aspects of pre-Soviet Russia as seem relevant to later developments. It developed as an academic discipline essentially after the Second World War, particularly in the United States (where the main centres are the Russian Institute at Columbia and the Russian Research Center at Harvard), although such studies had been pursued in Russia itself, and by Russian *émigrés* and individual foreign scholars, since the 1920's. Specialized Sovietological periodicals in English are *Soviet Studies* (University of Glasgow), *Soviet Survey* (London), Soviet Affairs series of *St Antony's Papers* (Oxford), *Problems of Communism* (Washington) and the *Bulletin of the Institute for the Study of the Soviet Union* (Munich).

The most comprehensive exposition of the main trends in Sovietology has been given by D. Bell, 'Ten Theories in Search of Reality: the Prediction of Soviet Behaviour in the Social Sciences' (*World Politics*, vol. x, No. 3, April 1958). He distinguished ten basic theories of Soviet reality, grouping them into four categories as follows:

(*a*) *Characterological theories:* (1) anthropological (Mead, Gorer, Dicks), analysing contemporary Soviet behaviour in terms of personality shaped by the cultural pattern; (2) psycho-analytical (Leites), seeing in the Bolshevik character a reaction against the moods of the 19th-century Russian intelligentsia, which is prompted by fears of death and latent homosexuality.

(*b*) *Sociological theories:* (3) the social system theory (Bauer, Inkeles, Kluckhohn), which identifies typical functionally relevant behaviour patterns within the Soviet system and their effect on different social groups; (4) the ideal types theory (Moore, Rostow), which analyses the Soviet social system in relation to a number of models of power structure, e.g. traditional, rational-technical, political, etc.

(*c*) *Political theories:* (5) Marxist, or rather Trotskyist (Deutscher, Carr), according to which the Soviet state since the 1920's has been directed by the party leadership through a bureaucracy in the interests of the workers (since a nationalized economy has been maintained), although for particular historical reasons without active support from the workers; (6) neo-Marxist (Burnham, and also Milovan Djilas), which argue that a 'new class' of managers or collective bureaucracy has emerged to replace the former exploiting classes; (7) the totalitarian theory (Wolfe), which views the Soviet system as a direct confrontation of the all-powerful leader with the mass of the population, whom he rules by terror; (8) Kremlinology (Borkenau, Nikolaevsky), which is primarily concerned with the relationships within the ruling clique and the bases of their power among the second echelons of the apparatus.

(d) *Historical theories:* (9) the Slav theory (Berdyayev, Pares, Maynard), which maintains that the Soviet system is largely a continuation of traditional Russian forms and characteristics; (10) the geo-political theory (Kennan, Dinerstein), according to which Soviet foreign policy, and to some extent internal developments, result from the country's strategic position in the world.

To these four categories should be added the fifth category of pneumatological theories, which analyse Bolshevism as a spiritual phenomenon. The more important of these are the religious theory (Gurian), which considers Communism an earthly pseudo-religion, and the axiological theory (Redlich), which analyses Soviet society in terms of the realization of a hierarchy of values in which power takes the first place. Another interesting axiological theory is suggested by R. Conquest, according to whom developments in Soviet society are determined by the interplay of three sets of values, those of the bureaucrats, the theorists and the humanists. *See* N. Berdyayev, *The Origin of Russian Communism*, 1937, and *The Russian Idea*, 1947; Sir J. Maynard, *The Russian Peasant, and other Studies*, 1942; J. Burnham, *The Managerial Revolution*, 1943; Sir B. Pares, *A History of Russia*, 1947; 'X,' 'Sources of Soviet Conduct,' *Foreign Affairs*, vol. xxv, No. 4, July 1947; G. Gorer, *The People of Great Russia*, 1949; Barrington Moore, Jnr, *Soviet Politics—the Dilemma of Power*, Cambridge, Mass., 1950, and *Terror and Progress*, Cambridge, Mass., 1954; E. H. Carr, *History of Soviet Russia* (6 vols.), 1950–9; H. V. Dicks, 'Observations on Contemporary Russian Behaviour,' *Human Relations*, vol. v, No. 2, 1952; M. Mead, *Soviet Attitudes to Authority*, New York, 1952; W. Gurian, *Bolshevism, a Study of Soviet Communism*, Notre Dame, Indiana, 1952; W. W. Rostow, *The Dynamics of Soviet Society*, 1953; I. Deutscher, *Russia, What Next?*, 1953, *The Prophet Armed*, 1954, and 'Russia in Transition' in *Universities and Left Review*, vol. i, No. 1, 1957; F. Borkenau, 'Zur Methode der Sowjet-Forschung,' *Philosophisches Jahrbuch d. Görres-Gesellschaft*, Munich, 1953; N. Leites, *A Study of Bolshevism*, Glencoe, Illinois, 1954; G. Kennan, *Realities of American Foreign Policy*, Princeton, New Jersey, 1954; J. S. Reshetar, Jr., *Problems of Analysing and Predicting Soviet Behavior*, Garden City, N.Y., 1955; R. Bauer, A. Inkeles and C. Kluckhohn, *How the Soviet System Works*, Cambridge, Mass., 1956; B. D. Wolfe, *Six Keys to Soviet Power*, 1956; R. Redlich (ed.), *Ocherki bolshevizmovedeniya* (*Essays in Bolshevism-ology*), Frankfurt-am-Main, 1956; M. Djilas, *The New Class*, 1957; H. S. Dinerstein, *War and the Soviet Union*, 1958; H. H. Fisher (ed.), *American Research on Russia*, Bloomington, Indiana, 1959; A. Inkeles and R. A. Bauer, *The Soviet Citizen*, 1959; R. Conquest, *Common Sense on Russia*, 1960; R. F. Byrnes, 'Studies in Revolution,' *World Politics*, vol. xii, No. 4, July 1960. W. Leonhard, *Kreml ohne Stalin*, Cologne, 1960; A. Dallin (ed.), *Soviet Conduct in World Affairs*, New York, 1960.

Soviets ('councils'), organs of State power in Russia, which according to the 1936 constitution are the 'political basis' of the U.S.S.R.

The Supreme Soviet (q.v.) of the U.S.S.R., republican, provincial and local soviets are formally elected by universal, equal, direct and secret vote, though the elections are in practice fictitious since in every constituency there is only one candidate. Soviets first emerged during the revolution of 1905 (q.v.) as Soviets of Workers' Deputies, and appeared again in 1917 as Soviets of Workers' and Soldiers' Deputies. The principal soviets fell under Bolshevik influence as a result of the Kornilov (q.v.) affair. Led by Trotskiy, the Petrograd Soviet established a Military Revolutionary Committee through which the Bolsheviks seized power (*see* OCTOBER REVOLUTION). Since 1917 soviets have been regarded as organs of the Dictatorship of the Proletariat, and were suitably described by Stalin as 'transmission belts from the party to the masses.' *See also* LOCAL GOVERNMENT. *See* A. J. Sack, *The Birth of the Russian Democracy*, New York, 1918; M. Fainsod, *How Russia is Ruled*, Cambridge, Mass., 1953; O. Anweiler, *Die Rätebewegung in Russland, 1905–21*, Leyden, 1958; V. Gsovski and K. Grzybowski (eds.), *Government, Law and Courts in the Soviet Union and Eastern Europe*, vol. i, 1959.

Sovkhoz (Russian abbreviation for 'Soviet Economy'), State farms, agricultural enterprises which differ from collective farms (*see* KOLKHOZ) in that they are run like industrial enterprises with hired labour which is paid regular wages. In 1958 there were 6,002 *sovkhozes* (including 1,739 dairy, 1,936 grain, 816 vegetable, 622 pig and 610 sheep). The *sovkhozes* play a secondary role in agriculture compared to the *kolkhozes*, although their number has increased in recent years (4,000 in 1953, with 1,700,000 workers and 15·2 million hectares of arable land; 3·8 million workers and 52·5 million hectares in 1958), and they predominate in the areas brought under cultivation during the Virgin Land Campaign (q.v.). *See* H. Schwartz, *Russia's Soviet Economy*, 2nd ed., 1954.

Sovnarkhoz, *see* ECONOMIC COUNCILS.

Special Board, quasi-judicial body established in 1934, after the murder of Kirov, within the Commissariat for Internal Affairs (*see* N.K.V.D.) for summary decisions in cases of terrorism and other 'counter-revolutionary' offences. It had branches (*see* TROYKA) attached to the republic and oblast security administrations and in the principal forced labour camps. The extra-judicial powers of the security police reached their highest point in the Special Board, which was one of the main instruments of Stalin's terror. It was abolished in 1956. *See* S. Wolin and R. M. Slusser (eds.), *The Soviet Secret Police*, New York, 1957.

Special Settlers, official designation of people administratively banished to remote parts of the country for an indefinite time. Special settlers live in separate settlements or among the local inhabitants, in both cases under supervision of the M.V.D.; those in separate settlements are entirely administered by the M.V.D. They have no passports and are therefore unable to move out of their place of residence (*see* PASSPORT, INTERNAL) and are under other legal disabilities, though since the introduction of the 1936 constitution they are expected to take part in elections. There are no figures available of the number of special settlers, but they are numerous and make up a considerable proportion of the labour force in the newly industrialized areas. The practice was for the first time applied on a large scale during the collectivization of agriculture, when peasants who refused to join *kolkhozes* were often deported as special settlers. The next group were deportees in 1939–40 from the newly annexed territories of eastern Poland, the Baltic States, Bessarabia and northern Bukovina; these peoples were followed by the deportations of allegedly 'unreliable' peoples between 1941–4 (*see* BALKARS; CHECHENS; GERMANS; INGUSH; KALMYKS; KARACHAY; TATARS); since 1955 many people released from 'corrective labour camps' (q.v.) have become special settlers. Banishment as a special settler can be arbitrarily terminated, as in the case of many Poles after the agreement with the Polish Government in exile in 1941, and those native peoples who were rehabilitated by decree in 1957.

Specialists, *see* INTELLIGENTSIA.

Speculators, official pejorative term applied to those who engage in private trading. In fact the chronic shortage (sometimes only local) of many consumer goods inevitably results in private trading by enterprising individuals. This has been unlawful (except in the case of personal possessions and agricultural products from private gardens) since the suppression of private trade at the end of the New Economic Policy period. Cases of large-scale organized 'speculation,' or black market activity, involving the corruption of officials, frequently come to light, and in some instances in recent years speculators were reported in the Soviet press to have been sentenced to death.

Speranskiy, Aleksey Dmitriyevich (*b.* 1888), pathologist. Educated at Kazan' University, he was professor at Irkutsk University, 1920–3, and later worked in I. P. Pavlov's laboratory and in the Institute of Experimental Medicine; he is a member of the Academy of Sciences. In his *Nervous System in Pathology*, 1930, he advanced the theory that the nervous component is the leading factor in every pathological process, thus starting a new trend in pathology. His other main work is *Elements of the Construction of the Theory of Medicine*, 1935.

Speranskiy, Count Mikhail Mikhaylovich (1772–1839), deputy Minister of Justice from 1808. At the request of Alexander I he worked out a plan for reforming the state legislative and administrative system by the introduction of an elected State Duma and representative assemblies in local government. The plan began to be carried out (e.g. the establishment of the Council of State, q.v.) when in 1812 Speranskiy became involved in a political intrigue and was banished to Nizhniy Novgorod. He was appointed Governor-General of Siberia in 1819, and there effected a radical reform of the administration. Between 1826 and 1833 he codified the existing Russian laws—the first new code since that of Aleksey Mikhaylovich in 1649. *See* M. Raeff, *Michael Speransky, Statesman of Imperial Russia*, The Hague, 1957.

Spesivtseva, Olga (*b.* 1895), dancer who graduated from the Imperial School to the Mariinskiy Theatre in 1913, joining the Russian Ballet in 1916. In 1920 she was appointed ballerina, though suffering from ill health. In 1921 she danced for Diaghilev, returned to Russia, but left her native land finally in 1924, working with the Paris Opera till 1932. She rejoined Diaghilev for a short period in 1927 to create the role of *La Chatte*. Besides her association with the Paris Opera, she also visited London, 1929, Buenos Aires, 1932, and Australia, 1934, during the latter tour, however, showing symptoms of mental disease. Her last appearance was at Buenos Aires in 1937 and since that date she has been confined in an asylum in New York. Spesivtseva is one of the great classical dancers of the 20th century. Her most famous roles were *Esmeralda*, *Giselle* and *The Sleeping Beauty*. See S. Lifar, *The Three Graces*, 1959.

Sputnik (Russian for 'satellite'), popular name for the Russian artificial earth satellites. Russia was the first country to launch an earth satellite, on 4th October 1957, and two more successful launchings followed on 3rd November 1957 and 15th May 1958. The second satellite carried a dog which survived for several days and was then killed automatically and painlessly. The first artificial satellite of the sun was also launched in Russia, on 2nd January 1959. The following table gives comparative data on these satellites.

	I	II	III	IV (*artificial planet*)
Weight (kg.)	83·6	1	1,327	1,472
Weight of scientific apparatus (kg.)	1	508·3	968	361·3
Maximum height of orbit at beginning of rotation (km.)	947	1,671	1,881	197 mn [2]
Minimum height of orbit at beginning of rotation (km.)	227	225	226	156 mn [2]
Initial eccentricity of orbit	0·0518	0·0988	0·1115	0·148
Initial period of rotation (mins.)	96·17	103·75	105·95	about 450 days
Inclination of orbit to earth's equator	65·1°	65·3°	65·2°	about 0·1° [3]
Duration of existence (days)	92	162	691	not known
Duration of functioning of apparatus	about 3 weeks	2 weeks	up to 1 month [4]	not known

See L. V. Berkner (ed.), *Manual on Rockets and Satellites*, 1958; *Soviet Writings on Earth Satellites and Space Travel*, 1959; D. King-Hele, *Satellites and Scientific Research*, 1960.

Stakhanov Movement, largely fictitious (*see* FICTIONS) movement among workers and *kolkhoz* peasants intended to increase the productivity of labour. On the orders of the party authorities it was launched in 1935 by the coal-miner A. Stakhanov; selected workers, aided by assistants, were given particularly advantageous conditions of work and achieved remarkable production results which were then

[1] Data not published.   [2] Distance from the sun.
[3] Inclination of orbit to the ecliptic.
[4] One radio transmitter continued to function for over a year.

used to justify an increase in production targets for all workers. After the Second World War the practice was carried on under other names. It was exposed as fictitious after Stalin's death, but revived in the form of 'teams of Communist Labour.'

Stalin (real name **Dzhugashvili**), **Iosif Vissarionovich** (1879–1953), dictator of Russia and of the world Communist movement, the most accomplished totalitarian ruler of modern times. He was the son of a Georgian artisan and was educated at the Tiflis theological seminary, but in 1898 was expelled for his connections with the revolutionary movement. In the same year he joined the Russian Social Democratic Labour Party, and five years later its Bolshevik faction. Until 1913 he worked as an active but unimportant follower of Lenin in the underground movement in Transcaucasia, and was then co-opted by Lenin and Zinov'yev, who desperately needed collaborators, into the Bolshevik Central Committee. At the time this had little significance but it served to ensure his formal seniority when he returned from banishment (he was banished six times and escaped five) to Petrograd after the February revolution of 1917; he became second only to Kamenev in the capital's Bolshevik hierarchy, and editor of the party's newspaper *Pravda*. Together with Kamenev, Stalin took up a conciliatory attitude towards the Provisional Government, but on Lenin's return from abroad he fell in with his plans for a Bolshevik seizure of power.

From 1917 to 1923 Stalin was Commissar for Nationalities in the first Soviet Government, and simultaneously Commissar for Worker-Peasant Inspection (q.v.), 1919–23. He rose to the position of Lenin's closest collaborator (apart from Sverdlov) after the Brest-Litovsk treaty crisis, in which the Left Communists (q.v.) and Trotskiy were opposed to Lenin. Like other leading party men, Stalin was a high-ranking commissar in the Red Army during the civil war. He was a member of the Politburo from its foundation and became Secretary-General (q.v.) of the party's Central Committee in 1922. Shortly before his last illness, Lenin, concerned about Stalin's rudeness and high-handedness, was planning to remove him from this powerful position, but by the time of Lenin's death Stalin had already consolidated his grasp upon the apparatus of the party. During the inner-party struggle that followed he collaborated with Zinov'yev and Kamenev to defeat Trotskiy, making use of the slogan of 'building socialism in one country first' to counter Trotskiy's demand for 'permanent revolution'; thereafter he collaborated with Bukharin and Rykov to defeat the 'new opposition' of Zinov'yev and Kamenev and the 'combined opposition' of these two with Trotskiy (*see* LEFT OPPOSITION); his final blow to the oppositions of the immediate post-Lenin years was the defeat of Bukharin's and Rykov's Right Opposition (q.v.), in which he was assisted by Molotov, Voroshilov, Kaganovich, Ordzhonikidze and Kirov, whom he gradually promoted to the Politburo. Together with them he ruled from 1929 to 1934 as the undisputed leader of the successful clique, introducing the Five Year Plans (q.v.), the collectivization of agriculture (q.v.) and the so-called 'cultural revolution' (q.v., *see also* PURGES). In 1934 an opposition to Stalin's rule emerged among his own supporters, apparently headed by Kirov, and the latter's assassination (in circumstances which make the complicity of Stalin himself appear likely) set the stage for the abandonment of 'collective leadership' and a series of purges within the party and State apparatus that culminated in the Great Purge (q.v.), which was aimed at the extermination of all real or imaginary opponents.

Stalin's absolute personal rule was henceforth a reign of terror (*see* STALINISM). He became the official head of the Government in 1940, and in 1941 the chairman of the State Defence Committee (q.v.), Commissar (1946–7 Minister) for Defence and supreme commander-in-chief of the armed forces. During the war he assumed the ranks of marshal and later generalissimo, and interfered personally with the work of the military commanders. He outwitted Churchill and Roosevelt at the conferences of Teheran, Yalta and Potsdam, and at little cost obtained considerable advantages for the Soviet Union. The political atmosphere had been permitted to relax somewhat during the war, but from 1946 Stalinism was rigorously restored in Russia itself and was imposed upon the satellite countries of Eastern Europe. Extreme obscurantism, xenophobia, chauvinism and anti-Semitism (*see* DOCTORS' PLOT) characterized the final years of Stalin's rule. His works include *History of the Communist Party of the Soviet Union (Bolsheviks)*. *Short Course* (edited by Stalin), Moscow, 1939, and *Problems of Leninism*, 11th ed., Moscow, 1940. *See* D. Souvarine, *Stalin*, 1939; B. D. Wolfe, *Three who made a Revolution*, 1948, and *Khrushchëv and Stalin's Ghost*, 1957; I. Deutscher, *Stalin*, 1949; L. Schapiro, *The Communist Party of the Soviet Union*, 1960.

Stalin Prizes, *see* LENIN PRIZES.

Stalinabad (until 1929 **Dyushambe**), city in Central Asia, capital, cultural and an economic centre of Tadzhikistan, situated in the Gissar Valley. Population (1959) 224,000 (1939, 83,000), mostly Russians, Tadzhiks and Uzbeks. It has textile (cotton and silk) and food industries. The Tadzhik Academy of Sciences, a university (founded 1948) and other higher educational establishments are here. Formerly a village, Stalinabad became a town in 1925 and has been capital of Tadzhikistan since 1924.

Stalingrad: 1. Oblast of the R.S.F.S.R., situated in the south-east of European Russia, traversed by the lower course of the Volga and the middle course of the Don; it is a region of dry steppe, and there are large salt deposits (Lake El'ton). Area 44,100 sq. m.; population (1959) 1,849,000 (54 per cent urban), Russians and Ukrainians (until the war also Germans). There are engineering, timber, oil and gas extraction, chemical, food and textile industries; wheat, sunflowers and vegetables are cultivated (frequent droughts), and cattle and sheep raised. The Volga-Don Canal runs through the oblast, and a large hydro-electric station (2,300,000 kw.) is being built. Principal towns: Stalingrad, Volzhskiy, Kamyshin. Until its annexation by Muscovy, 1552–6, the area was virtually unpopulated. In 1942–3 it was partly occupied by the Germans.

2. (until 1925 **Tsaritsyn**). Administrative, economic and cultural centre of the oblast, situated on the right bank of the Volga. Population (1959) 591,000 (fourth on the Volga, twentieth in the U.S.S.R.;

1861, 7,000; 1897, 55,000; 1917, 133,000; 1939, 445,000; 2nd February 1943, 1,515; 1st January 1944, 250,000). It is a major industrial and transportation centre of the country, having a large engineering industry (tractors, river vessels), iron and steel, saw-milling (second after Archangel), chemical, food and light industries; it is a river port, standing at one end of the Volga-Don Canal, has five railway lines and an airport (eight regular passenger lines).

Stalingrad was founded as a Russian fortified town in 1589, and during the 17th–18th centuries was frequently besieged and captured by Cossack rebels. From 1862 it became an important centre of the timber trade and of water-rail transfer of Baku oil; industrial development dates from 1875, and especially from the 1930's (tractor plant). It has been a provincial centre since the 1920's, and 1931–4 was the administrative centre of the Lower Volga Kray. The town was destroyed during the great Battle of Stalingrad, 1942–3, but has since been rebuilt. A sword of honour was presented to the city in 1943 inscribed 'To the steel-hearted citizens of Stalingrad, the gift of King George VI, in token of the homage of the British people.' *See* A. Werth, *Year of Stalingrad*, New York, 1947.

Staliniri (until 1935 **Tskhinvali**), administrative and cultural centre of the South Ossetian Autonomous Oblast (Georgia), situated 53 m. north-west of Tiflis. Population (1959) 22,000. It has woodworking and cheese-making industries, and talcum powder is produced.

Stalinism, theory and practice of Stalin's near-totalitarian rule in the Soviet Union, the satellite states of eastern Europe and in the world Communist movement. Orthodox Communist propaganda denies that Stalinism exists as a distinct body of theory, maintaining that Stalin simply developed and enriched the teachings of Marx and Lenin; since the 20th congress of the Communist Party (q.v.) it is also permissible to say that Stalin made mistakes. The theory of Stalinism is in fact a combination of Leninism (*see* BOLSHEVISM; LENINISM) and National Bolshevism (q.v.) with new elements added by Stalin himself and by Molotov, Zhdanov, Vyshinskiy, etc.; these include the doctrines of the possibility of 'building socialism in one country' first, of the existence of a state even under full communism if there is 'capitalist encirclement' (q.v.), of Socialist Realism (q.v.) in literature and the arts, of the happy and prosperous life of the Soviet people, their moral and political unity and their unbounded love for the Communist Party, the security organs and for Stalin himself, and of Stalin as a universal genius, source of limitless wisdom and benevolence. Most of these doctrines were dogmatic postulates in form and fictitious in content (*see* FICTION), and were intended to enforce conformity in public behaviour and expression. In Stalin's lifetime the practical concomitants were the terror of the security organs (*see* M.G.B.; N.K.V.D.) and the fear of the concentration camp (*see* CORRECTIVE LABOUR CAMPS) awaiting the nonconformist. The disintegration of the Stalinist system in Russia began with the relaxation of terror after Stalin's death and Beria's fall, and was greatly accelerated by the denunciation of Stalin's crimes made in Khrushchëv's secret report to the 20th party congress (q.v.). However, such basic features of Stalinism as the monopoly of the

Communist Party in almost all spheres of life, the manipulation of fictions and the cult of the party leader remain. *See* A. B. Ulam, *The Unfinished Revolution*, New York, 1960.

Stalino: 1. Oblast of the Ukraine, comprising the western part of the Donets Basin in the north and a part of the Sea of Azov lowland in the south; it has large deposits of coal, also salt, mercury and building materials. Area 10,300 sq. m.; population (1959) 4,265,000 (86 per cent urban), Ukrainians and Russians. It is a highly industrialized area—coal-mining, iron and steel, engineering, chemical and other industries; grain cultivation, market gardening and dairy farming are also carried on. The oblast has a dense railway network. Principal towns: Stalino, Makeyevka, Gorlovka, Zhdanov, Kramatorsk, Yenakiyevo, Chistyakovo, Konstantinovka, Slavyansk, Artëmovsk. Until its annexation by Russia from the Crimean Khanate in 1739 (*see* NEW RUSSIA) the area was virtually unpopulated. Salt has been mined since the late 17th century, coal since the 1770's, the engineering industry was established in the 1870's and the chemical industry in 1889. Since the 1870's industrial expansion has been rapid; the industries suffered severely during the civil war and the Second World War (German occupation 1918 and 1942–3), but were restored and further developed on both occasions.

2. (until 1924 **Yuzovo**, or **Yuzovka**). Administrative, economic and cultural centre of the oblast, the largest industrial centre of the Donets Basin and one of the largest in the U.S.S.R. Population (1959) 701,000 (third in the Ukraine, tenth in the U.S.S.R.; 1914, 49,000; 1923, 32,000; 1926, 174,000; 1939, 466,000; 1945, 392,000); together with its twin city of Makeyevka and several smaller towns, the population of the Stalino conurbation exceeds a million. It has large iron and steel, coal-mining, engineering (mining and power-generating equipment), chemical and other industries. Stalino was founded in 1869 as a result of the construction of the metallurgical plant by the New Russia Metallurgical Company (headed by the Welshman John Hughes—hence the name); it was the administrative centre of the whole Donets region, 1932–8.

Stalinogorsk (until 1934 **Dobriki**), town in the Tula Oblast (central Russia), situated 20 m. south-east of Tula. Population (1959) 107,000 (1939, 76,000). It is the second industrial centre of the Moscow Lignite Basin (after Tula), and has a large chemical industry (explosives, fertilizers, sulphuric acid, etc.) and an important power-station. The town was founded in 1930.

Stalinsk (until 1932 **Kuznetsk**, or **Novokuznetsk**), city in the Kemerovo Oblast (southern Siberia), chief industrial centre of the Kuznetsk Basin, situated on the Southern Siberian Railway. Population (1959) 377,000 (third in Siberia; 1926, 4,000; 1939, 166,000; 1945, 223,000). The Kuznetsk iron and steel plant is among the largest in the world, and second only to Magnitogorsk in Russia; there are also ferro-alloy and aluminium plants, heavy engineering, chemical, light and food industries, and a big electric power-station. Stalinsk was founded as a Russian fortified town in 1617; an ironworks was built in 1771 and closed down in the 1860's. The Kuznetsk plant was built 1929–32, and a new town around it, Novokuznetsk, which soon absorbed the old Kuznetsk. Another iron and steel plant, the Western Siberian, is under construction.

Stanislav (Ukrainian **Stanyslav**, Polish **Stanisławów**): 1. Oblast in Galicia (Western Ukraine), situated largely in the Carpathian foothills, partly covered by oak and beech forests; there are deposits of oil and salt. Area 5,400 sq. m.; population (1959) 1,098,000 (23 per cent urban), mostly Ukrainians (those in the mountains belonging to the Hutsul tribe), before the war also Poles and Jews. Grain and potatoes are cultivated, cattle and pigs raised, and there are sawmilling, oil-extraction and food industries; many old crafts are carried on, especially by the Hutsuls (wood-carving, carpet weaving, embroidery). Principal towns: Stanislav, Kolomyya, Galich. For history *see* GALICIA.

2. Administrative and economic centre of the oblast, situated 75 m. south-east of L'vov. Population (1959) 66,000 (before the war mostly Jews and Poles). It has oil-refining, woodworking and food industries, and is an important railway junction. The town has interesting buildings of the 18th century. Stanislav was founded in 1662, belonged to the Potocki family until 1801 and was a flourishing commercial centre (Armenian merchants); in 1919 it was capital of the Western Ukrainian Republic.

Stanislavsky (real name **Alekseyev**), **Konstantin Sergeyevich** (1863–1938), great actor and director. The son of a wealthy Moscow merchant, he directed from 1877 to 1887 the group of amateurs known as the 'Alekseyev circle,' and thereafter until 1898 directed a number of plays for the Society of Art and Literature. In 1898, together with V. I. Nemirovich-Danchenko, he founded the Moscow Art Theatre. This theatre, with its team of outstanding actors and Chekhov's and Gor'kiy's plays as the backbone of its repertoire, enabled Stanislavsky to develop to the full his views on acting which became known as the Stanislavsky system. Although it was based on the realistic tradition in the Russian theatre which went back to Shchepkin (q.v.), the Stanislavsky system appeared as something new and even revolutionary in comparison with the canons of the Malyy Theatre. Realistic form was to be a by-product of the actor's emotional involvement, of his 'reliving' the part, and Stanislavsky developed a special technique of 'reliving.' It was this tendency to identify the theatre with life that prompted the most gifted of Stanislavsky's pupils, Meyerhold and Vakhtangov (qq.v.), to return to the idea of a 'theatrical' or 'representational' theatre. Stanislavsky himself experienced a certain influence of Symbolism, which swept over Russian artistic life after the revolution of 1905. The officially sponsored modernism (*see* BOGDANOVISM) of the early years of the Soviet regime made Stanislavsky and his theatre appear old-fashioned and 'bourgeois,' while the partial restoration of traditional forms in social and cultural life from the early 1930's (*see* STALINISM; ZHDANOV) led to the elevation of a dogmatized and fictionalized (*see* FICTIONS) form of the Stanislavsky system to the official position of the true form of Socialist Realism (q.v.) in the theatre. Whereas Stanislavsky's genuine ideas have greatly influenced modern acting, both in Russia and abroad, the use made of his system during the last period of

Stalin's rule all but killed the Russian theatre. *See also* THEATRE. *See* his *My Life in Art*, 1924; *An Actor Prepares*, 1936; *Stanislavsky Produces Othello*, 1948; *Stanilavsky on the Art of the Stage*, 1950; *Building a Character*, 1950; also D. Magarshack, *Stanislavsky, a Life*, 1950; N. M. Gorchakov, *Stanislavsky Directs*, New York, 1954; I. V. Kostetskiy, *Sovetskaya teatral'naya politika i sistema Stanislavskogo*, Munich, 1956; T. Cole and H. K. Chinoy (eds.), *Actors on Acting*, 1960.

Stankevich, Nikolay Vladimirovich (1813–40), inspirer and leader of the main philosophical circle in Moscow in the 1830's, to which belonged both the future Westernists (q.v.) Bakunin, Belinskiy, Granovskiy, Katkov (qq.v.), etc., and the future Slavophiles K. S. Aksakov and Samarin (qq.v.). *See* E. J. Brown, 'The Circle of Stankevich,' *American Slavic and East European Review*, vol. xvi, No. 3, 1957.

Starets ('Elder,' plural **Startsy**), revered monk, spiritual tutor of younger monks, in the Orthodox Church. During the 19th century some Startsy of the Optina Pustyn' (q.v.) had much influence upon members of the lay intelligentsia, including Dostoyevskiy and V. S. Solov'ëv.

Starov, Ivan Yegorovich (1744–1808), architect. He was a master of the classical style, which he reduced to simpler, more severe forms than those of Bazhenov and Kazakov (qq.v.). His most notable work was the Tauric Palace, St Petersburg, built for Potëmkin, 1783–8. It is chiefly famous for its gigantic colonnaded hall which set the fashion for the widespread use of columns in Russian interiors (*see* ARCHITECTURE; ARCHITECTURE, ECCLESIASTICAL). *See* Tamara Talbot Rice, *Russian Art*, 1949; G. H. Hamilton, *The Art and Architecture of Russia*, 1954.

Stasov, Vasiliy Petrovich (1775–1848), architect, master of an extremely severe and simple classical style marked by a use of ancient Greek elements and flat, unadorned expanses of wall. Notable works are the barracks of the Paul Regiment and the Court Stables in St Petersburg, the Orangery at Tsarskoye Selo and the Provision Stores in Moscow. *See* G. H. Hamilton, *The Art and Architecture of Russia*, 1954.

Stasov, Vladimir Vasil'yevich (1824–1906), son of V. P., art critic and historian who was educated, like Serov and Tchaikovsky, at the School of Jurisprudence in St Petersburg. From 1851 to 1854 he lived abroad, and in 1872 was appointed Director of Fine Arts. Besides drafting the libretto of Borodin's *Prince Igor* he did much to publicize the work of the Russian national composers (*see* KUCHKA), and his biographical materials of the leading musical figures are of considerable importance. His aesthetical writings (*Twenty-five Years of Russian Art*; *The Tracks of Russian Art*; *Art in the Nineteenth Century*, etc.) had great influence on contemporary Russian art. His collected works were published in three volumes, St Petersburg, 1894; a fourth volume, dedicated to Count Tolstoy, was added in 1905.

State Capitalism, economic system under which the State owns the means of production and runs the economy on the capitalist principle, that is, aiming at the maximum profit. Lenin applied the term to the measures for regulating the economy by the State during the First

World War, and considered State capitalism to be the final stage in the development of the capitalist economy before the bourgeois state is replaced by the Dictatorship of the Proletariat (q.v.). The term State capitalism was also applied by Lenin to the State's role in the mixed State and private companies of the New Economic Policy period. The use by many sovietologists (see SOVIETOLOGY) of the term State capitalism to describe the Soviet economy is erroneous, since maximum profit is not normally the guiding principle.

State Control, supervision of efficiency in the administration, including the economic administration. This has been exercised since 1920 successively by the Commissariat for Worker-Peasant Inspection (q.v.), the Soviet Control Commission, 1934-40, the Commissariat (from 1946 Ministry) of State Control, and, since 1957, the Commission of Soviet Control attached to the Council of Ministers, whose chairman is an *ex officio* member of the latter body. The State Control system functions independently of the local administration, though it is of course subject to the supervision of the party organizations; it is regarded as of considerable importance and has often been headed by prominent party men, including Stalin and Molotov. Before the establishment of the Soviet regime there was an equivalent apparatus under a State Controller, but its functions were restricted to supervision of government efficiency.

State Defence Committee, supreme authority with unlimited powers that existed during the Second World War, consisting first of Stalin (chairman), Molotov (vice-chairman), Voroshilov, Beria and Malenkov; other members were co-opted later.

State Farms, see SOVKHOZ.

State Planning Commission, see GOSPLAN.

Stavropol': 1. (1937-43 Ordzhonikidze). Kray of the R.S.F.S.R., situated in North Caucasus in the northern foothills of the main Caucasian range and the dry steppes to the north-east; there are very rich deposits of natural gas. Area 31,100 sq. m.; population (1959) 1,886,000 (30 per cent urban), chiefly Russians and Ukrainians, also some Circassians and Karachays (the Karachay-Circassian Autonomous Oblast lies within the kray). Wheat and sunflowers are cultivated, cattle and sheep raised, and there are gas extraction and various food industries. The Mineral Waters group of spas is situated in the kray. Principal towns: Stavropol', Pyatigorsk, Kislovodsk, Cherkessk.

2. (1935-43 **Voroshilovsk**). Administrative, economic and cultural centre of the kray. Population (1959) 140,000 (1914, 60,000; 1939, 85,000). It has varied food, wool and leather industries, and is the starting-point of a natural gas pipeline to Moscow. Stavropol' was founded as a Russian fortress in 1777 and has been a provincial capital almost continuously since 1822; it was occupied for a time by the Germans during the Second World War.

Steklov, Vladimir Andreyevich (1863-1926), outstanding mathematician. Educated at Khar'kov University, he taught there and at St Petersburg University, was a member of the Academy of Sciences from 1912, and its vice-president from 1919. His main works were devoted to mathematical physics, where he solved a number of fundamental problems, as well as to general problems of mathematical analysis and to mechanics.

Stepanakert (formerly **Khankendy**), administrative centre of the Mountainous-Karabakh Autonomous Oblast (Transcaucasia), situated 60 m. south-east of Kirovabad. Population (1959) 20,000, mostly Armenians. It has silk and wine industries. Stepanakert has been a town since the late 1920's.

Stephen of Perm', Saint (1340–96), Illuminator of the Komi people and a saint of the Orthodox Church. He constructed an alphabet for the Komi people, and translated into Komi some parts of the Bible.

Stepnoy, *see* ELISTA.

Stepnyak (real name **Kravchinskiy**), **Sergey Mikhaylovich** (1852–95), member of Land and Freedom, the underground Populist organization. In 1878 he assassinated the chief of the *gendarmes*, Mezentsev, and lived subsequently in Switzerland and England. *See* his *Underground Russia*, New York, 1883, *The Russian Storm Cloud*, 1886, *The Career of a Nihilist*, 1889, and *King Stork and King Log* (2 vols.), 1895.

Sterlitamak, town in Bashkiria, situated on the River Belaya, 75 m. south of Ufa. Population (1956) 49,400 (1946, 55,000). It has chemical, engineering and food industries, and the Ishimbay oilfields are near by. Sterlitamak was founded in 1766, was capital of Bashkiria, 1920–1922, and of Sterlitamak Oblast within Bashkiria, 1952–3 (now abolished).

Stilyagi (singular **stilyaga**, from the Russian word for 'style'), Russian equivalent of 'Teddy Boys,' though unlike their English counterparts the *stilyagi* usually come from the Soviet upper or intellectual classes, and their nonconformism is to some extent an expression of conscious opposition to the existing social and political conditions. However, serious oppositional elements among the intellectual youth do not join the *stilyagi*, although for some time in the mid 1950's the party propaganda represented them as such in order to discredit them. *See also* HOOLIGANISM. *See* A. Kassof, ' Youth versus the Regime: Conflict in Values,' *Problems of Communism*, vol. vi, No. 3, May–June 1957.

Stoletov, Aleksandr Grigor'yevich (1839–96), physicist. Educated at Moscow University, he did post-graduate work in Heidelberg (under Kirchhoff), Berlin, Göttingen and Paris, and taught at Moscow University from 1866. His work was chiefly concerned with electricity and magnetism, and he acquired international repute with his study of the discharging effect of light. In his popular writings Stoletov propagated materialist views.

Stolypin, Pëtr Arkad'yevich (1862–1911), statesman, Governor of Grodno, 1902, of Saratov, 1903, and from 1906 Minister of the Interior and then also chairman of the Council of Ministers. Stolypin carried out a dual policy of firm suppression of the revolution of 1905 (q.v.) on the one hand, and on the other of implementing reforms intended to remove the causes of discontent. He did not hesitate to take unpopular measures, such as dissolving the Duma, or even unconstitutional ones, such as altering by imperial decree in 1907 the electoral system. His best work was done in the field of agrarian reform between 1906 and 1911: he made it possible for peasants to leave the village communities (*see* MIR) and settle in separate farms (over two million homesteads, about one-eighth of the total, left the communities between 1907 and 1916), and to buy land through the Peasant Land Bank (q.v.), and assisted peasants from over-populated areas of European Russia to settle as colonists in Siberia and Russian Central Asia. Stolypin, a liberal conservative, was beset by opposition from both the extreme Right and from the radicals. He was assassinated by a Socialist Revolutionary terrorist who was also a police agent. See *Memoirs of Count Witte* (trans. E. Yarmolinsky), New York, 1921; V. I. Gurko, *Features and Figures of the Past. Government and Opinion in the Reign of Nicholas II*, 1939; D. W. Treadgold, *The Great Siberian Migration*, Princeton, New Jersey, 1957; R. Hare, *Portraits of Russian Personalities between Reform and Revolution*, 1959.

Strakhov, Nikolay Nikolayevich (1828–96), philosopher, literary critic, publicist, a follower of A. Grigor'yev's (q.v.) philosophy of 'soil-boundness,' friend and philosophical mentor of Dostoyevskiy, later a friend of L. N. Tolstoy. In his many works (e.g. *The Struggle against the West in our Literature*) he showed strong Slavophile influences. A scientist by training, Strakhov was a leading anti-Darwinist in Russia. *See* V. V. Zenkovsky, *A History of Russian Philosophy*, vol. i, 1953; E. J. Simmons (ed.), *Continuity and Change in Russian and Soviet Thought*, Cambridge, Mass., 1955.

Stravinsky, Igor Fëdorovich (*b.* 1882), composer, pianist and con-ductor. He studied law at St Petersburg University until 1905, meeting Rimsky-Korsakov in 1901 and taking lessons from him in 1907. He became associated with Diaghilev in 1908 and subsequently received many commissions which had far-reaching results. In 1925 he visited America as conductor and performer, in 1934 became a French citizen (having resided mainly in France since the First World War) and in 1939 settled in the United States. His works comprise many ballets, including *The Firebird*, 1910, *Petrushka*, 1911, *The Rite of Spring*, 1913, *Pulcinella*, 1920, *Les Noces*, 1923, *Apollon Musagètes*, 1928, *Le Baiser de la Fée*, 1928, *The Card Party*, 1937, *Orpheus*, 1947, and *Agon*, 1958; operas, including *The Nightingale*, 1914, *Mavra*, 1922; *Oedipus Rex*, 1927, and *The Rake's Progress*, 1951; choral works, including *Symphony of Psalms*, 1930; orchestral works, including several symphonies, concertos, etc.; chamber music; piano music; vocal music, etc. Stravinsky is undoubtedly the most influential composer of the 20th century. Though he left his native land at a relatively early age, Russian folk music proved a constant source of inspiration and a determining factor in the evolution of his highly personal harmony. A veritable chameleon, Stravinsky has attempted every kind of musical style, harmony and form, ranging from the dissonances and pulsific rhythms of *The Rite of Spring*, the 'neo-classicism' of *Pulcinella*, the pious solemnity and austerity of the *Symphony of Psalms*, to essays in dodecaphonic music. Strikingly original in his musical thought, a master of orchestra-tion and of unusual yet effective sonorities, Stravinsky has con-tinued to produce compositions unfailingly for half a century. The fact that each new opus is greeted by considerable controversy is in itself a tribute to Stravinsky's unflagging powers of invention and freshness of thought. His services to ballet are unequalled. *See* his *Chronicle of my Life*, 1936; R. Myers, *Introduction to the Music of Stravinsky*, 1950; E. W. White, *Stravinsky, a Critical Survey*, 1957; R. Vlad, *Stravinsky*, 1960.

Strikes are not specifically forbidden in the Soviet Union, although the right to strike is not included among the basic rights of the citizens in the constitution. However, since they are detrimental to the fulfilment of the economic plan, which is regarded as a quasi-law, organizing a strike is tantamount to challenging the authority of the State; it also challenges the basic postulate that the interests of the Soviet state and the workers are identical. However, strikes do appear sporadically and are sometimes reported in the Soviet press, though the actual word strike is avoided. Although illegal, the first large strikes took place in Russia in the late 1870's and eighties (e.g. the strike at the Morozov textile factory in Orekhovo-Zuyevo in 1885) and prompted the first modern factory laws in the country. Waves of strikes occurred in the late nineties and the years immediately preceding the revolution of 1905 (q.v.); they were used and in part organized by the Social Democrats for political purposes. The revolutionary year of 1905 witnessed almost continuous strikes, which combined into a general political strike in October, forcing the emperor to grant a constitution. Some of the strikes during the revolutionary period of 1905–7 were transformed by the revolutionary parties (*see* RUSSIAN SOCIAL DEMOCRATIC LABOUR PARTY; SOCIALIST REVOLUTIONARIES) into uprisings. Strikes diminished in the following years but flared up again in 1912–14. The February revolution (q.v.) of 1917 was preceded by another strike wave in which economic demands were soon ousted by political ones.

Strikes continued throughout 1917 and were frequent during the period of War Communism (q.v.), culminating in the strikes in Petrograd at the time of the Kronstadt uprising. They were later suppressed in the nationalized enterprises, but during the period of the New Economic Policy (q.v.) the Communist-dominated trade unions sometimes organized strikes in private enterprises, particularly as a means of pressure upon foreign concessionaries (*see* CONCESSIONS). During Stalin's rule any attempts at strikes were dealt with very severely, but they became more frequent again with the general relaxation after his death. The great strikes in the main forced labour camp areas in 1953–5 played an important part in forcing the authorities to disband most of the camps. The last known important strikes occurred during the general unrest of 1956, including sit-down strikes at some of the largest Moscow works. *See also* TRADE UNIONS.

'Stroganov School,' distinctive style of icon-painting at the end of the 16th and beginning of the 17th centuries, created by masters working for the Stroganov family. The icons, painted for the personal use of the artistically inclined Stroganovs, excel by their small 'handy' size, miniature technique of painting and by the jewel-like quality of their colours. The ornamental and rich treatment of icons of this style betrays oriental influences. Some of the masters who painted icons for the Stroganovs simultaneously worked in the czar's workshops in Moscow. The best known of the masters of the school is Prokopiy Chirin (died in the mid 17th century). All icons executed on the orders of the Stroganov family have inscriptions to that effect.

Stroganovs, northern Russian merchant family who in the reign of Ivan the Terrible were granted the right to establish saltworks in the Urals. They had their own towns there, using Cossack mercenaries as guards; one of these, Yermak (q.v.), acquired the Siberian Khanate for Muscovy by conquest in the early 1580's. *See* B. Nolde, *La Formation de l'Empire Russe*, vol. i, Paris, 1952.

Strogovich, Mikhail Solomonovich (*b.* 1894), jurist, corresponding member of the Academy of Sciences since 1939 and head of the section for criminal law and procedure in its Institute of Law. He joined the Communist Party in 1943. Chief works: *The Doctrine of Material Truth in Criminal Procedure*, 1947; *Criminal Prosecution in Soviet Criminal Law*, 1951; *The Verification of Legality and Justifiability of Court Sentences*, 1956. In the discussion which preceded the legal reform (q.v.) of 1958, Strogovich was prominent among those who advocated greater guarantees of fair trial.

Strumilin (real name **Strumillo-Petrashkevich**), **Stanislav Gustavovich** (*b.* 1877), economist and statistician of Polish descent. He became a Social Democrat in 1897, a Menshevik in 1903, and has been a Communist Party member since 1923. He held leading positions in the State Planning Commission and the Central Statistical Administration, 1921–37 and 1943–51, at the same time teaching at various higher educational establishments in Moscow. Strumilin has been a member of the U.S.S.R. Academy of Sciences since 1931, and deputy chairman of its Council for the Study of Productive Forces since 1946. Main works: *Wealth and Labour*, 1905; *The Time Budget of the Russian Worker and Peasant in 1922–3*, 1924; *Problems of the Economics of Labour*, 1925; *The Workers' Life in Figures*, 1926; *Outlines of Soviet Economics*, 1928, 2nd ed., 1930; *Problems of Planning in the U.S.S.R.*, 1932; *Ferrous Metallurgy in Russia and the U.S.S.R.*, 1935; *Industrial Revolution in Russia*, 1944; *History of Ferrous Metallurgy in the U.S.S.R.*, vol. i, 1954; *On the Planning Front* (collection of articles), 1958. *See* R. W. Davies, 'Some Soviet Economic Controllers—I: Strumilin,' *Soviet Studies*, vol. xi, No. 3, Jan. 1960.

Struve, Pëtr Berngardovich (1870–1944), economist, sociologist and politician of German descent. He was the principal theorist of Marxism in Russia during the 1890's (*see* LEGAL MARXISTS), and in 1898 drafted the manifesto of the Social Democratic Labour Party. He soon left social democracy, and became leader of the liberal intelligentsia's constitutional movement, from 1902 to 1905 editing its journal *Liberation* abroad. He returned to Russia in 1905, joined the Constitutional Democratic Party, and became a member of the 2nd Duma in 1907. He played a prominent part in the Vekhi (q.v.) movement and maintained that the liberals should co-operate with the Government. He was Minister of Foreign Affairs in General Wrangel's government in the Crimea during the civil war, later emigrating and participating in the activities of the moderate Right.

See his *Economy and Price* (2 vols.), Moscow, 1913–16, *Social and Economic History of Russia*, Paris, 1952 (both available only in Russian), 'Past and Present of Russian Economics' in *Russian Realities and Problems* (ed. J. D. Duff), 1917, and 'Medieval Agrarian Society in its Prime: Russia' in the *Cambridge Economic History of Europe*, vol. i, 1941; L. W. Haimson, *The Russian Marxists and the Origins of Bolshevism*, Cambridge, Mass. 1955; G. Fischer, *Russian Liberalism. From Gentry to Intelligentsia*, Cambridge, Mass., 1958.

Struve, Vasiliy Yakovlevich (1793–1864), astronomer of German origin, the founder of the Russian astronomical school. He supervised the building of the Pulkovo Observatory, which under his direction, 1839–63, acquired the reputation of 'the astronomical capital of the world.' His main works were concerned with micrometrical and statistical studies of stars, and the measurement of a 25° 20′ Russian-Scandinavian arc of the meridian.

Sub-Carpathian Russia, official name of Transcarpathia when it was part of Czechoslovakia, 1919–39.

'Subjective Method,' in social sciences, combining the search for factual correctness ('truth as verity') with moral evaluation ('truth as justice') from a subjective anthropocentric point of view, was developed and adhered to by sociologists and historians of the Populist persuasion (Lavrov, Mikhaylovskiy, Kareyev, qq.v.). *See* T. G. Masaryk, *The Spirit of Russia* (2nd ed.), vol. ii, 1955; J. H. Billington, *Mikhailovsky and Russian Populism*, 1958.

Suchan, town in the Maritime Kray, situated 60 m. east of Vladivostok. Population (1956) 48,900. It has been an important coalmining centre since 1896, and is a railway junction. Suchan was founded in 1932 through the fusion of several mining settlements.

Sudebnik, name of the first two law codes of Muscovy, issued in 1497 and 1550. They mainly contain provisions relating to the courts of law and procedure, and were aimed at the centralization of judicial power in the state.

Sukachëv, Vladimir Nikolayevich (*b.* 1880), botanist and geographer. Educated at the Institute of Forestry in St Petersburg, he later taught there, as well as in Leningrad and Moscow universities, etc. He is a Member of the Academy of Sciences (since 1943), president of the All-Union Botanical Society (since 1946) and of the Moscow Society of Naturalists (since 1955). He joined the party in 1937. Sukachëv has worked out a typology of forests and formulated the concept of biogeocenosis, i.e. the biological community together with its habitat. After Stalin's death he took a leading part in exposing the fallacious nature of Lysenko's (q.v.) claims. This incurred the displeasure of Khrushchëv, and Sukachëv was dismissed in 1959 from his posts as director of the Academy of Sciences' institute for the study of forests and as editor of the *Botanical Journal*.

Sulimov, *see* CHERKESSK.

Sultan-Galiyev, Mirza (1880's–?), Volga Tatar National Bolshevik politician. Educated at the Russo-Tatar Teachers' Seminary in Kazan', he was a teacher of Russian in reformed Muslim schools in the Caucasus. After the February revolution of 1917 he was active in the all-Russian Muslim movement which supported the Provisional

Government, belonging to its left wing, but towards the end of the year he joined the Bolsheviks. After their seizure of power he rose rapidly and in 1920 became Stalin's right-hand man in the Commissariat for Nationalities. However, he soon developed an ideology of his own, culminating in the demand for a dictatorship of colonies and semi-colonies over the colonial powers. He was arrested in 1923 and branded as a 'bourgeois nationalist'; arrested again in 1929, he disappeared in the following year. *See* A. Bennigsen and C. Quelque-jay, *Les Mouvements nationaux chez les musselmans de Russie. Le 'Sultangalievisme' au Tatarstan*, Paris and The Hague, 1960.

Sumgait, town in Azerbaydzhan, situated on the Caspian Sea shore 25 m. north-west of Baku. Population (1959) 52,000. It is the centre of the Azerbaydzhan metallurgical industry (pipe-rolling mill and aluminium plant) and also has a chemical industry (synthetic rubber plant). Sumgait was founded in 1949.

Sumy: 1. Oblast in north-eastern Ukraine, situated on the border of the central Russian upland, partly in the black earth belt. Area 9,400 sq. m.; population (1959) 1,512,000 (32 per cent urban), Ukrainians and Russians. Wheat, maize, sugar-beet, potatoes and hemp are cultivated, pigs and cattle raised, and there are varied food, also engineering and chemical, industries. Principal towns: Sumy, Konotop, Romny. The area belonged to Pereyaslavl' Principality in the Middle Ages, became Lithuanian in 1362 and Muscovite in 1503. In 1941–3 it was occupied by the Germans.

2. Administrative and economic centre of the oblast, situated 90 m. north-west of Khar'kov. Population (1959) 97,000 (1914, 52,000; 1926, 44,000). It has sugar, engineering, chemical (fertilizers) and woollen industries. Sumy was founded by Cossack settlers from the Polish-held part of the Ukraine in 1652, and was an important trade centre in the 18th and 19th centuries. Industrial development dates from the 19th century (when it became the main centre of the sugar industry in the left-bank Ukraine). The town has been provincial capital since 1939.

Supreme Courts exist in the U.S.S.R. as a whole and in each Union and Autonomous Republic. They are ostensibly elected by the respective Supreme Soviets for five years and are responsible to the Supreme Soviets and their presidia. They normally act as courts of appeal, but also as first instance courts in cases of extreme importance. They supervise the work of lower courts and give them directives often amounting to binding interpretations of the law (although this function is reserved by the constitution to the presidium of the Supreme Soviet), and can initiate legislation. The U.S.S.R. Supreme Court consists of the civil, criminal and military colleges, the latter heading the hierarchy of the Military Tribunals (q.v.). It can act as the court of appeal from the supreme courts of Union Republics only when the latter's decisions contradict all-Union law or the interests of other republics. The chairman of the U.S.S.R. Supreme Court, who has extensive procedural powers, is usually not a lawyer but a high-ranking party official. Before the seizure of power by the Bolsheviks in 1917, the functions of the highest court in the country were exercised by the Senate (q.v.). After it was abolished the Commissariat of

Justice (*see* JUSTICE, MINISTRY OF) was given some of the supervisory and directing functions; they were then gradually transferred to the supreme courts, which were established at the beginning of the 1920's in the Union Republics and in 1924 for the whole U.S.S.R.

Supreme Soviet, ostensibly (according to the Stalin constitution of 1936) the highest organ of State power in the U.S.S.R. It consists of two chambers—the Soviet of the Union and the Soviet of Nationalities (qq.v.)—of approximately equal size (600 odd deputies each). Both chambers are elected simultaneously for five years; each chamber elects separately its chairman, deputy chairman and standing committees (on legislative proposals, finance and foreign affairs); at a joint meeting both chambers elect the Presidium (q.v.) of the Supreme Soviet, appoint the Chairman of the Council of Ministers, and confirm the composition of the Government. The Supreme Soviet usually meets once or twice in the year for a few days. A fixed item on the agenda is the budget; in addition a number of laws may be passed and ordinances (*see* UKASE) of the Presidium confirmed, and there are sometimes speeches by the Foreign Minister or Prime Minister on the Government's foreign policy and questions by the deputies on such aspects of foreign affairs as, for example, banning atom bombs. Sessions of the Supreme Soviet are theoretically public, but there is no public gallery in the ordinary sense and only reporters, foreign diplomats and foreign guests are normally admitted. All decisions without exception are passed unanimously, and in fact the Supreme Soviet sessions are purely ceremonial gatherings. There is some evidence that the standing committees, which meet in private, have some scope for genuine discussion. Supreme Soviets also exist in the Union and Autonomous Republics (qq.v.). The establishment in 1936 of the Supreme Soviet, with its democratic, parliamentary forms, at first raised, both in Russia and abroad, great hopes for a genuine democratization of the Soviet regime, but it proved to be one of the main elements of the fiction (q.v.) of Soviet democracy, designed to prevent the re-emergence of democratic tendencies; on the other hand the reintroduction of democratic forms has acquainted the mass of the people with them. *See further under* COMMUNIST PARTY OF THE SOVIET UNION; CONSTITUTION; DEMOCRACY; DEPUTIES; ELECTIONS; SOVIETS. *See* M. Fainsod, *How Russia is Ruled,* Cambridge, Mass., 1953.

Surkhan-Dar'ya, southernmost oblast in Uzbekistan, divided from Afghanistan by the Amu-Dar'ya River; there are deposits of coal, oil and salt. Area 7,800 sq. m.; population (1959) 426,000 (15 per cent urban), mostly Uzbeks, Tadzhiks and Turkmens, also Afghans, Arabs, Persians and Russians. Cotton, grain, fruit and grapes are cultivated, sheep (Astrakhan and Gissar breeds) and horses (Karabair breed) raised, and there are oil- and cotton-processing industries. Administrative centre Termez. For history *see* BUKHARA KHANATE; SOGDIANA; TRANSOXANIA. In 1960 the neighbouring Kashka-Dar'ya (q.v.) Oblast was fused with Surkhan-Dar'ya Oblast.

Surkov, Aleksey Aleksandrovich (*b.* 1899), poet, a party member since 1925. He acquired considerable popularity during the Second World War for his patriotic poems. In 1953 he became secretary of the party organization in the Writers' Union (q.v.) and in the follow-ing year first secretary of the union itself, displaying great zeal in fighting the opposition to the party among the writers (*see* INTELLEC-TUAL OPPOSITION). His position became extremely difficult after the expulsion of Pasternak (q.v.) from the union, and at the 3rd Writers' Congress in 1959 he was replaced by Fedin (q.v.). *See* J. Lindsay (trans.), *Russian Poetry, 1917–55*, 1957.

Suslov, Mikhail Andreyevich (*b.* 1902), party official. The son of a peasant from the Volga region, he joined the party in 1921, having since 1918 been active in the local Committee of the Poor (q.v.) and in the Komsomol. He was sent by the party to study at a Workers' Faculty in Moscow and later at the Plekhanov Institute of National Economy and the Economic Institute of Red Professorship. Active in the struggle against the oppositions of the late 1920's, he was appointed to the apparatus of the Central Control Commission (*see* COMMITTEE OF PARTY CONTROL) and took a leading part in the party purge of 1933–4. During the Great Purge (q.v.) he rose quickly, becoming a secretary of the Rostov Oblast party committee in 1937 and first secretary of the Ordzhonikidze (now Stavropol') Kray committee, and in 1941 a member of the party's Central Committee. He was a high-ranking political officer during the war, and in 1944 was sent as a plenipotentiary of the central authorities to Lithuania to restore the Soviet regime there; in this capacity he was responsible for mass deportations. In 1946 he became the head of the Agitation and Propaganda Department of the Central Committee and in the following year a secretary of the Central Committee, which post he has since occupied continuously. After Zhdanov's death in 1948 Suslov took over his position as the informal leader of the Cominform, and continued to specialize in foreign affairs, in particular in relations with foreign Communist parties after the Cominform's dissolution. In 1949–50 he was also editor-in-chief of *Pravda*. Since 1954 he has been chairman of the Foreign Affairs Committee of the Soviet of the Union (q.v.). He became a member of the Central Com-mittee's Presidium (q.v.) in 1955. Although generally considered to be a doctrinaire Communist, Suslov was reported in 1957 to have taken an active part in defeating the 'anti-party group' (q.v.).

Suvorin, Aleksey Sergeyevich (1844–1912), journalist and publisher. From 1876 he published *Novoye Vremya* (*New Time*), the first cheap popular right-wing newspaper in Russia; besides this he published cheap editions of the classics, etc. His *Diary*, partly published in Russia in 1923 (French trans. *Journal intime de A. Souvorine*, Paris, 1927), is an interesting record of the epoch.

Suvorov, Count Aleksandr Vasil'yevich (1730–1800), generalissimo, the greatest Russian soldier. He distinguished himself in the Seven Years War and the Russo-Turkish wars, and in 1768 and 1794 led the Russian forces in Poland. When Paul I joined the anti-French coalition in 1798 Suvorov's task was to arrest the French advance in Italy; he defeated the French in a series of brilliant attacks, and conquered northern Italy. Having been transferred to Switzerland, he was surrounded by the French because of confusion in the allied command, but escaped disaster through one of the most intrepid feats in military history, the march through the St Gotthard. *See* W. L. Blease, *Suvorov*, 1920.

Suzdal', town in the Vladimir Oblast (central Russia), situated 23 m. north of Vladimir. Population (1956) 7,900. It is a treasury of architectural monuments of the 13th–17th centuries. Suzdal' has been known since 1024, was capital of central Russia, 1095–1157, of Suzdal' Principality from 1238 and became Muscovite in the mid 15th century.

Sverdlov, Yakov Mikhaylovich (1885–1919), politician of Jewish origin, joined the Social Democratic Labour Party in 1901 and was active, 1902–17, as a professional revolutionary in the Bolshevik organizations, always adhering rigidly to Lenin's policy; he was co-opted into the central committee in 1913. Sverdlov became the party's chief organizer after the February 1917 revolution, and soon after the Bolsheviks' seizure of power he succeeded Kamenev as chairman of the All-Russian Central Executive Committee of the Soviets, thus becoming titular head of the state. For a period in 1918–19 Sverdlov, together with Stalin, was Lenin's closest collaborator.

Sverdlovsk: 1. Oblast of the R.S.F.S.R. situated mainly on the eastern slopes of the Ural Mountains and the neighbouring part of the West Siberian lowland, largely covered with coniferous forests; there are rich deposits of iron ore, copper and other non-ferrous metals, gold, platinum and precious stones. Area 74,400 sq. m.; population (1959) 4,048,000 (76 per cent urban), chiefly Russians (since the 16th century). It is the most important industrial area of the Urals (engineering, iron and steel, non-ferrous metallurgy, chemical, timber and woodworking industries); grain, potatoes and vegetables are cultivated and dairy farming carried on (Tagil breed); an old stone-carving craft is still practised. Principal towns: Sverdlovsk, Nizhniy Tagil, Kamensk-Ural'skiy, Serov, Pervoural'sk, Krasnotur'insk, Asbest, Revda. The area was annexed by Russia as part of the Siberian Khanate in the 16th century. Industrial development dates from the early 18th century and received new impetus during the 1930's and the Second World War, when many factories from western parts of the country were evacuated to the oblast.

2. (until 1924 **Yekaterinburg**). Administrative centre of the oblast, one of the principal economic and cultural centres of the U.S.S.R. Population (1959) 777,000 (first in the Urals, ninth in the U.S.S.R.; 1913, 87,000; 1920, 68,000; 1926, 140,000; 1939, 423,000). It has large heavy engineering industries (metallurgy, electrical equipment) and chemical and varied food and light industries; it is an important centre of transportation (seven railway lines, airport). Sverdlovsk is the seat of the Urals branch of the U.S.S.R. Academy of Sciences, 1932, and among its higher educational establishments are a university (founded 1920, abolished 1925, re-established 1931), a polytechnic institute, 1925, and a mining institute, 1914. It has several interesting buildings of the 19th and 20th centuries. Sverdlovsk was founded as a metal works and fortress in 1721 and became the administrative and commercial centre of the Urals mining industry and an important cultural centre of the Urals region (mining school

1723, Society of Mining Technicians 1825, museum 1834, municipal theatre 1843). It was also a centre of commerce (trade in West Siberian grain, lard, cattle and iron) and flour milling in the late 19th and early 20th centuries. In 1918 ex-Emperor Nicholas II and his family were shot here by the Bolsheviks.

Svobodnyy (till 1924 **Alekseyevsk**), town in the Amur Oblast (Far East), situated on the River Zeya and the Trans-Siberian Railway 105 m. north of Blagoveshchensk. Population (1959) 57,000. It has varied engineering (agricultural equipment, several repair works) and saw-milling industries and is a local cultural centre. Svobodnyy was founded in 1904 and until the 1930's was a commercial centre. From the 1930's to the mid 1950's it was the administrative centre of the forced labour camps in the Amur region.

Svod Zakonov ('Code of Laws'), code promulgated in 1833 which essentially remained in force until the Bolshevik seizure of power in 1917. It was largely drawn up by Speranskiy (q.v.) on the basis of his *Complete Collection of Laws of the Russian Empire*, containing all enactments since the Ulozheniye (q.v.) of 1649. The Svod Zakonov presented Russian laws in a modern form derived from the Napoleonic codes. *See* H. J. Berman, *Justice in Russia*, Cambridge, Mass., 1950.

Syktyvkar (until 1930 **Ust'-Sysol'sk**), capital of the Komi Autonomous Republic and cultural centre of the Komi people, situated on the River Vychegda 200 m. north of Kirov. Population (1959) 64,000 (1939, 24,000), Russians and Komi. It has timber, ship-repairing, food, leather and shoe industries. Syktyvkar has been known since the late 16th century, and during the following two centuries had a flourishing grain and fur trade. It has been a place of banishment.

Symphony. Although symphonies were written by Russian composers at the end of the 18th century (by Bortnyanskiy, for example) and the beginning of the 19th, unlike the early Russian operas (*see* OPERA) they were of little importance. It was not until the second half of the 19th century with the appearance of the Kuchka (q.v.) that the first real symphonies came into being. Of 'the Five,' three composers, Balakirev, Borodin and Rimsky-Korsakov, paid special attention to symphonic writing, though it is significant of the Russian School as a whole that, although clearly owing much to Western models (especially Schumann), each symphony departs in some way from conventional practice. Borodin was responsible for two symphonies, No. 1 in E flat major, 1867, and No. 2 in B minor, 1869–76, both of which are programmatic. Their vitality, freshness and harmonic innovation place them in a class apart from Western works; also of importance is the presence of oriental features (especially in the third movement of the B minor symphony). Of the three symphonies by Rimsky-Korsakov, outstanding is the symphonic suite *Antar*, 1868. This too is written to a programme and abounds in oriental features, besides making use of authentic folk melodies. Balakirev contributed two symphonies, No. 1 in C major, 1866–98 (an undeservedly neglected work), and No. 2 in D minor, 1908. The second symphony has a 'Romanza' as its second movement and a 'Polonaise' as its finale. Contemporary with the Kuchka are the six symphonies of Tchaikovsky (seven including *Manfred*) which constitute the backbone of 19th-century Russian symphonism. Though influenced by the French ballet composers Massenet, Delibes and Bizet, Tchaikovsky succeeded in achieving a compromise between nationalism, intensity of emotion and orchestral virtuosity. Much of his music was written to a programme, often subjective in character. Of slight importance are the eight symphonies of Glazunov which continued the traditions of the nationalist school, though paying greater attention to questions of form. Among the remaining composers of the late 19th century, Rakhmaninov's three symphonies are not without merit, particularly the second in E minor, 1907; Skryabin was the composer of five symphonies of mystical content.

The transition from nationalist to Soviet music was effected by Glière, who, though continuing 19th-century traditions, gradually adapted his style to suit the requirements of the new regime. Though primarily an orchestral rather than a symphonic composer, Glière's influence as a teacher has been of the greatest importance. Among the flourishing generation of Soviet composers may be mentioned Shaporin, Knipper, Shebalin, Khachaturyan, Kabalevskiy, Myaskovskiy, Prokof'yev and Shostakovich (qq.v.). The two latter are undoubtedly the most important Soviet symphonic composers of the present generation, Prokof'yev favouring a mixture of lyricism, dynamic force and the grotesque, Shostakovich a combination of satire, rhythmic vitality and melodic wealth. The main difference between the work of pre-revolutionary and Soviet composers seems to lie in the fact that the Russian composer of today is obliged to write music in conformity with definite ideological principles, any departure from which results in the discrediting of the composer (*see* SOCIALIST REALISM). Consequently, in comparison with the heterogeneous tendencies in Western symphonic music, Soviet music is characterized by its relative uniformity, conservatism and comprehensibility. Unlike the average Western symphony, however, its Soviet counterpart sometimes assumes gigantic proportions, thus continuing the long-established Russian tradition of love of pageantry and splendour. *See* G. Abraham, *Eight Soviet Composers*, 1943; R. Moisenko, *Realist Music*, 1949.

Syndicalism, as a trend of political thought, appeared in Russia at the turn of the 20th century in the form of Makhayevism (q.v.). At the same time Syndicalist tendencies became strongly felt in the labour movement, finding their expression in such organizations as the Group for the Self-emancipation of the Working Class and the Workers' Organization, 1900–3, both in St Petersburg; the latter was the most determined opponent of Lenin's Iskra (q.v.) within Russian social democracy. There was also a Syndicalist trend among Russian Anarchists, and syndicalist-minded people took an active part in setting up and guiding trade unions from 1905 onwards. The heyday of Syndicalism came after the Bolshevik seizure of power, when Lenin adopted the Syndicalist slogan of workers' control (q.v.) in industry, which in its practical implementation was workers' management, however inefficient. The Worker's Opposition (q.v.) of 1920–1, in so far as it sought to perpetuate and further elaborate and consolidate this workers' management, was rightly branded as a Syndicalist deviation. Syndicalist ideas have again been rather popular, as a counter-weight to the monopoly of political power in the hands of the party, in the opposition circles of the late 1940's and 1950's, particularly among the 'True Leninists' (*see* IDEOLOGY). *See* L. Schapiro, *The Origin of the Communist Autocracy*, 1955, and *The Communist Party of the Soviet Union*, 1960; S. V. Utechin, 'Bolsheviks and their Allies after 1917: the Ideological Pattern,' *Soviet Studies*, Oct. 1958.

Syr-Dar'ya, river of Central Asia which rises in the Tien-Shan Mountains and flows north-westerly through Kirgizia, Uzbekistan and Kazakhstan to the Aral Sea. It has a large drainage area and its main tributaries are on the right bank; these tributaries are used for irrigation, and the river flows through the fertile Fergana Valley (q.v.).

Syzran', town in the Kuybyshev Oblast, situated on the right bank of the Volga 80 m. west of Kuybyshev. Population (1959) 148,000 (1914, 46,000; 1939, 78,000; 1956, 169,000). It is an important centre of industry and transport (engineering, oil extraction and processing, food industries; port, five railway lines). Syzran' was founded in 1683, and was important as a centre of the grain trade from the mid 19th century until the 1920's. Its oil and engineering industries have been developed since the war.

T

Tadzhikistan, Union Republic of the U.S.S.R. situated in the south-east of Central Asia bordering on Afghanistan (along the upper course of the Amu-Dar'ya) and China; it is a mountainous country, including the Pamir and the mountain ranges to the north and west; there are lead, zinc, cadmium, silver, arsenic, bismuth, oil, ozokerite and coal deposits in the Fergana Valley, and gold in southern Tadzhikistan. Area 55,000 sq. m.; population (1959) 1,980,000 (twelfth among Union Republics of the U.S.S.R.; 1939, 1,484,000; 33 per cent urban). The ethnic composition in 1959 was: Tadzhiks, 53 per cent; Uzbeks (chiefly in the valleys), 23 per cent; Russians, 13 per cent, Tatars, 2·9 per cent. The principal crop is cotton grown in the valleys, al-though grain crops (wheat and barley) take up a far larger area; lucerne, fruit (apricots) and grapes (raisins) are also cultivated and there is sericulture; sheep (the mountain Darvaz, large Gissar and Astrakhan breeds), goats, horses (Lokay and Karabair breeds), camels, donkeys and yaks (in the Pamir) are kept. The main industries are concerned with cotton and silk processing; there is also mining and some metal-working. Most industries are concentrated in Stalinabad and the Leninabad area. There is a railway line connecting Stalinabad with the Trans-Caspian Railway at Bukhara, and high-ways from Stalinabad to the Pamir and from there to Osh in the Fergana Valley; otherwise roads are few and air transport is therefore important. The capital of the republic is Stalinabad. Tadzhikistan includes the Leninabad Oblast in the north and the Mountainous-Badakhshan Autonomous Oblast in the east; the rest of the republic is not now divided into oblasts, but in the 1940's and fifties there were Stalinabad, Kulyab, Garm, Kurgan-Tyube and Ura-Tyube oblasts.

For history *see* BUKHARA KHANATE; KOKAND KHANATE; SOG-DIANA; TRANSOXANIA; TURKESTAN. Tadzhikistan was formed in 1924 in the process of the National Delimitation of Central Asia (q.v.) as an Autonomous Republic within Uzbekistan; in 1929 it was raised to the status of a Union Republic and the western part of the Fergana Valley, with Leninabad, was included in it. Through-out the 1920's and early thirties the anti-Bolshevik Basmachi (q.v.) guerrilla movement operated in Tadzhikistan, its activities being facilitated by the country's mountainous character and the proximity of the Afghan frontier. To control the population better the Soviet authorities resorted in the 1930's to resettling the Tadzhiks, who mostly inhabited the mountainous areas of central Tadzhikistan, in the hitherto sparsely populated area along the right bank of the Amu-Dar'ya; this resettlement policy was continued after the Second World War. *See* P. Luknitsky, *Soviet Tajikistan*, Moscow, 1954, and the journal *Central Asian Review*.

Tadzhiks, Iranian-speaking people who live chiefly in Afghanistan

531

but also in Soviet Central Asia, where they number (1959) 1,400,000, constituting a majority in the Tadzhik Republic and a sizable minority in Uzbekistan. There are three distinct ethnic groups among the Tadzhiks: first, and most numerous, the Tadzhiks of the oases (Fergana, Zeravshan and Gissar valleys)—people of an old civilization, both agricultural and urban, who before the 1920's formed the Tadzhik-speaking element in the Sart (q.v.) population; secondly, the mountain Tadzhiks, who are Sunni Muslims and inhabit the mountainous areas of Kukhistan, Darvaz and Karategin in eastern Tadzhikistan: these are comparatively primitive, and because of their isolation remained more or less independent of the various powers who held sway in Central Asia, only being finally annexed to the Bukhara Khanate, with Russian help, in the 1880's; thirdly, the small tribes of the Pamir (Mountainous-Badakhshan Autonomous Oblast), who speak their own dialects and are not yet assimilated: these are Ismaili Muslims and until the 1930's they succeeded in smuggling out of the country their religious dues to the Aga Khan. For history *see* CENTRAL ASIA; SOGDIANA; TRANSOXANIA; TURKESTAN.

Taganrog, port on the Sea of Azov in the Rostov Oblast 40 m. west of Rostov. Population (1959) 201,000 (1939, 189,000). It is a major centre of industry: iron and steel (since 1897), engineering (boilers, combine harvesters, machine tools, aircraft), leather and food industries. Taganrog was founded in 1689 by Peter the Great, destroyed in 1712 after the Pruth Treaty with Turkey, and rebuilt, 1769–74. It was bombarded by the Allies in 1855 and occupied by the Germans in 1918 and 1941–3. Until overtaken by Odessa, Taganrog was the principal Russian port in the Black Sea area.

Tagantsev, Nikolay Stepanovich (1843–1923), jurist. Educated at St Petersburg University, he was professor there in the School of Jurisprudence, became a senator in 1887, head of the senate's (q.v.) criminal appeal department in 1897, and from 1906 was member of the State Council (q.v.) by appointment. For twenty-two years (1881–1902) he played the leading role in the commission which drafted the new Criminal Code (*see* Codes of Law). In his many works (*On Crimes against Life according to Russian Law*, 2 vols., 1870–1; *Course of Russian Criminal Law*, 3 vols., 1874–80; *Lectures in Criminal Law*, 2 vols., 1902; *The Death Penalty*, 1910, etc.) Tagantsev, adhering to the classical school of criminal law, advanced liberal and humane views on the treatment of criminals and advocated abolition of capital punishment.

Tairov (real name **Kornblit**), **Aleksandr Yakovlevich** (1885–1950), actor and director. Studying law at St Petersburg University he worked as actor and producer in various theatres in St Petersburg, Riga and Moscow from 1905 until 1914, when he founded the Kamernyy (i.e. Chamber) Theatre in Moscow. He headed this theatre until 1946, when he was dismissed as the artistic director, although he continued to produce plays there until 1949. Tairov's repertoire was highly cosmopolitan; his productions were famous for their charm, music and beauty, and in conscious opposition to Stanislavsky (q.v.) he held that form and technique rather than 'reliving' the part should be in the foreground of the individual actor's and the whole cast's consciousness. From 1930 onwards, however, he gradually succumbed to the official pressure for Socialist Realism (q.v.), and by the time his theatre was closed in 1950 his earlier tradition had almost vanished. *See further under* THEATRE.

Talas: 1 (or **Taraz**). Ancient town of Central Asia, now Dzhambul (q.v.).

2. Former oblast in Kirgizia which included the upper part of the River Talas valley, now abolished.

Taldy-Kurgan, former (1944–59) oblast of Kazakhstan, now absorbed by Alma-Ata.

Tallinn ('Danish Town,' Russian **Tallin,** formerly German **Reval,** Russian **Revel'**), capital, economic and cultural centre of Estonia, a fortified port on the southern coast of the Gulf of Finland. Population (1959) 280,000 (1897, 65,000; 1914, 131,000; 1939, 160,000). It has large and varied engineering (shipbuilding, electrical and mechanical equipment), woodworking, textile, printing and food industries. The Estonian Academy of Sciences (established 1946) is here, and there are several higher educational establishments, also notable buildings of the 13th–early 20th centuries. Tallinn has been known since 1154, became Danish in 1219, Livonian 1346, Swedish 1561 and Russian in 1710 (naval base and provincial capital). It was occupied in 1918 and 1941–4 by the Germans, and was capital of independent Estonia, 1919–40, also of Tallinn Oblast within the Estonian Republic, 1952–3, now abolished.

Talysh, Iranian-speaking people who inhabit the south-western shores of the Caspian Sea, numbering about 110,000, about 80,000 in Soviet Azerbaydzhan, where the majority are bilingual and are being assimilated by the Azerbaydzhanis; only few described themselves as Talysh in the 1959 census. They are Shiah Muslims, chiefly cattle-breeding peasants. A Talysh khanate was established in the 18th century, semi-independent from Persia; it became Russian in 1813, and in 1826 was abolished.

Tambov: 1. Oblast of the R.S.F.S.R., situated south-east of Moscow in the Oka-Don lowland, with black earth soil and some mixed forests. Area 13,200 sq. m.; population (1959) 1,547,000 (26 per cent urban). Grain, potatoes, sunflowers and sugar-beet are cultivated, dairy cattle (Red Tambov breed) and pigs raised, and there are food, engineering and textile industries. Principal towns: Tambov and Michurinsk. An important anti-Bolshevik peasant rising (*see* ANTONOV UPRISING) took place here in 1920–1.

2. Administrative and the main economic and cultural centre of the oblast, situated 60 m. north-east of Voronezh. Population (1959) 170,000 (1914, 53,000; 1939, 106,000). It has engineering (railway equipment, aircraft), food and chemical industries, and is a railway junction. Tambov was founded as a fortified town in the Muscovite southern defence line (against the Crimean Tatars) in 1636 and became provincial capital in 1779; before 1917 it was a flourishing centre of trade in grain and cattle.

Tamm, Igor' Yevgen'yevich (*b.* 1895), physicist. Educated at Moscow University, he has taught there since 1934 and has been a member of the Academy of Sciences since 1953. His work is mainly devoted to quantum mechanics, the theory of radiation and cosmic rays, and the interaction of nuclear particles. He formulated in 1930 the quantum theory of the dispersion of light in solid bodies; developed a theory of dispersion of light by electrons; established in 1932 the theoretical possibility of special conditions of electrons on crystal surfaces; and in 1937 developed a theory of radiation of electrons moving at high speed in atmosphere. Tamm shared with P. A. Cherenkov and I. M. Frank the Nobel Prize for Chemistry in 1958. *See* J. G. Crowther, *Soviet Science*, 1936.

Taneyev, Aleksandr Sergeyevich (1850–1918), nationalist composer and teacher, who studied under Rimsky-Korsakov and Petrov in St Petersburg, and with Reichel in Dresden. He served as a member of the Imperial Geographical Society's folk music commission. Works comprise three symphonies; two operas (*Cupid's Revenge*; *The Snowstorm*); orchestral and chamber music, etc. His work suffers from extreme academicism.

Taneyev, Sergey Ivanovich (1856–1915), pianist, composer and outstanding teacher, who attended Moscow Conservatory, studying under Langer, Hubert, N. Rubinshteyn and Tchaikovsky; nephew of Aleksandr. He succeeded Tchaikovsky as professor of harmony and instrumentation at the Conservatory in 1880, becoming director in 1885. His monumental work *Invertible Counterpoint* appeared in 1909. Works comprise *Orestes* (a musical trilogy, *première* St Petersburg, 1895); four symphonies; orchestral works, including an *Overture on a Russian Theme*, 1882; much chamber music; piano, organ music; vocal music, etc. Taneyev is one of the greatest Russian contrapuntists, but this factor also tends to make his work coldly unemotional. His deep interest in 16th-century music overrode any national tendencies. *See* G. Abraham and M. D. Calvocoressi, *Masters of Russian Music*, 1936.

Tarnopol, *see* TERNOPOL'.

Tartu (Russian Yur'yev 1030–1224 and 1893–1918, **Derpt** 1704–1893, German **Dorpat**), town and chief cultural centre of Estonia, situated 100 m. south-east of Tallinn. Population (1959) 74,000. It has food, engineering and saw-milling industries. There is a university, founded in 1632 by Gustavus Adolphus of Sweden (closed 1710, reopened 1802 by Alexander I), where the language of instruction was German until 1895, Russian till 1918, and since then has been Estonian; its library (established 1802) is the largest in the Baltic Republics. There is also a botanical garden, 1803, and an observatory, 1809. Tartu was founded by Yaroslav the Wise in 1030 on the site of the Estonian village Tarpatu, and belonged variously to the Livonian Order, Muscovy, Poland and Sweden; it has been Russian since 1705 except for Estonia's period of independence, 1919–40, and was occupied by the Germans in 1918 and 1941–4. The peace treaties between Soviet Russia and Estonia and Finland were signed here in 1920. Tartu was capital of Tartu Oblast within the Estonian Republic in 1952–3, now abolished.

Tashauz: 1. Oblast in Turkmenia, comprising the western part of the Khorezm oasis and the adjacent eastern part of the Kara-Kum

Desert. Area 29,100 sq. m.; population (1959) 295,000 (24 per cent urban), mostly Turkmens and Uzbeks. There is cotton growing in the Khorezm oasis, and horse (Yomud breed) and sheep (Astrakhan breed) raising. For history *see* KHIVA; KHOREZM.

2. Administrative centre of the oblast, situated in the Khorezm oasis on the Chardzhou–Kungrad railway. Population (1959) 37,000, Turkmens, Uzbeks and Russians. It has a cotton-processing industry and is a local cultural centre.

Tashkent: 1. Oblast of Uzbekistan comprising the Tashkent oasis in the middle course of the Syr-Dar'ya River and the adjacent mountainous area to the north-east, traversed by the Tashkent Railway; there are deposits of copper and coal. Area 7,900 sq. m.; population (1959) 2,263,000 (57 per cent urban), mostly Uzbeks and Russians. This is the main industrial area of Central Asia, with engineering, metallurgical, chemical, coal-mining, textile and food industries; there are two big hydro-electric stations. Cotton, lucerne, rice, fruit and grapes are cultivated, and sericulture carried on. Principal towns: Tashkent, Chirchik, Angren. For history *see* KOKAND KHANATE; TRANSOXANIA; TURKESTAN.

2. (medieval **Shash**). Administrative centre of the oblast and capital of Uzbekistan, the principal economic and cultural centre of Central Asia. Population (1959) 911,000 (the largest city east of the Urals; 1897, 156,000; 1914, 272,000; 1939, 550,000), chiefly Russians and Uzbeks. It has large engineering (agricultural and mining equipment), textile and food industries, and many small hydro-electric stations in the town and its surroundings. The Uzbek Academy of Sciences (formed 1943) is here, and has a number of research institutes for cotton growing, irrigation, sericulture, etc.; there is a university (founded 1919) and more than a dozen other higher educational establishments.

Tashkent was founded in the 7th century as a trading centre on the route from Transoxania to China, and was taken by the Chinese in 659, who held it for a brief period. It shared the turbulent history of Turkestan. In the 19th century Tashkent was a bone of contention between Bukhara and Kokand until its conquest by the Russians in 1864. A new European town was built beside the old oriental one, and the differences between the two parts have not yet disappeared. Tashkent became the main centre of Russian trade in Central Asia and the seat of the Governor-General of Turkestan. In 1917 the Tashkent Soviet, in which the Bolsheviks gained the ascendance, proclaimed the Soviet power in Turkestan, and during the civil war Tashkent was the main stronghold of the Bolsheviks in Central Asia. It became the capital of the Turkestan Autonomous Republic in 1918, was included in Uzbekistan in the process of the National Delimitation of Central Asia (q.v.), and became its capital in 1930.

T.A.S.S. (abbreviation for Telegraphic Agency of the Soviet Union), official Soviet news agency, attached to the U.S.S.R. Council of Ministers and subordinated in its work to the Propaganda Department of the Central Committee of the party. It was founded in 1925 and is the only news agency in the U.S.S.R., handling both internal and foreign news.

Tatar Autonomous Republic lies in the east of European Russia in
a lowland area traversed by the middle Volga and lower Kama; there
are very rich deposits of oil and natural gas. Area 26,200 sq. m.;
population (1956) 2,847,000 (42 per cent urban), mostly Tatars and
Russians (since the 16th century), also some Chuvash and Mordva.
It has large oil, engineering, chemical, woodworking and fur industries; grain, sunflowers and potatoes are cultivated, and horticulture (apples) and dairy farming are carried on. Principal towns:
Kazan' (capital), Zelenodol'sk, Bugul'ma, Chistopol', Al'met'yevsk.
The republic was established in 1920; for the early history of the
area *see* VOLGA BULGARIANS.

Tatars, three Turkic-speaking Sunni Muslim peoples who in 1959
numbered together 5 million.

(1) The Kazan' or Volga Tatars live mostly in the Volga area and
the Urals (mainly in the Tatar and Bashkir Autonomous Republics,
where they formed 47 per cent and about 25 per cent of the population
respectively), though there are also considerable colonies in Moscow
and other central Russian towns, in Leningrad, the Donets Basin, and in
the towns of Western Siberia and Kazakhstan. They are the most
advanced of the Muslim and Turkic-speaking peoples of the U.S.S.R.
They originated in a mixture between the Volga Bulgarians (q.v.) and
the Turkic-speaking, predominantly Kypchak (*see* CUMANS) element
in the Golden Horde (q.v.). After the latter's disintegration in the mid
15th century they formed the Kazan' and Astrakhan' (qq.v.) khanates, which were both conquered by Muscovy a century later. Although
there was Russian colonization, and some attempts at compulsory
baptism, Russian-Kazan' Tatar relations have on the whole been
good, with much intermarriage and assimilation (many noble Russian
families are of Tatar descent). Tatar merchants and officials played
an important part in the Russian advance into Central Asia. In the
late 19th and early 20th centuries Kazan' Tatars led in the modernist
movement among the Muslims of Russia, and after the February
revolution (q.v.) of 1917 they were the dominant force in the All-
Russian Muslim Council which supported the Provisional Government. Tatar Nationalists and National Bolsheviks advocated in
1917–19 the establishment of an autonomous Volga-Urals state,
including Tatars, Bashkirs, Chuvash and Mari, but (partly because
of opposition from the Bashkirs) a small Tatar Autonomous Republic
was formed. M. Sultan-Galiyev (q.v.), a Tatar National Bolshevik,
was the most highly placed Muslim in the Communist Party in 1919–
1923 and exercised considerable influence on the party's policy
towards national minorities.

(2) Siberian Tatars, numbering only about 70,000, live scattered in
small groups in Western Siberia. They are the remnants of the chief
ethnic element of the Siberian Khanate (q.v.).

(3) Crimean Tatars lived until 1945 in the Crimea, which before the
Second World War was a Tatar Autonomous Republic, although
Tatars made up less than a quarter of its population. Crimean Tatars
are linguistically and culturally closely related to the Turks of Turkey.
Of about 1 million population of the Crimea at the time of its conquest
by the Russians, 300,000 emigrated to Turkey immediately after

annexation, and 150,000 after the Crimean War. A Crimean Tatar, I. B. Gasprinskiy (q.v.), was the most outstanding advocate of pan-Turkism in Imperial Russia from the 1880's. In 1917–20 the dominant political force among the Crimean Tatars was the National Party, a socialist party which advocated federal structure for Russia and cultural autonomy for the national minorities. On the other hand, Admiral Kolchak (q.v.), the anti-Bolshevik leader in the civil war who stood for 'Russia one and indivisible,' was a Crimean Tatar. In 1945 all Crimean Tatars were deported (for alleged collaboration with the Germans) to Uzbekistan and Kazakhstan. Unlike most other peoples similarly deported, they were not rehabilitated in 1957. Before the 1920's the name Tatar was used by the Russians for several other Turkic peoples of Russia, notably the Azerbaydzhanis, Nogays and Khakas (qq.v.). *See* W. Kolarz, *Russia and her Colonies*, 1952; R. Pipes, *The Formation of the Soviet Union*, Cambridge, Mass., 1954; C. W. Hostler, *Turkism and the Soviets*, 1957; R. Conquest, *The Soviet Deportation of Nationalities*, 1960; S. A. Zenkovsky, *Pan-Turkism and Islam in Russia*, 1960; A. Bennigsen and C. Quelquejay, *Les Mouvements nationaux chez les musselmans de Russie. Le 'Sultangalievisme' au Tatarstan*, Paris and The Hague, 1960.

Tatishchev, Vasily Nikitich (1686–1750), historian, geographer and administrator, one of Peter the Great's collaborators in implementing his reforms. As head of the mining administration in the Urals he did much to develop the area. His *History of Russia from the Earliest Times* in five volumes laid the foundation of modern historiography in Russia. *See* R. Portal, *L'Oural au XVIIIe siècle*, Paris, 1950.

Tats, *see* IRANIANS.

Tauria, medieval name of the Crimea. It is also used locally to denote the neighbouring part of the mainland which is bordered in the north by the lower Dnieper, a steppe lowland that is a rich agricultural region belonging to Kherson and Zaporozh'ye oblasts.

Taxation. Indirect taxation is far more important in the Soviet system than direct, the principal form of it being the turnover tax (q.v.), which accounted for 45·3 per cent of total State revenue in the 1958 budget. Import and export tariffs are relatively unimportant, making up about 2 per cent of total budget revenue. Of direct taxes, the profits (q.v.) tax levied on State enterprises (which may, however, be considered an indirect tax on consumers) takes the first place (20·1 per cent of total revenue in 1958), followed by the income-tax (q.v.); the agricultural tax (q.v.), various fees and local rates are comparatively unimportant. All direct taxes, excluding profits tax, made up 10·2 per cent of revenue in 1958. Obligatory deliveries and sales by contract of agricultural products until 1958 were in fact a tax in kind, and to the extent that the present fixed purchase prices for agricultural products are below those of the *kolkhoz* market (q.v.), agricultural procurement (q.v.) is still a form of taxation. Until the issue of non-negotiable State loans (*see* GOVERNMENT BONDS) was stopped in 1958, subscription to them was also a form of direct taxation. Krushchëv's recent statements that taxation is to disappear are misleading, since in fact they only refer to income-tax. *See also* BUDGET. *See* F. D. Holzman, *Soviet Taxation*, Cambridge, Mass., 1955; L. M.

Herman, 'Taxes and the Soviet Citizen,' *Problems of Communism*, vol. viii, No. 5, 1959.

Taymyr, peninsula in northern Siberia between the Kara and the Laptev seas. Cape Chelyuskin (77° 43′ N.) is the northernmost point in Asia.

Taymyr National Okrug, in the Krasnoyarsk Kray (northern Siberia), comprises the Taymyr peninsula and the adjacent mainland and islands. Area 332,100 sq. m.; population (1959) 33,000 (60 per cent urban), mostly Russians, also Yakuts and Samoyeds. Nickel, copper, uranium and coal are mined; other activities of the inhabitants are fishing, reindeer raising and fur trapping. The okrug was formed in 1930; its administrative centre is Dudinka. The area is one of rapid economic development, based until the mid 1950's upon forced labour. *See also* NORIL'SK.

Tayshet, town in the Irkutsk Oblast (southern Siberia), an important junction on the Trans-Siberian Railway situated 360 m. north-west of Irkutsk. Population (1939) 17,000. A large iron and steel plant is to be built here. From the 1930's to the mid 1950's Tayshet was the administrative centre of the forced labour camps whose inmates were constructing the Tayshet–Lena railway; serious riots took place in the camps in 1954.

Tbilisi, *see* TIFLIS.

Tchaikovsky, Pëtr Il'ich (1840–93), composer, who studied at the School of Jurisprudence, St Petersburg, and in 1862 entered the St Petersburg Conservatory, being appointed professor at Moscow Conservatory in 1865. In 1877 he made a disastrous marriage and resigned his professorship the following year. He made his début as conductor at St Petersburg in 1887 with a programme of his own compositions. In 1888 he undertook a successful international tour as conductor, meeting Brahms, Grieg, Dvořák, Gounod, Massenet and Paderewski. He visited America in 1891, journeyed to England to receive an honorary degree at Cambridge, returned to Russia and died of cholera in St Petersburg. Works comprise eleven operas, including *Eugene Onegin*, 1877–8, *The Sorceress*, 1885–7, and *The Queen of Spades*, 1890; three ballets—*Swan Lake*, 1875–6, *The Sleeping Beauty*, 1888–9, and *The Nutcracker*, 1891–2; choral works; ecclesiastical music; many orchestral works, including six symphonies (seven with *Manfred*, 1885); the overture-fantasy *Romeo and Juliet*, 1880; *Italian Capriccio*, 1880; overture *The Year 1812*, 1880; three piano concertos; violin concerto; chamber music; many piano works and songs; arrangements, etc. Tchaikovsky's music is essentially personal and direct, the result of his own experience and suffering. His work is of consummate artistry, though marred by certain idiosyncrasies which tend to monotony. Nevertheless, his gifts of lyrical melody, his vivid imgaination, his love of dramatic or fantastic subjects (admirably suited to ballet), his rhythmic drive and his skill in writing for the orchestra and voice amply compensate for any occasional deficiencies. Tchaikovsky's debt to Russian folk music is often underestimated. *See* H. Weinstock, *Tchaikovsky*, New York, 1943; G. Abraham, *Tchaikovsky: a Symposium*, 1954.

Teachers. The number of teachers (including part-time) in primary and secondary schools rose from 280,000 in 1914–15 (present-day frontiers) to 1,900,000 in 1958–9, and the pupil-teacher ratio fell from 34 to 16. Teachers of the upper classes of full secondary schools are supposed to have higher education (in fact 84·7 per cent in 1958–9); those of classes 5–7 were until recently trained in special Teachers' Institutes giving a two-year course on the basis of nine or ten years of general secondary education; but these institutes have now been abolished and the aim is to train teachers for these classes in full Pedagogical Institutes (in fact 34 per cent with higher education and 52 per cent trained at Teachers' Institutes in 1958–9); teachers for the primary classes 1–4 are required to have professional secondary education which is acquired in pedagogical schools (in fact 90·6 per cent with secondary education, mostly pedagogical, in 1958–9). The appointment, transfer and dismissal of teachers is formally centralized in the hands of the oblast educational authorities and Union Republic ministries of education, but in fact is carried out by the rayon educational authorities. Teachers' salaries are graded according to their level of education, the classes they are teaching, experience and the type of locality (urban or rural). The starting salary of a primary schoolteacher is about 580 roubles per month before deductions (£14 10s.), the average salary of secondary school teachers 800–1,100 roubles per month (£20–£25). Many village schoolteachers receive free accommodation and fuel. Teachers belong to the privileged social category of 'specialists,' but within this category they occupy the lowest position. The All-Russian Teachers' Council, formed in 1917 by various teachers' associations, opposed the educational policy of the Bolshevik Government, advocated freedom of education, and was consequently suppressed. The present Union of Educational Workers is, like all trade unions, merely an adjunct of the Communist Party. An All-Union Pedagogical Society was founded in 1959. *See* S. V. Utechin, 'Education in the U.S.S.R.,' *Political Quarterly*, Oct.–Dec. 1958; K. Mehnert, *Der Sowjetmensch*, 5th ed., Stuttgart, 1959; G. Z. F. Bereday and J. Pennar (eds.), *The Politics of Soviet Education*, 1960.

Technical Repair Stations, *see* M.T.S.

Technicum, name given in the U.S.S.R. to professional secondary schools devoted to technical studies in the widest sense, including agricultural and commercial subjects. In a loose sense the term is often used to describe any professional secondary school. *See further under* EDUCATION.

Technology. The first known modern technological achievement in Russia was the construction of a serviceable steam engine by the 18th-century mechanic Polzunov (q.v.). Power engineering thus borne produced a remarkable crop of outstanding experts in the early 20th century (*see* ALEKSANDROV, I. G.; GRINEVETSKIY, RAMZIN). Electrical engineering had as its pioneers in Russia Yablochkov and Lodygin (qq.v.), and radio Popov (q.v.). The utilization of nuclear energy was directed during the 1950's by Kurchatov (q.v.). Theoretical problems of mechanical engineering were dealt with by, among others, Krylov and Artobolevskiy (qq.v.). The Russian school of metallurgy has been best represented by D. K. Chernov, M. A. Pavlov, Baykov and Bardin (qq.v.). Pal'chinskiy (q.v.) was probably the most outstanding mining engineer, Sikorsky and Tupolev (qq.v.) are the most famous aircraft designers. The technical problems of railway transport have been given much attention since the earliest days of railways, and in recent years Obraztsov (q.v.) has been a prominent expert in this field.

Technological theory and the best enterprises in the U.S.S.R. are comparable to the best in more advanced industrial countries, but there are many inefficient and obsolete enterprises, and the variety and quality of mass-produced goods are often poor. *See also* AUTO-MATION; MECHANICS; and entries on various branches of industry. *See* J. G. Crowther, *Soviet Science*, 1936; Lyubov (ed.), *Problems of Metallography and the Physics of Metals*, New York, 1957; *Soviet Research in Glass and Ceramics*, New York, Consultants Bureau, 1957; A. D. Galanin, *The Theory of Thermal-Neutron Nuclear Reactors*, New York, 1958; A. Tastin, 'Soviet Technology Reviewed and Revisited,' *Soviet Studies*, vol. xi, No. 2, Oct. 1959; W. B. Walsh, 'Some Judgments on Soviet Science,' *Russian Review*, vol. xix, No. 3, July 1960. Complete 'cover-to-cover' translations of the following journals exist in English: *Works Laboratory*; *Metals and Heat Treatment of Metals*; *Radio Engineering*; *Radio Engineering and Electronics*; *Journal of Abstracts: Metallurgy*; *Machine Tools and Cutting Tools*.

Telavi, town in Georgia situated 58 m. north-east of Tiflis, the centre of a notable wine-producing area (*see* KAKHETIA). Population (1939) 13,000. The ruins of an ancient fortress and palace have been preserved and are surrounded by several monasteries and churches of the 6th–16th centuries, formerly much visited by pilgrims. Telavi was founded in 893, and from the 17th century was capital of Kakhetia.

Television. There were 62 television transmitters in the U.S.S.R. in 1958, whose output in that year was about 38,000 hours; there are a number of relay stations for relaying the Moscow transmissions, and a whole network of such relay stations is being constructed. There were 3 million television sets in 1958 (400 in 1940, 200 in 1945, 15,000 in 1950); the total number of daily viewers was estimated at about 10 million in 1958. Experimental television transmissions were started in the U.S.S.R. in 1931 and the first centres began working in Moscow and Leningrad in 1938; the third centre started functioning in 1951 in Kiev.

Temir-Tau (until 1945 **Samarkand**), town in the Karaganda Oblast (Kazakhstan), an industrial satellite situated 22 m. north of Karaganda. Population (1959) 54,000 (1939, 5,000), mainly Russians. It has iron and steel and chemical (synthetic rubber, soda) industries, and a large thermal power-station. Temir-Tau was founded in the 1930's as a workers' settlement in connection with the building of the power-station, and became a town in 1945. The new Karaganda iron and steel plant now being built at Temir-Tau will be one of the largest in the U.S.S.R. A strike of the building workers in 1959 led to serious clashes with the security troops.

Terek, river in the Caucasus which rises south of Kazbek Mountain. It crosses the main Caucasian range by way of Dar'yal gorge and flows north-west until it reaches the lowland, then east into the Caspian Sea. Length 350 m.

Termez, town in Uzbekistan, administrative centre of the Surkhan-Dar'ya Oblast, situated on the Amu-Dar'ya River and the Bukhara–Stalinabad railway line, on the Afghan frontier. Population (1959) 22,000. It is the centre of a fine-fibre cotton-growing area, a local cultural centre, and the hottest place in the U.S.S.R. (maximum temperature +50° C.).

Ternopol' (Ukrainian **Ternopil'**, Polish **Tarnopol**): 1. Oblast in Galicia (western Ukraine), situated on the Volhynia-Podolia upland north of the River Dniester, a ravinous area in the black earth belt; there are deposits of lignite. Area 5,400 sq. m.; population (1959) 1,088,000 (16 per cent urban), mostly Ukrainians, some Jews (before 1946 also Poles). Wheat, sugar-beet and sunflowers are cultivated, cattle and pigs raised, and there are varied food industries. For history *see* GALICIA.

2. Administrative centre of the oblast, a major railway junction situated 78 m. south-east of L'vov. Population (1959) 52,000 (1939, 50,000), before the war half Jewish. It has some food industries. Ternopol' was founded as a fortress in 1540 and became an important trade centre; it has been provincial capital since 1921. In 1944 bitter fighting took place and the town was largely destroyed.

Terror has been the principal method of the Communist dictatorship throughout its history. From the Bolshevik seizure of power in 1917 (*see* OCTOBER REVOLUTION) until the introduction of the Stalin constitution in 1936 the regime was openly terroristic, described as the Dictatorship of the Proletariat (q.v.), which was defined by Lenin as 'power won and maintained by the violence of the proletariat against the bourgeoisie, power that is unrestricted by any laws.' A new justification for the continued practice of terror was advanced by Stalin in 1937, when he said that, with the victory of socialism, the class struggle sharpens rather than diminishes. This last theory was rejected at the 20th party congress (q.v.) in 1956, but the intellectual opposition (q.v.) was soon reminded by the official spokesmen that the Soviet regime is still in some sense a dictatorship. In practice both preventive and punitive terror were employed until Stalin's death (*see* COLLECTIVIZATION OF AGRICULTURE; PURGES; SECURITY ORGANS), but only the latter seems to have been used since 1953, apart from the practice of 'criticism and self-criticism' (q.v.). The new law on 'State crimes' promulgated in 1958 retains terroristic punishments for all 'political' crimes (q.v.). *See* B. Moore, Jnr, *Soviet Politics—the Dilemma of Power*, Cambridge, Mass., 1950, and *Terror and Progress*, Cambridge, Mass., 1954; M. Fainsod, *How Russia is Ruled*, Cambridge, Mass., 1953, and *Smolensk under Soviet Rule*, 1959; W. Leonhard, 'Terror in the Soviet System,' *Problems of Communism*, vol. vii, No. 6, Nov.–Dec. 1958; J. N. Hazard, *The Soviet System of Government*, 2nd ed., Chicago, 1960; H. McClosky and J. E. Turner, *The Soviet Dictatorship*, 1960.

Textile Industry. In 1958 total fabric production was 7,418 million metres (2,848 in 1913, 4,436 in 1940, 6,860 in 1956); of this 5,789 million metres were cotton fabrics, 845 million silk, 481 million linen and 303 million woollen. In 1958, 36 metres of fabric were produced per head of population (20 in 1913, 19 in 1928, 23 in 1940; the 1913 figure does not include the considerable amount of home-made fabrics). In 1958 the domestic output of cotton fibre was 1·5 million tons, of which 0·3 million tons were exported (mainly to Poland, East Germany and Czechoslovakia), the U.S.S.R. taking second place in cotton export after the U.S.A. In the same year 0·1 million tons of cotton were imported, mainly long-fibre cotton from Egypt. In 1958, 320,000 tons of wool were produced; 14,000 tons were exported and at the same time 57,000 tons imported in 1957. The textile industry is largely concentrated in central Russia (the main centres are Moscow, Ivanovo and Kostroma) and in Leningrad. *See* A. S. Becker, *Cotton Textile Industry of the U.S.S.R.*, Washington, D.C., 1955.

Theatre, in Russia, owes its inception to the Latin and Polish mystery or morality plays, which were imported into the Ukraine towards the end of the 16th century. Performances of these were given by students at the Kiev Academy, who carried them outside the confines of their academic cloisters. With the passage of time these old moralities became secularized, and various 'stock' or *commedia dell' arte* characters were introduced to give a more popular flavour. The most original of the native Kievan school of playwrights were St Demetrius of Rostov (1651–1709) and Theophan Prokopovich (q.v., 1681–1736), both of whom produced verse dramas based on religious subjects and patterned on the accepted baroque styles of the classical Italian theatre.

German influences, however, predominated in central Russia. Itinerant German players performed regularly in the so-called German Suburb of Moscow. In 1672 Czar Alexis, on the encouragement of his courtier, Artamon Matveyev, invited the German Lutheran pastor Dr I. G. Gregori to form an amateur company. German verse dramas and moralities were translated into Church Slavonic and performed before the court, thus providing some diversion from the usual fare of jesters, jongleurs and mountebanks who moved from one princely court to another.

Peter the Great created State-subsidized theatres in both Moscow and St Petersburg. French dramatic models superseded the German, and Molière and Racine were introduced to polite Russian society of the period. On a more popular level, an English rope-dancer named Maddox created a great sensation when he appeared in St Petersburg in 1715. The dominance of visiting foreign companies was challenged, however, by the emergence of a talented group of Yaroslavl' amateurs under the inspiration of F. Volkov (q.v., 1729–63), a local merchant; he has justly been described as 'the father of the Russian Theatre.' The fame of Volkov's productions led to an invitation from the Empress Elizabeth to perform at the Imperial Court in 1752. The union between the merchant Volkov and the court dramatist Sumarokov (1718–77) led to the creation of the first permanent theatre in Russia in 1756. Among the most talented in Volkov's company of actors was the famous tragedian I. A. Dmitrevskiy

(1734–1821)—'the Garrick of Russia,' whose performances in the typical Franco-Russian *comédie larmoyante* were received with great acclaim.

Parallel with the growth of State-supported theatres was the enterprise shown by a number of aristocratic patrons, such as the princes Gagarin and Shakhovskoy, in the creation of so-called 'serf theatres.' A leading member of the old nobility, Count Sheremetev, went so far as to marry the leading lady of his company, and in 1806 an account is given of the sale of some seventy-four performers of both sexes for the sum of 32,000 roubles by a Prince Volkonskiy. The most eminent of these serf actors was M. Shchepkin (q.v., 1788–1863), who founded the Russian school of realistic acting.

The 18th century, as well as the first half of the 19th, confirmed the predominance of the actor over the dramatist (an analogous situation prevailed in the British theatre, for example, between about 1840 and 1900). The romantic movement which had swept over Europe found its expression in the Russian theatre: 'Gothic' importations arrived from France and Germany (it may be noted that a similar 'romantic' urge seized Stanislavsky on the eve of the October revolution of 1917 when he produced Byron's *Cain*). Shakespeare, who was to become 'our flesh and blood,' as Turgenev said at the tricentenary celebrations in Moscow in 1863, was represented by the Hamlet of P. Mochalov (q.v., 1800–48), the leading Russian tragic actor of this period, whose sensitivity and artistry was compared to that of Edmund Kean. Foreign influences still dominated the Russian theatre (despite the verse dramas of Pushkin, whose *Boris Godunov*, published in 1831, was not produced until 1870). The 'Gothic' vogue was followed by the introduction of foreign and later native 'vaudevilles' (light comedies and sketches), the titles of which are indicative of their *genre*: *Two Orphans, Thirty Years, or the Life of a Gambler*, etc. Chekhov contributed a number of such vaudevilles before turning his attention to serious drama.

The emergence of the social dramas of Gogol' and A. N. Ostrovskiy (qq.v.) demanded the creation of a realistic style of acting, as opposed to the declamatory style then prevalent. Among the founders and exponents of this style were such celebrated actors and actresses as I. V. Samarin (1817–85), V. N. Davydov (1849–1925), M. G. Savina (1854–1915), G. N. Fedotova (1846–1925), A. Ye. Martynov (1816–60) and others. Contact with foreign players and companies provided a fruitful ground of comparison. The famous Italian actors Ernesto Rossi and Tomaso Salvini played in St Petersburg, as did Sarah Bernhardt and Coquelin. Perhaps the most marked influence on the theatre of the period was made by the visit of the ducal players belonging to the Meiningen theatre company, whose attempts to produce scenic simplicity and some characterization contrasted favourably with the scenically overburdened Russian stage and the false declamatory manner of some of its leading artists. Stanislavsky, who was quick to see the faults of the Meiningen players, nevertheless paid a tribute to their influence.

Like most Russian theatrical innovators, K. S. Stanislavsky (1863–1938) entered the theatre as an amateur. In 1898 he founded the Moscow Art Theatre in conjunction with V. I. Nemirovich-Danchenko (1858–1943). The new theatrical venture opened with *Czar Fёdor*, an historical drama by Count A. K. Tolstoy. This met with considerable success; the second production, *The Merchant of Venice*, however, was poorly received, and the theatre was threatened with financial and artistic bankruptcy. It offered to revive Chekhov's abortive *The Seagull*, which had had a resounding failure when it was produced at the Imperial Theatre in St Petersburg in 1896. *The Seagull* revival, a new and brilliant production which did not altogether please Chekhov, established the Moscow Art Theatre as the home of Chekhovian drama (*Uncle Vanya, The Cherry Orchard* and *The Three Sisters* followed in succession, culminating in the death of its 'founder-dramatist' in 1904). The leading actors of the original theatre company were Chekhov's wife, A. O. Knipper-Chekhova (b. 1870), V. I. Kachalov (1875–1948), I. M. Moskvin (1874–1946) and L. M. Leonidov (1873–1941); among the younger actors of the theatre company were N. P. Khmelёv (1901–45) and A. K. Tarasova (b. 1898)—the leading Chekhovian actress in the post-revolutionary period.

The development of the so-called Stanislavsky system, with its emphasis on engaging the subconscious strata in an actor's development of his role, did not preclude the great director from employing *avant-garde* scenic decorators such as Benois (q.v.) and stage directors such as Gordon Craig (who is best remembered for his production of *Hamlet* in 1911 at the Moscow Art Theatre, and for the impression some of his more outrageous theories made on Stanislavsky).

After the revolution of 1905 (q.v.) both Stanislavsky and younger directors such as V. Meyerhold, Ye. Vakhtangov (qq.v.), who had worked with Stanislavsky but had diverged from the mainstream of their mentor's method of production, and A. Tairov (q.v.) increasingly turned from the drama of Chekhov, Gor'kiy and other Russian dramatists to Shaw, Maeterlinck, Ibsen, Hamsun and others. Thus once again the Russian theatre turned to foreign sources, both to revive itself and to create in itself new perspectives of dramatic expression and scenic techniques. While Tairov moved towards the 'theatre theatrical' or 'art for the theatre's sake'—and created strange Cézannesque sets of cones and triangles, in which he set his actors moving in slow expressionistic movements—Meyerhold sought to fuse the various streams of futurism, expressionism and symbolism which had made their appearance in music and painting into a novel theatrical idiom. It was an adventure which led to his persecution and death.

Meyerhold's discoveries received an impetus from the October revolution (q.v.) of 1917. In his 'constructivist' and 'bio-mechanics' techniques he tried to embody the Machine Age in the theatre, by a whole paraphernalia of moving lifts and platforms, open girders and spotlights. A new plasticity was demanded of the actors. The liberating influence of the revolution was to be felt in the theatre.

The Soviet Government, itself occupied by graver political matters, showed a remarkable tolerance (within political limits) towards the theatre and its techniques and forms. The decree of 9th November

1917 put all theatres under the control of the Commissariat of Education (then under the enlightened commissar, Lunacharskiy, q.v.), and later, in August 1919, they were nationalized. Even as late as 1925 the Central Committee of the party, while claiming every right to decide on the *content* of a dramatic work, made no attempt to prescribe its essential form.

By 1930 the situation had changed dramatically: two plays by the Soviet 'poet laureate' Mayakovskiy (q.v.)—*The Bed Bug* and *The Bath House*—both satirizing Soviet bureaucracy, produced by Meyerhold, with music by Shostakovich (q.v.), were banned from the stage. A similar blow fell on the more favoured Moscow Art Theatre (whose 'realism' was believed by the authorities to contain a splinter of the essential truth) for its production of M. Bulgakov's play *The Days of the Turbins*. This latter play was revived shortly before the Second World War as a gesture of 'national solidarity': it had drawn a very sympathetic portrait of opponents of the Soviet regime, but in reconsidering it Stalin discovered that that was a 'proof of the invincible might of Bolshevism.'

But the drastic action of the early thirties was a prelude of things to come. By now both form and content had to conform to the obligatory standards of Socialist Realism (q.v.). Meyerhold had this to say about the new trend at the 1st Congress of Theatre Producers in 1939: 'This pitiful and sterile something which aspires to the title of Socialist Realism has nothing in common with art. Yet the theatre is art, and without art there can be no theatre. Go to the Moscow theatres and look at the colourless, boring productions which are all alike and which differ only in their degrees of worthlessness. No longer can one identify the creative signature of the Malyy Theatre, of the Vakhtangov Theatre, of the Kamernyy Theatre or of the Moscow Art Theatre. . . . Was this your aim? If so you have committed a horrible crime. You have washed the child down the drain along with the dirty water. In your effort to eradicate formalism you have destroyed art.' A few days after this speech Meyerhold and his actress wife disappeared in the final phases of the Great Purge (q.v.).

The Second World War brought a measure of relaxation to the theatre, as to other fields of internal life. Plays of patriotic motifs, historical dramas and foreign plays engaged the attention of the soldier audiences and the privileged theatregoers in Moscow (seats were difficult to obtain). A new note of lyricism crept into the productions of some Soviet directors, such as Stanislavsky's promising actor-producer Yurly Zavadskiy's *Othello* at the Mossoviet Theatre, which matched the colours of Titian in the costumes and lighting of the play. The Moor of the actor Mordvinov took on a 'humanized' interpretation to fit the mood of the day (without any of the anti-colonial overtones of 'black' versus 'white' of earlier productions). Elegant, well-costumed productions of foreign classics such as Wilde's *An Ideal Husband* were performed at the Moscow Art Theatre.

The end of the war saw a return of repressive measures against the theatre, first in August 1946, when the veteran director Tairov was dismissed from his post as chief director of the theatre he had founded: the director of the Leningrad Comedy Theatre, N. P.

Akimov, was similarly disgraced. This decree, inspired by Zhdanov (q.v.), was followed in January 1948 by attacks on 'cosmopolitan dramatic critics' of Jewish origin, by the closure of the Yiddish Chamber Theatre and by the death of the celebrated Jewish actor-director S. M. Mikhoels (q.v.) a few months later in mysterious circumstances.

It is not surprising, therefore, that the *Literary Gazette* in April 1950 quoted a director as saying: 'We must now only stage plays about which we are dead sure.' Few directors of theatres could be found who would give their immediate and unqualified support for a new play without first obtaining the 'unanimous' approval of the theatre's 'artistic council' (and above all the State censor). 'In our theatre it often takes longer to read a play than to write one,' comments the *Literary Gazette*, urging directors to abandon their caution.

The death of Stalin in 1953 brought little immediate change in the theatre. The short-lived premiership of Malenkov brought into the open the so-called 'non-conflict' theory, with which certain dramatists and producers sought to insure themselves against attack. A literal interpretation of Malenkov's plea to dramatists to fight 'against everything that is negative' brought a new spate of banned plays and disgraced editorial boards. The most significant and widespread changes in the theatre did occur, however, after Khrushchëv's secret speech denouncing Stalinist excesses (*see* TWENTIETH PARTY CONGRESS), and posthumous reparation was offered to Meyerhold: a commission was appointed to collect and preserve various of his writings, sketches, etc. Mayakovskiy's banned *The Bath House* and *The Bed Bug* were restaged, and the *enfant terrible* of the Russian theatre, N. Okhlopkov (q.v.), a pupil of Meyerhold, staged his long-awaited *Hamlet* which he had matured for over ten years, refusing to produce it during Stalin's lifetime. But despite the 'thaw' and the soul-searchings, *Kommunist* was quick to point out (in February 1958) to the editors of the leading theatrical magazine *Teatr* the dangers of taking 'a wrong standpoint' in assessing the fight against formalism in the 1930's; 'In particular, the whole of the creative work of Meyerhold is assessed apologetically, and his influence on the development of the progressive theatre abroad is exaggerated.' Nor did the same journal approve of the tentative attempts to revaluate Stanislavsky's system: 'Out of false objectivism the editorial [i.e. of *Teatr*] permitted statements which manifestly discredit the principles of realism in theatrical art and condone formalistic tendencies.'

More recently (December 1959) *Soviet Culture* has complained that the repertoire of the Moscow Art Theatre and other leading theatres is overladen with foreign plays. It instances the fact that in nine months of 1958, 229 performances were given of foreign plays as against 94 of plays by contemporary Soviet authors; the record of the Malyy Theatre shows that in the same period foreign plays were given 253 performances as against 102 of plays by native dramatists.

Thus the Russian theatre in its post-1917 evolution has passed through three distinct stages of elation, purgation and stagnation. Despite the widespread and generous financial and material support which the Soviet Government gives to the country's five hundred odd theatres, its two children's theatres and seventy puppet theatres, the theatre has failed to create its own classic, or the perfect archetype— the *Everyman* of its age. Caught between the prevailing political climate, with its emphasis on expediency and survival, and the demands of the free creative spirit in this most exacting of all arts, the Russian theatre may yet find that the latter will prove the most enduring signpost to the future. *See* K. S. Stanislavsky, *My Life in Art*, 1924; H. Carter, *The New Spirit in the Russian Theatre*, 1929; R. and G. Fülöp-Miller, *Russian Theatre*, Philadelphia, 1930; N. Houghton, *Moscow Rehearsals*, New York, 1936; D. Tutaev, *In Search of Everyman*, New York, 1947; J. Jelagin, *Taming of the Arts*, New York, 1951; M. Bradshaw (ed.), *Soviet Theaters, 1917–41*, New York, 1954; P. Yershov, *Comedy in the Soviet Theatre*, New York, 1956; N. I. Gorchakov, *Theater in Soviet Russia*, New York, 1957; J. Ruehle, 'The Soviet Theatre,' *Problems of Communism*, Nov.–Dec. 1959 and Jan.–Feb. 1960.

Theodosia, *see* FEODOSIYA.

de Thomon, Thomas (1760–1813), architect, a French aristocratic refugee whose great contribution to the waterfront *ensemble* of St Petersburg was his severe and majestic Exchange with its two rostral columns. The composition dominates the Neva, facing the Winter Palace on one side and the Fortress of Sts Peter and Paul on the other (*see also* ARCHITECTURE). *See* G. H. Hamilton, *The Art and Architecture of Russia*, 1954.

Tien-Shan (Russian **Tyan'-Shan'**): 1. Mountain system of Central Asia which stretches north-east from the Pamir to the western fringe of the Gobi Desert and forms a part of the frontier between the U.S.S.R. and Sinkiang. The principal range forms the border ridge of the High Plateau of Eastern Asia, and includes the Peter the Great, Trans-Alay, Kokshal-tau and Sary-yassy ranges. The highest peaks (Victory, 24,406 ft; Khan-Tengri, 23,620 ft) and the largest glaciers of the Tien-Shan system are in this range, which can be crossed by passes at an elevation of between 10,000 and 14,000 ft.

2. Oblast of Kirgizia comprising the central part of the Tien-Shan mountainous system; there are coal and iron ore deposits. Area 19,500 sq. m.; population (1959) 137,000 (19 per cent urban), almost entirely Kirgiz. The main occupation of the inhabitants is sheep and horse keeping; there is also some oats and barley cultivation, and wild animal hunting. Administrative centre Naryn.

Tiflis (Georgian **Tbilisi**), capital of Georgia, an important industrial and cultural centre of the U.S.S.R. situated on both banks of the River Kura. Population (1959) 694,000 (first in Transcaucasia, eleventh in the U.S.S.R.; 1897, 160,000; 1917, 264,000; 1939, 519,000), Georgians, Armenians and Russians. It has varied engineering (machine tools, equipment for food and textile industries, radio and telegraph equipment, etc.), food and light industries, and is an important centre of transportation (four railway lines, airport, the Georgian Military Road to Ordzhonikidze in North Caucasus). The Georgian Academy of Sciences is here (established in 1935 as the Georgian branch of the U.S.S.R. Academy of Sciences, raised in status 1941), and there is a university, 1918, a conservatoire, 1917, an arts academy (established as a school of painting in 1875, transformed 1922), a public library, 1850, a Georgian (former Caucasian) museum, 1867, and an opera and ballet theatre, 1851. The city is a treasury of Georgian architecture, including 5th–7th-century churches (St David's and Anchiskhat churches, and the Zion Cathedral), the Lurdzhi monastery church (12th century), the Metekhi Castle, 1278–93, and the Anchiskhat bell-tower, 1675; there are also interesting buildings of the 19th and 20th centuries.

Tiflis has been known since the 4th century, and has been the capital of Georgia or East Georgia since the 6th century. In 1801 it became Russian, and until 1882 was the residence of the Viceroy of the Caucasus. In 1917–18 it was capital of the anti-Bolshevik Transcaucasian Federation, in 1918–20 of independent Georgia, in 1922–36 of the Transcaucasian Federal Republic within the U.S.S.R., and in 1951–3 of Tiflis Oblast (now abolished) within the Georgian Republic. Tiflis is an old centre of Georgian culture (printing press 1709, philosophic seminary 1755, theatre in the 1790's, first newspaper 1819), and was the cultural centre of the whole of Transcaucasia during the 19th–early 20th centuries (first Russian paper in 1828, Russian theatre 1845, Armenian theatre in the 1860's). Politically it was one of Russian social democracy's main strongholds.

Tighina, see BENDERY.

Tikhomirov, Lev Aleksandrovich (1852–1923), politician and publicist. He was a member of the executive committee of the Narodnaya Volya (q.v.) organization, emigrated in 1883 and edited abroad the official journal of the organization. He renounced his revolutionary views in 1888, was later allowed to return to Russia, and became a leading publicist of the extreme Right. His book on the theory of absolute monarchy is one of the principal works in the field. See D. Footman, *Red Prelude,* 1944; R. Hare, *Portraits of Russian Personalities between Reform and Revolution,* 1959.

Tikhonov, Nikolay Semënovich (b. 1896), poet. He belonged to the 'Serapion Brothers' group (see ZAMYATIN) and began publishing in the early 1920's. Later he fell under the influence of Pasternak's poetry, but by 1930 had identified himself politically with the Soviet regime. During the war he was a senior war correspondent and was made chairman of the Writers' Union (q.v.) in 1944, but was removed in 1946, in the course of Zhdanov's campaign to reimpose strict party control over cultural life, and replaced by Fadeyev (q.v.). However, he was later made chairman of the Soviet Peace Committee. His verse, most of which is on political subjects, is of high quality and shows some resemblance to that of Kipling. See G. Struve, *Soviet Russian Literature, 1917–50,* Norman, Oklahoma, 1951; M. Slonim, *Modern Russian Literature,* New York, 1953; J. Lindsay (trans.), *Russian Poetry, 1917–55,* 1957.

Tiksi, port in the Tiksi Bay of the Laptev Sea, near the Lena delta on the Northern Sea Route. It was founded in 1934 and has some importance as a supply base for northern Yakutia.

Tilsit, see SOVETSK.

Timber. The forested area is about 722 million hectares, i.e. about 32 per cent of the total area of the U.S.S.R. and about one-fifth of the total forested area of the world. Up to 80 per cent consists of coniferous species. Three-quarters of the forested area is in Siberia and the Far East, but only one-quarter of the felling of timber. The timber industry is largely concentrated in the centre and north of European Russia and in the Urals, where the forests are more easily accessible; in central Russia and the Ukraine the forests are rapidly disappearing through excessive exploitation. Timber haulage amounted to 376 million cubic metres in 1958 (61 in 1913, 62 in 1928, 246 in 1940, 168 in 1945, 342 in 1956), one-third being firewood. Between 50 and 60 per cent of work in timber felling and haulage is mechanized. The production of wood pulp was 2·1 million tons in 1958, and of paper 2·2 million tons (0·2 in 1913, 0·3 in 1928, 0·8 in 1940, 2·0 in 1956). The largest saw-milling plants are in Archangel and Stalingrad. The woodworking and furniture industry is concentrated in Moscow, Leningrad, Gomel', Tyumen' and Tomsk, while paper is chiefly produced in Leningrad, Novgorod, Vologda, Gor'kiy and Perm' oblasts.

Timiryazev, Kliment Arkad'yevich (1843–1920), botanist, professor of Moscow University. His main work was concerned with photosynthesis (*Sun, Life and Chlorophyll*, 1923). He was one of the main champions of Darwinism in Russia (*Charles Darwin and his Teaching*, 1865). Timiryazev finds favour with Communists for his mechanistic philosophy, which is represented in propaganda as materialist, and also because he rejected the early findings of modern genetics and can thus be used as a prop for Lysenko's (q.v.) views.

Timoshenko, Semën Konstantinovich (*b.* 1895), Marshal of the Soviet Union (since 1940), born in Bessarabia, of Ukrainian parentage. He commanded a division in Budënnyy's First Cavalry Army during the civil war, and the Red Army units in the war with Finland, 1939–40. In 1940 he replaced Voroshilov as Commissar for Defence, introducing harsh regulations for conduct in the army. After the German invasion of the Soviet Union in 1941 Timoshenko was appointed commander on the western front, but both here and subsequently, when he commanded various army groups, did not prove very successful. Since the war he commanded various military districts in Russia until his retirement in 1960.

Tiraspol', town in the Moldavian Republic, situated on the left bank of the Dniester and the Odessa–Kishinëv railway. Population (1959) 62,000 (1910, 35,000; 1926, 18,400), Russians, Ukrainians, Moldavians and Jews. It is a centre of a market-gardening and wine-producing area, has varied food industries and is a local cultural centre. Tiraspol' was founded as a Russian fortress in 1792 on the site of a Moldavian village. It was the capital of the Moldavian Autonomous Republic within the Ukraine, 1929–40.

Tkachëv, Pëtr Nikitich (1844–85), publicist and revolutionary, leader of the Russian ' Jacobins.' He took part in the underground revolutionary circles of the 1860's and early seventies (including the notorious Nechayev circle which is depicted in Dostoyevskiy's *The Possessed*), at the same time contributing to the radical journals. To escape arrest in the Nechayev affair he emigrated, and published in Geneva the journal *Alarm Bell*, in which he expounded his ideas of a seizure of power by a revolutionary minority for the purpose of implementing socialist reforms through the State machinery. These ideas were influential in the Narodnaya Volya (q.v.) party and later in the Fokin (q.v.) organization. Adopted by Lenin, they became one of the cornerstones of Bolshevism. *See* M. Karpovich, 'A Forerunner of Lenin: P. N. Tkachëv,' *Review of Politics*, No. 6, Notre Dame, Indiana, 1944; J. H. Billington, *Mikhailovsky and Russian Populism*, 1958.

Tobol, navigable left tributary of the River Irtysh in south-western Siberia, rising in the Turgay plateau and flowing north-east through a fertile area rich in mineral resources which is now being rapidly cultivated and industrialized (*see* KUSTANAY). Length 1,000 m.

Tobol'sk, town in the Tyumen' Oblast (Western Siberia), river port on the Irtysh. Population (1956) 35,300. It is the centre of a lumbering and dairy-farming area, and is the supply point for the northern part of the Tyumen' Oblast; it has some industry (shipbuilding, saw-milling, fishing) and the old craft of bone-carving is still practised. It is an important local centre of culture (theatre, founded 1705, local museum). Tobol'sk was founded near the old capital of the Siberian Khanate by Russian Cossacks in 1587; from 1596 to 1824 it was capital of Siberia, and a provincial capital until 1923. It has been a place of banishment, including that of Nicholas II, 1917–18. Mendeleyev was born and went to school in Tobol'sk.

'**Tolkach**' (Russian 'pusher'), colloquial name for a person who is adept at string-pulling (*see* BLAT) and is making a career of it in the service of an enterprise, being formally employed as 'supply agent,' 'representative,' etc. *Tolkachi* are officially disapproved of, but in fact are necessary to the smooth running of enterprises and the fulfilment of plans (*see* PLANNING) in the conditions of extreme bureaucratization which exist in the Soviet economy. Since the reform of the economic administration in 1957 the role of unofficial connections in economic management, and consequently of the *tolkachi*, has further increased. *See* J. S. Berliner, *Factory and Manager in the U.S.S.R.*, Cambridge, Mass., 1957.

Tolstov, Sergey Pavlovich (*b.* 1907), archaeologist and ethnographer. Educated at Moscow University, he was head of its ethnography department 1939–51, has been a corresponding member of the Academy of Sciences since 1953, director of its Institute of Ethnography since 1953 and editor of *Soviet Ethnography* since 1946. He joined the Communist party in 1944. Since 1937 Tolstov has headed the combined archaeological and ethnographic Khorezm expedition; his extensive excavations have led to the discovery of the ancient Khorezm civilization (*Ancient Khorezm*, 1948).

Tolstoy, Count Aleksey Nikolayevich (1883–1945), novelist and playwright, a leading representative of National Bolshevism (q.v.). He first became known before the 1917 revolution as a Neo-Realist, supported the Whites in the civil war, emigrated, but subsequently joined the Change of Landmarks movement and returned to Russia in 1923. The Communists first regarded him with suspicion, as being a fellow traveller (q.v.), but from the mid thirties he held a favoured position as a pillar of Stalinism, and assisted in the creation of the

Stalin cult (*Bread*, 1937). His chief works are the trilogy on the life of the intelligentsia between 1914 and 1921, *The Road to Calvary*, 1921–1941 (trans. 1946), and the historical novel *Peter I*, 1929–45 (incomplete trans. 1936).

Tolstoy, Count Lev Nikolayevich (1828–1910), great novelist and moral philosopher. He was orphaned at the age of 9, studied at Kazan' University but left before graduating to follow for some years a life of pleasure. He joined the Russian forces in the Caucasus in 1851 and fought against Shamil', and took part in the heroic defence of Sevastopol' during the Crimean War. On arrival in St Petersburg in 1855 he was welcomed with admiration in the literary circles of the capital—by Turgenev, Nekrasov, Goncharov, Ostrovskiy, Chernyshevskiy and others—as a new star in Russian literature. During his time in the Caucasus he had written autobiographical stories (*Childhood*, 1852; *Boyhood*, 1854) and some war stories, in which were already foreshadowed the main features of his future work and his chief contributions to literature—the detailed psychological analysis and the purity of moral sense. These early works were followed by *Tales of Sevastopol'*, 1855, *Youth* (the third part of the autobiographical trilogy), 1857, etc. He travelled widely in western Europe in 1857 and 1860, devoting the second trip to a study of educational methods, and was repelled by its materialism. Tolstoy spent much of his time and energy during the 1860's and seventies upon educational activities, directing a school on his estate (Yasnaya Polyana in Tula province), publishing a magazine and writing textbooks as a pioneer of 'free education.' This period, too, was that of his most intensive literary work: from 1863 to 1869 he was engaged upon *War and Peace*, often held to be the greatest novel in the world, a panorama of Russian society on the eve of and during the Patriotic War against Napoleon in 1812; and from 1873 to 1877 he worked upon *Anna Karenina*, a vigorous and encyclopaedic portrayal of Russia after the emancipation of the serfs. By the time the latter was completed Tolstoy was facing a spiritual crisis and in the following years resolved it by developing a new religious and social philosophy, known as Tolstoyism, which was based upon the belief that the central message of Christ lay in the words 'that ye resist not evil.'

The renunciation of violence and wealth, self-improvement, and love to all living things are the main tenets of Tolstoyism (*A Short Exposition of the Gospels*, 1881; *What I Believe In*, 1883; *A Confession*, 1884; *What Are We To Do?*, 1886). In *What is Art?*, 1896, Tolstoy maintained that art is a means of 'infecting' other people with the feelings the artist has experienced, and rejected the 'superfluous detail' of his own great realistic works. His new philosophy was illustrated and propagated to a greater or lesser degree by all his subsequent imaginative creations (long stories: *The Death of Ivan Il'ich*, 1884, *Kreutzer Sonata*, 1889, *Master and Man*, 1895, *Hadji-Murad*, 1896–1904; the novel *Resurrection*, 1889–99; the plays *The Power of Darkness*, 1886, *Fruits of Enlightenment*, 1890, *The Living Corpse*, 1900; and many popular stories). Excommunication and government animosity resulted from his rejection of Church and State.

The fame of his teachings soon crossed the frontiers of Russia, and for the last fifteen or twenty years of his life Tolstoy was probably the most revered man in the world. Though Yasnaya Polyana became a place of pilgrimage, Tolstoy himself felt increasingly estranged both from it and from his family; he quitted Yasnaya Polyana in secret and died of pneumonia at a small railway station ten days later. Tolstoy the writer has had a deep influence on subsequent literature; Tolstoy the thinker has proved much less influential and his only great disciple was Gandhi. His collected works are being issued in Russia in 90 volumes (60 have appeared 1928–56). Many translations exist, the standard English version being by L. and A. Maude (21 vols.), 1928–37. *See also* R. Rolland, *Tolstoy* (trans. B. Miell), 1911; M. Gorky, *Tolstoy, Chekhov and Andreyev*, 1923; A. Maude, *The Life of Tolstoy* (2 vols.), 1930; J. Lavrin, *Tolstoy, an Approach*, 1944; E. J. Simmons, *Leo Tolstoy*, 1949; G. Steiner, *Tolstoy or Dostoyevsky, an Essay in Contrast*, 1960.

Tomsk: 1. Oblast of the R.S.F.S.R., situated in Western Siberia, traversed by the River Ob' and largely covered by swampy coniferous forests. Area 122,400 sq. m.; population (1959) 750,000 (47 per cent urban), chiefly Russians, some Tatars and Khanty. There are lumbering, wood-processing, metal-working, food and fur-trapping industries; grain and flax are cultivated and dairy farming is carried on. It has been an area of banishment and labour camps (*see* NARYM).

2. Administrative, economic and cultural centre of the oblast, on the River Tom' (a tributary of the Ob'). Population (1959) 249,000 (1914, 112,000; 1926, 92,000; 1939, 145,000). It has engineering, chemical and woodworking industries. The oldest university in Siberia, 1888, is here, also a polytechnical institute, 1900. Tomsk was founded as a fortified town in 1604, and was an important trade and transportation base (on the crossing of river and overland ways) for the further Russian advance into Siberia; it was a provincial capital, 1782–1925, the business centre of a gold-mining area from the 1830's, and from the late 19th century till the 1930's the main cultural centre of Siberia. Its industrial development has taken place since the 1930's and especially since the war.

Torg (originally 'market'), State agency for internal trade in consumer goods; the word usually appears as part of the portmanteau names of different agencies. Each *torg* deals in a particular class of goods. They are subordinated to the Ministries of Trade of the respective Union Republics, and administer chains of shops. All *torgs* and their subordinate shops work on the *khozraschët* (q.v.) principle.

Torgsin (Russian abbreviation for 'Trade Syndicate'), State trading organization with branches in all principal towns which existed from the late 1920's until 1936, a period of acute shortage of food and consumer goods. Jewellery, silver cutlery, gold or silver watches, etc., could be sold at the Torgsin in exchange for food and clothing; pre-revolutionary gold or silver coins, and foreign currency, could also be used at their face value. It was unwise to visit a Torgsin too frequently, since one would be suspected of having a large horde of valuables. Murders were sometimes committed, and graves robbed, in order to acquire gold teeth and rings for exchange at a Torgsin.

Totalitarianism, in the modern sense of a political movement aiming at complete domination by a single centralized party over all socially relevant activities, first appeared in Russia with the emergence of the Leninist trend (*see* LENINISM) within Russian social democracy. Lenin succeeded in creating a totalitarian-minded Bolshevik Party (*see* BOLSHEVISM) and attaining political monopoly of this party. Stalin, following the logic of Lenin's ideas and resorting to the extremes of terror (q.v.), came near to the realization of the totalitarian idea (*see* STALINISM), but failed in the end, notably in relation to religion and the family. The experience of Stalinism would seem to suggest that the totalitarian ideal is altogether unrealizable. After Stalin's death the system of Communist Party (q.v.) control became somewhat less rigid, but the principle itself has been firmly maintained. Totalitarian tendencies also existed in earlier Russian thought—e.g. the 15th–16th-century Church party headed by Joseph of Volokolamsk, or Chernyshevskiy (q.v.) and his followers —but Berdyayev's (q.v.) contention that Russian history consisted essentially of a series of approximations to the totalitarian ideal is exaggerated. *See* H. Arendt, *The Origins of Totalitarianism*, New York, 1951; J. L. Talmon, *The Origins of Totalitarian Democracy*, 1952; C. J. Friedrich (ed.), *Totalitarianism*, Cambridge, Mass., 1954; R. Lowenthal, 'Totalitarianism Reconsidered,' *Commentary*, June 1960.

Towns. The town status is officially recognized or conferred by the presidium of the Supreme Soviet of a Union Republic, though the reasons for such recognition are not entirely clear. The only obvious criterion is that the majority of the inhabitants should be engaged in non-agricultural occupations. But within the category of non-agricultural settlements the distinction between towns proper and urban settlements (q.v.) is not apparent; generally speaking it is size, but there is no definite limit and many towns are smaller than the larger urban settlements. According to the 1959 population census there were 1,694 towns: 222 with population of under 5,000; 284 with population 5,000–10,000; 889 with population 10,000–50,000; 151 with population 50,000–100,000; 123 with population 100,000–500,000; and 25 with a population of 500,000 and over. The following are the principal towns of the country, with a population of over 200,000 (in thousands):

Moscow	5,032	Sverdlovsk	777
Leningrad [1]	3,300	Stalino	701
Kiev	1,102	Tiflis	694
Baku [1]	968	Chelyabinsk	688
Gor'kiy	942	Odessa	667
Khar'kov	930	Dnepropetrovsk	658
Tashkent	911	Kazan'	643
Novosibirsk	887	Perm'	628
Kuybyshev	806	Riga	605

[1] Including numerous urban settlements which are subordinated to the city council.

Rostov-on-Don	597	Zhdanov	284
Stalingrad	591	Vladivostok	283
Saratov	581	Izhevsk	283
Omsk	579	Prokop'yevsk	282
Ufa	546	Tallihn	280
Minsk	509	Kemerovo	277
Yerevan	509	Lugansk	274
Alma-Ata	455	Kalinin	261
Voronezh	454	Orenburg	260
Zaporozh'ye	435	Archangel	256
L'vov	410	Penza	254
Krasnoyarsk	409	Kirov	252
Yaroslavl'	406	Tomsk	249
Karaganda	398	Groznyy	240
Krivoy Rog	386	Vilnius	235
Stalinsk	377	Murmansk	226
Irkutsk	365	Nikolayev	224
Makeyevka	358	Stalinabad	224
Tula	345	Frunze	217
Nizhniy Tagil	338	Kishinev	214
Ivanovo	332	Kaunas	214
Khabarovsk	322	Ryazan'	213
Barnaul	320	Bryansk	206
Krasnodar	312	Ul'yanovsk	205
Magnitogorsk	311	Kursk	203
Astrakhan'	294	Kaliningrad	202
Gorlovka	293	Taganrog	201

Towns are administered by town councils (*see* SOVIETS) under the supervision of the town party committees. Most towns are subordinated to rayon (q.v.) authorities, but the bigger and more important towns (603 in 1958) are subordinated directly to the provincial or Union Republic authorities, and Moscow and Leningrad are directly subordinated to the government of the R.S.F.S.R. Larger towns are subdivided for administrative purposes into a number of rayons. The town councils are responsible for roads and parks, etc., power, water and sewage services, education and health, and partly for housing; in the larger towns they administer the majority of houses, though these are owned by the State. *See* G. Jorré, *The Soviet Union, the Land and its People*, 3rd imp., 1955; M. Tikhomirov, *The Towns of Ancient Rus*, Moscow, 1959.

'Toz' (Russian abbreviation for 'Partnership for the Cultivation of Land'), rudimentary form of collective farming practised in the 1920's which consisted of a number of peasants pooling their draught animals and mechanical equipment in order to cultivate their land together, though its tenure remained individual. The practice was neither widespread nor compulsory, though it was encouraged by the authorities. During the collectivization of agriculture the *tozes* were abolished and replaced by *kolkhozes* (q.v.).

Trade officially exists in three forms of 'socialist' trade: State, cooperative and *kolkhoz* (*see* KOLKHOZ MARKET). The State and cooperatives (chiefly consumers' co-operatives, but also production co-operatives) engage in both wholesale (officially defined as trade between enterprises, q.v.) and retail trade. State trade is primarily organized for urban areas, while the bulk of rural trade is carried on by co-operatives. All the officially recognized forms of trade are regulated by the authorities, State and co-operative through direct planning, and the *kolkhoz* market by manipulating the supply of goods in State and co-operative shops. However, the bureaucratic machinery for regulating trade is frequently inefficient, causing shortages even when supplies are plentiful, and sometimes surpluses. Apart from the officially recognized forms of trade, there still exists private trading (*see* SPECULATORS). During the period of War Communism (q.v.) an attempt was made to abolish internal trade altogether; it was again permitted with the introduction of the New Economic Policy (q.v.), and although private trade was again suppressed by 1930 trade is considered an integral part of the socialist economy. Stalin's suggestion in 1952 that trade should soon give way to direct exchange of goods has been rejected since his death. *See further under* FOREIGN TRADE; PRICES; RETAIL TRADE.

Trade Unions. There were 47 trade unions at the beginning of 1957 with a total membership of 49 million; a fusion in June reduced their number to 23. All unions are formed on the industrial principle of organization, that is, with employees of a particular branch of the economy or administration belonging to the same union; there are no craft or general unions. Membership is open to all workers, employees, students and pupils of professional secondary and Vocational Technical schools; agricultural workers, that is those employed at the *sovkhozes* (q.v.) and Technical Repair Stations (*see* M.T.S.), may be trade union members, but *kolkhoz* (q.v.) peasants may not, since they are not wage-earners but officially co-owners of the farms. Independent professional people such as writers, etc., have their own professional associations (q.v.). Formally the structure of the trade unions is based on the principle of democratic centralism (q.v.), with primary organizations in factories and offices electing their committees (or organizers in case of fewer than 25 members) and territorial committees, and the central committee of each union being elected at conferences or congresses. Trade Union Councils exist to co-ordinate the activities of different unions on the provincial and republic levels. The highest body is the All-Union Central Council of Trade Unions, elected at a general Trade Union Congress which by statute is held every four years. In fact all trade union activities are controlled by the party organizations on all levels, and all the more important appointments are decided upon by the cadres (q.v.) departments of the party committees (*see also* NOMENCLATURE).

Ostensibly Soviet trade unions have all the normal trade union functions, and even go through the formality of collective agreements (q.v.). The higher level trade union committees form an integral part of the party and government apparatus, and as such take part in handling problems of concern to the trade unions. Lower level trade union organizations, however, are usually active and helpful in securing to their members their rights in matters of pay, etc., but they may not initiate demands for wage increases. Apart from these normal trade union functions, Soviet trade unions administer the State social insurance fund (since the abolition of the Commissariat of Labour in

1930), that is, the paying of sickness benefits and the financing and administering of health resorts. One of the chief tasks of the trade unions is to organize socialist emulation (q.v.) and such campaigns as the Stakhanov movement (q.v.) and the current campaign for setting up 'teams of communist labour,' etc., which are often detrimental to the interests of union members. The unions are charged with the political indoctrination of their members, but also do valuable work in the field of recreation and sport.

A law of 1874 forbidding societies which stimulated hatred between employers and workers hindered the development of trade unions in Russia, and such organizations of trade union type as existed from the 1870's were mostly illegal, though some were more successful in the 1890's. The first legal mass organizations of a trade union type were those set up by Zubatov and Gapon (qq.v.) in 1901–3 (see also POLICE SOCIALISM); these gave valuable experience to their members, which was utilized in the first genuine trade unions which were established (chiefly as craft unions) during the revolution of 1905 (q.v.); by 1907 membership numbered about 250,000, and by the time of the Bolshevik seizure of power (see OCTOBER REVOLUTION) in 1917 it was over 2 million. From the beginning there developed rivalry for influence in the unions between the Bolsheviks, Mensheviks, Economists (see ECONOMISM) and syndicalists (see SYNDICALISM). Lenin viewed the trade unions solely as a tool of the party (see LENINISM) and used the English word 'trade-unionism' as a term of abuse. The Mensheviks, particularly the so-called 'liquidationists' (see LIQUIDATIONISM), were much closer to appreciating the real nature of trade-unionism, and were more influential in the unions, sometimes maintaining their influence until the early 1920's. Because of this, to by-pass the official trade union leadership, the Bolsheviks created, in 1917, a network of factory committees under their own leadership, which were of assistance during the October revolution. Between 1917 and 1922 the unions were brought, sometimes forcibly, under complete Bolshevik control, though there were disagreements among the Bolsheviks themselves about the correct policy towards them, with Trotskiy, Bukharin and the Workers' Opposition opposing Lenin's line. See also LABOUR DISCIPLINE; LABOUR DISPUTES; STRIKES. See I. Deutscher, Soviet Trade Unions, 1950; S. M. Schwarz, Labor in the Soviet Union, New York, 1951; H. Seton-Watson, The Decline of Imperial Russia, 1952; M. Fainsod, How Russia is Ruled, Cambridge, Mass., 1953; M. Dewar, Labour Policy in the Soviet Union, 1917–28, 1956; T. T. Hammond, Lenin on Trade Unions and Revolution, 1893–1917, New York, 1957.

Transbaykalia, or **Dauria,** mountainous region in south-eastern Siberia between Lake Baykal in the west and Amur Oblast in the east, with forested ranges and steppe valleys, rich in mineral resources. It was annexed by Russia in the 17th century. See BURYAT AUTONOMOUS REPUBLIC; CHITA.

Transcarpathia, oblast in Western Ukraine adjacent to the Hungarian and Czechoslovak frontiers, situated on the southern slopes of the Carpathian Mountains and the neighbouring lowland in the south-west; there are deposits of salt and lignite. Area 4,900 sq. m.;

population (1959) 923,000 (28 per cent urban), chiefly Ukrainians and Hungarians. Maize, wheat and potatoes are cultivated, there is viniculture and horticulture, livestock is raised, and there are timber, wood-processing, salt- and coal-mining, and food industries. The mountainous part of the oblast attracts many tourists. Principal towns: Uzhgorod (administrative centre) and Mukachevo. The area belonged to Hungary from the 11th century, to Czechoslovakia (as an autonomous unit), 1919–39, to Hungary again, and from 1944 to the U.S.S.R., being formally ceded by Czechoslovakia in 1945. *See* J. B. Heisler and J. E. Mellon, *Under the Carpathians*, 1946; F. Nemec and V. Moudry, *The Soviet Seizure of Sub-Carpathian Ruthenia*, Toronto, 1955.

Transcaspian Oblast, former administrative unit which included most of the present Turkmen Republic except the Turkmen parts of the Amu-Dar'ya and Khorezm oases, with Ashkhabad as administrative centre. It was formed after the Russian conquest of the area in 1869–85, and abolished in 1924 when the Turkmen Republic was formed.

Transcaucasia, area bounded by the main Caucasian range in the north, the U.S.S.R. frontiers with Turkey and Persia in the south, and the Black and Caspian seas in the west and east, comprising the Union Republics of Armenia, Azerbaydzhan and Georgia. The latter joined Russia voluntarily, but the other parts of Transcaucasia were captured in the 19th century from Persia and Turkey, on the whole with the consent or even support of the inhabitants. The pre-revolutionary period of Russian rule was one of economic and cultural advance and the emergence of a native intelligentsia with autonomist views. Transcaucasia left Russia after the Bolshevik seizure of power (*see* TRANSCAUCASIAN FEDERATION), but was conquered in 1920 by the Red Army assisted by local Communists. A Transcaucasian Union Republic existed until 1936, when it was broken up into the Union Republics of Armenia, Azerbaydzhan and Georgia. The area is an important producer of oil, manganese ore, tea, citrus fruits and wine. Transcaucasians, especially Armenians and Georgians, have played a significant role in Russian political life during the 19th and 20th centuries.

Transcaucasian Federation, short-lived state established in 1917 after the Bolshevik seizure of power, declared in April 1918 to be an independent democratic republic. Georgian Mensheviks, the Azerbaydzhani party Mussavat (q.v.) and the Armenian party Dashnaktsutyun (q.v.) dominated its legislative assembly, which consisted of Transcaucasian members of the All-Russian Constituent Assembly (q.v.). In May 1918 the federation dissolved into the republics of Armenia, Azerbaydzhan and Georgia as a result of the unfavourable international situation: the Turkish invasion to gain possession of the territories ceded to her by Soviet Russia in the treaty of Brest-Litovsk, and conflicts between the parties that arose from the predominantly pro-Turkish attitude of the Mussavat. After the three republics had been conquered by the Red Army, a Transcaucasian Socialist Federal Soviet Republic was formed in 1922, becoming a Union Republic of the U.S.S.R. in the same year. In 1936 this republic was abolished and Armenia, Azerbaydzhan and Georgia were established as Union Republics. *See* F. Kazemzadeh, *The Struggle for Transcaucasia*, New York, 1951; R. Pipes, *The Formation of the Soviet Union*, Cambridge, Mass., 1954.

Transnistria, name applied by the Rumanians to the Rumanian zone of occupation, 1941–4, in the south-west Ukraine between the rivers Dniester (Rumanian Nistrul) and Southern Bug; Odessa was the capital.

Transoxania (Latin rendering of the Arabic Mawara'nnahr), medieval name of the region in Central Asia between the rivers Amu-Dar'ya (Oxus) and Syr-Dar'ya and the adjacent area east of the middle course of the Syr-Dar'ya. This region, known in antiquity as Sogdiana (q.v.), was conquered by the Arabs in 672–709. The authority of the caliphate was challenged by the pseudo-prophet Mukanna, who led a strong religious and social movement in the 770's and eighties, and by the indigenous dynasty of Samanids in 875–999, whose capital was Bukhara. After the fall of the Samanids the region belonged successively to the ephemeral states of Kara-khanids, Seljukids and Karakitay, and for a few years to Khorezm. In 1220 Transoxania was conquered by Genghis Khan, and later belonged to the Chagatay *ulus* of the Mongol empire. Timur, a native of Transoxania, again made it the nucleus of a great empire with Samarkand as capital. His successors ruled the country until it was conquered by the Uzbek nomads under Sheybani Khan in 1500–7. For later history *see* BUKHARA KHANATE. During the 9th–11th centuries Islam became the religion of the majority of the population in Transoxania, replacing Zoroastrianism, Nestorian Christianity and Manichaeism, and Bukhara and Samarkand were among the chief centres of Islamic learning and art. Both Arabic and native Iranian were used by the scholars and poets. Penetration by large numbers of Turkic-speaking nomads after the fall of the Samanids resulted in the Turkicization of a part of the sedentary population, and the creation of a Turkic literary language known as Chagatay which was used in Central Asia until after 1917. *See* V. V. Barthold, *Four Studies on the History of Central Asia*, vols. i and ii, Leyden, 1956.

Transport. Freight traffic by all means of transportation (excluding by horse) was 1,604·8 milliard ton-kilometres in 1958 (114·5 in 1913); total passenger traffic (excluding by horse and by civil aviation) was 206·4 milliard passenger-kilometres (27·6 in 1913). Of total freight traffic in 1958, railways accounted for 81·2 per cent (57·4 per cent in 1913), water (inland and sea) transport 11·9 per cent (42·2 per cent in 1913), motor transport 4·8 per cent (0·1 per cent in 1913) and pipelines 2·1 per cent (0·3 per cent in 1913). *See further under* CIVIL AVIATION; RAILWAYS; RIVER TRANSPORT; ROAD TRANSPORT; SHIPPING. *See* H. Hunter, *Soviet Transportation Policy*, Cambridge, Mass., 1957; *The Soviet Seven Year Plan* (introduction by A. Nove), 1960.

Transport Courts, special courts for criminal cases connected with railways or water transport; established in 1930–4, they were abolished in 1957.

Trans-Siberian Railway, longest railway in the world, running from Chelyabinsk in the Urals to Vladivostok on the Pacific, 4,388 m. The railway was constructed between 1891 and 1915, most of it with great speed between 1891 and 1899. Russian colonization of Siberia and the Far East was greatly facilitated by the railway. During its construction important geological prospecting took place (of the Kuznetsk, Karaganda, Ekibastuz and Cheremkhovo coal basins, and the Amur and Kolyma gold deposits) which laid the foundations of Siberia's future industrial expansion. A through service operates from Moscow to Peking over the Trans-Siberian and the Changchun railways. Electrification of the line is in progress, and has already (1960) been completed as far as Irkutsk. *See* D. W. Treadgold, *The Great Siberian Migration*, Princeton, N.J., 1957.

Troitse-Sergiyeva Lavra, monastery of the Holy Trinity, the largest Russian Orthodox monastery, founded by St Sergius of Radonezh *c.* 1340. It is situated 44 m. north of Moscow and is now within the town of Zagorsk. There are outstanding architectural monuments of the 15th–18th centuries: the Cathedral of the Holy Trinity, built in the Early Muscovite style, 1423, the Cathedral of the Assumption, 1559–85, the baroque bell-tower, 1741–70, etc. The monastery was an important religious, cultural and political centre from the 14th to 17th centuries, and supported the centralistic policies of the Muscovite princes and czars. In 1920 it was abolished and transformed into a museum. It has housed the Moscow Theological Academy from 1814 to 1918 and since 1948, and is the residence of the Patriarch.

Troitsk, town in the Chelyabinsk Oblast (Urals), situated 85 m. south of Chelyabinsk. Population (1959) 76,000. It has food (flour mills, meat packing) and light industries; several engineering plants and a big thermal power-station are under construction. It is an important railway junction and a local cultural centre; in the vicinity there are several sanatoria treating tubercular and other patients with koumiss. Troitsk was founded as a Russian fortress in 1743 and had a lively trade with Central Asia.

Troitskosavsk, *see* KYAKHTA.

Trotsk, *see* CHAPAYEVSK.

Trotskiy (real name Bronshteyn), Lev Davidovich (1879–1940), politician of Jewish birth who joined the Social Democratic movement in 1896, was banished to Siberia, escaped abroad and joined the Iskra (q.v.) organization. He became a Menshevik at the party split in 1903 and maintained that Lenin's organizational principles would result in a one-man dictatorship. As chairman of the St Petersburg Soviet he played a leading role in the 1905 revolution, was once more arrested and banished, and again escaped abroad, where he continued his opposition to Lenin's dictatorial tactics and attempted to reconcile all the factions and groups of Russian social democracy. Together with Martov he led the internationalist wing of the Mensheviks during the First World War, was expelled from France for pacifist propaganda, and lived in the U.S.A. He left for Russia after the February 1917 revolution, but for several weeks was held by the British at Halifax, Nova Scotia. In Russia Trotskiy soon joined the Bolsheviks and became Lenin's chief supporter in organizing the October revolution. He headed the St Petersburg Soviet and its Military Revolutionary Committee, and carried out the seizure of power in the capital. Commissar for Foreign Affairs, 1917–18, he represented Soviet Russia at Brest-Litovsk (q.v.), but opposed the conclusion of the treaty and resigned; 1918–25 Commissar for War, the chief organizer and leader of the Red Army during the civil war; 1919–27 a Politburo member, repeatedly opposing Lenin.

Trotskiy was deprived of power in Russia itself and in the world Communist movement by Stalin, Zinov'yev and Kamenev after Lenin's death, but persisted in fighting back, later joining forces with Zinov'yev and Kamenev in the 'combined opposition' (see LEFT OPPOSITION) until his expulsion from the party in 1927, banishment to Central Asia in 1928 and expulsion from Russia in 1929. During the Great Purge (q.v.) he was accused of espionage and subversive activities on behalf of foreign intelligence services, and was eventually murdered by Soviet agents in Mexico City, where he passed the last years of his life. In several countries followers of Trotskiy still exist as Communist splinter groups, and they constitute an important political party in Ceylon. See his *Our Revolution*, 1918, *The Defence of Terrorism*, 1921, *Literature and Revolution*, 1925, *My Life*, 1930, *The History of the Russian Revolution* (3 vols.), 1932–3, *The Revolution Betrayed*, 1937, *The Stalin School of Falsification*, 1937, *Stalin*, 1946, and *Diary in Exile 1935*, 1958; B. D. Wolfe, *Three who made a Revolution*, 1948; S. Salazar, *Murder in Mexico*, 1950; E. H. Carr, *The Interregnum, 1923–4*, 1954; I. Deutscher, *The Prophet Armed*, 1954, and *The Prophet Unarmed*, 1959; I. Don Levine, *The Mind of an Assassin*, 1960; L. Schapiro, *The Communist Party of the Soviet Union*, 1960.

Troubles, Time of (1598–1613), period between the extinction of the House of Rurikids and the establishment of the House of Romanov when there was widespread popular and Cossack unrest, invasions by Sweden and Poland, and five czars in Moscow at different times whose claims were doubtful (including an impostor and a Polish prince). The Time of Troubles came to an end with the expulsion of the Poles from Moscow by a volunteer army under K. Minin and Prince Pozharskiy, and the election of Michael Romanov as czar.

Troyka ('triumvirate'), colloquial name for three-man commissions set up by the security organs (q.v.) for the quick disposal of 'counter-revolutionary' cases through summary death or concentration camp (see CORRECTIVE LABOUR CAMP) sentences. In 1934–53 the *troykas* acted as branches of the Special Board (q.v.). The practice is said to have been abolished after Stalin's death and Beria's fall in 1953 and was officially abolished by the legal reform (q.v.) of 1958. See S. Wolin and R. M. Slusser (eds.), *The Soviet Secret Police*, New York, 1957; H. J. Berman, 'Soviet Law Reform—Dateline Moscow 1957,' *Yale Law Journal*, vol. lxvi, No. 8, July 1957; D. J. R. Scott, *Russian Political Institutions*, 1958.

Trubetskoy, Prince Nikolay Sergeyevich (1890–1938), son of Sergey, philologist and philosopher, professor at Vienna University from 1923. He studied the Slavonic, Finnish and Caucasian languages and was a protagonist of a new approach in linguistics—phonology, the science of vocal sounds. He was an ideological leader of the Eurasians (q.v.), 1921–8, and in *To the Problem of Russian Self-Knowledge*, 1927, he sets out his views on the Asiatic elements in the origins and culture of Russia. *See* his *Principes de Phonologie*, Paris, 1949; N. O. Lossky, *History of Russian Philosophy*, 1952; V. V. Zenkovsky, *A History of Russian Philosophy*, vol. ii, 1953.

Trubetskoy, Prince Sergey Nikolayevich (1862–1905), philosopher, professor at Moscow University, editor of the leading philosophical journal *Problems of Philosophy and Psychology*. He played a prominent role in the constitutional movement prior to the revolution of 1905, and became famous for his address to Nicholas II as spokesman of a *zemstvo* and municipal deputation. He attempted to combine in his works the Hegelian rationalistic idealism with the mysticism of V. Solov'ëv. His writings include *Metaphysics in Ancient Greece*, 1890, *On the Nature of Human Consciousness*, 1891, *The Foundations of Idealism*, 1896, *The Doctrine of Logos and its History*, 1900, and *Belief in Immortality*, 1908. *See* O. Trubetskaya, *Knyaz' S. N. Trubetskoy*, New York, 1953.

Trubetskoy, Prince Yevgeniy Nikolayevich (1863–1920), brother of Sergey, a legal philosopher (follower of V. Solov'ëv) and liberal politician. He was a professor at Kiev and Moscow universities, and edited *Moscow Weekly*. His principal works are *Religious and Social Ideal of Western Christianity in the Fifth Century, St Augustine*, 1892, *Religious and Social Ideal of Western Christianity in the Eleventh Century, Gregory VII and his Contemporaries*, 1897, *The Philosophy of Nietzsche*, 1904, *The Philosophy of Vl. Solov'ëv* (2 vols.), 1913, *Lectures on the Encyclopaedia of Law*, 1916, *The Metaphysical Assumptions of Knowledge*, 1917, and *The Meaning of Life*, 1918.

Trudoviks ('Labourists'), parliamentary party in the State Duma. It did not exist outside the Duma, and was largely parliamentary representation for the Socialist Revolutionaries and Popular Socialists. The Deputies were mostly peasants or intellectuals of peasant origin, including some village priests. The leader of the party in the 4th Duma was Kerenskiy.

'Trust,' code name for a G.P.U. operation which was carried out in the 1920's with the purpose of undermining efforts at underground anti-Soviet activities. The chief exploit of the 'Trust' was the visit of a monarchist *émigré* leader, Shulgin (q.v.), to the Soviet Union, where he met G.P.U. agents masquerading as members of a large monarchist underground movement. The discovery of the true nature of the 'Trust' soon afterwards was a severe blow to the idea of an underground movement.

Trusts, units of economic management combining a number of horizontally integrated enterprises, that is, enterprises producing similar products. *See also* ENTERPRISE; INDUSTRIAL MANAGEMENT.

Tsar, *see* CZAR.

Tsaritsyn, *see* STALINGRAD.

Tsarskoe Selo, *see* PUSHKIN.

Tsiolkovskiy, Konstantin Eduardovich (1857–1935), pioneer in rocketry and the theory of cosmic travel, a school-teacher by profession. Though regarded as a crank in his own time, he laid the foundations, 1903, for much of the later work in this field.

Tuapse, town in the Krasnodar Kray, a port on the Black Sea. Population (1956) 34,100. It has oil-refining, engineering (oil industry equipment, the largest ship-repair plant in the Black Sea area) and food industries; oil is exported (pipeline from Groznyy). Tuapse was founded in 1838 as a fort and saw much fighting in 1942.

Tugan-Baranovskiy, Mikhail Ivanovich (1865–1919), economist of Ukrainian parentage, professor at St Petersburg University. He was one of the chief Legal Marxists (q.v.) in the 1890's but later endeavoured to combine Marxism with marginal analysis. In 1918 he was Minister of Finance in the Ukrainian government of Hetman Skoropads'kyy. His main works are *Crises in Contemporary England,* 1894, *Russian Factory, Past and Present,* 1898 (7th ed. 1938), and *Fundamentals of Political Economy,* 1909.

Tuition Fees at present are only charged in certain categories of educational establishments, e.g. boarding-schools (q.v.) and some adult education institutions. All tuition fees were abolished immediately after the October revolution in 1917, but were reintroduced, except in primary schools, during the period of the New Economic Policy, when they were graded according to the official social class of the parents. Fees were again abolished in the early 1930's, but reintroduced once more in 1940 for the three upper classes of secondary schools, for professional secondary schools and for higher educational establishments. They were again abolished in 1957.

Tukhachevskiy, Mikhail Nikolayevich (1893–1937), Marshal of the Soviet Union. Of noble origin, he was educated at a military school, and from 1914 took part in the world war as an officer. In 1918 he joined the Bolshevik Party and volunteered for the Red Army, where he immediately made a spectacular career—army commander in 1918–19, commander of all Red forces in the Caucasus at the beginning of 1920, and in the West (against Poland) later on. In 1921 he commanded the government forces against the Kronstadt uprising and against Antonov (qq.v.), later headed the Military Academy, commanded the Western and Leningrad military districts, and was deputy chief, 1924, and chief of staff, 1925–8, of the Red Army. From 1931 he was Deputy Commissar for Military and Naval Affairs and deputy chairman of the Revolutionary Military Council, becoming in 1935 one of the first five Marshals of the Soviet Union; he was the most influential military personality of the time. During the Great Purge (q.v.) in 1937 he was accused of heading a military conspiracy, and together with a number of other generals was tried in secret and shot. His reputation was rehabilitated in 1958. At the time of the Soviet-Polish War Tukhachevskiy developed the doctrine of spreading socialist revolution by force of Soviet arms. *See* N. Rutych, *KPSS u vlasti,* Frankfurt-am-Main, 1960.

Tula: 1. Oblast of the R.S.F.S.R., situated south of Moscow on the Central Russian upland, with some mixed forests in the north and black earth soil in the south; there are deposits of lignite (*see* MOSCOW LIGNITE BASIN), iron ore and various building materials. Area 9,900 sq. m.; population (1959) 1,912,000 (61 per cent urban). There are metal-working (since the 16th century), coal-mining and chemical industries, grain and potato cultivation, dairy cattle and pig raising. Principal towns: Tula, Stalinogorsk.

2. Administrative and economic centre of the oblast, the main industrial centre of the Moscow Lignite Basin, situated 120 m. south of the capital. Population (1959) 345,000 (1917, 157,000; 1920, 128,000; 1939, 285,000). It has large iron and steel (two plants), engineering (arms, machine tools, transportation equipment) and other metal-working industries. The town is an important railway junction. A 16th-century kremlin has been preserved, and the famous country house of L. Tolstoy, Yasnaya Polyana, is near by. Known since 1146, Tula belonged to Ryazan' Principality, became Muscovite in 1503 (frequently raided by the Crimean Tatars) and provincial capital in 1775. It is an old centre of the metal-working industry (supplying arms to the Muscovite government from 1595), the largest in Russia until overtaken by the Urals in the 18th century; until the 1920's it was the second largest town in central Russia. In 1941 German forces approached Tula but were repulsed.

Tungus, a number of small peoples mostly living in Siberia and the Russian Far East who speak Tungus (or Tungus-Manchu) languages, and number (1959) 45,200. The most numerous of them are the Evenki (q.v.). They are reindeer breeders, hunters and fishers, and practise the animistic religion of Shamanism.

Tupolev, Andrey Nikolayevich (*b.* 1888), aircraft designer, lieutenant-general in the air force, member of the Academy of Sciences. Educated at the Moscow Higher Technical School, where he studied under N. Ye. Zhukovskiy, he took the initiative in 1916 in setting up the Aerodynamic Aircraft Design Bureau which later developed into the Central Institute of Aerodynamics and Hydrodynamics. Since then he has designed or directed the building of about a hundred civil and military aeroplanes, including the famous ANT 25 in the 1930's and the modern TU 104 and TU 114. Tupolev was arrested in 1938 at the height of the Great Purge (q.v.) and his name was not mentioned in public until his release and rehabilitation in 1943. However, while in prison he was allowed to continue his work.

Tura, capital of the Evenki National Okrug in the Krasnoyarsk Kray (central Siberia), situated on the lower Tunguska River (a right tributary of the Yenisey). Population (1956) 2,100. Tura was founded in 1927 as a 'cultural base' by the Committee of the North (q.v.).

Turgenev, Ivan Sergeyevich (1818–83), first Russian author to gain an international reputation. His chief works are *Sportsman's Sketches,* 1847–52, a series of stories of Russian peasants which, with the vigour of its attacks on serfdom, made a deep impression upon Russian educated society; and the novels *Rudin,* 1856, *A House of Gentlefolk,* 1859, *On the Eve,* 1860, *Fathers and Children,* 1862, *Smoke,* 1867, and *Virgin Soil,* 1877, which portrayed from a liberal point of view the psychology and the intellectual searchings of Russian society in the 1830's–1870's. Turgenev lived mostly in Germany and France after 1855; and in Paris, where he lived from 1870, he became widely popular, the French translations of his works bringing him worldwide fame. *See* his *Works,* trans. by Constance Garnett (14 vols.), 1894–9; *Literary Reminiscences* (trans. D. Magarshack), 1958;

A. Yarmolinsky, *Turgenev*, 1926 (2nd ed., New York, 1959); D. Magarshack, *Turgenev, a Life*, 1954; R. H. Freeborn, *Turgenev, the Novelist's Novelist*, 1960.

Turkestan: 1. (properly Turkistan). Obsolescent name for the geographical and historical area in Asia which comprises the Central Asian Union Republics of the U.S.S.R. together with southern Kazakhstan (formerly known as Russian Turkestan), Sinkiang (Eastern or Chinese Turkestan) and the northern part of Afghanistan (Afghan Turkestan). The term has been known since the 9th century, when it was used by the Iranians of Central Asia to denote the area, inhabited by Turkic-speaking nomads, between the Muslim Transoxania (q.v.) and China, i.e. chiefly the present-day southern Kazakhstan, Kirgizia and Sinkiang. After the Uzbek conquest of Transoxania the term Turkestan was extended to cover the latter. The Uzbeks transferred the capital from Samarkand to Bukhara, but were unable to preserve the political unity of the area. Not only did Khorezm reassert its independence, but by the beginning of the 18th century the rest of Turkestan broke up into a number of separate principalities, the most important of which proved to be the Kokand Khanate (q.v.). In 1740 Bukhara and Khorezm were conquered by the Persians, but soon regained independence. The whole of western Turkestan was conquered by the Russians in a series of campaigns between 1864 and 1885. It was annexed to Russia and ruled by a Governor-General of Turkestan (resident in Tashkent), except for the Khorezm and Bukhara khanates which, reduced in size, became Russian protectorates. In 1916 there was an anti-Russian uprising in Turkestan prompted by the mobilization of the native population, who had hitherto been exempt from military service, for work in the rear of the fighting troops. In November 1917 an autonomous government of Turkestan was formed at a congress in Kokand of Muslim organizations and Russian anti-Bolshevik representatives, but this 'Kokand autonomy' as it came to be known was suppressed by the Red Guards and the Cheka early in 1918, and a Turkestan Autonomous Soviet Republic formed which existed until the so-called National Delimitation of Central Asia (q.v.). Throughout 1918–24 the main concern of the Soviet authorities in Turkestan was the struggle against the Basmachi (q.v.) guerrilla movement. *See* E. D. Sokol, *The Revolt of 1917 in Russian Central Asia*, Baltimore, 1954; V. V. Barthold, *Four Studies on the History of Central Asia*, vols. i and ii, Leyden, 1956; A. G. Park, *Bolshevism in Turkestan*, New York, 1957; M. Holdsworth, *Turkestan in the Nineteenth Century*, 1959; F. Maclean, *A Person from England and Other Travellers*, 1959; R. A. Pierce, *Russian Central Asia, 1867–1917*, Berkeley and Los Angeles, 1960; S. A. Zenkovsky, *Pan-Turkism and Islam in Russia*, Cambridge, Mass., 1960.

2. Town in the South Kazakhstan Oblast on the Orenburg–Tashkent railway, about 145 m. north of Tashkent. Population (1956) 40,000. It is the centre of a cotton-growing area, and has some cotton-processing industry. The 15th-century mausoleum built at Timur's command in memory of the Muslim saint Khodzha-Akhmet Yasevi is still standing in the old Uzbek part of the town, and is a place of

pilgrimage for the Muslims of Central Asia. The larger, new part of the town is chiefly occupied by Russians and Kazakhs. Turkestan, known in antiquity as Khazret and in the Middle Ages as Yasy, was for many centuries an important centre of crafts and commerce on the trade route from Central Asia to the north.

Turkmenia, Union Republic of the U.S.S.R., situated in the south-west of Central Asia bordering on the Caspian Sea, Persia and Afghanistan; the southernmost point of the U.S.S.R. (35° 8′ N.) lies in the republic, which is chiefly desert lowland with the Kopet-Dag range in the south. There are oil, ozokerite, sulphur and glauber salt (in the Kara-Bogaz-Gol bay of the Caspian Sea) deposits. Area 188,500 sq. m.; population (1959) 1,516,000 (46 per cent urban; 1939, 1,252,000), Turkmens (61 per cent in 1959), mostly in the rural parts, also Russians (17 per cent), Uzbeks (8 per cent), Kazakhs (5 per cent), etc. The settlers, living mostly in the towns and along the Persian and Afghan frontiers, include Russians, Ukrainians, Armenians and Azerbaydzhanis. There is oil extraction and refining near the Caspian Sea shore, and there are chemical (glauber salt, ozokerite, iodine and bromide), light (cotton, silk, wool, leather and Astrakhan sheepskin) and some food industries; a carpet-weaving craft is widely practised. Cotton and silk are cultivated on irrigated land in the oases, and sheep (Astrakhan breed) and horses (Akhal-Teke and Yomud breeds) are pastured in the deserts. Turkmenia is traversed by the Trans-Caspian Railway, with branches from Chardzhou to Khorezm along the left bank of the Amu-Dar'ya and from Mary to the Afghan frontier. The capital of the republic is Ashkhabad, and there are three oblasts (Mary, Chardzhou and Tashauz) which comprise oases and their surrounding deserts; in the 1940's and fifties there were also Ashkhabad, Krasnovodsk and Kerki oblasts. For history *see* Buk-hara Khanate; Khorezm; Margiana; Turkestan. The area, except the Amu-Dar'ya and Khorezm oases, was conquered by Russia in 1869–85. In 1918 the Bolshevik power was overthrown in Turkmenia and a Trans-Caspian government set up in Ashkhabad, enjoying some British support. Bolshevik rule was re-established by 1920, and in the National Delimitation of Central Asia (q.v.) in 1924 the Turkmen Republic was formed. *See* P. Skosyrev, *Soviet Turk-menistan*, Moscow, 1956, and the journal *Central Asian Review*.

Turkmens, Turkic-speaking people mainly inhabiting the oases of the Turkmen Republic; a small number live in the south of Uz-bekistan and Tadzhikistan, and about 15,000 in the Stavropol' Kray (North Caucasus). In 1959 they numbered 1 million. The Turkmens are a Muslim people and engage chiefly in animal husbandry and agriculture; their carpet-weaving craft is well known, and Turkmen horses are still famous, though their breeding has declined since the advent of Russian rule. Unlike other Central Asian peoples, Turkmens still retain tribal and clan divisions. They are the direct descendants of the medieval Oguz tribes (to whom the Seljuk and Osman Turks also belonged). Until the 1880's the Turkmens were partly under varying degrees of domination by Khorezm, Bukhara and Persia, and partly independent, but they had no government authorities of their own. They were then semi-nomadic and one of their chief occupations was raiding Persia in order to capture people to be sold as slaves in Khiva and Bukhara. Russian rule was established over all Turkmens during the first half of the 1880's, with fierce resistance from one tribe, the Teke of the Akhal oasis (the Ashkhabad area); the other tribes remained passive or even sided with the Russians.

Turks. Most of the Turkic-speaking peoples live in Russia and all four branches of the family are represented. The North-western, or Kypchak, branch comprises the peoples living in the Volga area, the Urals, Western Siberia, the north of Central Asia and the North Caucasus—Tatars, Bashkirs, Altays, Kazakhs, Kara-Kalpaks, Kirgiz, Kumyks, Nogays, Karachays and Balkars. The North-eastern branch comprises those living in eastern and southern Siberia —Yakuts, Khakas, Tuvinians and Shorians. To the south-eastern or Kashgar, branch belong the Uzbeks and Uygurs (most of the latter live in Chinese Turkestan), and to the south-western, or Oguz, branch belong the Turkmens, Azerbaydzhanis, Crimean Tatars, Gagauz and Karaim. The Chuvash, whose language also belongs to the Turkic family, are outside the four main groups. The original home of the Turks was the area south and east of the Altay Mountains, which in the 6th century formed the nucleus of the first large Turkic empire, including most of Central Asia and southern Siberia. From the 6th century onwards the Turks gradually penetrated the steppes and deserts of Central Asia and the southern part of European Russia (*see* CUMANS; KHAZARS; VOLGA BULGARIANS), from time to time forming ephemeral states which imposed their rule on the Iranian-speaking sedentary population; the most important of these states was the great Seljuk empire of the 11th century. The Mongol conquest of Central Asia and European Russia led in fact to a firmer Turkic domination. The supremacy of the Golden Horde (q.v.) over the Russian principalities lasted for two and a half centuries, while in Central Asia there was unbroken Turkic rule from then onwards until the area was annexed to Russia in the 19th century. During this period in Central Asia the process of Turkicization of the Iranian inhabitants continued, and the Turkic-speaking peoples now make up the overwhelming majority of the indigenous population there. *See* Sir O. Caroe, *Soviet Empire: the Turks of Central Asia and Stalinism*, 1953; S. Wurm, *Turkic Peoples of the U.S.S.R.*, 1954; V. V. Barthold, *Four Studies on the History of Central Asia*, vols. i and ii, Leyden, 1956; C. W. Hostler, *Turkism and the Soviets*, 1957; R. Loewenthal, *The Turkic Languages and Literature of Central Asia, a Bibliography*, The Hague, 1957; S. A. Zenkovsky, *Pan-Turkism and Islam in Russia*, Cambridge, Mass., 1960.

Turksib, abbreviation for Turkestan-Siberian Railway, the important railway which connects the Trans-Siberian and the Orenburg–Tashkent lines. It runs through Novosibirsk Oblast, Altay Kray and south-eastern Kazakhstan. It was built 1913–30 and was acclaimed by the Communists as the first great achievement of the Five Year Plan.

Turnover Tax, sales tax levied primarily on consumer goods and calculated as the difference between two wholesale prices (q.v.)— that paid by wholesalers to the producers, and by retailers to the wholesalers—which are both independently fixed by the authorities, minus trade discount. The average rate of turnover tax was 54·7 per cent of the retail price in 1953 (77·8 per cent in 1947). For a long time the rates were highest, and possibly still are, for bread (rye bread, 86 per cent in 1940, 60–72 per cent in 1953). In the case of food, the burden of turnover tax is borne by the peasants (since the procurement prices, *see* AGRICULTURAL PROCUREMENT, paid by the State for agricultural products were until 1953 generally, and in some cases may still be, below cost). There are both progressive and regressive elements in the turnover tax system, but the overall effect is regressive. The largest receipts from the tax come from grain products and alcohol, and 46 per cent of the total budget revenue was in 1959 derived from it.

Turnover tax was introduced in 1930, replacing sixty-one different taxes. A token turnover tax was levied on producers' goods until 1949, when it was abolished except for oil and oil products, gas and electricity, where it functions as a differential rent. Consumer goods exempt from turnover tax are the main meat and milk products, mass-produced furniture, mass-produced children's clothing and footwear, printed matter and medicine. *See also* TAXATION. *See* F. D. Holzman, *Soviet Taxation*, Cambridge, Mass., 1955; L. M. Herman, 'Taxes and the Soviet Citizen,' *Problems of Communism*, vol. viii, No. 5, 1959.

Turukhansk, obsolete name of a vast territory in northern Siberia along the lower Yenisey (Krasnoyarsk Kray), annexed to Russia in the early 17th century. The area is rich in mineral resources; from the 19th century it was a place of banishment, and from the 1930's to the mid 1950's of forced labour camps.

Tushino, former town in the Moscow Oblast, a suburb 9 m. north-west of the capital, on the Moscow–Riga railway. Population (1959) 90,000. It has a textile industry (since 1867). The Central Air Club of the U.S.S.R. is in Tushino and there is a sports airfield where yearly displays have taken place on Air Fleet Day (19th August) since 1933. In 1608–9 the second Pseudo-Dimitriy, a pretender to the Muscovite throne, resided in Tushino, which was then a village. In 1960 Tushino was absorbed by Moscow.

Tuva, Autonomous Oblast of the R.S.F.S.R. (not included in a kray), situated in southern Siberia adjacent to Outer Mongolia; it is a partly forested mountainous area, traversed by the upper Yenisey, with deposits of gold, coal and salt. Area 66,400 sq. m.; population (1959) 172,000 (29 per cent urban), mostly Tuvinians and Russians (since the 19th century). Sheep, goats and cattle are raised, and there is some industry. Administrative centre Kyzyl. The area was Chinese, 1757–1912, became a Russian protectorate in 1914, a 'People's Republic' in 1921, and was annexed by the U.S.S.R. in 1944. *See* W. Kolarz, *The Peoples of the Soviet Far East*, 1954.

Tuvinians, Turkic-speaking people living in the Tuva Autonomous Oblast (southern Siberia) and numbering (1959) 100,000; they are Lamaist Buddhists. The Tuvinians mostly engage in animal husbandry and hunting, and are now collectivized. *See* W. Kolarz, *The Peoples of the Soviet Far East*, 1954.

Tvardovskiy, Aleksandr Trifonovich (*b.* 1910), poet of peasant origin. He reported the collectivization of agriculture for local papers, and was a war correspondent during the Second World War; his best long poems result from these experiences—*Muravia Country*, 1936, portraying the yearning of the peasant for his plot of land, and *Vasiliy Tërkin*, 1946, a brilliant picture of the Russian private soldier. As editor of *Novyy Mir* (q.v.) he was foremost in initiating the post-Stalin thaw in the field of letters by publishing chapters of his poem *Far Distances*, in which he exposed the mechanism of ensuring authors' conformity under the Soviet regime (*see* FICTIONS), and several nonconformist articles by young critics, including Pomerantsev's 'On Sincerity in Literature,' which substituted the criterion of sincerity for that of the 'party spirit' (*see* PARTYNESS). Tvardovskiy was dismissed from the editorship in 1954, but remained prominent in the intellectual opposition (q.v.), and was reinstated as editor in 1958. *See* J. Lindsay (trans.), *Russian Poetry, 1917–55*, 1957.

Twentieth Congress of the Communist Party (February 1956), first congress held after the death of Stalin, one of the main landmarks in the political development of the post-Stalin period. The proceedings of the congress, especially Khrushchëv's famous speech at the secret session which was devoted to a denunciation of Stalin, signified that the party leadership did not want to be regarded as committed to the Stalinist tradition (*see* STALINISM). Khrushchëv's speech, which although not published was read at meetings throughout the country, by removing many of the Stalinist fictions (q.v.), made possible public criticism of various aspects of the Soviet reality and greatly facilitated the development of vocal opposition, both in the Soviet Union and in the satellite countries. Following as it did the curbing of the powers of the security organs (q.v.), Khrushchëv's speech precipitated the revolutionary crisis of October–December 1956 in the Communist countries and stimulated 'revisionist' (*see* REVISIONISM) tendencies in the Communist parties; it also resulted in a considerable loss of membership and morale in Communist parties outside the Soviet orbit. *See* B. D. Wolfe, *Khrushchëv and Stalin's Ghost*, 1957.

Tyumen': 1. Oblast of the R.S.F.S.R., situated in Western Siberia, traversed by the River Ob', a swampy area extending through tundra, forest and wooded steppe zones; there are deposits of natural gas. Area 554,300 sq. m.; population (1959) 1,094,000 (32 per cent urban), chiefly Russians (since the 16th century), also Tatars in the south and Khanty, Mansi and Nenets in the north (the Yamal-Nenets and Khanty-Mansi National Okrugs lie within the oblast). Dairy and grain farming is carried on in the south, hunting, fishing and reindeer raising in the north; there are also timber, food and engineering industries. Principal towns: Tyumen', Tobol'sk. The area formed the core of the Siberian Khanate and was annexed to Russia in 1581. It has been a place of banishment and labour camps.

2. Administrative, economic and cultural centre of the oblast, the oldest Russian town in Siberia. Population (1959) 150,000 (1914, 50,000; 1926, 50,000). It has shipbuilding, engineering (timber industry equipment), wood-processing, leather and food industries, and is an important river-railway transport point. Tyumen' was founded

on the ruins of a Tatar town in 1586, and until the building of the Trans-Siberian Railway was the 'Gateway to Siberia.'

Tyutchev, Fëdor Ivanovich (1803–73), poet, diplomat and censor, who produced brilliant metaphysical poems (*Silentium!*, 1833) and later political poems in a nationalist and pan-Slavic vein. *See* R. Hare, *Pioneers of Russian Social Thought*, 1951; N. V. Riasanovsky, *Nicholas I and Official Nationality in Russia, 1925–55*, Berkeley and Los Angeles, 1959.

U

Udmurt Autonomous Republic, of the R.S.F.S.R., situated in the east of European Russia, between the rivers Kama and Vyatka, a hilly plain partly covered with coniferous forests and many swamps. Area 16,400 sq. m.; population (1959) 1,333,000 (44 per cent urban), mostly Udmurts, Russians (since the 15th century) and Tatars. There are engineering, iron and steel (since the 18th century) and timber industries; coarse grain and flax are cultivated, and dairy farming carried on; a big hydro-electric station is under construction on the Kama. Principal towns: Izhevsk (capital), Sarapul, Votkinsk. The area belonged partly to the medieval Volga Bulgarian state and the Kazan' Khanate, partly to the Vyatka Republic; it became Muscovite in the 15th–16th centuries. In 1920 the Votyak Autonomous Oblast was formed, renamed Udmurt in 1932; it became a republic in 1934.

Udmurts (formerly known as **Votyaks**), Finnish-speaking people who live in the Udmurt Autonomous Republic and neighbouring areas, numbering (1959) 623,000. They are Orthodox Christians by religion, and are chiefly peasants, now collectivized. *See* W. Kolarz, *Russia and her Colonies*, 1952.

Ufa, capital of the Bashkir Autonomous Republic (Urals), situated on the River Belaya. Population (1959) 546,000 (fourth in the Urals; 1914, 103,000; 1920, 93,000; 1939, 258,000), mainly Russian, also Tatar and Bashkir. It is a major industrial centre, with engineering (aircraft engines, electric and oil-industry equipment), oil-refining (pipelines from the Tuymazy and Ishimbay fields), wood-processing and varied light and food industries; it is also an important transportation centre. The city is the residence of the religious head of the Muslims of European Russia and Siberia (since 1788), and the Bashkir branch of the U.S.S.R. Academy of Sciences is situated here. Ufa was founded as a Russian fortress in 1574, becoming a town in 1586 and serving as a fur-collecting centre; it has been a provincial centre since 1862, and was an important centre of trade in agricultural products during the 19th century. Some industry has existed since the 1870's, but industrial development became rapid during the 1930's and especially after the Second World War. The Socialist Revolutionaries overthrew the Bolsheviks in Ufa in 1918, and the Ufa Directory (q.v.) was soon established; the town was taken in 1919 by the Red Army, and in 1922 was included in the Bashkir Republic against the will of the Bashkirs and made its capital. It was the administrative centre of Ufa Oblast within the Bashkir Republic, 1952–3, now abolished.

Ufa Directory, ephemeral anti-Bolshevik government established in 1918 at the State Conference in Ufa which had been summoned by the Committee of Members of the Constituent Assembly (q.v.); it was soon overthrown by Admiral Kolchak.

Ugrian Languages, group of three languages which are related to the Finnish group and are often regarded together with this as one Finno-Ugrian family. The Ugrian languages are Magyar and those of two small Siberian peoples, the Khanty and the Mansi.

Ukase, ordinance of the Presidium of the U.S.S.R. Supreme Soviet or the Supreme Soviets of the republics. The term is of medieval origin and was applied to the ordinances of the Muscovite czars and Russian emperors before 1917. It was revived in the Stalin constitution of 1936, possibly as a part of the general policy of reintroducing Russian national symbols.

Ukhtomskiy, Prince Aleksey Alekseyevich (1875–1942), physiologist, professor at Leningrad University, member of the Academy of Sciences. Continuing the work of his teacher Vvedenskiy, he advanced the theory of a dominant as a general working principle not limited to the nervous system, and the theory of rhythm adoption. *See* R. A. Bauer, *The New Man in Soviet Psychology*, Cambridge, Mass., 1952.

Ukraine (Ukrainian **Ukrayina**), Union Republic of the U.S.S.R. which lies in the south-west of European Russia north of the Black Sea and the Sea of Azov, bordered on the west by Rumania, Hungary, Czechoslovakia and Poland. It is the second largest republic of the U.S.S.R. (after the R.S.F.S.R.) in population (1959, 41,869,000; 1939, 40,469,000) and third largest (after the R.S.F.S.R. and Kazakhstan) in size (area 232,100 sq. m.). The capital of the Ukraine is Kiev, and it is divided into twenty-five oblasts. It lies largely in the Poles'ye, Dnieper and Black Sea lowlands of the Russian plain and in the Volhynia-Podolia, Dnieper and Donets uplands; in the west are the Carpathian Mountains, and in the south the Crimean Mountains. The Dnieper, Dniester, South Bug and Severskiy Donets (a tributary of the Don) are the chief rivers. The soils and vegetation form three latitudinal zones: mixed forests in the north (*see* POLES'YE), wooded steppe with beech and oak forests, and steppe, the two latter having mostly fertile black earth soil. There are vertical vegetation zones in the Carpathian and the Crimean mountains. The climate is moderately continental, considerably warmer than that of central Russia, and the southern shore of the Crimea has a Mediterranean climate. The Ukraine is rich in natural deposits: iron ore (*see* KERCH; KRIVOY ROG), manganese (*see* NIKOPOL'), coal (*see* DONETS BASIN), natural gas (*see* DASHAVA; SHEBELINKA), oil (*see* DROGOBYCH), mercury, salts, etc.

Population. The density of population in the Ukraine is slightly lower than that of the Moldavian Republic, but higher than elsewhere in the U.S.S.R.; it is highest in the industrial Donets Basin followed by the wooded steppe belt, the Poles'ye and the steppe zone; 46 per cent of the population is urban, 2 per cent less than the U.S.S.R. average. Ethnically Ukrainians form the bulk (76 per cent) of the population, followed by Great Russians (18 per cent) and Jews (2 per cent), both living in towns throughout the Ukraine; outside the towns the Russians live chiefly in the Crimea (forming the majority there), the Donets Basin and other areas adjacent to the R.S.F.S.R., and the southern oblasts. Before the Second World War Jews and the

Polish minority in Western Ukraine were much more numerous (Poles now form 1 per cent of the total), and German and Czech colonies also existed then. There are still small colonies of Bulgarians, Greeks and Gagauz in the south. Some Moldavians, Rumanians and Hungarians (in Transcarpathia) live in the west. The Tatars of the Crimea were deported to Central Asia in 1944 and were not re-habilitated by the decree of 1957.

Economy. Industry and agriculture are both highly developed in the Ukraine. Engineering takes first place in industry, followed by metallurgy, chemicals, coal-mining and the sugar industry. The principal grain crops are wheat, barley, rye and oats, while sugar-beet and sunflowers are also widely grown; cotton cultivation, which began in the 1930's, proved disappointing and has been abandoned. Orchards are very common. Animal husbandry concentrates chiefly upon pigs, cattle and poultry. There is a dense transportation net-work, railways being by far the most important means of transport. Five principal areas of economic specialization can be distinguished in the Ukraine: (1) the south-east (Stalino, Lugansk, Dnepropetrovsk and Zaporozh'ye oblasts), with coal-mining, metallurgy, chemicals and heavy engineering (*see* DONETS BASIN; SOUTHERN INDUSTRIAL REGION); (2) the north-east (Khar'kov, Poltava and Sumy oblasts), with large and varied engineering; (3) the south (Odessa, Nikolayev, Kirovograd, Kherson and Crimea oblasts), chiefly agricultural, with food and agricultural engineering industries, large seaports and ship-building; (4) the central (Kiev, Chernigov, Zhitomir, Cherkassy, Vinnitsa and Khmel'nitskiy oblasts), with varied agriculture, especially sugar-beet cultivation, sugar and other food and light industries, and diverse engineering; (5) the west (Rovno, Volhynia, Ternopol', L'vov, Stanislav, Chernovtsy and Transcarpathia oblasts), with varied but comparatively less developed industries (food and light, oil and natural gas extraction, some engineering).

History. The steppes of the southern Ukraine were populated by Scythians in antiquity, and there in the 8th–7th centuries B.C. Greek settlers founded many colonies (*see* CHERSONESUS), which later fell under Roman domination. The whole country was under the Goths in the 4th century A.D., but these were defeated at the onset of the Huns' invasion of Europe. From the early Middle Ages the forested and wooded steppe zones were inhabited by East Slav tribes—the Polyane, Severyane, Drevlyane, Volhynians, etc.—who, after a brief period of Khazar domination, were included in the Kievan state (*see* KIEVAN RUSSIA), the capital and chief centres of which were in the Ukraine; the steppe remained the home of the nomadic Pechenegs and Cumans. The centre of gravity shifted to the western Ukraine (*see* GALICIA AND VOLHYNIA, KINGDOM OF) after the disintegration of the Kievan state and especially after the Tatar conquest (*see* GOLDEN HORDE) in the 13th century. By the middle of the 15th century Lithuania dominated most of the Ukraine, though in the south-east the Crimean Khanate was established. In 1569 the Lithuanian-held lands became Polish, and the struggle soon devel-oped in the religious and cultural (*see* BRATSTVO) as well as in the social and economic spheres between the local Russian Orthodox population and the Polish Catholics. The Cossacks (q.v., *see also* Sich) were particularly militant, and during the 17th century won independence from Poland for the central Ukraine (*see* Hetmans; Khmel'nyts'kyy), entering a union with Muscovy in 1654. The almost complete internal autonomy which this central Ukrainian area at first enjoyed was gradually whittled down during the 18th century and finally abolished by Catherine II. The Ukraine to the west of the Dnieper (except Kiev) remained Polish until the Polish partitions of the 1790's; the Black Sea shores were taken by Russia from Turkey during the 18th century (*see* New Russia; *for history* of Bukovina, Crimea, Galicia and Transcarpathia *see* these articles).

A nationalist trend, demanding autonomy for the Ukraine, developed at the beginning of the 20th century, and after the February revolution of 1917 the Provisional Government granted this autonomy, recognizing the authority of the Ukrainian Central Rada (Council) over the central Ukraine. The Rada, headed by Hrushevs'kyy (q.v.), proclaimed an independent Ukrainian Republic after the Bolshevik seizure of power, and during the civil war the Ukraine was one of the most fiercely contested areas, witnessing German occupation and diverse Ukrainian nationalist (*see* Ukrainian Directory), White Russian (*see* Denikin; Wrangel), Communist and Anarchist (*see* Makhno) governments and authorities. The Ukrainian Soviet Republic was first proclaimed in December 1917, and it became one of the four original Union Republics when the U.S.S.R. was formed in 1922. In the early years the Communist Party collaborated with the nationalists in a policy of 'Ukrainization,' but since the late 1920's actual or alleged Ukrainian nationalists have been severely persecuted, especially during the Great Purge (q.v.). Nevertheless, 'bourgeois nationalist deviations' persisted, receiving new impetus from the German occupation during the Second World War; nationalist guerrillas (*see* Bandera) operated in the western Ukraine annexed from Poland in 1939—for several years after the end of the war. The Ukrainian Soviet Republic has separate representation at the United Nations. *See* W. E. D. Allen, *The Ukraine: a History*, 1940; M. Hrushevsky, *A History of the Ukraine*, 1941; C. A. Manning, *Ukrainian Literature*, Jersey City, 1944, *The Story of the Ukraine*, New York, 1947, and *Twentieth Century Ukraine*, New York, 1951; W. H. Chamberlin, *The Ukraine*, 1945; J. S. Reshetar, *The Ukrainian Revolution, 1917–20*, Princeton, 1952; R. E. Pipes, *The Formation of the Soviet Union*, Cambridge, Mass., 1954; B. Dmytryshyn, *Moscow and the Ukraine, 1918–53*, New York, 1956; J. A. Armstrong, *The Soviet Bureaucratic Élite. A Case Study of the Ukrainian Apparatus*, 1959; V. Markus, *L'Ukraine Soviétique dans les relations internationales, 1918–1923*, Paris, 1959; M. Kostiuk, *Stalinist Rule in the Ukraine*, 1960.

Ukrainian Directory, short-lived (1918–19) Ukrainian nationalist government, made up of people of differing political opinions and led first by the author V. Vynnychenko, then by S. Petlyura, commander of the Ukrainian nationalist forces; it soon disintegrated.

Ukrainians, East Slav people, closely related to the Great Russians and Belorussians, who inhabit the Ukraine and can also be found all over Russia, especially in the North Caucasus, the lower Volga area, the Altay Kray and the Maritime Kray in the Far East, numbering in all (1959) 37 million. The majority of Ukrainians are Orthodox, but inhabitants of Galicia and Transcarpathia are Uniate Catholics and there is a considerable cultural cleavage between them and the bulk of the Ukrainians. There are several distinct small ethnical groups of the Ukrainian people in the Carpathian Mountains area, notably the Hutsuls (q.v.).

Ukrainian as an ethnic name was first adopted by the romantic intellectual movement in the early 19th century (from the name of the 17th-century Cossack state 'Little Russian Ukraine'), and became universally used in the 1920's. Before then they called themselves simply Russians, but among Great Russians they were known as Little Russians (since the 17th century). The Ukrainians are the descendants of the East Slav tribes which inhabited the southern part of Kievan Russia (q.v.) in the early Middle Ages. After the Mongol conquest a large part of the population moved west to Galicia and Volhynia (qq.v.), but when the Tatar danger receded they spread eastwards again, gradually colonizing the whole of the present territory of the Ukraine. The final stage of this process was the colonization of New Russia (q.v.) in the 19th century. Already in the Kievan period some distinctive features in Ukrainian speech can be identified in the written sources, and during the 14th–16th centuries, under Lithuanian and Polish domination, the Ukrainian population began to develop a separate identity and some degree of national consciousness. The Ukrainian community was organized in the Cossack units (see COSSACKS; SICH) and in religious brotherhoods (see BRATSTVO). The Cossacks, led by Khmel'nyts'kyy (q.v.), in a series of campaigns, won independence from Poland in the mid 17th century and established a state of their own which comprised the central part of the present-day Ukraine. Unable to stand alone, they chose union with Muscovy, which was concluded in 1654 in Pereyaslav, and which resulted in a strong Ukrainian cultural influence in Muscovy during the 17th and early 18th centuries. Although there were attempts at severing the union (see MAZEPA), it became firmly rooted and made possible the 'all-Russian' national idea of the imperial period, to which Ukrainians greatly contributed (see PROKOPOVICH).

The abolition by Catherine II, in the process of creating a centralized administration, of the Ukrainian institutions of hetman and Sich offended Ukrainian pride, and from the early 19th century a romantic literary and national movement began to grow which became known as the Ukrainophile movement. The most outstanding Ukrainian poet, Shevchenko (q.v.), contributed much to the growth of Ukrainian national consciousness. Publications in Ukrainian, except folklore, were forbidden by the Russian Government after the Polish uprising of 1863, and this prohibition remained in force until the revolution of 1905 (q.v.). A nationalist conception of Ukrainian history was developed by Hrushevs'kyy (q.v.). Several left-wing Ukrainian parties were formed after the revolution of 1905, while Ukrainians continued to take full part in the all-Russian political life. For further history see UKRAINE. See J. A. Armstrong,

Ukrainian Nationalism, New York, 1955; G. S. N. Luckyj, *Literary Politics in the Soviet Ukraine, 1917–34*, New York, 1956; *Ukrainian Review*, Munich.

Ulanova, Galina Sergeyevna (*b.* 1910), prima ballerina. Studying with Vaganova, she graduated in 1928 and appeared with great success in the following year. Ulanova is distinguished by her supreme artistry, her technical perfection and her great sensitivity to musical atmosphere. Although comparatively unknown outside the Soviet Union until recent years, she has established herself as one of the greatest dancers of her day, a reputation merited not only by her stage roles in *The Sleeping Beauty* and *Les Sylphides*, but by her performances in the films *Giselle* and *Romeo and Juliet*. She went into semi-retirement early in 1960. *See* V. M. Bogdanov-Berezovsky, *Ulanova and the Development of the Soviet Ballet*, 1952.

Ulan-Ude (formerly **Verkhneudinsk**), capital, economic and cultural centre of the Buryat Autonomous Republic (western Transbaykalia), situated on the Trans-Siberian Railway. Population (1959) 174,000 (1926, 29,000; 1939, 126,000), mostly Russians. It is a major centre of industry (locomotives, glass, leather and food), and is the starting-point of the railway line to Peking via Ulan-Bator. Ulan-Ude was founded as a Russian fort in 1666 and became a town in 1775, with an annual fair attended by merchants throughout Siberia. For a short time in 1920 it was capital of the Far Eastern Republic.

Ulozheniye, code of laws enacted by the Zemskiy Sobor (q.v.) in 1649, consisting of nearly 1,000 articles divided into twenty-five chapters. Almost a third of them were concerned with courts and procedure, the rest with substantive law, public, private and criminal. The Ulozheniye sought to stabilize the social and political conditions after the Time of Troubles (*see* TROUBLES, TIME OF); one of its main provisions was the final establishment of serfdom (q.v.). It remained in force until the promulgation of the Svod Zakonov (q.v.) in 1833. *See* G. Vernadsky, *Medieval Russian Laws*, New York, 1947; H. J. Berman, *Justice in Russia*, Cambridge, Mass., 1950.

Ul'yanovsk: 1. Oblast of the R.S.F.S.R., situated astride the middle course of the Volga, largely on the upland of the right bank; it has black earth soil and is partly covered with mixed forests. Area 14,500 sq. m.; population (1959) 1,118,000 (36 per cent urban), chiefly Russians (since the 16th century), also some Tatars, Mordva and Chuvash (the two latter being the original inhabitants of the area). Grain, sunflowers and potatoes are cultivated, market gardening and cattle breeding carried on, and there are food, engineering, timber and textile (woollen fabrics) industries. Principal towns: Ul'yanovsk and Melekess.

2 (until 1924 **Simbirsk**). Administrative and economic centre of the oblast, situated on the right bank of the Volga. Population (1959) 205,000 (1920, 77,000; 1923, 68,000; 1939, 98,000). It has engineering (cars, machine tools), saw-milling and food industries, and is an important transportation centre (four railway lines, river port). There is a rich library, founded in 1830. The town is the birth-place of Lenin, and there is a Lenin Museum. Ul'yanovsk was founded as a fortified town and starting-point of the Muscovite Simbirsk defence

line in 1648, and became provincial capital in 1780. Industrial development dates from the Second World War.

Under-developed Countries, economic assistance to, *see* ECONOMIC AID.

Unemployment officially does not exist in the Soviet Union, since it is considered a characteristic of capitalist society. However, the published figures of the numbers of wage and salary earners show considerable seasonal fluctuations, amounting to several million, and clearly reveal seasonal unemployment. Temporary unemployment between jobs also exists, since there is no general provision or machinery for immediate re-employment of a person who has been dismissed or left his job, nor is there automatic employment of school leavers. There is also considerable concealed unemployment among the rural population, mainly owing to the existence of the *kolkhoz* (q.v.) system under which all *kolkhoz* members must be officially employed whether or not there is work for them to do.

Ostensibly unemployment was once and for ever eliminated in 1930, when unemployment benefit was abolished. Labour exchanges were gradually abolished during the following years and in 1933 the Commissariat of Labour itself ceased to exist. Since then it has been impossible to register as unemployed; job seekers can to a certain extent resort to the services of the general information bureaux which exist in the larger towns and to advertisements by newspapers or by posters; the offices for organized recruitment of labour also to some extent act as employment exchanges, and in recent years the majority of those recruited have been urban industrial workers with previous employment. A particularly acute problem of large-scale juvenile unemployment arose in the years 1955–8, when large numbers of secondary school leavers without any trade qualifications were unable to enter higher educational establishments and were either unwilling or unable to find manual jobs. This problem has become less serious with the educational reform of 1958 and the establishment of youth employment commissions in larger towns. The introduction of automation has in recent years led to instances of redundancy and consequent unemployment. *See* S. M. Schwarz, *Labor in the Soviet Union*, New York, 1951; A. Maxwell, ' Juvenile Unemployment in the U.S.S.R.,' *Soviet Survey*, Oct.–Dec. 1958.

Ungvár, *see* UZHGOROD.

Uniates, usual name for the Catholics of the Slavo-Byzantine rite. This denomination is officially forbidden in the Soviet Union, and only exists among *émigrés*, but in fact there is no doubt that a large number of Ukrainians living in Galicia and Transcarpathia regard themselves as Uniates. The Uniates originated with the recognition in 1594 by the Orthodox bishops in Poland of the Pope's authority, though they retained most of the external features of the Orthodox Church, such as the rite and the use of Church Slavonic as the ritual language. After the partitions of Poland in the 18th century, the union with Rome was abrogated in the territories annexed to Russia, but the denomination remained intact in the Austrian-held provinces, where, with the emergence of the Ukrainian national movement, it gradually came to be regarded as the national denomination of the Ukrainian population. After the annexation of the western Ukrainian territories by the Soviet Union in 1939–46, the Uniates, on both ideological and national grounds, opposed the Soviet regime and were in 1946 officially reincorporated into the Russian Orthodox Church; some bishops of the Orthodox Church must share the blame for this forcible reincorporation. *See also* RELIGION. *See* W. Kolarz, *Religion in the Soviet Union*, 1961.

Union for the Liberation of the Ukraine, nationalist organization aiming at the secession of the Ukraine from Russia. It was founded during the First World War by *émigrés* in Austria, with the assistance of the Austrian authorities, and revived as an underground organization in the 1920's, when it numbered among its members several leading Ukrainian intellectuals. It was broken up by the G.P.U. in 1929, and the trial of its actual or alleged members in 1930 was a part of the campaign of persecution against the old intelligentsia (*see* PURGES).

Union of Soviet Socialist Republics (abbreviated U.S.S.R.), official name of the Russian state. It was adopted in 1922 at a congress of representatives of the four Soviet republics then in existence—the Russian Soviet Federative Socialist Republic (R.S.F.S.R.), the Ukraine, Belorussia and Transcaucasia—and at this congress the U.S.S.R. was officially founded as a federal state. The avoidance of any national association in the choice of a name for the state was deliberate, since eventually the U.S.S.R. was intended to embrace the whole world. In 1925 Turkmenia and Uzbekistan were admitted as Union Republics, having been formed as a result of the National Delimitation of Central Asia (q.v.) in the previous year. Several Autonomous Republics were later raised to the status of Union Republics (Tadzhikistan 1929, Kazakhstan and Kirgizia 1936, Karelia and Moldavia 1940). In 1936 the Transcaucasian Republic was broken up into the Union Republics of Armenia, Azerbaydzhan and Georgia. The annexation of the Baltic States (q.v.) in 1940 led to the establishment of Estonia, Latvia and Lithuania as Union Republics. In 1956 Karelia was again demoted to the status of an Autonomous Republic. Despite some differences in the law of individual republics, the federal structure of the U.S.S.R. is largely fictitious, since throughout the country real power is in the hands of the highly centralized Communist Party of the Soviet Union (q.v.). *See further under* ADMINISTRATIVE TERRITORIAL DIVISIONS; AUTONOMOUS REPUBLIC; FEDERALISM; UNION REPUBLIC. *See* W. Kolarz, *Russia and her Colonies*, 1952; M. Fainsod, *How Russia is Ruled*, Cambridge, Mass., 1953; R. Pipes, *The Formation of the Soviet Union*, Cambridge, Mass., 1954.

Union of Zemstvos, organization formed after the beginning of the First World War by the local government bodies (*see* ZEMSTVO) to organize and co-ordinate additional medical services for the army in the field. Beginning with this task, the union developed into a part of the general movement among the liberal elements in the country to organize themselves so that they might replace the existing right-wing government, which they considered incapable of leading the country successfully during the war. Their chairman, Prince L'vov, did in fact become the first Prime Minister in the Provisional Government (q.v.) after the February revolution of 1917. *See* F. A. Golder, *Documents of Russian History, 1914–17*, 1927; P. Gronsky and N. Astrov, *The War and the Russian Government*, New Haven, 1929; M. T. Florinsky, *The End of the Russian Empire*, New Haven, 1931; V. I. Gurko, *Features and Figures of the Past. Government and Opinion in the Reign of Nicholas II*, 1939.

Union Republic, constituent republic of the Soviet Union, of which there are now fifteen (Armenia, Azerbaydzhan, Belorussia, Estonia, Georgia, Kazakhstan, Kirgizia, Latvia, Lithuania, Moldavia, R.S.F.S.R., Tadzhikistan, Turkmenia, Ukraine and Uzbekistan). Theoretically they are sovereign states and can at any time leave the Union. The government of each Union Republic is modelled after the all-Union government, though the republican Supreme Soviets have only one chamber. There are some insignificant differences in the legal codes of the different republics. The administrative functions of the republican governments, especially in the economic field, were very restricted under Stalin, but in consequence of the policy of decentralization embarked upon by the party leadership after Stalin's death their powers have been considerably increased. The theoretical right of the Union Republics to separate relations with foreign states is purely fictitious, and the separate representation of the Ukraine and Belorussia in the United Nations is the result of an agreement with the Western powers aimed at increasing the number of votes at the disposal of the Soviet Government. The right to secede is also purely fictitious, since on one hand the effective control in each republic is in the hands of the party organization, which is bound by party discipline to the central party leadership, and on the other hand any suggestion of secession is regarded as treason and punished accordingly. The external symbols of statehood —anthem, flag, etc.—are artificial, with little or no relation to tradition. Some of the Union Republics are parts of the former Russian Empire which seceded and became independent states after the Bolshevik seizure of power and were reannexed during the civil war (the Ukraine, the Transcaucasian Republics) or later (the Baltic States, q.v.); others were created by the Soviet Government through administrative reorganization (e.g. the National Delimitation of Central Asia, q.v.). *See* ADMINISTRATIVE TERRITORIAL DIVISIONS. *See* M. Fainsod, *How Russia is Ruled*, Cambridge, Mass., 1953; R. Pipes, *The Formation of the Soviet Union*, Cambridge, Mass., 1954; V. Aspaturian, *The Union Republics in Soviet Diplomacy*, Paris, 1960.

Universities form numerically a small part of higher education (q.v.) establishments, 40 out of 766, and in 1955–6 (the last year for which full figures are available) university students (excluding correspondence) numbered 115,652, or about 9 per cent of all students at higher education establishments. The universities have no autonomy and do not differ from other establishments of higher education, except by the subjects studied, traditional prestige and a certain tendency to continue the tradition of the pursuit of knowledge for its own sake. As a rule the universities are devoted to the study of the humanities and natural sciences, though some of them also have medical and technological faculties. University education developed late in Russia, and the first Russian university was founded in the middle of the 18th century. In the 19th century the number of universities increased, and they soon developed into seats of learning and study comparable to the universities of Western Europe. They usually consisted of four faculties—physics and mathematics, history and philology, law, and medicine. They were all State institutions, but their relations with the authorities oscillated during the century between autonomy and complete subordination to the Ministry of Education. Women were not admitted until 1917, but private Higher Women's Courses existed (from the 1870's) in the university cities which were closely connected with the universities, and in fact gave their students university education. According to the 1906 constitution, universities were represented by elected members in the Council of State (q.v.). Their autonomy became complete after the February revolution of 1917, but it was again abolished when the Bolsheviks seized power. Several new universities were founded during the civil war by both the Reds and the Whites, and national universities were established in Georgia and Azerbaydzhan during their short independence. The 1920's witnessed a decline of universities. The Communist authorities were generally hostile to them. The practice of political and social discrimination between applicants, the disorganization of secondary education, the emigration or dismissal of many eminent scholars, were followed by the splitting up of universities into separate institutes, in the process of which most universities disappeared by 1930 (e.g. none were left in the Ukraine). But from 1931 a new period of growth of university education began; most of the closed universities were reopened, new ones founded in the 1930's and forties in Union Republics where there had been none before, and several Autonomous Republics received universities in the 1950's. At first universities were confined to natural sciences, but from the mid 1930's the scope of university education has been constantly expanding. However, throughout the 1930's and again in the late forties and early fifties universities suffered from the recurrent waves of terror against the intelligentsia: many of their teachers were shot or sent to concentration camps, and the Far Eastern University in Vladivostok was even abolished as a result of the Great Purge (q.v.). Universities have always been nests of nonconformity in Russia. Student 'disorders' of a political nature played an important part in the opposition movements before 1917 and again in 1956. A list of existing universities, with dates of foundation, is given below:

Vilnius	1578	Kiev	1834
Tartu	1632	Odessa	1865
L'vov	1661	Chernovtsy	1875
Moscow	1755	Tomsk	1888
Kazan'	1804	Saratov	1909
Khar'kov	1805	Rostov-on-Don	1915
Leningrad	1819	Perm'	1916

Gor'kiy	1918	Kazakh (Alma-Ata)	1934
Voronezh	1918	Petrozavodsk	1940
Irkutsk	1918	Uzhgorod	1945
Dnepropetrovsk	1918	Kishinev	1945
Tiflis	1918	Tadzhik (Stalinabad)	1948
Azerbaydzhan (Baku)	1919	Turkmen (Ashkhabad)	1950
Latvian (Riga)	1919	Kirgiz (Frunze)	1951
Yerevan	1920	Yakutsk	1956
Central Asian (Tashkent)	1920	Chernigov	1957
Urals (Sverdlovsk)	1920	Kabarda-Balkar (Nal'chik)	1957
Far Eastern (Vladivostok)	1920	Mordva (Saransk)	1958
Belorussian (Minsk)	1921	Bashkir (Ufa)	1958
Uzbek (Samarkand)	1933	Daghestan (Makhachkala)	1958

See D. Odinets and P. Novgorodtsev, *Russian Schools and Universities in the World War*, New Haven, 1929; N. DeWitt, *Soviet Professional Manpower*, Washington, D.C., 1955; A. G. Korol, *Soviet Education for Science and Technology*, 1957; D. Grant (ed.), *The Humanities in Soviet Higher Education*, Toronto, 1960.

Ural (until 1775 **Yaik**), navigable river which forms part of the boundary between Europe and Asia; it rises in the Ural Mountains and flows south, then west, then again south into the Caspian Sea. Length 1,580 m.; principal ports: Ural'sk and Gur'yev. The banks of the Ural were colonized by Cossacks from the 17th century.

Ural-Kuznetsk Combine, large industrial project carried out in the 1930's with the intention of combining the iron ore of the Urals and the coking coal of the Kuznetsk Basin (q.v.) (distance over 1,200 m.) for the production of iron and steel. The idea had been mooted before the First World War and the first practical steps were taken during it, but the final decision was taken at the 16th congress of the party in 1930. During the Second World War the combine was the principal industrial base of the country.

Ural Mountains (ancient **Hyperborei,** or **Rhipaei Montes**), range of mountains forming part of the boundary between Europe and Asia and separating the Russian plain from the West Siberian lowland. The chain of mountains stretches for 1,500 miles from the Arctic Ocean to the Central Asian deserts; they are old and much eroded, especially the central Urals. The highest peak is Mt Narodnaya in the north (6,200 ft). The Ural Mountains are rich in mineral resources—iron ores, copper, aluminium, asbestos, gold, platinum, nickel, chromium, etc. In the adjacent lowlands large deposits of salt, coal and oil are found.

Urals, The, one of the chief industrial areas of the U.S.S.R., comprising the central and southern parts of the Ural Mountains and the adjacent lowland to the west and east; there are many forests. Area 290,000 sq. m.; population (1959) 16,527,000 (nearly 10 million urban), principally Russians (over 80 per cent), also Bashkirs, Tatars and Udmurts. Its rich natural resources (iron ore, non-ferrous, precious and rare metals, salts, precious stones, coal, oil and building materials) form the basis of its great mining, metallurgical, engineering and chemical industries. The chief cities (over 200,000 inhabitants) are Sverdlovsk, Chelyabinsk, Perm', Ufa, Nizhniy Tagil, Magnitogorsk, Izhevsk and Orenburg, and the region is divided into the Sverdlovsk, Perm', Chelyabinsk and Orenburg oblasts and the Bashkir and the Udmurt Autonomous Republics. Russian advance into the Urals began from Novgorod in the 11th century; 1479 saw the beginnings of rapid colonization, and industrial development (iron mining and working) dates from the early 18th century. The Urals was the largest producer of pig-iron in the world around the year 1800, and in Russia it was foremost until outstripped by the Southern Industrial Region (q.v.) in 1895. The development of industry received new impetus from the Five Year Plans and the Second World War, when it was the chief base of the country's war effort. Limited power resources restrict further industrial development in the Urals, and the area is therefore scheduled for the priority construction of atomic power-stations. *See* R. Portal, *L'Oural au XVIIIe siècle*, Paris, 1950; B. Nolde, *La Formation de l'Empire Russe*, vol. i, Paris, 1952.

Ural'sk, administrative, economic and cultural centre of the West Kazakhstan Oblast, situated on the River Ural and the Saratov–Orenburg railway. Population (1959) 105,000 (1939, 67,000), mostly Russians. Its chief industries process animal products, and there is also flour milling and some engineering (wind motors). Ural'sk was founded in the early 17th century as the centre of the Ural Cossacks' community, and was called Yaitskiy Gorodok until it was renamed in 1775 after the suppression of the Pugachëv uprising. It was an important centre of trade and food industries on the border of European Russia and the Kazakh steppes, and became a provincial centre in 1868.

Ura-Tyube, town in the Leninabad Oblast of Tadzhikistan, situated on the highway from Leninabad to the Zeravshan Valley and further to Stalinabad. Population (1956) 22,700. It is the main wine-producing centre in Tadzhikistan. Ura-Tyube was known in antiquity as Kyropolis. It was the centre of Ura-Tyube Oblast in 1945–7, now fused with Leninabad.

Urban Settlements, administrative unit such as a workers' settlement (q.v.), health resort, etc., with a mainly non-agricultural population but without the official status of a town. They are administered by settlement soviets which are subordinated either to the rayon soviet or to that of a nearby town. Urban settlements vary in size from a few hundred inhabitants to 50,000, but are usually transformed into towns before the population reaches the latter figure.

Urgench, administrative centre of the Khorezm Oblast (Uzbekistan), situated on the left bank of the River Amu-Dar'ya and on the Chardzhou–Kungrad railway. Population (1959) 43,000 (1939, 22,000). It has cotton-processing and food industries.

Uryankhay, *see* Tuva.

Ushinskiy, Konstantin Dmitriyevich (1824–70), most outstanding Russian educational theorist, who laid the foundations of modern primary educational methods in Russia.

U.S.S.R., *see* Union of Soviet Socialist Republics.

Ussuriysk (Nikol'sk-Ussuriysk till the 1930's, then **Voroshilov** till 1958), town in the Maritime Kray (Far East), about 70 m. north of Vladivostok. Population (1959) 104,000 (1914, 52,000; 1926, 35,000).

It has soya-oil, sugar and other food industries, and is a junction of the Trans-Siberian and Chinese Eastern railways. Ussuriysk was founded in 1866, became a town in 1898, and was administrative centre of the Ussuri Oblast within the Far Eastern Kray, 1933–43.

Ust'-Kamenogorsk, town in southern Siberia, administrative, economic and cultural centre of the East Kazakhstan Oblast, situated on the River Irtysh and a branch of the Turksib Railway. Population (1959) 117,000 (1939, 20,000), Russians. It is a major centre of non-ferrous metallurgy (large lead and zinc plant), and also has chemical and food industries; there is a large hydro-electric station, of which Malenkov was made manager after the expulsion of the 'anti-party group' (q.v.) from the Central Committee in 1957. Ust'-Kamenogorsk was founded as a Russian fortress in 1720, became a town in 1868, and provincial centre in 1939. The heavy industrial development dates from the Second World War.

Ust'-Ordynskiy: 1. Buryat National Okrug, within the Irkutsk Oblast (southern Siberia). Area 8,100 sq. m.; population (1959) 133,000 (15 per cent urban), Buryats and Russians. Grain is cultivated and cattle are raised. The National Okrug was established in 1937.

2. Urban settlement, administrative centre of the okrug, situated 43 m. north-east of Irkutsk. Population (1956) 7,000.

Ust'-Sysol'sk, see SYKTYVKAR.

Uyezd, former territorial administrative unit, larger than the present rayon. They were abolished in the late 1920's, but continued to exist in the Baltic States and Bessarabia until the late 1940's.

Uygurs, Turkic-speaking people who live chiefly in Chinese Turkestan but form a national minority in Soviet Central Asia (where they numbered 95,000 in 1959)—in Semirech'ye (Alma-Ata oblast of Kazakhstan) and in the Fergana Valley. They are Muslims, chiefly engaged in agriculture. In the 8th–9th centuries there was a large and powerful Uygur state in eastern Turkestan, but after its decline the name Uygur fell into disuse and was only revived in Soviet Central Asia by National Bolsheviks (see NATIONAL BOLSHEVISM) in the 1920's. The name has also now been adopted in Chinese Turkestan, which is officially called the Uygur-Sinkiang National Area.

Uzbekistan, Union Republic of the U.S.S.R. lying in the central part of Central Asia with deserts in the north-west (adjacent to the Aral Sea), a chain of fertile and densely populated oases roughly along latitudes 40°–42° (Khorezm, Zeravshan, Tashkent, Fergana Valley), and a mountainous area between Zeravshan and the middle course of the River Amu-Dar'ya; there are large deposits of natural gas near Bukhara, brown coal near Tashkent and oil in the Fergana Valley, also rich deposits of copper, lead and rare metals near Tashkent. Area 158,100 sq. m.; population (1959) 8,106,000 (fourth among the Union Republics of the U.S.S.R.; 1939, 6,336,000; 34 per cent urban). In 1959 the ethnic composition was as follows: Uzbeks, 62 per cent; Russians, 14 per cent; Tatars, 5·5 per cent; Tadzhiks, 4 per cent; Kazakhs, 4 per cent; Kara-Kalpaks, 2 per cent; there are also Koreans (2 per cent), etc.

The principal feature of the republic's economy is cotton production, both cultivation and industries associated with it. Cultivated land takes up about one-ninth of the area, and over a half of it is irrigated. The irrigated land is chiefly used for cotton and other industrial and fodder crops, while the non-irrigated land is almost entirely taken up by grain crops. The cotton-growing area was more than doubled between 1913 and 1941, and the cotton crop was nearly trebled. Uzbekistan's share in the total cotton production of the country increased from 36 per cent in 1913 to about 60 per cent in 1950; the republic is also the biggest silk-producing area of the U.S.S.R. (about one-half of the total). Fruit and grapes (for raisins) are also produced on a large scale. The main branch of animal husbandry is the breeding of Astrakhan sheep (two-thirds of the skins produced in the U.S.S.R.). Engineering and metal-working industries (mostly agricultural machinery and cotton-processing equipment) employ one-third of all industrial workers and are chiefly confined to Tashkent and the surrounding area, Samarkand and Andizhan; industry has developed especially since the Second World War, when many factories were evacuated here from western parts of the country. Coal and oil extraction have been developed since the 1930's, and the natural gas deposits are now to be exploited. The chemical industry of the republic is largely concentrated upon fertilizers. Uzbekistan is chiefly served by the Trans-Caspian Railway, with its branches to the Fergana Valley, Stalinabad and the Khorezm oasis; navigation on the Amu-Dar'ya also plays an important though diminished role. The capital of the republic is Tashkent (since 1930, prior to that date Samarkand), and it is divided into the Tashkent, Samarkand, Bukhara, Fergana, Andizhan, Khorezm, and Surkhan-Dar'ya oblasts and the Kara-Kalpak Autonomous Republic. For history *see* BUKHARA KHANATE; KHOREZM; KOKAND KHANATE; SOGDIANA; TRANSOXANIA; TURKESTAN. The Uzbek Republic was formed in 1924 during the National Delimitation of Central Asia (q.v.), and included Tadzhikistan as an Autonomous Republic; the latter became a Union Republic in 1929. The Kara-Kalpak Autonomous Republic was transferred from the R.S.F.S.R. to Uzbekistan in 1936. Throughout the 1920's and early thirties Uzbekistan was the main centre of the anti-Bolshevik Basmachi (q.v.) guerrilla warfare. The Great Purge (q.v.) of the late 1930's was very severely felt in Uzbekistan, which until then had been ruled by National Bolsheviks (*see* NATIONAL BOLSHEVISM). *See* the journal *Central Asian Review* published by the Central Asian Research Centre in London.

Uzbeks, most numerous Turkic-speaking people in Central Asia, numbering (1959) 6 million (4·8 million in 1939), inhabiting Uzbekistan and living in considerable numbers in the adjacent parts of Tadzhikistan, Kirgizia, Kazakhstan and Turkmenia. The Uzbek people as now understood are a recent and even somewhat artificial creation. In the late 14th and the 15th centuries Uzbeks were the politically dominant and most convinced Muslim element in the Golden Horde (q.v.); after its break-up the Uzbeks under Sheybani Khan moved south-east and conquered the ancient civilized areas of

Central Asia (*see* TRANSOXANIA; TURKESTAN). From then until the Russian conquest in the 19th century the Uzbek nomads were the politically dominant section of the population of the Bukhara, Khorezm and Kokand khanates (qq.v.). The National Delimitation of Central Asia (q.v.) and the establishment of the Uzbek Republic brought about the extension of the name Uzbek to include the Turkic-speaking part of the sedentary Sarts (q.v.), the true heirs to the ancient civilization of Central Asia, whose towns of Bukhara and Samarkand have traditionally been among the leading Islamic centres of the world. This amalgamation resulted in the intensified assimilation of the Uzbek tribesmen with the Sarts, whose language is now known as the Uzbek language, though there are still numerous tribal groups not yet assimilated. *See* V. V. Barthold, *Four Studies on the History of Central Asia*, vols. i and ii, Leyden, 1956; S. A. Zenkovsky, *Pan-Turkism and Islam in Russia*, Cambridge, Mass., 1960.

Uzhgorod (Ukrainian **Uzhhorod**, Czech **Užhorod**, Hungarian **Ungvár**), administrative, cultural and an economic centre of the Transcarpathian Oblast (western Ukraine). Population (1959) 47,000 (1939, 30,000), Ukrainians, Hungarians, Jews. It has food, engineering and woodworking industries. There is a university, 1946, and there are interesting buildings of the 12th–18th centuries. Uzhgorod was the centre of both the Ukrainian and the Russophile movements in Transcarpathia during the 19th century; it has been capital of Transcarpathia since 1919.

Uzlovaya, town in the Tula Oblast (central Russia), an important railway junction on the Moscow–Donbas line, about 30 m. south-east of Tula. Population (1959) 54,000 (1939, 18,000). It is a coal-mining centre in the Moscow Lignite Basin and has various industries connected with railway maintenance.

V

Vakhtangov, Yevgeniy Bagrationovich (1883–1922), actor and director of Armenian origin. A pupil of Stanislavsky (q.v.), he belonged to the Moscow Art Theatre from 1911, working as an actor and producer in its First Studio (from 1912) and in his own Third Studio (from 1920), which in 1926 was renamed the Vakhtangov Theatre. In his four classical productions (Chekhov's *Wedding*, 1920, Maeterlinck's *St Antony's Miracle*, 1921, Strindberg's *Eric XIV* and Gozzi's *Princess Turandot*, 1922) he embodied his vision of a modern mystery play. This tradition was preserved in the Vakhtangov Theatre until the 1930's. *See further under* THEATRE. *See* J. Jelagin, *Taming of the Arts*, New York, 1951.

Valaam (Finnish **Valamo**), small island in the north of Lake Ladoga with the famous Valaam Russian Orthodox monastery which dates from the 12th or 14th century. It was an important frontier fortress, frequently ruined by the Swedes. The monastery had extremely strict rules and compulsory work, and developed model dairy and garden farming; it was a place of pilgrimage. From 1918 to 1940 Valaam belonged to Finland; the monks left in 1940.

Valuyev, Count Pëtr Aleksandrovich (1814–90), Minister of the Interior, 1861–8, and chairman of the Committee of Ministers (q.v.), 1877–81. He took an important part in evolving and implementing the Great Reforms (q.v.), especially in establishing the *zemstvos* (q.v.). In 1863 Valuyev advanced a constitutional scheme providing for a consultative assembly made up of some elected and some appointed ministers; the scheme was again taken up in 1880 by Loris-Melikov (q.v.), but not put into practice.

Varangians, Norsemen who in the 9th century raided the eastern shores of the Baltic, penetrated into the interior and established the great trade route to Byzantium along the River Dnieper. According to the chronicles a number of East Slav and some Finnish tribes invited the Varangians in 862 to come and rule their country, thus founding the first Russian dynasty of Rurikids (q.v.).

Varga, Yevgeniy Samoylovich (*b.* 1879), economist, a Hungarian by birth, member of the Academy of Sciences since 1939. He joined the Hungarian Social Democratic Party in 1906; in 1919, without formally joining the Communist Party, was Commissar for Finance and later chairman of the Supreme Council of National Economy in the Hungarian Communist Government. He settled in Moscow in 1920, joined the Communist Party and was active in the Communist International and the Communist Academy, heading the latter's Institute for World Economy and World Politics from 1927. This institute and the journal *World Economy and World Politics* which Varga edited, were closed in 1947 when Varga was accused in the official press of 'serious mistakes of a bourgeois-reformist character,' particularly in his book *Changes in the Economy of Capitalism as a Result of the Second World War*, 1946.

Vasilenko, Sergey Nikiforovich (1872–1956), composer and conductor who studied at the Moscow Conservatory; his teachers included Taneyev, Ippolitov-Ivanov and Safonov. In 1906 he was appointed professor there. His works comprise operas; ballets; orchestral works; concertos, including one for balalaika; chamber and vocal music, etc.; he also wrote many compositions for folk instruments, and a number of literary works. Like Ippolitov-Ivanov, Vasilenko was deeply interested in the folk music of the Soviet republics, especially that of Uzbekistan, and much of his music is devoted to arrangements of folk-songs, etc., which also had an influence on his own composition. *See* his *Stranitsy vospominaniy*, Moscow, 1948.

Vasil'yevskiy, Vasiliy Grigor'yevich (1838–99), historian, professor at St Petersburg University, member of the Academy of Sciences from 1890, editor, 1890–9, of the *Journal of the Ministry of Education*, one of the main scholarly periodicals in Russia. An authority on the internal, particularly the economic, history of Byzantium, Vasil'yevskiy was the founder of the Russian school of Byzantine studies (among his works were *Materials for a History of the Byzantine State* and *The Legislation of the Iconoclasts*).

Vasnetsov, Viktor Mikhaylovich (1848–1927), painter, studied at the Academy of Arts. An outstanding representative of the Slavic revival, Vasnetsov returned to the earliest Russian history in his search for subject-matter. His reconstructions of the distant past were true in detail to the results of archaeological research, but his methods were those of a pedestrian realist and he never realized his ambition to recapture the spirit of the heroic times of the Varangian (q.v.) warriors. His greatest commission, paintings for the new Church of St Vladimir at Kiev, also proved a comparative fiasco artistically. However, some of his paintings on themes deriving from fairy-tales and folk epics possess a certain nostalgic charm.

Vavilov, Nikolay Ivanovich (1887–1942), botanist and geneticist, professor at Saratov University, later director of the All-Union Institute of Plant Breeding, 1924–40, and of the Academy of Sciences' Institute of Genetics, 1930–40, member of the Academy of Sciences from 1929, president of the Academy of Agricultural Sciences from its foundation in 1929 until 1935 (vice-president 1935–40), president of the All-Union Geographical Society, 1931–40, Fellow of the Royal Society. Through expeditions to all corners of the world he built up a unique collection of cultivated plants. He determined the main areas of origin of domesticated plants and animals, established the existence of parallel series of forms in different species ('The Law of Homologous Series in Variation,' *Journal of Genetics*, vol. xii, 1922), and suggested a classification of types of immunity of plants to infectious diseases. Highly respected in the academic world, Vavilov opposed Lysenko's (q.v.) unrealistic claims (though he had supported his experiments), and in consequence was deposed as the head of the Academy of Agricultural Sciences, arrested in 1940, and died in the Kolyma (q.v.) concentration camps. His reputation was rehabilitated after Stalin's death. *See* J. G. Crowther, *Soviet Science*, 1936; E. Ashby, *Scientist in Russia*, 1947; J. S. Huxley, *Soviet Genetics and World Science*, 1949; J. Langdon-Davies, *Russia Puts the Clock Back*, 1949.

Vavilov, Sergey Ivanovich (1891–1951), physicist, brother of N. I. Educated at Moscow University, he taught there (professor from 1929), was a member of the Academy of Sciences and director of its Physical Institute from 1932 (president from 1945), head of the State Optical Institute, 1932–45, plenipotentiary of the State Defence Committee (q.v.), 1941–5, chief editor of the second edition of the *Large Soviet Encyclopaedia*, 1947 ff. His own work was chiefly concerned with luminescence in condensed systems (solutions, etc.). In 1934 he explained the so-called Cherenkov effect. *See* J. G. Crowther, *Soviet Science*, 1936.

Veche, town assembly of medieval Russia which acquired absolute power in Novgorod, Pskov and Vyatka, elsewhere sharing authority with the local prince.

'Vekhi' ('Landmarks'), symposium published in 1909 by a group of politicians and philosophers (including Struve, Berdyayev, Bulgakov, Frank and Gershenzon, qq.v.) which marked the liberation of progressive thought in Russia from the mystique of revolution. The name in its wider application covers this whole trend of thought, most of whose leaders had been Marxists in the 1890's, though others (e.g. Novgorodtsev, Trubetskoy, qq.v.) had been Hegelians. Under the influence of Dostoyevskiy and V. Solov'ëv both groups evolved towards Christianity and Idealism. *See* T. G. Masaryk, *The Spirit of Russia*, vol. ii, 2nd ed., 1955; L. Schapiro, 'The Vekhi Group and the Mystique of Revolution,' *Slavonic and East European Review*, vol. xxxiv, No. 82, Dec. 1955.

Velikiy Ustyug, town in the Vologda Oblast (northern Russia), situated on the River Sukhona about 42 m. south-west of Kotlas. Population (1956) 35,800. It has some industry (shipbuilding, hog bristles), and a famous silver craft is still practised. There are interesting buildings of the 17th–19th centuries. Velikiy Ustyug has been known since 1218, and until the 17th century was the largest town and commercial centre of northern Russia.

Velikiye Luki, town in the Pskov Oblast (north-western Russia), situated on the Moscow–Riga railway. Population (1959) 59,000 (1939, 35,000). It has some industry and is an important railway junction. Velikiye Luki was founded in 1166 and was an important fortress and trading point of the Novgorod Republic; in 1478 it became Muscovite. The town was largely destroyed during fierce fighting in 1942–3; it was the administrative centre of Velikiye Luki Oblast, 1944–58, now abolished.

Venden, *see* CESIS.

Venetsianov, Aleksey Gavrilovich (1780–1847), painter, studied under Borovikovskiy (q.v.). In the early 1820's he withdrew to his country estate Safonkovo (Tver' province) and devoted himself to the artistic study of peasant life. Venetsianov was a poor draughtsman and far from being expert in perspective. But despite his technical faults he created the most original *genre* painting of his time, free of all sentimentality and anecdotal contents. His peasants are dignified and serene as they toil and lead their simple life in communion with placid nature. Venetsianov succeeded in bringing out the peculiar atmospheric light of the great Russian plain. At Safonkovo he organized a school of painting and many of his pupils were serfs.

Verkhneudinsk, see ULAN-UDE.

Verkhne-Ural'sk, town in the Chelyabinsk Oblast (Urals), situated on the River Ural about 40 m. north of Magnitogorsk. Population (1956) 11,000. It is the main centre of food production for Magnitogorsk. Until the mid 1950's there was an 'isolator' (q.v.) here for important political prisoners, which may still exist. Verkhne-Ural'sk was founded as a fortress in 1734.

Verkhoyansk, town in Yakutia (north-eastern Siberia), situated on the River Yana 656 m. north-east of Yakutsk. Population (1956) 1,800 (1951, 3,000), chiefly Russian. It is the 'cold pole' of the northern hemisphere (lowest reading—83·6° F.). It is the centre of a cattle-breeding and fur-trapping area, and tin-mining takes place in the vicinity. Verkhoyansk was founded in 1638 and has been a place of banishment.

Vernadskiy, Vladimir Ivanovich (1863–1945), scientist and thinker, one of the founders of geochemistry and the founder of bio-geo-chemistry. He also set up many academic bodies (Commission for the Study of Natural Productive Forces in Russia, 1915, Ukrainian Academy of Sciences, 1918, Institute of Radiology, 1922, etc.). Vernadskiy was active in the *zemstvo* (q.v.) movement, the Council of State (q.v., as elected member for Moscow University) and the Constitutional Democratic Party (q.v.). Opposed to the Bolsheviks, he was on the White side, 1917–21, living in Kiev and Simferopol', but after the civil war returned to his academic work in Petrograd. He remained consistently anti-Marxist, building his own natural philosophy largely on the ideas of N. F. Fëdorov (q.v.).

Vernyy, see ALMA-ATA.

Vertov, Dziga (real name **Kaufman, Denis Arkad'yevich**) (1896–1954), film director, founder of the film documentary whose work fore-shadowed the television documentary. He was at first an extreme realist, advocating only 'factual' films against established indoor techniques with actors, and wished to depict 'daily life in the raw.' He laid the foundations of editing and montage techniques which influenced foreign exponents of documentary film-making as well as leading Soviet directors. Vertov founded an extremist school of film-makers which in 1922 issued a manifesto denouncing 'artificial' art. In the early 1930's he was denounced by the authorities as a Formalist (*see* FORMALISM), and during the Great Purge (q.v.) he disappeared, but was again allowed to direct three films in 1942–4. His chief films were: *Anniversary of the Revolution*, 1918, *History of the Civil War*, 1921, the documentary series *Kino-Pravda*, 1922–5, and *Kino-Eye*, 1924, *One Sixth of the World*, made in 1926 as an ad-vertisement film for Soviet goods, *Man with a Camera*, 1929, *Three Songs of Lenin*, 1934, and *The Cradle Song*, 1937. *See also* CINEMA.

Veselovskiy, Aleksandr Nikolayevich (1838–1906), literary historian, an outstanding representative of the comparativist school in Russia.

His tradition was strong among Soviet historians of literature, particularly the Formalists (*see* FORMALISM), but in 1947, during the party onslaught on 'cosmopolitanism' among the Soviet intelligentsia (*see* ZHDANOV), the origins of this evil in literary theory were attributed to Veselovskiy. In 1956 his name was 'rehabilitated.'

Vichuga, town in the Ivanovo Oblast (central Russia), situated on the railway line Ivanovo–Kineshma 41 m. north-east of Ivanovo. Population (1959) 51,000. It is a major centre of the cotton industry, and has been famous for its cloth and linen since the first half of tho 17th century. The first large cotton mill was founded here in 1812 by a serf. Vichuga became a town in 1925 when three industrial villages were fused. The Stakhanov movement (q.v.) in the textile industry was started here in 1935.

Viipuri, *see* VYBORG.

Vikings, *see* VARANGIANS.

Village is the main type of rural settlement in the U.S.S.R. There are two words in Russian for village, roughly corresponding to 'village' and 'hamlet,' though now that few churches remain in the countryside there is no obvious distinction between the two. There are no official limits to the size of a village, and in the south the Ukrainian villages, and particularly those of the Cossacks (q.v.), often have several thousand inhabitants (the largest of them over 20,000); the size of villages generally decreases from the south to the north, and in the north of European Russia they are usually quite small. In the north and south villages are normally situated along the rivers, while in the centre they are spread over the watersheds. The typical plan of a village is linear, the village containing a few long streets, but in the Ukraine they are commonly built in a disorderly fashion without any definite plan. The houses are generally bigger (often with two or three storeys) and constructed of wood in the north, while in the south they are smaller, have one storey and are built of unbaked brick and whitewashed. After the collectivization of agriculture (q.v.) a small village would normally form one collective farm (*see* KOLKHOZ), while a large one would be divided into several; however, since the amalgamation of many small collective farms during the 1950's, a large village usually forms one *kolkhoz* and smaller villages are grouped together. Khrushchëv's idea of transforming villages into 'agricultural towns' (*see* AGRO-TOWNS) has been implemented on a small scale since 1957. Newly built rural settlements, e.g. in the Virgin Land area (*see* VIRGIN LAND CAMPAIGN), are not normally called villages but settlements and do not resemble traditional villages in their layout. The village was the basic unit of peasant self-government (*see* MIR) until 1917. The village as such is not now an administrative unit, and a 'village soviet' normally administers several villages. *See also* KHUTOR. See G. Jorré, *The Soviet Union, the Land and its People*, 3rd imp., 1955.

Village Poor, Committees of, *see* COMMITTEES OF THE POOR.

Vil'na, *see* VILNIUS.

Vilnius (Polish **Wilno**, formerly Russian **Vil'na**), capital, economic and cultural centre of Lithuania. Population (1959) 235,000 (1914, 193,000; 1921, 123,000; 1941, 235,000), Lithuanian and Russian (before the war mainly Poles and Jews). It has engineering, wood-working and light industries, and is an important railway junction (five lines); many old crafts are still carried on. It is the seat of the Lithuanian Academy of Sciences, 1941, and has a university (founded 1578, as a Jesuit academy, raised to university status 1803, abolished 1832, re-established 1919); there are many notable buildings of the 14th–19th centuries. Vilnius has been known since the 12th century and became capital of Lithuania in 1323. It was at first predominantly Orthodox and Russian (Belorussian), but became Catholic and Polish in the 17th century; during the 17th–19th centuries it was the principal seat of Jewish culture in Europe. Vilnius became Russian in 1795 and was the residence of the governor-general of the Lithuanian and Belorussian provinces; during the 19th century it was a centre of the Polish national movement, and of social democracy from the 1890's. The town was occupied by the Germans, 1915–18 and 1941–4; from 1918 it was the official capital of independent Lithuania, but in fact it was annexed by Poland, 1920–39. When the Soviet army occupied it in 1939 it was returned to Lithuania, but annexed by the U.S.S.R., together with the rest of the country, in 1940. From 1950 to 1952 it was the administrative centre of Vilnius Oblast (now abolished).

Vil'yams (Williams), Vasiliy Robertovich (1863–1939), agrobiologist and soil specialist of American parentage, professor at Moscow Agricultural Academy, member of the Academy of Sciences; he joined the Communist Party in 1928. Vil'yams advanced the theory of a 'single soil-forming process' and propagated a system of crop rotation with grasses as universally applicable irrespective of local conditions. This dogmatic approach, supported by the authorities and reflected in the planning, did considerable harm to agriculture and was abandoned after Stalin's death. Lysenko (q.v.) has claimed that Vil'yams's theories are a component part of the 'Michurinist' agrobiology.

Vinnitsa (Ukrainian **Vynnytsya**): 1. Oblast in the Ukraine, situated in the Volhynia-Podolia upland, bordering on Bessarabia, in wooded steppe country traversed by the Southern Bug. Area 10,300 sq. m.; population (1959) 2,141,000 (17 per cent urban), Ukrainians (before the war also Jews). Sugar-beet and wheat are cultivated, cattle raised, and there are food and light industries. The area belonged to Volhynia, became Lithuanian in 1393, Polish in 1569 and Russian in 1793.

2. Administrative, economic and cultural centre of the oblast, situated on the Southern Bug about 120 m. south-west of Kiev. Population (1959) 121,000 (1914, 48,000; 1939, 93,000). It has chemical (fertilizers), engineering (electrical equipment and instruments), textile and food industries. Vinnitsa has been known since the 14th century, was the residence of the Ukrainian Directory (q.v.) in 1918, and became provincial capital in 1920.

Vinogradoff, Sir Paul (Pavel Gavrilovich) (1854–1925), historian, professor of history at Moscow University. He resigned in 1902 because of conflicts with the authorities, and from the following year was professor of jurisprudence at Oxford. His main works dealt with the history of medieval institutions in Western Europe, particularly

England; he was also the author of several textbooks on history which were very popular in Russia. *See* his *Self-Government in Russia*, 1915; *Outlines of Historical Jurisprudence* (2 vols.), 1920–3; *Feudalism*, 1922; *Villainage in England*, 1927; *Growth of the Manor*, 2nd ed., 1932.

Vinogradov, Viktor Vladimirovich (*b.* 1895), linguist, professor of Moscow University, member of the Academy of Sciences since 1946, head of its section of Literature and Language since 1950, director of its Institute of Linguistics 1950–4 and of the Institute of Russian Language since 1958. He has published many works on grammar, style, lexicology and phraseology of the Russian language, including *Essays in the History of Russian 16th–19th centuries Literary Language*, 1934, and *The Russian Language. Grammatical Doctrine of the Word*, 1947; the latter was attacked in the official press. Vinogradov took an active part in restoring the standards of theoretical linguistics in Russia after the condemnation of Marrism (*see* MARR) in 1950.

Virgin Land Campaign, measures for the cultivation of virgin lands and reclamation of waste lands which were initiated by Khrushchëv in 1953 with the intention of securing an adequate supply of grain. It has mainly affected Western Siberia, North Kazakhstan and the southern Urals, where new settlers from European Russia, mainly semi-compulsorily recruited young people, have been brought. By 1956, 87,500,000 acres had been cultivated. Since then efforts have largely been concentrated on the intensification of farming within these areas rather than on further extension of the area under cultivation. *See* W. A. D. Jackson, 'The Virgin and Idle Lands of Western Siberia and Northern Kazakhstan: a Geographical Appraisal,' *Geographical Review*, vol. xlvi, No. 1, 1955; J. A. Newth, 'State Farms in the Kazakh S.S.R.,' *Soviet Studies*, vol. x, No. 3, Jan. 1959.

Vishnevskiy, Aleksandr Vasil'yevich (1874–1948), surgeon, professor at Kazan' University, from 1934 director of the surgical clinics of both the Central Institute for improving the qualifications of physicians and the All Union Institute of Experimental Medicine, director of the Institute of Surgery of the Academy of Medical Sciences, 1946. He introduced several new methods for the treatment of inflammation processes and traumatic shock (novocaine block, etc.); his methods were extensively used during the Second World War.

Vitebsk: 1. Oblast in northern Belorussia, a moraine area traversed by the Western Dvina and partly covered by mixed forests. Area (1959) 10,800 sq. m.; population (1959) 935,000 (38 per cent urban), mostly Belorussians, before the war also Jews. There are flax cultivation, dairy farming and pig breeding, and textile, food, metal-working and woodworking industries. Principal towns: Vitebsk, Orsha, Polotsk.

2. Administrative, economic and cultural centre of the oblast, situated on the Western Dvina. Population (1959) 148,000 (1913, 109,000; 1920, 80,000; 1939, 167,000). It has textile, engineering (machine tools) and food industries, and is a railway junction. There are interesting buildings of the 12th–19th centuries. Vitebsk has been known since 1021, became capital of Vitebsk Principality in 1101,

Lithuanian in 1320 and Russian in 1772 (provincial capital). Fierce fighting took place in 1944.

Vitim, navigable right tributary of the River Lena in Siberia, which rises in the Transbaykalian mountains. Length 1,200 m.; chief port Bodaybo. Its lower course crosses the rich Vitim gold-mining area which has been the site of several labour camps.

Vitte, *see* WITTE.

Vize, Vladimir Yul'yevich (1888–1954), leading figure in Arctic studies. As a geographer he participated in G. Ya. Sedov's attempt to reach the North Pole in 1912–14. He was a pioneer in sea ice studies, and also wrote much on the history of exploration. Between 1910 and 1937 he took part in fourteen Arctic expeditions, and he played a leading part in the organization of the North Polar Drift Expedition in 1937 (*see* PAPANIN). From 1930 until his retirement he was deputy director of the Arctic Institute in Leningrad, and he had great influence upon Soviet scientific work in the Arctic during the 1930's. See *Polar Record*, vol. vii, No. 50, 1955.

Vladikavkaz, *see* ORDZHONIKIDZE.

Vladimir: 1. Oblast of the R.S.F.S.R., situated east of Moscow, a region of forested lowland with large deposits of peat. Area 11,100 sq. m.; population (1959) 1,402,000 (57 per cent urban). There are large engineering, textile and glass-working (since the 16th–17th centuries) industries, and old handicrafts (linen, silk, woodworking) are carried on. Grain and potatoes are cultivated and there is market gardening (Vladimir cherries) and dairy farming. Principal towns: Vladimir, Kovrov, Murom, Gus'-Khrustal'nyy.

2 (or **Vladimir-na-Klyaz'me**). Administrative, economic and cultural centre of the oblast, situated about 120 m. east of Moscow. Population (1959) 154,000 (1914, 47,000; 1920, 24,000; 1939, 67,000). It has large engineering (tractors, automobile parts) and chemical industries. The town is a treasury of Russian art of the 12th–early 19th centuries, including the magnificent cathedrals of the Assumption (built 1158–61) and of St Demetrius (1193–7), which contain frescoes by Rublëv, and the beautiful church of the Intercession at nearby Bogolyubovo. Vladimir was founded as a castle by Vladimir Monomakh around the year 1100, was capital of central Russia, 1157–1238 (the Grand Principality of Vladimir), became Muscovite in 1364 and provincial capital in 1778. Industrial development dates from the 1930's. The notorious 'isolator' (q.v.) for important political prisoners was situated here from the late 1930's until the mid 1950's and may still exist.

Vladimir, Saint (Vladimir I) (956–1015), patron saint of Russian Christians, Grand Prince of Kiev from 980. He was baptized before his marriage to the sister of the Byzantine emperor, and in 988 made Christianity the official religion, summoning Greek clergy to evangelize the country. His feast is on 15th July.

Vladimirtsov, Boris Yakovlevich (1884–1931), orientalist, professor at Leningrad University, member of the Academy of Sciences. His works were devoted to the study of Mongol language, literature, ethnography and history. In his *Social System of Mongols*, 1934, he developed a concept of 'nomadic feudalism.'

Vladivostok, administrative and economic centre of the Maritime Kray, the chief cultural centre of the Russian Far East, situated on the western shore of the Sea of Japan in Peter the Great's Bay. Population (1959) 283,000 (1897, 29,000; 1914, 120,000; 1926, 108,000; 1939, 206,000), Russians (until 1937 also Chinese and Koreans). It is the terminus of the Trans-Siberian Railway (5,732 m. from Moscow) and the Northern Sea Route, centre of communications for Russian Pacific territories, the largest Russian port in the Pacific and the principal base of the Pacific fleet. It has engineering (shipbuilding and mining equipment), fishing, whaling and varied food industries; there is the Far Eastern branch of the U.S.S.R. Academy of Sciences, and the Far Eastern University (founded 1899 as the Oriental Institute, university from 1920, abolished 1939, reopened 1956). Vladivostok was founded as a port in 1860, became a town in 1875 and capital of the Maritime region in 1888; it developed rapidly as a free port (supplies for the Russian Far East and transit from Manchuria), naval base and fortress, and until the 1930's had a markedly international character. It was used for allied supplies in both world wars, and from 1918 until 1922 saw allied occupation under Japanese leadership and was the seat of various pro- and anti-Bolshevik governments.

Vlasov, Aleksandr Vasil'yevich (*b.* 1900), architect, member of U.S.S.R. Academy of Architecture, designer of Gor'kiy Park of Rest and Culture, Moscow. He was the chief architect of Kiev, 1944–50, and thereafter chief architect of Moscow. *See also* ARCHITECTURE.

Vlasov, Andrey Andreyevich (1900–46), general, leader of the anti-Communist movement among Soviet prisoners of war and civilian deportees in Germany during the Second World War. Of peasant birth, Vlasov joined the Red Army in 1919; he was military adviser to Chiang Kai-shek, 1938–9, and distinguished himself in the defence of Kiev and Moscow, 1941–2. Captured in 1942, he was induced by Russian sympathizers among German officers to play the leading part in the Russian anti-Communist movement. A 'Committee for the Liberation of the Peoples of Russia' was established in November 1944 with Vlasov as chairman; he had no authority over Russian units in the German Army until January 1945. He surrendered to the Americans in May 1945, was handed over to the Soviet authorities and executed. *See* G. Fischer, *Soviet Opposition to Stalin,* Cambridge, Mass., 1952; J. Thorwald, *Wen sie verderben wollen,* Stuttgart, 1952; G. Reitlinger, *The House Built on Sand: the Conflicts of German Policy in Russia, 1939–45,* 1960.

Vocational Training, of workers, is organized in three forms: (1) in apprenticeships at factories and other places of work; this system is extensive, and about 2·5 million new workers are claimed to have been trained yearly during the 1950's; (2) at Vocational Technical Schools established by the educational reform of 1958 on the basis of former Trade Schools and other schools of the State Labour Reserves system (*see* LABOUR RESERVE); these schools are fee-paying (except for orphans, etc.), but the pupils receive apprentices' wages; (3) in secondary schools where 'polytechnical education' since the 1958 reform includes compulsory vocational training.

Voguls, *see* MANSI.

Volga (ancient **Rha**), longest river (2,300 m.) and one of the
principal waterways of Europe, rising in the Valday upland north-
west of Moscow and flowing eastwards to Kazan' and then south into
the Caspian Sea, where it forms a large delta. Low left and high right
banks are typical of the river, particularly where it flows along the
Volga upland between Gor'kiy and Stalingrad. It is ice-free for
between 150 and 250 days a year, is fed chiefly by water from melting
snow, and therefore has high and long spring floods. The chief
tributaries are the Kama (left) and the Oka (right), both of which are
longer than the Rhine. Total drainage area 533,000 sq. m. Nearly all
the Russian plain landscape zones, from forest to semi-desert (below
Stalingrad), are traversed by the Volga, in whose basin are two of the
principal industrial areas of the country—the Moscow area between
the Volga and the Oka, and the Urals in the basin of the Kama.
There are large oil, natural gas, oil shale (*see* VOLGA-URALS OIL
AREA), salt and peat deposits. The river is navigable almost throughout its course, and has over 70 navigable tributaries, the total length
of the waterways exceeding 16,000 miles.

Two-thirds of all goods, and more than half of all passengers,
transported on the internal waterways of Russia are carried by the
Volga and its tributaries; the principal goods transported are timber,
oil, mineral building materials, grain and salt. The chief ports are
Gor'kiy, Kazan', Kuybyshev, Stalingrad, Astrakhan', Saratov,
Yaroslavl' and Rybinsk, mainly industrial cities standing on the
river where it is crossed by railways. Artificial waterways connect the
Volga with the Baltic and White seas (*see* VOLGA-BALTIC WATER-
WAY; WHITE SEA-BALTIC CANAL), the Don (*see* VOLGA-DON CANAL)
and Moscow (*see* MOSCOW-VOLGA CANAL). The Volga has emerged as
one of the major sources of power supply in the country through the
construction of the Volga, Stalingrad, Gor'kiy and other large hydro-
electric stations, whose high dams transform the river into a series of
artificial reservoirs (*see* KUYBYSHEV; RYBINSK RESERVOIR) with
lake-like conditions of navigation. Pollution, and the construction of
these dams, have since the 1930's depleted the former fish resources
of the river. The Volga formed part of the trade route from northern
Europe to Central Asia during the Middle Ages; on its banks arose the
medieval states of the Volga Bulgarians, the Khazars, the Golden
Horde and the Kazan' and Astrakhan' khanates. The region between
the upper Volga and the Oka formed the cradle of Muscovy, which
during the 16th century absorbed the entire Volga basin. *See also
under* the names of the principal Volga cities.

Volga-Baltic Waterway, artificial waterway which connects the
River Volga with the Baltic via the Rybinsk Reservoir, lakes Onega
and Ladoga and a number of small rivers and canals. Built in 1810,
it has been known as the Mariinskiy Waterway, but with the reconstruction now in progress it has become known as the Volga-Baltic
Waterway.

Volga Bulgarians, medieval Turkic-speaking people, ancestors of
the present-day Chuvashes and Volga Tatars, who lived on the middle
Volga and Kama, having come there from the steppes north of the

Sea of Azov in the 7th century. They belonged originally to the Hun confederation, then established a separate state with Bulgar as its capital; they were under Khazar suzerainty until the 10th century, independent until 1236, and then under the suzerainty of the Golden Horde until the 15th century. The state later existed as the Kazan' Khanate.

Volga-Don Canal, artificial waterway which connects the Volga (near Stalingrad) with the Don, built 1947–52, largely by forced labour. Length 63 m. The first attempt at constructing such a canal was made by the Turks in 1569, and from the time of Peter the Great plans for building it were repeatedly made. *See* P. A. Warneck, 'The Volga-Don Navigation Canal,' *Russian Review,* Oct. 1954.

Volga German Republic, established in 1918 as an Autonomous Workers' Commune, in 1924 transformed into an Autonomous Republic. More than half the population were Volga Germans descended from German colonists who settled on both banks of the lower Volga (near Saratov) during the 1760's in the reign of Catherine II. The republic was abolished by a decree of the Soviet Government after the German invasion in 1941, and the German inhabitants were deported to Siberia; they were not included in the decree on the rehabilitation of deported peoples in 1957. *See also* GERMANS. *See* W. Kolarz, *Russia and her Colonies,* 1952.

Volga-Urals Oil Area (formerly known as the Second Baku), principal oil-producing area of the country, situated between the middle Volga and the Urals. Oil extraction was started in the 1930's, and by 1955 production was more than double that of the old Baku oilfields. The Tatar-Bashkir oilfields are the chief centre.

Volhynia (Russian and Ukrainian **Volyn'**): 1. Area in north-western Ukraine comprising the Volhynia, Rovno and Zhitomir oblasts, with the Poles'ye lowland in the north and the Volhynia-Podolia upland in the south. The region belonged to the Kievan state from the 9th century, from 988 as a principality which later became independent. From 1199 to 1340 it was fused with Galicia, and was then Lithuanian, becoming Polish in 1569, Russian in 1793–5, again partly Polish 1919–39; it was occupied by the Germans in 1918 and 1941.

2. Oblast of the Ukraine, the westernmost of the Volhynia area, bordering on Poland; it has deposits of lignite and peat. Area 7,800 sq. m.; population (1959) 890,000 (24 per cent urban), mostly Ukrainians, also Jews and Poles before the war. Grain and potatoes are cultivated, and cattle, pigs and bees kept; there are also food and timber industries, and peat and lignite extraction. Principal towns: Lutsk (administrative centre) and Kovel'.

Volkhov, river flowing north from Lake Il'men' into Lake Ladoga. Length 130 m. Novgorod stands on the Volkhov, which was part of the trade route from Scandinavia to Byzantium in the Middle Ages.

Volkov, Fëdor Grigor'yevich (1729–63), merchant and actor who in 1751 founded the first Russian provincial public theatre in Yaroslavl'.

Vologda: 1. Oblast of the R.S.F.S.R., situated in northern Russia, stretching from Lake Onega and the Rybinsk Reservoir to the Northern Dvina River; it is a rolling plain partly covered with coniferous forests and many swamps. Area 56,200 sq. m.; population (1959) 1,307,000 (35 per cent urban). There is dairy farming (Yaroslavl' breed), flax cultivation, and linen-milling, lumbering, paper-milling, woodworking and metal-working industries; old crafts (Vologda lace) are still practised. Principal towns: Vologda, Cherepovets, Velikiy Ustyug. The area was colonized in the 11th century by Novgorod, and became Muscovite in 1462. It has been a place of banishment since the 15th century.

2. Administrative, economic and cultural centre of the oblast, situated on the Moscow–Archangel and Leningrad–Perm' railways. Population (1959) 138,000 (1914, 45,000; 1939, 95,000). It has engineering (shipbuilding, timber industry equipment), linen-milling and dairy industries, and at nearby Sokol there is a large paper plant. There are many architectural monuments of the 16th–early 19th centuries, also an Institute of Dairying. Vologda has been known since 1147, became Muscovite in 1347, and in the 15th–early 18th centuries was an important trading point on the route to Siberia and Western Europe.

Vol'sk, town in the Saratov Oblast, situated on the right bank of the Volga about 80 m. north-east of Saratov. Population (1959) 62,000. It has a large cement industry (since 1896). Vol'sk has been known since the 17th century and became a town in 1780.

Vol'skiy, Stanislav (real name **Sokolov, Andrey Vladimirovich**) (1880–?), politician and philosopher, a Social Democrat. After the split in the Russian Social Democratic Party he joined the Bolsheviks and during the revolution of 1905 conducted the weavers' strike in the Ivanovo-Voznesensk area and was one of the leaders of the Moscow uprising. In 1908 he headed the left-wing Bolsheviks in Moscow and next year joined the radical Bolshevik sub-faction 'Vperëd' (q.v.). In his book *Philosophy of Struggle*, 1909, Vol'skiy aimed at providing Marxism with a new ethical doctrine based on the principles of Bogdanovism (q.v.). In the following years he tended towards Anarcho-Syndicalism, advocating 'socialism of feeling' in addition to 'scientific socialism.' After the February revolution of 1917 he was on the editorial board of Gor'kiy's Social Democratic internationalist paper *New Life*, and worked in the military section of the Petrograd Soviet. He opposed the Bolshevik seizure of power and emigrated in 1919, but returned the following year and gave up politics.

Volzhskiy, town in the Stalingrad Oblast situated on the left bank of the Volga opposite Stalingrad. Population (1959) 57,000. It was founded as a workers' settlement in the 1950's in connection with the construction of the Stalingrad hydro-electric station, and became a town in 1954.

'Voprosy Filosofii' (*Questions of Philosophy*), chief philosophical journal, published since 1947 by the Institute of Philosophy of the Academy of Sciences. Its chief editors have been high-ranking party propagandists (M. N. Kedrov, D. I. Chesnokov, M. D. Kammari and, since 1959, A. F. Okulov). It was founded in connection with Zhdanov's (q.v.) campaign against 'objectivism' in philosophy (*see* ALEKSANDROV, G. F.). With the beginning of the intellectual 'thaw' after Stalin's death, *Voprosy Filosofii* published a few 'revisionist' articles (*see* REVISIONISM), for which it was soon called to task. Its scholarly level has in recent years considerably improved.

Vorkuta, town in the Komi Autonomous Republic, situated in the extreme north-east of European Russia, the centre of the Pechora coal basin. Population (1959) 55,000. (This figure refers to the town in the narrower sense, i.e. the central part of the area administered by the Vorkuta Town Council, which includes several mining settlements; the total population of Vorkuta was stated in 1957 to be 160,000; before the dissolution of the forced labour camps it was estimated at over 300,000.) The town has a large coal-mining industry (since the 1930's) and is a local cultural centre. Vorkuta was founded in 1932 as the centre of a large forced labour camp area, and became a town in 1943. The big strike in 1953 of Vorkuta camp inmates played an important role in the political development of the post-Stalin era: it served as a model for a series of strikes in the other main camp areas, and was thus one of the causes of the penal reform of the mid 1950's. *See* J. Scholmer, *Vorkuta,* 1954.

Voronezh: 1. Oblast of the R.S.F.S.R., situated south-east of Moscow, and traversed by the Don, which separates the central Russian upland in the west and the Oka-Don lowland in the east; it is a ravinous area, with rich black earth soil and a few oak forests. Area 20,200 sq. m.; population (1959) 2,363,000 (35 per cent urban), Russians and Ukrainians. Wheat, sunflowers and sugar-beet are cultivated, and there is intensive livestock breeding (Russian trotters originated here); there are also engineering, chemical, building materials and food industries. Principal towns: Voronezh and Borisoglebsk. Until Russian colonization in the 16th century the area was virtually unpopulated; in 1919–22 it was the scene of anti-Bolshevik guerrilla warfare, and in 1942–3 was partially occupied by the Germans.

2. Administrative centre of the oblast and the principal economic and cultural centre of the central black earth region. Population (1959) 454,000 (1920, 90,000; 1923, 79,000; 1939, 344,000). It has varied engineering (agricultural and food industry equipment, excavators, Diesel motors, etc.), chemical (synthetic rubber, oil cracking) and food industries. There is a university (established in 1918 on the basis of the evacuated Tartu University) and several other higher educational establishments, including an agricultural institute (founded in 1913). Voronezh was founded as a Muscovite frontier fortress against the Tatars in 1586, was the industrial base (shipbuilding, etc.) for Peter the Great's Azov campaign, 1695–6, and became provincial capital in 1711; it has been an important commercial and cultural centre since the 1830's, and was capital of the central black earth region, 1928–34. It saw fierce fighting in the civil war and the Second World War, being severely damaged in the latter.

Vorontsov, Vasiliy Pavlovich (1847–1918), economist and publicist, a liberal Populist. In his works—*The Fate of Capitalism in Russia,* 1882, *The Peasant Commune,* 1892, *Progressive Trends in Peasant Economy,* 1892, *The Fate of Capitalist Russia,* 1907, etc.—Vorontsov, while accepting Marx's theory of capitalist development in Western

Europe, argued that in Russia capitalism was neither desirable nor likely to develop, and its function of developing the country's productive forces should and could be performed through a direct transition to social forms of production, of which there already existed such embryonic forms as the peasant commune (*see* MIR) and the *artel'* (q.v.). Though his main thesis proved erroneous, there was much that was sound in Vorontsov's view that Marxism was ill suited as a theoretical framework for the study of the Russian peasant economy. *See also* NEO-POPULISM.

Voroshilov, *see* USSURIYSK.

Voroshilov, Kliment Yefremovich (*b.* 1881), politician, Marshal of the Soviet Union (since 1935). As a metal-worker in the Donbas, he joined the Bolshevik faction of the Social Democratic Labour Party in 1903 and was active in underground work. He took some part in establishing the Cheka (q.v.) after the Bolshevik seizure of power in 1917. He distinguished himself both militarily and politically during the civil war and became a member of the party's Central Committee in 1921. Siding with Stalin in the inner-party struggle that followed Lenin's death, he was appointed Commissar for War and the Navy in 1925, and a Politburo member in the following year. He was relieved of the post of Commissar of Defence in 1940, following the Soviet-Finnish war, but appointed a deputy prime minister. Voroshilov was a member of the State Defence Committee (q.v.) during the Second World War, but failed as a commander in the field. He headed the Soviet Control Commission in Hungary, 1945–7. From Stalin's death in 1953 until his retirement in 1960 on grounds of ill health he was Chairman of the Presidium of the U.S.S.R. Supreme Soviet, i.e. titular head of state.

Voroshilovgrad, *see* LUGANSK.

Voroshilovsk (until 1931 **Alchevsk**), town in the Lugansk Oblast of the Ukraine, about 25 m. south-west of Lugansk. Population (1959) 98,000 (1926, 16,000; 1939, 55,000). It is situated amidst rich coal deposits and is a major centre of the iron and steel and coking industries of the Donets Basin. It was founded in 1895.

Vostokov (real name **Osteneck**), **Aleksandr Khristoforovich** (1781–1864), philologist of Baltic German parentage, chief librarian at the Rumyantsev Museum (now the Lenin Library) in Moscow, member of the Academy of Sciences. His *Discourse on the Slavonic Language*, 1820, *Russian Grammar*, 1831, *Description of Russian and Slavonic Manuscripts of the Rumyantsev Museum*, 1842, etc., are among the fundamental works in Slavonic philology.

Voting, *see* ELECTIONS.

Votkinsk, town in the Udmurt Autonomous Republic, situated 38 m. north-east of Izhevsk. Population (1959) 59,000 (1939, 39,000), chiefly Russians. It has a large engineering plant. The town is the birth-place of Tchaikovsky and his old home is a museum. Votkinsk was founded as an ironworks in 1759 and became a town in the 1930's. In 1918 the workers of Votkinsk overthrew the Bolsheviks and formed the Votkinsk division which fought on the side of the Whites.

Votyaks, *see* UDMURTS.

Voyeykov, Aleksandr Ivanovich (1842–1916), geographer, the founder of Russian climatology. Educated at St Petersburg and Göttingen universities, he taught at Moscow and St Petersburg, travelled widely in western Europe, the Americas, India and other Asian countries, set up and directed the meteorological commission of the Russian Geographical Society (organizing a network of amateur observers), and founded, 1891, and edited the *Meteorological Herald*. In his fundamental work *Climates of the Globe, especially of Russia*, 1884, Voyeykov gave a classification of climates and analysed the climate-forming factors. He was the first to use the method of balances in the study of geographical phenomena; he was also a pioneer of palaeo-climatology.

Voznesenskiy, Nikolay Alekseyevich (1903–50), Communist of lower middle class origin, joined the party in 1919, was trained at the Sverdlov Communist University, 1921 ff., and in the Economic Institute of Red Professorship, 1928–31, worked in the party apparatus and became a member of the Committee of Party Control (q.v.) in 1934. From 1935 he worked with Zhdanov in Leningrad, and during the Great Purge (q.v.) rose spectacularly to chairman of the Gosplan (q.v.) in 1938 and a deputy prime minister in 1939; during the war he was a member of the State Defence Committee (q.v.). A member of the party's Central Committee from 1939, Voznesenskiy became a candidate member of the Politburo in 1941 and a full member in 1947. After the death of Zhdanov in 1948 Voznesenskiy, as head of the Zhdanovite faction in the party leadership, fell victim to Malenkov's persecution of Zhdanovites (*see* LENINGRAD CASE), and he was dismissed from all his posts in 1949, arrested and shot on Stalin's orders. *See* his *The Economy of the U.S.S.R. during World War II*, Washington, D.C., 1948; B. D. Wolfe, *Khrushchëv and Stalin's Ghost*, 1955.

Vperëd ('Forward'), radical sub-faction of the Bolsheviks founded by Bogdanov, Lunacharskiy and Maksim Gor'kiy in 1909. It comprised the majority of the left-wing Marxist intellectuals who had joined Lenin in 1904 (*see* BUREAU OF THE MAJORITY COMMITTEES) and had largely constituted the Bolshevik leadership during the revolution of 1905, as well as many of the better-educated worker members of the Bolshevik faction. The ideological basis of the group was Bogdanovism (q.v.), and its main tactical disagreement with Lenin was over the latter's insistence on participation in the Duma, which the Vperëdists considered harmful to the revolutionary cause. The group soon split up and lost significance as an organized body. In 1917 some of its leaders, including Lunacharskiy, joined the Mezhrayontsy (q.v.). *See* L. Schapiro, *The Communist Party of the Soviet Union*, 1960.

Vrangel', *see* WRANGEL.

Vrubel', Mikhail Aleksandrovich (1856–1910), painter, studied at the Society for the Encouragement of Arts and at the Academy of Arts, 1880–4, after taking a degree in law at St Petersburg University. He exhibited with the Mir Iskusstva (q.v.). Vrubel' was the first Russian painter of the late 19th century to break completely with the ideas of the Peredvizhniki (q.v.). Art was to him not a social service but a self-contained region of human endeavour, and elements of art were not just means of communicating a message but were significant in themselves. His short career was an essay in freedom of expression. During his years at the academy he studied early Russian icons, which were then completely neglected. He visited Venice, and restored frescoes in the ancient church of St Cyril at Kiev; he also designed murals on themes from Russian epics. He transplanted Pan to Russian birch wood, and gave that Greek god the pale blue eyes, high cheek-bones and large-jointed calloused hands of a Russian peasant. He visited Spain, only to bring back studies of the gipsies he had known in Russia. He found his ultimate symbol in Lermontov's (q.v.) 'Demon,' whose unfathomable despair strained his imagination to the utmost. In 1905 Vrubel' went mad and spent the last years of his life in an asylum. His importance for Russian art is hard to overestimate. His search for the absolute was not less intense than the similar experiences of Gauguin or van Gogh, and it prepared the soil for such great masters as Kandinskiy, Malevich and Chagall.

Vvedenskiy, Nikolay Yevgen'yevich (1852–1922), physiologist, professor at St Petersburg University, a Populist (*see* POPULISM) revolutionary in his youth. A pupil of Sechenov (q.v.), Vvedenskiy concentrated on and developed the theory of parabiosis (main work, *Stimulation and Narcosis*, 1901). He founded a fruitful school of physiological research in Russia, headed after his death by Ukhtomskiy (q.v.).

Vyatka, *see* KIROV.

Vyborg (Finnish **Viipuri,** Swedish **Viborg**), town in the Leningrad Oblast, situated on the Gulf of Finland about 75 m. north-west of Leningrad. Population (1959) 51,000 (1939, 73,000), Russians, before the war Finns and Swedes. It is an important centre of industry and transport (agricultural machinery; seaport, five railway lines, Saima canal). Vyborg was founded as a castle in 1293, became a town in 1403, and was an important fortress on the Russian frontier. It became Russian in 1710 (provincial capital), but was included in Finland in 1811. In 1940 it was ceded to the U.S.S.R. (being included in the Karelo-Finnish Republic), but was again Finnish 1941–4. The town suffered severely during the Second World War.

Vysheslavtsev, Boris Petrovich (1877–1954), philosopher and psychologist; he became professor at Moscow University in 1917 but was expelled from Russia in 1922 together with other leading intellectuals. He worked in the Russian Academy of Religion and Philosophy in Berlin, and was later active in the oecumenical movement. In his main work, *Ethics of the Transformed Eros*, Vysheslavtsev applied the findings of the depth psychologists to ethical problems. His *Philosophical Misery of Marxism* is a brief but penetrating analysis.

Vyshinskiy, Andrey Yanuar'yevich (1883–1955), lawyer and politician of Polish descent who joined the Social Democratic Labour Party in 1902 and adhered to the Mensheviks after the 1903 split. He played an active role in the 1905 revolution, and in 1920, when it was clear that the Bolsheviks had established their power, he joined them. He was a lecturer, and subsequently professor and rector, at Moscow University from 1921, and from 1928 to 1931 was head of the higher education department in the Commissariat of Education. In 1931 he became procurator of the Russian Federal Republic, of the U.S.S.R. in 1935, and deputy chairman of the Council of People's Commissars in 1939. During the show trials in Moscow, 1928–38, Vyshinskiy was prominent as chairman of the court in the Shakhty and Industrial Party trials, and as public prosecutor in the Metro-Vickers trial, 1933, and the three chief trials of the Great Purge (q.v.). Soviet legal science was dictated by Vyshinskiy from 1937: he was the leading exponent of Stalinism (q.v.) in legal theory and practice, and postulated that confession by the accused was adequate proof of guilt. He was deputy Minister of Foreign Affairs (under Molotov) from 1940 to 1949 and again 1953–5, and Minister 1949–53; he had no influence upon policy in these roles, acting simply as mouthpiece for Stalin and the Politburo. *See* M. S. Calcott, *Russian Justice*, New York, 1935; A. Y. Vyshinsky (ed.), *The Law of the Soviet State* (trans. H. W. Babb), New York, 1948; J. N. Hazard (ed.), *Soviet Legal Philosophy*, Cambridge, Mass., 1951; H. Kelsen, *The Communist Theory of Law*, 1955.

Vyshniy Volochëk, town in the Kalinin Oblast (central Russia), situated 74 m. north-west of Kalinin. Population (1959) 66,000 (1939, 64,000). It has textile and glass industries (since the 19th century). Vyshniy Volochëk is an old commercial centre and was especially important 1709–1810, when it stood upon the only artificial water-way connecting the Baltic Sea and the Volga.

W

Wages. Four wages systems are now in use in the U.S.S.R.: time wages, piece wages, piece wages with bonuses, and progressive piece wages, the last two being the most common. There are separate scales for each trade, usually expressed in coefficients by which the rate fixed for the lowest grade is to be multiplied. The difference between the lowest and the highest rate (usually for the 10th grade) is in all cases very considerable. The calculation of piece wages is usually based on the norm (q.v.), i.e. the expected output per shift which gives the right to the standard rate of pay. This structure of wages was established in the 1930's and no substantial changes were formally made (except for raising the norms) for two decades. In fact in most industries the wages are higher than those laid down by the official scales. A special Committee on Labour and Wages was formed after Stalin's death (whose chairman is an *ex-officio* member of the Council of Ministers) to rationalize and simplify the wage structure. With the gradual introduction of automation in industry, time wages, all but banned in the 1930's, are again becoming more widely applied.

Wages are normally paid monthly, though there is usually an advance in the middle of the month roughly corresponding to two weeks' wages. Minimum wages (in pre-1961 roubles) were fixed in 1956 at 300–350 roubles per month in the towns and 270 roubles in the countryside, but are supposed to be raised to 500–600 roubles by 1965. The monthly average for all wages and salaries was 790 roubles in 1958, and is supposed to be increased by 26 per cent to 995 roubles by 1965. It is officially claimed that real incomes (counting wages and social services) of workers and employees in 1958 were 3·7 times higher than in 1913 and 55 per cent higher than in 1950; a further increase of 40 per cent is intended by 1965. These claims are difficult to check and seem exaggerated. *See* J. G. Chapman, 'Real Wages in the Soviet Union, 1928–52,' *Review of Economics and Statistics*, May 1954; M. Yanowitch, 'Trends in Differentials between Salaried Personnel and Wage Workers in Soviet Industry,' *Soviet Studies*, vol. xi, No. 3, Jan. 1960; *The Soviet Seven Year Plan* (introduction by A. Nove), 1960.

War Communism, name by which the Bolshevik Government's social and economic policy from 1918 to 1921 is known. The policy had two aims: to support the Bolshevik effort during the civil war, and to accomplish the transition to conditions of communism. In practice the policy included nationalization of industry and trade, wages in kind for workers and employees, compulsory food deliveries by the peasants and obligatory labour service by the bourgeoisie. As a result discontent became rife and several uprisings took place in 1921 (*see* ANTONOV; KRONSTADT); the policy of War Communism was ended and the New Economic Policy (q.v.) put into effect. *See* M. Dobb, *Soviet Economic Development since 1917*, 1948; E. H. Carr,

The Bolshevik Revolution, vol. ii, 1952; H. Schwartz, *Russia's Soviet Economy*, 2nd ed., 1954.

Wenden, *see* CESIS.

West Kazakhstan Oblast is situated in the extreme north-west of the republic, bordering on the Volga region; it is dry steppe lowland, traversed by the River Ural. Area 58,300 sq. m.; population (1959) 383,000 (30 per cent urban), mainly Russians and Ukrainians in the north, Kazakhs in the south, also Tatars. Wheat and millet are cultivated in the north, and cattle, sheep and camels kept in the south. Industry is concentrated in Ural'sk, the administrative centre of the oblast. The area formed part of the traditional 'gateway to Europe' for the nomadic peoples of Asia; in the 13th–15th centuries it belonged to the Golden Horde and then to the Nogay Khanate. Russian Cossacks from the Volga began to settle on the banks of the Ural in the 16th century. The Kazakh Junior Hundred was formed east of the Ural in the 17th century, and in the following century, pressed by the Kalmyks and the Turkmens, it sought Russian protection. In 1803 a part of the Junior Hundred was permitted to settle between the Ural and the Volga in the western part of the present oblast.

Westernism, trend in Russian 19th- and 20th-century thought (philosophy, historiography, jurisprudence, politics) maintaining either that Russian conditions are essentially similar to those of Western Europe, or should imitate them, or both. The term Westernism originated in the 1840's when the Westernists were opposed by the Slavophiles (q.v.). *See also* POLITICAL THEORY. *See* R. Hare, *Pioneers of Russian Social Thought*, 1951; T. G. Masaryk, *The Spirit of Russia* (2 vols.), 2nd ed., 1955.

White Army, name by which the anti-Bolshevik forces during the civil war (q.v.) are generally known.

White Russia, *see* BELORUSSIA.

White Sea, gulf of the Barents Sea, frozen from September to May. Area over 30,000 sq. m.; chief port Archangel. The principal rivers flowing into the White Sea are the Northern Dvina, the Mezen' and the Onega. On the Solovetskiy Island in the sea there is a famous former monastery which until the 1950's was a concentration camp.

White Sea-Baltic Canal, artificial waterway which connects the White Sea with Lake Onega, and through it with the Baltic Sea and the Volga. Length 142 m., including 32 m. of canals. The idea of constructing the canal was first mooted in Peter the Great's time, and in 1915–16 surveying was carried out. It was built in 1931–3 by forced labour.

Williams, *see* VIL'YAMS.

Witte, Count Sergey Yul'yevich (1849–1915), statesman of German origin who became Minister of Transport in 1892 and was Minister of Finance, 1892–1903. In the latter capacity his policy of protectionist tariffs, large foreign loans and extensive railway construction did much to encourage Russia's industrial development. As Prime Minister, 1903–6, he negotiated the Portsmouth peace treaty with Japan (having previously opposed the emperor's Far Eastern policy which led to the Russo-Japanese War, q.v.), and advised Nicholas II to grant a constitution that would provide for a legislative Duma. Witte was a moderate conservative and was thus the object of suspicion both from the liberals and from the extreme right, including the emperor, who suddenly dismissed him. Subsequently, as an independent member of the Council of State (q.v.), he opposed Stolypin, despite the fact that the latter's policy was largely a continuation of Witte's own. *See* his *Memoirs* (trans. A. Yarmolinsky), New York, 1921; V. I. Gurko. *Features and Figures of the Past. Government and Opinion in the Reign of Nicholas II*, 1939; R. Hare, *Portraits of Russian Personalities between Reform and Revolution*, 1959; T. H. von Laue, 'Factory Inspection under the Witte System: 1892–1903,' *American Slavic and East European Review*, vol. xix, No. 3, Oct. 1960.

Women have legally the same rights and duties as men, and any discrimination, such as unequal pay, is forbidden. The employment of women for certain kinds of heavy work is also forbidden, and employed women are entitled to extra paid maternity leave; *kolkhoz* (q.v.) women and girls (from the age of 12) are under the same obligations of work in the *kolkhoz* as men and boys. In 1958 women formed 46 per cent of all wage and salary earners (27 per cent in 1929); they made up 45 per cent of people employed in industry, 30 per cent in building, 85 per cent in the health services, 67 per cent in education and 49 per cent in the government, party, etc., apparatus; in the *kolkhozes* the bulk of the work during the Second World War and the following decade was done by women. Of all people with higher education, women formed in 1957 52 per cent (compared with 28 per cent in 1928); they made up 29 per cent of all technologists, 32 per cent of jurists and 75 per cent of physicians. There is general social equality of women except among the Muslim peoples. The equality in employment frequently turns out to be unfavourable to women, since the regulations excluding them from heavy work are inadequate and often disregarded, and in recent years this problem has been raised in the press, the critics objecting both to the unfair practices and to their glorification in the official propaganda. As elsewhere women in the Soviet Union have in general tended to be a conservative and stabilizing factor, and in particular it was largely owing to them that the Communist attempts to undermine the family in the 1920's and early thirties were defeated. The conservative element within the family is especially strengthened by the fact that, with most women having to work for financial or other reasons, the grandmothers play an important role in the care of small children (e.g. religious interests among children are usually attributed to the influence of grandmothers). Traditionally in Russia, although women's social position was inferior to that of men, their legal position in regard to property was equal. Women played an important part in the revolutionary movement of the 19th century (e.g. S. Perovskaya in the Narodnaya Volya, Vera Zasulich in social democracy, Ye. Breshko-Breshkovskaya among the Socialist Revolutionaries). *See also* ABORTION; CHILDREN; FAMILY; MARRIAGE; POPULATION. *See* E. J. Simmons (ed.), *Through the Glass of Soviet Literature*, New York, 1953; W. Petersen, 'The Evolution of Soviet Family Policy,' *Problems of Communism*, vol. v, No. 5, Sept.–Oct. 1956.

Work-day Unit (*trudoden'*), measure of work in the collective farms (*see* KOLKHOZ) which is used as a basis for the distribution (in cash and kind) of a *kolkhoz*'s income among its members. Such distribution is normally made yearly, but in order to ameliorate the hardship thus caused a system of regular advance payments is now officially recommended to those *kolkhozes* which are capable of making them. The work-day unit does not correspond to a day's work, but is credited for a particular amount of work. Different rates apply for different kinds of work, so that the fulfilment of a day's norm may correspond to anything between 0·5 and 2·5 units. Bonuses for *kolkhoz* teams over-fulfilling their norms are also calculated in work-day units. A work-day unit has no fixed value, this being calculated as a ratio of any distributable residue (after sales to the State—*see* AGRICULTURAL PROCUREMENT—contributions to *kolkhoz* funds, etc.) of the collective farm's product and its monetary profit in a given year to the total number of work-day units credited to the members. Since *kolkhozes* are economically very unequal there are great variations in the value of work-day units. *See also* PEASANTS. *See* R. Schlesinger, 'The New Structure of Soviet Agriculture,' *Soviet Studies*, vol. x, No. 3, Jan. 1959; A. Nove, 'The Incomes of Soviet Peasants,' *Slavonic and East European Review*, vol. xxxviii, No. 91, June 1960.

Worker-Peasant Inspection, Commissariat of, existed 1920–34 to control the administrative apparatus and to guard against bureaucratization. The first commissar was Stalin. It was replaced in 1934 by the Commission of Soviet Control.

Workers' Control, form of management in industry practised during the period of War Communism (q.v.). It was in fact an unsuccessful workers' administration through factory committees. The enthusiasts of workers' control saw in it the beginnings of socialism, and were rightly accused, especially by Mensheviks, of adhering to syndicalism. *See further under* INDUSTRIAL MANAGEMENT.

Workers' Faculties, special faculties attached to many higher educational establishments during the period 1919–41 to prepare for higher education for those with no secondary education. The system formed part of the so-called cultural revolution (q.v.) and its effect was greatly to lower academic standards in the universities and other higher educational establishments. Workers' Faculties were abolished in pursuance of Zhdanov's 'restoration' policy in education.

Workers' Opposition, semi-syndicalist opposition within the Bolshevik Party which was formed in 1920 by a number of prominent worker Communists, especially trade union leaders, headed by Shlyapnikov and Kollontay (the only intellectual member). The oppositionists criticized the bureaucratic control of industry by the Government and the central party organs, and advocated the establishment of an All-Russian Congress of Producers to run the country's economy. The opposition was condemned at the 10th party congress, 1921, and it was on this occasion that the resolution was taken forbidding factions within the party and authorizing the Central Committee to expel any members guilty of 'factionalism.' The Workers' Opposition was alleged to have continued during the following year, and most of its leaders were expelled from the party; some of its adherents continued to form oppositional groups on similar but more extreme lines. All known leaders of the Workers' Opposition except Kollontay disappeared during the Great Purge (q.v.). *See* L. Schapiro, *The Origin of the Communist Autocracy*, 1955, and *The Communist Party of the Soviet Union*, 1960.

Workers' Settlements, type of urban settlement (q.v.) usually situated near and associated with an industrial undertaking or construction project.

World War I, Russian Campaigns:

East Prussia, 1914. At the urgent request of France, Russia undertook to invade East Prussia in addition to her planned offensive against Austria, despite the eleventh-hour change of plan involved. Two armies under General Zhilenskiy (commanding the north-western front)—the First (General Rennenkampf) and Second (General Samsonov)—crossed the frontier in mid August, before organization was complete or their rear services ready, the First Army being directed westward and the Second to the south-west. They were opposed only by the German Eighth Army (General von Pritwitz). After a frontier skirmish a pitched battle was fought by the First Army at Gumbinnen which resulted in a strategic victory for the Russians, since the Germans withdrew with heavy casualties and the nerve of the German commander was broken—he declared that he must withdraw behind the River Vistula. He and his Chief of Staff were dismissed and replaced by Hindenburg and Ludendorff. Rennenkampf had made no attempt to pursue the German army. Consequently Samsonov's Second Army, weary, half starved, incompetently commanded and out of supporting distance from the First, suffered one of the most crushing defeats of the war at Tannenberg (27th–29th August); irreplaceable losses in officers, N.C.O.s and equipment had a crippling effect upon Russia for the rest of the war. Rennenkampf, alarmed at the turn of events, withdrew rapidly, making no effort to succour Samsonov (who committed suicide) and leaving his troops to fend for themselves. The Russian corps evaded destruction, but by mid September their withdrawal from East Prussia was complete, and the campaign in that theatre concluded.

Poland and Russia, 1914. The ineptitude of the Austrians outmatched that of the Russians. In a country of bad communications, with poor intelligence on both sides, inconclusive fighting took place in August between the armies of Ivanov and von Hoetzendorff; the latter, having withdrawn towards the River Dunajec, had early to call on his German allies for help. The situation was temporarily restored by German reinforcements, and Przemysl (a fortress which frequently changed hands) was retaken from the Russians, who, however, also reinforced, took the offensive in October, moving towards Silesia; by late November the front was stabilized for the winter. On the outer wings (a second Russian invasion of East Prussia being included in the general advance) the Austro-German forces must have been overwhelmed had the Russian armies not been so short of ammunition and equipment, and had not their intentions been clear to the enemy through intercepted wireless messages sent *en clair*. This Russian offensive compelled the transfer of eight enemy divisions from the western front.

1915. The Russians had once more been forced to evacuate East Prussia by late February, but farther south they counter-attacked. The German Supreme Headquarters, fearing a Russian advance into Hungary, decided that Austria must be assisted in a major offensive. The Russian Third Army (General Dimitriyev) was broken by a general assault in May; by September, Lemberg, Warsaw, Kovno and Grodno had fallen, and though they evaded envelopment 325,000 prisoners were lost. On 8th September the Czar assumed command of all the Russian armies, with Alekseyev as Chief of Staff. By the end of the month the front was stabilized for the winter on the line Riga-Lake Naroch'-Baranovichi-junction of the River Bug with the Carpathians.

1916. The Russian armies were reorganized in three groups, under (north to south) generals Kuropatkin, Evert and Brusilov. The last —the most successful Russian commander of the war—attacked in early June, compelling the Austrians who faced him to withdraw with the loss of 450,000 prisoners, and reaching Lutsk on the River Styr'. The entire Austro-German force was in jeopardy, but the planned attacks by the other two Russian groups failed to materialize, and though a German counter-offensive achieved little and Brusilov made considerable further gains during the summer, he had shot his bolt by early October owing to lack of ammunition and the exhaustion of his troops. Operations ceased for the winter.

1917. After the fall of the monarchy in the February revolution (q.v.) the Provisional Government (q.v.) decided to continue the war, with Kerenskiy as Minister of War (from May) and Brusilov as supreme commander-in-chief (in July and August, being succeeded by Kornilov and by Kerenskiy himself in September). A general attack took place on 31st July, but discipline was failing and the German counterstroke met little resistance. Both sides settled down in trenches early in September. Riga soon capitulated, and, following the October revolution (q.v.), hostilities were formally suspended on 2nd December. In Finland 20,000 Russians laid down their arms, and it was occupied by the Germans. The only military achievement of Kerenskiy's offensive was the retention on the Russian front of enemy divisions badly required in the West.

Campaign against the Turks in the Caucasus. This was the most successful of all Russian campaigns of the war, in a theatre with a most rigorous climate. After preliminary fighting the Turkish Third Army attacked in mid December 1914, but was crushingly defeated in the Russian counter-attack, losing 30,000 men killed and a whole corps by surrender. In September 1915 the Grand Duke Nicholas took command of the Army of the Caucasus, and opened a successful offensive in January 1916, taking Erzerum, Trebizond and Erjingian in February, April and July respectively. By then, however, the Russians had outrun their pack—their only—transport. Though the Turks were in full retreat they were later reinforced, the front was stabilized and the campaign came virtually to an end. *See also* BREST-LITOVSK, TREATY OF. *See* B. Pares, *Day by Day with the Russian*

Army, 1914–15, 1915; B. Gourko, *Russia in 1914–17*, 1918; Sir E. Ironside, *Tannenberg. The First Thirty Days in East Prussia*, 1925; F. A. Golder, *Documents of Russian History, 1914–17*, 1927; J. E. Edmonds, *A Short History of World War I*, 1951.

World War II, Russian Campaigns. The German invasion of Russia, which broke the Nazi-Soviet Pact (q.v.), was launched on 22nd June 1941. By November the Germans had swept forward to Leningrad, besieging but failing to take the city, had overrun the Ukraine and the industrial Donets Basin, and were a threat to Moscow itself. Throughout their retreat the Russian armies followed a rigorous scorched-earth policy, on the express orders of Stalin. However, the extreme severity of the winter brought the German advance to a halt, Marshal Zhukov—the most outstanding Russian commander of the war—was able to beat off the threat to Moscow, and the Germans were steadily forced back, with Rostov-on-Don being retaken after bitter fighting, and Marshal Konev's forces making progress in the Tula region. A German offensive in the spring of 1942 was anticipated by Marshal Timoshenko, who launched a strong attack in the Khar'kov region, where a long-drawn-out struggle followed (May–June) and Timoshenko's forces suffered heavy losses. In the south, however, Sevastopol' (after a heroic defence) and the rest of the Crimea were lost in July, the German forces advanced towards the Volga and the Caucasus, and by August the great battle for Stalingrad had begun. For several months the siege of this city overshadowed all other operations; it was almost completely destroyed in the fierce fighting and bitter Russian defence, and the most critical point was reached in late September, when the Russian garrison in the city was almost overwhelmed. However, the intervention of the 13th Guards division, under Rodimtsev, temporarily restored the situation; in November a Russian offensive was begun, and by the end of January 1943 the besieging German Sixth Army under von Paulus (who himself was captured) had been annihilated—a catastrophic loss in men, equipment and prestige for the Germans. The destruction of the German Sixth Army at Stalingrad released large Russian forces in the south, and by mid February Kursk, Rostov and Khar'kov were retaken, though the last, together with most of the Donets Basin, was soon lost again in a strong German counter-offensive. Fearing a second encirclement in the Caucasus, the German High Command ordered the army there to withdraw, thus losing valuable grain resources. The Russians were also active further north, retaking Velikiye Luki (the pivot of the German fronts towards Moscow and Leningrad), Rzhev and Vyaz'ma between January and March.

In the early summer of 1943 a carefully prepared German attack was launched against the Kursk-Orël salient, but after heavy fighting this was defeated, with enormous losses in men and equipment, the Russians retaking Orël in early August, and Khar'kov soon after. The Russian offensive was broadened and by September Taganrog, Poltava, Bryansk and Smolensk had been retaken. The momentum of the Russian recovery now seemed irresistible; they sealed off the Crimea, retook Kiev and Zhitomir (November), improved their position in the Leningrad area, and early in 1944, after the capture of Nikolayev and Krivoy Rog, wiped out the German positions in the Dnieper bend. In March the Russian armies crossed the rivers Southern Bug, Dniester and Prut, taking Odessa in mid April, but in the Crimea Sevastopol' was not retaken until May. They resumed the offensive in June in Belorussia, by mid July the German armies in the Baltic States were under a grave threat (being forced to abandon Pskov and Narva), and in September–October the Baltic States were reoccupied by Russian forces. The Germans were also suffering even more acute reverses in Poland, and by the end of July Russian troops were ten miles east of Warsaw. When the Warsaw uprising began on 1st August, however, the Russians remained stationary and did not advance to support General Bor's 'Home Army,' which, having counted on Russian assistance, was left to face the Germans in the city alone. In the south Rumania was overrun by Malinovskiy's and Tolbukhin's troops, and surrendered in August 1944. War was declared on Bulgaria, which despite her immediate request for an armistice was occupied by Tolbukhin, while through co-operation between Soviet forces and Tito's partisans the Germans were expelled from Yugoslavia.

By the turn of the year the Russians were sweeping forward along a vast front across Poland and further south towards Budapest. The final offensive against Germany was undertaken on three main fronts, the northern under Rokossovskiy, the centre under Zhukov and the southern under Konev; during January and February 1945 Tilsit, Breslau and Poznan fell. The Soviet forces were temporarily halted on the Oder line, but advanced both on their right flank (taking Königsberg early in April) and through Hungary, capturing Vienna on 13th April. Other Russian armies crossed the Oder and the Neisse to take part in the siege of Berlin, and on 25th April Russian and American troops met on the Elbe. Berlin surrendered to the Russians on 2nd May 1945. *See also* COMMUNIST DICTATORSHIP; POTSDAM CONFERENCE; YALTA CONFERENCE. *See* W. E. D. Allen and P. Muratoff, *The Russian Campaigns of 1941–3*, 1944, and *The Russian Campaigns of 1944–5*, 1945; T. Plievier, *Stalingrad*, Munich, 1947; Strategicus, *A Short History of the Second World War*, 1950; *Stalin's Correspondence with Churchill, Attlee, Roosevelt and Truman*, 1958.

Wrangel, Pëtr Nikolayevich (1878–1928), general. He served in the Russo-Japanese War and First World War. He joined Kaledin (q.v.) in July 1917, and after the latter's suicide early in 1918 joined the anti-Bolshevik forces of General Denikin (q.v.); on Denikin's defeat by the Bolsheviks in November 1919 Wrangel was left in command of the disorganized army. With French assistance he advanced against the Bolsheviks for a time but was soon forced into a retreat which ended with the evacuation of his forces from Sevastopol' in 1920 (*see further under* CIVIL WAR). Thereafter Wrangel lived in exile in Belgium. *See* his *Always with Honor*, New York, 1958.

Writers' Union, professional organization for representing and defending the interests of authors and ensuring their ideological and political conformity; the latter task is carried out by the party organization within the union. It has provincial and local branches;

branches in each Union Republic are grouped into the Writers' Union of that republic, which in turn is affiliated to the central Writers' Union. The organization was formed in 1932 by a decision of the Central Committee of the party, which simultaneously dissolved all existing literary associations. The new organization united the two categories who had previously been distinguished as 'proletarian writers' (*see* R.A.P.P.) and 'fellow travellers' (q.v.) under the common designation of 'Soviet writers.' At its first congress in 1934, which was addressed by Zhdanov on behalf of the Central Committee, the doctrine of Socialist Realism (q.v.) was adopted as binding for all members of the union. During both the Great Purge and the 'anti-cosmopolitan' campaign of 1949–50 the Writers' Union was used for the vilification of its own members. The 2nd congress, held in 1955 more than twenty years after the first, witnessed sharp exchanges between those subservient to the party and the more independent-minded writers. During the next four years the machinery of the union, headed by Surkov (q.v.), was chiefly used for attempting to stamp out the opposition among the writers to the domination of the party. An R.S.F.S.R. Writers' Union, dominated by provincial nonentities, was established to counteract the influence of the rebellious Moscow and Leningrad writers. In 1958 the union expelled Pasternak (q.v.). At the 3rd congress, 1959, which was addressed by Khrushchëv, a policy of reconciliation (officially called 'consolidation') between the party authorities and the writers appears to have been worked out, and Surkov was replaced by the more sympathetic K. A. Fedin (q.v.). *See also* INTELLECTUAL OPPOSITION. *See* H. M. Hayward, 'Soviet Literature in the Doldrums,' *Problems of Communism*, vol. viii, No. 4, July–Aug. 1959; R. Hingley, 'The Soviet Writer's Congress,' *Soviet Survey*, No. 29, July–Sept. 1959.

Y

Yablochkina, Aleksandra Aleksandrovna (*b.* 1866), actress of the Malyy Theatre in Moscow (from 1888), of a theatrical family and herself on the stage from the age of 6. She was at her best in the classical roles, Desdemona, Sof'ya in Griboyedov's *Woe from Wit*, etc. From 1916 she was chairman of the Russian Theatrical Society.

Yablochkov, Pavel Nikolayevich (1847–94), electrical engineer. Retired as a military engineer, he lived mostly in Paris after 1875. In 1875–6 he invented the first serviceable electric arc-lamp, the so-called 'Yablochkov candle' (Fr. patent 1876), which was widely used throughout the world until the mid 1880's when it was replaced by Edison's greatly superior incandescent lamp. Yablochkov made several other electrical inventions, but died in poverty.

Yablonovyy, range of mountains in Transbaykalia, dividing it into western and eastern parts. Length nearly 1,000 m.; highest peak Mt Sokhondo, 8,050 ft.

Yadrintsev, Nikolay Mikhaylovich (1842–94), ethnographer, historian and publicist, the founder of Siberian Regionalism (q.v.). In 1882 he published *Siberia as a Colony*, the first systematic treatment of the subject from a Siberian point of view; he also founded and edited, first in St Petersburg and later in Irkutsk, an influential newspaper, the *Eastern Review*. In 1889 he discovered the location of Genghis Khan's capital Karakorum, and the Orkhon Inscriptions.

Yagoda, Genrikh Grigor'yevich (1891–1938), Communist of Jewish origin. He became deputy chairman of the G.P.U. (q.v.) in 1924 and Commissar for Internal Affairs (*see* N.K.V.D.) in 1934. He was Stalin's chief agent in the security organs and conducted the early purges (q.v.), but was accused by Stalin of slackness and replaced by Yezhov in 1936. Yagoda was Commissar for Posts and Telegraphs, 1936–7, but was arrested in 1937, was one of the chief defendants at the show trial of the 'Anti-Soviet Bloc of Rightists and Trotskiyites' (q.v.) and was shot.

Yakutia, Autonomous Republic within the R.S.F.S.R., situated in Eastern Siberia, a mountainous region in the east, south and west, lowland in the north and centre, traversed by the rivers Lena, Yana, Indigirka and Kolyma, largely covered by coniferous forests and having an extremely cold climate (*see* VERKHOYANSK); there are large deposits of coal, iron ore, gold and diamonds. Area 1,188,300 sq. m.; population (1959) 489,000 (49 per cent urban), mostly Yakuts and Russians (the latter since the 17th century). The activities of the inhabitants include gold- and coal-mining, livestock breeding, grain cultivation and fur trapping. Principal towns: Yakutsk and Aldan. The Autonomous Republic was formed in 1922, but the Bolsheviks only established final control in the area (against the Whites) in the following year. Yakutia has been a place of banishment since the

19th century and of labour camps from the 1930's to the mid 1950's; it is the site of important construction projects, although the dissolution of many camps resulted in a decrease of economic activity. *See* W. Kolarz, *The Peoples of the Soviet Far East*, 1954; K. Staf, *Yakutia as I saw It*, Moscow, 1958.

Yakuts (own name **Sakha**), Turkic-speaking people, the most numerous of the northern peoples of Russia, who live in the Lena Basin and neighbouring areas of Eastern Siberia, numbering (1959) 236,000 (1926, 241,000). They are sedentary, chiefly livestock breeders. The Yakuts have been known since the 14th century, when they came from the south and wiped out, expelled or conquered the Tungus and Paleo-Asiatic inhabitants. They have been subject to Russia since the 17th century.

Yalta, town in the Crimean Oblast, situated on the southern coast of Crimea 55 m. east of Sevastopol'. Population (1956) 34,100. It has been the principal centre of the Crimean health resorts since the 1880's (about 300,000 tourists and patients yearly); there are also tobacco and wine industries, and a film studio. At nearby Nikita there is a famous botanical garden (founded 1812). Yalta was an ancient Greek colony. In 1945 the Yalta Conference took place in nearby Livadiya. *See* M. P. Chekhova, *The Chekhov Museum in Yalta*, Moscow, 1958.

Yalta Conference, conference between Churchill, Roosevelt and Stalin held near Yalta in February 1945 to prepare for the final defeat and subsequent occupation of Germany. The Western Allies obtained Stalin's promise to enter the war against Japan, and the U.S.S.R. actually declared war on 8th August, only six days before Japan's surrender. At the conference Stalin achieved considerable gains for the Soviet Union while giving very little away. *See further under* FOREIGN POLICY; REFUGEES.

Yamal-Nenets National Okrug, within the Tyumen' Oblast (Western Siberia), comprises a large tundra area astride the lower Ob' and the Ob' Bay, including Yamal Peninsula. Area 289,600 sq. m.; population (1959) 63,000 (35 per cent urban), chiefly Russians (since the 16th century) and Nenets. The activities of the inhabitants are fishing, reindeer raising and fur trapping. Administrative centre Salekhard. Prior to the mid 1950's it was an area of banishment and labour camps.

Yanzhul, Ivan Ivanovich (1846–1914), economist and publicist of Ukrainian parentage, an early representative of the Solidarist trend in Russia. He was professor at Moscow University, and the first factory inspector of the Moscow industrial area, 1882–7, later an academician. Yanzhul was greatly influenced by English thought and practice, which he popularized in Russia, especially Christian Socialism, the role of public opinion and public initiative, social surveys and social legislation, the university extension movement, etc. Among his chief works are *English Free Trade* (2 vols.), 1876, 1882, *Factory Life in the Moscow Province*, 1884, *Essays and Studies: a Collection of Articles on National Economy, Politics and Legislation* (2 vols.), 1884, *In Search of a Better Future. Social Essays*, 1893, *Industrial Syndicates or Entrepreneurs' Associations for Regulating*

Production, especially in the U.S.A., 1895, and three volumes of his reminiscences, 1907–11.

Yaroslav I, the Wise (1019–54), prince of Kiev. *See* KIEVAN RUSSIA.

Yaroslavl': 1. Oblast of the R.S.F.S.R., situated in central Russia north of Moscow; it is a lowland region traversed by the Volga (with the Rybinsk Reservoir in the north-west) and partly covered with mixed forests. Area 14,400 sq. m.; population (1959) 1,395,000 (58 per cent urban). There are engineering and textile industries, and varied old crafts are carried on; there are two hydro-electric stations on the Volga. Flax and potatoes are cultivated, and dairy farming (Yaroslavl' breed) is carried on. Principal towns: Yaroslavl', Rybinsk, Rostov.

2. Administrative, economic and cultural centre of the oblast, the oldest Russian town on the Volga. Population (1959) 406,000 (1917, 125,000; 1920, 76,000; 1939, 309,000). It is an important centre of industry and transport, with large engineering (cars and lorries), chemical (synthetic rubber, oil refining), textile (since 1722) and other industries, a river port and four railway lines. There is magnificent architecture of the 13th–17th centuries, including 17th-century churches in the original Yaroslavl' style. Yaroslavl' was founded by Prince Yaroslav the Wise at the beginning of the 11th century, became capital of Yaroslavl' Principality in 1216, Muscovite in 1463 and provincial capital in 1777. In the 16th and 17th centuries it was a flourishing commercial centre on the Moscow-Archangel route; industrial development dates from 1564 (shipyards). Until the construction of the Moscow-Volga Canal, 1937, Yaroslavl' was Moscow's Volga port. The first provincial theatre in Russia was established here in 1750, and in 1803 one of the earliest educational institutions of university level, the Demidov Juridical Lyceum (transformed into Yaroslavl' University 1918, later abolished).

Yaroslavskiy, Yemel'yan (real name **Gubel'man, Miney Izrailevich**) (1878–1943), politician of Jewish birth who joined the Social Democratic Labour Party in 1898 and was active in the party's underground organizations as a firm supporter of Lenin; he was imprisoned and banished for several years. Yaroslavskiy was active in the Bolshevik seizure of power; in 1918 he belonged to the Left Communists (q.v.) and subsequently became a protagonist of Stalinism, especially in the falsification of the history of the party; he was also an outstanding Militant Atheist (*see* ATHEISTS, MILITANT) and edited the journal *The Godless*. *See* his *Religion in the U.S.S.R.*, 1932, *Landmarks in the Life of Stalin*, 1942, *Twenty-five Years of Soviet Power*, 1943; and also the official *History of the Communist Party in the Soviet Union (Bolsheviks): Short Course*, 1943, which was largely written by Yaroslavskiy.

Yashin (real name **Popov**), **Aleksandr Yakovlevich** (*b.* 1913), author. He attracted attention at the end of 1956 with the publication in the second issue of *Literary Moscow* (a collection of oppositional writings, *see* INTELLECTUAL OPPOSITION) of his short story 'The Levers,' which describes the dullness and unreality of party life (*see* FICTIONS) on the level of the village committee. *See* J. Lindsay (trans.), *Russian*

Poetry, 1917–55, 1957; E. Stillman (ed.), *Bitter Harvest*, New York, 1959.

Yegor'yevsk, town in the Moscow Oblast, situated 72 m. south-east of the capital. Population (1959) 59,000 (1939, 56,000). It has a large textile industry (since the 1820's). Yegor'yevsk has been known as a village since 1462, and became a town in 1778.

Yekaterinburg, *see* SVERDLOVSK.

Yekaterinodar, *see* KRASNODAR.

Yekaterinoslav, *see* DNEPROPETROVSK.

Yelets, town in the Lipetsk Oblast (central Russia), situated 70 m. north-west of Voronezh. Population (1959) 78,000 (1914, 58,000; 1926, 36,000; 1939, 51,000). It has food and engineering industries, and an old lace-knitting craft is still practised. Yelets was founded in 1146; prior to 1917 it had a flourishing grain trade, the first grain elevator in the country being built here in 1888.

Yelgava, *see* JELGAVA.

Yelisavetgrad, *see* KIROVOGRAD.

Yelizavetpol', *see* KIROVABAD.

Yenakiyevo (from 1920's **Rykovo,** 1935–43 **Ordzhonikidze**), town in the Stalino Oblast (Ukraine), situated 28 m. north-east of Stalino. Population (1959) 92,000 (1939, 89,000). It has large coal-mining, iron and steel (since 1897) and chemical industries. Yenakiyevo was founded in 1883.

Yenisey, river in central Siberia which rises in two headstreams in the Sayan Mountains and flows north into the Yenisey Bay (long estuary) of the Kara Sea. Length, from confluence of headstreams, 2,100 m.; from the source of the Selenga in the Yenisey drainage area, 3,700 m.; drainage area over 1,000,000 sq. m. The Yenisey is a mountain river with rocky shores and rapids in its upper reaches; from below Krasnoyarsk to Dudinka it divides the West Siberian lowland and the Central Siberian plateau, and is a mighty stream with few islands and a wide valley. Its main tributaries are the Angara, Podkamennaya Tunguska and Nizhnyaya Tunguska; principal ports: Dudinka, Igarka, Krasnoyarsk. The Yenisey is navigable almost throughout its course, the main goods carried being timber, grain and coal; it is accessible to seagoing vessels as far as Igarka (*see* IGARKA; NORTHERN SEA ROUTE). The great energy resources of the river are to be utilized by the construction of hydro-electric stations above Krasnoyarsk (4,200,000 kw., begun 1956) and later at Yeniseysk, possibly even more powerful. The river was first visited by Russians in the 16th century, and since the 17th its basin has been colonized by them. It has been an area of banishment (since the 17th century), labour camps, and now of rapid industrialization.

Yeniseysk, town in the Krasnoyarsk Kray (central Siberia), situated on the Yenisey 217 m. north of Krasnoyarsk. Population (1959) 16,000 (1914, 12,000). Founded in 1618, the town was a trading and administrative centre of the Yenisey Basin in the 17th–18th centuries. A huge hydro-electric station (projected capacity 5,000,000 kw.) is planned for construction here.

Yerevan (formerly Russian **Erivan'**), capital, economic and cultural centre of Armenia, situated on the River Razdan. Population (1959) 509,000 (1914, 33,000; 1926, 65,000; 1939, 204,000; 1956, 385,000), mostly Armenians. It has large aluminium, engineering (machine tools, watches, electrical equipment, etc.), chemical (synthetic rubber, tyres, plastics), building materials, food, light and printing industries. The Armenian Academy of Sciences, 1943, is here, and there is a university, 1920. Yerevan has been known since the 7th century, and from 1440 belonged variously to Persia and Turkey; in 1827 it became Russian (provincial capital), and 1918–20 was capital of independent Armenia.

Yermak (*d.* 1584), Cossack ataman (i.e. 'headman'), known as the conqueror of Siberia. Yermak was in the service of the merchant family of Stroganovs (q.v.), and in 1581, commanding 840 Cossacks and soldiers, invaded the Siberian Khanate and conquered its capital, thus enabling Muscovy (q.v.) to annex Western Siberia.

Yermolova, Mariya Nikolayevna (1853–1928), famous tragic actress of the Malyy Theatre in Moscow, of a theatrical family. Her repertoire included Shakespeare (Ophelia and Lady Macbeth), Schiller (Joan of Arc and Mary Stuart), Racine, Hugo, Lope de Vega, Ibsen, Ostrovskiy (q.v.) and others.

Yesenin, Sergey Aleksandrovich (1895–1925), poet of peasant origin who became the protégé of Blok (q.v.) in 1913 and soon achieved popularity as the most gifted of the group of 'peasant poets.' Politically he was under Populist influence, and in 1917 became a Left Socialist Revolutionary. In the following years he was the leader of the Imagist literary group. He led a debauched life, marrying Isadora Duncan in 1921 and being divorced by her two years later. In 1925, disillusioned by the Soviet regime, which he felt to be alien to his beloved 'peasant Russia,' he committed suicide. His poetry, in whose images are intermingled rural Russia and religious themes, though extremely popular, was frowned upon by the authorities until after Stalin's death. *See* G. Struve, *Soviet Russian Literature, 1917–50*, Norman, Oklahoma, 1951; G. Ivanov, *Peterburgskiye zimy*, New York, 1952; M. Slonim, *Modern Russian Literature*, New York, 1953; J. Lindsay (trans.), *Russian Poetry, 1917–55*, 1957; R. Poggioli, *The Poets of Russia, 1890–1930*, Cambridge, Mass., 1960.

Yevpatoriya (until 1783 **Gözlev**), town in the Crimean Oblast, situated on the Black Sea shore 50 m. north-west of Simferopol'. Population (1959) 57,000 (1914, 32,000), before 1945 partly Tatar. It is an important beach and mud health resort, especially for children, and has some fishing and wine industries. Yevpatoriya was an ancient Greek colony, became Turkish in 1478 and Russian in 1783. Since 1837 it has been the spiritual centre of the Crimean Karaim.

Yevtushenko, Yevgeniy Aleksandrovich (*b.* 1933), poet. He attracted great attention in 1956 with the publication of his long poem *Zima Railway Station*, which depicts the spiritual and political confusion and searchings of a young man in post-Stalin Russia. He was expelled from the Komsomol and attacked by the official critics after the publication of this poem, but has continued to publish. Through the inwardness and the nonconformity of his poetry he has become very popular among the young generation. *See* R. Conquest (ed.), *Back to*

Life, 1958; M. Futtrell, 'Evgeny Evtushenko,' *Soviet Survey*, No. 25, July–Sept. 1958; E. Stillman (ed.), *Bitter Harvest*, New York, 1959.

Yeysk, town in the Krasnodar Kray (North Caucasus), a port on the Taganrog Bay of the Sea of Azov. Population (1959) 55,000 (1860, 20,000). It is a health resort (mineral waters, mud, beach) and has engineering (printing presses, machine tools) and food industries. Yeysk was founded in 1848 as a seaport.

Yezhov, Nikolay Ivanovich (1895–?1939), one of the most sinister figures of the Stalinist period. Of a poor family, he joined the Communist Party after the seizure of power, but did not become prominent until 1934, when he became a member of the Central Committee and of its Organizational Bureau. He was soon appointed chairman of the Commission of Party Control (referred to as the party's 'intelligence service,' *see* COMMITTEE OF PARTY CONTROL), and in 1936 became Commissar for Internal Affairs (*see* N.K.V.D.) with the specific task of directing the Great Purge (q.v.), the bloodiest period of the Communist regime, known in Russia as the Yezhovshchina. He was succeeded by Beria in 1938 soon after he had become a candidate member of the Politburo, and was appointed Commissar for River Transport, but disappeared in 1939. At the 20th party congress (q.v.) in 1956 Khrushchëv, in his secret report, described Yezhov as a degenerate, and it was later said that he had paid the penalty for his crimes. *See* B. D. Wolfe, *Khrushshchëv and Stalin's Ghost*, 1957.

Yezhovo-Cherkessk, *see* CHERKESSK.

Yoshkar-Ola (formerly **Tsarëvokokshaysk**, 1919–27 **Krasnokokshaysk**), capital and cultural centre of the Mari Autonomous Republic, situated about 80 m. north-west of Kazan'. Population (1959) 88,000 (1939, 27,000), mostly Russians. It has wood-processing and food industries. Yoshkar-Ola was founded by the Russians as a fortified town and administrative centre of the Mari country in 1578.

Young Guard ('Molodaya Gvardiya'), underground organization of young Russians, Komsomol members (numbering about one hundred), which existed September–December 1942 in the town of Krasnodon in the Ukraine during the German occupation. The group showed much heroism but was betrayed by an informer and most of its members were arrested, tortured and murdered. The novelist Fadeyev (q.v.) describes it in *The Young Guard*.

Yur'yev, *see* TARTU.

Yuzhno-Sakhalinsk (Japanese **Toyohara**), administrative, cultural and an economic centre of Sakhalin Oblast, situated near the southern end of Sakhalin Island. Population (1959) 86,000, mostly Russians. It has paper, various food and some light industries, and a railway repair shop. It became the centre of South Sakhalin Oblast in 1946 and of Sakhalin Oblast in 1947.

Yuzovka, *see* STALINO.

Z

Zagorsk (until 1930 **Sergiyev**), town in the Moscow Oblast, situated 44 m. north east of the capital. Population (1959) 73,000 (1939, 45,000). It is the centre of an old (since the 15th century) wood-carving and toy-making craft. The famous Trinity Monastery of St Sergius (*see* TROITSE-SERGIYEVA LAVRA) was founded here in 1337, and is now a museum and the residence of the Patriarch of Moscow. Originally an extramural settlement of the monastery, Zagorsk became a town in 1917.

Zak, Yakov Izrailevich (*b.* 1913), pianist and teacher. He studied at Odessa Conservatory under Starkova till 1932 and at Moscow under Neuhaus till 1935. From 1935 he had taught at Moscow Conservatory, being appointed professor in 1947. A virtuoso pianist of wide tastes, he specializes in the music of Chopin.

Zakharov, Andreyan Dmitriyevich (1761–1811), architect who studied at the Academy of Arts, St Petersburg. He is notable for his superb reconstruction of the main Admiralty building, St Petersburg, the tower of which, with its gilded, needle-like spire, is the nodal point of the three main 'perspectives' or streets. His treatment of the building is marked by gracefulness combined with an imposing majesty. *See also* ARCHITECTURE. *See* Tamara Talbot Rice, *Russian Art*, 1949; G. H. Hamilton, *The Art and Architecture of Russia*, 1954.

Zakharov, Vladimir Grigor'yevich (1901–56), composer and folk music specialist, who studied at the Rostov-on-Don Conservatory under N. Z. Heifetz until 1927. He taught in a music school and was a frequent broadcaster; he became musical director of Pyatnitskiy's Russian folk choir in 1932. His works include a violin concerto; orchestral works; many songs, including *And Who Knows*, 1939; and many arrangements for folk orchestra (*see* FOLK MUSIC). Zakharov's work is the exact counterpart of that of Aleksandrov and Dunayevskiy (qq.v.). His music is strongly influenced by folk-song and is characterized by melodic purity, humour, and freshness of harmony. His treatment of folk polyphony is highly individual.

Zampolit, Russian abbreviation for 'Deputy Commander for Political Affairs,' the name since 1942 of the former Military Commissars. *See* COMMISSAR.

Zamyatin, Yevgeniy Ivanovich (1884–1937), writer. In his youth he was a Bolshevik, but soon left the party. He began writing as a Neo-Realist, taking as his subjects provincial life in pre-revolutionary Russia, English society (*The Islanders*, 1918; he had been in England on an official mission during the First World War) and conditions in Russia during the civil war. For several years after 1917 he lectured and conducted classes on prose writing in Petrograd, transmitting the stylistic tradition of Leskov and Remizov; in 1921 a number of young writers influenced by him formed the 'Serapion Brothers'

617

group, among them Zoshchenko, Fedin, Kaverin and Tikhonov (qq.v.). In the 1920's he concentrated upon the basic inhumanity of communism, beginning with his famous novel *We* (written in 1920 but never published in Russia, though it became well known in literary circles), clearly influenced by Dostoyevskiy and H. G. Wells, in which he drew a picture of the future totalitarian society that became the model for both Huxley and Orwell. He continually denounced the servility and conformism of many of the writers. At the time of the quasi-dictatorship of the 'proletarian writers' (*see* AVERBAKH; R.A.P.P.) Zamyatin was no longer able to publish his writings. As the result of a courageous letter to Stalin he was permitted to emigrate in 1932; he lived in Paris and died there embittered both by the incomprehension he met with among Russian *émigrés* and by the state of Europe. He has not, unlike many other writers, been 'rehabilitated' since the 20th party congress. *See* W. B. Edgerton, 'The Serapion Brothers,' *American Slavic and East European Review*, vol. vii, No. 1, 1949; G. Struve, *Soviet Russian Literature, 1917–50*, Norman, Oklahoma, 1951; M. Slonim, *Modern Russian Literature*, New York, 1953; V. Zavalishin, *Early Soviet Writers*, New York, 1958.

Zaporogians, see COSSACKS.

Zaporozh'ye (Ukrainian **Zaporizhzhya**): 1. Oblast in southeastern Ukraine, between the Dnieper bend and the Sea of Azov, largely black earth lowland steppe with deposits of lignite. Area 10,500 sq. m.; population (1959) 1,466,000 (57 per cent urban), Ukrainians and Russians (before the war also Jews and Germans). There are large metallurgical, engineering, chemical and food industries; wheat, sunflowers and cotton are cultivated, and market gardening (melons) carried on. Principal towns: Zaporozh'ye, Melitopol', Berdyansk. The first non-nomadic people to settle in the area were the Ukrainian Cossacks, who established the Sich community on the Dnieper bend in the late 16th century (for further history see NEW RUSSIA). From 1917 to 1921 the region was the centre of Makhno Anarchist movement.

2 (until 1921 **Aleksandrovsk**). Administrative, economic and cultural centre of the oblast, situated on the Dnieper. Population (1959) 435,000 (sixth in the Ukraine; 1914, 51,000; 1939, 282,000; 1956, 381,000). It is a major industrial centre (iron and steel, aluminium, chemicals, agricultural machinery, cars, electrical equipment) and a transportation centre (river port, airport, four railway lines). There is a large hydro-electric station (see DNEPROGES). Zaporozh'ye was founded as a fortress in the defence line against the Crimean Tatars in 1770; it saw much fighting in 1918–19, and suffered severely during the Second World War (occupied 1941–3).

Zarudnyy, Sergey Ivanovich (1821–87), jurist, head of the law department of the State Council from 1861 and a senator from 1869. He was prominent in the judicial reforms of 1864 (see GREAT REFORMS) which overhauled and modernized the judicial system, introducing trial by jury in criminal cases, the independence of judges and examining magistrates, and public court proceedings.

Zelenodol'sk, town in the Tatar Autonomous Republic, situated on the left bank of the Volga 25 m. west of Kazan'. Population (1959) 60,000 (1939, 30,000), mostly Russians. It has large saw-milling and woodworking (plywood, railway sleepers, etc.) industries, and is the junction of the Moscow–Kazan' and the Volga railways.

Zelinskiy, Nikolay Dmitriyevich (1861–1953), chemist. Educated at New Russia (Odessa) and Göttingen universities, he was professor at Moscow University, a member of the Academy of Sciences from 1929, president of the Moscow Society of Naturalists, 1935–41. He studied isomerism, catalysis of organic combinations (particularly important was his work on the chemistry of petroleum), the structure of albuminates, and adsorption (a carbon gas-mask in 1915). Among his many pupils were Chugayev, Nesmeyanov and Nametkin (qq.v.).

Zemlya i Volya, see POPULISM.

Zemskiy Sobor ('Assembly of the Land'), assembly of representatives of the boyars, clergy, merchants, towns and districts in 16th–17th-century Muscovy whose duty was to decide upon important measures of state policy; at first it was appointed, but later elected. The Zemskiy Sobor of 1612 put an end to the Time of Troubles (see TROUBLES, TIME OF) and arranged to meet regularly. Peter the Great abolished it. See J. L. H. Keep, 'The Decline of the Zemskiy Sobor,' *Slavonic and East European Review*, vol. xxxvi, No. 86, Dec. 1957.

Zemstvo, colloquial name of institutions of local government which were established in 1864 in the course of the Great Reforms (q.v.). District *zemstvos* were elected on a restricted franchise, and they elected the provincial *zemstvos*. The activities of the *zemstvos* were supervised by provincial governors, but they had authority in economic and educational matters, public health, etc. The liberal and radical intelligentsia found the *zemstvos* to be the most appropriate field for their practical work, and the constitutional movement prior to the revolution of 1905 (q.v.) chiefly expressed itself through the *zemstvos*. They were prominent in the war effort and in demands for a responsible government during the First World War (see UNION OF ZEMSTVOS). The sphere of *zemstvo* authority was widened after the February revolution (q.v.) of 1917, but they were abolished after the Bolshevik seizure of power and replaced by the soviets (q.v.). See P. G. Vinogradoff, *Self-Government in Russia*, 1915; G. Fischer, *Russian Liberalism, from Gentry to Intelligentsia*, Cambridge, Mass., 1958.

Zeravshan Valley, valley of the River Zeravshan in the Uzbek and Tadzhik Union Republics of Central Asia. It is one of the chief oases of Central Asia (both Bukhara and Samarkand are situated in it) and one of the ancient centres of civilization there (see SOGDIANA).

Zhdanov (until 1948 **Mariupol'**), city in the Stalino Oblast (Ukraine), situated on the northern coast of the Sea of Azov. Population (1959) 284,000 (1914, 45,000; 1939, 222,000), Russians and Ukrainians (before the war also Greeks). It is a major centre of industry, with large iron and steel plants (using ore from Kerch') and engineering and other industries, and is the seaport of the Donets Basin. Zhdanov was founded by Greek colonists in 1775 and became a seaport in 1780; its industrial development dates from the

1890's and was especially rapid during the 1930's. The town suffered much during the Second World War (occupied 1941–3).

Zhdanov, Andrey Aleksandrovich (1896–1948), politician who joined the Bolsheviks in 1915, 1924–34 headed the party organization in Nizhniy Novgorod, and 1934–44 in Leningrad. He was also secretary of the Central Committee from 1934, becoming a candidate member of the Politburo in 1935 and a full member in 1939. In his capacity as secretary of the Central Committee Zhdanov was in charge of ideological affairs, and the ideological elements of Stalinism (q.v.) were largely his creation. He introduced the obligatory school of Socialist Realism (q.v.) in the arts, replaced the historiographical school of Pokrovskiy by that of Grekov, and directed the post-war campaigns against Western cultural influences, 'formalism' in the arts and 'objectivism' in scholarship. Zhdanov was prominent in the defence of Leningrad when it was besieged during the Second World War and in the establishment of the Cominforn in 1947. *See* E. J. Simmons (ed.), *Through the Glass of Soviet Literature*, New York, 1953; R. W. Mathewson, *The Positive Hero in Russian Literature*, New York, 1958.

Zhelyabov, *see* NARODNAYA VOLYA.

Zhitomir (Ukrainian **Zhytomyr**): 1. Oblast of the Ukraine, the easternmost of the three oblasts situated in Volhynia (q.v.), partly covered with pine and oak forests and with large deposits of building materials. Area 11,500 sq. m.; population (1959) 1,603,000 (26 per cent urban), mostly Ukrainians, also Russians and Jews (before the war Poles and Germans). Grain, potatoes and sugar-beet are cultivated, cattle raised, and there are food, timber and stone-quarrying industries. Principal towns: Zhitomir, Berdichev.

2. Administrative, economic and cultural centre of the oblast, situated 80 m. west of Kiev. Population (1959) 105,000 (1891, 70,000; 1914, 93,000; 1926, 68,000; 1939, 95,000), before the war half Jewish. It has woodworking (furniture, musical instruments) and food industries, is the centre of a hop-growing area and an important railway junction. Zhitomir has been known since 1240, belonged to Kiev Principality, became Lithuanian in 1320, Polish in 1569 and Russian in 1793 (provincial capital 1804). In 1943–4 it witnessed fierce fighting.

Zhmud', *see* SAMOGITIA.

Zhukov, Georgiy Konstantinovich (*b.* 1896), Marshal of the Soviet Union, Russia's most outstanding military leader during the Second World War. Of peasant origin, he joined the Red Army in 1918 and the Communist Party in the following year. He first became known for his successful operations against the Japanese on the Mongolian-Manchurian frontier in 1939. During the Second World War he was at first Chief of the General Staff and subsequently Deputy Commissar of Defence and deputy supreme commander-in-chief of the Soviet armed forces. He was prominent in the planning of Soviet operations, often co-ordinating the actions of a number of army groups (in the defence of Moscow, 1941, the battle of Stalingrad, 1942, the relief of Leningrad, 1943, and the advance to the west, 1943–4); on occasions he took personal command of an army group, e.g. in the final advance on Berlin. On 8th May 1945 he received the surrender of the German High Command in Berlin, and in 1945–6 headed the Soviet Control Commission in Germany. In 1946 he was removed by Stalin, who resented his great popularity, and after a brief period as Commander-in-Chief Land Forces and Deputy Minister of the Armed Forces he was sent into a kind of honourable banishment as the commander of a military district in Russia. He again became a First Deputy Minister of Defence upon Stalin's death in 1953, and two years later Minister of Defence. He was the first professional soldier to enter the real seat of power in the country when he became a candidate member of the Presidium (q.v.) of the Central Committee in 1956. Siding with Khrushchëv against Stalin's chief lieutenants Malenkov, Kaganovich and Molotov, he became a full member of the Presidium upon their expulsion in 1957 (*see* ANTI-PARTY GROUP). However, he was himself expelled from the Presidium and the Central Committee and dismissed as Minister of Defence a few months later for his attempts to undermine the position of the Communist Party in the armed forces (*see* COMMISSAR). Since then his role in the Second World War has again been played down in the official propaganda. *See* P. Ruslanov, 'Marshal Zhukov,' *Russian Review*, vol. xv, No. 2, April 1956.

Zhukovskiy, Nikolay Yegorovich (1847–1921), professor of theoretical mechanics at the Moscow Higher Technical School and Moscow University, the 'father of Russian aviation.' He is the author of many works on theoretical and applied mechanics and mathematics, those on hydrodynamics and aerodynamics being the most numerous and important. He worked out a formula for calculating the lifting power of an aeroplane, 1905, developed the whirlwind theory of the propeller, 1912–18, etc. Together with a group of his pupils he set up the Central Aero-Hydrodynamic Institute, 1918, and the Military Air Academy. *See also* AIRCRAFT; CHAPLYGIN; TUPOLEV.

Zhukovskiy, Vasiliy Andreyevich (1783–1852), poet who led the Russian Romantic school (the ballad *Svetlana*, 1911), and a translator of Schiller, Byron, Firdousi and Homer. He was tutor to Alexander II and frequently used his position at court to intercede for opponents of the regime, such as the Decembrists, although he did not agree with them. *See* N. V. Riasanovsky, *Nicholas I and Official Nationality in Russia, 1825–55*, Berkeley and Los Angeles, 1959.

Zinin, Nikolay Nikolayevich (1812–80), chemist, one of the founders of the Russian chemical school. Educated at Kazan' University, he worked for a year under Liebig in Giessen, and was later professor at Kazan' and at the Medico-Surgical Academy in St Petersburg, and a member of the Academy of Sciences. He achieved the transformation of nitrobenzol into aniline and a number of other syntheses which greatly influenced Butlerov and Borodin (qq.v.). Zinin was among the founders, 1868, and the first president of the Russian Chemical Society (now called after Mendeleyev).

Zinov'yev (real name **Radomysl'skiy**), **Grigoriy Yevseyevich** (1883–1936), politician of Jewish birth who joined the Social Democratic Labour Party in 1901, and its Bolshevik faction in 1903. After the

1905 revolution he emigrated, became a Central Committee member in 1907, and from 1909 to 1917 was Lenin's chief lieutenant in directing the Bolshevik organization; he accompanied Lenin on his return to Russia after the February 1917 revolution, but was associated with Kamenev in opposing Lenin's policy of a Bolshevik seizure of power. He was chairman of the Petrograd Soviet after the October revolution, became a candidate member of the Politburo in 1919, was a full member, 1921–6, and was chairman of the executive committee of the Communist International from 1919 to 1926. In the internal party conflict which followed Lenin's death, Zinov'yev first sided with Kamenev and Stalin agaiñst Trotskiy, but after the latter had been defeated associated with him and Kamenev against Stalin (*see* LEFT OPPOSITION). After he had been overcome by Stalin and Bukharin, Zinov'yev was deprived of all his offices and was several times expelled from the party. He was sentenced to ten years' imprisonment in 1935 for 'moral complicity' in the assassination of Kirov, was tried again at the first of the show trials of the Great Purge (q.v.) in 1936, and was executed. *See* E. H. Carr, *The Interregnum, 1923–4*, 1954, and *Socialism in One Country, 1924–6*, vol. i, 1958; L. Schapiro, *The Communist Party of the Soviet Union*, 1960.

Zinov'yevsk, *see* KIROVOGRAD.

Ziolkovsky, *see* TSIOLKOVSKIY.

Zlatoust, town in the Chelyabinsk Oblast (Urals), situated 60 m. west of Chelyabinsk. Population (1959) 161,000 (1926, 48,000; 1939, 99,000). It is an important industrial centre, producing special steels, tools, precision instruments and agricultural machinery; an old craft of metal engraving is still carried on. Zlatoust was founded as an ironworks in 1754 and by 1811 was a centre of side-arms production. In 1918 workers overthrew the Bolsheviks in the town; in 1927 the shock-workers' movement (q.v.) was started here.

Zoshchenko, Mikhail Mikhailovich (1895–1958), satirical writer of Ukrainian parentage. He joined the 'Serapion Brothers' (*see* ZAMYATIN) in 1921, and soon gained great popularity with his short stories depicting the bewilderment and disbelief of the 'little man' in the midst of the grandiose fiction (q.v.) of the 'construction of socialism.' In 1946 Zhdanov selected Zoshchenko as the main target of his attacks when he began his campaign for imposing absolute party control over cultural life; Zoshchenko was expelled from the Writers' Union and lived in obscurity until his death. *See* his *Russia Laughs* (trans. H. Clayton), Boston, 1935; *The Woman Who Could Not Read* (trans. E. Fen), 1940; *The Wonderful Dog* (trans. E. Fen), 1942; *see also* R. A. Domar, 'The Tragedy of a Soviet Satirist: the Case of Zoshchenko' in E. J. Simmons's (ed.) *Through the Glass of Soviet Literature*, New York, 1953.

Zubatov, Sergey Vasil'yevich (1864–1917), head of the Moscow branch of the Okhrana (q.v.) who introduced Police Socialism (q.v.) in Russia. With the help of some former Social Democrats and some Moscow University professors he founded in 1901 the Society of Mutual Help of Workers in Mechanical Production—the first legal trade union in Russia. Under police protection this society flourished and was imitated in Minsk, Odessa and St Petersburg (*see* GAPON).

Zubatov was able to control the movement in Moscow, but else-where it got out of hand and was used by Social Democrats for revolutionary purposes. Zubatov was forced to resign in 1903. *See* K. Tidmarsh, 'The Zubatov Idea,' *American Slavic and East European Review*, vol. xix, No. 3, Oct 1960.

Zyryanovsk, town in the East Kazakhstan Oblast, one of the main mining centres of the Oriferous Altay. Population (1959) 54,000 (1939, 16,000), mainly Russians. Polymetallic ores (lead, zinc, etc.) have been mined here since 1794.

Zyryans, *see* KOMI.

APPENDIX

Academy of Sciences. There were 163 full members, 366 corresponding members and 45 foreign members at the end of 1962. Keldysh (q.v.) succeeded Nesmeyanov as president of the academy in 1961, while the political supervision of the academy is in the hands of Fedoseyev. The academy's branch in Moldavia was transformed into a separate republican academy in 1961.

Anti-Party Group. Voroshilov's (q.v.) membership in the group was revealed at the 22nd party congress in 1961, when he, Bulganin, Saburov and Pervukhin (qq.v.) were dropped from the Central Committee; Molotov, Kaganovich and Malenkov (qq.v.) were stated in 1964 to have been expelled from the party.

Anti-Semitism. More than half of those sentenced to death in 1961 and 1962 for alleged embezzlement and currency offences (*see* CAPITAL PUNISHMENT) were Jews.

Capital Punishment. In 1961 the death penalty was extended to cover embezzlement of State property, counterfeiting money and attacks upon officials by 'incorrigible criminals,' and in 1962 to the offences of taking bribes, rape and attacks upon the police or members of People's Squads (q.v.). In the early 1960's the death penalty has been frequently inflicted upon people alleged to have been guilty of embezzlement, sabotage and currency offences.

Censorship of dispatches sent by foreign correspondents and radio reporters was relaxed in 1961.

Central Committee. At the 22nd party congress in 1961, 175 members and 155 candidate members of Central Committee were elected—the largest Central Committee in the party's history.

Communism. The new party programme adopted at the 22nd party congress in 1961 is aimed at achieving by 1980 what is variously described as the creation of material conditions for Communism or the basic construction of Communism. Both the programme and such public discussion of problems of the transition to Communism as does take place are mainly devoted to the exegesis of the views that Khrushchëv has been propounding since 1956.

Economic Councils. To counteract 'localist' tendencies in economic management, republican councils of national economy were established in 1960 in the R.S.F.S.R., the Ukraine and Kazakhstan; a single economic council formed for the four Union Republics of Central Asia in 1962; and the U.S.S.R. Council of National Economy set up, also in 1962. Another move in the same direction was the creation in 1961 of 17 regional groupings of Economic Councils with an embryonic co-ordinating machinery in each. Most economic councils were enlarged in 1963, and their jurisdiction now usually extends over two to four oblasts.

Foreign Policy. The Congo crisis, which began in July 1960, brought from the Soviet Union ineffective attempts to support M. Lumumba and, after his murder, the dissident Stanleyville premier M. Gizenga. But more importantly, it called forth a sustained and vituperative attack by the Soviet Union upon United Nations policy in the Congo, upon the Secretary-General, Mr Dag Hammarskjold (including unsuccessful efforts in the Security Council and the General Assembly to secure his removal), and attempts to gain support—which was not forthcoming—in the United Nations for the Soviet 'troika' proposal, i.e. the division of the office of Secretary-General between three men, one from the West, one from the Communist bloc and one neutral. In the summer of 1961 the 'Berlin crisis' was revived. In June Mr Khrushchëv renewed his demands for a German Peace Treaty and a Berlin settlement; in August, owing to an unprecedented number of refugees from East Germany arriving in West Berlin during the preceding months, the border between the two parts of the city was closed by the East German Government; and this was followed by Soviet allegations of the misuse of the allied air corridors to West Berlin and unsuccessful attempts to interfere with their use by the Western powers. But again this 'crisis' died down, though the border between East and West Berlin remains closed and Mr Khrushchëv has continued to talk on occasions of a German Peace Treaty and a Berlin settlement; discussions on the latter point have continued intermittently between the Soviet Foreign Minister and the American Secretary of State. In July 1962, after protracted discussions lasting sixteen months, the Soviet Union, together with Britain, France and the United States, signed a four-teen-power agreement guaranteeing the neutrality of Laos.

Negotiations with the U.S.A. and Britain on banning nuclear tests continued intermittently from 1958 despite the Soviet Union's breaking of the three-year unofficial moratorium on such tests in the autumn of 1961 which was followed by American tests in the spring of 1962. These negotiations resulted in the conclusion in 1963 of a treaty which banned tests on the earth's surface and in the atmosphere, though no agreement could be reached on banning underground tests. Negotiations on the general question of controlled disarmament have been resumed, but have so far remained fruitless.

An important turning point in the relations between the U.S.S.R. and the U.S.A. was the Cuban crisis of 1962 when, in the face of President Kennedy's firmness, the Soviet Government yielded and agreed to withdraw its ballistic missiles from Cuba.

Relations between the Soviet Union and other Communist countries have varied in recent years. There is some evidence that the renewal of the 'Berlin crisis' in 1961 may have been due as much or more to the intransigence of the East German regime as to the desire of the Soviet Government. Sino-Soviet relations have deteriorated rapidly. Serious ideological differences between the two countries became apparent during 1960, especially over Mr Khrushchëv's rejection of Stalinism, which is openly attacked by the Chinese authorities, and over the Chinese Communists' insistence upon the inevitability of war with 'capitalist' states. Since then the Soviet Union has withdrawn much technical assistance, including skilled personnel and advisers, from China. Relations between the Soviet Union and Albania deteriorated during 1960, also apparently over the issue of rejecting Stalinism, and reached an open breach with the breaking off of diplomatic relations in December 1961, since when the two governments have not hesitated to attack each other in public statements and in the press.

Gagarin, Yuriy Alekseyevich (*b.* 1934), the first cosmonaut. Born in a *kolkhoz* peasant family, he was educated at a trade school, secondary technical school and aviation school. A Soviet Air Force pilot from 1957, he joined the Communist Party in 1960. On 12th April 1961 he undertook the first flight in a space ship, circling the earth once and landing at a predetermined place in the Soviet Union. He was promoted from senior lieutenant to major and made a Hero of the Soviet Union.

Keldysh, Mstislav Vsevolodovich (*b.* 1911), scientist, president of the U.S.S.R. Academy of Sciences. He graduated from Moscow University in 1931, became a member of the Academy of Sciences in 1946, of its Presidium in 1953 and a vice-president in 1960. He joined the Communist Party in 1949, and is a Hero of Social Labour and laureate of Stalin and Lenin prizes. His work is devoted to vibration theory, aerodynamics and other fields of mechanics and applied mathematics, and he apparently took a leading part in organizing research on rocketry and space flights. He succeeded Nesmeyanov (q.v.) as president of the academy in 1961.

People's Squads, quasi-voluntary formations, consisting mostly of young people, whose function is to assist the militia (q.v.) in maintaining public order. They began to be formed in 1957–8 and in 1959 a formal decision of the Central Committee of the party and the Council of Ministers prescribed that they should be set up at all major industrial and transport enterprises, building sites, *sovkhozes, kolkhozes* (qq.v.), educational establishments, etc. The People's Squads are directly subordinated to the local party committees, which shows that their function is primarily a political rather than a police one. The ideological justification for them is that this is one of the forms of the transferring of administrative functions from the State organs to 'social' organizations (*see under* COMMUNISM). Many cases have been reported of excesses by these squads and of armed attacks upon them. There is little enthusiasm for the squads and in many cases they now appear to exist only on paper. *See also* CAPITAL PUNISHMENT, HOOLIGANISM.

Stalin. Many of Stalin's crimes were denounced at the 20th party congress (q.v.) in 1956; this process continued at the 22nd congress in 1961, when it was voted that Stalin's body should be removed from the Lenin Mausoleum, and since then all places that had been named after Stalin have had their names changed.

NOTES

NOTES

NOTES

NOTES

NOTES

NOTES

NOTES

NOTES

NOTES

NOTES

NOTES

NOTES